Lecture Notes in Computer Science   1896
Edited by G. Goos, J. Hartmanis and J. van Leeuwen

Springer
*Berlin
Heidelberg
New York
Barcelona
Hong Kong
London
Milan
Paris
Singapore
Tokyo*

Reiner W. Hartenstein
Herbert Grünbacher (Eds.)

Field-Programmable Logic and Applications

The Roadmap to Reconfigurable Computing

10th International Conference, FPL 2000
Villach, Austria, August 27-30, 2000
Proceedings

Springer

Series Editors

Gerhard Goos, Karlsruhe University, Germany
Juris Hartmanis, Cornell University, NY, USA
Jan van Leeuwen, Utrecht University, The Netherlands

Volume Editors

Reiner W. Hartenstein
University of Kaiserslautern, Computer Science Department
P. O. Box. 30 49, 67653 Kaiserslautern, Germany
E-mail: hartenst@rhrk.uni-kl.de

Herbert Grünbacher
Carinthia Tech Institute
Richard-Wagner-Str. 19, 9500 Villach, Austria
E-mail: hg@cti.ac.at

Cataloging-in-Publication Data applied for

Die Deutsche Bibliothek - CIP-Einheitsaufnahme

Field programmable logic and applications : the roadmap to
reconfigurable computing ; 10th international conference ; proceedings
/ FPL 2000, Villach, Austria, August 27 - 30, 2000. Reiner W.
Hartenstein ; Herbert Grünbacher (ed.). - Berlin ; Heidelberg ; New
York ; Barcelona ; Hong Kong ; London ; Milan ; Paris ; Singapore ;
Tokyo : Springer, 2000
   (Lecture notes in computer science ; Vol. 1896)
   ISBN 3-540-67899-9

CR Subject Classification (1998): B.6-7, J.6

ISSN 0302-9743
ISBN 3-540-67899-9 Springer-Verlag Berlin Heidelberg New York

This work is subject to copyright. All rights are reserved, whether the whole or part of the material is concerned, specifically the rights of translation, reprinting, re-use of illustrations, recitation, broadcasting, reproduction on microfilms or in any other way, and storage in data banks. Duplication of this publication or parts thereof is permitted only under the provisions of the German Copyright Law of September 9, 1965, in its current version, and permission for use must always be obtained from Springer-Verlag. Violations are liable for prosecution under the German Copyright Law.

Springer-Verlag Berlin Heidelberg New York
a member of BertelsmannSpringer Science+Business Media GmbH
© Springer-Verlag Berlin Heidelberg 2000
Printed in Germany

Typesetting: Camera-ready by author, data conversion by Steingräber Satztechnik GmbH, Heidelberg
Printed on acid-free paper   SPIN 10722573   06/3142   5 4 3 2 1 0

Preface

This book is the proceedings volume of the 10th International Conference on Field-Programmable Logic and its Applications (FPL), held August 27 - 30, 2000 in Villach, Austria, which covered areas like reconfigurable logic (RL), reconfigurable computing (RC), and its applications, and all other aspects. Its subtitle "The Roadmap to Reconfigurable Computing" reminds us, that we are currently witnessing the runaway of a breakthrough. The annual FPL series is the eldest international conference in the world covering configware and all its aspects. It was founded 1991 at Oxford University (UK) and is 2 years older than its two most important competitors usually taking place at Monterey and Napa. FPL has been held at Oxford, Vienna, Prague, Darmstadt, London, Tallinn, and Glasgow (also see: http://www.fpl.uni-kl.de/FPL/).

The New Case for Reconfigurable Platforms: Converging Media. Indicated by palmtops, smart mobile phones, many other portables, and consumer electronics, media such as voice, sound, video, TV, wireless, cable, telephone, and Internet continue to converge. This creates new opportunities and even necessities for reconfigurable platform usage. The new converged media require high volume, flexible, multi-purpose, multi-standard, low power products adaptable to support evolving standards, emerging new standards, field upgrades, bug fixes, and, to meet the needs of a growing number of different kinds of services offered to zillions of individual subscribers preferring different media mixes.

The traditional name (FPL) of this conference no longer indicated its entire scope, which had been substantially extended and also covered evolvable and adaptable systems, coarse grain reconfigurable (sub)systems, their synthesis methods and applications, their indispensable role in System-on-Chip (SoC) development, as well as RC as an emerging new paradigm, threatening to shake up the general foundations of computer science: computing in space vs. computing in time. Several keynotes of this conference covered such aspects of the configware wave rolling in.

What was new at FPL 2000? With a number of papers FPL 2000 was beginning to bridge the gap between the RL & RC club and the Evolvable Hardware (EH) scene having its own conferences. Until a few months before the conference, network processors had only been subject of NDAs, creating a frustrating difference between usage and publications - frustrating to people interested in studying the technical issues of the high growth rate Internet business. FPL 2000 was the first conference at which this gap was filled by a number of papers, not only on network processors, but also on SoC design for next generation mobile wireless communication.

Goals. FPL 2000 had the goal of providing a preview of what we can expect in the new millennium, and, a roadmap to next generation reconfigurable systems (RS) and their application: hardware, configware, software and application development tools, IP core usage, SoC design, as well as RS technology. It was an important goal of the conference, to bring together experts, users, newcomers, and students from industry and academia.

Growing acceptance. The size of FPL conferences has increased rapidly, from 90 (FPL 1998) to 144 (1999). From 1999 to 2000 the number of papers submitted more than doubled. Our goal for FPL-2000 was to keep this growth rate and to reach an attendance 200 or beyond. The advance program was compiled from 131 papers, which came from 30 different countries:

Germany:	23	France:	5	Mexico:	3	Switzerland:	2	Ireland:	1
US:	20	Austria:	4	Netherlands:	3	Argentina:	1	Norway:	1
UK:	15	Czech Rep.:	4	Brazil:	2	Australia:	1	Portugal:	1
Japan:	12	Canada:	3	China:	2	Belgium:	1	Slovakia:	1
Spain:	7	Greece:	3	Finland:	2	Belarus:	1	Slovenia:	1
Poland:	5	India	3	Sweden:	2	Estonia:	1	Thailand:	1

Accepted. The program committee accepted for presentation 64 regular papers, 21 posters, and 10 student papers. Another 6 papers were invited papers or (invited) keynotes. Each submitted paper had been sent to four reviewers to meet the goal of an average of at least three reviews per paper. We gratefully acknowledge the organizational work done by staff at the Carinthia Tech Institute at Villach.

Acknowledgments. We would like to thank the authors for submitting first versions and for preparing the final versions of the accepted papers, as well as the members of our Program Committee and all other reviewers listed on the next page. We especially express our thankfulness to Thomas Hoffmann from Kaiserslautern University for managing the review process and for assembling the proceedings volume, as well as Michael Herz and Ulrich Nageldinger for supporting him whenever needed. We gratefully acknowledge the excellent cooperation with Alfred Hofmann of Springer-Verlag, being FPL's official publisher now for the 8th year.

June, 2000   Herbert Grünbacher, General Chair
                                                            Reiner Hartenstein, Program Chair

Program Committee:

Nazeeh Aranki, Jet Propulsion Laboratory, USA
Peter Athanas, Virginia Tech, USA
Samary Baranov, Ben Gurion University Negev, Israel
Jürgen Becker, Darmstadt University of Technology, Germany
Neil Bergman, Queensland University of Technology, Australia
Eduardo Boemo Scalvinoni, University of Madrid, Spain
Gordon Brebner, University of Edinburgh, Scotland
Klaus Buchenrieder, Infineon Technologies AG, Germany
Michael Butts, Synopsys, Inc., USA
Stephen Casselman, Virtual Computer Corp., USA
Bernard Courtois, TIMA Laboratory, France
Andre DeHon, California Institute of Technology, USA
Carl Ebeling, University of Washington, USA
Hossam Elgindy, University of Newcastle, Australia
Norbert Fristacky, Slovak Technical University, Slovakia
John Gray, Algotronix Ltd., UK
Manfred Glesner, Darmstadt University of Technology, Germany
Herbert Grünbacher, Carinthia Tech Institute, Austria
Stephen Guccione, Xilinx Inc., USA
Richard Hagelauer, Kepler-University of Linz, Austria
Wolfgang Halang, University of Hagen, Germany
Reiner Hartenstein, University of Kaiserslautern, Germany
Scott Hauck, University of Washington, USA
Michael Herz, University of Kaiserslautern, Germany
Thomas Hoffmann, University of Kaiserslautern, Germany
Brad Hutchings, Brigham Young University, USA
Udo Kebschull, University of Leipzig, Germany
Andres Keevallik, Tallinn Technical University, Estonia
Andreas Koch, TU Braunschweig, Germany
Tom Kean, Algotronix Ltd., UK
Dominique Lavenier, Los Alamos National Laboratory, USA
Jason Lohn, NASA Ames Research Center, USA
Wayne Luk, Imperial College, UK
Patrick Lysaght, Strathclyde University, Scotland
Reinhard Männer, University of Mannheim, Germany
Bill Mangione-Smith, University of California at Los Angeles, USA
John McCanny, The Queen´s University of Belfast, Northern Ireland
George Milne, University of South Australia, Australia
Toshiaki Miyazaki, NTT Laboratories, Japan
Ulrich Nageldinger, University of Kaiserslautern, Germany
Viktor Prasanna, University of Southern California, USA
Jonathan Rose, University of Toronto, Canada

Zoran Salcic, University of Auckland, New Zealand
John Schewel, Virtual Computer Corp., USA
Hartmut Schmeck, University of Karlsruhe, Germany
Christian Siemers, University of Applied Sciences Heide, Germany
Moshe Sipper, EPFL, Lausanne, Switzerland
Stephen Smith, Altera Corp., USA
Rainer Spallek, Dresden University of Technology, Germany
Adrian Stoica, Jet Propulsion Laboratory, USA
Kalle Tammemäe, Tallinn Technical University, Estonia
Jürgen Teich, University of Paderborn, Germany
Lothar Thiele, ETH Zürich, Switzerland
Stephen Trimberger, Xilinx Corp., USA
Kjell Torkelsson, Ericsson Telecom AB, Sweden
Ranga Vemuri, University of Cincinnati, USA
Roger Woods, The Queen's University of Belfast, Northern Ireland
Hiroto Yasuura, Kyushu University, Japan

Reviewers:

Hideharu Amano, Keio University, Japan
Theodore Antonakopoulos, University of Patras, Greece
Jeffrey Arnold, Adaptive Silicon, Inc., USA
Utz Baitinger, University of Stuttgart, Germany
Erich Barke, University of Hannover, Germany
Don Bouldin, University of Tennessee, USA
Ansgar Bredenfeld, GMD, Germany
Jordi Carrabina, Universitat Autònoma de Barcelona, Spain
Andrei Dinu, De Montfort University, UK
Adam Donlin, Edinburgh University, Scotland
Dietmar Fey, University of Siegen, Germany
Masahiro Fujita, University of Tokyo, Japan
Ulrich Golze, TU Braunschweig, Germany
Costas Goutis, University of Patras, Greece
Jörg Henkel, NEC Inc., USA
Sorin Huss, Darmstadt University of Technology, Germany
Hideyuki Ito, NTT Network Innovation Lab., Japan
Andreas Kirschbaum, Continental Teves AG, Germany
Rainer Kress, Infineon Technologies AG, Germany
Holger Kropp, University of Hannover, Germany
Helena Krupnova, INPG, France
Parag Lala, University of Arkansas, USA
Rudy Lauwereins, Université Catholique de Louvain, Belgium
Liam Marnane, University College Cork, UK
Tsutomu Maruyama, University of Tsukuba, Japan
Friedrich Mayer-Lindenberg, TU Hamburg-Harburg, Germany
Masato Motomura, NEC Corporation, Japan
Klaus Müller-Glaser, University of Karlsruhe, Germany
Wolfgang Nebel, University of Oldenburg, Germany

Adam Pawlak, Silesian University of Technology, Poland
Toomas Plaks, South Bank University, UK
Miodrag Potkonjak, University of California at Los Angeles, USA
Bernard Pottier, University of Brest, France
Franz J. Rammig, University of Paderborn, Germany
Wolfgang Rosenstiel, University of Tübingen, Germany
Eduardo Sanchez, EPFL, Lausanne, Switzerland
Alexander Sedlmeier, Infineon Technologies AG, Germany
Micaela Serra, University of Victoria, Canada
Dimitrios Soudris, Democritus University of Thrace, Greece
Joern Stohmann, Infineon Technologies AG, Germany
Toshinori Sueyoshi, Kumamoto University, Japan
Russell Tessier, University of Massachusetts, USA
Anne-Marie Trullemans-Ankaert, Université Catholique de Louvain, Belgium
Klaus Waldschmidt, University of Frankfurt, Germany
Norbert Wehn, University of Kaiserslautern, Germany
Markus Weinhardt, Imperial College, UK

Steering Committee:

Manfred Glesner, Darmstadt University of Technology
John Gray, Algotronix Ltd., UK (lifetime honorary member)
Herbert Grünbacher, Carinthia Tech Institute, Austria
Reiner Hartenstein, University of Kaiserslautern, Germany
Andres Keevallik, University of Tallinn, Estonia
Wayne Luk, Imperial College, UK
Patrick Lysaght, Strathclyde University, Scotland

Industrial Liaisons:

Axel Sikora, BA Lörrach, Germany

Michal Servit Award Committee:

Gordon Brebner, University of Edinburgh, Scotland
Manfred Glesner, Darmstadt University of Technology, Germany
John Schewel, Virtual Computer Corp., USA (Sponsor)
Hartmut Schmeck, University of Karlsruhe, Germany
Hiroto Yasuura, Kyushu University, Japan

Student Papers:

Peter Zipf, University of Siegen, Germany
Thomas Hoffmann, University of Kaiserslautern, Germany

Table of Contents

Invited Keynote

The Rising Wave of Field Programmability 1
Makimoto, T.

Tightly Integrated Design Space Exploration
with Spatial and Temporal Partitioning in SPARCS 7
Govindarajan, S.; Vemuri, R.

Network Processors

A Dynamically Reconfigurable FPGA-Based Content Addressable
Memory for Internet Protocol Characterization 19
Ditmar, J.; Torkelsson, K.; Jantsch, A.

A Compiler Directed Approach to Hiding Configuration Latency in
Chameleon Processors 29
Tang, X.; Aalsma, M.; Jou, R.

Reconfigurable Network Processors Based on Field Programmable
System Level Integrated Circuits 39
Iliopoulos, M.; Antonakopoulos, T.

Internet Connected FPL 48
Fallside, H.; Smith, M.J.S.

Prototyping

Field Programmable Communication Emulation
and Optimization for Embedded System Design 58
Renner, F.-M.; Becker, J.; Glesner, M.

FPGA-Based Emulation: Industrial and Custom Prototyping Solutions 68
Krupnova, H.; Saucier, G.

FPGA-Based Prototyping for Product Definition 78
Kress, R.; Pyttel, A.; Sedlmeier, A.

Implementation of Virtual Circuits by Means of the FIPSOC Devices 87
Cantó, E.; Moreno, J.M.; Cabestany, J.; Lacadena, I.; Insenser, J.M.

Dynamically Reconfigurable I

Static and Dynamic Reconfigurable Designs for a 2D Shape-Adaptive DCT 96
Gause, J.; Cheung, P.Y.K.; Luk, W.

A Self-Reconfigurable Gate Array Architecture 106
Sidhu, R.; Wadhwa, S.; Mei, A.; Prasanna, V.K.

Multitasking on FPGA Coprocessors 121
Simmler, H.; Levinson, L.; Männer, R.

Design Visualisation for Dynamically Reconfigurable Systems 131
Vasilko, M.

Verification of Dynamically Reconfigurable Logic 141
Robinson, D.; Lysaght, P.

Miscellaneous I

Design of a Fault Tolerant FPGA 151
Bartzick, T.; Henze, M.; Kickler, J.; Woska, K.

Real-Time Face Detection on a Configurable Hardware System 157
McCready, R.

Multifunctional Programmable Single-Board CAN Monitoring Module 163
Pfeifer, P.

Self-Testing of Linear Segments in User-Programmed FPGAs 169
Tomaszewicz, P.

Implementing a Fieldbus Interface Using an FPGA 175
Lías, G.; Valdés, M.D.; Domínguez, M.A.; Moure, M.J.

Technology Mapping and Routing & Placement

Area-Optimized Technology Mapping for Hybrid FPGAs 181
Krishnamoorthy, S.; Swaminathan, S.; Tessier, R.

CoMGen: Direct Mapping of Arbitrary Components into LUT-Based FPGAs 191
Abke, J.; Barke, E.

Efficient Embedding of Partitioned Circuits onto Multi-FPGA Boards 201
Chandra Jain, S.; Kumar, A.; Kumar, S.

A Placement Algorithm for FPGA Designs with Multiple I/O Standards 211
Anderson, J.; Saunders, J.; Nag, S.; Madabhushi, C.; Jayaraman, R.

A Mapping Methodology for Code Trees onto LUT-Based FPGAs 221
Kropp, H.; Reuter, C.

Biologically Inspired Methods

Possibilities and Limitations of Applying Evolvable Hardware
to Real-World Applications 230
Torresen, J.

A Co-processor System with a Virtex FPGA for Evolutionary Computation 240
Yamaguchi, Y.; Miyashita, A.; Maruyama, T.; Hoshino, T.

System Design with Genetic Algorithms 250
Bauer, C.; Zipf, P.; Wojtkowiak, H.

Implementing Kak Neural Networks on a Reconfigurable Computing Platform 260
Zhu, J.; Milne, G.

Compact Spiking Neural Network Implementation in FPGA 270
Maya, S.; Reynoso, R.; Torres, C.; Arias-Estrada, M.

Invited Keynote

Silicon Platforms for the Next Generation Wireless Systems -
What Role Does Reconfigurable Hardware Play? 277
Rabaey, J.M.

Invited Papers

From Reconfigurability to Evolution in Construction Systems:
Spanning the Electronic, Microfluidic and Biomolecular Domains 286
McCaskill, J.S.; Wagler, P.

A Specific Test Methodology for Symmetric SRAM-Based FPGAs 300
Renovell, M.

Mobile Communication

DReAM: A Dynamically Reconfigurable Architecture
for Future Mobile Communication Applications 312
Becker, J.; Pionteck, T.; Glesner, M.

Fast Carrier and Phase Synchronization Units for Digital Receivers
Based on Re-configurable Logic 322
Blaickner, A.; Nagy, O.; Grünbacher, H.

Software Radio Reconfigurable Hardware System (SHaRe) 332
Revés, X.; Gelonch, A.; Casadevall, F.; García, J.L.

Analysis of RNS-FPL Synergy for High Throughput DSP Applications:
Discrete Wavelet Transform 342
Ramírez, J.; García, A.; Fernández, P.G.; Parilla, L.; Lloris, A.

Dynamically Reconfigurable II

Partial Run-Time Reconfiguration Using JRTR 352
McMillan, S.; Guccione, S.A.

A Combined Approach to High-Level Synthesis
for Dynamically Reconfigurable Systems 361
Zhang, X.-j.; Ng, K.-w.; Luk, W.

A Hybrid Prototyping Platform for Dynamically Reconfigurable Designs 371
Rissa, T.; Niittylahti, J.

Task Rearrangement on Partially Reconfigurable FPGAs with
Restricted Buffer 379
ElGindy, H.; Middendorf, M.; Schmeck, H.; Schmidt, B.

Design Space Exploration

Generation of Design Suggestions for Coarse-Grain
Reconfigurable Architectures 389
Hartenstein, R.; Herz, M.; Hoffmann, Th.; Nageldinger, U.

Mapping of DSP Algorithms on Field Programmable Function Arrays 400
Heysters, P.M.; Smit, J.; Smit, G.J.M.; Havinga, P.J.M.

On Availability of Bit-Narrow Operations in General-Purpose Applications 412
Stefanović, D.; Martonosi, M.

A Comparison of FPGA Implementations of Bit-Level
and Word-Level Matrix Multipliers 422
Grover, R.S.; Shang, W.; Li, Q.

A New Floorplanning Method for FPGA Architectural Research 432
Wolz, F.; Kolla, R.

Miscellaneous II

Efficient Self-Reconfigurable Implementations Using On-chip Memory 443
Wadhwa, S.; Dandalis, A.

Design and Implementation of an XC6216 FPGA Model in Verilog 449
Glasmacher, A.; Woska, K.

Reusable DSP Functions in FPGA´s 456
Andrejas, J.; Trost, A.

A Parallel Pipelined SAT Solver for FPGAs 462
Redekopp, M.; Dandalis, A.

A Multi-node Dynamic Reconfigurable Computing System
with Distributed Reconfiguration Controller 469
Touhafi, A.

Applications I

A Reconfigurable Stochastic Model Simulator
for Analysis of Parallel Systems 475
Yamamoto, O.; Shibata, Y.; Kurosawa, H.; Amano, H.

A CORDIC Arctangent FPGA Implementation
for a High-Speed 3D-Camera System 485
Bellis, S.J.; Marnane, W.P.

Reconfigurable Computing for Speech Recognition:
Preliminary Findings 495
Melnikoff, S.J.; James-Roxby, P.B.; Quigley, S.F.; Russell, M.J.

Security Upgrade of Existing ISDN Devices by
Using Reconfigurable Logic 505
Ploog, H.; Schmalisch, M.; Timmermann, D.

The Fastest Multiplier on FPGAs with Redundant Binary Representation 515
Miomo, T.; Yasuoka, K.; Kanazawa, M.

Optimization

High-Level Area and Performance Estimation
of Hardware Building Blocks on FPGAs 525
Enzler, R.; Jeger, T.; Cottet, D.; Tröster, G.

Balancing Logic Utilization and Area Efficiency in FPGAs 535
Tessier, R.; Giza, H.

Performance Penalty for Fault Tolerance in Roving STARs 545
*Emmert, J.M.; Stroud, C.E.; Cheatham, J.; Taylor, A.M.;
Kataria, P.; Abramovici, M.*

Optimum Functional Decomposition for LUT-Based FPGA Synthesis 555
Qiao, J.; Ikeda, M.; Asada, K.
Optimization of Run-Time Reconfigurable Embedded Systems 565
Eisenring, M.; Platzner, M.

Invited Keynote

It's FPL, Jim - But Not as We Know It!
Opportunities for the New Commercial Architectures 575
Kean, T.

Invited Paper

Reconfigurable Systems: New Activities in Asia 585
Amano, H.; Shibata, Y.; Uno, M.
StReAm: Object-Oriented Programming
of Stream Architectures Using PAM-Blox 595
Mencer, O.; Hübert, H.; Morf, M.; Flynn, M.J.

Architectures

Stream Computations Organized for Reconfigurable Execution (SCORE) 605
Caspi, E.; Chu, M.; Huang, R.; Yeh, J.; Wawrzynek, J.; DeHon, A.
Memory Access Schemes for Configurable Processors 615
Lange, H.; Koch, A.
Generating Addresses for Multi-dimensional Array Access
in FPGA On-chip Memory 626
Döring, A.C.; Lustig, G.
Combining Serialisation and Reconfiguration for FPGA Designs 636
Derbyshire, A.; Luk, W.

Methodology and Technology

Multiple-Wordlength Resource Binding 646
Constantinides, G.A.; Cheung, P.Y.K.; Luk, W.
Automatic Temporal Floorplanning with Guaranteed Solution Feasibility 656
Vasilko, M.; Benyon-Tinker, G.
A Threshold Logic-Based Reconfigurable Logic Element
with a New Programming Technology 665
Aoyama, K.; Sawada, H.; Nagoya, A.; Nakajima, K.
Exploiting Reconfigurability for Effective Detection
of Delay Faults in LUT-Based FPGAs 675
Krasniewski, A.

Compilation and Related Issues

Dataflow Partitioning and Scheduling Algorithms for WASMII,
a Virtual Hardware 685
Takayama, A.; Shibata, Y.; Iwai, K.; Amano, H.

Compiling Applications for ConCISe:
An Example of Automatic HW/SW Partitioning and Synthesis 695
Kastrup, B.; Trum, J.; Moreira, O.; Hoogerbrugge, J.; van Meerbergen, J.

Behavioural Language Compilation with Virtual Hardware Management 707
Diessel, O.; Milne, G.

Synthesis and Implementation
of RAM-Based Finite State Machines in FPGAs 718
Sklyarov, V.

Applications II

Evaluation of Accelerator Designs for Subgraph Isomorphism Problem 729
Ichikawa, S.; Saito, H.; Udorn, L.; Konishi, K.

The Implementation of Synchronous Dataflow Graphs
Using Reconfigurable Hardware 739
Edwards, M.; Green, P.

Multiplexer Based Reconfiguration for Virtex Multipliers 749
Courtney, T.; Turner, R.; Woods, R.

Efficient Building of Word Recognizer in FPGAs
for Term-Document Matrices Construction 759
Bobda, C.; Lehmann, T.

Short Papers

Reconfigurable Computing between Classifications and Metrics -
The Approach of Space/Time-Scheduling 769
Siemers, C.

FPGA Implementation of a Prototype WDM On-Line Scheduler 773
Cheng, W.W.; Wilton, S.J.E.; Hamidzadeh, B.

An FPGA Based Scheduling Coprocessor for
Dynamic Priority Scheduling in Hard-Time Systems 777
Hildebrandt, J.; Timmermann, D.

Formal Verification of a Reconfigurable Microprocessor 781
Sawitzki, S.; Schönherr, J.; Spallek, R.G.; Straube, B.

The Role of the Embedded Memories in the Implementation
of Artificial Neural Networks 785
Gadea, R.; Herrero, V.; Sebastia, A.; Mocholí, A.

Programmable System Level Integration
Brings System-on-Chip Design to the Desktop 789
Lafayette, G.L.

On Applying Software Development Best Practice to FPGAs
in Safety-Critical Systems 793
Hilton, A.; Hall, J.

Pre-route Assistant: A Routing Tool for Run-Time Reconfiguration 797
Blodget, B.

High Speed Computation of Lattice gas Automata with FPGA 801
Kobori, T.; Maruyama, T.; Hoshino, T.

An Implementation of Longest Prefix Matching
for IP Router on Plastic Cell Architecture 805
Shiozawa, T.; Imlig, N.; Nagami, K.; Oguri, K.; Nagoya, A.; Nakada, H.

FPGA Implementation of an Extended Binary GCD Algorithm
for Systolic Reduction of Rational Numbers 810
Mătăsaru, B.; Jebelean, T.

Toward Uniform Approach to Design of Evolvable
Hardware Based Systems 814
Sekanina, L.; Sllame, A.M.

Educational Programmable Hardware Prototyping
and Verification System 818
Trost, A.; Zemva, A.; Zajc, B.

A Stream Processor Architecture Based on the Configurable CEPRA-S 822
Hoffmann, R.; Ulmann, B.; Völkmann, K.-P.; Waldschmidt, S.

An Innovative Approach to Couple EDA Tools
with Reconfigurable Hardware 826
Hatnik, U.; Haufe, J.; Schwarz, P.

FPL Curriculum at Tallinn Technical University 830
Tammemäe, K.; Evartson, T.

The Modular Architecture of SYNTHUP, FPGA Based PCI Board
for Real-Time Sound Synthesis and Digital Signal Processing 834
Raczinski, J.-M.; Sladek, S.

A Rapid Prototyping Environment for Microprocessor Based System-on-Chips
and Its Application to the Development of a Network Processor 838
Brinkmann, A.; Langen, D.; Rückert, U.

Configuration Prefetching for Non-deterministic Event Driven
Multi-context Schedulers 842
Noguera, J.; Badia, R.M.

Wireless Base Station Design
Using a Reconfigurable Communications Processor 846
Phillips, C.

Placement of Linear Arrays 849
Fabiani, E.; Lavenier, D.

Author Index 853

The Rising Wave of Field Programmability

Tsugio Makimoto

Hitachi, Ltd. New Marunouchi Bldg., 5-1, marunouchi 1-chome Chiyoda-ku,
Tokyo, 100-8220 Japan

Introduction

There have been alternating cycles of standardization and customization in the semiconductor industry, which I first noticed in 1987. It later appeared in Electronics Weekly (U.K.) in January 1991 under the name of Makimoto's wave. As shown in Fig. 1, there have been changes in direction roughly every ten years.

A prediction was made, more than ten years ago, that field programmability would become a leading technology during the standardization cycle that would start around 1997. Today, the prediction has come true and we are seeing a rising wave of field programmable technologies.

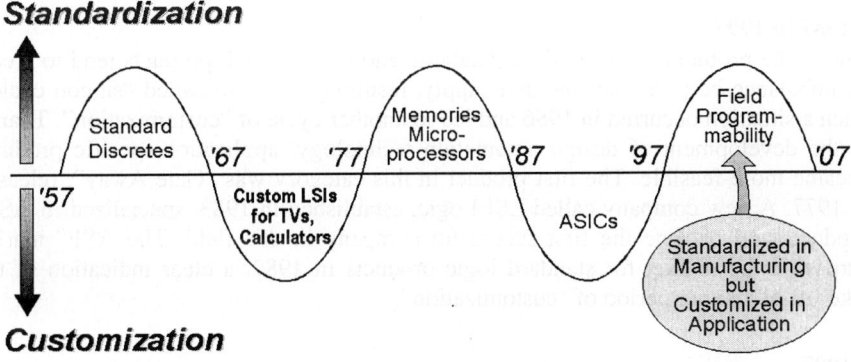

Fig. 1. Makimoto's Wave

Historical Review

•1947 to 1957
The big bang of the semiconductor industry occurred in 1947, when the transistor was invented by William Shockley, Walter Brattain, and John Bardeen at Bell Telephone Laboratories. The following ten years were mostly devoted to researching and refining devices for mass production.

• 1957 to 1967
This decade saw the take-off of the semiconductor industry based on discrete devices, such as transistors and diodes. Because these devices were interchangeable, a cycle of "standardization" began.

• 1967 to 1977
The IC chip was invented in 1958 by Jack Kilby of Texas Instruments. The actual take-off of the chip industry started after several years of incubation, around 1967. Circuits were customized for specific applications, so a cycle of "customization" began. A key product developed during this period was the electronic calculator, and custom chips had to be designed and built to differentiate the calculator functions. As the "calculator war" escalated, the life cycles of calculator chips became shorter, and production volumes decreased, resulting in decreased operational efficiency. That was the end of the "customization" cycle.

• 1977 to 1987
The cycle of customization led to the microprocessor being invented and introduced to the market in 1971 by Intel. Processor chips made it possible to provide different types of calculator functions flexibly by means of a "program" stored in a memory chip. By about 1977, the combined market for microprocessor and memory chips reached 1 billion dollars, showing the clear take-off of the cycle of "standardization".

• 1987 to 1997
One of the problems with product standardization is that such products tend to create an imbalance between demand and supply, resulting in the so-called "silicon cycle". Such a situation occurred in 1986 and led to another cycle of "customization". Thanks to the development of design automation technology, application-specific products became more feasible. The first product in this category was "Gate Away", released in 1977. A new company called LSI Logic, established in 1983, specialized in ASIC products and became the first successful company in this field. The ASIC market surpassed the market for standard logic products in 1987, a clear indication of the take-off of another period of "customization".

• 1997 -
In the past several years, we have observed the emergence of a new market segment, the "Digital Consumer (DC)" market, which includes cellular phones, digital cameras, and game machines. In the consumer market, fine tuning to each specific segment is a strong requirement and the life cycle of products tends to be shorter. New technologies are required for satisfying the requirement. Makimoto's wave indicates the need for field programmable technologies around 1997 to respond to individual market requirements while keeping operational efficiency, leading to the next cycle of "standardization".

It is evident that the prediction has come true since we are now observing a rising wave of field programmability. For example, the FPGA market surpassed the low-density GA market (less than 10K gates) in 1995 and surpassed the total GA market in 1999. Another example is our own experience. Hitachi has been promoting the flash memory on chip MCU called F-ZTAT™, to provide more flexibility based on field programmability. The product was introduced to the market in 1996 and exceeded the milestone figure of 1M/month in 1997, corresponding to the start of new "standardization" cycle.

Semiconductor Pendulum and Acting/Reacting Forces

Imagine a long pendulum swinging back and forth between standardization and customization. There are various forces acting on and reacting to the pendulum, as shown in Fig. 2.

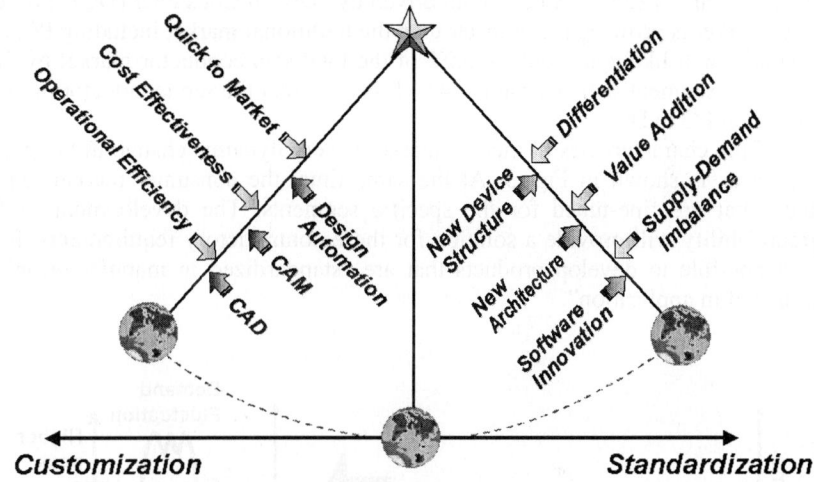

Fig. 2. Semiconductor Pendulum

When the pendulum swings too far toward standardization, there will be such reacting forces as

- Need for differentiation
- Need for value addition
- Market confusion due to supply-demand imbalance

On the other hand, when the pendulum swings too far toward customization, there will be such reacting forces as

- Better operational efficiency
- Improved cost effectiveness
- Faster time to market

Various kinds of semiconductor technologies act on the pendulum. For example, the invention of the microprocessor pushed the pendulum towards standardization around 1977. That was based on innovations in architecture and software. Another example is the progress of design automation technology around 1987, which pushed the pendulum back towards customization.

Today's rising trend of standardization (1997-) depends on innovations in device structures as well as in architectures.

Shift in Market Structure: from PC to DC

PCs have been the major driving force of the chip industry for the past two decades. However, we are observing a new trend driven by "Digital Consumer (DC)" products. The DC market is growing much faster than the traditional market including PCs. The DC segment will likely account for 35% of the total semiconductor market by 2004, while the PC segment will be around 24%. It is clear that the semiconductor market is shifting from PC to DC.

One of the characteristics of the DC market is very dynamic change in the product life cycle, as is shown in Fig. 3. At the same time, the consumer market requires products that are fine-tuned for the specific segments. The development of field programmability will provide a solution for these contradictory requirements. It will make it possible to develop products that are "standardized in manufacturing" but "customized in application".

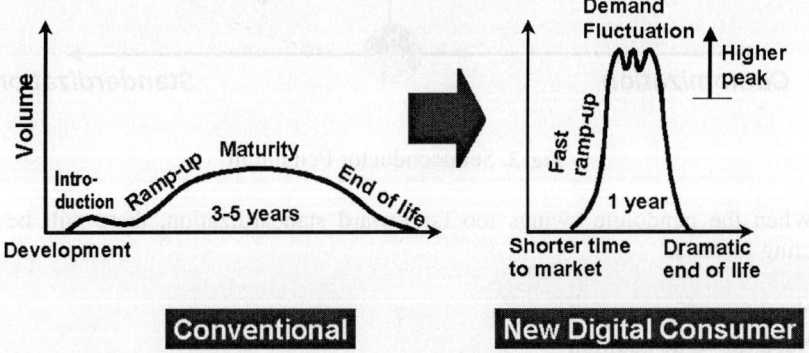

Fig. 3. Dramatic Change in Product Lifecycle

Field Programmable Technologies

There are various different kinds of field programmable devices, some already on the market and others in the laboratory. They use various kinds of non-volatile schemes, including fuse, anti-fuse, EPROM/FEPROM, flash memory, and NV-RAM.

The development of non-volatile (NV) RAM is accelerating. Figure 4 shows the operating principles of two types of NV RAM, namely FRAM and MRAM. NV-RAM will provide a powerful means for achieving a "flexible chip" once the cost and reliability issues have been solved.

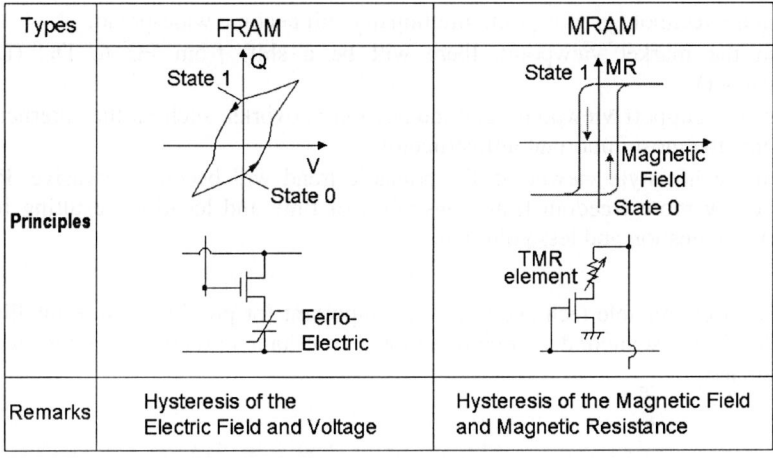

Fig. 4. NV-RAM Technology

Innovation in architectures is also a hot area in the field of programmable technology. The concept of re-configurability will create a new category of semiconductor products: Application-Specific Programmable Products (ASPP). The idea was presented by Jordan Selburn at the 1998 Dataquest Conference. Simply stated, ASPPs are Application-Specific Standard Products (ASSP) with embedded programmable logic that provide hardware flexibility.

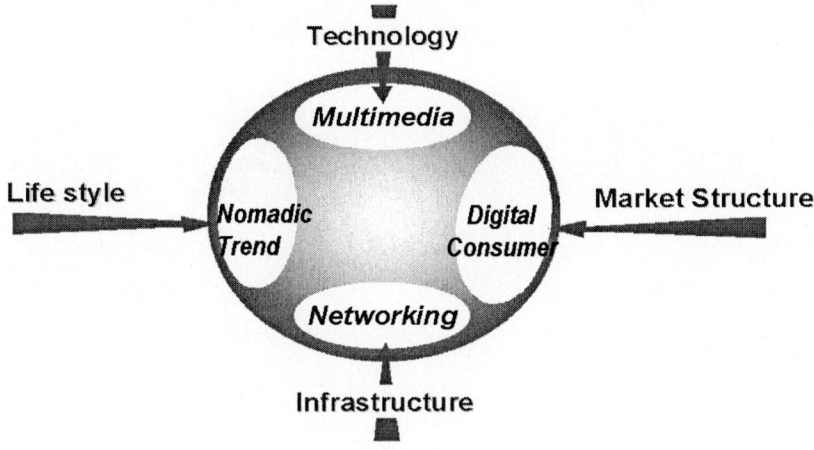

Fig. 5. Future Vision

Future Outlook

Figure 5 shows a vision of our future society in the coming century. Various viewing angles are needed to visualize it.

- From the technology viewpoint, multimedia will become widespread.
- From the market viewpoint, there will be a shift from PC to DC (Digital Consumer).
- From the support viewpoint, communication networks, such as the Internet, will become the most important infrastructure.
- From the life-style viewpoint, the nomadic trend will become pervasive. People will enjoy more freedom from constraints of time and location, resulting in less traffic congestion and less pollution.

Field programmable technology is very important for providing more intelligence and flexibility to semiconductor chips and will contribute to realizing the vision of our future society.

Tightly Integrated Design Space Exploration with Spatial and Temporal Partitioning in SPARCS *

S. Govindarajan and R. Vemuri

Department of ECECS, University of Cincinnati, Cincinnati, OH 45221
sriram@ececs.uc.edu, ranga.vemuri@uc.edu

Abstract. This paper describes the tight integration of design space exploration with spatial and temporal partitioning algorithms in the SPARCS design automation system for RCs. In particular, this paper describes a novel technique to perform efficient design space exploration of parallel-process behaviors using the knowledge of spatial partitioning. The exploration technique satisfies the design latency constraints imposed by temporal partitioning and the device area constraints of the RC. Results clearly demonstrate the effectiveness of the partitioning knowledgeable exploration technique in guiding spatial partitioning to quickly converge to a constraint satisfying solution. Results of design automation through SPARCS and testing designs on a commercial RC board are also presented.

1 Introduction

The Reconfigurable Computer (RC) consisting of multiple FPGA devices, memory banks, and device interconnections, offers a variety of resources but limited in hardware. Figure 1 shows an overview of the SPARCS [1, 2] design automation system for RCs, consisting of a synthesis framework that interacts with a partitioning environment. The RC is viewed as a co-processor that is controlled by a host computer. The SPARCS system accepts a behavioral specification in the form of a Unified Specification Model (USM) [3]. The USM can capture a parallel-process specification in VHDL [4] into a collection of *tasks*, *logical memories* and *flags*.

Temporal partitioning in SPARCS uses the inter-task dependencies to derive a temporal schedule consisting of a sequence of temporal segments where each segment is a subgraph of the USM. The temporal partitioner attempts to minimize the *delay* [1, 2] of the temporal schedule by selecting a latency constraint (L_i) on each temporal segment i. The temporal partitioner ensures that: (i) the collection of tasks in each temporal segment after synthesis will fit within the RC, and (ii) the memory requirements for each temporal segment are within the available physical memory on the RC.

Spatial partitioning in SPARCS involves partitioning each temporal segment such that: (i) the set of tasks in each spatial partition after synthesis will fit within the corresponding device; (ii) the latency constraint is satisfied; (iii) the logical memories are mapped to the physical memory banks on the RC; (iv) the flags and the memory buses are routed through the interconnection network on the RC. It is imperative that spatial partitioning that follows temporal partitioning be done with utmost care so as to satisfy the RC and design constraints. Henceforth, we will use the term *partition* to denote a spatial partition.

Both temporal and spatial partitioning require design estimates that are used to evaluate the partitioning costs. In order to generate efficient Register-Transfer Level (RTL) designs

---

* This work is supported in part by the US Air Force, Wright Laboratory, WPAFB, under contract number F33615-97-C-1043.

that implement the given behavior, HLS and partitioning techniques need to carefully select implementations that best satisfy the constraints. The RC synthesis framework in SPARCS allows tight integration of the partitioning environment with a design space exploration engine through an Exploration Control Interface (ECI). The ECI consists of exploration/estimation methods that a partitioning tool may call to select *design points* (possible implementations) and obtain estimates. After the partitioning and exploration is completed, the ¡back-end HLS tool is constrained by the selected design points to synthesize RTL designs that satisfy these estimates.

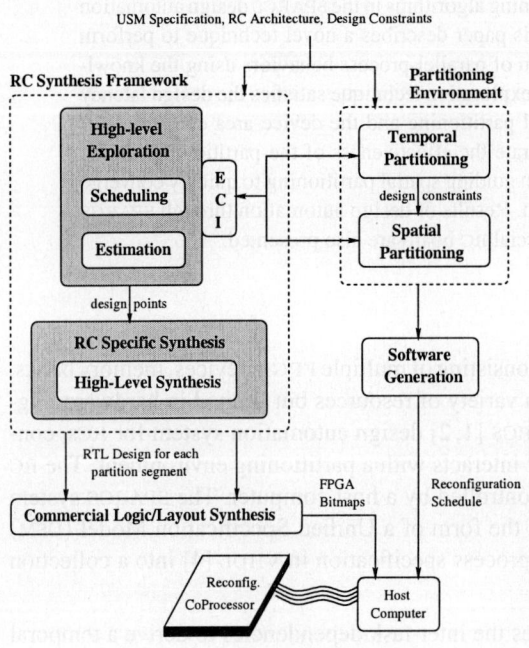

Fig. 1. SPARCS Design Flow

In the *traditional heterogeneous model* of integrated HLS and spatial partitioning, the partitioner invokes a HLS estimator to obtain the area/latency of each spatial partition. Several heterogeneous systems, such as *SpecSyn* [5], *Chop* [6] and *Vulcan I* [7], focussed on providing good design estimates while not performing complete HLS. Later, researchers (COBRA-ABS [8], *Multipar* [9]) developed a completely *homogeneous model*, wherein HLS and partitioning are performed in a single step. The COBRA-ABS system has a Simulated Annealing (SA) based model and *Multipar* has an ILP based model for synthesis and partitioning.

However, unification of spatial partitioning and HLS into a homogeneous model adds to the already complex sub-problems of HLS, leading to a large multi-dimensional design space. Therefore, the cost (design automation time) of having a homogeneous model is very high, i.e, either the run times are quite high (COBRA-ABS [8]) or the model cannot handle large problem sizes (*Multipar* [9]). The traditional heterogeneous model, although less complex, also has a significant drawback of performing exploration on a particular partition segment, *which is only a locality of the entire design space*.

In this paper, we propose a *spatial partitioning knowledgeable exploration technique* that combines the best flavors of both the models. The exploration technique has the capability to simultaneously explore the design space of multiple spatial partitions. This enables exploration and spatial partitioning to generate constraint satisfying designs in cases where the traditional heterogeneous model fails. In [10], we introduced the idea of a partitioning-based exploration model for single-threaded behavioral specifications. In this paper, we extend this to parallel-process (USM) specifications and present the integration of design space exploration with spatial and temporal partitioning in the SPARCS [1] system.

The rest of the paper is organized as follows. Section 2 describes the proposed partitioning knowledgeable exploration model for a USM specification. Section 3 presents the exploration algorithm in detail and describes the ECI. Section 4 presents the integration with the temporal and spatial partitioning in SPARCS. Section 5 presents results comparing the traditional and proposed exploration techniques and test results on a commercial RC. Finally, we present a summary in Section 6.

2 Partitioning Knowledgeable Exploration Model for the USM

The USM embodies a *task graph* that consists of a collection *tasks* (N_{tasks}) and edges representing dependencies (flags) between them. Each task is a CDFG consisting of *blocks* of computation and edges representing control flow. Each block in a task in-turn has a simple data flow graph, while the collection of blocks (in a task) represent a single-thread of control. The collection of tasks the USM represent a parallel control-thread model.

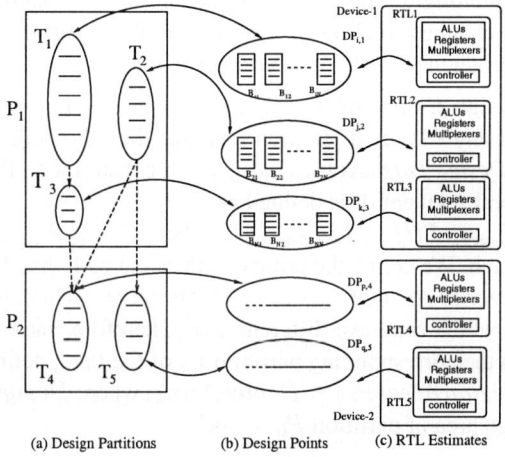

Fig. 2. The USM exploration model

Definitions for Partitioned Task Graph: We define following terms with respect to our partitioned task graph model:
- A *partition* $P_i \subseteq N_{tasks}$, is a subset of tasks in the task graph.
- A *configuration* C_{set} is a set of mutually exclusive partitions of all the tasks. $C_{set} = \{P_i\}$ such that $(\forall T_i \in N_{tasks} : \exists P_k : T_i \in P_k) \wedge (\forall P_i, P_j \in C_{set} : P_i \cap P_j = \emptyset)$
- A *design point* $DP_{i,k}$ corresponds to a specific implementation i of a task k. A design point is essentially a collection of *schedules* [11], one for each block in the CDFG of the task.
- A $L(t)$ is the latency of the task t, defined as the number of clocks cycles per input vector.
- $L_{min}(t)$ is the fastest latency of the task t, corresponding to the ASAP schedules of all its blocks.
- $L_{max}(t)$ is the slowest latency of the task t, corresponding to the slowest (smallest resource bag) schedules of all its blocks.
- $A_{min}(t)$ and $A_{max}(t)$ represent the smallest and largest design areas of task t corresponding to the slowest and fastest schedules, respectively.
- A *design space* of a task t is the set of all possible design points bounded by $L_{min}(t)$

and $L_{max}(t)$. Further, the design space of a partition is the union of the design spaces of all tasks in that partition.

For the partitioned USM shown in Figure 2(a), $C_{set} = \{P_1, P_2\}$, where $P_1 = \{T_1, T_2, T_3\}$ and $P_2 = \{T_4, T_5\}$. Figure 2(b) shows the design points corresponding to each task. From each design point, an RTL design for the corresponding task can be synthesized. In addition, the RTL resource requirements for each individual block of any task is also maintained. Thus, for each design point detailed RTL design estimates are maintained. As shown in Figure 2(c), each partition P_i is synthesized as a collection of RTL designs for the corresponding device in the RC. Note that the blocks belonging to a task share all the datapath resources and a single finite state machine controller.

The exploration model currently does not share hardware between tasks, instead, performs an efficient allocation of the device area to the tasks that are assigned to that partition. In addition, the exploration model attempts to minimize design latency by exploiting the task-level and operation-level parallelism. Nevertheless, the model can be changed to allow sharing by simply modifying the RTL estimation mechanism and introducing a suitable controller model [12].

Design Constraints: The goal of the exploration process is to generate design points for any USM configuration such that the following constraints are best satisfied:
- *Design Latency*($L_{constraint}$): is a constraint on the set of tasks belonging to one temporal segment. It is defined as:
$\sum_{t \in CP} L(t) \leq L_{constraint}$, where $CP \subseteq N_{tasks}$, is the *critical path* of tasks in the graph. We define the critical path as the path that determines the largest total latency.
- *Device Area*($DeviceArea_k$): The target architecture consists of multiple devices each of which can have different area. Therefore, each device k imposes an area constraint on the corresponding partition P_k of the USM, defined as:
$DesignArea(P_k) \leq DeviceArea_k$, where $DesignArea(P_k)$ is the estimated RTL design area of partition P_k.

The exploration engine is also constrained by a *component library* from which resources (ALUs) are selected for scheduling and binding. The user may specify a specific component library for each task.

3 The Exploration Algorithm and the ECI

The exploration algorithm is shown in Figure 3. Given a subset of partitions $P_{set} \subseteq C_{set}$, the algorithm determines the set of tasks $T_{set} = \cup_{P_k \in P_{set}} P_k$ that need to be explored. *The goal of the algorithm is to generate design points for the tasks in T_{set} such that the design constraints are best satisfied*. For each task $t \in T_{set}$, the algorithm initially generates a design point $DP_{fast,t}$ corresponding to the fastest schedule. Therefore, initially each task would have a worst case area but least latency ($L_{min}(t)$). The design points (or schedules) for the rest of the tasks $N_{tasks} - T_{set}$ are left untouched.

The algorithm performs exploration in a loop (lines 4-21), where each iteration *relaxes* or *tightens* the schedule of a task. Relaxing a task corresponds to a latency increase and an area reduction, and tightening works vice versa. During each iteration, the *critical path* and the *design costs* are evaluated. The algorithm maintains the *best solution* (S_{best}, a collection of design points $\forall\, t \in T_{set}$) obtained so far, defined as the one that has the least *total AreaPenalty* $= \sum_{P_k \in C_{set}} AO(P_k)$, where the *Area Overshoot* $AO(P_k) = \begin{cases} \Delta A_k & \text{if } \Delta A_k > 0 \\ 0 & \text{otherwise} \end{cases}$, and $\Delta A_k = DesignArea(P_k) - DeviceArea_k$.

At the core of the exploration algorithm is a collection of cost functions that determine the task to be selected for relaxation (T_r) or tightening (T_t). Using these cost functions the tasks in T_{set} are sorted to form a priority list (P_{list}). While selecting a task for relaxation, the priority list is traversed from left to right, and for tightening from right to left. Each cost function captures an essential aspect of the partitioning knowledgeable exploration model and these functions collectively guide the exploration engine in finding a constraint satisfying design. These cost functions have been listed in the order in which they are applied for sorting the list of tasks:

Partition Area Violation (PAV_t): represents the area violation of the partition to which the task belongs.
$PAV_t = \frac{DesignArea(P_k) - DeviceArea_k}{DeviceArea_k}$,
and $t \in P_k$. The tasks are ordered in increasing PAV_t such that, tasks belonging to the most occupied device are selected for relaxation and tasks belonging to the least occupied device are selected for tightening. Note that all tasks belonging to the same partition will have the same PAV.

Algorithm: USM_Exploration
Input: Design constraints and P_{set}
Output: $\forall P_j \in P_{set}, \forall T_i \in P_j : DP_i$
Begin
1 $T_{set} = \{T_i \mid T_i \in P_i, \forall P_i \in P_{set}\}$
2 $\forall T_i \in T_{set}$: Initialize(T_i)
3 Iteration = 0 // *relax-tighten loop*
4 **while** (Iteration < UpperBound)
5   Compute *critical path*
6   Compute *design costs*
7   Update S_{best}
8   **if** (design fits) **then exit**
9   T_{list} = sorted T_{set}, using costs:
10   1. Decreasing PAV_t
11   2. Increasing C_t
12   3. Increasing LA_t cost
13   Select T_r from T_{list} for Relaxation
14   Select T_t from T_{list} for Tightening
15   **if** ($T_r \neq \emptyset$) **then**
16   Relax(T_r)
17   **else if** ($T_t \neq \emptyset$) **then**
18   Tighten(T_t)
19   **else exit**
20   **end if**
21 **end while**
22 **if** (design did not fit)
23   Restore using S_{best}
24   Re-compute *CP and costs*
25 **end if**
End

Fig. 3. USM Exploration Algorithm

Criticality (C_t): A critical task ($C_t = 1$) belongs to the critical path. Between the set of tasks that belong to one partition, those that do not fall on the critical path are ordered before those that are on the critical path ($C_t = 0$). This is because, non-critical tasks are good candidates for relaxation, since the design latency will not be increased. Similarly, critical tasks are good candidates for tightening, since the design latency will be decreased.

Latency-Area Tradeoff (LA_t): This is the most important cost function that determines the task that is selected among those have equal PAV_t and C_t. For a task t, and the corresponding design point $DP_{i,t}$, we define the latency-area tradeoff cost as follows: $LA_t = \mathcal{L}_{norm}(DP_{i,t}) + \mathcal{A}_{norm}(DP_{i,t})$, where $\mathcal{L}_{norm}(DP_{i,t}) = (\frac{\mathcal{L}(DP_{i,t}) - L_{min}(t)}{L_{max}(t) - L_{min}(t)}) * 100$, and $\mathcal{A}_{norm}(DP_{i,t}) = (\frac{A_{max}(t) - \mathcal{A}(DP_{i,t})}{A_{max}(t) - A_{min}(t)}) * 100$

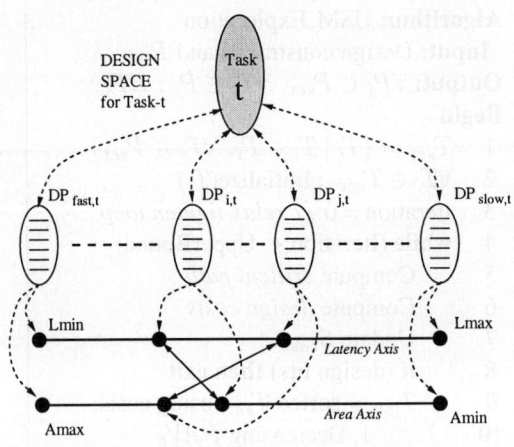

Fig. 4. Design Space of a Task

We will explain this cost function using the pictorial view of the design space of a task shown in Figure 4. For a task t, the set of all design points can be ordered in the latency axis from its $L_{min}(t)$ to $L_{max}(t)$. Correspondingly, the design points for the task t can be ordered on the area axis from $A_{max}(t)$ to $A_{min}(t)$. As shown in Figure 4, for any two design points $DP_{i,t}$ and $DP_{j,t}$ their ordering in both the latency and area axis need not be the same. However, the issue of concern is *how close or far a design point is from the respective bounds*. The cost $\mathcal{L}_{norm}(DP_{i,t})$ is a metric for measuring the distance of the design point $DP_{i,t}$ from the *latency lower bound* $L_{min}(t)$. Similarly, the cost $\mathcal{A}_{norm}(DP_{i,t})$ is a metric for measuring the distance of the design point $DP_{i,t}$ from the *area upper bound* $A_{max}(t)$. Both the costs have been *normalized* within their ranges such that they can be summed up to provide a *closeness factor* (LA_t) of the design point with respect to the latency and area lower bounds.

A low value LA_t implies that the tasks' current area is close to its upper bound and the current latency is close to its lower bound. This means that tasks with low LA_t are good choices for relaxation so that their latency can be increased and their area can be reduced. Similarly, tasks with high LA_t are good choices for tightening. The tasks in priority list are ordered in increasing values of LA_t.

After these costs are applied and the priority list is ordered, the algorithm selects a task for relaxation or tightening. If there exists a task whose latency can be relaxed and still remains within the bound, then algorithm relaxes it, otherwise a task is selected and tightened. In order to relax or tighten a task, the algorithm invokes the block-level exploration algorithm [10]. The block-level algorithm, based on the internal cost metrics of the task, selects and re-schedules the *best block* [10] within that task. For scheduling a task, we use a low-complexity time-constrained scheduling algorithm [13]. The criteria for the relaxation and tightening a task are: (i) the tasks' latency should remain within the bounds, and (ii) the design latency should remain within the given constraint ($\sum_{T_i \in CP} Latency(T_i) \leq L_{constraint}$).

The relax-tighten loop stops when any one of these conditions are met: (i) the design fits – all device area constraints are satisfied, (i) none of the tasks can be relaxed or tightened, or (iii) A lot of exploration time (iterations) has been spent. This is provided so that the exploration time can be cut-off for large design spaces. At the end of the relax-tighten loop, if the design did not fit the best solution is restored.

3.1 The Exploration Control Interface

The Exploration Control Interface (ECI) facilitates tight integration with any partitioning algorithm. The interface consists of a collection of exploration and design area estimation methods that generate design points and area estimates for the current USM configuration. *These methods can be collectively used to control the trade-off between the time spent in exploration and the amount of design space explored.* Here, we present ECI methods and their correlation to the exploration algorithm.

Explore Design(P_{set}): This method invokes the exploration algorithm on the given P_{set}. The method generates a schedule for each task in $P_{set} = \{T_i \mid \forall P_k \in P_{set}, T_i \in P_k\}$, and estimates the design areas of all partitions in P_{set}, such that the constraints are best satisfied. *Since the exploration engine maintains the current configuration of the entire USM, it can find constraint satisfying solutions where a traditional exploration/estimation technique would fail.*

Explore Partition(P_k): This method also invokes the exploration algorithm on $P_{set} = \{P_k\}$. This method is equivalent the *traditional* exploration technique that only performs a *local search* of the design space of one partition. Hence, this is a more constrained method that may not be able to satisfy the design latency and device area constraints as well as the *Explore_Design()* method.

Explore Task(t): This method invokes the block-level exploration algorithm [10] on all blocks in task t. The goal of the algorithm to generate a set of schedules for all blocks in the task t such that the area constraint on partition $P_k \ni t$ and design latency are best satisfied.

Estimate Design(P_k): When this method is invoked there always exist a design point for each task $t \in P_k$. This method performs a post-scheduling estimation to estimate RTL design area of each task. Currently, the partition area is computed as the sum of all task areas. If a shared datapath is implemented, then the estimation method need may be modified accordingly.

4 Integrating Exploration and Partitioning in SPARCS

In this section, we will describe the integration of design space exploration with temporal and spatial partitioning algorithms in SPARCS.

4.1 Interaction with Temporal Partitioning

The ideal approach is to integrate the temporal partitioner with a spatial partitioner and let the spatial partitioner determine the RC hardware utilization dynamically. For temporal partitioners that are based on optimal models such as ILP, such as in SPARCS [14], this approach will be time consuming and impractical. In SPARCS, the temporal partitioner assumes a lumped model of the RC (summed device area and memory space) and without considering the effects of spatial partitioning in detail. Nevertheless, SPARCS incorporates a detailed feedback to temporal partitioning, in the case when spatial partitioning fails on any temporal segment.

The lumped RC area is set as a constraint to the exploration engine and all tasks are placed in one partition. The *Explore_design()* method is invoked several times with varying design latency constraints at equidistant points within the bounds on the *entire design latency* (for all tasks). For each invocation of *Explore_design()*, a design point is generated for each task. Thus, prior to temporal partitioning in SPARCS, several design points are generated for each task in the USM. This enables the temporal partitioner to contemplate multiple implementations of a task, while trying to optimize design latency. At the end of temporal partitioning, a latency constraint is imposed on each temporal segment such that the entire *design delay* (see Section 1) is minimized.

4.2 Interaction with Spatial Partitioning

Following temporal partitioning, each temporal segment is spatially partitioned by the SPARCS system. During partitioning, the ECI enables a tight interaction in order to perform efficient design space exploration.

The spatial partitioning system [1, 15] consists of two partitioning algorithms: (i) A Simulated Annealing (SA-based) and (ii) Genetic Algorithm (GA-based). Figure 5 presents an abstract template representing both algorithms. The bold line numbers indicated places of *dynamic* interaction between the partitioner and the exploration engine. Initially, one (or more) random configuration(s) are generated and the exploration engine generates design points for these. The loop in line-4 represents the outer-loop of the GA *generations* or the SA *temperatures*. The loop in line-5 represents the inner-loop of the GA *population size* or the SA *iterations per temperatures*.

```
Algorithm: Template for GA or SA
1   C_current = Random Initial Configuration
2   ExpEngine.Initialize(C_current)
3   Gen/Temp = Initial Generation or Temp.
4   while (Gen/Temp < Final Value)
5       while (PopSize/Iters < Max Value)
6           C_new = Perturb(C_current)
7           for each (Temporal Seg. G_i ∈ USM)
8               ExpEngine.SetConfig(G_i, C_new)
9               ExpEngine.SetLatency(L_i)
10              ExpEngine.USM_Exploration()
11              ExpEngine.Estimate_Design()
12          end for
13          if (acceptable(C_new,Temp))
14              C_current = C_new
15          end if
16      end while   // PopSize/Iter loop
17  end while   // Gen/Temp loop
```

Fig. 5. Partitioner Template: GA/SA-based

In order to achieve efficient memory utilization, *the spatial partitioning of all temporal segments ($G_i \in USM$) are performed simultaneously* by the USM spatial partitioner [1, 15]. For this purpose, these algorithms maintain a *super-configuration* that is the set of all configurations (spatial partitions) over all temporal segments. During each iteration, the algorithms generate a new super-configuration (C_{new}) by perturbing the existing super-configuration ($C_{current}$). Note that for each temporal segment $G_i \in USM$, there exists a configuration in C_{new} and $C_{current}$.

For each temporal segment G_i, the lines 8-9 pass the current configuration of G_i to the exploration engine and set the corresponding latency constraint L_i. Then, the exploration algorithm is invoked on a temporal segment and the design areas of all spatial partitions in that temporal segment are estimated. This way, exploration and estimation are performed for all temporal segments ($G_i \in USM$) in a sequence. During the spatial partitioning process, when any configuration is accepted (at line-14) by the GA or SA, the exploration engine is again invoked (the same way) to generate new design points and estimates design areas.

Note: For experimentation, we developed two versions for each partitioning algorithm. The first one represents the *traditional* model of exploration where at any time during spatial partitioning (at line-10) only the single-partition exploration in performed using the *Explore_Partition()* method. The other version represents the *proposed* model where at line-10 always the multi-partition exploration is performed using the *Explore_Design()* method. Thus, the proposed model always performs a *partitioning knowledgeable exploration* on multiple spatial partitions, whereas the traditional model performs a local search on individual spatial partitions.

5 Results

First, we present results demonstrating the effectiveness of the multi-partition exploration technique as compared to the traditional model of exploring a single partition. Then, we present results of some designs that were synthesized through SPARCS and tested on a commercial RC board.

5.1 Exploration Results from GA-/SA-Based Spatial Partitioners

We have run a number of experiments on a constructed DCT [16] example consisting of 12 tasks. Each task has four vector products and the design space varies from 5 to 20 clocks and on the area axis from 120 to 5,200 CLBs. It can been seen that the design space of the entire design is very large; $(20-5)^{12}$ possible design points, or latency combinations for all tasks. We also constructed a 12-task FFT [16] example that has a very small design space of about 30 design points.

We have considered the *Wildforce* [17] target architecture consisting of four FPGA devices, with fixed and programmable interconnections and 32 K memory banks. The DCT example uses two memory segments with 16 words each for the input and the output 4x4 matrices. The there are eights flags that synchronize the execution of the tasks. The twelve tasks in the DCT example were temporally partitioned into two segments with the 9 tasks in one and three in the other. We ran both the GA and SA spatial partitioners on a *Sun Workstation* with a 128MB RAM and a 143 Mhz *Sparc-5* processor. Both partitioners have a built-in wildforce-specific router and memory estimator [15], that handle the interconnection and memory constraints.

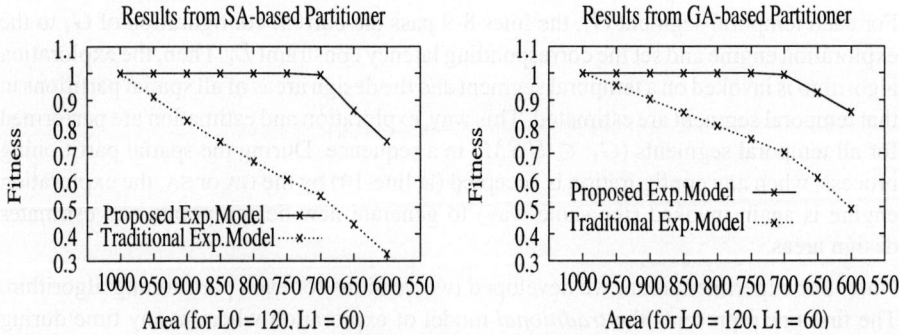

Fig. 6. USM Exploration and Partitioning Results for DCT

We fixed the latency constraints of the two temporal segments at their upper bound values (120 and 60 clocks) and ran both the partitioning algorithms (SA and GA) by varying the device area constraint. Figure 6 shows two plots of the results from the SA-based and the GA-based partitioners. Each plot has the device area constraint on the x-axis and solution *fitness* [1, 15] on the y-axis. Fitness is a measure of the solution quality in terms of the area, memory and interconnect constraints. Any solution always satisfies the latency constraint. A fitness value of 1 indicates that all constraints are satisfied and a *lower fitness* value indicates a *higher violation* of constraints.

Each plot, has two curves representing the solutions generated by invoking the traditional single-partition (dashed lines) and proposed multi-partition exploration models (solid lines) during spatial partitioning. As shown in both plots, for an area constraint of 1000 CLBs(and higher), both exploration models of exploration found constraint satisfying solutions. As we tighten the area (lower than 1000 CLBs), the SA and GA versions that perform a multi-partition exploration find constraint satisfying solutions whereas their traditional counterparts do not. In fact for the traditional models, we can see that the solution quality becomes poorer (fitness < 1) with tighter area constraints. For all these cases, the proposed model found a solution in a few seconds to minutes, whereas, the traditional model could not even after running for over 4-6 hours. This shows that the solution found by the multi-partition exploration does even exist in the local search space of the traditional single-partition exploration.

For the FFT example, both models of exploration generate similar results which can be explained as follows. FFT is not as compute-intensive as the DCT example and each FFT task has only two or three possible implementations with little variation in the design area and latency. This provides no leverage to exploration engine to perform a latency-area trade-off on the tasks. Due to the very limited set of available design points, both exploration models converge easily to the best possible solution.

5.2 Onboard Testing

Figure 7 tabulates results of two designs that were automatically partitioned and synthesized by SPARCS for the *Wildforce* board [17], from *Annapolis Micro Systems*. The FFT design was temporally partitioned into two temporal segments with nine tasks in the first segment and three tasks in the second temporal segment. Using the USM partitioning and exploration environment, both temporal segments were spatially partitioned into the four *XC4013* devices on the board. The spatial partitioning and exploration process completed in 130 seconds on a 143 Mhz *Sun Sparc-5* processor with 128 MB RAM. For DCT, there was no necessity for temporal partitioning since all tasks fit within the four *XC4013*s on Wildforce. The spatial partitioning and exploration process completed in less than a minute on a 143 Mhz *Sun Sparcs-5* processor with 128 MB RAM.

Design Name	TP No.	No. of Tasks	Area (CLBs) Est.	Area (CLBs) Actual	Latency (clks) Constraint	Latency (clks) Actual
FFT	1	9	1541	1392	162	161
	2	3	705	545	82	82
DCT	1	4	2112	2222	84	76

Fig. 7. DCT and FFT tested on Wildforce

These example were further synthesized through commercial logic (*Synplicity*) and layout (*Xilinx M1*) synthesis tools to generate the FPGA bitmaps. These design were loaded and successfully executed on the *Wildforce* board. After behavioral modeling, the complete design automation process including simulations and testing using the SPARCS tools was performed within a day, for each example.

6 Summary

This paper describes the tight integration of design space exploration with spatial and temporal partitioning algorithms in the SPARCS system [1]. In particular, this paper proposes a *spatial partitioning knowledgeable exploration technique* for parallel-process behavioral specifications. The exploration technique has the capability to simultaneously explore the hardware design space of multiple spatial partitions. This enables exploration and spatial partitioning to generate constraint satisfying designs in cases where the traditional exploration model fails. In [10], we introduced the idea of a partitioning-based exploration model for single-process behavioral specifications. In this paper, we extend the model to handle parallel-process (USM, [3]) specifications. Results are presented to demonstrate the effectiveness of the exploration technique and design automation process using SPARCS.

References

1. I. Ouaiss, S. Govindarajan, V. Srinivasan, M. Kaul and R. Vemuri. "An Integrated Partitioning and Synthesis System for Dynamically Reconfigurable Multi-FPGA Architectures". In *Proceedings of the 5th Reconfigurable Architectures Workshop (RAW), Lecture Notes in Computer Science 1388*, pages 31–36, April 1998.

2. S. Govindarajan, I. Ouaiss, V. Srinivasan, M. Kaul and R. Vemuri. "An Effective Design System for Dynamically Reconfigurable Architectures". In *Proceedings of Sixth Annual IEEE Symposium on FPGAs for Custom Computing Machines (FCCM)*, pages 312–313, Napa, California, April 1998. IEEE Computer Society. ISBN 0-8186-8900-5.
3. I. Ouaiss, S. Govindarajan, V. Srinivasan, M. Kaul and R. Vemuri. "A Unified Specification Model of Concurrency and Coordination for Synthesis from VHDL". In *Proceedings of the 4th International Conference on Information Systems Analysis and Synthesis (ISAS)*, July 1998.
4. IEEE Standard 1076-1993. *IEEE Standard VHDL Language Reference Manual*.
5. D. D. Gajski, F. Vahid, et al. . "Specification and Design of Embedded Systems". In *Prentice-Hall Inc.*, Upper Saddle River, NJ, 1994.
6. K. Kucukcakar, and A. Parker. "CHOP: A constraint-driven system-level partitioner". In *Proceedings of the Conference on Design Automation*, pages 514–519, 1991.
7. R. K. Gupta and G. De Micheli. "Partitioning of funtional models of synchronous digital systems". In *Proceesings of the International Conference on Computer-Aided Design*, pages 216–219, 1990.
8. A. A. Duncan, D. C. Hendry and P. Gray. "An Overview of the Cobra-ABS High-Level Synthesis System for Multi-FPGA Systems". In *Proceedings of FPGAs for Custom Computing Machines (FCCM)*, pages 106–115, Napa Valley, California, 1998.
9. Y. Chen, Y. Hsu, and C. King. "MULTIPAR: Behavioral partition for synthesizing multiprocessor architectures". In *IEEE Transactions on VLSI systems*, volume 2, No. 1, pages 21–32, March 1994.
10. S. Govindarajan, V. Srinivasan, P. Lakshmikanthan and R. Vemuri. "A Technique for Dynamic High-Level Exploration During Behavioral-Partitioning for Multi-Device Architectures". In *Proceedings of the 13th International Conference on VLSI Design (VLSI 2000)*, 2000. Received the best paper award.
11. D. D. Gajski, N. D. Dutt, A. C. Wu and S. Y. Lin. *"High-Level Synthesis: Introduction to Chip and System Design"*. Kluwer Academic Publishers, 1992.
12. J. Roy, N. Kumar, R. Dutta and R. Vemuri. "DSS: A Distributed High-Level Synthesis System". In *IEEE Design and Test of Computers*, June 1992.
13. S. Govindarajan and R. Vemuri. "An Efficient Clustering-Based Heuristic for Time-Constrained Static-List Scheduling. In *Proceedings of the IEEE Design, Automation and Test in Europe, DATE Conference*, 2000.
14. M. Kaul and R. Vemuri. "Temporal Partitioning combined with Design Space Exploration for Latency Minimization of Run-Time Reconfigured Designs". In *Design, Automation and Test in Europe, DATE*, pages 202–209. IEEE Computer Society Press, 1999.
15. Vinoo Srinivasan. *"Partitioning in Reconfigurable Computing Environments"*. PhD thesis, University of Cincinnati, ECECS Department, 1999.
16. L. B. Jackson. *"Digital Filters and Signal Processing"*. Kluwer Academic Publishers, second edition, 1989.
17. Wildforce multi-FPGA board by Annapolis Micro Systems, Inc. . "http://www.annapmicro.com".

A Dynamically Reconfigurable FPGA-Based Content Addressable Memory for Internet Protocol Characterization

Johan Ditmar[1], Kjell Torkelsson[1], Axel Jantsch[2]

[1]CadLab Research Center, Ericsson Radio Systems, Stockholm, Sweden.
{johan.ditmar, kjell.torkelsson}@era.ericsson.se
[2] Department of Electronics, Royal Institute of Technology, Stockholm, Sweden.
axel@ele.kth.se

Abstract. Internet Protocol (IP) characterization is the process of classifying IP packets into categories, mainly depending on information in the header. This report describes the implementation of an FPGA-based dynamically reconfigurable Content Addressable Memory (CAM) for IP version 6 (IPv6) characterization. This CAM is characterized by a large width of the search word, a relatively small number of CAM words (i.e. several 100's) and the fact that these words may contain 'don't cares'. The CAM is updated by dynamic reconfiguration and has a novel architecture that allows the space, that each single CAM word occupies, to be variable. A priority mechanism has been developed which allows also to explicitly assign a priority to a CAM entry. This way, CAM words can be added/deleted in a more efficient way.

1 Introduction

The Internet Protocol (IP) provides the basis for interconnections on the Internet. Its application field grows very rapidly as well as the number of users. In the future, IP will not only be used to interconnect computers, but all kinds of equipment will use this protocol to communicate with each other including base stations for cellular communication. Due to the increasing demand for high bandwidth, much effort is spent to make faster IP handling systems. Not only speed, but also flexibility is an important factor here, since new standards and applications have to be supported at all times. A way to gain speed and flexibility is to move critical software functions to reconfigurable hardware.

1.1 Internet Protocol Characterization

One of these critical functions is IP characterization, as done in firewalls and routers. IP characterization is the process of classifying packets into categories that require special treatment. A subset of IP characterization is IP filtering. IP filtering is a security feature that restricts IP traffic by permitting or denying packets by applying certain rules. This way, users can be restricted to specific domains or applications on the Internet. To do characterization, IP headers that reach a router need to be compared to patterns stored in a table, and an output that classifies a packet should be generated. Nowadays, this table is stored in memory and matching is done entirely in software. Due to growing requirements, software-based search algorithms become too slow [6,9] and alternative implementations need to be considered. One alternative is to use a Content Addressable Memory.

1.2 Content Addressable Memories

Content Addressable Memories (CAMs) are memory devices in which search operations can be performed in constant time, independent of the number of locations in the memory. Searches are done by comparing a *search word* which is supplied to the CAM with the contents of a memory in the CAM. If the contents of a location match the search word, the match is signalled and the address of the matching location is returned. For IP characterization, the contents of the CAM words may contain 'don't cares' as well, allowing 'wild-card' matching.

1.3 FPGA-Based CAM Implementation

Commercial high-speed CAMs are available, but these do not have the required width for IP characterization of over 300 bits. In this paper, we implement a CAM in a Field Programmable Gate Array (FPGA) that is wide enough. Since FPGAs are already used in IP handling systems, the CAM can be integrated with other logic on the same chip. It also allows us to add logic to the CAM to extend its functionality, such as counters for acquiring statistical data.

For IP characterization, fast searches are required, while the contents of the CAM stay constant over a longer period. Instead of integrating logic on the FPGA to change the contents, the CAM is updated by generating a programming bitstream in software during system operation and reconfiguring the FPGA. This is called *dynamic reconfiguration*.

Several other FPGA-based CAMs have been proposed that are not dynamically reconfigurable [1,4]. These CAMs are either too slow when searching for wide expressions or can not contain enough CAM words. Furthermore, they have no mechanism for dealing with multiple matches.

When using dynamic reconfiguration, the logic for adding/deleting CAM words can be omitted. A novel architecture has been developed that allows the space for each CAM word to be variable. This way, our CAM implementation is able to store more CAM words and search for wide expressions with enough performance. A priority mechanism has been implemented that decides what address to return when multiple CAM words match. Traditional implementations of priority mechanisms are inefficient when adding/deleting CAM words or have a large impact on the search speed. Our implementation tackles these problems, by setting the priority of each CAM word via the FPGA configuration as well.

2 Requirements

2.1 An IPv6 Packet Header

An IP packet is of variable length and consists of one or more headers and a payload. The headers contain information about addressing and control. The payload is the data encapsulated in the IP-packet, following the headers. It contains a higher level protocol (TCP, UDP) packet with its own header and payload.
Figure 1 shows the structure of an IPv6 base header [5]. The source and destination address are the IP addresses of the originator and the intended recipient of the packet and their size is 128 bits compared to 32 bits for IP version 4 (IPv4). Due to the increased size of the IP addresses, incoming packets should be matched with significantly more data than in current IPv4 systems.

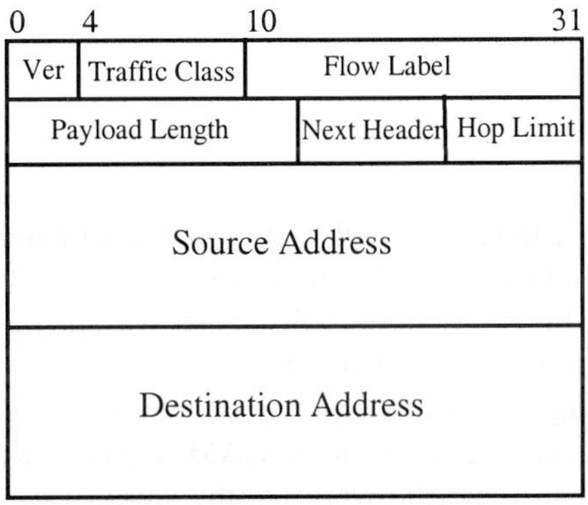

Field	Number of bits
Source Address	128
Destination Address	128
Incoming Link	6
Outgoing Link	6
Next Header	8
Traffic Class	6
TCP/UDP Source Port	16
TCP/UDP Destination Port	16
TCP/UDP Syn/Ack	1
Total number of bits:	315

Fig. 1. An IPv6 Header Diagram.

Table 1. Information that is used for IP characterization

IP characterization is based on some fields in the header, some fields in the higher level protocol that is encapsulated in the payload of the IP packet, and information from the router.

2.2 CAM Size

Table 1 gives an overview of the fields of which the contents of the CAM consist. The total number of bits that the CAM should be able to match, is 315 bits.
The maximum number of bits that needs to be stored in every CAM location is therefore large, but most locations store a lot of 'don't cares' as well. This has two reasons:
- Not all fields that characterize a packet are used for matching a CAM word. An example is filtering packets from a certain host. In this case only the source address of the forbidden IP packets needs to be matched. Another example is matching the IP version to count the number of IP version x packets that arrive, which only needs four bits to be stored.

- IP addresses are often not completely specified, meaning that the packet is to be sent to a net or subnet rather than a host. This means that the 128 bit source and destination address fields stored in the CAM words often have 'don't cares' at the end.

The number of CAM words that should be stored in the CAM is the order of 100.

2.3 Performance

The CAM is to be used in a communication channel that has a bandwidth of 622 Mbits/s. The time available for characterizing an IP packet is equal to the time it takes to transfer this packet over the communication channel. Since the communication channel is used to transfer voice and video as well, latency should be minimized where possible and buffering is therefore not desirable. To calculate the performance requirements, we therefore use a minimum packet datagram length of 40 bytes, which is equal to an IPv6 header only. The minimum search rate of the CAM should then be:

$$\frac{622 \cdot 10^6}{8 \cdot 40} = 1.9 \cdot 10^6 \text{ searches/s}$$

2.4 Priority

As mentioned before, the input of the CAM can contain both source and destination address and other information. In some cases, this other information may take priority over the addressing information altogether. This priority effect also exists with hierarchically structured addresses, that contain 'don't cares'. Here, one part of an address takes priority over another part in the matching decision, depending on which address has fewest 'don't cares' [6]. This means that in case two or more CAM words give a match for a certain input, the index of the most specific word i.e. the word, whose address contains fewest 'don't cares' should be returned. This requires a priority mechanism for the CAM words.

3 Design Methodology

3.1 Hardware Environment

The implementation of the CAM is targeted to Xilinx Virtex XCV1000 FPGA at speed grade 4. This FPGA is situated on a PCI card, the RC1000-PP made by Embedded Solutions. This board is used in a PC with a 450 MHz Pentium II processor and 320 MB RAM, running Windows NT.

3.2 Design Tool Flow

The design tool flow describes the tools that have been used and the data flow between them and is shown in Figure 2. It consists of a static and a dynamic part. The static part is used to implement the logic that is not dynamically changed.

A FPGA-Based Content Adressable Memory for Intenet Protocol Characterization

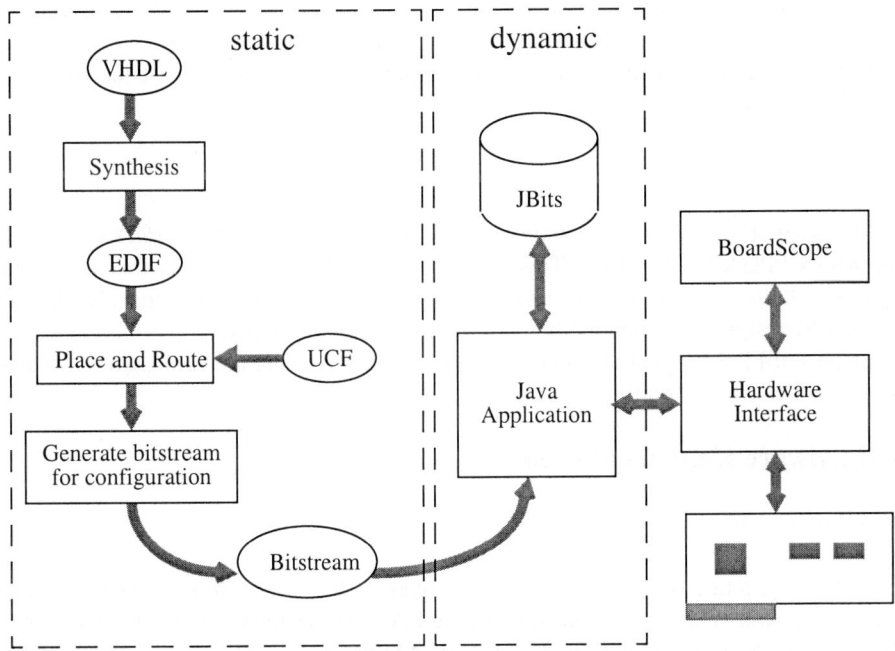

Fig. 2. Design tool flow

This includes I/O and logic that interfaces to the dynamic part. Furthermore it initializes the dynamic part of the design, by generating a basic structure that will be reconfigured in a later phase. Instead of generating this basic structure, one should ideally be able to use a *module based design* concept, where parts of the FPGA area are reserved for reconfigurable structures. This area should be empty and have ports that connect the dynamically reconfigurable structure to the other parts of the circuit (i.e. board interface and 'random' logic). There is however no support for this in present tools. The static part is designed using Synplify for VHDL synthesis in combination with tools available from Xilinx for place and route and bitstream generation. The locations of all components that are to be dynamically reconfigured are constrained in a User Constraints File (UCF).

The dynamic part of the design controls the reconfiguration of the FPGA during operation of the application and a tool called JBits is used for this. With JBits, the programming bitstream of the FPGA can be altered with relatively simple commands as explained in Section 3.3. The JBits functionality is used in a Java application, that implements the user interface of the CAM and controls the reconfiguration. This application is communicating with the hardware using the *Xilinx Hardware Interface* (XHWIF) [7]. It permits simple porting of JBits to the hardware. It includes methods for reading and writing bitstreams to FPGA's, incrementing the on-board clock and reading and writing to and from the on-board memory.

Via the hardware interface, the vendor specific C-functions for communicating with the board can be used in the user Java application.

BoardScope is a tool that presents a graphical representation of the FPGA configuration and the state of instantiated flip flops by reading back a configuration from the FPGA. This is very useful for debugging purposes, since simulation of the dynamic part is not possible.

3.3 JBits

JBits is a set of Java classes which provide an *Application Program Interface* (API) into the Xilinx FPGA bitstream [8]. This interface operates either on bitstreams generated by design tools, or on bitstreams read back from actual hardware. This provides the capability to design and dynamically modify the logic on an FPGA.
Examples of FPGA logic that can be reconfigured this way are the configuration of the lookup tables and the routing.

4 Hardware Implementation

4.1 Global Structure

The global structure of a CAM is given in Figure 3. It consists of a *match field* and a *priority encoder*. The match field contains the CAM words and has logic that compares the incoming search term with each of these CAM words. Each location in the CAM is connected to an output that tells whether or not a match occurred at that location.

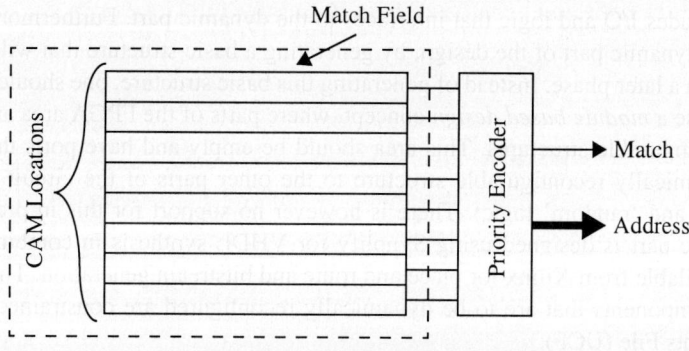

Fig. 3. Global structure of the CAM

These outputs are connected to the priority encoder, that looks if a match occurred and returns the address of the matching location that has highest priority.

4.2 Match Field

As mentioned in Section 2.2, the words that are stored in the CAM usually contain many 'don't cares'. If the contents of the memory locations include these 'don't cares', all CAM locations are of equal size and consume equal number of resources. In the CAM that we implement, these 'don't cares' are left out so that the size of the CAM locations varies per CAM word and becomes smaller in many cases. This is done by

dividing each CAM word in 5 *match blocks* of 64 bits each. These match blocks are then concatenated with shift registers in between, leaving out those blocks that merely contain 'don't cares'. This way, 64 bits are matched at a time and by placing the *reduced* words in a certain way, more of them can be stored in the CAM.
Figure 4 gives an example of how a CAM word is reduced.

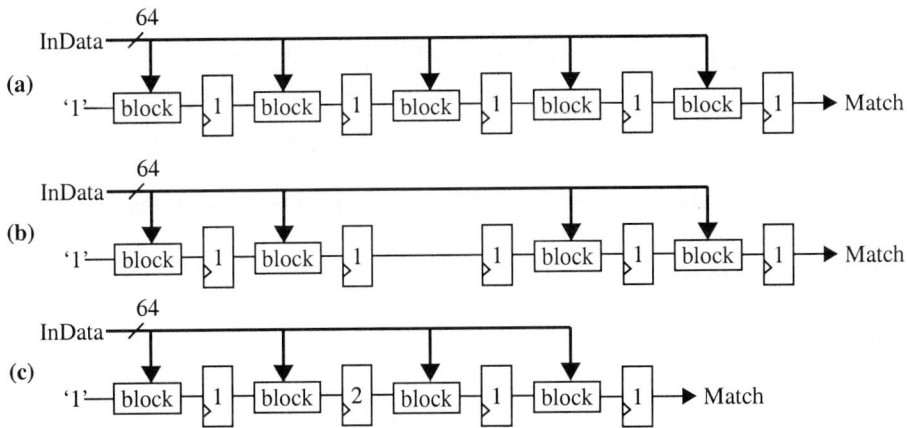

Fig. 4. Mapping of a full CAM word (a) and a reduced CAM word (b,c) to match blocks (depicted with 'block') and shift registers

Figure 4 (a) shows a CAM word that is not reduced. *InData* is the data that is to be compared with the contents of the words in the CAM and 64 bits are matched at a time. Each match block compares the incoming data with its own contents and if they match, then the output value of the preceding match block is propagated and loaded into the shift register that follows the match block. In case there is no match, a '0' is propagated. A complete match takes 5 clock cycles. If a certain match block merely contains 'don't cares', then this block always propagates the value stored in the previous shift register and is logically a wire. This is shown in figure 4 (b) for the third block. This block is then omitted and the length of the shift register following the second block is incremented to make sure that the last two blocks are still matched in clock cycle 4 and 5, see Figure 4 (c).

To utilize the space that is gained by using this mechanism, all the match blocks and shift registers are placed in a chain in the match field as shown in Figure 5.

Every match block has the choice of continuing a CAM word by propagating the result of the previous match block or to start a new CAM word by propagating a '1' in case of a match. This is modelled by a switch in the figure.

Since CAM words can start and end at any location in the chain, it should be able to connect the output of every match block to the priority encoder. This is done by dividing the chain of match blocks into groups of 4 match blocks each. Within a group, the outputs of the match blocks are connected to two 4-input multiplexers that connect to two inputs of the priority encoder. This way, two CAM words can end and connect to the priority encoder within one group and the maximal number of CAM locations is half the number of match blocks.

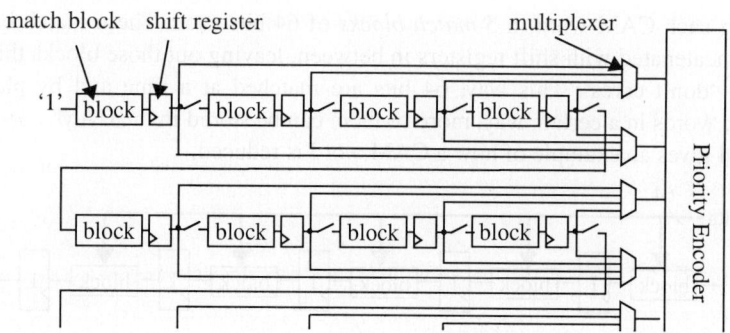

Fig. 5. Physical structure of CAM. The 64-bits input that is connected to each match block has been left out for sake of clarity.

4.3 Priority Encoder

Since the contents of the CAM words contain 'don't cares', there is a possibility that two or more words give a match at the same time. As mentioned in 2.4, the CAM words should be prioritized and the address of the CAM word with the highest priority should be returned. Two priority schemes are possible [9]:

- Inherent priority: inherent priority exploits the CAMs predictable ordering when reading multiple matched data. In this case, the system stores the CAM words in order of priority. By using a priority encoder, the top address of the CAM has the highest priority and the bottom address has the lowest priority.
- Explicit priority: the inherent priority can be replaced with an explicit priority field added to each CAM word. In case of a multiple match, the address of the CAM word with the highest explicit priority as stored in the priority field is returned.

The advantage of explicit priority is that updating the CAM becomes easier, since new CAM words can always be added at the end. With inherent prioritizing, it's necessary to reserve a location reserved by moving other CAM words and updating the memory that is addressed by the CAM. To implement explicit priority, several schemes are possible. One way to do explicit encoding is by adding an explicit priority field to each CAM word [10]. This mechanism is not very efficient and the matching process can take many clock cycles, depending on the number of possible explicit priority values. Using dynamic reconfiguration, other implementations are possible. One of these possibilities is using a regular priority encoder in combination with a switch box. This switch box routes every output of the CAM to the correct input of the priority encoder and the configuration of the switch box is controlled by JBits. Although this method is efficient in time, it would consume too much hardware for the CAM size at hand. This problem has been solved by reducing the number of *priority values*. The number of priority values is the number of different explicit priority values that a CAM word can have. In case of an inherent priority encoder, this is equal to the number of locations. By reducing this number, the amount of hardware is reduced, but there is a risk that more priority values than available are needed for a certain CAM configuration. To solve this, a combined explicit/inherent priority encoder has been implemented, where the priority can be set to one of eight values for each CAM word, but in case two entries have the same explicit priority, their priority is determined inherently.

5. Results

Table 2 shows the speed and utilization of four different CAM implementations. The first three CAMs A-C contain the match field as described before. This match field has 512 match blocks and since each word may consume 5 blocks, the CAM is able to contain 102 320-bits words. A maximum of 256 words can be stored, if these can be reduced efficiently by leaving out 'don't cares'. The match field was combined with different encoding mechanisms. Implementation A uses inherent priority and implementation B uses explicit priority with eight priority values, followed by an inherent priority encoder. Implementation C contains the same match field, but does not use a priority mechanism. This CAM only outputs one bit, that is high when one or more CAM words match. This is useful for IP filtering, where the CAM only has to return one bit that tells whether an IP packet is accepted or not. Implementation D is a CAM, that contains another type of match field where 'don't cares' cannot be left out. In this implementation, all CAM words consume equal amount of resources and this CAM can contain 128 CAM words of 320 bits each. This CAM was combined with an inherent priority encoder.

CAM	Priority Mechanism	Max. No. CAM Words	Utilization [%]	f [MHz]	Search Speed [Msearches / s]
A	Inherent	256	47	19.1	3.8
B	Explicit/Inherent	256	49	17.2	3.4
C	None	256	40	45.9	9.4
D	Inherent	128	51	35.4	7.1

Table 2: Speed and utilization of different CAM implementations.

From these results it follows that all CAM implementations meet the performance requirements of 1.9 Msearches/s. Furthermore it becomes clear that the priority encoder is responsible for the delay and that when priority is not needed, a search speed of 9.4 Msearches/s can be achieved. The performance of the CAM with explicit priority is similar to that of the same CAM with just inherent priority.
If the size of each CAM location is not made variable, the maximum number of CAM words that can be stored becomes smaller, but the search speed becomes higher because a smaller priority encoder is needed. Partial reconfiguration is not supported and every time the contents of the CAM change, the entire FPGA is reconfigured. This does not have much influence on the performance of the CAM, since its contents are not updated very often in this application (i.e. a few times per day).

6. Conclusions

Dynamic reconfiguration is a good way to implement FPGA-based CAMs. We have shown that a highly flexible circuit can be implemented, that allows an efficient mapping of the CAM. Since critical functions (searching the CAM) and non-critical functions (changing the CAM) can be separated and implemented in hardware and software, respectively, the final hardware implementation becomes both faster and smaller than regular FPGA implementations.

Different CAMs have been implemented using this method and it was shown that all of them meet the requirements for IP characterization. Depending on the implementation, a search speed between 3.4 and 7.1 million searches/s was achieved, while the required speed was 1.9 million searches/s. Without a priority mechanism, a search speed of 9.4 million searches/s was accomplished. It has also been shown that adding explicit priority to the CAM does not lead to significant hardware costs or performance decrease, while adding/deleting CAM words becomes more efficient.

All CAM implementations consume about half of the FPGA resources and the number of CAM words can therefore be increased and/or related logic can be integrated on the same chip.

References

[1] A. McEwan, J. Saul, A. Bayley, "A High Speed Reconfigurable Firewall Based On Parameterizable FPGA-based Content Addressable Memories", *Proceedings of the International Conference on Parallel and Distributed Processing Techniques and Applications (PDPTA)*, 1999.
[2] M. Defossez, "Content Addressable Memory (CAM) in ATM applications", *Xilinx Application Note 202*, 1999.
[3] J. Brelet, B. New, "Designing Flexible, Fast CAMs with Virtex Slices", *Xilinx Application Note 203*, 1999.
[4] J. Brelet, "Using Block SelectRAM+ for High-Performance Read/Write CAMs", *Xilinx Application Note 204*, 1999.
[5] S. Deering, R. Hinden, *Internet Protocol, Ver. 6 Specification*, RFC 2460, 1998.
[6] M. Mansour, A. Kayssi, "FPGA-based Internet Protocol Version 6 Router", Proc. of IEEE International Conference on Computer Design, p. 334, vol. 2, 1998.
[7] S. Guccione, D. Levi, "Run-Time Parameterizable Cores", *Proceedings of the 9th International Workshop of Field Programmable Logic and Applications FPL '99*, p. 215, Springer Lecture Notes in Computer Science, 1998.
[8] Xilinx Inc, "JBits Xilinx Reconfigurable Computing Platform", *JBits 2.1 Tutorial*, 1999.
[9] A.J. McAuley, P. Francis, "Fast Routing Table Lookup Using CAMs", *Proceedings of IEEE Infocom '93*, p. 1382, 1993.
[10] S. V. Kartalopoulos, "An Associative RAM-based CAM and Its Application to BroadBand Communiactions Systems", *IEEE Transactions on Neural Networks*, p. 1036, vol. 9, 1998.

A Compiler Directed Approach to Hiding Configuration Latency in Chameleon Processors

Xinan Tang, Manning Aalsma, and Raymond Jou

Chameleon Systems, Inc.
161 Nortech Parkway
San Jose, CA 95134
tang@chameleonsystems.com

Abstract. The Chameleon CS2112 chip is the industry's first reconfigurable communication processor. To attain high performance, the reconfiguration latency must be effectively tolerated in such a processor. In this paper, we present a compiler directed approach to hiding the configuration loading latency. We integrate multithreading, instruction scheduling, register allocation, and prefetching techniques to tolerate the configuration loading latency. Furthermore, loading configuration is overlapped with communication to further enhance performance. By running some kernel programs on a cycle-accurate simulator, we showed that the chip performance is significantly improved by leveraging such compiler and multithreading techniques.

1 Introduction

With the rapid progress of reconfigurable computing technology, the new generation of reconfigurable architectures support runtime configuration to execute general-purpose programs efficiently [10, 7, 13, 6]. Runtime configuration becomes an essential feature to allow reconfigurable machines to compete with the main-stream RISC, VLIW, and EPIC machines.

However, the runtime reconfiguration latency can be significant. To maximize program execution performance, such loading overhead must be minimized. Various techniques have been proposed to reduce/tolerate the configuration latency. Configuration caching [10], prefetching [8], and compression [9] are named as a few. In this paper, we propose a compiler directed approach that exploits chip hardware to tolerate the configuration latency. We believe that effectively hiding the configuration latency is the key to achieving high performance on Chameleon like processors.

In our approach, four major techniques [11], *multithreading, instruction scheduling, register allocation*, and *prefetching* are leveraged to *hiding* the configuration loading latency. Our experimental results show that such an integrated approach can double performance and it is very effective in hiding the reconfiguration latency.

In Section 2, we briefly introduce the Chameleon chip and the compiler environment. In Section 3, we formulate and explain the latency-tolerance problem.

In Section 4, we present the compiler based integrated solution. In Section 5. we report experimental results and analyze the performance impacts. Finally, related work is reviewed in Section 6, and future work is discussed in Section 7.

2 Chameleon Hardware Model and Software Environment

The Chameleon reconfigurable chip is a processor based reconfigurable architecture. We briefly describe the Chameleon hardware model and the software environment in this section.

2.1 Chameleon Architecture Model

The Chameleon chip provides a platform for high-performance telecommunication and datacommunication applications[4]. It is a processor-based reconfigurable architecture, in which a RISC core, the reconfigurable fabric, a fast bus, the memory system, and IO are built in a single chip. Fig. 1(a) gives an abstract architecture model of Chameleon CS2112 chips.

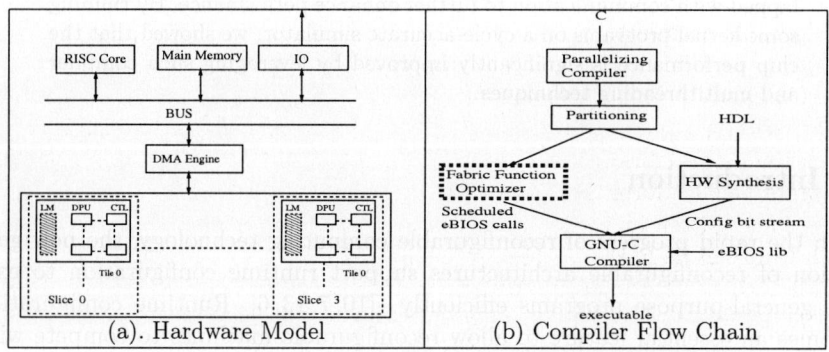

Fig. 1. Abstract hardware and software models for Chameleon chips

A 32-bit RISC core is used as a host processor. It schedules computation-intensive tasks onto the programmable logic. The programmable logic (fabric) is an array of 108 data path units (DPU). Each DPU can be dynamically reconfigured to execute one of eight instructions. The 108 DPUs are divided into four *slices* and each slice is further partitioned into 3 *tiles*. In each tile there are nine DPUs, of which seven are 32-bit ALUs and two are 16-bit multipliers. The inputs to a DPU can be changed on the cycle base. All instructions are executed in one cycle. Each DPU can have maximum 8 instructions stored in the control unit (CTL), and the next instruction is determined by the CTL within the same cycle. By loading a new configuration bit stream, the reconfigurated DPUs can perform new computation. In addition, there are 8Kbytes of *local memory* (LM) for each slice and a DPU can read/write 32 bits in two cycles. Inside the chip, a high-speed bus links the core, the fabric, the main memory, and other IO devices together.

A config bit stream is stored in the main memory. It is loaded onto the fabric at runtime by DMA. Each slice has two planes for bit streams. An *active* plane executes the working bit stream and a *back* plane contains the next config bit stream. Switching from the back plane to the active one takes one cycle. Therefore, the back plane can be effectively used as cache for loading configuration.

Since the CS2112 chip is a loosely coupled reconfigurable architecture, it requires to move a large chunk of data from the main memory to the fabric local memory to cover the configuration and communication latency. Therefore, the granularity of program to be executed on the fabric is best at the function level. Unlike fine-grained reconfigurable architectures such as PRISC [12] and Chimaera [7], the Chameleon fabric is very efficient at executing medium-grained functions that contain tens or even hundreds of instructions. At such a medium-grain level, loading a config bit stream may take up to hundreds of cycles if there is a cache miss. Thus, effectively to tolerate the loading latency is the key to attaining high performance on the Chameleon chip.

2.2 Chameleon Software Environment

Fig.1(b) outlines the Chameleon software environment. Like other compilers for reconfigurable architectures [3, 5, 16, 2], it mainly consists of two compilers. An optimizing compiler takes a C program and partitions the program into two parts: (1) code suitable to run on the RISC core; (2) code profitable to execute on the reconfigurable fabric. The RISC part is then compiled by a GNU C compiler and the fabric one is passed to a hardware (HW) synthesis compiler in an intermediate form. For the efficiency reason, the HW compiler also takes in programs written in Verilog and generates config bit streams. The config bit stream can then be linked with other compiled code to form an executable.

To launch a function onto the fabric, an eBIOS (runtime system) is designed to support: (1) multithreaded execution between the core and the fabric; (2) communication and synchronization between the core and the fabric. To hide the configuration latency, the sequence of eBIOS calls must be carefully scheduled to exploit parallelism. The fabric-function optimizer is an optimization module that performs (1) eBIOS call scheduling; (2) static resource allocation to make full use of available hardware resources. In the following, we will focus on the latency tolerant techniques employed in the fabric-function optimizer.

3 Problem Statement

To run a function on the fabric, the call is replaced by a series of equivalent eBIOS calls to perform: (1) loading a config bit stream; (2) moving data in DMA; (3) firing the fabric. The scheduling problem studied in this paper is to place a series of calls into a proper order so that (1) control and data dependences are obeyed. (2) total program execution time is minimized. To minimize total execution time, the configuration overhead must be minimized. Thus, if the configuration overhead is reduced, the total execution time is also effectively reduced.

Formally, we can formulate the problem as follows: *given a series of fabric function calls* $F = f_1, ..., f_n$, *each f_i has its parameter list l_i, and its corresponding config bit stream c_i. Find a schedule S that consists of a series of eBIOS calls so that the total execution time on the processor is minimized.*

In this paper, F can be a *fork/join* series, and function f_i has only one config bit stream c_i. Therefore, partially reconfiguration is not considered. Fig. 2(a) lists a series of four function calls, f_1, f_2, f_3 and f_4. In the series, functions f_2 and f_3 can run in parallel.

f1; fork f2; f3; join; f4	1| #pragma cmln mac(\\ 2| in x[N],in y[N],\\ 3| out *z) 4| 5| mac(x, y, &z); 6|	1| LOAD_CONFIG(mac_bits); 2| WAIT_FOR_CONFIG(); 3| DMA_MOVE(X, 4*N, LM_1); 4| WAIT_FOR_DMA(); 5| DMA_MOVE(Y, 4*N, LM_2); 6| WAIT_FOR_DMA(); 7| FIRE_FABRIC(); 8| WAIT_FOR_FABRIC(); 9| SCALAR_MOVE(&z, DPU_1);	1| LOAD_CONFIG(mac_bits); 2| DMA_MOVE(X, 4*N, LM_1); 3| DMA_MOVE(Y, 4*N, LM_2); 4| WAIT_FOR_CONFIG(); 5| WAIT_FOR_DMA(); 6| FIRE_FABRIC(); 7| WAIT_FOR_FABRIC(); 8| SCALAR_MOVE(&z, DPU_1);
(a) sequence.	(b) C call	(c) schedule 1	(d) schedule 2

Fig. 2. Fork/join program representation and eBIOS schedules.

Let's see an example that shows the scheduling impacts. Fig. 2 (b), a C call is indicated to the scheduler in the pragma line (lines 1-3), which says function mac has two input arrays and one output scalar. Two eBIOS schedules are listed in Fig. 2 (c) and (d) respectively.

Schedule 1 listed in Fig. 2 (c) first loads the config bit stream of mac (lines 1-2). Then two input arrays are sent to the fabric using DMA (lines 3, 4, 5, and 6). Next, the fabric is fired (line 7). After the completion of running (line 8), the scalar result is retrieved (line 9). However this schedule is not an effective one. First, it does not issue any DMA operation after configuration loading; Second it does not pipeline the DMA issuing operations. Schedule 2 listed in Fig. 2 (d) is better by pipelining two type of operations: loading a configuration and moving data in DMA (lines 1-3). Moreover, it reduces one synchronization (WAIT_FOR_DMA). Thus a better schedule will have significant performance impacts. In the following, we will discuss how a 'good' schedule can be found out.

4 Scheduling Algorithm and Compiler Optimizations

Since the problem formulated is NP-*Complete*, feasible algorithms require the use of heuristics. We will first introduce the multithreaded eBIOS, and then present our heuristic scheduling algorithm. Finally a series of compiler optimizations are also described.

4.1 Multithreaded Runtime System

The eBIOS is a runtime system that supports the *fork/join* style of parallelism. A master thread runs on the RISC core and other slave threads can run concurrently on the fabric. To support such an execution model, the eBIOS must support *split-phased* (asynchronized) transactions between the core and the fabric [15]. Particularly, the following operations are *non-blocking* in terms of the RISC core execution: (1) **LOAD_CONFIG:** loading a config bit stream onto the fabric; (2) **DMA_MOVE:** moving data between the main memory and the fabric; (3) **FIRE_FABRIC:** activate computation on the fabric.

However, such multithreaded execution inadvently adds to the programming complexity. It is essential for the scheduling algorithm to find a good schedule to guarantee: (1) the 'right' combination of eBIOS calls that is dead-lock free; (2) the 'best' schedule that has minimized execution time.

4.2 Heuristic Scheduling Algorithms

A two-level heuristic is used to solve the scheduling problem. First, we aggressively schedule eBIOS calls that belong to the same function call. Second we hoist up certain operations between two neighbor function calls to exploit parallelism.

Fig. 3(a) gives a list scheduling based algorithm that arranges the eBIOS calls within the same function-call boundary. Given an input function f_i, parameter list l_i, and config bit stream c_i, The algorithm works as follows. After issuing load config bit stream (line 2), the algorithm sorts the input parameter list l_i into four sublists (line 3): (1) l_i^1 is an input array list; (2) l_i^2 is an output array list; (3) l_i^3 is an input scalar list; (3) l_i^4 is an output scalar list. The purpose of such sorting is to facilitate handling data dependences between parameters and the function call. For list l_i^1, we further sort it into a *decreasing* order according to the length of input array (line 5). Then, we take each input array from the sorted list and issue DMA_MOVE operation one by one (lines 7 and 8). The reason of issuing longer DMA operations earlier is to use their execution time to cover the DMA setup costs of shorter DMA operations.

```
1  | RTS_schedule(f_i, l_i, c_i) {
2  |   select(LOAD_CONFIG) for c_i;
3  |   (l1,l2,l3,l4) = sort_parameter_list(l_i);
4  |   if (|l1| > 0) { /* Input arrays */
5  |     sort l1 into a non-ascending order;
6  |     foreach array input in sorted l1 {
7  |       select (DMA_MOVE, READ);
8  |     }
9  |   }
10 |   select(WAIT_FOR_CONFIG);
11 |   foreach scalar input in l3 {
12 |     select(SCALAR_MOVE, READ);
13 |   }
14 |   if (|l1|)
15 |     select(WAIT_FOR_DMA);
16 |   select(FIRE_FABRIC);
17 |   select(WAIT_FOR_FABRIC);
18 |   if (|l2| > 0) { /* output arrays */
19 |     sort l2 into a non-ascending order;
20 |     foreach array output in sorted l2 {
21 |       select (DMA_MOVE, WRITE);
22 |     }
23 |   }
24 |   foreach out scalar in l4 {
25 |     select(SCALAR_MOVE, WRITE);
26 |   }
27 |   if (|l2| > 0)
29 |     select(WAIT_FOR_DMA);
30 | }
```

Fig. 3. Scheduling algorithms for eBIOS calls

Next, operation WAIT_FOR_CONFIG is issued to guarantee that the config bit stream arrives on the fabric. After that scalar parameters can be sent onto the fabric (lines 11-13). The reason of DMA first and scalar second is that a config bit stream may modify some DPU registers while DMA operations can run in parallel with loading configurations. Then, we check whether the previously issued DMAs have finished (line 15). Afterwards, we can start fabric computation (line 16), and wait for its completion at line 17. Then we continue to process output parameters accordingly (lines 18-29 shown in the right).

In summary, the heuristics used in the scheduling algorithm are as follows: (1) overlap loading a config bit stream and DMA operations (lines 2-9); (2) pipeline DMA operations to cover up their setting up costs (line 4-9, and 18-23); (3) use DMA operations to hide scalar operations (lines 11-15, and 24-29). The time complexity of the algorithm is $O(nlogn)$ assuming $|l_i| = n$. Most of time is spent on sorting l_1^i and l_2^i into a proper order.

For scheduling eBIOS calls from multiple function call sites, the resource conflict analysis should be done first. Two concurrent functions f_i and f_j are resource free if (1) the combined number of slices used is less than 4; (2) the intersection of the slice set is empty; (3) the intersection of the DMA set is empty. Otherwise two functions have to be executed sequentially due the resource constraints.

The minimum scheduling cluster (MSC) of function f_i is defined as:

$$MSC_i = \begin{cases} \{f_{i+1}, \ldots, f_{i+k}\} & \text{if } free(f_i, f_{i+1}) \& \ldots \& free(f_i, f_{i+k}) \& conflict(f_i, f_{i+k+1}) \\ \{f_{i+1}\} & \text{otherwise} \end{cases}$$

Ideally, function f_i should be scheduled together with other functions within the same MSC_i. To make the scheduling tractable, only two neighbor function calls are considered, $MSC_i = \{f_{i+1}\}$. This is based on the fact that there are only two config planes on the Chameleon CS2112 chip. Furthermore, we only hoist up the config loading operation in between the firing fabric and the waiting for its completion. Thus, we try to use fabric computation time of one function to overlap configuration loading for another function.

4.3 Compiler Optimizations

In addition to scheduling, other compiler optimizations are also applied to reduce execution time.

Function inlining is a technique to replace a call with the function body to reduce the stack manipulation overhead. By inlining the original C call with a series of eBIOS calls, the actual parameters are directly bound to the eBIOS calls and the program execution time is reduced significantly.

Static resource allocation is a technique similar to register allocation. The resources that a fabric function needs are slices and DMA channels. If resources for a fabric function can be statically allocated for a fabric function, the overhead of dynamic resource allocation such as address computation can be eliminated completely.

Synchronization between the core and the fabric must be done to enforce certain order. For example, WAIT_FOR_CONFIG waits for the config loading to finish and WAIT_FOR_DMA waits for DMAs to finish. There is an *autonomous* working mode in the CS2112 chip in which synchronization is done by hardware automatically. Our scheduling algorithm can identify such a case and eliminate unnecessary synchronization when the autonomous mode can be applied.

5 Experimental Results

To test the efficacy of heuristic algorithms, we use kernel benchmarks to measure the effectiveness of our scheduling algorithm and compiler optimizations. The major results are as follows: (1) the eBOS scheduling algorithm can dramatically increase program execution performance up to 60% (see Section 5.1); (2) the prefetching algorithm can boost performance up to 30% (see Section 5.2); (3) by using the autonomous mode, performance can be further increased by up to 15% for certain benchmarks (see Section 5.3);

Table 1 lists main characteristics of benchmarks used. Benchmarks fht, fir24, and pngen are kernels for CDMA systems. The DMA is used in all benchmarks. The length of a config bit stream is given in Kilo bytes. We expect that the longer of a config bit stream, the more effective of our scheduling algorithms.

The simulator used is a commercial cycle-accurate simulator, ModelSim. Since we simulate the entire chip at the RTL level, timing information is guaranteed to be cycle accurate. During the experiment, function-inlining is always applied since it definitely enhances performance.

Table 1. Benchmark Description

Name	Description	Bit Stream Length	DMA Channels	
			input	output
mac	vector product	0.9K	2	0
addvec	vector addition	1.1K	2	1
fht	hadamard function	2.1K	1	1
fir	FIR filter	2.1K	8	0
fir24	24 tap	$\simeq 5.0K$	> 1	≥ 1
pngen	PN generator	$\simeq 5.0K$	> 1	≥ 1

5.1 Effects of eBIOS Scheduling

Table 2. Performance of the eBIOS scheduling algorithm.

	schedule	mac	addvec	fht	fir	fir24	pngen	ave.
	O0	3303	3577	3518	6007	4705	8021	
time	O1	3074	3326	3529	4375	4323	6955	
	O2	1612	2048	2446	2472	3069	5535	
	0,1	7	7	-0	27	8	13	10
imp(%)	1,2	48	38	31	43	29	20	35
	0,2	51	43	30	59	35	31	42

Table 2 lists program execution performance for programs generated by different scheduling algorithms. O0 means a naive scheduling algorithm in which each config loading and DMA operation is issued sequentially. O1 means applying the scheduling algorithm. O2 means using the static slice allocation on top of O1. The first three rows give corresponding execution times measured in cycles and the next three rows list the improvement rate, computed by

$$Imp_{i,j} = (T_{Oi} - T_{Oj})/T_{Oi} \qquad (1)$$

From Table 2, we can see that on average imp is 10% when the scheduling algorithm is applied ($imp_{0,1}$ row). Benchmark fir has the highest improvement rate (27%) since the number of DMAs used is the biggest (8). However benchmark fht has a negligible negative impact. The reasons are two fold. First, the number of DMAs are smaller (1 input and 1 output). Second, pipelining config loading and DMA operations may cause the bus contention. This result indicates that the scheduling algorithm will have a big performance impact if more DMAs are used and the bus contention is not an issue.

When applying the static resource allocation ($imp_{1,2}$ row), the performance of all benchmarks is increased. The reason is that after the static resource allocation is applied the critical path of entire program execution is reduced. Therefore, the optimization impact becomes more visible.

In general, the combined improvement rate is 42%. This shows that the combined scheduling algorithm has a significant impact on performance.

5.2 Effects of Prefetching

Table 3(a) lists the performance impacts of the the prefetching based scheduling algorithm on the two combined benchmarks, mac-addvec (mac+addvec) and fir24-pngen (fir24+pngen). The experiment was done by turning on/off option $-O3$. When option $-O3$ is *off*, all functions in two test cases run sequentially. When option $-O3$ is *on*, mac-addvec runs in parallel since there is no resource conflict but fir24-pngen is forced to run sequentially since there is resource conflict. However loading config bit stream for pngen is prefetched to the back planes. Therefore, loading config bit stream for function pngen runs in parallel with the execution of function fir24 on the fabric.

Table 3. Performance of Compiler Optimizations.

O3	mac-addvec	fir24-pngen	ave.
off	3301	8231	
on	3048	5812	
conflict	no	yes	
imp(%)	7.66	29.39	18.53

(a) prefetching

Auto	mac	addvec	fht	fir24	Ave.
no	1612	2048	2446	3069	
yes	1510	1739	1966	2735	
imp(%)	6.0	15.0	20.0	11.0	13.0

(b) autonomous mode

In Table 3(a), row off corresponds to program execution time when the prefetching algorithm is not applied. Row on corresponds to execution time when the algorithm is applied. Row conflict indicates whether there is resource conflict. Row imp gives the performance improvement rate.

From Table 3(a), we can see that on average performance is increased by almost 19% when the prefetching based scheduling algorithm is applied. Comparatively, fir24-pngen has bigger performance improvement over mac-addvec, 29.39% vs. 7.66%. The reasons are two fold. First, the fabric running time of fir24-pngen is longer than that of mac-addvec. Second, the length of the config bit stream of fir24-pngen is also longer that that of mac-addvec(See Table 1). Therefore, prefetching the config bit stream of fir24-pngen is more rewarding.

5.3 Effects of Using the Hardware Feature

Table 3 (b) lists program execution performance before and after the fabric autonomous execution feature is applied. This experiment is done based on $O2$ optimization. The *yes/no* rows in Table 3 (b) give execution time of a program *using/not using* the hardware feature correspondingly. Only four benchmarks are qualified for such an optimization. On average, execution performance is improved by 13%. The improvement rate of the benchmarks that have output DMAs (addvec, fht, and fir24) is bigger than the one that does not have (mac). The reason is that an extra synchronization for output DMAs was also eliminated. This suggests that the hardware feature should be exploited whenever possible.

6 Related Work

In compiling for reconfigurable architectures, most of work focuses on the code partitioning and parallelizing loops [3, 5, 16, 2]. On these machines [10, 7, 13, 6], the processor usually stalls when a configuration is loaded. The performance impact of prefetching has been studied by Hauck et. al. [8]. However the communication overhead is not considered in the study. Viswanath et. al. [14] did a quantitative case study on the effects of the communication overhead, and they identified the importance of reducing such overhead. Bondalapati et. al. [1] proposed a general model mapping loops onto the reconfigurable architecture. Our problem formulation is different from theirs by considering the fork/join tree and communication cost. In this paper, we propose a compiler-directed approach to hiding the 'interface' latency, including the reconfiguration and communication latencies. To the best of our knowledge, this is the first integrated effort to leverage compiler and multithreading techniques to solve this problem. We believe that our approach can also be applied to other similar architectures.

7 Conclusions and Future Work

We have developed a compiler-directed approach, combining compiler optimization and multithreading techniques, to hide the configuration loading latency. We have implemented the list scheduling based algorithm that find a 'best' schedule for a series of eBIOS calls. The experimental results are very encouraging, and performance has been significantly improved by applying the integrated method. The future work will be: 1) continue to improve the scheduling algorithms; 2) design advanced resource allocation schemes; 3) investigate better prefetching algorithms. We will also experiment on our chips with real applications.

References

1. K. Bondalapati and V. K. Prasanna. "mapping loops onto reconfigurable architectures". In *Proc. of Inter. Workshop on Field Programmable Logic and Applications*, Sep. 1998.
2. M. Budiu and S. C. Goldstein. "fast compilation for pipelined reconfigurable fabric". In *Proc. of ACM/SIGDA Inter. Symposium on FPGA*, 1999.
3. T. J. Callahan and F. John Wawrzynek. "instruction level parallelism for reconfigurable computing". In Hartenstein and Keevallik, editors, *Inter. Workshop on Field-Programmable Logic and Applications*. Lecture Notes in Computer Science, LNCS 1482,Springer-Verlag, Aug. 1998.
4. Chameleon Systems, Inc. http://www.chameleonsystems.com/, 2000.
5. M. Gokhale and J. Stone. "NAPA C: Compiling for a hybrid risc/fpga architcture". In *Proc. of the IEEE Symposium on FCCM*, Apr. 1998.
6. S. C. Goldstein, H. Schmit, M. Moe, M. Budiu, S. Cadambi, R. R. Taylor, and R. Laufer. PipeRench: A coprocessor streaming multimedia acceleration. In *Proc. of ISCA-26*, pages 28–39, Atlanta, Geor., May 1999.
7. S. Hauck, T. W. Fry, M. M. Hosler, and J. P. Kao. "the chimaera reconfigurable functional unit". In *Proc. of the IEEE Symposium on FCCM*, Apr. 1997.
8. S. Hauck, T. W. Fry, M. M. Hosler, and J. P. Kao. ""configuration prefetch for single context reconfigurable coprocessors"". In *Proc. of ACM/SIGDA Inter. Symposium on FPGA*, Feb. 1998.
9. S. Hauck, Z. Li, and E. J. Schwabe. "configuration compression for the xilinx xc6200 fpga". In *Proc. of the IEEE Symposium on FCCM*, Apr. 1998.
10. J. R. Hauser and J. Wawrzynek. "garp: A mips processor with a reconfigurable coprocessor". In *Proc. of the IEEE Symposium on FCCM*, Apr. 1997.
11. S. S. Muchnick. *Advanced Compiler Design and Implementation*. Morgan Kaufmann Publishers, 1997.
12. R. Razdan. *PRISC: Programmable Reduced Instruction Set Computers*. PhD thesis, Harvard University, Division of Applied Sciences, Boston, 1994.
13. C. R. Rupp, M. Landguth, T. Garverick, E. Gomersall, H. Holt, J. M. Arnold, and M. Gokhale. "the napa adaptive processing architecture". In *Proc. of the IEEE Symposium on FCCM*, Apr. 1998.
14. S.K.Rajamani and P.Viswanath. "a quantitative analysis of the processor-programmable logic interface". In *Proc. of the IEEE Symposium on FCCM*, Apr. 1997.
15. X. Tang and G. R. Gao. Automatically partitioning threads for multithreaded architectures. *Journal of Parallel and Distributed Computing*, 58(2):159–189, Aug. 1999.
16. M. Weinhardt and W. Luk. "pipeline vectorization for reconfigurable systems". In *Proc. of the IEEE Symposium on FCCM*, Apr. 1999.

Reconfigurable Network Processors Based on Field Programmable System Level Integrated Circuits

Marios Iliopoulos and Theodore Antonakopoulos

Department of Electrical Engineering and Computers Technology
University of Patras, 26500 Rio – Patras
Greece
antonako@ee.upatras.gr

Abstract. The increasing demand of networking applications has imposed a new category of electronic circuits that integrate powerful CPU processing, networking and system support functions in a single, low cost chip. These integrated circuits, called Network Processors, are optimized for tasks such as access protocol implementation, data queuing and forwarding, traffic shaping and Quality of Service (QoS) support. This paper presents the use of Field Programmable System Level Integrated Circuits that combine the flexibility of programmable cores and the high performance of dedicated hardware, to implement network processors used for medium access protocols.

1 Introduction

Network Processors should offer flexibility, programmability, performance and low cost while being able to shorten time-to-market cycles for new networking products. However, these requirements contradict since network processors that consist of programmable cores may offer flexibility and less time-to-market but usually they have poor performance and increased cost. On the other hand, network processors that contain dedicated hardware offer high performance and low cost, but are less flexible and have higher time-to-market cycles [1]. Another solution is to use a programmable core supported by dedicated hardware in order to increase the efficiency and performance of programmable cores. Although this solution is easily adaptable to newer versions of the supported protocol, it still suffers from decreased flexibility, since dedicated hardware restricts the usage of the chip to a specific application.

Latest trends in network processors design combine RISC processor cores with reconfigurable hardware in an attempt to solve the trade-off of high performance and flexibility. A new emerging technology developed towards this approach is called Field Programmable System Level Integrated Circuits (FPSLICs) [2] and combines an 8-bit RISC microcontroller (AVR), reconfigurable hardware using Field Programmable Gate Array (FPGA) cells and SRAM, thus it can offer a single chip solution for complete systems.

This paper presents the use of FPSLIC architecture as a vehicle to implement reconfigurable network processors that are able to implement low complexity access protocols. This is because the 8-bit AVR processor is considered „weak" for the demands of complex network protocols, but it can still be used for networking applications such as 10Mbps Ethernet MAC, Point-to-Point Protocol controllers, home control networking, etc. On the other hand, the same basic idea supported by a 32-bit powerful microprocessor (such as an ARM processor core) and more reconfigurable logic will enable the implementation of network processors capable of supporting higher data rates and more complex protocols such as the IEEE 802.11, Bluetooth and 100Mbps Ethernet.

This paper makes use of a parametric architecture called General Network Architecture (GNA) [3] that directly maps network functions into a set of customizable hardware blocks that are interconnected through flexible interfaces. Section 2 introduces the FPSLIC architecture, the general network architecture and how GNA is mapped to an FPSLIC device. Section 3 demonstrates the implementation of a 10Mbps Medium Access Controller using general network architecture and one FPSLIC device. Finally, section 4 describes the implementation of more powerful network devices using the FPSLIC architecture and distributed processing.

2 Introduction to FPSLIC and GNA Architectures

In order to understand the use of FPSLICs for implementing reconfigurable Medium Access processors, we will describe in brief the FPSLIC architecture (section 2.1), the General Network Architecture (section 2.2), and how the GNA architectural blocks map to the FPSLIC device resources.

2.1 The FPSLIC Architecture

As illustrated in Figure 1, the initial version of FPSLIC contains the AVR microprocessor core, which is an 8-bit RISC processor with single-clock instructions, approaching 1 MIPS/MHz and 32 general purpose registers. The AVR core is supported by peripherals such as flexible timer/counters, a Real-time Counter, UARTs, programmable Watchdog Timer with internal oscillator, a 2-wire serial port interface and programmable I/O ports. The FPSLIC also contains 36K bytes of SRAM for program execution and data storage.

The reconfigurable part of FPSLIC is an SRAM based FPGA module with configurable Dual Port RAM cells. The FPGA has user programmable I/Os for interfacing to external world and may support low to medium complex devices (10K to 40K gates).

The AVR and the FPGA module communicate using three different interfaces: a control interface, 16 interrupt lines and a dual port RAM. The control interface decodes AVR address lines and control signals for accessing 16 memory mapped registers implemented in the FPGA, thus it can be used for implementing custom peripherals and/or directly controlling FPGA functions. AVR's interrupt controller can accept 16 programmable interrupt lines, which are produced by the FPGA.

Finally, the AVR and the FPGA can also communicate through a dual port RAM which can be read/written by both the AVR and the FPGA allowing shared memory implementations.

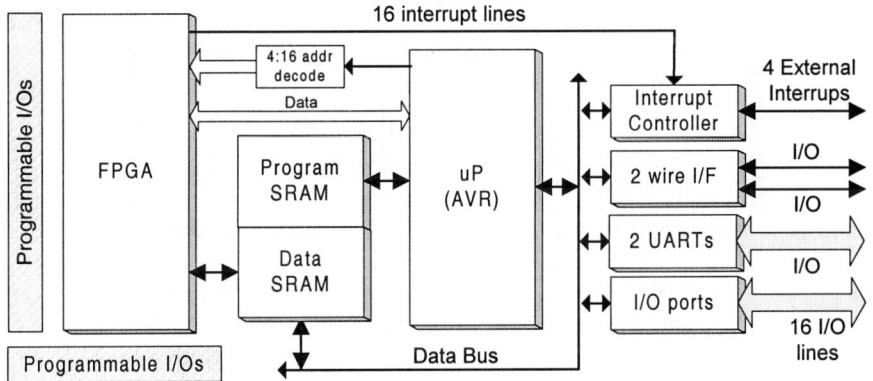

Fig. 1. The FPSLIC architecture

2.2 The General Network Architecture (GNA)

The FPSLIC resources are exploited by using the General Network Architecture (GNA) [3], which is a parametric architecture for realizing Medium Access Protocols. The General Network Architecture consists of customizable hardware blocks that are interconnected through flexible interfaces according to the dataflow illustrated in figure 2. The customizable hardware blocks perform *bit-serial functions* that process the serial bit-stream, *parallel functions* that process the parallel data, *event processing functions* that recognize the network events, and *control functions* that synchronize all the above blocks and consist of control registers, and state machines.

According to figure 2, the received serial data are passed through the bit-serial and parallel operations before they are stored into buffers and processed by the protocol's functions implemented in firmware. The whole process is controlled by the state machines block, which transacts with the above functions and the events coming from the network. Similarly, in the transmit direction, the data coming from the buffers are transformed through parallel and bit-serial operations into a bitstream, which is transmitted over the network. The processor core configures/controls the GNA blocks and collects status information through a control interface.

There are two main blocks in the architecture, the Receiver section which contains all the receive related functions, and the Transmitter section that contains all the transmit related functions. The control section contains all the control registers that are programmed/read by the microprocessor through a separate control interface. The control interface can be a custom microprocessor interface or a standard bus.

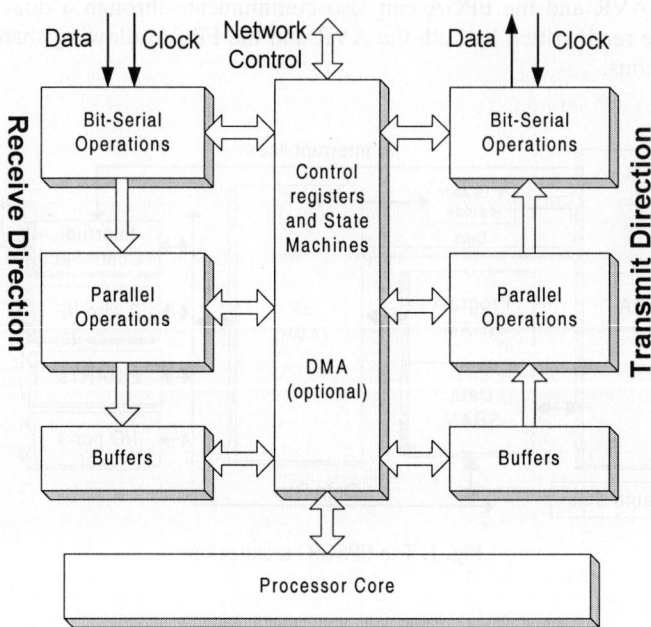

Fig. 2. The General Network Architecture

The data movement from/to the memory is accomplished through a dedicated path, either transparently without processor intervention by using a DMA engine, or by using direct processor read/writes without any DMA support.

The bit-serial functions block contains an array of bit-serial functions that are interconnected in such a way that each of them can work cascaded or in parallel with the others through configurable interconnections. In the receive direction the bit-serial functions block gets input from the network and gives output to a serial-to-parallel shift register. In the transmit direction the bit-serial functions block gets input from a parallel-to-serial shift register and outputs to the network. The parallel functions block contains an array of functions connected to configurable interconnections as in the bit-serial functions block. The parallel functions block interfaces with the shift register and local FIFOs.

The events section monitors network events and informs the state machines section which controls and collects status from all the other blocks in the architecture. FIFOs are parameterized according to network buffering requirements and are connected to the DMA engine blocks or to the control registers section depending on the data path implementation.

Using the FPSLIC, all network related functions i.e. the bit-serial, parallel functions and the state machines contained in the GNA are implemented into the programmable logic, while the RISC processor implements all the control and management functions of the protocol. The FPSLIC's dual port SRAM, which is accessible by both the reconfigurable logic and the microprocessor can be used for temporary data storage while control and status information can be exchanged through the control and interrupt logic provided. Host transactions can be accomplished either by using the integrated UARTs, or through a custom host interface implemented in the programmable logic. With the integration of the program SRAM, FPSLIC does not require external memory devices, except from a serial FLASH for downloading program data into its internal memory.

3 Application Example – 10 Mbps Ethernet MAC Controller

A 10Mbps Ethernet MAC controller is used to implement the access protocol as defined in [4]. In the receive direction the MAC controller searches for Start-of-Frame Delimiter (SFD) at the beginning of each packet, qualifies the frame length and the received address and verifies the CRC. Also, it observes any receive code violations or carrier events that may occur and keeps a status vector for each packet received. In the transmit direction the MAC controller adds to the supplied frame a seven-bytes preamble and one-byte SFD, performs padding on frames having fewer than 60 bytes and appends the CRC. Also, the MAC controller performs the carrier sense, collision detection and the back-off algorithm and reports the status of the transmission using a status vector for each packet.

The application of GNA and FPSLIC for the implementation of a 10Mbps MAC controller is illustrated in figure 3. The general network architecture is customized in this case for supporting a 10 Mbps Ethernet network interface card.

The network functions implemented in the reconfigurable part of the chip consist of a receiver section and a transmitter section. The receiver section consists of a CRC-32 check module (bit-serial function), preamble detect, SFD detect modules (parallel functions) and the receive state machine which controls all the receive blocks using information from the control registers and network events (carrier sense, collision detect module). It produces write enable and address signals for writing the received data in the common dual port RAM module. On the other hand, the transmitter section consists of a CRC-32 generation module and a transmit state machine which controls the data flow to the network. It receives information from the control registers and network events and produces address and control signals for reading data from the dual port RAM.

Queue management, statistics gathering, buffer descriptors, control frame generation/detection, back-off and other MAC functions are performed by state machines implemented in software and executed by the AVR microcontroller.

An ISA interface, implemented in the FPGA, offers the appropriate host interface for reading/writing data and passing control, configuration information to the MAC. The full system is completed by an external I^{2}C flash for AVR program downloading and power up FPGA configuration, plus an Ethernet 10Mbps physical device.

In a typical reception procedure using the FPSLIC-MAC the receive block recognizes the start of packet (preamble) and the start of data (SFD) and stores the incoming parallel data to a buffer in the Dual Port RAM while sending an interrupt to the AVR processor. The AVR processes the packet header and constructs a receive buffer descriptor in the dual port RAM memory. When reception is completed, AVR causes an interrupt to the host indicating that a valid packet is stored at the location indicated by the buffer descriptor. In the transmit direction, the host stores the data to be transmitted in the dual port RAM and constructs a transmit buffer descriptor. The AVR appends the preamble, the SFD and the padding if needed and initiates a transmission. According to the status information received by the events processing block, it either marks the transmission as successful or retransmits the packet if a collision is detected performing the appropriate back-off algorithm. The transmission state machine appends the CRC and sends the data over the channel.

The implementation of the above 10Mbps MAC showed a problem in the FPSLIC architecture which was the limited addressing capability of the AVR processor to the FPGA part through the static microcontroller interface that uses only 2 address bits (directly address 4 registers and indirectly addresses 16 registers). A solution was to use the general purpose I/Os of the AVR processor to externally extend the address space for interfacing to the FPGA section.

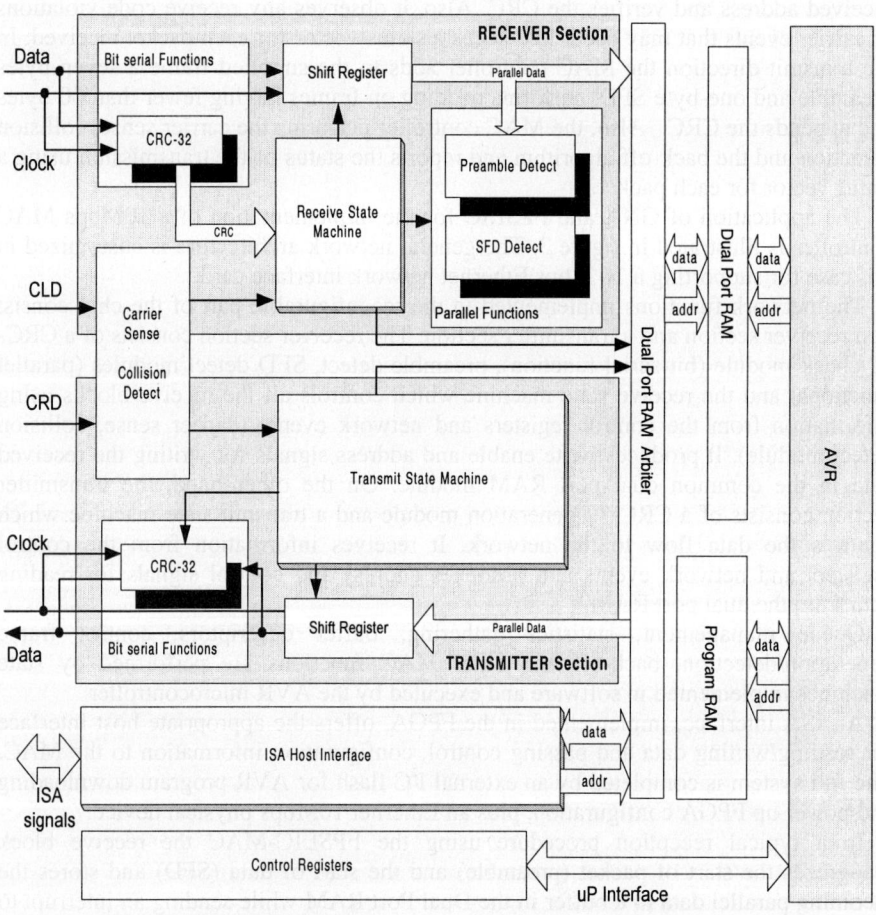

Fig. 3. Block diagram of an Ethernet MAC controller

4 Extending FPSLIC Capabilities

Due to the limited performance of the AVR 8-bit microcontroller, more demanding network architectures require powerful microcontrollers. One solution is to use more than one FPSLIC devices, implementing a distributed network processing solution. An architecture like the one illustrated in figure 4 is able to implement more complex network devices for processing at higher data rates and for supporting more demanding protocols.

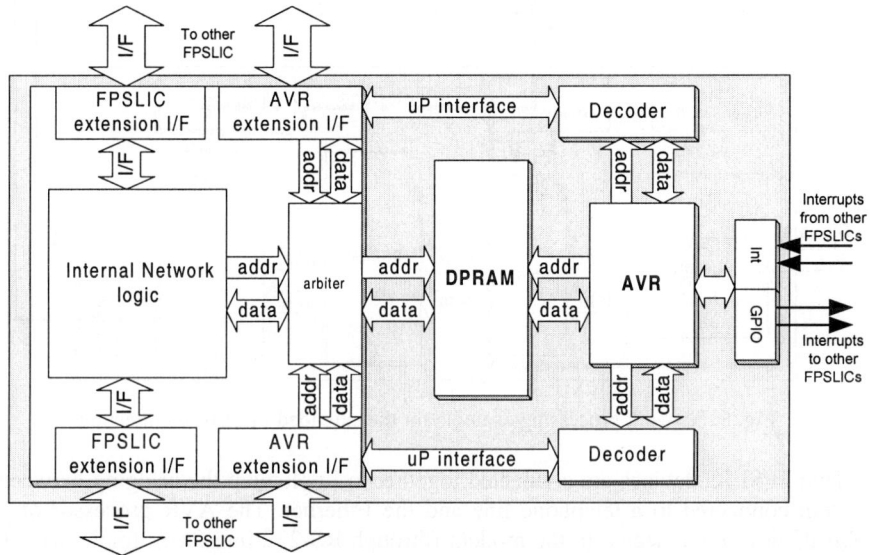

Fig. 4. FPSLIC configured for extension

The idea is based on connecting the configurable parts of two or more FPSLIC devices to produce a more powerful device with common memory space and to off-load protocol complexity by using more than one AVR processors. The communication between AVRs takes place through GPIOs, interrupts and a control path that is implemented in the reconfigurable logic illustrated as the AVR extension interface. Using the AVR extension interface, the AVR can also access the DPRAM of adjacent FPSLIC devices. The configurable part of the FPSLIC is extended through the FPSLIC extension interface.

An architecture containing two FPSLIC devices like the one shown in figure 5, can be used to implement access protocols requiring full duplex operation. Each AVR processor is attached to one direction (transmit or receive). The AVR processors execute code that controls the respective direction, while exchanging information through the AVR extension interfaces using either control registers or the dual port RAMs that can be accessed by both AVR cores (dashed line). A host interface can be implemented in the reconfigurable part of one of the FPSLIC devices while still having access to the dual port RAM of the other device through the FPSLIC extension interface.

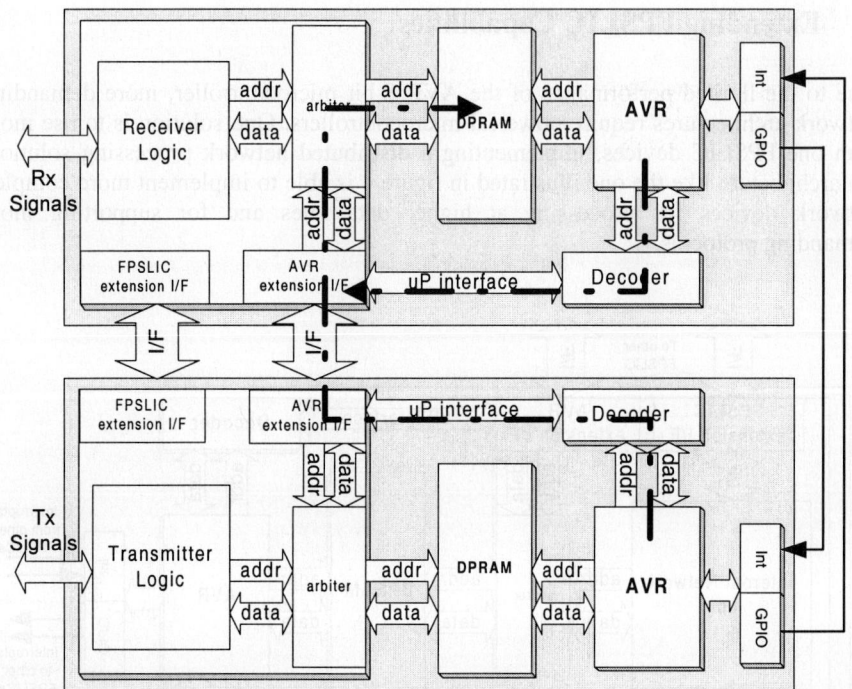

Fig. 5. Network processing example for the extended FPSLIC architecture

Two FPSLIC devices are connected together to implement the bridging between a modem connected to a telephone line and the Ethernet. The AVR processor of the FPSLIC device connected to the modem (through RS-232 interface), implements the PPP protocol and stores the data to the DPRAM of the FPSLIC connected to the Ethernet. The FPSLIC MAC processes the data according to the IEEE 802.3 protocol and transmits them over the Ethernet. In the other direction, the FPSLIC MAC processes the data from the Ethernet and passes them to the other FPSLIC device that performs the appropriate protocols in order to be sent over the telephone line.

5 Conclusions

The configurable nature of an FPSLIC device together with the general network architecture gives the network designer the flexibility to implement different access protocols based on the same platform, which consists of the microprocessor development tools and a HDL model of the General Network Architecture. In this paper we presented the use of FPSLIC architecture for implementing low complexity reconfigurable network processors and how this architecture can be extended to implement more powerful, distributed network processing tasks.

References

1. Nicholas, Cravotta, *Network processors: The Sky's the Limit*, EDN Magazine, November 1999, pages 108-119.
2. ATMEL, AT94 Series Field Programmable System Level Integrated Circuit, Advance Information.
3. Marios Iliopoulos, Theodore Antonakopoulos, *A Methodology of Implementing Medium Access Protocols Using a General Parameterized Architecture,* 11th IEEE International Workshop on Rapid System Prototyping, June 2000, France.
4. ANSI/IEEE Std 802.3-1996: *Carrier Sense Multiple Access with Collision Detection (CSMA/CD) access method and physical layer specifications*

Internet Connected FPL

Hamish Fallside[1] and Michael J. S. Smith[2]

[1]Xilinx Inc, 2100 Logic Drive, San Jose, CA 95124, USA
hamish@xilinx.com

[2]University of Hawaii at Manoa, 2540 Dole Street, Honolulu, HI 96822, USA
msmith@eng.hawaii.edu

Abstract. In this paper we explore the design of internet-based systems using field-programmable logic (FPL). We describe results from designing a hardware platform that connects FPL directly to an internet. This hardware platform comprises an FPGA; an Ethernet interface; storage for static and dynamic configuration; and nonvolatile configuration logic. An important feature of our hardware platform design is the implementation of network protocols that allow transfer of both application and configuration data to and from an FPGA across an internet. We provide quantitative comparisons between the implementation of network protocols in programmable logic and implementations using general-purpose processors.

Introduction

There is a growing demand for small, low cost, low power, flexible computing devices or appliances that attach directly to internets. For example, there are marketing forecasts that non-PC devices will account for almost 50 percent of internet connected devices by 2002 and that sales of such internet appliances will likely exceed the number of PCs sold by 2005 [1]. These internet connected devices or appliances are a potential application for field-programmable logic (FPL). The ability to use FPL and the Internet to reprogram hardware remotely would enable re-programmable switches, routers, and firewalls; multipurpose hardware devices; remote debugging and instruction; field upgrades and fixes; support for new and changing standards; and many other applications [2–6]. We set out to explore the role of FPL in such internet applications.

Currently PCs dedicate special hardware to control peripherals (memory, disks, video, even for mouse and keyboard) yet there is no special hardware to control what may become the most important peripheral of all: the Internet. Instead, we typically use a large and inefficient operating system running on a processor that is highly optimized for arithmetic and data processing. The complex pipelines and large arithmetic and floating-point units of modern microprocessors remain largely unused during communication. We wondered what was the most appropriate design for internet applications: processors (general or special purpose), dedicated hardware, programmable hardware, or a combination of any or all of these with software.

There are three types of questions we set out to answer:
- Engineering. Can we replace conventional microprocessor and software by dedicated internet hardware? What performance can we achieve?
- Economic. What is the cost? Does it make economic sense to dedicate hardware to the Internet as a peripheral?
- Technology. If the economics make sense, what is the appropriate technology?

We built a hardware platform to explore the answers to these questions; particularly the trade-offs between hardware and software implementations of an increasingly important function: internet connectivity. In this paper we answer the first group of engineering questions by explaining how we designed one solution. We do not have complete answers to the remaining questions (yet), but in this paper we begin to address these issues in a quantitative manner.

There are two ways to communicate over a channel: in a dedicated or shared manner. In a shared network such as the Internet, data is divided up into packets and each packet travels separately from source to destination. We focus on the Internet in this paper, though our work applies to any packet-shared network: wired or wireless.

The Internet is built around a set of protocols, which are methods and algorithms that handle the data packets. The most commonly used protocols established over the last 20 years are the Transmission Control Protocol (TCP) and the Internet Protocol (IP). TCP and IP are usually thought of as separate layers, but normally implemented together in software, called the TCP/IP stack, that runs on a general-purpose processor. However, the Internet runs on many layers of software and hardware, not just the TCP/IP stack. Comer [7] and Stevens [8] explain the software fabric of the Internet.

If the Internet is a road and a connected device is a car, you could think of the TCP/IP stack as the car engine. The hardware layer below the TCP/IP stack is the media access controller (MAC), the gearbox and brakes of the car. The hardware layer below the MAC that connects to the cables of the Internet is the physical layer (PHY), the wheels of the car. There will be different PHY layers depending on whether we use cable, wireless, or fibre, for example. However, the connection between the MAC and different PHY layers is very similar (and often identical), and is called the media-independent interface (MII). The digital MII is the interface between special (often mostly analog) PHY circuits and the digital systems that implement the MAC and TCP/IP stack. We have been unable to find good reference materials that explain the (mostly hardware) MAC and PHY layers, other than the datasheets from companies that make these components (see [9], for example). The definitive reference is the IEEE standard 802.3.

If we wish to add internet connectivity to a device, we must decide how to implement the MAC layer and protocol processing, such as the TCP/IP stack, either in programmable logic, dedicated hardware, processor plus software, or some combination of these. In order to make these decisions we must be able to measure the advantages and disadvantages of each approach. Kumar et al. have examined benchmark suites for configurable computing systems [10], but we need measurement techniques for network processing. There is little published work in this area and we decided to establish some metrics ourselves before designing out hardware platform.

In the following section we establish some complexity measures for a MAC as well as a software plus processor implementation of a TCP/IP stack. TCP and IP may not be the most important protocols (and certainly not the only protocols) for future internet applications, but in this paper we use the TCP/IP stack to make our complexity estimates, because few devices use other protocols.

We will examine three example designs using a PIC, an 8051 microcontroller, and a Sparc microprocessor to estimate average as well as lower and upper bounds for the amount of hardware and software required to implement a MAC and TCP/IP stack. At the end of this paper, we will compare the figures for these example designs with our FPGA hardware implementation.

Bounds on Protocol Processing

In June 1999 a small web server was implemented in 512 12-bit instructions (256 instructions for the TCP/IP functions) using a programmable microcontroller (a Microchip 12C509A, often called a PIC [11]) and a 24LC256 EEPROM (256 kbit). This web server used the Serial Line Internet Protocol (SLIP) in order to communicate with a host computer (bypassing the need for an Ethernet MAC). This PIC-based design supported a web site with approximately 32 small files (located in the external EEPROM) [12].

Though few details of this particular design are available, it is reasonable to conclude that it used „stateless TCP/IP" instead of a conventional TCP/IP stack. Stateless TCP/IP uses precomputed packets to drastically simplify the stack design. Nevertheless, we will use this PIC-based design to establish a lower bound on the complexity of an implementation of a very simple form of TCP/IP stack using software plus processor.

We can make an estimate of gate size (in four-transistor NAND gate equivalents) if we were to implement the PIC-based design using an ASIC or FPGA. We have used metrics from [13, Chapter 15] to estimate the number of gates used by the components, the ALU and datapath, for which we have area, but not gate size estimates. We used a conversion factor of $5 \times 10^{-4} / \lambda^2$ for a standard-cell ASIC implementation. The parameter λ measures the feature size and permits gate size measurements to be made from area measures, independently of the process generation.

The 12C509A PIC contains a processor, 1024 by 12 bits of EPROM memory, and 41 bytes of data memory [11]. Table 1 shows the estimates of the gate counts for each of the components in the 12C509A PIC. The total gate count estimate is 16.4 kgate (including onboard program and data memory) or 4.5 kgate (excluding program memory). This estimate is definitely a lower bound because some of the TCP/IP tasks (constructing packet headers, for example) have been precomputed and stored in the external EEPROM.

Table 2 shows the PIC-based design gate estimates translated to the Xilinx Virtex FPGA family. The Virtex parts contain static RAM (called Block RAM) that are separate from the CLBs. (The CLB, or Configurable Logic Block, is the basic unit of logic in a Xilinx static RAM-based FPGA. One Virtex CLB contains four logic cells plus four flip-flops organized as two slices.) Each Block RAM is a synchronous dual-port 4 kbit RAM. The 12 kbit of EPROM onboard the 12C509A PIC thus translates to four blocks of Virtex RAM. We will explain the figures used to estimate the size of the MAC presently.

Table 1. Microchip 12C509A PIC Gate Size Estimates.

PIC component	Area/kλ^2	kgates	Notes
ROM program memory [11]		12	1024 x 12 bits, 1 gate per bit
EEPROM data and control memory [11]		0.5	41 bytes, 1 gate per bit
8-bit ALU [13]	330	0.2	Estimate for a simple 8-bit processor, 2901 equivalent
Instruction decode		2	Estimate for a simple 8-bit processor
8-bit datapath	2400	1.2	Registers and Muxes
Timers (estimate)		0.5	Registers and Muxes
Total		16.4	

Our average bound design uses a typical implementation of a MAC and a TCP/IP stack in an embedded system with an 8051 microcontroller. A commercial 8051 core (an 8-bit machine) occupies approximately 500 CLBs in a Xilinx Virtex FPGA (this figure is for the processor core and excludes program memory) [14]. The synthesizable 8051 soft core from Synopsys requires 10–13 kgate [15]. These two measurements of the size of an 8051 give us a conversion factor (biased towards circuits such as microprocessors) of approximately 20 gates/CLB that we will use in this paper. (Any attempt to compare ASIC and FPGA capacities in gates is fraught with problems, but we are using these figures here for no more than back-of-the-envelope calculations.) Additional space for code is required to implement the TCP/IP stack and an Ethernet MAC in our 8051 based example. We can estimate the code requirements as follows:

- A typical embedded TCP/IP stack requires approximately 25 kbyte of code (see [16], for example).
- A full-featured commercial Ethernet MAC core occupies about 800 Virtex CLBs [17], or about 16 kgate.
- A basic Ethernet MAC requires about 4 kgate [13], or about 200 Virtex CLBs.
- Driver code for the Ethernet and a real-time operating system (RTOS) to handle the 8051 interrupts is also required. A typical RTOS requires a minimum of 4 kbyte of code to perform task management and handle interrupts (see [18], for example, for figures for an ARM7 processor).

Table 2 shows that the 8051 based design totals 10 kgate (excluding program and data memory). Table 2 also includes a lower estimate of 25 kbyte of ROM and 4 kbyte of RAM for program and data memory, which translates to 58 Virtex RAM blocks.

Our upper bound design uses a Sparc processor. The Leon embedded Sparc compatible processor requires 1800 Virtex CLBs (36 kgate) [19]. A TCP/IP stack for a Sparc compatible processor requires approximately 25 kbyte [16]. Again, this is in addition to the approximately 10 kbyte memory requirement of a Sparc compatible RTOS (see [18] for figures for a Sparc-lite processor). Table 2 shows the Sparc-based design totals 36 kgate (excluding program and data memory) and would require about 70 blocks of RAM if implemented in a Virtex FPGA.

Table 2. Processor implementation summaries.

Resource	PIC	8051	Sparc	Notes
Gates (kgate)	4.5	10	36	
ROM (kbyte)	1.5	25	25	1024 x 12 bits
RAM (kbyte)	0	4	10	
Virtex BRAM	3	58	70	4 kbit per block RAM
Virtex CLBs	425	700	2000	Include 200 CLB for simple Ethernet MAC

Our estimates for implementing the lower bound (PIC), average (8051), and upper bound (Sparc) solutions for internet protocol processing in FPGA logic are summarized in Table 2. The smallest member of the Virtex family, the XCV50, contains 384 CLBs and eight blocks of RAM; the XCV1000 contains 6144 CLBs and 32 blocks of RAM. The lower bound PIC-based design fits in a single Virtex device, as the memory requirements are three RAM blocks. The other two designs would require external RAM.

Details of Our Hardware Platform Design

Figure 1 is a block diagram of our hardware platform, the Demonstation. The Ethernet interface to the Demonstation is a PHY chip [9]. The analog portion of the PHY chip is the only thing preventing us from connecting a Xilinx FPGA physically to the Ethernet cable.

We use the Xilinx byte-wide SelectMap interface to configure the FPGA [20]. Data from a 1 Mbyte parallel ROM is written to the SelectMap interface of the FPGA at power-up by a configuration controller, implemented in a nonvolatile CPLD. The FPGA then takes control of the configuration controller.

Two banks of asynchronous byte-wide SRAM, each 1 MB, are connected to the FPGA. One of these SRAM banks connects to both the FPGA and the configuration controller. This allows the FPGA to load configuration data from the Internet and then write that data to SRAM. When a configuration file has been assembled in SRAM, the FPGA instructs the configuration controller to reconfigure the FPGA using the data in SRAM. Using this scheme, FPGA reconfiguration may be either full or partial.

All the hardware implementations of embedded web servers or TCP/IP stacks (that we are aware of) either use a serial protocol or require a computer or router to connect to a shared network. These are important differences, both of which are often ignored, from a direct internet connection. The Demonstation interfaces directly with the packet-switched multiple-access Ethernet physical layer. In addition, our design permits dynamic reconfiguration over the Internet, without the need for an attached computer, and this (as far as we know) is also unique.

Constructing the Internet in layers (software or hardware) allows each layer to be changed. Applications use the Internet protocols to transfer data. These protocols are defined by the Requests for Comments (RFC) [21]. The FPGA must implement an application that is capable of file transfer using the network protocols to move data to and from the Demonstation.

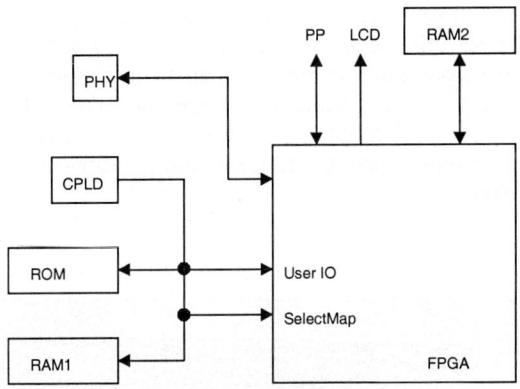

Fig. 1. Block diagram of the Demonstation.

One application that uses TCP is the File Transfer Protocol (FTP). We could use FTP to transmit configuration and data to the FPGA, but to simplify things, we started with the Trivial File Transfer Protocol (TFTP), which is less complex than the FTP. TFTP uses the Universal Datagram Protocol (UDP) rather than TCP. Taken together, UDP and TFTP function in a similar fashion to TCP, and as a subset of FTP.

The MAC currently supports 10BaseT, but the PHY device will also support 100BaseT, and provides full Carrier Sense, Multiple Access, Collision Detect (CSMA/CD), and Ethernet II and IEEE 802.3.

The IP layer provides IP address checking and the IP header checksum. In our TFTP implementation no defragmentation is performed on received IP datagrams (fragmentation occurs when a datagram is too large for a network between the source and destination). Defragmentation is generally regarded as being undesirable, because loss of a single fragment means that the entire datagram will be discarded [8]. TFTP uses a maximum data block size of 512 bytes, and thus datagrams will not be fragmented on an Ethernet. We did implement a simple defragmentation design in approximately 100 Virtex CLBs as an experiment.

The UDP layer performs a checksum on the message contained within the IP datagram, and provides source and destination port numbers for the applications that use it. TFTP on the Demonstation implements a write-request server to a client. TFTP sends a response message back to the client for each message received. This return message is usually an acknowledgement of data received or an error message. Data received over the Internet from the client is written to the SRAM (RAM1 in Fig. 2) on the Demonstation. Once the last data message is acknowledged the TFTP layer signals the configuration controller to initiate reconfiguration of the FPGA.

Results

Our Demonstation hardware platform successfully performs reconfiguration of Virtex devices across 10 Mbit/s Ethernet using TFTP in a few seconds. The actual reconfiguration time depends heavily upon network loading. TFTP transmits data in 512 byte messages and each message has to be acknowledged before the next can be transmitted. This gives a theoretical maximum throughput of 8 Mbits/s. Our measured TFTP results give reconfiguration times of up to a minute for the largest Virtex devices (which require up to 8 Mbit of configuration data). TCP has a theoretical maximum throughput of 1.2 Mbyte/s [22] with measured sustained rates at 90% of this value. We would thus expect to reduce reconfiguration times slightly using TCP over 10 MB/s Ethernet.

Fig. 2. The Demonstation platform. Top left is the Ethernet interface: cable connector, transformer and PHY chip. Bottom left is a prototyping area. Bottom right is an LCD panel, and parallel port (PP) for debugging. Above the LCD is a socket for a Virtex FPGA. Next to the FPGA socket (above right and below left) are two banks of SRAM (RAM1 and RAM2). To the right of the FPGA socket are the power regulators. The configuration controller, a nonvolatile CPLD, is on the underside of the board.

The worst case timing for our design occurs when a full-length frame (containing 1500 bytes of data) is followed by a minimum length frame (with 46 bytes of data). Frames are separated by an inter-frame gap (IFG) of 9.6 μs. In the worst case we have to move 1500 bytes from the MAC buffer to SRAM before we can process the next frame. So we have 67.2 μs to process and store 1500 bytes, or 44.8 ns per byte. Our design meets this timing constraint using a system clock of 50 MHz, giving us two clock cycles per byte to process and store each byte.

For 100BaseT Ethernet there would be 15.4 μs to process a full-length frame, which requires a clock frequency of 146 MHz. The increased data rate could be implemented by adding another receive buffer and/or by increasing the data path sizes within the stack.

Table 3. FPGA implementation summary. The design results in this table were obtained using Synplify synthesis software with the Xilinx Alliance tools version 2.0. The CLB and RAM block counts are for the Virtex FPGA family.

Protocol/layer	VHDL lines	CLBs	RAM blocks
MAC	3000	200	6
IP	2000	150	0
UDP	4000	175	3
TFTP	2400	133	0
Total	11400	658	9

The complete FPGA protocol stack contains a total of nine block RAMs and 658 CLBs (or about 13,000 gates by the simple conversion metrics we have used here). Table 3 summarizes the details of the various protocol and application layers implemented in the FPGA.

We can compare the breakdown of VHDL and hardware for the Demonstation protocol stack shown in Table 3 to an analysis of network protocol software for Unix [22]. About 40% of the Unix code is dedicated to TCP; 20% to IP; 20% to network utilities (error checking and so on); and 10% to UDP and ARP (a protocol for address resolution) combined. These estimates hold for both the number of lines of C code and number of procedures in each protocol layer. One thing these figures tell us is that we should expect to write another 5000 lines of VHDL code and use at least 200 Virtex CLBs (or about 4 kgate) to implement a TCP layer.

We have tried to compare the results shown in Table 3 with other implementations, but we believe we are the first to implement a protocol stack in an FPGA and the first to design a platform that implements reconfiguration over the Internet. Probably the closest work to ours is a product announced by iReady aimed at internet FAX machines [23]. The custom iReady chip is built by Seiko and uses 67 kgate for a network protocol stack (for the point to point protocol, PPP, using a serial port together with support for IP, TCP, UDP, and two sockets) and 20 kbyte for network buffers. The iReady chip is thus not able to connect directly to the Internet, but does implement a TCP/IP stack. From brief discussions with iReady, we believe one reason for the large difference between their implementation (67 kgate) and ours (13 kgate) is due to the fact that their chip has been designed and tested to work with many different routers and switches, incurring additional overhead.

In the introduction we explained that we set out to answer three sets of questions. In this paper we have presented answers to the first set of engineering questions. We can replace conventional microprocessor and software by FPL in internet applications. We can implement internet reconfiguration. We can reconfigure an FPGA containing several hundred thousand gates in a reasonable time across the Internet.

In the introduction we also posed economic and technology questions for which we do not yet have answers. We have included very brief remarks on the issues of costs and power because we find these are questions that we are asked repeatedly when discussing our project.

We made no cost estimates before building Demonstation and cost did not influence our design. The current platform is dominated by the cost of the Virtex part, but low-cost alternatives, such as the Xilinx Spartan FPGAs, are equally suitable.

Perhaps more telling is that there is no other way to implement the ability to reconfigure hardware using an internet. In situations where remote reconfiguration is valuable (such as satellites, for example) cost may be less of a factor.

The 8051 design gives us the ability to estimate power dissipation of an average embedded TCP/IP stack implementation. The Dallas Semiconductor 8051 consumes about 5 mW/MHz [24]. In the Xilinx Virtex family, the 8051 core runs at about 30 MHz. At 30 MHz the Dallas 8051 consumes 150 mW. We can quickly estimate that an 8051 core running in a Virtex part at 30 MHz would consume more than this. Our current Virtex implementation draws nearly 1 A total while using three different supply voltages (5V, 3.3V, and 2.5V). The Demonstation includes FPGA, CPLD, static RAM, LCD, parallel port, and PHY chip, and we made absolutely no effort to minimize the power consumption of the present platform design.

We presented an FPGA implementation of the network protocols required to connect hardware to an internet. We compared our design with other possible implementations using standard processors. We have demonstrated that FPL can be used to provide network protocols and applications that are currently implemented using software and a general-purpose microprocessor. Complete details of the XCoNet project are documented on the Web [25].

References

1. IDC http://www.idc.com:8080/Press/Archive/jun15c.htm
2. Brebner, G. and N. Bergmann. 1999. Reconfigurable Computing in Remote and Harsh Environments. Ninth International Workshop on Field Programmable Logic and Applications (FPL99).
3. Lockwood, J. W., J. S. Turner, and D. E. Taylor. 2000. Field Programmable Port Extender (FPX) for Distributed Routing and Queuing. Eighth ACM International Symposium on Field-Programmable Gate Arrays (FPGA00).
4. Maly, K., C. Wild, C. M. Overstreet, H. Abdel-Wahab, A. Gupta, A. Youssef, E. Stoica, R. Talla, and A. Prabhu. Interactive Remote Instruction: Initial Experiences. 1996. Proceedings of the Conference on Integrating Technology into Computer Science Education.
5. McHenry, J., P. Dowd, T. Carrozzi, F. Pellegrino, and W. Cocks. 1997. An FPGA-Based Coprocessor for ATM Firewalls. The Fifth Annual IEEE Symposium on Field-Programmable Custom Computing Machines (FCCM97).
6. Miyazaki, T., K. Shirakawa, M. Katayama, T. Murooka, A. Takahara. 1998. A Transmutable Telecom System. International Workshop on Field Programmable Logic and Applications (FPL98).
7. Comer, D. E. 1995. Internetworking with TCP/IP Vol. I: Principles, Protocols, and Architecture. 3rd edition. Prentice Hall. ISBN: 0132169878.
8. Stevens, W. R. 1994. TCP/IP Illustrated, Vol. 1. The Protocols. Addison-Wesley. ISBN: 0201633469.
9. Level One Ethernet Transceiver. See http://www.level1.com/product/pdf/lxt970ad.pdf
10. Kumar, S., L. Pires, S. Ponnuswamy, C. Nanavati, J. Golusky, M. Vojta, S. Wadi, D. Pandalai, and H. Spaanenburg. 2000. A Benchmark Suite for Evaluating Configurable Computing Systems—Status, Reflections, and Future Directions. Eighth ACM International Symposium on Field-Programmable Gate Arrays (FPGA00).
11. Microchip. See http://www.microchip.com/Download/Lit/PICmicro/12C5XX/40139e.pdf
12. IPIC. See http://www-ccs.cs.umass.edu/~shri/iPic.html
13. Smith, M. J. S. 1997. Application-Specific Integrated Circuits. Reading, MA: Addison-Wesley. ISBN 0201500221. TK7874.6.S63.

14. Dolphin Flop805X Core. See
   http://www.support.xilinx.com/products/logicore/alliance/dolphin/flip805x-pr.pdf
15. Synopsys 8051 Core. See http://www.synopsys.com/products/designware/8051_ds.html
16. SuperTask RTOS. See http://www.ussw.com/products/supertask.
17. CoreEl Fast MAC Cores. See
    http://www.xilinx.com/products/logicore/alliance/coreel/cs1100.pdf
18. Express Logic ThreadX RTOS. See http://www.expresslogic.com/threadx.html. ThreadX on an ARM7 is about 4 kbyte. ThreadX on an ARC processor is 4-25 kbyte.
19. ESA, European Space Agency Leon SPARC V8 Development. See
    http://www.estec.esa.nl/wsmwww/leon/
20. Xilinx Virtex family datasheet. See http://www.xilinx.com/partinfo/ds003.pdf and application note on parallel configuration, http://www.xilinx.com/xapp/xapp137.pdf
21. RFC 691 FTP, RFC 768 UDP, RFC 783 TFTP, RFC 791 IP, RFC 793 TCP. See http://www.cis.ohio-state.edu/htbin/rfc/rfcXXX.html
22. Comer, Douglas E. and. David L. Stevens. 1998. Internetworking With TCP/IP: Design, Implementation, and Internals. 3rd edition. Vol 2. Englewood Cliffs, NJ: Prentice Hall. ISBN: 0139738436
23. iReady Internet Tuner. See http://www.iready.com/products/internet_tuner.html
24. Dallas Semiconductor. See http://www.dalsemi.com/DocControl/PDFs/87c520.pdf
25. XCoNET. See http://www-ee.eng.hawaii.edu/~msmith/XCoNET/XCoNET.htm

Field Programmable Communication Emulation and Optimization for Embedded System Design

Frank-Michael Renner, Jürgen Becker, and Manfred Glesner

Institute of Microelectronic Systems,
Darmstadt University of Technology,
Karlstrasse 15,
D-64283 Darmstadt, Germany
{renner,becker,glesner}@mes.tu-darmstadt.de

Abstract. The generation of application-specific communication architectures is a time consuming and error prone task in embedded system design. In most design environments the evaluation of generated communication structures is done by cosimulation only. In this paper we present an approach to architecture-precise embedded system communication emulation using a reconfigurable rapid prototyping platform, hardware monitoring of the emulated communication structure as well as local and global communication architecture optimization techniques[1].

Keywords: Hardware/software codesign, architecture-precise rapid prototyping, real-time embedded systems, field programmable emulation

1 Introduction

One of the key issues in hardware/software codesign, the generation of suitable interprocess communication interfaces determines amount and type of communication between different components of a digital system. In obtaining full benefit of high performance components, the problem of communication is one of the main obstacles. Most of the computationally intensive algorithms have to deal with an immense amount of data. Not the processing components itself but the quality of the interfaces and the throughput of connections between these components is the main bottleneck of the system [1].

In most design environments for mixed hardware/software systems the embedded system specification is partitioned into separate hardware and software processes where the communication between these processes is either neglected, estimated very roughly or assumed to be fix [9]. Current communication generation approaches either support point-to-point communication, shared memory communication [10], a common bus [2], or a similar fixed architecture [4]. Other approaches are limited to an interface conversion between different and incompatible protocols [3]. Only a few approaches realizing flexible, application specific

---
[1] This work is supported by the German Research Foundation (DFG) within the Research Program "Rapid Prototyping of Embedded Systems with Hard Time Constraints"

communication structures, are under development [11], where the communication estimation is included within the automated hardware/software system partitioning to reduce communication overhead and to trade off fast but expensive protocols with slower and cheaper ones.

The key problem is to validate the generated communication structure against the requirements afterwards. This is normally done by cosimulation [13, 14] due to the lack of architectural prototyping systems. Architectural Prototyping is a promising new method driven by technology advances as well as by the progress in synthesis techniques which tries to bridge the gap between prototypes of the (executable) system specification and implementation details of the final product. There is a first industrial platform available for fast breadboarding of system designs at approximately 20 MHz (*MP 4 System Explorer* [12]). Considering the trend in nowadays complex system designs of re-using previously designed modules (also termed IP-modules) such as processors, memories or I/O circuitries, the interfacing of the components has to be covered especially by an architectural prototyping system.

Here, a new architecture-precise communication emulation and optimization approach is described which is part of the design flow within the codesign environment *DICE* [8]. An automated communication architecture synthesis (see section 3) generates for a given hardware/software partitioning an optimized communication topology to determine how the different components are to be connected. The target architecture is not restricted to a special application or system structure. Based on communication and timing constraints as system requirements and communication performance models [6] a thorough analysis of different communication architectures currently using direct, buffered and bus-based communication is performed. The derived communication structure along with the hardware and software processes are transfered to the real-time prototyping environment *REPLICA* (see section 2) for communication emulation, validation and optimization (see section 4).

2 Target System for Architecture-Precise Prototyping

REPLICA [5] (**R**ealtime **E**xecution **P**latform for **I**ntermodule **C**ommunication **A**rchitectures) is a rapid prototyping system focusing on realistic interprocessor/intermodule communication emulation (see figure 1). The system is integrated within the hardware/software codesign environment for real-time embedded systems called *DICE*. A description of this codesign environment can be found in [8]. The rapid prototyping system facilitates design space exploration and validation of derived communication structures. The reconfigurable system architecture allows prototyping of different topologies, communication types and protocols.

REPLICA is based on a scalable and reconfigurable system architecture. As depicted in figure 2 a), a minimal system consists of a backplane, up to six processing modules and optionally an interface module between each processing module and the backplane. The backplane (*BP*) can be configured for

Fig. 1. The real-time execution platform *REPLICA*

different interconnect topologies generated during communication synthesis. A non-blocking switch matrix has been chosen as interconnection device. During the prototyping step this device imposes no restrictions on the topologies which can be implemented and elaborated. The final application system will implement the optimal communication structure including the interfaces between the hardware and software components and will not suffer from the interconnection costs introduced by the switch matrix.

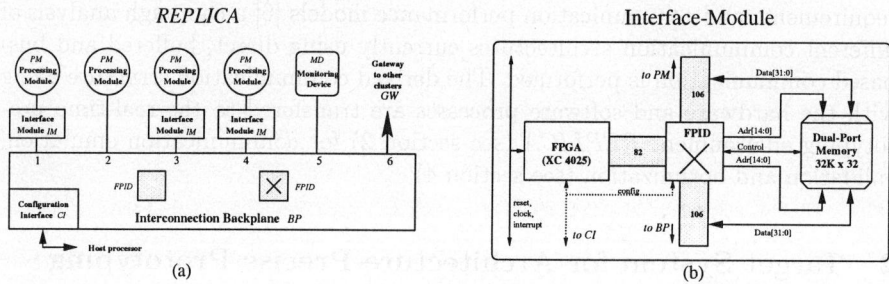

Fig. 2. Reconfigurable architecture of *REPLICA* and an interface module (*IM*)

The communication type and the protocol of the communication connections to be prototyped may require additional hardware resources such as memory and glue logic synchronization circuits. These components will be mapped on interface modules (*IM*) providing additional FPGAs and dual port ram (DPRAM) for realizing these communication links (see figure 2 b).

REPLICA can be used in conjunction with various processing modules (*PM*), including a floating point signal processor board with up to four Texas Instruments TMS320C40 processors, a RISC microcontroller board based on the Motorola Power-PC505, a microcontroller board based on a Siemens C167 and an

FPGA-based emulation system with a capacity of 50K gates and a typical emulation frequency of 5-10 MHz.

The integrated hardware monitor *HarMonIC* (**Har**dware **Mon**itor for **I**nterprocess **C**ommunication) [5] extracts real-time measured communication data about I/O-channel activities for performance evaluation and enhancement of arbitrary communication channels within the system.

HarMonIC is a central and passive hardware monitor and can be connected to any signal of the emulated target system using crossbar switches. The architecture of the hardware monitor enables the access of these signals without changing the functional or timing behavior of the emulated system (non-intrusive). The event driven concept of the monitoring device exists of two separate phases, the *online* and the *offline* phase (see Figure 3).

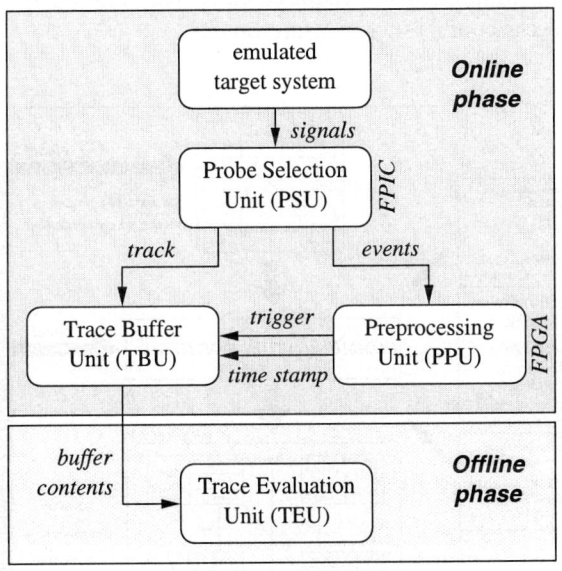

Fig. 3. Block digram of *HarMonIC*

Within the *online* phase of *HarMonIC* all events are detected and recorded in real time, i.e. synchronous to the system clock. All units of the online phase are realized in hardware to guarantee real time behavior without missing any event to be detected.

The recorded information are analyzed and evaluated within the *offline* phase. As the information is buffered, this must not be executed in real time. The Trace Evaluation Unit (*TEU*) is realized in software and offers the flexibility needed to analyze the measured data.

3 Communication Synthesis and Optimization

After partitioning a mixed VHDL/C specification or a given system description consisting of hardware, software and IP components, a hardware/software system of several cooperating processes and abstract communication functions is derived [8]. Software components have to be mapped to software execution platforms, like microcontrollers, microprocessors and DSPs, while hardware components are implemented using FPGAs or ASICs. The interprocess communication, which is modeled in the specification phase using abstract *send* and *receive* functions, must be physically realized by generating an optimized communication structure between these components and by replacing the abstract communication functions. We define a communication structure as *feasible*, if it is efficient enough to fulfill the hard real-time constraints and to use only the ports available by the given hardware and software execution units. In addition, the *optimized* communication structure minimizes the required area, the number of necessary ports and potential access conflicts when using busses.

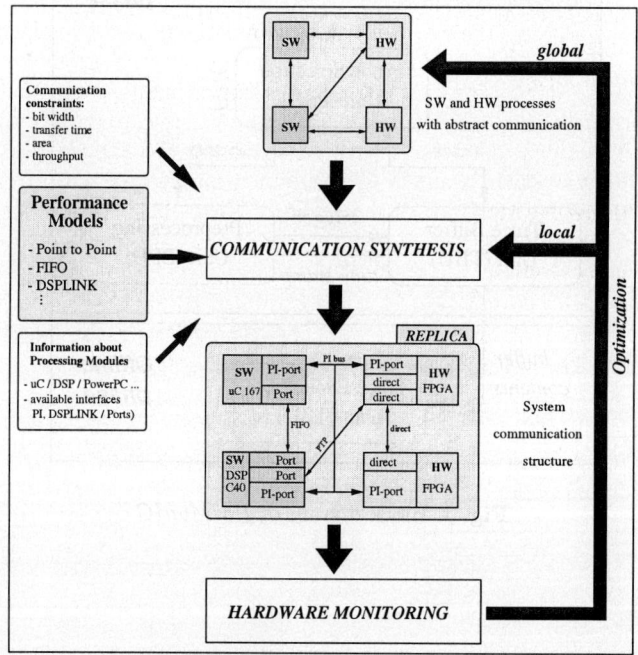

Fig. 4. Communication architecture synthesis and optimization flow

During communication synthesis (see figure 4), an optimized communication structure of the complete embedded system is generated within the following steps:

- An arbitrary number of processes can be mapped manually to specific processors, e.g. data flow oriented parts should be mapped to DSPs and control flow dominated processes to microcontrollers. An optimized mapping of the remaining processes is determined automatically during the communication synthesis step.
- Under consideration of the communication and timing constraints the performance estimation of transfer delays related to different communication links under investigation is performed.
- The communication synthesis algorithms determine an optimized communication structure regarding the given timing constraints and port limitations of the processing modules. If the port limitations are violated, a bus-based structure for non-critical ports is generated. Transfers with high throughput or with tight real-time constraints are realized using the existing ports while the remaining transfers are mapped to the generated busses.

A detailed description of the underlying communication synthesis algorithms can be found in [7]. To emulate the generated communication structure the abstract *send* and *receive* functions are replaced with the according hardware and software drivers to access the physical communication structure. The communication drivers are part of a *communication library* to support automated communication architecture synthesis. Additional items of this library include communication performance models [6] used to estimate the communication overhead during communication synthesis and VHDL descriptions for additional logic when implementing special connections.

During communication emulation within the embedded system environment the generated communication structure is monitored using the hardware monitor *HarMonIC*. The measured communication data is used to further optimize the generated communication structure. In a *local* optimization loop the necessary depths of the buffered communication links are adjusted to the needed amount of memory cells and the initial worst-case arbitration scheme of a bus-based communication type is improved using the measured communication data as well. If the communication activity excels the capacity of the communication structure due to heavy interaction with the environment a better system partitioning is initiated within the *global* optimization loop.

4 Communication Emulation and Optimization - An Example

Figure 5 illustrates the feasibility of this approach. The example application consists of three processes: one controlling process realized in software (*Ctrl*) and two hardware processes *PSrc* and *PSink*.

The designer is able to preselect manually specific processing modules to execute certain processes, or he can leave this decision to the communication synthesis algorithm. First the communication overhead is estimated using communication performance models. Details of the performance models and estimation results are given in [6]. The communication estimation results are used to

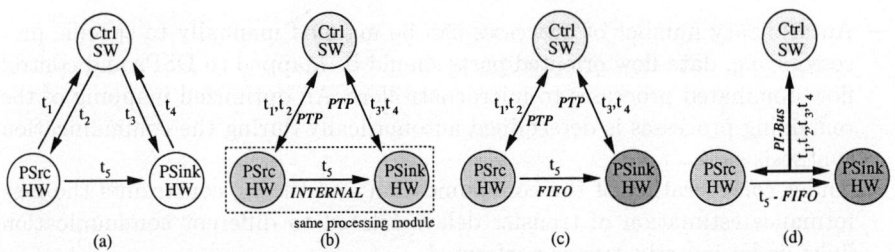

Fig. 5. Automated communication structure generation for example application

determine an optimized communication structure efficient enough to fulfill the communication constraints while obeying the limited port resources and minimizing the additional area introduced by the communication structure.

In figure 5 (b) both hardware processes are mapped to the same processing module by the communication synthesis algorithms in order to minimize the area introduced by the communication structure. Here, all communication constraints are fulfilled and the amount of port resources was not exceeded. The software process *Ctrl* is mapped to a Siemens C167 microcontroller, while the hardware processes *PSrc* and *PSink* are mapped to an FPGA. The same result is obtained when the number of port resources are not sufficient due to communications between the hardware processes, or the transfer delay time is too large using external transfers. For communication emulation the abstract communication functions are replaced with the specific hardware and software drivers to access the physical communication structure. C-processes and VHDL components to access the point-to-point connections replace the abstract *send* and *receive* functions. The communication architecture graph generated during communication synthesis is used to configure the rapid prototyping system *REPLICA*. The hardware monitor *HarMonIC* is configured automatically and monitors the emulated communication structure. The measured communication data is used to validate the communication structure against the communication constraints given by the designer.

If the user maps the hardware processes to different FPGAs manually, the resulting communication graph due to the communication synthesis algorithm is shown in figure 5 (c). Again, all communication constraints are fulfilled and the amount of port resources was not exceeded. The asynchronous communication between the processes *PSrc* and *PSink* is realized using a FIFO connection. The configuration of *REPLICA* is shown in figure 6.

The point to pint connections between *Ctrl*, *PSrc* and *PSink* is realized using the reconfigurable switches (FPIC) on the corresponding interface modules (IM) and the backplane (BP). In addition, the realization of the FIFO connection requires memory resources which are available on the interface modules. The *FIFO sentinel* (see figure 7) observes the ports of the connected processes, guards the addressing of the dual port memory for the FIFO connection and provides additional information to the hardware monitor for optimization purposes.

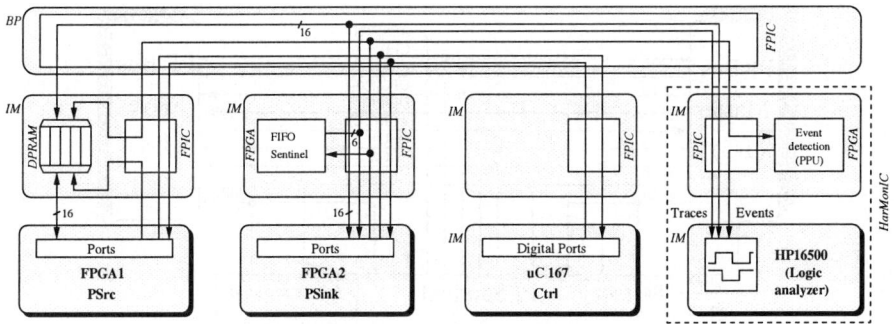

Fig. 6. Emulation of the application communication structure with *REPLICA*

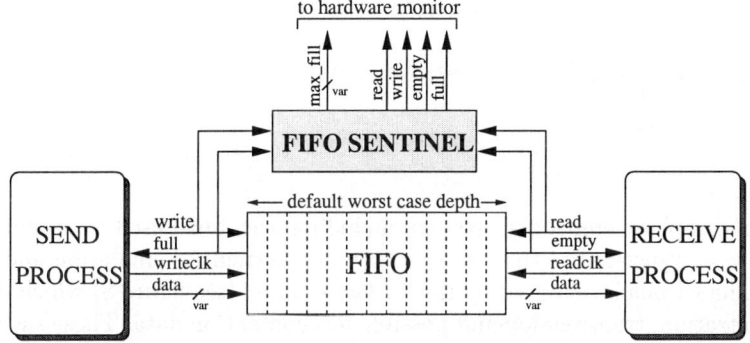

Fig. 7. FIFO based communication observation using the *FIFO sentinel*

In addition to the timing of the communication transfers during emulation, the FIFO sentinel monitors the maximum FIFO depth needed by the hardware/software system. This data is used within the optimization loop to minimize the area introduced by the FIFO depth. The *sentinel* is realized for all buffered communication types (FIFO, LIFO, DPRAM, Shared Memory).

To demonstrate the emulation of a bus-based communication structure, the number of available port resources of the software processing module was reduced to one external port for the communication synthesis algorithms. As we need two transfer channels from the software process, a PI bus is inferred connecting all processes. Transfers with high throughput and tight timing constraints are mapped to the remaining ports. As no ports remain for the software process, only transfer t_5 with high data throughput is mapped to the remaining ports of the hardware processing modules. Transfers t_1 to t_4 are mapped to the PI bus. Thus, the initial PI bus arbitration priority order is { **Ctrl** – *uC167*, **PSrc** – *FPGA2*, **PSink** – *FPGA3*}.

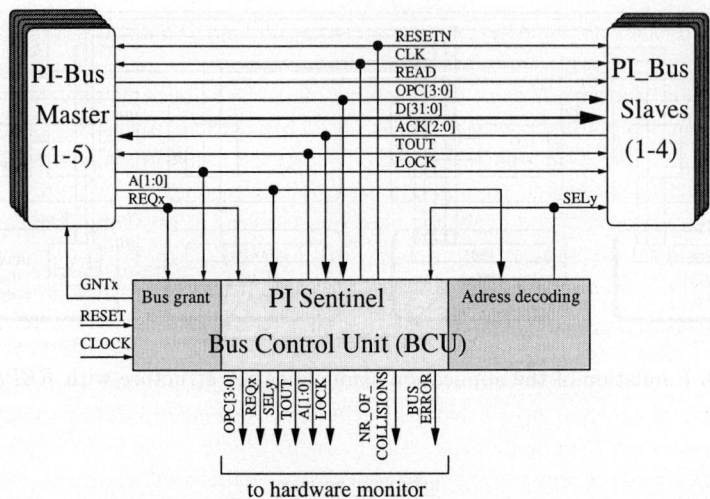

Fig. 8. PI bus observation using the *PI sentinel*

The complete embedded system including the bus-based communication structure is transfered to the rapid prototyping system for emulation and evaluation. The PI bus is observed by the *PI bus sentinel* (see figure 8) which collects bus arbitration, transmission and possible bus contention data. These signals are transferred to the hardware monitor. The measured bus activity data is used in the *local* optimization loop to adapt and optimize the arbitration scheme or to generate a second PI bus to avoid bus contention and thus unpredictable data transfer latencies. If the *local* optimization of the generated bus-based communication structure does not satisfy the communication constraints, a better system partitioning is initiated within the *global* optimization loop.

5 Conclusions

In this paper we described an approach to communication emulation and optimization using different field programmable devices (e.g. crossbar switches, FPGAs). In contrast to embedded system cosimulation a *realistic* architecture-precise prototype including its communication structure is emulated within the embedded system environment. With the measured real-time data of the hardware monitor the communication structure can be optimized regarding memory depths as well as bus priorities to minimize bus contentions.

Future work include the design of additional communication types and automation of the hardware prototype generation including the replacement of the abstract communications functions by reconfigurable hardware implementations. In addition, the measured monitor data will be used to automatically initiate a better hardware/software system partitioning, if communication bottlenecks exceed the capacity of the possible automatically generated communication structure.

References

1. Yen, T.-Y. and Wolf, W.: Hardware-Software Co-Synthesis of Distributed Embedded Systems. Kluwer Academic Publishers (1997), ISBN 0-7923-9797-5
2. Ortega, R. B. and Borriello, G.: Communication Synthesis for Distributed Embedded Systems. In: Proc. of the Int. Conference on Computer Aided Design. San Jose, USA (1998)
3. Passerone, R. and Rowson, J.A. and Sangiovanni-Vincentelli, A.: Synthesis of Interfaces between Incompatible Protocols. In: Proc. of the 35th Design Automation Conference. San Francisco, USA (1998)
4. Baganne, A. and Philippe, J.-L. and Martin, E.: A Formal Technique for Hardware Interface Design. In: IEEE Transactions on Circuits and Systems, 45(5) (1998)
5. Kirschbaum, A.: A Rapid Prototyping Approach for communication architectures in embedded systems. PhD dissertation, Darmstadt University of Technology (1998), ISBN-3-928973-47-9
6. Renner, F.-M. and Becker; J. and Glesner, M.: Communication Performance Models for Architecture-precise Prototyping of Real-time Embedded Systems. Int. Journal of Design Automation for Embedded Systems, 5(3) (2000)
7. Renner, F.-M. and Becker; J. and Glesner, M.: Automated Communication Synthesis for Architecture-precise Rapid Prototyping of Real-time Embedded Systems. Proc. of the 11th Int. Workshop on Rapid System Prototyping, Paris, France (2000)
8. Hollstein, T. and Becker, J. and Kirschbaum, A. and Renner, F.-M. and Glesner, M.: DICE - An Interactive Approach to Hardware/Software Co-Design of Heterogeneous Real-Time Systems. In: Proc. of the Baltic Electronic Conference, Tallinn, Estonia (1998)
9. Kumar, S. and Aylor, J.H. and Johnson, B.W. and Wulf, W.A.: The Codesign of Embedded Systems: A Unified Hardware/Software Representation. In: Kluwer Academic Publishers (1996)
10. Henkel, J. and R. Ernst: High-Level Estimation Techniques for Usage in Hardware/Software Co-Design. In: Proc. of the Asia and South Pacific Design Automation Conference, Yokohama, Japan (1998)
11. Knudsen, P.V. and Madsen, J.: Communication Estimation for Hardware/Software Codesign. In: Proc. of the 6th Int. Workshop on Hardware/Software Codesign, USA (1998)
12. Courtoy, M.: Rapid System Prototyping for Real-Time Design Validation In: Proc. of the 9th Int. Workshop on Rapid System Prototyping, Leuven, Belgium (1998)
13. Bishop, W.D. and Loucks, W.M.: A heterogeneous environment for hardware/software cosimulation. In: 30th Annual Simulation Symposium (1997)
14. Passerone, C. and Lavagno, L. and Sansoe, C. and Chiodo, M. and Sangiovanni-Vincentelli, A.: Trade-off evaluation in embedded system design via co-simulation. In: Proc. of the Asia and South Pacific Design Automation Conference (ASP-DAC '97), Chiba, Japan (1997)

FPGA-Based Emulation:
Industrial and Custom Prototyping Solutions

Helena Krupnova and Gabriele Saucier

Institut National Polytechnique de Grenoble/CSI,
46, Avenue Felix Viallet, 38031 Grenoble cedex, France
{bogushev,saucier}@imag.fr

Abstract. The given paper presents the state of the art in the FPGA-based logic emulation. The analysis of the existing emulation solutions is performed according to the following classification : (1) large emulation systems (Quickturn [26], Ikos [16], MentorGraphics [21]); (2) semi-custom rapid prototyping boards (Aptix [3], Simutech [24]); (3) custom prototyping solutions (Transmogrifier2 [20], Weaver [6], Replica [18], FPGA vendors demonstration and prototyping boards [31], [2], microprocessor-based boards, etc.). Each system is exposed in terms of its capacity, architecture, used FPGAs and performance.

1 Introduction

Designers say today that up to 80% of the project development time is spent at the verification step. Moving towards the System On a Chip makes the verification gap even wider than the design gap. Among the currently available verification possibilities are (1) formal verification (2) simulation (3) accelerated simulation (4) emulation and (5) rapid prototyping. Each verification method plays its own role in the design process. Simulation is not expensive and good for initial block-by-block verification of the design, and is widely supported by different abstraction level commercial simulators. Formal verification allows the verification with high level of confidence and is good for maintaining functional equivalence at different stages of the flow and eliminating regression simulations. When the performance of the simulation becomes insufficient to insure the desired test coverage, the accelerated simulation takes place, which is implemented by reinforcing the workstation performance by connecting it to the hardware emulation boards. Working up to 10,000 times faster than simulation, the FPGA-based emulation allows to significantly extend the verification coverage. Logic emulation fills a wide verification gap between simulation and actual silicon steps. When the FPGA implementation achieves the speed of 10-20 MHz, one can speak about the rapid prototyping. Working close to the real speed, the rapid prototyping provides an extensive, "live" test coverage and can be extremely useful for subjective eye/ear evaluation of an electronic product. The term "rapid" has two meanings - (1) the prototype is obtained rapidly and (2) the prototype works rapidly.

According to their role and their characteristics, the FPGA-based prototyping platforms can be classified in three major categories : (1) high-capacity commercial emulators represented by the three market leaders - Quickturn [26], Ikos [16] and MentorGraphics [21]; (2) semi-custom platforms like Aptix [3] and Simutech [24]; (3) custom platforms, basically issued from the university research projects and industry/university cooperation ([9], [6], [18]). The first category covers the logic emulation field, and the last two categories are basically related to the rapid prototyping. The emulation can also be viewed from two points : functional emulation and real-time emulation. Due to its moderate performance, the first category is related to the functional emulation, and the last two categories can be related to both, functional and real-time emulation.

The given paper presents the current status of the FPGA-based emulation and rapid prototyping and gives an overview of the existing solutions and their tradeoffs.

2 Commercial Emulation Systems

The common characteristics of the commercial emulation systems are their high capacity - they consist of hundreds of FPGAs placed on boards which are combined into racks, chassis, etc. Quickturn and Ikos emulators use Xilinx FPGAs and MentorGraphics/MetaSystems emulators use the custom emulation chips. Due to the big number of FPGAs and the complexity of the partitioning problem (caused by the high Size/IO pin ratio), the FPGAs in the emulators are typically filled by 10-30%. And it is known that more FPGAs are used, the smaller is the performance. Because of the board delay due to partitioning, the typical emulation frequency is situated in the range of 1-3 MHz. According to the reported experience ([25]), reasonable emulation speed for several million gates design is 200-300KHz.

An emulation system can be evaluated by the following criteria. The most obvious is the capacity in terms of FPGA density and memory size. But the estimation is not obvious in terms of the methodology. Evaluating a single FPGA capacity is already an ambiguous task, which is confirmed by the multitude of notions : ASIC gate, PLD gate, typical gate, system gate, average gate. The task is complicated when memory capacity is added, and if memory is used for logic or product terms (Altera Flex10K and Apex20K [1]) or if logic is used as memory (Xilinx 4000 and Virtex [29]). In addition, due to the internal routing complexity, FPGAs can be successfully filled up to the fixed ratio (often 0.9). In its turn, due to the complexity of multi-FPGA partitioning, an emulator can be successfully filled up to a certain ratio. When evaluating the memory capacity, multiple levels of memory hierarchy should be usually taken into account : (1) embedded FPGA memory resources, (2) dedicated memory chips on the FPGA boards, (3) dedicated memory boards. The emulation software usually offers the specific memory primitives. In general case, the design memories should be manually wrapped up to establish the correspondence between the functionalities offered by the memory primitives and the functionality required by the design memories.

The next important criterion is the performance. The area/speed tradeoff in the emulation technology is made possible by using the time-division multiplexing techniques, like in Ikos VirtualWires technology ([4], [27]). By multiplexing the FPGA I/O pins and partially sacrificing performance, the FPGA filling ratio can be increased, thus reducing the required amount of hardware and diminishing the per emulation gate dollar cost. The emulation frequency prediction is not a trivial task. Because changing emulation frequency changes the design speed in a non linear way due to the fact that some devices, that were stalled at the lower frequency can operate normally when slightly increasing the frequency ([25]). Thus, increasing the frequency 2 times may actually increase the performance 10 times.

Another issue is the clock generation strategy. A common feature of the commercial emulation systems is that they rebuild the timing of the design to solve the potential clocking problems. User clocks are linked to the emulation clocks and transformed into the clock enables. Gated clocks are eliminated and the asynchronous parts of the design are identified. Analog devices should be extracted from the emulated design and implemented outside.

In addition, the interface between the emulator and the target system, the ability to incorporate standard components and cores should be also taken into account. As the emulation is designed for design debugging, the debugging facilities constitute an important part of an emulator. They are represented by the number of observable signals, depth of the sample storage, the way of introducing probes, possibility to connect to the logic analyzer or to use the embedded logic analyzer, stimulus entries, etc. A key point is whether the design should be recompiled when changing the set of observed signals. Because the compilation corresponds to the FPGA place and route, it is a very time consuming process and the speed of the compilation usually determines the turnaround of debugging iterations. The incremental compilation provides a significant speed up for different debugging iterations.

An important criteria which the emulation engineer should be aware of before the emulation project is launched is the emulation time vs. setup time. Very often the real emulation time is the minor part compared to setting up compilation scripts, converting test vectors, solving library problems, writing memory wrappers and solving problems with non-emulatable design portions.

Table 1 presents a comparative analysis of industrial emulation systems including their architecture, interconnect structure, capacity and frequency of emulation. This table covers both large emulation systems and semi-custom emulation platforms.

The emulation market is shared between three market leaders.

Quickturn offers three emulation products : CoBALT, System Realizer and Mercury ([26]). CoBALT is a processor-based emulator supporting designs of up to 8 million gates. System Realizer is the FPGA-based emulator for designs in the range of 100K to 3 million gates. Mercury is the next gener-

Table 1. Industrial emulation systems.

	Aptix	Simutech	IKOS	QuickTurn	MentorGraphics
Product Name	MP3, MP3C, MP4 System Explorer	Rave Prototyper	Avatar-8, VirtuaLogic-8	System Realizer, Mercury, CoBALT	Celaro, SimExpress
Architecture	plug&play adapter support MP3: 3 FPIC (1024pins each) MP4: 4 FPIC (1024pins each)	Up to 31 Core Boards connected via backplane	Xilinx 4062 FPGAs, 1 to 6 emulation modules per system	Xilinx FPGAs, Mercury uses also RISC micro-processors, CoBALT consists of an array of inter-connected micro-processors	proprietary custom emulation chip (Meta Systems)
Interconnect	hierarchical through FPICs : MP3 : mixed MP4 : folded clos architecture	via bus (time multi plexed)	time multiplexing with VirtualWires, nearest neighbor mesh	partial crossbar, custom interconnect chip	fractal routing archi-tecture
Capacity	up to 20 FPGAs	scalable up to 31 slots 1 FPGA per slot	up to $4*10^6$ gates	up to $3*10^6$ gates for System Realizer, up to $10*10^6$ gates for Mercury	up to $26*10^6$ gates (Celaro) up to 1M gates (SimExpress)
Frequency	20-35MHz	5 MHz	500KHz to 2MHz	1-3MHz	1-3MHz
Open/Closed	open	open	closed	closed	closed

ation FPGA-based emulation system with up to 10 M gates capacity which in addition includes microprocessors capable to implement non-synthesizable design portions and test-benches.

A prototype of one of the actual Quickturn emulators, called RPM was presented in [30]. In RPM, the FPGAs are hard wired together on large PCBs, called emulation-module boards. Each FPGA is connected to all its nearest-neighbor FPGAs in a regular array of signal-routing channels. All emulation-module boards are connected through backplane connectors onto one large array of FPGAs. Another prototype, called Realizer, was described in [7]. It is composed of logic boards, each logic board has 14 XC3090 FPGAs with 128 pins each used for interconnect, and 32 XC2018 FPGAs used as crossbar chips. A second-level crossbar of 64 XC2018 chips interconnects up to 8 logic boards. A partial crossbar interconnect structure is used.

IKOS Systems ([16]) offers two emulation systems : Avatar-8 and VirtuaLogic-8 (Avatar-8 being a replicant of VirtuaLogic-8 not including the debugging facilities). IKOS emulation is based on a VirtualWires technology ([27], [4]), which overcomes pin limitations by intelligently multiplexing each physical wire among multiple logical wires and pipelining these connections at the maximum clocking frequency of the FPGA. Wire multiplexing requires scheduling of virtual wires to physical wires, which results in creating a finite-state machine, and also synthesizing multiplexer/demultiplexer logic and registers. Hardware overhead is largely compensated by increasing logic utilization ratio. The emulation clock is broken into a number of microcycles determined by a free-running μCLK. The microcycles are grouped into sequential phases to support combinational paths that extend across multiple chips. This is performed by the timing resynthesis step, which replaces the user's clock by a single global synchronous clock. The emulation speed is determined as the product of the virtual clock cycle time by the number of virtual cycles in one cycle of the user's clock. The cycle time of the virtual clock is chosen to be the inter-FPGA traversal time. The number of virtual cycles is equal to the number of FPGA crossings in the longest combinatorial path. By solving the pin limit problem VirtualWires approach increases the FPGA utilization ratio from 10-30% in hard wired systems to over 45%.

Mentor Graphics ([21]) offers two emulators : SimExpress (first generation tool) and Celaro (the second generation tool). The architecture used in SimExpress and Celaro is based on a full custom chip specifically designed for emulation. The full custom chip comprises an entire emulator, including programmable elements, interconnect matrix, logic analyzer, clock generators, memory interface, and I/O channels. An interconnect matrix guarantees that the propagation delays between any two programmable elements within the chip are fixed and predictable. All programmable element outputs are connected to the on-chip signal probing circuitry, without relying on the compiler to perform the routing, and, consequently, consuming precious interconnection resources otherwise available to the user logic. A bank of I/O channels connects the emulator-on-a-chip to all other emulators-on-a-chip in the system, via a fractal routing network.

The emulation case study presented in [14] compares the implementation of the design in SystemRealizer and SimExpress emulators. The experimental evaluation shows that the design is compiled more quickly in the SimExpress system, but the emulation runs faster in SystemRealizer. This is due to the fact that SimExpress compilation flow benefits from the speed of the dedicated synthesis and place and route software. In the same time, as the custom emulation chip contains the embedded logic analyzer and probing facilities, it cannot run as fast as commercial FPGAs. Table 2 presents the tradeoffs between the different emulation solutions, and namely the FPGA-based emulation, time-multiplexed emulation, μProcessor based emulation and custom-chip based emulation.

Table 2. Emulation Tradeoff Analysis.

FPGA-based Hardware Emulators	Time-Multiplexed Emulators	μProcessor Based Emulators	Custom-Chip Based Emulators
+ high execution speed	- limited speed	-slow emulation speed	- reduced speed
- compilation is CPU-intensive	+ faster compilation	+fast compilation	+ faster compilation
- poor debugging capabilities	+ 100% visibility	- limited visibility	+ 100% visibility
- high cost	+ higher device filling, less FPGAs required, smaller cost	- high cost	- high cost
+ automatic timing-correct partitioning	+ automatic timing-correct partitioning	N/A	+ automatic timing-correct partitioning
+ high capacity	+ high capacity	+ high capacity	+ high capacity

3 Rapid Prototyping

The basic differences between the big emulation systems and the rapid prototyping systems is that the latter have (1) no more than 20 FPGAs on the board (usually no more than 10); (2) the typical FPGA filling can go up to 60-80%; (3) the performance can go up to 20-30 MHz; (4) the user can plug in the latest available FPGAs. Considering the recent achievements regarding the increased FPGA capacity, the last issue makes the capacity of the rapid prototyping platforms comparable to the capacity of the big commercial emulators. The basic difficulty with rapid prototyping platforms is the software implementation flow, and namely the partitioning step. In large commercial emulators mapping the design, partitioning, place and route is done automatically. On the contrary, mapping the design on the rapid prototyping boards is entirely the user task. Open boards can require "designing for emulation" to reach the required performance which includes the following aspects: (1) timing-driven FPGA synthesis; (2) partitioning; (3) clock handling (the clocking schemes are often limited to four to eight low-skew hardware clock networks); (4) external I/O and bus resources handling.

FPGA pin limitation remains the basic issue and in many cases the implementation is impossible without pin multiplexing. The recently appeared Rave platform from Simutech ([24]) solves the partitioning problem by using the natural system partitioning in bus-connected components and also uses the time-multiplexing for realizing system communication. Another difficult point of the rapid prototyping boards compared to the large emulation systems is the debugging. The number of signals which can be probed is usually limited to a fixed number and the debugging and observability strategy should be taken into account during the partitioning step.

Aptix ([3]) System Explorer MP3, MP3C and MP4 boards ([3], [8], [28]) are based on a flexible open emulator architecture that incorporates FPGA-based emulation with all other system components. The System Explorer architecture is based on Aptix's Field Programmable Interconnect Chip (FPIC) and Field Programmable Circuit Board (FPCB) technologies. System components are plugged on the FPCB directly or mounted in modules, connections between the components are then routed through the FPICs. The Aptix MP3 FPCB uses a mixed crossbar-based interconnect architecture. The MP3 FPCB contains 3 FPIC devices, and each FPIC device is connected to the defined region of user holes for plugging FPGAs. The number of used FPGA devices depends on the FPGA package pin numbers. The Aptix MP4 board is based on a folded-clos interconnect architecture. The difference with the MP3 architecture is that on the MP4 boards each FPGA is connected to all the crossbar chips, while on the MP3 board the FPGAs are split into subsets and each subset connects to the selected FPIC. To route two nets, the signal has to traverse one (if two FPGAs are placed within the same FPIC region) or two (if the FPGAs are placed into different FPIC regions) FPICs. The optimal routing delay through an FPIC is about 4ns. Depending on the routing path and the fanout, net delay can go up to 30ns and higher.

The entire implementation flow starting from synthesis to placement and routing of FPGAs should be performed using commercially available tools. Actually Aptix provides three-level software support. First, the Axess tool performs the placement of the components on the board and generating the FPIC programming files. The Explorer tool encapsulates the Axess tool, as well as the FPGA vendor place and route tools. It can manage the load balancing between multiple processors if multiple hosts and multiple place and route licenses are available. Finally, the recently announced Expedition tool will encapsulate the Explorer tool as well as the HDL synthesis and partitioning tools. Prototyping case studies using an Aptix board can be found in [5], [12].

Simutech recently announced the Rave platform ([24]) which is designed for evaluation and verification of IP blocks in a System On a Chip context. The Rave Prototyper system consists of a rack which can receive up to 31 CoreBoards connected via a backplane by using the bus interface. Each CoreBoard contains 2 FPGAs - one implements the bus interface and is called the "Traffic Cop", and the second one is a "user FPGA". The customers can manufacture their own CoreBoards containing the IP blocks or cores.

The communication between different CoreBoards is realized by the time multiplexed 128-bit bus. The innovative feature of the Rave Prototyper is the possibility of the remote access via internet.

4 Custom Prototyping Boards

Custom prototyping boards can be classified according to the different axes: (1) prototyping platforms vs. design platforms; (2) single FPGA vs. multi FPGA; (3) distribution: systems that exist in a unique copy vs. systems distributed inside a big semiconductor company vs. commercially available systems; (4) application domains - hardware/software co-design, pure hardware prototyping, reconfigurable computing, applications development, test, simulation acceleration; (5) routing architectures - mesh, crossbar, bus based systems; (6) origin - university boards vs. industrial boards. The information about a big number of FPGA-based proprietary prototyping systems is available in [13], [15] as well as in [10]. It is difficult to make direct comparisons between the custom prototyping boards because they are designed for specific needs and their architectures are often tailored according to their application areas. Three categories of the custom prototyping systems are detailed in this section: (A) systems that are issued from the university research projects as well as the industry/university cooperation; (B) processor-based prototyping and design platforms; (C) commercially-available small-capacity prototyping boards.

The examples of the university custom prototyping systems are Transmogrifier-2 system ([20]), REPLICA rapid prototyping system ([18]), WEAVER prototyping environment ([6], [17]) and PCI-based board presented in [9]. These systems are developed for the research purposes in hardware-software co-design area, as well as for pure hardware prototyping.

The processor-based platforms usually contain one or two FPGAs and a free hole area. They are mainly designed to allow the customers to develop the peripheral devices and to test the applications. The examples of such a systems are STM-MDT prototyping boards based on ST microprocessors ([19]), HSDT200, HSDF100 ARM Emulation Boards from SIDSA ([23]), EVM40400, ICE63200 Atmel AT91 microcontroller based boards from Europe Technologies ([11]), VELOCITY RSP7 Rapid Silicon Prototyping System based on ARM microcontrollers from Philips ([22]).

The third category includes a big number of boards centered around the recently announced Xilinx ([31], [32]) and Altera ([2]) prototyping board offers. These offers include prototyping and demonstration boards from device manufacturers (Xilinx Prototype Board, Altera System-on-a-Programmable-Chip development board), as well as a long list of the boards proposed by the third party partners (PROC10K, PROC20K from Gidel, Constellation from Nova Engineering, Megalogic System 100 from Princeton Technology Group, XT1000 from Tensilica, DIGILAB 10K10, DIGILAB 20Kx240 from El Gamino for Altera; Xilinx Development System from Avnet, Virtual Workbench H.O.T.II from

VCC, XESS Corporation boards, Wildstar from Annapolis Microsystems, DIME Modules from Nallatech for Xilinx, etc.).

5 Conclusions

FPGA-based logic emulation is a moving domain. The most important factor which currently biases the emulation evolution is the rapid FPGA capacity growth. The future of the concrete emulation platform depends on the way the system can benefit from the progress made regarding the FPGA capacity. Due to the fast FPGA capacity evolution, very often the capacity of the Aptix board filled with the latest FPGAs, approaches to the capacity of the large commercial emulators, and it may happen that an entire custom multi-FPGA system designed several years ago can be replaced now by a single FPGA. From the other side, low progress has been made regarding the FPGA pin capacity. Compared to 10 to 20 times increase in the FPGA logic capacity, the I/O pin number increased only 2 to 3 times. In the same time, the circuit bus width increases (128-bit buses). This leads to the generalization of the pin multiplexing usage. The progress regarding the emulation frequency is quite slow and is also related to the evolution of the FPGAs: from one side, the latest FPGAs are faster, and from the other side, due to the increased capacity, less partitioning is required and fewer board traversals are needed between the FPGAs. Finally, the FPGA-based emulation still requires complex software flows and manual intervention to prepare the design for emulation.

References

1. Altera Device Data Book, Apex 20K Programmable Logic Device Family Data Sheet, *1999*.
2. Altera Development Boards, *//www.altera.com/html/mega/boards.html*.
3. Aptix Home Page, *//www.aptix.com/*.
4. J. Babb, R. Tessier, M. Dahl, S.Z. Hanono, D. M. Hoki, A. Agrawal, "Logic Emulation with Virtual Wires", *IEEE Trans. Computer-Aided Design of Integrated Circuits and Systems 16/6* (1997): 609-626.
5. V. Bhatia, S. Shtil, "Rapid Prototyping Technology Accelerates Software Development for Complex Network Systems", *Proc. RSP* (1998): 113-115.
6. T. Buchholz, G. Haug, U. Kebschull, G. Koch, W. Rosenstiel, "Behavioral Emulation of Synthesized RT-level Descriptions Using VLIW Architectures", *Proc. RSP* (1998) : 70-75.
7. M. Butts, J. Batcheller, J.Varghese, "An Efficient Logic Emulation System", *Proc. ICCD* (1992) : 138-141.
8. M. Courtoy, "Rapid System Prototyping for Real-Time Design Validation", *Proc. RSP* (1998) : 108-112.
9. J. P. David, J. D. Legat, "A 400Kgates *Mbytes SRAM multi-FPGA PCI system", *Proc. Intl. Workshop on Logic and Architecture Synthesis* (1997) : 113-117.
10. Design & Reuse Design Platform Catalog, *//www.design-reuse.com/PROTO_PLATFORM/proto_platform_1.html*.
11. Europe Technologies EVM 40400 Application Notes, *//www.europe-technologies.com/evm40400_appnotes.htm*.

12. T. Fujimoto, T.Kambe, "VLSI Design and System Level verification for the Mini-Disk", *Proc. 33rd Design Automation Conf.* (1996): 491-496.
13. S. Guccione, "List of FPGA-based Computing Machines", //www.io.com/˜guccione /HW_list.html (1983).
14. K. Harbich, J. Stohmann, E. Barke, L. Schwoerer, "A Case Study : Logic Emulation - Pitfalls and Solutions", *Proc. RSP'99* (1999) : 160-163.
15. S. Hauck, "The Roles of FPGAs in Reprogrammable Systems", *Proc. of the IEEE, Vol. 86, No. 4* (1998) : 615-639.
16. IKOS Home Page, //www.ikos.com/.
17. U. Kebschull, G. Koch, W. Rosenstiel, "The WEAVER Prototyping Environment for Hardware/Software Co-Design and Co-Debugging", *Proc. DATE, Designer Track* (1998) : 237-242.
18. A. Krischbaum, S. Ortmann, M. Glesner, "Rapid Prototyping of a Co-Processor based Engine Knock Detection System", *Proc. RSP'98* (1998) : 124-129.
19. P. Kuntz, "Proprietary FPGA Prototyping Boards at STMicroelectronics", *Proc. Sixth Training on SoC Design Using Design and Prototyping Platforms*, April 19-20, 2000, Grenoble, France.
20. D. M. Lewis, D. R. Galloway, M. Ierssel, J. Rose, P. Chow, "The Transmogrifier-2: A 1 Million Gate Rapid Prototyping System", *Proc. ACM/SIGDA Int. Symp. on Field Programmable Gate Arrays* (1997) : 53-61.
21. Mentor Graphics Accelerated Verification/ Emulation page, //www.mentorg.nl/av/index.html
22. Velocity : Rapid Silicon Prototyping System, //www-us.semiconductors.philips.com/ technology/ velocity.
23. SIDSA ARM Emulation Boards, //www.sidsa.com/ARM.htm.
24. Simutech Home Page, //www.simutech.com/.
25. G. Stoler, "Validation of Complex designs by Means of Prototyping", *Fifth Training on Validation of Complex Systems Through Hardware Prototyping, Training Materials*, Grenoble (2000).
26. Quickturn Home Page, //www.quickturn.com.
27. R. Tessier, J. Babb, M. Dahl, S.Z. Hanono, A. Agrawal, "The Virtual Wires Emulation System: A Gate-Efficient ASIC Prototyping Environment", *Proc. ACM/SIGDA Int. Symp. on Field Programmable Gate Arrays* (1994).
28. H. Verheyen, "Emulators ease design prototyping", *Electronic Products*, Jan. 1996.
29. "Virtex-E Field Programmable Gate Arrays Data Sheet, 1999",
30. S. Walters, "Computer-Aided Prototyping for ASIC-based systems", *IEEE Design&Test of Computers, No 6* (1991) : 4-10.
31. Xilinx Prototyping Platforms, //www.xilinx.com /products /protoboards /protoboards.htm.
32. Xilinx Prototype Platforms User Guide for Virtex and Virtex-E Series FPGAs, *Xilinx Data Sheet DS020, December 1999*.

FPGA-Based Prototyping for Product Definition

Rainer Kress, Andreas Pyttel, and Alexander Sedlmeier

Infineon Technologies AG, Advanced Design Methods
D-81730 Munich, Germany
{Rainer.Kress|Andreas.Pyttel|Alexander.Sedlmeier}@infineon.com

Abstract. The design process of large integrated circuits at system-level is divided into three major parts: functional design, architectural design, and integration. This paper concentrates on the functional design in which the final product is defined. Further, the algorithms describing the functionality of the system are refined. The paper shows the hardware/software prototyping of filter algorithms for multi-standard mobile phones.

1 Introduction

According to Sematech, the design process has a productivity increase of about 21% per year [1]. In the same time span, the technology has a productivity increase of about 58%. The gap between these two rates of progress requires improved methodologies for system design. This paper shows how FPGAs can help in the functional design process to refine the specification of systems-on-chip.

An advanced system design flow is divided into three major parts: functional design, architecture design, and integration. In figure 1, the two refinement loops are shown for the functional and architectural design. Both loops are independent of each other which means that the functionality is independent of the architecture used. In this paper we concentrate on the high-level part of the design flow from specification to register transfer level.

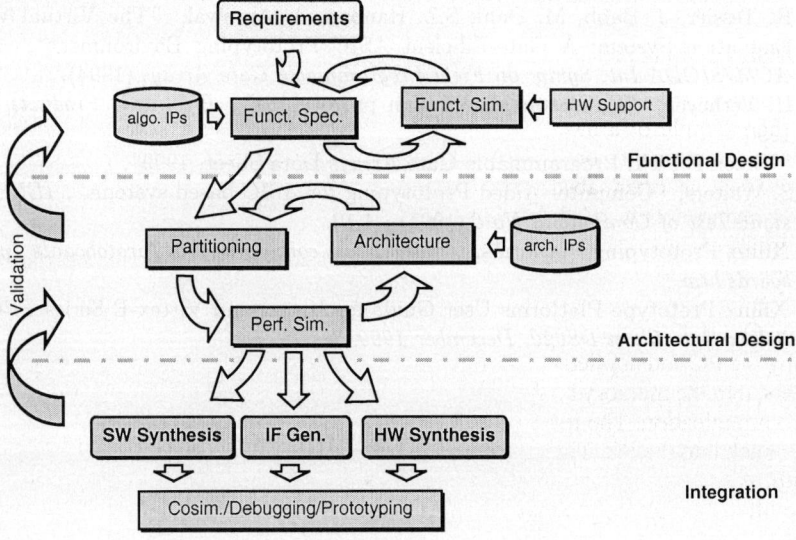

Fig. 1. System-level design flow

R.W. Hartenstein and H. Gruenbacher (Eds.): FPL 2000, LNCS 1896, pp. 78-86, 2000.
© Springer-Verlag Berlin Heidelberg 2000

Functional design captures the behavior of a system. Starting from requirements engineering where the marketing and the product definition groups talk with the customer, an initial system description is produced. This system description is translated into an executable specification. Available, in-house or external, algorithmic intellectual property (IP) can speed-up the design process by reusing those IPs. The executable specification allows us to analyze the system. Prototyping with FPGAs at this level of the design process can increase the speed of execution so that the customer gets a look and feel of the system. In most cases the implementation of the prototype is completely different from the final implementation of the system. Nevertheless, in most cases, the prototype is able to run at a similar speed as the final implementation and it is used for early debugging and for product definition and tuning. For example, different algorithms or parameters can be tested showing different trade-off solutions to the customer.

Architectural design selects a class of suitable architectures for the given specification. Those architectures may be microprocessors, controllers, digital signal processors, ASICs, FPGAs, and an interconnection scheme. Furthermore, schedulers and operating systems are treated as architecture components as well. These components are candidates for the implementation of the behavior. The components may come from an internal or external library of IPs or they are designed later. In an early performance analysis the designer can check if the design meets the constraints. If it does not, the target architecture needs to be changed. This is done in the architecture refinement loop.

Integration synthesizes the software and hardware components. It generates the necessary interfaces and cosimulates the architecture at a detailed level. Prototyping at this step can help debugging.

This paper concentrates on the product planning phase in which the functionality of the system is planned and captured. The hardware/software prototyping of filter algorithms for multi-standard mobile phones serves as an example. The paper is organized as follows: first, the design flow of the prototyping system is explained. Then, we focus on description of the interfaces with Handel-C. Finally, the prototype itself is shown and debugging strategies are discussed.

2 Design Flow

A prototype is a preliminary working example or a model of a product, component or system (figure 2). It is often abstract or lacking some details of the final version. In our case, the prototype consists of a PC and an FPGA

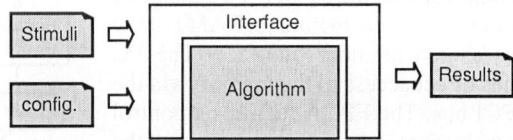

Fig. 2. Control flow of the prototype

board. Both are connected via a PCI-bus. A memory buffer between the PC and the FPGA allows communication via a shared memory interface scheme. Stimuli generated by the PC and applied to the algorithm hosted in the FPGA are transferred via the PCI-bus into the memory buffer. An interface handles the protocol for the shared memory communication. The results generated are transferred via a second shared memory buffer back into the PC. Thus the PC software can analyze the results and generate new stimuli. A logic analyzer connected to the FPGA observes and records internal states of the filter. The configuration of the FPGA board and the logic analyzer is handled by the PC.

The following sections describe the design flow of the algorithm prototyping. This flow comprises three main tasks:
- Algorithm development and synthesis to register-transfer level
- Interface generation
- FPGA integration

2.1 Algorithm Development

The development of the algorithm starts with capturing the functionality in Cadence´s Signal Processing Worksystem (SPW). SPW is a block-oriented design, simulation, and implementation environment for electronic systems. Common application areas for SPW include wireless and wired communications, multimedia, and networking. SPW enables the user to specify, capture, and simulate the complete system design at multiple levels of abstraction (e.g. algorithms, hardware and software architectures, HDL).

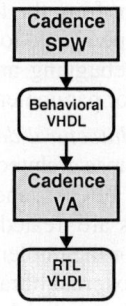

The SPW description of the algorithm is refined, e.g. from floating-point numbers to fixed-point representation. Then the refined algorithm is synthesized by the high-level synthesis tool called Visual Architect (VA). VA translates algorithms on the behavioral level to a hardware description language (HDL) on the register transfer level (RTL). The produced RTL-VHDL netlist consists of components that are described in a generic library (GLIB). The VHDL netlist of the algorithm design is mapped to the FPGA. Figure 3 shows the algorithm development part of the design flow.

Fig. 3. Algorithm development and refinement

2.2 Interface Generation and FPGA Integration

The PC communicates with the FPGA hardware via a shared memory. It provides the stimuli and reads back the results, while the prototyped algorithm runs on the FPGA. Two banks of random access memory (RAM) serve as shared memory interface. The PC has direct access to the memory via the PCI bus. The FPGA requires a control mechanism to read and write to the interface memory.

The FPGA integration combines the RTL VHDL netlist of the algorithm generated by VA and the memory interface. This interface could have been written in VHDL. However, Handel-C was considered to be a better choice. The advantages of using Handel-C will be described in section 3.2.

Handel-C is a programming language designed to enable the compila-

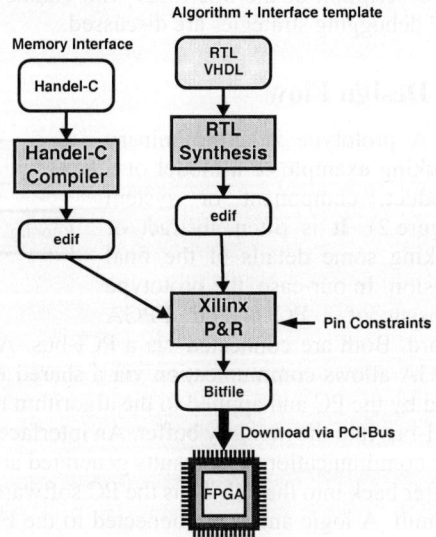

Fig. 4. FPGA Integration

tion of programs into synchronous hardware. It seamlessly integrates with the C code running on the PC and it fits well into the VHDL environment. The following section will introduce the reader into the concepts of Handel-C.

Figure 4 shows the FPGA integration design flow. The top-level VHDL file integrates the algorithm to be prototyped as well as the interface via component instantiation. The design of the algorithm, which is implemented in VHDL, is further refined during RTL synthesis. The interface, however, which is implemented in Handel-C and compiled to edif, is integrated by black-box instantiation. This method is used to integrate cores that only exist as netlist format (e.g., xnf or edif), rather than VHDL. During synthesis the component is treated as black-box, regarding only its interfaces. The Xilinx place-and-route software finally merges the edif netlists and maps them to the FPGA.

2.3 Handel-C

Handel-C [2] is aimed at compiling high level algorithms directly into gate level hardware. It is an extended subset of C that is tailored to implementing hardware. Programs written in Handel-C translate into circuitry on a FPGA. Since the Handel-C syntax is based on conventional C, programmers who are familiar with C recognize almost all constructs in the Handel-C language.

Sequential programs can be written in Handel-C just as in conventional C. Additional parallel constructs allow the programmer to exploit the inherent parallelism of his application. The Handel-C environment comes with a simulator and a compiler.

Handel-C simulator. The simulator can display the state of every variable (register) in the program at every clock cycle. If required, the simulation steps and the number of simulated cycles that are under program control can be shown. Optionally, the source code that was executed at each clock cycle as well as the program state may be displayed. Both assist the programmer in the debugging of the source code.

Handel-C compiler. The compiler allows designs expressed in Handel-C to be compiled into two main netlist formats: XNF files for the Xilinx devices or EDIF files which may be used with either the Xilinx or Altera devices.

Key features. The most important features of the Handel-C language are highlighted in the subsequent paragraphs.

Parallel constructs and bitwidth. Handel-C is based on the syntax of ANSI C. Therefore, programs designed for Handel-C are inherently sequential. Since the target is hardware the designer should try to make use of the features of hardware, such as parallelism and variable data sizes. Handel-C provides various features that C does not. Statements can execute in parallel using the par{} construct which allows code to be highly parallelized, and hence performs faster. Unlike in C, integers in Handel-C can be of any width, signed or unsigned. All operators are strictly checked by the compiler.

Synchronization. When expressions are evaluated in parallel, communication between the parallel statements have to be considered. Handel-C provides the design construct "channel" for synchronization. This construct is only available in the simulator mode. There are no means to map channels to real hardware.

A channel has an associated type (signed or unsigned), as well as a width, and can either be written to or read from. The communication is synchronized, and will only occur when there is exactly one reader and one writer. Having more than one writer or reader connected to a channel at a time causes a semantic error.

The Handel-C simulator has very simple timing semantics. Assignments take one clock cycle. This means that expressions take no cycles to evaluate, nor does the control logic for statements. The only exception to this rule is channel communication, which can take anything from one cycle upwards. Communication blocks until there is both a reader and a writer. A read or write to a channel must wait until it has a partner.

Memories and arrays. Arrays come in three forms: RAM, ROM or simple arrays. The simple arrays do not allow random access. They are merely syntactic sugar for using multiple variables. A RAM or ROM is a typed area of memory that is accessed by an index. The difference between the two is that RAM elements can be assigned a value, whereas ROM elements are fixed. A RAM or ROM in Handel-C has restrictions attached to its use. The data bus of a memory can only hold a single value at a time, and thus a single memory location can be accessed at each clock cycle only.

Macro expressions and macro procedures. To aid the programmer, Handel-C provides macros similar in concept to the `#define` directives used by C pre-processors. These directives perform more than just textual manipulation of the source. Macros are divided into two categories, *expressions* and *procedures*.

Macro expressions themselves are further divided into two categories, shared and non-shared expressions. The syntax for both is similar. It is shown in figure 5:

```
macro expr expr1(a) = a + 1;
shared expr expr2(a) = a + 2;
int 8 var1, var2;
var1 = expr1(var2);
var2 = expr2(var1);
```

Fig. 5. Shared/non-shared expressions

Shared expressions generate hardware only once the compiler producing the necessary multiplexers for the inputs if there are any, whereas non-shared expressions generate hardware each time they are used, and consequently do not need any multiplexers.

It is in the responsibility of the programmer to ensure that shared macro expressions with parameters are not used by different sections of code in the same clock cycle. Non-shared expressions, as they generate hardware for each invocation, can be used without restrictions.

Macro procedures are declared and used with the syntax shown in figure 6. Hardware is generated for each time the procedure is used. Any number of parameters is allowed, but macro procedures cannot be recursive. However they are allowed to use recursive expressions if required. Macro procedures are mainly used to divide Handel-C code into particular sections.

```
macro proc mp(n) {
par {
    a = a + n;
    b = b - n;
    }
}
unsigned 8 a, b;
void main() {
    mp(6);
}
```

Fig. 6. Macro procedures

Similarities with C. Handel-C does not support as many different data types such as C does. The only data types supported are integers and characters. But unlike C, the user can specify the width of integers. This is possible as the implementation is mapped to hardware.

Handel-C Highlights. As illustrated in the above paragraphs, Handel-C makes it possible for software developers who are not experienced in hardware design to create hardware implementations. This establishes an easy possibility for software designers to be part of the large embedded systems market where performance optimized hardware is required.

3 Prototyping Platform

The prototyping platform consists of the RC1000-PP FPGA board (section 3.1), which is plugged into a PCI slot of a Pentium II PC running at 400 MHz. Via the PCI interface, data can be transferred between the PC and the FPGA board. This data transfer is supported by a library of driver functions, which comprise the configuration of the FPGA, the transfer of user data, and the programming of the clock generator.

Internal states of the design can be measured by means of a logic analyzer, whose probing cable is connected with the board. The logic analyzer is connected with the PC via ethernet, allowing for the results to be read back (figure 7).

The HP 16702A logic analyzer works with a HP unix operating system. It has a graphical user interface based on the CDE desktop. A web server is running on the device, which enables access via internet. Therefore, designer groups can collaborate from different locations.

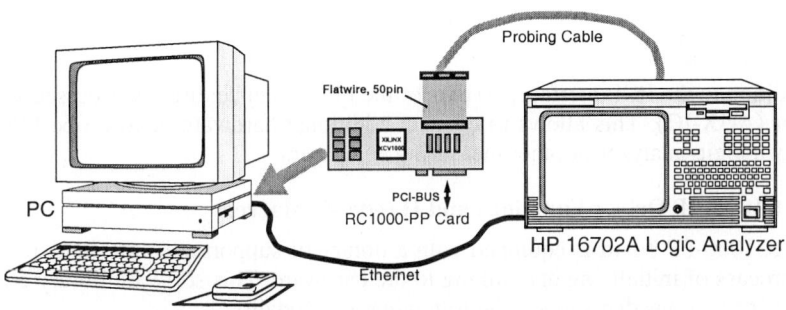

Fig. 7. Prototyping Environment

3.1 The RC1000-PP Board

The RC1000-PP board (figure 8) is a PCI bus plug-in card for PCs. It has one large Xilinx FPGA and four banks of memory with 2 MBytes each. All four memory banks are accessible by both the FPGA and any device on the PCI bus. Another feature is the programmable clock generator, which supports 2 clock signals with a range of 400 kHz to 100 MHz. The board that is used in our example is equipped with a Xilinx XCV1000 FPGA. There are 3 methods of transferring data or communicating between the FPGA and any PCI device, via the PLX PCI9080 PCI controller chip.

- Bulk data transfers between the FPGA and PCI bus are performed via the memory banks. Synchronization between the FPGA and the other device is done using one of the following communication methods.
- There are two unidirectional 8-bit ports, called control and status, for direct communications between the FPGA and PCI bus. Semaphores indicate when data has been written or read.
- The User I/O pins GPI and GPO are both connected to the FPGA to provide for single-bit communications.

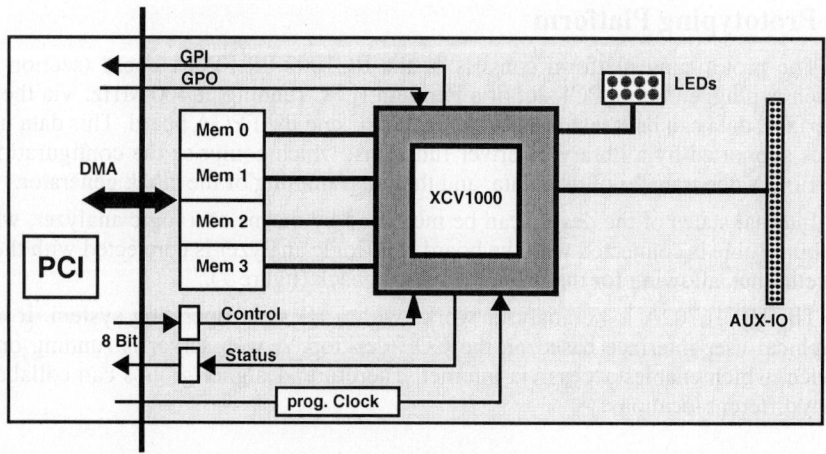

Fig. 8. Schematic view of the RC1000-PP Board

In addition to the PCI interface, 50 pins of the FPGA can be directly accessed via a connector (AUX-IO). This allows to connect additional hardware or to probe FPGA signals by a logic-analyzer or other measuring equipment.

3.2 RC1000-PP Driver Functions and Handel-C Macros

The RC1000-PP board is equipped with a library of support software that simplifies the process of initializing and talking to the hardware. This software library comprises driver functions that support the following functionality:

- Initialization and selection of a board
- Handling of FPGA configuration files
- Control of the programmable clocks
- Data transfer between PC and the RC1000-PP board
- Function to help with error checking and debugging

These library functions can be included by the user in a C or C++ program, which runs on the host PC and performs data transfer via the PCI bus.

The SRAM of the RC1000-PP board is divided into four banks. The whole address space can be accessed by the PC via DMA. To avoid conflicts with the FPGA, which can also access the memory, a semaphore mechanism is implemented in the C-code library. This mechanism is realized by the functions *RequestMemory* and *ReleaseMemory*. Both functions take a 4bit mask as an argument indicating the number of the respective memory bank. This allows to protect each memory bank individually.

On the FPGA side, corresponding functionality to access memory, the semaphores, and the 8-bit ports (control and status) are implemented as Handel-C macros. These macros are located in a header file that can be included using the C-Preprocessor. The macros which access the semaphores have the same syntax as the functions of the C library. The memory access is performed by 4 macros, one for each RAM bank. The read macro needs only 2 parameters: the register to read data into and the respective memory address. Similarly, the write-macro requires the address and an expression that describes the data to be written. In addition the Handel-C macros already include the FPGA pin locations of the data, address, and control pins of the memory chips.

The configuration of the FPGA can be either done via file access, or by including the bitfile into the C code. In the latter case configuration is faster. The RC1000-PP board has two clock generators with a programmable frequency. One of the clock generators can be started, stopped, or run in single step mode, supported by library functions. This is very helpful for debugging purposes.

3.3 Debugging

Programmable hardware enables the addition of specific logic to the original application for debugging support. The specific logic can be removed after the circuit has been debugged. There are several ways to instrument code for debugging purposes. The instrumentation can be performed at different design levels: the behavioral level, register-transfer level, and gate level. Four possibilities of the instrumentation are explained in the following:

- *Interrupt*: a running application can be stopped by disabling the system clock for all registers.
- *Single step processing*: the design can run in single-step mode, where the registers are only enabled during one clock cycle. (e.g., via the clock enable signal).
- *Data path register tracing*: the registers may be traced by using a scan-path chain, which connects all registers. In scan-path mode, the register values are piped through the chain, while the design that is debugged halts.
- *Breakpoint*: a breakpoint stops the design in a state corresponding to a specific instruction of the source code. Breakpoints are identified by comparing the controller state with a given breakpoint identifier. The encoding of the breakpoint identifier is determined during synthesis.

4 Application

The application which demonstrates the advantages of the prototype is chosen from the mobile radio communication area. Radio propagation in the mobile radio environment is described by highly dispersive multipath caused by reflection and scattering. The paths between base station and mobile station may consist of large reflectors and/or scatterers located some distance to the mobile station, giving rise to a number of waves that arrive in the vicinity of the mobile station with random amplitudes and delays. Close to the mobile station, these paths are further randomized by local reflections or diffractions. Since the mobile station will be moving, the angle of arrival must also taken into account since it affects the doppler shift associated with a wave arriving from a particular direction. Various filter algorithms are available that help reducing those unwanted effects.

The application consists of several digital filters and a memory interface. All components are implemented in a Xilinx XCV1000 FPGA (figure 9).

The digital filter components have four filter-taps. The design has an eight bit data input and eight bit data output. Via the data input, the filter coefficients can be configured by a load signal. The design is pipelined and requires a new stimulus value every six clock cycles.

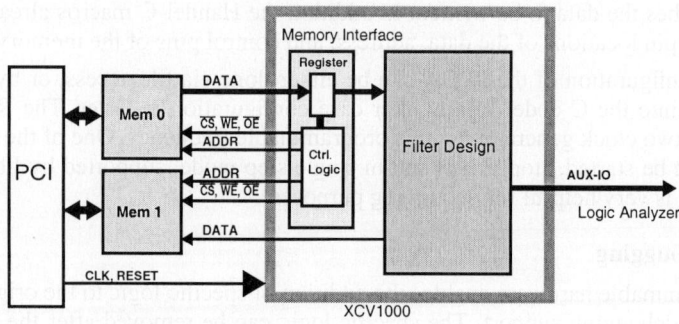

Fig. 9. Design of the Application

The task of the memory interface is to provide stimuli for the filter at the given time, and to store the result. It consists of a data register, which stores the 9 bit input values, and control logic. The controller algorithm starts with requesting the memory banks 0 and 1 for access by the FPGA. It runs in a loop from start address to the maximal address. In this loop, every 6 clock steps, a new input value is loaded from bank 0 into the data-register and simultaneously a result value is written to bank 1. The signals that control read or write access are set accordingly. Finally, both memory banks are released.

The 50-bit auxiliary interface enables the direct access to FPGA-pins. Via these pins, internal states of the design can be observed by the logic analyzer (figure 7).

The design of the memory interface is generic, i.e., it can be used for different design prototypes by changing only a few parameters of the interface. Therefore, the code of the interface can be automatically generated, according to the properties of the filter design. The turn-around time for complex designs is about three hours from changes in the SPW description to the FPGA implementation. The designer just has to start a script. Then he receives the final netlist automatically.

Reasons for using this prototyper in an industrial environment are real-time aspects that can be achieved. A complete system, e.g., a mobile radio station cannot be built with software only. Simulators are definitely to slow. One main advantage of FPGA against DSP is the simpler and tighter integration of additional modules for the high frequency part or other analog modules. Further, our prototyping system is seamlessly extensible via the 50-pin IO port of the RC1000 PP board.

5 Conclusions

The application of an FPGA-based prototyping platform for product planning has been presented. Real-time aspects that have been achieved show the usefulness of this approach. A main advantage of FPGA approach against DSP use is the tighter integration of additional hardware modules. The prototyping system is modular and can be easily extended.

References

1. N. N.: The International Technology Roadmap; Sematech, 1999
2. M. Bowen: Handel-C Language Reference Manual, Embedded Solutions Ltd., 1999

Implementation of Virtual Circuits by Means of the FIPSOC Devices

E. Cantó[1], J.M. Moreno[1], J. Cabestany[1], I. Lacadena[2], and J.M. Insenser[2]

[1]Departament of Electronics Engineering, Technical University of Catalunya (UPC),
c/ Gran Capitá s/n, 08034 Barcelona, Spain.
`canto@eel.upc.es`
[2]SIDSA, PTM, Torres Quevedo 1, 28760 Tres Cantos (Madrid), Spain.
`lacadena@sidsa.es`

Abstract. This paper will explain a systematic technique for the implementation of a synchronous circuit into the DRFPGA (dynamic reconfigurable FPGA) included in the FIPSOC devices, taking advantage of their properties of dynamic reconfiguration. The circuit to be implemented is partitioned using a set of temporal bipartitioning rules, and each partition is mapped on a separated context, sharing both contexts the same hardware resources. The time-multiplexed execution of both contexts constitutes a virtual circuit.

1 Introduction

Custom computing machines (CCM) can be used for many computationally intensive problems. Architectural specialization is achieved at the expense of flexibility, because they are designed for one application and are inefficient for other application areas. Reconfigurable logic devices achieve a high level of performance on a wide variety of applications. The hardware resources of the device can be reconfigured once a function is completed for another different one, achieving a high level of performance on a wide variety of computations. A step forward is run-time reconfiguration or dynamic reconfiguration, where hardware resources can be reconfigured while the system is in normal execution, increasing the efficiency of the system.

A large number of applications have been proposed and developed, exploiting the advantages of dynamically programmable logic devices. Some of them are reconfigurable processor units (RPUs), adaptive signal processing, self-repairing and evolvable hardware [1][2][3], artificial neural networks [4][5], and others. Another perspective to take profit of dynamic reconfiguration capabilities is to partition a large computing design on a limited set of hardware resources, so that a partition is being executed while another partition is being configured, improving the functional density of the implementation. This last approach will be used as the goal of this paper.

The organization of this paper is as follows. In the section 2 we will introduce the DRFPGA of the FIPSOC devices. In the section 3 we will describe the dynamic implementation of a circuit and the concepts of micro-cycle, macro-cycle and virtual circuit. It will be also described a systematic temporal bipartitioning technique useful for the implementation of synchronous circuits on a FIPSOC device in section 4.

Finally, in section 5 it will be reported the conclusions obtained from the simulation of basic combinational and sequential circuits.

2 The FIPSOC Dynamic Reconfiguration

The FIPSOC [6][7] is a new family of Dynamically Reconfigurable FPGA devices. This device includes a 8051 microcontroller core, a DRFPGA, a configurable analog block (CAB) which includes a programmable A/D, D/A acquisition/conversion section, RAM memory for the configuration bits and/or for general purpose user programs and some additional peripherals. The programmable digital section consists of an FPGA, whose building blocks have been termed DMCs (digital macro cells). The DMC, whose internal structure is depicted in Fig. 1(a), is a large granularity, 4-bit wide programmable cell that contains a combinational block and a sequential block interconnected through an internal router. Both combinational and sequential blocks have 4 bit outputs, plus some extra outputs for macro modes. The DMC output block has four bit outputs individually multiplexing combinational or sequential outputs, plus two auxiliary outputs.

The combinational block is implemented with four 16-bit Look Up Tables (LUTs), than can be programmed to provide any combinational logic function. Each two LUTs constitute a tile, which has six inputs and two outputs. The combinational block can be used either as RAM, as a 4 to 1 multiplexer, or as a 4-bit adder/subtractor macro mode with carry signals.

The sequential block is composed of four registers, which can be configured independently as different types of D flip-flop or D latches, with different clock or enable polarities and synchronous or asynchronous set/reset signals. It also contains macro modes for a 4-bit up/down counter with load and enable, and a 4-bit shift register with load and enable.

Both combinational and sequential blocks can be configured in static or dynamic modes. Dynamic mode provides two time independent contexts that can be swapped with a single signal. The contents of the registers are duplicated so that they can be stored when active context is changed and restored back when the context becomes active again. Also each configuration bit is duplicated, so as to provide dynamic reconfiguration capabilities. The combinational block is organized in two independent tiles, whose functionality depends on the operation mode, static or dynamic. In static mode each tile of the combinational block includes two 16-bit LUTs sharing two inputs that can be programmed to implement two 4-bit boolean functions, or they can grouped to implement one 5-bit boolean function, or can be used as a 16x2 bits RAM. In dynamic mode each tile can implement two 3-bit boolean functions without shared signals, a 4-bit boolean function, or a 8x2 bits RAM. Static and dynamic modes for sequential block have the same functionality.

As depicted in Fig. 1(b), there is a physical isolation between active configuration bits and the mapped memory, which can be used for storing the configuration of the two contexts, or as a general purpose RAM once its contents have been transferred to the active context. A new scheme for reconfiguring DMCs was introduced to the FIPSOC circuitry enabling a faster reconfiguration time. Each DMC has two inputs (IA3 for the context swap trigger and IB3 for the context index) accessible for any of their outputs able to trigger a new context swap, reducing context swap time to just one clock cycle.

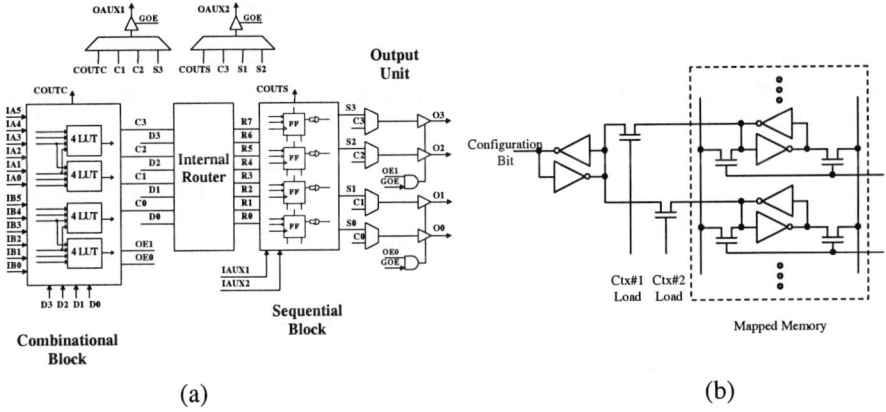

Fig. 1. (a) Internal structure of a DMC. (b) Isolation scheme between configuration memory and mapped memory.

3 The Dynamic Implementation

A dynamic reconfigurable FPGA allows a large circuit (the static implementation) to be implemented on a smaller physical device, sharing the hardware resources with a time-multiplexed scheduler and dynamic reconfiguration, improving the logic density factor [8]. The dynamic implementation is also named virtual circuit because of the analogy between it and a virtual memory, where a program can be larger than the physical memory, mapping portions of the virtual memory to the physical memory when needed [9].

The process to follow is to execute a temporal partitioning of the circuit to obtain a set of temporal independent partitions (contexts), so each partition is executed by the hardware resources of the DRFPGA independently from the others during a micro-cycle [10]. One partition will be the active context in the programmable logic while the remaining ones will be virtual contexts (their configuration bits are in memory, but not yet used) during a micro-cycle. In the next micro-cycle a virtual context will be the new active one and the old active context will become virtual, and so on. The ordered set of micro-cycles is a macro-cycle and it corresponds with the clock-cycle of the static implementation of a synchronous circuit. When the last micro-cycle has finished a new macro-cycle will be executed, as depicted in Fig. 2. Each context will provide a set of cut-signals (communication signals to the next contexts) as a function of their primary inputs (the inputs of the virtual circuit) and other cut-signals (outputs from others contexts). A virtual circuit will be equivalent to its static implementation if it produces a set of output vectors (at the end of the macro-cycle) identical to the set obtained with the static implementation (at the end of the clock cycle), for any set of input vectors.

The benefit of a dynamic implementation over the static one is an improved functional density. Functional density [8] measures the computational throughput for a hardware circuit area, and is defined as the inverse of the cost function $D=1/C$, traditionally measured as $C=A \cdot T$, where A is the area of the implementation and T is the time required for a clock cycle. A better functional density means a more intensive use of hardware resources for a fixed time. An ideal temporal bipartitioning will divide the circuit into two balanced partitions, each one with one half of the static implementation size and delay, maintaining the same functionality. The functional density of the dynamic implementation will double the static one, if the additional cost for reconfiguration is negligible.

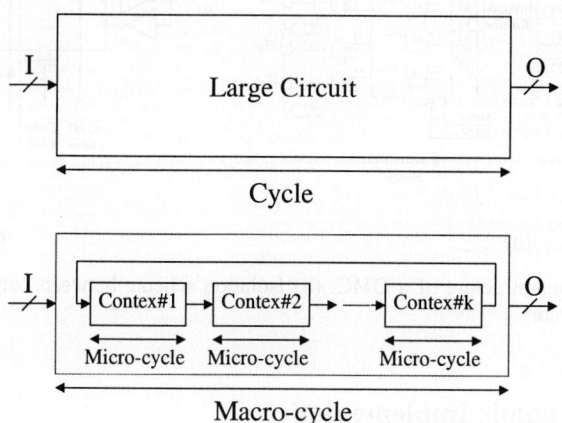

Fig. 2. The static implementation of a large circuit is partitioned on a set of ordered contexts, constituting a dynamic implementation.

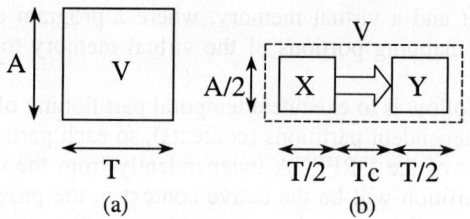

Fig. 3. Area and delay for a (a) static implementation and for an (b) ideal dynamic implementation of a circuit V.

The temporal partitioning of a circuit must accomplish a temporal independence principle, ensuring that each partition can be executed in its time-slot independently from the others. This principle is resumed in that all inputs of a context have been calculated previously. As a consequence of this principle it will be generated a unidirectional cut between every ordered couple of contexts. The reconfiguration scheme included in the DRFPGA of the FIPSOC device permits to share signals between different time-slots using their flip-flops/latches as buffers for communications. The only extra time penalty will be given by the need to change the active context, minimizing extra time in the cut. The dynamic implementation in their hardware resources contains two contexts, but the study of the benefits of adding contexts versus the area cost concluded than the number of contexts on a DRFPGA should be small [11][12], because DRFPGAs with more contexts need to devote more area to their communications.

4 The Temporal Bipartitioning Technique

We will describe a temporal bipartitioning technique for the DRFPGA of the FIPSOC device, although it can be used for any DRFPGA containing standard latches and multi-context FFs (FFs that are able to backup and restore their contents between context swaps), without employing special buffer resources used by another solutions [9][11][12]. We distinguish the nets connecting the hardware resources into combinational and sequential nets. Each net is constituted by an unique source (a logic unit or a primary input) and one or more destinations (logic units or primary outputs). A combinational net is the one whose source is a combinational resource (i.e., LUTs) or is a primary input of the circuit. This approach makes than the primary inputs must be available during the execution of both contexts. A sequential net is the one whose source is a sequential resource (i.e., DFFs).

The temporal independence principle for a combinational net is accomplished as follows. The source must write the net value in the same or in a previous micro-cycle than the micro-cycle used by the destinations to read the net value, within the same macro-cycle. We denote the micro-cycle containing the context 1 and 2 as m_1 and m_2 respectively, and the macro-cycle in execution as M_T.

As depicted if Fig. 4(a) if the source (c_o) and destinations (v_1, v_2) of a combinational net are placed in the same context, the destinations read the net value written by the source inside the same micro-cycle and macro-cycle, avoiding the use of a buffer resource for communication. In Fig. 4(b) there is a combinational net with at least one of their destinations is placed in a later micro-cycle than the micro-cycle containing its source. In this case it must be used an additional buffer resource for the transmission of its value between both micro-cycles on the same macro-cycle. The buffer resource is a standard D latch enabled by the complementary value of a context

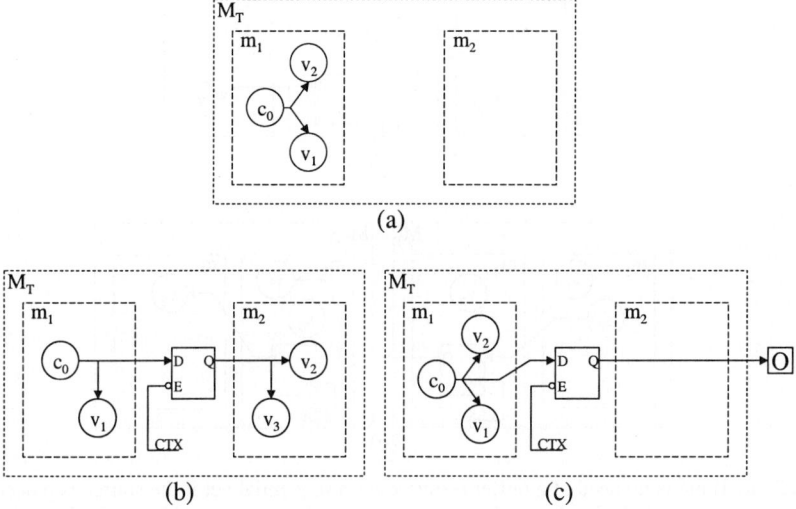

Fig. 4. (a) There is no buffer resource for a combinational net if source and destinations are placed in the same micro-cycle. (b) It is necessary a buffer resource if at least one destination is in a later micro-cycle than the source. (c) The same if the source of a primary output net is contained in the first context.

index signal (ctx=0 for m_1 and ctx=1 for m_2). This signal ctx is internally generated by the logic or externally provided. In the same way, an additional buffer resource must be used if a primary output net is placed in context 1, as depicted in Fig. 4(c), assuring that every primary output will be available at the end of a macro-cycle.

The temporal independence principle for a sequential net is accomplished as follows. The source must read their input nets in a previous macro-cycle than macro-cycle used to write its output net value. That is, the destinations must read the value of the net in the next macro-cycle than the macro-cycle used by the source to read the value of their input nets.

As depicted in Fig. 5(a) it is not needed a buffer resource if all the destinations (v_1, v_2) of a net are placed in the first context (m_1) and the source (s_0) is placed in the second context (m_2). In this situation, the value of the net is written by its source in the same micro-cycle and macro-cycle than the used ones by the destinations to read the net value. In Fig. 5(b) the source is placed in m_2 and at least one of the destinations is placed in the same context it will be necessary to transmit the net value through m_1 using an additional buffer resource. The buffer resource will be a multi-context DFF

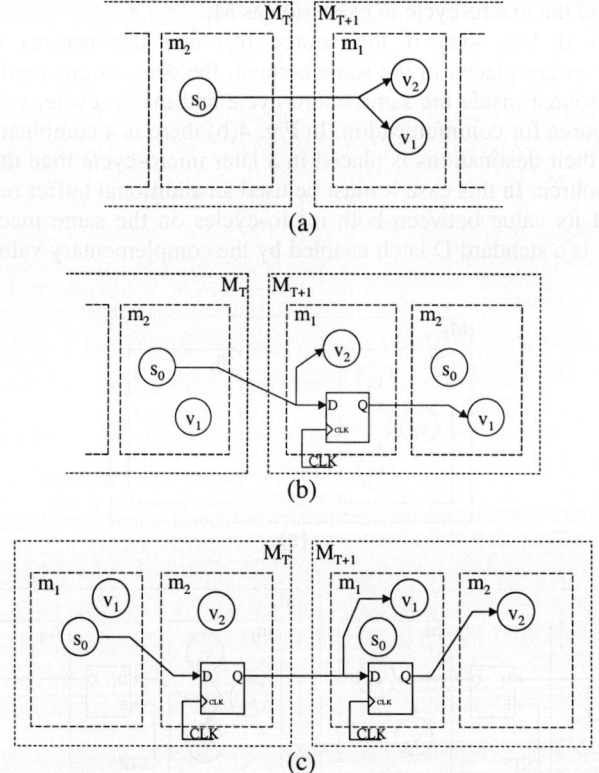

Fig. 5. (a) There is no need of a buffer resource for a sequential net if the source is placed in the second context and all the destinations are placed in the first one. (b) One buffer resource is needed if the source is placed in the second context and at least one of the destinations is also placed in the second context. (c) It will be needed two buffer resources if the source is placed in the first context and at least one of the destinations is placed in the second context.

and it will be placed in the first context and its clock will be attached to a clock signal (clk) that doubles the frequency of the ctx signal. In Fig. 5 (c) the source is placed in the first context and at least one of the destinations is placed in the second one, needing two additional buffer resources to transmit the net value through both context (m_1 and m_2), and they can share the same physical hardware resource.

5 Simulation Results and Conclusions

A pure combinational circuit and a pure synchronous sequential circuit were temporal partitioned and simulated using a VHDL compiler for the verification of the proposed temporal bipartitioning technique.

The combinational circuit used is an 8-bit parity detector. The gates were mapped into the combinational block of the DMC, sharing each pair of gates the same reconfigurable LUT, as depicted in Fig. 6 (a). It was added four additional static D-latches (represented in the figure as small squares) for the buffering of the combinational nets between contexts. The whole dynamic implementation will require just one DMC, with the combinational block configured in dynamic mode and the sequential block configured in static mode.

In Fig. 6 (b) is depicted the waveform of the simulation results obtained for a set of input vectors. The signals o0 and o4 were joined in the representation because o0 doesn't have sense during the execution of the second micro-cycle, and o4 doesn't have sense during the first one. The same explanation applies to the pair of signals o1-o5 and o2-s. The signal o3 doesn't have sense during the execution of the second context. For this particular example of partition it is not necessary to maintain the input vector during the execution of the second context, because there is no primary

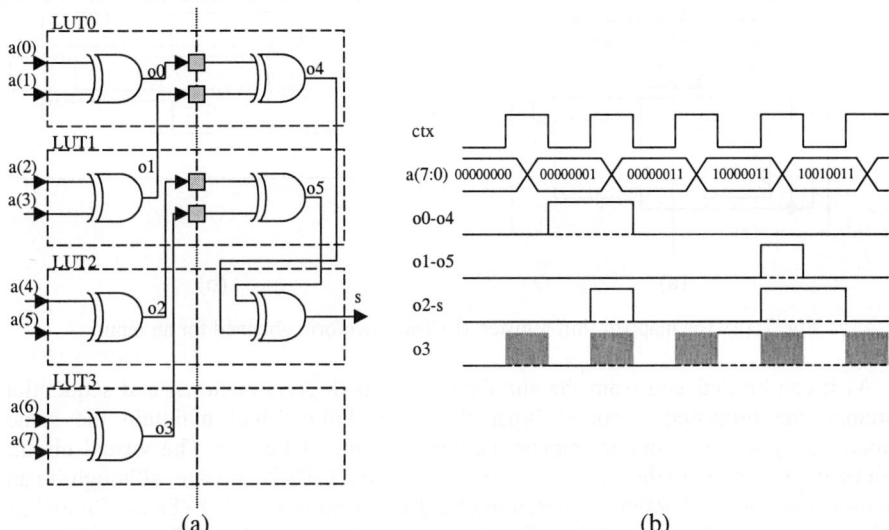

Fig. 6. (a) The mapped parity detector. (b) The waveform obtained for a set input vectors.

input in the second context. For another partition or for a generic circuit it will be necessary to maintain the input vector during the whole execution of the first context, and during the second one. The output will be obtained from the pair o2-s at the end of the execution of the second context.

The sequential circuit used for the simulation is a 4-bit shift register. The flip-flops were mapped in the sequential block of the DMC, sharing each pair of flip-flops the same multi-context DFF, as depicted in Fig. 7(a). Two DFFs (represented in the figure as small squares) were added for the buffering of the sequential net (q1) between contexts, sharing a new multi-context DFF. The whole dynamic implementation will require just one sequential block of a DMC, because it just needs three DFFs configured in dynamic mode.

Fig. 7(b) depicts the waveform that shows the results of the simulation for a particular input. The context index signal (ctx) is obtained from a clock signal (clk) used for the trigger of the DFFs at one half of its frequency. The DFFs placed in the second context will be triggered by the rising edge of clk when the second context is in execution (ctx=1). On the same way the DFFs placed in the first context will be triggered by the rising edge of clk when this context is active (ctx=0). The signal q1 will cross two contexts before reaching its destination flip-flop, delaying the signal q2 two cycles of clk. Because there are no primary inputs in the first context it would be unnecessary to maintain the input during the execution of this context, although it was maintained in this example.

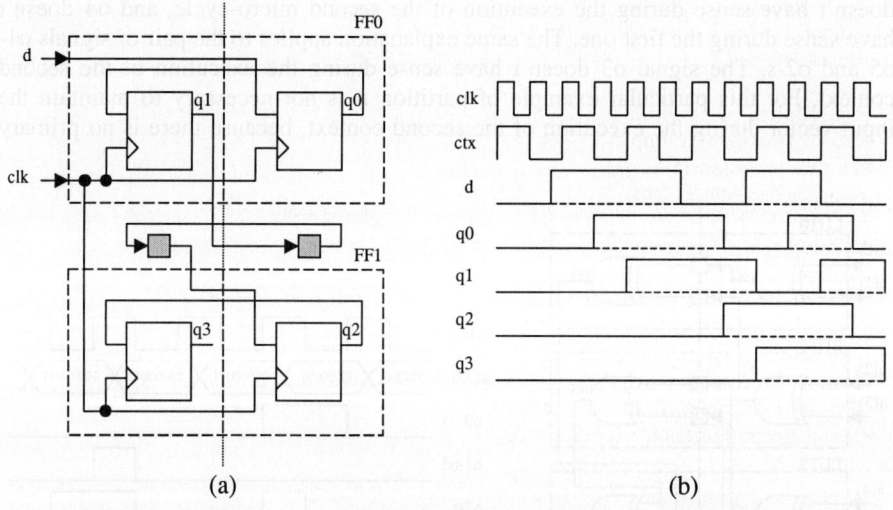

Fig. 7. (a) The mapped shift register. (b) The waveform obtained for an input.

As it can be deduced from the simulations for both combinational and sequential circuits, the proposed temporal bipartitioning technique will maintain the same functionality of the dynamic implementation than the static one. The virtual circuit can be implemented in the DRFPGA contained on the FIPSOC device, although it can be used also for any DRFPGA containing hardware resources able to be configured as D-Latches and multicontext DFFs. The benefits of sharing different functional blocks the same hardware resources will provide a cost-effective implementation of a circuit.

Our current work is concentrated in the exhaustive benchmarking process of the bipartitioning algorithm. This process will consider large-scale real circuits whose functionality will be mapped in the FIPSOC devices using dynamic reconfiguration techniques, so as to determine the corresponding increase in functional density. Furthermore, the proposed bipartitioning algorithm is being included within the FIPSOC CAE environment.

References

1. J.M. Moreno, J. Madrenas, J. Cabestany, E. Cantó, R. Kielbik, J. Faura, J.M. Insenser, "Realization of Self-Repairing and Evolvable Harware Structures by Means of Implicit Self-Configuration", Proceedings of the First NASA/DoD Workshop on Evolvable Hardware (EH'99), pp. 182-187, Pasadena, California, July 1999.
2. J.M. Moreno, J. Madrenas, J. Faura, E. Cantó, J. Cabestany, J.M. Insenser, "Feasible Evolutionary and Self-Repairing Hardware by Means of the Dynamic Reconfiguration Capabilities of the FIPSOC Devices", Evolvable Systems: From Biology to Hardware, M. Sipper, D. Mange, A. Pérez-Uribe (eds.), pp. 345-355, Springer-Verlag, 1998.
3. J. Madrenas, J.M. Moreno, J. Cabestany, J. Faura, J.M. Insenser, "Radiation-Tolerant On-Line Monitored MAC Unit for Neural Models Using Reconfigurable-Logic FIPSOC Devices", 4th IEEE International On-Line Test Workshop, pp. 114-118, Capri, Italy, July 1998.
4. J.M. Moreno, J. Madrenas, J. Cabestany, E. Cantó, J. Faura, J.M. Insenser, "Dynamically Reconfigurable Strategies for Implementing Artificial Neural Networks Models in Programmable Hardware", Proceedings of the 6th Conference Mixed Designs of Integrated Circutis and Systems (MIXDES'99), pp. 379-384, Kraków, Poland, June 1999.
5. J.M. Moreno, J. Cabestany, E. Cantó, J. Faura, J.M. Insenser, "The Role of Dynamic Reconfiguration for Implementing Artificial Neural Networks Models in Programmable Hardware", Engineering Applications of Bio-Inspired Artificial Neural Networks, J. Mira, J.V. Sánchez Andrés (eds.), pp. 85-94, Springer-Verlag, 1999.
6. J. Faura, C. Horton, P. van Doung, J. Madrenas, J.M. Inserger, „A Novel Mixed Signal Programmable Device with On-Chip Microprocessor". Proceedings of the IEEE 1997 Custom Integrated Circuits Conference (1997) 103-106.
7. J. Faura, J.M. Moreno, M-A. Aguirre, P. Van Doung, J.M. Insenser, „Multicontext Dynamic Reconfiguration and Real-Time Probing on a Novel Mixed Signal Programmable Device with On-Chip Microprocessor", Field-Programmable Logic and Applications, W. Luk, Y.K. Cheung, M. Glesner (eds.) pp. 1-10, Springer-Verlag, 1997.
8. Michael J. Wirthlin, Brad. L. Hutchings, „Improving Functional Density Using Run-Time Circuit Reconfiguration". IEEE Transactions on VLSI Systems, Vol. 6, No. 2, pp. 247-256, June 1998.
9. Huiqun Liu and D.F. Wong, „Circuit Partitioning for Dynamically Reconfigurable FPGAs". International Symposium on Field Programmable Gate Arrays, Monterrey, CA, pp. 187-194, Feb. 1999.
10. Steve Trimberger, „Scheduling Designs into a Time-Multiplexed FPGA", International Symposium on Field Programmable Gate Arrays, pp. 153-160, Feb. 98
11. D. Chang, M. Marek-Sadowska, „Partitioning Sequential Circuits on Dynamically Reconfigurable FPGAs", International Symposium on Field Programmable Gate Arrays", pp. 161-167, Feb. 98
12. D. Chang, M. Marek-Sadowska, „Partitioning Sequential Circuits on Dynamically Reconfigurable FPGAs", IEEE Transatcions on Computers, Vol. 48, No. 6, pp. 565-578, June 1999.

Static and Dynamic Reconfigurable Designs for a 2D Shape-Adaptive DCT

Jörn Gause[1], Peter Y. K. Cheung[1], and Wayne Luk[2]

[1] Department of Electrical and Electronic Engineering,
Imperial College of Science, Technology and Medicine,
London SW7 2BT, United Kingdom
{j.gause@ic.ac.uk, p.cheung@ic.ac.uk}

[2] Department of Computing,
Imperial College of Science, Technology and Medicine,
London SW7 2AZ, United Kingdom
wl@doc.ic.ac.uk

Abstract. This paper presents two reconfigurable design approaches for a two dimensional Shape-Adaptive Discrete Cosine Transform (2D SA-DCT). The SA-DCT is an example of a new type of multimedia video processing algorithm where the computations performed are data dependent. A static design, where the configuration does not change during execution of the task, is presented. The use of a data dependence graph (DDG) is proposed which represents the computations and input signals required to calculate a particular output signal depending on a variable input parameter. By re-structuring the DDG and exploiting possible sharing of FPGA resources for different entities within the SA-DCT, it is demonstrated that the area required for an implementation can be significantly reduced. An alternative dynamic approach is also introduced where the FPGA's configuration may change over time. This is well suited to using dynamically reconfigurable logic but suffers from long reconfiguration time if current FPGAs are used.

1 Introduction

Multimedia processing is characterised by very high processing demands. Typical multimedia applications entail combined processing of various data types including video, audio, speech, images, 2D/3D graphics, and text. The video processing tasks are clearly the most computationally intensive. In addition, many novel multimedia processing algorithms involve growing diversity and decreasing predictability in the computation flow. This calls for hardware architectures with increased flexibility at run-time [1].

MPEG-4 has been developed as the new standard for audio-visual coding in multimedia applications [2]. An example of a novel MPEG-4 video processing tool is the Shape-Adaptive Discrete Cosine Transform (SA-DCT) which was introduced by Sikora and Makai in [3]. The algorithm has been included in the MPEG-4 Video Verification Model [4], as an alternative to the standard block-based DCT which is widely used in the MPEG-1, MPEG-2, H.261, and H.263 standards. The SA-DCT is applied for coding arbitrarily shaped object segments contained within an 8×8 image block, specifically in blocks with at least one transparent pixel.

Due to the arbitrary shape of the object within an 8×8 image block, a hardware implementation of a two dimensional SA-DCT (2D SA-DCT) is not as straightforward as the implementation of the standard 8×8 DCT where the transform is always carried out on eight pixels per row and eight pixels per column. In contrast, for the SA-DCT, the calculations performed, and hence the hardware required to accomplish these calculations, depend on the number of pixels occupied by the object within the 8×8 block. Hence, flexible and efficient architectures and implementations are required to adapt to these constraints.

Reconfigurable logic devices, notably (SRAM based) Field Programmable Gate Arrays (FPGAs), are suitable for dealing with these adaptability requirements as a trade-off between the speed of ASICs and the flexibility of software [5]. They can be configured for a variety of applications with high processing demands and reconfigured for other applications if necessary. This makes FPGAs very appropriate for the implementation of many MPEG-4 modules in general, and for the SA-DCT in particular.

An architecture of a 2D SA-DCT based on time-recursion has been presented in [6]. However, this architecture does not present the best solution in terms of computational requirement and has the disadvantage of numerical inaccuracy due to its second-order recursive structure. An architecture which can perform a DCT-N for variable length N, $2 \leq N \leq 8$, has recently been proposed in [7]. This design allows efficient sharing of hardware resources for different N but increases the hardware cost compared to an implementation of a single DCT-N for only one particular N.

The purpose of this paper is to investigate suitable designs for an SA-DCT implementation using reconfigurable logic. A generic one dimensional SA-DCT architecture consisting of a static module with a time-constant structure and a dynamic module which can change its structure at run-time is proposed. Employing the proposed 1D SA-DCT architecture, a 2D SA-DCT can be implemented on FPGAs using two different approaches. In this paper, a static design is presented, where the configuration data for all possible computations is loaded once, after which it does not change during execution of the task. The use of a data dependence graph (DDG) is proposed which represents the computations and input signals required to calculate a particular output signal depending on a variable input parameter. By re-structuring the DDG and exploiting possible sharing of FPGA resources for different entities within the SA-DCT, it is demonstrated that the area required for an implementation can be reduced considerably. The results of an implementation based on Distributed Arithmetic on an Altera FLEX10KE FPGA will be presented. A dynamic approach is also introduced where the FPGA's configuration may change over time. It will be shown that this is well suited to using dynamically reconfigurable logic but suffers from long reconfiguration overhead if currently available FPGAs are used.

Section 2 describes the algorithm of the 2D Shape-Adaptive DCT. A generic architecture of the 1D SA-DCT is proposed in Sect. 3 which is used for both, a static and dynamic realisation approach of the 2D SA-DCT. These designs are presented in Sect. 4. In Sect. 5, the implementations of both static and dynamic approach are discussed. Finally, a conclusion follows in Sect. 6.

2 2D Shape-Adaptive DCT

The Shape-Adaptive DCT algorithm is based on predefined orthogonal sets of DCT basis functions. The basic concept of the method for coding an arbitrarily shaped image foreground segment contained within an 8×8 reference block is outlined in Fig. 1 [4]. The required two dimensional SA-DCT is usually separated into two one dimensional SA-DCTs, a vertical SA-DCT followed by a horizontal SA-DCT.

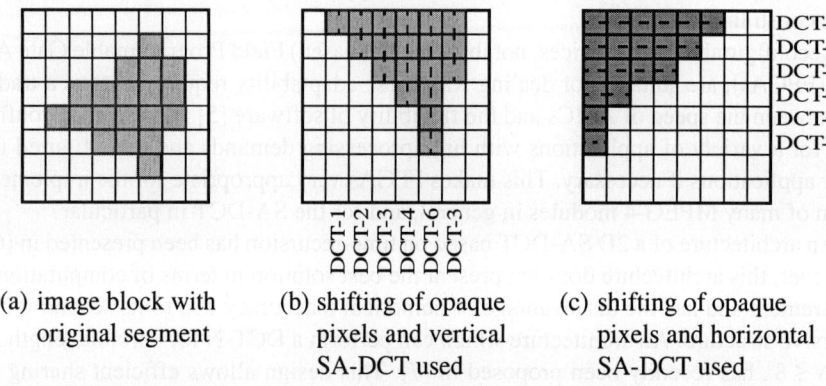

(a) image block with original segment

(b) shifting of opaque pixels and vertical SA-DCT used

(c) shifting of opaque pixels and horizontal SA-DCT used

Fig. 1. 2D SA-DCT method

An example of an image block segmented into foreground (shaded) and background (light) region is shown in Fig. 1(a). To perform the vertical SA-DCT, the number of foreground (or opaque) pixels of each of the eight columns of the image block is calculated, and the columns are shifted and aligned to the top of the 8×8 block (Fig. 1(b)). Depending on the vector size N (number of opaque pixels) for each particular column of the segment, a DCT of size N (DCT-N) is performed on the column data vector $\underline{x} = [x_0 \, x_1 \, ... \, x_{N-1}]^T$ which results in N vertical DCT-coefficients $\underline{c} = [c_0 \, c_1 \, ... \, c_{N-1}]^T$ according to [4]:

$$\underline{c} = \sqrt{\frac{2}{N}} \cdot \underline{DCT-N} \cdot \underline{x} \,. \qquad (1)$$

The DCT transform matrix $\underline{DCT\text{-}N}$ is defined as:

$$\underline{DCT-N}(p, k) = \alpha(p) \cdot \cos\left[p\left(k + \frac{1}{2}\right) \cdot \frac{\pi}{N}\right], \qquad (2)$$

for k, p = 0, 1, ..., N-1, and $\alpha(p) = \begin{cases} \sqrt{\frac{1}{2}} & p = 0 \\ 1 & p \neq 0 \end{cases}$

Hence, a particular element c_p of $\underline{c}$ can be calculated as a sum of N products using

$$c_p = \sqrt{\frac{2}{N}} \sum_{k=0}^{N-1} DCT-N(p,k) \cdot x_k \ . \tag{3}$$

For example, the right-most column of the object in Fig. 1 is transformed using a DCT-3. To execute the horizontal SA-DCT, the length of each row of the intermediate block (after vertical SA-DCT) is calculated and the rows are shifted to the left border of the 8×8 block as shown in Fig. 1(c). A horizontal DCT adapted to the size of each row is then performed using (1) and (2).

3   Proposed Architecture for 1D SA-DCT

We propose a generic one dimensional (1D) SA-DCT consisting of two main parts, as shown in Fig. 2. Firstly, the opaque pixels in each column or row have to be shifted to the top or left, respectively, and the number of opaque pixels N per column or row has to be counted (module *Shift & Count*). In the second part, module *DCT-N*, a multiplication of an $N \times N$ constant coefficient matrix with an input vector comprising the values of the N shifted pixels, is performed according to (1) and (2). Whereas module *Shift & Count* is *static*, that is exactly the same module is used for all input signals of the SA-DCT, the module *DCT-N* is *dynamic* since its structure can change at run time depending on N.

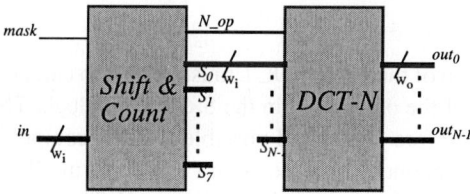

Fig. 2. Proposed generic 1D SA-DCT architecture

The inputs of module *Shift & Count* are the value of one pixel and a mask bit which is 1 if the pixel is opaque and 0 if the pixel is transparent. One pixel value and its respective mask bit are shifted in at a time. The mask bit *mask* is used to count the number of opaque pixels N within each column or row and to shift their values to the first N output registers. Outputs of the module are a) N_op, which represents the number of opaque pixels N per column or row, respectively, and b) the eight pixel values of one column or row arranged so that outputs S_0 to S_{N-1} carry the opaque pixel values.

Module *DCT-N* has as inputs N_op and the first N outputs of module *Shift & Count*, $S_0 ... S_{N-1}$, which are the values of the opaque pixels of the processed column or row (see Fig. 2). Within module *DCT-N* a constant matrix - vector multiplication of size N according to equation (1) is performed. N_op can be interpreted as a control signal which selects the actual DCT-N computation accomplished as sketched in Fig. 3. For $N\_op = 0$, no computations are necessary. Outputs are the N DCT coefficients of the opaque pixels.

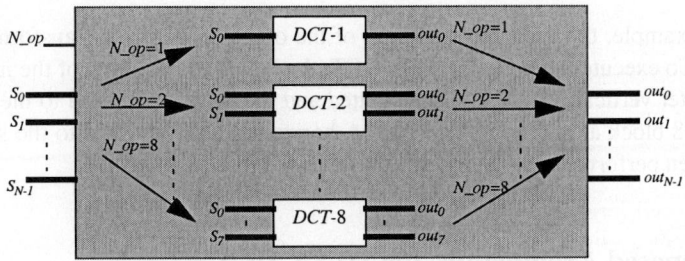

Fig. 3. Generic structure of module *DCT-N*

4 Reconfigurable Design for 2D SA-DCT

The generic architecture for the 1D SA-DCT suggested in Sect. 3 has been used for a reconfigurable design of the 2D SA-DCT. Two general approaches are presented, a *static* design where the configuration is loaded once, after which it does not change during execution of the entire task, and a *dynamic* design where the FPGA's configuration may change over time.

4.1 Static Design

A static implementation of the 2D SA-DCT must be able to calculate the right result for every possible shape of the object within the 8×8 image block. The configuration data of the FPGA must therefore contain all possible DCT-N computations for $1 \leq N \leq 8$. In a straightforward implementation the circuit can perform all eight DCT-N calculations in parallel and select the outputs depending on N. The main disadvantage of this approach is the large amount of hardware necessary to implement all eight DCT-Ns, even though only one DCT-N is required at a time. For an efficient FPGA implementation it is therefore necessary to share hardware resources throughout different DCT-N entities as much as possible. Hence, the relationship between the DCT-size N and the structure of the data flow of the *DCT-N* module has to be investigated to find a representation which allows a more area efficient implementation.

We propose the use of a *data dependence graph* (DDG) which represents the computations and input signals required to calculate a particular output signal depending on a variable input parameter. A DDG consists of coloured nodes and directed edges. The nodes represent independent computations or tasks. If two nodes have the same colour, their respective calculations result in the same output signal. Only one of the computations marked by the same colour can be performed at a time, determined by the variable input signal. The edges of the graph directed towards the nodes show which input signals are required for the particular operation represented by the node whereas the edges directed away from the nodes point at the output of this operation. The edges are labelled by a value of the variable input signal. For a particular value of the variable parameter, the computation flow uses only the edges and respective nodes labelled by this value. Nodes of the DDG can be grouped into blocks. A block can be thought of as a hardware entity. By re-structuring the DDG and re-grouping nodes, hardware resources can be shared more efficiently.

Figure 4 shows the DDG of a part of the *DCT-N* module (for $N = 1, 2$, and 3), before and after re-structuring and re-grouping. The graph shows which computations and which input signals have to be used to calculate a particular output signal depending on N. The signals s_k ($k = 0 \ldots 7$) stand for the inputs, here the values of the opaque pixels, and the signals c_p ($p = 0 \ldots 7$) represent the outputs. A node of the DDG denoted DCT-N(p) symbolises the computations performed, in this case the multiplication of the pth row vector of matrix <u>*DCT-N*</u> with input vector $\underline{s} = [s_0 \, s_1 \ldots s_{N-1}]^T$, resulting in the pth output c_p of DCT-N according to equation (3). Different dashed line patterns are used for the edges to distinguish between different N. Every computation is to be performed only for one specific N. For instance, DCT-2(1) calculates output c_1 of DCT-2 (that is $N=2$) using inputs s_0 and s_1. Whilst c_1 does not exist for $N=1$ (DCT-1 has only one output c_0), it can also be output of DCT-3 (for $N=3$) where s_0, s_1, and s_2 are used as input signals.

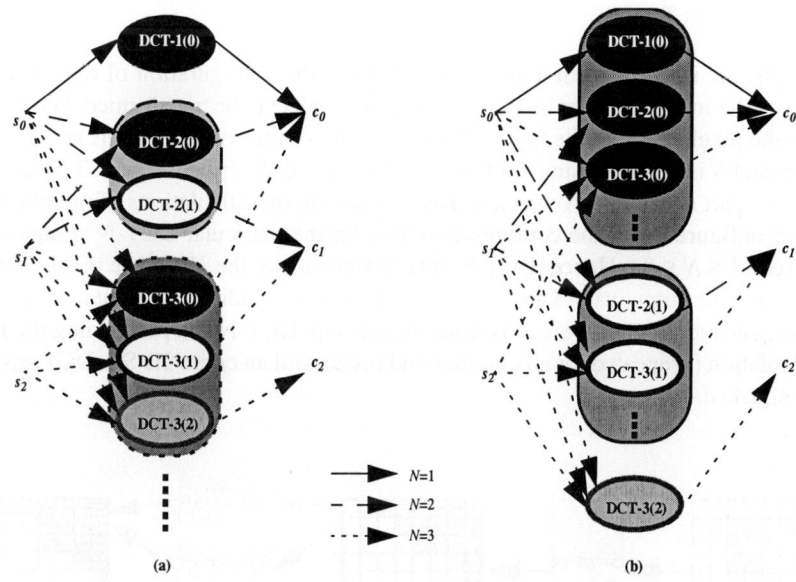

Fig. 4. Restructuring of data dependence graph

In Fig. 4(a) the DDG is arranged in a way so that nodes (operations) marked with the same N are grouped together into blocks. In this case, the computations of every block are necessary only for one particular value of N. For an SA-DCT hardware implementation in this manner only the results of one of eight blocks are used at a time while the others are not required, even though all eight blocks exist and produce outputs. Within one block all computations are required at the same time and each computation produces a different output value, therefore sharing of hardware resources is difficult. In fact, for a 1D SA-DCT design in this manner, all possible 36 multiply and accumulate (MAC) calculations according to (3) have to be implemented (one for DCT-1, two for DCT-2, and so on) separately.

An alternative way of grouping nodes into blocks is shown in Fig. 4(b). Here, all nodes labelled with the same p, that is computations which produce the same output, are placed into the same group. Hence, every output signal is produced only by one particular block, no output selection is necessary. The signal N is used to select the right computation required to calculate a particular output, in contrast to a design according to Fig. 4(a) where N is used to select the right outputs amongst the computation results of all blocks. Each block contains at most one computation for which the result is required at a time. This allows intensive hardware resource sharing within one block while using blocks in parallel. For a 1D SA-DCT implementation in this manner, only eight MAC units, which is the minimum needed to implement a DCT-8 with eight outputs, and a decoder which selects the right constants of the *DCT-N* matrix, depending on N, need to be implemented. Hence, the number of MAC modules, and therefore the hardware cost, can be reduced significantly to approximately 22%.

4.2 Dynamic Design

In a dynamic implementation of the 2D SA-DCT the configuration of the FPGA depends on the input data, that is on the shape of the object to be transformed. While reading in the pixel values of the first column, the values of the opaque pixels are shifted to the top and N is counted using module *Shift & Count* as described in Sect. 3. Depending on N, the part of the FPGA which is used to perform the calculations of module *DCT-N* is reconfigured with the configuration data for the particular DCT-N computations required ($1 \leq N \leq 8$). Hence, DCT-N is performed using the N opaque pixel values as inputs, and the output values are stored. This process of reading in the data, shifting and counting N, reconfiguring the device for the relevant DCT-N and performing the DCT-N calculation is repeated for all columns and rows, until an entire 2D SA-DCT has been accomplished.

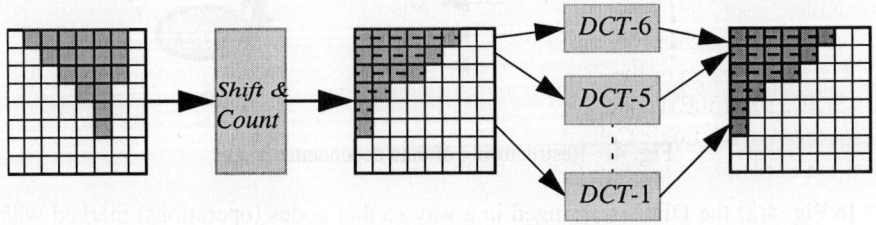

Fig. 5. Example of dynamic 1D (horizontal) SA-DCT

This approach is well suited to using dynamically reconfigurable logic within a custom computing machine (CCM). An example of a dynamic implementation of a horizontal SA-DCT is illustrated in Fig. 5. The top row of the object has six opaque pixels, that is $N=6$ for this row. Hence, module *DCT-N* is instantiated as *DCT-6*, that is the FPGA is reconfigured to perform a DCT-6. After sending back the computation results, a DCT-5 for the second row of the object has to be performed. Therefore, the FPGA has to be reconfigured with the configuration data for a DCT-5. This is repeated for all rows of the object. Sixteen reconfigurations are necessary to perform a complete 2D SA-DCT in this manner.

5 FPGA Implementation and Results

We first analyse how to efficiently implement a general constant matrix - vector multiplication as required for each DCT-N calculation and then how to incorporate those computations into an SA-DCT architecture. A very efficient method of computing this multiply and accumulate (MAC) operation, especially for FPGAs, is to use Distributed Arithmetic [8], where the MAC calculations are performed in a bit-serial manner. The technique is based on storing pre-calculated scalar products for all possible bit patterns of the input signals in a ROM. By exploiting symmetries within the *DCT-N* matrices the number of ROM address bits can be reduced to $\lceil N/2 \rceil$ and the number of required ROM words can be decreased to $2^{\lceil N/2 \rceil}$ [9]. Distributed Arithmetic can make extensive use of look-up tables (LUTs) and/or embedded ROMs which are part of modern SRAM based FPGAs, such as Altera FLEX 10K [11] or Xilinx Virtex [12], and hence make them ideal for this type of computations. No multipliers are necessary. This is especially important for FPGAs since they are very efficient for shift and add operations but are generally inefficient for implementing parallel multipliers [10].

For a static SA-DCT implementation using Distributed Arithmetic, effective hardware resource sharing according to Fig. 4(b) can be achieved by using the same ROM for more than one DCT-N, with N forming part of the ROM address instead of selecting the outputs at the end. The signal N is three bits wide since it can have eight different values in the range 1 through 8. If N is used as part of the ROM address, the ROM size will become $2^3 = 8$ times as large. Since $\lceil N/2 \rceil$ address bits are required to select the right matrix coefficients depending on the input signals, no more than seven bits are required for the entire 1D SA-DCT to address the ROMs. Because the minimum address width of embedded ROMs within many modern FPGAs such as Altera FLEX10K [11] and Xilinx Virtex [12] is at least eight bits, the number of ROMs required is not increased. In fact, the embedded ROM blocks can be utilised more efficiently.

The static design of the 2D SA-DCT for MPEG-4 has been implemented on an Altera FLEX 10K130E device [11], in compliance to the MPEG-4 Verification Model [4]. 3721 (55%) of the Logic Cells (LCs) and all 16 EABs have been employed. A schematic of the implemented circuit is shown in Fig. 6. The module *Transpose* is used for the necessary matrix transposition between vertical and horizontal SA-DCT. The circuit runs at 47 MHz with a throughput of one value per two clock cycles. Using this clock frequency, a complete 2D SA-DCT can be performed in 4.47 µs.

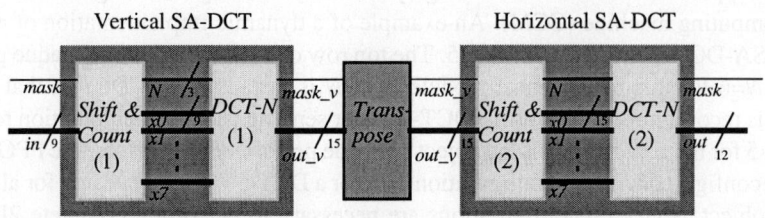

Fig. 6. Implementation of 2D SA-DCT

For the dynamic design, all eight possible instances of the DCT-N module have been implemented for Altera FLEX 10KE devices. The problems of the dynamic approach are the long configuration time of current FPGAs and the high number of reconfigurations necessary for a considerably small amount of processing time of a DCT-N computation. Provided that all possible values of N have the same frequency of occurrence, it takes on average approximately 21 ms to reconfigure an appropriate Altera FLEX 10K FPGA [11] compared to only 167 ns to compute one DCT-N. In this case the reconfiguration overhead would be approximately 125,000. Even with (partially) dynamically reconfigurable devices such as Xilinx XC6200 or Virtex FPGAs [12] the overhead is still large. For a Virtex FPGA, the average partial reconfiguration time for a DCT-N is about 420 µs, still 2,500 times longer than the time to compute a DCT-N. It takes 1.51 µs to compute a complete 2D SA-DCT if all parts of the dynamic design can work at their highest clock frequency and the reconfiguration time is not taken into account. Hence, to make the dynamic design quicker than the static design, the time for all 16 reconfigurations needs to be smaller than 2.96 µs, that is, 185 ns for one reconfiguration.

Reducing the reconfiguration time could be possible by using context switching FPGAs where a number of different configurations, which can be selected very rapidly, are stored on-chip [13]. An approach to reduce the number of reconfigurations could be realised by consecutively passing through all contour blocks of the object for a given N and performing the DCT-N operation only for this particular value of N. However, this approach introduces irregular data processing and memory usage.

6 Conclusion

We have presented two reconfigurable design approaches for a 2D Shape-Adaptive DCT, an example of a new type of multimedia video processing algorithm where the computations performed are data dependent. A static design, where the configuration data does not change during execution of the task, has been presented. The proposed use of a data dependence graph (DDG) allows a structured method for optimising sharable resources. By re-structuring the DDG and exploiting possible sharing of FPGA resources for different entities within the SA-DCT, it has been demonstrated that the area required for an implementation can be significantly reduced. An alternative dynamic approach has also been presented where the FPGA's configuration may change over time. This is well suited to using dynamically reconfigurable logic but suffers from long reconfiguration overhead if currently available FPGAs are used.

Current and future work includes the development of a generic reconfigurability model in order to determine the conditions under which dynamic reconfiguration would be more attractive than static reconfiguration. Possible model parameters include the number and size of independently reconfigurable units, and the number, size, computation time and reconfiguration time of independent computations and their probability of occurrence, as well as the probability that one computation follows another.

Acknowledgements. This work was supported by the Department of Electrical and Electronic Engineering, Imperial College, and Sony Broadcast & Professional Europe.

References

1. Pirsch, P., Stolberg, H.-J.: VLSI Implementations of Image and Video Multimedia Processing Systems. IEEE Trans. Circuits Syst. Video Technol. **8** (1998) 878-891
2. MPEG Group: Overview of the MPEG-4 Standard. ISO/IEC JTC1/SC29/WG11 N2725 (1999)
3. Sikora, T., Makai, B.: Low Complexity Shape-Adaptive DCT for Generic Coding of Video. Proc. Workshop on Image Analysis and Image Coding (1994)
4. MPEG Group: MPEG-4 Video Verification Model Version 15.0. ISO/IEC JTC1/SC29/WG11 N3093 (1999)
5. Haynes, S.D., Stone, J., Cheung, P.Y.K., Luk, W.: Video Image Processing with the SONIC Architecture. IEEE Computer **33** (2000) 50-57
6. Le, T., Wendt, M., Glesner, M.: VLSI-Architecture of a Time-Recursive 2-D Shape-Adaptive DCT Processor for Generic Coding of Video. Proc. Intern. Conf. on Signal Processing Applications and Technology (1997) 1238-1242
7. Le, T., Glesner, M.: A New Flexible Architecture for Variable Length DCT Targeting Shape-Adaptive Transform. Proc. IEEE International Conference on Acoustics, Speech, and Signal Processing **4** (1999) 1949-1952
8. Peled, A., Liu, B.: A New Hardware Realization of Digital Filters. IEEE Trans. Acoust., Speech, Signal Process. **22** (1974) 456-462
9. Sun, M.T., Wu, L., Liou, M.L.: A Concurrent Architecture for VLSI Implementation of Discrete Cosine Transform. IEEE Trans. Circuits Syst. **34** (1987) 992-994
10. Haynes, S.D., Cheung, P.Y.K.: A Reconfigurable Multiplier Array For Video Image Processing Tasks, Suitable For Embedding In An FPGA Structure. Proc. IEEE Symposium on FPGAs for Custom Computing Machines (1998) 226-234
11. Altera Inc.: FLEX 10KE Embedded Programmable Logic Family Data Sheet (1999)
12. Xilinx Inc.: Virtex^{TM} 2.5 V Field Programmable Gate Arrays (2000)
13. Chang, D., Marek-Sadowska, M.: Partitioning Sequential Circuits on Dynamically Reconfigurable FPGAs. IEEE Trans. on Computers **48** (1999) 565-578

A Self-Reconfigurable Gate Array Architecture *

Reetinder Sidhu[1], Sameer Wadhwa[1], Alessandro Mei[2], and Viktor K. Prasanna[1]

[1] Department of EE-Systems, University of Southern California,
Los Angeles CA 90089, USA
sidhu@halcyon.usc.edu, sameer@halcyon.usc.edu,
prasanna@ganges.usc.edu

[2] Department of Mathematics, University of Trento
38050 Trento (TN), Italy
mei@science.unitn.it

Abstract. This paper presents an innovative architecture for a reconfigurable device that allows single cycle context switching and single cycle random access to the unified on-chip configuration/data memory. These two features are necessary for efficient self-reconfiguration and are useful in general as well—no other device offers both features. The enhanced context switching feature permits arbitrary regions of the chip to selectively context switch—its not necessary for the whole device to do so. The memory access feature allows data transfer between logic cells and memory locations, and also directly between memory locations.

The key innovation enabling the above features is the use of a mesh of trees based interconnect with logic cells and memory blocks at the leaf nodes and identical switches at other nodes. The mesh of trees topology allows a logic cell to be associated with a pair of switches. The logic cell and the switches can be placed close to the memory block that stores their configuration bits. The physical proximity enables fast context switching while the mesh of trees topology permits fast memory access. To evaluate the architecture, a point design with 8×8 logic cells was synthesized using a standard cell library for a 0.25 μm process with 5 metal layers. Timing results obtained show that both context switching and memory access can be performed within a 10 ns clock cycle. Finally, this paper also illustrates how self-reconfiguration can be used to do basic routing operations of connecting two logic cells or inserting a logic cell by breaking an existing connection—algorithms (implemented as configured logic) to perform the above operations in a few clock cycles are presented.

1 Introduction

By exploiting the reconfigurability of devices such as FPGAs, significant performance improvements have been obtained over other modes of computation for several applications. Such a device provides configurable logic whose functionality is governed by bits written into its configuration memory, which is typically SRAM. Thus device functionality can be quickly reconfigured to suit application requirements by writing appropriate bits into the configuration memory—this is the key advantage of reconfigurable computing over other modes of computation.

In most cases however, reconfiguration of the device, whether at compile time or at runtime, is performed externally. Much greater performance gains and a high degree of flexibility can be obtained if the device can generate configuration bits at runtime and use them to modify its own configuration—the ability of a device to do so is what we call *self-reconfiguration*.

Self-reconfiguration is a powerful feature that allows configured logic to adapt itself as the computation proceeds, based on input data and intermediate results. It can be used for simple tasks such

---

* This work was supported by the National Science Foundation, Grant CCR-9900613. Alessandro Mei was supported by MURST, "Progetto Giovani Ricercatori 1998".

as reconfiguring the constant in a KCM (constant coefficient multiplier)—a self-reconfigurable device can do so on its own, which is faster than reconfiguring the device from an external source. Self-reconfiguration can also be used for non-trivial tasks such as constructing an FSM for string matching [6], or evolving genetic programs [5]. The above applications achieve efficient computation through a fine-grained interleaving of computation and configuration which would not be possible without a self-reconfigurable device.

A self-reconfigurable device needs to be able to store multiple contexts of configuration information and context switch between them. Also, it should allow configured logic to access the configuration memory. The configured logic can then perform self-reconfiguration by modifying configuration memory contents of a particular context and then switching to that context. Hence for efficient self-reconfiguration, it is crucial that the device should enable configured logic to perform

- fast context switching,
- fast random access of the configuration memory,

Even for applications that do not use self-reconfiguration, the above two features can be useful—the former reduces reconfiguration overhead while the latter allows configuration memory to be used for data storage as well.

So far, no device architecture has been designed specifically to support self-reconfiguration. Existing devices offer at most one of above two features—none offers both. Devices such as the Sanders CSRC [4] can switch contexts in a single clock cycle but provide only serial configuration memory access—it can take hundreds of clock cycles to access a particular location [3]. On the other hand, a device like the Berkeley HSRA [9] provides fast random access to the configuration memory (which can thus be used for data storage too) but requires hundreds of clock cycles to switch context—a complete reconfiguration takes about 5 μs [2].

In this paper we present an innovative architecture (Section 2) that supports both single cycle context switching (Section 2.8) as well as single cycle random memory access (Section 3.1), thus providing both features necessary for efficient self-reconfiguration. Further, the context switching feature permits arbitrary regions of the chip to selectively context switch—it is not necessary for the whole device to do so. The memory access feature permits data transfer with single source multiple destinations, and—with restrictions—multiple sources and destinations. In addition, the architecture has a simplicity and regularity that makes it efficient for configured logic to generate configuration bits for self-reconfiguration. This is demonstrated by describing how self-reconfiguration can be used to do basic routing operations such as connecting two logic cells or inserting a logic cell by breaking an existing connection (Section 4). Finally, implementation results are presented (Section 5) followed by conclusion and future directions (Section 6).

2 Architecture

2.1 Overview

The Self-Reconfigurable Gate Array (shown in Figure 1) consists of a rectangular[1] array of *PEs*. Each PE consists of a *logic cell* and a *memory block*. A logic cell contains a 16-bit LUT and a flip-flop. A memory block can store one or more configuration contexts as well as data for the configured logic. PEs are connected to each other through direct connections to 4 nearest neighbors as well as a *mesh of trees network*. As shown in Figure 1, it consists of a complete binary tree along each row and column of the array, with PEs at the leaves of the trees and identical *switches* at the non-leaf nodes.

The mesh of trees is a well studied network in parallel processing [1]. It has useful properties such as a small diameter and a large bisection bandwidth. The mesh of trees is also suitable for

---

[1] Henceforth we assume, for convenience, an array size of $N \times N$ where N is a power of 2 ($N = 2^n$) although it is not a fundamental limitation.

VLSI implementation since it permits area efficient layout of the PEs in a 2D mesh. The mesh layout also makes possible local, nearest neighbor interconnections. Also, since the area occupied by the mesh of trees network grows only logarithmically with PE array size, the architecture can be efficiently scaled to bigger devices. There is, however, a much more important reason for using this network. It is the use of the mesh of trees with memory blocks and logic cells at its leaves and switches at the non-leaf nodes, that makes it possible for context switch and memory access operations to be performed in a single clock cycle, as explained below.

We first describe the *ownership* relation that exists between PEs and switches. Consider any row of the PE array. It consists of N PEs and $N-1$ switches. We associate with each PE, the switch that succeeds it in the in-order traversal of the tree. The above associations are made for each row and column tree. As a result each PE is associated with two[2] switches—a row switch and a column switch. Switches associated with a PE are owned by that PE.

A configuration context contains bits that configure all the logic cells and all the switches in the mesh of trees network. The configuration contexts are stored in memory blocks. Each memory block not only stores configuration bits for the logic cell in that PE, but also for the switches owned by that PE. In the VLSI layout, a PE and its switches can be placed close to each other[3]. This makes it practical to have a dedicated wire for each configuration bit to be transferred from a memory block of the logic cell and switches—the large number of wires required (about 80) is not a problem as they are very short in length. All memory blocks locally transfer data simultaneously over their dedicated wires (the context address is broadcast to all PEs). In this manner a context switch operation can be performed in a single clock cycle (please see Section 2.8 for a detailed explanation).

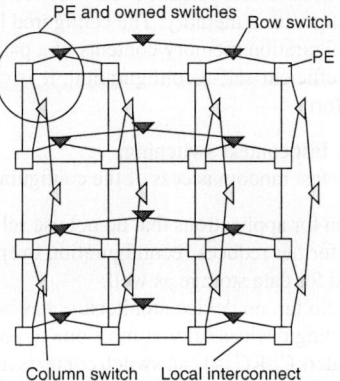

Fig. 1. SRGA architecture is based on a mesh of trees interconnect with PEs (containing a memory block and logic cell each) at the leaves and identical switches at other nodes.

A memory access operation transfers data between rows or between columns of PEs. The source and destination are the logic cells and/or the memory blocks of the PEs. Each memory block is implemented as a random access memory that can read or write a single bit every clock cycle (the address used by the memory blocks is broadcast to all PEs). Also, as mentioned earlier, memory blocks are located only at the leaf nodes of the mesh of trees network. Thus an N-bit data word can be transferred between rows over column trees or between columns over row trees. In this manner a memory access operation can be performed in a single clock cycle (please see Section 3.1 for a detailed explanation).

2.2 Interconnection Network

The interconnection network of the proposed device consists of 2 parts—the *logic interconnection network* (LIN) and the *memory interconnection network* (MIN). The mesh of trees network mentioned above is composed of a part of the LIN and all of the MIN as described in the following sections. Section 2.3 describes the switch at each non-leaf node of the mesh of trees network.

Logic Interconnection Network The LIN serves the same purpose as the interconnection network in a typical FPGA—that of connecting together the logic cells as specified by the config-

---

[2] The exceptions are PEs in the right column which do not have an associated row switch and PEs in the bottom row which lack an associated column switch.

[3] The tree of switches is "flattened" with the $N-1$ switches placed in a single row (or column) adjacent to their owner PEs.

uration bits controlling the network switches. All LIN wires are in pairs. Each wire always carries signals in a single direction and wires forming a pair carry signals in opposite directions.

The network consists of 2 types of interconnections. One type are the local connections between each logic cell and its 4 nearest neighbors. These are direct connections—they do not pass through any switches. The other type of connections are in the form of a mesh of trees with PEs at leaf nodes and switches at others.

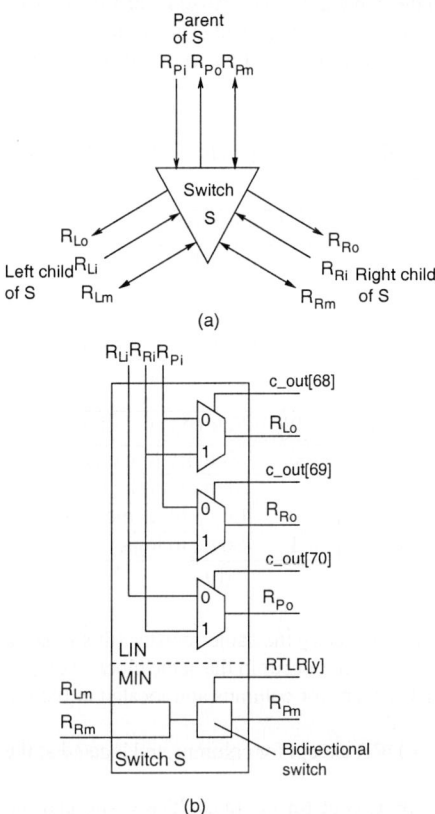

Memory Interconnection Network The MIN is used for performing data transfers during the memory access operations. Unlike the LIN, the wires are not in pairs—a single wire is used for each connection, and it may carry signals in either direction. The MIN also forms a mesh of trees network with PEs at the leaf nodes and switches at the remaining ones.

2.3 Switch

For each non-leaf node of the mesh of trees network there is an switch, the structure of which is shown in Figure 2. Each switch is connected to 2 child nodes and a parent node. Both child nodes are either switches or logic cells while the parent node is a switch.

For the LIN part of the switch, each connection is a pair of wires and so it has 3 inputs and 3 outputs. As shown, each output can be connected to either of 2 inputs via the muxes. The switch thus allows any input to be connected to any output without any restriction, except connecting an input to its output pair. Such a connection would only route a signal back where it came from, which is not useful. To configure the LIN part of the switch, 3 bits are required—1 for the control input of each of the 3 muxes.

For the MIN part of the switch, each connection is a single wire. The wires from the child nodes are permanently connected together and are connected to the parent wire through a bidirectional switch. By opening all switches at a particular level, a memory tree can be broken into multiple smaller trees.

Fig. 2. (a) Switch input and output connections. (b) Internal details. Column switches have identical structure. Please see Figure 4 for connections with owner PE.

2.4 Registers

The SRGA contains a number of registers that are accessed by the configured logic for performing context switch and memory access operations. The registers are shown in Figure 3 and described below.

The SRGA contains 3 global registers—their contents are broadcast to all PEs. They are described below.

Operation Register (OR) It is a 2-bit register that specifies what operation (if any) shall be initiated in the next clock cycle, as shown in Table 1(a).

Memory Operation Register (MOR) It is also a 2-bit register that specifies (if the OR indicates a memory operation in the next clock cycle) source and destination of the data transfer as shown in Table 1(b).

Context and Memory Address Register (CMAR) It specifies (depending on OR contents) the context to switch to or the memory address to be accessed in the next clock cycle. It consists of 2 fields. Bits $0 : \log_2 nc - 1$ form the *context field* of the CMAR—only these bits need to be specified when the CMAR is used for a context switch. The remaining $\lceil \log_2 cs \rceil$ bits form the *offset field*. This field (along with the context field) is utilized when the CMAR is used to specify a memory address. nc is the number of contexts and cs is the configuration word size—that is, the number of bits required to configure a logic cell and its 2 owned switches (each memory block thus stores $nc \times cs$ bits).

The SRGA contains 4 periphery registers—they are located along the boundary of the $N \times N$ PE array. Each register is N-bits long.

Table 1. (a) OR operations, (b) MOR operations.

OR[1]	OR[0]	Operation
0	0	No operation
0	1	Context switch
1	0	Row memory access
1	1	Column memory access

(a)

MOR[1]	MOR[0]	Source and destination
0	0	Memory to memory
0	1	Memory to logic (read)
1	0	Logic to memory (write)
1	1	Logic to logic

(b)

Source Row Register (SRR) It is located along the left side of the PE array. A set bit implies that the corresponding PE row will be the source for the next row memory access.

Destination Row Register (DRR) It is located along the right side of the PE array. A set bit implies that the corresponding PE row will be a destination for the next memory access operation.

Row Mask Register (RMR) It is located along the bottom of the PE array. A set bit indicates that, during a row memory access, no data transfer will take place for the corresponding column. The RMR and the DCR are physically the same register (this is not a problem as both a row and column memory access cannot occur in the same clock cycle).

Source Column Register (SCR) Same as SRR except for columns and located at the top of the array.

Destination Column Register(DCR) Same as DRR except for columns and located at the bottom of the array.

Column Mask Register (CMR) Same as RMR except for columns. The CMR and the DRR are physically the same register.

The SRGA contains 2 memory mapped registers. Each has N^2 bits—1 bit in each of the N^2 memory blocks. These registers can be accessed by the configured logic using memory access operations.

Context Switch Mask Register (CSMR) If the CSMR bit in a PE is set, the PE does not switch contexts even when a context switch operation occurs. Thus the CSMR enables the context switch operation to be controlled for each PE thus providing flexibility in context switching.

Data Restore Mask Register (DRMR) If the DRMR bit in a PE is set, it prevents the flip-flop contents of the logic cell in the PE from being restored when a context switch operation occurs. Thus, the DRMR enables data sharing between logic configured on different contexts.

2.5 PE

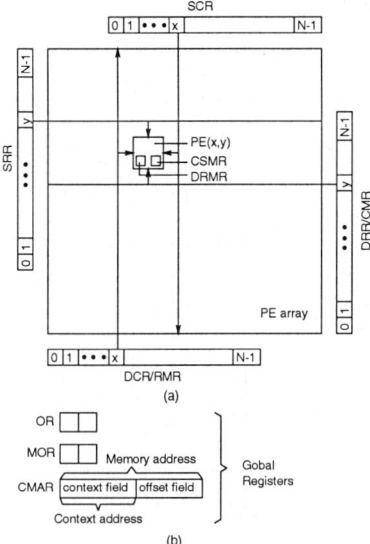

Fig. 3. (a) PE connections to periphery and memory mapped registers. (b) Global registers.

Fig. 4. PE structure.

Figure 4 shows the structure of a PE (and also the connections to the 2 switches owned by it). The PE receives various signals from registers described in the preceding section. These are used by the control logic shown on the top of the figure to generate wr_mem, wr_log and switch_context which are used during context switch and memory access operations as described in Section 3.

The LIN nearest neighbor connections (N_i, E_i, S_i, W_i, N_o, E_o, S_o, W_o) and the row tree and column tree connections (R_i, C_i, R_o, C_o) are connected to the logic cell and so are the MIN connections (the bidirectional R_m and C_m are converted to the unidirectional R_{mi}, C_{mi}, R_{mo} and C_{mo}). The memory block supplies configuration bits to the logic block over the wires c_out[0:67] and to the 2 owned switches over c_out[68:73]. These (c_out[0:74]) are the large number of short wires for transferring configuration bits mentioned in Section 2.1.

For memory reads and writes, the memory block is connected to the row and column MIN trees through d_in and d_out. The context_state and DRMR signals are used to restore logic cell flip-flop contents when context switching (as described in Section 2.8).

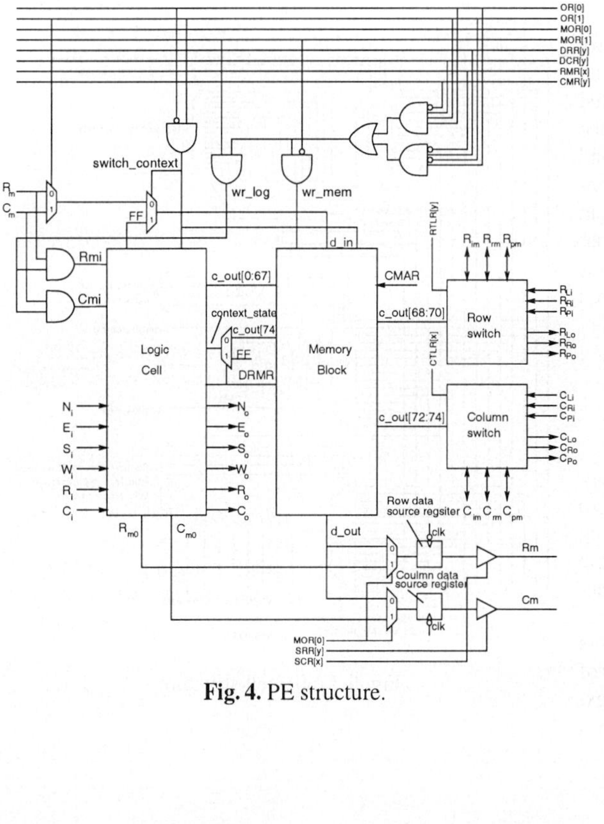

The 2 muxes at the bottom are used to select either the logic cell or memory block output to drive the MIN when the PE is a source in a memory access operation. The tristate buffers are used since the MIN wires are bidirectional.

2.6 Memory Block

Figure 5 shows the structure of a memory block. The memory cell array is internally arranged as nc columns of $cs (=75)$ bits each. Thus each column can store a configuration word. This arrangement enables all cs bits of a configuration word to be read out in a single clock cycle (and registered in c_out). Also, in case of a memory read or write operation, a single bit can be read from or written to the memory cell array. As should be clear from the figure, the CSMR and DRMR can also be accessed through memory operations. The CCR stores the address of the current context and is used during context switching as described in Section 2.8.

2.7 Logic Cell

Figure 6 shows the structure of a logic cell. It consists of a 16-bit LUT and a flip-flop. The LUT can implement 2 boolean functions of 3 inputs (with outputs $L1_o$ and $L2_o$) or a single boolean function of 4 inputs (output $L0_o$).

As can be seen, the mux $M0_i$ enables any of the inputs received by the logic cell to be used as input $L0_i$ of the LUT—the inputs $L1_i$, $L2_i$ and $L3_i$ are driven by muxes $M1_i$, $M2_i$ and $M3_i$ respectively which are identical to $M0_i$. Similarly, the output N_o of the logic cell can be connected to any of the inputs or any of the outputs of the LUT or flip-flop. Identical muxes $M1_o$–$M7_o$ drive the other outputs of the logic cell.

The complete flexibility in configuring connections allows the LUT and flip-flop to be used while other signals are routed though the logic cell. Also, since each mux has similar inputs and requires 4 control bits, the configuration word format (shown in Figure 7) is simple and regular, which considerably eases generation of configuration bits required for self-reconfiguration.

2.8 Context Switch Operation

Performing a context switch operation from current context a to another context b involves saving the state of context a, restoring the state of context b and replacing the configuration bits of context a with those of b in registers that determine the functionality of the configurable logic. A context switch operation completes in a

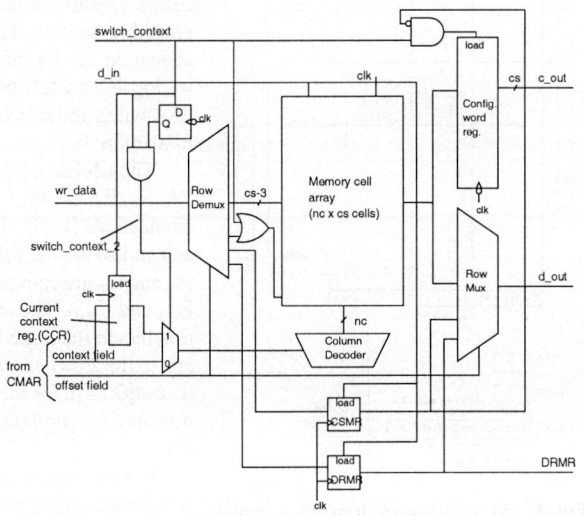

Fig. 5. Memory block structure.

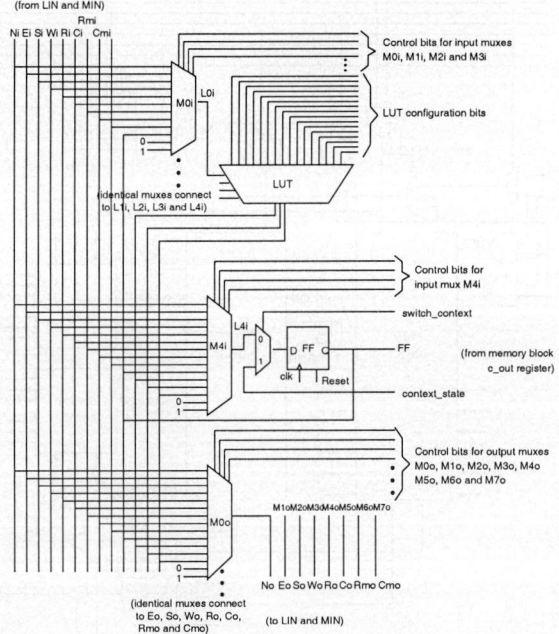

Fig. 6. Logic cell structure.

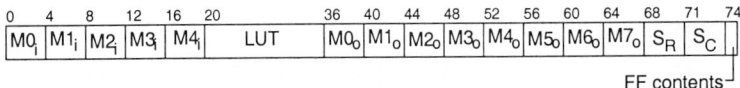

Fig. 7. Configuration word format.

single clock cycle. The context state consists of the $N \times N$ bits stored in the logic cell flip-flops (FF in Figure 6). The registers that determine the functionality of the configurable logic are the configuration word registers in each memory block (shown in Figure 5). The state of context b is restored only in those PEs which have their DRMR (Data Restore Mask Register) bit reset—in other PEs, the context a state is retained. In this manner data can be shared between contexts. Also, only those PEs switch to context b which have their CSMR (Context Switch Mask Register) bit reset—other PEs retain context a. In this manner, arbitrary regions of the $N \times N$ PE array may switch contexts while remaining regions retain the current context. In order to have static logic (logic that does not change on context switches) using above approach, it needs to be configured only on one context. This is more efficient than the static logic mode in [8] which required the same logic to be configured in all contexts. Also, the proposed approach permits multiple contexts to be active in different regions of the PE array at the same time.

3 Basic Operations

For a context switch to occur, some logic on the currently active context (context a) needs to write into the CMAR (explained in Section 2.4) the address of the context to switch to (context b) and into the OR the bits 01—writing these bits into the OR initiates a context switch operation in the next clock cycle. At the positive edge which marks the beginning of the next clock cycle, the CMAR and OR contents are registered and broadcast to all the memory blocks.

In each memory block (shown in Figure 5), in the first half of the clock cycle, the configuration word for context b is loaded into the configuration word register as follows. The switch_context signal is 1 while the switch_context_2 signal is 0. As a result the context field of the CMAR gets applied to the column decoder selecting the column corresponding to context b for loading into the configuration word register. Also its load enable input (EN) is 1 (assuming that the CSMR bit is 0). Therefore at the negative clock edge at the end of the first half of the clock cycle, the configuration word register gets loaded with the configuration word for context b.

During the second half of the clock cycle, context a state is saved and context b state is restored as follows. The signal switch_context_2 becomes 1 applying contents of the current context register (which contains the value a) to the column decoder. The signal row_select[cs-1] also becomes 1. These signals together select for writing the memory cell that stores FF contents for context a. Also the value of d_in, the data input to the memory array is the output of FF. Thus at the end of the second half of the clock cycle, the contents of FF get stored in bit 73 of the configuration word (shown in Figure 7) for context a. At the same clock edge, the switch_context signal ensures that FF gets loaded with the context_state signal. The value of context_state is either the FF contents saved in the configuration word of context b (if DRMR is 0) or the current contents of FF (if DRMR is 1). Also at the same clock edge, the current context register is loaded with the value in the context field of the CMAR (b) which would then be used to save the state of context b at the next context switch. In this manner, the context switch operation is performed in a single clock cycle.

3.1 Memory Access Operations

A memory access operation transfers data between rows or between columns of PEs. The source and destination of data are the logic cells and/or the memory blocks in the PEs. Data transfers can occur from memory blocks to logic cells (memory read), from logic cells to memory blocks (memory write) or directly from memory block to memory block[4]. Each data transfer is of an N-bit word, with each PE in the source row (or column) contributing 1 bit. Transfer of any arbitrary subset of the N-bits can be done using the mask registers RMR and CMR. All memory access operations complete in a single clock cycle. In the first half of the clock cycle, data is read out of the memory blocks or the logic cells of the source PEs. In the second half, the data bits are broadcast over the column (or row) memory trees and written into the logic cells or memory blocks of the destination PEs.

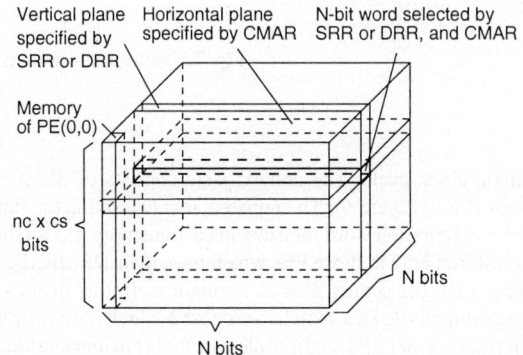

Fig. 8. Selection of an N-bit data word along a row.

The operation is a read, write or memory transfer operation depending on the contents of the MOR. For all operations, OR contains 10 indicating a row memory operation. Also a single 1 bit in the SRR indicates the source row while the 1 bits in the DRR specify the destination rows. The CMAR contains the memory address and the RMR is used to mask any bits, if required. Figure 8 shows the selection of an N-bit word of data along a row. The SRR or DRR selects a vertical plane while the CMAR specifies a horizontal bit-plane—the selected bits are at their intersection. Writing 10 in the OR register initiates the operation in the following clock cycle.

Memory Read Operation The MOR contains 01 which indicates that the source is memory blocks (address of the N-bit memory word specified by the SRR and the CMAR as shown in Figure 8) while the destination is logic cells (specified by the DRR).

In the first half of the clock cycle, in each memory block, the CMAR contents are applied to the row demux, the column decoder and the row mux, causing the required data bit to be output on d_out (please see Figure 5). At the negative clock edge, d_out is registered in the column data source flip-flop (shown in Figure 4).

Since the SRR bit for the source row is 1, the tristate buffers in the source row PEs are enabled, driving the flip-flop contents onto the corresponding memory column trees (described in Section 2.2). In this manner, in the second half of the clock cycle, the N-bit word is broadcast over the N column memory trees.

Finally, in each PE in the destination rows (rows for which DRR is 1), the wr_log signal (shown in Figure 4) is asserted causing the bit broadcast over its corresponding column memory tree to be available as the C_{mi} input to the logic cell. As can be seen from Figure 6, the C_{mi} input can be used by the logic in various ways—as an input to the LUT, the flip-flop FF, the muxes $M0_o$ to $M7_o$ connected to the logic cell outputs, or any combination thereof. The outputs of any of the above that use C_{mi} as input, stabilize by the end of the second half of the clock cycle, thus completing the memory read operation.

---

[4] Data transfer between logic cells is also supported by the MIN but is not discussed since the LIN is more suitable for connecting logic cells.

Note that for PEs in non-destination rows, C_{mi} is 0 because wr_log is not asserted. The same is true for those columns of destination row PEs for which the corresponding bit of the mask register RMR is 1.

Memory Write Operation The MOR contains 10 which indicates that the source is logic cells (specified by the SRR), while the destination is memory blocks (address specified by the DRR and CMAR). In the first half of the clock cycle in each PE, the C_{mo} output of the logic cell is applied to the input of the column source data flip-flop which registers it at the negative clock edge. As shown in Figure 6, any of several wires inside a logic cell may be connected to C_{mo} by appropriately configuring mux $M7_o$.

At the negative clock edge, C_{mo} is registered in the column data source flip-flop (shown in Figure 4). Since the SRR bit for the source row is 1, the tristate buffers in the source row PEs are enabled, driving the flip-flop contents onto the corresponding memory column trees (described in Section 2.2). In this manner, in the second half of the clock cycle, the N-bit word is broadcast over the N column memory trees.

Finally, in each PE in the destination rows, the wr_mem signal (shown in Figure 4 is asserted causing the bit broadcast over its corresponding column tree to be available as the d_in input to the memory block. Also, the CMAR contents are applied to the row demux and the column decoder of the memory array (shown in Figure 5), selecting the memory cell into which d_in will be written. At the positive clock edge, d_in gets written into the memory array, thus completing the memory write operation.

Note that for PEs in non-destination rows, wr_mem is not asserted, preventing any memory write from taking place. The same is true for those columns of destination row PEs for which the corresponding bit of the mask register RMR is 1.

Memory to Memory Data Transfer Operation The MOR contains 00 which indicates that the source is memory blocks (address specified by the SRR and CMAR) and the destination is also memory blocks (address specified by the DRR and CMAR). Note that the CMAR is used for both source and destination addresses. Thus this operation is useful only if source and destination are on the same horizontal memory slice (shown in Figure 8).

In the first half of the clock cycle, data bits are read from the source row memory blocks into the corresponding column data source flip-flops as explained in Section 3.1. In the second half of the clock cycle, the data bits get written into the memory blocks of the destination PEs as described in Section 3.1. In this manner, the memory to memory data transfer operation is performed in a single clock cycle. As usual, the RMR can be used to prevent the transfer of any of the N bits.

4 Basic Routing Operations Using Self-Reconfiguration

Modification of configured logic using self-reconfiguration typically occurs as follows. Active context (a) decides that some logic on it needs to be modified. Context a then writes certain parameters (in a predetermined location—flip-flops or memory) that specify the reconfiguration required. It then switches to context b. Logic configured on context b reads the supplied parameters and uses them to generate the required configuration bits. Next, it writes the bits to appropriate locations in the memory (these locations store configuration bits for context a). Finally, context b switches back to context a, which now continues processing using logic that has been modified through self-reconfiguration.

In this section, we first look at the problem of connecting 2 logic cells in the same row. Since the SRGA architecture is symmetric w.r.t rows and columns, connecting 2 logic cells in the same column can be done in a similar manner. Next, we extend the operation to perform insertion of a logic cell between 2 logic cells previously connected (Section 4.2), and connecting two logic cells which are not in the same row or column (Section 4.3).

4.1 Connecting 2 logic cells in the same row

The problem is to connect the output of a logic cell to the input of another in the same row, using only row tree wires[5]. The LIN row tree to be used for the routing is a complete binary tree containing $N - 1$ switches (since each row has N PEs). Thus creating the required connection means appropriately configuring a subset of the $N - 1$ switches. As can be seen from Figure 9, connections need to be created up the tree starting

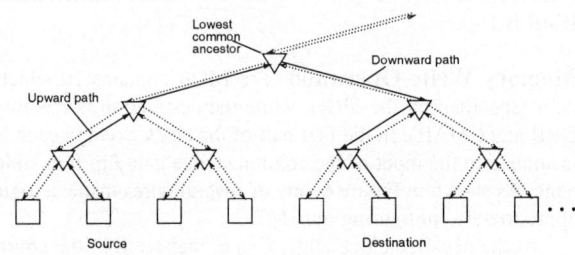

Fig. 9. Connection between 2 logic cells using row switches.

from the source logic cell, and then down the tree till the destination logic cell is reached. The highest node through which the connection passes is the *least common ancestor* of the source and destination logic cells.

To create the connection, the context which requires the routing (a) needs to specify to the context that will perform the routing, the following information:

- The context address c ($0 \leq c < nc$) on which the routing is to be performed (typically it would be a itself).
- The row number y ($0 \leq y < N$) in which the logic cells to be connected are located.
- The column numbers x_s and x_d ($0 \leq x_s, x_d < N$) of the source and destination logic cells respectively.

The first 2 parameters are used to determine the memory locations in which the configuration bits will be written. Each switch is configured using 3 bits (see Figure 2) which are stored in the memory block of the PE that owns the switch. The required memory locations are thus $N - 1$ columns of 3 bits each— each column is associated with one of the $n - 1$ switches. Since all the

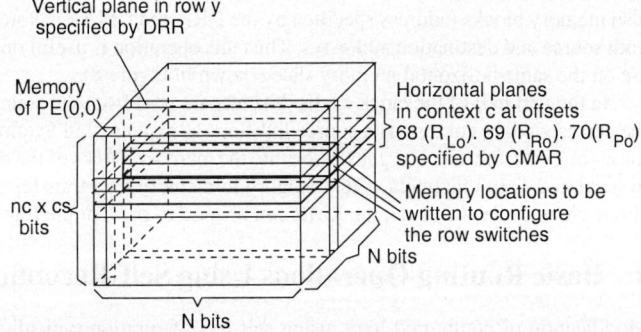

Fig. 10. Memory locations that configure switches of row y in context c. See Figure 7 for offset values.

switches (and hence their memory blocks) are in the same row, the memory locations that need to be written are 3 rows of $N - 1$ bits each. Figure 10 shows these locations and how they are accessed. The DRR uses the supplied row y to specify the vertical bit plane. The CMAR uses supplied context c as the contents of its context field while the offset field contains 68, 69 or 70 to access one of the 3 horizontal planes (corresponding to muxes driving the R_{Lo}, R_{Ro} and R_{Po} outputs respectively, as shown in Figure 2). The memory locations that control the switches of the muxes in row y in context c are at the intersections of the planes.

---

[5] Connecting using only local, nearest neighbor wires is a much simpler problem. Also the routing delay would be linear compared to logarithmic in case of tree switches.

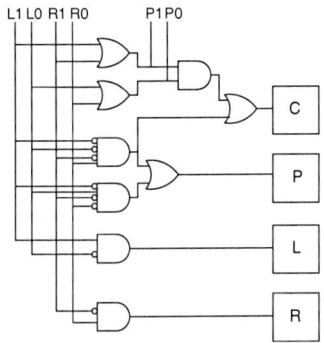

Fig. 11. Logic module structure.

The remaining parameters (x_s and x_d) are used to compute the configuration bits to be written to the locations determined using the first 2 parameters. We now look at the problem of computing these bits. Each of the $N-1$ switches is configured by 3 bits. However, looking at Figure 9, it can be seen that each switch to be configured receives a single input and supplies a single output. Thus only a single mux needs to be configured for each switch. Therefore, we compute 4 bits for each switch—bits L, P, R specify respectively whether the mux driving the left child (R_{Lo}), right child (R_{Ro}) or parent (R_{Po}) outputs is to be configured, and bit C specifies with what value.

The logic used to compute the bits required consists of $N-1$ identical logic modules, one module corresponding to each row switch. Each module generates the 4 bits (L, R, P and C) for its corresponding switch. Figure 11 shows the structure of the logic module. Each module requires 5 logic cells. Just as the switches to be configured are arranged as complete binary tree, so also we configure the $N-1$ logic modules as a complete binary tree—each module and the switch it represents are in the same position in their respective trees. The edges of the logic module tree consist of 2 unidirectional links from each child node to its parent. The lowest level modules are connected to flip-flops—a pair of flip-flops represents each logic cell.

Computation starts by setting the flip-flops corresponding to the source and destination logic cells to contain 01 and 10 respectively. Each logic module receives 2 bits from each child node. If it receives 01 from one child and 00 from the other, it is on the upward path (see Figure 9). Thus it needs to configure the parent mux and hence writes a 1 into it. Based on whether the 01 was received from the left or right child, 0 or 1 is written to the C flip-flop (see Figure 2). The logic module passes the received 01 to its parent. If a node receives a 10 input from one child and 00 from the other, then it is on the downward path. The left or right mux needs to be configured and a 1 is written to the L or R flip-flop depending upon which child node the 10 was received from. In both cases, input from parent needs to be selected and hence 0 is written to the C flip-flop. The module passes 10 to its parent. Finally, if a module receives a 01 from one child and 10 from the other, it represents the switch which is the least common ancestor of the source and destination logic cells. A 1 is written to the L or R flip-flop depending upon whether the 10 was received from the left or right child. Also, a 1 is written to the C flip-flop since the left input needs to be connected to the right mux or vice versa. The logic module passes neither 01 or 10 to its parent.

The module logic shown in Figure 11 performs the above functions. Since only combinational logic is required to compute configuration bits, the signals travel up the tree and bits in all logic module are computed in a *single clock cycle*[6]. The subsequent task of writing configuration bits into the memory becomes very simple if the computed bits for a switch are located in the same column in which they are to be written. Therefore we map logic modules to $(N-1) \times 5$ logic cells, each module located in the column in which are to be written the 3 bits that configure the switch it represents.

Routing of the modules thus placed to connect them in a complete binary tree can be efficiently performed. Figure 12 shows how an $N-1$ ($N=8$) node tree, with 2 logic cells per node can be configured with a single upward link from each child node to its parent. Since the required logic modules have 5 logic cells (and hence the tree requires 5 rows), they can be connected as a tree with 2 upward links from each child node to its parent.

---

[6] The clock period increases logarithmically with tree size.

Finally, the computed bits (L, R, P and C bits in all modules) are used to configure the switches. As discussed above, there are 3 ($N - 1$) bit memory locations, 1 each for the control bits of the muxes driving the R_{Lo}, R_{Ro} and R_{Po} outputs. Each clock cycle, the one of L, R or P bits in all the $N - 1$ logic modules are inverted and written to the RMR and the C bits of all $N - 1$ logic modules are written to the location addressed by DRR and CMAR as discussed previously.

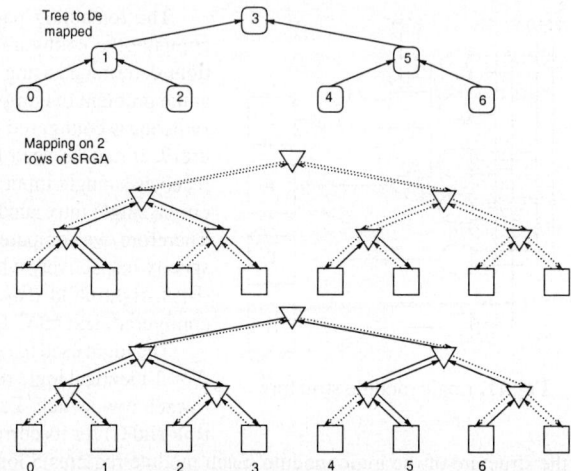

Fig. 12. Mapping of a complete $N - 1$ node binary tree (with a unidirectional link from each child node to its parent) onto 2 rows of N logic cells. Each node consists of 2 logic cells.

In this manner, in only 3 clock cycles, the configuration bits to perform the routing operations are written. Thus, a connection between 2 logic cells in the same row (or column) can be created in a constant number of clock cycles—it does not depend upon the size of the row. The length of the clock cycle would depend upon the row length but it would grow only logarithmically with row length (since signals only need to propagate up the tree of logic modules). A related observation is that several such connections can be created in a row (or column) in parallel time if they occur in separate subtrees.

4.2 Inserting a logic cell between 2 connected logic cells in the same row

The output of logic cell l_s is connected to the input of logic cell l_d in the same row, using only row tree switches. The problem is to insert another logic cell l_i, also in the same row into the connection between l_s and l_d. Doing so requires breaking the above connection and creating 2 new connections—from the output of l_s to the input of l_i, and from the output of l_i to the input of l_d.

The input parameters are x_i (column of l_i) and all the parameters required for the row routing operation described in Section 4.1. The required operation can be very simply implemented using 2 invocations of the above mentioned row routing operation. It is invoked once with row and destination column parameters x_s and x_i, and with x_i and x_d the second time.

It should be noted that the above operations overwrite row switch configurations which had created a connection between x_s and x_d—thus the original connection need not be explicitly broken. In this manner, the logic cell insertion operation can be efficiently performed in a constant number of clock cycles.

4.3 Connecting 2 logic cells not in the same row or column

The problem is to connect the output of logic cell l_s to the input of logic cell l_d, when l_s and l_d are neither in the same row or same column. Let the location of l_s and l_d be (x_s, y_s) and (x_d, y_d). The required connection can be created by first connecting the output of l_s to the input of the logic cells at (x_d, y_s) (or (x_s, y_d)) and then connecting the output of the intermediate logic cell to the input of l_d. The former operation is the row routing operation described in Section 4.1 while the latter is its column counterpart which can be performed in a similar manner. In addition, the logic cell at (x_d, y_s) needs to be configured to connect the connections along the row and column trees. This can be easily done by configuring the 4 bits that control $M5_o$ to connect the input R_i to its output C_o. The logic cell can still be used for other purposes. In this manner, logic cells can be efficiently connected even if they are not in the same row or same column.

5 Implementation

Table 2. Area estimates for the 8 × 8 SRGA design.

Component	Area (μm^2)
Switch	311
Logic cell	7741
Memory block	81797
PE	90881
2 × 2 array	363018
4 × 4 array	1480095
8 × 8 array	5925859

The complete SRGA architecture presented in Section 2 was described in several thousand lines of Verilog code. The description was at the RTL level with several components explicitly instantiated. It was then synthesized using a library of standard cells for a 0.25 μm process with 5 metal layers. The synthesized design can store 8 configuration contexts and has an array size[7] of 8 × 8. The timing estimates are expected to increase slightly[8] after place and route. However, delays due to loading and fanout are accounted for in the results shown.

As can be seen from Table 2, most of the area in a PE is taken by the memory block. Its area of 81797 μm^2 for a memory size of only ($nc \times cs = 8 \times 77 =$) 616 bits is quite poor even for SRAM. The reason is that the current implementation uses 2 standard library cells to implement a single memory cell[9]. By designing a custom memory cell, we expect to reduce the area taken by a PE (and hence the array) by about half.

Table 3. Timing estimates for the 8 × 8 SRGA design.

Operation performed	Time required (ns) (first half)	(second half)	Total time (ns)
Context switch	4.76	4.26	9.02
Memory read	5.09	3.83	8.92
Memory write	5.78	3.15	8.93
Memory to memory	5.09	3.15	8.24
Min. clock cycle	5.78	4.26	**10.04**

Table 3 shows the times required (in both halves of the clock cycle) to perform the context switching operation—please see Section 2.8 for a description of what happens in each clock cycle half. The results obtained through implementation demonstrate that the SRGA is capable of context switching in a single clock cycle.

Table 3 also shows the times required (in both halves of the clock cycle) to perform the memory read, memory write, and memory to memory data transfer operations—please see Section 3.1 for what happens in each half of the clock cycle for the above operations. Again, the times obtained show that the SRGA can perform memory access operations in a single clock cycle. The bottom row of the table shows the minimum time required for each half of the clock cycle (obtained by selecting the maximum times in their corresponding columns) and also the total clock cycle time of 10.04 ns. Thus the SRGA design can be expected to operate in the range of 80-100 MHz without optimization. Since the SRGA design has been shown to perform single cycle context switch and single cycle memory access, while operating at a reasonable clock speed, the chief claims made for the proposed architecture have been validated by the implementation.

6 Conclusion and Future Directions

This paper presented the detailed description of an innovative reconfigurable device architecture that performs single cycle context switching as well as single cycle memory access to the unified on-chip configuration/data memory. These 2 features were realized through the novel use of a mesh of trees interconnect with logic cells and memory blocks at the leaves and identical switches at the other nodes. Timing estimates obtained from an SRGA design synthesized using a standard cell library demonstrated that the architecture could perform both above features while operating at a reasonable clock speed.

---

[7] Synthesis of larger array sizes failed due to large database sizes.
[8] Unless design is optimized for speed. Results shown are for unoptimized design.
[9] The standard memories created by memory generators were not found suitable as the required memory block needs extra logic to handle the context switch operation.

The SRGA architecture is suitable for a large class of reconfigurable computing applications since it reduces the reconfiguration overhead and provides fast on-chip memory for data storage. But more important is the ability of the SRGA to perform efficient self-reconfiguration—it is made possible by the fast context switching and memory access capabilities. Self-reconfiguration is a powerful feature since it enables the reconfigurable device to modify its own configuration logic at runtime without any external intervention. This power is demonstrated by showing how the SRGA can perform basic routing operations very efficiently using self-reconfiguration—part of the efficiency is due to the simplicity and regularity of the interconnection structure. Further, significant speedups using self-reconfiguration have been obtained for string matching [6][7] and genetic programming [5] applications. The above applications require the self-reconfigurable device to provide fast context switching and memory access, which are precisely the characteristics of the SRGA.

Following are the future directions we plan to explore:

Interconnect As mentioned in Section 2.2, for efficient mapping of various types of logic, the interconnection resources of the SRGA may need to be increased. This can be done by adding more wires to each row and column tree, by connecting same level nodes in a tree, or by connecting row and column trees through non-leaf nodes. Note that all the above can be done while preserving the basic mesh of trees structure with identical switches.

Clocking Logic configured on different contexts would typically operate at different clock frequencies. Support needs to be added to the SRGA to enable configuration contexts to specify the required frequency and accordingly alter operating frequency after a context switch.

Switches Another feature being considered is the addition of configurable logic and/or a flip-flop to each switch. This would enable efficient mapping of muxes and decoders and would also help in retiming. Routing using self-reconfiguration would also become more efficient.

References

1. F. Thomson Leighton. *Introduction to Parallel Algorithms and Architectures*. Morgan Kaufmann, 1992.
2. S. Perissakis, Y. Joo, J. Ahn, A. DeHon, and J. Wawrzynek. Embedded dram for a reconfigurable array. In *Proceedings of the 1999 Design Automation Conference*, Jun. 1999.
3. S. M. Scalera. Personal communication, 1998.
4. S. M. Scalera and J. R. Vazquez. The design and implementation of a context-switching fpga. In *Proceedings of IEEE Workshop on FPGAs for Custom Computing Machines*, pages 78–85, Napa, CA, April 1998.
5. R. P. S. Sidhu, A. Mei, and V. K. Prasanna. Genetic programming using self-reconfigurable FPGAs. In *Field Programmable Logic and Applications - 9th International Workshop, FPL'99*, volume 1673 of *Lecture Notes in Computer Science*. Springer Verlag, 1999.
6. R. P. S. Sidhu, A. Mei, and V. K. Prasanna. String matching on multicontext FPGAs using self-reconfiguration. In *FPGA '99. Proceedings of the 1999 ACM/SIGDA Seventh International Symposium on Field Programmable Gate Arrays*, pages 217–226, Feb. 1999.
7. R. P. S. Sidhu, S. Wadhwa, A. Mei, and V. K. Prasanna. A self-reconfigurable gate array architecture. In *Submitted to IEEE Transactions on Very Large Scale Integration (VLSI) Systems*.
8. Steve Trimberger, Dean Carberry, Anders Johnson, and Jennifer Wong. A time-multiplexed FPGA. In *Proceedings of IEEE Workshop on FPGAs for Custom Computing Machines*, pages 22–28, Napa, CA, April 1997.
9. W. Tsu, K. Macy, A. Joshi, R. Huang, N. Walker, T. Tung, O. Rowhani, V. George, J. Wawrzynek, and A. DeHon. High-speed, hierarchical synchronous reconfigurable array. In *Proceedings of the International Symposium on Field Programmable Gate Arrays*, pages 69–78, Feb. 1999.

Multitasking on FPGA Coprocessors*

H. Simmler[2], L. Levinson[1], and R. Männer[2]

[1] Weizmann Institute of Science, Rehovot, Israel 76100
[2] University of Mannheim, B6, 26; 68131 Mannheim, Germany,
simmler@ti.uni-mannheim.de

Abstract. Multitasking on an FPGA-based processor is one possibility to explore the efficacy of reconfigurable computing. Conventional computers and operating systems have demonstrated the many advantages of sharing computational hardware by several tasks over time. The ability to do run-time configuration and readback of FPGAs in a coprocessor architecture allows investigating the problems of implementing realistic multitasking. This paper explores the control software required to support task switching for an application split over the host processor – coprocessor boundary as well as the requirements and features of context saving and restoring in the FPGA coprocessor context. An FPGA coprocessor designed especially to support multitasking of such applications is described.

1 Introduction

FPGAs for custom computing machines have shown remarkable speedups for several classes of algorithms in the past years. Main reasons for high speedups are deep pipelines and parallel execution of the algorithms. In the case of FPGA coprocessors like Pamette [1], microEnable [2] or VCC HOT [3] a high datarate between the host CPU bus and the coprocessor is also an important factor in achieving high speedups. The overall performance of these FPGA coprocessor systems must be measured as a combination of execution time and data transfer from and back to the host CPU memory.

One ongoing field of research is the run time reconfiguration (RTR) of FPGAs. Most RTR approaches use these coprocessor boards as a base platform, due to the high datarate needed for the FPGA control.

RTR makes use of the reconfigurability of the FPGAs. Algorithms which use more FPGA resources than available can simply be split into parts which are then executed sequentially [4]. This is one possible use of reconfiguration. Another possibility is to execute several algorithms, that do not require all FPGA resources, in parallel in one FPGA, i.e. true multitasking [5]. A hardware manager on the CPU takes over the multitasking control and the data transfers. Due to the multiple usage of the CPU-to-FPGA coprocessor connection for the parallel executed tasks, the overall performance for each task is reduced and

---

* Work supported by the German-Israeli Foundation for Scientific Research and Development

logic must be added to each task to arbitrate the shared resource. A similar bottleneck is the interface to external RAM or other external devices, because these externals can be used by only one task at a time. Also each FPGA task has only a fraction of the total FPGA resources for its execution.

These bottlenecks suggest adopting a simpler usage of RTR that can be compared to a batch operation [6]. Each single task is managed through a "Virtual Hardware Manager" which is connected to the task processes. This batch method provides exclusive access to any external device and the full CPU-to-FPGA communication bandwidth. This is preserved by the execution of only one task at a time. Therefore the whole performance can be achieved for each task at the price of a possibly higher latency from start to end of execution. This can happen, because the tasks are scheduled by a special scheduling policy like first-come-first-served or shortest-task-first.

The cited RTR approaches used either total or partial overlay techniques to manage the tasks. However long tasks may block execution for minutes or even hours. A task manager must thus be able to suspend the ongoing execution of one task to avoid these blocking situations. Such a preemptive multitasking environment works like modern operating systems and must be able to extract and reconstruct the status of the FPGA designs for each task swap. A task manager suspends the ongoing execution of one task and uses the released FPGA resources to execute another task [7]. This makes it possible to build a multitasking system where each running task receives a defined time slot for its execution on the FPGA coprocessor. With the overlay technique, the FPGA design of each task must simply be loaded during initialization. With multitasking, in contrast, the FPGA design state of the preempted task must be extracted and reconstructed for each task swap.

The ideas of FPGA multitasking and the proof-of-concept implementation were briefly presented in [7]. This paper shows a more detailed list of the necessary requirements and presents the latest measurements made with a Xilinx XCV400 device. Furthermore the effects for supporting multitasking are presented and a new FPGA coprocessor board architecture is outlined. The following Section 2 lists numerous requirements needed to perform task switching and describes the task switch in more detail. Section 3 provides a brief overview of the Client-Server Model that manages the execution of several tasks. Some new architectural features especially for multitasking support are shown in Section 4. Section 5 describes the current status of our project and some recent measurements followed by the conclusions in Section 6.

2 Task Switching

Essential for implementing multitasking on FPGA coprocessors is the ability to suspend the execution of an ongoing task *and* to restore a previously interrupted task.

Such a task switch can be compared to a task switch on modern CPU's [8]. All CPU registers that define the current task's state, e.g. flag registers, control registers and code and data descriptors, are saved into a special segment when a task switch is triggered by the operating system. This is necessary to continue the process from exactly the same state when it is later re-scheduled for execution. Then the register contents of another process to be re-started are restored to the CPU registers and this process continues execution. In case of an Intel Pentium II 104 bytes have to be stored [9].

A FPGA design normally does not have a code or data descriptor like a CPU. Rather, an FPGA holds data in several registers scattered over the FPGA. For example, data pipelines keep all data words of each single pipeline stage in separate registers, so that they are available at each clock cycle. Therefore, all used registers, latches and internal memory of an FPGA design must be saved to enable later restoration of the task. This can require up to 350 kBytes for a modern FPGA device such as the Xilinx XCV1000 [10]. In addition to saving all used register bits, there are other requirements which are listed below.

2.1 Requirements

As the central element of an FPGA coprocessor, the **FPGA** itself must provide some necessary features.

First, one must be able to extract the current state of all registers and internal memories. The determination of the internal register status is done by analyzing the readback bitstream of the FPGA. Therefore the FPGA must provide a readback bitstream that includes them. Secondly, one must be able to either preset or reset all registers and memory bits when a task is restored. This is necessary to restore the FPGA task to the state prior to the task switch. A detailed description of this task extraction and task reconstruction will be given in Section 2.2.

In addition to the requirements on the FPGAs, the **coprocessor board** must provide two features: Obviously configuration and readback of the FPGA must be supported. But to be useful, this configuration and readback must be sufficiently fast to keep task switch times reasonably small. The second requirement is complete control of the clock. Stopping the clock allows freezing the task in the current state, so that the readback can get a snapshot of all register and RAM settings at that time. Moreover, the ability to do task switching of FPGA tasks not only depends on the features of FPGA and coprocessor, but also imposes requirements on the FPGA design to be executed on the FPGA. Special attention is required when the FPGA task uses more than one clock. All clocks are constrained to be integer multiples of the slowest clock and in phase. The task must be interrupted only between cycles of this slowest clock. This ensures that when the clocks are restarted in phase no clocks are lost and all relative timings are preserved.

FPGA designs must not implement latches or registers by means of combinatorial logic loops. The state of such storage elements can neither be read back nor initialized since their state is not accessible to the configuration and readback systems of the FPGA.

A problem occurs when accessing external RAM on the coprocessor board where the address and the corresponding data are transferred on different clock cycles (e.g. synchronous and pipelined RAM [11],[12]). Allowing a task switch at any time can lead to a switch right after an addressing phase of the external RAM. The restored FPGA design will then read invalid data, because the addressed data was already presented at the RAM output. This situation can be seen at the top of Figure 1. To avoid task switches in this situation additional interface logic must generate a signal indicating when it is safe to stop the clock and to switch the task. This TS_Signal is generated by the FPGA design and can be used as an input signal of the Virtex capture block[1] [10]. Additionally to enabling the capture block also the clock has to be stopped to freeze the complete task. This is necessary because the capture block only captures the design state but does not prevent it from further accessing external devices like RAM. This can be seen at the bottom of Figure 1.

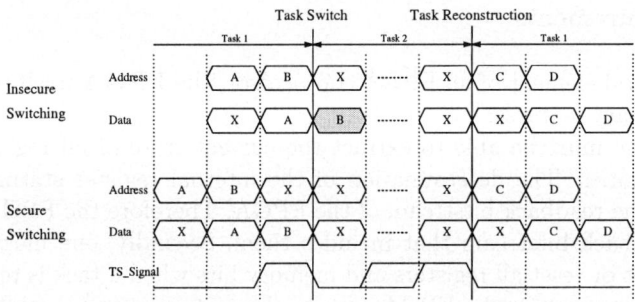

Fig. 1. External RAM access during a task switch.

Similar difficulties have to be handled when an external data source or destination is connected. A complete handshake mechanism for the data transfer is essential to guarantee proper operation. The handshake signals must be held inactive whenever the connected task is swapped out. The same logic as for the external RAM can be used here to signal the critical time when a task switch must not be made.

As mentioned before, it is essential to stop the FPGA design on a single clock and, in case of external RAM and I/O devices, only at a non-critical time.

Besides the FPGA requirements, the switchable FPGA designs and the clock control of the coprocessor boards, the **task- or hardware manager software** also imposes requirements. The task or hardware manager software must be able to extract all important state bits from the readback bitstream and must save them for their later restoration. Usually, e.g. with the Xilinx Virtex series, the readback bitstream is not suitably formatted for use as a configuration bitstream. For restoration a new download bitstream must be generated by merging the

---

[1] This capture block is mandatory for reading the status of the design.

extracted current state with the original configuration bit stream. The following Section 2.2 describes this state extraction and reconstruction process in detail.

2.2 Design State Extraction and Reconstruction

State extraction of a FPGA design and reconstruction of this state are the two key features to enable task switching on FPGAs. The aim of the state extraction is to ascertain all register and RAM contents that are used by the design. On the other hand, state reconstruction is to recreate the previously extracted state for each resource used in the FPGA.

State extraciion of a stopped FPGA design is done by filtering all status information bits out of the readback bitstream. In order to extract these state bits, their bit positions within the readback stream must be known. Configuration information is filtered, because the logic cell configurations and their interconnections will not change at all during a task switch. The extracted state bits are then stored and form the basis for the reconstruction. Storing only the relevant information will also reduce the amount of status bits by $\approx 90\%$[2].

Task reconstruction is done by correctly setting the state of each single register or latch, and of each RAM bit in the configuration bitstream. This initialization state is normally included in the netlist file or given in an extra constraints file. Vendor specific place and route tools will then place the netlist, do all the routing and finally generate a configuration bitstream for download into the FPGA device. This whole place and route process can take, e.g., hours and is therefore unacceptable for preparing a reconstructed configuration for dynamic task switching. A direct manipulation of the configuration bitstream avoids this lengthy place and route procedure. Such a bitstream manipulation can be done for two reasons: First a task switch does not change any logic functionality or connections in the FPGA design. Secondly, the initialization information is directly coded by single bits in the configuration bitstream. All bit positions for each initialization bit in the bitstream must also be known to enable this direct and fast manipulation of the initialization states. In practice, the original bitstream is taken and each initialization bit is changed accordingly to the previously extracted register state. This is done for all used registers and RAM bits. Finally the manipulated bitstream is used to configure the FPGA. The result is then the reconstruction of the FPGA state at the moment of the task switch.

3 Client Server Model

All state extraction and bitstream manipulation must be done by a central unit in the host software system, the **Hardware Management Unit** (HMU). To

---

[2] For the Xilinx XCV400 device and 91% for the XCV1000.

achieve best performance the HMU must be part of the operating system itself. For a proof of concept, however, a client-server model including this HMU is sufficient and was built with only little effort for achieving good performance.

The client–server implementation was built for WinNT and uses the microEnable FPGA coprocessor [2] which includes a PCI interface, a Xilinx XC4028EX device and SRAM memory. The server is implemented as a multithreaded program that has exclusive access to the coprocessor and handles all service functions such as configure or readback. The client–server communication is bidirectional. Passing data and commands is based on interprocess communication and shared memory. A round–robin scheduling strategy was implemented within the HMU and special attention was given to the DMA tranfers to avoid blocking situations by very long DMA transfers. The measurements were done with one registered design to demonstrate the design reconstruction. Another design used external RAM to show the data consistence during swapped out FPGA design.

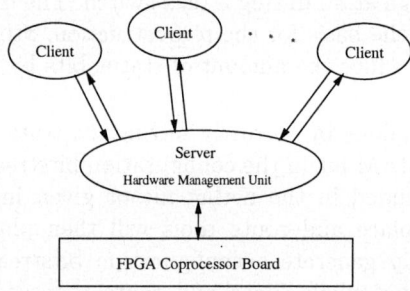

Fig. 2. Client–Server model architecture.

The possibility of task switching was successfully shown with the client–server model. However task switch efficiency was not very good because of the absence of a fast configuration and readback capability. The XC4028 was configured within ≈80 ms and readback takes ≈800 ms. The design extraction and state reconstruction for the complete FPGA was performed in 18 ms and 13 ms respectively on a 166MHz Pentium. Several important conclusions relating to configuration and to external RAM were made with this client–server model. First, the configuration/readback interface must be as fast as possible to reduce the task switch time to a minimum. Secondly, save/restore of external RAM during a task switch additonally increases the time and must be avoided.

4 An FPGA Coprocessor Designed for Multitasking

An FPGA coprocessor specifically designed to support multitasking has been outlined. The experience of the client server model and the proof-of-principle system was incorporated into the new coprocessors architecture. The coprocessor can also be used as a modern single task FPGA coprocessor. Its most important features are:

- Fast configuration and readback capability.
  As described in Section 2.1 the time needed for a readback and for configuring the FPGA has the main influence on the system overhead during a task switch. Therefore it is essential to use a fast configuration interface.
  The new Xilinx Virtex (XCV300 through XCV800) was chosen as the FPGA device because of its eight bit parallel interface that can run at a maximum speed of 66MHz. It provides both configuration and readback. An estimated time of ≈ 12 ms for a task switch with configuration and readback is expected for the XCV400.
- A memory switch to avoid additional memory swapping.
  The client–server model can handle only one FPGA design at a time that has access to the external RAM. Assuming that there can be more than one design with this RAM access, the memory contents constitute part of the dynamic state that must be swapped out and back by the task switch. For several megabytes of memory, this dramatically increases the time to switch tasks. In order to avoid this additional overhead the new architecture includes a RAM switch and eight individual RAM blocks. Figure 3 shows the connection scheme of this RAM switch for several tasks. This RAM switch allows the HMU to simply disconnect RAM blocks that are assigned to a task to be suspended by a task switch. The RAM blocks of the following task to be re-activated are then connected to the same FPGA interface and the newly restored task can start execution.

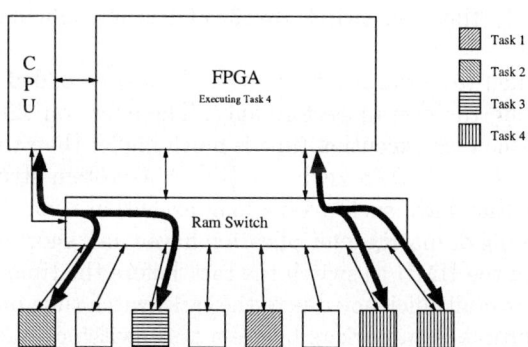

Fig. 3. RAM switch connection scheme. *The figure shows the coprocessor FPGA executing Task 4 and in parallel the HMU accessing the RAM of Tasks 2 and 3.*

- Direct RAM access during task execution.
  The RAM switch also can connect some or all RAM blocks, which are currently not used by the running task, directly to the CPU-to-coprocessor connection.

This feature enables the HMU to prepare the next task for execution by transferring its input data to its RAM block in parallel to the currently running task. This optimizes the utilization time of the FPGA. Figure 4 illustrates this in a time diagram.
– Simple data sharing between concurrent tasks.
  The mentioned relationship between a task and a RAM block can be expanded in such a way that one or more RAM blocks can be accessed by two tasks. Therefore data transfer between two concurrent tasks can be implemented easily as well as RTR with several subdesigns.

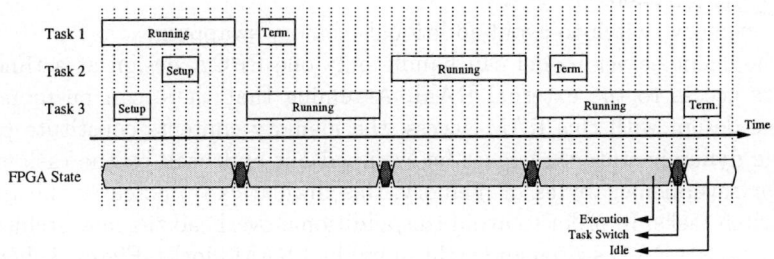

Fig. 4. Task execution timing diagram.

It must be mentioned that all running tasks can make use of the maximum performance of external FPGA interfaces like the RAM interface and the CPU-to-FPGA connection. Therefore they retain the same performance at the interfaces and only the task switch overhead has an influence on the overall performance.

The time needed to perform a task switch has to be added to the execution time for calculating the overall performance. The effect on this performance is only negligible if the task execution time is much higher than the estimated task switch time of ≈ 12 ms. A DES keybreak [13] or a protein structure prediction [14, 15] are tasks that have such a very long execution time. Other algorithms like image processing or matrix multiplication have much shorter execution times and would require the HMU to switch the task before the time slot is over. This will result in less overall efficiency due to the task switch time but can be avoided by processing multiple data packets before a task switch occurs.

5 Current Status

The multitasking FPGA coprocessor described above is almost ready for construction.

Recent measurements done with another Virtex FPGA coprocessor board[3] have shown that a XVC400 FPGA can be configured within 12.4 ms and read-

---
[3] microEnableII; PCI based card with one XCV400 device.

back can be performed within 14.4 ms using the SelectedMap interface. Due to the increased amount of bits[4], the time needed for manipulating the bitstream is about 2.7 times higher on the same 166MHz Pentium. Measurements on a modern PentiumIII/600MHz have shown that only restoring the complete XCV400 bitstream can be done in ≈7.5 ms. Additional tests with the extraction/reconstruction library and real hardware were also successfull for the reconstruction of registered designs whereas the reconstruction of internal RAM will be tested in the future. Extracting the status bits from the readback bitstream was successfully shown for FPGA designs using register and internal RAM.

Concerning the HMU, the client server model has been implemented and successfully run. Some detailed planning has begun to include the manager architecture directly into the operating system. Linux has been chosen for this because it is an open system and allows the necessary modifications.

For demonstration and measurements, several algorithms are already implemented or currently under development for the new multitasking architecture. Most of them, like the protein structure prediction, have long execution times, but there are also some algorithms, such as image processing, with much shorter execution times.

6 Conclusion

This paper describes the possibility of performing multitasking of FPGA designs. The idea is to share the FPGA resources among several tasks through the use of pseudo multitasking, much as computer operating systems emulate multitasking on a single CPU.

Even though parallel execution of several tasks in the same FPGA is possible, there are several advantages for multitasking: e.g. switching between the FPGA designs of several tasks will retain the full communication data rate between the CPU and the FPGA. Although the total data rate over time is the same for parallel execution and multitasking, in the case of multitasking the I/O resources are totally dedicated to the current FPGA design. Therefore the application is not concerned with sharing these resources.

Secondly, in contrast to the overlay technique for sequential execution of several algorithm steps with different FPGA designs, the hardware manager does not need to wait until pipelines, FIFOs, etc. are completely empty. Multitasking allows switching the FPGA design at almost any time without loosing data.

The third advantage concerns programming of the FPGA design. Each FPGA design has the complete set of I/O resources available. The programmer does not need to care about resource sharing and so writing FPGA designs is much easier.

The disadvantages are almost the same as in modern multitasking operating systems. Only one task at a time is allowed to execute[5]. The completion of com-

---

[4] XC4028EX has ≈668 kBits; XCV400 has ≈1.75 MBits.
[5] On a single processor computer.

putations is delayed. Full efficiency cannot be achieved due to the task switching overhead.

The described client–server model was implemented to demonstrate this task switching principle for FPGAs. This model together with two FPGA designs, especially designed to check the feasibility of task switching on FPGAs, have shown that it works for the XC4000 series. Additional tests and measurements with Virtex devices have shown that it can be done within a reasonable time.

The lessons from this experience and measurements have been incorporated into the design of a new architecture, containing specific multitasking support features. Some of these important features have been described in this paper.

References

1. Mark Shand: PCI Pamette V1. DEC, Systems Research Center, Palo Alto, USA. 1997. http://www.research.digital.com/SRC/pamette
2. K.-H. Noffz and R. Lay: microEnable, Silicon Software GmbH, Mannheim, Germany. 1999. http://www.silicon-software.com
3. Virtual Computer Corporation: VCC H.O.T. II, Virtual Computer Corporation, Reseda, USA. 1997. http://www.vcc.com
4. R. Hudson, D. Lehn and P. Athanas: A Run-Time Reconfigurable Engine for Image Interpolation, IEEE Symposium on FPGAs for Custom Computing Machines, Los Alamitos, California. April 1998. Page 88-95.
5. G. Brebner: The Swappable Logic Unit: A Paradigm for Virtual Hardware, IEEE Symposium on FPGAs for Custom Computing Machines, Los Alamitos, California. April 1997. Pages 77–86.
6. J. Jean, K. Tomko, V. Yavagal, R. Cook and J. Shah: Dynamic Reconfiguration to Support Concurrent Applications, IEEE Symposium on FPGAs for Custom Computing Machines, Los Alamitos, California. April 1998. Pages 302–303.
7. H. Simmler, L. Levinson and R. Männer: Preemptive Multitasking on FPGAs. IEEE Symposium on FPGAs for Custom Computing Machines, Los Alamitos, California. April 2000. *unpublished*.
8. J. Nehmer and P. Sturm: Systemsoftware. dPunkt.Verlag. 1998.
9. Intel: Intel Architecture Software Developer's Manual, Volume 3, Intel Inc.. 1999. http://www.intel.com/design/product.htm
10. Xilinx Inc.: Virtex 2,5V Field Programmable Gate Arrays, Xilinx. San Jose, California 95124. 1999.
http://www.xilinx.com/products/virtex.htm
11. IDT: Fast Static Rams and Modules, IDT Inc. 1999.
http://www.idt.com/products/sram/Welcome.html
12. Samsung: SRam Products, Samsung Semiconductor Inc.. 1999
http://www.usa.samsungsemi.com/products/browse/ntramsram.htm
13. T. Kean and A. Duncan: DES Key Breaking, Encryption and Decryption on the XC6216, IEEE Symposium on FPGAs for Custom Computing Machines, Los Alamitos, California. April 1998. Pages 310–311.
14. H. Simmler, E. Bindewald, R. Männer: Acceleration of Protein Energy Calculation by FPGAs, Proc. Int'l Conf. on Mathematics and Engineering Techniques in Medicine and Biological Science. CSREA Press, June 2000. *unpublished*.
15. E. Bindewald, et.al.: Ab inition protein structure prediction with MOLEGO, Proc. 7th Int'l Conf. on Intelligent Systems for Molecular Biology. 1999.

Design Visualisation for Dynamically Reconfigurable Systems

Milan Vasilko

Microelectronic Systems Research Group
School of DEC, Bournemouth University, Talbot Campus
Fern Barrow, Poole, Dorset BH12 5BB, UK
M.Vasilko@computer.org

Abstract. This paper presents the results of experimentation with a design visualisation for dynamically reconfigurable systems. Several techniques have been developed, which provide visualisation of temporal and spatial characteristics of a design with one or more configurations. The presented visualisation techniques are capable of supporting the design space exploration for both reconfigurable and partially reconfigurable systems. The practicality of these techniques has been verified on their implementation in the DYNASTY Framework.

1 Introduction

Design visualisation is an integral part of many engineering design methodologies. In VLSI computer-aided design, design visualisation provides circuit designers with an abstract view of design characteristics in a form appropriate for a particular design abstraction. At high-level, design abstraction hides the design complexity in order to provide a manageable design model (e.g. a data-flow or a finite state-machine graph). On the other hand, at low-level it is necessary to provide detailed design information needed for an accurate analysis of its qualities (e.g. in a detailed layout view).

Traditional visualisation tools, such as schematic or state diagram editors, floorplanners and layout editors, allow designers to define a structure, connectivity, and behaviour of a design, but also to analyse the design functionality, performance, feasibility, reliability and other characteristics.

Unlike designers of static, non-reconfigurable systems, designers of dynamically reconfigurable system are required to analyse numerous design characteristics simultaneously. The search for a good design solution requires the analysis of numerous temporal and spatial design properties, including the design latency, throughput, configuration time, spatial conflicts, sharing of reconfigurable resources in different configurations, impact of placement on FPGA configuration time, size of configuration data, power consumption, etc.

While most of the research into design techniques for reconfigurable systems focuses on algorithmic, methodological or design entry issues, very little work has been devoted to reconfigurable design space visualisation. Luk and Guo in [1] describe a visualisation environment for reconfigurable libraries, which allows designers to track execution of pipelined computations. User interfaces of some commercial FPGA tools (e.g. Atmel FPGA layout editor or Xilinx ChipScope) allow consideration of logic and routing resources in multiple configurations. Recently, several academic tools have been proposed which provide a 2D view of configurations in a reconfigurable system (e.g. [2]).

This paper presents visualisation techniques developed as a part of the DYNASTY Framework [3]. These techniques were developed with the aim to support reconfigurable design space exploration, manipulation and analysis from the system-level down to the layout-level.

The composition of this paper is as follows. The following section summarises the relevant features of the DYNASTY Framework. In Section 3 we discuss the requirements for the reconfigurable design visualisation and present our implementation of the proposed techniques. Section 4 presents two examples of design visualisation using the new techniques. The paper concludes with a summary of features provided by the presented visualisation tools.

2 DYNASTY Framework

DYNASTY Framework [3] was developed as a CAD environment to support research into novel design techniques for Dynamically Reconfigurable Logic (DRL) systems. The Framework implements a *temporal floorplanning* based design methodology. A typical DYNASTY design flow is shown in Fig. 1.

The Framework uses an integral design representation, which combines models from behavioural, architectural and physical levels. This design representation, together with the available design manipulation and visualisation tools, allows simultaneous DRL design space exploration in both temporal and spatial dimensions. More details about the DYNASTY Framework and the temporal floorplanning can be found in [3].

2.1 Design Manipulation

One of the key features of the DYNASTY Framework is its combination of design manipulation and visualisation tools, which allows manipulation at multiple design abstraction levels.

Two basic tools are provided for the manipulation of the design and library entities within the DYNASTY Framework:

- *Design Browser* tool allows the designer to analyse the design structure at behavioural, architectural (register-transfer) and layout levels. A selected design abstraction model can be viewed graphically using the respective model viewer (e.g. CDFG[1] viewer in Fig. 2). Furthermore, a variety of DYNASTY algorithms can be invoked from the Design Browser to perform transformations and calculations on the selected design object.

---
[1] Control/Data Flow Graph - a behavioural abstraction model used in DYNASTY

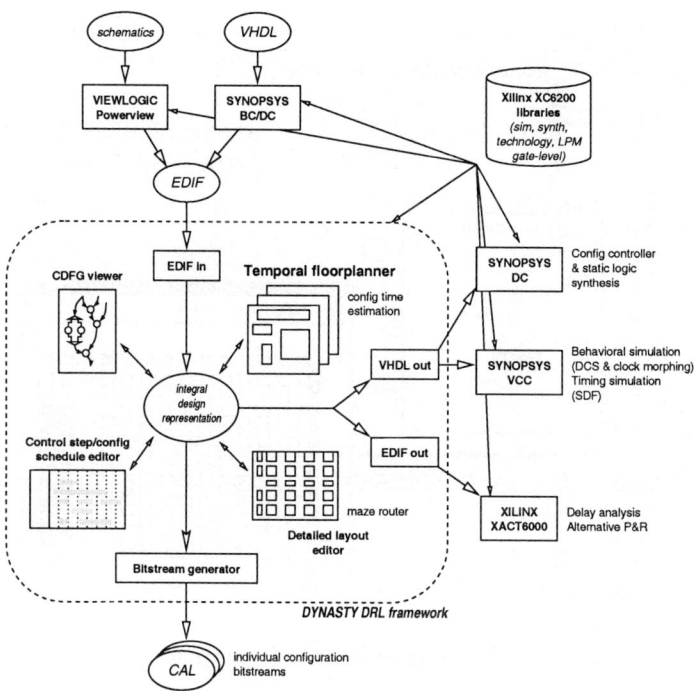

Fig. 1. Temporal floorplanning-based design flow in the DYNASTY Framework [3].

- *Library Server Browser* tool provides an interface between library servers and the designer. Each library server can include: cell and parametric module libraries, technology-specific design or estimation algorithms, target technology device models and other technology-specific characteristics. Using the Library Browser interface designers can view the contents of the library servers and select from the options available for the target technology (e.g. the type of a configuration overhead estimation algorithm).

Both Design and Library Server Browser tools are shown in a typical DYNASTY design session in Fig. 2.

In order to avoid unnecessary design iterations, the effects of design manipulation have to be indicated to the designer during the manipulation process. Reconfigurable design visualisation techniques described in the following section allow designers to analyse the effects of these changes visually.

3   Reconfigurable Design Visualisation

An ideal design visualisation system should be able to present all the necessary design information to the designer. Design tools for static systems provide visualisation of many common design characteristics (e.g. structural informa-

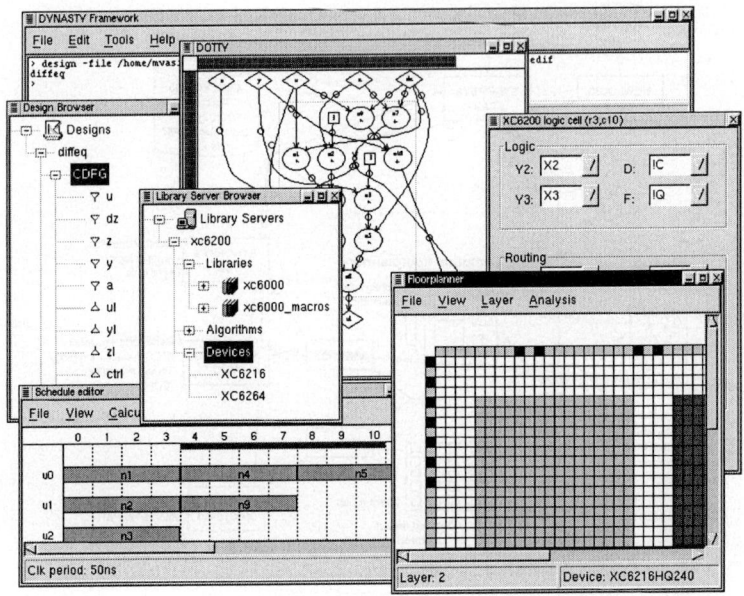

Fig. 2. A typical DYNASTY session.

tion, overall timing, and others). In the following we will concentrate only on visualisation of the design characteristics specific to reconfigurable systems.

In the design methodology implemented in the DYNASTY Framework we have aimed to visualise the following reconfigurable design properties:

- configuration partitioning
- reconfiguration overhead effects
- spatial conflicts (overlaps) between blocks in different configurations
- design execution and configuration schedule

Furthermore, our goal was to support different DRL technologies and therefore the visualisation techniques should not be technology-specific. The following sections outline the techniques developed to accommodate the above visualisation requirements using the Floorplanner and the Schedule Editor tool.

3.1 Configuration Partitioning

During configuration partitioning, an input behavioural design model is split into sets representing individual configurations. It is convenient to manipulate the design at this level as the direct relevance between the behavioural model elements and the resulting configuration partitions can be easily established.

On the other hand, the execution latency of the design depends on the time necessary for the configuration of all design blocks. This time depends on the features and the performance of a configuration interface available in the target reconfigurable technology.

In order to provide visualisation of both of these design conditions the DYNASTY Floorplanner tool provides two alternative views:

- *Configuration view* represents partitioning of the design into configurations. Such a view is useful in the early design stages when a designer needs to perform this partitioning on a behavioural design model. At this stage, only the configuration sequence with a design block granularity is determined, while the actual cycle-accurate execution schedule can be calculated at a later stage. An example of a configuration view in the 3D Floorplanner tool is shown in Fig. 3(a).
- *System clock view* is a cycle-true display of the design activity. This view includes visualisation of both execution and configuration processes for all design blocks. The cycle-true schedule is recalculated by the library server as the design is being manipulated. An example of a system clock view is shown in Fig. 4(a).

3.2 Reconfiguration Overhead Effects

In the DYNASTY Framework, the reconfiguration overheads are calculated by a technology-specific algorithm in the library server. In its current implementation, the Framework supports DRL designs with only one configuration controller. Period of reconfiguration is indicated in the Schedule Editor window using a red bar in the top part of the schedule display (seen as dark grey in Fig. 2). In the Floorplanner, the configuration of individual blocks is indicated using a pyramid (in a 3D view) or a triangle (in a 2D view). The number of pyramids/triangles in the vertical direction indicates the configuration latency as a number of system clock cycles.

Using these techniques a designer can assess the configuration overheads for the current placement, partitioning, execution schedule and system/configuration clock period in a DRL design.

3.3 Spatial Conflicts (Overlaps) between Blocks in Different Configurations

A dual approach was implemented to visualise possible spatial conflicts:

- If the conflict was caused by manipulation outside the Floorplanner tool (e.g. by changing a library module allocated to a behavioural model element), the conflicting floorplan blocks are highlighted.
- During manipulation of the blocks within the Floorplanner an on-line checking of data dependencies and block positions has been implemented, which will reject all placements generating a spatial conflict.

3.4 Design Execution and Configuration Schedule

Due to the interdependencies between the execution and configuration design scheduling, the visualisation of both schedules have been merged into a single Schedule Editor tool. The Schedule Editor displays the overall execution schedule, which combines the execution and the configuration latencies of the individual design blocks. Schedule steps are identical to the system clock cycles. If the configuration clock is different from the system clock, the configuration latencies are scaled to the system clock units. Any data dependency conflicts between the blocks can be seen in the Schedule Editor window.

3.5 2D versus 3D Floorplanner

The Floorplanner tool has been designed to provide design visualisation in both 2 and 3 dimensions. While the 3D floorplan view well represents the overall design characteristics, its manipulation may become tedious for large designs. Using the 2D Floorplanner designers can examine each of the layers individually and also in the locations which are difficult to see in a 3D view. The 2D Floorplanner is also better suited for exploration of desired sharing between configuration layers (a designer can display multiple layers to examine their similarities).

4 Design Visualisation Examples

We demonstrate the capabilities of the visualisation techniques presented in this paper using two simple examples. Due to the restricted space, the examples here will use only the 3D Floorplanner tool. Model dynamically reconfigurable FPGA architectures based on the Xilinx XC6200 technology [4] have been used for the implementation of these examples.

4.1 Laplace Filter Operator

The first example is a simple Laplace operator for a spatial filter used in image processing. The 3×3 Laplace operator implements the following computation [5]:

$$gm_{(1,1)} = 4 \times i_{(1,1)} - (i_{(1,2)} + i_{(2,1)} + i_{(2,3)} + i_{(3,2)})$$

where (r, c) represent row and column pixel coordinates in the operator mask. Data-flow graph for this operation is shown in Fig. 3(b).

Let us consider an implementation of the Laplace operator on a resource-limited FPGA architecture (20×20 array). The size of this reconfigurable array does not allow for the entire Laplace operator to be implemented in a single configuration. The designer may opt to consider an alternative implementation, where the data-flow computation is "folded" over several configurations.

In this case, the designer would construct a 3D floorplan from the blocks derived from the behavioural model of the design. The main objective in this case is to minimise the design execution latency. The latency is determined by

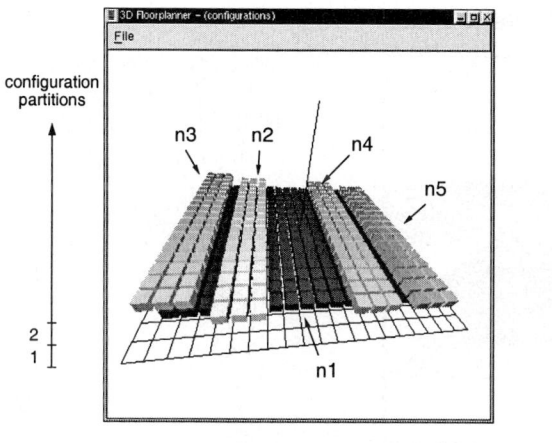 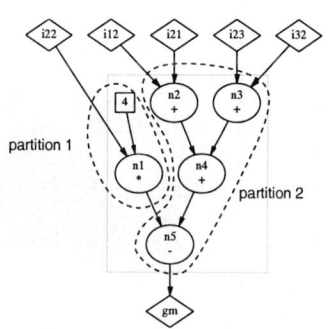

(a) 3D floorplan (configuration partition view).

(b) Data-flow graph.

Fig. 3. Laplace operator 3D floorplan and data-flow graph after scheduling. Each layer in the 3D floorplan represents one design *configuration* as partitioned by a designer.

both module execution latency and the configuration latency[2]. While module execution latency is fixed for a given module type, the configuration latency can be reduced if module resources can be shared among configurations. The designer needs to identify those design solutions, where the configuration latency is minimised.

First, the design modules would be partitioned into individual configurations. The 3D Floorplanner tool in a configuration view can be used to visualise such an initial solution (Fig. 3(a)). Once an initial partitioning was achieved, the designer would aim to minimise configuration overhead with a module placement which would maximise resource sharing. The actual execution latency can be measured in Schedule Editor and can be seen in the 3D floorplan using the system clock view (Fig. 4(a)).

4.2 Pattern Matcher

This example shows how a designer can observe the reduction of the configuration time as a result of sharing the reconfigurable logic resources. We use a comparator circuit (Fig. 5(a)) from a simple pattern matcher [6] as an example.

Figure 5(b) shows two configurations from Fig. 5(a) each with a different match pattern. After configuration estimation algorithm has analysed sharing

---

[2] In order to maintain clarity of the presented examples, the configuration clock period was chosen so that the number of system clock cycles needed for configuration does not exceed four. Selection of the ratio between the system and configuration clock will normally depend on design objectives and constraints.

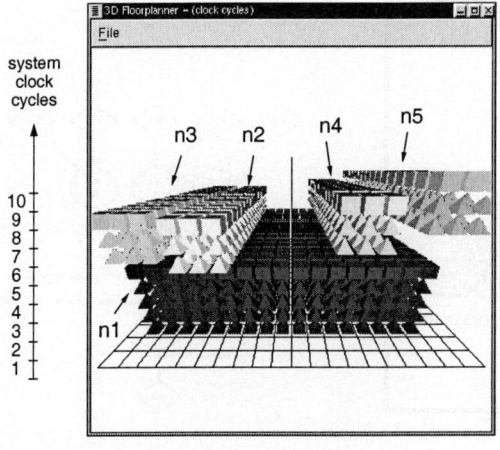 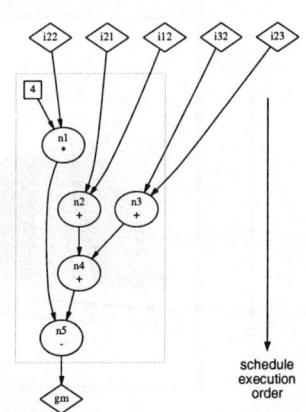

(a) 3D floorplan (system clock view).

(b) Scheduled data-flow graph.

Fig. 4. Laplace operator 3D floorplan and data-flow graph after scheduling. Each layer in the 3D floorplan represents one *system clock cycle*; a pyramid indicates that a block is being reconfigured and a cube denotes its execution.

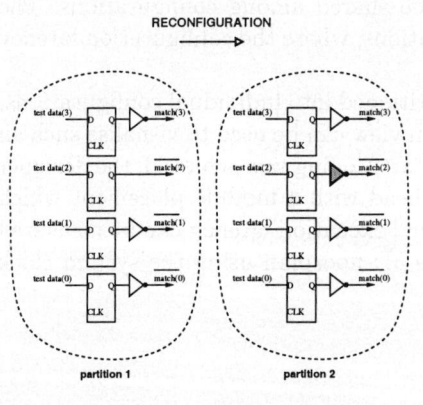 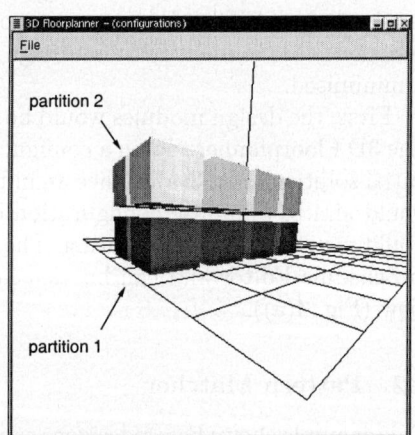

(a) Schematic diagram.

(b) 3D floorplan (configuration partition view).

Fig. 5. Reconfigurable 4-bit comparator in a pattern matcher circuit.

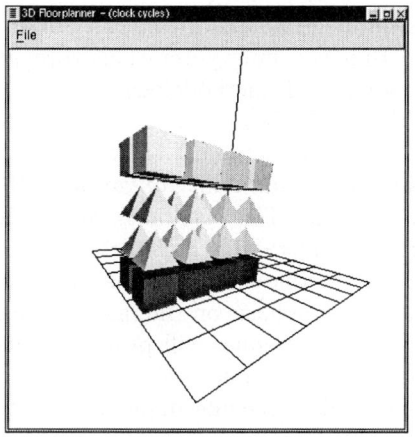 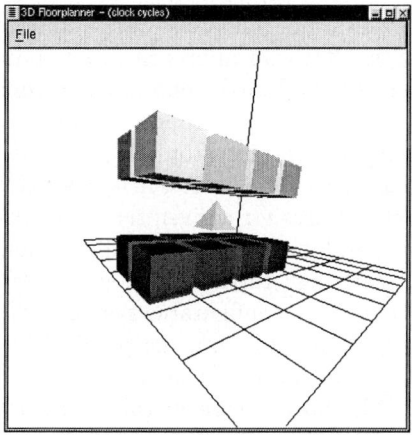

(a) Two configurations before configuration overhead optimisation.

(b) After configuration overhead optimisation: only one block needs to be reconfigured.

Fig. 6. Reconfigurable 4-bit comparator in a pattern matcher circuit (system clock cycle view).

possibilities between the two configurations, the system clock view of the 3D Floorplanner indicates that only one floorplan block needs to be reconfigured (Fig. 6(b)). This provides the designer with immediate information about the qualities of such a placement.

5 Conclusions

We have presented design visualisation techniques suitable for CAD tools targeting dynamically reconfigurable systems. All of these techniques have been prototyped in our DYNASTY Framework. The presented solutions offer the following features:

- Rich visual design presentation allows easier analysis and understanding of the design characteristics. This contributes to the reduction of the overall number of design iteration needed to find a suitable design solution.
- Design manipulation through the visual interface allows direct and intuitive modification of design properties.
- Design analysis is coupled with the design manipulation and thus the impact of various design decisions can be calculated and visualised during the manipulation process.

The combination of the DRL design visualisation techniques and the temporal floorplanning design methodology provides a rapid development route for

DRL systems. With the help of library server estimation algorithms and design visualisation, numerous design alternatives can be evaluated in the early design stages. Such an approach avoids blind and time-consuming iterations through the FPGA place & route tools, common in some DRL methodologies.

Furthermore, an open architecture of DYNASTY library servers allows implementation of custom DRL architecture models. In combination with the visualisation capabilities, it is possible to evaluate the suitability of various DRL architectures for a given set of behavioural problems. This capability will aid in the development of future application-specific reconfigurable architectures.

Although further development of automatic synthesis and estimation algorithms for reconfigurable systems will reduce the emphasis on the manual DRL design manipulation, the presented visualisation techniques will provide an intuitive visual aid for analysis of the automatically generated designs.

The future work in this area can be expected to include improvements to the DRL design tool user interfaces. A 3D design abstraction offers possibilities for more interactive interfaces based on virtual reality and other interactive technologies.

Acknowledgements

The author is grateful to Xilinx, Inc. and Xilinx Development Corp. for donations which made work on some of the aspects of the DYNASTY Framework possible.

References

1. W. Luk and S. Guo, "Visualising reconfigurable libraries for FPGAs," in *Proc. 31st Asilomar Conference on Signals, Systems and Computers*, pp. 389–393, IEEE Computer Society, 1998.
2. K. Bondalapati and V. K. Prasanna, "DRIVE: An interpretive simulation and visualisation environment for dynamically reconfigurable systems," in *Field-Programmable Logic and Applications* (P. Lysaght, J. Irvine, and R. Hartenstein, eds.), LNCS 1673, (Glasgow, UK), pp. 31–40, Springer-Verlag, Aug. 30–Sept. 1, 1999.
3. M. Vasilko, "DYNASTY: A temporal floorplanning based CAD framework for dynamically reconfigurable logic systems," in *Field-Programmable Logic and Applications* (P. Lysaght, J. Irvine, and R. Hartenstein, eds.), LNCS 1673, (Glasgow, UK), pp. 124–133, Springer-Verlag, Aug. 30–Sept. 1, 1999.
4. Xilinx, *XC6200 Field Programmable Gate Arrays*. Xilinx, Inc., Apr. 1997. Version 1.10.
5. J. P. Heron and R. F. Woods, "Architectural strategies for implementing an image processing algorithm on XC6200 FPGA," in *Field-Programmable Logic: Smart Applications, New Paradigms and Compilers, (FPL '96 Proceedings)* (R. W. Hartenstein and M. Glesner, eds.), LNCS 1142, pp. 317–326, Springer-Verlag, 1996.
6. P. Foulk and I. Hodson, "Data folding in SRAM configurable FPGAs," in *IEEE Workshop on FPGAs for Custom Computing Machines* (D. A. Buell and K. L. Pocek, eds.), Napa, CA, USA: IEEE Comput. Soc. Press, Apr. 5–7, 1993.

Verification of Dynamically Reconfigurable Logic

David Robinson and Patrick Lysaght

Dept. Electronic and Electrical Engineering
University of Strathclyde
204 George Street
Glasgow, G1 1XW
United Kingdom

Fax: +44 (0) 141 552 4968
d.robinson@eee.strath.ac.uk

Abstract. Conventional FPGA design assumes a one-to-one mapping between circuits and device resources. In contrast, dynamically reconfigurable designs map many circuits to shared device resources. Each many-to-one mapping can be decomposed into sequences of temporal, one-to-one mappings. The verification of dynamically reconfigurable logic is complicated by the need to verify that each constituent mapping is correct and that its sequencing with respect to time and other circuits is also correct. In this paper, we introduce new design tools for verifying dynamically reconfigurable logic. The tools extend the capabilities of the Dynamic Circuit Switching (DCS) CAD framework for dynamically reconfigurable logic. The verification capabilities include new design rule checks, design violation monitoring, and the extension of coverage analysis and performance profiling techniques to dynamically reconfigurable designs.

1 Introduction

Verification is among the biggest problems in modern circuit design. The importance of verification reflects the high cost of recovering from any design errors, but most especially those errors that are discovered latest in the design cycle [1]. Although errors in FPGA designs can be remedied more readily than those in other ASIC designs, it is important to integrate verification from the outset of the design flow. In particular it is important to perform accurate functional verification before progressing to the costly physical-implementation stage.

Dynamic reconfiguration extends the standard verification problem. It increases the complexity of the verification task by making functional verification dependent on physical implementation parameters [2]. The use of dynamic reconfiguration changes what was a time-invariant, one-to-one mapping between circuit components and FPGA resources into a time-dependent, many-to-one mapping. Therefore the physical interaction between dynamic tasks must be considered early in the design process; even before the final physical properties of the tasks are known [3].

Simulation is the most established method of verifying design functionality. With simulation, the designer is responsible for creating appropriate testbenches with adequate sets of test vectors. He is also responsible for identifying and debugging any errors that may be arise. This paper reports on the development of new techniques for verifying dynamically reconfigurable logic. Their aim is to assist the designer by providing him with tools specifically designed to ease the task of verifying dynamic behaviour. The tools extend the capabilities of the Dynamic Circuit Switching (DCS) CAD framework [3] by incorporating task status registers (TSRs) and active monitors. These tools enable a range of new verification capabilities including design rule checks, design violation monitoring, and the extension of coverage analysis and performance profiling techniques to reconfigurable designs.

Section 2 defines the terminology used throughout the rest of the paper. In section 3, a review of DCS is presented to outline it current capabilities for verifying dynamically reconfigurable logic. In section 4, the extension of DCS to include task status registers and active monitors is reported. Section 5 presents the new design rule checks and design violation monitoring capabilities and their role in verifying dynamically reconfigurable systems. Section 5 describes performance profiling and coverage analysis for reconfigurable logic. Section 7 concludes the paper.

2 Terminology

In the remainder of the paper we have used the following terminology extensively. Some of these terms have appeared in previous papers [5] while some are introduced here. A *reconfiguration condition* is a predefined condition associated with a dynamic task that must be satisfied before the task may be reconfigured. A dynamic task can undergo two types of reconfigurable operation, namely *activation* or *deactivation*. Activation occurs when the configuration data for the dynamic task is used to configure the FPGA. Deactivation occurs when the dynamic task is removed from the FPGA device. It can be subdivided into two types; *controlled deactivation* and *uncontrolled deactivation*. The first describes the case where the dynamic task is deliberately removed from the array by overwriting it with configuration data created specifically for this purpose. Dynamic tasks are overwritten to ensure that all allocated resources are left in a safe state to prevent conflict with the remaining circuitry. This is achieved by loading a safe configuration that encloses the dynamic task's footprint. Uncontrolled deactivation occurs when a dynamic task is removed by overwriting it with a new dynamic task. This approach is most appropriate when the footprint of the new dynamic task completely covers that of the dynamic task that it is overwriting.

Three sets are defined to represent the status of a reconfigurable dynamic task. The *active set* describes the set of tasks that are currently active in the circuit. Those tasks that are not currently active are members of the *inactive set*. The *transition set* contains tasks that are in the process of being reconfigured and as such, are neither in the active set or the inactive set.

The *reconfiguration latency* of a dynamic task is the time between a reconfiguration condition being satisfied and the task being completely activated or deactivated. The *reconfiguration interval* is the period of time that dynamic tasks spend in the transition set. A *mutex set* (an abbreviation of **mut**ually **ex**clusive set) is a collection of dynamic tasks, no two elements of which can be present in the active set simultaneously as they require common resource. It is an error if more than one dynamic task in a mutex set is in the active set [3].

3   Dynamic Circuit Switching

A partial flow for dynamically reconfigurable designs represented within DCS is depicted in Fig. 1. The initial design has two principal components. The first of these is the hardware description language (HDL) description (currently DCS uses VHDL). The VHDL files describe the individual circuits in the design. The dynamic behaviour of the reconfigurable circuits is captured separately in a reconfiguration information file (RIF). DCSim automatically transforms the VHDL and RIF data into a representation that can be simulated by a conventional VHDL simulator.

DCSim creates a behavioural model of the dynamic execution of reconfigurable tasks and integrates this with all the other components of the complete design. It introduces two classes of simulation artefacts, isolation switches and schedule control modules (SCMs), to model dynamic circuit behaviour. Each dynamic task is surrounded by isolation switches on its primary inputs and outputs to allow it to be switched into or out of the active simulation model. Hence the term dynamic circuit switching (DCS). Associated with the isolation switches are schedule control modules that control the state of the switches. Reconfiguration control is distributed among the SCMs: collectively they are responsible for determining the correct sequence of task activation and deactivation [4].

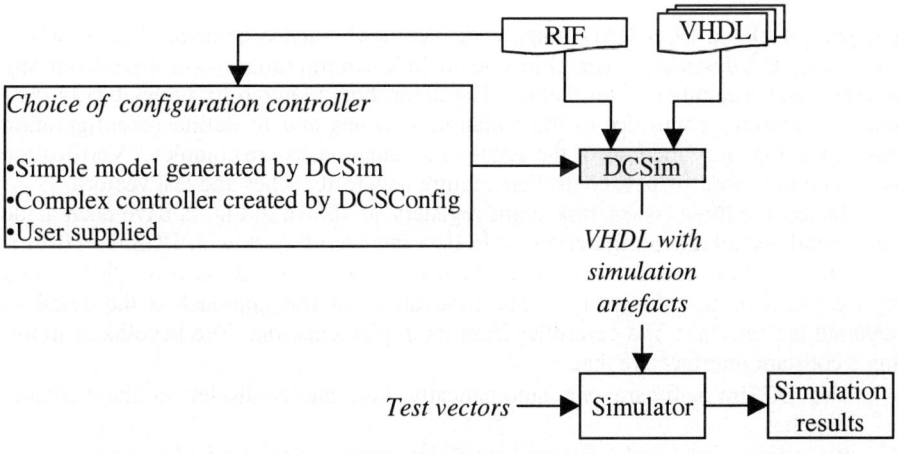

Fig. 1. DCS design flow

After processing by DCSim the design is functionally verified by simulating it with any VHDL simulator that complies with the IEEE language standards. The testbench is created by the designer. After successful execution of the testbench, DCS has enabled the designer to verify that:

1. The circuit components and their interconnections have been correctly captured
2. The static tasks of the design operate correctly
3. The reconfiguration information has been correctly captured
4. The reconfigurable tasks operate correctly when active
5. The sequencing of reconfigurable tasks is correct
6. Those tasks that are not being reconfigured during periods of dynamic reconfiguration continue to operate correctly

Note that the last four entries in the list are associated exclusively with the use of dynamic reconfiguration.

The next step in the DCS design flow is to replace the SCM simulation artefacts with a dedicated reconfiguration control circuit that is synthesised from the RIF. In fact, the RIF is first annotated with new information in the form of synthesis constraints. The constraints serve to guide the behavioural synthesis of the reconfiguration controller by the DCSConfig tool as shown in Fig. 1. DCSConfig is used to synthesise reconfiguration controllers and is one of the programs within the DCS framework. The new system description is re-simulated to verify the correctness of the reconfiguration controller. The original testbench, including the actual output responses, is re-used to accelerate verification. A third option is for the user to specify his own control algorithm so that other software, hardware and hybrid control strategies are permitted in addition to the hardware controllers that we have described earlier

4 Extending DCS

Experience of the DCS CAD framework has highlighted a number of areas where extensions are desirable. The ability to include configuration controllers from any source poses a number of problems. The algorithms required to automatically connect an arbitrary controller to the isolation switches and to define reconfiguration conditions that are functions of the status of dynamic tasks are complex. Verification is also complicated, as new controllers require new testbenches and test vectors.

To resolve these issues, task status registers, as shown in Fig. 2, have been made an integral part of all configuration controllers intended for use with DCSim. Historically, these status registers were first included in the configuration controller created by the DCSConfig software [5]. The motivation for this approach is the desire to separate the interface of a controller from its implementation. The benefits of defining a constant interface are that:

- The DCSim software can automatically link the controller to the isolation switches
- Reconfiguration conditions can be defined using a uniform set of properties
- Testbenches can be designed independently of a particular controller's complexity and implementation

Each dynamic task in a design is assigned a unique status register, maintained by the configuration controller. Table 1 lists the status flags that are contained in a status register.

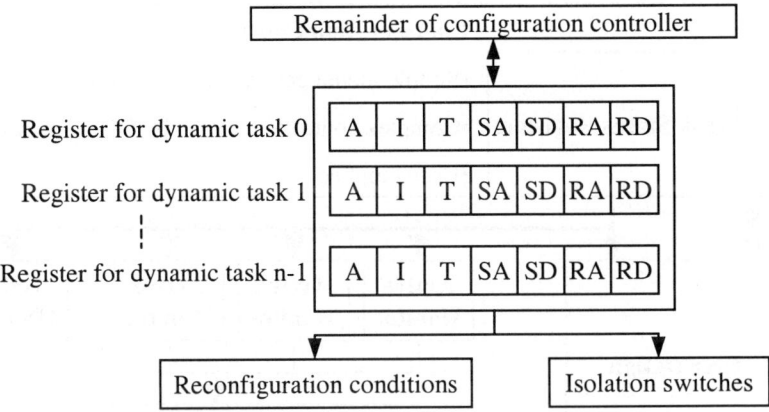

Fig. 2. Task status registers for a design with n dynamic tasks

Table 1. Information represented in the task status registers

Active (A)	Set when the task is in the active set, i.e. present on the array. It is cleared for all other conditions
Inactive (I)	Set when the task is in the inactive set, i.e. not present on the array and not in transition.
Transition (T)	Set when the task is in the transition set
Scheduled for Activation (SA)	Set when the configuration controller has scheduled the task for activation
Scheduled for Deactivation (SD)	Set when the configuration controller has scheduled the task for deactivation
Request Activation (RA)	Set when the activate reconfiguration condition has been satisfied
Request Deactivation (RD)	Set when the deactivate reconfiguration condition been satisfied

The reconfigurable behaviour of dynamic tasks is exposed in a consistent manner through their status registers. The standardisation of the status registers is exploited by a new class of testbench component called active monitors. These are added to the testbench to provide a structured form of gathering information and responding to it during simulations. Active monitors examine the status registers for particular sequences of events, and then respond by performing pre-defined actions. The events, and the response to these events, are completely controlled by the designer. The extended DCSim software contains four examples of active monitors: mutex set monitoring, coverage analysis, performance profiling and latency violation detection. These are explained in detail in the remainder of the paper. Fig. 3 shows the structure of a design that has been processed by DCSim.

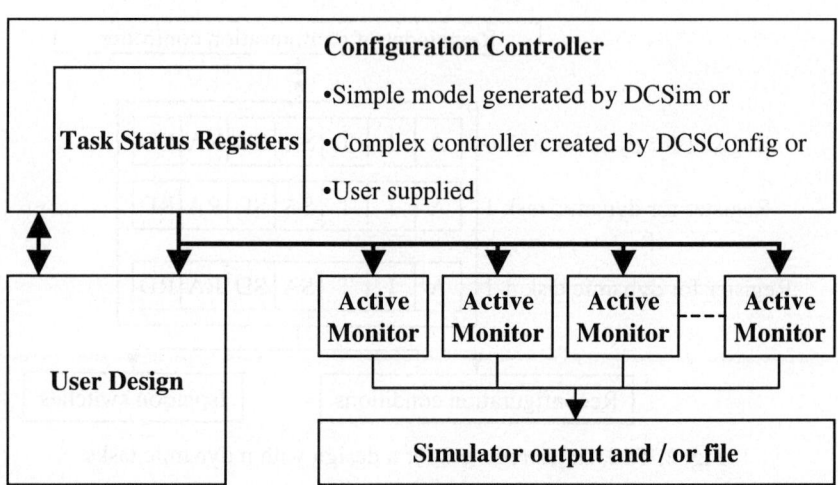

Fig. 3. Structure of design processed by DCSim

5 Active Monitors for Design Verification

Verification and debugging of dynamically reconfigurable logic can be improved by including active monitors that detect errors during simulation and display diagnostic messages. Two active monitors for verification are included in the DCS CAD framework.

Verifying Reconfiguration Sequencing
If two or more elements in a mutex set were to activate simultaneously, the physical implementation of the associated circuits on the device array could be corrupted, Fig. 4. The reconfiguration controller interprets the reconfiguration sequence and conditions to control when dynamic tasks activate and deactivate. It must be carefully designed to ensure that the mutually exclusivity of dynamic tasks is always preserved. The consequences of an error can range from sporadic and subtle failures of operation, to physical damage to the FPGA.

To automatically detect reconfiguration-sequencing errors, DCSim automatically creates an active monitor. This can detect both errors and potential errors in the reconfiguration sequence. By tracking the progression of an error from initial cause to physical manifestation, the debug process is simplified. Detecting errors in the reconfiguration sequence requires knowledge of the mutex sets. Once these sets are defined, the status registers for these tasks can be monitored to detect sequencing errors. A reconfiguration-sequencing monitor can perform seven different tests. The tests are pre-assigned to one of three levels of severity. These levels map to the VHDL keywords *note*, *warning* and *error*. The *note* level corresponds to a condition that may cause problems if not corrected by the system, but is not currently causing an error. These are highlighted to direct the designer towards the simulation time when the conditions that caused an error first began to appear. The *warning* level represents a condition that is in progress that may cause errors, depending on the system architecture and the nature of the dynamic task. The *error* level represents an error that has actually occurred. The level of severity that is to be detected by the active monitor can be set by the designer before the design is processed by DCSim. The levels are shown below along with the states that the monitors react to. A brief explanation of each state is also provided.

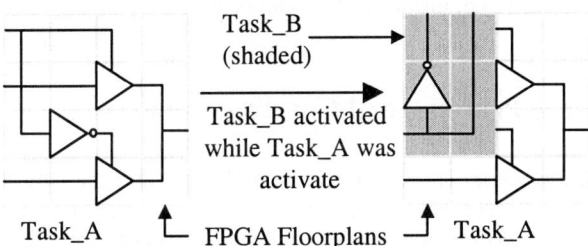

Task_A and Task_B are mutually exclusive as they are mapped to common resources. Here, Task_B has partially overwritten Task_A, corrupting the tri-state control lines

Fig. 4. A potential error due to multiple active dynamic tasks that should remain mutually exclusive in time

Note
Dynamic task scheduled for activation when already active
- The activation has not been started at this stage and can still be cancelled by the configuration controller

Dynamic task scheduled for deactivation when not active
- The deactivation has not been started at this stage and can still be cancelled by the configuration controller

Dynamic task scheduled for both activation and deactivation
- This will only result in an error if the configuration controller performs these in the wrong order

Dynamic task scheduled for activation when another in the mutex set is active and not scheduled for deactivation
- The activation has not been started at this stage and can still be cancelled by the configuration controller

Warning
Dynamic task undergoing controlled deactivation when not active
- Unless there are no active tasks in the mutex set, and the functions of any deactivate information already present can be replicated, this will cause an error

Dynamic task activating when already active
- If the dynamic task is sequential, and a reconfiguration removes state information, then this will corrupt the dynamic task. This will not be an error if the dynamic task is purely combinatorial, or the FPGA retains state information during a reconfiguration

Error
Multiple tasks active in mutex set
- Multiple dynamic tasks that are simultaneously active cause an error

Verifying Reconfiguration Timing Constraints
If dynamic reconfiguration is used to implement a real-time system, then the reconfiguration latencies must also meet defined timing constraints. DCSim can create an active monitor to automatically detect violations of these constraints. This component measures the reconfiguration latency of each task and compares it to maximum and minimum bounds. If these bounds are violated, an error condition can be reported to the designer, and if desirable, the simulation can be halted.

6 Performance Profiling and Coverage Analysis

Two further active monitors have been added to DCSim that are valuable for design verification, but do not take part directly in the process. Performance profiling provides a useful method of obtaining values for reconfiguration latencies, and provides the designer with a tool for analysing the reconfigurable behaviour of a design. Coverage analysis is used to optimise the set of test vectors by locating tasks that are not adequately exercised during test and tasks that are tested excessively.

Reconfiguration Performance Profiling
In all but the simplest systems, analytically predicting the values of the reconfiguration latencies is difficult. The reconfiguration latency for a dynamic task is determined by a number of different factors. Values for these become available at different points in the design process. The overheads from the configuration controller are typically not known until late in the functional design stage and the sizes of the dynamic tasks' bitstreams are unknown until after placement and routing.

An alternative to analytically determining the reconfiguration latencies is to calculate a value empirically. During simulation, an active monitor is used to create a profile of the reconfiguration latencies for each dynamic task. After a number of simulation runs with different sets of stimuli, the data can be analysed statistically to calculate minimum, median and maximum values. This information can be reported to the designer, along with any other relevant statistical information; e.g. number of measurements or standard deviation. This requires a post-processing stage because only raw data is collected during simulation. In addition to the reconfiguration latencies of the dynamic tasks, other latencies that relate to the configuration controller can be measured. Examples include the time taken to acknowledge a reconfiguration request or the time taken to process such a request. Note that the data collection has been automated. The final analysis of the data is not automated in the current revision of the tools.

Reconfiguration Coverage Analysis
Any verification strategy that relies on simulation is dependent on the quality of the test vectors used to stimulate the design. Reconfigurations that never occur in simulation cannot be tested. On the other hand, a set of test vectors that stimulates sections of the design too many times, simply prolongs the verification phase without performing any extra tests. Coverage analysis is used to empirically measure of the quality of set of simulation test vectors.

The reconfiguration sequence of mutex elements can be represented by a finite state machine. Each state represents an active task. Transitions between states are controlled by the reconfiguration conditions of the constituent dynamic tasks. To completely test the reconfigurable behaviour of a design, the following conditions have to be tested.

Table 2. Capabilities of reconfiguration coverage analysis

States	Detect which tasks have not been activated or deactivated
Transitions	Detect which transitions between tasks have not been exercised
Sequences	Detect which sequences of tasks have not been exercised

Each instance of a condition is assigned a counter that is incremented every time the instance is executed in the simulation. At the end of a simulation, a value of zero represents a condition that has not been tested, and a value of greater than one represents a condition that has been tested multiple times. Currently, DCSim implements the first of these tests.

7 Conclusions

This paper has presented extensions to the DCS CAD framework that increase its capabilities as a verification environment. At the core of these extensions is the automatic inclusion of task status registers in the configuration controller. This provides a consistent interface to the controller so that reconfiguration sequences can be created without knowledge of the controller architecture, and testbenches can be reused even after a controller is changed.

The introduction of active monitors provides an extensible method of performing simulation-time diagnostics. By monitoring the task status registers, certain errors can be automatically detected, and diagnostic information recorded. Two monitors for detecting reconfiguration sequencing errors and reconfiguration timing constraint violations have been included in DCSim. Active monitors have also been used to extend the standard techniques of performance analysis and code coverage to reconfigurable designs.

There is little prior work on verification of dynamically reconfigurable logic. Although new simulators are being reported [8][7][6], they function better as tools for exploring the high-level design space. In general, they are too abstract for detailed design verification. Those simulators that are suitable for verification require highly detailed models of the FPGA and access to the bitstreams for dynamic tasks [9]. Consequently they are most applicable after physical design has been completed. Formal verification techniques remain promising, but are still at an early stage of development [10].

The DCS CAD framework is currently the only verification environment that can be used for both functional simulation and timing simulation and has been extended with new verification capabilities specifically for dynamically reconfigurable logic.

References

[1] Avant! Corporation, "Formal Techniques Help Shoulder the Verification Burden" Electronics Journal Technical, Aug. 1998
http://www.avanticorp.com/Avant!/EJ/Technical/Articles/Item/0,1058,88,00.html
[2] B. L. Hutchings, "Exploiting Reconfigurability Through Domian-Specific Systems", in Field-Programmable Logic and Applications, W. Luk, P.Y.K. Cheung and M. Glesner (editors), pp. 193-202, London, England, Sept 1997
[3] D. Robinson, G. McGregor and P. Lysaght, "New CAD Framework Extends Simulation of Dynamically Reconfigurable Logic", in Field Programmable Logic and Applications, R. Hartenstein and A. Keevallik (Eds.), pp 1-8, Tallinn, Estonia, Sept. 1998
[4] P. Lysaght and J. Stockwood, "A Simulation Tool for Dynamically Reconfigurable Field Programmable Gate Arrays", in IEEE Transactions on VLSI Systems, Vol.4, No. 3, pp. 381-390, 1996
[5] D. Robinson and P. Lysaght, "Modelling and Synthesis of Configuration Controllers for Dynamically Reconfigurable Logic Systems using the DCS CAD Framework", in Field Programmable Logic and Applications, P. Lysaght, J. Irvine and R. Hartenstein (Eds.), pp 41-50, Glasgow, Scotland, Aug. 1999
[6] W. Luk, N. Shirazi and P.Y.K. Cheung, "Modelling and Optimising Run-time Reconfigurable Systems", in IEEE Symposium on Field Programmable Custom Computing Machines, K. L. Pocek and J. Arnold (Eds.), pp. 167-176., Los Alamitos, California, USA, April 1996
[7] D. Gibson, M. Vasilko and D. Long, "Virtual Prototyping for Dynamically Reconfigurable Architectures using Dynamic Generic Mapping", in Proceedings of VIUF Fall '98, Orlando, Florida, USA, Oct. 1998
[8] M. Vasilko and D. Cabanis, "A Technique for Modelling Dynamic Reconfiguration with Improved Simulation Accuracy", in IEICE Transactions on Fundamentals of Electronics, Communications and Computer Sciences, Nov. 1999
[9] Gordon Brebner, "CHASTE: a Hardware/Software Co-design Testbed for the Xilinx XC6200", in Reconfigurable Architectures Workshop, R. W. Hartenstein and V. K. Prasanna (Eds.), Geneva, Switzerland, April 1997
[10] K. W. Susanto and T. Melham, "Formally Analysed Dynamic Synthesis of Hardware", in Theorem Proving in Higher Order Logics: Emerging Trends: 11th International Conference (TPHOLs'98), Canberra, Australia, Sept. 1998

Design of a Fault Tolerant FPGA

T. Bartzick, M. Henze, J. Kickler, and K. Woska

University of Siegen,
Institute of Technical Computer Science,
57068 Siegen, Germany
{bartzick/henze/kickler/woska}@ti.et-inf.uni-siegen.de

Abstract. In this paper we introduce our fault tolerant FPGA and explain the fault tolerant features of our FPGA. They result from the block structure, the cell structure, and the intrablock routing along with a global state machine for testing. The state machine along with comparator detects single stuck-at-zero/one faults in the cell structure and mask them on block level.

1 Introduction

Nowadays designers of fault tolerant systems must plan the fault absorbing features manually. By having a fault tolerant platform for the hardware the designer can concentrate on the layout of the system itself and the development effort is reduced [BZW00]. FPGAs are often used as hardware platforms in a system. Therfore we implement a fault tolerant FPGA in connection with the hardware/software codesign group in our institute.

A prerequisite to the design of our FPGA is the reporting of faults to the superior RCU[1] [ZBW00]. The RCU controls the programming and the reconfiguration of the FPGA.

Our FPGA automatically detects faults in the cells. This runtime testing does not delay the functionality. If a fault is detected it may be necessary to restore a consistent status of the FPGA. Thus it is possible to store the status of the FPGA. Our FPGA can be used as a non fault tolerant FPGA by running the FPGA in this mode most of the resources needed for the fault tolerance can be used for functional purposes.

This paper is further divided into three sections. Section two describes our FPGA. The third section explains the test function. An outlook is given in section four.

2 The Structure of the FPGA

The FPGA consist of 256 cells and 32 IOBs. The cells are arranged in 8x8 blocks, each block having 2x2 cells. The IOBs are bidirectional.

---
[1] Reconfiguration Control Unit

2.1 Block Structure

As shown in figure 1 a block of the FPGA consists of three standard cells (A, B, C) and one special cell (X). With four cells in a block the addressing is easy and the test is relative quick. Additionally the block has a comparator unit to detect faults and a RAM block (not in figure 1). Here the configuration data which controls the multiplexers in the cells, the cell functionality and the block routing are stored.

The block and thus the FPGA can work in two modes: In non fault tolerant mode each of the four cells execute a function. In fault tolerant mode three cells execute a function and one cell is tested.

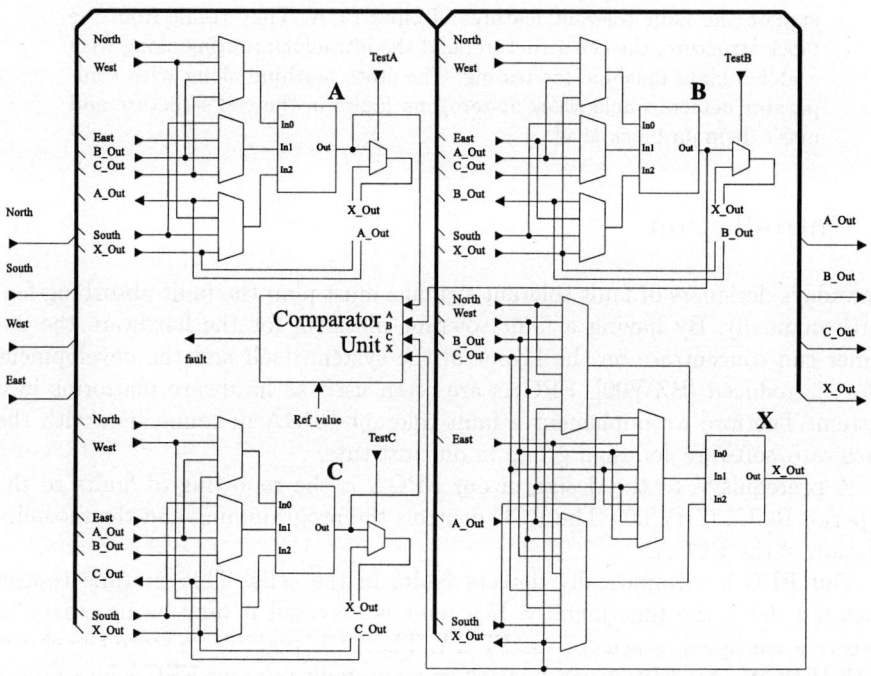

Fig. 1. The Block Structure

Standard Cell and X Cell As shown in figure 2 each cell has two LUTs[2], five multiplexers, one flipflop (*FF*), one latch and a checkup unit. The LUTs are used to perform the functions of the cell and multiplexers route the different signals through the cell. The result of a cell operation, further called status, can be stored in the latch and the checkup unit tests the storing and restoring of the cells status.

---

[2] Look Up Table

The Inputs of a cell address both LUTs. Multiplexer *M0* selects between the two functions programmed in the LUTs. Multiplexer *M1* is used to select either the *M0* output or another cell's flipflop input *FF* (*M1_Out*) for this cell's *FF* input (*fromM1_A* for example) and is controlled by the tester. Multiplexer *M2* selects between combinatorial and sequential behavior of the cell. The output signal of the cell can be stored in the latch if *checkpoint* is true. Thus the stored status can be restored using the signal *rollback*. This is necessary if a fault was detected. *Checkpoint* and *rollback* are global signals. Thus the cell status of every cell is stored or restored in the same moment. The checkup unit tests if the saving or restoring of the cell status was successful. If fault was detected during the storing or restoring of the cell status a fault is signaled to the RCU. Otherwise the system continues. Multiplexer *M4* has a special function. In test mode, *M4* is used to switch between combinatorial and sequential testing. Otherwise configuration data is routed through *M4*.

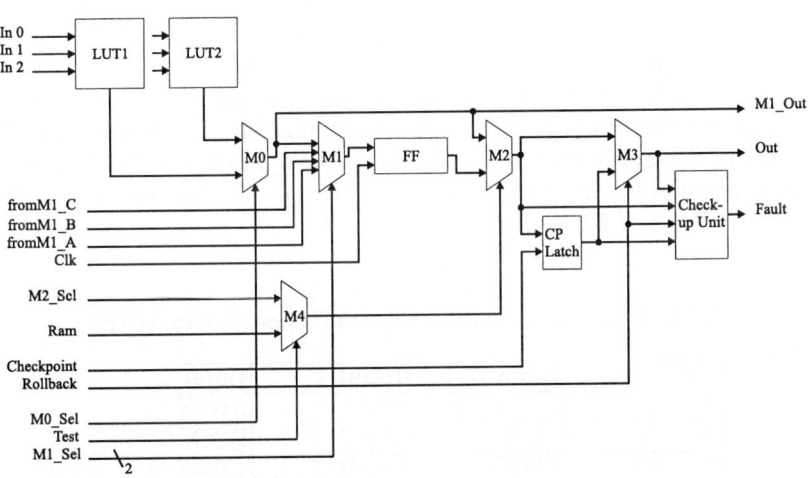

Fig. 2. The Special Cell

Comparator The comparator is a separate block unit consisting of two multiplexers connected to an antivalency. It compares the output of the tested cell with a reference value from the test control logic. Additionally it is possible to compare the X cell output with a standard cell output.

The output of the three standard cells and the X-cell are routed into the first multiplexer. A multiplexer switches the signal which is compared to a signal selected by the second multiplexer. This can be either the reference value or the X cell output. The comparation is done by the antivalency-gate. The output of the comparator unit is forwarded to the RCU.

2.2 Blockrouting

Every block has four inputs North, South, West, and East, from the interblock routing and four outputs, one from each cell, to the interblock routing. The interblock routing routes the signals between the blocks. The inputs and outputs are combined to a bus structure that is connected to each cell in the block.

In testmode the output of the tested cell is replaced with the output of the X cell. Three multiplexers connect either the cell output or the special cell output to the block output and the intrablock routing. The inputs of the standard cells are connected to 4:1 multiplexers. These multiplexers control the routing to the cell input. The inputs of the X cell are connected to 8:1 multiplexers. The X cell can replace another cells function, so it must have access to the input signals of all other cells in the block. Table 1 shows the inputs of the multiplexers for the three cell inputs.

The three routing multiplexers of a standard cell require 3x2 bits to select the inputs. The three X cell multiplexers require 3x3 bits, because they must route all eight block signals (see table 1). In test mode the X cell uses the 6 Bit routing-RAM of the tested cell. The missing three bits are connected to 0 or 1.

Furthermore the block contains several wires to transmit the next value of the flipflop into the X cell. Three wires from the $M1\_Out$ of each standard cell are connected to the multiplexer $M1$ in the X cell (see figure 2, $fromM1\_\{A, BorC\}$). In the standard cells $M1\_Out$ from the X cell is connected to multiplexer $M1$ to restore the value in FF (see figure 2).

Table 1. Cell input routing. (N)orth,(W)est,(S)outh, (E)ast

Cell	Input 0	Input 1	Input 2
A	NWBC	SEBC	AWSX
B	NWAX	SEAC	BESX
C	NWAX	SEAB	CWSX
X	NWBCNWAX	SEBCACAB	AWBECWSX

2.3 Ramblock and Programming

To program the FPGA the RCU applies a 10 bit address word and an 8 bit data word to the FPGA. The first six bits of the address word define the block to be programmed. A row and a column decoder are controlled by three bits each. Every block is connected to two decoder output lines respective to their position in the FPGA. If the row and the column line of a block are active, it is addressed and the data word is written to it. Inside a block four bits of the address word specify the byte to be written (see table 2).

Table 2. Ramblock programming

Address [9:6]	Function
0000 - 0111	LUT A1,A2,B1,B2,C1,C3,X1,X2
1000	CS-MUX select of A,B,C and X
1001 - 1100	Intrablock routing
1101 - 1111	Interblock routing
1001 bit[7]	Testmode

3 Cell Test

Blocks are tested, if a configuration bit of the block is set to "1". This bit defines if the block is run in test mode. To enable the test mode, this bit must be set to "1", it is initialized with a "0". So all unused blocks are ignored during test. The test of the FPGA takes place in 32 clock cycles and is independent of the number blocks in the FPGA, because each block is tested simultaneously. For each cell of a block eight cycles are necessary to test the combinatorial and sequential path against stuck-at-zero (s-0) and stuck-at-one (s-1) faults.

The following example demonstrates, the test of a single cell (here cell A) (see figures 1 and 2). The X cell of the block takes over the functionality of cell A during test.

Before testing, cell A's unused LUT is programmed with a test pattern and the cell functionality is copied to the unused LUT of cell X. The next clock cycle causes both cells to switch to these newly programmed LUTs. The value stored in A's flipflop ($M1\_Out$) is routed to X's flipflop by selecting $fromM1\_A$ as cell X's flipflop input (mux $M1$). Now X can perform the functionality of A. Simultaneously the block multiplexers route the inputs and outputs of cell A to cell X. So the whole block keeps its original functionality during test.

To test a cell, the LUT is programmed with a test pattern. The RAM architecture of the LUTs support - besides writing and copying the program data - writing two fixed data words to the LUTs. The s-0 test uses an AND pattern "10000000" and routes the signal "1" to the three cell inputs. The s-1 test uses an OR pattern "11111110" and routes a "0" to the inputs. If one of the input lines or the path to the cell's output has a s-0 fault a "0" will be visible at the cell output. The output of the cell is compared with the expected value by a comparator and signals a fault to the RCU by activating a row and a column fault report line. Every block row and every block column of the FPGA share a common report line. So the RCU is able to determine where the fault occurred. If no fault is detected the cell functionality is switched from combinatorial to sequential mode one clock cycle later. Now the flipflop data is routed to the cell output to be compared with the reference value. After both LUTs of the cell are tested the original configuration is restored, while testing switches to another cell. When all cells are tested, the RCU saves the status of the FPGA by storing all cell outputs in special latches ($CP\ LATCH$).

If a fault is detected the RCU stops the test sequence for the whole FPGA and cell X replaces the defect cell, which remains in test mode and does not affect the user circuit. If an fault is detected in cell X, the original configuration is used and cell X is ignored. Now the RCU has several possibilities of fault handling [ZBW00]. It can use the data stored in *CP Latch* to restore the FPGA to the last status. Second, it is able to reprogram the FPGA with regard on the defect block. Before restarting the test with the new configuration the test mode bit of the defect cell's block configuration memory is set to "0" so no more faults are reported from this block.

The multiplexers select lines controlling the test sequence and the RAM control signals are generated by a 5 bit state machine counting from 0 to 31. All Signals generated thereof are identical for all blocks. The RCU produces two control signals to hold the state and to reset the machine.

4 Future Work

By now the block structure, intrablock routing, cell structure and the cell test are implemented in VERILOG. The simulation of these has shown, that our FPGA detects 100% of s-0 and s-1 single faults in the combinatorial and sequential datapath. Additionally some s-0 and s-1 in the select lines to the multiplexers are detected. Development of the interblock routing and input/output units is not finished, but this doesn't affect the test architecture in general. An additional address bit will be needed to address the input/output units. Further it should be possible to route the 5 bits of the test state machine to the user circuit as a counter. Thus the user has an additional resource.

References

[ASH+99] Abramovici, Stroud, Hamilton, Wijesuriya, and Verma. *Using Roving STARs for On-Line testing and Diagnosis of FPGAs in Fault-Tolerant Applications*. Intl. Test Conference, Atlantic City, NJ, 1999.

[BZW00] Christine Bauer, Peter Zipf, and H. Wojtkowiak. *Integration von Fehlertoleranz im Codesign*. In Proc. Third ITG/GI/GMM-Workshop, 2000.

[DeH96] André DeHon. *Dynamically Programmable Gate Arrays : A Step Toward Increased Computational Density*. Proceedings of the 1996 Canadian Workshop of Field Programmable Devices, 1996.

[ZBW00] Peter Zipf, Christine Bauer, and H. Wojtkowiak. *A Hardware Extension to Improve Fault Handling in FPGA-Based Systems*. Design and Diagnostic of Electronic Circuits and Systems Workshop (DDECS 2000), Smolenice Castle, Slovakia, April 5-7, 2000.

Real-Time Face Detection on a Configurable Hardware System

Rob McCready

Department of Electrical and Computer Engineering
University of Toronto
Toronto, ON, Canada M5S 3G4
mccready@eecg.toronto.edu

Abstract. We present the design of a real-time face detection system and its implementation on a configurable hardware platform. The system works at 30 frames/second, which is the full frame rate of the video camera. A new detection algorithm was developed that is both robust and extremely efficient in hardware. The image is filtered and then passed through a neural-network-like face detector. Only simple operations are required to calculate the result. The detection accuracy achieved is comparable to other methods from the recent literature. The hardware face detection system is approximately 1000 times faster than the same algorithm running in software on a modern processor.

1 Introduction

Human beings use vision as the primary means for gathering information about and navigating through their surroundings. Providing this same ability to automated systems would be a major step towards having them operate effectively in our world. The branch of vision research that deals with analysis of the human face has attracted particular attention over the last decade. Two active areas of automated vision research are face recognition and expression analysis. Before these methods can operate in open environments, however, we first need to be able to reliably distinguish faces from complex backgrounds. This is the task known as face *detection*: to locate the positions of human faces in an image given the many potential variations in lighting, background and facial appearance. Since face detection is only a first step before recognition and other tasks, it needs to be done particularly quickly.

Most previous research in face detection has focussed on efficient implementations in software, as most vision researches do not have the resources or experience required to build custom hardware. In this paper we develop a highly-parallel real-time hardware implementation of a face detection algorithm on a configurable hardware platform. Configurable hardware provides a fast prototyping environment and allows experimentation not feasible with a custom hardware implementation.

In the following section we give a brief overview of the target hardware system. In Section 3 we describe the face detection algorithm. Section 4 discusses the hardware design and implementation results, and Section 5 concludes.

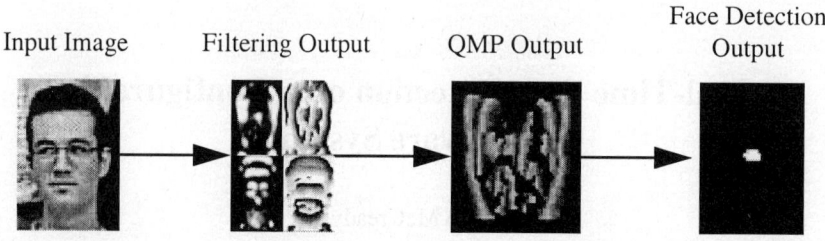

Fig. 1. Face detection processing sequence

2 Hardware Platform: The Transmogrifier-2a

The Transmogrifier-2a [6] is an extensible programmable hardware architecture containing from one to sixteen boards in power-of-two increments. Each board contains two Altera 10K100 FPGAs, 4 ICube FPIDs for inter-chip and inter-board routing, 8 MB of SRAM in 4 independent banks, and other housekeeping and programmable clocking circuitry. Its major uses are as a fast prototyping tool for large hardware designs and as a platform for reconfigurable computing research. In addition, the circuits produced are large enough to provide critical benchmarks for ongoing research into next-generation FPGA architectures. Video input and output cards are attached to I/O connectors on two of the boards. This allows the image data to be read directly from the camera and face detection results to be displayed on an attached monitor with no need for a separate intervening computer. The system clock frequency is set at 12.5 MHz in order to reliably use the off-chip SRAM.

3 Face Detection Algorithm

A number of widely-varying face detection approaches have been proposed in the literature: principal components templates [1]; neural network classifiers [2][3]; shape models with local texture descriptors [4]; and many more. Most of these methods are either inherently serial or require too much hardware to implement. We developed a face detection method that is both robust and efficient in hardware. In this section we first describe the goals of the algorithm, and then give an overview of our approach.

3.1 Goals

Our primary goal was to design an robust detection approach that would also be fast and compact when implemented in hardware. This translates into using a small number of simple mathematical operations, and ensuring that these can be performed in parallel with little control circuitry.

Accurate face detection is difficult because of the many possible sources of variation in face appearance. As is common in current face detection methods, to simplify the problem we assume that all faces will be approximately upright and facing the camera. Faces may, however, appear at any location in the image and at nearly any size. There is no limit on the number of faces that may be present.

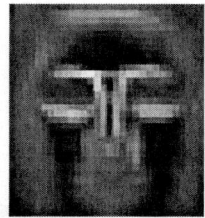

Fig. 2. Normalized probability of intensity transition

3.2 Algorithm Overview

The general structure of the algorithm is illustrated in Figure 1. Each image in the video sequence is filtered, and the output of the filters is converted to a more efficient format called QMP. This is passed to a neural-network-like classifier which performs face detection. Detection of multiple face sizes is achieved by successively shrinking the input image and repeating the detection process. As the image shrinks, the fixed-size classifier finds faces which were previously too large. The smallest detectable face is 32 pixels high by 30 pixels wide, which is the size of the face classifier input, and the largest is 160 pixels high by 150 pixels wide.

3.3 Image Filtering and the QMP Format

The first step illustrated in Figure 1 is image filtering. The filtering process is a simple 2-D convolution operation. The two filters we use, called "G2" and "H2", are useful for a range of machine vision tasks [5]. When used together they have analysis properties similar to *sin* and *cos*, in that their outputs at a given point in the image may be combined into a response *magnitude* and a response *phase*. The response phase in particular is a very useful measure of local image texture that is invariant with respect to common lighting variations. After filtering, the phase is coarsely quantized into a set of bins. In addition to the phase bins there is a bin for the case of low response magnitude, as at low magnitude the phase becomes very noisy. This format is called Quantized Magnitude/Phase (QMP). QMP is critical to the efficiency of the system. Not only is it cheap to calculate and store, it greatly reduces the size of the face detection hardware by removing the need for any multiplications in the classifier network.

3.4 Face Classifier

To handle facial variation the algorithm uses a modified neural network classifier trained from a large number of face and non-face examples. From an efficiency perspective, there are two important aspects of the classifier. The first is that using QMP as input to the classifier removes the need for multiplications. The second aspect is that in practice only a single neuron is required to perform reasonably accurate face detection. Other detection strategies based on neural networks using pixel values as input require several layers of neurons for a total of 20 neurons or more [2]. Together, QMP and the single neuron save an immense amount of hardware: the use of QMP alone reduces the hardware area by 75%.

The face model is illustrated in Figure 2, which is a graphical representation of the

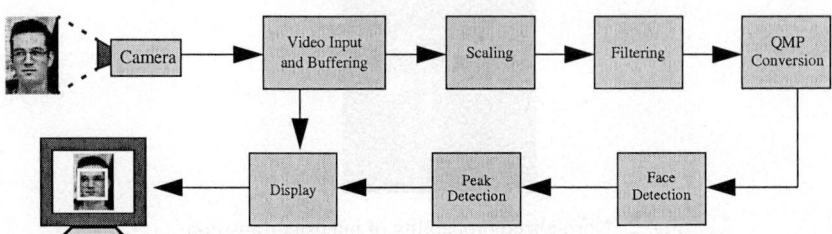

Fig. 3. Block diagram of face detection hardware

likelihood of a strong intensity transition at each point in the face region. Using this model the algorithm achieves approximately 87% accuracy on a test set of face images.

4 Hardware Implementation

Figure 3 shows a block diagram of the system. Data flows in from the video input to the scaling unit and then to the filters. Filter results are converted into QMP format and passed to the face detection unit, which calculates face detection results. These results pass through a peak detector which finds local maxima, and the location of any maxima are finally passed to the display unit where the marked face locations are merged with the original input and shown on the monitor. In this section we briefly describe each of units in the system and then present performance results.

4.1 Video Input and Scaling

The video input unit receives data from an external frame grabber board containing a Brooktree 812 chip. In order to avoid interlace tear on moving objects, only the odd field is used and pixels are horizontally averaged to produce a 320x240 final image. As pixels arrive from the camera they enter a scaling stage which iteratively shrinks the image by a factor of 1.25 until the required scale range has been searched.

4.2 Filtering and QMP Conversion

From the video input and scaling units, pixels are passed through the G2 and H2 filters. Rather than hand-crafting the filter hardware, we developed a set of software tools. One tool generates a set of filters of a specified size and optimizes the filter coefficients such that each may be expressed as the sum or difference of two powers of two. This allows us to use no more than one adder or subtractor to calculate the multiplication of a pixel with a coefficient value. Other tools take the optimized coefficients and emit a filter hardware description in the Altera AHDL language. In the process, adder pyramids are constructed which minimize the size and number of intermediate adders and registers. These tools were extremely useful during the design process, as they allowed us to change filter parameters with little manual re-design.

The QMP conversion unit takes the filter results and calculates a QMP representation. The final result is quantized into only 4 phase bins, so only two fixed multiplications and three compares are required to find the correct phase bin number. Checking for low magnitude requires two 3-bit squaring units, one 7-bit adder, and three compare operators.

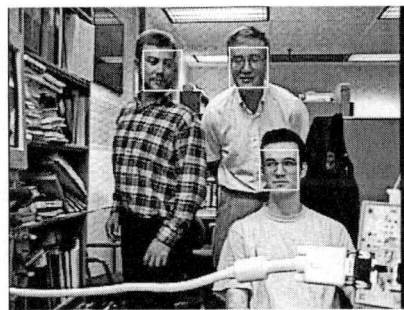 

Fig. 4. Face detection hardware output showing multi-scale detection and two different face markers

4.3 Face Detection

The two QMP units pass their results to the Face Detection Unit (FDU), which implements the face classifier. It is by far the largest unit in the system, and consists of 32 row units spread among 8 FPGAs. The FDU keeps track of the 30x32 rectangular area of face detection results that will be affected by the next incoming QMP value, maintaining these results in a large bank of registers. When the QMP value arrives, the detection results are updated and the contents of the registers are shifted to the left. This adjusts the results to prepare for the next QMP value. While results are not needed they are stored in on-chip buffers. Each row unit handles one row of detection results, performing the required result updating, shifting, and buffering.

4.4 Peak Detection and Display

The peak detection unit receives face probabilities from the FDU and finds peaks in the result surface, since each face will produce some response at more than one adjacent location. Peak detection uses a 3x3 grid of comparators. If the center value is greater than or equal to its eight neighbors, the location is counted as a peak and is passed on to the display unit. In practice this method works well. The display unit marks the locations on the original input image and displays the results on an attached monitor.

4.5 Implementation Results

The system is implemented using 9 boards of a TM-2a system. It operates at the full camera frame rate of 30 frames per second, and can detect any number of faces at any location and nearly any scale. This is approximately 1000 times faster than the same algorithm running in software, and approximately 3000-6000 times faster than the reported speed of comparable software systems. Figure 4 shows actual output from the face detection hardware as extracted from a memory bank on the TM-2a.

In total, the system uses 31500 Altera Logic Cells (LCs). Approximately 14000 of these LCs are used by the FDU, and a further 5000 are used by the filtering hardware.

5 Conclusions and Future Work

Our goal was to implement a robust, fast face detection system on the TM-2a, and this has been achieved. We designed a face detection approach that is comparable in detection accuracy to other current methods and is also fast and compact when implemented in hardware. The hardware system runs at the full frame rate of 30 frames/second, meets all functionality goals, and requires only just over half of the TM-2a system. This leaves plenty of room for future improvement.

This project has demonstrated the usefulness of the Transmogrifier-2a hardware and CAD architecture for fast prototyping of real-time vision algorithms in hardware. The detection system was built from scratch by a single researcher in only five months. By reducing the hardware development time to only approximately five times that of a similarly optimized software system, configurable logic allows vision researchers to explore hardware approaches to real-time vision that they otherwise would not attempt.

6 Acknowledgments

The author is very grateful to his supervisor, Prof. Jonathan Rose. Without Prof. Rose's guidance and support, this work would not have been possible. The author would also like to thank Marcus van Ierssel, David Galloway, and Mark Bourgeault for their aid with the software and hardware used in the implementation.

References

[1] B. Moghaddam and A. Pentland, "Probabilistic Visual Learning for Object Detection", International Conference on Computer Vision, Cambridge, MA, June 1995.
[2] H. A. Rowley, S. Baluja, and T. Kanade, "Rotation Invariant Neural Network-Based Face Detection", Computer Vision and Pattern Recognition, 1998, pages 38-44.
[3] H. Schneiderman, T. Kanade. "Probabilistic Modeling of Local Appearance and Spatial Relationships for Object Recognition", IEEE Conference on Computer Vision and Pattern Recognition (CVPR), pp. 45-51. 1998. Santa Barbara, CA.
[4] M.C. Burl, T.K. Leung and P. Perona, "Face Localization via Shape Statistics", Int. Workshop Face and Gesture Recognition, 1995, Zurich, Switzerland
[5] W. T. Freeman and E. H. Adelson, "The design and use of steerable filters", IEEE Trans. on Patt. Anal. and Mach. Intell., 13(9):891-906, 1991.
[6] D. Lewis, D. Galloway, M. van Ierssel, J. Rose, P. Chow, "The Transmogrifier-2: A 1 Million Gate Rapid Prototyping System," in IEEE Trans. on VLSI, Vol. 6, No. 2, June 1998, pp 188-198.

Multifunctional Programmable Single-Board CAN Monitoring Module

Petr Pfeifer

A Student of Department of Measurement,
Faculty of Electrical Engineering, Czech Technical University in Prague
Technicka 2, 16627 Praha 6, Czech Republic
xpfeifer@fel.cvut.cz

Abstract. This paper presents PC-104/CAN design of a programmable single-board multifunctional card, intended for an access to the CAN controllers from industrial version of the ISA bus (PC/104) and event time-stamping by signal changes from controllers and dedicated ISA signals. This paper shows one of possible solutions in a nearly single-chip design.

Keywords: Student Papers, FPL2000, programmable device, ALTERA, FLEX6000, EPF6016, CAN, SJA1000, PC/104

1 Introduction

At a Department of Measurement of Faculty of Electrical Engineering a system for the Controller Area Network (CAN) bus traffic and additional physical quantities monitoring in cars was developed. Because of many functions, very small usable board size, reliability and design rating for an industrial usage in the extended temperature ranges, the usage of a programmable device as a heart of the design was the necessity. In similar cases, the usage of a programmable device is the best way. FLEX6000 family device was my choice for bellow described application.

2 FLEX6000 Programmable Logic Device Family Description

2.1 Device Description

Programmable devices described further are produced by ALTERA Corporation. The main features of this product are register-rich, look-up table (LUT) based architecture, usable gates range from 10,000 to 24,000 gates, built-in low-skew clock distribution tree, individual tri-state output enable and slew-rate control for each pin, fast paths from register to input/output pins, multi-volt input/output interface operation and low power consumption. The devices have SRAM reconfigurable elements, which give designers the flexibility to quickly change their designs during prototyping and design testing. To download configuration, the device needs a configuration device – usually an appropriate serial EPROM or EEPROM. Designers can also change functionality during operation via in-circuit reconfiguration. The device has built-in Joint Test Action Group (JTAG) boundary-scan circuitry compliant with the IEEE Std. 1149.1-1990 and it can be configured via this interface too.

In the described design the EPF6016TI144-3 device was used, because of 5.0V supply voltage support for all the internal circuits, industrial temperature range, minimal 500 flip/flops and about 100 usable input/output pins requirement. This device has 16,000 typical design gates capability, contains 880 logic elements (LEs) and has total 144 pins in the Thin QFP package. Each logic element includes a 4-input look-up table, which can implement any 4-input function, a register and dedicated paths for carry and cascade chain functions, used for easy design pipelining without consuming more logic elements. Logic elements are combined into groups called logic array blocks (LABs); each LAB contains 10 LEs. Signal interconnections within LE and to and from device pins are provided via routing structure, a series of fast, continuous row and column channels that run the entire length and width of the device. Each input/output pin is fed by an I/O element (IOE) located at the end of each channel. Each IOE contains a bi-directional input/output buffer with slew-rate and tri-state control.

2.2 Design Development Software

For the described design the Altera's MAX+PLUS® development system for Windows was used. This software provides automatic place-and-route. All the design functions were written in the Altera Hardware Description Language (AHDL). An example written in this language is shown bellow.

Example of an AHDL program

```
%
   This example shows possible realization of an ISA memory address
   decoder(mapper). A card seems like a 16-bit fast memory mapped
   device.
%
CONSTANT Base_Address = 2*H"0D8";      % Base address D800:0000 %
SUBDESIGN Card_address_decoder
{
   SA[19..11]     = INPUT;    %ISA address lines                  %
   SMEMRD         = INPUT;    %ISA read memory below 1MB request  %
   SMEMWR         = INPUT;    %ISA write memory below 1MB request %
   MEMCS16        = BIDIR;    %16-bit device addressed signal     %
   OWS            = BIDIR;    %fast device addressed signal       %
VARIABLE
BEGIN
   % Open-collectors are realized by tri-state output drivers %
   MEMCS16 = TRI(0,(SA[19 .. 11]==Base_Address)&(!SMEMR#!SMEMW));
   OWS     = TRI(0,(SA[19 .. 11]==Base_Address)&(!SMEMR#!SMEMW));
END;
}
```

Because of the slowest and therefore the cheapest chip used, not only the automatic fitting could be used, but the direct functional LEs placing of all the time-critical logical functions was necessarily.

3 Design and Design Elements Description

Goal-directed development was finished successfully. Thanks to the programmable device usage, the board is very simple and the design is synoptical.

3.1 Board Design Description

The last version of described board contains four CAN controllers, one-chip oscillator (EPSON) and the programmable device with a configuration device only. No additional active devices are required. The PC/104 format board (approximately 9x9.5cm) contains only several terminating resistors and standard de-coupling capacitors. All the devices, active or passive, are in the SMT version (size 0805 mainly). All of this together makes the board very simple. Thanks to the device selection, also the board power consumption is very low (current consumption of all the board is about 130mA at 5V/24MHz clock, without access from ISA bus). The design was realized on four-plane board, to meet the EMC (Electromagnetic Compatibility) requirements and for easy design. The chip and connector locations at board are shown at Figure 1; Figure 3 is photography of the realized PC/104 card.

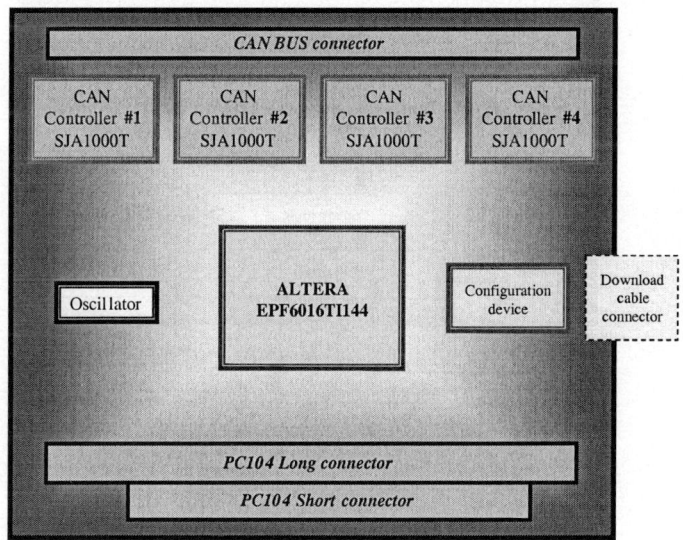

Fig.1. Chips and connectors locations at the CAN PC/104 board

3.2 The Functions of the Programmable Device

The programmable device provides many very important functions. Their overview can be found at the Fig. 2 in a simplified form. Because of the device address mapping, the device realizes fast address decoder. Especially /MEMCS16 and any less /EndXFrame (/0WS) signals are time critical. The address decoder drives all of the next device parts also, and allows that all of the registers in 2KB blocks are relocatable. The next function of the programmable device is a simple ISA-CAN controllers bus bridge. Because of multiplexed bus used to control CAN SJA1000T controllers, the bi-directional multiplexer is implemented, which is driven by address decoder and appropriate ISA's signals, like Memory Read and Memory Write. All the registers of the CAN controllers are mapped to the PC address memory, each register at even address. Not only 16-bit access is required, the 8-bit access at even addresses is supported as well. When the 16-bit access is executed, high eight data bits are cleared when from ISA is read, only low eight bits are used when written. The distribution of four independent clock signals for all the CAN drivers in the used programmable logic device is a matter of course.

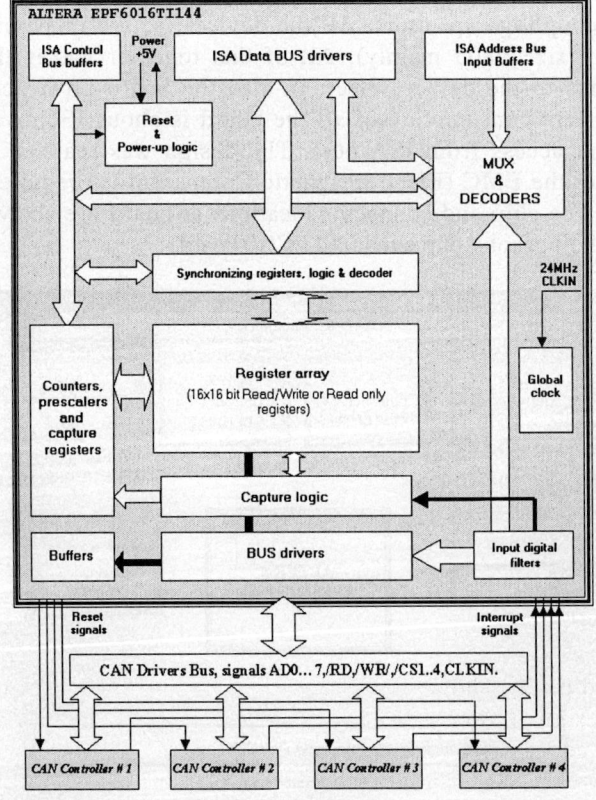

Fig. 2. Principle block diagram of all important functional blocks of the design implemented in the programmable logic device

The programmable device contains register array, accessible from ISA bus. Because of different ISA and board clock frequencies, the synchronizing register is used as a simple bridge. It was the big problem of the design, because of real ISA signals is not so good and used programmable device is rather slow. However, reading built-in registers must be safe at any time. When a read access to the register area is executed, a content of the appropriate register in the register array is latched to the bridge register only in time, when it does not changes its own state, to prevent the system malfunction or the busses collision. Minimal access time is design dependent, in case of the 24MHz oscillator usage it is about 42 ns. Thus it is the maximal time delay, after which the data of the appropriate register is latched to the bridge register and hold to the end of read cycle in the output buffers. The second case, when a write access to the register area is executed, an actual contents of ISA data bus is latched to the auxiliary bridge register. Its content is rewritten to the appropriate addressed register subsequently, in the right time, when connected flip-flops in the register array do not change their own states.

The register array contains four capture registers, each for relative CAN controller. This capture registers hold actual time, when the relative CAN controller generates an interrupt signal, simply a time mark or stamp of a selected CAN bus event. All of the interrupt conditions are user selectable via CAN controller registers. Very similar functionality have another three capture registers, which are controlled by arbitrary selected interrupt signal transition on ISA control bus. The logical OR product of all enabled interrupt sources is send to arbitrary selected interrupt line on the ISA control bus (8 selectable IRQ lines) to invoke interrupt request and to call interrupt service routine.

The programmable device contains a lot of counters, dividers and prescalers. All parts of this block generate many important signals and determine the device timing. Likewise described interrupt product an additional programmable counter was built in, which works in the same manner. This counter generates interrupt request in arbitrary time period (typically 1ms) to realize the bus load function. The time stamp base frequency and the bus-load interrupt delay/frequency are arbitrary configurable via Prescalers Configuration Register in a wide ranges.

In spite of the design complexity, the report file of the software development system shows only 40 % usage of all resources.

4 Conclusion

The described design shows typical usage of modern programmable devices to maximize design power and capability and to minimize design power consumption and design size requirements. It meets all modern trends. In the next design we want to implement all the four CAN controllers, with several limitations naturally. However, in that time and that situation the described design certainly was the most functional and cost effective solution.

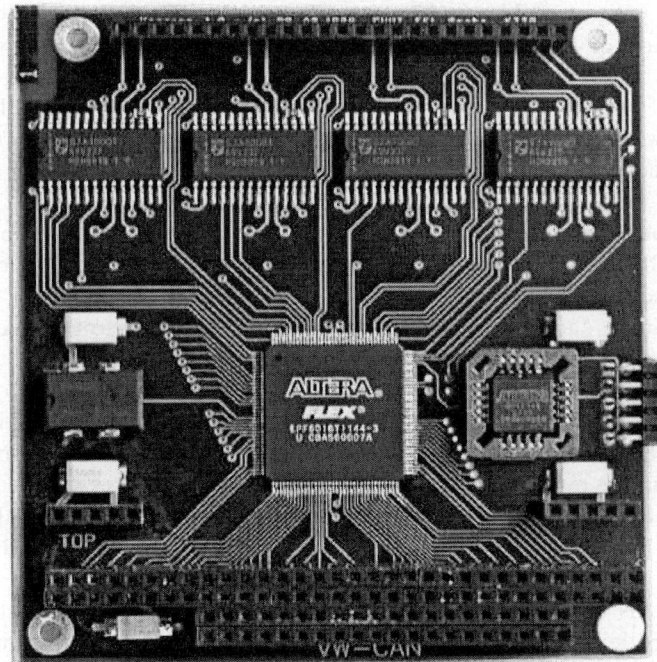

Fig.3. Photography of the realized PC/104 card
(The final design has the configuration device soldered directly to the PCB, download connector is not used.)

Acknowledgment

The development of the described design was supported by the CTU and Skoda-Volkswagen project and by the research program "Decision Making and Control for Manufacturing". Described board is a part of a larger and complex measurement system.

I would like to thank to Ing. Jiri Novak, Ph.D., the leader of my project, for many important reminders and guidance.

References

1. ALTERA Device Data Book 1999, Altera Corporation 1999,pp.411-467,821-982
2. SJA1000 Stand-alone CAN controller, DATA SHEET, PHILLIPS, 4.11.1997
3. Snorek,Richta:Pripojovani periferii k PC,Grada Publishing,pp.68-177
4. MAX+PLUS® II AHDL, Altera Corporation 1995
5. http://users.supernet.com/sokos/
6. http://www.pc104.com
7. http://www.altera.com/html/literature/lan.html

Self-Testing of Linear Segments in User-Programmed FPGAs

Pawel Tomaszewicz

Warsaw University of Technology
Nowowiejska 15/19, 00-665 Warsaw, Poland
ptomasze@tele.pw.edu.pl

Abstract. A method for the development of a test plan for BIST-based exhaustive testing of a circuit implemented with an in-system reconfigurable FPGA is presented. A test plan for application-dependent testing of an FPGA is based on the concept of a logic cone and linear segment. Linear segments that satisfy single- or multi-generator compatibility requirement can be combinationally-exhaustively tested concurrently and are merged into a test block. Two methods for merging logic cones and linear segments are proposed. Experimental results are presented.

1 Introduction

Testing of FPGAs and other user-programmable devices requires solutions that differ from those applicable to mask-programmable. Some of the proposed FPGA test techniques are based on the concept of built-in self-test (BIST). For example, with the technique proposed in [1], [5], selected programmable logic blocks (PLBs) are temporarily configured to generators or compactors to pseudoexhaustively test other PLBs (after the test is completed these test-supporting modules are configured back to their normal operation mode). This way self-test capability is achieved without any area overhead or performance penalty.

Testing procedures are generally based on checking as many modes of FPGA operation as possible. Thus they give a reasonable chance that, after programming, the device will operate correctly in the field, regardless of a specific function implemented by the user. A chip manufacturer normally carries out such testing procedures and they are unrelated to the system design.

The user is however interested whether or not an FGPA device, configured to implement a user-defined function, will operate correctly in the system. To achieve that, an FPGA should also be tested after programming. In contrast to the manufacturing test, such testing must exercise only one specific configuration of the circuit.

In this paper, we discuss several issues associated with application-dependent testing of FPGAs. Based on the concept of combinationally exhaustive testing and proposed model for such testing [4], we developed a tool for decomposition of a user-programmed circuit into several units, each exercised in an individual test session.

We present results produced by this tool and discuss problems encountered during the circuit decomposition.

2 Self-Testing of FPGA-Based Circuits

We present a method for the development of a test plan for BIST-based exhaustive testing of a circuit implemented with an in-system reconfigurable FPGA. We test only these resources which are used to implement the user-defined function. The user-defined logic is decomposed into a number of sections and each section is exercised using the remaining components of the FPGA temporarily configured into test pattern generators and test response compactors. The test procedure based on the concept of combinationally exhaustive testing [4], guarantees a functionally exhaustive at-speed testing for the combinational portions of the circuit. It means that during testing all possible binary vectors that can occur in normal operation at the input of each combinational logic block are generated. During each test test session a part of FPGA which undergoes the testing is placed in the same PLBs as during the normal operation mode.

2.1 Model of an FPGA-Based Circuit

A logic cone (LC) is a single-output subcircuit whose inputs are fed by clocked outputs of PLBs or by the boundary (I/O logic) of the FPGA. The only memory element in a logic cone can be a flip-flop located at its output. If there is no such a flip-flop, then the output of the cone must feed the FPGA boundary. If a logic cone has an output flip-flop, then this flip-flop can feed some PLBs included in the cone. Thus, a logic cone is, in general, a sequential circuit. Each FPGA-based circuit can be uniquely decomposed into a number of logic cones.

A linear segment is a network of logic cones. If such a network is provided with all possible input vectors, then every logic cone in this network is provided with all input patterns that can occur in the normal circuit operation. These logic cones are therefore functionally exhaustively tested. A maximal linear segment (MLS) is a linear segment whose set of vertices is not a proper subset of the set of vertices of any other linear segment [3]. For an MLS an exhaustive test pattern generator (ETPG) is placed on all its inputs. A test response compactor (TRC), such as a multiple-input signature analyser, collects the stream of data occurring on all the segment outputs. MLSs with feedbacks decomposed into linear segments without feedback and one extra test session is added to perform test of remaining connections in FSMs [6].

2.2 Computing a Group of Linear Segments

After MLSs are computed self-test requirements have to be check. There are two basic limitations of self-test procedure: test time and memory necessary to store self-test session configurations. The test time consists of two main factors: time required to reconfigure the device and time required to perform test for loaded configuration. The first factor depends on the number of test sessions. The second one depends on the length of the longest ETPG for each test session. The amount of memory required to store configurations depends on the number of the test sessions.

Two linear segments can be merged and supplied by a common generator if they satisfy single-generator compatibility (s-compatibility) requirement [6]. Two linear segments are s-compatible if they do not feed each other. The concept of s-compatibility can be generalised to an arbitrary number of linear segments. If there is a group of linear segments and each two of these segments are s-compatible, then this group of linear segments is internally s-compatible.

In some cases, the length of a generator required to supply a group of s-compatible MLSs does not satisfy the test time. In these cases concurrent testing of several linear segments using several test pattern generators can be performed. Such testing is related to the concept of multiple-generator compatibility (m-compatibility). Multi-output linear segments are m-compatible, i.e. can be C-exhaustively tested concurrently with each linear segment supplied by an ETPG if each linear segment is internally s-compatible and if they are fully disjoint.

3 Strategies of Test Development

The first strategy aims at the minimisation of the number of the test sessions. For this purpose the s-compatibility of MLSs concept is exploited. The result of s-compatibility procedure is groups of MLSs those can be tested concurrently. The most important parameter of the group is the length of the ETPG required to perform combinationally exhaustive test. To reduce the length of the test pattern generators m-compatibility concept is subsequently applied.

The other approach is to exploit the m-compatibility relation as the first step of MLSs grouping. As a result we obtain, compared to the previous method, a larger number of test blocks. In order to minimise the number of test sessions the concept of s-compatibility is then applied. The procedure of merging of s-compatible groups of MLSs can increase the length of required test generators. To avoid too large increase in the test generator length, a special parameter is introduced that controls the maximal acceptable length of the generator. In this approach there is a trade-off between the number of the test blocks and the length of the test pattern generators.

Merging two MLSs is possible if they are in a compatibility relation. Partitioning the set of MLSs into test blocks can be based on the concept of the non-compatibility graph and the graph colouring algorithm. As a result, we receive the number of colours that corresponds to the number of test sessions.

During the merging of MLSs, we have to check the limitation on the test time for each test block. The other limitation is associated with resources needed to implement the BIST logic. Therefore, we also have to check if a sufficient number of PLBs and enough routing resources not included in the blocks under test exist in the FPGA to implement ETPGs and one or more TRCs.

4 Experimental Results

The objective of our experiment is to find the minimal number of test sessions for a given user-defined circuit and meet limitation on the time. Designs done by students in advance courses on digital systems taught at our Institute have been examined (Table 1). Computer aided engineering system Altera MAX+plus II ver7.21 Student Edition was used. All the designs used in the experiment were compiled for Altera FLEX EPF10K20RC240-4 device. The assumption was made that only information generated by the compiler, given in a report file as a network of FPGA cells, can be used. It means that the test development procedure did not rely on a high-level description of a user-defined circuit.

Table 1. Linear segments computation algorithm using S-M method – experimental results

Project name	# MLS	Max. width of MLS	Max. width of s-comp. test block	Max. width of m-comp. test block	# Colours
Alarm	25	72*	72*	72*	5
Calosc	81	36*	47*	47*	30*
Caly	7	13	13	13	3
Chiptrip	24	12	22	16	9
Core1	26	13	13	13	13*
Kurka	24	10	22	11	3
Mainauto	36	13	69*	69*	2
Manager	73	15	108*	15	4
Wilenski	59	21	81*	21	4

An algorithm of computing linear segments was implemented by the author and used in analysis of several designs. After pre-processing of an input file each design is decomposed into linear segments. Next the S-M algorithm is applied in which first s-compatibility relation is checked for every two linear segments. As a result, a non-s-compatibility table that constitutes the input data for the algorithm of graph colouring is computed. Next the m-compatible procedures are applied to reduce the maximal length of the ETPG.

From Table 1 it can be seen that in some cases S-M procedure produces results for which the requirements on quality of the test (the length of ETPG is equal to the maximal width of s-compatible test block) are still not met. For such cases, an application of M-S method can improve results considerably. In this method first the m-compatibility relation is applied to find MLSs that can be controlled by separate generators. It guarantees that the length of each ETPG is minimal. However, the number of test session obtained in that way is often not acceptable. To reduce the number of test sessions the s-compatibility procedure is applied. This process is controlled by the parameter w (width) that determines the acceptable length of the ETPG. Two test blocks cannot be merged if the length of the longest ETPG in the constructed block exceeds w. This procedure merges m-compatible groups. The M-S method allows the constructor to control the trade-off between the number of test sessions and the maximal length of ETPG.

In the experiments whose results are the acceptable number of test sessions was assumed not to exceed $p = 10$. This parameter is closely connected with the maximal time needed for reprogramming of FPGA and the size of memory necessary to store the configuration for every test session. For the FLEX 10K architecture, which uses SRAM configuration elements, the entire reconfiguration process requires less than 200 ms [2].

Another assumption was made on the time limitation for one test session. In FPGAs, it is possible to implement circuits clocked with 100 MHz. The ETPG with the length of 32 ($w = 32$) produces about $4,295 \cdot 10^9$ test patterns. It means that with 100 MHz clock the exhaustive test can be performed within about 43 seconds. The projects that do not meet these test assumptions are denoted with an asterisk (*).

As can be seen in the Table 1, the project *mainauto* does not meet the specified requirements. For this example, the M-S method was applied and results are presented in Fig. 1.

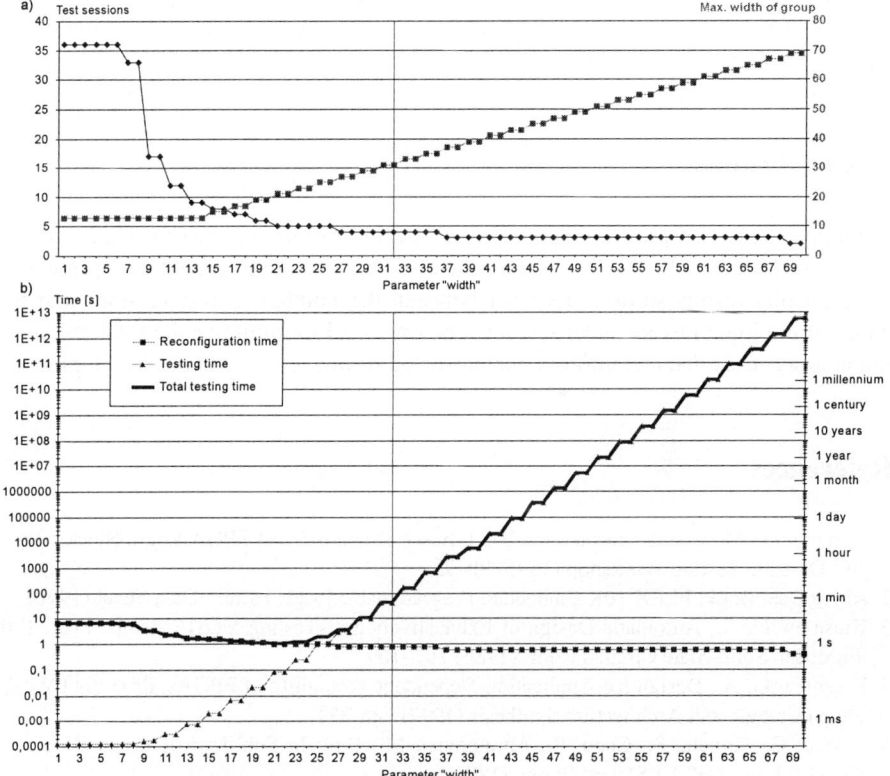

Fig. 1. Application of the M-S method for *mainauto* project

The number of test sessions and the maximal width of the test block (length of the largest ETPG) were obtained by the M-S method for the parameter w in range 1 to 69 (Fig. 1a). With the growth of parameter w the number of test sessions decreases and the maximal width of block increases. The total test time depends on both the number of test sessions and the maximal width of test block and can be described by following formula:

$$TotalTestTime = ReconfigurationTime \bullet NumberOfTestSessions + TestTime, \quad (1)$$

$$TestTime = \sum_{i=1}^{p} TestTime_i,$$

where $TestTime_i$ is the test time for test session i, and

$$TestTime_i = ExhTestTime(\max_{j=1,\ldots,r(i)} WidthOfMLS_{ij}),$$

where $ExhTestTime(q) = 2^q / ClockFrequency$, is the time required for generating an exhaustive sequence of test patterns by a q-bit generator.

It can be seen that for the assumed parameter $w = 32$ the solution is not optimal, because for parameter $w = 27$ a solution exists which has the same number of test sessions ($p = 4$) and ten times smaller total test time (Fig. 1b). In Fig. 1 the solution obtained for parameter $w = 69$ corresponds to solution obtained with S-M method. This solution has minimal number of test sessions but the c-exhaustive testing of the largest test block is not feasible.

5 Conclusions

In this paper, we propose a method for self-testing of circuits implemented with in-system reconfigurable FPGAs. Two strategies of test development are presented. Experimental results show a trade-off between the number of test sessions and the width of the logic blocks under test must be exploited to minimise the total test time. Some procedures that can improve the presented results are now under development.

References

1. Abramovici, M., Lee, E., Stroud, C.: BIST-Based Diagnostics of FPGA Logic Blocks, Proc. 3rd On-Line Testing Workshop (1995) 90–92
2. Altera Data Book, FLEX 10K Embedded Programmable Logic Family Data Sheet (1996)
3. Krasniewski, A.: Automatic Design of Exhaustively Self-Testing VLSI Circuits, Proc. 12th European Solid-State Circuits Conf. (1986) 167–169
4. Krasniewski, A.: Design for Application-Dependent Testability of FPGAs, Proc. Int'l Workshop on Logic and Architecture Synthesis (1997) 245–254
5. Stroud, C., Konala, S., Chen, P., Abramovici, M.: Built-In Self-Test of Logic Blocks in FPGAs, Proc. 14th VLSI Test Symp. (1996)
6. Tomaszewicz, P., Krasniewski, A.: Self-Testing of S-Compatible Test Units in User-Programmed FPGAs, Proc. 25th EUROMICRO Conf., Vol. I (1999) 254-259

Implementing a Fieldbus Interface Using an FPGA

G. Lías, M.D. Valdés, M.A. Domínguez, and M.J. Moure

Instituto de Electrónica Aplicada „Pedro Barrié de la Maza".
Departamento de tecnología electrónica.
University of Vigo.
Lagoas-Marcosende. 36200. Vigo. Spain.
glias@dte.uvigo.es

Abstract. Fieldbuses are serial communication buses frequently used in industrial applications. There are a lot of different commercial solutions making difficult the compatibility between the equipment of different manufacturers. In this way to change an equipment implies to change the fieldbus too with the consequent economic losses. To avoid this problems this paper proposes the implementation of the fieldbus protocol in a reconfigurable device. Using reconfigurable devices it is possible to modify the protocol of a communication bus without changing its hardware support. Due to the diversity of commercial fieldbuses this work is centered on the implementation of a FPGA based interface for WorldFIP, one of the most popular fieldbuses.

1 Introduction

The wide use of microprocessors based control systems to supervise manufacturing processes promoted the development of different industrial communication buses called fieldbuses [1]. Unlike parallel or backplane buses whose objective is to guarantee the high speed data communication between physically near devices, fieldbuses are oriented to serial data transference in discrete processes (automobile, food, capital goods, household appliances, etc) and continuous ones (metallurgy, electricity, water, gas, etc). The arise of fieldbuses was motivated by the following factors:

- The need to reduce cable wiring.
- The bigger data integration of the plants in the industries information systems.
- The growing of the processing capability of sensors and actuators.
- The tendency to decentralize the processing resources in order to create distributed systems.
- The demand of standard connections (open connections) to facilitate the development of systems as well as to guarantee the compatibility of products.

2 FPGA and Fieldbuses

The implementation of fieldbus interfaces using SRAM FPGAs carries out a lot of advantages derived from its reconfiguration capability. Among those the most important are:
- The interface can be easily adapted when little changes in the bus definition occur (frame format, transmission headers, change of the transmission line code, etc) avoiding the characteristic economic loss associated to the equipment renewal.
- The FPGA programming code can be easily improved to add new functions when it is necesary.
- Little changes should be required to switch between fieldbuses with similar physical layers like, for example, CAN and WorldFIP.

Taking into account these advantages the development of reconfigurable fieldbus interfaces results in a very interesting project. This paper describes the implementation of a WorldFIP interface using a SRAM FPGA. WorldFIP is a very popular fieldbus commonly used in the industry.

2.1 The FPGA Required for This Application

The objective of this project is the implementation of the minimum services provided by the WorldFIP protocol. These services are: buffer writing, buffer reading, redundancy bits generation and buffer transfer.
A high speed FPGA is not required because fieldbuses operates at low frequencies. Nevertheless, the use of a FPGA with low propagation time it is desired to obtain the maximum operation frequency. By other side, when many variables must be registered, it is wiser to use a FPGA with embedded memory blocks in order to simplify the design. Bearing these two aspects in mind (speed and memory capacity) the FGPA FLEX 10K20RC240-4 of Altera was chosen [2].
The design was specified using VHDL so it could be easily implemented in other FPGAs. The programming environment used was MAX PLUS II.

3 The Working System

Figure 1 shows a block diagram of the system used to develop this project. A brief description of each part of the system is given below.

3.1 Bus Arbitrator

In the WorldFIP protocol the information exchange is carried out by means of variables [3]. A variable can be consumed by several stations but produced by only one. A single number called identifier is given to each variable. The bus arbitrator mission is to broadcast a variable identifier to all nodes, triggering the node producing that variable to place its value on the network. Once the variable value is on the network all modules who need that information consume it simultaneously. Also, the arbitrator is the responsible of the non-periodic variables transference and bus management.

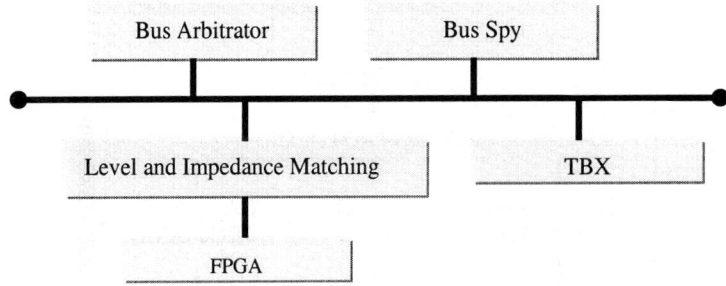

Fig. 1. Block diagram of the working system.

3.2 Bus Spy

This is a special device used to capture all the frames traveling through the bus. It is used by the system designer to verify the properly working of the implemented WorldFIP interface. It only produces its presence variable.

3.3 TBX

An input/output simulating module used by the system designer to verify the properly working of the interface when more than one device is connected to the bus.

3.4 Level and Impedance Matching

This circuit consist in a special chip called CREOL which drives the signals used to capture the data frames (Carry Detect Output, Request To Send, etc), a tranformed used for impedance matching and a filter for noise reduction.

4 The Implemented Interface

The WorldFIP interface is implemented using the FLEX 10K20RC240-4. It requires two clocks, one of 10 MHz that corresponds with the system clock and another one of 2 MHz used to control the data sending. These clocks are generated using two external oscillators. The system clock cannot be directly connected to the FPGA because it must drive a great number of gates distorting the signal. To avoid this problem the main oscillator (10MHz) is connected to internal FPGA global buffer which distributes the clock signal through the gates. The embedded memory blocks

are used to implement two databases and a variable index. In all cases memories have been configured as cycle shared double port RAM [4] working in synchronous mode for writing operations and in asynchronous mode for reading operations.
The implemented WorldFIP interface consist of (see figure 2):

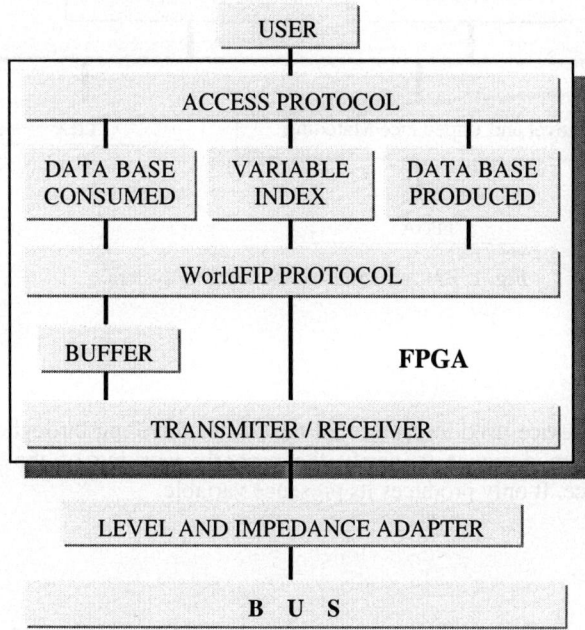

Fig. 2. The implemented WorldFIP interface.

4.1 Transmitter/Receiver

- The transmitter.

The function of the transmitter is to send the data adding the frame starting sequence (FSS) and the frame end delimiter bits (FED) established by the WorldFIP protocol (EN 50170). The transmitter is driven by a 2 MHz clock oscillator because the bus uses Manchester coding with a transmission rate of 1 Mbps (logic levels must be changed twice per bit).

- The receiver.

The function of the receiver is to translate the frames traveling through the bus and to deliver them, as a succession of bytes, to the receiving buffer checking the corresponding FCS (Frame Check Sequence). It is fed by a 10 MHz oscillator and takes 5 samples per half symbol. This frecuency guaranties the correct sampling of any frame.

4.2 Receiving Buffer

This device is used to temporarily store the last frame received that would be processed later by the WorldFIP protocol. A cycle shared double port RAM configuration was selected because both the receptor and the WorldFIP protocol may access the buffer at the same time.

4.3 WorldFIP Protocol

The function of this block is to process the frames stored in the reception buffer, that is, to check if the requested identifier is consumed or produced by the device and to carry on with the necessary actions. It could be divided into three parts (see figure 3):

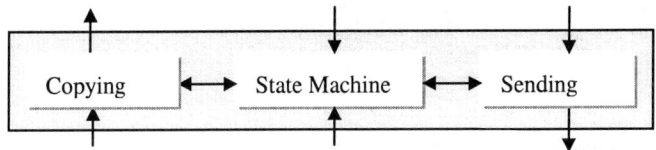

Fig. 3. WorldFIP protocol structure.

- Copying Block:
This block is used to transfer the frame stored in the receiving buffer to the consumed database.
- Sending block:
This part of the system is used to send the frames stored in the produced database.
- State Machine:
The previous blocks need information about the variables. This information is produced by the state machine which searches an identifier number in the variable index and translates it into the required signals.

4.4 Consumed and Produced Databases

These databases contain the value of the produced and consumed variables respectively. As in the case of the receiving buffer we have chosen a shared cycle double port RAM because the variable access protocol and the WorldFIP protocol use these databases at the same time.

4.5 Identifier Index

It is a database (cycle shared double port RAM) containing all the identificator managed information, a reference indicating if they are consumed or produced (C/P) and their address in the database. Figure 4 shown the format of the index's entries.

4.6 Variable Access Protocol

It is the responsible of the access to the variables permitting the creation and initialization of the produced and consumed identifier databases from an external circuit. In addition it allow to read and write the variables. This block enables the system to change the access protocol without changing the design.

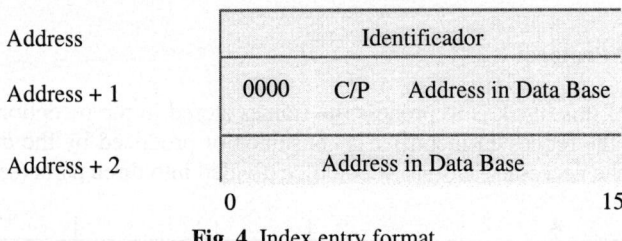

Fig. 4. Index entry format.

4.7 System's Technical Overview

All functional blocks contained in this system were developed as state machines, except the identifier index, which is divided into two parts, a cycled shared double port RAM and a state machine used to search for the information stored into the memory. The final system uses the 82% of the logic resources of the FPGA (logic Cell Blocks) and the 74% of the interconnection resources. With these usage rates simple communication interfaces can be implemented but when more functions are needed the use of a bigger FPGA is necessary.
Due to the diversity of commercial FPGAs it is possible to choice the suitable one for an specific application taking into account your economic resources.

5 Conclusions

The extended use of fieldbuses in industrial plants has created the need to develop communications interfaces easily adaptable to different standards. This project has proved that such interfaces can be efficiently implemented and modified using an FPGA.

References

1. Poza F., „Contribución al estudio de sistemas de comunicaciones industriales mediante técnicas de descripción formal", *Doctoral Thesis*, University of Vigo, Spain. 1997.
2. ALTERA Data Book, Altera Corporation, San José (CA), 1998.
3. EN 50170 Standard, WorldFIP, France.
4. "Implementing Dual-Port RAM in FLEX 10K Devices", Application Note 65, Altera Corporation, San José (CA), February 1996.

Area-Optimized Technology Mapping for Hybrid FPGAs

Srini Krishnamoorthy, Sriram Swaminathan, and Russell Tessier

Department of Electrical and Computer Engineering
University of Massachusetts
Amherst, MA. 01003
sikrishn@ecs.umass.edu

Abstract. As integration levels in FPGA devices have increased over the past decade, the structure of programmable logic resources has become more diversified. Recently, Altera Corporation has introduced a new family of LUT-based FPGAs that have been augmented with user-configurable programmable logic array blocks (PLAs). In this paper a novel FPGA technology mapping approach is described that automatically partitions user designs into netlist subgraphs appropriately-sized for implementation on both types of available user resources. The subgraphs are subsequently mapped to assigned target resources. It is shown that fast *estimation* of *post-minimization* product term counts plays an especially important role in the mapping of designs to PLAs.

1 Introduction

Recent innovations in FPGA architecture have led to the development of new FPGA families that combine diverse sets of logic resources on the same silicon substrate. To support wide fan-in, low logic-density subcircuits, such as finite state machines, several contemporary *hybrid* FPGA architectures [7] contain SRAM-configurable programmable logic arrays (PLAs), product term based structures optimized for area-efficient design implementation [6]. When coupled with fine-grained look-up tables, PLAs provide an integrated programmable resource that can be used in many digital system designs to support control logic for LUT-based datapaths.

In this paper, the general technology mapping problem for hybrid FPGAs is described and an automated mapping algorithm for hybrid FPGAs which optimizes design area is presented. While previous work in hybrid technology mapping has focused on single-output logic cones [7] [8], our heuristic approach uses the concept of Maximum Fanout Free Subgraphs (MFFSs) [5] to quickly identify circuit regions that are well-suited to PLA implementation. To evaluate an input design, a flow-based search is performed on the input netlist to locate design subcircuits that contain high fan-in but require limited logical area. After subgraphs are ranked and clustered, PLA subgraphs and the remaining portion of the original design are mapped to PLAs and LUTs respectively. While our approach is specifically optimized to target Altera APEX20KE FPGAs, it is general enough to be easily adapted to other hybrid programmable architectures as well. Subgraph evaluation for PLA implementation is significantly complicated by the limited number of product terms available in each PLA. For successful PLA implementation, subgraphs must meet both I/O limitations *and* product term limitations. While it is possible to quickly evaluate subgraph Pterm counts prior to PLA optimization, these counts may differ substantially from final counts found after PLA optimization using logic minimization approaches. To aid in subgraph evaluation we have developed a product term *estimator* that can accurately predict the post-minimization product term count of subgraphs without performing time-consuming full logic minimization.

Quartus, Altera's software tool for mapping circuits to APEX20KE devices can map a given circuit to either LUTs or PLAs, but it cannot automatically partition circuits to target both LUTs and PLAs. We have used our subgraph based partitioning tool, *hybridmap*, to partition a given circuit into both LUTs and PLAs. The output of this tool is fed to Quartus to complete mapping to APEX20KE devices containing both LUTs and PLAs.

2 Background

Technology mapping for LUT-based devices has been explored extensively since the introduction of commercial FPGAs fifteen years ago. The existing approaches can roughly be categorized as tree-based, flow-based [3], and cut-based [4] mapping. The most extensively-used approach, flow-based mapping, has been applied to both LUT-only [3] and LUT/ROM-based FPGA architectures and is adapted in this paper for LUT/PLA-based devices. While memory blocks not used to implement memory functions can be leveraged to implement combinational functions with extended logical depth [5] [10], limited memory input counts currently restrict the breadth of logic functions that can be implemented. As a result, wide fan-in subcircuits such as finite state machines must be migrated into accompanying device LUTs in many design implementations, motivating a design migration to newer hybrid LUT/PLA devices.

Recently, Kaviani [7] [8] has investigated both the architectural parameters of hybrid FPGA architecture and supporting technology mapping approaches. In the architectural study it was shown that *low-fanout* PLAs make area-efficient replacements for small numbers of lookup tables and are well-suited to implement logic nodes with wide fan-in and sparse logical density. The described technology mapping approach for these hybrid LUT/PLA architectures applies partial collapsing and partitioning to isolate wide fan-in logic nodes with single outputs. Input sharing is then used to determine which nodes should be combined into the PLA. In contrast to the Kaviani architecture, the Altera APEX20KE contains PLAs with relatively large numbers of product terms (up to 32) and outputs (up to 16) in relation to input count (32). The structure of the PLA is largely influenced by a desire to allow the circuitry forming the PLA to operate either as a PLA *or* as a small memory containing 2048 SRAM bits [6]. In Section 5, it will be shown that as the number of outputs increase in a PLA, product term sharing becomes an important issue in efficient PLA mapping. As a result *subgraph-based* rather than single-output node-based approaches that consider both input *and* product term counts are appropriate for mapping to wide-fanout PLAs.

3 Problem Definition

For single-output PLAs well-known two-level minimization techniques can be employed to map designs to minimized sum-of-products representations [2]. More extensive combinational node search approaches are needed to determine which multi-fanout subgraphs are appropriate for implementation in PLAs. In our *hybridmap* system a search is optimized to locate wide-fanin local subgraphs of logic embedded within a design netlist that require a minimal product term count (e.g. ≤ 32). By extracting this circuitry from the LUT-implementation space, more design logic can be squeezed into an FPGA device or a smaller device can be used for the same design. Following allocation of portions of the user design to specific FPGA resources, individual technology mapping tools are used to optimize each design portion to a PLA or collection of LUTs independently.

The same terminology that has previously been used in [10] and [5] to describe graph operations involved in technology mapping will be applied in this paper. Input to the technology mapping system is a combinational circuit, represented as a directed acyclic graph $G(V, E)$ containing combinational nodes V and interconnection edges E. For each node v in G, a *cone*, rooted at v, consists of v and at least one of its predecessors. If all edges driven by nodes in the cone (except for the root) fan out to other nodes in the cone, the cone is said to be *fan-out free*. The fan-out free cone rooted at v containing the largest possible number of nodes is the *maximum fan-out free cone* or $MFFC(v)$. The concept of a fan-out free cone can be further extended to subgraphs if multiple nodes are considered to form a *root set*, S. A *fan-out free subgraph*, $FFS(S)$, is a subgraph containing S and a number of predecessors in which all edges driven by nodes in the subgraph (except S) fan out to other nodes in the subgraph. The maximum fan-out free subgraph, $MFFS(S)$, is the fan-out free subgraph rooted at S that contains the largest number of nodes. A subgraph that contains no more that d inputs can be characterized as *d-feasible* and a subgraph that contains no more than m product terms after logic minimization can be characterized as *m-packable*. For a specific device, a subgraph is considered *PLA-feasible* if the number of subgraph inputs and outputs are each less than the number of PLA inputs (i_m) and outputs (o_m) and the number of product terms needed to implement the subgraph is fewer than the number (p_m) found in a PLA.

4 Methodology

Hybridmap uses a collection of new heuristics and existing technology mapping tools to perform hybrid technology mapping. The high-level flow of the steps taken by our tool is shown in Figure 1. Initially, the circuit under consideration

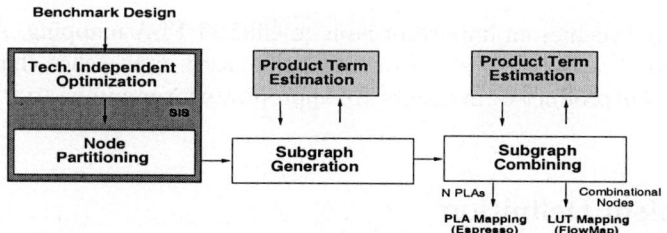

Fig. 1. Software Flow

is represented as a directed acyclic graph containing combinational nodes. Technology independent optimization is performed by *SIS* [9] using the optimization scripts *script.rugged* or *script.algebraic* to reduce the logic complexity of input designs. As a second preprocessing step, the *SIS* kernel extraction tool, *xl_split* [9] is used to recursively split wide-fanin nodes into multiple nodes, each possessing input counts which meet PLA i_m constraints.

Following preprocessing, a multi-step graph-based analysis of circuit nodes is performed to locate suitable subgraphs for PLA implementation. As a first step, a graph traversal starting from each graph node, v, is performed. For each traversal, a breadth-first search is used to locate fan-out nodes that are direct graph descendents of v. This traversal leads to identification of the subgraph root set associated with v. Following the breadth-first search, a maximum fan-out-free subgraph based on the root set is determined by tracing backward from the root set along fan-in edges until all inclusive nodes and edges are identified. After MFFS evaluation for all graph nodes v, all isolated subgraphs are ranked based on input and product term count. An important tool in product term evaluation is Pterm *estimation* which estimates the post-minimization product term count that could be expected by applying logic minimization tools such as *Espresso* [2]. To promote full PLA utilization, individual subgraphs are clustered based on input and product term sharing to determine the final collection of subgraphs to be implemented in PLAs. The three steps that form the core of our system flow, subgraph generation, product term estimation, and subgraph combining, are described in greater detail in the next two sections. Additional algorithm details can be found in [11].

4.1 Subgraph Generation

Identification of feasible PLA subgraphs starts as a localized circuit DAG search designed to locate collections of shared nodes that drive PLA outputs and have limited fanout. These nodes form a subgraph root set and serve as a basis for the identification of fan-in signals and nodes that may be absorbed into PLAs. To promote product term reuse, nodes in the root set ideally share numerous fan-in signals and fan-in nodes. The heuristic used to identify root set nodes in our system is similar to the root set determination algorithm outlined in [5]. For each node v in G, a transitive fan-out set is determined by traversing the fan-out of v in a breadth-first fashion until a prespecified tree depth, n is reached. As shown in Figure 2a for $n = 2$, this node set includes all combinational nodes that are driven by v and all direct successors of these nodes. At intermediate points in the search the covered tree that contains the largest number of nodes while still driving no more than o_m outputs is saved. Following search completion the leaves of the saved tree are designated as the root set. In Figure 2a the darkly-shaded leaf nodes can be identified as the root set of this traversal. Given the feed-forward nature of this step, root set determination across all V nodes in graph G can be completed in $O(V)$ time.

Once a root set has been determined, an inverse traversal of G starting from S is performed to determine the MFFS associated with the root set. At each iterative step of the post-order DAG traversal a test is made to determine if candidate node fan-out is limited to other current subgraph nodes. When no other nodes that meet this criteria can be located or the fan-in to the subgraph exceeds i_m, inverse graph traversal is terminated. As shown in Figure 2b, all predecessors of the root set contained by an MFFS can be targeted to a PLA since intermediate signals driven by the subgraph are not needed outside the subgraph. For worst case traversal, the algorithm will require $O(E)$ time to evaluate MFFSs for each DAG node in G, where E is the number of edges in G.

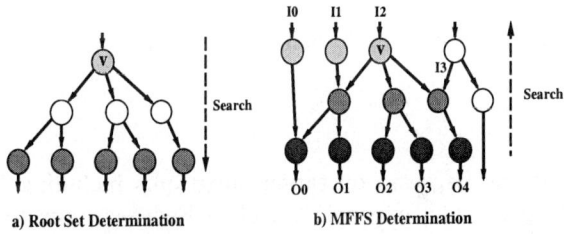

Fig. 2. Root Set and MFFS Determination

4.2 Product Term Estimation

As described in Section 1, PLA structures in hybrid FPGA devices are well-suited to the implementation of wide fan-in, low logic-density circuit constructs such as finite state machines. In considering a set of subgraphs with equivalent input and output characteristics, it is therefore desirable to select subgraphs with limited product term counts over those with larger counts. To illustrate the range of product term counts that can be found in subgraphs with approximately (within 1 or 2) $i_s = 32$ inputs and $o_s = 16$ outputs, product term counts for 168 disjoint subgraphs extracted from the benchmarks listed in Table 3 were derived and plotted in Figure 3. In the figure it can be seen that 34% of subgraphs contain less than 32 product terms and that many of these m-packable subgraphs contain Pterm counts quite close to the 32 Pterm boundary. Through experimentation it has been determined that after two-level minimization, product term counts can vary significantly from original values. As a result to select subgraphs that minimize post-minimization product term count, a heuristic tool based on Espresso has been developed that can estimate to within 10% accuracy the post-minimization product term count of subgraphs on average in less than 10% of the time taken by Espresso. Our estimation tool performs the same basic

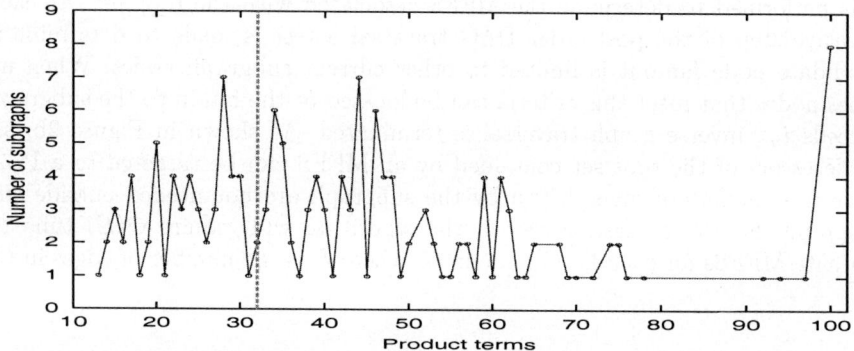

Fig. 3. Pterm Count for Subgraphs with $i_s = 32$, $o_s = 16$

PLA optimizations as Espresso on target subgraphs including Pterm sharing, Pterm covering, and graph expansion. Unlike Espresso, our tool significantly limits the reduction search space by restricting Pterm expansion and output complementation to only those combinations most likely to lead to an overall Pterm reduction. These minimizations are illustrated through use of examples. The input required by Espresso is an encoded truth table, as shown in Figure 4. Each row indicates a product term (or *cube*) with true (1), complemented (0) or don't care (-) conditions and each output column represents a single output. For circuits containing large numbers of outputs (e.g. 32) *don't care* expansion by Espresso (Fig 4) can lead to a large search space. In performing estimation, we choose to expand only a single cube at a time. The minimizations listed above (cube sharing, Pterm covering, graph expansion) are then applied incrementally to reduce Pterm count. A second approach uses lookup tables to programmably invert PLA outputs. During the minimization process, for a n output subgraph, only n complementations are considered compared to the 2^n complementation patterns tried by Espresso. Each output is complemented starting from the one driven by the most Pterms. As shown in the example, by choosing to complement only the first output, the logic expressed by the first three Pterms is now covered by the fourth.

Before expansion		After expansion		Before complement		After complement	
Input	Output	Input	Output	Input	Output	Input	Output
		010011	100	--0---	10	-01-0-	11
01-011	100	011011	100	-1----	10		
011010	010	011010	010	----1-	10		
0100-1	001	010011	001	-01-0-	01		
		010001	001				

Cube Expansion Example   Output Complementation Example

Fig. 4. Minimization Examples

4.3 Subgraph Combining

Following graph reduction, all resulting subgraphs under consideration can feasibly be implemented in a target PLA. Multiple, smaller subgraphs may be combined together through bin packing to form combined implementations that still meet i_m, o_m, and p_m PLA requirements. Merged subgraph combinations are evaluated using the following cost equation which encourages the growth of wide fan-in subgraphs while penalizing overly Pterm-dense combinations:

$$Cost_{jk} = feas(j,k) \times \frac{c \times i_{jk}}{d \times p_{jk}} \quad (1)$$

where c and d are scaling constants and i_{jk} and p_{jk} are merged subgraph input and Pterm counts respectively. A merged subgraph is judged to be feasible if input, output and post-minimization Pterm counts are less that available PLA counts. While input and output limits are straightforward to evaluate, possible product term merging across subgraphs may require additional invocation of the product term estimator to eliminate combined graphs that overflow product term counts from consideration. Given r target PLAs, following combining the r feasible subgraphs that cover the most inputs while minimizing the number of internal product terms are selected. Selected subgraphs are extracted from the original subgraphs and optimized by a full pass of Espresso. The remainder of the circuitry is mapped to four-input look-up tables using FlowMap [3].

5 Results

Hybridmap has been implemented and applied to 11 MCNC logic synthesis benchmarks. All experiments were performed on a 250MHz Sun UltraSparc with 320 MB of memory. To measure the importance of subgraph-based technology mapping for hybrid FPGAs, the number of output signals driven by each product term across 150 mapped subgraphs was determined for subgraphs with over a range of subgraph outputs counts (o_s). In Figure 5 shared output values greater than one indicate that product terms are shared across a number of outputs and that subgraph analysis approaches are necessary to consider subcircuits that drive multiple outputs simultaneously. For low PLA output counts, little product term sharing occurs but as the number of PLA outputs increase, sharing becomes more prevalent. Such product term sharing would indicate a need for subgraph rather than cone-based optimization. In Section 4.2, an al-

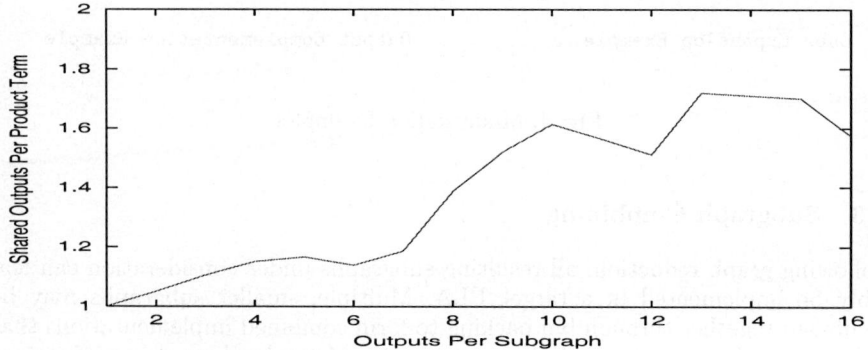

Fig. 5. Average Outputs Driven by Each Product Term

gorithm for fast product term estimation was outlined that can estimate the post-minimization product term count of a subgraph prior to the application of Espresso. A total of 15 subgraphs with input and output values close to 32 and 16 (the I/O counts of PLAs in APEX20KE) were evaluated for each MCNC benchmark and averaged results appear in Table 1. On average, the estimator determined a product term count that was within 3.7% of the total determined by Espresso in a small fraction of Espresso run time. The maximum error found by the estimator for any single design was determined to be 7 product terms. The run times of the estimator are small enough to allow for the Pterm evaluation of a small set of subgraphs during the subgraph generation and combining steps.

To test the quality of *hybridmap* in reducing LUT utilization, four large benchmarks were mapped to the APEX20KE family. Quartus was used to map the partitioned circuit created by hybridmap onto the APEX20KE devices. From Table 2 it can be seen that PLAs can effectively be used to reduce the overall LUT count in a mapped design allowing area for additional design circuitry to be implemented in leftover LUTs. By automatically mapping subgraphs to PLAs about 10% additional LUTs may be mapped to a target device versus a mapping that uses LUTs only. As a final experiment, *hybridmap* was compared to recent results reported in [8] for hybrid devices containing relatively low-fanout PLAs with $i_m = 16$ inputs, $o_m = 3$ outputs, and $p_m = 10$ Pterms. As shown in Table 3 even though the subgraph-based tools were designed to target PLAs with wide fanout, the results from *hybridmap* were competitive with previously-reported work. The inputs used for these experiments were previously used in [8] and were obtained from Kaviani.

Table 1. Comparison of Estimator with Espresso

Circuit Name	Orig. Pterms	Espresso Pterms	Espresso Time (s)	Estimator Pterms	Estimator Time (s)	Ave. Diff (Pterms)	Max. Error (Pterms)
apex4	32	25	772	25	2	0	0
cordic	29	26	21	29	1	3	3
cps	21	20	347	20	2	0	0
frg2	45	39	726	39	1	1	3
misex3	27	26	1384	26	12	0	0
sbc	45	35	268	40	9	5	7
scf	27	21	52	21	13	0	1
spla	43	25	106	25	11	0	0
total	269	217	3676	225	51	-	7

Table 2. Hybrid Mapping for the APEX20KE Architecture

Circuit	APEX Device	LUTs-only Quartus 4-LUTs	Hybrid PLAs	Hybrid Left Over 4-LUTs
spla	20KE100	1769	10	1648
pdc	20KE100	2303	10	2168
frisc	20KE100	2294	10	2025
des	20KE100	1150	10	1038

Table 3. Comparison with Node-based Hybrid Mapping

Circuit	# of 4-LUTs	Node-based PLAs	Node-based 4-LUTs	Hybridmap PLAs	Hybridmap 4-LUTs
s1423	154	19	72	19	95
frg2	324	30	123	30	107
x3	282	25	98	25	109
dalu	357	27	106	27	104
sbc	266	26	105	26	124
cps	520	53	209	53	221
s1488	219	21	81	21	85
scf	300	33	126	33	116
apex2	905	90	366	90	355
alu4	666	69	286	69	245
Total	3993		1572		1561

6 Conclusions

Recent advances in FPGA architecture and technology have made programmable devices with hybrid logic resources a reality. In this paper we have outlined heuristic techniques to automatically identify portions of a design netlist that are appropriate for implementation in PLA-based logic resources found in Altera APEX20KE devices. By integrating our search method with a fast product term estimator it is possible to quickly identify wide-fanin, low logic density subgraphs that are well-suited to PLA implementation.

Acknowledgements

We are thankful to Alireza Kaviani for providing us with the circuits that were previously used in [8].

References

1. *APEX 20K Data Sheet.* Altera Corporation, 1999.
2. R. Brayton, A. Sangiovanni-Vincentelli, G. Hachtel, and C. McMullin. *Logic Minimization Algorithms for Digital Circuits.* Kluwer Academic Publishers, Boston, MA, 1984.
3. J. Cong and Y. Ding. FlowMap: an Optimized Technology Mapping Algorithm for Delay Optimization in Lookup-table Based FPGA Designs. *IEEE Transactions on Computer-Aided Design of Integrated Circuits and Systems*, 13:1–12, Jan. 1994.
4. J. Cong, C. Wu, and Y. Ding. Cut Ranking and Pruning: Enabling a General and Efficient FPGA Mapping Solution. In *ACM 7th International Symposium on Field-Programmable Gate Arrays*, Monterey, Ca., Feb. 1999.
5. J. Cong and S. Xu. Technology Mapping for FPGAs with Embedded Memory Blocks. In *ACM 6th International Symposium on Field-Programmable Gate Arrays*, Monterey, Ca., Feb. 1998.
6. F. Heile and A. Leaver. Hybrid Product Term and LUT Based Architectures Using Embedded Memory Blocks. In *ACM 7th International Symposium on Field-Programmable Gate Arrays*, Monterey, Ca., Feb. 1999.
7. A. Kaviani and S. Brown. The Hybrid Field-Programmable Architecture. *IEEE Design and Test of Computers*, pages 74–83, Apr. 1999.
8. A. Kaviani and S. Brown. Technology Mapping Issues for an FPGA with Lookup Tables and PLA-like Blocks. In *ACM/SIGDA 8th International Symposium on Field-Programmable Gate Arrays*, Monterey, Ca., Feb. 2000.
9. E. Sentovich. *SIS: A system for sequential circuit analysis.* Tech. Rep. UCB/ERL M92/41, Electronics Research Laboratory, University of California, Berkeley, may 1992.
10. S. Wilton. SMAP: Heterogeneous Technology Mapping for Area Reduction in FPGAs with Embedded Memories. In *ACM 6th International Symposium on Field-Programmable Gate Arrays*, Monterey, Ca., Feb. 1998.
11. Srini Krishnamoorthy, Sriram Swaminathan and Russell Tessier. *Area-Optimized Technology Mapping for Hybrid FPGAs.* UMass Amherst ECE Dept Tech. Report TR-CSE-00-4, 2000

CoMGen: Direct Mapping of Arbitrary Components into LUT-Based FPGAs

Joerg Abke and Erich Barke

Institute of Microelectronic Systems,
University of Hannover, Appelstr. 4,
D-30167 Hannover, Germany
{abke, barke}@ims.uni-hannover.de,
http://www.ims.uni-hannover.de/~abke/public

Abstract. Rapidly growing design complexities and short time-to-market demands strengthen the need for fast and efficient functional verification and rapid prototyping. In this paper we present CoMGen (**Co**nfigurable **M**odule **Gen**erator) which implements arbitrary components ranging from flattened gate-level to pre-described parameterizable module descriptions into Look-Up Table (LUT)-based Field Programmable Gate Arrays (FPGAs). CoMGen targets a wide variety of today's FPGAs and is based on generic LUT and flip-flop models. The module descriptions can be given in the popular hardware description language Verilog. Several tools exist for either only gate-level implementations or register transfer-level oriented module generation. CoMGen combines both while providing a fast, efficient and highly configurable mapping environment. It extends a universal module generator [1] in many terms. This paper provides a survey of CoMGen and its concept. The second part states very promising results for flattened gate-level netlists and gives an outlook on our current and future research.

1 Introduction

Today's implementation and verification demands are basically short time-to-market aspects, tremendously cut re-design cycles and first silicon success for several million-gate designs. Additionally, new methodologies involving third party Intellectual Property (IP) have to be considered. These demands strengthen the need for fast and efficient implementation of rapid-prototyping and functional verification by logic emulation [2]. In contrast, traditional synthesis leads to long runtimes and does not explore regular structures, which are contained in datapath components. Importantly, synthesis does not make extensive use of pre-defined and optimized module specifications as available on the IP-market.

Module generators are known to overcome the synthesis problem. Most module generators depend on or are optimized for specific FPGA devices [11]. A more flexible generator concept based on a generic logic block model has been proposed in [12], [13] which has been extended to a library of module generators [14]. However, this library only comprises combinational modules. Additionally, the library is limited to dedicated component architectures, which makes it inflexible. Further components ranging from new architectures to complete soft- and hard-macros, also known as IP-blocks, have to be coded in a programming language consuming a long development process. This is in contrast to short time-to-markets demands. Another methodology, Structured Design Implementation (SDI) [4], [5], [6] takes the bit-slice structure of datapath components into account. It is also based on a set of module generators, which is tightly coupled to the implementation system. Thus, SDI belongs to the class library of generators methodologies. However, it has some drawbacks. The module's architecture is coded within the generator. Hence, it is inflexible in terms of supporting further components. Additionally, it relies on its own proprietary input format SNF. It does not consider controller elements, which are neccessary for design automation starting at behavioural-level. It also assumes a fixed on-chip topology, targets only the Xilinx XC4000 family, and has no automatic decomposition for components which exceed the resources of one single FPGA. However, it proves the concept of structured implementation support for fast and efficient mapping into LUT-based FPGAs.

Also, commercially available tools consist of module libraries [3]. However, they are also restricted to a dedicated FPGA architecture and do not support prototyping environments consisting of heterogenous FPGAs. A different synthesis methodology that maps RTL structures directly into various types of FPGA devices has been presented in [8]. This approach considers the structure of each component that is synthesized onto FPGAs without using the gate-level. However, it does not include multipliers, which are important components in datapaths.

In this paper, we present the highly configurable module generator CoMGen, that generates arbitrary modules for LUT-Based FPGAs. It implements soft-macros as well as hard-macros using a macro description which is given in the widely used hardware description language Verilog [15]. We have extended the idea of a universal module generator for combinational modules [1] in many terms. First, this generator approach implements any kind of macro and gate-level netlist into a logic-cell-based FPGA. Second, the components' definitions are given in Verilog. Third, the generation includes both sequential and combinational module parts.

The parameterizable modules, which we define as soft-macros, are generated according to the LPM (**L**ibrary of **P**arameterized **M**odules) standard [7]. However, they are not limited to it. Module definitions beyond the standardized LPM notification can be added to CoMGen's library easily. Hard-macros can also be incorporated into the environment.

Our approach overcomes the problem of long development cycles for new components as well as the drawback of modules which are directly coded within the source. Furthermore, the combinational module part can be implemented either area optimized or delay optimized.

The paper is organized as follows. Section 2 introduces the CoMGen system. In Section 3 the generic logic block model is described. Section 4 introduces the process of module specification and instantiation. CoMGen's technology mapping of combinational and sequential modules is given in Section 5. Section 6 presents experimental results. Finally, Section 7 concludes this paper including aspects of our further research of CoMGen.

2 CoMGen Overview

A detailed overview of CoMGen is given in Figure 1. All parts of the grey-shaded tile are included in CoMGen. A module generation is launched by either a structural Verilog netlist or a direct module request, which can be done manually

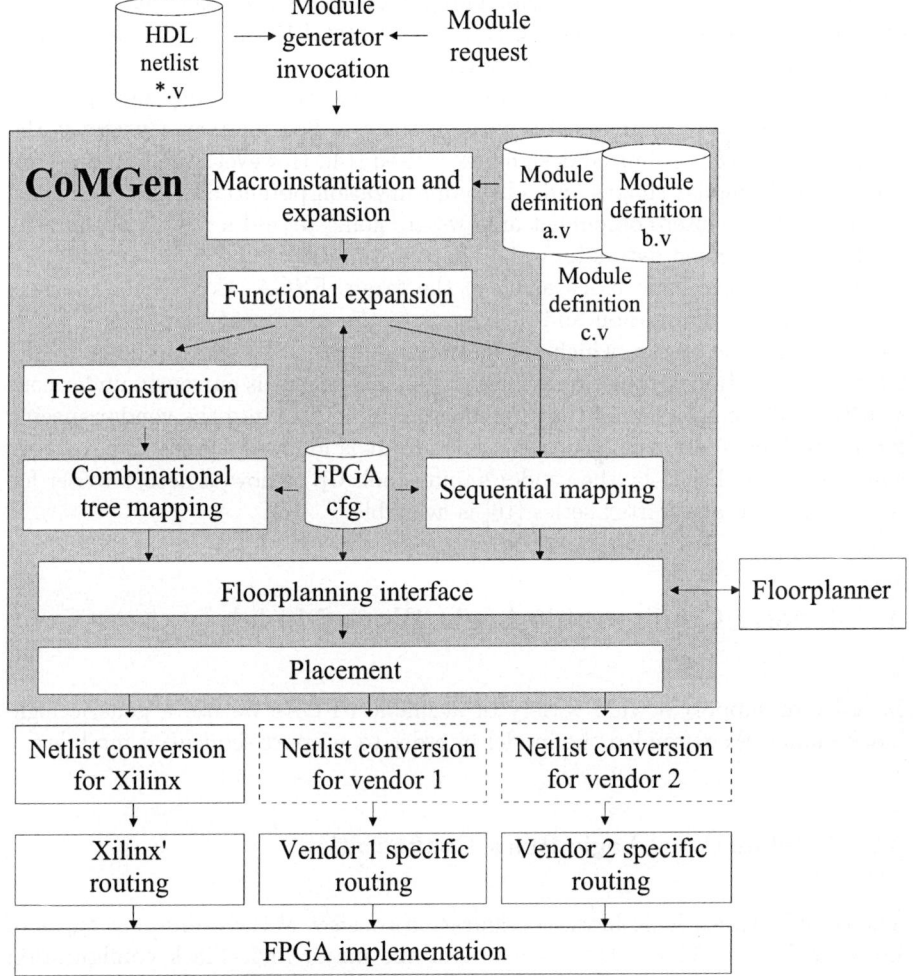

Fig. 1. CoMGen System Overview

or by an automatic tool as presented in [14]. A given Verilog netlist may also contain structural parts like glue-logic or pre-defined modules such as described in [9].

The module generation starts with the macro-instantion and expansion. Within this step, the parameterized instances are expanded to modules which contain structural and logical information. The structural and logical information is defined in the module definitions. All definitions are given in Verilog netlist format in order to provide an easily and rapidly extendable library.

The module information enters the functional expansion where further logic can be added in order to meet the needs of the module's sequential parts and the given FPGA technology. A detailed description of this procedure is given in Section 3.2. The technological data is provided by the FPGA configuration.

The combinational logic is transfered into the internally used logic representation of logic trees in the next step. This is followed by the tree mapping where the trees are mapped into the LUTs of the target FPGA. Additionally, logic optimization such as fixed operand reduction is done within this step.

Both combinational and sequential logic is fed to the floorplanning interface. This interface communicates with an external floorplanner. Currently, the floorplanner of the optimized design flow is used [14]. However, due to its restriction to quadrangular shapes and a high optimization potential of the CoMGem-approach on the inter-component area we are going to add a new floorplanner.

The floorplanner determines the shape's dimension and location for each component on the logic block array of the target FPGA. CoMGen's interface gets this shape information and delivers it to the placement step. Here, CoMGen assigns logic blocks, which are clustered out of LUTs and flip-flops, to the logic block locations of the target FPGA. The placement is currently under construction. The conversion of the implementation netlists into the vendor specific format is done apart from the CoMGen core. It is followed by the final routing which is accomplished by the vendor's route tool. Up to now, a netlist writer for Xilinx' XC4000 and Virtex series [16] is available.

3 Generic Configurable Logic Block Model

In order to support a wide variety of available FPGAs we use a generic logic block model. We extended the model in order to support sequential modules.

3.1 Combinational Logic Block Configuration

The combinational logic block configuration consists of three different types of Look-Up Tables. These three types cover the major logic block configuration modes of today's FPGAs. These combinational modes are described in detail in [1].

3.2 Sequential Logic Block Configuration

In order to support a wide variety of sequential logic block features a flexible sequential model, that is shown in Table 1, has been developed. The signals fall into four groups. These are the data signals, the clock signals, the asynchronous and the synchronous control inputs. The implementation method for sequential parts can be found in Section 5.2.

Table 1. The Sequential Model

Signal	Description
Data	
Q	Data out
D	Data in
Clock signals	
T	Toggle
L	Level-triggered
QL	Level-triggered (inverted)
C	Edge-triggered
QC	Edge-triggered (inverted)
MS	Two-edge-triggered
QMS	Two-edge-triggered (inverted)

Signal	Description
Asynchronous signals	
ASet	Asynchronous set
AClear	Asynchronous reset
En	Clock enable
Synchronous signals	
SSet	Synchronous set
SClear	Synchronous reset
SLoad	Synchronous load

4 Module Description Using Verilog

Verilog is one of the most widely used hardware description languages. In order to support fast development of further modules, Verilog has been selected for the implementation description. This choice enables circuit designers to extend their own hard- or soft-macros by using our mapping environment. Thus, a circuit designer is able to verify by emulation or to build an FPGA-prototype of any digital circuitry with our approach instantaneously using a description he is familiar with. It is commonly accepted that the lack of such a description has mostly prevented circuit designers from using modern verification and prototyping techniques.

The specification as well as the definition parts consist of standardized Verilog at a structural level.

4.1 Module Instantiation

Module instantiation is performed as in any standard hardware description. As an example, Figure 2 shows a 32 by 32 Bit unsigned multiplier that refers to a multiplier module braun32x32 in the structural definition library with 32 by 32 Bit inputs. Additionally, a structural module description can be given to the generator as presented in Section 6.1.

```
'define BUS_SIZE        32
'define MUL             braun32x32

module mul ( p, a, b );
output  ['BUS_SIZE*2-1:0]       p;
input   ['BUS_SIZE-1:0]         a;
input   ['BUS_SIZE-1:0]         b;

'MUL mul( p, a, b );
endmodule
```

Fig. 2. Module Instantiation of a 32 by 32 Bit Multiplier

4.2 Module Definition

Any module can be described in a structural way to CoMGen by a module definition. The module definition includes a structural netlist of the component. It can be given as a hard-macro or as a parameterizable component. Additionally, it will include the component's architectural information in order to support the placement, inter-module and decomposition optimization, which are currently under construction. The module definition of the parameterizable Braun-multiplier braun is given in Figure 3. This definition contains further module instantiations, which are defined in the same way.

5 Technology Mapping into Logic Blocks

5.1 Combinational Logic Mapping

This unique mapping approach is based on tree mapping of 2-to-1 multiplexors [1]. It has been extended to trees of multiplexor-, or- and and-nodes in order to optimize the mapping of arbitrary combinational logic. The mapping is oriented towards both soft- and hard-macros. Thus, it is not comparable to traditional mapping and logic optimization. Modules are described in a dedicated manner and optimized according to CoMGen's implementation strategy. Nevertheless, the strategy includes parts of traditional logic optimization (i.e. fix operand reduction), but it also considers decomposition of modules.

5.2 Sequential Logic Mapping

The implementation of a flip-flop or a latch from a model into the FPGA technology is accomplished in two steps. First, a check for availability is undertaken. Second, a compilation of the available components according to the given needs is done. If the target FPGA does not provide a needed feature, the implementation is arranged by the available flip-flop or latch and additional combinational logic is added. However, some signals can not be assembled just by adding further logic. The decision whether an extension is possible or not is done internally

```
//------------------------------------------------------------
// FUNCTION:  unsigned multiplier (Braun)
// PREDEFINE:
//     <A>                      bit size of operant a (>2)
//     <B>                      bit size of operant b (>2)
//
// PARAMETER:
//     p[ A+B-1 : 0 ]           result
//     a[ A-1   : 0 ]           operant a
//     b[ B-1   : 0 ]           operant b
//------------------------------------------------------------
module 'MAIN ( p, a, b );
output   ['A+'B-1:0]      p;
input    ['A-1:0]         a;
input    ['B-1:0]         b;
wire     [('A-1)*'B-1:0]  c;     // A-1 * B
wire     [('A-2)*'B-1:0]  s;     // A-2 * B
wire     ['B-1:0]         x;

         assign p[0]          = a[0]&b[0];
         assign s['A-3:0]     = a['A-2:1]&{'A-2{b[0]}};
         assign c['A-2:0]     = 0;
         assign x             = {'B{a['A-1]}}&b;

         'csadd csa[0:'B-2] (s[('A-2)*'B-1:'A-2],p['B-1:1],
               c[('A-1)*'B-1:'A-1], x['B-2:0], s[('A-2)*('B-1)-1:0],
               c[('A-1)*('B-1)-1:0], a['A-2:0], b['B-1:1]);
         'endadd add (p['A+'B-1], p['A+'B-2:'B],{x['B-1],
               s[('A-2)*'B-1:('A-2)*('B-1)]},
               c[('A-1)*'B-1:('A-1)*('B-1)]);
endmodule
```

Fig. 3. Module Definition of a Parameterizable Braun-Multiplier

using a two-dimensional non-compatibility matrix. For short, an asynchronous set can not be implemented by an available synchronous set. However, it is evident how to extend a simple D-type flip-flop with synchronous set and reset by adding additional control logic to the data input. In general, asynchronous control signals must be provided by the target FPGA if it is used in the generator in order to avoid gated-clock paths.

6 Experimental Results

This section gives experimental mapping results for arbitrary descriptions and for generated descriptions. Due to the ongoing work on packing, placement and decomposition we limit our experimental results to mapping. Thus, meaningful results for sequential parts because of their correlation to packing and placement strategies have not been obtained, yet.

6.1 Mapping a Gate-Level Component

Table 2. Experimental Results for Gate-Level Netlists (XC4000-Series)

Netlist	#CLBs		runtime (s)	
	M1.5	CoMGen	M1.5	CoMGen
booth_4x4	40	36	8.91	0.74
booth_8x8	121	121	11.14	2.01
booth_16x16	410	396	19.35	7.26
booth_24x24	871	807	29.14	22.09
booth_32x32	1428	1346	57.52	39.29
adder_8+8	17	23	8.45	0.33
adder_16+16	46	55	9.1	0.69
adder_32+32	108	130	10.87	1.64
wallace_4x4	12	12	8.09	0.15
wallace_8x8	57	50	8.73	0.47
c17	1	1	5.6	0.07
c432	28	51	8.23	0.6
c880	58	71	8.93	1.07
c6288	569	423	15.9	18.62
c7552	416	491	18.36	36.34
$\sum$	4072	4022	—	—
$\emptyset$	271	268	15.22	8.76

Some experiments have been done by mapping gate-level netlists of different kinds in order to show the potential of CoMGen's mapping of glue-logic. Table 2 presents the CLB utilization of Xilinx' M1.5.25 `map` and of CoMGen with optimization for speed. The netlists for multipliers and adders have been obtained from a generator for VLSI implementation [9], [10]. All other combinational circuits are taken from the ISCAS85-benchmark suite. The comparison has been performed on a Sun Ultra-Sparc 10 workstation running at 440 MHz. The sum of user and system time of the process is given as runtime in seconds. The CLB utilization, which has been obtained by CoMGen, is in average comparable to those of M1.5. Although CoMGen does not perform a full logic optimization its results in terms of CLB consumption are highly acceptable. CoMGen outperforms Xilinx' runtimes for 13 circuits in total and significantly in average. This outstanding result is due to the well tailored and speed optimized implementation of CoMGen.

6.2 Mapping a Module

Results of different combinational shifter and rotator modules with word-width n can be found in Table 3.

Table 3. CLB Utilization for Rotator and Shifter (XC4000-Series)

n	#CLBs rotator	shifter
4	5	5
8	14	18
16	35	35
32	84	130

Up to now, Braun and Pezaris multipliers, adder, subtractor, multiplexor, combinational shifter, divider and shift register modules have been implemented according to the LPM standard [7]. Optionally, they can be pipelined as defined in LPM.

7 Conclusion and Further Research

A unique new approach of mapping both combinational and sequential circuits by using the configurable module generator CoMGen is presented in this paper. CoMGen's flexibility and high configurability offer a wide area of application. Because of its Verilog module definition interface it can be easily extended to user's demands. CoMGen aims both at fast generator based mapping at RT-Level and customized circuit implementation either at RT or at gate-level. Former mapping methodologies were only dedicated to one level. Moreover, we are going to target both datapath and controller implementations in order to implement high-level synthesis designs. The definition library can provide many different module structures which have to be selected by a high-level synthesis tool.

The mapping results which have been presented in this paper encourage us to complete a unique and flexible mapping environment that is dedicated to today's million-gates complexities of FPGAs in the era of pre-defined macrocells for implementing a whole system-on-FPGA.

Currently, packing, placement and floorplanning methodologies are under construction. This will be driven by component's definition (i.e. bit-slices and levels), signal-flow direction and inter-module optimizations. It will also consider component's decomposition. Additionally, carry path elements are in focus of our further research activities in order to make use of all FPGA features. Further research will also extend the module definition.

References

1. J. Abke, E. Barke, and J. Stohmann. A Universal Module Generator for LUT-Based FPGAs. In *Proc. of the 10th IEEE Int'l. Workshop on Rapid System Prototyping*, pages 230–235. IEEE Computer Society, 1999.
2. L. Geppert. Electronic Design Automation. *IEEE Spectrum*, Jan. 2000.
3. J. Hwang, C. Patterson, S. Mohan, E. Dellinger, S. Mitra, and R. Wittig. Generating Layouts for Self-Implementing Modules. In *Proc. of the 8th Int'l Workshop on Field-Programmable Logic and Applications*, pages 525–529, 1998.
4. A. Koch. Module Compaction in FPGA-based Regular Datapaths. *Proc. of the 33th ACM/IEEE Int'l Conference on Design Automation (DAC)*, pages 471–476, 1996.
5. A. Koch. Structured Design Implementation – A Strategy for Implementing Regular Datapaths on FPGAs. *FPGA*, pages 151–157, 1996.
6. A. Koch. *Regular Datapaths on Field-Programmable Gate Arrays*. PhD thesis, Technical University of Braunschweig, Germany, 1997.
7. LPM 210: Library of Parameterizable Modules Module Specification. http://www.edif.org/lpmweb/documentation/210cells.htm.
8. A. R. Naseer, M. Balakrishnan, and A. Kumar. Direct Mapping of RTL Structures onto LUT-Based FPGA's. *IEEE TCAD*, 17(5):624–631, July 1998.
9. J. Pihl and J.-E. Øye. A Web-Based Arithmetic Module Generator for High Performance VLSI Applications. In *Proc. of the Int'l Workshop on IP Based Synthesis and System Design*, 1998.
10. J. Pihl and E. Sand. Arithmetic Module Generator for High Performance VLSI Designs. http://modgen.fysel.ntnu.no.
11. S. Riedel, H.-J. Brand, and D. Müller. Module Generation from the Implementation Viewpoint. *IWLAS*, 1996.
12. J. Stohmann and E. Barke. An Universal CLA Adder Generator for SRAM-Based FPGAs. *6th Int'l Conference on Field Programmable Logic and Applications*, pages 44–54, 1996.
13. J. Stohmann and E. Barke. A Universal Pezaris Array Multiplier Generator for SRAM-Based FPGAs. *Int'l Conference on Computer Design*, pages 489–495, 1997.
14. J. Stohmann, K. Harbich, M. Olbrich, and E. Barke. An Optimized Design Flow for Fast FPGA-Based Rapid Prototyping. *8th Int'l Conference on Field Programmable Logic and Application*, pages 79–88, 1998.
15. D. E. Thomas and P. R. Moorby. *The Verilog Hardware Description Language*. Kluwer Academic Publishers, 4th edition, 1998.
16. Xilinx. *The Programmable Logic Data Book*. Xilinx, Inc., 1998.

Efficient Embedding of Partitioned Circuits onto Multi-FPGA Boards

Sushil Chandra Jain[1], Anshul Kumar[1],
and Shashi Kumar[2]

[1] Department of Computer Science & Engineering,
Indian Institute of Technology, New Delhi
{scjain,anshul}@cse.iitd.ernet.in
[2] School of Engineering, Jönköping Univ.,
P.O. Box 1026, 55 111 Jönköping, Sweden
Kumar.Shashi@ing.hj.se

Abstract. Multi-FPGA boards(MFBs) are extensively used by the designers for logic emulation, rapid prototyping, custom computing and low volume sub-system implementation. Efficient use of an MFB does not only require a good routing topology, but also a good set of CAD tools to partition the given circuits and embed them on the MFB. Khalid et al[1] have shown that among the MFB topologies, hybrid series of architectures containing fixed FPGA-FPGA connections and programmable connections through Field Programmable Interconnect Devices(FPIDs) are better than other architectures. Programmable connections can connect different pairs of FPGAs under program control, but require additional wires, extra delays etc. compared to fixed connection.

An MFB, to be used in rapid prototyping, is expected to emulate a large number of digital circuits. To accommodate the routing requirement generated by partitioning them, MFB is required to have significantly large number of programmable connections. In this paper, we have shown that an efficient embedding tool can substantially reduce the requirement of programmable connections. The paper presents an optimal as well as a fast heuristic for embedding. Our methods can work with a large class of hybrid routing topologies.

1 Introduction

Because of the flexibility and programmability offered by Field Programmable Gate Arrays(FPGAs), these have become cost effective implementation alternatives in the areas of reconfigurable computing, hardware emulation, rapid prototyping and low volume sub-systems. As the capacity of a single FPGA is often inadequate to accommodate a large digital circuit, multi-FPGA boards(MFBs) are commonly used. The routing topology between FPGAs of an MFB may include fixed FPGA-FPGA connections and/or programmable connections through Field Programmable Interconnect Devices(FPIDs). A fixed connection is a dedicated connection between a pair of FPGAs and requires a single wire. A programmable connection provides a flexible connection between any pair of FPGAs connected to FPID, but requires two wires, two extra-pins on FPID, additional delay etc. Hence, it involves much higher cost than a fixed connection. Khalid et al[1] have shown that there is a trade-off between the routing flexibility provided and the extra cost in *hybrid architectures* containing both FPGA-FPGA fixed connections and FPGA-FPID-FPGA programmable connections. Therefore, it is important to select an interconnection topology of FPGAs and FPIDs for an MFB which offers the right combination of cost and routing flexibility.

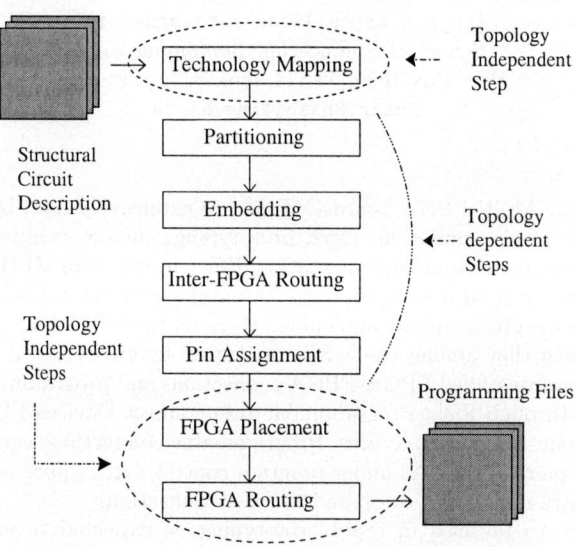

Fig. 1. The Design Flow for MFBs

For emulating a digital circuit using an MFB, it is required to be processed through several stages. Fig. 1 shows these processing steps as described by Hauck et al[2]. We have added annotations to the figure to indicate which steps are dependent on the topology and which are not. Also, we have separated the partitioning and embedding steps as these steps may be done simultaneously or separately. In this paper, we focus on the second topology dependent step namely *embedding* of post-partitioned circuits onto *hybrid architectures*.

Except for topologies, which have identical connections between all pairs of FPGAs like Hybrid Complete Graph Partial Crossbar(HCGP), embedding problem is non-trivial. Fig. 2 shows two embeddings of the same partitioned circuit onto the same MFB. This MFB consists of 4 FPGAs, each having 10 I/O pins, and 2 FPIDs. Fixed connection part of the MFB connects FPGAs in a *Linear Array with end around connections* with each neighbour connected through 4 wires, whereas programmable connection part connects each FPID with each FPGA through 2 wires. Each of the 4 parts satisfies the maximum pin constraint i.e. no part has connection requirement more than 10. An *embedding function* **F**, which

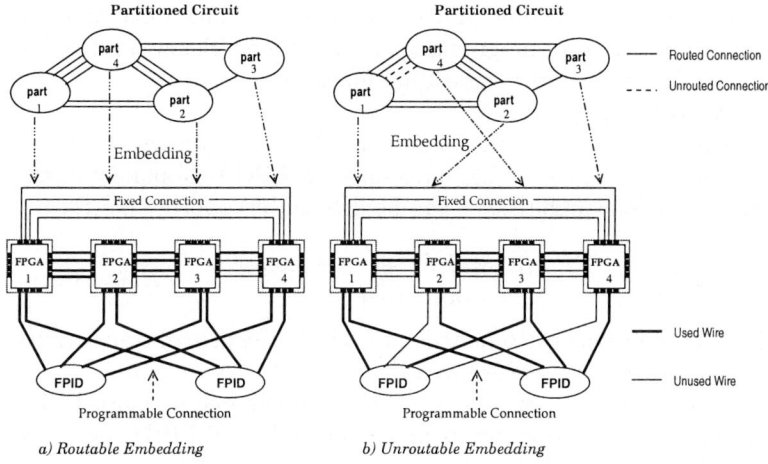

Fig. 2. Examples of Routable & Unroutable Embedding

maps the FPGA number to embedded part number i.e. $\mathbf{F}(fpga\#) \to (part\#)$ can be used to represent the embedding. Embedding-1 shown in Fig.2(a) with $\mathbf{F}(1,2,3,4) \to (1,4,2,3)$ is routable, whereas embedding-2 shown in Fig.2(b) with $\mathbf{F}(1,2,3,4) \to (1,2,4,3)$ is not routable.

In this paper, we discuss solutions to this important embedding problem. Heuristic solutions to the embedding problem have been reported in[1-4], but the solutions are applicable for only one or a few specific topologies. Our solution is general and takes MFB topology as a parameter. We describe a branch and bound based optimal algorithm as well as a fast heuristic to solve this parameterized embedded problem. A tight lower bound on the requirement of number of programmable connections is used to efficiently guide both these algorithms.

The rest of this paper is organized as follows: In the next section, we formulate the embedding problem. Section 3 describes optimal and heuristic based algorithms. Experimental setup has been elaborated in section 4, followed by results and discussions in section 5 and finally by conclusions in section 6.

2 The Embedding Problem Formulation

The problem of embedding is that of finding a mapping of an n-way partitioned circuit onto n FPGAs. The objective is to find one of many possible mappings, which is routable for the given routing architecture. We assume that the embedding step is taken up when the partitioner has partitioned the circuit satisfying the pin constraints of FPGAs. This, however, does not ensure that a routable embedding for a given routing topology exists. An embedding algorithm is expected to find a routable embedding whenever it exists. Since programmable connections offer additional delay, it is desirable to use the fixed connections as much as possible and use programmable connections only when essential. Therefore, we actually view the embedding problem as that of finding a mapping function, which minimizes the use of programmable connections. Below we describe some notations and formulation for embedding function.

Routing Architecture

Let us consider an MFB containing n FPGAs with a hybrid routing topology. Let N be the number of I/O pins on each FPGA. Topology of the fixed connection part of the architecture can be defined by topology matrix C, where

$$C_{ij} = \begin{cases} 1, if\ FPGA_i\ \&\ FPGA_j\ are\ connected \\ 0, \quad\quad\quad\quad otherwise \end{cases} \forall i,j = 1..n \quad (1)$$

We assume the topology to be regular such that degree of connectivity of all FPGAs is same. The degree d is given by $d = \sum_j C_{ij}\ \forall i = 1..n$.

Programmable connection part of MFB contains one or more FPIDs. But for simplicity of presentation, we assume a single logical FPID connected symmetrically to all FPGAs. Let $\overline{P}$ denote the number of I/O pins of each FPGA connected to the FPID and $\overline{Q}$ denote the number of fixed connections between each connected pair of FPGAs. Clearly, $\overline{P} + \overline{Q}.d \leq N$. Let X denote the $n \times n$ fixed FPGA-FPGA connectivity matrix and S denote the $n \times 1$ FPGA-FPID connection vector. Then X can be given by $X = \overline{Q}.C$ and S can be given by $S = \overline{P}.U$. Where U is the unit vector of size n having each element equal to 1.

Inter-Part Connectivity Matrix

We represent the interconnection requirement of a partitioned circuit by a matrix A, where A_{ij} = number of wires required between part$_i$-part$_j$ $\forall i,j = 1..n$.

Embedding Function

Embedding can be described by an embedding function $\mathbf{F}$ such that $\mathbf{F}(i) = j\ \forall i, j = 1..n$, where j^{th} part is embedded onto i^{th} FPGA . FPGA to FPGA connection requirement can be described by another matrix E. The function $\mathbf{F}$ relates A and E such that $E_{rs} = A_{F(r)F(s)}$. We can also represent E as a function of A and F as $E = \Phi(A, F)$.

Routability Condition

An embedded circuit with connection requirement matrix E is routable on a given MFB with parameters X and $\overline{P}$, if there are sufficient interconnections (fixed or programmable) for all pairs of parts. We denote this condition by $R(X, \overline{P}, E)$. This can be expressed using switch configuration matrix L as follows, where L_{ij} denotes the connection between FPGA$_i$-FPGA$_j$ routed through FPID.

$$R(X, \overline{P}, E) = 1,\ if\ \exists L\ |\ L.U \leq S\ \&\ X + L \geq E \quad (2)$$

where $\leq$ and $\geq$ denote element by element inequality.

To simplify this we define a difference operator $\sim$ for non-negative numbers a and b as $a \sim b = \max(a - b, 0)$. We extend the use of $\sim$ operator to matrices with non-negative elements to mean element by element application of the scalar operator.

Since the elements of L are non-negative, $X + L \geq E \Rightarrow L \geq E \sim X$. L satisfying the condition of (2) will exist if $(E \sim X).U \leq S$. Therefore,

$$R(X, \overline{P}, E) = [(E \sim X).U \leq S] = \left(\sum_j (E_{ij} \sim X_{ij})\right) \leq \overline{P}\ \forall i$$

$$= \max_i \left(\sum_j (E_{ij} \sim X_{ij}) \right) \leq \overline{P} \qquad (3)$$

Exploring Embedding Space

Equation (3) describes routability condition for one embedding solution. Therefore, the problem of embedding a partitioned circuit A can be defined as that of finding an F which satisfies $R\left(X, \overline{P}, \Phi(A, F)\right)$. That is to find
$$F \mid \max_i \left(\sum_j \left(A_{F(i)F(j)} \sim X_{ij} \right) \right) \leq \overline{P}.$$

An embedding algorithm is complete if it finds a routable embedding if it exists. As discussed in the beginning, we are interested in finding an embedding which tries to use the fixed connections as much as possible and uses programmable connections only when essential. Therefore, we actually view the embedding problem as that of finding F, which minimizes the use of programmable connections. For expressing this, we introduce P_{min} defined as
$$P_{min}(X, E) = \min P \mid R(X, P, E).$$
From (3), $P_{min}(X, E) = \max_i \left(\sum_j (E_{ij} \sim X_{ij}) \right)$.

The optimal value of P for all embeddings is given by

$$P_{opt}(X, A) = \min_F P_{min}(X, \Phi(A, F)) = \min_F \max_i \left(\sum_j \left(A_{F(i)F(j)} \sim X_{ij} \right) \right) \qquad (4)$$

Clearly, this embedding is valid if $P_{opt}(X, A) \leq \overline{P}$ and optimal embedding is given by $F_{opt}(X, A) = F \mid (P_{min}(X, \Phi(A, F)) = P_{opt}(X, A))$.

Eq (4) describes the optimum value of P i.e. minimum programmable connections over all possible embeddings.

3 Optimal and Heuristic Algorithms

The embedding problem is essentially an *assignment* problem. However, the objective function is quite different from that used in the typical *Linear/ Quadratic Assignment* problem[5]. We have, therefore, developed new solution for this. Our solutions to the problem of finding F_{opt} are based on an efficient method to compute lower bounds on the values of P_{opt}. These lower bounds are used to guide a greedy heuristic solution as well as an optimal branch and bound solution. Further, a good initial embedding for both these solutions is also based on this lower bound computation.

Lower Bound and P_{opt}

Equation (4) can be rewritten in the following form
$$P_{opt}(X, A) = \min_G \left(\max_i \sum_j \left(A_{ij} \sim X_{G(i)G(j)} \right) \right), \text{ where } G \text{ is } F^{-1}.$$
Let us define

$$P_{LB}^i(X, A) = \min_G \sum_j \left(A_{ij} \sim X_{G(i)G(j)} \right) \qquad (5)$$

This represents the minimum number of programmable connections needed as far as i^{th} part is concerned in isolation. Each row of X has d non-zero elements with a value $\overline{Q}$ and $(n-d)$ zero elements. Therefore, the subscript $G(i)$ of X can be replaced by i in equation (5).i.e. $P_{LB}^i(X,A) = \min_G \sum_j (A_{ij} \sim X_{iG(j)})$.

$P_{LB}^i(X,A)$ can now be easily computed observing that $\sum_j (A_{ij} \sim X_{iG(j)})$ is minimum when G permutes i^{th} row of X in such a way that its d non-zero elements are aligned with the highest d elements of A. P_{LB}^i can be used to define a lower bound of P_{opt} as

$$P_{LB}(X,A) = \max_i P_{LB}^i(X,A) \leq P_{opt}(X,A)$$

The notion of these lower bounds can be extended to a situation when the circuit is partially or fully embedded during the iterative process of embedding. The partial or full embedding done so far constrains the permutations which are allowed, that is, during lower bound computation, only those elements in X are permuted which are free.

Initial Embedding

Lower Bound ideas are used to compute a good initial embedding. $P_{LB}^i(X,A)$ is computed for all i. The part numbers are sorted in decreasing order of $P_{LB}^i(X,A)$ values and this order is denoted by vector B. We choose initial embedding as $G[i] = B[i]$, that is, $B[i]^{th}$ part is embedded onto i^{th} FPGA. This initial embedding works well if FPGA numbering is such that i^{th} FPGA has $(i-1)^{th}$ FPGA and $(i+1)^{th}$ FPGA as neighbours as far as possible.

3.1 Heuristic Based Solution

Our heuristic starts with the initial embedding and iteratively improves it by exchanges which result in the reduction of requirement of programmable connections.

For i^{th} FPGA of n FPGAs in MFB, let $neighb(i)$ is a set of topological neighbour FPGAs and $far(i)$ is a set of non-neighbour FPGAs. Let CB be current bound. Function $exchange(i,j)$ swaps the embedded parts within i^{th} and j^{th} FPGAs. Steps involved are given below:

step 1: Do Initial Embedding and set upper limit on iteration#.
  Set $CB \leftarrow P_{LB}(X,A)$.
step 2: $\forall i = 1..n-1$ and $\forall j > i$ do $\{exchange(i,j)$,
  if $CB \geq P_{LB}(X,A)$ $CB \leftarrow P_{LB}(X,A)$ else revert $exchange\}$.
step 3: Pick k^{th} FPGA, with i^{th} part embedded on it with highest $P_{LB}^i(X,A)$.
step 4: $\forall i \in neighb(k)$ and $\forall j \in far(k)$ do
  $\{$ $exchange(i,j)$; if $(CB \geq P_{LB}(X,A))$ then $CB \leftarrow P_{LB}(X,A)$
  $\{$ if $(P_{LB}^i(X,A)$ is not max. for k^{th} FPGA with embedded i^{th} part)
    then   go to   step 5$\}$
  else revert $exchange\}$.
step 5: Increment iteration#. if (upper limit has reached) *or*
  (no improvement in last two iterations) exit else step 3.

3.2 Branch and Bound Optimal Solution

In this solution, we maintain the best solution obtained so far in the variable *Best* and use this to bound our search for a better embedding. The initial embedding provides the starting best solution and its programmable connection requirement as the starting *bound*.

Let *freeset* be a set of parts yet to be embedded. For i^{th} FPGA, $visited(i)$ be a set of parts embedded but unembedded because of non-promising branch. Let $embed(i,r)$ embeds r^{th} part onto i^{th} FPGA and $unembed(i)$ unembeds i^{th} FPGA and returns unembedded part#. The detailed steps are as follows:

step 1: Let *Best* be initial embedding done and *Bound* be its $P_{LB}(X, A)$. Set index $i = n$ for FPGA#. Obviously *freeset* & $visited(i)$ will be empty $\forall i = 1..n$.

repeat
  loop
    step 2: (**A Solution**) if (*freeset* is empty) { if ($P_{LB}(X, A)$ <*Bound*)
        Best ← Current solution, *Bound* ← $P_{LB}(X, A)$} step 5
    step 3: (**Pruning**)   If ($P_{LB}(X, A) \geq$ *Bound*) then step 5.
    step 4: (**Embedding**) Increment i. Pick part $r \in (freeset - visited(i))$,
        $embed(i,r)$, *freeset* -= $\{r\}$, set $visited(j)$ empty $\forall j > i$.
  end loop
step 5: (**Unembedding**)
repeat $\{r \leftarrow unembed(i)$, *freeset* += $\{r\}$, $visited(i)$ += $\{r\}$, Decrement $i\}$
  until $((freeset - visited\,(i+1))\, not\, empty)$.
until $i = 0$.

4 Experimental Setup

4.1 Test Circuits

To test our algorithms, we took circuits from two sources.
1. MCNC Benchmark Circuits
    We took digital circuits from MCNC benchmark suite[6]. These circuits are small to medium sized real circuits. Cong et al[7] have shown that FlowMap provides better delay and number of LUTs optimization compared to Chortle-d, MIS-pga-delay and DAG-Map algorithms in case of LUT based FPGAs. We have used FlowMap algorithm of SIS package for technology mapping.
2. Synthetic Circuits
    Large sized circuits were synthetically generated using *circ/gen* package of Univ. of Toronto[8]. Fig.3 shows this process. In this process, some parameters of technology mapped digital circuits are identified by *circ* package based on structural properties of the circuit and expressed in a language known as *gen script*. Scaled version of the circuit can be generated by *gen* package using gen script and scaling factor. The generated circuits are called clones. MCNC benchmark circuits were used as seeds to generate the clones.

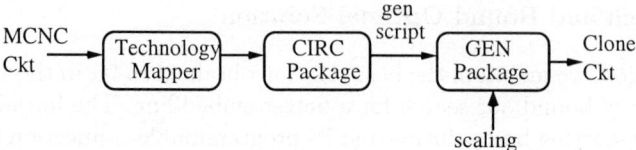

Fig. 3. Clone Circuit Generation

4.2 Partitioner

Partitioning of the circuit is topology dependent step. Since our objective is to analyze the effect of topology orientation in embedding, we decided to use topology independent partitioner. We found *khmetis* partitioner from Univ. of Minnesota[9] suitable as it provides many command line parameters to control quality of parts.

After partitioning, we generated connectivity matrix A. The output of *khmetis* partitioner is hyperedges spanned over one or more parts. Each hyperedge spanned over m-parts can be assumed as a clique such that each part becomes a node and weight of edge can be estimated as $\frac{2}{m}$. A_{ij} value of A matrix can be obtained by summing weights of all the connecting edges rounded off to nearest integer.

5 Results and Discussion

The two embedding algorithms discussed in section 3 were tested on 11 real circuits and 10 clones generated using *circ/gen* package[8]. Table 1 & 2 show the results of the circuits. Each entry in the table represents minimum fraction of programmable connections required. Lower bound and initial computations are very fast as they give results within a minute. Using initial embedding, results from heuristic can be obtained within a minute. Even branch and bound algorithm takes less than 10 minutes in almost all the cases (except in case of S38417 and *Toroidal Mesh*, where it takes nearly 3 hours) and gives optimal result. We have observed particularly in case of S38417 and *Toroidal Mesh*, that random embedding as start embedding did not give optimal results even running branch and bound algorithm for 3 days, but with initial embedding results came out within 3 hours.

Here we report results for two simple and commonly used topologies namely *Linear Array with end around connection* and *Toroidal Mesh*. The number of FPGAs chosen is 16. The I/O pin count of FPGAs were taken from Xilinx XC4000 series. Most of the circuits were mapped onto XC4013 FPGAs containing 192 I/O pins.

We make the following observations from the results:

1. Lower bounds calculated are very close to optimal values. For the chosen 11 real circuits, lower bound is same as optimal in case of *Linear Array* and

Table 1. P Calculations for MCNC Benchmark Circuits

CKT	Type	Linear Array				Toroidal Mesh			
		Lwr Bnd	Rndm	Huristic	B & B	Lwr Bnd	Rndm	Huristic	B & B
C6288	16-Mult	.161	.213	.161	.161	.109	.192	.125	.109
C7552	ALU	.098	.197	.151	.098	.052	.192	.104	.062
dsip	Data Encr	.067	.119	.067	.067	.057	.109	.057	.057
mm30a	Minmax	.078	.140	.078	.078	.057	.119	.057	.057
mult32a	Multiplier	0	.026	0	0	0	.026	0	0
mm9b	Minmax	.098	.135	.098	.098	.067	.119	.067	.067
s13207	Logic	.338	.546	.343	.338	.213	.421	.250	.234
s38417	Logic	.234	.317	.234	.234	.177	.296	.177	.177
t481	Logic	.171	.182	.171	.171	.140	.151	.140	.140
too_large	Logic	.302	.343	.302	.302	.239	.302	.239	.239
s5378	Logic	.229	.328	.229	.229	.156	.307	.156	.156
Avg of %age diff		0%	48.8%	5.0%	-	-2.2%	84.1%	8.1%	-

Table 2. P Calculations for Clone Circuits

CLONE	Linear Array				Toroidal Mesh			
	Lwr Bnd	Rndm	Huristic	B & B	Lwr Bnd	Rndm	Huristic	B & B
dsip_clone_1	.072	.125	.072	.072	.057	.109	.057	.057
dsip_clone_2	.135	.171	.135	.135	.093	.161	.093	.093
dsip_clone_3	.583	.682	.583	.583	.447	.572	.463	.463
k2_clone	.406	.416	.406	.406	.343	.354	.343	.343
t481_clone	.166	.182	.166	.166	.135	.161	.135	.135
too_large_clone	.369	.375	.369	.369	.307	.322	.307	.307
s3593_clone_1	.718	.773	.718	.718	.585	.671	.605	.585
s3593_clone_2	.652	.699	.652	.652	.519	.613	.519	.519
example_seq	.606	.892	.658	.614	.445	.791	.583	.523
s38417_clone	.613	.750	.630	.630	.437	.696	.509	.492
Avg of %age diff	-0.4%	21.0%	0.7%	-	-2.9%	34.0%	1.8%	-

hardly 2.2 % lower on average in case of *Toroidal Mesh*. For clone circuits, lower bound is 0.4 % lower than optimal on average in case of *Linear Array* & 2.9 % lower than optimal on average in case of *Toroidal Mesh*.

2. We observe that our exchange based heuristic algorithm substantially decreases the requirement of programmable pins, as compared to starting random embedding, for both routing topologies and for both real and cloned circuits. Because of the smaller size of our problem, it also gives results which are very close to the optimal. For example, the heuristic requires on average 5.0% more programmable connections than the optimal embedding for *Linear Array* topology for real circuits as against 48.8% required by random embedding.

6 Conclusions

For efficient embedding of partitioned circuit onto an MFB, embedding algorithm must use the routing architecture details of MFB. In this paper, we have presented an optimal algorithm as well as an iterative heuristic for MFBs with hybrid routing architecture. The other tools, required to generate partitioned circuits, were obtained from different sources namely technology mapper from UCLA[7], circuit clone generator from Univ. of Toronto[8] and partitioner from Univ. of Minnesota[9]. Results have demonstrated significant reduction in programmable connection requirement. However, algorithms assume single FPID and regular topology in routing architecture. The approach described in the algorithms can be easily extended to multiple FPIDs and irregular topologies by suitably modifying routability condition and bounding function. Since, the fraction of programmable connections in each FPGA may not be the same, minimization of sum or average of programmable connections may be used as objective function.

References

1. Mohammed A.S. Khalid, *Routing Architecture and Layout Synthesis for Multi-FPGA Systems*, Ph.D. thesis, University of Toronto, Department of Electrical and Computer Engineering,University of Toronto,10 King's College Road,Toronto, Ontario Canada M5S 3G4, 1999.
2. Scott Hauck, *Multi-FPGA Systems*, Ph.D. thesis, University of Washington, Deptt of Comp Sc and Engg, Univ of Washington, Seatle, 1995.
3. J. Babb et al, "Logic Emulation with Virtual Wires," *IEEE Trans. on CAD*, vol. 16, no. 6, pp. 609–626, June 1997.
4. K. Roy-Neogi and C. Sechan, "Multiple-FPGA Partitioning with Performance Optimization," *International Symposium on FPGAs*, pp. 146–152, 1995.
5. Panos M. Pardalos, Franz Rendl and Henry Wolkowicz, "The Quadratic Assignment Problem: A Survey and Recent Developments," *American Mathematical Society Publications - DIMACS Volume Series*, vol. 16, 1994.
6. S. Yang, "Logic Synthesis and Optimization Benchmarks User Guide Version 3.0," Microelectronics Centre of North Carolina, January 1991.
7. Cong, J. and Y. Ding, "FlowMap: An Optimal Technology Mapping Algorithm for Delay Optimization in Lookup-Table Based FPGA Designs," *IEEE Trans. on Computer-Aided Design*, vol. 13, no. 1, pp. 1 – 12, 1994.
8. M. Hutton et al, "Characterization and Parameterized Random Generation of Digital Circuits," *Proceedings of the DAC, Las Vegas*, pp. 94–99, 1996.
9. George Karypis and Vipin Kumar, "hMETIS* - A Hypergraph Partitioning Package Version 1.5.3," Computer Science Dept.,University of Minnesota, Minneapolis, MN 55455, 1998.

A Placement Algorithm for FPGA Designs with Multiple I/O Standards

Jason Anderson, Jim Saunders, Sudip Nag, Chari Madabhushi,
and Rajeev Jayaraman

Xilinx, Inc.
2100 Logic Drive
San Jose, CA 95124 USA
{janders, jims, sudip, chari, rajeev}@xilinx.com

Abstract. State-of-the-art FPGAs possess I/O resources that can be configured to support a wide variety of I/O standards [1]. In such devices, the I/O resources are grouped into banks. One of the consequences of the banked organization is that all of the I/O objects that are placed within a bank must use „compatible" I/O standards. The compatibility of I/O standards is based on each standard's supply and reference voltage requirements. For designs that use more than one I/O standard, the constraints associated with the banked organization lead to a constrained I/O pad placement problem. Meeting these constraints with a minimal deleterious effect on traditional objectives like minimizing wirelength turns out to be quite challenging. In this paper, we present a placement algorithm that operates in the context of these constraints. Our approach uses a combination of simulated annealing, weighted bipartite matching and constructive packing to produce a feasible I/O placement. Results show that the proposed algorithm produces placements with wirelength characteristics that are similar to the placements produced when pad placement is unconstrained.

1 Introduction

Increasingly fast system clock speeds and modern bus and low-voltage applications have resulted in the proliferation and acceptance of new I/O standards. To keep pace with these developments, programmable logic vendors have recently introduced FPGAs with flexible I/O resources that may be configured to operate according to a wide variety of I/O standards [1]. For example, the XILINX® Virtex™-E FPGA family has I/O resources, called SelectI/O™ resources, that are capable of supporting 20 different I/O standards.

In the Virtex-E FPGA, multiple I/O blocks are grouped together into banks. As a result of the underlying hardware architecture associated with the banked I/O organization, there are restrictions regarding the I/O standards that may be combined together in a single bank. FPGAs are commonly used in applications where they communicate with several devices and buses. Consequently, it has become commonplace for a single FPGA design to use multiple I/O standards. This yields a constrained placement problem as a user's I/O objects must be placed in a way that does not violate the rules regarding the I/O standards that can be used together in the same bank. In this paper, we use the term „I/O block" to refer to a physical I/O resource or slot. We use the term „I/O object" to refer to an I/O instance in a user's design.

The difficulty of the constrained I/O placement problem is suggested by the example depicted in Figure 1. The figure shows three different placements of a design's I/O objects and core logic. I/O objects with different shading are incompatible and cannot be placed together in the same bank. We assume that there is a single I/O bank per chip edge. Figure 1(a) depicts the placement that might be achieved in the absence of the constraints associated with the banked I/O organization. Figure 1(b) depicts a good constrained I/O placement in which one group of compatible I/O objects is spread between two banks. The placement in Figure 1(c) would be the result if we placed I/O objects using the naïve approach of taking each group of compatible I/O objects and placing them together in a single bank. Notice that the naïve placement in Figure 1(c) has many more long connections than the placement in Figure 1(b), which suggests that the naïve placement is an inferior placement. A human designer would need to have an intimate knowledge of a circuit's connectivity to be able to make intelligent decisions about how I/O objects should be allocated to banks. Clearly, the difficulty of this problem warrants the development of an algorithm to provide an automatic solution.

In this paper, we present a novel placement algorithm that has been developed for FPGA designs that use multiple I/O standards. Commercial CAE tools must be robust enough to deal with such problems and to our knowledge, this paper represents the first published solution. Our approach uses a combination of simulated annealing, weighted bipartite matching, and constructive packing to generate an I/O placement that does not violate the I/O „banking" rules. Our algorithm is currently being used in the XILINX placement tools for Virtex and Virtex-E FPGAs.

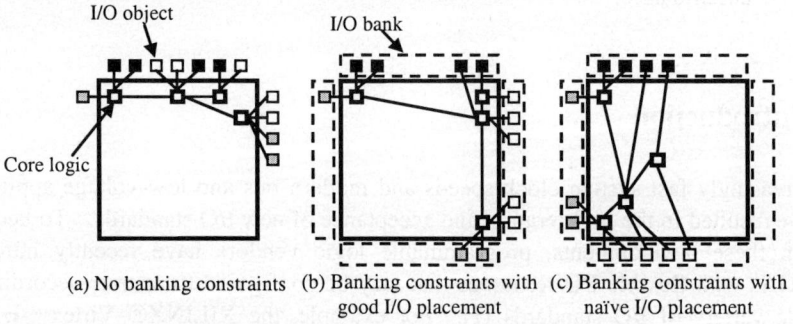

Fig. 1. Difficulty of constrained I/O placement problem

2 Background

In this section, we provide background on I/O standards and the architecture targeted by our algorithm. Following this, we discuss simulated annealing-based placement.

2.1 I/O Standards and Banking Rules

The I/O standards supported by current FPGAs differ from each other in several ways. Some I/O standards require the use of a differential amplifier input. When such standards are used, an external reference voltage, *Vref*, must be provided to the amplifier by the user. Using the differential amplifier allows I/O voltage swings to be reduced, which results in faster switching. A second characteristic is that some standards require a specific supply voltage, *Vcco*, to power the I/O blocks. Figure 2 shows the voltage requirements for some of the I/O standards supported by the Virtex-E FPGA. Notice that *Vref* requirements are associated with input I/O objects; whereas, both input and output I/O objects may have *Vcco* requirements. As shown, bidirectional I/O objects of a particular standard have both the input requirements and the output requirements of that standard.

I/O Standard	Direction	*Vref* Req.	*Vcco* Req.
Peripheral Component Interface (PCI)	Input	Not Req.	3.3V
	Output	Not Req.	3.3V
	Bidirectional	Not Req.	3.3V
Gunning Transceiver Logic (GTL)	Input	0.8V	Not Req.
	Output	Not Req.	Not Req.
	Bidirectional	0.8V	Not Req.
High-speed Transceiver Logic Class I (HSTL_I)	Input	0.75V	Not Req.
	Output	Not Req.	1.5V
	Bidirectional	0.75V	1.5V

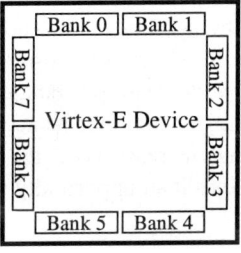

Fig. 2. Some I/O standard voltage requirements (left); organization of Virtex-E FPGA (right)

In the Virtex and Virtex-E FPGAs, the *Vref* and *Vcco* voltages are supplied externally and connect to special pins that serve groups of I/O blocks, called *banks*. All of the I/O blocks in a bank are served by a single *Vref* voltage and a single *Vcco* supply voltage. Virtex-E FPGAs have two I/O banks per chip edge or eight banks in total, as shown in Figure 2. Clearly, the banking of *Vref* and *Vcco* voltages leads to restrictions regarding the I/O standards that may be combined within the same bank: two I/O objects that, because of their I/O standards, require different *Vref* or different *Vcco* voltages cannot legally be used together in the same bank. For example, using the data in Figure 2, we see that an input I/O object that uses the GTL standard cannot be placed in the same bank as an input I/O object that uses the HSTL_I standard because these two standards require different *Vref* voltages.

In Virtex-E, each bank has multiple *Vcco* pins and multiple *Vref* pins. All of the *Vcco* pins in a bank are dedicated pins that cannot be used for user I/O signals. They must be connected to the same supply voltage. On the other hand, the *Vref* pins in a bank may be used to accommodate user I/O signals, if the bank does not contain any user I/O object that is configured to use a standard that needs a reference voltage.

The notions of *Vref* and *Vcco* voltage requirements should make the rationale for the banked I/O organization apparent: if it were possible to configure each I/O block independently, each I/O block would need to have access to separate user-supplied

Vref and *Vcco* voltages. This would greatly increase the number of pins that are committed to receiving *Vref* and *Vcco* and would limit the number of pins available for user I/O signals. The banked organization provides a reasonable trade-off between I/O flexibility and the number of I/O blocks available to the user. We expect that any FPGA supporting multiple I/O standards will employ a banked I/O organization.

2.2 Simulated Annealing-Based Placement

The first step of our placement algorithm uses simulated annealing [2]. Simulated annealing has been applied effectively in many combinatorial optimization problems. Recently published work has shown that simulated annealing produces good results in the FPGA placement domain [3]. A simulated annealing-based placer begins with a random placement of logic blocks and I/O objects. Following this, the random placement is improved iteratively, by choosing pairs of logic blocks or I/Os to swap. The „goodness" of each swap is evaluated using a cost function. The cost function used is typically designed to minimize estimated wirelength and timing cost. Swaps that decrease placement cost are always accepted. However, swaps that increase cost may or may not be accepted, depending on probabilities. By accepting some swaps that increase cost, the algorithm permits a limited amount of hill-climbing which gives it an opportunity to free itself from local minima.

3 A Placement Algorithm for FPGA Designs with Multiple I/O Standards

The flow of our placement algorithm is as follows: We begin by applying simulated annealing to place a user's I/O objects and core logic blocks. In Section 3.1, we describe a new annealing cost function that contains a component that is directed at resolving the banking rule violations that may be present for designs that use multiple I/O standards. After simulated annealing, we greedily improve the I/O placement using a weighted bipartite matching approach, as described in Section 3.2. Following this, if the I/O placement has no banking rule violations, the placement algorithm terminates. Otherwise, we use a constructive packing algorithm to assign I/O standards to banks in a feasible way. Our packer is described in Section 3.3.

3.1 Simulated Annealing-Based Placement

The annealing cost function we employ takes into account wirelength, timing cost, and the banking violations that result from illegal I/O placements. The function we use is:

$$PlacementCost = \alpha \cdot WirelengthCost + \beta \cdot TimingCost + \gamma \cdot BankingViolationCost \qquad (1)$$

where α, β and γ are scalar constants that reflect the importance of each term. During placement, when core logic blocks are moved, only the values of the wirelength cost and the timing cost may be affected; whereas, I/O movements may affect the values of all three terms of equation 1.

We estimate wirelength using a metric that is based on each net's bounding box. Timing cost is determined in conjunction with user-specified timing constraints. Timing analysis and slack allocation [4] are used to determine a delay slack for each source-to-sink connection. Connection slacks are then translated into a cost function that represents the importance of placing a particular source and sink close together.

The banking rule violation cost in equation 1 is determined by summing the violations for each bank:

$$BankingViolationCost = \sum_{i \in B} BankCost_i \qquad (2)$$

where B is the set of all I/O banks. Violations within a bank may occur as a result of *Vref* conflicts or *Vcco* conflicts. A *Vref* conflict occurs when a bank contains I/O objects that, because of the standards they use, would require multiple *Vref* voltages to be applied to the same bank. *Vcco* conflicts are defined similarly. The cost of a bank, i, is the sum of the *Vref* conflict cost and the *Vcco* conflict cost:

$$bankCost_i = vrefConflictCost_i + vccoConflictCost_i . \qquad (3)$$

Banks that contain no I/O objects have no conflicts and are assigned a cost of zero.

To compute the *Vref* conflict cost for a bank, i, we first define the notion of a bank's *prevailing Vref*. The prevailing *Vref* for a bank is simply the *Vref* voltage requirement that is most common in the bank. That is, it is the *Vref* voltage that is required by the greatest number of I/O objects in the bank. More formally, the prevailing *Vref* for a bank i is:

$$prevailingVref_i = v \mid v \in VREF, NIO_{v,i}^{VREF} = max_{v' \in VREF}(NIO_{v',i}^{VREF}) \qquad (4)$$

where VREF represents the set of *Vref* voltages used by the I/O objects in the design and $NIO_{v,i}^{VREF}$ represents the number of I/O objects in bank i that use I/O standards requiring a *Vref* voltage of v. When determining the prevailing *Vref* for a bank, we break ties between multiple *Vrefs* arbitrarily. Banks that do not contain I/O objects that require a *Vref* have a *Vref* conflict cost of zero. Otherwise, for a bank, i, the *Vref* conflict cost is given by:

$$vrefConflictCost_i = \sum_{v' \in VREF, v' \neq prevailingVref_i} NIO_{v',i}^{VREF} + NIO_i^{VREF\_BLOCK} \qquad (5)$$

where $NIO_i^{VREF\_BLOCK}$ represents the number of I/O objects in bank i that are currently placed in I/O blocks that can receive a user-supplied *Vref* voltage. Recall that in the Virtex and Virtex-E FPGAs, the I/O blocks that receive *Vref* voltages are not dedicated and can be used for user I/O signals if the bank containing them does not contain any I/O objects that require a *Vref* voltage. In essence, equation 5 states that the *Vref* conflict cost for a bank is the number of I/O objects in the bank that require a *Vref* other than the bank's prevailing *Vref* plus the number of objects placed in I/O blocks that can receive user-supplied *Vref* voltages.

Although not described in this section, we cost *Vcco* violations similarly to *Vref* violations. That is, we compute a prevailing *Vcco* voltage for each bank and from this, compute the number of *Vcco* conflicts for each bank.

3.2 I/O Placement Improvement

Following the simulated annealing-based placement, we enter an I/O placement improvement phase where we use a weighted bipartite matching formulation to improve the placement of I/Os relative to the core logic. In general, the connectivity of I/O objects to core logic is much greater than the connectivity between I/Os. Consequently, we can assume that the cost of placing an I/O object in an I/O block is independent of where other I/O objects are placed as long as the core logic is fixed. Thus, the cost of placing an I/O object in an I/O block can be represented using a static cost function, which allows us to apply weighted bipartite matching to the problem.

A bipartite graph, $G(V,E)$, is a specific type of graph with the property that the vertex set, V, can be partitioned into two vertex sets, V_1 and V_2 such that each edge $(u,w) \in E$ indicates that $u \in V_1$ and $w \in V_2$ [5]. In a weighted bipartite graph, each of the edges has an associated weight or cost. A matching, M, is a set of edges such that no two edges in M have a common vertex. The weight of a matching, M, is simply the sum of the weights of the edges in set M. In the weighted bipartite matching problem, the goal is to find a matching with minimum weight [6][7].

In our case, the first vertex set, V_1, corresponds to the set of I/O objects being placed. The second vertex set, V_2, corresponds to the set of the available I/O blocks. That is, set V_2 represents the potential placement locations for the objects in set V_1. There is an edge from each vertex in set V_1 to every vertex in set V_2. The cost assigned to each of these edges is:

$$edgeCost_{i,j} = \Delta \cdot \alpha \cdot WirelengthCost + \Delta \cdot \beta \cdot TimingCost + \rho \qquad (6)$$

where $i \in V_1$ and $j \in V_2$ and $\Delta \cdot \alpha \cdot WirelengthCost$ and $\Delta \cdot \beta \cdot TimingCost$ represent the changes in wirelength cost and timing cost, respectively, if I/O object i were moved from its current position to the I/O block j. Let b represent the bank containing I/O block j. The final term, ρ, is defined as follows:

$\rho = \infty$: if I/O object i requires a *Vref*, v, and $prevailingVref_b \neq v$.

$\rho = \infty$: if I/O object i requires a *Vref*, v, and $prevailingVref_b$ has no value.

$\rho = \infty$: if I/O block j can receive a *Vref* and $prevailingVref_b$ has a value.

$\rho = 0$: all other cases.

For clarity we describe the values of ρ only for *Vref* violations. The purpose of the ρ term is to maintain an I/O placement that does not violate the I/O banking constraints.

After formulating the problem, we find a minimum cost matching, M, which corresponds to an assignment of I/O objects to I/O blocks. If the cost of the matching is non-infinite, then the I/O placement is feasible and our placement algorithm terminates. However, if the minimum cost matching solution has infinite cost, then the annealing step has failed to produce a feasible assignment of prevailing *Vrefs* and prevailing *Vccos* to banks. In this case, we execute a constructive packing step to remedy this infeasibility. In the next section, we describe the packing step.

Our matching formulation is able to repair minor banking rule violations in the annealing placement. Consider the example depicted in Figure 3. The left side of the figure shows an I/O placement after simulated annealing. In this case there are two banks, each containing three I/O blocks. There are six I/O objects to place: three that require a *Vref* voltage of A (labelled A) and three that require a *Vref* voltage of B (labelled B). The annealing placement contains banking rule violations as there is an object labelled B in bank 1 which has a prevailing *Vref* of A. In our matching formulation, each of the objects that require *Vref* A will have an infinite cost edge to all of the I/O blocks in bank 2. Similarly, each of the objects that require *Vref* B will have an infinite cost edge to all of the I/O blocks in bank 1. For this simplified case, the minimum cost matching will have non-infinite cost and it will appear similar to that shown on the right side of Figure 3, which is free of rule violations.

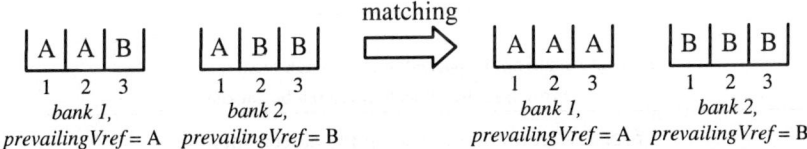

Fig. 3. Example that shows how matching can repair minor banking rule violations

3.3 Constructive Packing

We enter a constructive packing step if the minimum cost matching found in the previous step has infinite cost. In the packing step, we view each bank as a „bin" and pack I/O objects into bins using a simple bin packing algorithm. The goal of this step is to re-assign a prevailing *Vref* and a prevailing *Vcco* voltage to each bank. We expect that annealing and matching will produce a feasible I/O placement in the majority of cases. The packing step will generally be applied only in very difficult cases, which correspond to designs that use many different *Vref* and *Vcco* voltages.

The bin packing algorithm we use is given in Figure 4. Each of the bins in our formulation has an associated prevailing *Vref*, a prevailing *Vcco,* and a capacity. We begin by initializing each of the bins. This involves setting each bin to be empty and setting the prevailing *Vref* and prevailing *Vcco* voltage of each bin to be unassigned. Next, we sort the I/O objects according to their expected packing „difficulty". For example, the group of I/O objects that require both a *Vref* voltage and a *Vcco* voltage impose the most constraints and therefore these will be packed first.

After sorting the I/O objects, we take each object, i, in turn and sort the bins in decreasing order of their affinity to object i. The affinity of a bank, b, to an I/O object, i, that requires a *Vref* voltage, v, and a *Vcco* voltage, o is:

$$affinity_{i,b} = NIO_{v,b}^{VREF} + NIO_{o,b}^{VCCO} . \qquad (7)$$

Equation 7 says that the affinity of a bank to an I/O object, i, is the number of I/O objects in the bank that require the same *Vref* voltage as object i plus the number objects in the bank that require the same *Vcco* voltage as object i. When computing affinity, we take the values of $NIO_{v,b}^{VREF}$ and $NIO_{o,b}^{VCCO}$ from the annealing placement. By doing so, we establish a preference for assigning prevailing *Vref* and prevailing *Vcco* voltages to banks in a way that is similar to the annealing placement. The effect of this is that we mitigate the potential damage to the quality of the annealing result.

---

bankList ← list of all bins (banks).
Initialize bins in *bankList*.
ioList ← sorted list of all I/O objects to place (in order of decreasing packing difficulty).
For each I/O object, i, in *ioList*
    Sort *bankList* in order of decreasing affinity to I/O object i.
    For each bank, b, in *bankList*
        If object i can be added to bank b then
            Add object i to bank b.
            break.
    If object i could not be packed into any bank then
        Error case: I/O objects could not be packed.

Fig. 4. Algorithm for packing I/O objects into banks

After sorting the bins according to their affinities, we employ a greedy approach where we take each bin in turn and check whether the I/O object being packed can be added to the bin. To determine if an I/O object can be added to a bin, we compare the *Vref* and *Vcco* requirements of the I/O object to the prevailing *Vref* and *Vcco* voltage associated with the bin. We do not permit any intermediate illegal packing configurations: for an object to be packed in a bin, it must be compatible with the bin's prevailing *Vref* and *Vcco* assignment. We also do not permit a bin's capacity to be exceeded. When an I/O object is added to a bin, the bin's prevailing *Vref* and prevailing *Vcco* may be affected. Each bin's prevailing voltage values may change from unassigned to a specific value only once; prevailing voltage values will never change from one specific value to another specific value. If we find an I/O object that could not be packed into any bin, automatic placement is deemed unsuccessful. For such cases, we recommend that the user pre-place I/O objects in a feasible manner.

After the packing is complete, we discard its assignment of I/O objects to banks (bins) and use only its prevailing *Vref* and prevailing *Vcco* voltage assignments. We then re-execute the I/O improvement phase of Section 3.2 using these new prevailing voltage values.

4 Experimental Results

To evaluate the quality of result produced by our placement algorithm, we apply it to the problem of placing designs that require multiple I/O standards. The designs that we use in our experiments are Virtex-E customer circuits of various sizes with various I/O standard requirements. We evaluate placement quality using the metric of estimated wirelength. Placement wirelength is estimated by summing the half-perimeter bounding box of the pins of each net.

In this experiment, we place each design twice. We first place each design in an unconstrained manner, ignoring all banking constraints on I/O object locations. Following this, we use our algorithm to place each design, ensuring that banking constraints are strictly obeyed. We then compare the wirelength of these two placements. The aim of this experiment is to investigate how well our algorithm is able to deal with the constraints associated with the banked I/O organization. Another way to view the experiment is from the hardware architecture viewpoint: it addresses the question of whether the banked I/O organization has a deleterious effect on placement wirelength.

The characteristics of our circuits and the experimental results are given in Table 1. Column 2 of the table shows the size of each circuit in terms of the number of slices and I/O objects it uses. Each Virtex-E slice contains two four-input look-up-tables, two flip-flops, as well as other specialized circuitry. Column 3 of the table shows the number of different *Vref* and *Vcco* voltages used by each circuit. The number of *Vref* and *Vcco* voltages used by each circuit reflect the difficulty of each problem as they relate directly to additional constraints on the I/O placement.

Table 1. Characteristics of the benchmark circuits and experimental results

Circuit	# slices/ # I/Os	# Vrefs/ # Vccos	Additional moves (constrained) (%)	Est. wirelength (unconstrained)	Est. wirelength (constrained)	Additional wirelength (%)
Circ1	593/130	2/1	15.2%	4564	4990	9.3%
Circ2	2792/133	1/2	4.7%	28187	28347	0.5%
Circ3	6816/162	2/2	2.3%	113348	122335	7.9%
Circ4	11177/254	2/2	2.2%	235208	236392	0.5%
Circ5	4608/202	2/2	8.3%	36689	36496	-0.5%

We use the same simulated annealing schedule for both the unconstrained and the constrained placement runs. However, because of the non-deterministic nature of the annealing algorithm and the differences in the cost functions used in the two runs, the number of moves made in each of these runs is slightly different. Column 4 of Table 1 shows the percentage increase in the number of annealing moves made in the constrained placement run versus the unconstrained run. Columns 5 and 6 of the table show the wirelength of the unconstrained and constrained placement runs, respectively. Column 7 shows the amount of additional wirelength needed when banking constraints are obeyed versus when banking constraints are ignored. The constructive packing step discussed in Section 3.3 was not necessary to generate a feasible I/O placement for any of the designs considered.

The results in Table 1 show that our placement algorithm deals very effectively with the constraints imposed by the banked I/O organization. Specifically, the results show that the quality of placements produced when banking rules are obeyed is not significantly different than the quality of placements produced when banking rules are ignored. For all of the circuits considered, adherence to banking rules did not impact circuit wirelength by more than 10%.

5 Conclusions

The key contribution of this paper is to present a placement algorithm for FPGA designs that use multiple I/O standards. The proposed algorithm is unique in that it combines simulated annealing, weighted bipartite matching and bin packing heuristics. The simulated annealing step places a user's core logic and I/O objects using a cost function with a component that is directed at removing I/O banking rule violations. Following simulated annealing, I/O placement is improved using a weighted bipartite matching approach. If annealing and matching fail to produce a feasible I/O placement, the algorithm enters a constructive packing step where I/O objects are packed into banks in a feasible way. Experimental results show that the proposed algorithm deals with the placement constraints effectively, with minimal impact on total estimated wirelength.

References

1. Xilinx Inc., „Virtex™-E 1.8V Field Programmable Gate Arrays," *Product Data Sheet*, http://www.xilinx.com, 2000.
2. S. Kirkpatrick, C. Gelatt and M. Vecchi, „Optimization by Simulated Annealing," *Science*, May 13, 1983, pp. 671 – 680.
3. A. Marquardt, V. Betz and J. Rose, „Timing-Driven Placement for FPGAs," *Proc. ACM/SIGDA Int. Sym. on Field Programmable Gate Arrays*, 2000, pp. 203 – 213.
4. J. Frankle, „Iterative and Adaptive Slack Allocation for Performance-driven Layout and FPGA Routing," *Proc. of the 29th ACM/IEEE Design Automation Conference*, 1992, pp. 536 – 542.
5. T. Cormen, C. Leiserson and R. Rivest, „Introduction to Algorithms," *McGraw-Hill Book Company*, New York, 1994.
6. R. Tarjan, „Data Structure and Network Algorithms," CBMS-NSF Regional Conference Series in Applied Mathematics, *Society for Industrial and Applied Mathematics (SIAM)*, Philadelphia, 1983.
7. M. Fredman and R. Tarjan, „Fibonacci Heaps and Their Uses in Improved Network Optimization Algorithms," *Journal of the Association for Computing Machinery*, Vol. 34, No. 3 July 1987, pp. 596 – 615.

A Mapping Methodology for Code Trees onto LUT-Based FPGAs

Holger Kropp and Carsten Reuter

Institut für Theoretische Nachrichtentechnik und Informationsverarbeitung,
Universität Hannover,
Appelstr. 4, 30167 Hannover, Germany
kropp,reuter@mst.uni-hannover.de
http://www.mst.uni-hannover.de/~kropp

Abstract. One important algorithm for data compression is the variable length coding that often utilizes large code tables. Despite the progress modern FPGAs made, concerning the available logic resources, an efficient mapping of those tables is still a challenging task. In this paper, we describe an efficient mapping methodology for code trees onto LUT-based FPGAs. Due to an adaptation to the LUT's number of inputs, for large code tables a reduction of up to 40% of logic blocks is achievable compared with a conventional gate-based implementation.

1 Introduction

Data compression techniques are essential to reduce costs for transmission or storage of data. Important applications using data compression are in the field of common video or audio processing schemes, for example CCITT visual telephony (H.263) [1] or MPEG [2]. These schemes demand flexible hardware, suitable to meet real–time constraints.

Besides traditional standard– and full–custom cell implementation style, an implementation on modern LUT-based FPGAs becomes an alternative. They have low non–recurring costs and allow a flexible design realization. Due to the technological progress, these FPGAs, e.g. Xilinx's Virtex [3], Altera's APEX [6] or Lattice' VANTIS [7] architectures, provide a large number of logic, flip-flops (FF), memory, and routing resources. Clock frequencies of approx. 200 MHz can be achieved. Hence, it is possible to implement data compression algorithms with high throughput rate on LUT–based FPGAs.

Video processing schemes consist of different algorithm classes. Low-level algorithms are characterized by their deterministic number of arithmetic operations and data. Typical low-level algorithms are filters or transformations that require a lot of operators like adders, subtractors, and multipliers. Modern FPGA architectures have features, e.g. Fast Carry Logic, enabling a dedicated realization of arithmetic operators [5] [4] that are used for efficient modules or IPs.

In contrast to common low-level algorithms, high-level algorithms are very control intensive tasks. Improving the throughput by parallel processing is often not possible. A typical high-level algorithm in the field of video processing is the Huffman tree-based variable length code (VLC). In particular, a data dependent conversion of a symbol into a code word requires large code tables, imposing a substantial problem for an FPGA implementation. In case of VLC and tree–based data compression codes, so far, only a few prototype implementations exist. They are usually not adapted to modern FPGA architectures.

This work presents a methodology for an efficient mapping of tree–based codes on LUT–based FPGA architectures, targeting a high utilization of LUTs inputs and FFs. Furthermore, it allows an adaptation to different LUT sizes on an architectural level.

The paper is organized as follows. In section 2 tree–based codes are introduced and State–of–the–art implementation techniques are presented. Section 3 describes our methodology for an improved FPGA implementation. Results will be provided in section 4. Section 5 provides concluding remarks.

2 Tree-Based Codes

So called variable length codes represent a lossless data compression technique. The goal is a reduction of the total average code word length, by coding source symbols with a higher probability using short code words and less frequent symbols using long code words. During encoding, source symbols from a source alphabet of m elements $a_i (i = 1..m)$, are mapped onto code words from the code alphabet $\{0, 1\}$. The assignment of code words to source symbols is based on the probabilities $P(a_i)$ of the source symbols.

The *term tree–based code* comes from a common visualization method of codes using binary trees. The classic coding scheme is Huffman coding [8]. Figure 1 shows a Huffman tree for the symbol alphabet *E, L, H, O, !*, and their corresponding probabilities. Every leaf is labeled with the probability of the corresponding symbol. In this binary tree, each left branch contains the code bit '0' and each right branch the '1'. In order to determine the code for a specific symbol string, one has to traverse from the entry point (root node) to the specific leaf. The code words are obtained by concatenating the bits at the branches. For example the string "HELLO!" is encoded as '110 10 0 0 1111 1110' (spaces are added for readability).

If a code word should be decoded, the decoder starts at the entry point of the code tree. First, it reads the leftmost bit of the code string, bit '1', in the example, and traverses through the correspondent branch, i.e. the right one. This procedure has to be continued until the last bit is reached. Each time the decoder detects a leaf, a specific symbol is decoded and the decoder starts at the entry point again.

Note that the encoder has to transmit the code bits in reverse order, to provide the bits for the decoder in the right order. A reverse Huffman tree for the "HELLO!" example is given in Figure 2. In contrast to the tree in Figure 1, symbols can either be nodes or leafs. Therefore, for m symbols we have m entry points. The encoding procedure starts at the corresponding entry point and runs bottom up to the top node (root). The symbol results by concatenating the bits at the branches. For example, the first symbol "H" of the string "HELLO!" is encoded as '110'.

In general, there are several ways to implement tree–based encoders. The following paragraph illustrates current approaches.

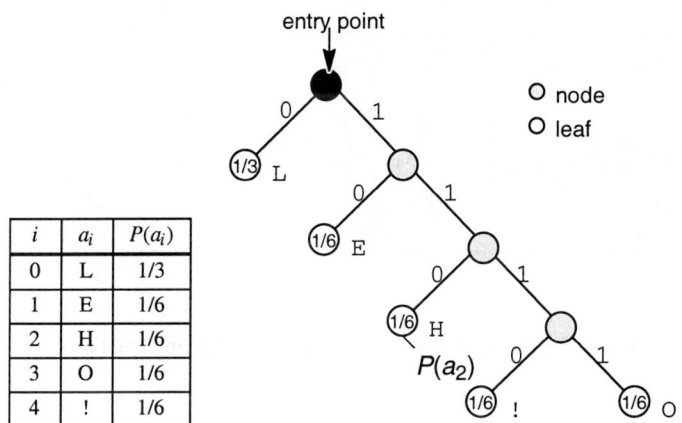

Fig. 1. A Huffman tree for the example "HELLO!"

i	a_i	$P(a_i)$
0	L	1/3
1	E	1/6
2	H	1/6
3	O	1/6
4	!	1/6

2.1 State–of–the–Art

In case of full–custom and standard–cell designs only a few dedicated hardware implementations for tree encoders were published [9][10].

In [9] a simple scheme is proposed for mapping Huffman trees onto memory. Additionally, a small 8-bit ALU, a stack, which performs data reversal, and some more registers are necessary.

The architecture in [10] is a direct mapping of the reverse code tree onto a structure of gates and FFs, depicted in Figure 1. Additionally, an input decoder is necessary, addressing each entry point. Due to its simple elements, architecture [10] is more suitable for an LUT-based implementation, than architecture [9].

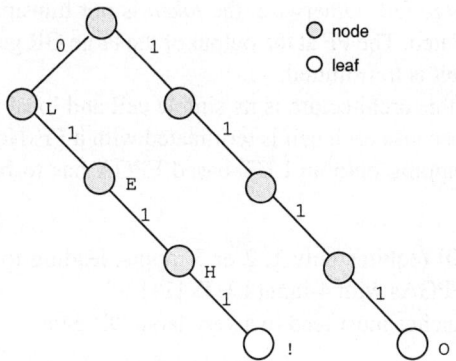

Fig. 2. Reverse Huffman tree for the example "HELLO"

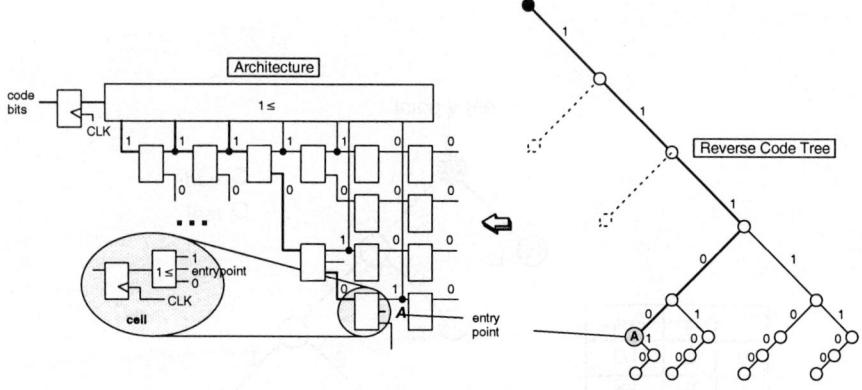

Fig. 3. Reverse Huffman tree and appropriate architecture [10]

The proposed architecture [10] is illustrated in Figure 3. On the right hand side, a part of a reverse Huffman tree is shown. Each node is mapped onto a simple cell, which contains an OR gate and a FF.

The tree consists of two node types:

- single nodes, that have exclusively a 0– or an 1–branch
- binary nodes, that have a 0– and an 1–branch.

Each node type can have an additional entry point for a specific symbol. Concerning the mapping process, a single node contains no or one 2–input OR gate, respectively. A binary node contains one 2–input or one 3–input OR gate, respectively.

The output of a cell's FF corresponds to branches, labeled with '0' or '1'. All FF outputs, that correspond to a 1–branch, are connected with the large OR gate above. Note during encoding it is important, that the whole architecture contains only a single '1', the so called *token*. A *token* is inserted via a specific entry point and stored by a FF. Each clock cycle it is passed to the following cell (corresponding to the successor node within the tree). Every time the *token* passes a cell with an '1' output, an '1' is generated at the output of the large OR. Otherwise, the *token* is not transmitted to the large OR gate, and a '0' is generated. The FF at the output of the large OR guarantees, that at each clock cycle one code bit is transmitted.

The advantage of this architecture is its simple cell and local routing structure and the high throughput, because each cell is terminated with a FF. Nevertheless, under the assumption, that a mapping onto an LUT–based FPGA has to be performed, several drawbacks exist:

- a basic cell of [10] requires only 1, 2 or 3 inputs, leading to a poor utilization of commonly used FPGAs with 4-input LUTs [11]
- all possible 1–branches must feed to a very large OR gate.

In order to derive an efficient parameterizable mapping that targets different LUT–sizes, the following methodology has been developed.

3 Mapping Methodology

This section describes the principles of our methodology for an efficient LUT mapping of code trees, based on the architecture of [10]. An implementation of the whole architecture requires following units, which are depicted in Figure 4:

- an entry point decoder
- the reverse code tree
- a large OR for *token* detection

Our methodology is focussed on the reverse code tree and the large OR.

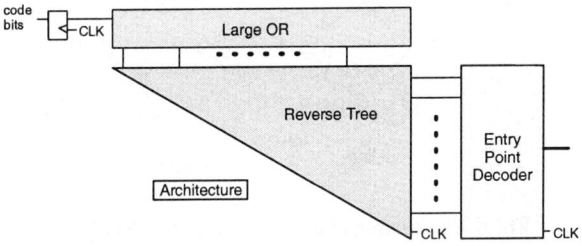

Fig. 4. Block diagram of the code tree architecture

In order to model different LUT-sizes, first we have chosen a simple cell model from the University of Toronto[11], called basic logic element (BLE). Each BLE consists of a K–input LUT, a flip flop (FF), and a multiplexor. Figure 5 shows these BLEs, which can be combined to a logic cluster to model logic cells [11] of different FPGA architectures.

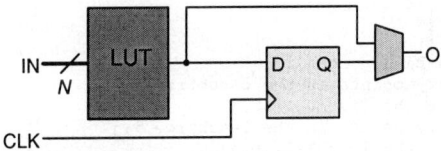

Fig. 5. Basic logic element [11]

Our goal is to overcome the drawbacks of [10] by merging nodes (so called *projection*), leading to an improved LUT utilization and an overall reduction of necessary BLE resources. The methodology is illustrated with the help of Figure 6. It shows a reverse code tree. The distance between a node and the root node is characterized by a node's level, j. The root node has level $j=0$ and the leaves at the lowest level have the index $j=lmax$. Where $lmax$ is equivalent to the maximum code word length. The additional index i describes the position of a node within a level from right to left.

It is assumed, that the code tree is traversed bottom up, i.e. a node's successor has the level index j-1. Its predecessor has a level index j+1. Subtrees of a node i,j, reachable

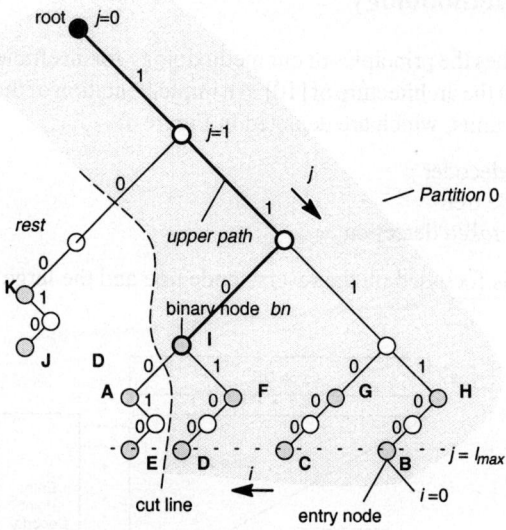

Fig. 6. Partitioning of a reverse code tree (STEP1)

via the 0-branch, are called $0\text{-}subtree,i,j$. E.g., nodes A and E are elements of the 0-$subtree,1,3$ of node I. The subtrees which belong to a 1-branch are called $1\text{-}subtree,i,j$. The methodology is divided into two steps. In a first step ("STEP1") the code tree is partitioned into p partitions, and in a second step ("STEP2") the merging process of nodes of the same level j as well as their mapping onto BLEs has to be performed, such that the number of used LUT inputs becomes a maximum.

```
STEP1: Partition the tree
repeat{
   for(j=lmax downto 0){
     for(i=0 upto imax){
       if(node i,j is a binary node){
          search all entry points in the 0-subtree,i,j
          store them into the list 0-list,j
          search all entry points in the 1-subtree,i,j
          store them into the list 1-list,j
       }
     }
   search the first K entry nodes at level j
   traverse the path from the K'th entry node up to the 0-branch of a binary node bn
   cut the path at this 0-branch
   traverse the path from bn to the root node and cut all 0-branches adjacent to this path
   }
   p = nodes and branches, right from the cut line
   rest = nodes and branches, left from the cut line
   root path = path from bn to the root node
   concatenate upper path and rest
}
until the whole tree has been partitionated
```

In STEP1, to determine each partition $K-1$ entry nodes are considered. It starts with the leaf $i=0$ at the right side of the code tree in level $j=lmax$. Note the entry points in the specific subtrees are essential for STEP2. According to a $0\text{-}subtree,i,j$ or a $1\text{-}subtree,i,j$

an entry point is stored in 0-*list,j* or 1-*list,j*, respectively. The algorithm for STEP1 is as follows:

In STEP2, for each partition p, nodes of one level j are merged into one BLE j, i.e., the algorithm works like a projection of nodes at a specific level j into one BLE. This reduces the number of BLEs to $p \cdot lmax$ BLEs. Each LUT is configured as K–input OR in best case. All 0– and 1–branches between nodes at level j and their predecessor nodes at level $j+1$ are merged into a single line. This line connects the output of BLE $j+1$ with the input of BLE j. In order to generate a '1' at the code output every time the *token* passes a 1–branch, all BLE outputs, representing a possible 1–branch, must be an input of the large OR gate (see fig. 4).

Note that the merging of several 0– and 1–branches into one BLE input or output, respectively, results in errors at the code output. Therefore, additional BLEs are required, to mask or pass the *token*, corresponding to the used entry points in the underlying subtree. Considering, that only one *token* is allowed in the whole tree architecture, some logic is required, which resets the FFs. The algorithm for STEP2 is as follows:

```
STEP2: Perform the mapping of the p subtrees onto the BLEs
foreach partition{
  for(j=lmax downto 0){
    assign possible entry node at level j to one LUT input
    assign LUT output to D-input of the FF in BLE j
    if(j<lmax){
      //collect all node branches into one single line at level j
      assign BLE j+1 output to one LUT input in BLE j
      if(1-list,j not empty){
        //logic to pass or mask the token
        if(#entries in 0-list,j > #entries in 1-list,j){
          (OR(each element in list,j) AND output BLE j)
        } else {
          (NOR(each element in 1-list,j) AND output BLE j)
        }
        assign BLE j output to an input of large OR gate
      }
    }
    consider reset of FF in BLE j
  }
}
```

4 Results

Our methodology was implemented in a C++ program, that enables the parsing of VLC code tables and the mapping onto LUT-based FPGA architectures. Furthermore, the program generates a netlist in BLIF- or XNF-format. The mapping process targets to map the whole architecture, including the code tree, the entry point decoder, and the large OR (see Figure 4). The program was applied on 5 VLC code tables of the video coding standard H.263 [1]. Table 1 shows the results in terms of number of BLEs with 4-input LUTs. To compare our implementation with [10], the percentage of improvement is given. All code tables have a different number of entry points (*#entries*), nodes, 1–nodes (in %), and maximal code word length *lmax*.

For large code tables, with a relation of 0– and 1–nodes not close to 50%, an improvement up to 40% is achievable. Hence, to derive results for large code tables and different FPGAs, we varied the number of LUT's inputs. Figure 7 shows the results for

Table 1. Implementation results of different VLC tables for 4-input LUTs

VLC table	#nodes	#1-nodes	#entries	#BLEs	Improvements
transform coefficients (TCOEFF)	332	16%	102	309	36%
motion vector data (MVD)	269	13%	64	217	40%
block pattern intra pict.(BPC_I)	20	15%	9	27	13%
block pattern chrom. pred. pict.(BPC_P)	51	14%	21	69	23%
block pattern lum. (BPY)	30	37%	16	50	-2%

the largest VLC table *TCOEFF*. K is varied from 3 to 8. It is obvious, that with increasing LUT sizes the number of necessary BLEs decreases significantly, from 22% for K=3 downto 58% for K=8.

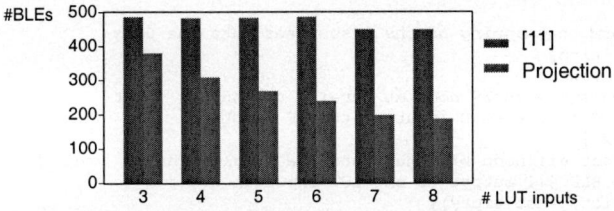

Fig. 7. Implementation results for K–input LUTs

5 Conclusion

An FPGA mapping methodology for large code tables which are important for tree–based codes has been presented. First, an adequate architecture was chosen to implement reverse code trees. Then an adaptation targeting LUT–based FPGAs had to be performed, that consists of two major steps. In step 1 a suitable code tree partitioning is done with respect to LUT's inputs. The main idea of step 2 is to project as many nodes as possible into one logic element in order to maximize the LUT utilization.

The mapping methodology was implemented in a tool using C++. To consider different FPGA architectures, the number of LUT's inputs (K) is parametrizeable.

It is possible to reduce the required number of logic elements in an FPGA with 4–input LUTs by approx. 40%, compared to an implementation technique that does not take advantage of LUT adaptation.

Acknowledgments

The work presented is supported by the Deutsche Forschungsgemeinschaft, DFG, under contract number Pi–169/7.

References

1. ITU-T Draft Recommendation H.263, "Video coding for low bitrate communication," 1995.
2. ISO–IEC IS 13818, "Generic Coding of Moving Pictures and Associated Audio," 1994.
3. Xilinx Inc., *http://www.xilinx.com/products/virtex.htm*, 2000.
4. Xilinx Inc., *Core Solutions Data Book*, 1997.
5. Altera Co., *Data Sheet FLEX10K*, 1995.
6. Altera Co., *http://www.altera.com/html/products/apex.html*, 2000.
7. Vantis Inc., *Preliminary: Vantis VF1 Field Programmable Gate Array*, 1998.
8. D. A. Huffman, "A Method for the Construction of Minimum-Redundancy Codes," *Proc. IRE 40*, Sept. 1952, pp. 1098-1101.
9. H. Park, and V.K. Prasanna, "Area Efficient VLSI Architectures for Huffman Coding" *IEEE Trans. on Circuits and Systems-II*, Nr. 9 Vol. 40, Sept. 1993, pp.568-575.
10. A. Mukherjee, N. Ranganathan, and M. Bassiouni, "Efficient VLSI Design for Data Transformation of Tree-Based-Codes" *IEEE Trans. on Circuits and Systems*, Nr. 3 Vol. 18, Mar. 1991, pp.306-314.
11. V. Betz, J. Rose, "How Much Logic Should Go in an FPGA Logic Block?" *IEEE Design and Test of Computers*, Nr. 1 Vol. 15, Jan.-Mar. 1998, pp.10-15.
12. H. Kropp, C. Reuter, P. Pirsch, "The Video and Image Emulation System VIPES," *Proc. 9th Int'l Works. Rapid System Prototyping*, June 1998, pp. 177–175.

Possibilities and Limitations of Applying Evolvable Hardware to Real-World Applications

Jim Torresen

Department of Informatics
University of Oslo
PO Box 1080 Blindern
N-0316 Oslo, Norway
jimtoer@ifi.uio.no

Abstract. Evolvable Hardware (EHW) has been proposed as a new method for designing systems for real-world applications. This paper contains a classification of the published work on this topic. Further, a thorough discussion about the limitations of the present EHW and possible solutions to these are proposed. EHW has been applied to a wide range of applications. However, to solve more complex applications, the evolutionary schemes should be improved.

1 Introduction

Evolvable hardware (EHW) has recently been introduced as a new scheme for designing systems for real-world applications. It was introduced for about seven years ago [1] as a new method for designing electronic circuits. Instead of manually designing a circuit, only input/output-relations are specified. The circuit is automatically designed using an adaptive algorithm. In this algorithm, a set (population) of circuits – i.e. circuit representations, are first randomly generated. The behavior of each circuit is evaluated and the best circuits are combined to generate new and hopefully better circuits. The evaluation is according to the behavior initially specified by the user. After a number of generations, the fittest circuit is to behave according to the initial specification. The most commonly used evolutionary algorithm is genetic algorithm (GA) [2]. The algorithm – which follows the steps described above, is illustrated in Fig. 1.

In GA, each individual circuit is often named chromosome or genotype and shown by a circled "+" in the figure. A circuit can be represented in several different ways. For digital circuits however, gate level representation is most commonly used. That is, the representation contains a description of what kind of gates are applied and their inter-connections. For FPGA technology, this is normally equal to a subset of the configuration bit string. The most computational demanding part of GA is usually the evaluation of each circuit – typically named fitness computation. This involves inputing data to each circuit and computing the error given by the deviation from the specified correct output.

Randomness is introduced in the selection and thus, not only the fittest circuits are selected – as seen in the figure. However, the probability of a circuit

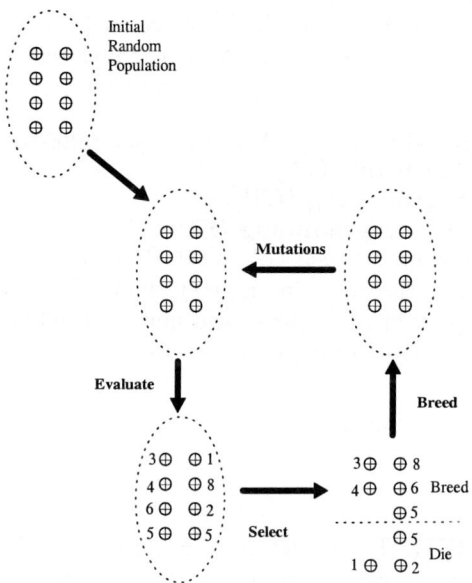

Fig. 1. The genetic algorithm.

being selected for breeding decreases with decreasing fitness score. In breeding, the parameters of the pairwise selected circuits are exchanged to generate – for each couple, two new offsprings – preferably fitter than the parents. Some of the best circuits may as well be directly copied into the next generation. Mutations may also occur and introduce changes in the chromosomes, making them slightly different from what could be obtained by only *combining* parent chromosomes. One loop in Fig. 1 is named one *generation*.

A number of industrial applications has arrived based on EHW. These are classified in this paper. The paper further includes a discussion of the properties of the present EHW and proposal of possible new directions for EHW applied to real-world applications. Much work has been undertaken on various topics related to EHW. Some considers modeling of biological systems without any specific application in mind — e.g. artificial life research. Such studies are not considered in this paper.

The next section contains a classification of EHW research based on a given classification framework. This is followed by a discussion about the limitations and possibilities in using EHW for real-world applications in Section 3. Conclusions are given in Section 4.

2 A Framework for Classifying EHW

EHW research is rapidly diverging. Thus, to understand the EHW field of research, a classification framework would be beneficial. This is presented below. The many degrees of freedom in EHW could be represented in a multidimensional space. However, here a list format is prefered.

Evolutionary Algorithm (EA). A set of major algorithms exists:
- **Genetic Algorithm (GA)**
- **Genetic Programming (GP)**
- **Evolutionary Programming (EP)**

The major difference between GA and GP is the chromosome representation. GA organizes the genes in an array, while GP applies a tree of genes. Both schemes apply both crossover and mutation, while EP – which has no contraints on the representation, uses mutation only.

Technology (TE). Technology for the target EHW:
- **Digital**
- **Analog**

Building Block (BB). The evolution of a hardware circuit is based on connecting basic units together. Several levels of complexity in these building blocks are possible:
- **Analog comp. level.** E.g. transistors, resistors, inductors and capacitors.
- **Gate level** E.g. OR and AND gates.
- **Function Level** E.g. sine generators, adders and multipliers.

Target Hardware (THW). In EHW, the goal is to evolve a circuit. The two major alternatives for target hardware available today are:
- **Commercially available devices.** FPGA (Field Programmable Gate Arrays) are most commonly used. They consist of a number of reconfigurable digital gates, which are connected by entering a binary bit string into the device. This string specifies how the gates are connected. Field-Programmable Analog Arrays (FPAA) are available as well. They use the same programming principle as FPGAs, but they consist of reconfigurable analog components instead of digital gates.
- **Custom hardware.** ASIC (Application Specific Integrated Circuit) is a chip fully designed by the user.

Fitness Computation (FC). Degree of fitness computation in hardware:
- **Offline EHW (OFL).** The evolution is simulated in software, and only the elite chromosome is written to the hardware device (sometimes named extrinsic evolution).
- **Online EHW (ONL).** The hardware device gets configured for each chromosome for each generation (sometimes named intrinsic evolution).

Evolution (EV). Degree of evolution undertaken in hardware:
- **Off-chip evolution.** The evolutionary algorithm is performed on a separate processor.
- **On-chip evolution.** The evolutionary algorithm is performed on a separate processor incorporated into the chip containing the target EHW.
- **Complete HW evolution.** The evolutionary algorithm is implemented in special hardware – i.e. not running on a processor.

Scope (SC). The scope of evolution:
- **Static evolution.** The evolution is finished before the circuit is put into normal operation. No evolution is applied during normal operation. The evolution is used as a circuit optimizing tool.
- **Dynamic evolution.** Evolution is undertaken while the circuit is in operation and this makes the circuit online adaptable.

Table 1. Characteristics of EHW applied to real-world applications.

Application	EA	TE	BB	THW	FC	EV	SC
Adaptive Equalizer [3]	GA	D	Neuron	Custom	ONL	On-chip	S
Ampl. and Filter Design [4]	GA	A	T/R/L/C	Custom	OFL	Off-chip	S
Analog Circuit Synthesis [5]	GP	A	R/L/C	Custom	OFL	Off-chip	S
Character Recognition [6]	GA	D	Gate	Comm.	OFL	Off-chip	S
Clock Adjustment [7]	GA	D	Gate	Custom	ONL	Off-chip	S
Digital Filter Design [8]	GA	D	Gate	–	OFL	Off-chip	S
IF Filter Tuning [9]	GA	A	Filter	Custom	ONL	Off-chip	S
Image Compression [10]	GA	D	Pixel	Custom	OFL	On-chip	D
Multi-spect. Image Rec. [11]	GA	D	Function	Comm.	OFL	Off-chip	S
Number Recognition [12]	GA	D	Gate	Comm.	OFL	Off-chip	S
Prosthetic Hand [13]	GA	D	Gate	Custom	ONL	Complete	S
Road Image Rec. [14]	GA	D	Gate	Comm.	OFL	Off-chip	S
Robot Control [15]	GA	D	Gate	Comm.	ONL	Complete	D
Robot Control [16]	GA	D	Gate	Comm.	ONL	Off-chip	S
Sonar Classification [17]	GA	D	Gate	Comm.	OFL	Off-chip	S

Table 1 summarizes the characteristics of the published work on EHW applied to real-world applications. The applications are mainly in the areas of classification, control and parameter tuning. A major part of them are based on digital gate level technology using GA as the evolutionary algorithm. However, promising results are given for analog designs, where evolution is used to find optimal parameters for analog components. The applicability of analog technology is further discussed in Section 3.2. About half of the experiments are based on custom hardware – or simulation of such. It is more common to put only the fitness evaluation (ONL), than the whole evolution (On-chip/Complete), on the *same* chip as the target EHW. This is reasonable, since the fitness evaluation is – as mentioned earlier, the most computational demanding part of the evolution. Many topics are relevant when discussing the EHW applicability. Several of these topics are discussed in the next section.

3 EHW Used in System Design

This section presents some of the limitations of EHW as they may be important to explain why EHW is not widely used today. Further, possible promising ways of applying EHW and evolutionary schemes are proposed.

3.1 Application of Evolvable Hardware

There are many real-world applications. Many of them may be solved *without* EHW. Thus, one would like to analyze what properties of applications make them of interest to apply EHW. That is, what a given application requires of an implemented system.

First, the scope of evolution should be determined. It must be decided if it is required that the system is online adaptable during execution or not. To make an online adaptable system, dynamic evolution should be applied. So far, only a few examples exist of dynamic evolution [10, 15]. Dynamic evolution provides a new scheme for designing systems adaptable to changes in the environment as well repairing failures in the system itself. The adaptability feature of EHW would probably be more exploited in future systems, since this feature is normally not found in traditional hardware systems. If the architecture of the system is not changing during normal operation, static evolution is used. This may still be interesting if the evolved circuit is performing *better* than a traditionally designed device. So far, only a few applications [17] using *digital* designed systems have arrived where this has been proved. However, Koza has given many successful examples of analog electric circuit synthesis by genetic programming [5]. Another example is tuning of analog filter circuits [9].

Second, if digital technology is to be used, it must be determined if there are real-time performance constraints in the application. That is, if fast – specially designed, hardware is required to run the application. If there are no such constraints, computer simulations would be a better choice. However, special demands like cost, circuit size, power consumption or reliability could still require special hardware. E.g. for high volume products, the cost could be reduced by using evolvable hardware compared to computer simulations on COTS[1] hardware. There are some successful examples showing the benefit of using EHW in real-time systems. This include image compression [10] and an prosthetic hand controller [18]. Both these are based on custom hardware.

To summarize, the directions for promising use of evolvable hardware could be when applied in online adaptable systems requiring special hardware implementations to run the application successfully. E.g. the embedded systems market is large and would probably benefit from such a technology. Further, for applications where an evolved circuit performs better[2] than a traditionally designed system should be successful as well. The important issue is that hardware

---

[1] Commercial Off The Shelf.
[2] The circuit would have to be validated based on what is the *most* important issue (e.g. cost, circuit size or power consumption) for the given application.

development in general is more time consuming and expensive than software development. Thus, when implementing an application in special hardware, there should be something to gain from it.

3.2 Evolvable Hardware Technology

One of the device families used as EHW are the Field Programmable Gate Arrays (FPGAs). Many of the limitations of applying such devices as EHW were resolved by the introduction of the Xilinx XC6200 devices. Whereas the configuration bit string coding is normally kept secret by the manufacturer, this is freely available information for the XC6200. Unfortunately, Xilinx has decided to end the production of these devices.

One area within EHW research is analog design [19]. As the world is analog in nature there would always be a need for interfacing the analog environment. However, in contrast to digital design, most of the analog circuits are still handcrafted by the experts of analog design [20]. Unfortunately, the number of people with knowledge about analog design has diminished as the vast field of digital design and computer science has appeared. Thus, EHW could be a means for making analog design more accessible. A few years ago there arrived several Field-Programmable Analog Arrays (FPAA). Experiments with online fitness evaluation in these kinds of devices have been undertaken [21,22]. The simple initial experiments are promising. However, the limited precision of the devices leads to noise that could limit the design of large or high-precision systems. The problem would be how to make such a system behave deterministically. More details about FPGAs and FPAAs applied as EHW are given in [19].

Lack of commercial hardware that can be applied as EHW may explain why as much as half of the works presented in Table 1 is based on custom hardware.

3.3 EHW as a Digital Design Tool

Digital design is an area where software tools move in the direction of providing the designer a high level input interface. The input is usually either schematic drawings and/or hardware description language code. The software performs the automatic synthesis down to the target hardware. The optimization ability of evolutionary schemes could prove to be valuable in design development tools offering input at a higher level than today. The evolutionary method should provide the following features:

1. The development time of a digital system is reduced. One would have to specify the input/output-relations rather than designing the explicit circuit. However, the problem is how to be able to cover every possible input/output relation rather than using an explicit HDL or schematic specification.
2. More complex systems can be designed. So far only small and simple circuits have been evolved. However, as new design schemes – like incremental evolution, are developed it should be possible to evolve complex circuits and systems [23].

In normal digital design, one would normally design the system for every possible combination of the inputs. However, for more complex systems, this is a near impossible task. To prove that a circuit is working correctly one would have to simulate every possible combination of the inputs. If this is an unobtainable task, one would at least try to review the design to be convinced that the design will not fail at any event. Reviewing an evolved complex system is not an easy task. Moreover, experiments have shown that evolving a circuit by using a limited number of rows in a truth table is extremely difficult [24].

These issues seem to be a bottleneck for applying evolutionary design methods as a substitute to manual digital design techniques. These are today based on using complex system designing tools offering the designer *macro* blocks, which maps effectively onto the target hardware. Few experimental results indicate that evolutionary techniques will outperform traditional digital design in the near future. To make EHW more applicable, the EHW could probably benefit from using macro blocks more complex than those that already have been applied in function level evolution.

3.4 Noise Robustness and Generalization

The gate level version of EHW is basically applying two-level signals. In comparison to neural network modeling using 32-bit floating point values, digital EHW could not normally provide the same noise robustness and generalization [6]. To improve the representation ability of EHW, each signal could be coded by a variable number of bits - using multi-valued logic [25]. This is applied in [13, 17]. If the input patterns to the system are in digital format, it would probably be interesting to investigate an architecture where an increased number of bits is used towards the output of the system. That is, the *number* of bits used for representation signals in each layer increases from input to output. This would correspond to providing more accuracy for the higher levels of the system. Detecting the values of a small number of pixels in a picture could be undertaken with a coarse accuracy compared to detecting larger objects in an image. Another option to improve the signal coding is to include time in the coding approach. That is, to attain the value of a signal, it must be observed for a certain time.

3.5 Evolving Complex Systems

The work described in Section 2 is mainly based on circuits with a limited number of building blocks. Thus, the applications have limited complexity. To solve more complex applications, the limitation in the chromosome string length must be solved [26, 27]. A long string is required for representing a complex system. However, a larger number of evolutionary generations are required as the string increases. This often makes the search space *too* large and explaines why only small circuits have been evolvable so far. Thus, work has been undertaken to try to diminish this limitation.

There are several ways of solving this problem:
- Dividing the GA.
- Compressing the chromosome string.
- Increasing the building block complexity.
- Dividing the application.

Various experiments on dividing the GA computation and using parallel processing have been undertaken [28]. The schemes involve fitness computation in parallel or a partitioned population evolved in parallel. This approach requires that GA finds a solution if it is allowed to compute enough generations. When small applications require weeks of evolution time,there would probably be strict limitations on the systems evolvable even by parallel GA.

One approach to compressing the chromosome string is by using variable length chromosome [12]. Increased building block complexity is e.g. by using higher level functions as building blocks instead of gates. Most work is based on using fixed functions as building blocks. Results from experiments using this approach are found in [29].

Dividing the application is based on the principle of divide-and-conquer. It was proposed for EHW as a way to incrementally evolve the application [23]. The scheme is called increased complexity evolution, since a system is evolved by evolving smaller sub-systems. Increased building block complexity is also a part of this approach, where the building blocks are becoming more complex as the system complexity increases. Experiments show that the number of generations required for evolution by the new method can be substantially reduced compared to evolving a system directly in one operations [6]. Considerable future work on this topic is anticipated [30]. The result of this will probably show the applicability of EHW to complex real-world applications.

3.6 The Future of EHW

Several applications have arrived based on EHW. This is both in digital and analog target technology. There seem to be two major directions for the future: First, evolution can be applied to tune the parameters of a circuit. Second, the evolution can be applied to make online adaptable real-time systems. However, the evolutionary schemes would have to be improved to overcome the limitations described in this paper. It seems like evolution will be introduced as a substitute to traditional analog design earlier than it is applied in traditional digital design.

4 Conclusions

This paper has contained a study of the characteristics of EHW applied to real-world applications. Further, limitations and possibilities of the EHW approach have been discussed. There seems to be a number of applications using analog target hardware. For the digital based applications, only small systems have been evolvable. The major reason for this seems to be the lack of schemes for evolving complex digital systems. This will be an important future research issue.

Acknowledgements

The author would like to thank the group leader Dr. Higuchi and the researchers in the Evolvable Systems Laboratory, Electrotechnical Laboratory, Japan for inspiring discussions and fruitful comments on my work, during my visit there in January-April 2000.

References

1. T. Higuchi et al. Evolvable hardware: A first step towards building a Darwin machine. In *Proc. of the 2nd Int. Conf. on Simulated Behaviour*, pages 417–424. MIT Press, 1993.
2. D. Goldberg. *Genetic Algorithms in search, optimization, and machine learning*. Addison Wesley, 1989.
3. M. Murakawa et al. The grd chip: Genetic reconfiguration of dsps for neural network processing. *IEEE Transactions on Computers*, 48(6):628–638, June 1999.
4. J.D. Lohn and S.P. Colombano. A circuit representation technique for automated circuit design. *IEEE Trans. on Evolutionary Computation*, 3(3):205–219, September 1999.
5. J. R. Koza et al. *Genetic Programming III*. San Francisco, CA: Morgan Kaufmann Publishers, 1999.
6. J. Torresen. Increased complexity evolution applied to evolvable hardware. In Dagli et al., editors, *Smart Engineering System Design: Neural Networks, Fuzzy Logic , Evolutionary Programming, Data Mining, and Complex Systems, Proc. of ANNIE'99*. ASME Press, November 1999.
7. E. Takahashi et al. An evolvable-hardware-based clock timing architecture towards gigahz digital systems. In *Proc. of the Genetic and Evolutionary Computation Conference*, 1999.
8. J. F. Miller. Digital filter design at gate-level using evolutionary algorithms. In *Proc. of the Genetic and Evolutionary Computation Conference*, 1999.
9. M. Murakawa et al. Analogue EHW chip for intermediate frequency filters. In M. Sipper et al., editors, *Evolvable Systems: From Biology to Hardware. Second Int. Conf., ICES 98*, pages 134–143. Springer-Verlag, 1998. Lecture Notes in Computer Science, vol. 1478.
10. Sakanashi et al. Evolvable hardware chip for high precision printer image compression. In *Proc. of 15th National Conference on Artificial Intelligence (AAAI-98)*, 1998.
11. R. Porter et al. An applications approach to evolvable hardware. In *Proc. of the First NASA/DoD Workshop on Evolvable Hardware*, 1999.
12. M. Iwata et al. A pattern recognition system using evolvable hardware. In *Proc. of Parallel Problem Solving from Nature IV (PPSN IV)*. Springer Verlag, LNCS 1141, September 1996.
13. I. Kajitani and other. An evolvable hardware chip and its application as a multi-function prosthetic hand controller. In *Proc. of 16th National Conference on Artificial Intelligence (AAAI-99)*, 1999.
14. J. Torresen. Scalable evolvable hardware applied to road image recognition. In *Proc. of the 2nd NASA/DoD Workshop on Evolvable Hardware*. Silicon Valley, USA, July 2000.

15. D. Keymeulen et al. On-line model-based learning using evolvable hardware for a robotics tracking systems. In *Genetic Programming 1998: Proc. of the Third Annual Conference*, pages 816–823. Morgan Kaufmann, 1998.
16. A. Thompson. Exploration in design space: Unconventional electronics design through artificial evolution. *IEEE Trans. on Evolutionary Computation*, 3(3):171–177, September 1999.
17. M. Yasunaga et al. Evolvable sonar spectrum discrimination chip designed by genetic algorithm. In *Proc. of 1999 IEEE Systems, Man, and Cybernetics Conference (SMC'99)*, 1999.
18. I. Kajitani et al. An evolvable hardware chip for prosthetic hand controller. In *Proc. of MicroNeuro'99*, pages 179 – 186, 1999.
19. J. Torresen. Evolvable hardware — The coming hardware design method? In N. Kasabov and R. Kozma, editors, *Neuro-fuzzy techniques for Intelligent Information Systems*, pages 435 – 449. Physica-Verlag (Springer-Verlag), 1999.
20. O. Aaserud and I.R. Nielsen. Trends in current analog design: A panel debate. *Analog Integrated Circuits and Signal Processing*, 7(1):–, 1995.
21. S. J. Flockton and K. Sheehan. Intrinsic circuit evolution using programmable analogue arrays. In M. Sipper et al., editors, *Evolvable Systems: From Biology to Hardware. Second Int. Conf., ICES 98*, pages 144–153. Springer-Verlag, 1998. Lecture Notes in Computer Science, vol. 1478.
22. R. S. Zebulum. Analog circuits evolution in extrinsic and intrinsic modes. In M. Sipper et al., editors, *Evolvable Systems: From Biology to Hardware. Second Int. Conf., ICES 98*, pages 154–165. Springer-Verlag, 1998. Lecture Notes in Computer Science, vol. 1478.
23. J. Torresen. A divide-and-conquer approach to evolvable hardware. In M. Sipper et al., editors, *Evolvable Systems: From Biology to Hardware. Second Int. Conf., ICES 98*, pages 57–65. Springer-Verlag, 1998. Lecture Notes in Computer Science, vol. 1478.
24. J. F. Miller and P. Thomson. Aspects of digital evolution: Geometry and learning. In M. Sipper et al., editors, *Evolvable Systems: From Biology to Hardware. Second Int. Conf., ICES 98*, pages 25–35. Springer-Verlag, 1998. Lecture Notes in Computer Science, vol. 1478.
25. T. Kalganova et al. Some aspects of an evolvable hardware approach for multiple-valued combinational circuit design. In M. Sipper et al., editors, *Evolvable Systems: From Biology to Hardware. Second Int. Conf., ICES 98*, pages 78–89. Springer-Verlag, 1998. Lecture Notes in Computer Science, vol. 1478.
26. W-P. Lee et al. Learning complex robot behaviours by evolutionary computing with task decomposition. In Andreas Brink and John Demiris, editors, *Learning Robots: Proc. of 6th European Workshop, EWLR-6 Brighton*. Springer, 1997.
27. X. Yao and T. Higuchi. Promises and challenges of evolvable hardware. In T. Higuchi et al., editors, *Evolvable Systems: From Biology to Hardware. First Int. Conf., ICES 96*. Springer-Verlag, 1997. Lecture Notes in Computer Science, vol. 1259.
28. E. Cantu-Paz. A survey of parallel genetic algorithms. *Calculateurs Parallels*, 10(2), 1998. Paris: Hermes.
29. M. Murakawa et al. Hardware evolution at function level. In *Proc. of Parallel Problem Solving from Nature IV (PPSNIV)*. Springer Verlag, LNCS 1141, September 1996.
30. J.R. Koza. Future work and practical applications of genetic programming. In *Handbook of Evolutionary Computation*, page H1.1:3. IOP Publishing Ltd and Oxford University Press, 1997.

A Co-processor System with a Virtex FPGA for Evolutionary Computation

Yoshiki Yamaguchi, Akira Miyashita, Tsutomu Maruyama,
and Tsutomu Hoshino

Institute of Engineering Mechanics and Systems, University of Tsukuba
1-1-1 Ten-ou-dai Tsukuba Ibaraki 305-8573 JAPAN
yoshiki@darwin.esys.tsukuba.ac.jp

Abstract. In this paper, we show that a co-processor system with a Virtex FPGA can achieve high performance in evolutionary computations by utilizing the two features of the FPGA. First, agents in evolutionary computation models which are usually expressed using short bit-strings can be stored in distributed select RAMs of Virtex FPGAs very efficiently. Second, the partial reconfiguration and readback functions of the FPGAs make it possible to exploit more parallelism without thinking about circuits for data I/O. The preliminary results of a model base on Iterated Prisoner's Dilemma showed that the system can achieve high performance because of the two features.

1 Introduction

In evolutionary computations, same sequences of operations are repeatedly applied to a large number of individuals (agents), and this procedure occupies the most of the computation time of evolutionary computations. Therefore, by applying the procedure to more agents in parallel using dedicated hardwares, we can expect more performance gain, but on the other hand evolutionary computations require floating point operations for controlling population of the agents though the computation time for them is very small. The circuit for the floating operations requires a lot of hardware resources, but the performance by the circuits is often worse than microprocessors. Thus, co-processing systems with a microprocessor and FPGAs are necessary for efficient processing of evolutionary computations.

Xilinx Virtex FPGAs are very suitable for evolutionary computations because of the following features. First, distributed select RAMs of the FPGAs can store bit strings very efficiently, which are usually used for the data structure of the agents in the evolutionary computations. This makes it possible to implement more agents on one FPGA, and exploit more parallelism. Second, the partial reconfiguration and readback functions of the FPGAs make it possible to use all the hardware resources for the agents without thinking about the circuits for data transfer between each agent on the FPGA and the microprocessor. Furthermore, with these functions we can access the data in distributed select RAMs very efficiently, which can be accessed only sequential by user circuits. Transferred data by the partial reconfiguration and readback includes extra informations, but the software overheads for accessing FPGAs on PCI bus are larger than the transfer time for the extra informations.

In this paper, we show that a co-processor system with a Virtex FPGA can achieve high performance in an evolutionary model based on Iterated Prisoner's Dilemma. The behavior of the model is very complex, and many interesting behaviors by the model have been reported. The behavior of the model is very sensitive to the parameters used in the model. However, the relationship between the parameters and the interesting behaviors has not been studied yet, because of the huge computation time required by the model.

This paper is organized as follows. Section 2 introduces an evolutionary computation model based on Iterated Prisoner's Dilemma. Section 3 describes the co-processing system, and preliminary evaluation results are discussed in section 4. In section 5, conclusions are given.

2 Evolution Model Based on Iterated Prisoner's Dilemma

2.1 Iterated Prisoner's Dilemma

The Prisoner's Dilemma, which is classified as a two-person non-zero sum game, is an experimental and theoretical model for investigating the problem of cooperation [5]. In the game, two agents (A and B) select one of the following moves; C (Cooperate) or D (Defect), and get each payoff according to their moves, as shown in table 1.

Table 1. Payoff Matrix for the Prisoner's Dilemma

A \ B	Cooperate	Defect
Cooperate (C)	Reward A:3 / B:3	Sucker A:0 /B:5
Defect (D)	Temptation A:5 / B:0	Punishment A:1 /B:1

In Iterated Prisoner's Dilemma, this selection of the moves is repeated. If the number of the repetition is limited and known, the game is very simple. Rational agents always select D because expected payoffs by D is higher than that of C. However, if the number of repetition of the game is unknown or unlimited, cooperative strategies have chances to get higher payoffs. When the games are played between many agents, cooperative agents can get 3 point in average each other, while a defective agent gets 5 point when played with cooperative agents, but only 1 point when played with defective agents. Therefore, the best strategy strongly depends on the environment which the agents belong to.

2.2 Lindgren's Evolution Model

Lindgren's evolution model is a very simple model based on the IPD[2, ?]. The followings are the features of the model.

1. **games based on IPD**
   (a) Each agent has a 32-bit table for its strategy, and a history of moves of the game (5 moves at maximum). Figure 1 shows the structure of an agent.
   (b) The next move of each agent is decided by reading out the value (C=0, D=1) of the strategy table using the history as an address of the table, as shown in figure 2.
   (c) Moves of an agent are transferred to its opponent with some error rate, as shown in figure 2.
   (d) Each agent plays IPD games with all other agents (round-robin).
2. **population dynamics**
   Agents that earned more payoffs will be copied according to its payoffs. Therefore, agents with less payoffs may be deleted.
3. **mutation**
   The value and length of the strategy table are changed with some probability.

The procedures above are repeated many times (one cycle is called a generation), and agents with various strategies appear and disappear throughout the simulation of the model.

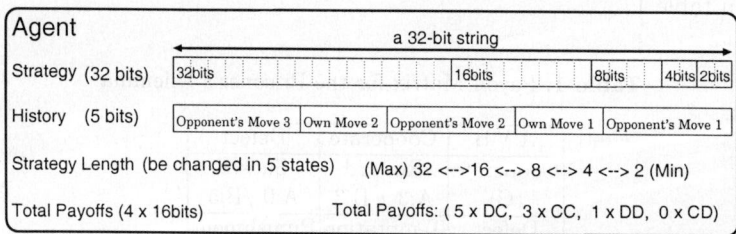

Fig. 1. Structure of an Agent

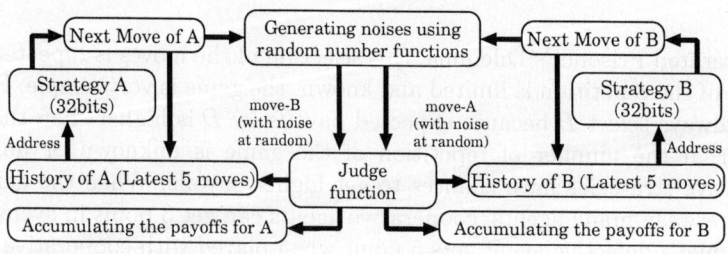

Fig. 2. Overview of a Game in Lindgren's Model

2.3 Features of the Computation of the Model

In the Lindgren's model, all agents play IPD games with all other agents. Thus, the order of the computation of the naive implementation is $N \times N$ (N is the number of agents). However, by grouping agents which have same strategy, and playing games between the groups, we can reduce the order of the computation to $g \times g$ (g is the number of groups of the agents).

Within the reasonable ranges of parameters of the Lindgren's model, most of the groups do survive into the next generation though the number of agents in each group may be changed by the population dynamics. Thus, by memorizing the results of games in previous generations, we can reduce the number of games drastically. In each generation, games only between new agents created by the mutations in the generation and agents from previous generation (agents which survived the population dynamics) are played.

Thus, the order of the computation of the games becomes $g \times n$ (n is the number of new agents), and the order of computation for updating payoffs of agents in each group becomes

1. update of payoffs of agents from previous generation
   $g \times d$
   (d is the number of groups whose number of agents are changed) +
2. update of payoffs for new agents
   $2 \times g \times n + n \times n$

When g is small, the number of agents in each group is relatively large, and almost all of the number of agents in the groups are changed in each population dynamics. Thus, d becomes very close to n, which means that the computation order is almost $n \times n$. However, when g is large, the number of agents in each group becomes small (total number of agents is N and fixed) and is not changed frequently, and d becomes relatively small compared with n.

Table 2 shows a time profiling result and the execution time per one call of each function in a C program for this model on Pentium-III 750MHz (the number of agents N is 512, and the number of the repetition in a IPD game is 8192). In this table, *IPD_game* can be easily implemented on hardwares, and high performance gain is expected. However, other functions require floating point operations (values of payoffs shown in the table 1 are all integers, but we need to change the values in order to investigate the relationship between the payoffs and the behaviors of the model). Therefore, we decided to use a microprocessor for processing those functions. With this co-processing system, we can execute *IPD_game* and *update_payoffs_of_agents_from_previous_generations* in parallel with a FPGA and a microprocessor respectively.

3 Co-processing of the Model with FPGA and Microprocessor

3.1 Virtex FPGA and the FPGA Board

We implemented the model using a FPGA board (ADC RC1000 by Alpha Data) with one Xilinx Virtex XCV1000. Figure 3 shows the block diagram of the PCI

Table 2. Time Profiling of a C program for the Model (Pentium-III 750MHz)

function name	percentage	time per call(msec)
IPD_game	99.73	0.3818
update_payoffs_of_agents_from_previous_generations	0.0944	0.0370
update_payoffs_of_agents_for_new_agents	0.0556	0.0218
population_dynamics	0.0581	0.0228
mutation	0.0622	0.0244

board. The board has four memory banks (32 bits width and 2MBytes per each block (8MBytes in total)), which can be accessed by a processor via PCI bus, and by the FPGA. The FPGA on the board can be configured through PCI bus, which means that high speed configuration is possible.

This external memories can be used for two purposes below.

1. temporal buffer for data transfer between the FPGA and the microprocessor, and
2. storing pseudo random numbers.

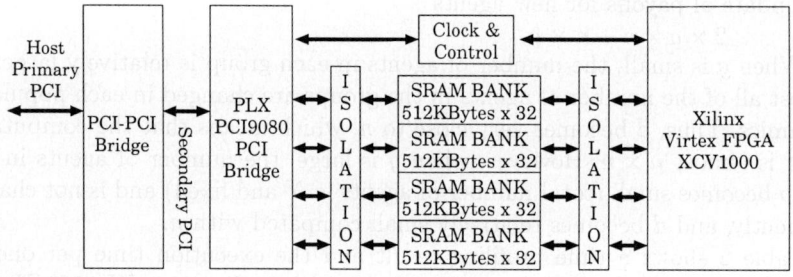

Fig. 3. PCI Board with Virtex FPGA

Xilinx Virtex FPGAs are very suitable for the model because of the following features. First, distributed select RAMs of the FPGAs can store bit strings very efficiently, which are used for the data structure of the agents. Second, the partial reconfiguration and readback functions of the FPGAs make it possible to use all the hardware resources for the agents without thinking about the circuits for data transfer between each agent on the FPGA and the microprocessor.

3.2 Implementation of Agents Using Distributed RAMs

Figure 4 shows the block diagram of the circuit for one IPD game. As shown in the figure, only strategy of each agent and counters for accumulating the number of their pairs of moves (*CC* means both players selected *C*) are implemented on the FPGA because the following reasons.

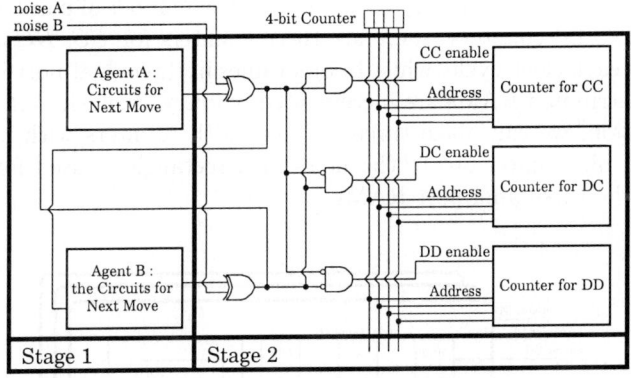

Fig. 4. circuits for playing IPD game

1. Strategy of each agent on the FPGA is duplicated so that its length becomes 32 bits. The length is necessary only for mutations which are executed on the microprocessor.
2. Values of payoffs are changed frequently and floating point values may be used in order to investigate the relation ship between the payoffs and the behavior of the model. Therefore, the circuit counts only the number of pairs of the moves. We need only the number of three pairs because the number of the repetition in a IPD game is fixed (the number of CD is $8192 - DC - DD - CC$).

The circuit is pipelined into two stages. Figure 5 and 6 show the details of each stage.

Figure 5 shows the circuit for selecting a next move of each agent. In the circuit, a strategy of an agent is stored in distributed RAMs. Five logic cells are used for keeping previous five moves and the value is given to the distributed RAMs as address.

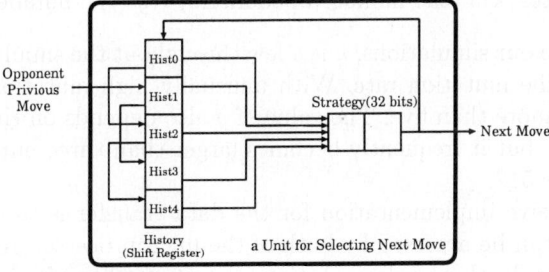

Fig. 5. circuits for selecting a next move using distributed RAMs

Figure 6 shows the circuit for accumulating the number of pairs of the moves. In the figure, 5 bit counters (there are three counters for CC, DC and DD) are incremented each clock cycle, while 16 bits values in three dual-port RAMs which consist of distributed RAMs are incremented in every 16 clock cycles. With this implementation, we can make three 16 bits-width counters with only 30 logic cells. A four bit counter out of the bold-lined rectangle is used for generating address for the three dual-port RAMs.

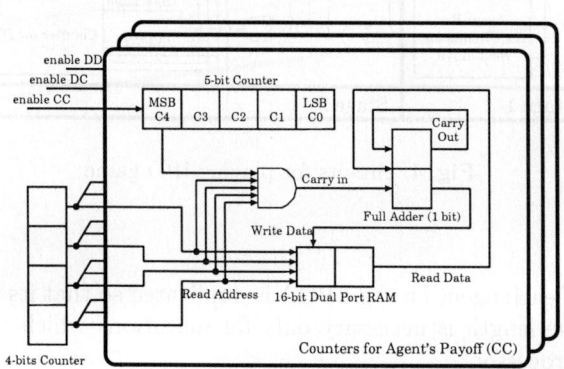

Fig. 6. circuits for accumulating agents' payoff using distributed RAMs

3.3 Data Transfer between the FPGA and the Microprocessor

The amount of data which has to be transferred between the microprocessor and the FPGA is as follows.

1. microprocessor to FPGA
   $n \times$ 4 Bytes (strategy) + 1 bit (trigger to start computation)
   (n is the number of new agents)
2. FPGA to microprocessor
   2 Bytes $\times$ 3 (the number of counters) $\times g$ (the number of groups)

According to our simulations, n is a few throughout the simulations, although it depends on the mutation rate. With unusually high mutation rate, it sometimes becomes more than five. The value of g also depends on the parameters of the simulations, but it frequently becomes larger than three hundreds when the population N is 512.

The most naive implementation for the data transfer is to use the external SRAMs which can be accessed by both of the microprocessor and the FPGA as temporal buffers. In this implementation, circuits for transferring data between the SRAMs and the circuits in the figure 5 and 6 become necessary. The system performance is decreased by these circuits because of the following reasons.

1. **data transfer time**
   In the circuits shown in the figure 5 and 6, strategies of agents and the number of the pairs of their moves are stored in distributed RAMs, which can be accessed only sequentially. Furthermore, we need to transform the bit-sequences to 16(32) bits data so that the microprocessor can read them as 16(32) bits data. (This operation can be executed by the microprocessor, but its speed is much slower than the FPGA).
2. **size of the circuit for data transfer**
   The size of the data transfer circuits is not small. First, more than a few hundreds of circuits for IPD games can be implemented on the FPGA. Therefore, we need an address decoder which can specify one of a few hundreds of circuits. Second, the circuit for data transformation described above requires a lot of hardware resources if we try to reduce its time.

Xilinx Virtex FPGAs support partial reconfiguration and readback functions. By these functions, we can directly access to the data in distributed RAMs without any circuits for data transfer. We can use all hardware resources on the FPGA for IPD games.

The data transfer speed by the functions is slower than the speed by external SRAMs because of the limited I/O width (8 bit), and extra data are transferred when we use these functions. However, software overheads for accessing the FPGA on PCI bus are relatively large, and the speed down by the slow transfer speed and by sending more amount of data is not critical.

4 Evaluation Results

According to our simulation of the evolutional model, the number of groups (g) is about 430 at maximum when the total number of agents (N) is 512.

When we use the external SRAMs for data transfer, we could not implement so many circuits for IPD games on one XCV1000. Therefore, we added two LUTs (for another strategy) and one 1-bit selector to the figure 5. By this modification, we can compute two games with one circuit though the computation times become twice. This circuit runs at 33 MHz. Figure 7 shows the result of time analysis when g (number of the groups) is 384, and n (number of the new agents) is 2. In the figure 7, the computation for the IPD games still occupies the most of the computation time. The data transfer time is relatively large even if only 9 Byte (4 Byte × 2 + 1 bit) is sent to the FPGA because of the software overheads. Speed gain compared with Pentium-III 750MHz is 213 times.

When we use the partial reconfiguration and readback functions, we can implement 480 circuits for IPD games, and it runs at 30 MHz. Therefore, we can process all the IPD games at once. Figure 8 shows the estimated timing analysis result (the functions are still under development). In the figure 8, times for the parts covered with oblique lines are estimated based on accessing time from microprocessor to the FPGA and transfer speed of configuration data. The expected speedup is more than 440 times.

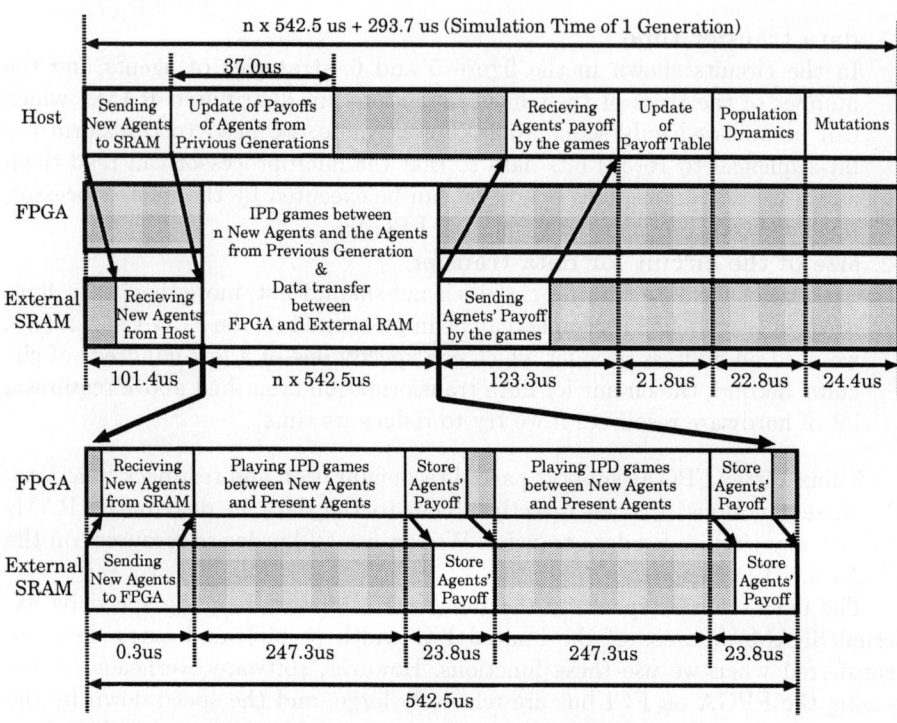

Fig. 7. Timing Analysis 1 (256 parallel × 2)

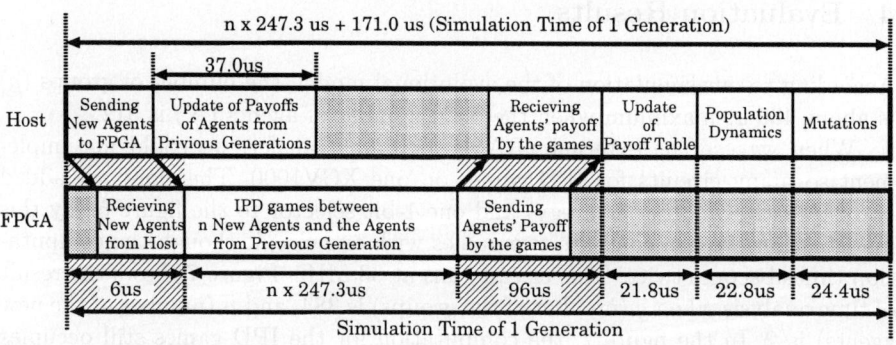

Fig. 8. Timing Analysis 2 (480 parallel)

5 Conclusions

In this paper, we showed that a co-processing system with a Virtex FPGA can achieve high performance gain because of the distributed select RAMs and the partial reconfiguration and readback functions.

The speed gain for functions which are executed by one Virtex XCV1000 is more than one thousand times compared with Pentium-III 750MHz, though the total performance gain remains about 200 times (when we use the partial reconfiguration and readback functions, more than 400 times of speed gain is expected). This is caused by the slow data transfer speed between the FPGA on the PCI bus and the microprocessor, and some functions which have to be executed sequentially on the microprocessor. We need more tightly coupled system for higher performance which can fully utilize high performance of the FPGA.

The partial reconfiguration and readback functions on the system is now under development and we could not measure the exact time, but it is clear that by these functions we can achieve higher performance by processing more agents in parallel.

References

1. Henry Styles and Wayne Luk, "Customising Graphics Applications: Techniques and Programming Interface", Field-Programmable Custom Computing Machines, 2000.
2. K. Lindgren, "Evolutionary Phenomena in Simple Dynamics", Artificial Life II, pp.295-312, 1991.
3. K. Lindgren and M. G. Nordah, "Cooperation and Community Structure in Artificial Ecosystems" Artificial Life 1, pp.15-37, 1994.
4. T.Maruyama, T.Funatsu and T.Hoshino, "A Field Programmable Gate-Array System for Evolutionary Computation" FPL'98 pp.356-365
5. W. Poundstone, "Prisoner's Dilemma : John von Neumann, Game Theory, and the Puzzle of the Bomb.", Oxford University Press, 1993.

System Design with Genetic Algorithms

C. Bauer, P. Zipf, and H. Wojtkowiak

Universität Siegen
Fachbereich Elektrotechnik und Informatik
Fachgruppe Technische Informatik
D-57068 Siegen / Germany
bauer@ti.et-inf.uni-siegen.de

Abstract. There are various ways to use genetic algorithms in system design. In this paper we present two approaches: genetic algorithms for partitioning the system into hardware and software and using genetic algorithms for implementing hardware on an FPGA. By using genetic algorithms for the partitioning of the system it is possible to integrate fault tolerance automatically into the system. Developing hardware with genetic algorithms provides the possibility to create various alternatives, usable in the partitioning phase. Also fault ignoring implementations can be developed.

1 Introduction

Nowadays system design is getting more and more complex, too complex for a designer to survey all relevant aspects of the design. It is especially difficult to involve fault tolerance measures in the design without consuming too much resources of the system. But fault tolerance is a often required characteristic of the system. To ease the design process hardware software codesign is a commonly used design methodology.

In hardware software codesign the keyphase is the partitioning of the system into the hardware and the software components. To find the best solution has shown to be a very complex problem. We also try to involve fault tolerance measures into this step. For this we use genetic algorithms. They are able to scan the solution space and they provide natural fault tolerance.

For the partition phase various alternatives are needed for the hardware and the software modules. To gain as different implementations as possible we try to also develop the hardware module with genetic algorithms. So we can leave the traditional ways of implementing a function and get new insights about more optimal implementations of functions. Genetic algorithms provide more than one solution at the same time, usable for the partition phase. To get a rating for the genetic algorithm we use a Verilog model of the FPGA XC6216.

The first part of this paper describes the partitioning with genetic algorithms and the second part the development of a function on an FPGA with genetic algorithms.

2 System Design

Hardware software codesign supports the designer in the implementation especially of a larger system. He only needs to specify the system in a specification language. A fully automated codesign system uses the description, identifies the modules, decides which modules are to be implemented in hardware and which in software and produces an adequate description for them. Usually the output is in the form of a hardware description language and software code.

The partitioning is a keyphase in the codesign process. Deciding which components are implemented in hardware and which in software has proven to be difficult to automate. But partitioning is not only a decision, whether the component should be realized in hardware or in software. In addition there is the possibility of extended partitioning. Not only the hardware software decision for an element of the system is made, but also the way the element is to be implemented is chosen. Functions can be realized in different variants. Components, that differ in speed, area etc., are able to perform the same functionality and even different algorithms for one function may be available.

Partitioning takes place at different levels of the system. Larger components can perform the same function as a group of simpler components. We use a specification of the system in the form of a data flow graph as shown in figure 1. The nodes of the graph signify the smallest parts of the system, the functional elements. The elements are parts of the systems that cannot be further divided into smaller parts.

The possible parts of a system realized as one block are called modules. Modules stand for either functional elements or more complex subsystems. In the partitioning process it has to be decided which modules, simple elements, or subsystems are better suited for the function. Finding the optimal solution for partitioning the system in the solution space turns out to be a complex covering problem. For this problem we use genetic algorithms, which have the advantage of additional fault tolerance measures.

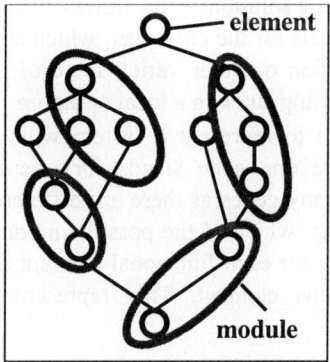

Fig. 1 The Data Flow Graph

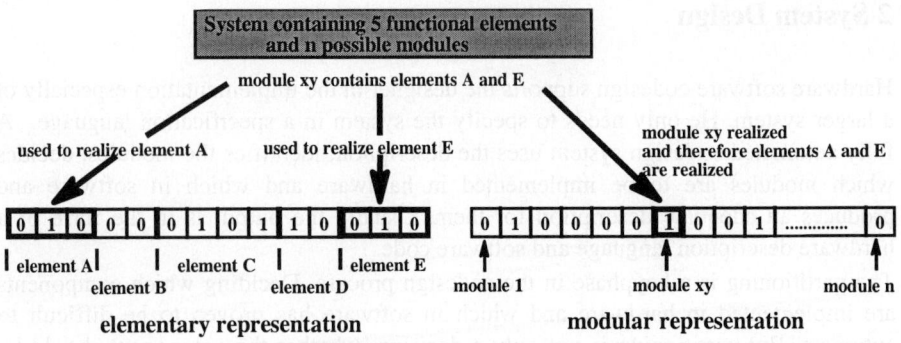

Fig. 2 Elementary versus Modular Trepresentation

3 Partitioning the System with Genetic Algorithms

To use the potential of the partitioning algorithm all elements and parts of the system must be known. The algorithm uses the cost, the time, the needed amount of fault tolerance and, with complex modules, the elements they include. The user defines them in a file, which is processed in the partitioning step. One method to generate different alternatives is shown in chapter 4. For scheduling the modules the order of functional elements is also needed and is also listed in the file. All modules are represented in a genetic algorithm deciding which of them is used for the realization of the system.

3.1 Representation of the System

A genetic algorithm finds a solution for a problem by developing a pool of random solutions towards an acceptable one. One possible solution is called a chromosome and is an individual of the pool of solutions, the population. Individuals are improved by various operators, especially the fitness function, crossover and mutation. These functions are applied to the chromosomes of one generation and create a new, expectedly better, generation of solutions. The fitness function rates the individuals and with this chooses individuals for the crossover, which combines some individuals to get a new one. The mutation operator varies some of these new individuals to prevent the algorithm from getting stuck in a local optimum.

There are several possibilities to represent a system with a chromosome. In [5] a representation is used, where one gene stands for one functional element. The chromosome consists of as many genes as there are different elements in the system specification. Each gene marks, which of the possible modules realizes this element. The length of the genes varies for each functional element depending on the number of modules implementing this element. This representation will be called an „elementary representation".

Another possibility to represent a system with a chromosome is to use one bit for each module, which is called the „modular representation" of a system (see figure 2). A „1" in a gene means the realisation of this module, with a „0" the module is not contained in the system. This has the consequence that all possible modules must be described in advance with all their characteristics by the designer. A later addition of possible modules results in a modification of the chromosome length and therewith in a modification of the settings of the algorithm.

Also a chromosome of the modular representation is larger than one of the elementary. But one great advantage of the modular representation is the availability of the natural fault tolerance of genetic algorithms. In contrast to the elementary representation there is a direct relation between mutations and faults. The natural fault tolerance of genetic algorithm comes from the gathering of the individuals on so called fitness plateaus. With the progression of the genetic algorithm the individuals become more and more similar. And they become more and more „fit", i.e. the value the fitness function returns changes for the better. Thus the individuals are somewhat similar and most of them have a good fitness. If a change, i.e. a mutation, occurs in one individual, it mostly changes toward another individual, different only in some bits. So the fitness of the mutated individual still is a good one. A change of a bit from „1" to „0" means, that the module is no longer contained in the system. This can be seen as a fault of the module, it no longer fulfils its function. But the fitness has likely not worsen. So the system still is functioning, it is insensitive toward faults.

To implement active fault tolerance within the system, there must be a possibility to insert redundancy, i.e. duplicate modules, and encode this in the chromosome. To get more than one representation of a module a new fault tolerant module is created, which stands for the multiple implementation of the old module. From different implementation alternatives for one module a number of fault tolerant modules can be extracted by combining this alternatives. It has to be considered, that in software it is only reasonable to combine different implementations of the module. In hardware a similar implementation can be used to form a fault detecting or fault masking module. We do not regard the combination of hardware and software modules because of the more difficult result comparison. With increasing numbers of alternatives the number of new modules rises significantly. Be n_{hi} the number of hardware alternatives and n_{si} the number of software alternatives of module i, then there are $n_{hi}^3 + n_{hi}^2 + n_{si}^3 - 2n_{si}^2 + n_{si}$ newly generated fault tolerant modules.

Within the elementary representation the new modules must be appended to the original list of modules. The number of alternatives of a functional element grows with $O(n_{hi}^3 + h_{si}^3)$. But the length of the chromosome only increases by $\log_2$ of this term.

In the modular representation another strategy for implementing fault tolerance is required. Fault masking requires at least three implementations of a module. If the number is limited to this, fault tolerant modules have a simple representation in the modular representation. Each module can be implemented, 0, 1, 2 or 3 times in the system, which is coded with two binary digits. To get a fault tolerant module representation only two bits instead of one for one module is needed. This new representation has the ability to represent all modules in a fault detecting or fault masking way. The length of the chromosome is only doubled in comparison to the old representation. Wether the modules for the fault tolerance are similar or different implementations decides the fitness function on the basis of how many different modules with the same functionality are realized.

3.2 The Fitness Function

The fitness function specifies the individuals that are more likely to spread their genes into the next generation by giving them a greater fitness value. To determine the fitness of one individual several qualities of the modules must be considered. The time and the cost of the modules can simply be added to the fitness value. The cheaper a module is and the less time it needs, the better the system and therefore the better the fitness of the individual. We use the fitness as an reciprocal value: Individuals with a lower fitness value are more likely to survive.

In the modular representation it is possible that one functional element is not covered by a module and the system does not fulfil its specified functionality. This is impossible in the elementary representation, because each gene corresponds to one module realizing this element. Because of the desired full range functionality of the system we have to add a penalty for each missing functional element. This is done by simply adding a penalty value to the fitness value.

If one functional element is implemented more than once in the system, this solution cannot be considered as optimal. The time this module needs for the execution and the cost of this module is added several times to the fitness value so that the fitness gets worse. If multiple implementations are desired because of fault tolerance aspects, the fitness has to be adapted. We use a factor for the desired fault tolerance. The fitness is divided by this factor, if the corresponding module is implemented more than once in the module representation or if the fault tolerant module is used in the elementary representation. With this factor the user can define, what amount of cost or time he is willing to invest into the fault tolerance. The greater this factor is the less interesting are the additional costs and time.

With these conditions the fitness is described as follows:

$$\frac{cost+cost\_time\_weighting \cdot time}{1+\frac{fault\_tolerance}{100}}+penalty$$

- cost: The added cost of all included modules plus the cost for all additional components for fault detection and masking.
- time: the added execution time of all included modules plus the execution time for all additional components for fault detection and masking.
- cost_time_weighting: A factor to set different weighting between cost and time influence in the fitness of the individual.
- fault_tolerance: The added fault tolerance factor of all modules, that have been defined to require fault tolerance.
- penalty: This value is set, whenever not all functional elements have been included in the system by this chromosome. The value can be changed in order to get different results off the algorithm.

To get the real execution time of the system, we have to consider the Data Flow Graph. This graph defines the execution order of the functional elements. In the final system realization not only functional elements are implemented but also complex modules. But these modules do not occur in the Data Flow Graph. We have to merge the functional elements of the original graph in such a way that the elements and modules that are coded by the chromosome are contained (see figure 3). This is possible, if every functional element is only realized once in the system. Two or three realizations are allowed for fault tolerance. This condition is automatically fulfilled in the elementary representation. The modular representation has to take some sanctions to determine which modules constitute the modular graph.

With the new modular graph the modules building the system are defined and every module has its successor. The next step to calculate the system time is the scheduling. The hardware is realized in a way, that all hardware modules can be executed in parallel and so only the scheduling of the software has to be considered. The start time of every software module is determined by adding the execution times of all predecessors on a direct path from the initial module to the actual module. If there is more than one way the longest alternative is chosen. We assume a one processor system, hence only one software module can be executed at a time. Software modules may clash with the starting time of other software modules. In this case the module that started later is delayed and gets a new starting time. The starting times of all successors have to be recalculated.

The user of the genetic algorithm can define several parameters. With the cost–time–weighting factor he can strengthen the influence of either the execution time or the cost of the system. If there is a maximum for time or cost the algorithm takes this into consideration. This is especially useful, if the hardware is a Field Programmable Gate Array (FPGA) with limited hardware resources. For each component a fault tolerance factor between 1 and 10 is given by the user. The larger the value, the more likely all individuals of the population choose the fault tolerant version of the component. Values greater than 10 restrict the genetic algorithm too much. In a system with more than one processor the algorithm can allow more than one software component to be executed at a time. The number of the processors is defined by the user. Variation of the penalty factor for the absence of a functional unit changes the searching width of the genetic algorithm and the number of generations needed to find an adequate solution.

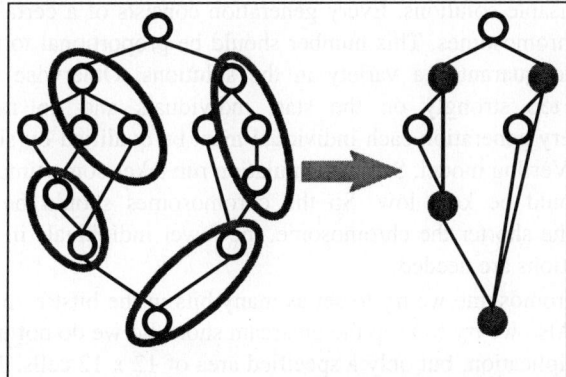

Fig. 3 Converting the elementary graph into the modular graph

4 Implementing Hardware with Genetic Algorithms

In our codesign approach FPGAs are used for the realization of the designed hardware parts. There are many different ways to implement a given design on an FPGA. Especially if the FPGA is not used completely, that is not all cells or all routing resources are used, the number of alternatives for the design is very high. To find the most suitable solution we use genetic algorithms. Since we want to use many characteristics of FPGAs for fault tolerance measures, we use the Xilinx FPGA XC6216 with all its features.

The rating of a found solution is very difficult, so we need to investigate it on the FPGA itself. The FPGA must be programmed with the bitstream from the genetic algorithm and the result must be evaluated. The Xilinx XC6216 has 4096 cells and therefore there are too many alternatives to code them in a genetic algorithm. Also the rating of the received results is very difficult. By testing the output of the FPGA you get only a binary rating: it fulfils its functionality or not. Since we also wanted to automatize the algorithm we did not use a real FPGA but a Verilog model ([3], [8]). With this model we are able to get the value of internal lines of the FPGA and therefore improve the rating of the implementations. Also the genetic algorithm can automatically start the simulation and get the result the FPGA returns.

Alternatively we can use a simplified model of the configured cicuit that is extracted from the configuration bitstream by a softwaretool we implemented. This way, the simulation is faster but missing some details, like the control logic of the FPGA.

The problem we tried to implement with genetic algorithms on a XC6216 is a simple multiplication with only small numbers. The genetic algorithm starts with a random bitstream to program the FPGA. This bitstream is then improved by the algorithm to form a solution satisfying the specification.

4.1 The Bitstream

To configure a complete XC6216 with 4096 cells and all routing resources, each cell with the surrounding routing resources is programmed with 9 Bytes, so a bitstream of 9 x 4096 Byte is needed. This bitstream is developed by the genetic algorithm as a chromosome. The longer a chromosome in a genetic algorithm, the more generations are needed to get usable solutions. Every generation consists of a certain number of individuals resp. chromosomes. This number should be proportional to the length of the chromosome to guarantee a variety in the solutions. Otherwise the obtained solutions depend too strongly on the start individuals and do not cover all possibilities. In every generation each individual must be qualified by simulating the bitstream with the Verilog model. Since a simulation run takes some time, the number of simulations should be kept low. So the chromosomes should be as short as possible, because the shorter the chromosome, the fewer individuals in a generation and the less generations are needed.

To get a shorter chromosome we try to set as many bits in the bitstream with a fixed value as possible. Also we try to keep the bitstream short. So we do not use the whole FPGA for the multiplication, but only a specified area of 12 x 12 cells. 12 x 12 gates are sufficient to implement the multiplication. The area in the FPGA ranges from row 52 to row 63 and from column 0 to column 11 (see figure 4). Only these 12 x 12 = 144 cells are configured by the genetic algorithm and therefore are available for the multiplication. Using only this part of the FPGA reduces the bitstream to 144 x 9 = 1296 Bytes. With the Verilog model of the FPGA we are able to simulate only these cells by instantiating only these blocks. For later verification of the solution the bitstream can be simulated in the complete model.

Most of the Bytes for one cell are used for programming the switches of the routing resources. But only the cells at the edges of a 4x4 and a 16x16 Block have access to these switches. The cells inside the blocks do not use these Bytes. So these Bytes need not to be programmed and are left out in the bitstream. The Bytes programming the routing switches contain some unused bits, bits that are not assigned to a multiplexer. These Bits can be set to a default value. The same applies to the Bytes programming the IOBs. These Bytes are only used in the cells of row 62 and column 1. And by defining the input and output pins in advance, these Bytes can be predefined. Our multiplication problem requires only combinatorial solutions. So we can the combinations of the cell to the 4 not using the internal flipflop. With all the default values the size of the chromosome can be reduced to less than 5000 bits. The bits of the chromosome are splitted into groups and inserted into the bitstream between the predefined bits.

In the first version of our algorithm, we want to test its usability. So we reduced the routing resources to a minimum by using only the neighbourhood lines and the Fast–Lane–4. All Bytes programming the Fast–Lanes–16 and the chip length lines were left out. This decreased the download time of the bitstream and the length of the generated chromosome to approx. one half.

4.2 The Rating

The fitness function of the genetic algorithm loads the developed bitstream into the Verilog model of the FPGA by starting the Verilog simulator. To the inputs of the

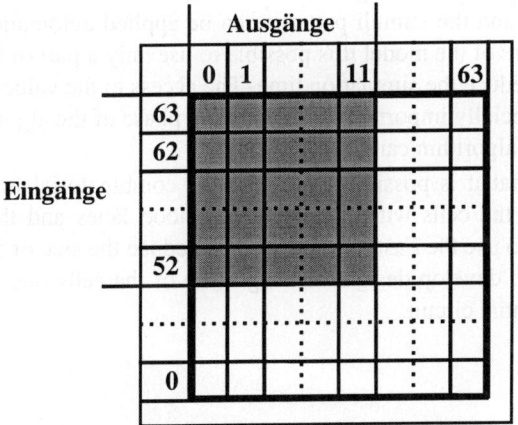

Fig. 4 The Allocation of the FPGA

FPGA stimuli patterns are applied. The patterns are all combinations of the multiplied bit words. The values on the output pins are loaded back into the evaluation function of the genetic algorithm and are compared with the expected values. The greater the difference between the expected value and the real one the worse the fitness value gets. By generating the fitness value it has proven, that not only the recieved result must be considered. Also the variation of the single bits is important. So we used a combination between a horizontal fitness for the variation and a vertical fitness for the correct result.

At the beginning of the algorithm the population only consists of random individuals. There is a great gap between a random bitstream and a reasonable configuration that produces at least some changing output bits. To bridge this gap, we also rate some internal lines of the chip, the Fast–Lanes over 4 Cells. Lines with a not defined value („z" or „x") raise the fitness of a chromosome. So the individuals converge toward a solution, that performs a function at the output.

Even with all the restrictions we made to the bitstream, one run of the genetic algorithm takes quite a time. The recieved results showed, that the flipflops in the cell have a too large influence on the result. So we left the flipflops unused in the programming.

4.3 Results

With the usage of the genetic algorithm it is possible to generate different alternatives for a hardware realization. Taking the example described above you can delete cells in the used area of the FPGA and thus simulate a fault. Alternatives that leave defined cells out can be developed by the genetic algorithm. The algorithm only uses the specified cells of the model. The different alternatives can be used for a fault tolerant system by reconfiguring the FPGA after a fault in one cell has occurred.

Also the genetic algorithm is able to generate alternatives that need smaller or larger areas of the FPGA. These alternatives can be taken into account from the partitioning algorithm of the codesign environment.

As shown above, it is a great advantage to use the Verilog model for verifying the developed bitstreams. The Verilog simulation can be started from within the genetic algorithm program and the stimuli patterns can be applied automatically. Due to the hierarchical structure of the model it is possible to use only a part of the FPGA for the evaluation and so reduce the simulation time. The access to the values of internal lines of the FPGA is especially important for the starting phase of the algorithm. With it the convergence of the algorithm can be improved.

We have shown, that it is possible to develop an combinatorial implementation by programming only the cells with their neighbourhood lanes and the Fast–Lanes–4. The next steps are to use the FastLanes as well, to reduce the size of the occupied area in the FPGA and to develop designs leaving some of the cells out. Also we want to implement a sequential circuit.

5 Conclusion

With our approach it is possible to partition a system automatically and insert fault tolerance measures. The fault tolerance measures are at one side the natural fault tolerance of the genetic algorithm and on the other side active fault tolerance specified by the user. Furthermore we can generate different implementations for a hardware module with one run of the genetic algorithm. It is possible to specify these alternatives in a way that they use particular cells of the FPGA only. They can be used by an external unit ([9]) to bypass detected faults in the FPGA hardware by not using the faulty cells for the function.

For future use we want to simplify the usage of the Verilog model by accessing it via the Verilog Programming Language Interface. At the time being one run of the model takes about 30 seconds. Regarding the needed number of runs for the genetic algorithm this is much too long. As another alternative to gain time it is imaginable to rewrite the Verilog model in a high level programming language like C or C++. The access from the genetic algorithm program would be much faster, but some implementation details would be lost. A third possibility, already imlemented, is the above mentioned extraction of the function from the bistream. With this the functionality of the generated bitstream can be obtained very fast.

References

[1] C. Bauer, P. Zipf, H. Wojtkowiak. Fault Tolerance with Genetic Algorithms in Hardware Software Codesign. In Elektronik Praxis: HighSys '99

[2] C. Bauer, P. Zipf, H. Wojtkowiak. Integration von Fehlertoleranz im Codesign. In Proc. Third ITG/GI/GMM-Workshop, 2000

[3] A. Glasmacher. Entwurf und Implementierung der Zellmatrix eines FPGAs als Verilogmodell. Studienarbeit, Universität Siegen, 2000

[4] E. Maehle and F.-J. Markus. Fault-tolerant dynamic task scheduling based on dataflow graphs. In Proc. 2nd Annual Workshop on Fault-Tolerant Parallel and Distributed Systems, 1998

[5] D. Sahe, R. S. Miha and A. Basu. Hardware software partitioning using genetic algorithm. In VLSI Design, 1997

[6] A. Thompson. Evolving fault tolerant systems. In First IEE/IEEE International Conference on Genetic Algorithms in Engineering Systems, Sheffield, 1995

[7] A. Thompson. Evolutionary techniques for fault tolerance. In Proc. UKACC Int. Conf. on Control 1996

[8] K. Woska. Entwurf und Implementierung der Steuerlogik eines FPGAs als Verilogmodell. Studienarbeit, Universität Siegen, 2000

[9] P. Zipf, C. Bauer, H. Wojtkowiak. A Hardware Extension to Improve Fault Handling in FPGA-Based Systems. In Proc. DDECS , 2000

Implementing Kak Neural Networks on a Reconfigurable Computing Platform

Jihan Zhu and George Milne

cisjz@cs.unisa.edu.au, milne@cis.unisa.edu.au

Advanced Computing Research Centre, School of Computer and Information Science, University of South Australia. Mawson Lakes, Adelaide, South Australia 5095, Australia

Abstract. The training of neural networks occurs *instantaneously* with Kak's corner classification algorithm CC4. It is based on *prescriptive* learning, hence is extremely fast compared with iterative supervised learning algorithms such as backpropagation. This paper shows that the Kak algorithm is hardware friendly and is especially suited for implementation in reconfigurable computing using fine grained parallelism. We also demonstrate that on-line learning with the algorithm is possible through dynamic evolution of the topology of a Kak neural network.

1 Introduction

Neural networks are parallel, distributed information processing systems in which learning replaces programming. Neural networks have a pre-specified layered structure composed of interconnected neurons, together with a learning algorithm to adapt both the strength of the interconnections (i.e. the weights) and the way the neurons are connected (i.e. the topology). Parallelism, modularity and dynamic adaptation are the three main computational characteristics of neural networks, which respectively refer to: neurons in the same layer process information simultaneously; each neuron performs the same type of computation (i.e. the whole network can be partitioned into an assembly of basic modules); both weights and the topology of a network are adjusted dynamically. These computational characteristics suggest that a highly concurrent and flexible hardware architecture is ideal for implementing neural networks. We argue that neural networks map nicely to FPGA based reconfigurable computing architecture as we can exploit concurrency and can rapidly reconfigure to adapt their weights and topologies.

The successful realization of artificial neural networks in reconfigurable computing has been very limited, however, due to the difficulties in implementing learning algorithms. There are two main reasons for this. The first is related to the nature of the learning algorithms while the second is related to the granularity and the complexity of learning algorithms. There is a clear need to identify suitable learning algorithms for implementing neural networks on reconfigurable computing platforms.

The training of neural networks is a complex task with most design approaches depending heavily on simulation. Part of the difficulty lies with the empirical nature of the supervised learning algorithms such as backpropagation where topologies and weights are explored through a process of trial and error[1]. This often involves building prototypes with different neural topologies and initial sets of weights, and then simulating these prototypes in software for many iterations until a network is found to have performed satisfactorily according to some training criterion. Because neural computation is computationally intensive, this empirical process can be extremely time-consuming.

Although the hardware acceleration of the traditional learning algorithms permits some parallelism to be exploited[2, 3], the whole training process still remains iterative and empirical. Furthermore, the learning algorithms are not hardware friendly because of the costly multiplications needed for computing the dot-product between the weights and the inputs to at least integer precisioned granularity. Due to their complexity, a faithful realization of the learning algorithms in FPGA-based reconfigurable hardware leads to huge designs which often do not fit onto the limited hardware resource. Also, such implementations are difficult to scale up with increased precision and neuron counts. Although implementations of neural networks based on bit stream arithmetic[4, 5] simplify the costly multiplications, appropriate learning algorithms have yet to be devised to support on-chip learning. As a consequence, training must be done off-line.

Instantaneously trained neural networks (ITNN) as proposed by Kak[6, 7] use a *prescriptive* learning algorithm which determines both the topology and weights of the network just by a simple inspection of the training samples. This is a major improvement over traditional learning algorithms because no costly iterations are needed. The model of ITNN is motivated by a biologically plausible mechanism for short-term memory in which biological learning occurs instantaneously. The learning algorithm used with the ITNN is called the corner classification algorithm CC4 (referred to as the Kak algorithm hereafter). Comparative studies in software simulation have shown that the Kak algorithm is up to 200 times faster than the backpropagation algorithms with comparable generalization capability in pattern recognition and prediction tasks[8].

In this paper, we show that the Kak algorithm is well suited for implementation in reconfigurable computing using fine grained parallelism. We also demonstrate that online learning with the algorithm is possible by dynamic evolution of the topology of a Kak neural network. Section 2 describes the Kak algorithm. Section 3 presents an implementation for the Kak algorithm on a reconfigurable computing platform. Section 4 demonstrates a possible implementation strategy for evolvable hardware-based incremental learning with ITNN. Section 5 presents the conclusions.

2 Learning in ITNN

ITNN models the biological short-term memory in which all training samples are faithfully represented in hardware memory by allocating one neuron for each training sample. In ITNN, each hidden neuron acts as a correlator to its own training sample, which produces a high correlation score to its own training sample, and does not correlate with all other training samples. The network as a whole is a logical combination of those correlators and hence maps for the training samples to their desired classifications.

2.1 Specification of ITNN Topology and Weights

Given a training sample set, the Kak algorithm determines directly the topology and weights of an ITNN. An example of an ITNN is illustrated in Fig. 1. The Kak algorithm assumes a three layer feed-forward neural architecture consisting of binary neurons.

These three layers are the input, hidden and output layers. A bias neuron is introduced to the input layer so that the threshold values for all hidden neurons are set to 0 for simplicity. The bias neuron receives a constant value of 1 as input and is therefore is always stimulated. The required number of input neurons is the length of the input vector plus 1 for the bias neuron. The number of hidden neurons equals the number of samples in the training set (i.e. each hidden neuron represents one training sample). The required number of output neurons equals the desired number of outputs.

With the topology of the network specified, assigning weights for the network is done by simply inspecting the training samples. Let x_{ij} be the jth bit of the ith input vector which is n bits long including the extra bit for the bias input. Since every bit in the input vector corresponds to one neuron in the input layer, and every training sample corresponds to one neuron in the hidden layer, j, i are also the indices for neurons in the input and hidden layers respectively. The assignment for weights w_{ij} from the jth input neuron to the ith neuron in the hidden layer is defined according to the equation(1):

$$w_{ij} = \begin{cases} 1 & \text{if } x_{ij} = 1 \\ -1 & \text{if } x_{ij} = 0 \\ r-s+1 & \text{if } j = n \end{cases} \quad (1)$$

when $j = n$ the bias weights $w_{in} = r-s+1$, where s is the total number of 1s in the ith input training vector and r is the desired radius of generalization. Similarly, let o_{ik} be the kth desired output for the ith input vector, and k be the index for the neurons in the output layer, then the assignment for weights v_{ik} from neurons in the hidden layer to neurons in the output is given according to equation (2):

$$v_{ik} = \begin{cases} 1 & \text{if } o_{ik} = 1 \\ -1 & \text{if } o_{ik} = 0 \end{cases} \quad (2)$$

Fig. 1 demonstrates the results of prescribing weights and topology for the ITNN to perform an example of input-output mapping tabulated in Table 1, assuming $r = 0$.

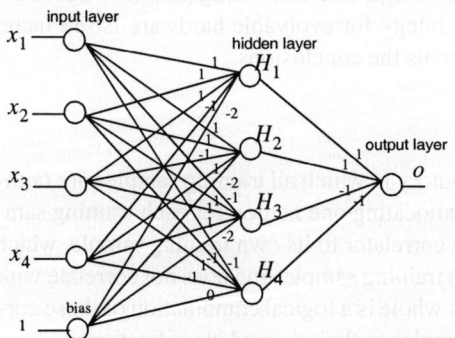

Table 1: Input/output mapping

input				output
x_1	x_2	x_3	x_4	o
1	1	1	0	1
1	1	0	1	1
0	1	1	1	0
0	0	1	0	0

Fig. 1 An example of learning in ITNN.

2.2 Learning and Generalisation with ITNN

The Kak algorithm can be considered from two perspectives: the radius of generalization $r > 0$ and $r = 0$. When $r = 0$, the ITNN does not generalize, it merely remembers the training samples. This is obvious because the way the weights have been assigned ensures each hidden neuron acts as a filter which is only correlated with its own training sample and is not correlated to all other training samples. ITNN generalizes when $r > 0$. The value r is called the radius of generalization because it sets a tolerance: if the *hamming distance* between an input vector and its corresponding weight vector is less than r then the probing input vector is treated as being sufficiently close to the stored training sample and will trigger the same response from the network. It is also relevant to point out that an ITNN can be trained to perform real valued input-output mappings if the real values are coded into binary format.

3 Implementation

The ITNN model is based on biological short-term memory which is characterised by two aspects: instantaneous learning and limited capacity. The second aspect, limited capacity, comes about because each hidden neuron is used to represent one sample in the training set. This aspect presents difficulty to the hardware implementation of ITNN because the size of the hidden layer is $O(t)$ where t is the number of the training samples. When there are many training examples the ITNN size can be very large. The following strategies are used to alleviate this difficulty:
- increasing FPGA gate efficiency and the modularity of the implementation by serializing the computation of a neuron,
- efficient use of hardware resources by re-using the same hardware for both the training stage and the execution stage, and
- time-multiplexing hardware neurons.

These strategies are discussed after the overall implementation plan has been described.

3.1 An Overview of the Implementation

The implementation is carried out on a Space2 reconfigurable computing platform [9, 10] which consists of a DEC Alpha host machine and a coprocessing board composed of an array of up to eight Xilinx XC6200 series FPGA chips[11]. Each chip has 64x64 logic cells, each of which comprises a two-input logic gate and an optional D-type flip-flop. A key characteristic of the Space2 machine is that it is rich in registers whose states can be accessed from any part of computing surface, with gates which are capable of being dynamically or partially reconfigured. The implementation strategies described here are also applicable to recent technologies such as Xilinx Virtex series FPGAs[12] which are much larger and are capable of partial reconfiguration.

The implementation consists of software and hardware components. The software component runs on the host and has the following tasks:
- loading the training data set into the main memory,
- specifying ITNN topology from the given training set,
- compiling the topology specification into hardware neural components,
- loading pre-compiled (placed and locally routed) neural hardware components into the FPGA computing surface, and assembling the ITNN at run-time,
- conducting the training of ITNN, and

- scheduling the execution and managing temporary values if time-multiplexing of the hardware neurons is deemed necessary.

The hardware components consist of a set of pre-compiled hardware neurons and glue logic. The design of the pre-compiled hardware neurons is described in later subsections. The training samples are held in memory, one sample per row, which are in the form of input/desired-output data-pairs, for example (input 1 1 0 1, output 1 0).

The implementation is divided into two stages: training and execution. The training stage is relatively simple and mainly involves assigning the weights and calculating the bias weights. The execution stage processes the input samples and generates neural network responses to the inputs. The data paths for these two stages are different. In the training stage, training data from the input patterns is fed in column-wise: starting from the LSB, in a bit-serial / word parallel fashion, one clock cycle per column. In the execution stage, input vectors from the testing set are fed in row-wise in a bit-serial / sample parallel fashion. The data paths are illustrated in Fig. 2.

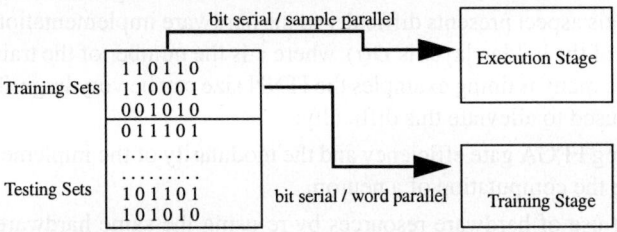

Fig. 2 Data paths for ITNN training and execution

3.2 Implementation of the ITNN Hidden Neurons

To achieve better FPGA gate efficiency and to realize the implementation of ITNN on a limited FPGA resource we have arranged to have the training and execution stages share the same hardware. Furthermore, the computation in an ITNN neuron is serialized to achieve high modularity within the design, and hence make the run-time compilation and assembly of ITNN from neural modules possible.

At the execution stage, because ITNN uses binary neurons, the computation of the dot-product between the inputs and the weights for a neuron can be implemented by using simple logic gates. The dot-product for neuron i is defined in equation (3):

$$y_i = \sum_{j=0}^{n-1} x_{ij} w_{ij} + 1 \cdot w_{bias} \tag{3}$$

where n is the length of the input vector including the bias. Since the input x_{ij} is a binary variable and the weight w_{ij} (excluding the bias) only has two possible values: -1 and 1, the computation in (3) is reduced to binary additions/subtractions plus a constant integer bias weight.

It is obvious that a straightforward implementation of the above computation may lead to irregular and costly designs because weights vary from one neuron to another. To achieve regularity and gate efficiency, the above computation has to be serialized and absorbed into a loadable up/down binary counter with the bias weight used as the preset to the counter and the weights (i.e. the training input vector x_{ij} in this case) used as the up/down signal.

There is an additional benefit from the above serialization of the computation. Notice that, in the training stage, the same counter can be used for calculating s (i.e. the sum of all +1s in a training vector) needed to compute the bias weights. If we use $r+1$ as the preset to the counter, feed the serialized input vector to the CE port of the counter and let the counter count down, then at the end of training cycle the result stored in the counter will be the bias weight (i.e. $r-s+1$). Thus the same hardware neuron can be used for both the training and execution stages. All the binary numbers for the computation are represented and interpreted in two's compliment format.

The implementation of the ITNN hidden neuron is illustrated in Fig. 3. In the execution stage, the signal *training* is set to low. Each input sample is presented in parallel and serialized by using a parallel-to-serial converter (PSC). The output bit-stream from the PSC is distributed to every neuron in the hidden layer, and connected to the CE port of every counter. In each neuron, the weights stored in the weight register are used to set the up / down signal of the counters. The weight register is connected serially to the up signal port of the counter. The calculation for the dot-product between the input vector and the weights is implemented as a loadable, cascadable binary counter with the bias weight as the preset to the counter. The threshold unit is implemented as the logic operation $\overline{Q_3} \cdot (Q_0 + Q_1 + Q_2)$. It takes n cycles for the above computation to complete, where n is the length of the input vector.

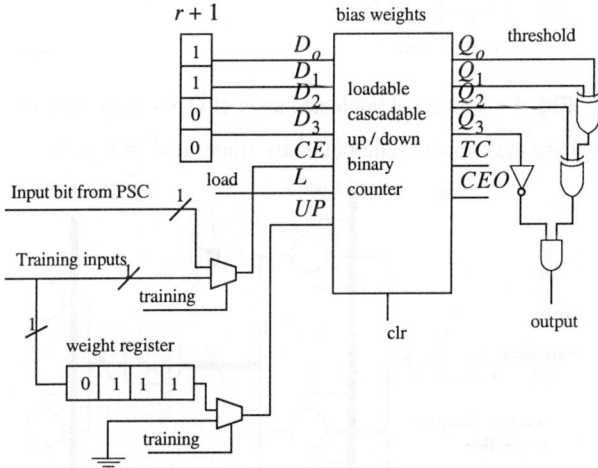

Fig. 3 A bit-serial implementation of ITNN hidden neuron

In the training stage, the signal *training* is set to high. Column-wise training data is fed in and aligned with each neuron in the hidden layer, one column per cycle. The training data bits are stored in the weight registers as the weights, and are also fed to the CE port of each counter to calculate the value s needed for the bias weights. The up signal is held low so that the counter counts down. The counter is preset to $r+1$. The training also takes n cycles (i.e. the length of the input vectors).

The size of the counters is decided when the topology of the ITNN is specified, if the input vectors are n bits long then at least a m bit counter is need such that $n \leq 2^{m+1} - 1$ to ensure there is no over-flow. The register for holding the generalization radius r is also m bits long. The weight registers are n bits long.

3.3 Implementation of the Output Neurons

The implementation for output neurons is also serialized to achieve gate efficiency and modularity; the outputs from the hidden neurons are serialized by a PSC. An ordinary up / down counter is used to implement the dot-product between the weights and the outputs from the hidden neurons. The output bit stream from the PSC is connected to the CE port of the counter. The up signal port of the counter is connected to a weight register which stores the desired outputs for each training sample used as the weights. During the training, the desired outputs are fed straight into the weight register. The implementation of the output neuron is illustrated in Fig. 4.

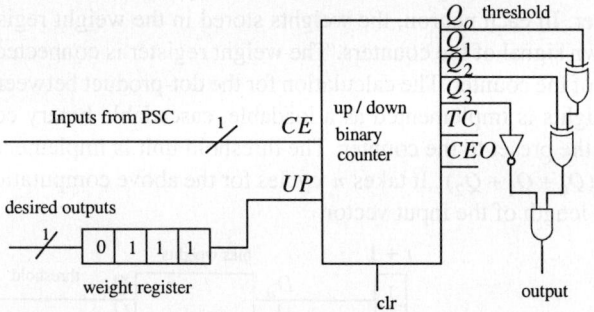

Fig. 4 A bit serial implementation of ITNN output neuron

The overall implementation and data paths are illustrated in Fig. 5.

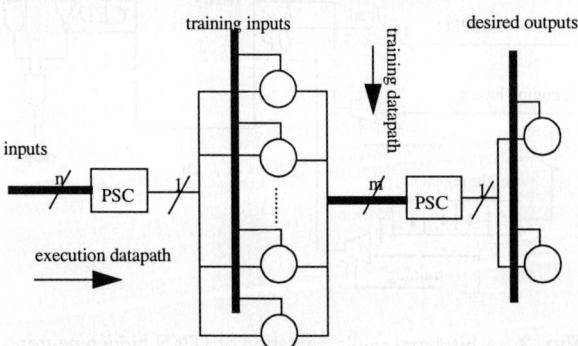

Fig. 5 Abstract illustration of the Implementation strategy and data paths

3.4 Multiplexing Hardware Neurons

The size of the ITNN hidden layer increases linearly with the number of training samples. Because FPGA resources are limited, there will be cases when the specified ITNN will not fit in the available FPGA resources. To scale up the implementations of ITNN gracefully with increased precision and neuron counts, we have used a strategy to time-multiplex the hardware neurons. The same hardware neurons are time-shared with different partitions of the training samples. This arrangement is only possible with ITNN because of its localized learning (i.e. one input sample is used to train its corresponding hidden neuron). Thus, the partitioning training sample set is equivalent to partitioning the neurons in the hidden layer. In other supervised training algorithms such as back-propagation, one training sample is used to train all hidden neurons and, to ensure training accuracy, all training samples must be used for training.

The task of partitioning the training set and time-multiplexing of hidden neurons is managed and scheduled in software. If the overall size of the specified ITNN does not fit into the available FPGA resources, the training sample set is partitioned into p smaller training sets so that an ITNN with reduced hidden layer size (labelled as ITNN_p) can be implemented on the available FPGA resource, and time-shared by the p partitioned training sets. The hardware for ITNN_p is shared for the partitioned training sets in sequential steps. The specified ITNN is thus implemented as the combined results of ITNN_p running p times sequentially.

During training, the partitions of the training sets are presented one by one to the ITNN_p. Weights and the bias are read and stored by the host after each step. During the execution stage, appropriate weights including a bias weight for each partition are written to the neurons in the hidden layer by the host. Because the computation in the output neuron is serialized, the effect of time-multiplexing of hidden neurons on the output neurons is minimal. Only the appropriate weights from the current hidden neurons to the output neurons need to be written at each time step by the host. An example of a dual partitioning time-multiplexing scheme is illustrated in Fig. 6.

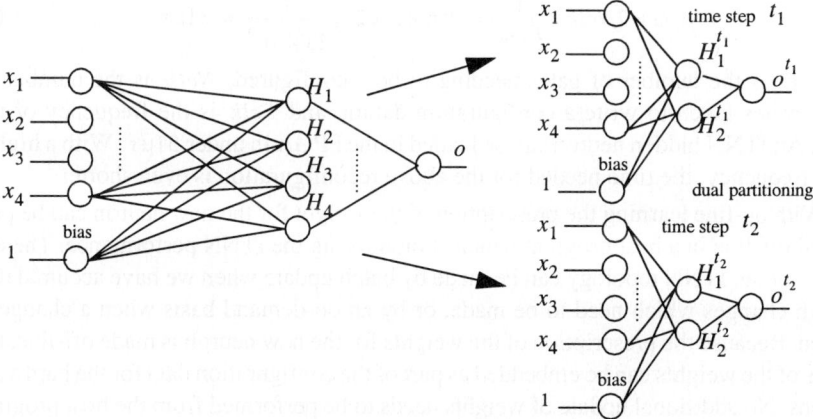

Fig. 6 A dual partitioning time-multiplexing scheme

Ten 64-bit-input neurons can be implemented with one XC6216 chip, hence 80 such neurons can be realized on a Space2 machine[10]. A reasonable size application with 160 training samples can be handled by using the dual partitioning scheme. With Xilinx's largest chip, the XVC812E (which contains 56x84 CLBs), 72 such neurons can be implemented, seven times as many as can be realized on a XC6216 chip. However, with large applications where hundreds of training samples may be required, the time-multiplexing scheme is still applicable and is crucial in implementing ITNNs.

4 On-Line Learning with ITNN

Although the Kak algorithm with its prescriptive learning overcomes the problem of using costly empirical and iterative simulation methods to find the correct topology and weights for neural networks, the performance of a trained ITNN is only as good as the training set used for specifying the ITNN in the first place. The performance depends heavily on the numbers of training samples available, the representativeness of the samples and the quality of the samples (whether noisy data is present in the sample set). Furthermore the stability-plasticity dilemma (i.e. preserving learned knowledge, while continuing to incorporate new) still exists with the Kak algorithm. One solution to the problem is to use on-line learning to incorporate new training examples that have to be learned or to eliminate bad samples which have already been learned. In the Kak algorithm, this means adding or eliminating neurons from the hidden layer, and hence modifying both the respective weights between neurons and the topology of the network itself. Because of the localized learning of the Kak algorithm, this can be easily implemented as adding or off-loading hardware neurons to and from the FPGA computing surface through partial or dynamic reconfiguration.

The XC6200 series FPGA chips have a dedicated processor interface which allows a user to directly write to the configuration RAM of the chip and change the functions of the cells. The functionality of a cell is encoded by two bytes. The XC6216 chip has a 32-bit data bus, hence each write cycle can change the functions of 2 adjacent cells. Combining this feature with the ITNN neuron, and assuming a clock frequency of 33 MHz, the total time, T, taken to load a 256 gate ITNN neuron (with 64 bits-input) is:

$$T = G \times 2Nclk \times \frac{1}{Fclk} = 256 \times 2 \times 2 \times \frac{1}{33 \times 10^6} = 31 \mu s \qquad (4)$$

where G is the number of gates needing to be reconfigured, $Nclk$ is the number of clock cycles taken to write a configuration datum, and $Fclk$ is the frequency of the clock. An ITNN hidden neuron can be loaded in the FPGA in under $31 \mu s$. With a higher clock frequency, the time needed for the above reconfiguration is even shorter.

With on-line learning the prescription of the weight for the new neuron can be performed off-line in a host program which is monitoring the ITNN performance. The evolution of the ITNN topology can be made by batch update when we have accumulated enough changes which need to be made, or by an on-demand basis when a change is needed. Because the prescription of the weights for the new neuron is made off-line, the values of the weights can be embedded as part of the configuration data for the hardware neurons. No additional update of weights needs to be performed from the host program to the FPGA once the hardware neurons are loaded.

5 Conclusion

In this paper we have presented the Kak algorithm and ITNN as a viable alternative to traditional costly and iterative neural network learning algorithms for reconfigurable hardware implementation. The instantaneous learning ability of the Kak algorithm and its binary arithmetic nature make ITNN well suited for implementation on FPGA based fine-grained reconfigurable computing platforms. The localized learning with the Kak algorithm leads to extremely flexible ITNN architecture which makes on-line learning possible through topology adaptation. To achieve better gate efficiency and modularity we serialized the computation in the hardware neuron, and absorbed it into a loadable up/down counter. The scalability of problem with the ITNN is overcome by using a time-multiplexing strategy which is equivalent to partitioning the training set. On-line learning is proposed to improve ITNN's performance and to overcome the stability-plasticity dilemma. This mechanism is achieved by topology adaptation through dynamically allocating or deleting neurons from the hidden layer of ITNN.

Acknowledgments

J. Zhu is supported by a Postgraduate Award Scholarship from the Australian Government. This work is also supported by a grant from the Australian Research Council.

References

1. Hush, D.R. and B.G. Horne, *Progress in supervised neural networks: what's new since Lippmannn?* IEEE Signal Processing Magazine, IEEE Press, 1993. **10**(1), p. 8-39.
2. Eldredge, J.G. and B.L. Hutchings, *Density Enhancement of a Neural Networks Using FPGAs and Run-Time Reconfiguration.* Proc. of IEEE Workshop on FPGAs for Custom Computing Machines, IEEE Computer Society Press, 1994, p. 180-188.
3. Hadley, J.D. and B.L. Hutchings, *Design Methodologies for Partially Reconfigured Systems.* Proc. of IEEE Symposium on FPGAs for Custom Computing Machines, IEEE Computer Society Press, 1995, p. 78-84.
4. Lysaght, P., et al., *Artificial Neural Network Implementation on a Fine-Grained FPGA.* Proc. of the 4th International Workshop on Field-Programmable Logic and Applications, LNCS 849, Springer, 1994, p. 421-431.
5. Gschwind, M., et al., *Space Efficient Neural Network Implementation.* Proc. of the 2nd ACM Symposium on Field-Programmable Gate Arrays, ACM, 1994, p. 23-28.
6. Kak, S.C., *On generalization by neural networks.* Journal of Information Sciences, Elsevier Science Inc., 1998. 111, p. 293-302.
7. Tong, K.-W. and S.C. Kak, *A New Corner Classification Approach to Neural Network Training.* Journal of Circuits, Systems, Signal Processing, Burkh auser Boston, 1998. 17, p. 459-469.
8. Raina, P., *Comparison of learning and generalization capabilities of the Kak and the backpropagation algorithms.* Journal of Information Sciences, Elsevier Science Inc., 1994. 81, p. 261-274.
9. Milne, G., et al., *Realising massively concurrent systems on the SPACE Machines.* Proc. of IEEE Workshop on FPGAs for Custom Computing Machines, IEEE Computer Society Press, 1993, p. 26-32.
10. Gunther, B.K., *SPACE 2 as a Reconfigurable Stream Processor.* Proc. of the 4th Australian Conference on Parallel and Real-Time Systems, Springer, 1997, p. 74-84.
11. Xilinx, *XC6000 FPGAs*, 1997, Xilinx, www.xilinx.com.
12. Xilinx, *Virtex-E 1.8V Extended Memory FPGAs*, 2000, Xilinx, www.xilinx.com.

Compact Spiking Neural Network Implementation in FPGA

Selene Maya, Rocio Reynoso, César Torres, and Miguel Arias-Estrada

National Institute for Astrophysics, Optics and Electronics
Tonanzintla, Puebla, Mexico
ariasm@inaoep.mx
http://cseg.inaoep.mx/~ariasm

Abstract. An FPGA based Artificial Neural Network is proposed. The neuron is based on a spiking scheme where signals are encoded in a stochastic pulse train. The neuron is composed of a synaptic module and a summing-activation module. The architecture of the neuron is characterized and its FPGA implementation is presented. The basic spiking neuron is used to implement a basic neural network. An extension of the neuron architecture to include an address-event protocol for signal multiplexing in a single line is proposed. VHDL simulations and FPGA synthesis results are discussed.

1. Introduction

Neural Networks covers different applications ranging from pattern recognition and image processing, to robotic applications. While software implementation is useful for investigating the capabilities of neural network models, they are not adequate for real-time processing in the context of large networks or on-line learning. In order to overcome these drawbacks a specific hardware architecture implemented in FPGA technology is proposed. The architecture exploits the inherent parallelism of neural networks combined with a spiking scheme for data encoding.

Two main approaches to hardware implementation of neural networks have been explored: analog and digital. Both of these establish trade-offs among three parameters: accuracy, silicon area and processing speed. The analog implementation lacks of accuracy and generally requires large design cycles. On the other hand, VLSI digital technology has progressed and several tools make easier and shorter the design process, specially with programmable logic technology. With recent advances in FPGA devices it has been possible to implement complex and high performance systems with short cycle designs. The drawback of digital implementation is that it is area consuming, reducing the amount of neurons in a single chip. The approach we follow adopts a spiking neuron model that uses a pulse code scheme to represent the signal strength.

The advantage of using a pulsing scheme is: a) a considerable reduction of the hardware complexity for the arithmetic operators, thus a reduced silicon area per neuron and, b) the reduction of the interconnections in the communication scheme since only one line is required to transmit the output of a neuron.

The proposed architecture is intended for high-density neural network implementation on a single FPGA, in the order of 1000's of neurons. A hierarchical and modular design is proposed in order to make it flexible and scalable. The communication scheme explored is based on the Address Event Protocol, in order to establish an efficient point to point communication, multiplexing pulses from other neurons. The Address Event Protocol has shown its functionality in neuromorphic chip interconnections [1]. Communication protocols like address event is necessary to maximize interconnection resources of the FPGA and allow correct timing among neurons for the pulse codification.

The rest of the paper is organized as follows. Section 2 introduces pulsed neural networks; section 3 presents the proposed FPGA based neuron module which functionality is characterized using VHDL simulations. Section 4 presents a simple neural network based in our pulsing neuron. Section 5 discusses the architecture extension to incorporate an address-event protocol to communicate neurons in large networks. Finally some conclusions are given.

2. Pulsed Neural Networks

Contemporary neurocomputing technology has taken its models of information processing and management from the biological nervous systems, the signals between the neurons are of electrical nature, except the message transmission process (synapse), which is mostly a chemical phenomenon. Another useful biological fact is that some neurons perform in a mode in which they generate a stream of action potentials when they are triggered themselves. In this case the frequency is proportional to the amplitude of the input signal received. This second property justifies the introduction of the well known stochastic or pulsed neural networks.

In general all artificial neural networks (ANN), consist of a basic neuron model composed of weighted inputs (through a synapse), and a summing-activation function as an output [1].

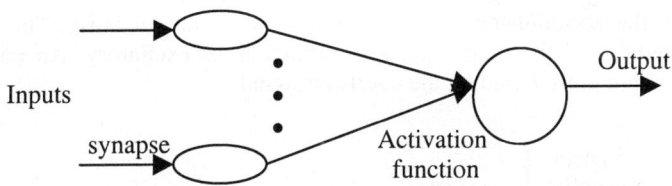

Fig. 1. Generic Neuron Structure

The function of the synapse is to multiply its input by a weight value to produce an output. A neuron activation function is a nonlinear thresholding function on the sum of the output of its synapses.

A stochastic ANN uses the same general organization of all the ANN; the difference is that it uses stochastic pulse trains for signal representation and computation.

The pulse coupled neural networks (PCNN) [1][2] models are based on abstractions of important properties of biological neurons. The two fundamental properties of the PCNN are the use of streams of stochastic pulses and the way to combine or operate them [3]. In PCNN, an operand x, i.e. an activation or a weight, is always normalized, and is represented by a stream of pseudo-random binary pulses $x_{(n)}$, generated every clock step. The probability of occurrence of a bit equal to 1 in $x_{(n)}$ is equal to the normalized value of the corresponding operand. Neural operations are performed using basic logic gates with streams of pulses as their inputs.

The connectivity requirements of the PCNNs are low (only one line is required to transmit the output of a neuron), and they are suitable for hardware implementation. PCNN are excellent for dynamical control, (rather than chaotic behavior), a PCNN will spontaneously desynchronize rather than remaining fixed in a synchronization lock for all time, this allows a PCNN to exhibit many more dynamical regimes, and to be a much more complex and versatile processing system.

3. FPGA-Based Pulsing Neuron Architecture

Reconfigurable Field Programmable Gate Arrays (FPGAs) [2] provide a reprogrammable HW resource that can be exploited to great advantage for ANNs. They are readily available at reasonable cost and have a reduced HW development cycle. High-speed, i.e., fully-parallel ANNs require a tremendous number of multipliers [4]. Practical implementations of ANNs are possible only if the amount of circuitry devoted to multiplication is significantly reduced, one way to do it is to use bit-serial stochastic computing techniques with the advantage that the multiplication of two probabilistic bit-streams can be accomplished with a single 2-input logic gate. This makes it feasible to implement large, dense, fully parallel networks with digital techniques that achieve a high-level of performance.

The proposed Pulsing Neuron Model is composed of a synapse module and a summing-activation module.

The synapse module is shown in figure 2. It consists of an accumulator (adder-register) that sums the weights each time it receives an input pulse [5]. Depending on the weight, the accumulator overflows producing an output pulse. The sign of the weight determine if the output pulse is inhibitory or excitatory. An edge detector forms the output pulse based on the overflow signal.

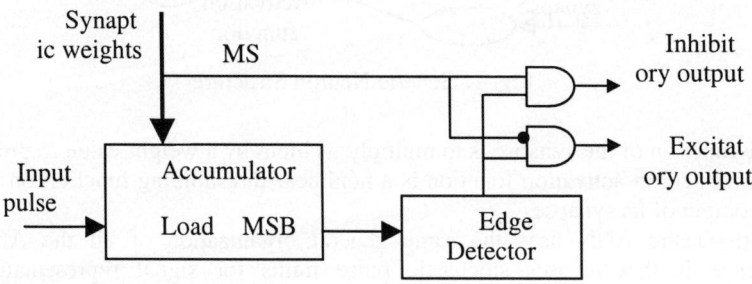

Fig. 2. Synapse module.

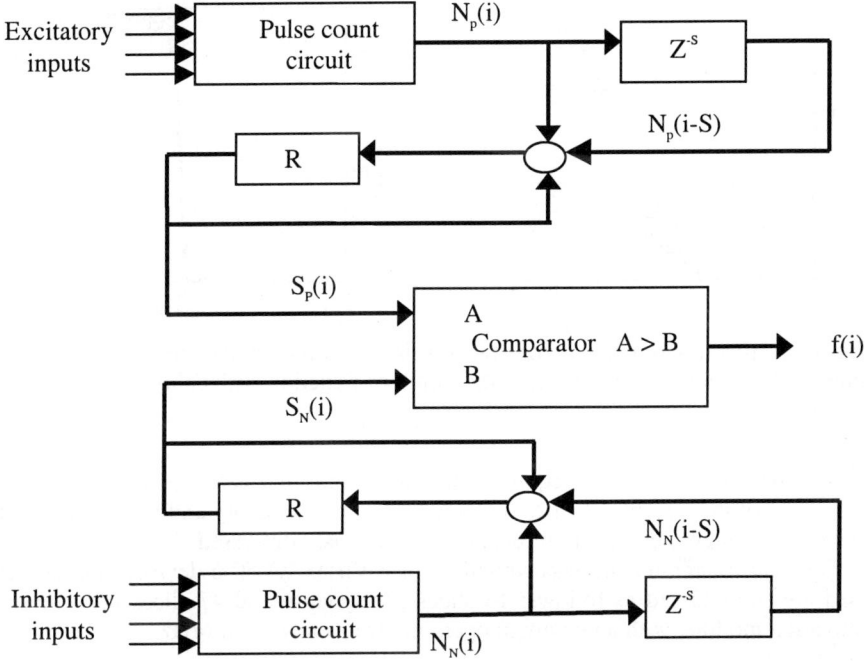

Fig. 3. Summing-Activation module. The module has inhibitory and excitatory circuits and a comparator block that produces an output pulse when the excitatory signals are larger than the inhibitory.

The summing-activation module concentrates the inhibitory and excitatory pulses from all the synapses in the neuron [6], as shown in figure 3. The module counts the pulses with counter circuits. The counters are triggered by the pulses from the synapses but, to avoid missing counts due to coincident pulses from different synapses, there is extra circuitry, which decorrelate those pulses. The decorrelation circuit delays the output from the counter, and subtracts it from the current output. Then, final counts from the inhibitory and excitatory summing circuits are compared producing a pulse if the excitatory sum is larger than the inhibitory sum.

The neuron model was implemented with the VHDL language and the neuron was characterized. The response of the neuron is shown in figure 4. The neuron presents a modified sigmoid response, which can be mathematically approximated by:

$$1/(1 + exp(a * x + b)) \qquad (2)$$

Where:

$$x = w * \{input\ signal\} + \{bias\} \qquad (3)$$

The slope of the linear part of the curve can be adjusted by increasing the number of delay elements in the delay block of the summing-activation module (figure 3). This corresponds to modify the constant a in equation 1.

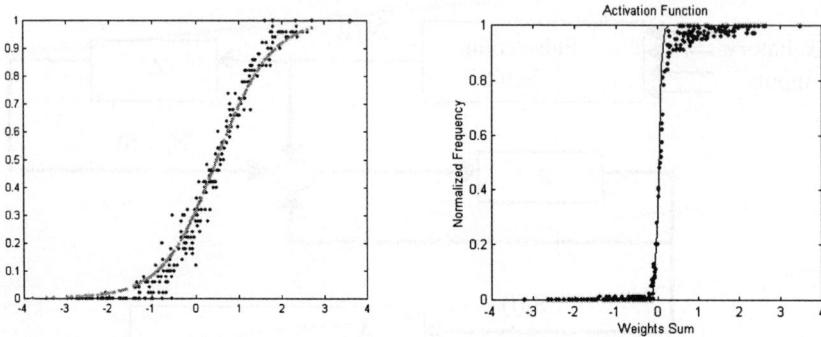

Fig. 4. Activation functions from the Pulsing Neuron Implementation. a) Function without delay in the summing-activation unit. b) Function with delay in the summing-activation unit.

In order to reduce the required chip area and to overcome system noise, a restriction of the weight values to the range [-1,1] is mandatory and is solved adapting the modified sigmoid activation function as previously discussed.

The neuron architecture was compiled for a Virtex XV50-6 device. The resources used are summarized as follows: 13 slices per synapse and 47 slices per summing-activation module, with a maximum operating frequency of 90 MHz.

4. Networks of Pulsing Neurons

The pulsing neuron was used to implement the XOR problem network as a way to validate it. The network consists of 3 neurons: two hidden layer neurons and one output neuron. Training was done offline using Matlab with the modified sigmoid response modeled from the VHDL results. Learning was done with backpropagation, and the slope of the activation function was adjusted in the hardware implementation in order to guaranty weights in the [-1.0, 1.0] interval. The activation function used is shown in figure 4b. Results of the XOR network are shown in figure 5.

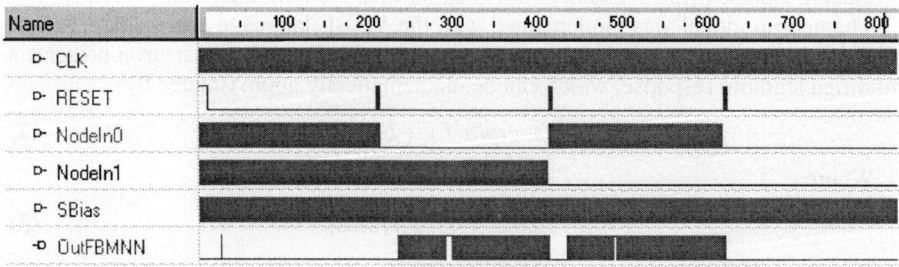

Fig. 5. XOR network output. The input nodes are pulse trains in NodeIn0 and NodeIn1. The output of the network is pulse coded in OutFBMNN.

The XOR network was compiled for a Virtex XV50-6 device. The resources used are 240 slices, and a maximum operating frequency of 90 MHz. The limiting factor is the number of synapses per neurons since they increase the area requirements. Under the architecture proposed, the weights are integrated into the synapse, with an external weight encoding, the synapse area requirements would decrease.

5. Interconnection Issues in Large Networks

The power of neural networks come from the non-linear properties of neurons, and the network interconnections. Interconnections become the bottleneck during hardware implementation due to limited resources in FPGAs.

A way to circumvent this problem is to incorporate the address-event protocol [7] into the pulsing neural networks. The address-event allows communicating several discrete events in a single line. A pulsing neuron output can send its activity signal as an event containing only its address or position in the network. Several inputs to the same neuron can be multiplexed into a single input line, and the corresponding synapse can be processed in the same pulse counting module. The address-event protocol decorrelates overlapping events by sending them to a FIFO. The proposed extension to incorporate the address-event protocol in networks of pulsing neurons is illustrated in figure 6.

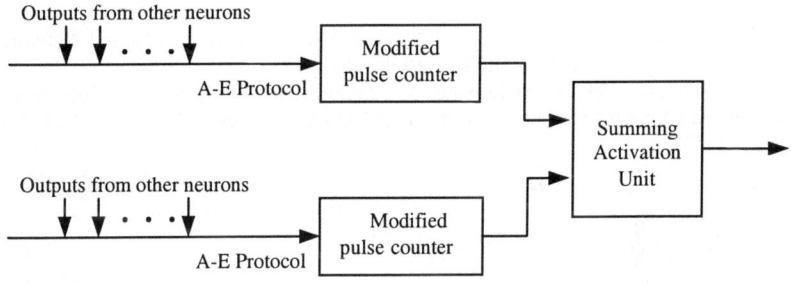

Fig. 6. Address-event protocol integration in the pulsed neural network architecture

6. Conclusions

A pulsing neuron architecture for FPGA implementation was developed. The neuron architecture is composed of a synapse module and an summing-activation module. The neuron was validated in a small neural network and its FPGA resource occupation was obtained. The neuron needs improvements in order to compact the size of the synapse and to incorporate an external mechanism for weight storage.

The address-event protocol is introduced as an alternative for building large networks multiplexing the interconnection resources in the FPGA. Further work will explore other pulse coding schemes, like pulse phase modulation, to reduce the bandwidth requirements in the interconnection lines, increasing the number of possible interconnection links among neurons.

Acknowledgements

Thanks to Dr. Juan Jaime Vega Castro for his invaluable advice.

This project is supported by the Consejo Nacional de Ciencia y Tecnologia of Mexico (CONACYT), under project #J32151-A.

References

1. IEEE Transactions on Neural Networks. "Special issue on pulse coupled neural networks", Vol. 10, No. 3 (1999)
2. Bade, S. and Hutchings, B.: FPGA-Based Stochastic Neural-Implementation. IEEE Workshop on FPGAs for Custom Computing Machines, Napa, CA, (1994) 189-198
3. Beuchat, J.-L.: Réalisation materielle de réseaux neuronaux en logique stochastique. Technical Report, (1996) http://diwww.epfl.ch/~jlbeucha/neural_html/projet2.html
4. Moerland, P. and Fiesler, E.: Neural network adaptations to hardware implementations. Handbook of neural computation, release 97/1, IOP Publishing Ltd and Oxford University Press, (1997)
5. Hikawa, H.: Frequency-Based Multilayer Neural Network with On-Chip Learning and Enhancement Neuron Characteristics. Transactions on Neural Networks IEEE, Vol. 10, No. 3, (1999) 545-553
6. Hikawa, H.: Learning Performance of Frequency-Modulation Digital Neural Network with On-Chip Learning. WCCI '98 -- IJCNN (1998) 557-562
7. Lazzaro, J., Wawrzynek, J., Mahowald, M., Sivilotti, M., Gillespie, D.: Silicon auditory processors as computer peripherals. IEEE Transactions On Neural Networks, Vol. 4, No. 3, (1993) 523-527

Silicon Platforms for the Next Generation Wireless Systems - What Role Does Reconfigurable Hardware Play?

Jan M. Rabaey

Berkeley Wireless Research Center
University of California at Berkeley
tel: (510) 666 3111
jan@eecs.berkeley.edu

Abstract. Wireless communication and networking is experiencing a dramatic growth, and all indicators point to an extension of this growth in the foreseeable future. This paper reflects on the demands and the opportunities offered with respect to the integrated implementation of these applications in the "systems-on-a-chip" era. It is demonstrated that the combined need of flexibility and energy-efficiency makes a compelling case for the use of reconfigurable architectures.

1. Introduction

Progress in wireless information systems, as envisioned by the 3rd generation and beyond, puts tremendous pressure on the underlying implementation technologies. Silicon technology has witnessed an unprecedented growth cycle in the last few decades, which will with high probability extend into the next few as well. The increasing complexity of silicon implementations closely follows a path prescribed by Moore's law. Yet, it is commonly observed that the complexity of wireless systems outpaces the technology evolution predicted by Moore's law. As a result, the implementation of future wireless systems will require novel thinking with respect to the implementation architectures and their relation to the applications at hand.

The wireless infrastructure and mobile components pose a set of stringent implementation requirements that are often considered to be contradictory:

- Reducing the cost in a multi-standard, evolutionary and adaptive environment requires flexible and evolvable solutions, which are often translated into software-programmable architectural implementations
- Yet these solutions often do not offer the performance and energy-efficiency that is required for the state-of-the art wireless algorithms and networks. The latter are more easily offered by semi-custom solutions, but these tend to lack the required flexibility.

As a result, the architectural community has been exploring a variety of novel architectures and implementation approaches, such as VLIW processors, processors with accelerators and reconfigurable processors.

This paper will first discuss the opportunities offered by the progress in semiconductor technology. This is followed by an exploration of the needs of future wireless systems. It will then progress into an overview of the different solutions, and provide clear metrics in how to evaluate and compare the options. Actual values for metrics such as flexibility, cost, performance and energy-efficiency will be offered with the aid of some actual benchmark examples.

2. The System-on-a-Chip

The continued progress of semiconductor technology has enabled the "system-on-a-chip" to become a reality, combining a wide range of complex functions on a single die. Integrated circuits that merge core processors, DSPs, embedded memory, and custom modules have been reported by a wide range of companies. Projections of future integration densities suggest that this trend will surely continue in the next decade.

One of the most dramatic consequences of this super-integration is a fundamental change in the use of computation in our society. In the pc-era, computation was mostly confined to the desktop or server box. The possibility of performing millions (or billions) of operations in a module of a cubic cm has broken that lock, and complex computation is now emerging in a ubiquitous fashion, ranging from set-top boxes, consumer media components, appliances, and sensor and monitor devices. This revolution in the way in computation is performed is extremely exciting, and opens the door for many novel opportunities, some of which we cannot even envision today.

Yet at the same time, the "system-on-chip" approach introduces some major challenges that have to be addressed for the technology to become a viable undertaking. First of all, one has to address the economics of the production and realization process of these complex designs that can integrate billions of transistors on a single die:

- The cost of production facilities and mask making has increased significantly. This has lead to a major increase in the NRE (non-recurring engineering) costs of a design, and translates into a higher entry barrier for a new design start to be economically attractive.
- A larger number of physical effects (such as capacitive and inductive coupling introduced by interconnect wires) have come to the foreground in the design of these deep-submicron devices. This negatively impacts the design process. Realizing a correct design in a reasonable amount of time is becoming increasingly harder.
- While the complexity of the designs is increasing from year-to-year, the productivity of the integrated-circuit designer is not keeping pace.

All these observations, combined with an intense pressure to reduce the time-to-market, are causing a shift in the design paradigm. If one can define a common hardware denominator that can be shared across multiple applications, volume increases and overall costs may eventually be (much) lower than in the case when the chip is customized for the application. This approach has been dubbed **platform-**

based design [1]. The applicability and hence the reusability of a single platform is inherently determined by its **flexibility**, i.e. its capability of covering a range of functionalities and applications [2].

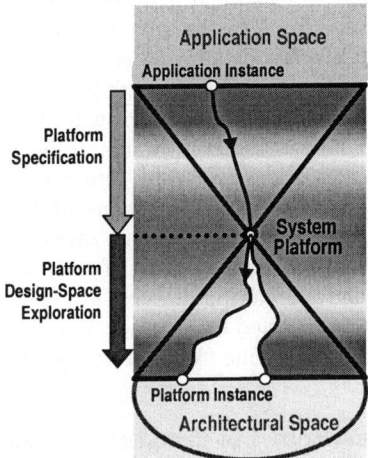

Fig. 1. The system platform concept creates a common solution between the constraints of the application and architectural abstractions [1].

The most flexible platforms are the software programmable components. Here, flexibility is achieved using a "machine" capable to perform a set of instructions specified by the instruction set architecture (ISA). Microprocessors and, to a certain degree, DSPs, are examples of such. A systems engineer might be naturally drawn to these software-programmable platforms because of their ultimate flexibility. Yet, the embedded applications, targeted by these SOCs, impose a different set of design metrics and constraints than the pure performance goals, set by the traditional software platforms. For instance, in the world of wireless networks, cost and energy dissipation are the dominant factors determining the potential success of a given implementation. These broader metrics as well as the specific properties of the addressed applications are the main causes for the differentiation in the architectural space that we witness today.

The definition of the system platform can be considered the result of a push-and-pull process between the application engineers — who desire independence of the implementation architecture while meeting stringent implementation metrics — and the architecture designers and/or semiconductor companies — who want maximum reuse of their designs. This is illustrated in Figure 1. The position of the equilibrium point depends upon the tightness of the design constraints as well as cost determining factors such as volume and market.

3. Trends in Wireless Systems

The world of wireless communications and networking has experienced an unprecedented growth in the last decade. The number of wireless subscribers has grown exponentially between 1990 and 1998, matching remarkably well a Fibonacci sequence as shown in Figure 2 This trend is expected to continue well into the next decade. While most of the volume in the wireless traffic is due to voice communications at present, a shift towards data traffic is slowly but surely emerging, a shift which is expected to materialize in full force with the deployment with the so-called 3rd generation of wireless systems. In fact, the growth of wireless networking closely mirrors and complements the evolution towards fully-distributed and ubiquitous computation systems, already discussed in the introduction of this paper. It is my conjecture that the major growth in wireless systems, after the deployment of a wide-area 3rd generation network, will be in the home, office, and building environment, providing connectivity between the myriad of distributed sensor, information processing, computation, and monitoring devices, as well as providing access to the existing high-bandwidth networks and the internet. Wireless technology is clearly the preferred approach towards solving the **"last-meter" problem** in information access and distribution.

An analysis of the characteristics of these next-generation systems reveals some dominant requirements that have to be met for the technology to be viable:

1. The abundance of wireless services with varying data-rate and quality of service requirements will create a spectrum shortage. This can only be addressed by increasing the spectral efficiency of modems (in bits/sec/Hz/m^3), and by reconsidering the way spectrum is allocated to services — in other words, the standardization process. Fortunately, advances in communication theory provide us with solutions to both of these problems. Techniques such as multi-antenna diversity, beamforming, and multi-user detection and cancellation can provide dramatic increases in spectral efficiency, while opening the door for a peaceful co-existence of uncoordinated wireless services in the same band without effecting the quality-of-service. This approach, which we have dubbed the universal spectrum-

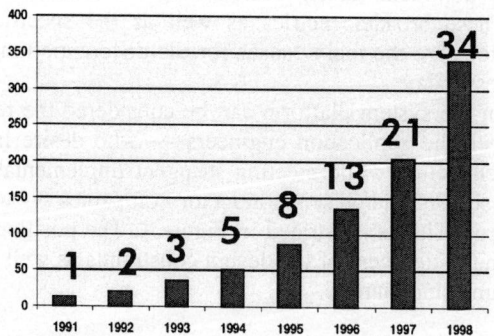

Fig. 2. Growth in wireless subscribers over the world (source: Goldman-Sachs).

	Wide-band CDMA			FDMA Multiple Antenna
	Matched Filter	Blind MMSE	Exact Decorrelator	SVD
Performance Bits/sec/Hz	1	2	2	6
Multiplications	124	496	230,000	736
Memory	248	1240	640,000	2120
ALU	124	502	240,000	800
Word Length	8-bit	12-bit	16-bit	16-bit

Fig. 3. Computational complexity of some advanced wireless communication algorithms.

sharing radio, does come at a price in computational complexity. Figure 3 illustrates the computational costs of some of the mentioned algorithms. This growing appetite for computational cycles is confirmed in the picture of Figure 4, which shows the growth in computational complexity over the generations of wireless systems. In fact, the complexity has grown faster than the computational capabilities of silicon, as predicted by Moore's law: It may hence be stated that the wireless implementation platforms of the future have to provide tremendous real-time computational capabilities. Fortunately, most of the complexity resides in a few structured and regular computational kernels that are easily parallelized and that are amenable to stream-based processing.

2. Achieving the deep penetration of wireless services, as envisioned in the ubiquitous wireless scenario, requires a steep reduction in cost and energy dissipation of the wireless modem. To be successful, modem costs below 5$ and energy consumption below 1 mW have to be targeted. While integration is certainly an important help in that direction, further improvements in both implementation and energy efficiency are needed.

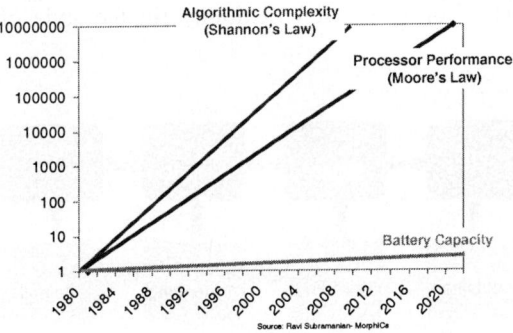

Fig. 4. Algorithmic complexity as required by various generations of wireless systems outstrips Moore's law.

In summary, the implementation platform for the wireless system of the future requires a seamless combination of the contradictory requirements of high performance, flexibility, low energy consumption, and low cost.

4. Architectures for Wireless Systems

The definition of such a platform requires an in-depth understanding of the modem functions and their properties. As shown in Figure 5, a radio receiver (or transmitter) typically combines a data pipe, which gradually transforms the bit-serial data stream coming from the A/D converter into a set of complex data messages, and a protocol stack, that controls the operation of the data pipe. Data-pipe and protocol stack differ in the types of computations to be performed, and in the communication mechanisms between the functional modules. In short, they exhibit fundamentally different models of computation. In addition, the different modules of the data and protocol stacks operate on time and data granularities that vary over a wide range. For instance, the physical layer of the radio manipulates individual bits at rates in the high MHz range, while the application layer processes complex data structures at rates that are in the low Hz range.

Devising a homogeneous architecture that efficiently deals with this range of computational models and data and time granularities is extremely hard, if not impossible. It is hence safe to predict that the architectural platform for wireless applications will combine a heterogeneous collection of computational modules, each of which targets a specific computational model and level of data granularity.

This raises immediately the question of how to select the constituent components that make up this heterogeneous fabric, given the wide range in architectural options. Ultimately, this process boils down to an elaborate trade-off in the flexibility-efficiency-performance-cost space. Only an extensive profiling of the applications or algorithms can help to determine the required bounds on performance and flexibility, or, even more importantly, to outline the dominant computational patterns and the model of computation. While this effort might seem to be excessive, the pay-back can be dramatic, as is illustrated in Figure 6. Based on a number of benchmark studies, this plot compares some architectural alternatives in the energy efficiency/flexibility space. The impact of providing full flexibility (in the style of the Von Neuman

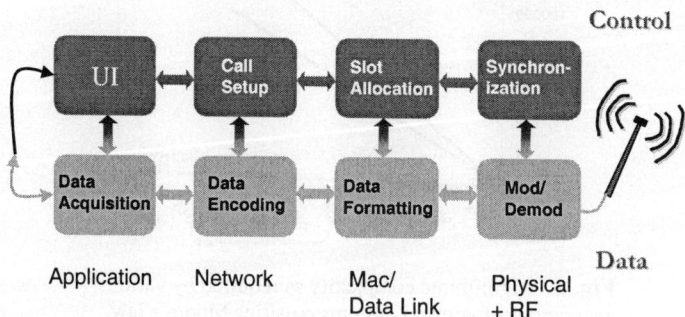

Fig. 5. Functional components of wireless transceiver.

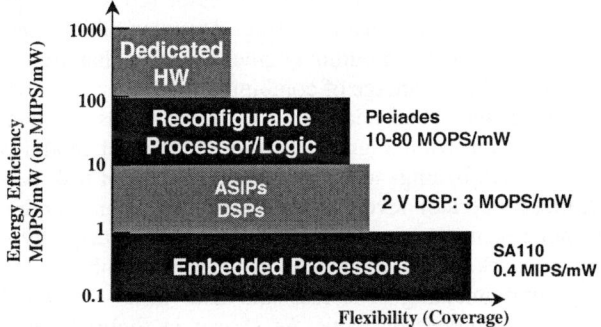

Fig. 6. Analysis of energy efficiency versus flexibility trade-off for a number of common architectural styles (for a 0.25 micron CMOS process).

machine, exemplified by the embedded microprocessor) is quite staggering, and results in three orders of magnitude in "inefficiency" compared to the fixed custom implementation of the same function. Another interesting observation is that the gap between the two can be closed by the introduction of "domain-specific" architectures, such as DSPs and ASIPs (Application-Specific Instruction Processors).

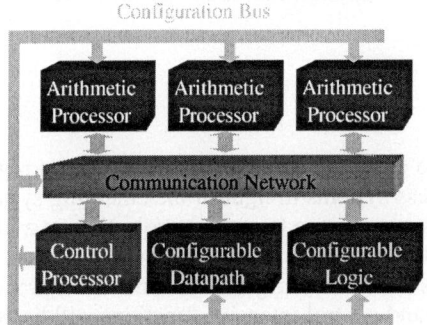

Fig. 7. Berkeley Pleiades Reconfigurable Architecture.

It is fair to state that one of the most interesting and unexpected results of the "system-on-a-chip" has been a renaissance in the field of processor architecture. Rather than being a pure "board-on-a-chip", the tight integration of computation and communication, combined with the redefined metrics of embedded applications, has led to a wide range of new (or revised) architectural approaches that attempt to exploit the specific properties of a limited application domain. Examples of these are the configurable instruction-set processor, the embedded very-long instruction set processor (VLIW), the very-short instruction set processor (or the vector processor), and the reconfigurable processor.

The latter is perhaps the most innovative entry in the computer architecture field in the last decade. Rather than the "multiplexing-in-time" concept, advocated in the instruction-set processor, the reconfigurable processor relies on a "programming-in-space" approach. Using programmable wiring, parametrizable functional units are connected to form a dedicated computing engine. For tasks that are semi-stationary in time, this approach has the advantage of combining flexibility and efficiency. Various approaches have been published addressing different levels of data, operator, and reconfiguration rate granularity. Figure 7 shows an abstract model of the Berkeley Pleiades approach, which belongs to the architectural class of task-based reconfiguration at the arithmetic operator level. It combines a traditional embedded processor with an array of heterogeneous computational modules, connected by a reconfigurable communication network. The approach efficiently combines two models of computation — communicating processes and data flow — with the latter being implemented on the co-processor array. As shown in Figure 6, the reconfigurable approach effectively succeeds in bridging the gap between the DSP and the custom design approach in terms of energy efficiency - by trading in some flexibility.

The advent of the SOC has furthermore focused the spotlight on the importance of a well-founded interconnect strategy. Most often, all interest in the design process is focused on the selection and conception of the computational elements. How to connect them together might be just as important. The traditional bus approach tends to be inefficient and unpredictable, definitely in the presence of real-time constraints. The "communication-based design" methodology might very well be one of the most important breakthroughs in design-methodology for SOC.

5. Summary

In this paper, we have collected a number of observations regarding the needs of the next-generation wireless systems in light of the emerging system-on-a-chip approach. Based on this analysis, we venture to make a projection on a plausible implementation platform for the wireless modem of the future, which is shown in Figure 8. While its computational core is formed by a group of embedded processors (general purpose and/or DSP), all data and control intensive functions will be performed by an array of configurable data and control processors, each of which is optimized for a particular

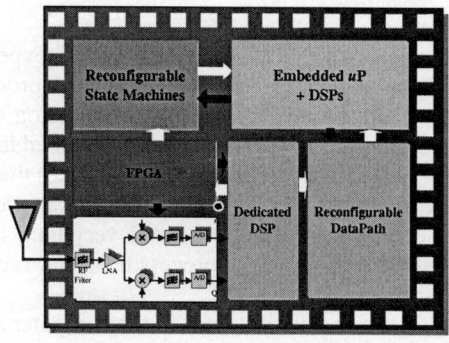

Fig. 8. Plausible implementation fabric for "software-enabled" radio.

model of computation, and a specific data and time granularity. The analog components are kept as simple as possible with digital processing compensating for the resulting imperfections.

References

1. A. Ferrari and A. Sangiovanni-Vincentelli, "System Design: Traditional Concepts and New Paradigms", Proceedings ICCD 1999.
2. J. Rabaey et al, "Heterogeneous Reconfigurable Systems", Proceeding VLSI Signal Processing Workshop, November 1997, Manchester, England.

From Reconfigurability to Evolution in Construction Systems: Spanning the Electronic, Microfluidic and Biomolecular Domains

John S. McCaskill and Patrick Wagler

GMD - German National Research Center for Information Technology
Schloss Birlinghoven, St. Augustin (Bonn)
D-53754, Germany
McCaskill@gmd.de, Patrick.Wagler@gmd.de

Abstract. This paper investigates configurability, reconfigurability and evolution of information processing hardware in conventional and unconventional media. Whereas current electronic systems have an advantage in terms of processing speed, they are at a definite disadvantage in terms of plasticity, true hardware reconfiguration and especially reconfiguration and evolution of the hardware construction system itself. Here molecular computers, including the control of chemical reaction synthesis, hold the promise of being able to achieve these properties. In particular, combinatorially complex families of molecules (such as DNA) can direct their own synthesis. The intermediate level of microfluidic systems is also open to reconfiguration and evolution and may play a vital role in linking up the electronic and molecular processing worlds. This paper discusses opportunities for and advantages of reconfiguration across these various levels and the possibility of integrating these technologies. Finally, the threshold level of construction control required for iterative bootstrapping of nanoscale construction is discussed.

Introduction

Biological systems exhibit an exquisite interplay between hardware and software, between (re)construction and operation and between function (phenotype) and inheritance (genotype). In this paper, we wish to explore a perspective on reconfigurable hardware going beyond the traditional electronic context, exploring both the microscale potential of solid and liquid phase systems and the nanoscale capabilities of biomolecular systems. Based on experience with these three levels of hardware within the context of evolution research in our laboratory, there are two basic messages in the paper: the first is a persisting distinction between a functional machine and its blueprint or description, arising from the necessity of generic solutions to the construction problem. The second is the existence of a natural progression, from fixed to reconfigurable and then to evolvable hardware, depending on the timescale, effort and autonomy of the reconfiguration process.

Electronically reconfigurable hardware is now largely based on the current generation of SRAM controlled Field Programmable Gate Arrays (FPGAs). The dynamically reconfigurable chips developed by Algotronix and then Xilinx [1] allowed first experiments in true evolution of synchronous digital and asynchronous analog electronic circuits [2] using the technology developed for rapid reconfiguration. Already a number of remarkably powerful computers (*e.g.* POLYP [3]) have been built using these devices. Evolvable electronic hardware in which large populations of variously configured such devices are selected to perform externally specified functions have been investigated by Tangen [4]. Their special potential advantage over simulation-based optimization is the ability to handle intractably complex or physically not well characterized problems, *i.e.* they can evolve to function on-line in a real-world, real-time environment.

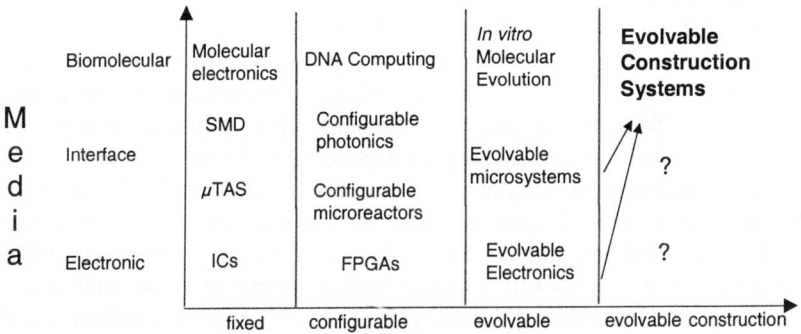

Construction flexibility

Fig. 1. Towards evolvable construction systems. Evolvable Construction is an emerging technology spanning the electronic, mechanical and biological fields. It is distinct from the familiar fields of Evolutionary Algorithms (which abstracts evolutionary principles to solve complex optimization problems) and Genetic Programming (which employs evolution to solve programming tasks). Evolvable Hardware is concerned with the evolution of complex machines, from molecular machines like self-replicating molecules to electronic machines like computers. Evolvable construction systems are capable of controlling their own construction as well as some measure of computation as an integral part of their functioning. Current electronic "evolvable hardware" involves reconfiguration through a fixed construction system. Biochemical and microreactor systems offer possibilities to co-evolve the construction system itself. Such systems may also lead to new electronic architectures. [Abbreviations: IC Integrated Circuit, µTAS Micro Total Analysis System, SMD Single Molecule Detection, FPGA Field Programmable Gate Array].

Although purely electronic systems have become attractive in terms of reconfiguration speed, mechanical and molecular reconfiguration opens up the possibility of rapid redesign of the entire hardware system. This is not only important in real-world applications with interfaces to microscopic systems, but also generically for the problem of evolving new hardware. In this paper we shall propose an increasing research effort on the theory and technology of reconfigurable and thereafter evolvable construction systems: ideally the redesign of the hardware construction system itself should be at the focus of current technology. This appears impossible within the conventional electronic production technology, involving huge factories and large processors with normed interfaces. A shift to the molecular computing framework reveals that computer constructing systems or even self-construction systems may be open to iterative redesign and evolutionary optimization. Incidentally, this is one of the major attractions of the young field of DNA Computing [5]. Moreover, we propose a threshold level of construction complexity, beyond which a bootstrapping process (akin to the bootstrapping compilers for iterative rounds of software design) can lead to increasingly sophisticated hardware construction systems. We argue that some important basic steps in this direction have already been taken and perhaps the threshold is not so far off.

Molecular information processing involves hardware construction and signal processing simultaneously. The hardware is customized to the current task and sometimes its construction is the current information processing task. Biomolecular systems use both programmed synthesis and iterative design improvement, *i.e.* both molecular manufacturing and evolvable hardware. Certainly these properties will be crucial in attempts to harness the immense parallelism of biomolecular systems for complex nanoscale engineering, but they also may reveal important insights into computing as such. The utility of the universal computer concept is tied to the idea of a clear separation between hardware and software. There are two major biological differences between hardware and software although both are implemented in molecular terms. One concerns the fundamental difficulty of generically copying hardware, leading to the distinction between hardware and its description in terms of a lower dimensional (typically linear) representation. This was pointed out by von Neumann [6] even before the publication of the structure of DNA. The other, less fundamental one concerns differences in the lifetime and construction time scales for different structures: with shorter lived structures such as messenger RNAs or immunoglobulins playing a similar role to software in electronic computations.

This paper is structured as follows. After a review of progress from reconfigurable to evolvable hardware in the three domains (we are briefest with the electronic level as this is most familiar to the common theme of this conference), we discuss techniques for linking up these domains and the potential advantages of doing so. It concludes with a discussion of the significance and potential of this approach.

Evolvable Electronic Hardware

This field is the closest to reconfigurable electronic devices and has been well reviewed in the literature. Indeed there have been several international conferences devoted primarily to this subject [7, 8]. Here we wish to concentrate on two main issues for evolvable electronic hardware which motivate an investigation of alternative media for complex evolution. They are not the conventional problems of component size and energy consumption, although the overhead (factor of 10) associated with the two level architecture of current reconfigurable FPGAs means that these aspects are already beginning to strike hard technology barriers. Rather, they concern the issues of true hardware evolution and our ability to iteratively optimize the construction process itself.

Chip construction is an enormously complex task, from the production of pure crystalline silicon ingots, through multilayer endowment and wet or dry etching technologies all the way to packaging. The instruments used to perform this processing include melt foundries, wafer saws, mask aligners etc, so that it is currently impossible to envisage an autonomous evolution of the construction process itself. The design process also contains labor intensive design entry (supported by CAE and CAD systems) and whole suites of conversion, optimization and fault checking software, for which the creation of successive versions require the full gambit of modern programming technologies and user intervention. In short, the whole construction process involves a relatively large and rigid set of methodologies whose incremental testing and evolution appears impossible.

The problem of departing from this set of tools, even within the very restricted virtual hardware context of dynamically configurable FPGAs, has become apparent in the work on evolvable electronic hardware. The Xilinx 6000 series [1] introduced the novel property of random access configuration cells, controlling the programmable interconnect and function blocks in the FPGA. Previous FPGA technologies (such as XC4000) utilized a less resource consuming shift register to access the configuration cells, which meant that only whole chip configuration was available and this serially, so that typical reconfiguration times down to a fraction of a second resulted. Because of the complexity of chip design data, it did not initially make sense to allow FPGA processed data to directly reconfigure the chips. Most of the work on evolvable hardware with the (already extinct) family of dynamically reconfigurable chips, involved externally controlled dynamics of populations of competing alternative chip designs which were downloaded to the devices for *in situ* evaluation.

In our lab, Tangen designed and evaluated a completely evolving system in configurable hardware in which modular design descriptions, providing a dense encoding of the configurable logic in a portion of one FPGA (XC6000), are processed by the very same logic array which they are reconfiguring [4]. Here we drew on biological information encoding, in which genes are processed by the functional proteins they encode for. In particular, not the chip designs themselves, but their string encodings are proliferated and processed by the spatially resolved population of logic circuits which they collectively encode. This also provides a coherent conceptual framework for the exploitation of co-evolution effects in the iterative optimization of electronic circuits. In contrast with the work of Thompson [2], this work was conducted within the purely digital and synchronous mode of operation, which results in enhanced controllability of the evolution process.

As in previous work with NGEN [9], Tangen extended the genetic population size by having local configurations stored in external SRAM chips flowing continuously into and out of the FPGAs. This allowed a larger virtual space to be simulated in hardware. An array of 8 boards each with 8 agent FPGAs was used in the experiments on POLYP. True hardware evolution with this character is difficult, and was compounded by the withdrawal of technical support from the Xilinx 6000 series. The problem of autonomous routing of electronic signals is a severe one in the framework of FPGAs. The extensive iterative global optimization by simulating annealing, used to obtain complete functional placement and routing, presents a barrier to locally autonomous design. Effective routing by string recognition in DNA based computation provides a more effective locally controllable way of changing such interconnect, as will be seen below. In any case, for the electronic level new techniques are necessary. We think that the clear separation between copyable structures (such as chip design encodings) and non-copyable structures as introduced above will remain central in evolvable electronic structures. Finally, it may also prove possible to create self-organizing electronic structures either on surfaces or in solution using some of the techniques of molecular electronics and this will open up new possibilities for reconfigurable electronic hardware. For the moment however, these developments are still a fair way off. By way of example, a new procedure for the dynamic construction of capillaries or wires inside microchannels (Fabrication using Laminar Flow or FLO) was developed by Kenis et al. [10].

Fixed, Reconfigurable and Evolvable Microfluidic Hardware

Microfluidics provides a potential bridge between the world of evolving biomolecular reactions and reconfigurable electronic hardware. Microreactors already allow the controlled investigation of many reactions in small volumes in parallel and microflow systems have been constructed for integrated total analysis (μTAS [11, 12]). The main research content of this paper is to outline the steps from fixed microreactors to evolvable ones via reconfigurable hardware. To some extent a development paralleling the electronic development towards FPGAs and beyond can be envisaged. We make some concrete proposals for a continuous path to complex evolvable microreactors in this section, at the same time reviewing some interesting techniques which may be used to implement reconfiguration. As in electronics, reconfigurability separates into reconfigurable processors and reconfigurable connections. Since mixing is a common elementary step in microreactors, the emphasis of this paper is on reconfigurable connections.

We begin with an analysis of fixed microreactor construction via photolithography. The traditional microfabrication technologies to produce microfluidic reactors are wet-chemical anisotropic etching of single-crystalline silicon (bulk micromachining) [13, 14], or dry-etching processes by means of low-pressure plasma or ion beams (surface micromachining) [15]. Further techniques such as microstructuring photosensitive glass [16], laser micromachining, mechanical micromilling or micro spark erosion all yield irreversible fixed microstructures. A common procedure for rapid prototyping of microfluidic devices is based on three main steps. First a master is created by photolithographic patterning of a positive relief photoresist, using a high-resolution transparency as the photomask [17]. A polymer (polydimethylsiloxane,

PDMS) is then cast against the master. Curing the polymer and releasing it from the master yields a replica containing the microchannels required. Then the channels are sealed irreversibly by oxidizing the PDMS mold and a glass slide in a plasma and bringing them into contact. This is the direct approach: rapid disposable production to allow reconfiguration.

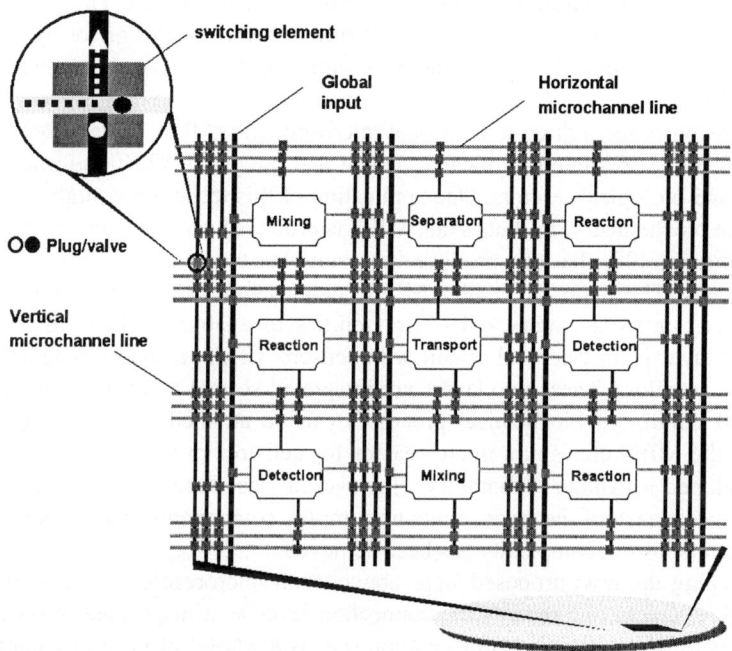

Fig. 2. Programmable and reconfigurable reactor network. A reconfigurable microfluidic chip can take a number of different forms, with once off or dynamically reconfigurable connections and/or processing elements. The diagram shows how a reconfigurable interconnect can be established in a fluidic system, using a two layer technology (dark channels are on the lower layer) and a system of photoactivated or magnetically controlled plugs or microvalves (see blowup). As in conventional FPGAs, connection resources can be local (not shown), long-line or global and the processing elements can also be used to assist the connections. Dynamically configurable processing elements that have already been implemented include mixers and strand transfer devices. Valves should be made to operate bistably in order to avoid control overhead.

A first step towards proper reconfiguration lies in separating components into a fixed (highly optimized) set containing most of the structural information and a smaller, simpler and variable set which can be used in the final processing step to customize designs. We would like this second set to involve enough combinatorial complexity that a large family of microreactors can be generated. Of course, the separation into mask generation and structure transfer is also to this end, allowing a wide range of microreactors to be built, but the mask processing steps stand at the beginning of the processing and so all the complex structuring tasks have to be performed on each wafer. One obvious procedure is to separate out layers with complex devices from much simpler connection layers, the latter determining the way in which devices from the fixed layers are connected. The connection layer structures are varied with little effort from trial to trial, keeping the complex devices constant. This is a strategy which may be used for hybrid electronic and microfluidic systems or for hybrid optical-microfluidic systems. It is also consistent with emerging standards in microsystem technology [18].

Ikuta has proposed a three-dimensional micro-integrated fluid system (MIFS) [19] in 1994. A MIFS is a micro-fabricated device that integrates VLSI and microscopic chemical and biological reactors. One application of this technology might be to programmable biochemistry. In Ikuta's lab, MIFS is produced using the integrated harden polymer process [20] that can produce very complex three-dimensional polymer or metal devices. The upper layer of a MIFS contains miniaturized elements such as pipes, valves, micro-actuators and other facilities to enable biochemical reactions. The lower layer is an electrical circuit with sensors, CPUs, memory, gate-arrays, or drivers for actuators. These two layers are integrated so that real-time sensing, computing and control of biochemical processes can be attained within a single chip. Based on the MIFS concept, a micro reactor for cell free protein synthesis [21] has been developed in Kitano's laboratory. However, a clear focus on reconfiguration is not discernible: each of the layers contains complex components and no clear separation in manufacturing complexity has been achieved.

Even taking the next proposed steps above, such microreactors are not really reconfigurable, unless one regards the connection layer as a disposable resource. The next step is to allow "flash" reconfiguration (*i.e.* as a whole) of the entire connection layer or at least of a combinatorially significant set of junctions. This can be achieved using photoinitiated polymerization but here in a grid of etched channels. The polymers flow into and fill the grid from a small number of connections and a photomask then determines the channels which are to be blocked by the polymerized material. Relatively low precision masks of approx. 50 μm resolution are sufficient, so that they can be generated dynamically and computer controlled by a DMD (Digital Mirror Device), customized to reflect ultraviolet light [22]. The use of DMDs like this was also part of a project proposal in DNA Computing (McCaskill *et al.* 1997). This step in the direction of reconfigurable microfluidics has a parallel in precursors to FPGAs such as EPLDs or EPROMs.

To attain truly dynamically switchable microfluidic connections, some form of microvalves would appear essential. We should emphasize that even comparatively slow switching timescales of seconds to minutes would be useful if high density arrays of simply controllable microvalves can be achieved. Almost all procedures in microvalve construction have resulted in components on the scale from 0.2 to 2 mm. To attain complex microfluidic circuit connections *via* series of valves, of order 10^4 such valves are desired. In order to achieve efficient control of such valves, they should be bistable, so that they can be serially reconfigured and maintain their state when the control signal is removed. Simple microvalves for high density applications were developed [23]. These were based on hydraulic control, which allows addressing via multi-valve cascades. However, they were not bistable and although smaller, turned out to have maximum packing densities in the 0.5mm range. More work is needed in this direction.

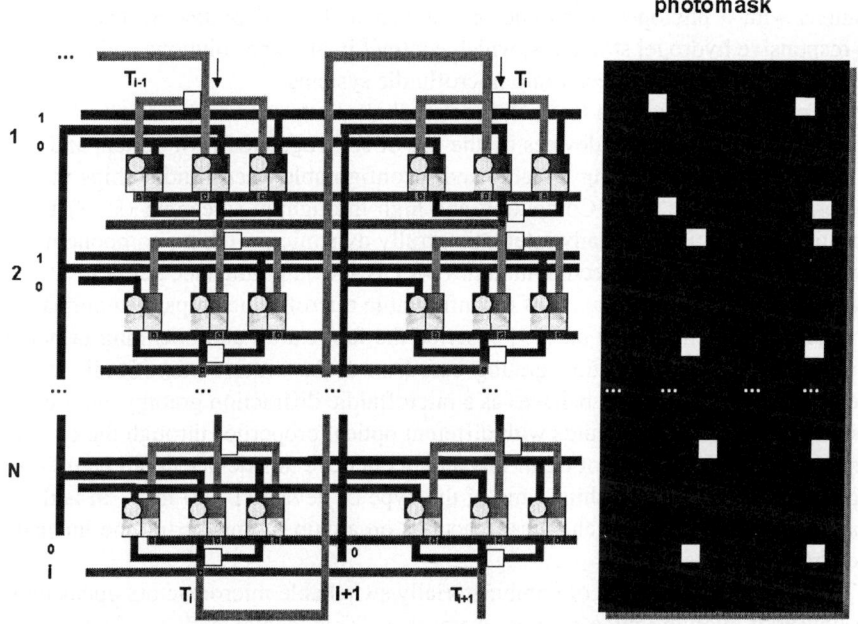

Fig. 3. Optically programmable valves for DNA-Computing. Optically programming configurations for DNA-Computing. Each module shown is an active component, allowing magnetically directed transfer for specific DNA strands (which bind to the complementary sequences immobilised to the magnetic beads). The channel network is similar for different instances of the maximal clique problem, which the network is designed to solve. Maximal clique is a hard graph theoretic problem on N nodes, for which the decision problem is NP-complete. The graph instance being tackled can be encoded in an NxN binary matrix and the microreactor optically configured to include or exclude the alternating side modules in each triple by a mask which directs the polymerization of channel-blockers. This same problem is currently being configured optically by photosensitive immobilization of specific DNA to beads

Going beyond simple valves, magnetic beads may be used to create externally switchable mixing and molecular transfer devices. In addition to magnetically switchable mixing devices [24], we have designed bistable magnetically switchable binding devices [25]. Here magnetic beads transfer specific molecules from one chamber to the next in a bistable arrangement, so that a serial or parallel control by external magnets is possible. Other techniques of interest in configuring specific molecular transfer along channels include electro-osmosis [26] and electrophoresis [27]. Both these techniques have led to integrated microfluidic devices, but their role in reconfigurable microreactors has not yet been explored.

BEEBE et. al. recently presenting a new dynamic method to produce valves within microchannels for local flow control [28]. The fabrication procedure combines lithography, photopolymerization and microfluidics and starts by filling transparent microchannels with a photopolymerizable prepolymer and a photoinitiator. The resulting pH-responsive hydrogel structures, which contract in alkaline solutions and expand in acids, can be integrated directly into microfluidic systems.

One potential application for such functional elements can be the autonomous flow control inside microfluidic devices by the use of self-regulated flow sorters and shut-off valves. We suggest using variable and reconfigurable microfluidic chips in combinatorial chemistry, DNA Computing and high throughput screening (HTS) for diagnostics. Our group is already integrating truly dynamic-switching-components in a network of microfluidic selection modules for DNA-Computing (see below).

Another potential application of reconfigurable microfluidic chips is to optical signal processing. Schueller et al. [29] describe the fabrication and operating principles of a reconfigurable diffraction grating based on a elastomeric microfluidic device. The array of microchannels behaves as a microfluidic diffraction grating and it can be reconfigured by pumping fluids with different optical properties through the channels to modulate the diffraction of light. The authors believe this device could be used - as a result of the shortly switching time of this type of device (1-500 ms) - in real-time monitoring of evolution of chemical reactions on a chip by measuring the intensities of diffracted beams.

The further development of combinatorially switchable microreactors opens up the possibility of evolving microreactors themselves. This idea extends the first proposal by Kitano [30] who based his proposal on Ikuta's (see above) electronically controlled microreactors. Using evolutionary programming techniques, he proposed to evolve MIFS clusters complex enough to evolve specific chemical substances and long RNA chains, which can be incorporated into biochemical systems such as the DNA computing systems proposed by Adleman in 1994 [31]. Our own approach to using reconfigurable microfluidic hardware to solve DNA Computing problems is based instead on the combinatorial switching network idea. Instead of the molecular transfer modules based on magnetic beads, our architecture also permits the use of the reconfigurable photo-polymerization technique shown above. A diagram showing the optical configuration of a microflow system, by photo-initiated polymerization leading to specific channel blocking, to solve the maximal clique problem is shown in Figure 3.

Such dynamically reconfigurable microreactors can be programmed much akin to the programmable electronic devices which paved the way for evolvable electronic hardware. Optical coupling of microreactors with electronic hardware also allows a fine-grained reconfigurability to be achieved (see below). We expect these reconfigurable microreactors to be invaluable in building general molecular construction systems based on self-replication.

Evolvable Biomolecular Hardware

Cells synthesize a vast array of biomolecular structures and devices encoded by DNA. They do this using the protein translation apparatus and sophisticated self assembly procedures. Utilizing the "cell factory" is already an accepted component of current research programs [32], but involves all of the constraints and uncertainties of dealing with cellular complexity. The question as to whether cells are capable of universal computation has already been answered in the affirmative (*e.g.* ciliates [33]). Recent research on novel principles for *in vivo* DNA based computers have enabled this thesis to become concrete [34]. The immediate question facing computer scientists and biotechnologists alike is can these systems be programmed: biotechnology would like to see programmable real-world functionality, *e.g.* concrete molecular output; computer scientists would like to see efficient parallel algorithms for difficult combinatorial problems. However, the really exciting thing about biological systems is the way in which they deal with the issue of design: finding the algorithms to solve new difficult tasks or problems. Part of this answer has to do with evolution.

Results in *in vitro* evolution over the past decade suggest that a great potential exists in evolving molecular structures in chemically well-defined environments outside cells. Even simply in terms of numbers, whereas 10^{10} is a lot of cells in the lab, *in vitro* molecular evolution experiments can cope easily with 10^{15} molecules or more. Molecular biology has progressed to the point where sequence programmable and evolvable molecular systems have been constructed as cell-free chemical systems using biomolecules such as DNA and proteins [35]. Typically, *in vitro* amplification of biomolecules shows major evolution on the time-scale of hours in the laboratory. Rapid sequencing and fluorescence detection allows at least part of these changes to be monitored in real time. The process is sped up through the short generation times of less than a minute and the huge populations of 10^{15} or more molecules. Synthetic and naturally occurring molecules are placed in environments with exotic resources, in which the problem of survival takes on new structural and organisational dimensions. Progress has also been made in programming the environmental selection conditions to reflect artificial targets: either construction or information processing targets. Examples include the evolution of ribozymes [36], enzymes using transition state analogues as targets and the formulation of selection chains based on hybridisation reactions to reflect externally defined combinatorial optimisation problems [25].

Biochemical ecosystems rely on the chemical coupling between different biopolymers being amplified *in vitro* in laboratory experiments. The simplest examples of these biochemical ecosystems involve predator-prey [37] and co-operative or symbiotic relationships between different amplifying species [38]. Such systems enable the evolutionary processes associated with the emergence of organisational forms, capable of stably integrating many different types of molecules, to be analysed in the laboratory. The first steps of distributing evolving information on two different molecules have already proved surprising. Spatial pattern formation in such systems appears to play a crucial role in stabilising the evolution of complex assemblies of molecules [35]. This work draws together the fields of spatial self-organization (*e.g.* Turing patterns) with evolutionary self-organization (*e.g.* quasispecies).

As these "in vitro" systems increase in sophistication, the goal of attaining general programmable molecular construction systems appears tangible. Already, the first such systems which extend evolution from the simple optimisation of individual molecules to systems of interacting molecules have been established. While self-replicating molecular systems have also been designed based purely on small organics [39], evolvable molecular systems currently employ enzymes extracted from bacterial cultures as catalysts. Enhancements in *in vitro* protein translation [40] and more particularly the evolution of RNA catalysts [41] (ribozymes) is beginning to open up the possibility that complete construction systems can be achieved in which all informational macromolecules are generated by the system itself. This research is not only relevant to the origin of life, but to the capability of bootstrapping construction as the final stage in reconfigurable hardware as discussed in above.

It is possible that DNA Computers will form the first truly evolvable computing hardware. Artificially programmed selection via hybridization to programmed DNA sequences allows combinatorial optimization to be performed with populations of DNA molecules. This field of DNA Computing already plays a many-faceted role within computer science and complexity theory [5], only a few years after the initial experimental demonstration by Leonard Adleman [31]. DNA Computing does not dispense with the need for sophisticated algorithms, since the solution of hard combinatorial problems by brute force search requires an exponentially large quantity of DNA. Incidentally, it is still unclear whether alternative computing paradigms such as Quantum Computing can be scaled more effectively in practice. Independently of this, however, DNA Computing provides unique opportunities to evolve hardware and even complete construction systems.

The idea of programming DNA Computers as configurable hardware using dataflow architectures is already proving fruitful [25]: instead of constructing universal DNA hardware or hardware only suited for a given problem instance, DNA computers can be built which solve all problem instances (up to a maximum size) belonging to a specific problem family. Our approach is to configure the computers for the problem family through an appropriate microflow reactor and then to configure each different individual problem instance using only optical patterns by biochemical photolithography. More sophisticated configurable and evolvable microfluidic systems will enable still more flexible reconfigurable architectures (*e.g.* for arbitrary problems) to be constructed. Finally, the link up with electronic hardware will allow hardware design and computation tasks to be partitioned effectively to exploit both the advantages of high speed serial processing and massively parallel computation.

Multilevel Reconfigurability: Linking the Domains

The interface between the molecular and electronic information processing worlds has also seen rapid progress in the last decade. The fluorescent labeling of biomolecules has enabled single molecules of DNA, even short pieces, to be observed [42]. We have developed a single molecule tracker using our configurable hardware and a strip detector (developed in Bonn) to analyze spatially resolved photon bursts from diffusing biomolecules in real time [42]. Application of this detector to a range of molecular information processing tasks is possible by adapting the configurable hardware. Single molecules as information processing machines provide vast savings in energy and potentially enable huge parallel computers, as in the field of DNA computing. On the other hand, we expect photochemical patterning of molecular systems in microfluidic devices, as proposed in [25], to provide the mainstay of high density input to hybrid molecular systems.

How far are we still from bootstrapping construction systems? Work on ribozymes suggest that increasingly complex self-reproducing systems of molecules are near at hand. We need more research on configurable mechanisms of controlling computation and communication between macromolecules. We hope that our own program on configurable microreactors will contribute. The linkup with electronic systems may well prove to be a next step, rather than an essential prerequisite in this development, despite the fact that progress in molecular electronics, which may allow self-organizing circuits, is currently very promising. While it would be exceedingly brave to hazard a guess at the future shape of computation, we are confident that evolvable construction systems will play an increasing role in the coming decades. We can expect to see an ever increasing interchange between molecular biology, nanotechnology, microsystems, electronics and information technology in the transition from reconfigurable systems to fully evolvable ones.

Acknowledgements

The authors would like to thank D. van Noort and U. Tangen for a careful reading of the manuscript. The setup support of the German Ministry of Science (FKZ 01SF9952) is also gratefully acknowledged.

References

1. XC6200-field programmable gate arrays data sheet, Xilinx 1 1-73
2. Thompson, A. "An evolved circuit intrinsic in silicon, entwined with physics" *Lect. Not. Comp. Sci.* 1259 (1996) 390-405
3. Tangen, U, McCaskill, J.S. Hardware evolution with a massively parallel dynamically reconfigurable computer: Polyp. In Sipper, M., Mange, D. and Perez-Uribe, A., eds., ICES'98 Evolvable Systems: From Biology to Hardware, volume 1478, Springer-Verlag Heidelberg (1998) 364-371
4. Tangen, U. "Self-Organisation in Micro-Configurable Hardware" to be published in Bedau, M.A., McCaskill, J.S., Packard, N., Rasmussen, S. eds. "Artificial Life VII: Proceedings of the 7. International Conference" Aug. 2-7 2000
5. Paun, G., Rozenberg, G., Salomaa, A. "DNA Computing – new computing paradigms" Springer-Verlag (1998) Berlin Heidelberg
6. von Neumann, J. (1956) "Theory of Self-Reproducing Automata" Urbana: Burks, A.W. University of Illinois Press.

7. *Lecture Notes in Computer Science* ICES 98 Sipper, M., Mange, D., Perez-Uribe, A. eds. (1998) and ICES 96 Higuchi, T., Iwata, M., Liu, W. eds. (1996) Springer-Verlag Berlin
8. Sanchez, E., Tomassini, M. eds. "Towards Evolvable Hardware – The Evolutionary Engineering Approach" (1996) Springer-Verlag Heidelberg
9. McCaskill, J.S., Maeke, T., Gemm, U., Schulte, L. and Tangen, U. "NGEN: A massively parallel reconfigurable computer for biological Simulation: Towards a self-organizing computer" *Lect. Not. Comp. Sci.* 1259 (1996) 260-276
10. Kenis, P.J.A., Ismagilov, R.F., Whitesides, G.M. "Microfabrication inside capillaries using multiphase laminar flow patterning" *Science* 285 (1999) 83–85
11. Harrison, D.J., Fluri, K., Fan, Z., Effenhauser, C.S., Manz, A. *Science* 261 (1993) 895
12. Manz, A., Becker, H. "Microsystem Technology in chemistry and Life Science", Topics in Current Chemistry, Vol.194, Springer-Verlag, Heidelberg (1998)
13. Köhler, M in "Etching in Microsystem Technology" Wiley-VCH (1999)
14. Peterson, K.E. *Proc. IEEE* 70 (1982) 420
15. Muller, R.S. *Sensors and Actuators* A21 (1990) 1
16. Dietrich, T.R., Abraham, M., Diebel, J., Lacher, M., Ruf, A. *J. Micromech. Microeng.* 3 (1993) 187
17. Quin, D, Xia, Y., Whitesides, G.M. "Rapid prototyping of complex structures with feature sizes larger than 20 μm *Adv. Mat.* 8 (1996) 917–919
18. Schuenemann, Bauer, G., Schaefer, W., Leutenbauer, Grosser, V., Reichl, H. Modularization of Microsystems and Standardization of Interfaces In Reichl, H., Obermeier, E. eds., Micro System Technologies 98 6th International conference on micro-, electro-, opto-Mechanical Systems an Components, VDE-Verlag GmbH Berlin (1998) 141-146
19. Ikuta, K., Hirowatari, K., Ogata, T. "Three Dimensional Micro Integrated Fluid System (MIFS)" fabricated by stereo lithography" *Proc. of. IEEE International Workshop on Micro Electro Mechanical Systems (MEMS '94)* (1994) 1–9
20. Ikuta, K., Hirowatari, K. "Real three dimensional micro fabrication unsing stereo lithography and metal molding" *Proc. of. IEEE International Workshop on Micro Electro Mechanical Systems (MEMS '93)* (1993) 42–47
21. Ikuta, K., Maruo, S., Fukaya, Y and Fujisawa, T. "Biochemical IC chip toward cell free DNA protein synthesis" *Proc. of. IEEE International Workshop on Micro Electro Mechanical Systems (MEMS '98)* (1998) 131–136
22. Cerrina, F., Yue, Y. http://www.xraylith.wisc.edu/dna_chips/index.html
23. Bräutigam, R., Steen, D., Ehricht, McCaskill, J.S. Isothermal Biochemical Amplification in Miniaturized Reactors with integrated Micro Valves, Microreaction Technology, Proceedings of the third International Conference on Microreaction Technology, Frankfurt a.M., (1999) Springer-Verlag, Berlin
24. McCaskill, J.S. Schmidt, K. Patent PCT/EP98/03942 "Switchable dynamic micromixer with minimum dead volume" WO 99/01209
25. McCaskill, J.S. "Optically Programming DNA Computing in Microflow Reactors" Preprint GMD - German National Research Center for Information Technology Schloss Birlinghoven, St. Augustin March 2000
26. Asbury, C.L., van den Engh, G. "Trapping of DNA in non-uniform oscillating electric fields." *Biophys. J.* 1 (1998) 1024-30
27. Manz, A. "The secret behind electrophoresis microstructure design" in Widmer, E., Verpoorte, Banard, S. eds. Proceedings of the 2nd International Symposium on μTAS" (1996) pp. 28-30, Basel

28. Beebe, D.J., Moore, J.S, Bauer, J.M., Yu, Q., Liu, R.H., Devadoss, C., Jo, B.-H. *Nature* 404 (2000) 588–590
29. Schueller, J.A., Duffy, D.C., Rogers, J.A., Brittain, S.T., Whitesides, G.M. "Reconfigurable diffraction gratings based on elastomeric microfluidic devices" *Sens. Actuators* 78 (1998) 149-159
30. Kitano, H. "Morphogenesis for Evolvable Systems" In Sanchez, E., Tomassini, M. eds. "Towards Evolvable Hardware – The Evolutionary Engineering Approach" (1996) Springer-Verlag Heidelberg pp.99-117.
31. Adleman, L.M. "Molecular computation of solutions to combinatorial problems" Science 266 (1994) 1021–1024
32. Web address: http://www.cordis.lu/fp5/home.html
33. Landweber, L. F., Kuo, T.-C., Curtis, E.. Evolution and Assembly of an Extremely Scrambled Gene, Proc. Natl. Acad. Sci. (2000).
34. "DNA VI –Sixth International Meeting in DNA Based Computers" Conference Proceedings Condon, A., Rozenberg, G. eds. June 13-17 (2000) Leiden Center for Natural Computing
35. McCaskill, J.S. "Spatially Resolved *in vitro* Molecular Ecology" Biophysical Chemistry 66 (1997) 145-158
36. Wright, M. C., Joyce, G.F. "Continuous in vitro evolution of catalytic function." *Science* 276(5312) (1997) 614-617
37. Wlotzka, McCaskill, J.S. "A molecular predator and its prey: Coupled isothermal amplification of nucleic acids" *Chemistry and Biology* Vol.4, No. 1 (1997) 25-33
38. Ehricht, R., Ellinger, T., McCaskill, J.S. "Cooperative amplification of templates by cross hybridisation (CATCH)" *European Journal of Biochemistry* 243 (1997) 358-364
39. Luther, A., Brandsch, R., von Kiedrowski, G. "Surface-promoted replication and exponential amplification of DNA analogues." *Nature* 396 (1998) 245 - 248
40. Alimov, A.P., Khmelnitsky, A.Yu, Simonenko, PN, Spirin AS, Chetverin AB „Cell-free synthesis and affinity isolation of proteins on a nanomole scale." *Biotechniques* 28(2) (2000) 338-44
41. Doudna, J. A., Usman, N. et al. "Ribozyme-catalyzed primer extension by trinucleotides: a model for the RNA-catalyzed replication of RNA." *Biochemistry* 32(8) (1993) 2111-2115
42. McCaskill, J.S. Abschlussbericht BMBF Teilprojekt "In-vitro Evolution in Mikroreaktoren und Geräteentwicklungen" (1999) FKZ 0310799

A Specific Test Methodology for Symmetric SRAM-Based FPGAs

M. Renovell

Laboratoire d'Informatique, Robotique et Microélectronique de Montpellier
LIRMM-UM2 161 Rue Ada 34392 Montpellier France
renovell@lirmm.fr   Tel (33)467418523   Fax (33)467418500

Abstract. This paper describes a test methodology for symmetric SRAM-based FPGAs. From a fundamental point of view, a test methodology for FPGAs differs from the test methodology for ASICs mainly due to the configurability of such flexible devices. In the paper, the FPGA architecture is first analyzed identifying the test problems specific to FPGAs as well as the test properties. This architecture is divided into different architectural elements such as the logic cells, the interconnect cells and the RAM cells. For each architectural element appropriated fault models are proposed, and test configurations and test vectors are derived targeting the proposed fault models.

1. Introduction

Programmable logic in the form of Field-Programmable Gate Arrays (FPGAs) has become now a widely accepted design approach for low- and medium-volume computing applications. Low development costs and inherent functional flexibility have spurred the spectacular growth of this technology [1-2]. There are many FPGA types but a widely used is the static-RAM based FPGA architecture. In such a programmable circuit, an array of logic cells and interconnection cells can be configured in the field to implement a desired designed function, this is usually called In-System Configurability (ISC).

Testing for conventional digital ICs is a difficult and important task [3-24]. And testing for FPGAs is an even more complex problem. Indeed, the classical test approaches used for digital ASICs fail when applied to FPGAs. The main reason is because symmetric FPGAs have an heterogeneous architecture mixing interconnect elements, logic elements and RAM elements. Another important reason is because each of these elements is made in a non-classical way.

Concerning the heterogeneous architecture for example, we can observe that digital ASICs usually include a few number of large blocks as illustrated in figure 1.a. Each block is of a specific nature: a random logic block, a RAM block, buses... In a classical digital test approach, a specific test technique is consequently used for each block according to its nature. On the contrary, a symmetric FPGA can be viewed as composed of a large number of small blocks, all the blocks are identical but

heteregeneous including: logic modules, RAM cells and interconnect elements as illustrated in figure 1.b. In the blocks, these heterogeneous elements are strongly interconnected making the usual test techniques difficult to apply. As the matter of fact, a typical heterogeneous FPGA block can be viewed as a recollection of all the problems encountered in testing:
  a) Sequential elements (flip-flops),
  b) Mixed architecture (logic/interconnect/RAM),
  c) Multiple representation level (module/gate/transistor)
  d) Fault model definition (stuck/short/open/memory..).

To face these difficulties, a practical solution consists in conceptually dividing the heterogeneous block into different homogeneous sub-blocks as represented in figure 2. An interesting possible solution can be to divide the heterogeneous block into the following homogeneous sub-blocks:
  a) The logic cell,
  b) The interconnect cell,
  c) The RAM cells.

Then, a specific and adequate test approach can be applied to each homogeneous cell according to its nature. But, it is obvious that each specific test approach must take into account the connection of the considered cell with the other ones. For example, the test approach proposed for the RAM cells must account for the connections between the RAM cells and the logic cells and interconnect cells.

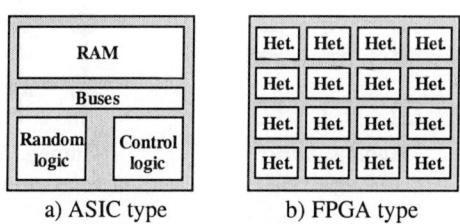

a) ASIC type   b) FPGA type

Fig.1. Homogeneous ASIC vs Heterogeneous FPGA

Testing for FPGAs is clearly not easy but on the other side, symmetrical FPGAs have important test properties that must absolutely be considered and used. As previously mentioned, almost all the blocks into the FPGAs are identical. That means that the small block is repeated forming a regular two-dimensional mxm array. From the test point of view, regular structures present some properties that simplified the test process.

Finally, applying the above conceptual division to the whole FPGA means that we have to propose a specific test approach for:
  a) a two-dimensional array of logic cells,
  b) a two-dimensional array of interconnect cells,
  c) a two-dimensional array of RAM cells.

The works published in the literature usually follow this practical test strategy and target one of the above defined arrays [3-24]. As an example, Inoue and al. address the problem of testing the array of look-up table in [13], Huang and al. address the problem of testing the array of logic cells in [20]. Following this practical divide and conquer test strategy, the author has proposed first a test procedure targeting the array of interconnect cells [4,5,8], second another test procedure targeting the array of logic cells in [6,7,10], third a test procedure for the array of LUT/RAM modules in [9,11], and finally a test procedure for the array of interconnect/logic interface cells in [12].

In this paper the test of the two-dimensional array of interconnect cells is presented in section 2, the test of the two-dimensional array of logic cells in section 3 and the test of the two-dimensional array of RAM cells in section 4. Finally section 5 concludes

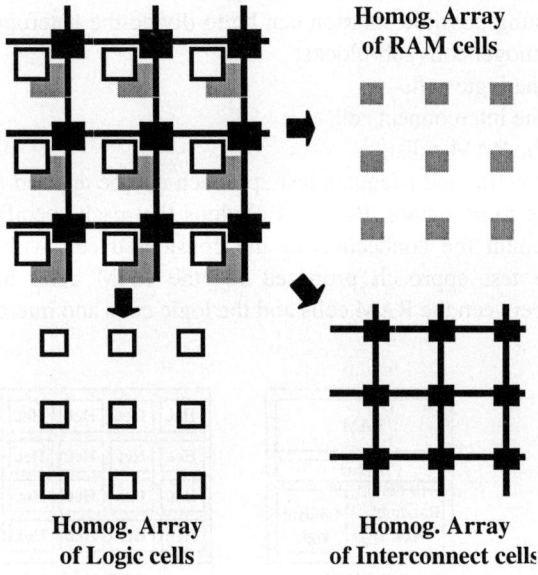

Fig. 2. Homogeneous Sub-Arrays

2. Testing the Array of Interconnect Cells

This section is devoted to the test of the interconnect cells. This problem has been discussed in detail by the authors in [4,5,8,10]. The interconnect structure is composed of a mxm array of « Switch Matrix » interconnected by k metal lines. This regular array is illustrated in the simplified example of figure 3 where m=5 and k=4.

A switch matrix is a programmable connecting element receiving k lines on each side. The lines are connected to the switch matrix pins called North pins $(N_1...N_k)$, East pins $(E_1...E_k)$, South pins $(S_1...S_k)$ and West pins $(W_1...W_k)$. Inside the Switch Matrix, some pairs of pins can not be connected and are called non-connectable pins. Some pairs of pins can be connected and are called connectable pins. Figure 3 gives an example of switch matrix with 4 pins on each side. In figure 3 the connectable pins are linked by a dotted line. Figure 3 gives also an example of configuration where some connectable pins are connected (full lines). In the remainder of the paper we consider as an example that any set of pins with the same (resp. different) number i are connectable (resp. non-connectable). The considered set of connectable pins illustrated in figure 3 corresponds to the Xilinx 4000 family.

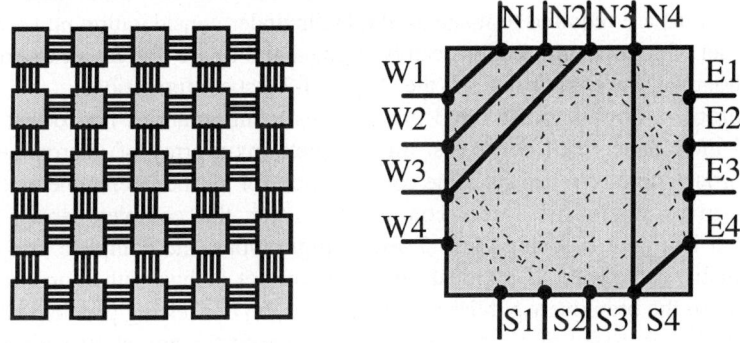

Fig. 3. Array of interconnect cells and Switch Matrix

It is now necessary to define adequate fault models for this particular interconnect cells and lines. Due to the nature of the elements, we consider fault models classically used for interconnections i.e. Opens and Shorts. Figure 4 gives the list of assumed faults with their particular names.

	For any Line	For any pair of Lines	For any pair of Conn. Pins	For any pair of Non-Conn. Pins
Fault Type	Open	Short	Short	Short
Name	**Line-Open**	**Permanent-Connection**	**Permanent-Connection**	**Permanent-Disconnection**

Fig. 4. Fault models for the Interconnect Cells

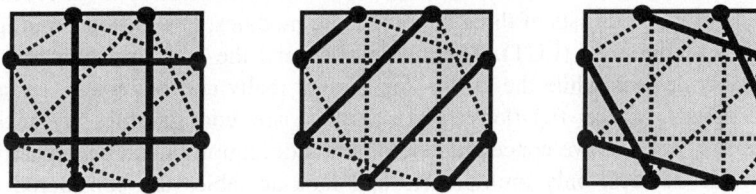

Fig. 5. Test Configurations for a single interconnect cell

Obviously, the faults concerning the non-connectable pins are independent of the switch matrix configuration while faults concerning the connectable pins depend on the switch matrix configuration. A test configuration that connects for example pins N4 and S4 makes the Permanent-Connection fault between connectable Pins N4 and S4 redundant and so, untestable. While a test configuration that does not connect the pins make the fault non-redundant. We have demonstrated that a minimum of 3 test configurations are required to make all the faults under consideration non-redundant. Several set of 3 test configurations can be defined and figure 5 gives an example with the Orthogonal, the Diagonal-1 and the Diagonal-2 test configurations.

The problem now is to use the 3 previous test configurations not to test a single isolated interconnect cell but to test the complete mxm array of interconnect cells. The approach here is to use the same configuration for all the interconnect cells. This method gives obviously 3 test configurations for the complete array that are illustrated in figure 6. Using these 3 test configurations, the complete array can be conceptually considered as a global bus. The concept of bus with shorts and opens allow to use the previously published works about the bus testing problem [26-28]. It has been demonstrated that a n bits bus can be tested for any short and open with $\log_2(n)$ vectors. For the considered array, the resulting number of test vectors is: $\log_2(2km)$.

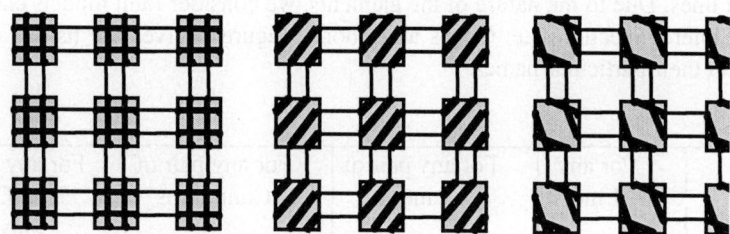

Fig. 6. Test Configurations for the array of interconnect cells

3. Testing the Array of Logic Cells

This section is devoted to the test of the logic cells. This problem has been discussed in detail by the authors in [6,7,10]. This section summarizes the main results. The logic cells usually consists of three types of logic modules: D flip-flops, multiplexers and look up table units (LUT). The multiplexers and the look-up tables are typical configurable devices while the D flip-flop are not really configurables. In fact, the control signals of the flip-flop (reset, clock...) are configurables by means of multiplexers. Because we concentrate here on the definition of test configuration for configurable devices, only multiplexers and look-up tables are considered in this section.

In figure 7, we have an example of FPGA 4-to-1 multiplexer. In a typical FPGA representation, the data inputs E0,E1,E2,E3 are represented because they are

Operation Inputs while the 2 bit address A0 and A1 are not represented because they are Configuration Inputs not available during normal operation. In practice the internal logic structure can vary or is not really known, and so the fault model associated to this device is the stuck-at of the 6 different inputs E0,E1,E2,E3,A0,A1 and the single output S.

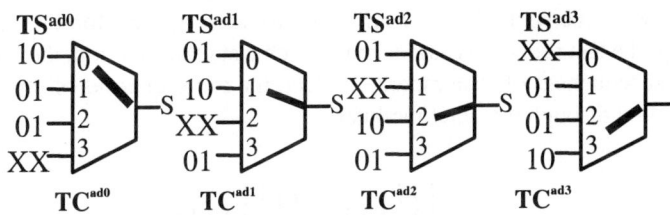

Fig. 7. Test of the Multiplexer

It can be demonstrated that all the stuck-at-0/1 of the inputs and output of the FPGA multiplexer can be detected by using 4 test configurations. As the matter of fact, a test configuration is associated to each multiplexer address. For each test configuration, a sequence of 2 test vectors is applied. These 4 test configurations are illustrated in figure 7 where the configurations are symbollicaly represented by a connection between an input and ouput. In a more general way, we can say that a multiplexer with 2^n addresses (n address bits) require 2^n test configurations.

Assuming now that the LUT is a particular type of multiplexer, the test conditions are identical for the multiplexer and the LUT. Hence, we can use the vectors previously defined for the multiplexer. In such conditions, we found that the exclusive-OR and complemented exclusive-OR vectors must be applied on the LUT configuration inputs and an exhaustive sequence of 2^n vectors must be applied on the LUT operation Inputs. This is equivalent in defining 2 test configurations called TC^{XOR} and TC^{XNOR} and defining 2 corresponding test sequences called TS^{XOR} and TS^{XNOR}. The 2 test configurations are symbollically represented by a XOR ($\oplus$) or XNOR symbol inside the LUT in figure 8.

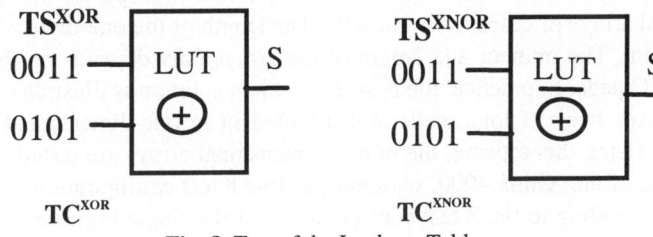

Fig. 8. Test of the Look-up Table

The test configurations and test vectors defined for the isolated multiplexer and LUT are now used to define test configurations and test vectors for the logic cell. The logic cell is an interconnection of modules such as multiplexers, LUTs and flip-flops and so, a test configuration of a logic cell is an aggregate of the test configurations of the modules as illustrated in figure 9 with the Xilinx 4000 logic cell [25]. In order to 'cover' all the test configurations of all the modules in the cell, several test configurations must obviously be defined for the logic cell. We demonstrated that using our technique, only 8 test configurations are required for the Xilinx 4000. Concerning, the test sequences associated to each test configuration, they are obtained from the test sequences of each module. In fact, the test sequences of the modules are simply justified through the other modules.

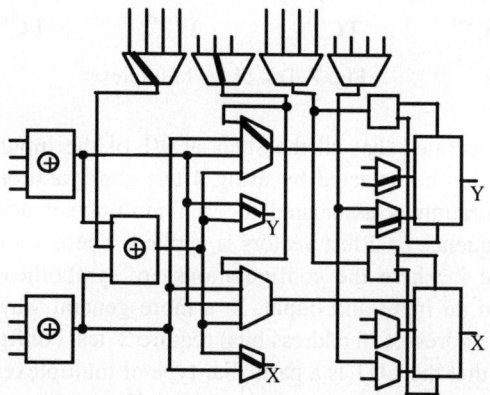

Fig. 9. Example of logic cell test configuration

The minimization of the number of Test Configuration using the module Test Configurations leads to only 8 Test Configurations for completely testing the complex XILINX 4000 CLB. The problem now is to define Test Configurations and Test Sequences for the mxm array of logic cells. In case of an array of logic cells, the problem consists in controlling and observing the whole logic cells. Individual access to each logic cell is not possible in practice. Indeed, a FPGA does not have enougth I/O pads to control and observe each logic cell in parallel from outside.

For these reason, the logic cells are interconnected in a special way forming one-dimensional arrays of cascaded logic cells. The length of the one-dimensional array is not important. The number and length of the arrays only depends on the number of available I/O pads. In practice, the most convenient solution is illustrated in Figure 10 where a mxm array of logic cells is distributed in m one-dimensional arrays of m logic cells. Using this scheme, the m one-dimensional arrays are tested in parallel. In the example of the Xilinx 4000, we simply define 8 test configurations for the whole array corresponding to the 8 test configurations of the single logic cell. At this point, it must be noted that the complete Test Procedure has been simulated using an iterrative array of 4 CLBs giving 100% coverage of the assumed fault models. These simulations validate the proposed test configurations and test sequences.

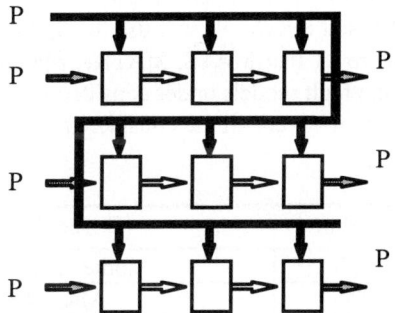

Fig. 10. One-Dimensional array principle

4. Testing the Array of RAM Cells

This section is devoted to the test of the array of RAM cells that are embedded in the LUT/RAM modules. The LUT/RAM module is assumed to be part of a logic cell and it is assumed to be configured in RAM mode. This problem has been discussed in detail by the authors in [9,11]

Considering first a single isolated module in RAM mode, the module operates as a classical RAM and any type of existing RAM test can be used. This is very interesting because the problem of RAM testing has been investigated for a long time and very mature algorithms exist [29-30]. A well-known class of test algorithms for RAM circuits are the MARCH algorithms. The RAM fault models usually considered in the march tests are:

- SAF: The stuck-at fault can be defined as follows: The logic value of a stuck-at cell or line is always 0 or 1 and cannot be changed to the opposite value.

- AF: The address decoder faults concern faults in the address decoder. Different types of faults are usually considered. The first fault assumes that no cell will be accessed with a certain address. The second fault assumes that a certain cell is never accessed. The third fault assumes that multiple cells are accessed simultaneously with a certain address. And finally, the last fault assumes that a certain cell can be accessed with multiple addresses.

- TF: The transition fault is a special case of the SAF. It is defined as follows. A cell or line which fails to undergo a $0 \rightarrow 1$ transition when it is written is said to contain an up transition fault; similarly, a down transition fault is the impossibility of making a $1 \rightarrow 0$ transition.

- CF: The coupling fault involves 2 cells and can be defined as follows. A write operation which generates a up or down transition in one cell changes the contents of a second cell. Different types of coupling faults are usually considered. The inversion coupling fault (CFin) assumes that an up or down transition in one cell inverts the contents of a second cell. And the idempotent coupling fault (CFid) assumes that an up or down transition in one cell forces the contents of a second cell to a certain value, 0 or 1.

Note that DRAM circuits are more sensitive to CF than SRAM circuits. Dealing in this paper with SRAM based FPGA, we will use the SAF, AF and TF fault models. It can be observed in Figure 11 that MATS, MATS+, Marching 1/0 and MATS++ are able to detect some of the fault models under consideration. It seems interesting to use the MATS++ test because it covers all the considered fault models and the number of test vectors is very low.

Algorithm	Covered Fault
MATS	some AFs, SAFs
MATS+	AFs, SAFs
Marching 1/0	AFs, SAFs, TFs
MATS++	AFs, SAFs, TFs

Fig. 11. March tests

Note that only one test configuration is required to test a single module in RAM mode. Considering now the complete array of LUT/RAM module, the approach used here is similar to the one used in the previous sections for the logic cells and the interconnect cells i.e. all the LUT/RAM modules in the array have the same test configurations. This method gives obviously 1 test configuration for the complete array. In order to guarantee full controllability and observability of each module, we propose to connect the output of the LUT/RAM module in RAM mode to the input of the DFF included in the logic cell. The output of the Dff is connected to the data in of the following LUT/RAM module. This particular test configuration called pseudo shift register is illustrated in figure 12 with m=3.

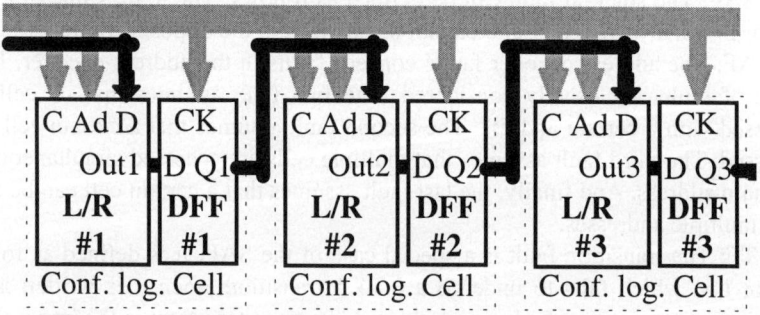

Fig. 12. The pseudo shift register

In this unique test configuration, the common primary inputs connected to every module include the control signals (Read/Write, Enable..) and address inputs of the LUT/RAM module, and the clock (CK) of the Dffs. The Read/Write control signal and the Dff clock can be adequately used to shift a value from the primary data input to the primary output, through the Dffs and through the modules. In this configuration, the MATS++ algorithm can be adapted taking into account the shift trough the different cells: This adaptation is called the shifted MARCH++ algorithm.

5. Conclusion

This paper gives a general overview of a structural test approach proposed for testing RAM-based FPGA taking into account their configurability. The SRAM-based FPGA architecture is first discussed identifying the specific FPGA test problems as well as the FPGA test properties. The FPGA architecture is then conceptually divided into different architectural elements such as the logic cells, the interconnect and the RAM cells. For each architectural element appropriated fault models are proposed, and test configurations and test vectors are derived targeting the fault models under consideration.

References

[1] S.D. Brown, R.J. Francis, J. Rose, S.G. Vranesic, «Field-Programmable Gate Arrays», Kluwer Academic Publishers, 1992.
[2] S.M. Trimberger (ed), «Field-Programmable Gate Array Technology», Kluwer Academic Publishers, 1994.
[3] C. Jordan and W.P. Marnane, «Incoming Inspection of FPGAs», Proc. of IEEE European Test Conference, pp. 371-377, 1993.
[4] M. Renovell, J. Figueras and Y. Zorian, «Testing the Interconnect Structure of Unconfigurated FPGA», IEEE European Test Workshop, pp. 125-129, Sète (Montpellier), FRANCE, June 1996
[5] M. Renovell, J. Figueras and Y. Zorian, «Test of RAM-Based FPGA: Methodology and Application to the Interconnect», 15th IEEE VLSI Test Symposium, pp. 230-237, Monterey, CA, USA, May 1997.
[6] M. Renovell, J.M. Portal, J. Figueras and Y. Zorian, «Test Pattern and Test Generation Methodology for the Logic of RAM-Based FPGA», IEEE Asian Test Symp., pp. 254-259, Akita, Japan, November, 1997.
[7] M. Renovell, J.M. Portal, J. Figueras and Y. Zorian, «Testing the Configurable Logic of RAM-based FPGA», IEEE Int. Conf. on Design, Automation and Test in Europe, pp. 82-88, Paris, France, Feb 1998.
[8] M. Renovell, J.M.Portal, J. Figueras and Y. Zorian, «Testing the Interconnect of RAM-Based FPGAs», IEEE Design & Test of Computer, Vol. 15, n°1, pp.45-50, January-March 1998.
[9] M. Renovell, J.M. Portal, J. Figueras and Y. Zorian, «SRAM-based FPGAs: Testing the RAM mode of the LUT/RAM modules», IEEE European Test Workshop, pp.,146-151, Barcelone, Spain, May 1998.

[10] M. Renovell, J.M. Portal, J. Figueras and Y. Zorian, "*Minimizing the Number of Test Configurations for different FPGA Families* ", IEEE 8th Asian Test Symposium ATS99, pp. 363-368, Nov. 16-18, Shanghai, China, 1999.

[11] M. Renovell, J.M. Portal, J. Figueras and Y. Zorian, «SRAM-Based FPGA: Testing the LUT/RAM modules», IEEE International Test Conference, pp. 1102-1111, Washington, DC, USA, Oct. 18-23, 1998.

[12] M. Renovell, J.M. Portal, J. Figueras and Y. Zorian, "*Testing the Configurable Interconnect/Logic Interface of SRAM-Based FPGA's* ", IEEE Int. Conf. on Design, Automation and Test in Europe DATE99, pp. 618-622, March 10-12, Munich, Germany, 1999.

[13] T. Inoue, H. Fujiwara, H. Michinishi, T. Yokohira and T. Okamoto, «Universal Test Complexity of Field-Programmable Gate Arrays», 4th Asian Test Symposium, pp. 259-265, Bangalora, November 1995, India.

[14] H. Michinishi, T. Yokohira, T. Okamoto, T. Inoue, H. Fujiwara «A Test Methodology for Interconnect Structures of LUT-based FPGAs», IEEE 5th Asian Test Symposium, pp. 68-74, November 1996.

[15] H. Michinishi, T. Yokohira, T. Okamoto, T. Inoue, H. Fujiwara «Testing for the Programming Circuits of LUT-based FPGAs», IEEE 6th Asian Test Symposium, pp. 242-247, November 1997.

[16] T. Inoue, S.Miyazaki and H. Fujiwara «Universal Fault Diagnosis for Lookup Table FPGAs», IEEE Design & Test of Computer, special Issue on FPGAs, pp.39-44, January-March 1998.

[17] M. Abramovici and C. Stroud, «No-Overhead BIST for FPGAs», 1st IEEE International On-line Testing Workshop, pp. 90-92, Nice, FRANCE,1995.

[18] C. Stroud, P. Chen, S. Konala, M. Abramovici, «Evaluation of FPGA Ressources for Built-In Self Test of Programmable Logic Blocks», Proc. of 4th ACM/SIGDA Int. Symposium on FPGAs, pp. 107-113, 1996.

[19] M. Abramovici, C. Stroud, «ILA BIST for FPGAs: A Free Lunch with Gourmet Food», 2nd IEEE International On-line Testing Workshop, pp. 91-95, Biarritz, FRANCE,1996.

[20] W.K. Huang and F. Lombardi, «An Approach for Testing Programmable/ Configurable Field Programmable Gate Arrays», 14th IEEE VLSI Test Symposium, pp. 450-455, Princeton, NJ, USA, May 1996.

[21] F. Lombardi, D. Ashen, X.T. Chen, W.K. Huang «Diagnosing Programmable Interconnect Systems for FPGAs», FPGA'96, pp. 100-106, Monterey CA, USA, 1996.

[22] D.G.Ashen, F.J.Meyer, N.Park and F.Lombardi, «Testing of Programmable Logic Devices (PLD) with Faulty Resources», IEEE International Workshop on Defect & Tolerance in VLSI Systems, pp.76-84, Paris, October 1997.

[23] W.K. Huang, F.J. Meyer, N. Park and F. Lombardi, «Testing Memory Modules in SRAM-based Configurable FPGAs», IEEE International Workshop on Memory Technology, Design and Test, August, 1997.

[24] M. Hermann and W. Hoffmann, «Fault modeling and test generation for FPGAs», in R.W. Hartenstein and M.Z. Servit (eds), Lecture Notes in Computer Science, Field Programmable Logic, Springer-Verlag, pp. 1-10, 1994.

[25] Xilinx, «The Programmable Logic Data Book», San Jose, USA, 1994
[26] W.H. Kautz, « Testing for Faults in Wiring Networks » IEEE Transactions on Computers, Vol. C-23, No. 4, pp. 358-363, 1974.
[27] P. Goel and M.T. McMahon, «Electronic Chip-in Place Test» Proc. of International Test Conference, pp. 83-90, 1982.
[28] N. Jarwala and C.W. Yau, «A New Framework for Analyzing Test Generation and Diagnosis Algorithms for Wiring Networks » Proc. of International Test Conference, pp. 63-70, 1989.
[29] M.S. Abadir and J.K. Reghbati, «Functional Testing of Semiconductor Random Access Memories », ACM Computing Surveys, 15 (3), pp. 175-198, 1983.
[30] A.J. Van de Goor, «Testing Semiconductor Memories: Theory and Practice , John Willey & Sons, 1991.

DReAM: A Dynamically Reconfigurable Architecture for Future Mobile Communication Applications

Jürgen Becker, Thilo Pionteck, Manfred Glesner

Darmstadt University of Technology
Institute of Microelectronic Systems
Karlstr. 15, D-64283 Darmstadt, Germany
Fax: ++49 6151 16 4936
e-mail: {becker, pionteck, glesner}@mes.tu-darmstadt.de

Abstract. *The development of current and future broadband access techniques into the wireless domain introduces new and flexible network architectures with difficult and interesting challenges, e. g. access mechanisms, energy conservation, error rate, transmission speed characteristics of the wireless links and mobility aspects. This paper discusses first the major challenges in hardware architecture design of reconfigurable system-on-a-chip solutions for the digital baseband processing in future mobile radio devices. The focus of the paper is the introduction of a new dynamically reconfigurable hardware architecture tailored to this application area. Its performance issues and potential are discussed by the implementation of a flexible and computation-intensive component of future mobile terminals.*

1. Introduction

Flexible and high bandwidth demanding mobile communication systems of the next generation present a various set of challenging problems to system designers in the wireless industry. The combination of advances in integrated circuit technology and novel system-level solutions can contribute efficiently to the widespread commercialization of mobile high-speed communication systems. In the last years, the fast technological development in *very large scale integration* (VLSI) possibilities has brought the notion to single *system-on-a-chip* (SoC) solutions. Thus, the implementation of various functions required by different abstraction layers of a wireless mobile network should result in a highly integrated single-chip in the future. The design of digital systems for mobile baseband processing involves several heterogeneous areas, covering on one side the various aspects in communication system theory and application, e. g. the Data Link Control (DLC) layer specifications of future mobile standards, the radio network (RN) architecture (broadcast, fading channel etc.), and the specifications of applied physical (PHY) layer techniques (modulation, coding etc.).

Future mobile communication systems, e.g. third generation (3G) systems, will not only offer the same old services with improved quality, but in addition these devices will have to offer many new exciting services, which will range from internet browsing to real-time multimedia communication applications. Moreover, next generation mobile terminals should also support new services that will soon emerge when the system is deployed. The upcoming future standards should also allow the introduction of such new services easily. Thus, the design of a corresponding mobile system has to reflect all these forecasted services and flexibility. At the same time the mobile devices should realize all services within the physical and operational requirements of the given mobile system infrastructure. In addition, the mobile terminal has to provide an acceptable power consumption in order to be feasible for multimedia terminal operation. Finally, the *time-*

to-market and low price requirements have to be fulfilled in order to be competitive. Currently, most of the microelectronic system solutions in mobile communication are a combination of ASICs, microcontrollers, and Digital Signal Processors (DSP) devices. Reconfigurable hardware architectures have been proved in different application areas [1] [2] [7] to produce at least one order of magnitude in power reduction and increase in performance. In our approach the potential to integrate application-tailored coarse-grained dynamically reconfigurable architectures into SoC-solutions for future generations mobile terminals is described and demonstrated by the performance values of analyzed computation-intensive application parts within future mobile communication systems. The proposed reconfigurable SoC-architecture provides, for the selected application area, more flexibility than ASICs and better performance values than DSPs, or even today´s fine-grained commercial reconfigurable devices [11]. The major goal addressed here is to evaluate flexibility versus power/performance trade-offs, either by releasing the DSP for other tasks, or by migrating functionality from ASICs to our coarse-grained reconfigurable hardware architecture.

The paper is structured as follows: in section 2 an algorithm performance analysis is performed motivating the design of application-specific cost-effective, low power and high-performance SoC implementations in next generation´s mobile communication systems. Section 3 provides a detailed description and introduction of the new developed dynamically reconfigurable hardware part of such SoCs, including its evaluated performance issues and implementation status. The usefulness of this new coarse-grained parallel array architecture is illustrated in section 4 by the implementation analysis of a computation-intensive application part within future mobile terminals, e. g. a flexible CDMA-based RAKE-receiver.

2. Algorithm Performance in Mobile Communication Systems

2nd generation (2G) mobile communication systems, i.e. GSM and IS-95 standards, had been defined and optimized to provide operation for a certain application. On the other hand, 3G systems, i.e. based on the UMTS standard, will be defined to provide a transmission scheme which is highly flexible and adaptable to new services [16]. This vision adds a new dimension to the challenges within the digital baseband design, since the final microelectronic systems must be able to support this flexibility and adaptability. In addition, the cost of the final system is closely related to the number of components assembled on board. The reduction in costs is not only gained by reducing the costs of components, but also by reducing the costs of assembling and testing of the final system. The *time-to-market* introduction and the reduction of cost are the most important factors in determining the success of final products, especially in this application area. In the literature there are many proposed solutions listed to handle these flexibility requirements. Concepts such as *Software Radios* are discussed in detail [5] [6]. Since within such concepts the necessary overall system performance is missing [8] [9], alternative solutions have to be developed. For computation-intensive functions with flexibility requirements found in mobile communication applications, reconfigurable hardware offers an alternative solution to the software programmable DSPs. The DSP has been the basis of the hardware implementation of digital communication applications for the last fifteen years or more. But during the last five years, reconfigurable computing has emerged as a new hardware implementation methodology, with a very promising performance, also for arithmetic data-paths applications that dominate the digital communication [1] [2] [7]. These relatively new hardware architecture concepts can provide increased system performance at lower cost and risk of system implementation. Thus, the so-called structural programmable or reconfigurable logic combines the flexibility of general-purpose DSPs with speed, density, and low cost of ASIC solutions. Therefore, the enhancement of reconfigurable hardware to increase system performances within the here viewed application area can be resumed:

- in some application parts programmable logic substitutes ASIC implementations partly or entirely, and/or
- computation-intensive functions are migrated from the DSP processor to the reconfigurable hardware part, e. g. to save power and to release the DSP processor for other functions.

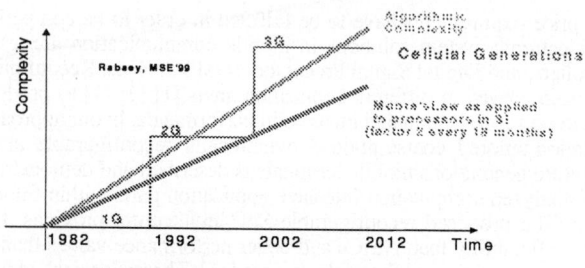

Application beats Moore's law

Fig. 1: Estimated performance requirements in major signal processing tasks for next generation UMTS-based mobile receiver architectures [14] [18]

Signal Processing Task (384 kbs)	DSP-Load [MIPS]
digital filters (RRC, channelization)	~ 3600
searcher, synchronization (frame, slot, delay path estimation)	~ 1500
RAKE-receiver	~ 650
maximal ratio combining (MRC)	~ 24
channel estimation	~ 12
Turbo-coding	~ 52
Total	**~ 5838**

Table 1: Examples of digital baseband processing requirements

In addition, there are many operational challenges, such as battery life, easy and flexible terminals to exploit dynamically different and new services, e.g. also by downloading upgrades and new services or protocols from the internet and configure the hand-held devices according to these downloaded codes. Flexibility can be defined as the ability of the mobile terminal to support many modes of operation, e.g. voice, audio, video, navigation, data transmission etc.. This also means, for example, that the mobile device has to have the ability to operate within different standards, such as GSM, UMTS, and IS-95. Adaptability is the ability of the mobile terminal to easily and quickly accommodate a new service. In figure 1 the DSP software performance requirements for the major signal processing tasks in next generation´s UMTS receiver is given, according to [14]. Relative to GSM, UMTS and IS-95 will require intensive layer 1 related operations, which cannot be performed on today´s processors [18]. Thus, an optimized hardware/software partitioning of these computation-intensive tasks is necessary. Since today´s low power DSPs cannot achieve such a performance, the DSP load has to be reduced to release it for added value applications and to save power. Therefore, some selected computation-intensive signal processing tasks have to be migrated from software to hardware implementation, e.g. to ASIC or reconfigurable hardware SoC parts. The herewith introduced new coarse-grained reconfigurable hardware architecture could provide the necessary implementation issues for computation-intensive tasks with flexibility requirements in operation and implementation (see section 4).

3. An Application-Tailored Dynamically Reconfigurable Architecture

As explained in the previous sections, next generation´s mobile communication systems will provide the customer with a large variety of different services, whereas some of them are not known yet. In addition, known services have large spectrum of requirements, e.g. different data

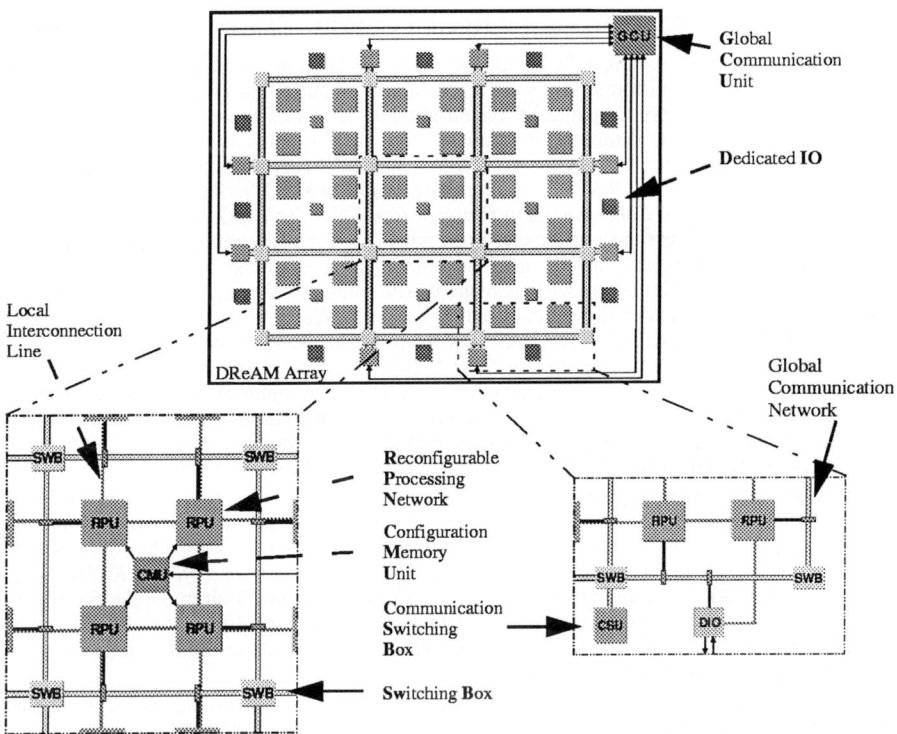

Fig. 2: Hardware Structure of the Dynamically Reconfigurable DReAM Architecture

rates, different quality of services (QoS), and real-time services etc.. For preparing future mobile terminals and its microelectronic components to cope with all these challenges, we developed a new coarse-grained and dynamically reconfigurable architecture.

The proposed *Dynamically Reconfigurable Architecture for Mobile Systems (DReAM)* consists of an array of parallel operating coarse-grained *Reconfigurable Processing Units (RPUs)*. Each RPU is designed for executing all required arithmetic data manipulations for the data-flow oriented mobile application parts, as well as to support necessary control-flow oriented operations. The complete DReAM array architecture connects all RPUs with reconfigurable local and global communication structures (see figure 2). In addition, the architecture will provide dynamic reconfiguration possibilities for the RPUs as well as for the interconnection structures, e.g. only partly and during run-time while other parts of the reconfigurable architecture are active. In the following, the design, structure and performance issues of the major hardware components in the DReAM architecture are explained. As shown in figure 2, the DReAM architecture consists of a scalable array of RPUs that has 16-bit fast direct local connections between neighboring RPUs, whereas each four RPU sub-array shares one common *Configuration Memory Unit* (CMU). The CMU holds configuration data for performing fast dynamic reconfiguration for each of these four RPUs and is controlled by one responsible CSU. Each CSU controls two CMUs and performs a fast dynamic RPU reconfiguration in one cycle by a burst mode configuration data transfer. Moreover, four global interconnect *Switching Boxes* (SWB) are controlled by one CSU. The detailed hardware structure of the SWBs and the related global as well as local inter-RPU communication mechanisms are described in [12].

3.1 Hardware Structure of the Reconfigurable Processing Unit (RPU)

The dynamically *Reconfigurable Processing Units* (RPUs) are the major hardware components of the DReAM architecture They are responsible for controlling 16-bit or 8-bit arithmetic data manipulations and are dynamically reconfigurable. In contrast, the CLBs (*Configurable Logic Blocks*) of today's commercially available fine-grained and universal FPGA-chips are operating on the 1-bit level [11]. As shown in figure 3 each RPU consists of: two *reconfigurable Arithmetic Processing* Units (RAPs), one *Spreading Data Path* (SDP), one *RPU-controller*, two *dual port RAMs*, and one *Communication Protocol Controller* for 2 independent outputs. Each RAP can perform all necessary arithmetic operations (8-/16-bit) identified in the above mentioned examined application parts of mobile communication systems. For repeated operation execution only one configuration set is necessary. The multiplication and MAC operation can performed with a fixed operand, resulting in a higher performance, or with two variable inputs. Independent of the configuration the RAP unit adapts onto the input data stream in order to achieve best performance. One *Spreading Data Path* (SDP) for the execution of CDMA-based spreading tasks is designed and implemented in each RPU (see figure 3). This SDP unit can be used together with the adding operations of 2 RAPs for implementing efficiently fast complex PN-code correlation operations. Such spreading operations are required often in CDMA-based communication systems with QPSK-modulation (*Quadrature Phase Shift Keying*).

The *RPU-controller* is responsible for guiding all data manipulations and transfers inside the RPU, as well as to determine from which local neighbour RPU or global interconnect line input data is consumed. Moreover, the *RPU-controller* performs together with the CMU and its controller the fast dynamic reconfiguration of the RPU. The two 8-by-16 bit *dual port RAMs* within each RPU are used as look-up-table (LUT) when performing the fast 8-bit multiplication operations. In addition, both can be used as normal data memories, or one of these two RAMs can be used, if necessary, with FIFO-behavior, e. g. for buffering intermediate results within the data-driven and asynchronously operating DReAM architecture.

The *Reconfigurable Arithmetic Processing* Units (RAP) unit is built around fast 8-/16-bit integer multiplier operators, as shown in figure 4. The multiplier is designed to provide a very high speed constant/variable multiplication (i.e. one of the operands is constant for some time interval) and small compact design by using modified Look-Up Table (LUT) multiplication procedure. According to [14] most of the multiplication within the mobile system are fixed operand operation. The main idea of the LUT multiplication is to generate all possible multiplication of the fixed operand Y (8-/16-bit constant) and store them in the LUT, then use the variable operand X

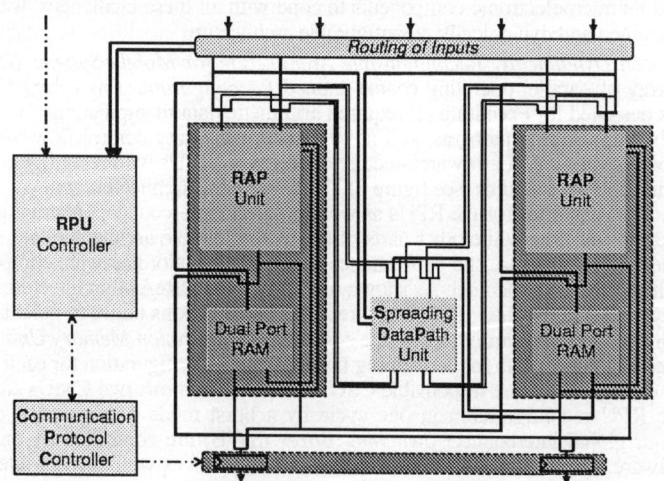

Fig. 3: Hardware Structure of the *Reconfigurable Processing Unit* (RPU)

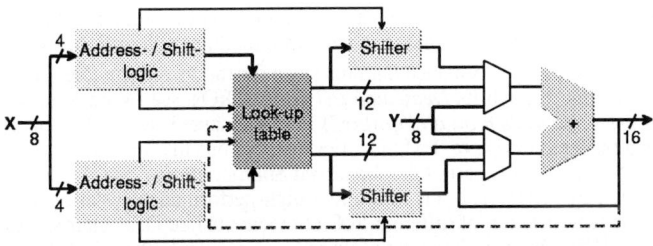

Fig. 4: Hardware Data Path of *Reconfigurable Arithmetic Processing Unit* (RAP)

as the address to the LUT, so providing the result R=X*Y within one cycle (pipelined, see figure 4). Note, the RAP unit can adapt automatically it's speed according to the operand nature, i.e. whenever the Y-operand is constant for some period of time, the RAP unit will increase its speed drastically. For further details about the RAP data path structure, its performance and area properties see [15], whereas the implementation is based on a 0.35 µm CMOS standard cell process. To perform complex or normal CDMA-based spreading tasks a configurable *Spreading Data Path* (SDP) unit is implemented in every RPU. As shown in figure 3, the unit can be used with the two adders in the RPU to perform a complex correlation function, e. g. found in (*Quadrature Phase Shift Keying*) QPSK-modulation, or it can perform one- or two-channel normal correlations, e. g. found in (*Binary Phase Shift Keying*) BPSK-modulation. It is mainly designed to perform a complex correlation operation for QPSK-scheme on 8 bit data words with serial PN-code. The SDP can also be utilized in many other functions, e.g. despreading, synchronization, etc. The *RPU-controller* is a FSM-based control unit that is responsible for guiding all operations for data manipulations and transfers within the RPU. In addition to the typical controlling tasks, the controller supports also conditional operations implementations. Moreover, the *RPU-controller* performs, together with the CMU and its controller, the fast dynamic reconfiguration of the RPUs. Two *dual port RAMs* are available within each RPU, which are used as look-up-tables when performing fast integer/constant multiplication operations. In addition, both RAMs can be used as a normal data memories or asynchronous FIFOs.

3.2 Efficient Inter-RPU and Intra-SoC Communication Mechanisms

The performance of applications mapped onto the DReAM array architecture depends strongly on the efficiency and speed of the local and global inter-RPU communication mechanisms. Since the coarse-grained RPUs implement control and datapath parts, e. g. loop structures, an advanced asynchronous synchronization and communication mechanism is required. Here, an efficient data communication protocol has be specified and implemented, in contrast to today's fine-grained FPGA-architectures, where simple point-to-point bitlevel connections can be switched between configurable logic blocks (CLBs) [11].

In the DReAM array architecture, each RPU is locally connected to it's four neighbours (North, East, South, and West) through 16-bit fast direct connection lines. In addition, it can be connected to the global lines through a SRAM-based switching box (SWB, see figure 2). The data-driven communication mechanism inside the DReAM array architecture is realized by an efficient hand-shaking protocol for unidirectional point-to-point connection between two RPUs. The inter-RPU communication protocols can be distinguished into local communication between neighbouring RPUs, and global communication between any two distanced RPUs.

For local communication between a half-interleaved handshake is implemented (1-cycle delay, and for global inter-RPU communication a fully-interleaved handshake is used (2-cycle delays). This has to be done due to the difference in length between the local and the global interconnect wires, resulting in different communication signal delays. The global interconnect structure realized by the above described SWBs implemented in DReAM can be partly and dynamically reconfigured within one cycle during run-time by the *Communication Switching*

Units (CSUs, see figure 2). For more details about the inter-RPU communication protocols incl. the corresponding synchronization signals and hardware modules within DReAM see [12].

The realization of a high performance data interface for the reconfigurable DReAM architecture for communicating through its *Dedicated I/O Units* (DIOs, see figure 5) to other hardware components on the same *system-on-a-chip* (SoC) is implemented by an efficient connection of the SoC bus via a buffered bridge to the DIOs. For the SoC bus the *Advanced high Performance Bus* (AHB) is used. The AHB is part of the *Advanced Microcontroller Bus Architecture* (AMBA) which was designed by ARM. The bus acts like a high-performance system backbone bus and supports the efficient connection of different SoC components like DSP, microcontroller and on-chip memory. The DReAM array itself is not directly connected to the AHB. Instead, the DIOs are connected via a read and a write bus to a AHB bridge. This AHB bridge is responsible for transfering the data from the DReAM array to the AHB and vice versa. The bridge includes buffers for each DIO. This is important for the overall system performance as the AHB is 32 bit wide and the read and write busses from the bridge to the DIOs is only 16 bit wide, thus making a buffering of data mandatory. The data throughput of the AHB bridge can increased to 800Mb/s in using a 64 bit wide AHB and pipelining, which satisfies future baseband processing needs. From the AHB side the bridge acts as a slave. For each DIO a port with a unique address is provided. It is also possible to prioritizitate some DIOs during runtime. Thus it is possible to increase the data rate for some DIOs which is required for some data intensive applications like a RAKE receiver. For the connection from the bridge to the DIOs there exist a read and a write bus. The bridge acts like a master for these two busses. If a DIO is configured as a input port it will only receive data from the write bus and if it is configured as a output port, it will write its data onto the read bus. The data transfer via the read and write bus is triggered by the bridge and is controlled independ-

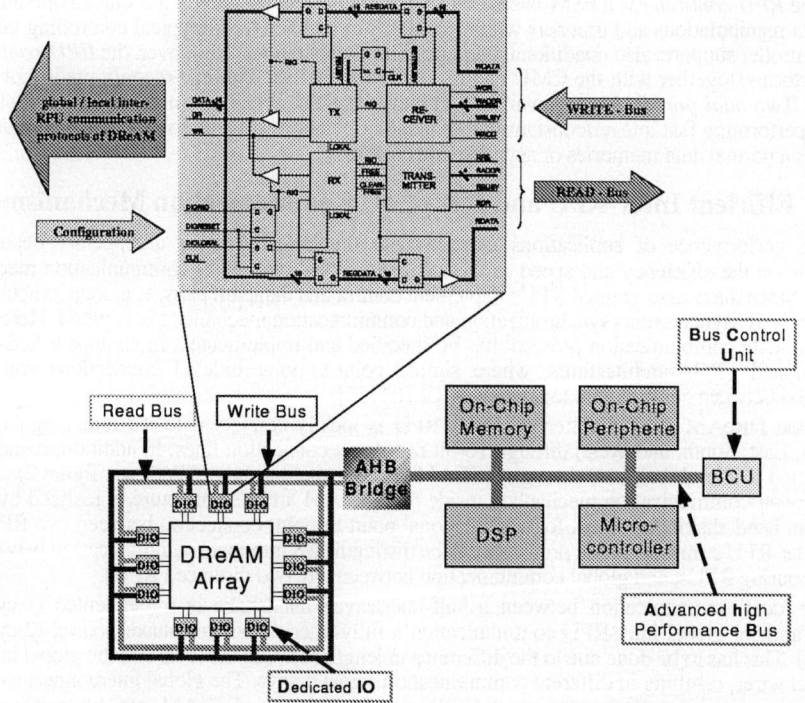

Fig. 5: Efficient Interface of the DreAM Array to other SoC components

ently from each other. The DIOs themselves are connected via the local and the global communication network to the DReAM array.

4. Application: Flexible CDMA-Based Receiver Implementation

The following example of a computation-intensive RAKE-receiver component from future mobile communication systems is mapped manually onto DReAM. For future CDMA-based mobile communication systems RAKE-receivers are essential while consuming a huge computation performance [14]. ASIC implementations could provide such a performance [10], but are not flexible enough to adapt to the various situations and services in the next generation of wireless communication systems. In DS-CDMA systems the data signal is multiplied by a PN-sequence with much higher bandwidth than the data signal. Thus, the Spread Spectrum (SS) signal is well matched for multipath channel, i.e. more than one copy of the transmitted signal will arrive at the receiver with different time delays. If the time delay between the received copies is more than one chip duration, then a RAKE-receiver (with n fingers, where n is the number of potential signal copies) can resolve and then combine the signals according to their SNR (*signal-to-noise-ratio*), dependent on the actual channel and mobility situation. The received data signal for each finger can be found as a complex correlation (QPSK-modulation) of the binary delayed signal y(t) and the conjugate of the PN-code (*pn**)[10]:

$$r = \sum_{n=0}^{L-1} \int_0^T y\left(t - \frac{n}{W}\right) c_n^*(t) pn^*(t) dt$$

where cn^* is the complex conjugate of the weighting factor for each finger. A RAKE-finger despread the received signal with a correlator. The despreaded signal is then multiplied by a complex amplitude to correct phase-error and to weight each finger according to *Maximal-Ratio-Combining* (MRC) strategy. The received data is first converted from the analog to the digital domain (ADC) and then 4 times oversampled. Every four data samples in the two branches Inphase (I) and Quadrature (Q) are loaded to the RAM. Then, the synchronization unit block select the appropriate sample from the I- and Q-branches in order to reduce the phase-difference between the I- and Q-branches. The data coming out of every finger is weighted according to it's SNR level. The data of all fingers are then combined before dumping the data to the demodulator. More signal processing can take place afterwards (e.g. de-interleaving and decoding). The number of Rake-fingers depend on the channel-profile and the chip-rate, e. g. the higher the chip rate, the more resolvable paths [13]. IS-95 uses RAKE-receivers with four fingers [16]. We used MATLAB 5.2 for simulating a RAKE-receiver with four fingers for the data rate required in the next (third) generation mobile standard. For lower values of SNR the effect of increasing the number of fingers will increase the performance of the system. By increasing the number of fingers from three to five fingers, the performance of the receiver for 10dB SNR is equal to that of 15dB SNR. Thus, dependent of the SNR values of the transmitted signal and the required BER of the mobile service, the number of fingers have to be adapted. Moreover, the simulation results showed that 8-bit quantization produces more than three times improvement over 4-bit quantization. Although the demodulation is not implemented here, it is interesting to say that 8X8-bit multiplication for the demodulator causes very small degradation in the performance of about 0.25 dB relative to the unquantized case [10]. Dependent on these simulation results, the implementation of the RAKE-receiver on the DReAM architecture and possible dynamical reconfigurations during operation can be performed. For this mapping example, it is assumed that the channel tracker, which provides the gains for each finger, and the channel sounding is done outside the DReAM array. In later realizations, the channel tracker will also be mapped onto DReAM. In figure 6 the newest optimized mapping of a RAKE-receiver with four fingers oonto DReAM is shown. Notice that the PN-code generation is not shown in figure 6 in order to simplify discussion. The PN-code itself is created with the help of a shift-feedback-register.

At the top of figure 6 the mapping of one RAKE-finger onto DReAM is shown. The required four RPUs for one RAKE finger are arranged in such a way to take advantage of the fast local

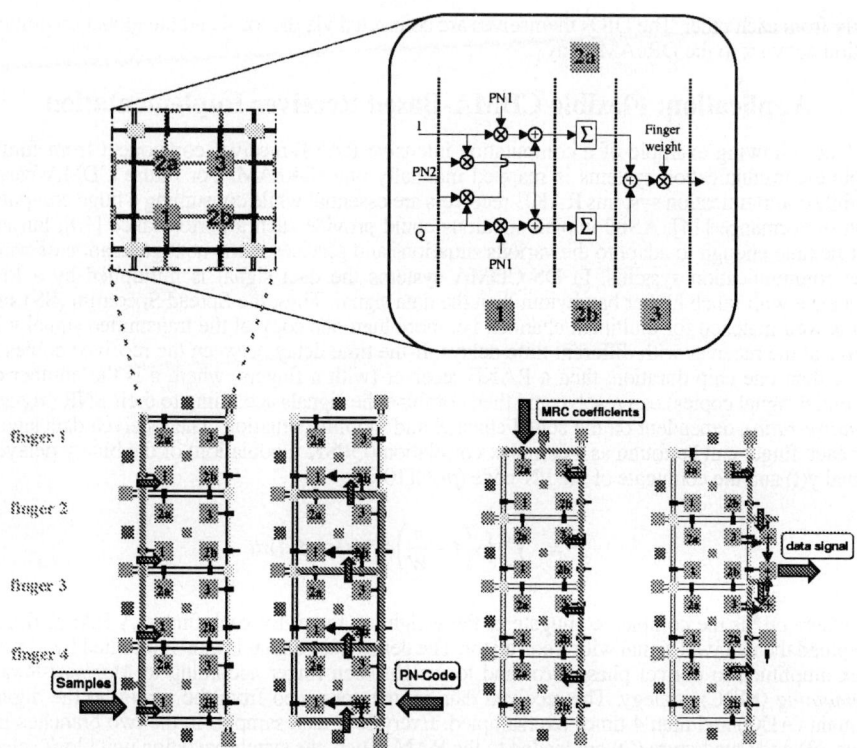

Fig. 6: CDMA-based Rake-receiver mapped to DReAM

interconnect lines. For the correlation operation itself only one RPU (1) is needed. Two additional RPUs (2a, 2b) are required in order to sum the partital results. The fourth RPU (3) is needed for adding the two sums of RPU 2a and RPU 2b and for the weighting. In the lower part of figure 6 the distribution of the different input signals (data samples, PN-code, MRC coefficient) is shown. If we assume a high data rate of 1.5 Mb/s, the data is despreaded by a PN-code of length 16 chips, resulting in chip rate for each finger of 24 Mchip/s. With a 4-time oversampling, this would result in 96 Msymbol/s. As only 1/4 of this data are required for the despreading, the decision which sample is the best is done outside the DReAM array which reduces the required data transports and thus leads to less power consumption. The communication network itself does not support broadcast and so the data samples, divided in Inphase (I) and Quadrature (Q), have to sent successively to the RAKE fingers. Therefore the communication network has to operate at least with 96 MHz (24 Mchips * 4 fingers). As the global communication network consists of two independent 16 bit wide busses, this is no problem in the actual implementation. The data samples are despreaded by the *Spreading Data Path* (SDP) unit inside RPU 1, which takes one clock cycle. As the despreading operation includes a summation, the data for the RPUs 2a and 2b are available after two clock cycles. Note, this operation is pipelined and even with a clock cycle of only 100 MHz DReAM is able to fulfill all timing requirements for such a computation-intensive RAKE-receiver. This is because of the high degree of parallelism which is possible with the DReAM array and the ability of runtime reconfiguration. The runtime reconfiguration is, for example, is required for the distribution of the PN-code and the MRC coefficients, as these data are transmitted via the same global communication lines.

5. Conclusions

The paper presented first an overview of the challenges and importance in realizing flexible microelectronic system solutions for future mobile communication applications. Therefore, a new coarse-grained dynamically reconfigurable architecture (DReAM) was introduced, including its potential for flexible SoC-solutions in adaptive air interface candidate systems for the digital baseband processing in modern wireless communication systems. The parallel hardware architecture structure of DReAM, incl. its application-tailored operation implementations, was discussed in detail. DReAM is tailored to future mobile signal processing, providing an acceptable trade-off between flexibility and application performance requirements. Future CDMA-based mobile communication systems have a huge amount of complex application parts, whereas their risk minimized and flexible implementation is very important, especially in the case of late specification changes (standards!). The usefulness of the introduced dynamically reconfigurable architecture for efficient and parallelized hardware/software SoC implementation was demonstrated by analyzing and implementing onto DReAM a computation-intensive mobile signal processing algorithm e. g. a CDMA-based RAKE-receiver application, resulting in providing the necessary performance and flexibility trade-offs. Power analysis and optimization as well as automatized IP-based application mapping methods will be the next steps of this project.

References

[1] P. Athanas, A. Abbot: Real-Time Image Processing on a Custom Computing Platform, IEEE Computer, vol. 28, no. 2, Feb. 1995.
[2] R. W. Hartenstein, J. Becker et al.: A Novel Machine Paradigm to Accelerate Scientific Computing; Special issue on Scientific Computing of Computer Science and Informatics Journal, Computer Society of India, 1996.
[3] R. W. Hartenstein, M. Herz, Th. Hoffmann, U. Nageldinger: KressArray Xplorer: A New CAD Environment to Optimize Reconfigurable Datapath Array Architectures; 5th Asia and South Pacific Design Automation Conference 2000, ASP-DAC 2000, Yokohama, Japan, January 25-28, 2000
[4] H. Erben, K. Sabatakakis: Advanced software radio architecture for 3rd generation mobile systems., Vehicular Technology Conference, 1998. VTC 98. 48th IEEE Published: 1998 Volume: 2 , Page(s): 825 -829 vol.2
[5] D. Efstathio, et al.: Recent Developments in Enabling Technologies for Software Radio, IEEE Comm. Mag., Aug. 1999. pp. 112-117.
[6] Mitola.: The software Radio Architecture., IEEE Communication Mag. , May 1995, pp. 26-38.
[7] J. Becker, A. Kirschbaum, F.-M. Renner, M. Glesner: Perspectives of Reconfigurable Computing in Research, Industry and Education; 8th International Workshop On Field Programmable Logic And Applications, FPL'98, Tallinn, Estonia, August 31-Spetmber 3, 1998, Lecture Notes in Computer Science, Springer Press, 1998
[8] David Nicklin :Utilising FPGAs in Re-configurable Basestations And Software Radios, Xilinx Inc. Electronic Eng. Mag.
[9] Gregory Ray Goslin: A Guide to Using Field Programmable Gate Arrays (FPGAs) for Appliccation-Specific Digital Signal Processing Performance, Xilinx Inc. 1995.
[10] Stephen D. Lingwood, et al. "ASIC Implementation of a Direct-Sequence Spread-Spectrum RAKE-Receiver.", IEEE 44th Vehicular Technology Conference, 1994.
[11] Xilinx Corp.: http://www.xilinx.com/products/virtex.htm.
[12] J. Becker, M. Glesner, A. Alsolaim, J. Starzyk: Fast Communication Mechanisms in Coarse-grained Dynamically Reconfigurable Array Architectures; Proc. of Second Int'l. Workshop on Engineering of Reconfigurable Hardware/Software Objects (ENREGLE'00, in conjunction with PDPTA 2000), June 23-24, 2000, Las Vegas, USA
[13] Jhong Sam Lee, et al.,: CDMA Systems Engineering Handbook.., Artech House, Boston. 1998.
[14] Peter Jung, Joerg Plechinger., "M-GOLD: a multimode basband platform for future mobile terminals",CTMC'99, IEEE International Conference on Communications, Vancouver, June 1999.
[15] A. Alsolaim, J. Becker, M. Glesner, J. Starzyk: Architecture and Application of a Dynamically Reconfigurable Hardware Array for Future Mobile Communication Systems; Proc. of IEEE Symposium of Field-Programmable Custom Computing Machines (FCCM'00), April 17-19, 2000, Napa, USA
[16] Tero Ojanpera, et. al.,: Wideband CDMA for Third Generation Mobile Communicatios., Artech House Pub., 1998.
[17] Manfred Glesner, Juergen Becker, Lukusa Kabulepa: Microelectronic Systems Design Perspective for future Radio Communication Applications; Invited Paper for 1999 Asia Pacific Symposium on Information and Telecommunication Technologies (APSITT'99), 30-31 August 1999, Ulaanbaatar, Mongolia
[18] Jan M. Rabaey: System Design at Universities: Experiences and Challenges; IEEE Computer Society International Conference on Microelectronic Systems Education (MSE'99), July 19-21, Arlington VA, USA
[19] J. Becker, L. Kabulepa, F.-M. Renner, M. Glesner: Simulation and Rapid Prototyping of Flexible Systems-on-a-Chip for Future Mobile Communication Applications; Proc. of 11th IEEE Int'l. Workshop on Rapid System Prototyping (RSP'2000), Paris, France, June 2000
[20] Jinn-Shyan Wang, Wayne Tseng, Hung-Yu Li: Low-Power Embedded SRAM with the Current-Mode Write Technique; IEEE Journal of Solid-State Circuits, Vol. 35, no. 1, January 2000

Fast Carrier and Phase Synchronization Units for Digital Receivers Based on Re-configurable Logic

A. Blaickner, O. Nagy, and H. Grünbacher

Carinthia Tech Institute - CTI
Richard-Wagner-Strasse 19, A-9500 Villach, Austria
a.blaickner@cti.ac.at, hg@cti.ac.at

Abstract. Wireless communication systems operate within a wide variety of dynamic ranges, variable bandwidths and carrier frequencies. New high density re-programmable logic arrays are a suitable technology basis providing sufficient processing power required by software radio concepts employing multiple standards and transmission schemes. For high speed wireless data transmission and access networks as used in multimedia communication systems fast signal synchronization and acquisition schemes are required. Within this work, programmable carrier phase synchronization units have been designed as FPGA based subsystems to be used in various re-configurable digital receiver concepts. The performance and the available processing capacity was investigated and verified within a rapid prototyping design flow environment.

Index Terms – Wireless, software radio, digital receiver, synchronization, FPGA, hardware/software co-design.

1 Introduction

The telecommunication field is still populated by numerous dedicated systems, which operate on different frequency bands and modulation schemes [8]. Third-generation wireless communication concepts address system solutions with multiple transmission capabilities, variable data rate and performance. In the absence of a single transmission standard, flexible user terminals and base stations offer attractive solutions.

The development of programmable digital communication systems and related transmitter / receiver architectures for several different air- / line- interface standards, modulation schemes and bandwidths, is encouraged by high density re-configurable VLSI devices. Programmable all-in-one multi-mode transmission systems, either to match regional standards, carrier frequencies and bandwidths, or to ensure a specific link quality and data rate become feasible. Within future intelligent multimedia network solutions, adaptive or cognitive system behavior, optimum channel selection, remote service and reloading capabilities are only a few promising features that make software radio receiver concepts to be expected a key technology in the future [7][5][8].

In this work architectures, theory, design and performance of synchronization units for future programmable transmission systems are presented.

2 On Software Radio and Digital Receiver Architectures

The ideal digital receiver, processing the complete signal bandwidth covered by multiple standards is not feasible. This is due to the high dynamic range, the sampling frequency and digital processing power required. Using programmable direct digital frequency synthesis (DDS), switched analogue subsystems, partial bandwidth digitization (A/D-conversion) and intermediate frequency filtering the receiver is still able to process multiple standards but in a realistic framework [8][7]. A general architecture of a software radio and a digital receiver is shown in Fig. (1),(2).

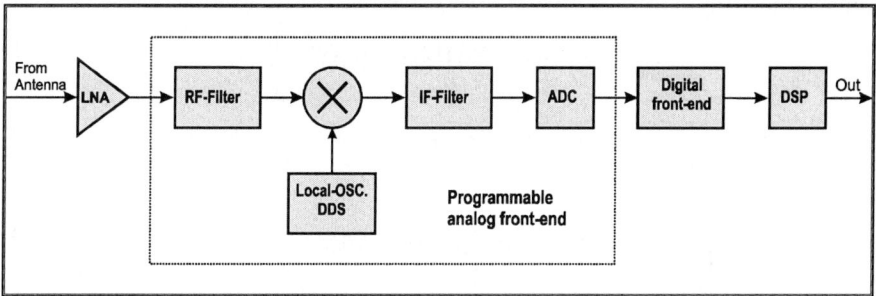

Fig. 1. Software radio receiver architecture.

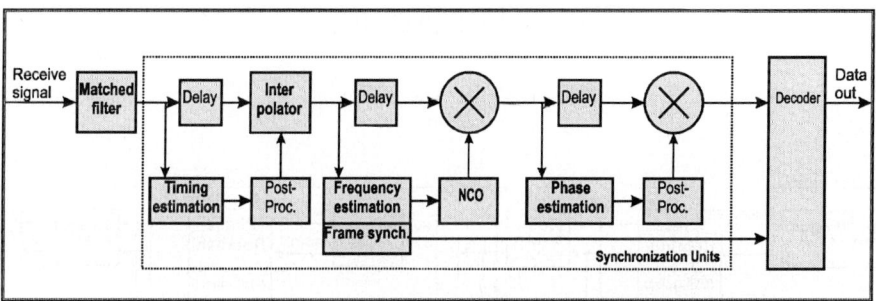

Fig. 2. Digital demodulator with carrier and phase synchronization units.

For multi-mode receiver applications fast and reliable synchronization algorithms are required. A main focus of this work was the design and verification of core functions and subsystems to be used within programmable receiver applications.

Fig. (2) shows, that a digital receiver requires several units for the estimation and processing of carrier-, phase- and timing offsets of the received signal. The estimates are used within the corresponding correction units as NCO-mixer, interpolator and phase rotator to compensate for the parameter offsets. The synchronization units may be used in various digital receiver architectures and transmission standards (e.g. coherent-, multicarrier-, spreadspectrum-communication, WLAN, HIPERLAN, xDSL, DVB). The design, realization and system performance of carrier phase synchronization units including computationally efficient processing elements, is presented in the following chapters.

3 Theoretical Framework

The estimation of signal parameters like carrier offset, phase offset or timing offset is mainly achieved by maximum likelihood estimation or a nonlinear operation approach. In most cases estimator algorithms can be derived by maximizing the likelihood function, Eq. (1) (2). The formulas can be interpreted as a measure of a multi-dimensional distance vector between the received signal vector r(t) and a trial vector s(t). The derived algorithms may be either used within feedback loops driving the estimated signal parameter to zero, or in a feed-forward oriented scheme, which requires the estimator to generate an unbiased parameter estimate for a direct offset compensation [9][4][10].

$$L(\tilde{\phi}) = C_1 \cdot \exp\left[-\frac{C_2}{N_0}\int_{T_0}|r(t) - s(t,\tilde{\phi})|^2 dt\right] \quad (1)$$

$$\Delta(\tilde{\Phi}) = \ln[L(\tilde{\phi})] = \left[-\frac{2C_2}{N_0}\int_{T_0}\mathrm{Re}[r(t)\cdot s^*(t,\tilde{\phi})]dt\right] \quad (2)$$

$$R(T_0,\tilde{\Phi}) = \mathrm{Re}\int_{T_0}[r(t)\cdot s^*(t,\tilde{\phi})]dt \quad (3)$$

For example the derivation of the correlation integral Eq. (3) with dR/dF=0, results in a feedback estimator for the carrier phase offset, as shown in Fig. (3a).

$$u_\theta(k) = \mathrm{Im}\left[\exp(-j\tilde{\theta})c_k^*p(k)\right] \quad (4)$$

$$\tilde{\theta}(k+1) = \tilde{\theta}(k) + K_\theta u_\theta(k) \quad (5)$$

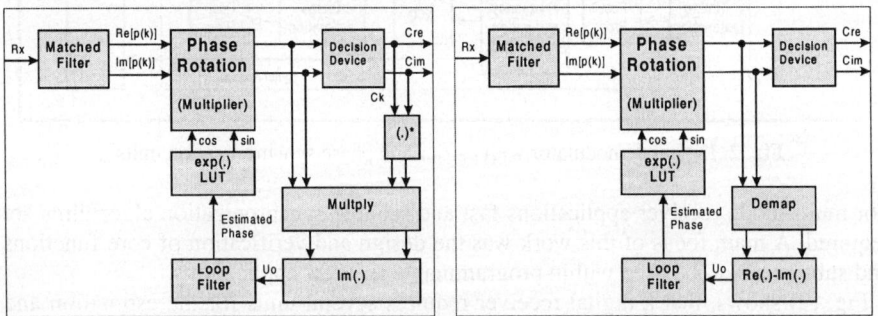

Fig. 3. Decision directed (a), non-data aided (b) feedback carrier phase synchronization units.

By taking a m-PSK symbols constellation to the power of M and by the introducing a non-linearity a feed-forward estimator scheme may be derived [9]. The algorithm is the digital equivalent to the analog X^M multiplier-synchronizer, except a non-linearity was introduced and shown in Fig. (4). These algorithms build the computational basis for the digital VLSI realizations presented.

$$\hat{\theta} = \frac{1}{M} \tan^{-1} \left(\frac{\frac{1}{N+1} \cdot \sum_N \mathrm{Im}[p^M(k)]}{\frac{1}{N+1} \cdot \sum_N \mathrm{Re}[p^M(k)]} \right), \quad \hat{\theta} = \frac{1}{M} \tan^{-1} \left(\frac{\frac{1}{N+1} \cdot \sum_N F(\rho) \sin(M(\theta_n + 2\pi n \Delta fT))}{\frac{1}{N+1} \cdot \sum_N F(\rho) \cos(M(\theta_n + 2\pi n \Delta fT))} \right) \quad (6)(7)$$

$$\hat{\theta} = \arg(x_n + j y_n) = F(\rho) \cdot \exp(iM\Phi_n) \quad (8)$$

$$F(\rho) = F(\sqrt{x_n^2 + y_n^2}) \ , \ e^{i\Phi_n} = \left(\frac{x_n + j \cdot y_n}{\sqrt{x_n^2 + y_n^2}} \right), F = ()^0, ()^1, ()^2 ; \quad (9)$$

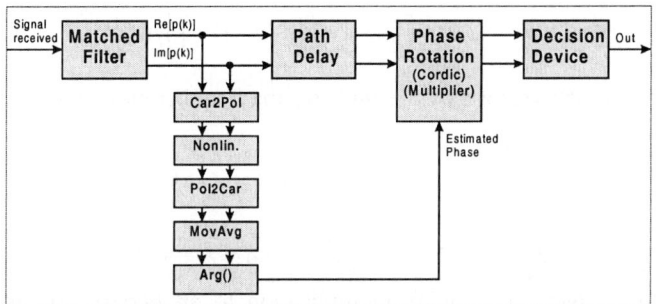

Fig. 4. Non-data aided feed-forward carrier phase synchronization unit.

For the frequency phase correction and the determination of the angular position of the symbols, computational efficient algorithms are available. One candidate to be used either for the rotation of phase vectors or the required cartesian to polar transform, is the *Cordic-* Algorithm (**CO**ordinate **R**otation on **DI**gital **C**omputer). The advantage is a reduced processing complexity but with the disadvantage of an induced high latency of the data path, due to the nature of the algorithm [1][2]. This fact makes the Cordic algorithm more suitable to feed-forward oriented synchronization structures, whereas for feedback synchronizers complex multipliers are preferable.

The Cordic algorithm can be used either in the so-called vectoring mode, where a given complex vector **r** is rotated by an angle a, or in rotation mode, that calculates the angle of the given input vector. The latter is used for the rectangular to polar transform. If a the vector is rotated by an angle α, the angle α can be expanded to α_i with $q_i, \in \{-1, +1\}$, and the error z_n, such that

$$\tilde{r} = r \cdot e^{j\alpha}, \quad \alpha = \sum_{i=-1}^{n-1} q_i \cdot \alpha_i + z_n \quad (10)(11)$$

and the sub-rotation angles α_i, take on the following values

$$\alpha_i = \begin{cases} \pi/2 & \text{for } i = -1 \\ \arctan(2^{-i}) & \text{for } i = 0,1,\ldots,n-1 \end{cases} \quad (12)$$

Note that α_i is approximately equal or less than 2^{-i} and the resulting angular expansion error is $|z_n| < 2^{-(n-1)}$. Substitution of Eq. (11) into Eq. (10) results into

$$\tilde{r} = r \cdot \prod_{i=-1}^{n-1} e^{j q_i \alpha_i} \cdot e^{j z_n} = r \cdot (j q_i) \cdot \prod_{i=0}^{n-1} e^{j q_i \alpha_i} \cdot e^{j z_n} \tag{13}$$

$$e^{j q_i \alpha_i} = \cos q_i \alpha_i + j \sin q_i \alpha = \cos \alpha_i \left(1 + j q_i 2^{-i}\right) \tag{14}$$

$$\tilde{r} = r \left(\prod_{i=0}^{n-1} \cos \alpha_i \right) \cdot (j q_{-1}) \cdot \left(\prod_{i=0}^{n-1} \left(1 + j q_i 2^{-i}\right) \right) \cdot e^{-j z_n} \tag{15}$$

The range of rotation angles is $\pm\alpha_{max}$, which can be seen from Eq. (11) and Eq. (12), where the second term is a scaling factor and can be pre-evaluated using

$$\alpha_{max} = \sum_{i=-1}^{n-1} \alpha_i \approx 190^\circ, \quad F_n = \prod_{i=0}^{n-1} \cos \alpha_i = \prod_{i=0}^{n-1} (1 + 2^{-2i})^{\frac{1}{2}} = \prod_{i=0}^{n-1} \left(1 + \frac{1}{4^i}\right)^{-(1/2)} \tag{16}$$

$$\tag{17}$$

For the rotation of the vector **r** by the angle α, the final iteration with (i=0,1,...,n-1) is

$$q_i = \begin{cases} -1 \text{ if } z_i < 0 \\ +1 \text{ if } z_i \geq 0 \end{cases} \quad r_{i+1} = \begin{cases} r_i \cdot j q_i & \text{if } i = -1 \\ r_i \cdot (1 + j q_i \cdot 2^{-i}) & \text{if } i \geq 0 \end{cases} \tag{18}$$

$$\tag{19}$$

$$z_{i+1} = z_i - q_i \alpha_i, \quad x_{i+1} = x_i - q_i \cdot y_i \cdot 2^{-i}, \quad y_{i+1} = y_i + q_i \cdot x_i \cdot 2^{-i} \tag{20}$$

The algorithm reduces a complex multiplication to an iterative set of operations consisting of binary shift and accumulation for each of x, y and z. Additional errors are introduced by implementation restrictions as quantization and finite iterations. Consider the vector $r_i = (x_i, y_i)$ at the i-th stage (i ≤ m) and width m is updated with the truncated value $r_i \cdot 2^{-i}$, but if (i > m) then $r_{i+1} = r_i$ updates a zero, due to the preceding right shifts. This shows that the maximum number of useful iterations is limited by m. Kota, Cavallaro [3] concluded that $n + \log n + 2$ bits are required to achieve n bits of accuracy after n iterations. Several investigations using different bus widths and iteration step counts have been carried out prior to the implementation. The error plots for a set of angles and vector lengths are shown in Fig. (5), (6) and (7) to the left and the error in [bits] are shown in Fig. (5), (6) and (7) to the right. The simulation results were obtained by varying the magnitude of **r** and the angle a in uniform steps.

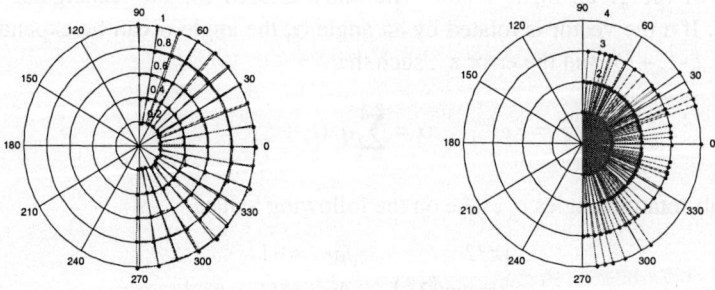

Fig. 5. Error plot, databus = 8bit, z-bus = 8bit, iterations (6), scaling off, rounding off.

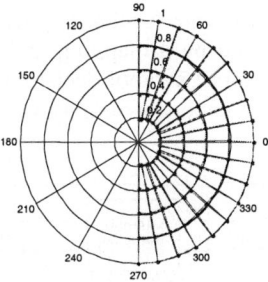 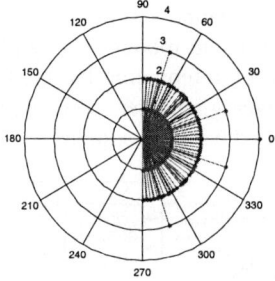

Fig. 6. Error plot, databus = 8bit, z-bus = 8bit, iterations (6), scaling on, rounding on.

A reduction of data path width is possible if the number of iterations is increased. The simulation results of a 10 stage Cordic processor with 10bit data paths are shown in Fig (7). Further improvements may be reached by reduction of the update error Dz. This could be solved by using a quasi floating-point method. A normalization scheme was introduced here, that utilizes all m bits of the z update path as long as possible and therefore prevents from being reduced to zero after certain iterations. The z-parameter is shifted by 2^i after every iteration, which requires a shift left operation only. The pre-calculated sub-rotation angles can be defined as $a^i = 2^i . a^i$ and stored in a table. This leads to an increase in accuracy, which is shown in Fig. (6) and Fig. (7). Another point is that shift operations are asymmetric with respect to positive and negative numbers. A solution used here, is to add the sign bit to the shifted value, which makes the operation symmetric (i.e. ceil (.), floor (.)).

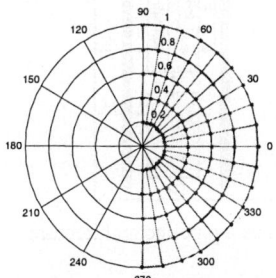 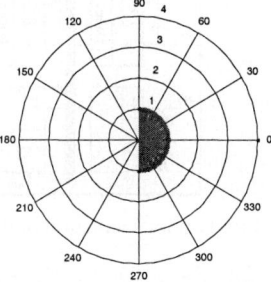

Fig. 7. Error plot, databus = 10bit, z-bus = 10bit, iterations (10), scaling on, rounding on.

4 System Architecture

The system architectures for the synchronizer units discussed are presented in Fig. (8). In the feed-forward synchronization unit a Cordic cell in so-called rotational mode is used for the rotation and correction of the modulation symbols. For the phase estimation itself a Cordic element combined with an averaging filter and a symbol mapping unit is used. The path delay compensates for the processing latency of the estimator stage.

As the available bandwidth of feedback loops is reduced by large delays in the processing pipeline a complex multiplier was chosen for the feedback synchronizers. The phase of the modulation symbols is either derived by a mapping and compare method or by referencing the modulation symbols against symbol decisions. In both cases an averaging filter stage and a lookup table with exponential unity vectors $\mathbf{e}^{j\xi}$ is provided in the feedback path.

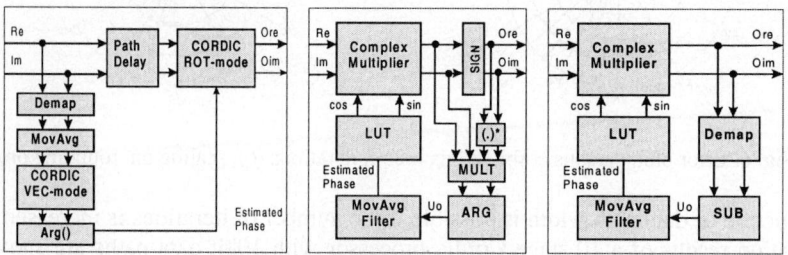

Fig. 8. Feedforward and feedback carrier phase synchronizer system architectures.

The Cordic cell itself is based on add, fix-shift and optional rounding operations and is realized as a parallel pipelined version. The pipeline architecture with the decoupled register stages is shown in Fig. (9).

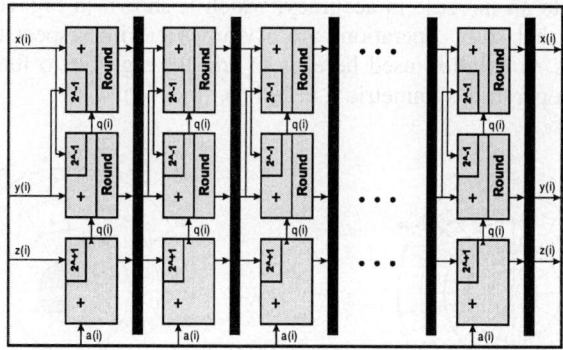

Fig. 9. Implementation of the Cordic algorithm as a pipeline architecture.

5 Performance Results

The following diagrams show simulated results of performance investigations. In Fig. (10) and Fig. (11) m-PSK modulated symbols are plotted in the scatter diagram-complex plane. The received m-PSK signal constellation with added white Gaussian noise is rotating caused by carrier and phase offsets and is shown in Fig. (10a) and Fig. (11a). The diagrams show 1024 samples of the received signal with carrier and phase offset errors and varying signal to noise ratios Eb/No=20dB, Eb/No=10dB. The scatter diagrams Fig. (10b) and Fig. (11b) present the phase and frequency corrected signal- and symbol constellation. The synchronized results are further processed by maximum likelihood detection and error decoding schemes - convolutional decoding.

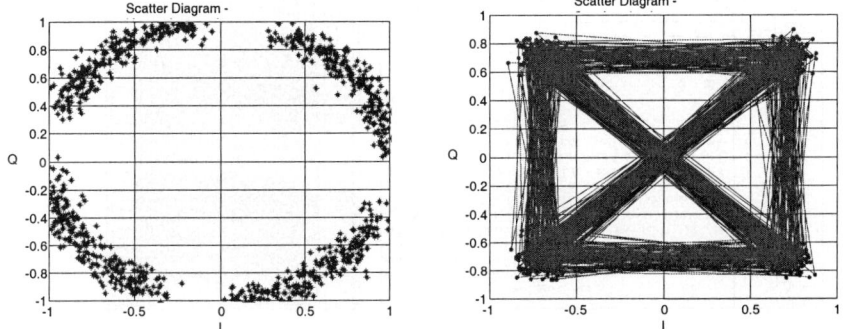

Fig. 10. Carrier phase synchronizer signals- input(a), corrected(b), Eb/No=20dB, 1024 samples.

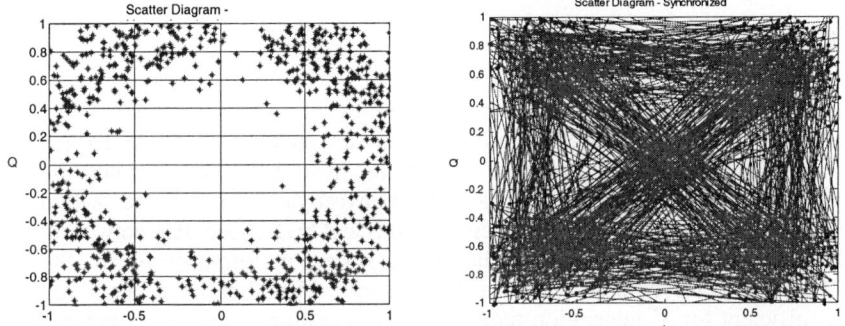

Fig. 11. Carrier phase synchronizer signals- input(a), corrected(b), Eb/No=10dB, 1024 samples.

The following figures Fig. (12) and Fig. (13) present the timing simulations and the FPGA layout and routing for the Flex10k and Apex20k technologies, that have been used within the project. The typical system clock signal period is 18ns / 8ns for Flex10k / Apex20k respectively. The Cordic pipeline requires 10 register stages each with a data bus width of 10 bits. The logic complexity required is ranging from 1900 up to 3300 logic cells and 1k byte of RAM-memory. Behavioral- and RTL- level descriptions have been used for the implementation.

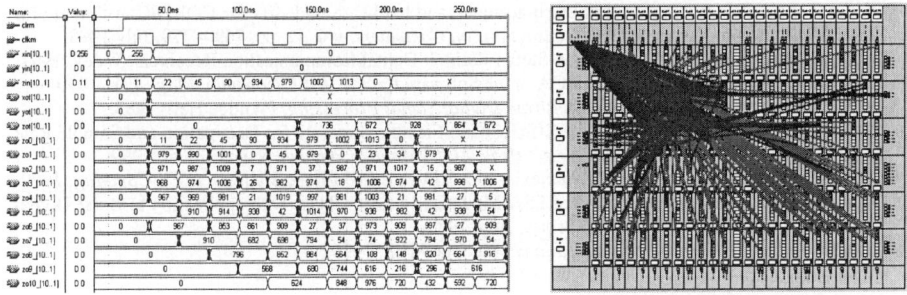

Fig. 12. Carrier phase synchronizer - timing simulation, layout and routing (Flex10K).

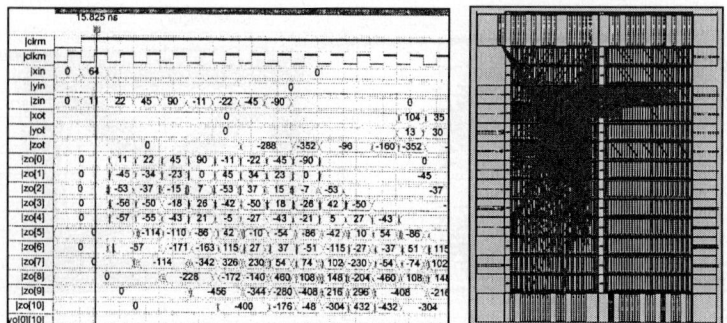

Fig. 13. Carrier phase synchronizer - timing simulation, layout and routing (Apex20K).

6 Conclusion

In this paper, various solutions of fast re-programmable synchronization units with the corresponding system architectures and the attained performance have been presented. Computational efficient Cordic units have been incorporated in the designs. The synchronization units have been investigated to be used within re-programmable communication system applications and high speed data networking. It was shown that using the Flex10k technology a system performance of 55 Msym/s, 110 Mbps and in the case Apex20k of 125 Msym/s, 250 Mbps have been reached. This is sufficient for 3rd generation mobile-, LAN- and high speed access networking and multimedia set-top box applications. Currently work on channel-processing, pulse-shaping, forward error correction and adaptive channel equalization is in progress.

References

[1] Y. H. Hu, "CORDIC-based VLSI architectures for digital signal processing, "*IEEE Signal Processing Magazine*, pp. 16 – 35, July 1992.
[2] J. Duprat and J.-M. Muller, "The CORDIC algorithm: New results for fast VLSI implementation," *IEEE Transactions on Computers*, vol. 42, pp. 168 – 178, February 1993.
[3] K. Kota and 3. R. Cavallaro, "Numerical accuracy and hardware tradeoffs for CORDIC arithmetic for special-purpose processors," *IEEE Transactions on Computers*, vol. 42, pp. 769 – 779, July 1993.
[4] Heinrich Meyr, Marc Moeneclaey, and Stefan Fechtel: Digital Communication Receivers, Wiley, 1997.
[5] M. Cummings and S. Haruyama, "FPGA in the Software Radio," *IEEE Commun. Mag.*, Feb. 1999.
[6] R. E. Crochiere and L. R. Rabiner, *Multirate Digital Signal Processing*, Prentice Hall, 1983.
[7] L. Lundheim and T. A. Ramstad, "An Efficient and Flexible Structure for Decimation and Sample Rate Adaptation in Software Radio Receivers," *Proc. ACTS Mobile Commun. Summit*, June 1999.
[8] T. Turletti and D. Tennenhouse, "Complexity of a Software GSM Base Station," *IEEE ComMag. 1999*.
[9] A. J. Viterbi, "Nonlinear Estimation of PSK-Modulated Carrier Phase with application to Burst Digital Transmission," *TACT Information Theory.*, July, 1983.
[10] Proakis, John, G., *Digital Communications*., Mc Graw Hill, 1996.

7 Biographies

Herbert Grünbacher, Prof. Dr., was born in Jochberg, Austria in 1945. He received his PhD degree from the Technical University Graz in 1979. After several years in the semiconductor industry he became Professor for Computer Engineering at the Vienna University of Technology. He is presently Director at Carinthia Tech Institute, Austria.
His research interest is system modeling, hardware-software co-design and VLSI system design.

Alfred Blaickner, Dr., was born in Salzburg, Austria, in 1958. His research activities began in 1986 within the Department of Communications at Graz University of Technology and the European Space Agency. In 1989 he joined Rohde & Schwarz, Germany. In 1995 he received his Ph.D. degree from Graz University of Technology. He is currently teaching courses in communications engineering and working on integrated circuit design and telecommunications projects. His research interests include digital communications, signal processing, and VLSI-system design. He is a member of IEEE.

Oliver Nagy, was born in Stuttgart, Germany, in 1977 and is studying at Carinthia Tech Institute, Austria. He is currently in his final year, working on his master thesis. His interests are in telecommunication systems, signal processing and VLSI design.

Software Radio Reconfigurable Hardware System (SHaRe)

Xavier Revés, Antoni Gelonch, Ferran Casadevall, and José L. García

Universitat Politècnica de Catalunya, Signal Theory and Communication Department
Jordi Girona 1-3, 08034 Barcelona (Spain)
{xreves, antoni, ferran}@xaloc.upc.es
garciam@teleline.es

Abstract. Recent requirements and evolution of personal communications systems will tend to increase the number of applications that will run over the same hardware/software. While an option is providing this platform with all the algorithms needed, a more suitable one is providing such a platform with the capacity to evolve, along time, from one function to another. Here we present a hardware platform with self reconfiguration abilities depending on system demand. The reconfiguration can be partial or complete within a short time to cope with the current application. This capability has an important effect on the software radio techniques applied to terminals and base stations as it will add extra value through a quick support to new standards and the incorporation of new software-designed applications.

1 Introduction

When working in mobile systems, the present third generation (3G) deploying has produced a substantial growth of services offered by network providers. Multiplicity of bands, data formats and rates, and processing demands in general will be common attributes. These diversity requires a quite complex structure with separate silicon for each possible standard. Another solution is using an application-multiplexed structure able to bear all this dispersion. It is clear that an aspect that can reduce implementation costs is reusing as many times as possible the same system in several applications. In this case, the second approach is quite reasonable when designing terminals from the point of view of the Software Radio techniques [1], [2], [3]. Those terminals must be capable of managing new and different standards and/or applications but with only part of them being executed concurrently. It's reasonable considering that different applications share part of the structure so it seems interesting to change only part of the processing structure. Also, software radios can reduce manufacturing costs and allow upgrading of the system as soon as different processing techniques and applications appear.

One important aspect in reconfigurable systems is the cost in terms of time, that is, the time spent on reconfiguring the system. In mobile communications area, reconfiguration times are not specially stressing when a user changes from one data stream format to another since a certain delay will be allowed. Perhaps a harder requirement should take this delay into account, like in the case where a mobile user changes from one standard protocol to another trying to maintain the current call. Moreover, we must not forget that an important design issue of this kind of systems is the scalability, that is, the capability to provide increasing processing power without increasing complexity.

By other hand, it is well known that Field Programmable Gate Arrays (FPGA) offer the possibility to designer of reshaping the application as many times as wished. Taking advantage of that, it is possible building hardware systems that change their functionality at any time. Also several options appear when focusing on what parts of the system can be modified or how you are actually doing it. Totally or partially reconfigurable FPGAs are suitable if the overall system flexibility is kept to allow, at least, working within the selected area. This can be accomplished using many different architectures where inherent FPGA flexibility can polish errors in the previous design stages. But choosing an adequate initial architecture can help reaching final objectives. One important aspect when designing the system architecture is the minimum reconfigurable block size. Each of these blocks must be small enough to avoid reconfiguration overhead when only a small part of the system is to be modified. Conversely, large blocks have the ability to simplify the architecture.

With this in mind, and considering the structures usually implemented in a typical radio link, a Reconfigurable Hardware System (SHaRe) was designed and built. This partially auto-reconfigurable platform is being presented in more detail further on.

The final objective of this research work was to develop a reconfigurable hardware platform, mixing FPGAs and DSP technology, able to test, in real time, the proposed third generation mobile system radio access technologies and evaluate its performance. This platform should be as flexible as possible to allow the characterisation by software of the different radio access techniques proposed. From the viewpoint of the Software Radio implementation requirements, the aggregate processing demand of a generic mobile cellular base station managing 30 users, without considering the IF processing demand, can be estimated around 150 MOPS (Million Operations per Second). This value include only the baseband, bitstream, source and the signaling processing demand. About the IF processing demand it is estimated around 2500 MOPS which is assumed, until now, carried out by special-purpose digital receiver chips.

2 SHaRe Platform Architecture

Considering all the previously commented ideas, our aim was building a system based on a set of blocks made of non-partially reconfigurable FPGA [4] of an undetermined size. Each of these blocks will include one or more clusters which will be the smallest reconfigurable portions of the system. Defining the blocks dimensions can be done on the basis of the knowledge of the set of possible applications (a priori knowledge) and associating every block with one ore more clusters. If those applications are not known the definition can be done on the basis of certain abstract criteria. The second approach requires to define a flexible platform that allowing the union of several clusters to accommodate a single block. Again the size of these clusters must be a trade-off between the available number of them and the range of valid sizes for each one. It cannot go unnoticed that a highly clustered system increases designer effort as the underlying hardware must be known and the desing must be partitioned. Conversely, a not much clustered system, although simplifies architecture and designer effort (must deal with fewer and larger FPGAs) can drift towards high reconfiguration cycles or towards scarcely used clusters what represents a lost of resources.

The final clustered architecture can be supported by an automation software at a high level language with a compiler having perfect knowledge of the underlying structure. This approach is out of the scope of this document, but the actual structure of the system being presented has grossly been thought as a tridimensional, simple but flexible, data, control and configuration flow so that the "only" task of the compiler would be to identify those data flows present into the design.

2.1 Defined Blocks

The proposed flat architecture for the FPGA network board (SHaRe) is shown in the Fig. 1. Three different modules are shown: the Peripheral and Processing Management (PPM) module, the VME [5] Interface and Programming (VIP) module and the Intensive Processing Unit (IPU) module. All them are constituted of several FPGAs as "intelligent" part. The modules are housed over a printed circuit board with a VME physical interface in 6U format which allow the scalability of the system. Notice the possibility of SHaRe to be connected to a typical VME backplane and to be concatenated with another VME compliant board.

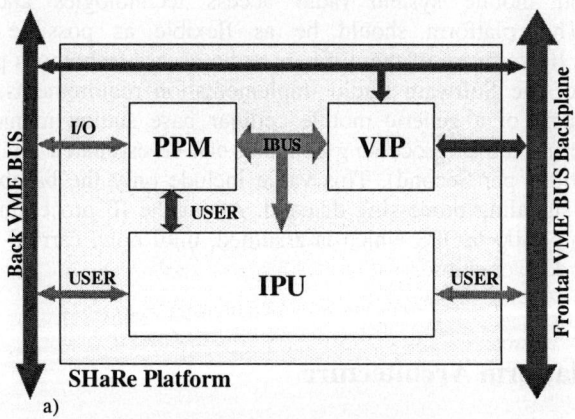

Fig. 1. General SHaRe block diagram

The most important block from the point of view of managing physical resources and system scalability is the VIP one. It provides support to the different buses defined in VME standard. The accessibility to all these buses together with the potential capabilities of the rest of elements gives the system the ability to build a complete VME structure (needless to say that without data sources or sinks that structure is useless) with transfer rates beyond 60Mbytes/sec.

The VIP module provides the necessary link between the VME bus and the inner part of the SHARE board through the internal bus (IBUS: Synchronous Burst User

Interface). It also manages the reprogramming facilities of the FPGAs included in the rest of modules. The VIP FPGA is the only one that starts-up automatically, and only automatically, (in normal operation) to make the system functional at power-up.

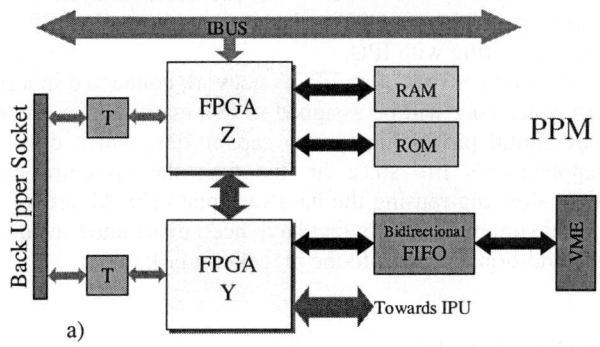

Fig. 2. PPM module internal structure

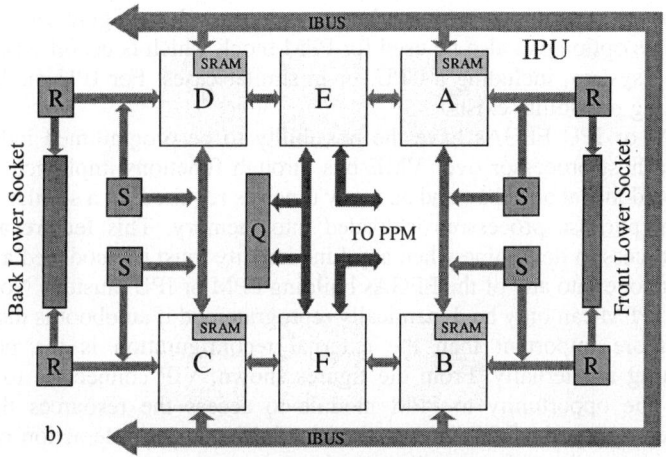

Fig. 3. IPU module internal structure

A simplified diagram of PPM and IPU appear in Fig. 2 and Fig. 3 respectively. PPM module is built around two FPGAs, and IPU one is basically made up of six FPGAs, each of them constituting a cluster. PPM module is designed to be able to perform CPU-like tasks and to communicate through serial/parallel ports to external environments. As the serial/parallel ports can be redefined, no limitations are introduced about used interface or speed (some FPGAs can easily reach 100Mbit/sec serial interfaces), thus allowing an easy migration to different communications protocols (e.g. Ethernet, X.25, RS232, IEEE-488 etc.) only adding the appropriate physical level link. This is because no drivers at physical level have been introduced to have available a wide range of possibilities. Then, the corresponding drivers, depending on the interface required, must be appended at the socket.

With regard to what has been called CPU-like tasks, the idea in mind is having the possibility to introduce a small processor core into one or both FPGAs to execute a rather simple managing program. The aim is not getting the performance of a commercial processor (otherwise placing one instead of the FPGA would have been a better approach) but being able to check how an FPGA working this way can help the system. For this purpose, up to 1Mbyte of SRAM and 512kbytes of ROM have been supplied. Not only managing or CPU tasks can be assigned to PPM but also signal processing tasks interacting with IPU.

The last block (IPU) consists of an FPGA network connected in a software-defined basis. The main processing will be assigned to this matrix. As a processing unit, will include most of digital processing system capabilities, which don't need to be the same along application's life since in this case the structure can be modified dynamically thus allowing reusing the hardware platform. Moreover, several SRAM blocks (up to a maximum of 256kbytes) have been distributed inside this network in order to provide additional support to the processing task.

2.2 Programming Methods

As mentioned above, VIP module programs itself at power-up as the corresponding FPGA acts as glue logic between buses and general configuration registers and utilities. This option can also be used for PPM block which is useful when building a stand-alone system, including a CPU, or in similar cases. For IPU module, no self-programming possibility exists.

All PPM or IPU FPGAs have the possibility to be programmed individually by means of a host processor over VME bus through functions implemented into VIP. This can be done, at any time and as many times as required, in a similar way as code for general purpose processors is loaded into memory. This feature allows to an external process to determine when any functionality must by modified and then load the correct code into any of the FPGAs building PPM or IPU clusters. Notice that any FPGA into PPM can only be dynamically reprogrammed if autoboot is disabled for it.

Much more important than the external reconfiguration is the possibility of implementing it internally. From the figures shown, VIP connection to the internal bus gives the opportunity to PPM module to access the resources that allow to program/reprogram the FPGAs over the board. The strong interaction of PPM with IPU allows it to monitor application-dependent variables for watching system evolution. Then, when a modification in any of the clusters into IPU is required, a programming cycle can be done. This ability is which we have called auto-reprogram. Of course PPM can participate in the application tasks, but the designer can take advantage of that capacity to build an auto-managed application.

Each IPU cluster may require several kilobytes of data. Storing mechanisms have been provided to PPM (the same resources that allow it to act as a CPU) to retain different configurations of more than one cluster. When the diversity of configurations required for the present application exceeds storage capabilities, more data can be found into VME domains through VIP IBUS-VME bridge.

In any case, reconfiguration is parallel to any processing since a dedicated programming bus has been installed on the board. At any point of the application some devices can be working while others are being reconfigured. A certain mechanism puts reconfiguracion on record so that working application may wait until a concrete part is ready.

2.3 Soft Radio Architecture

Until this point a description of SHaRe's architecture has been presented to allow a general understanding of the system. The blocks depicted have been considered flat representations of the ensemble. But the blocks can be reordered and represented in another way. This representation will give a hierarchical representation per layers of SHaRe and is shown in Fig. 4. It can be seen the presence of three layers. The lower one will perform basic system functions (modulation/demodulation, bitstream processing, etc.). This corresponds completely to IPU. The next level above will deal with higher system tasks (channel parameter extraction, synchronism functions, etc.) and is shared between IPU and PPM. Finally, the top level will manage the part of application running over the board. This task will be exclusively performed by PPM.

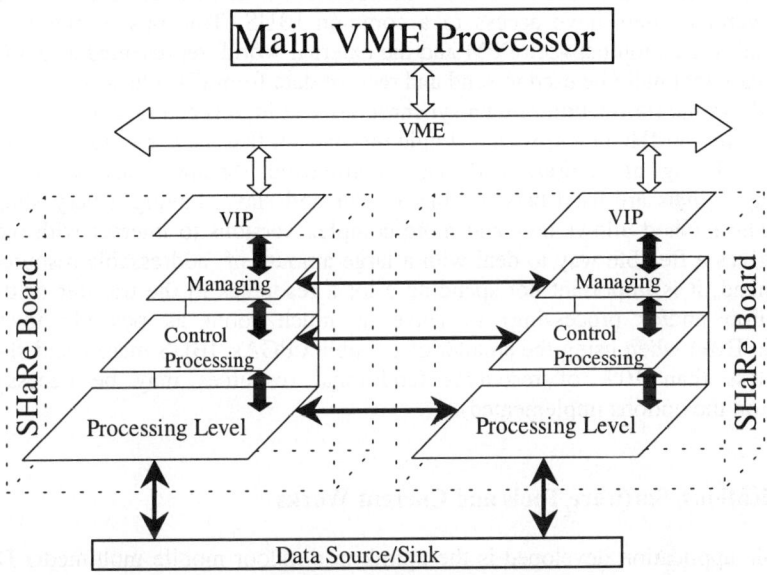

Fig. 4. SHaRe Hierarchy Stack

Viewing the architecture this way it can be understood that the system can modify parameters corresponding to any of the levels through data being received from either the channel or the system administrator. This approach is useful in a canonical Software Radio transceiver because evolution from environment analysis is a key point. Evolution is not only done online by the same system but is also done through system operation enhancement.

Another important aspect to highlight is the system scalability that provides SHaRe. Although it is given the complete set of resources to cope with a complex application, those can be insufficient for the current one. SHaRe gives a simple solution to this problem. A set of boards can be joined as showed in Fig. 4 getting a more complex system but also a more powerful processing machine. It is important to see that the hierarchical structure is kept.

2.4 Data Communication

As main paths of data between clusters we define dedicated paths allowing word transfer widths of up to 32 bits (if data is transferred synchronously several hundreds of megabytes per second can be achieved although generally not required), large enough for most of signal processing applications even if complex data are used. These datapaths are specially useful when signal sampling rates are high and give the structure the capability of sequentially concatenate different blocks, each one of them performing a different task, or implementing parallel paths with cross-passing information.

These dedicated paths would be the main data flow, but to transfer data at lower mean rates, as it can happen when sending control parameters or tables to be updated from time to time, a shared bus structure is acceptable. In our case, as observed in the figures, several clusters have access to a common IBUS. This bus is mainly for bidireccional interaction between PPM and the external world, represented as a VME bus, but it can optionally be used to send and receive data from IPU clusters.

IBUS allows the transaction of data synchronously at high speed rates (128Mbytes per second with 32MHz clock) with a simple mechanism that uses few resources into the FPGAs. Using an address and data multiplexed scheme, only some few handshaking signals are used between bus master and slave, having a very simple protocol. The method allows new and more complex versions to interact with older ones and gives a flexible way to deal with a large amount of addressable resources. By other hand, it is important not spending a lot a resources in the transfer of data (configuration and/or processing) to leave as much room as possible to the application. Even when using the smaller of possible FPGAs, IBUS master and slave occupies less than 10% of resources (additional resources may be necessary depending on the options implemented).

2.4 Applications, Software Tools and Current Works

An example application developed is the uplink in a indoor mobile multimedia DS-CDMA system which represents a system of complexity similar to that of WCDMA for UMTS. In the transmitter a maximum of 256kbps were allowed per user in eight different channels of 32kbps separated each other by Gold sequences. Data were spread at 4Mchips/sec and, after a QPSK modulation, translated to the digital to analog converter at a sampling rate of 32Msps. The receiver, after analog to digital conversion, performed the corresponding tasks of synchronization (lock and follow) and CDMA demodulation. The complete system gross processing demand is about 2Giga operations (some more complex than others) per second in the transmitter and about twice as much in the receiver. Most of processing capacity was used in channel and I/Q demodulator filtering in reception (32Msps and 9-11 bits). The whole transmitter could be inserted into a XC4013 FPGA. Also the synchronism algorithm and CDMA demodulation could be implemented into a XC4013. Notice that this is the smallest FPGA that can be placed over SHaRe. Reception I/Q demodulator and filtering was using almost three times more of space depending on the algorithm used. Using larger FPGAs and taking into account that the complexity (in terms of resources) of the system implemented does not increment as fast as the number of users does, it is deduced that over a single SHaRe board some tenths of users can be implemented.

By other hand, software tools are important when managing a complex hardware structure. The knowledge of every corner of the structure is hard for novel users but is the only way of doing it without an automated tool. At present developing and programming applications can be done through definition of the different cluster tasks and loading the code generated into FPGAs. The code is sent through a driver running on a Sparc processor card over VME bus with a Solaris operating system. The definition of FPGA code can be done by means of a hardware description language (VHDL).

At present, a tool based on IEEE 1149.1 (Boundary-Scan and Test Access Port) is being developed which will allow the user to test, debug and monitor applications remotely or locally with the help of analysis systems. This can be done from the top of the hierarchy presented before.

3 SHaRe Features

The main Share board features and performances are described in the Table 1. The most important features indicates us the capacity that the system has to communicate with the environment and the maximum processing capacity that can be obtained.

Table 1. SHaRe's set of features

Description	Feature
Host bus	VME64 (ANSI/VITA 1-1994)
	Up to 66Mbytes/sec.
Test Port	JTAG TAP (IEEE 1149.1)
Board's Devices	Up to 9 Xilinx® FPGA
Devices Family (5V or 3.3V)	Xilinx® XC4000E/EX/XL/XLA (4013-4085)
	Xilinx® Spartan/XL (30-40)
SRAM Memory per board	2 Mbytes maximum
ROM Memory per board	8 Mbits maximum
FIFOs input/output size	From 2k x 32 bits up to 64k x 32 bits
Number of MACs[1]	Up to 40 Giga MACs with larger devices
IBUS mean transfer speed over sustained transfer	Up to 110 Mbytes/sec with 32MHz clock.

4 Conclusions

Partially reconfigurable platforms with high processing capabilities can help supporting many standards and applications by reusing the same hardware. Software Radio techniques can take advantage of the efficiency of reconfigurable or self-

---

[1] Estimated peak capacity per full board based on a Xilinx® 16 bits FIR filter benchmark. (MAC: *multiply-accumulate*). One DSPTMS320C6x can perform about 0.5 Giga MAC/sec.

configurable platforms to improve system behaviour without lost of flexibility. The diversification of services, protocols and access topologies will require the introduction of clever multiband and multi-standard terminals able to implement new applications without hardware modification, so partially reconfigurable systems will likely be next generation terminals. In this paper a partially self-reconfigurable system (SHaRe, Fig. 5) has been presented based exclusively on FPGAs. As a testbed, SHaRe will allow checking multiple digital environments and, as a tool, will allow to add quickly and easily new improvements and functions into commercial mobile terminals by using hardware description languages (e.g. VHDL, Verilog) in a first step and even high level languages (like C/C++ or JAVA) for system-level description. SHaRe's properties make it suitable for checking auto-reconfiguration algorithms on the basis of self-evolution control.

Fig. 5. Frontal photograph of first SHaRe prototype

Acknowledgement

This work has been supported by CYCIT (Spanish National Science Council) under grant TIC98-0684

References

1. Joe Mitola. "The Software Radio Architecture". IEEE Communications Magazine. May 1995.
2. Srikathyayani Srikanteswara, Jeffrey H. Reed, Peter Athanas and Robert Boyle. "A Soft Radio Architecture for Reconfigurable Platforms". IEEE Communications Magazine. February 2000.
3. Mark Cummings, Shinichiro Haruyama. "FPGA in the Software Radio". IEEE Communications Magazine. February 1999.
4. XILINX XC4000E XC4000X Series Field Programmable Gate Arrays. Xilinx. May 1999.
5. VME bus Specification, ANSI/IEEE STD1014-1987. VITA 1987.

Analysis of RNS-FPL Synergy for High Throughput DSP Applications: Discrete Wavelet Transform

Javier Ramírez[1], Antonio García[1], Pedro G. Fernández[2],
Luis Parrilla[1], and Antonio Lloris[1]

[1] Dept. of Electronics and Computer Technology,
Campus Universitario Fuentenueva, 18071 Granada, Spain
{jramirez, agarcia, lloris, lparrilla}@ditec.ugr.es
[2] Dept. of Electrical Engineering,
Escuela Politécnica Superior, 23071 Jaén, Spain
pfernan@ujaen.es
http://ditec.ugr.es/

Abstract. This paper focuses on the implementation over FPL devices of high throughput DSP applications taking advantage of RNS arithmetic. The synergy between the RNS and modern FPGA device families, providing built-in tables and fast carry and cascade chains, makes it possible to accelerate MAC intensive real-time and DSP systems. In this way, a slow high dynamic range binary 2's complement system can be partitioned into various parallel and high throughput small word-length RNS channels without inter-channel carry dependencies. To illustrate the design methodology, novel RNS-based architectures for multi-octave orthogonal DWT and its inverse are implemented using structural level VHDL synthesis. Area analysis and performance simulation are conducted. A relevant throughput improvement for the proposed RNS-based solution is obtained, compared to the equivalent 2's complement implementation.

1 Introduction

FPL devices have recently generated interest for use in Digital Signal Processing systems due to their ability to implement custom solutions while maintaining flexibility through device reprogramming. These devices represent an alternative to DSPs and ASICs since a significant performance improvement over DSPs, with moderately low development cost, can be obtained while maintaining system programmability.

Furthermore, the number of applications requiring high-precision and high-bandwidth signal processing is constantly increasing and the development of structures for these systems is of growing interest. Traditional binary 2's complement arithmetic systems suffer from long carry propagation delays. Thus, the RNS [1, 2] (Residue Number System) is gaining relevance to solve the disadvantages of the carry propagation delay in binary adders and multipliers, so a number of tasks performed in the main DSP computation procedures can be accelerated through the use of efficient RNS arithmetic units improved for the MAC (Multiply and Accumulate) operation [3, 4]. In the RNS, in contrast to binary 2's complement weighted arithmetic, there is no performance degradation with increasing word-width. Arbitrary word-width RNS adders and multipliers maintain a constant throughput and do not suffer from carry propagation delay drawbacks. The RNS is a non-weighted and limited carry arithmetic numeric system whose parallelism between high throughput small word-length channels enables the design of high performance DSP systems.

An RNS implementation of an arithmetic-intensive application leads to several copies of the original system performing modular arithmetic and working over small dynamic ranges but globally handling the total one. Thus, it is possible to consider the mapping of RNS systems into FPL devices. However, the LUT (Look-Up Table) requirements for some RNS operations have been a serious obstacle for the development of such structures. The new programmable device families, such as Altera FLEX10K or APEX20K [5], Virtex [6] and Actel ProASIC [7], have overcome this problem by means of small built-in embedded memories and logic blocks with fast carry and cascade chains, thus enabling these devices for RNS arithmetic.

In this paper, the advantages of the use of RNS rather than FPL devices to implement arithmetic-intensive DSP applications is analyzed. To illustrate this, novel RNS-based architectures for multi-octave orthogonal DWT (Discrete Wavelet Transform) are implemented using structural VHDL synthesis. Area analysis and performance simulations are conducted leading to relevant throughput improvements compared to the equivalent binary 2's complement architectures.

2 Residue Number System Arithmetic

An RNS is defined by a set of L positive and pairwise relatively prime integers $\{m_1, m_2, ..., m_L\}$, called moduli. Let $M = \prod_{i=1}^{L} m_i$; thus, the ring of integers modulo M, $Z(M)$, represents the dynamic range of the RNS. Thus, any positive integer $X \in Z(M)$ is uniquely represented by the L-tuple $[x_1, x_2, ..., x_L]$ of its residues, where $x_i = X \bmod m_i$. Given two integers $X, Y \in Z(M)$, and their corresponding residue representations $[x_1, x_2, ..., x_L]$ and $[y_1, y_2, ..., y_L]$, arithmetic in the RNS is defined by:

$$X \circ Y \leftrightarrow \left[\left| x_1 \circ y_1 \right|_{m_1}, \left| x_2 \circ y_2 \right|_{m_2}, ..., \left| x_L \circ y_L \right|_{m_L} \right] \quad (1)$$

where o represents either addition, subtraction or multiplication. In this way, RNS arithmetic is defined over the direct sum of integer rings modulo m_i, $Z(m_i)$, and it is performed in parallel without dependencies between the residue digits.

Conversion from the residue representation $[x_1, x_2, ..., x_L]$ to its integer value X is based on the Chinese Remainder Theorem (CRT). The theorem states that there exists a unique $X \in Z(M)$ for a given residue representation and that it can be computed as:

$$\left| X \right|_M = \left| \sum_{j=1}^{L} \hat{m}_j \left| \frac{x_j}{\hat{m}_j} \right|_{m_j} \right|_M \qquad \hat{m}_j \equiv \frac{M}{m_j} \cdot \quad (2)$$

Thus, the RNS provides a fundamental methodology for the partitioning of large dynamic range systems into a number of smaller but independent channels over which computations are performed in parallel.

3 FPL Implementation of RNS-Based DSP Algorithms

To date, RNS design methodologies have been most successfully applied for Finite Impulse Response (FIR) filters, which can take full advantage of fast RNS arithmetic while avoiding the problems associated with scaling. Thus, those DSP algorithms that rely upon or can be formulated as convolution are the main target of this numeric system.

Given an input sequence, $x(n)$, a FIR filter is characterized by the convolution operation:

$$y(n) = \sum_{k=0}^{N-1} h_k x(n-k) \quad , \tag{3}$$

where $y(n)$ is the filter output, the h_k terms are the filter coefficients and N denotes the length of the filter. When (3) is encoded in RNS arithmetic, the equations to be computed are described by:

$$\left| y(n) \right|_{m_j} = \left| \sum_{k=0}^{N-1} h_k^j x_j(n-k) \right|_{m_j} \quad j = 1, ..., L \tag{4}$$

where h_k^j and $x_j(n-k)$ denote the residues of h_k and $x(n-k)$ modulo m_j, respectively and all operations and multiplications in (4) are defined as modulo m_j operations. In a digit-parallel design, each modulo m_j processor in (4) for $j = 1, 2, ..., L$ is implemented independently and the ensemble is operated in parallel for maximum performance. Thus, each modular FIR filter requires N multipliers and $N-1$ adders. Moreover, applications requiring a high number of taps can benefit from the use of DA (Distributed Arithmetic) in the RNS domain [3] to reduce memory use in parallel filter implementations.

3.1 Implementation of RNS Arithmetic Modules on FPL Devices

FPL devices providing embedded LUTs and dedicated logic blocks are potential solutions for this kind of RNS-based MAC-intensive algorithms. These devices consist of LEs (Logic Elements) and LUTs. Depending on the family, each LE includes one or more variable input size LUTs (typical are $2^6 \times 1$, $2^5 \times 1$, $2^4 \times 1$ or $2^3 \times 1$), fast carry propagation logic and one or more flip-flops. Likewise, LUTs allow us to build specialized memory functions such as ROM or RAM.

Specifically, each LE included in the Altera FLEX10K [5] device consists of a $2^4 \times 1$ LUT, an output register and dedicated logic for fast carry and cascade chains in arithmetic mode. A number of Embedded Array Blocks (EABs), providing a 2K-bit RAM or ROM and configurable as $2^8 \times 8$, $2^9 \times 4$, $2^{10} \times 2$ or $2^{11} \times 1$, are the cores for the implementation of RNS LUT-based multipliers. Other FPL device families supporting RNS arithmetic are Altera APEX20K, Actel ProASIC and Virtex. These devices allow the implementation of high throughput modular arithmetic DSP processors, so RNS-FPL merged solutions can achieve the demanding high-precision and high-bandwidth requirements of modern DSP technology.

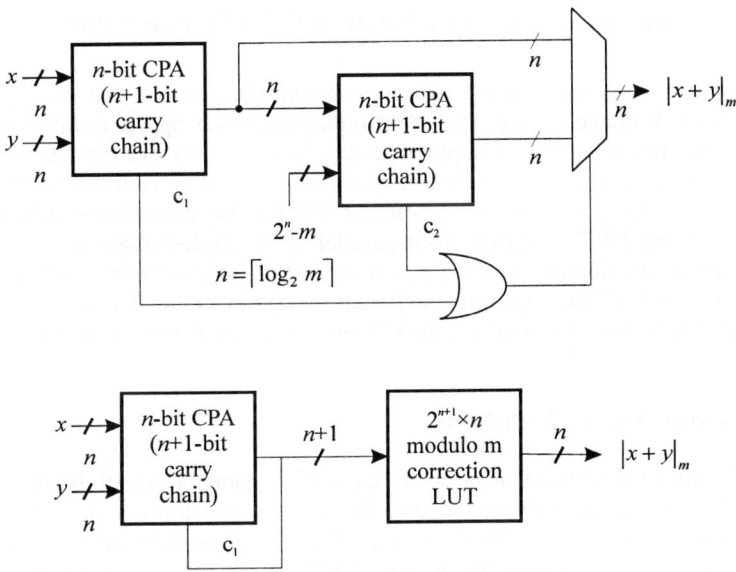

Fig. 1. FPL implementation of residue adders.

Several alternatives exist for the implementation of modular adders [8]. Specially oriented for FPLs and only using LEs is the adder that generates the two possible results and selects the correct one according to the carries. Another alternative is to add the input operands and then implement modulo reduction with a LUT. Fig. 1 shows FPL designs of both alternatives. The first of them does not use memory resources and takes full advantage of short carry chains. At the same time, registers provided by LEs make that pipelining does not require additional resources. Table 1 shows area usage and performance for the two adder designs using grade –4 FLEX10K devices.

Table 1. Performance given in MSPS (MegaSamples Per Second) and LEs and EABs required by 6-, 7- and 8-bit residue adders using grade –4 speed FLEX10K devices.

	6-bit moduli			7-bit moduli			8-bit moduli		
	LEs	EABs	MSPS	LEs	EABs	MSPS	LEs	EABs	MSPS
Two stage CPA	15	0	40.00	18	0	42.73	19	0	34.36
Two stage CPA (pipelined)	16	0	71.42	18	0	58.47	20	0	57.47
LUT-based	7	1	30.39	8	1	30.03	9	2	28.65
LUT-based (pipelined)	7	1	76.33	8	1	76.33	9	2	76.33

On the other hand, the throughput increase of LUT-based modulo multiplication over binary multiplication is even better than that of addition since a small synchronous EAB can be clocked at frequencies up to 70 MHz for a grade –4 speed FLEX10K device and is not prejudiced by the increasing precision of modern DSP technology.

4 FPL Implementation of RNS-Based DWT Filter Banks

In the last few years, many new transform techniques have arisen that are specifically oriented towards image coding. These techniques frequently appear as multiresolution analysis, time-frequency analysis, pyramid algorithms and wavelet transforms [9, 10]. They offer better compression ratios than DCT-based coding techniques and do not suffer from blocking artifact. Thus, different VLSI architectures have been reported [11, 12] for the DWT, ranging from parallel filter implementations to bit-serial, systolic arrays, distributed memory, etc. A novel FPL implementation of one-octave and two-octave RNS decomposition and reconstruction filter banks for the 1-D DWT and its inverse is shown to illustrate the FPL-RNS synergy described above.

4.1 Discrete Wavelet Transform

A signal can be expressed as a series expansion using a set of basis functions generated from a basic wavelet function by dilations and translations. The wavelet series expansion represents signals with a sequence of wavelet approximation and detail coefficients corresponding to the sampling in the time-scale space. The successive discrete approximation sequences are lower and lower resolution versions of the original, each sampled twice as sparsely as its predecessor. The DWT can be implemented by a tree-structured algorithm in the multiresolution analysis framework. Thus, the level J 1-D DWT decomposition of a sequence $x(n)$ is defined by the recurrent equations:

$$a_n^{(i)} = \sum_{k=0}^{M_L-1} g_k a_{2n-k}^{(i-1)} \qquad i = 1, 2, ..., J$$
$$d_n^{(i)} = \sum_{k=0}^{M_H-1} h_k a_{2n-k}^{(i-1)} \qquad a_n^{(0)} \equiv x(n) \qquad (5)$$

where the sequences $a_n^{(i)}$ and $d_n^{(i)}$ are the approximation and detail sequences at level i, and the g_k and h_k coefficients identify the wavelet family used. These equations correspond to an identical structure which consists of a pair of convolvers and decimators that is repeated at each decomposition level. The signal $x(n)$ can be perfectly recovered through its multiresolution decomposition { $a_n^{(J)}$, $d_n^{(J)}$, $d_n^{(J-1)}$, ..., $d_n^{(1)}$ }.

While there are different kinds of wavelet families, most applications make use almost exclusively of orthogonal wavelets. The perfect reconstruction property and the orthogonality conditions imposed on the wavelets mean that the high-pass decomposition and reconstruction filter coefficients h_k and $\overline{h}_k$ can be obtained from the low-pass decomposition and reconstruction filters g_k and $\overline{g}_k$, respectively:

$$h_k = (-1)^{k+1} g_{N-k-1}$$
$$\overline{h}_k = (-1)^{k+1} \overline{g}_{N-k-1} \qquad k = 0, 1, ..., N-1 \qquad (6)$$

where N is the number of taps of the analysis and synthesis FIR filters. Thus, orthogonality condition given in (4) can be exploited to halve the number of multipliers and adders in each octave of the analysis and synthesis multiresolution wavelet filters.

4.2 RNS Architectures for the Orthogonal Discrete Wavelet Transform

By substituting the orthogonality condition (4) in (3), the octave-i detail sequence $d_n^{(i)}$ can be expressed as:

$$d_n^{(i)} = \sum_{k=0}^{N-1} (-1)^{k+1} g_{N-k-1} a_{2n-k}^{(i-1)} = \sum_{k=0}^{N/2-1} g_{N-2k-2} a_{2n-2k-1}^{(i-1)} - \sum_{k=0}^{N/2-1} g_{N-2k-1} a_{2n-2k}^{(i-1)} . \quad (7)$$

Thus, the octave-i approximation $a_n^{(i)}$ and detail $d_n^{(i)}$ sequences can be computed sharing the N multipliers of the low-pass filter coefficients $\{g_0, g_1, ..., g_{N-1}\}$ in alternate cycles in accordance with:

$$a_n^{(i)} = \sum_{k=0}^{N-1} g_k a_{2n-k}^{(i-1)} \qquad i=1,2,...,J$$

$$d_n^{(i)} = \sum_{k=0}^{N/2-1} g_{N-2k-2} a_{2n-2k-1}^{(i-1)} - \sum_{k=0}^{N/2-1} g_{N-2k-1} a_{2n-2k}^{(i-1)} \qquad a_n^{(0)} \equiv x(n) \quad (8)$$

The same idea can be applied for the computation of the 1-D DWT in the RNS. By taking modulo m_j, (6) can be expressed as:

$$\left| a_n^{(i)} \right|_{m_j} = \left| \sum_{k=0}^{N-1} \left| g_k a_{2n-k}^{(i-1)} \right|_{m_j} \right|_{m_j} \qquad i=1,2,...,J$$

$$\left| d_n^{(i)} \right|_{m_j} = \left| \left| \sum_{k=0}^{N/2-1} \left| g_{N-2k-2} a_{2n-2k-1}^{(i-1)} \right|_{m_j} \right|_{m_j} - \left| \sum_{k=0}^{N/2-1} \left| g_{N-2k-1} a_{2n-2k}^{(i-1)} \right|_{m_j} \right|_{m_j} \right|_{m_j} \quad (9)$$

which allows us to synthesize an architecture that halves the number of LUT-based (Look-Up Table) modular multipliers of each octave channel. In this way, an octave-i modular decomposition level consists of N shared LUTs and two modular adder trees that compute the approximation and detail sequences. The LUTs are clocked at the input sample frequency and are used in alternate clock cycles to compute the products of the low-pass and high-pass filters. These products are added by two modular adder trees controlled by half of the input frequency out-of-phase clocks *clock1* and *clock2*. The resulting 1-D DWT RNS architecture for 8-tap decomposition filters is shown in Fig. 2.

In a similar way, the reconstruction algorithm involved in the IDWT (Inverse Discrete Wavelet Transform) can benefit from the relations between the synthesis filter coefficients $\overline{h}_k$ and $\overline{g}_k$ given in (4) to share the LUTs of only one filter. Each of the reconstruction stages consists of a pair of interpolators and convolvers that compute:

$$\hat{a}_m^{(i-1)} = \begin{cases} \sum_{k=0}^{N/2-1} \overline{h}_{2k+1}\hat{d}_{\frac{m}{2}-k}^{(i)} + \sum_{k=0}^{N/2-1} \overline{g}_{2k+1}\hat{a}_{\frac{m}{2}-k}^{(i)} & m \text{ even} \\ \sum_{k=0}^{N/2-1} \overline{h}_{2k}\hat{d}_{\frac{m-1}{2}-k}^{(i)} + \sum_{k=0}^{N/2-1} \overline{g}_{2k}\hat{a}_{\frac{m-1}{2}-k}^{(i)} & m \text{ odd} \end{cases} \qquad (10)$$

Introducing relation (4) and taking modulo m_j, (8) can be expressed as:

$$\left|\hat{a}_m^{(i-1)}\right|_{m_j} = \begin{cases} \left\|\left|\sum_{k=0}^{N/2-1}\left|\overline{g}_{N-2k-2}\hat{d}_{\frac{m}{2}-k}^{(i)}\right|_{m_j}\right|_{m_j} + \left|\sum_{k=0}^{N/2-1}\left|\overline{g}_{2k+1}\hat{a}_{\frac{m}{2}-k}^{(i)}\right|_{m_j}\right|_{m_j}\right\|_{m_j} & m \text{ even} \\ \left\|\left|\sum_{k=0}^{N/2-1}\left|\overline{g}_{2k}\hat{a}_{\frac{m-1}{2}-k}^{(i)}\right|_{m_j}\right|_{m_j} - \left|\sum_{k=0}^{N/2-1}\left|\overline{g}_{N-2k-1}\hat{d}_{\frac{m-1}{2}-k}^{(i)}\right|_{m_j}\right|_{m_j}\right\|_{m_j} & m \text{ odd} \end{cases} \qquad (11)$$

that leads to an architecture for the orthogonal 1-D IDWT in which the LUTs of the low-pass synthesis filter are shared to generate the low-pass and high-pass filter outputs as shown in Fig. 3. In this way, the N LUTs operate at the input rate producing $N/2$ partial products of each filter which are added by two modular adder trees clocked by out-of-phase clocks *clock1* and *clock2* at half of the sampling rate.

The proposed RNS VLSI architectures for the 1-D DWT and IDWT implement the analysis and synthesis filters respectively, halving the number of LUTs due to the orthogonality relations between the filter coefficients. With this scheme, the decimation and interpolation processes involved in the DWT and IDWT allow us to compute the two half of the input frequency outputs $\left|a_n^{(i)}\right|_{m_j}$ and $\left|d_n^{(i)}\right|_{m_j}$ and the twice the input frequency output $\left|a_n^{(i-1)}\right|_{m_j}$ with only half of the memory resources.

An additional resource requirement reduction can be obtained if only one modular adder tree clocked at the input frequency is used. However, this alternative reduces the performance of the system since the modular adder tree must operate at the input frequency.

4.3 Implementation over FPL Devices. Area Analysis and Performance Comparison

Two's complement arithmetic and RNS versions of the proposed 1-D DWT and IDWT architectures were implemented over FPL devices to compare hardware complexity and performance. Altera FLEX10K [5] devices were used.

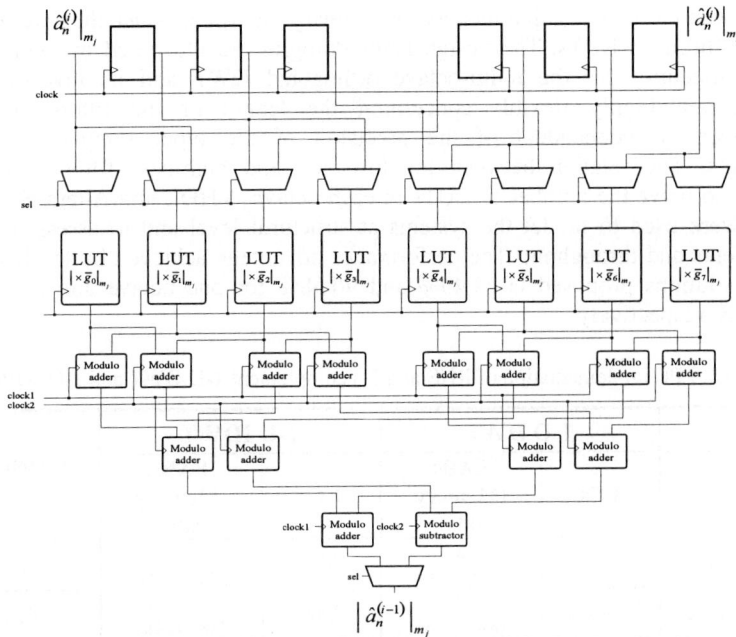

Fig. 3. Modulo m_j RNS architecture for the octave-i reconstruction filter bank.

One-level and two-level decomposition and reconstruction architectures were synthesized using VHDL to quantify parameters such as area and performance. 8-bit input samples and 10-bit filter coefficients were assumed, so that one octave and two octaves required 21- and 34-bit dynamic ranges, respectively. Table II shows the results obtained for each 6-, 7- and 8-bit RNS channel and for traditional arithmetic 1-D DWT and 1-D IDWT implementations over grade −4 speed FLEX10K devices. Hardware requirements were assessed in terms of the number of LEs and EABs while performance was evaluated in terms of the register-to-register path maximum delay. The performance advantage of the 6-, 7- and 8-bit RNS-based architectures proposed increased with the dynamic range considered. In this way, the performance is up to 23.45% and 96.58% better for one octave and two octaves, respectively, when compared to equally pipelined traditional arithmetic implementations.

5 Conclusion

The methodology to design RNS-enabled DSP architectures over FPL devices was assessed in this paper. The synergy between the RNS and modern FPL device families providing embedded LUTs can overcome the demanding high-precision and high-throughput obstacle of the traditional binary 2's complement arithmetic for modern real-time DSP applications. FIR filtering is the main target of this study since it can take full advantage of the RNS while avoiding the problems associated with scaling. When FPL devices are used for such systems, modular adders can benefit from the short carry chains and pipelining supported by LEs while modulo multipliers yield an even more throughput increase over binary multipliers since they are based in small synchronous LUTs. The design methodologies are illustrated by synthesizing RNS architectures for the multi-octave orthogonal DWT and its inverse. These structures are highly flexible concerning the length of the filters and their performance is independent of the precision of the input samples and filter coefficients. The relation between the low-pass and high-pass filter coefficients allows us to halve the number of LUTs in each octave. VHDL and Altera FLEX10K devices were used to model the systems at structural level and to assess hardware requirements and throughput. The performance advantage achieved by the RNS-FPL merged solutions proposed is 23.45% and 96.58% for one octave and two octave transforms, respectively.

Table 2. FPL implementation of RNS and 2's complement 1-D DWT and 1-D IDWT.

	1-D DWT		1-D IDWT		Throughput (MSPS)
	LEs	EABs (Memory bits)	LEs	EABs (Memory bits)	
6-bit channel	316	8 (8×6×64)	321	8 (8×6×64)	68.96
7-bit channel	362	8 (8×7×128)	367	8 (8×7×128)	67.11
8-bit channel	403	8 (8×8×256)	409	8 (8×8×256)	65.78
One-octave 21-bit (Binary)	1164	-	1173	-	55.86
Two-octave 34-bit (Binary)	3689	-	3705	-	35.08

Acknowledgements

The authors were supported by the Dirección General de Enseñanza Superior (Spain) under project PB98-1354. CAD tools and supporting material were provided by Altera Corp. under the Altera University Program.

References

1. M. Soderstrand, W. Jenkins, G. A. Jullien, and F. J. Taylor, *Residue Number System Arithmetic: Modern Applications in Digital Signal Processing*. IEEE Press Reprint Series. IEEE Press, 1986.
2. N. Szabo and R. Tanaka, *Residue Arithmetic and its Applications to Computer Technology*. McGraw-Hill, 1967.
3. A. García, U. Meyer-Bäse, A. Lloris and F. J. Taylor, "RNS Implementation of FIR Filters Based on Distributed Arithmetic using Field-Programmable Logic", *Proc. IEEE Int. Symp. on Circuits and Systems*, Orlando, FL, vol. 1, pp. 486-489, Jun. 1999.
4. J. Ramírez, A. García, P. G. Fernández, L. Parrilla and A. Lloris, "A New Architecture to Compute the Discrete Cosine Transform Using the Quadratic Residue Number System," *Proc. of 2000 IEEE Int. Symp. on Circuits and Systems*, Geneva, 2000, vol. 5, pp. 321-324.

5. Altera Corporation, *1998 Data Book*, Jan. 1998.
6. Xilinx Inc., *The Programmable Logic Data Book*, 1999.
7. Actel Corporation, *ProASIC 500K Family Data Sheet*, 2000.
8. M. A. Bayoumi, G. A. Jullien and W. C. Miller, "A VLSI Implementation of Residue Adders." *IEEE Trans. on Circuits and systems*, vol. 34, no. 3, pp. 284-288, Mar. 87.
9. G. Strang, T. Nguyen, *Wavelets and Filter Banks*, Wellesly-Cambridge Press, 1997.
10. M. Vetterli, J. Kovacevik, *Wavelets and Subband Coding*, Prentice Hall, 1995
11. C. Chakrabarti, C. Mumford, "Efficient Realizations of Encoders and Decoders Based on the 2-D Discrete Wavelet Transform," *IEEE Trans. VLSI Syst.*, vol. 2, no. 3, Sep. 1999.
12. M. Vishwanath, M. Owens, M. J. Irwin, "VLSI Architectures for the Discrete Wavelet Transform," *IEEE Trans. Circuits Syst. II*, vol. 42, no. 5, May 1995.

Partial Run-Time Reconfiguration Using JRTR

Scott McMillan and Steven A. Guccione

Xilinx Inc.
2100 Logic Drive
San Jose, California 95124
{Scott.McMillan, Steven.Guccione}@xilinx.com

Abstract. Much has been written about the design and performance advantages of partial Run-Time Reconfiguration (RTR) over the last decade. While the results have been promising, commercial support for partial RTR has lagged. Until the introduction of the Xilinx Virtex$^{(tm)}$ family of devices, no mainstream, commercial FPGA has provided support for this capability. In this paper we describe *JRTR*, a software package which provides direct support for partial run-time reconfiguration. Using a cache-based model, this implementation provides fast, simple support for partial run-time reconfiguration. While the current implementation is on the Xilinx Virtex family of devices using the *JBits* tool suite, this approach may be applied to any SRAM-based FPGA that provides basic support for RTR.

1 Introduction

Perhaps the greatest advantage to using SRAM based FPGAs is the ability to modify the configured circuit at any time. In the majority of cases, however, this capability is used exclusively in the design phase of a project. Once a design is tested and verified, it is seldom if ever changed. Over the last decade, researchers have explored using this ability to modify SRAM-based FPGAs to reduce circuit complexity, increase performance and simplify system design [1],[2],[3],[4]. In spite of these demonstrated advantages, these techniques have not found widespread acceptance. Much of the reason for this can be attributed to lack of both hardware and software support for partial reconfiguration.

With the introduction of the Xilinx Virtex family of devices [5], hardware support for partial run-time reconfiguration is available for the first time in a large, mainstream commercial device. In addition, the Xilinx *JBits* tool suite [6] provides the software support necessary to make use of all of the features of the Virtex architecture. While run-time reconfiguration has always been supported in *JBits*, simple and direct support for partial run-time reconfiguration has not. This paper describes *JRTR*, a model and software implementation that addresses this deficiency.

2 Run-Time Reconfiguration Hardware and Software

While all SRAM-based FPGA devices are capable of having their circuit configuration modified at any time, software tools, and even the information necessary to perform run-time reconfiguration has been largely unavailable commercially. This situation changed with the introduction of the Xilinx XC6200 family of devices [7]. This device family featured an open architecture, with all circuit configuration data exposed to the users. Unfortunately, with the exception of some small research tools such as *JERC6K* [8], *RAGE* [3] and *ConfDiff* [9], no commercially available software for the XC6200 device supported this run-time reconfiguration feature.

At Xilinx, the *JERC6K* work was transferred to the older and somewhat more limited *XC4000* family and renamed the *Xilinx Bitstream Interface* or *XBI* [6]. This software was later renamed *JBits* and supported direct construction and modification of circuits. Unfortunately, the *XC4000* family of devices only supports bulk configuration and contains no support for partial reconfiguration. Any changes to the device circuit configuration resulted in a halting of the device and a relatively slow reloading of the entire configuration bitstream. This was unacceptable for most applications.

More recently, the *JBits* software has been ported to the Xilinx *Virtex* family of devices. As with the *XC4000* family version, circuit configurations could be built and modified off-line, but reconfiguring the entire device resulted in the same sort of interruption as in the 4K version.

The recent addition of the *JRTR* software to the Virtex version of the *JBits* tool suite has resulted in direct support for partial reconfiguration. This support makes use of combined hardware and software techniques to permit arbitrarily small changes to be made directly to Virtex device circuit configuration data quickly and without interruption of operation.

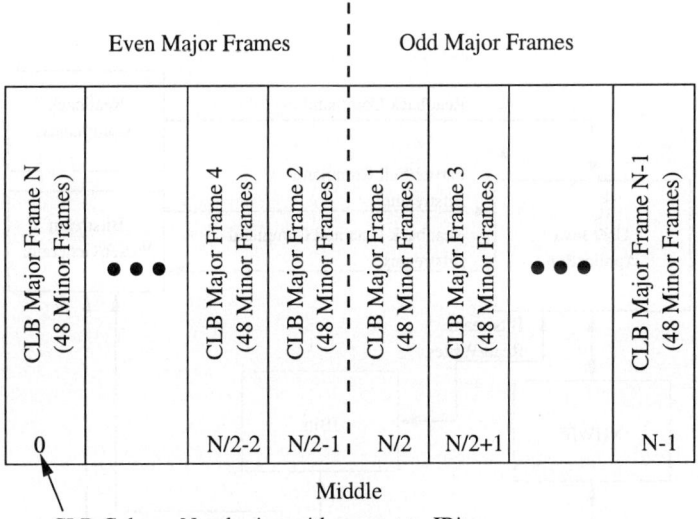

CLB Column Numbering with respect to JBits.
N = Number of CLB columns in device (e.g. for XCV800, N=84).

Fig. 1. The Virtex device configuration data organization.

3 Partial Reconfiguration in Virtex Device

As with most other FPGAs, the Virtex device can be viewed as a two-dimensional tiled array of *Configurable Logic Blocks* or *CLBs*. Associated with each CLB tile is some amount of logic and routing. In older device families such as the XC4000, the entire device would be configured using a single block of configuration data commonly referred to as a *bitstream*. This bitstream contained all of the data necessary to program the device into the desired configuration. If any piece of the configuration was to be changed, the entire configuration would have to be re-loaded.

While these earlier Xilinx device architectures were programmed using static data, the Virtex device configuration bitstream takes a packet-based approach. Here, the configuration bitstream consists of a sequence of command / data pairs of varying lengths that are used to read and write internal registers and configuration and state data. These commands operate on individual *frames* or column slices of the configuration memory. These frames are the smallest addressable units in the Virtex device configuration bitstream and may be accessed independently.

Figure 1 shows the Virtex device configuration data addressing scheme which uses major and minor frames. The major frame address refers to an entire CLB column containing a group of 48 minor frames. A minor frame refers to the individual columns of data used to program the device and represents the smallest grain of reconfigurability. To modify data within a CLB, affected data must be masked into frame(s) and re-loaded into the device. Reconfiguring an entire CLB requires this operation to be done on 48 contiguous minor frames within the device.

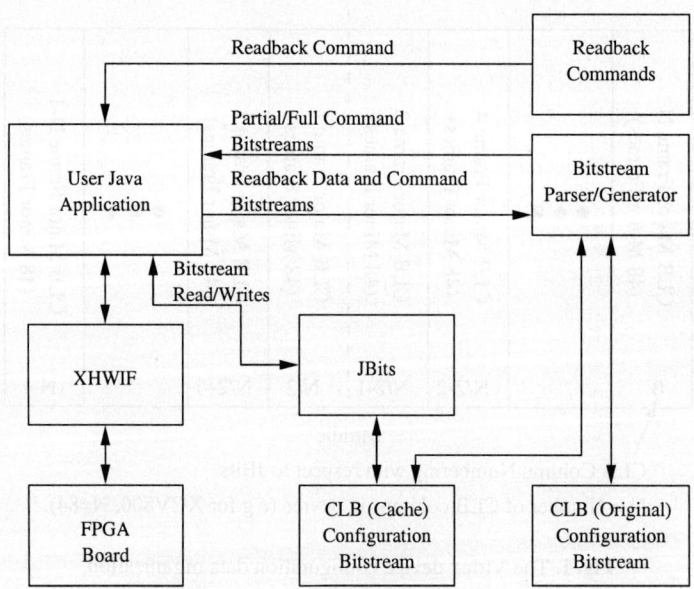

Fig. 2. An overview of the JRTR system.

4 The JRTR Interface

The *JBits* configuration bitstream Application Programming Interface (API) provides a set of Java classes to access and manipulate Virtex device configuration data. Currently, this data is manipulated in some piece of host memory, and later downloaded to hardware. Not coincidentally, this approach is nearly identical to the bulk download of the older XC4000 device family. This is because the current *JBits* for Virtex device software was essentially ported from the earlier XC4000 device version.

In order to better take advantage of the hardware support for partial run-time reconfiguration in Virtex device, the *JBits* API has been extended with the *JRTR* API. This interface provides a caching model where changes to configuration data are tracked and only the necessary data is written to or read back from the device.

Figure 2 shows the high level block diagram for the *JRTR* code. The existing *JBits* interface is still used to read and write bitstream files to and from disk and other external devices. But the *JRTR Bitstream Parser / Generator* is used to analyze the bitstream configuration data and to maintain both the data image and the access information.

The *JRTR* API is described in more detail in Table 1. The model for this code resembles a writeback cache in a traditional microprocessor system. Changes to the configuration bitstream are tracked each time the `get()` function call is used. This list of modified frames is eventually used to produce a set of packets to perform the necessary partial reconfiguration.

Table 1. The JRTR Application Program Interface.

Function	Description
parse()	Parses write and readback bitstream packet commands and overlays them onto the CLB and Block RAM (BRAM) configuration memories.
get()	Generates full or partial CLB and BRAM configuration packet streams.
clearPartial()	Clears the partial reconfiguration flag and forces a full reconfiguration only on the next get().
clearFull()	Clears the partial and full configuration flags and puts the object into an initial state.
writeClbCache()	Forces a write of the cache to the original CLB configuration.
getClbCache()	Returns a pointer to the CLB configuration stream. This will be used to synch up with the JBits object after parsing.

Figure 3 gives a typical code example of how *JRTR* is used. The current *JBits* interface is used to load in the configuration bitstream data from a file and then the data is parsed into a *JRTR* object with the `parse()` function call. The initial synchronization of *JBits* CLB configuration memory with the *JRTR* cache is somewhat more subtle, however. These two objects must reference the same memory location in order for the modifications made to the CLB configuration with *JBits* to be marked in the *JRTR* cache.

```
/* Parse <inputfile> bitstream */
JBits jBits = new JBits(deviceType);
jBits.read(inputfile);

JRTR jrtr = new JRTR(deviceType);
jrtr.parse(jBits.getAllPackets());

/* Sync JBits and parser cache */
jBits.setClbConfig(jrtr.getClbCache().get());

/* Download the full bitstream to device */
board.setConfiguration(jrtr.get());

/* Modify the CLB Cache with JBits. */
jBits.set(....)
.
.
.
jBits.set(....)

/* Download partial configuration data to device */
board.setConfiguration(jrtr.get());
```

Fig. 3. *JRTR* code to perform partial reconfiguration.

Once the configuration data is downloaded to the hardware, any number of *JBits* set() calls, including those in cores or other classes and subroutines, can be made. Once the new configuration is set to the desired state, the *JRTR* get() call is used to produce the minimum number of packets necessary to perform the partial reconfiguration of the device. These packets can then be directly downloaded to the hardware.

Currently the API provides fairly simple, but complete, control of the configuration caching. The user can produce partial configurations at any time, and load them into hardware. While this level of control is desirable in most applications, this API also provides the tools necessary to experiment with other more transparent models of partial run-time reconfiguration.

Figure 4, shows a representation of a typical *JRTR* cache after some configuration data has been modified. In this case, data in five different frames has been modified. When the partial reconfiguration packets are produced by *JRTR*, they will actually contain only four distinct packets. The two frames near the center of the device are contiguous in the Virtex device address space and will be grouped into a single packet, minimizing the reconfiguration overhead.

Table 1 describes each of the function calls in the *JRTR* API. While most of the API provides calls for housekeeping functions, the parse() and get() functions provide most of the needed functionality. The parse() function loads in a bitstream containing either full or partial configuration data and uses this to modify the *JRTR* internal cache. The get() function call returns the partial packets generated by *JRTR*

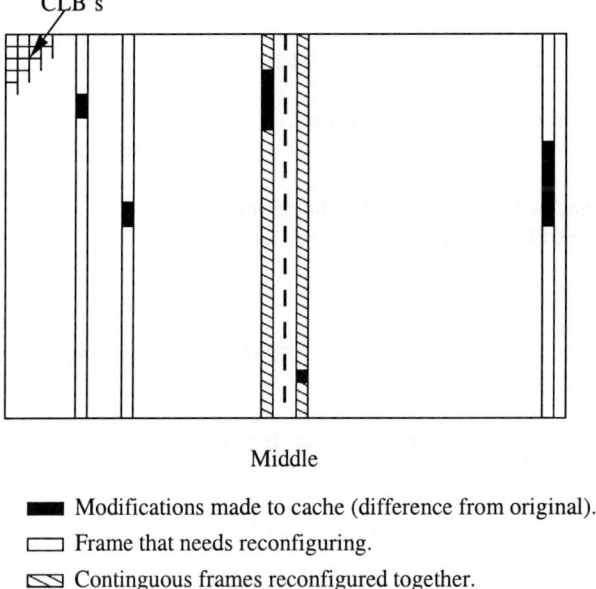

Middle

■ Modifications made to cache (difference from original).
☐ Frame that needs reconfiguring.
▨ Continguous frames reconfigured together.

Fig. 4. Partially reconfigured SRAM cells and their associated frames.

to provide the Virtex device bitstream packets necessary to partially reconfigure the device. Note that each `get()` function also clears all of the "written" markers in the cache. Only subsequent modifications to the device configuration will be tracked and returned by future `get()` calls. Explicit calls do exist, however, that will set or reset the cache, for applications that may require this level of control.

5 Partial Readback

As with configuration, the *JBits* API currently assumes a bulk model for readback. All configuration bits are read back in a single operation and accessed in the host memory. As with the configuration model, this is primarily for historical reasons. And as with configuration, *JRTR* also provides a model for partial readback. Because of the nature of readback, this model is somewhat different from that of configuration and is necessarily not cache-based. Explicit requests for frame data must be made to the hardware, and the requests are done sequentially, not as a single block of Virtex device packets.

The partial readback example below shows how the *JRTR Bitstream Parser / Generator* object can be used in conjunction with the *JRTR Readback Commands* to perform partial readback. As in the case of partial reconfiguration, the CLB cache state is maintained and kept in synchronization with the configured hardware.

Unlike reconfiguration, the readback process is somewhat iterative. A readback request packet is written to the hardware, then the data is read back. For multiple partial readbacks, this process of write / read must be repeated. While there is some overhead

```
/* Readback CLB columns 4 thru 10. */
byte readbackCommand[] =
   ReadbackCommand.getCols(DEVICETYPE, 4, 10);

/* Get the readback data length */
int readbackSize = ReadbackCommand.getReadLength();

/* Send readback command to hardware */
board.setConfiguration(readbackCommand);

/* Read back the data */
byte readbackBytes[] =
   board.getConfiguration(DEVICENUMBER, readbackSize*4);

/* Load the readback data */
jrtr.parse(readbackCommand, readbackBytes);

/* Synchronize the JBits and readback data */
jBits.setClbConfig(jrtr.getClbCache().get());
```

Fig. 5. A partial readback example.

associated with this process, it has still been demonstrated to provide speedups over the bulk readback approach.

Figure 5 gives an example of some partial readback code. Note that frame columns are explicitly requested. While hardcoded values are used in the example for clarity, these constants could also have been taken from *JBits* resource constants, requesting, for instance, the frame containing the first bit of the F LUT in Slice 0.

Again, the nature of readback is somewhat different and is typically used to read back flip flop state information, or occasionally embedded RAM. This means that for a flip flop, which is found in a single frame of the 48 per CLB, the savings in data read back from the hardware is a factor of 48. While the amount of data is reduced by more than an order of magnitude, actual wall clock performance will depend on the speed of the interface and various software overheads. Networked debug applications, for instance, have demonstrated as much as a factor of three increase in performance using *JRTR*. Clearly this effect is more pronounced for slower data links, where the amount of data transferred is the major component of overall system performance.

6 Implementation Issues

The implementation of frame addressing in Virtex device is somewhat unusual. Frame address zero is at the center of the device, with addresses growing from the center outward, alternating right, left. This results in an interleaving of the data in the configuration bitstream. If, for instance, two physically contiguous CLBs are read as a block, the data will actually be returned interleaved with the associated frames from the other half of the device. Figure 6 illustrates this graphically. In order to read the "even" frames in

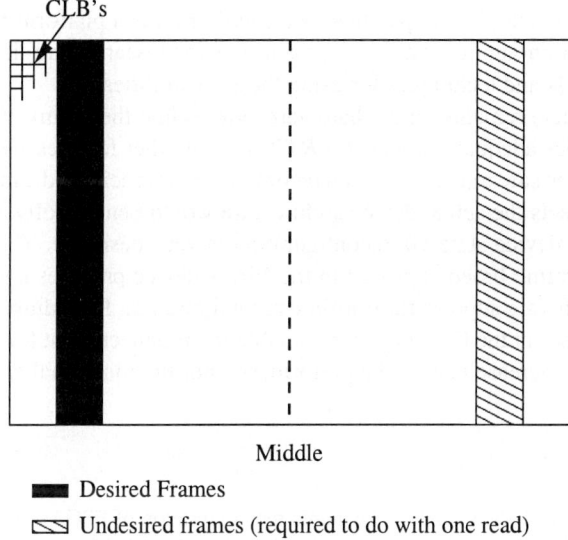

Fig. 6. Frame addressing in Virtex Device.

a single operation, an equal number of "odd" frames are also returned. This hardware feature of the Virtex device architecture makes grouping of contiguous frames difficult, and typically results in a factor of two penalty for blocks of data written to or read back from the device.

In addition to the odd / even addressing scheme, some other modifications to the Virtex device support for run time reconfiguration would be welcome. First, placing dynamic components such as flip flop outputs and embedded RAM in a distinct, contiguous address space would be useful. Since these are the only parts of the configuration bitstream capable of changing in normal operation, grouping these would simplify and enhance the performance of debug applications such as *BoardScope*. In addition, applications which only modify state, and not routing, would benefit.

State initialization is yet another issue. Being able to specify state of a flip flop when performing run time reconfiguration is crucial. Depending on a reset line of some sort is impractical in most cases. Lastly, design for partial reconfiguration at the silicon level presents some new challenges. Currently the sequence in which frames are reconfigured can result in intermediate states which are illegal or produce illegal results. Atomic operation of changes for any reconfigurable resource should be supported. In general, this means that all configurable MUXes and other such resources should reside in a single frame.

7 Conclusions

JRTR provides a simple and effective model and implementation to support partial runtime reconfiguration. Using a cache-based approach, partial run-time reconfiguration and readback has been implemented for the Xilinx Virtex family of devices and integrated into the *JBits* tool suite. It is hoped that *JRTR* will provide a platform not just for runtime reconfiguration application development, but for research and development into new software tools and techniques for using these capabilities.

Much work also remains on the hardware side. While the Xilinx Virtex device architecture provides adequate support for *RTR*, several other features are desirable. The ability to guarantee safe transitions when reconfiguring is crucial and simpler addressing which better reflects the actual device architecture would benefit software. In addition, the ability to set device state via reconfiguration is very desirable. That said, we also believe that the frame-based approach in the Virtex device provides a good balance of hardware and software support for run-time reconfiguration. Providing smaller grained addressing, perhaps at the CLB or programmable interconnect point level is likely to be overkill and may increase neither the performance nor the functionality.

References

1. Patrick Lysaght and John Dunlop. Dynamic reconfiguration of FPGAs. In Will Moore and Wayne Luk, editors, *More FPGAs*, pages 82–94. Abingdon EE&CS Books, Abingdon, England, 1993.
2. Herman Schmit. Incremental reconfiguration for pipelined applications. In Kenneth L. Pocek and Jeffrey Arnold, editors, *IEEE Symposium on FPGAs for Custom Computing Machines*, pages 47–55, Los Alamitos, CA, April 1997. IEEE Computer Society Press.
3. Jim Burns, Adam Donlin, Jonathan Hogg, Satnam Singh, and Mark de Wit. A dynamic reconfiguration run-time system. In Kenneth L. Pocek and Jeffrey Arnold, editors, *IEEE Symposium on FPGAs for Custom Computing Machines*, pages 66–75, Los Alamitos, CA, April 1997. IEEE Computer Society Press.
4. Steven A. Guccione and Delon Levi. Design advantages of run-time reconfiguration. In John Schewel, editor, *Reconfigurable Technology: FPGAs for Computing and Applications, Proc. SPIE 3844*, pages 87–92, Bellingham, WA, September 1999. SPIE – The International Society for Optical Engineering.
5. Steve Kelem. Virtex configuration architecture advanced users' guide. Xilinx Application Note XAPP151, version 1.1, Xilinx, Inc., July 1999.
6. Steven A. Guccione and Delon Levi. XBI: A java-based interface to FPGA hardware. In John Schewel, editor, *Configurable Computing: Technology and Applications, Proc. SPIE 3526*, pages 97–102, Bellingham, WA, November 1998. SPIE – The International Society for Optical Engineering.
7. Xilinx, Inc. *XC6200 Development System Datasheet*, 1997.
8. Eric Lechner and Steven A. Guccione. The Java environment for reconfigurable computing. In Wayne Luk and Peter Y. K. Cheung, editors, *Proceedings of the 7th International Workshop on Field-Programmable Logic and Applications, FPL 1997. Lecture Notes in Computer Science 1304*, pages 284–293. Springer-Verlag, Berlin, September 1997.
9. Wayne Luk, Nabeel Shirazi, and Peter Y. K. Cheung. Compilation tools for run-time reconfigurable designs. In Kenneth L. Pocek and Jeffrey Arnold, editors, *IEEE Symposium on FPGAs for Custom Computing Machines*, pages 56–65, Los Alamitos, CA, April 1997. IEEE Computer Society Press.

A Combined Approach to High-Level Synthesis for Dynamically Reconfigurable Systems

Xue-jie Zhang[1], Kam-wing Ng[1], and Wayne Luk[2]

[1] Department of Computer Science and Engineering
The Chinese University of Hong Kong
Shatin, N.T., Hong Kong
{xjzhang,kwng}@cse.cuhk.edu.hk
[2] Department of Computing, Imperial College
180 Queen's gate
London, England SW7 2BZ
wl@doc.ic.ac.uk

Abstract. In this paper, two complementary design models and related synthesis techniques are combined to capture behavioral and structural information in modelling and synthesizing a dynamically reconfigurable system. The proposed formulation is achieved by using finite domain constraints and related constraint-solving techniques offered by constraint logic programming. Our formulation represents operation-level temporal constraints and dynamic resource constraints in a unified model. Different synthesis tasks, such as temporal partitioning, scheduling and dynamic module allocation can be modelled in this framework, enabling the discovery of an optimal or near optimal solutions. Experiments have been carried out using a prototype of the high-level synthesis system implemented in CHIP, a constraint logic programming system. Current experimental results show that our approach can provide promising synthesis results in terms of the synthesis time and the number of reconfigurations.

1 Introduction

Dynamically reconfigurable systems change many of the basic assumptions in the high-level synthesis process[1][2]. The flexibility of dynamic reconfiguration (multiple configurations, partial reconfiguration, etc.) requires new methodologies and high-level synthesis algorithms to be developed as conventional high-level synthesis techniques do not consider the dynamic nature of dynamically reconfigurable systems[3].

Exploitation of the dynamically reconfigurable capability necessitates a temporal partitioning step in the high-level synthesis process. Temporal partitioning divides the specification into a number of specification segments to be executed one after another in the dynamically reconfigurable architecture. There exist many formulations of temporal partitioning using different optimization methods. Linear programming (LP) and integer linear programming (ILP) have been used to provide an optimal solution for the temporal partitioning problem[5][6][7]. Heuristic optimization methods have also been used since most of the problems are NP-complete[8]. However, while LP/ILP formulations usually suffer from the prohibitively long execution times, often heuristic methods can neither provide optimal results nor estimations of the quality of the final design.

We have developed a modelling technique for specifying the temporal dimension of systems[9][10][11]. Our approach uses an extended control/data flow graph (ECDFG) as the intermediate representation of a design. The CDFG is extended by abstracting the temporal nature of a system in terms of the sensitization of paths in the dataflow. Interested readers are referred to the original references for the details about ECDFG[9][10][11]. The ECDFG model has been used for abstracting, analyzing and synthesizing dynamically reconfigurable designs, but it currently does not model structural level designs.

An algorithm may have an extremely large number of possible reconfigurable implementations. There have been very few studies on specification and development methods for designs with elements reconfigurable at run time, and on assessing trade-offs in circuit speed, design size and reconfiguration overhead. A network model has been developed for specifying reconfigurable designs at the structural level and for mapping them into a variety of implementations with different trade-offs in performance and resource usage[12]. The associated methods and tool have been applied to a number of applications[13][14]. However, the static network-based model is specified at the structural level. At this lower level, the synthesis results can be suboptimal and harder to optimize.

The objective of our work is to address the above mentioned problems by combining two complementary design models and related synthesis techniques developed at the Chinese University of Hong Kong and at Imperial College. In this paper, we present a synthesis methodology which transforms an ECDFG-based description into a network with control blocks connecting together the possible configurations for each reconfigurable component. The combined approach makes it possible to extend our behavior model[9] with a structural level design model[12] for improving design quality while reducing development time. The proposed formulation is achieved by using finite domain constraints and related constraint-solving techniques offered by constraint logic programming. The finite domain constraints are used to model structural level designs for high-level synthesis of dynamically reconfigurable systems. Using finite domain constraints, it is possible to represent operations' temporal constraints and dynamic resource constraints in one unified model. Different synthesis tasks, such as temporal partitioning, scheduling and dynamic module allocation can also be modelled in this framework.

2 High-Level Synthesis Formulation Using Constraint Logic Programming

The high-level synthesis for dynamically reconfigurable designs is a multi-dimensional optimization problem consisting of some time-sharing and structuring decisions, such as temporal partitioning, scheduling and module allocation. Most of the design decisions are tightly interconnected. For example, a decision made during temporal partitioning may influence scheduling. These relations can be expressed by *constraints*. To find an optimal implementation for dynamically reconfigurable design, a huge amount of constraints between different design decisions must be quantified during synthesis. Moreover, previous research in high-level synthesis for dynamically reconfigurable systems concentrated on finding good heuristic methods for solving separate synthesis problems, but does not consider the impact of reconfiguration granularity on performance and reconfiguration overhead, yielding only one reconfigurable implementation with local optimal cost. A synthesis tool must be able to model these dependencies.

A programming paradigm supporting prototype development and constraints is *constraint logic programming* (CLP). CLP extends logic programming by a mechanism for constraint modelling and processing[15][16]. CLP systems offer a unified method for representing, analyzing and solving constraints. Constraints express relations between parameters of the problem. The idea of CLP is to restrict the search space as much as possible by constraints, and to search the remaining space in a moderate amount of time. The processes of constraint handling and search are intertwined. Each constraint is imposed but the execution is delayed until the constraint can be evaluated without anticipating any search decisions. When during the searching phase some parameters are restricted the relevant constraints are resumed and executed. Additionally this search can be done in a heuristic or problem-specific way.

In the following sections, we present a new formulation of high-level synthesis for dynamically reconfigurable systems using the CHIP system[18][17]. CHIP (Constraint Handling in Prolog) is a CLP language designed to tackle constrained search problems with a short development time and with good efficiency. It extends conventional Prolog-like logic languages by introducing three new computation domains: finite domains, booleans and rationals. Finite domain constraints are used in our approach to represent different time-sharing constraints and dynamic resource constraints in one unified model.

2.1 High-Level Synthesis as a CLP Problem

We assume that an ECDFG intermediate representation of the design has been created by a preprocessing step. As a preprocessing step, we determine the temporal templates and mobility ranges (ASAP and ALAP values) of all the operations in the ECDFG. We also estimate the upper-bound on the number of temporal partitions N by using a fast list-scheduling heuristic for building a finite domain constraints formulation[8].

To solve high-level synthesis problems for dynamically reconfigurable FPGAs using finite domain constraints, we need to view the ECDFG as constraints which have to be fulfilled to get a correct reconfigurable implementation. This requires an operation level modelling for the synthesis subproblem.

Definition 1. *An ECDFG is defined as $G = (V, E)$, where $V = \{v_1, ..., v_n\}$ represents operations. Operation nodes are atomic actions potentially requiring* use of reconfigurable logic. The edge set $E = \{(v_i, v_j) \subseteq V \times V\}$ represents dependencies between operations. An operation v_i, $(1 \leq i \leq n)$ is expressed as a tuple of four finite domain variables, $v_i = (TS_i, CS_i, CF_i, DU_i)$, where:

- TS_i is a temporal partition in which the operation v_i is placed,
- CS_i is a start time of the operation v_i,
- CF_i is a possible implementation of the operation v_i on a reconfigurable component, and
- DU_i is a duration of the operation v_i.

From the finite domain constraints point of view, a dynamically reconfigurable system can be represented by a CLP model. Each design subproblem is represented by an operation's parameter with a domain representing the alternatives of the decision. Thus, we can define our formulation of the high-level synthesis in terms of these domain constraints.

Definition 2. *A Constraint Satisfaction High-level Synthesis Problem (CSHSP) for a dynamically reconfigurable system is a 3-tuple $P = (M, D, C)$ where*

- $M = \{TS_1, ..., TS_n, CS_1, ..., CS_n, CF_1, ..., CF_n, DU_1, ..., DU_n\}$ *is a finite set of variables ,*
- $D = (TS, CS, CF, DU)$ *is a tuple of 4 finite sets of domains, and*
- C *is a set of constraints.*

The variables TS_i, CS_i, CF_i and $DU_i \in M$ take on the values from domains TS, CS, CF and DU respectively. For example, the specification $TS :: 1..N$ defines a domain variable TS which can take on values $1, 2, ..., N$. A constraint $c \in C$ between variables of M is a subset of the Cartesian product $TS_1 \times ... \times TS_n \times CS_1 \times ... \times CS_n \times CF_1 \times ... \times CF_n \times DU_1 \times ... \times DU_n$ specifying which values of the variables are compatible with each other. In practice, the constraints are defined by equations, inequalities, global constraints or programs. A detailed discussion of constraint representations will be given later.

A solution s to a CSHSP P is an assignment of values to all variables, such that it satisfies all the constraints and we write $P \models s$. There exist usually many solutions that satisfy the defined constraints. They have different quality which is defined by a related cost function.

2.2 Operation-Level Constraints

Operation-level constraint is a relation between two domain variables. It is used in our approach to specify different properties and restrictions imposed on related operations. The precedence relation imposed by a partial order of the ECDFG nodes is modelled by inequality constraints on the start time of operations. If there exists an arc from the operation v_i to the operation v_j then the following inequality constraint is imposed:

$$CS_i + DU_i \leq CS_j \qquad (1)$$

An operation v_i on which another operation v_j is dependent cannot be placed in a later temporal segment than the segment in which operation v_j is placed. The temporal partitioning order constraint is modelled as:

$$TS_i \leq TS_j \qquad (2)$$

We defined a temporal template T_e in our previous work[9]. The semantics is that T_e, where $T_e \subset V$, imposes the constraint:

$$CS_i = CS_{T_e} + o_i, \forall v_i \in T_e \qquad (3)$$

where CS_{T_e} and o_i denote the start time of the temporal template T_e and an integer cycle offset. In other words, if T_e is scheduled to control step CS_j, then every member operation, v_i, of T_e must be scheduled to control step, $T_j + o_i$. This locks all operations in T_e into a temporal pattern, which is useful because a temporal template collapses all the dependencies occurring in the different control paths. Temporal templates will be used to guide the clustering of ECDFG operations into groups which map to reconfigurations during synthesis.

2.3 Global Constraints

For more complex relations between domain variables, we have used three global constraints *cumulative*, *diffn* and *among* which are defined in the constraint logic programming system CHIP[17].

The *cumulative* constraint has been defined in CHIP to tackle more efficiently scheduling and placement problems. This constraint is defined in CHIP as follows:

$$cumulative([T_1, ... T_m], [D_1, ..., D_m], [R_1, ..., R_m], L) \qquad (4)$$

where $[T_1, ... T_m]$, $[D_1, ..., D_m]$ and $[R_1, ..., R_m]$ are non-empty lists of domain variables that have the same length m, and where L is an integer. The constraint *cumulative* holds if the following condition is true:

$$\forall i, \sum_{j|T_j \leq i \leq T_j + D_j - 1} R_j \leq L \qquad (5)$$

In our approach, we introduce dynamic resource constraint in terms of the *cumulative* constraint. From an interpretation point of view the *cumulative* constraint matches directly the dynamic resource constraint problem, where $T_1, ..., T_m$ correspond to the start time of the operations, $D_1, ..., D_m$ to the duration of the operations, and $R_1, ..., R_m$ to the area of configurable logic resource used by each operation. L represents the total resource capacity of a dynamically reconfigurable architecture. From Definition 1, substituting CS for $T_1, ..., T_m$, DU for $D_1, ..., D_m$ and CF for $R_1, ..., R_m$ in constraint (4), we obtain $cumulative(CS, DU, CF, L)$ which is imposed on all temporal segments.

The *diffn* constraint was introduced in CHIP in order to handle multidimensional placement problems. The *diffn* constraint takes as an argument a list of n-dimensional rectangles and assures that for each pair of $i, j (i \neq j)$ of n-dimensional rectangles, there exists at least one dimension k where i is after j or j is after i. The n-dimensional rectangles are defined by a tuple $[O_1, ..., O_n, L_1, ..., L_n]$, where O_i and L_i are respectively called the origin and the length of the n-dimensional rectangle in the i-th dimension. In our approach we have used *diffn* in defining constraints for temporal partitioning and dynamic resource binding. For example, two operations v_i and v_j cannot be assigned to the same resource configuration if their executions overlap. This constraint can easily be represented using the *diffn* constraint since operations can be modelled as rectangles as shown in Figure 1. An operation v_i is represented as a 2-dimensional rectangle with lower left corner at coordinates (CS_i, CF_i), length DU_i and height 1. In our previous work[11], we proposed a *configuration bundling*

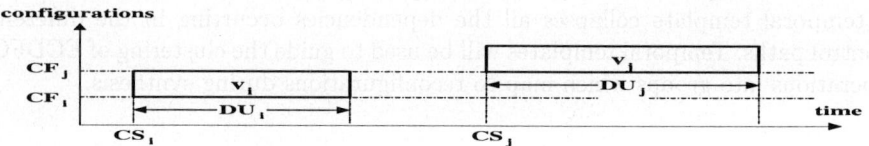

Fig. 1. An example of *diffn* constraint

driven module allocation technique that can be used for component clustering. The basic idea is to group configurable logic together properly so that a given configuration can do as much work as possible, allowing a greater portion of the task to be completed between reconfigurations. In [12], a logic block that can be configured to behave either as P or as Q is described by a network with P and Q sandwiched between two control blocks C and C'. To allow combining the above mentioned techniques for functional block reuse, components that can be configured to different behavior determine dynamically the resource binding. Modelling of dynamic resource binding can be accomplished by using *among* constraints. The *among* constraints are introduced in CHIP in order to specify the way values can be assigned to variables. One of the interesting features of the *among* constraint is that it allows us to express directly the number of times that a set of values is taken by a set of variables. We now give the semantics of the *among* constraints for modelling dynamic resource binding as follows.

$$among(N, [X_1, ..., X_s], [C_1, ..., C_s], [V_1, ..., V_m]) \qquad (6)$$

Here N is a domain variable, $[X_1, ..., X_s]$ is a list of domain variables, $[C_1, ..., C_s]$ and $[V_1, ..., V_m]$ are lists of integers. The constraint holds if the following conditions are both true: (1) $\forall i \in [1, m-1] : V_i < V_{i+1}$, (2) exactly N terms among $X_1 + C_1, ..., X_s + C_s$ take their value in the list of values $[V_1, ..., V_m]$.

Consider a simple example as shown in Figure 2. The example shows how to use the *among* constraint in order to model dynamic reconfiguration. The operations are clustered in 4 classes $\{1,3,6\}$, $\{2,4,7\}$, $\{5,10\}$ and $\{8,11\}$, each class containing all the operations requiring the same configurable logic resource[11]. For each configurable logic resource we create a domain variable that corresponds to the class of operations as indicated by the dynamic resources binding. All the previous variables are grouped in the list of variable DR. We express the fact that for each class we have to produce a fixed number operations by giving for each value (i.e. resource class) the number of times it should occur in the variables (i.e. operations requiring the same configurable resource class). This is directly expressed as one *among* constraint for each class. For example the constraint $among(2, DR, D0, [3])$ states that the third resource class should be reused 2 times by the list of variable DR. $D0$ corresponds to a list of 0's of same length as list DR.

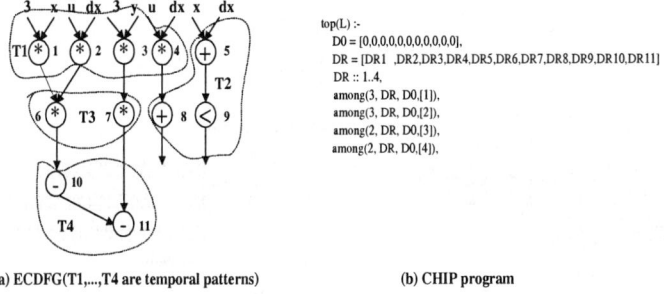

(a) ECDFG(T1,...,T4 are temporal patterns) (b) CHIP program

Fig. 2. An example of *among* constraint

3 Synthesis Methodology

A solution to a set of constraints is an assignment to all domain variables which satisfies all constraints, as described in Section 2. The assigned values are selected from the domain variables. There are usually many different solutions, and the goal of the synthesis process is to select a solution which minimizes a given cost function. The cost function is defined as a domain variable. The main objective of our approach is to partition a given ECDFG into subsequent reconfigurations and a static network with control blocks connecting together the possible configurations for each component so as to minimize the number of reconfigurations and overall latency. The cost function can be defined as follows:

$$minimum(Cost, [TS_i, CS_i]) \qquad (7)$$

Minimization of the domain variable *Cost* produces the fastest implementation satisfying the given constraints. To find an assignment to domain variables which minimizes the defined cost function is an optimization problem, and can be solved using different optimization methods. In this paper, we use a static-list scheduling heuristic. This is an established low-complexity technique, used for resource constrained scheduling[8]. The static-list scheduling algorithm searches for possible solutions by organizing the search space as a static priority list. In each node of the list, we assign new values to three domain variables (TS_i, CS_i, CF_i). The assignment of the values to selected domain variables triggers constraint propagation.

Consider a simple example as shown in Figure 3. Given are an ECDFG which consists of four temporal templates (labelled T1, T2, T3 and T4), and allocation resources which include 1 adder, 1 ALU and 2 multipliers as shown in Figure 3(a). Our synthesis system will output an RTL netlist with all the dynamically binding information as shown in Figure 3(b). The different gray boxes identify the operations that can be mapped to the same reconfigurable resource.

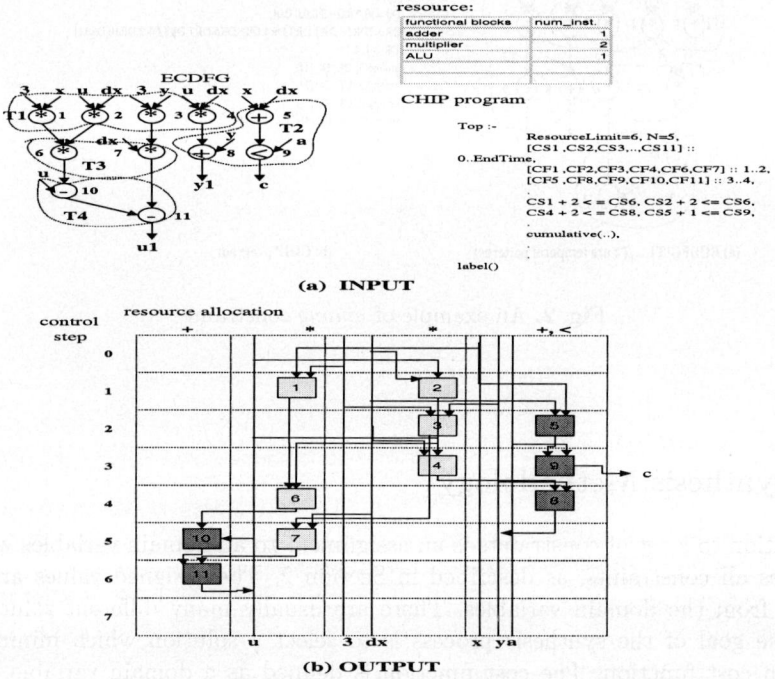

Fig. 3. An example illustrating the inputs and outputs of the synthesis system

4 Experimental Results

Experiments have been carried out using a prototype implementation of the high-level synthesis system implemented in CHIP 5.2[17], a constraint logic pro-

Table 1. Synthesis results

Benchmarks	Resource constraints	Number of partitions	Control Steps	Time (seconds)
EWF	1*(p), 2+, Area=6	18	25	6.5
	1*, 2+, Area=6	18	26	6.5
	2*, 2+, Area=10	9	24	6.5
	3*, 3+, Area=15	5	23	6.5
Differential Equation	1*(p),1A, Area=3	3	10	3
	2*(s),1+, 1A,Area=9	2	10	3

gramming system. This is a Prolog system with constraints solvers over finite and rational domains. All experiments have been run on a SPARCstation 20/61 machine.

We demonstrate our results on two high-level synthesis benchmarks: differential equation(DIFFEQ) and fifth order elliptic wave filter(EWF)[8]. The simplest example DIFFEQ has 11 operations and 16 variables, and EWF has 34 operations and 47 variables. In both experiments, it has been assumed that the delays of adder(+), ALU(A), single-cycle multipler(*(s)), multi-cycle multiplier(*) and pipelined multiplier(*(p)) are 1, 1, 1, 2, and 2 cycles respectively. Table 1 presents experimental results obtained with our synthesis system. An optimal assignment of temporal segments and a dynamic resource allocation can be obtained in only a few seconds. Our approach provides an effective way of combining different design constraints and solving them in one framework.

5 Conclusions

We have formulated the high-level synthesis problem for dynamically reconfigurable system using finite domain constraints and related constraints solving techniques offered by constraint logic programming. The problem of temporal partitioning and dynamic resource binding have been modelled using finite domain constraints. The constraint solving techniques are then used to find a solution to the imposed constraints. Current experimental results show that our approach can provide promising synthesis results in terms of the synthesis time and the number of reconfigurations.

Acknowledgments

Many thanks to George Constantinides, Arran Derbyshire, Richard Sandiford, Seng Shay Ping and Markus Weinhardt for their comments and suggestions. The work described in this paper was partially supported by the following grants: the Research Grant Council of the Hong Kong Special Administrative Region (Project No.: CUHK4408/99E), UK/HK Joint Research Scheme (Project No.: 6900825), UK EPSRC (Project No.: GR/54356 and GR/59658) and Yunnan Province Young Scholar Grant.

References

1. J. Villasenor, B. Schoner, K. Chia, C. Zapata and B. Mangione-Smith: Configurable Computing Solutions for Automatic Target Recognition, Proc. FCCM'96, IEEE Computer Society Press, 1996, pp. 70–79.
2. J.G. Eldrege and B.L. Hutchings: Run-time Reconfiguration: A Method for Enhancing the Functional Density of SRAM-Based FPGAs, J. VLSI Signal Processing, Vol. 12, 1996, pp. 67–86.
3. B.L. Hutchings and M.J. Wirthlin: Implementation Approaches for Reconfigurable Logic Applications, Field-Programmable Logic and Applications, LNCS 975, Springer-Verlag, 1995, pp. 419–428.
4. Y.L. Lin: Recent Developments in High-level Synthesis, ACM Trans. on Design of Electronic Systems, Vol. 2, No. 1, January 1997, pp. 2–21.
5. M. Kaul, R. Vemuri, S. Govindarajan and I. Ouaiss: An Automated Temporal Partitioning Tool for a Class of DSP Application, Proc. PACT'98, 1998.
6. M. Kaul and R. Vemuri: Temporal Partitioning Combined with Design Space Exploration for Latency Minimization of Run-time Reconfigured Designs, Proc. Data'99, 1999.
7. K.M.G. Purna and D. Bhatia: Temporal Partitioning and Scheduling Data Flow Graphs for Reconfigurable Computers, IEEE Trans. on Computers, Vol. 48, No. 6, 1999, pp. 579–590.
8. M. Vasilko and D. Ait-Boudaoud: Architectural Synthesis Techniques for Dynamically Reconfigurable Logic, Field-Programmable Logic and Applications, LNCS 1142, Springer-Verlag, 1996, pp. 290–296.
9. K.W. Ng, X.J. Zhang and G.H. Young: Design Representation for Dynamically Reconfigurable Systems, Proc. 5th Annual Australasian Conference on Parallel And Real-Time Systems (PART'98), Springer-Verlag (Singapore), 1998, pp. 14–23.
10. X.J. Zhang, K.W. Ng and G.H. Young: High-level Synthesis Using Genetic Algorithms for Dynamically Reconfigurable FPGAs, Proc. 23rd Euromicro Conference (EUROMICRO' 97), 1997.
11. K.W. Ng and X.J. Zhang: Module Allocation for Dynamically Reconfigurable Systems, Parallel and Distributed Processing, LNCS 1800, Springer-Verlag, 2000, pp. 932–940.
12. W. Luk, N. Shirazi and P.Y.K. Cheung: Modelling and Optimizing Run-Time Reconfigurable Systems, Proc. FCCM'96, IEEE Computer Society Press, 1996, pp. 167–176.
13. W. Luk, N. Shirazi and P.Y.K. Cheung: Compilation Tools for Run-Time Reconfigurable Designs, Proc. FCCM'97, IEEE Computer Society Press, 1997, pp. 56–65.
14. N. Shirazi, W. Luk and P.Y.K. Cheung: Automating Production of Run-Time Reconfigurable Designs, Proc. FCCM'98, IEEE Computer Society Press, 1998, pp. 147–156.
15. J. Jaffar and M.J. Maher: Constraint Logic Programming: A Survey, The Journal of Logic Programming, 1994.
16. K. Marriot and P.J. Stuckey: Programming with Constraints – An Introduction, The MIT Press, 1998.
17. CHIP, System Documentation, COSYTEC, 1996.
18. A. Aggoun and N. Beldiceanu: Overview of the CHIP Compiler System, Proc. 8th International Conference on Logic Programming, 1991, pp. 775–789.

A Hybrid Prototyping Platform for Dynamically Reconfigurable Designs

Tero Rissa and Jarkko Niittylahti

Digital and Computer Systems Laboratory,
Tampere University of Technology,
P.O. Box 553, FIN-33101 Tampere, Finland
tero.rissa@tut.fi, jarkko.niittylahti@tut.fi
fax: +358 3 365 4575

Abstract. This paper presents the architecture and the implementation of a novel general-purpose prototyping platform for dynamically reconfigurable designs[1]. Using dynamical reconfigurability the hardware can be reused even inside the data flow processing. This extends the capabilities of the hardware significantly. The presented platform enables rapid prototyping and verification of dynamic reconfiguration in large variety of designs in various applications. Due to its Linux-based operating system and versatile debugging and I/O capabilities, design time and effort to operate with the platform can be minimized. In this platform, dynamic reconfiguration is based on Atmel AT40K-series FPGA. The platform is the first one utilizing this FPGA architecture's abilities in dynamic reconfiguration.

1 Introduction

Dynamically reconfigurable systems have been subjected to intensive research. It has shown promising results [1], but there are still problems to be solved before it can be utilised in large volume applications. Currently, there are no prototyping platforms that would utilize all aspects of modern dynamically reconfigurable FPGA circuits or could be integrated to modern system development environments. On the other hand, design process is time consuming and requires engineer to go deeply into low-level implementation aspects.

The purpose of this prototyping platform is to lower the threshold to utilise dynamic reconfiguration as key implementation method of a designed system. As there is also necessity for advanced description method for dynamically reconfigurable systems, it can not be developed before there is a prototyping platform suitable to test different approaches in real applications.

1.1 Software, Custom Hardware, and Reconfigurable Computing

The software executed in a general-purpose microprocessor has its greatest benefit in flexibility. With software, virtually any task can be performed if the execution time is not limited. Processing units, i.e., microprocessors, can be manufactured in large quantities, therefore making them cheaper. However, in a microprocessor the tasks are di-

---

1. This project is funded by Nokia Research Center (NRC).

vided in small subtasks that can be executed with its arithmetic and logic unit (ALU). In the worst case, the execution of a subtask needs as much time as would be needed to execute whole task concurrently with different kind of hardware. Furthermore, contemporary digital circuits are based on CMOS technology, where power consumption is dominated by dynamic power consumption. This means that almost all of the power consumed in the circuit is due to the switching of the transistors. The software solution consumes more time to perform a specific task, but it also consumes more power than a concurrent hardware solution.

A concurrent hardware solution is often called as custom hardware. This is because of the hardware must be customised to the task. In this solution, an Application Specific Integrated Circuit (ASIC) is built. This chip consumes less power and its performance is significantly better than it would be in software implementation. However, ASICs take long time to manufacture and they are extremely expensive if only small quantities are needed. The greatest drawback is that after the chip has been manufactured, any changes to its hardware structure are impossible. As it is application specific, it can not be used in any other application than it was originally designed for.

The concept of reconfigurable computing is to make general-purpose devices that may be used to custom computing. These kinds of devices inherit the custom hardware's abilities in performance and power consumption due to the concurrency. They also are as flexible as software and can be manufactured in large quantities due the general nature. Furthermore, dynamic reconfiguration makes possible designs that were very difficult or even impossible to implement either in software or custom hardware. For example evolvable designs were impossible to implement with custom hardware and extremely slow with software. Fault tolerant designs, which can operate after physical (hardware) damage, can only be implemented with dynamically reconfigurable hardware.

Of course reconfigurable system can not inherit only the good features of software and custom hardware. The drawback in the reconfigurable systems is the overhead it must pay in order to gain the reconfigurability. This overhead appears in speed, size, and power consumption. Due to this overhead, reconfigurable architectures are in between the software and custom hardware in these three optimisation parameters. However, a reconfigurable architecture can always be changed after manufacture. This feature is not present in custom hardware. As a general rule, designs in reconfigurable architecture can be made to be better than software in terms of these three optimisation parameters, because it can be customised to the application.

1.2 Hybrid Systems

A hybrid system is a combination of software, custom hardware, and reconfigurable logic. The goal is to combine good characteristics of each technique in order to create a system that is superior compared to a system that would have used only one implementation method. The presented platform is an example of a hybrid system. The standard components as PCI-bridge, Ethernet-circuit, and memories, etc., represent custom hardware. There is seldom need to change functionality of this kind of circuitry and making those from scratch would require several man-months and could be considered as vain. In the most advanced systems, all these may be integrated to a singe chip as in [2].

In this board, the reconfigurable unit that is used to the actual calculation is naturally the FPGA. In addition to the FPGA, there is a CPLD, which controls various functions in the board. This gives flexibility in situations where the original setup is changed. The software part is not so obvious. The software component in the board is ARM7-based microcontroller. The operating system run on the controller schedules the tasks in the board, which takes most of the controllers resources. The controller may also be used to act as a software component of the system, but software component can also locate in another system, like personal computer or other development system. The data is then transferred to the card and manipulated with the reconfigurable hardware.

1.3 Related Work

The first reconfigurable prototyping platforms were based on Xilinx XC6200-series FPGA. The first reported platform, HADES, was implemented in ETH Zürich [3]. Since then, there have been various platforms utilising this FPGA-architecture. Most of the platforms did not support dynamic reconfiguration. However, for example Riley-2 from Imperial College [4], and RIFLE-62 from Bournemouth University [5] did support dynamic reconfiguration. For the platforms based on XC6200-series FPGAs, there were also complete environments for HW/SW co-design in reconfigurable systems as in [6]. In addition to academic projects, also commercial platforms were presented [7].

The XC6200-series FPGAs was designed in a manner, where every connection was uni-directional and there were no tri-state drivers. Therefore, all the configurations were legal and could not cause electrical conflict. This ability made this FPGA-series very suitable for prototyping of dynamically reconfigurable system, especially for evolvable designs. In the XC6200-series, only two FPGA members were released and production ended in the year 1998. Xilinx's next FPGA series, namely XC4000, did not support partial nor dynamic reconfiguration because of lack of commercial success that XC6200 received.

Currently, Xilinx has another FPGA, which support dynamic reconfiguration: the Virtex series. However, dynamic reconfiguration is different in Xilinx Virtex-series and Atmel 40K-series FPGAs. As 40K-series FPGA does not set a limitation to partial reconfiguration, Virtex is partitioned into 48 sections that can be configured separately. These sections, called frames, start from the bottom of the device and end to the top of the device, including all the I/O blocks and CLBs. The frame size is dependent of the device size. It ranges from 384 bits for a smallest one to 1248 bits for a largest Virtex FPGA. Currently, Xilinx's software does not support communication between these sections, if they are dynamically reconfigured. For this reason, the authors do not consider prototyping platforms that utilize Xilinx's Virtex-series FPGAs as prototyping platforms for dynamically reconfigurable systems in the same context as the presented platform.

2 System Architecture

The main system concept is to combine a microcontroller and a dynamically reconfigurable FPGA with the controller's external bus interface. Therefore, the microcontroller can directly access the FPGA as a part of its memory space. The block

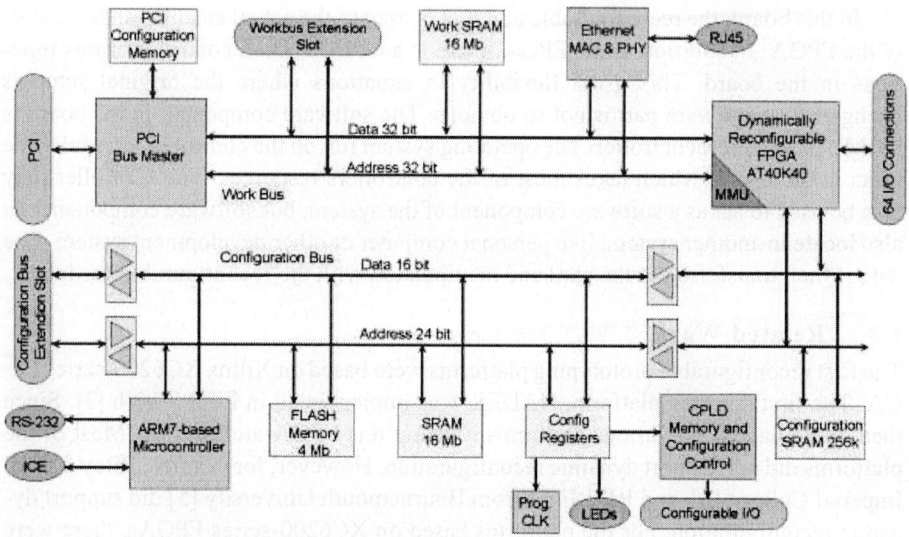

Fig. 1. The block diagram of the prototyping platform

diagram of the prototyping platform is presented in Fig. 1. The board has two individual busses. The Control Bus is mainly used by ARM7-based microcontroller. The FLASH memory is used to store configurations of the FPGA and the program of the controller. SRAM is naturally for work memory of the controller. Configuration Registers appear in controller's address space. They can be used to control the programmable clock generator, eight LEDs, and above all the configuration word of CPLD. This word determines for example the configuration mode of the FPGA.

The Configuration bus is divided in two sections with tri-state drivers. In normal operation, the controller has full access to FPGA and configuration SRAM. The controller is separated from the FPGA, when the FPGA configures itself from the memory, or data is written to configuration SRAM from external source, e.g., from Ethernet or PCI. The controller may also directly reconfigure the FPGA.

The main purpose of the Workbus is to provide working memory and I/O to the FPGA. PCI Bus Master provides 33 MHz PCI connection. The Ethernet-circuit provides both Media Access Control (MAC) and physical layers of IEEE802.3. The MMU on the FPGA is used to handle the arbitration of the Work Bus. There is an direct access from the Control Bus to the Work Bus, but not vice versa. However, the data from the Work Bus may be written to the Configuration SRAM and read from there. Both the Control Bus and the Work Bus are fully extendable with extension slots.

3 Implementation

Currently, the FPGA is Atmel AT40K40. The platform is pin-compatible with upcoming larger versions of this FPGA-family. The reconfiguration can be carried out in various manners. The fastest reconfiguration method is to write a 16-bit configuration word at frequency of 33 MHz. The reconfiguration time of 50 Kgate AT40K40 is 0.6

A Hybrid Prototyping Platform for Dynamically Reconfigurable Designs 375

Fig. 2. Photograph of card's top-side

ms. At partial reconfiguration, a functionality of a CLB can be changed in 0.1 us [8]. The structure of a cell is briefly introduced in Section 3.1.

The platform has a very versatile input and output capabilities. It is designed as a PCI Mezzanine Card (PMC), but it can also work stand-alone. Additionally, an Ethernet connection makes possible to use and reconfigure the platform via Internet. In addition to this, new software and reconfiguration data can be downloaded from In Circuit Emulator (ICE), RS-232 connection, PCI-connection, or user defined connection to FPGA. When the card is used as stand alone or in Common Mezzanine Card (CMC) environment, where the horizontal diameters are not limited according to the specification (for example in personal computer), the card can be expanded with external cards. The card has two data-address bus pairs. These can be used for direct extensions, such as external memory or a Digital Signal Processing (DSP) processor. There are also total of 76 sig-

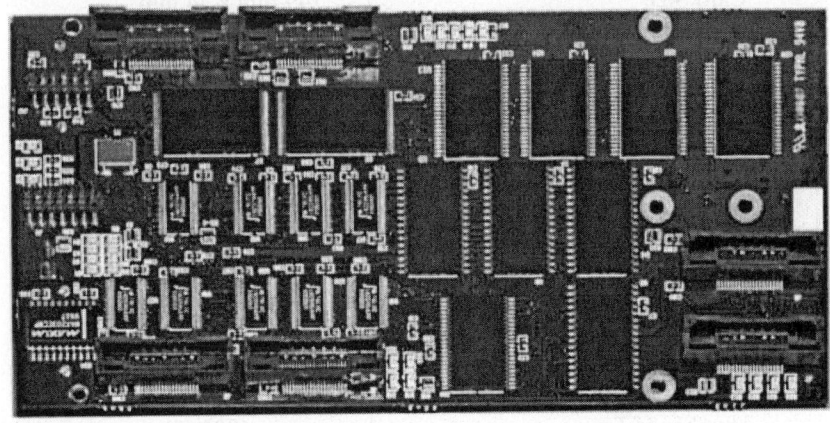

Fig. 3. Photograph of card's bottom-side

nals connected directly from FPGA to connectors that can be used to connect external devices to the card. 64 of them are in two dedicated pin-headers.

Fig. 2 illustrates the top-side of the card. PMC PCI connectors are in the right-hand side of the board, Ethernet and RJ-232 RJ-45 connectors in the left-hand side. In Fig. 3 there is the bottom side of the card. Extension connectors that appear in pairs in the borders of the card violates the PMC standard in height and may left unmounted if the space is limited. Table 1 lists some key statistics of the card's physical characteristics.

3.1 Atmel AT40K40-Series FPGA

Atmel 40K-series are SRAM-based dynamically reconfigurable FPGAs. Atmel 40K-series CLB, a cell, includes two 3-input LUTs and one D flip-flop. Therefore, it can be considered as fine-grained. The FPGA can be fully or partially dynamically reconfigured in several different modes. FPGA's structure is very suitable for compute-intensive, arithmetic functions due to its structure. Like in majority of commercial FPGA devices, AT40K-series FPGAs have horizontal and vertical interconnect lines, which are controlled by switch matrices. This kind of interconnection scheme is very inefficient for multiplication-oriented signal processing algorithms. Therefore, in this series FPGAs, each cell is connected to eight adjacent cells. This makes possible to carry out vector multiplications without using any bus resources. The FPGA architecture is fully symmetric. There are four times four cell blocks with distributed RAM blocks. The symmetric structure makes possible to move functional blocks inside the FPGA without synthesis and place and route.[9]

Table 1. Board physical statistics

Parameter	Value
Card Size	149 mm x 74 mm
Number of Layers	8
Count of True Vias	1073
Count of Buried or Blind Vias	1732
Smallest Drill Size	0.2 mm
Number of Pads	3473
Width of Trace	5 mils
Clearance Width	5 mils
Number of Traces	~4000

4 Operating System

In most of the existing prototyping platforms for reconfigurable systems, there is no Operating System (OS). However, an OS has much to offer, specially in general-purpose hybrid systems. In this platform, the OS handles different processes, memory management, and automates the reconfiguration.

The OS is based on ARM Linux. Linux is a Unix variant originally written by Linus Torvalds. Linux supports, amongst others, multitasking, virtual memory, shared libraries, demand loading, shared copy-on-write executables, proper memory management and TCP/IP networking. The ARM Linux is a port of Linux to ARM-processor based machines. The original port is mainly made by Russel King. The main benefits of this OS is that it offers ready and user-friendly interface to the system. The Linux has several drivers implemented that will be needed with the board. These include drivers for graphics, communication, sound, and protocol stacks like TCP/IP and ATM. Application level support is easy to be implemented in top of the OS. Easier use makes possible the utilization of the board in various applications. In the other hand, different applications will give new ideas how to utilise dynamic reconfiguration.

The idea of OS in dynamically reconfigurable system is not unique. For example, Siemens Corporation and University of Kaiserslautern have developed advanced OS to machines based on Xputer paradigm [10]. This OS enabled, amongst others, the dynamic software and hardware partitioning and pre-emptive interrupt handling. These abilities lack from the OS of the presented platform. It is possible to implement functions beforehand with software and hardware, and then make run-time decision which one will be used, but in order to make real dynamic alteration of HW/SW partitioning both hardware description and software code should be made with common language. This opposes problems that can not be solved with this platform. Even if there would be effective language, it should be possible to compile/synthesise in run time. Both of these are heavy tasks and can not be made at run time. Also the decision of the partition is not a simple task as pointed out in [11]. However, the OS in this platform has presynthesised building blocks that it may use to construct hardware functionalities at run time as suggested in [12]. The complexity of constructed functions is limited to regular structures with simple subcomponents. Pre-emptive change of tasks is impossible to be implemented with this FPGA-family because there is no possibility to save the context. Only switch of the hardware task may be made if there is space for the new task or previous task can be terminated.

5 Conclusions

The presented prototyping platform was designed and implemented at Tampere University of Technology in co-operation with Nokia Reseach Center. Currently, it is under testing and software development. The platform makes possible to explore dynamically reconfigurable designs in HW/SW environment. It can be integrated in large variety of existing prototyping environments in complex commercial systems or personal computers. It is also powerful as a stand-alone due to its Ethernet connection and its extensive input and output connections. Dynamic reconfiguration can not be introduced in large scale commercial systems before its benefits are verified in actual applications. The presented platform enables this possibility and in a short future, it will be integrated as a part of research and development environment for a wireless communication systems.

Acknowledgements

The authors would like to thank all the people in Nokia Research Center, especially Tero Kärkkäinen and his group, who have participated in the development of this prototyping platform.

References

[1]   R. W. Hartenstein, "The microprocessor is no longer general purpose: why future reconfigurable platforms will win," in *Proc. 2nd Ann. IEEE Int. Conf. on Innovative Systems in Silicon*, Austin, TX, USA, Oct. 8-10 1997, pp. 2-12.

[2]   Lu Guangming, H. Singh, Lee Ming-Hau, N. Bagherzadeh, F. J. Kurdahi, E. M. C. Filho, and V. Castro-Alves, "The MorphoSys dynamically reconfigurable system-on-chip," in *Proc. 1st NASA/DoD Workshop on Evolvable Hardware*, Pasadena, CA, USA, July 19-21 1999, pp. 152-160.

[3]   S. H.-M. Ludwig, "The design of a coprocessor board using Xilinx's XC6200 FPGA-an experience report," in *Proc. 6th International Workshop on Field-Programmable Logic and Applications*, Darmstadt, Germany, Sept. 23-25 1996, pp. 77-86.

[4]   P. I. MacKinlay, P. Y. K. Cheung, W. Luk, and R. Sandiford, "Riley-2: a flexible platform for codesign and dynamic reconfigurable computing research," in *Proc. 7th Int. Workshop on Field-Programmable Logic and Applications*, London, UK, Sept. 1-3 1997, pp. 91-100.

[5]   M. Vasilko and D. Long, "RIFLE-62: a flexible environment for prototyping dynamically reconfigurable systems," in *Proc. 9th IEEE Int. Workshop on Rapid System Prototyping*, Leuven, Belgium, June 3-5 1998, pp. 130-135.

[6]   G. McGregor, D. Robinson, and P. Lysaght, "A Hardware/Software Co-Design Environment for Reconfigurable Logic Systems," in *Proc. 8th Int. Workshop on Field-Programmable Logic and Applications*, Tallinn, Estonia, Aug. 31 - Sept. 3 1998, pp. 259-267.

[7]   J. Schewel, "A hardware/software co-design system using configurable computing technology," in *Proc. 1st Int. Parallel Processing Symp.*, Orlando, FL, USA, Mar. 30 - Apr. 3 1996, pp. 620-625.

[8]   Atmel, Inc., *AT40K Series Configuration*, Application Note, 1999.

[9]   Atmel, Inc., *AT40K FPGAs with FreeRAM*, Databook, 1999.

[10] R. Kress, R. W. Hartenstein, and U. Nageldinger, "An operating system for custom computing machines based on the Xputer paradigm," in *Proc. 7th Int. Workshop on Field-Programmable Logic and Applications*, London, UK, Sept. 1-3 1997, pp. 304-313.

[11] K. S. Chatha and R. Vemuri, "Hardware-software codesign for dynamically reconfigurable architectures," in *Proc. 9th Int. Workshop on Field-Programmable Logic and Applications*, Glasgow, UK, Aug. 30 - Sept. 1 1999, pp. 175-184.

[12] S. Sezer, J. Heron, R. Woods, R. Turner, and A. Marshall, "Fast partial reconfiguration for FCCMs," in *Proc. IEEE Symp. on FPGAs for Custom Computing Machines*, Napa Valley, CA, USA, Apr. 15-17 1998, pp. 318-319.

Task Rearrangement on Partially Reconfigurable FPGAs with Restricted Buffer

Hossam ElGindy[1], Martin Middendorf[2], Hartmut Schmeck[2], and Bernd Schmidt[2]

[1] School of Computer Science and Engineering, University of New South Wales, Sydney 2052, Australia
[2] Institute of Applied Computer Science and Formal Description Methods, University of Karlsruhe, D-76128 Karlsruhe, Germany

Abstract. Partially reconfigurable FPGAs can be shared among multiple independent tasks. When partial reconfiguration is possible at runtime the FPGA controller can decide on-line were to place new tasks on the FPGA. Since on-line allocation suffers from fragmentation, tasks can end up waiting despite there being sufficient, albeit non-contiguous resources available to service them. Rearranging a subset of the tasks executing on the FPGA often allows the next pending task to be processed sooner. In this paper we study the problem of placing and rearranging tasks that are supplied by input streams which have constant data rates. When such tasks are rearranged, the arriving input data have to be buffered while the execution is suspended. We describe and evaluate a genetic algorithm for identifying and scheduling feasible rearrangements when moving tasks are reloaded from off-chip and buffer size is limited.

1 Introduction

The ability to reconfigure parts of an FPGA while it is operating allows functional components/tasks to be swapped in and out as needed. If the requirements of tasks and their arrival sequence is known in advance, suitable arrangements of the tasks can be designed and sufficient resource can be provided to process tasks in parallel [6]. However, when placement decisions need to be made on-line, it is possible that a lack of contiguous free resource will prevent tasks from entering although sufficient resource in total is available. Tasks are consequently delayed from completing and the utilization of the FPGA is reduced because resources that are available are not being used.

When a new arriving task can not be allocated immediately it might be possible that it can be placed onto the FPGA after a proper rearrangement of a subset of the executing tasks. Three methods — two deterministic heuristics and a genetic algorithm — for solving this task rearrangement problem have been proposed in [1]. The goal of these methods is to increase the rate at which waiting tasks are allocated while minimizing disruptions to executing tasks that are to be moved.

In this paper we consider the task rearrangement problem for tasks that are supplied by continuous rate input data streams. Such tasks occur in several key application areas for FPGAs, e.g. video communications [7] and cryptographic applications [8]. When the execution of tasks is suspended during a rearrangement their input data streams have to be buffered. The amount of buffer that is needed depends on the data rate and the length of the period where the execution is suspended. Hence, the limited capacity of the buffer has to be taken into account when searching for good rearrangements. We describe a genetic algorithm to solve this task rearrangement problem. Our algorithm is an extension and modification of the genetic algorithm presented in [1] where input data streams have not been considered.

2 FPGA Model and General Placement Strategy

A partially reconfigurable FPGA is modelled as a rectangular array of reconfigurable logic and routing resources that may be partitioned among multiple independent tasks. Tasks are queued and processed in arrival order; they are assumed to be independent and to be contained within orthogonally aligned, non–overlapping, rectangular sub–arrays of the FPGA. Interdependent sub–tasks are assumed to be confined to the bounding box of the task. The time to load a task onto the FPGA is supposed to be proportional to its area. A controller can suspend the execution of a task and can reload this task at another location on the FPGA. We assume that every task is supplied by an input data stream arriving from off-chip at a constant rate. When the execution of a task is suspended an input buffer of fixed size stores the data arriving for this task (see Figure 1). The amount of buffer needed is the product of the data rate and the length of the time interval the execution is suspended (see Figure 2).

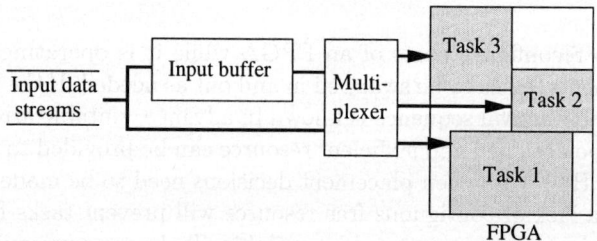

Fig. 1. FPGA with input buffer and three executing tasks

It is also assumed that sufficient resources are available on the FPGA for transmitting the input data from the input buffer to the tasks and for sending output data outside the FPGA. That is, besides the limited size of the input buffer no I/O requirements pose any further constraints on the placement of tasks. Furthermore, we allow tasks to be rotated by 90°. Without these assumptions the genetic algorithm can be adapted appropriately.

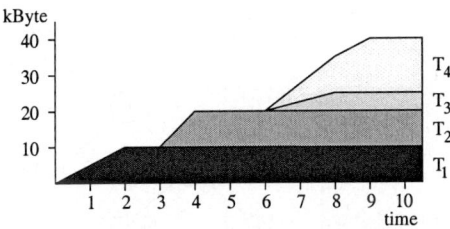

Fig. 2. Input buffer usage for suspended tasks: tasks T_1, T_2, T_3, T_4 have data rates 5,10,2.5,5 (in kByte/time unit) and are suspended in time intervals 0-2,3-4,6-8,6-9 respectively.

When a new task reaches the head of the queue the system checks if the total free space on the FPGA is at least the size of the task. When this is not the case the task is rejected due to lack of free space. Otherwise the system tries to place the task by a simple First Fit strategy. When this is not possible the genetic algorithm tries to find a rearrangement of the executing tasks that allows to place the waiting task. If the genetic algorithm finds a feasible rearrangement the task can be placed onto the FPGA. Otherwise the task is rejected by the genetic algorithm. When a task was rejected the system waits until some task on the FPGA stopped its execution. Then the system tries again to place the task as described above.

3 The Genetic Algorithm

Rearranging a subset of the executing tasks proceeds in two steps. The first step (see Section 3.1) identifies a rearrangement of the tasks executing on the FPGA that frees sufficient space for the waiting task. The second step (see Section 3.2) schedules the movements of the chosen tasks so as to minimize the amount of input buffer needed. Both subproblems, that is, to find a feasible rearrangement and the problem of scheduling the task rearrangement to realize our goals, are NP–complete [3, 4]. Our approach is to use a combination of two genetic algorithms one for each subproblem.

3.1 Search for Feasible Rearrangements

In this subsection we describe a genetic algorithm called R-GA for finding a feasible rearrangement of the tasks executing on the FPGA. The R-GA starts by creating an initial population of possible solutions by means of a specific initialization method. As long as the stopping condition has not been met a new generation is created. This involves determining the fitness of each individual by the application of an evaluation function. Individuals which represent desirable solutions (high fitness values) are selected with high probability to produce offspring. The children created by crossover and mutation operators are inserted

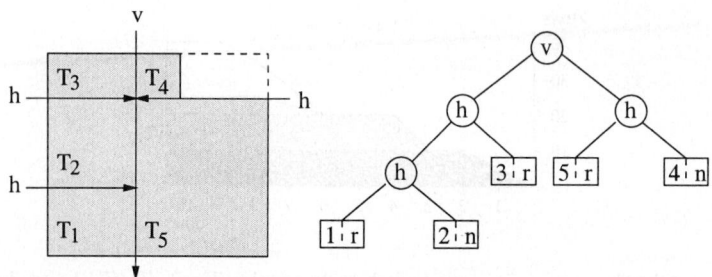

Fig. 3. Arrangement (left) with corresponding slicing tree (right)

into the new population thereby replacing other individuals with low fitness. In particular, R-GA has the following characteristics.

i) Representation: R-GA works only on the subset of possible arrangements that allow a specific genetic representation, called a slicing tree. Such a task arrangement — called a slicing task arrangement — is recursively defined as either a single task, or as a task arrangement for which there exists a vertical or horizontal line segment dividing it into two slicing task arrangements. Each slicing task arrangement can be represented by a slicing tree (see Figure 3). A leaf represents a task with fixed orientation. A parent node corresponds to the minimal bounding box containing two horizontally or vertically aligned patterns represented by the children. Such a pattern can be either a task or another bounding box. The leaves are labelled with the index of the task and its orientation (not-rotated (n), rotated (r)). Parent nodes contain the cut direction (vertical (v) or horizontal (h)).

ii) Initialization: An initial population is formed by individuals (fixed slicing trees) which are built bottom–up by random pairing, i.e. starting with the leaves, two randomly chosen nodes are linked together by a newly created parent node until a complete slicing tree is obtained.

iii) Evaluation: The evaluation function considers the ratio of the tasks completely allocated inside the FPGA border, the compactness of the arrangement, the total number of cells that have to be rearranged, the data rates of the input streams, and the actual input buffer usage.

iv) Crossover: The crossover operation is based on gene–pool crossover [5]. All proper subtrees of two parents are inserted into a gene–pool. A new individual is created from subtrees chosen from the gene–pool. Each subtree is evaluated by a rating function which considers the compactness and the number of tasks in the subtree. The subtree with the highest rate is chosen and all subtrees in the gene–pool containing at least one task of the selected subtree are removed. The next subtree is chosen as the highest ranked subtree of the remaining gene–pool. The two selected subtrees are combined by inserting one subtree at a node of the other subtree so that the resulting combined tree receives the highest possible rating. The complete slicing tree is obtained by repeatedly adding disjoint subtrees.

v) Mutation: Mutation changes the structure of a fixed slicing tree. If a tree was selected for mutation, one of three different mutation types is applied.

Exchange mutation swaps two randomly selected subtrees. Insertion mutation attaches a randomly chosen subtree at a randomly selected insertion node of the tree. Rotation mutation randomly selects a subtree whose corresponding task arrangement is rotated to the left or to the right by 90° or 180°.

3.2 Scheduling Task Rearrangements

The time needed to complete the rearrangement depends on the size of the tasks that have to be reloaded. We assume a task may continue executing until it is suspended prior to moving and that a task is resumed as soon as it has been reloaded. If its destination is not free when it is reloaded, the tasks occupying the destination are immediately suspended and removed.

We distinguish between the minimum possible cost of moving a task, and the actual cost of moving it. The minimum cost is the time needed to save and reload the task, which is unavoidable. However, the actual cost needs to account for the time a task is suspended while other tasks are being reloaded. The difference between the actual and minimum costs represents a scheduling delay. The input buffer usage depends on the data rates and the time tasks are suspended from execution.

For scheduling we use a genetic algorithm — called S-GA — where a schedule is represented by a string of integers corresponding to the task indices arranged in the order they are moved. For initialization, a set of randomly generated permutations of these indices is used. Since our goal is to minimize the buffer usage we applied an evaluation function calculating the total growth of buffer that is caused by the suspensions of executing tasks. The mutation operator swaps two randomly chosen task indices in the gene string. For crossover we use order crossover which is suited to genes that represent permutations. Order crossover chooses a pair of cut points at random and combines two parental gene strings by keeping the substring between the cut points and adding the missing genes in the order they appear in the other parent.

4 Test Results

To study the task rearrangement problem and the performance of the genetic algorithm we generated synthetic task sets. Sets of 3,000 tasks were created that are characterized by the following 5 independent, uniformly distributed random variables:

- Two variables representing the task side lengths were permitted to range from 1 to 32.
- The task service period was allowed to range from 1 to 1,000 time units (tu).
- The intertask arrival period was chosen between 1 tu and 10 tu. This value was chosen so that the queue always contains at least one task (cmp. [1]).
- One variable representing the data rate of the tasks input stream was chosen between 1 bit/tu and 20 kByte/tu.

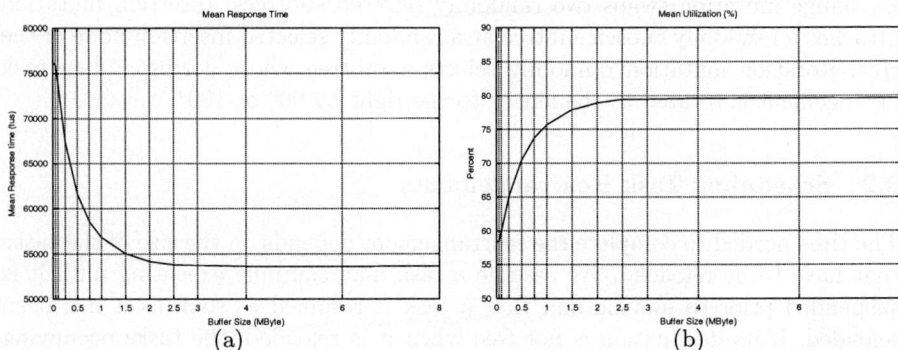

Fig. 4. Performance of GA: (a) mean response time, (b) mean utilization of FPGA area.

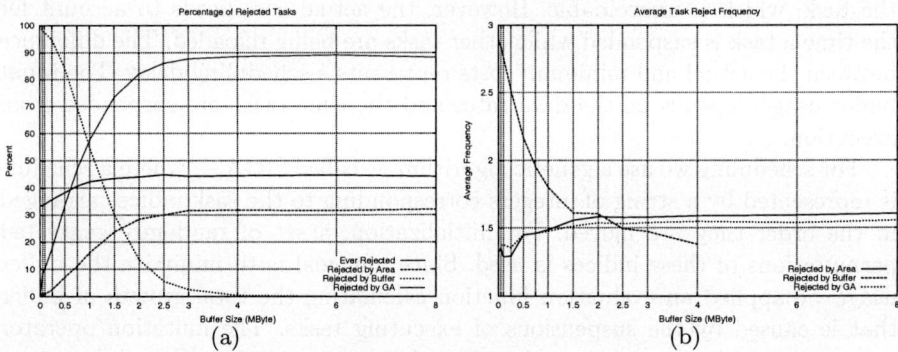

Fig. 5. Task rejections: (a) percentage of rejected tasks (the "ever rejected" curve represents the rate of tasks rejected at least once compared to the number of all tasks; the other three curves show rates that are compared to the number of tasks that have been rejected at least once), (b) average rejection frequency of rejected tasks for the different reasons (the frequency is computed with respect to the tasks which are rejected at least once for the particular reason).

The tasks were queued and placed in arrival order onto a simulated FPGA of size 64 × 64. The time needed to load a task was determined by the availability of space and the time used to configure the cells needed by the task. The configuration delay per cell was thus also a parameter and was set to 0.005 tus. Each experiment averaged the results of 5 runs.

For both GAs we maintained a population size of 50 over 500 generations. In order to build a new generation the 10 best individuals of the old generation survived while the others were replaced by new individuals. Mutation probabilities were set to 0.5 (with 1/3 chance for each mutation type in the R-GA). Crossover probabilities were set to 0.25 and 0.85 for R-GA and S-GA respectively.

Figure 4 (a) shows the mean response time, i.e. the time between task arrival at the tail of the queue and the task completion time. Note that the computation times of the GA are not included in the response times. The main reason is that our goal is to explore the general potential of task rearrangements for improving FPGA performance. Another reason is that parts of our algorithm (the R-GA) can potentially be run in the background. The curve in Figure 4 (a) shows that the mean response time declines rapidly as the buffer size grows until the minimum value is reached at a buffer size of 3 MByte. Thus, rearrangements can improve FPGA performance significantly when some amount of input buffer is available. Figure 4 (b) shows the mean utilization of the FPGA. The utilization raises from less than 60% up to almost 80% at buffer sizes of at least 3 MByte. A larger amount of buffer allows to rearrange tasks more often thereby improving FPGA utilization.

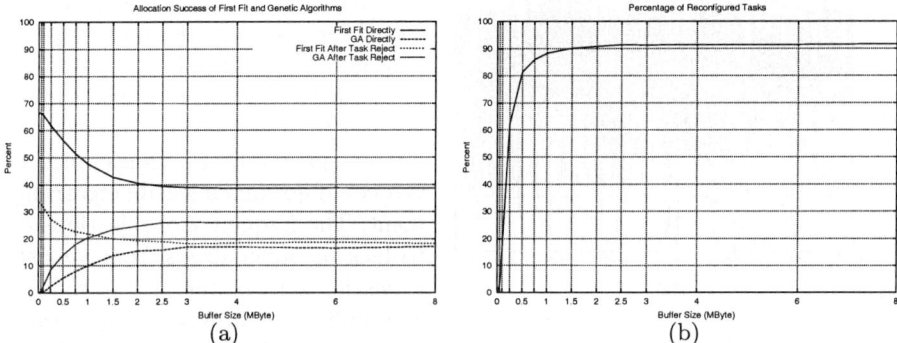

Fig. 6. (a) Rate of success of allocation (b) Percentage of reconfigured tasks.

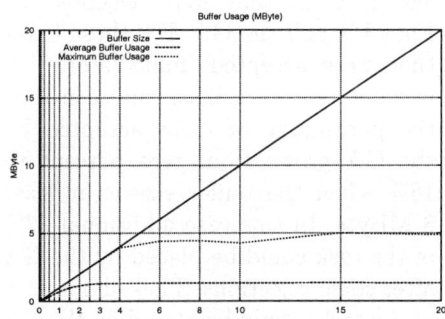

Fig. 7. Maximum and average buffer usage.

Figure 5 (a) compares the rates of tasks that were rejected for different reasons. It seems surprising that the percentage of tasks that were ever rejected (i.e. at least once) increases from about 34% at zero buffer to about 45% at a buffer size of at least 2 MByte. Recall that for larger buffers the utilization of the FPGA increases. Hence, in general it becomes more difficult to place the next task onto the array immediately after finishing the placement of the preceeding task. The curve describing the rate of tasks that are rejected due to a lack of free buffer starts at 100% for zero buffer since at least some buffer is needed for a rearrangement. But this rate declines quickly to less than 20% at a buffer size of 2 MByte and to almost 0% at a buffer size of at least 3 MByte.

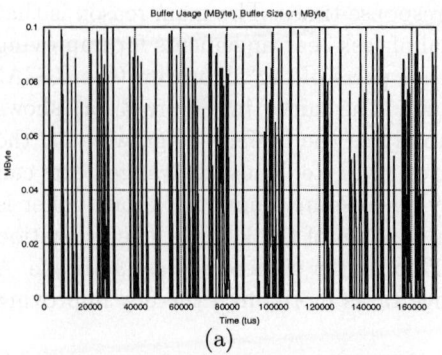

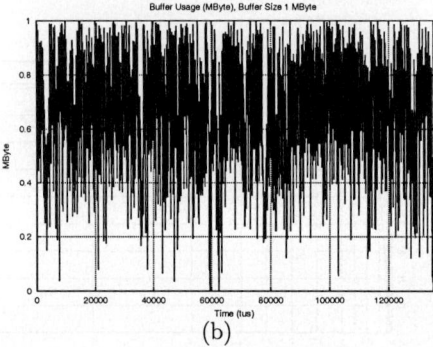

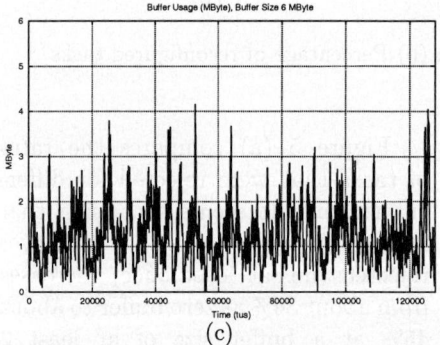

Fig. 8. Buffer usage: (a) buffer size 0.1 MByte, (b) buffer size 1 MByte, (c) buffer size 6 MByte.

Also at 3 MByte buffer size the percentage of tasks rejected at least once due to lack of space reaches its maximum value at about 32%. The rate of tasks rejected at least once by the GA also reaches its maximum value at about 89% for a buffer size of at least 3 MByte. Note that the sum of the values of the three curves for the reasons for rejecting a task can be more than 100 percent because some tasks are rejected several times and for different reasons.

The average number a task is rejected for a specific reason is depicted in Figure 5 (b). For buffer sizes of at least 2 MByte a rejected task is on average 1.6 times rejected due to lack of free space and 1.5 times since the GA could not find a feasible rearrangement. The frequency of rejections due to lack of buffer drops from almost 3 times for zero buffer to less than 1.5 at a buffer size of 3 MByte (no values are given for buffer sizes of at least 6 MByte since no task was rejected due to lack of free buffer in this case).

Figure 6 (a) compares the percentage of tasks that were accepted by First Fit and the GA. For those tasks that were accepted immediately, i.e. without rejection, it can be seen that the percentage of tasks accepted by the GA grows from zero percent to 18% when the buffer size is at least 3 MByte. In this case additional 27% of the task could be placed by the GA after some rejections. Thus about 45% of the tasks could be placed by the GA after doing some rearrangement when enough buffer is available.

The percentage of tasks that are rearranged is depicted in Figure 6 (b). Up to 92% of the tasks are rearranged with an average number of 5.7 rearrangements per task when there is enough buffer available.

The buffer utilization is shown in Figure 7. It can be seen that the maximum buffer size needed never exceeded 5 MByte. The average buffer usage was always less than 1.5 MByte. In Figure 8 the buffer usage is depicted in more detail for buffers of three different sizes. When buffer space is short (0.1 MByte) the buffer can be used only sometimes when simple rearrangements are possible that move only a few tasks with low input data rates (cmp. Figure 8 (a)). A buffer of 1 MByte can be used almost all the time but the high usage rate shows that the system might still profit from a larger buffer (cmp. Figure 8 (b)). Figure 8 (c) shows that a buffer size of 6 MByte is enough and with very few exceptions at least some buffer space is used all the time.

5 Conclusion

We proposed a method for a proper placement of tasks each supplied by a constant rate input data stream on dynamically and partially reconfigurable FPGAs. It was shown that rearranging some of the executing tasks often allows the next task to be placed sooner. For this it is necessary to enhance the FPGA with an additional input buffer. It is used to buffer the input data streams of those tasks that are suspended from execution during a rearrangement. The computation of a proper rearrangement and a corresponding schedule was done by a genetic algorithm. Test results on synthetic problem instances show that the average time between arrival of a new task and the time when its execution finished was reduced significantly by the genetic algorithm. This was possible since the utilization of the FPGA could be improved from 60% to 80% when enough input buffer space is available. An interesting problem for further study is to take the routing capabilities of different existing FPGAs into account and to study the problem on real world problem instances.

References

1. Diessel, O.; ElGindy, H.; Middendorf, M.; Schmeck, H.; Schmidt. B.: Dynamic Scheduling of Tasks on Partially Reconfigurable FPGAs. IEE-Proceedings – Computer and Digital Techniques, Vol. 147, No. 3, 2000.
2. Diessel, O. and ElGindy, H.: 'Run–Time Compaction of FPGA Designs', Luk, W. and Cheung, P.Y.K. and Glesner, M. (Eds.), Proc. 7th International Workshop on Field–Programmable Logic and Applications (FPL '97), Springer–Verlag, Berlin, Germany, 1997, pp. 131 – 140.
3. Diessel, O. and ElGindy, H.: 'Partial FPGA Rearrangement by Local Repacking.' Technical Report 97-08, Department of Computer Science and Software Engineering, The University of Newcastle, 1997.
4. Li, K. and Cheng, K.H.: 'Complexity of Resource Allocation and Job Scheduling Problems on Partitionable Mesh Connected Systems', Proceedings 1st IEEE Symposium on Parallel and Distributed Processing, IEEE Computer Society, Los Alamitos, CA, 1989, pp.358 – 365.
5. Mühlenbein, H. and Voigt, H.-M.: 'Gene pool recombination in genetic algorithms', Osman, I.H. and Kelly, J.P. (Eds.), Proc. Metaheuristics Int. Conf., Kluwer Academic Publishers, Norwell, 1995.

6. Teich, M.; Fekete, S. and Schepers, J.: 'Compile-Time Optimization of Dynamic Hardware Reconfigurations', Proc. Int. Conf. on Parallel and Distributed Processing Techniques and Applications (PDPTA'99), Las Vegas, U.S.A., 1999.
7. Villasenor, J.; Jones, C. and Schoner, B.: 'Video Communications Using Rapidly Reconfigurable Hardware,' *IEEE Transactions on Circuits and Systems for Video Technology*, 1995, **5** (6), pp. 565 – 567.
8. Vuillemin, J.E.; Bertin, P.; Roncin, D.; Shand, M.; Touati, H.H. and Boucard, P.: 'Programmable Active Memories: Reconfigurable Systems Come of Age,' *IEEE Transactions on Very Large Scale Integration (VLSI) Systems*, 1996, **4** (1), pp. 56 – 69.

Generation of Design Suggestions for Coarse-Grain Reconfigurable Architectures

R. Hartenstein, M. Herz, Th. Hoffmann, and U. Nageldinger

Computer Structures Group (Rechnerstrukturen), Informatik
University of Kaiserslautern, D-67653 Kaiserslautern, Germany
hartenst@rhrk.uni-kl.de - http://xputers.informatik.uni-kl.de - Fax: +49 631 205 2640

Abstract. Coarse-grain reconfigurable architectures have been a matter of intense research in the last few years. They promise to be more adequate for computational tasks due to their better efficiency and bigger speed. As the coarse granularity implies also a reduction of flexibility, a universal architecture seems to be hardly feasible. Based on the KressArray architecture family, a design-space exploration system is being implemented, which supports the designer in finding an appropriate architecture for a given application domain. By analysing the results of a number of different experimental mappings, the system derives suggestions how the architecture can be enhanced. This paper presents an analyser tool, which allows the generation of such suggestions using approximate reasoning based on fuzzy logic. The tool is flexible enough to support different data gathering methods and an extensible rule set.

1. Introduction

While early solutions in reconfigurable computing were based on fine-grained FPGAs, in the recent years also coarse-grain reconfigurable architectures have been developed, which are capable of implementing high-level operators in their processing elements, featuring multiple-bit wide datapath: [1], [2], [3], [4], [5], [6], [7]. The coarse-grain approach promises advantages over FPGA-like fine-grain architectures:

- Less configuration data is needed, since there are typically orders of magnitude less operators than in an FPGA.

- Routing structures transfer words instead of bits, thus needing less control signals and associated configuration storage. The lower amount of configuration data supports fast loading and dynamic partial reconfiguration.

- Coarse-grain architectures are much more area-efficient. This applies to both, operators and routing resources. Powerful operators like ALUs, MACs and others can be directly implemented in silicon, instead of being mapped onto zillions of CLBs surrounded by wide areas of fine grain routing resources.

- The coarse granularity is better suited for application development of computational tasks from a high-level language and similar sources.

To obtain sufficient flexibility for high production volume most future SoC implementations need some percentage of coarse grain reconfigurable circuitry [8]. Reconfigurable computing even has the potential to question the dominance of the microprocessor [9].

[10]. However, for the use of a coarse granularity some problems have to be solved to cope with the reduced flexibility compared to FPGA-based solutions:

- Processing elements of coarse-grain architectures are more "expensive" than the logic blocks of an FPGA. While it is possible for FPGA mappings, that a number of logic blocks is unused or cannot be reached by the routing resources, especially the latter situation is quite annoying for coarse-grain architectures due to the fewer number of processing elements.
- While the multi-bit datapath applies well to operators from high-level languages, operations working on smaller word-lengths and especially bit manipulation operations are weakly supported. If such operations occur, like e.g. in data compression algorithms, they may result in a complex implementation requiring several processing elements.

Due to these problems, the selection of architectural properties like datapath width, routing resources and operator repertory is a general problem in the design of coarse-grain architectures. Thus, a design space exploration is done in many cases, to determine suitable architectural properties. As the requirements to the architecture are mostly dependent on the applications to be mapped onto it, previous efforts use normally a set of example applications, e.g. DES encryption, DCT, or FIR filters. For examples such an explorations is described in [7] to determine the best bit width for ALUs of the architecture. According to this method, coarse-grain architectures are often targeted for specific application domains, like multimedia [2], [7] or DSP [4].

To find a suitable architecture for a given application domain, the KressArray Xplorer framework is being implemented at Kaiserslautern University [11], [12]. The framework uses the KressArray [5] architecture family as basis for an interactive exploration process. When a suitable architecture has been found, the mapping of the application is provided directly. The designer is supported during the exploration by suggestions of the system how the current architecture may be enhanced. This paper focuses on the tool which gives these suggestions.

The rest of this paper is structured as follows: The next section briefly sketches the KressArray architecture family. Then, the design space for the exploration process is described. In section 4, the general approach for an interactive design space exploration for

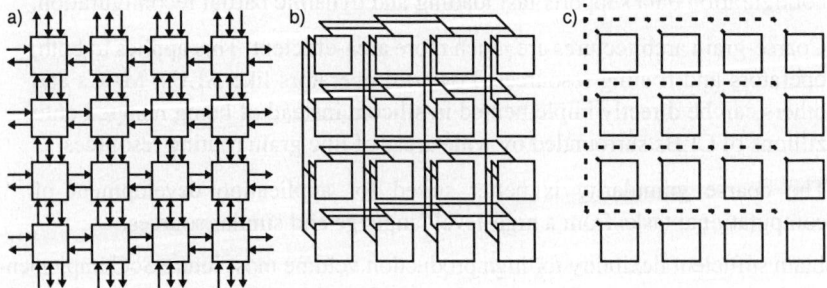

Figure 1: Three levels of interconnect for KressArray architectures: a) nearest neighbor links, b) backbuses in each row or column (for more examples see figure 2), c) serial global bus.

an application domain is presented. In the following section, some selected related work is sketched briefly. After this, a short overview on the KressArray Xplorer framework is given. The next section motivates our approach for the generation of design suggestions, followed by an overview on the implementation of this approach. Finally, the paper is concluded.

2. The KressArray Architecture Family

The KressArray family is based on the original mesh-connected (no extra routing areas, see figure 2 d, e) KressArray-1 (aka rDPA) architecture published elsewhere [5], [13]. An architecture of the KressArray family is a regular array of coarse grain reconfigurable DataPath Units (rDPUs), each featuring a multiple-bit datapath and providing a set of coarse grain operators. The original KressArray-1 architecture provided a datapath of 32 bits and all integer operators of C, the proposed system can handle also other datapath widths and operator repertories. The different types of communication resources are illustrated in figure 1. There are three levels of interconnect: First, a rDPU can be connected via nearest neighbor links to its four neighbors to the north, east, south and west. There are unidirectional and bidirectional links. The data transfer direction of the bidirec-

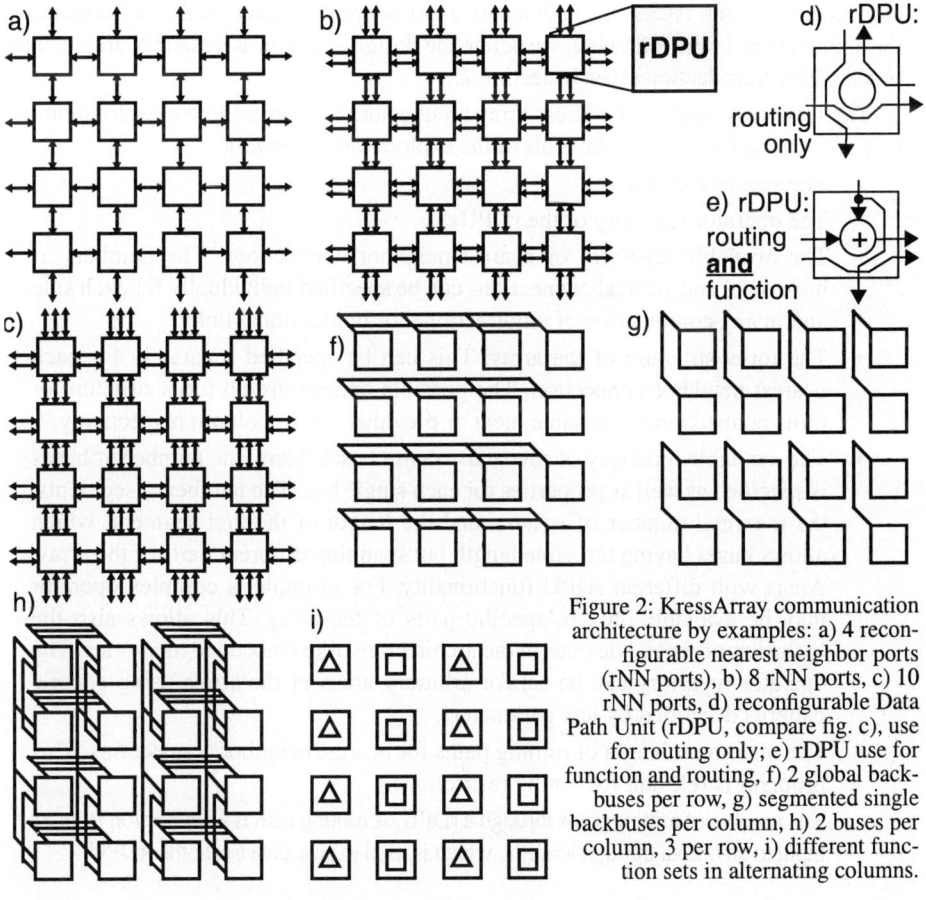

Figure 2: KressArray communication architecture by examples: a) 4 reconfigurable nearest neighbor ports (rNN ports), b) 8 rNN ports, c) 10 rNN ports, d) reconfigurable Data Path Unit (rDPU, compare fig. c), use for routing only; e) rDPU use for function and routing, f) 2 global backbuses per row, g) segmented single backbuses per column, h) 2 buses per column, 3 per row, i) different function sets in alternating columns.

tional ones is determined at configuration time. Second, there may be backbuses in each row or column, which connect several rDPUs. These buses may be segmented, forming several independent buses. Third, all rDPUs are connected by one single global bus, which allows only serial data transfers. This type of connection makes only sense for coarse grain architectures with a relatively low number of elements. However, a global bus effectively avoids the situation, that a mapping fails due to lack of routing resources. The rDPUs themselves can serve as pure routing elements, as an operator, or as an operator with additional routing paths going through. Some more communication architecture examples are shown in figure 2 [14].

The number and type of the routing resources as well as the operator repertory are subject of change during the exploration process. Typically, a trade-off has to be found between the estimated silicon area and the performance of the architecture. Examples for trade-off issues are sequential or parallel multiplication or the realization of complex operators like multiply-accumulate by one or multiple rDPUs.

3. The KressArray Design Space

The KressArray structure defines an architecture class rather than a single architecture. The class members differ mainly by the available communication resources and the operator repertory. Both issues have obviously a considerable impact on the performance of the architecture. In the following, we define the design space for KressArray architectures based on the introduction given in section 2.

The following aspects of a KressArray architecture are subject to the exploration process and can be modified by the tools of the exploration framework:

- The size of the array.
- The operator repertory of the rDPUs.
- The available repertory of nearest neighbor connections. The numbers of horizontal and vertical connections can be specified individually for each side and in any combination of unidirectional or bidirectional links.
- The torus structure of the array. This can be specified separately for each nearest neighbor connection. The possible options are no torus structure or torus connection to the same, next or previous row or column respectively.
- The available repertory of row and column buses. Here, the number of buses is specified as well as properties for each single bus: The number of segments, the maximal number of writers, and the length of the first segment, which allows buses having the same length but spanning different parts of the array. Areas with different rDPU functionality. For example, a complex operator may be available only in specific parts of the array. This allows also the inclusion of special devices in the architecture, like embedded memories. The operator repertory can be set for arbitrary areas of the array, using generic patterns described by few parameters.
- The maximum length of routing paths for nearest neighbor connections. This property is relevant for timing restrictions.
- The number of routing paths through a rDPU. A routing path is a connection from an input to an output through a rDPU, which is used to pass data to another rDPU.

- The interfacing architecture for the array. Basically, data words to and from the KressArray can be transferred by either of three ways: Over the serial global bus, over the edges of the array, or over an rDPU inside the array, where the latter possibility is mostly used for library elements.

In order to find a suitable set of these properties for a given application domain, an interactive framework is currently developed. The framework, called KressArray Xplorer, allows the user a guided design of a KressArray optimized for a specified problem. At the end of the design process, a description of the resulting architecture is generated.

4. Design Space Exploration

The global approach to design space exploration for a domain of several applications is shown in figure 3. First, all applications are compiled into a representation in an intermediate format, which contains the expression trees of the applications. All intermediate files are analyzed to determine basic architecture requirements like the number of operators needed. The main design space exploration cycle is interactive and meant to be performed on a single application. This application is selected from the set of applications in a way, that the optimized architecture for the selected application will also satisfy the other applications. This selection process is done by the user, with a suggestion from the system. For our current example setup to optimize the performance by exploring the communication architecture, we use the application with the worst regularity, as this is supposed to have the highest routing requirements. An approach to measure the regularity of an application has been published in [17].

The exploration itself is an interactive process, which is supported by suggestions to the designer, how the current architecture could be modified. The application is first mapped onto the current architecture. The generated mapping is then analyzed and statistic data is generated. Based on this data, suggestions for architecture improvement are created using a fuzzy-logic based approach described below. The designer may then chose to apply the suggestion, propose a different modification, return to a previous design version, or end the exploration. Some modifications allow the new architecture to be used directly for the next mapping step, while others will require a reevaluation of the basic architecture requirements and/or a reselection of the application for the exploration. Given our setup for performance optimization, a change to the routing resources should not require a reevaluation, as the current application is supposed to be the one with the worst routing requirements. In contrast to this, a change of the operator repertory for the rDPUs requires the replacement of subtrees in the dataflow graph, thus effecting the number of required rDPUs in the array as well as the complexity of all applications. Thus, for a change of the operator repertory, a reevaluation is required.

After the exploration cycle has ended, the final architecture has to be verified by mapping the remaining applications onto it. On the one hand, this step produces mappings of all applications to be used for implementation, while on the other hand, it is made sure that the architecture will satisfy the requirements of the whole domain.

5. Related Work

For most reconfigurable architectures, the designers did a thorough evaluation of different architectures. In [7], target application properties are considered to determine the datapath width for processing elements for the PipeRench architecture. The results are gained by evaluating several example applications mapped onto the architecture. In [15], Moritz et al. present a framework for architectural design space exploration of processors for the Raw Machine [6], considering application requirements. This approach is based on mathematical models, which have to be provided for the applications to be considered. Due to the switched interconnect of Raw, this work does not address requirements of routing resources.

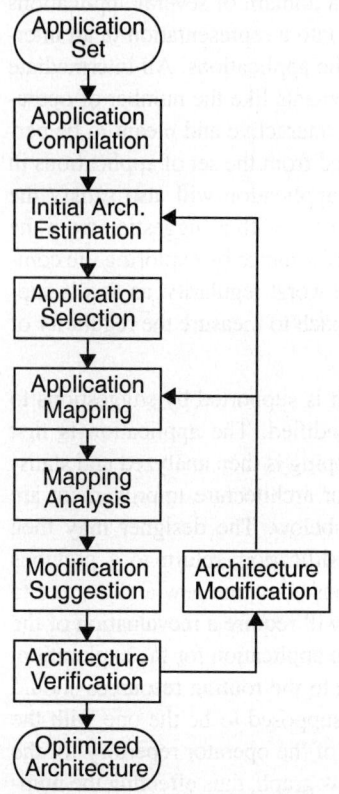

Figure 3: Global approach for domain-specific architecture optimization.

Other design exploration frameworks are found mostly in the area of VLSI design. One approach which comes closest to ours is described in [16]. The framework by Guerra et al. allows interactive design space exploration for datapath-intensive ASICs, starting from a high level description. This work also considers application properties like regularity, which has an impact on the routing requirements. Design guidance is generated, by polynomial functions and parameterized rules. However, we find the way the suggestions are generated not adequate for our purposes, as we expect the properties of the design, which are extracted not to be that clear. This is because of the use of heuristic algorithms on the one hand, and the possibility to explore heterogeneous structures with areas of different operator repertories on the other hand, as both may distort the characterizations extracted from the design. Further, the approach described allows optimization for a single application, while we target optimization for application domains consisting of several applications.

6. The KressArray Xplorer

This section will give a brief description of the components of the KressArray Xplorer, which is published elsewhere [12]. An overview on the Xplorer is shown in figure 4. The framework is based on a design system, which can handle multiple KressArray architectures. It consists of a compiler for the high-level language ALE-X, a scheduler for performance estimation, and a simulated-annealing based mapper. This system works on an intermediate file format, which contains the net list of the application, delay parameters for performance estimation, the architecture description, and the mapping information. The latter is added by the mapper at the end of the synthesis process. An architecture estimator determines the minimum architecture requirements in terms of operator numbers and suggests the application with the biggest complexity to an interac-

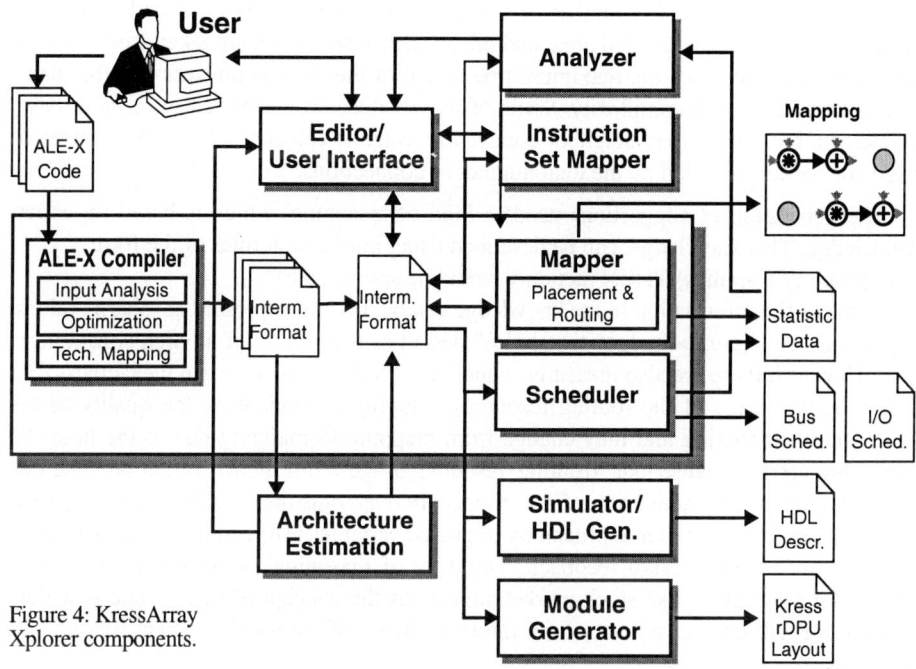

Figure 4: KressArray Xplorer components.

tive graphical user interface. This interface is also generally used to control all other tools. Further, it contains two interactive editors, an architecture editor, which allows to change the architecture independently by the design suggestions, and a mapping editor, which allows to fine-tune the result of the mapper. An analyzer generates suggestions for architecture improvements by information gathered from the mapping and other sources. An instruction mapper allows the change of the operator repertory by exchanging complex operators in the expression tree with multi-operator implementations. A simulator allows both simulation of the application on the architecture as well as generation of a behavioral HDL (currently Verilog) description of the KressArray. Finally, a Module Generator (planned) can be used to generate the final layout of a KressArray cell.

7. Generation of Design Suggestions

In this chapter, we will discuss the problem of the generation of design suggestions for our framework and motivate our approach, which is performed by the analyzer tool of the Xplorer framework. The problem of the generation of feedback on a given design can be split into several subproblems:

- Analysis of the current architecture and gathering of information. This includes the combination of data to gain derived information.
- Generation of suggestions from this information.
- Ranking of the suggestions after their importance.

In our approach, the basis for the information gathering step is the mapping produced by the design system. Data gathered includes the usage of buses and nearest-neighbor connections in percent, the number of serial bus connections, the estimated number of execution cycles, the estimated area, and others. Other properties are taken from the current application set, like the maximum tree height of the expression trees and the maximum estimated graph complexity. Some of these values are generated from more basic properties, e.g. the nearest neighbor connection usage is calculated from the number of used connections divided by the total number of connections.

The generation of suggestions needs a kind of reasoning, which is based on expert knowledge. This knowledge, can be described using implication rules of the form „IF (property x applies) THEN (action y would be appropriate)".

Some of the information in the knowledge can be directly expressed as 'sharp' values, e.g. the clause "(area > budget_threshold)" describes the quality, if an area constraint is met. However, there are also measures, which are affected with a certain inexactness. For example, the usage of the routing resources is highly dependent on the quality of the placement and routing and may change from mapping to mapping due to the heuristic algorithm used. A clause like "(routing_resource_usage > threshold)" might produce different results in subsequent runs of the mapper. To overcome these problems, we chose to model the properties in our approach by linguistic variables [18] and use fuzzy reasoning [19] to generate the design feedback. This way of reasoning has shown to give good results for other areas like stock-market advice. As the concept of fuzzy logic is widely known, we will only give a very brief informal sketch of the issues relevant for our system.

A *linguistic variable* describes a measure not by its numerical value, but by natural language terms, called *linguistic values*. E.g. for the routing resource usage the linguistic values could be ‚low', ‚mediocre', ‚high', and ‚full'. A measured value (in percent) of the usage is then transformed by describing, how much the numerical value applies to each linguistic value, by giving an according score between 0 and 1. E. g. a usage of 70% may lie between 'mediocre' and 'high', which is expressed by assigning a score of 0.4 to 'mediocre' and 0.6 to 'high' and 0 to the other values. The translation from the numerical value to the scores is typically done by *membership functions*.

By employing these concepts, it is possible to overcome the problems with uncertainty and describe knowledge in a more natural way, e.g.:
"IF (routing_resource_usage is 'high') AND (performance is 'low') AND (number_of_back_buses is 'low') AND (average_fan_out is 'high') THEN (add_back_bus='high')"

Note, that rules with 'sharp' values can also be modeled by this approach as a special case. Ranking of different suggestions can be included into the rules themselves, as the resulting suggestion is also a linguistic value with an associated score. For the final presentation of the suggestions to the user, the linguistic variables can directly be used.

8. Implementation of the Analyser Tool

The main tasks of the analyzer tool, according to the discussion in the previous section, are the gathering of information and the generation of suggestions using the methods described above. The gathering itself requires some flexibility, as there are several sources for the data. The current intermediate file containing the mapping is the main source, but other data, like performance estimation, is produced by other programs. Furthermore,

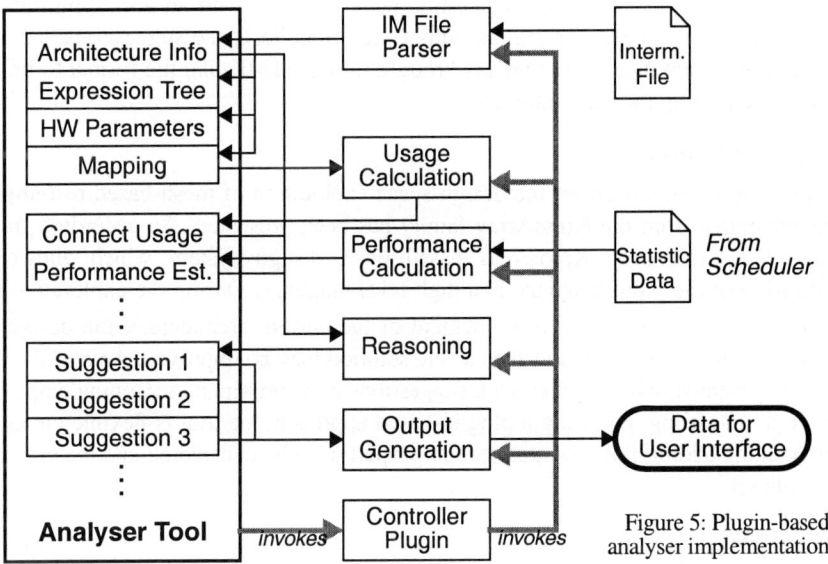

Figure 5: Plugin-based analyser implementation

both the ruleset as well as the information database have to be extensible. To manage all this, a plug-in concept has been chosen, which allows maximal flexibility. The general structure of the analyzer with example plug-ins is shown in figure 5.

The analyzer tool itself contains the data gathered by the plug-ins. The information gathered is supposed to be either numeric values or fuzzy sets. Such data can be dynamically generated by the analyzer and referenced by other plug-ins using a unique name. An exception are the expression tree, the architecture information, and the mapping, which are complex data structures created by analysis of the intermediate file. On start of the analyzer, the name of a plug-in is passed as argument, which is then invoked first to run the analysis process.

The plug-ins are loaded dynamically and can access all data stored at the analyzer. Basically, each plug-in has the capability to invoke other plug-ins as well as external programs. In both cases, arguments can be passed to the child plug-in or process. However, we considered it more convenient to employ dedicated controller plug-ins, which are invoked first by the analyzer and start the other plug-ins needed for the analysis. Such a controller plug-in is analogous to a shell script, except that it is included into the plug-in concept. The first plug-in invoked is the parser plug-in, which reads the intermediate file and builds the complex data structures in the analyzers. Following plug-ins work on these data structures to extract more information, like the usage of the routing connections or the average fan-out of the operators. Other plug-ins add to the database by running external programs or analyzing files from other programs, like the statistics from the scheduler, which contain a performance estimation.

As the fuzzy logic operations in the reasoning plug-in involve more complex computations, there is only one plug-in for all rules. The rule to be applied and the required values are passed as arguments to this plug-in. Typically, a whole ruleset is applied, which leads to several suggestions, with each suggestion being affected with an according ranking. After the ruleset has been applied, an output plug-in collects the suggestions and sorts them after their ranking. Then, they are brought into a HTML-like file format to be presented to the user by the User Interface.

9. Conclusions

An interactive approach for the design-space exploration of mesh-based reconfigurable architectures from the KressArray family has been presented. An according framework called KressArray Xplorer is based on a design system which allows the specification of the input language in a high-level language. During the exploration process, which is based on iterative refinement of the current architecture, the designer is supported by suggestions on how the current solution may be improved. An analyzer tool has been presented, which makes such suggestions by approximate reasoning employing fuzzy logic modeling. By using a plug-in-based approach, the tool is flexible enough to allow both the addition of new architecture properties to be considered and the extension of the rule set.

References

1. E. Mirsky, A. DeHon: „MATRIX: A Reconfigurable Computing Architecture with Configurable Instruction Distribution and Deployable Resources", Proc. FPGAs for Custom Computing Machines, pp. 157-166, IEEE CS Press, Los Alamitos, CA, U.S.A., 1996.
2. A. Marshall et al.: A Reconfigurable Arithmetic Array for Multimedia Applications; FPGA'99, Int'l Symposium on Field Programmable Gate Arrays, Monterey, CA, U.S.A., Febr. 21 - 23, 1999
3. C. Ebeling, D. Cronquist, P. Franklin: „RaPiD: Reconfigurable Pipelined Datapath", Int'l Workshop on Field Programmable Logic and Applications, FPL'96, Darmstadt, Germany, Sept 1996.
4. R. A. Bittner, P. M. Athanas and M. D. Musgrove: „Colt: An Experiment in Wormhole Runtime Reconfiguration"; SPIE Photonics East `96, Boston, MA, USA, November 1996.
5. R. Kress: „A Fast Reconfigurable ALUs for Xputers", Ph.D. thesis, Univ. Kaiserslautern, 1996.
6. E. Waingold et al.: „Baring it all to Software: Raw Machines", IEEE Computer 30, pp. 86-93.
7. S. C. Goldstein, H. Schmit, et al.: „PipeRench: A Coprocessor for Streaming Multimedia Acceleration"; Int'l Symposium on Computer Architecture 1999, Atlanta, GA, USA, May 1999.
8. J. Rabaey. "Low-Power Silicon Architectures for Wireless Communications"; Embedded Tutorial, ASP-DAC 2000, Yokohama, Japan, Jan. 2000
9. R. Hartenstein: "Der Mikroprozessor im Neuen Jahrtausend"; Elektronik, Januar 1000
10. R. Hartenstein (invited paper): The Microprocessor is no more General Purpose: why Future Reconfigurable Platforms will win; Int'l Conf. on Innovative Systems in Silicon, ISIS'97, Austin, Texas, USA, Oct 1997
11. R. Hartenstein, M. Herz, Th. Hoffmann, U. Nageldinger: „Mapping Applications onto Reconfigurable KressArrays"; International Workshop on Field Programmable Logic and Applications, FPL'99, Glasgow, Scotland, August/September 1999.
12. R. Hartenstein, M. Herz, Th. Hoffmann, U. Nageldinger: „Synthesis and Domain-specific Optimization of KressArray-based Reconfigurable Computing Engines", Asia and South Pacific Design Automation Conference, ASP-DAC 2000, Yokohama, Japan, January 2000.
13. R. Kress et al.: „A Datapath Synthesis System for the Reconfigurable Datapath Architecture"; Asia and South Pacific Design Automation Conference, ASP-DAC'95, Makuhari, Chiba, Japan, August 29 - September 1, 1995.
14. R. Hartenstein: "Reconfigurable Computing"; HighSys '99, Sindelfingen, Germany, Oct. 1999

15. C. A. Moritz, D. Yeung, A. Agarwal: „Exploring Optimal Cost-Performance Designs for Raw Microprocessors"; Int'l symposium on FPGAs for Custom Computing Machines, FCCM'98, Napa, CA, April 1998.
16. L. Guerra, M. Potkonjak and J. Rabaey: „A Methodology for Guided Behavioral-Level Optimization"; Proceedings of the 35th Design Automation Conference 1998 (DAC'98), June 15-19, 1998, San Francisco, CA, USA.
17. L. Guerra, M. Potkonjak and J. Rabaey: „System-Level Design Guidance Using Algorithm Properties"; IEEE VLSI Signal Processing Workshop, 1994.
18. W. Pedrycz: „Fuzzy Modelling - Paradigms and Practice"; Kluwer Academic Publishers, 1996.
19. B.R. Gaines: „Foundations of Fuzzy Reasoning"; Int'l Journal of Man-Machine Studies, Vol. 8, 1976.

Mapping of DSP Algorithms on Field Programmable Function Arrays

Paul M. Heysters, Jaap Smit, Gerard J.M. Smit, and Paul J.M. Havinga

University of Twente, depts. Computer Science & Electrical Engineering,
Enschede, the Netherlands
heysters@cs.utwente.nl

Abstract. This position paper[1] discusses reconfigurability issues in low-power hand-held multimedia systems. A *reconfigurable systems-architecture* is introduced, with a focus on a *Field Programmable Function Array* (FPFA). Application domain specific algorithms determine the granularity of FPFA processor tiles. Several algorithms are discussed and mapped onto a FPFA processor tile.

1 Introduction

In the next decade two trends will definitively play a significant role in driving technology: the development and deployment of personal mobile computing devices and the continuing advances in integrated circuit technology. The semiconductor technology will soon allow the integration of one billion transistors on a single chip [1]. This is an exciting opportunity for computer architects and designers; their challenge is to come up with system designs that efficiently use the huge transistor budget and meet the requirements of future applications. The development of personal mobile devices will give an extra dimension, because these devices have a very small energy budget, are small in size but require a performance that exceeds the levels of current desktop computers. The functionality of these mobile computers will be limited by the required energy consumption for communication and computation.

The way out is *energy efficiency:* doing more work with the same amount of energy. Traditionally, designers have been focused on low-power techniques for VLSI design. However, the key to energy efficiency in future mobile multimedia devices will be at the higher levels: energy-efficient system architectures, energy-efficient communication protocols, energy-cognisant operating systems and applications, and a well designed partitioning of functions between wireless device and services on the network.

Mobile computers must remain usable in a variety of environments. They will require a large amount of circuits that can be customized for specific applications to

---

[1] This research is supported by PROGRESS, the embedded systems research program of the Dutch organisation for Scientific Research NWO, the Dutch Ministry of Economic Affairs and the Technology Foundation STW.

stay versatile and competitive. *Reconfigurability* is thus an important requirement for mobile systems, since the mobiles must be flexible enough to accommodate a variety of multimedia services and communication capabilities and adapt to various operating conditions in an (energy) efficient way. Research has shown that adapting continuously the system and protocols can significantly improve the energy efficiency while maintaining a satisfactory level of performance [4].

Reconfigurability also has another more economic motivation: it will be important to have a fast track from sparkling ideas to the final design. If the design process takes too long, the return on investment will be less. It would further be desirable for a wireless terminal to have architectural reconfigurability whereby its capabilities may be modified by downloading new functions from network servers. Such reconfigurability would also help in field upgrading as new communication protocols or standards are deployed, and in implementing bug fixes [3]. One of the key issues in the design of portable multimedia systems is to find a good balance between flexibility and high-processing power on one side, and area and energy-efficiency of the implementation on the other side.

Finally, a major obstacle to designing one billion transistor systems is the physical design complexity, which includes the effort devoted to the design, verification and testing of an integrated circuit. A possible solution is to work with a highly regular structure since they only require the design and replication of a single processor tile and an interconnection structure. We have designed a reconfigurable architecture that is suitable for many DSP-like algorithms and yet is energy-efficient. In this paper we will show how various algorithms map on this architecture.

2 Reconfigurable Systems Architectures

The design of energy efficient hand-held multimedia computers cannot be done in isolation. The energy problem has to be considered at all layers of a system.

The interconnect of a system contributes significantly to the total energy consumption of a system. Experiments have demonstrated that in chip-designs, about 10 to 40% of the total power is dissipated in buses, multiplexers and drivers [5]. This amount can increase dramatically for systems with multiple chips due to large off-chip bus capacitance. Measurements on a Xilinx XC4003 FPGA show that at least 65% of a design's power is dissipated in the collection of interconnect resources and logic cell interface circuitry [3].

Multimedia applications have a high computational complexity. They also have regular and spatially local computations. Exploiting such locality of reference improves the energy efficiency of a system.

With high-speed wireless networks, many different architectural choices become possible, each with different partitioning of functions not only between the resources of the hand-held itself, but also between servers resident in the network. Partitioning is an important architectural decision, which dictates where applications can run, where data can be stored, the complexity of the mobile and the cost of communication services [4].

Our approach to cope with the challenges mentioned above is to have a reconfigurable systems-architecture, in combination with a QoS driven operating system. In our architecture locality of reference is exploited at several levels. The main philosophy used is that operations on data should be done at the place where it is most energy efficient and where it minimizes the required communication. This can be achieved by matching computational and architectural granularity.

In our architecture, we have an organization of a programmable *communication switch* surrounded by several autonomous modules. Modules communicate without involvement of the main processor. For example, an audio stream from the network can be sent directly to the audio module. In a system we differentiate three grain-sizes of operations:

- *fine grained* operations in the modules that perform functions like multiply and addition.
- *medium grained* operations are the functions of the modules. The functional tasks are allocated to dedicated (reconfigurable) modules (e.g. display, audio, network interface, security, etc.) [2].
- *course grained* operations are those tasks that are not specific for a module and that can be performed by the CPU module, or even on a remote compute server. This partitioning is mainly a task of the operating system.

In the remaining part of this paper we will focus on the fine-grained reconfigurable processing modules, and more specifically on the Field Programmable Function Array.

3 Field Programmable Function Array

Field-Programmable Function Arrays (FPFAs) are reminiscent to FPGAs, but have a matrix of ALUs and lookup tables [7] instead of Configurable Logic Blocks (CLBs). Basically the FPFA is a low power, reconfigurable accelerator for an application specific domain. Low power is mainly achieved by exploiting locality of reference. High performance is obtained by exploiting parallelism. A FPFA consists of interconnected *processor tiles*. Multiple processes can coexist in parallel on different tiles. Within a tile multiple data streams can be processed in parallel. Each processor tile contains multiple *reconfigurable ALUs*, local memories, a *control unit* and a *communication unit*. Fig. 1 shows a FPFA with 25 tiles; each tile has five ALUs.

The ALUs on a processor tile are tightly interconnected and are designed to execute the (highly regular) inner loops of an application domain. ALUs on the same tile share a control unit and a communication unit. The ALUs use the locality of reference principle extensively: an ALU loads its operands from neighboring ALU outputs, or from (input) values stored in lookup tables or local registers.

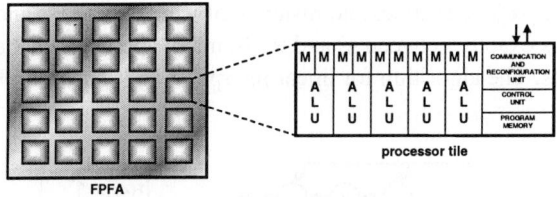

Fig. 1: *FPFA architecture.*

The FPFA concept has a number of advantages:

- The FPFA has a highly regular organisation, it requires the design and replication of a single processor tile, and hence the design and verification is rather straightforward. The verification of the software might be less trivial. Therefore, for less demanding applications we use a general-purpose processor core in combination with a FPFA.
- Its scalability stands in contrast to the dedicated chips designed nowadays. In FPFAs, there is no need for a redesign in order to exploit all the benefits of a next generation CMOS process or the next generation of a standard.
- The FPFA can do media processing tasks such as compression/decompression efficiently. Multimedia applications can for example benefit from such energy-efficient compression by saving (energy-wasting) network bandwidth.

3.1 Typical FPFA Algorithms

In this section we will study several widely used algorithms. These algorithms provide a means to bring together a set of requirements for the functionality of an FPFA-ALU. We will look into some algorithms from the digital signal-processing domain: linear interpolation, finite-impulse response filter and Fast Fourier Transform. Other algorithms of our interest include Viterby decoding, Turbo decoding and various computer graphics algorithms.

Linear Interpolation
It may be convenient (and energy efficient) to use tables for difficult calculations like square roots, division and sine. In order to keep the energy consumption low, such a table should be kept local and small. Interpolation between the function values from a table can be used to approximate a function value that is not in the table. The algorithm works as follows. For a value x ($x_0 \leq x < x_1$), two surrounding function values $F(x_0)$ and $F(x_1)$ are looked up in a table. With these values the in between function value $F(x)$ is calculated with:

$$F(x) = [F(x_1) - F(x_0)] \times x_{fraction} + F(x_0) \qquad (x_0 \leq x < x_1) \qquad (1)$$

$x_{fraction} = (x-x_0)/(x_1-x_0)$ determines the distance of x relative to x_0 and x_1. For example $x_{fraction}$ is ½ if x is exactly between x_0 and x_1. In many applications the $x_{fraction}$ values are known constants. The algorithm for linear interpolation is shown in Fig. 2.

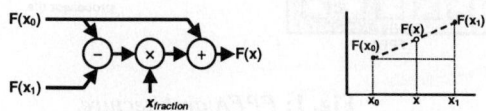

Fig. 2: *Linear interpolation.*

Finite-Impulse Response Filter

The finite-impulse response filter (FIR) is a frequently used algorithm in digital signal processing applications. Fig. 3 shows two implementations of a 4-tap FIR filter.

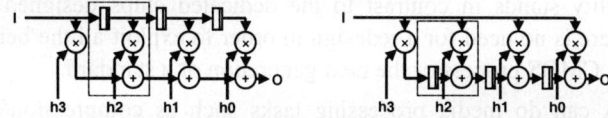

Fig. 3: *FIR filter.*

Each section contains a multiplication, an addition and a delay. As shown in Fig. 3, the left FIR filter uses three inputs and two outputs for every tap. The right FIR filter uses three inputs and one output. However, in the latter case, the input is routed to more than one tap.

Fast Fourier Transform

Fourier transform enables the conversion of signals from the time domain to the frequency domain (and vice versa). For digital signal processing, we are particularly interested in the Discrete Fourier Transform (DFT). The Fast Fourier Transform (FFT) can be used to calculate a DFT efficiently. FFT recursively divides a DFT into smaller DFTs. Eventually only basic DFTs remain. These DFTs have a number of inputs that is equal to the radix of the FFT. This is illustrated in Fig. 4 for a radix 2 FFT with N=8 input signals.

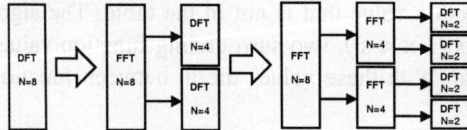

Fig. 4: *Recursion of a radix 2 FFT with 8 inputs.*

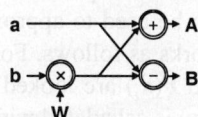

Fig. 5: *The radix 2 FFT butterfly.*

$$A = a + W \times b \equiv (a_{re} + a_{im}) + ((W_{re} \times b_{re} - W_{im} \times b_{im}) + (W_{re} \times b_{im} + W_{im} \times b_{re})_{im})$$
$$B = a - W \times b \equiv (a_{re} + a_{im}) - ((W_{re} \times b_{re} - W_{im} \times b_{im}) + (W_{re} \times b_{im} + W_{im} \times b_{re})_{im}) \quad (2)$$

The resulting basic DFTs can be calculated by a structure called a *butterfly*. The butterfly is the basic element of a FFT. Fig. 5 depicts the radix 2 butterfly; **a** and **b** are complex inputs and **A** and **B** are complex outputs. **W** is a complex constant called the *twiddle factor*. The radix 2 butterfly consists of a complex multiplication, a complex addition and a complex subtraction.

The FFT butterfly depicted in Fig. 5 can be written as Equation (2). A hardware algorithm for the radix 2 FFT butterfly has six inputs ($a_{re}, a_{im}, b_{re}, b_{im}, W_{re}, W_{im}$) and four outputs ($A_{re}, A_{im}, B_{re}, B_{im}$). Each input is used two times. Three subtraction, four multiplication and three addition operations are used.

3.2 ALU Datapath Design

After investigating the functionality required by an application domain, a suitable ALU can be designed. Based upon [9] and [7], we introduce an FPFA-ALU that can be used to implement the algorithms discussed in the previous section. This ALU – which is depicted in Fig. 6 – has 4 inputs (**a, b, c, d**) and 2 outputs (**O1, O2**). The input operands are all 16-bit, 2-complement numbers. The internal ALU datapaths are either 20 or 40 bits wide.

As can be seen in Fig. 6, three different levels can be distinguished in the ALU:

- *Level one* is a reconfigurable function block. The function blocks f_1, f_2 and f_3 in Fig. 6 each can perform five operations: add, subtract, absolute value, minimum and maximum. The result of level one is:

    $$Z1 = f_3(f_1(a,b), f_2(c,d))$$

    This means that most functions with four operands and five operations can be performed, e.g. $Z1 = abs((a+b)-max(c,d))$. The internal operands have a width of 19-bits + a sign-bit.[2]

- *Level two* contains a 19×19-bit unsigned multiplier and a 40-bits wide adder. The multiplier result is thus 38-bits + a sign-bit. An East-West interconnect connects neigbouring ALUs, which makes multiple precision arithmetic possible. A value on the East input can be added to the multiplier result. The result of a multiply-add (Z2) can be used as input for level 3 and for the ALU connected to the West output. We can represent the behaviour of level two as:

    $$Z2 = m_X[a|b|c|d|nop] \times m_Y[a|b|c|d|Z1|nop] [+|-] m_E[0:c|c:0|0:d|d:0|c:d|E|0|nop]$$

    m_X, m_Y and m_E are multiplexers (the output is one of its parameters and a colon denotes concatenation). In algorithms that do not use a multiply-add operation, the *nop* options can be used to bypass level 2.

---

[2] The carry signals are propagated to neigbouring ALUs to support extended precision of the operands. For clarity reasons these carry signals are *not* depicted in Fig. 6.

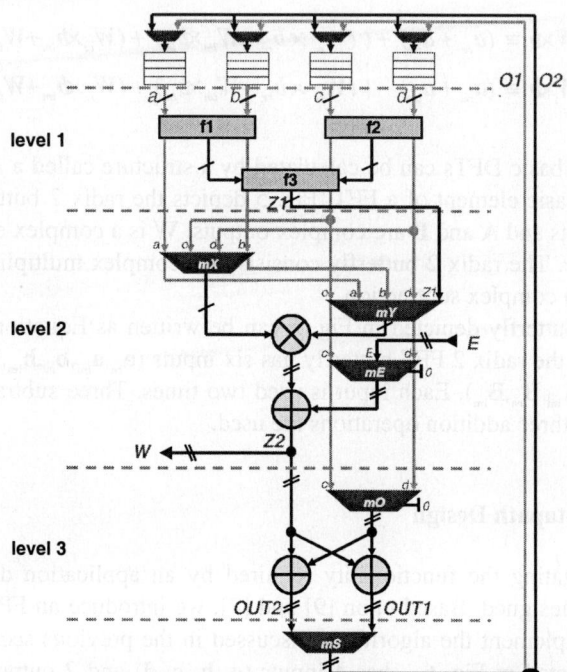

Fig. 6: *ALU datapath design.*

- *Level three* can be used as a 40-bit wide adder or as a butterfly structure:

   $OUT2 = m_o[0|c:0|0:c|d:0|0:d|c:d|nop] - Z2$
   $OUT1 = m_o[0|c:0|0:c|d:0|0:d|c:d|nop] + Z2$

   OUT2 and *OUT1* are both 40-bit wide.

The final multiplexer (m_s) selects which two 20-bit results are written back into the registers via its outputs **O1** and **O2**.

3.3 Processor Tile Datapath Design

A FPFA processor tile in Fig. 1 consists of five identical blocks, which share a control unit and a communication unit. An individual block contains an ALU, two memories and four register banks of four 20-bit wide registers. Because of the locality of reference principle, each ALU has two local memories. Each memory has 256 16-bit entries. A crossbar-switch makes flexible routing between the ALUs, registers and memories possible. Fig. 7 shows the crossbar interconnect between five blocks. This interconnect enables an ALU to write-back to any register or memory within a tile.

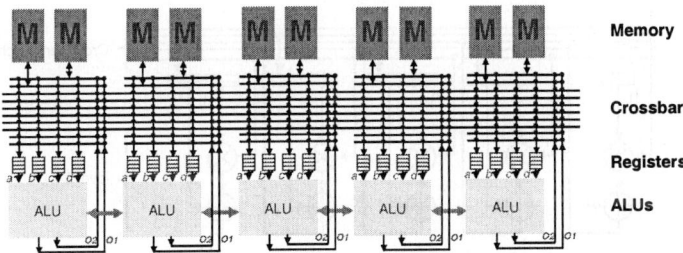

Fig. 7: *Crossbar-switch.*

Five blocks per processor tile seems reasonable. With five blocks there are ten memories available. This is convenient for the FFT algorithm, which has six inputs and four outputs. Also, we now have the ability to use 5×16=80-bit wide numbers, which enable us to use floating-point numbers (although some additional hardware is required). Some algorithms, like the FIR filter, can benefit substantially from additional ALUs. With five ALUs, a five-tap FIR filter can be implemented efficiently. The fifth ALU can also be used for complex address calculations and other control purposes.

3.4 Mapping of Algorithms

The FPFA-ALU has been designed with well-know DSP algorithms in mind. As an example, we will show how the algorithms presented in Section 3.1 can be mapped on the FPFA.

Linear Interpolation

The linear interpolation algorithm of equation (1) can be mapped to the ALU depicted in Fig. 6. Assume that operands $F(x_0)$, $F(x_1)$, and $x_{fraction}$ are available at inputs **d**, **c** and **a** respectively. Then $F(x) = [c - d] \times a + d$, which is calculated with the following behaviour:

$Z1 = c\text{-}d$
$Z2 = a \times Z1 + 0{:}d$
$OUT1 = Z2$

Finite-Impulse Response Filter

Fig. 8 shows the implementation for a five-tap finite-impulse response filter. When the FIR filter is started, every clock cycle an additional ALU is used, until all five ALUs are in use. Thus, the first result is ready after five clock cycles. Every subsequent cycle returns the next result.

Fast Fourier Transform

Fig. 9 shows how the FFT butterfly of Equation (2) can be calculated on four FPFA-ALUs.

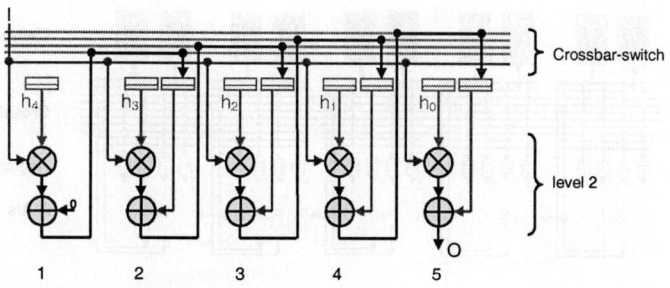

Fig. 8: *Five-tap finite-impulse response filter.*

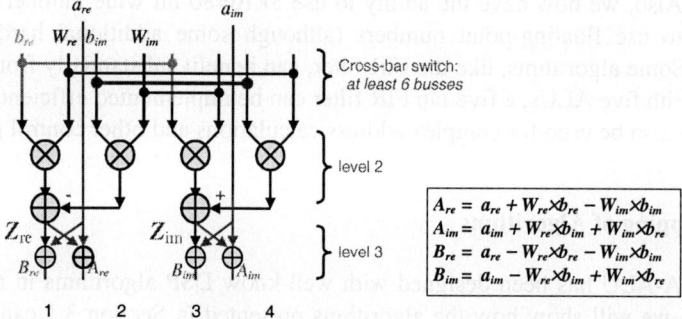

$$A_{re} = a_{re} + W_{re} \times b_{re} - W_{im} \times b_{im}$$
$$A_{im} = a_{im} + W_{re} \times b_{im} + W_{im} \times b_{re}$$
$$B_{re} = a_{re} - W_{re} \times b_{re} - W_{im} \times b_{im}$$
$$B_{im} = a_{im} - W_{re} \times b_{im} + W_{im} \times b_{re}$$

Fig. 9: *The radix 2 FFT butterfly.*

4 Discussion and Related Work

We intend to implement an energy-efficient mobile system based on the (reconfigurable) architecture presented in Section 2. Consequently, a whole new QoS model that can balance issues like energy budget, required performance and communication costs is required. We are also working on operating system extensions for energy efficiency. The operating system has to provide the flexibility required by the QoS model and it must exploit the flexibility of the systems architecture. The FPFA is part of the systems architecture. We believe that the architecture of the FPFA implies a good energy-efficiency. The minimization of the energy consumption of an architecture like the FPFA requires that the energy consumption due to arithmetic (logic), communication (wiring) and data storage (RAM) be balanced. It is shown in [8] how these concepts can be balanced to find a lower bound for the energy consumption of the FFT. We applied the design concepts again to design the FPFA such that it is energy efficient for a wide class of signal processing applications. In our current research, we are investigating the energy efficiency of various algorithms when executing on a FPFA architecture. We plan to build an experimental chip after we have demonstrated the efficiency of the architecture and evaluated various architectural alternatives. The interconnection network between the processor tiles is another topic of research.

To support a wide range of algorithms requires a lot of flexibility in the ALU. This has particular impact on level one of the FPFA-ALU datapath. The control of level one would require 15 control bits per ALU. To save on control bits, and to have more flexibility, we plan to implement the level one functionality by a reconfigurable block that is similar to Xilinx CLBs [11]. This also gives us the possibility to do bit-level logic functions. Having a reconfigurable block in level one means that the functionality of the ALU becomes partly reconfigurable. Note that such a reconfigurable block must be configured before the ALU can be used.

Unfortunately, space restrictions restrain us from giving a literature overview of the impetuous area of reconfigurable systems-architecture. However, we do want to mention the *Raw architecture* [10] of MIT and the *Imagine stream architecture* [6]. Raw has a mesh of identical processor tiles. Each tile has a tile processor, a static switch processor and a dynamic router. The tile processor is related to a 32-bit MIPS processor. The RAW group abandoned the idea to include reconfigurable logic in their processor tile, mainly because of the added complexity of the reconfigurable logic, its interface, and the software interface.

We distinguished three vertical levels in the ALU datapath. There are also architectures that use a horizontal approach, such as the Imagine stream architecture. This architecture has clusters of functional units. One cluster can for example contain three adders, two multipliers, one divide/square root unit, one 128-entry scratch-pad register file and one communication unit. All functional units in a cluster are connected to busses and can operate in parallel. In this architecture a multiply-add is performed by first completing a multiply and subsequently sending the result to an adder. So, the delay of a multiply-add is equal to the sum of the delay of a multiply and the delay of an addition. In our ALU, the multiplication and additions of level two and three can be done largely in parallel. This is illustrated in Fig. 10. The lesser significant bits of the result of a multiplier are known (or stable) prior to the more significant bits. As soon as the next bit of the multiplication result is known, the adder can calculate the next bit of its result. Clearly, the delay increase of a multiply-add in a leveled ALU is smaller than the delay of an individual addition.

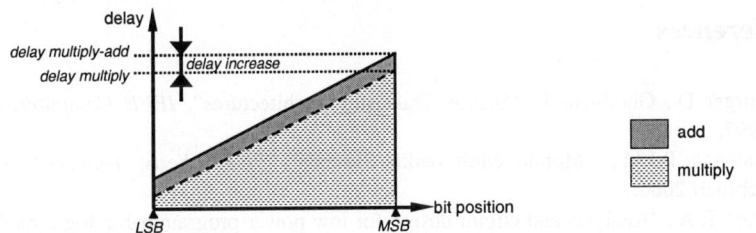

Fig. 10: *Delay increase for vertical leveled multiply-add operation.*

A vertically leveled ALU has a relatively long signal propagation time, which implies a relatively slow clock. The slower clock is a tradeoff; a vertically leveled ALU requires less clock ticks for particular operations (like the multiply-add) than a flat ALU. We showed above, that the FPFA-ALU can perform very complex functions in just one clock-tick.

The multiply-add functionality of level two of the ALU is not required for every algorithm (e.g. Viterby decoding). An unused multiplier consumes chip area and might even consume some energy. However, if we omit the multiplier, a severe performance penalty has to be paid for the algorithms that do require a multiplication. In future one billion transistor chip designs, the area of a multiplier is small compared to the area used for communication and local memory. Therefore, we believe that the benefits outweigh the penalty and that a multiply-add unit should be integrated in the FPFA-ALU. However, when not used, the multiply-add unit should not consume much energy.

5 Conclusion

The introduced FPFA architecture is aimed at fine-grained operations in hand-held multimedia computers. The architecture has a low design complexity, is scalable and can execute various algorithms energy efficiently, while maintaining a satisfactory level of performance. Several non-trivial algorithms have been mapped successfully on the FPFA processor tile. Examples from the digital signal-processing domain include linear interpolation, FIR filter and FFT.

In contrast to the FPFA, which is aimed at fine-grained 16-bit wide operations, the FPGA is aimed at bit level logic functions. As a consequence, operations like multiply-add are relatively expensive on a FPGA (i.e. they take a large area and thus consume a large amount of energy).

The ALU of a FPFA processor tile has four input operands. Most standard ALUs have two input operands. The extra inputs increase the functionality of the ALU and enable it to compute powerful functions like the linear interpolation efficiently.

The FPFA design has still many open issues, which include the control of a processor tile and the interconnect between processor tiles.

References

1. Burger D., Goodman J., "Billion-Transistor Architectures", *IEEE Computer*, September 1997.
2. Havinga P.J.M., "Mobile Multimedia Systems", *Ph.D. thesis, University of Twente*, Februari 2000.
3. Kuse E.A., "Analysis and circuit design for low power programmable logic modules", *Ms. Thesis, University of California at Berkeley*, December 1997.
4. Lettieri P., Srivastava M.B., "Advances in wireless terminals", *IEEE Personal Communications*, pp. 6-19, February 1999.

5. Mehra R., Rabaey J., "Exploiting regularity for low-power design", *proceedings of the international Conference on computer-aided design*, 1996.
6. Rixner S., Dally W.J., et al, "A Bandwith-Efficient Architecture for Media Processing", *Micro-31*, 1998.
7. Smit J., et al, "Low Cost & Fast Turnaround: Reconfigrable Graph-Based Execution Units", *Proceedings Belsign Workshop*, 1998.
8. Smit J., Huijsken, J.A, "On the energy complexity of the FFT", *Proceedings of the Patmos Conference, Oldenberg, Germany*, 1995.
9. Stekelenburg M., "Optimization of a Field Programmable Function Array", *Ms. thesis, University of Twente*, March 1999.
10. Taylor M., "The Raw Prototype Design Document", *Massachusetts Institute of Technology*, V1.3, February, 2000.
11. Xilinx, "Virtex^{tm}-E 1.8V Field Programmable Gate Arrays", *Advance Product Specification*, December, 1999.

On Availability of Bit-Narrow Operations in General-Purpose Applications

Darko Stefanović and Margaret Martonosi

Department of Electrical Engineering
Princeton University
Princeton NJ 08544, USA
{darko,mrm}@ee.princeton.edu

Abstract. Program instructions that consume and produce small operands can be executed in hardware circuitry of less than full size. We compare different proposed models of accounting for the usefulness of bit-positions in operands, using a run-time profiling tool, both to observe and summarize operand values, and to reconstruct and analyze the program's data-flow graph to discover useless bits. We find that under aggressive models, the average number of useful bits per integer operand is as low as 10, not only in kernels but also in general-purpose applications from SPEC95.

1 Introduction

The purpose of a *bit-set analysis* is to identify which bit positions in various values computed by a program carry essential information and which do not, and, consequently, which bit positions must be computed by instructions and which do not. A typical programming language does not allow one to express bit usage requirements, hence in a compile-time analysis they must be inferred by the compiler. A typical RISC instruction set is too crude to express arbitrary bit usage requirements (at most, it may express a few fixed sub-words), hence in a run-time analysis these requirements must be re-derived from the executing program. Once useful bit-sets are identified for each value, it may become possible to simplify the hardware that implements the program's instructions so that it will produce only the useful bit-sets. With luck, the smaller circuitry will also be faster; and, fitting a larger number of smaller circuits in the same silicon area allows potentially higher execution parallelism. Our goal is ultimately to apply the results as one of the criteria for code partitioning in hybrid fixed-configurable processors.

2 Background

In the early days of computing, narrow-width computation was available in hardware and programmers could write code by hand to exploit it. The integer types of C still support this at the programming language level, albeit in an ill-defined and non-portable manner. With the advent of RISC processors, uniform, word-width operation became the norm; and only recently have we seen support for sub-word operations again, in the multimedia extensions to RISC instruction sets.

During the last decade there has been interest in detecting and exploiting narrow operations through compiler analysis. Razdan and Smith [1, 2, 3] proposed a static analysis to narrow widths for use with a tightly-coupled configurable functional unit. Their analysis is a bit-wise abstract interpretation over the bit positions of each variable in an internal representation of the program, with forward and backward passes to characterize the generation and the use of bit positions.

More recently, Stephenson, Babb, and Amarasinghe [4], and independently Budiu, Goldstein, Sakr, and Walker [5] have constructed static analyses to identify narrow computation, for use in various settings. Stephenson's analysis *Bitwise* is an abstract interpretation that computes data ranges: the minimum and maximum value that may be assumed by variables in an internal representation based on SUIF [6]. This interval analysis is equipped with useful heuristics for recognizing loop induction patterns. It is integrated with powerful pointer and alias analyses [7]. Bit-width savings are reported to be 15–80% (static count) on a set of small (kernel) programs. In conjunction with silicon compilation, it achieves up to 86% reduction in silicon area on some programs.

Budiu's analysis *BitValue* is primarily a bit-wise analysis, somewhat similar to Razdan and Smith's, but it explicitly treats constantness (forward pass) and uselessness (backward pass). It operates on an internal representation, also based on SUIF. Underlying analyses (such as the alias analysis which affects recognized data dependences) are not as sophisticated as in *Bitwise*. *BitValue* analysis optionally includes an ad-hoc loop induction analysis. With both turned on, bit-set savings on the order of 29% (static count) and 30% (dynamic count) are reported on a set of programs from SPEC95 and Mediabench.

Brooks and Martonosi [8], on the other hand, use dynamic profiling to observe the set of operands presented to individual arithmetic instructions. Under the assumption that each operand's high-order bits can be elided to a single sign bit, they find that significant savings are possible in the number of bits needed for the representation, and in integer unit's consumed power, as much as 60%.

In short, previous research has demonstrated the availability of bit-narrow operands. However, different studies have assumed different definitions of which bit positions are useful. For instance, should only high-order bits be considered as potentially useless; or, should bits proven constant by analysis be considered useless; or, what is the granularity of usefulness decisions? As a result the effectiveness of different compile-time analyses cannot be compared, nor can the different definitions be compared. In this study we use run-time knowledge of observed values, so that our precision is a bound on that achievable by compile-time analyses. We are then able to compare different definitions of which bits are useful, and how they are tallied.

Our run-time program analysis incorporates data-flow graph reconstruction and propagation of bit-use information backward in the graph, which allows the elimination of bits as unused, unlike with instruction-by-instruction observations [8]. Since this feature can be turned on or off, we can evaluate the effectiveness of such an analysis.

The broader purpose of the tools built is to discover bit-narrow operands in general-purpose applications, their prevalence being one of the criteria for the selection of code sections for implementation in configurable hardware.

3 Run-Time Program Analysis

3.1 Data-Flow Reconstruction

The front-end of our tool is a modified version of the *sim-profile* tool of the SimpleScalar architectural simulation toolset [9], for the Alpha instruction set architecture as target (including multi-media extensions). We track the flow of data through an architecture's functional and storage units, and dynamically construct a data-flow graph. Our basic notion is that of a *value*: an instruction uses a number of input values and produces a number of output values. With each value we record the observed register contents—the raw bits of the value.

A value has a *type*, which is inferred dynamically from its usage. Ideally the type of a value is resolved to *integer* or *floating-point*. Occasionally this is not possible, so the type lattice includes the elements integer, floating-point, unknown, and conflict.

We keep track of a program's state, including both registers and memory. Each register contains at most one value. Registers that a program has not touched contain no value. When an instruction creates an output value and stores it in a register, we note that the register contains that value. When an instruction reads an input value from a register, we retrieve the value contained in the register. However, if no value is currently contained in the register, we make a fresh value: this allows tracking to start from initial externally defined register contents (and to restart after a system call). Memory on the Alpha is both byte-addressable and byte-accessible. Our memory model is a mapping from byte addresses to pairs: $a \mapsto \langle v, i \rangle$, where i is the offset of the byte at memory address a within a stored value v. A store instruction causes the mapping to be updated for a number of successive addresses. At any given time, a value is said to have a register presence if it is contained in any register, and to have a memory presence if any of its constituent bytes have a presence anywhere in memory.

The instructions executed by the program are represented by instruction *nodes*. Each node indicates the program address of the instruction, its class and opcode, and its input and output values. Unlike operation nodes in compilers, this is a run-time concept, and each dynamic execution of an instruction results in a distinct node. No instruction nodes are created for instructions identifiable as data transport: register moves and memory loads. In the case of memory loads, this means that the retrieved bytes are checked to see if they exactly match one entire stored value. The values are appropriately bypassed from the producing node to the ultimate using node. Thus the data flow of the computation is reconstructed independent of the data storage decisions and layout.

While instructions are simulated, new nodes and values are added to the graph. Bit-set analysis is performed on the oldest values, and upon analysis, the oldest values (and their nodes) are discarded. The difference between the oldest and the newest nodes, i.e., the lookahead that the bit-set analysis enjoys, also determines the amount of storage the simulator needs and its speed of simulation. With the current prototype implementation we can achieve lookaheads of a few million instructions.

3.2 Bit-Set Analysis

Our bit-set analysis comprises two independent components: analysis of the dynamic data-flow graph, and computation of a static summary.

The goal of dynamic data-flow graph analysis is to infer that certain bit positions of the analyzed values are not needed for subsequent computation. The main source of such information, in the Alpha instruction set, are logic instructions. For instance, consider an instruction SRL r1, 8, r2, which shifts the contents of r1 by 8 bits and stores the result in r2, and suppose that this instruction is the only use of the value present in r1. The instruction shifts the uppermost 7 bytes of r1 into the lowermost 7 bytes of r2, and writes zeroes into the uppermost byte of r2. The lowermost byte of r1 is discarded: it is not useful in this instruction. Since this instruction is the only use of the value in r1, the lowermost byte of that value need not be computed at all. The information flow in this analysis is backward: all the uses of a value, and their subsequent uses, etc., affect which bits of the value are truly needed. In case of finite lookahead, we conservatively assume that all values that have a presence (in registers or memory) at the time of analysis will have all their bits used by future computation. The result of dynamic data-flow graph analysis is an annotation *useful/useless* on the bits of each dynamic value.

We compute a static summary over all executions of each static instruction in the program, more precisely, of each operand of each static instruction. By observing the bit-values (0 or 1) assumed by a bit-position of an operand over all executions, we annotate a bit-positions with *Always-0* or *Always-1* if it is constant over all executions. If dynamic data-flow graph analysis is performed, we also statically summarize its results and annotate a bit-position with *Sometimes-useful* if it is useful on any execution. If dynamic data-flow graph analysis is not performed, *Sometimes-useful* is assumed for all bit-positions.

3.3 How Many Bits Are Useful: Definitions

Various bit-set analyses are meaningful only in the context of particular *assumptions* made about the hardware. Because of the static-summarizing step, our analyses are only valid under the assumption that the hardware executing a given static instruction remains unchanged for the duration of the program. This is by no means a universal assumption, but a reasonable one.

While the annotations *Always-0*, *Always-1*, and *Sometimes-useful* are convenient for computing the static summary, in interpreting the results it is more convenient to convert to a three-way classification of bits into N: never useful; C: sometimes useful and constant; and V: sometimes useful but not constant.

We offer several definitions that describe which bits are considered *useless* in an operand:
- Definition 1 (bit-wise, optimistic): All N and C bits. This definition reflects the savings possible in configurable hardware. In addition to eliminating all reference to outputs marked N, a circuit can be synthesized to provide C outputs as hard-wired 0 or 1. C inputs can be used directly to simplify the circuit description. (It is instructive to consider the interaction of the savings inferred in program analysis, and those in subsequent circuit synthesis [4].)
- Definition 2 (bit-wise, less optimistic): All N bits. If joint synthesis of circuit implementations corresponding to larger data-flow subgraphs is not possible, then wires carrying 0s and 1s, though known constants, are necessary, and this definition models that cost.

- Definition 3 (prefix bit-wise, optimistic): All leading N or C bits. This definition reflects the fact that customizing circuits to take advantage of isolated known-constant bits may not be as practical as generating a family of circuits for any operand width. (Particularly true when we consider narrow functional units for inclusion in a non-configurable processor.) Thus, only high-order bits are considered useless, leaving a contiguous string of useful low-order bits.
- Definition 4 (prefix bit-wise, less optimistic): All leading N bits. This definition is conservative both in the sense of definition 2 and of definition 3.
- Definition 5 (data range): All leading sign bits but one. This definition assumes that hardware circuits for widening (with sign extension) are inserted where necessary. In other words, useful bits are those needed for the 2's complement representation of the observed data range, exactly as in [8], and analogous to statically inferred data ranges in [4].

The definitions described which bits were considered useless; all *remaining* bits are useful, and are counted towards the totals we report in the results.

4 Experimental Setup

Our initial focus was on the Raw benchmark suite, in order to compare the results with those of [4]. We also examined a number of longer-running benchmarks, including SPEC95 (both integer and floating-point) and Honeywell ACS [10] suites. We summarize the relevant program characteristics in Table 1. The columns for integer operands refer to the integer values identified and analyzed by our tools.

Benchmarks were compiled on a Compaq (Digital) Alpha 21164 EV56 machine using native C and Fortran optimizing compilers. Each benchmark was simulated using our run-time analysis extensions to SimpleScalar/Alpha. The lookahead size was limited by the memory capacity of the simulator host machine and the memory overhead of the simulator to about 1.5 million instructions. This was sufficient to encompass entire executions of all but one Raw benchmark.

Results are reported for all integer operands. Whereas a bit-wise analysis can infer that certain bits are constant in floating-point operands, this is more difficult to exploit, and is generally eschewed for configurable hardware.

5 Results

Average bit requirements are shown in Figure 1, for the unweighted average, and in Figure 2 for the average weighted by each instruction's execution count. For each benchmark, seven bars are shown with average bit requirements computed according to different analysis modes. In order from the bottom upward in the graph: *def1/bp:* definition 1 of Section 3.3, with dynamic analysis ("back-propagation") as described in Section 3.2; *def2/bp:* definition 2 with dynamic analysis; *def3/bp:* definition 3 with dynamic analysis; *def4/bp:* definition 4 with dynamic analysis; *def1:* definition 1 without dynamic analysis; *def3:* definition 3 without dynamic analysis; *def5:* definition 5 (which does not involve dynamic analysis). To make the chart legible, we included only three of the 16 Raw benchmarks; the ones not shown behave similarly to *sor*.

Table 1. Properties of benchmarks.

Benchmark	Description	Source lines	Instructions executed	Integer operands (static)	Integer operands (dynamic)
Raw					
adpcm	Multimedia: audio compression	195	288672	1309	584829
bubblesort	Dense matrix	62	2993603	1211	7015682
convolve	Multimedia	74	34248	1383	71967
edge-detect	Multimedia	175	151124	1875	289721
histogram	Multimedia	115	862026	1416	2040775
intfir	Multimedia: Integer FIR filter	64	381020	1160	855144
intmatmul	Dense matrix: matrix multiplication	78	602363	1218	1472609
jacobi	Dense matrix	84	30652	1166	68270
life	Automata: Conway's game of life	150	1460919	1716	3552042
median	Multimedia: median filter	86	745383	1308	1347242
mpegcorr	Multimedia: kernel from MPEG-3	144	25958	1383	63115
newlife	Automata: Conway's game of life	119	736575	1627	1890671
parity	Multimedia	54	313236	1128	751227
pmatch	Multimedia: pattern matching	63	1403699	1178	3263404
sha	Encryption: secure hash algorithm	638	1030098	6572	3007709
sor	Dense matrix: Successive overrelaxation	60	1026951	1300	2516264
Honeywell					
microkernel	Two-dimensional discrete cosine tranform	169	248322172	7606	412699970
timing	CORDIC vector rotation algorithm	219	58295213	7627	104040721
versatility.compress	Wavelet image compression algorithm	528	56202163	8343	113693092
SPECint95 (train inputs)					
126.gcc-jump	GNU C compiler (jump.i input)	133049	202205526	150516	268594145
129.compress	Adaptive Lempel-Ziv coding	1422	46186413	6069	83526455
130.li	LISP interpreter running the Gabriel benchmarks	4323	192134942	9343	251585142

The kernels from Raw overall have very low bit requirements by any measure, with the exception of *sha* (which by design constructs numbers spread wide over the integer range). Larger programs from the Honeywell and SPEC95 suites tend to have higher bit requirements. These average bit requirements numbers could, in principle, be compared against those reported from static analyses, as in *Bitwise* and *BitValue*, with the expectation that our run-time analysis represents the limit to which the compile-time analysis may aspire; however, differences in the context of analysis preclude a *direct* numerical comparison.

In addition to averages, the distribution of bit requirements is of interest. For two characteristic programs, the *life* kernel from the Raw suite, and the *gcc* compiler, it is shown in Figures 3 and 4. We divide possible bit requirements into bins for 0, 1, 2, 3–4, 5–8, 9–16, 17–32, and 33–64 bits, and display them as a stacked bar graph. Each of the seven analysis modes results in a different bar; and again the operands may be counted (a) statically or (b) dynamically.[1]

In the average bit requirement plots, as well as in the detailed distributions, we note that models *def1/bp* and *def3/bp* produce nearly identical results; and similarly models *def2/bp* and *def4/bp*; and models *def1* and *def3*. Thus, the restriction of useless bits to the high-order prefix is of little significance.

---

[1] Drawing the seven exact distribution curves is less informative visually, because some of them are too close to one another to be discernible.

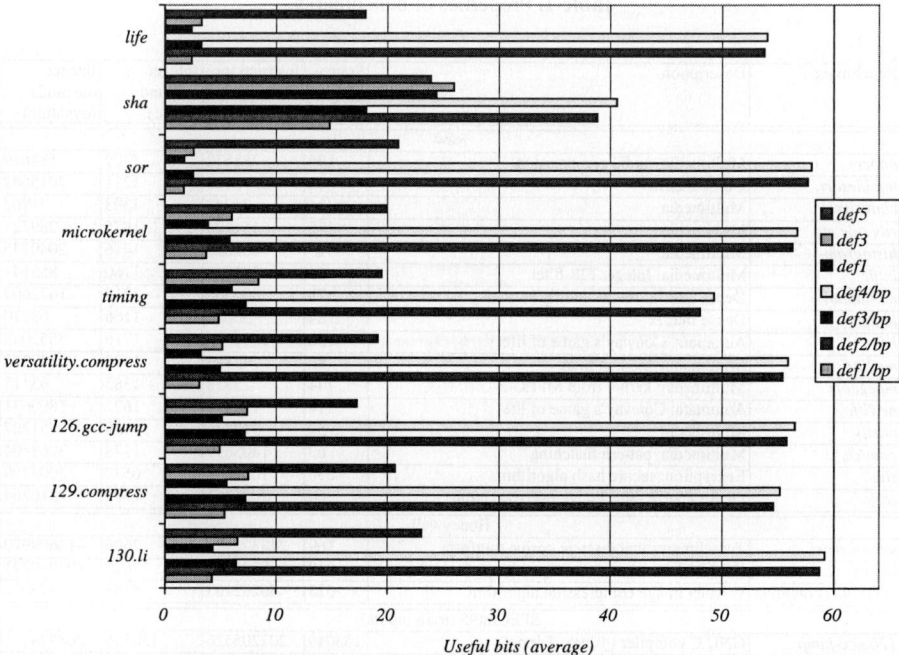

Fig. 1. Average useful bits, static operand count

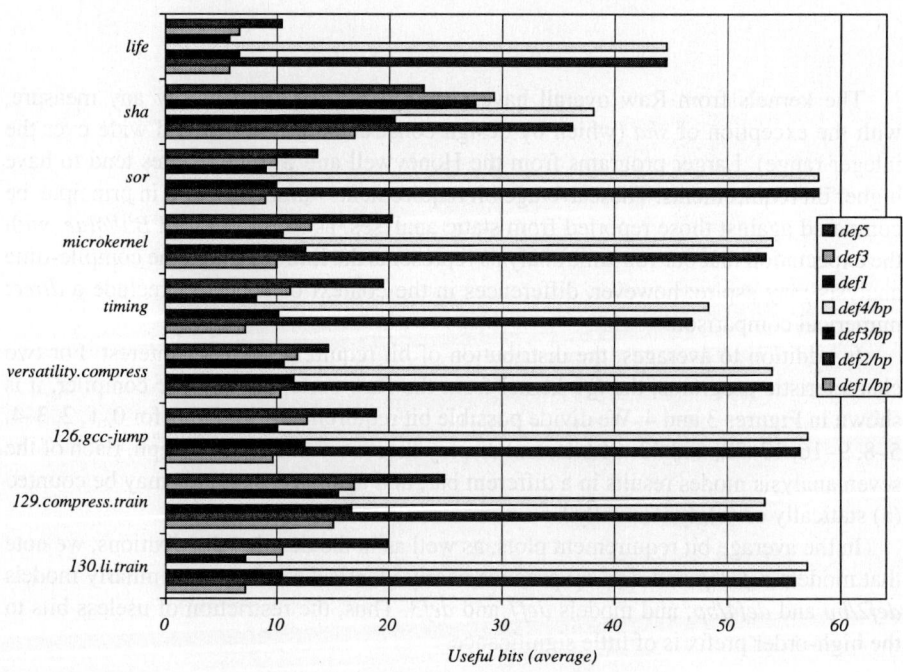

Fig. 2. Average useful bits, dynamic operand count

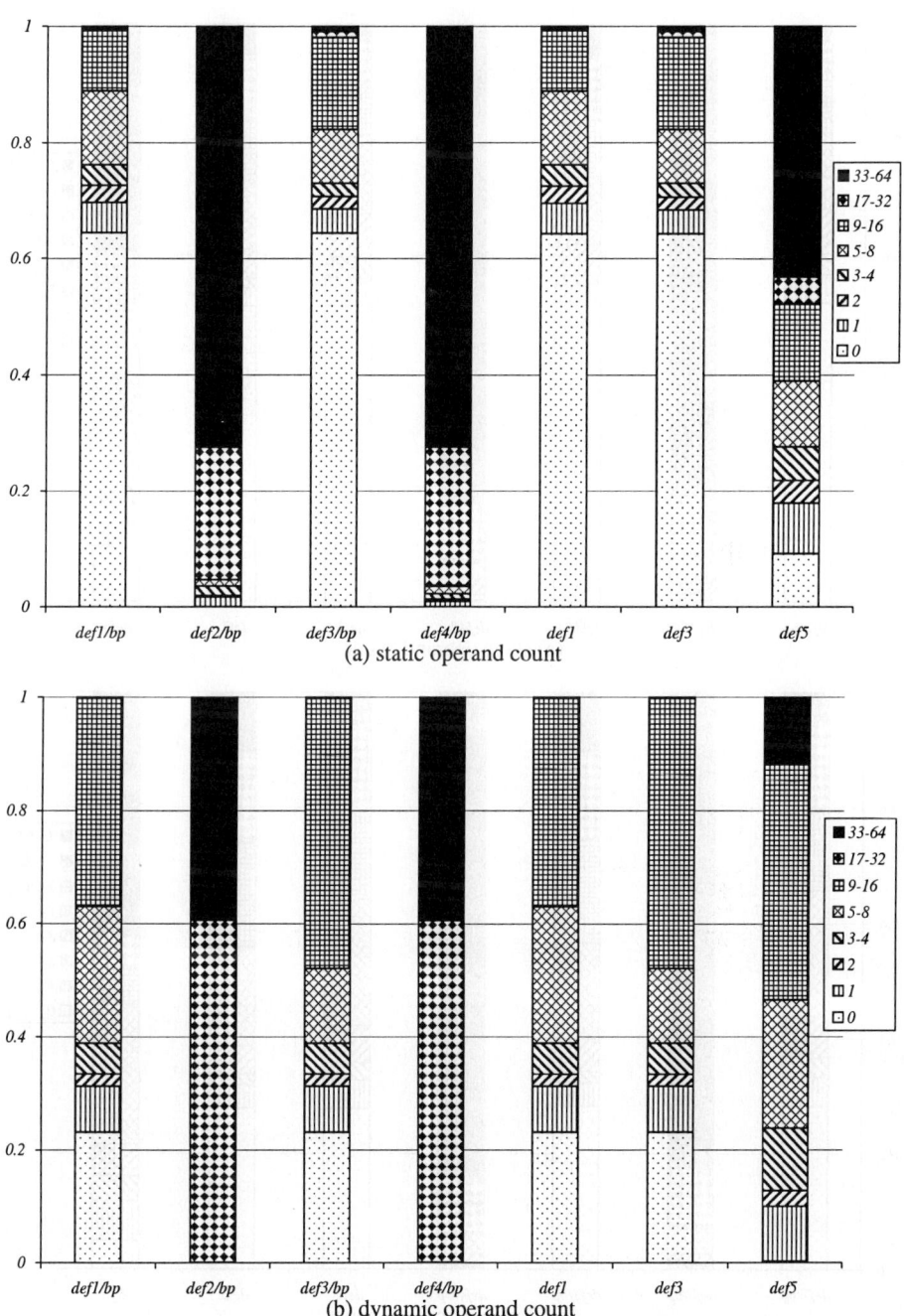

Fig. 3. Benchmark *life*: bit requirements distribution

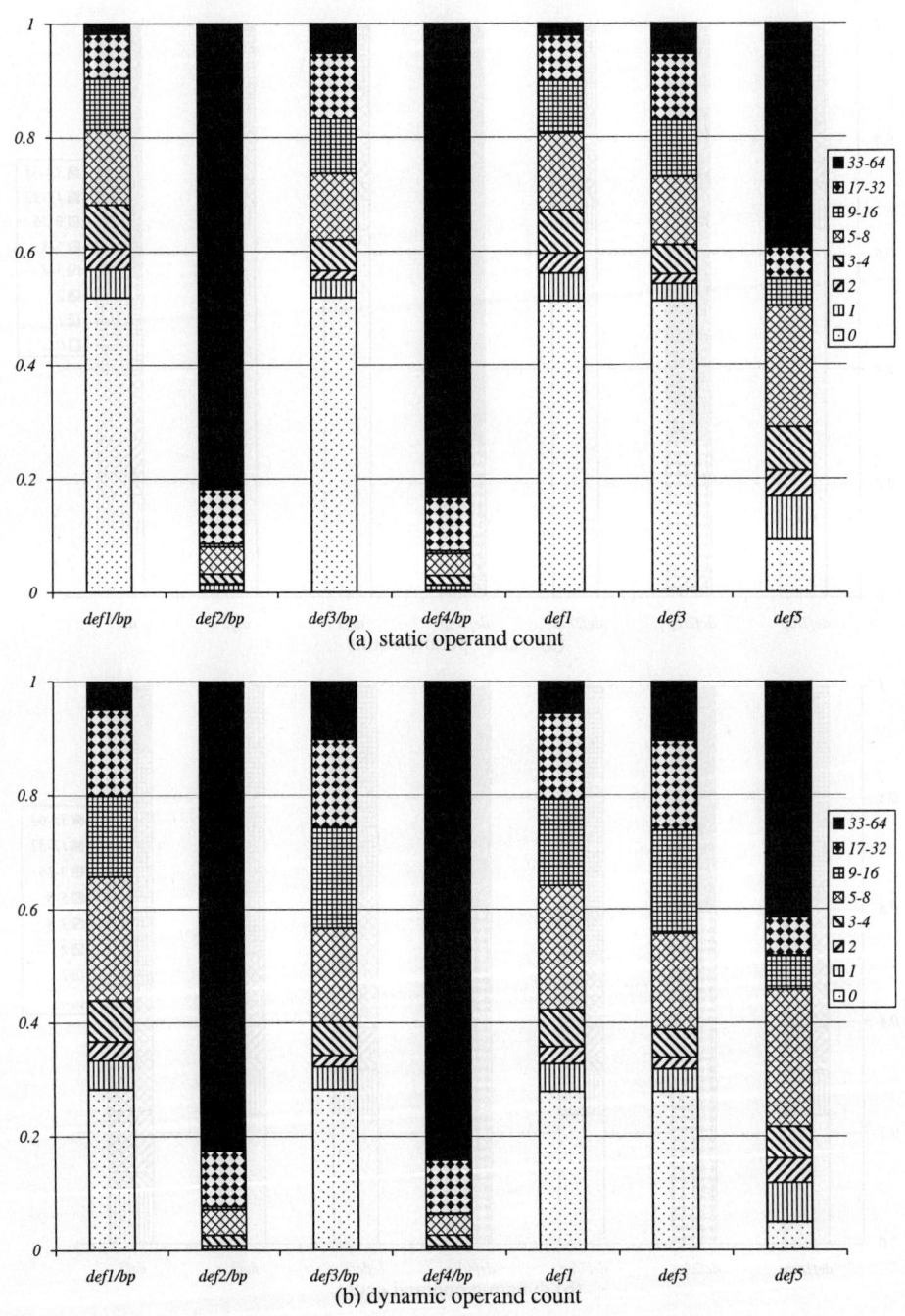

Fig. 4. Benchmark *126.gcc-jump*: bit requirements distribution

Comparing *def1/bp* with *def1*, or *def3/bp* with *def3*, we see that the additional savings that backward-propagated operand-use information gives are very small. This becomes quite clear when we compare *def1/bp* with *def2/bp*, or *def3/bp* with *def4/bp*, where we see that using constantness information makes a huge difference; models *def2/bp* and *def4/bp* make use *only* of the backward-propagated operand-use information, and this is scant.

Lastly, definition 5 is typically weaker than either 1 or 3, i.e., it considers more bits as useful. In light of the fact that greater savings are reported [4] from a static analysis using definition 5 than from another static analysis [5] using definition 3, we draw the conclusion that the difference in savings is not due to the use of differing definitions, but either to a more powerful compile-time analyses preceding the analysis of bit-sets, or to significantly different operand accounting.

To summarize, the number of bits that can be saved other than in the high-order prefix is small, by any definition. Analysis using backward flow over the dynamically reconstructed data-flow graph is not very powerful in inferring that bit-positions are not needed. The constantness information from observed operand values is much more informative.[2]

Acknowledgments. We would like to thank Jonathan Babb for valuable discussions on the design of *Bitwise* as well as for allowing us the use of the Raw benchmark suite. We thank David Brooks, Zhen Luo, and the anonymous reviewers for their comments.

References

[1] R. Razdan. *PRISC: Programmable Reduced Instruction Set Computers*. PhD thesis, Harvard University, Cambridge, Massachusetts, 1994.
[2] R. Razdan and M. D. Smith. A high-performance microarchitecture with hardware-programmable functional units. In *Micro-27*, Nov. 1994.
[3] R. Razdan, K. Brace, and M. D. Smith. PRISC software acceleration techniques. In *Proc. Int'l Conf. on Computer Design*, pages 145–149, Oct. 1994.
[4] M. Stephenson, J. Babb, and S. Amarasinghe. Bitwidth analysis with application to silicon compilation. In *PLDI 2000*, Vancouver, BC, June 2000.
[5] M. Budiu, S. C. Goldstein, M. Sakr, and K. Walker. BitValue inference: Detecting and exploiting narrow bitwidth computations. In *EuroPar 2000*, Munich, Germany, 2000.
[6] M. W. Hall, J. M. Anderson, S. P. Amarasinghe, B. R. Murphy, S.-W. Liao, E. Bugnion, and M. S. Lam. Maximizing multiprocessor performance with the SUIF compiler. *IEEE Computer*, Dec. 1996.
[7] J. Babb, M. Rinard, A. Moritz, W. Lee, M. Frank, R. Barua, and S. Amarasinghe. Parallelizing applications into silicon. In *FCCM '99*, Napa Valley, CA, Apr. 1999.
[8] D. Brooks and M. Martonosi. Dynamically exploiting narrow width operands to improve processor power and performance. In *5th HPCA*, Jan. 1999.
[9] D. Burger and T. M. Austin. The SimpleScalar tool set, version 2.0. *Computer Architecture News*, pages 13–25, June 1997.
[10] S. Kumar. Benchmarking tools and assessment environment for configurable computing. Submitted by Honeywell Technology Center to USA Intelligence Center and Fort Huachuca under Contract No. DABT63-96-C-0085, Sept. 1999.

---

[2]The corresponding compile-time backward analysis may be *relatively* more powerful, because the static inference of operand values is weaker.

A Comparison of FPGA Implementations of Bit-Level and Word-Level Matrix Multipliers

Radhika S. Grover, Weijia Shang, and Qiang Li

Department of Computer Engineering, Santa Clara University,
Santa Clara, CA, U.S.A.
rgrover@scudc.scu.edu
{wshang,qli}@sunrise.scu.edu

Abstract. We have implemented a novel bit-level matrix multiplier on a Xilinx FPGA chip where each processing element does a simple operation of adding three to six bits to generate one partial sum bit and one to two carryout bits. The speedup over word-level is possible because individual bits of a word do not have to be processed as a unit in a bit-level architecture. It is shown in a previous work that bit-level architectures for fixed point applications can be O(log p) times faster than the corresponding word-level architecture where p is the word length. In this paper we implemented the bit-level matrix multiplier on a Xilinx FPGA chip that is compared to a word-level matrix multiplier composed of highly optimized multiplier and adder macros available in the Xilinx Core generator library. The architecture presented in this paper is even faster than previous ones by breaking the critical path in the dependence graph into half. Our results show that speedup by a factor of 2 can be obtained in practice.

1 Introduction

Bit-level architectures consist of thousands of processing elements (PEs) that are connected in a regular topology, where each element processes from one to a small number of bits. Bit-level architectures have several advantages over word-level architectures. First, a bit-level architecture can be *O(log p)* times faster than the corresponding word-level architecture where *p* is the word length, for fixed point operations [1]. The speedup is possible because individual bits of a word do not have to be processed as a unit in a bit-level architecture. For example, in the bit-level matrix multiplier proposed in this paper which does $C = X \cdot Y$ with $c_{ij} = \sum_{k=1}^{r} x_{ik} y_{kj}$, the least significant bits of the *r* partial products can be added before the partial product is fully computed. In contrast, in a word-level matrix multiplier a product of two words has to be computed completely before it can be added to the next word-level product. Thus in a bit-level architecture the carry chain is broken by sending the partial sums and carries of a word to the accumulating operation instead of to the whole finished word. Yet another advantage is that bit-level architectures are suited for FPGA because each PE needs only a few full adders and flip-flops and bit-level processor arrays are simple, modular and regular. Therefore the method proposed here can be used to map algorithms to FPGA chips directly.

In [2], a novel approach for bit-level architectures design is presented. The first step in their approach is to derive the dependence structure that is considered in [2] as a function of dependence structures of word-level algorithms, dependence structures of arithmetic algorithms implementing word-wise operations and algorithm expansions. This way, the dependence structures of bit-level algorithms can be derived without using time-consuming general dependence analysis methods. The second step is to find a mapping with some optimization criterion, often, the total execution time. They illustrate their design using matrix multiplication as an example. Although their designs gain speedup over word-level architectures, the critical path in their design can be cut to half to gain more speedup. Also, in their design, adding more hardware does not necessarily result in speed-up.

The bit-level algorithm expansion, time and space mappings of the new dependence structure for the bit-level matrix multiplier have been discussed in detail in previous papers [3,4]. Hence, in this paper, we limit ourselves to giving a brief overview of the design and comparing the execution times of word and bit-level matrix multipliers. The design is implemented on a Xilinx 4000xl FPGA chip. Our results show a speedup over a word-level multiplier implemented using highly optimized word-level multiplier and adder macros from the Xilinx core generator library. The bit-level design presented here is shown to be very efficient for multiplying moderate size matrices.

The rest of the paper is organized as follows: Section 2 describes the design of the bit-level matrix multiplier including the structure of each PE in the array as well as the overall structure of the array. Section 3 describes briefly the word-level multiplier and adder macros in the Xilinx Core generator library and the Xilinx XC4000 FPGA family. Section 4 discusses the FPGA implementation of the designs and Section 5 presents the results. In Section 6 our conclusions are presented.

2 Bit-Level Matrix Multiplier Design

In this section the design of the bit-level matrix multiplier is presented. Also, the structure of the PEs in the array and the overall layout of the PEs is presented. For a detailed analysis of the design the reader is referred to [3,4].

Throughout this paper, *sets, matrices* and *row vectors* are denoted by capital letters; *column vectors* are represented by lower-case symbols with an overbar; and *scalars* are shown as lower-case letters. The *transpose* of a vector $\bar{v}$ is denoted as $\bar{v}^T$. Vector $\bar{0}$ denotes a row or column vector whose entries are all zeroes. The dimension of vector $\bar{0}$ and whether it denotes a row or column vector are implied in the context in which it is used.

Consider matrix multiplication $Z = X \cdot Y$ where X is $l \times r$ and Y is $r \times m$ and word size is p bits. Each element of Z is a sum of r products, i.e., $z_{j_1,j_2} = \sum_{j_3=1}^{r} x_{j_1,j_3} y_{j_3,j_2} = X_{j_1} \bar{y}_{j_2}$. To multiply one row of X with one column of Y requires a processor array with $p \times r$ or $p \times (r+1)$ PEs (where p is the word size in bits), depending on whether r is odd or even respectively. As an example suppose the row elements of X are $[x_{11}^3 x_{11}^2 x_{11}^1 \ x_{12}^3 x_{12}^2 x_{12}^1 \ x_{13}^3 x_{13}^2 x_{13}^1 \ x_{14}^3 x_{14}^2 x_{14}^1 \ x_{15}^3 x_{15}^2 x_{15}^1]$ and the column elements of Y are $[y_{11}^3 y_{11}^2 y_{11}^1 \ y_{21}^3 y_{21}^2 y_{21}^1 \ y_{31}^3 y_{31}^2 y_{31}^1 \ y_{41}^3 y_{41}^2 y_{41}^1 \ y_{51}^3 y_{51}^2 y_{51}^1]^T$. Each processor in the array adds three to six bits and contains a few one-bit registers used for storing data. The data elements of matrix Y are loaded into the registers of the PEs, with one bit stored in each PE prior to starting the execution. The carries and partial sums are pipelined and hence are stored in the registers of the PEs before traveling between PEs. The data elements of matrix X are broadcast to the PEs of the array. (Alternately, with a few simple modifications they could be pipelined between data elements, resulting in more clock cycles but a higher clock frequency). The longlines of the FPGA can be used to broadcast the data elements. A longline is an interconnect, running across the chip, that distributes high fanout signals with low skew.

Using a design method developed in [5,6], the bit-level architecture for the matrix multiplication presented in this paper is designed and has execution time of $O(r)$ (see [4] for details). Bit-level arrays are compared with word-level processor arrays for matrix multiplication in [1]. The latter can have either $O(r)$ PEs in order to have completion time $T_c = O(r^2)$, or $O(r^2)$ PEs with $T_c = O(r)$. Each word-level PE can use carry-save adders to implement its word-level multiplication, which requires $O(p \log p)$ space and $O(\log p)$ execution time [7]. On the whole, a word-level processor array may need either $O(rp \log p)$ space to get $O(r^2 \log p)$ execution time, or $O(r^2 p \log p)$ space to get $O(r \log p)$ time. Hence, the fastest bit-level design is $O(\log p)$ faster than the fastest word-level design. Using an example and a dependency graph, the basic idea of the design is presented first.

Example 1: This example shows the outputs of the PEs in each iteration when one row of matrix X is multiplied with one column of matrix Y and $p = 3$ and $r = 3$.

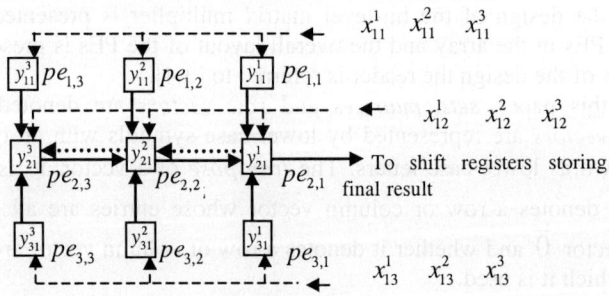

Fig. 1. Processor array structure to multiply one row by one column for $r = 3$, $p = 3$

The data elements of matrix Y, which are stored in each node, are shown in Fig. 1. The solid lines indicate flow of partial sums. The dotted lines indicate flow of carry (second order) and the dashed lines show the broadcasting of data elements of matrix X.

The execution when two 3 × 3 matrices with word size 3 bits are multiplied is presented next. Only the partial sums are shown; the lower and higher order carries are not shown in the table below. Also, assume that at time 1 the values of matrix Y have been stored into the PEs. Each array element output is represented as $x_{ab}^c \times y_{de}^f + pe_{i_1,i_2}^t$. The output of a PE at time t is represented as pe_{i_1,i_2}^t, where (i_1,i_2) is the index of the PE.

Table 1. Output of processing elements in Fig. 1 at different instants of times

Time	$pe_{1,1}$	$pe_{1,2}$	$pe_{1,3}$	$pe_{2,1}$	$pe_{2,2}$
2	$x_{11}^1 y_{11}^1$	$x_{11}^1 y_{11}^2$	$x_{11}^1 y_{11}^3$		
3	$x_{11}^2 y_{11}^1$	$x_{11}^2 y_{11}^2$	$x_{11}^2 y_{11}^3$	$x_{12}^1 y_{21}^1 + pe_{1,1}^2 + pe_{3,1}^2$	$x_{12}^1 y_{21}^2 + pe_{1,2}^2 + pe_{3,2}^2$
4	$x_{11}^3 y_{11}^1$	$x_{11}^3 y_{11}^2$	$x_{11}^3 y_{11}^3$	$x_{12}^2 y_{21}^1 + pe_{1,1}^3 + pe_{3,1}^3 + pe_{2,2}^3$	$x_{12}^2 y_{21}^2 + pe_{1,2}^3 + pe_{3,2}^3 + pe_{2,3}^3$
5				$x_{12}^3 y_{21}^1 + pe_{1,1}^4 + pe_{3,1}^4 + pe_{2,2}^4$	$x_{12}^3 y_{21}^2 + pe_{1,2}^4 + pe_{3,2}^4 + pe_{2,3}^4$
6				$pe_{2,2}^5$	$pe_{2,3}^5$
7				$pe_{2,2}^6$	

Time	$pe_{2,3}$	$pe_{3,1}$	$pe_{3,2}$	$pe_{3,3}$
2		$x_{13}^1 y_{31}^1$	$x_{13}^1 y_{31}^2$	$x_{13}^1 y_{31}^3$
3	$x_{12}^1 y_{21}^3 + pe_{1,3}^2 + pe_{3,3}^2$	$x_{13}^2 y_{31}^1$	$x_{13}^2 y_{31}^2$	$x_{13}^2 y_{31}^3$
4	$x_{12}^2 y_{21}^3 + pe_{1,3}^3 + pe_{3,3}^3$	$x_{13}^3 y_{31}^1$	$x_{13}^3 y_{31}^2$	$x_{13}^3 y_{31}^3$
5	$x_{12}^3 y_{21}^3 + pe_{1,3}^4 + pe_{3,3}^4$			

For e.g., from the above table, depicting the output of different processing elements at different instants of time, we can see that the output of $pe_{2,1}$ at time 3 is given by: $x_{12}^1 y_{21}^1 + x_{11}^1 y_{11}^1 + x_{13}^1 y_{31}^1$.

Fig. 2 represents the dependence structure for multiplying one column by one row of the matrices where $r = 3$ and $p = 3$. The higher-order carry is not shown.

The hardware realization of this design and the basic structure of each PE is described now. In Fig. 1, the processors in the second row add a maximum of six bits– the three partial sums from adjacent processors in the same column or row (shown by solid lines), the new partial product bit at the processor (dashed lines), the carry c (lower order) that is stored inside the PE from the previous computation (dashes and dots) and the carry c' (higher order) from the adjacent processor in the same row (dotted lines). In general, the structure of the PEs in the centre row is most complex as compared to the others. The structure of this PE for the center row (row number is $\frac{r+1}{2}$) where r is odd is shown in Fig. 3.

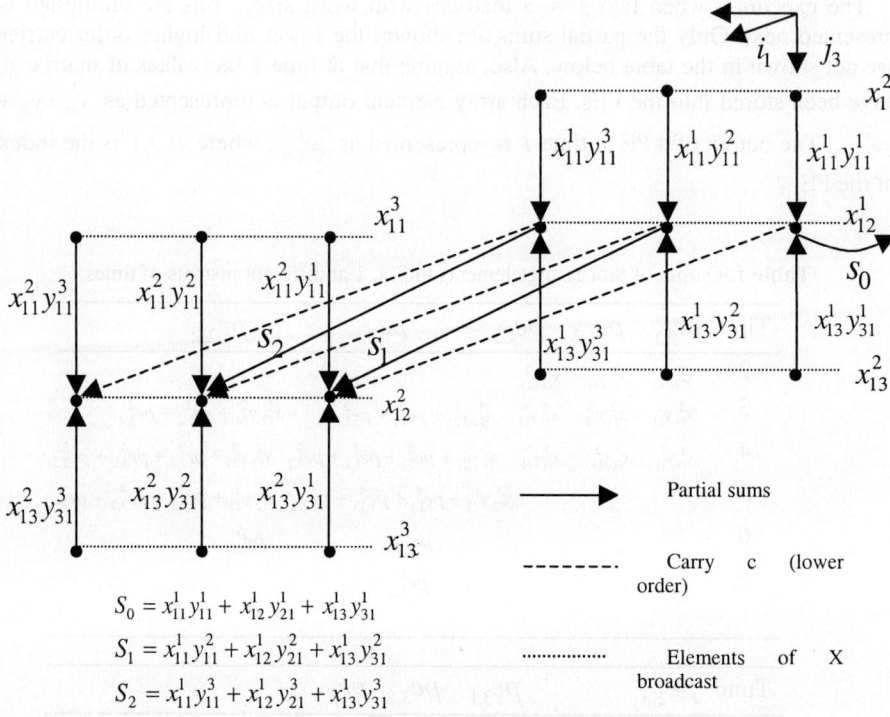

Fig. 2. Illustrates computations at various nodes in two iterations for $r = 3$ and $p = 3$

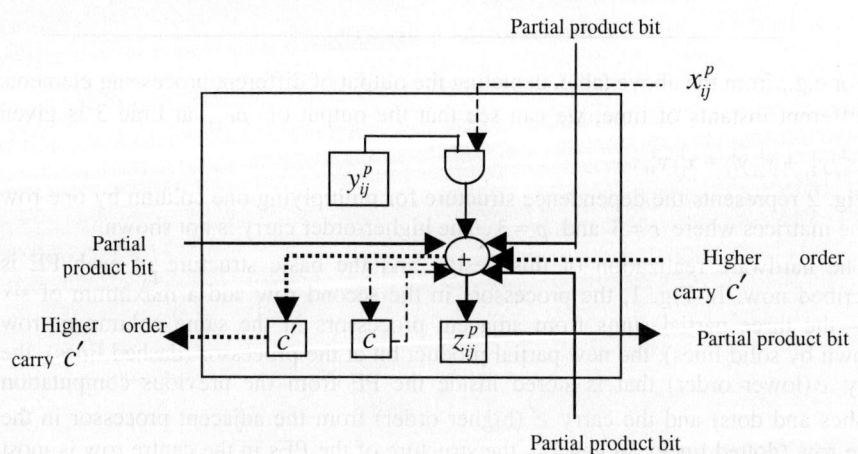

Fig. 3. Structure of PEs in the center row when r is odd

A maximum of four one-bit registers are required in each PE. One register stores a bit of input matrix Y. Another register holds the partial product bit that is to be sent to a neighboring PE. The third register holds the lower-order carry, which is added to the partial product bit of higher weight in the next clock cycle. The fourth register holds the higher-order carry, which is pipelined to the neighboring PE. An adder adds six input bits to produce a sum bit (which is pipelined as a partial product bit to an adjacent processor) and two carries. An *and* gate multiplies the input bit from matrix X with a bit from matrix Y. The remaining PEs that are not in the center row have the following general structure as shown in Fig. 4.

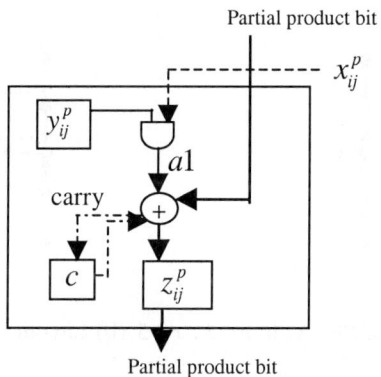

Fig. 4. Structure of PEs in all rows except the center row

The structure of the PEs in the first and last row can be further simplified by noting that there are no bits to be added in these PEs and the adder is not required. When r is even, no bits from matrices X and Y are broadcast to and stored in the center row of PEs respectively. The structure of the PEs in the center row, when r is even, is slightly different from that in Fig. 3. A register for storing a bit of input matrix Y and the *and* gate are not required. The adder needs to sum five bits in this case as no partial product bit from multiplying the input bits of matrices X and Y is generated here.

The number of PEs required to multiply one row by one column is $p \times r$, when r is odd, and $p \times (r+1)$ when r is even. The layouts of PEs for both cases when r is odd and even are shown below in Fig. 5. The shaded circles depict PEs, each of which stores a bit of matrix Y, whereas the unshaded circles represent PEs that do not store a bit of matrix Y. The dotted lines indicate the elements of matrix X that are broadcast to the various PEs. The partial sum bits are pipelined along the solid lines.

3 Xilinx XC4000x FPGA Family and Word-Level Macros in Xilinx Core Generator

In this section we briefly describe the Xilinx XC4000x family and the word-level macros in the Xilinx core generator library. Since up to four registers are used in a processor array, the design can be implemented on a Xilinx Virtex family chip, which contains four registers in a CLB. However, since the word-level multiplier and adder in the Xilinx core generator are available only for the Xilinx XC4000x family, the bit-level design is implemented on XC4000xl-3.

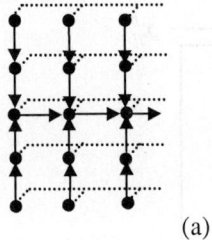 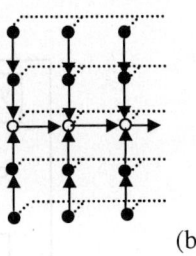

(a) (b)

Fig. 5. (a) Layout of PEs with $p = 3$, $r = 5$ (b) Layout of PEs with $p = 3$, $r = 4$

XC4000 [8] Series devices have a regular, flexible, programmable architecture of Configurable Logic Blocks (CLBs), interconnected by a powerful hierarchy of versatile routing resources, and surrounded by a perimeter of programmable Input/Output Blocks (IOBs). Each CLB contains function generators and two storage elements that can be used to store the function generator outputs. In general, the entire architecture is symmetrical and regular. It is well suited to established placement and routing algorithms. The word-level matrix multiplier is implemented using the following two macros from the Xilinx Core Generator library – Word Multiplier and Registered Adder [9].

The Registered Adder module accepts two input buses, A and B, and a carry-input (CI), adds them, and registers the sum, S. The input data buses can be either 2's complement signed or unsigned numbers. The output bus is 1-bit wider than the input operands to accommodate any carry-out that may be generated when adding the MSBs.

Table 2. Registered Adder Characterization Data

Input Width	CLB Count	Area Required for (Rows,Columns)	4000XL-3 (MHz)
4	4	4, 1	95
8	6	6, 1	87
16	10	10, 1	70
32	18	18, 1	55

The word-level multiplier, a parameterized module is a high-speed area-optimized implementation that multiplies an N-bit wide variable by an M-bit variable and produces an N+M bit result. An area-efficient, high-speed algorithm is used to give an efficient, tightly packed design. Each stage is pipelined for maximum performance. The total latency (number of clocks required to get the first output) is a function of the width of the B variable only. After an initial latency the multiplier produces a result every clock cycle.

Table 3. Multiplier latency

B Data Width	Latency (# Clocks)
6 to 8 bits	4
9 to 16 bits	5
17 to 32 bits	6

4 Implementation

The word and bit-level matrix multiplication designs were implemented on a Xilinx XC4000xl −3 chip. In both cases, the place and route tools *without any manual intervention* did the routing. Only a PERIOD timing constraint was used so that the design could be clocked at the fastest possible speed. The results have been obtained for the multiplication of a row vector with a column vector.

The word-level matrix multiplier uses two components from the Xilinx core generator library – multiplier and registered adder. Two word operands were multiplied by the multiplier in each cycle (after an initial latency) and added to the sum in the registered adder. The design was coded using Verilog HDL.

The Xilinx core generator library does not support Virtex at present for the word multiplier and registered adder. Hence we were forced to use XC4000 family. As discussed in Section 2, four registers are required for each PE. Most of the PEs in the bit-level design can be contained inside one Virtex CLB. For this reason the bit-level design implemented on the Virtex is expected to perform better.

We present below a listing of sample Verilog code for the design shown in Fig. 4. For the complete code listing the reader is referred to [4]. In the code below, *myreg* is a simple one-bit clocked register that transfers a bit from the register input to the output at the falling or rising clock edge and *fa* is a one-bit full adder.

5 Results

The following results were obtained for word-level matrix multiplication using macros from the Xilinx core generator library. The word size of the matrix elements is 8 bits. The resources required for the design are also given in terms of the total number of CLB look-up tables and flip-flops that are used.

```
module add3( s1, x, y, b, clk );
    input x, y, b, clk;
    output s1;
    and andg( a1, x, y1 );
    myreg regS( s1, sum, clk ) , regC( C, carry, clk ),
regY( y1, y, clk );    // clocked registers
    fa fa1( sum, carry, a1, C, b );
endmodule
    // Behavioural code for a one-bit full adder
module fa(Sout, Cout, a, b, c);
    input a, b, c ;
    output Sout, Cout;  reg Sout, Cout;
    always @( a or b or c )
        { Cout, Sout } = a + b + c ;
endmodule
```

Table 4. Results of word-level matrix multiplication, where multiplier inputs are 8 bits wide

Matrix size	Period (ns)	Frequency (MHz)	Look-up tables	Flip-flops	Computation time (ns)
8x8	14.96	66.8	141	113	210
16x16	14.96	66.8	141	113	330
32x32	15.93	62.76	141	113	590

Table 4 shows that the design operates at a frequency very close to the optimal one of 70 MHz described in the datasheet for the adder (with 16 bit inputs). The bit-level matrix multiplication yielded the following results:

Table 5. Results of bit-level matrix multiplication, where multiplier inputs are 8 bits wide

Matrix size	Period (ns)	Frequency (MHz)	Look-up tables	Flip-flops	Computation time (ns)
8x8	12.7	77.5	118	132	228.6
16x16	12.7	77.5	201	206	254
32x32	12.7	77.5	390	442	279.4

It can be seen from Table 5 that as the matrix size increases, a larger speedup is obtained. For matrix size of 32x32, a speedup of about 50% is obtained.

While no efforts were made to optimize the placement and routing of our design in this study, it will be the focus of future work. The bit-level design consumes larger amount of resources than the word-level design. The latter uses the area-optimized multiplier, which is highly optimized for low consumption of resources.

6 Conclusion

In this paper, we presented a bit-level design that is faster than previous designs. The bit-level design is implemented on a Xilinx FPGA chip and compared with a word-level design that uses components from the Xilinx library for matrix multiplication. Both the bit-level as well as the word-level designs are implemented on the Xilinx XC4000xl FPGA. The comparison indicates that significant speedup can be obtained by using bit-level architectures. Using matrix multiplication, we have shown how to map a bit-level parallel algorithm directly into an FPGA chip. Our future work includes optimizing the size of the PEs and developing a fully pipelined design, which can operate at much higher speeds.

References

1. C. W. Li and B. W. Wah, "Optimal Bit-Level Processor Arrays for Matrix Multiplication," *Proc. 11th Int'l Conf. on Systems Engineering*, Univ. of Nevada, NV, July 1996, pp. 596-601.
2. W. Shang, B. W. Wah, "Dependence Analysis and Architecture Design for Bit-Level Algorithms", *Intl. Conf. On Parallel Process.*, vol. I, pp30-38, 1993.
3. R. S. Grover, W. Shang, Q. Li, "An Improved architecture for bit-level matrix multiplication", To be published in Conf. Proc. *PDPTA '2000*, Las Vegas, USA, June 26-29,2000.
4. R. S. Grover, W. Shang, Q. Li, Technical Report number: coen00-01, *Department of Computer Engineering, Santa Clara University*, Santa Clara, CA 95053, May 2000.
5. Z. Yang, W. Shang and J. A. B. Fortes, "Conflict-Free Scheduling of Nested Loop Algorithms on Lower Dimensional Processor Arrays", *Proc. 6th IEEE Int'l Parallel Processing Symposium,* March 1992, Beverly Hills, CA, *pp.156-164.*
6. W. Shang and J. A. B. Fortes, "On Mapping of Uniform Dependence Algorithms into. Lower Dimensional Processor Arrays," *IEEE Trans. on Parallel and Distributed Systems*, Vol.3, No.3, May 1992, pp.350-363.
7. John L. Hennessy and David A. Patterson. Computer Architecture: A Quantitative Approach. Morgan Kaufmann Publishers, Inc., 1990.
8. XC4000E and XC4000X FPGA Series – Description v 1.6. *Xilinx Data Book*, 1999
9. CORE Generator & IP Modules - *Documentation & Data Sheets*, Xilinx, 1999

A New Floorplanning Method for FPGA Architectural Research

Frank Wolz and Reiner Kolla

Universität Würzburg, Lehrstuhl für Technische Informatik
{wolz,kolla}@informatik.uni-wuerzburg.de

Abstract. In this paper, we propose a new approach for solving discrete floorplanning problems. Using an abstract architecture model, our method is suitable especially for FPGA architectural research: Modules to be placed and the target architecture are modeled by periodic graphs. The objective is, to find a valid assignment of module nodes to slot nodes of the target architecture, such that a cost function on the placement will be minimized. We use an algorithm which is abstracted and derived from a traditional pattern matching technique.

1 Introduction

A typical application that deals with floorplanning of modules on given target architectures comes with the FPGA design process, where macro blocks realizing placed and routed subcircuits have to be assigned to architectural resources. While some tools are performing a cell–after–cell–assignment and afterwards global and detailed routing [TSO94,BR97], the increasing complexity of FPGAs in recent years led more and more to macro–strategies [YTK96,KRS97,SB97,EB99]. If we have a look on previous floorplanning methods, we recognize a common characteristic: macro blocks were always treated as "black boxes" and may not share any resources; overlappings were categorical forbidden. But this means also, that logic cells in macro blocks are generally regarded as "occupied". Dealing with very flexible routable logic blocks, this doesn't probably matter because we can choose very compact assignments anyway to reduce routing delays and need only to control routablility, i.e. to minimize the number of needed tracks along the cells. Placements of cell macros on more restricted routing resources, e.g. fine grain architectures, are often producing gaps of unused cells, where a lot of resources could be wasted. The now following approach to discrete floorplanning represents probably the first attempt working with overlappings of macro blocks on arbitrary target architectures to use free block–internal resources.

1.1 A New Approach

On contrary to a lot of previous approaches, our floorplanning method is simply based on abstract definitions of the target architecture and the modules to place. The only paradigm of our approach is derived from a relevant common characteristic of all field–programmable architectures: their regular (periodic) structure. For these purposes we choose the family of periodic graphs for modeling the architectures, where nodes represent programmable cells for logic and/or routing, and edges represent routing channels between two cells. The macros to place are also modeled by periodic graphs, but in this case, nodes and edges are representing "requirements" instead of "resources". A formal definition will be given later in section 3.1. At this level of abstraction, the floorplanning problem consists of the following discrete version: objects with properties characterizing some requirements have to be assigned some objects with properties describing resources of a target architecture. The assignment has to be valid such that no resources are exceeded and it should minimize a user–specified cost function. In the case of field–programmable architectures, such properties could be realized for example by the programmable bits of a logic cell: the resource properties of a cell are given by the set of its valid programming patterns and the requirement properties of macro subcircuits to implement are given by programming patterns for logic cells which then would implement the subcircuit on these cells. We will focus this application later in section 4. Target architecture and modules to place are forming regular structures of patterns and our floorplanning method is based on the simple recognition of property patterns offering feasible architecture resources. Before we can turn to an exact problem and algorithmic formulation in section 3, we first need to introduce some definitions and basics in periodic graphs and multidimensional pattern matching.

2 Definitions and Basics

2.1 Periodic Graphs

In respect of periodic graphs we generally keep terms and definitions as they are used at Höfting et al. [HW95], however, we regard a *finite* version of periodic graphs. A d-dimensional finite *periodic graph* G^X is described by a finite graph G (the so-called *static graph*) and an expansion vector $X = (x_1 \ldots x_d) \in \mathbb{N}^d$. A static graph is a directed graph and has edge labels $z \in \mathbb{Z}^d$. To construct the periodic graph G^X, we place an instance of the static graph G's node set in each cross point of an orthogonal $(x_1 \times \ldots \times x_d)$-grid, respectively. The edges of the periodic graphs are drawn as followed: Let v be a node of the static graph and let there exist an edge labeled y to a target node w. Let v_x be the corresponding node to node v in grid point with coordinates x. If the grid point $x + y$ exists, so there also exists an edge e of the periodic graph from v_x to the corresponding node of w at grid point $x + y$. If $y = 0$, we call e an *internal edge*, otherwise we call it an *external edge*. However, if the grid point $x + y$ does not exist, we define e as a *nil edge* with source node v_x and undefined target node. We use this term also for incoming nil edges. Let v be a node of a periodic graph based on the static graph G and let S be the subgraph in a grid point of a periodic graph based on the same static graph G. Then, the *corresponding node* of v in S, denoted by $C(v, S)$, is the node in S, that has been generated from the same node of G as node v. We similarly define *corresponding edges* $C(e, S)$. Figure 1 shows on its left side a static graph and on its right side the appropriate two–dimensional periodic graph with expansion vector $(4, 3)$. Note, that the periodic graph has also an offset: $(-1, -1)$.

2.2 Multidimensional Pattern Matching

We already mentioned, that we use a method derived from pattern matching to detect valid placements of modules on a target architecture. The pattern matching technique

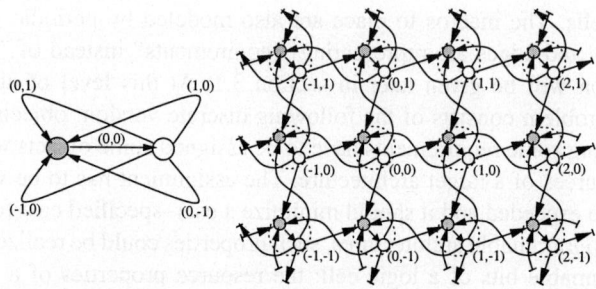

Fig. 1. Static Graph and Periodic Graph

has been adapted from Kedem et al. [KLP96], who comprise several frame works from the 1970s and 1980s. In this section, we explain the basic pattern matching technique on string arrays. Section 3.2 contains the derivation to our floorplanning problem.

Problem: Let T[$t_1 \ldots t_d$] and P[$p_1 \ldots p_d$] be two d-dimensional string arrays, where $t_i \in \{1 \ldots n\}$ and $p_i \in \{1 \ldots m\}$ for some fix $n, m \in \mathbb{N}$. Search all occurrences of pattern P[ ] in the text T[ ], which is the set of all vectors $(x_1 \ldots x_d)$, such that for all $(p_1 \ldots p_d)$ where $p_i \in \{1 \ldots m\}$ the equation P[$p_1 \ldots p_d$] = T[$p_1+x_1, \ldots, p_d+x_d$] holds.

Algorithm:

1. If $d = 1$, we solve the pattern matching problem by a known algorithm (e.g. Knuth–Morris–Pratt [KMP77]) and return a list of all occurrences of pattern P[ ] in text T[ ].
2. Else, if $d > 1$, we calculate the "characteristic function" $\chi_{d-1}[p_1 \ldots p_{d-1}]$ for P[$p_1 \ldots p_d$]: For all vectors $(p_1 \ldots p_{d-1})$, number the one–dimensional string chains P[$p_1 \ldots p_{d-1}$] consecutively in ascending order, such that equal chains get the same numbers.
3. For all $j = 1 \ldots (n-m+1)$ visit all subchains in each one–dimensional string chain T[$t_1 \ldots t_{d-1}$] starting at position j and having length m. If there exists a string array P[$p_1 \ldots p_{d-1}$] that matches this subchain, store the appropriate value of the characteristic function in a $(d-1)$-dimensional array T_{d-1}, that is: $T_{d-1}[t_1 \ldots t_{d-1}]$:= $\chi_{d-1}[p_1 \ldots p_{d-1}]$.
4. Solve the obtained matching problem with text T_{d-1}[ ] and pattern χ_{d-1}[ ] recursively. The result after return from recursion is a list L_{d-1} of $(d-1)$-dimensional vectors.
5. Construct the list L_d: for all $(q_1 \ldots q_{d-1}) \in L_{d-1}$, insert $(q_1 \ldots q_{d-1}, j)$ to L_d.
6. Increase j, i.e. regard next series of subchains (step 3).

Figure 2 shows an example of this recursive procedure for $d = 3, n = 3, m = 2$. The sequential version of this algorithm has time complexity $O(dn^d)$. However, we can solve the $(n - m + 1)$ subproblems in each recursion level in parallel, so time complexity reduces to $O(d \log m)$ on a maximum amount of $n^d / \log m$ processors.

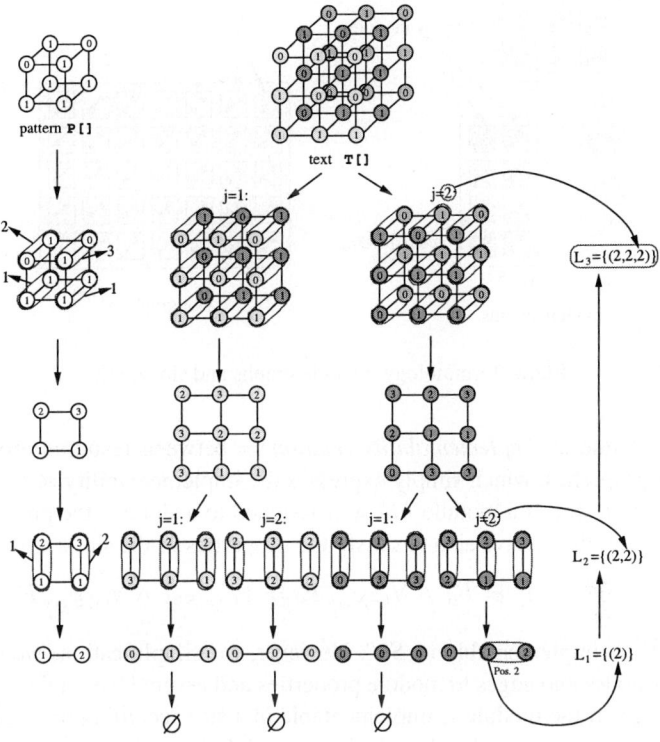

Fig. 2. Multidimensional Pattern Matching

3 Floorplanning by Pattern Matching

3.1 Problem Formulation

Let G^X be a periodic graph of dimension d, structurally described by the static graph G and let be $X \in \mathbb{N}^d$. We call G^X the *slot graph*. Let be S^x the duplicate of G in grid point x. Obviously, all S^x are isomorphic subgraphs. We call them *slots* with a unique resource property P_S. In the same way, we assign a property P_v to each node v in G^X a property P_e to each edge e, such that nodes (edges) that have the same corresponding node (edge) in the static graph get the same properties. Let be $y \in \text{span}(X)$ and $Y \in \mathbb{N}^d$, such that $y + \text{span}(Y) \subseteq \text{span}(X)$. We denote a periodic subgraph of G^X, which has its origin in grid point y and has expansion vector Y as $G^{(y,Y)}$. Let $U(G^X)$ be the set of all such periodic subgraphs of G^X. Let $\mathcal{M} = \{M_1^{X_1} \ldots M_n^{X_n}\}$ be a set of periodic graphs. We call them *module graphs*, each $M_i^{X_i}$ is also described by the static graph G. We call the subgraphs M_i^x in $M_i^{X_i}$ *modules* and assign some requirement properties A_i^x. Nodes v (edges e) of each periodic graph $M_i^{X_i}$ get properties A_v (A_e), but on contrary to the slots, modules and their nodes/edges may obtain different properties. Figure 3 visualizes our definitions: module graphs and the slot graph are based on the same static graph. Corresponding nodes are generated from the same node of the static graph.

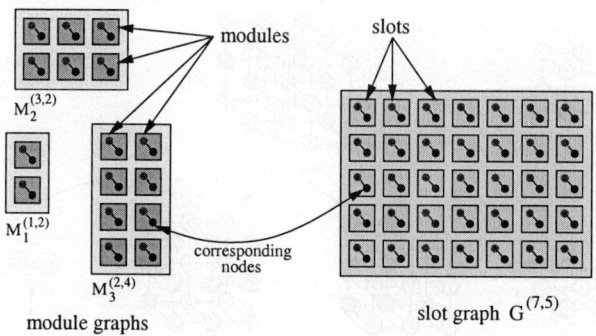

Fig. 3. Terminology: module graphs and slot graph

We now define an *implementability relation* $\models$ between resource properties and requirement properties, which simply expresses the implementability of a module, if it was assigned to a slot. If a module M_i^y was assigned to a slot S^x, the properties of the module's nodes (edges) have also to satisfy the properties of the slot's nodes (edges):

$$M_i^y \models S^x \iff A_i^y \models P_S \land \forall_{v \in V_{M_i^y}} P_v \models P_{C(v,S^x)} \land \forall_{e \in E_{M_i^y}} P_e \models P_{C(e,S^x)}$$

We say: "M_i^y is implementable in S^x". However, for simplification, we subordinate properties of nodes and edges to module properties and assume the implementability of nodes and edges if the module is implementable in a slot according to its property. Up to now, we are only able to decide, whether a module is implementable in a slot. But a slot could also be specified to accept the requirements of more than one module, so we have to extend our relation $\models$. For this case, we define an accumulating operation $\sqcup$ on the set of requirement properties and assume the closure of this set. Remember, that all slots have the same resource properties and that there only exists a solution of our floorplanning problem, if each module is implementable in a slot for itself. We then are able to define: a set M of modules M_i^x is a *compatible set*, if and only if the combination of their requirement properties is compatible to the slot's resource property:

$$M \text{ is } S\text{-compatible} \iff \left(\bigsqcup_{(i,x) \text{ where } M_i^x \in M} A_i^x \right) \models P_S$$

Now, a *placement* of module graphs from $\mathcal{M}$ on the slot graph G^X is a mapping $\varphi : \mathcal{M} \to U(G^X)$. Obviously φ induces also an assignment of the modules to slots: $\varphi_i : modules(M_i^{X_i}) \to slots(G^X)$. The set of modules which are assigned to slot S^x is:

$$M_\varphi^x = \left\{ M_i^y \in M_i^{Y_i} \mid M_i^{Y_i} \in \mathcal{M} \text{ and } \varphi_i(M_i^y) = S^x \right\}$$

Note, that φ is not necessarily injective. We also abstractly define a cost function $c : \varphi \mapsto \mathbb{R}$ that evaluates a placement. This cost function could be a measure composed by several different criteria. In most cases, the objective is to get very compact placements, so the cost function participates in the dilatation of a placement. The problem of discrete floorplanning on periodic graphs can now be formally described. Find a φ such that the following conditions hold:

a) $\forall_{x \in \text{span}(X)} M_\varphi^x$ is an S–compatible set
b) $c(\varphi)$ is minimized

3.2 Adaption to Pattern Matching

Property Containment Technique. Our floorplanning algorithm places m module graphs successively on a slot graph of dimension d, evaluates the placement and accepts or rejects a solution. The frame algorithm operates in a two-levelled branch&bound strategy. The first level selects the order in which the module graphs will be taken for placement. This step works in breadth first manner. The second level finds a valid placement by depth first search.

Frame Algorithm:

1. Select a permutation $\Pi = (\pi_1 \ldots \pi_m)$ of the module graphs (see below). If there has been taken a permutation Π' before, let k be the length of the longest common prefix of Π and Π'.
2. For all module graphs M_{π_j}, where $j = k+1 \ldots m$ do:
3. If $j \geq 2$, select the best placement as yet for module graphs $M_{\pi_1} \ldots M_{\pi_{j-1}}$ as a pre-placement.
4. Adjust the expansion of the slot graph (see below).
5. Perform the *property containment search* for module graph M_{π_j}. (If $j \geq 2$, consider the pre-placement of $M_{\pi_1} \ldots M_{\pi_{j-1}}$.)
6. Select a subset of valid placements, e.g. a set of most compact solutions, evaluate all solutions in this subset and select the best one.
7. Increase j, i.e. goto step 2.
8. If obtained a complete solution, save it on a heap.
9. Go to next permutation (step 1).

Property Containment Search. Only at the first level of recursion, the properties are checked themselves. Then, containments are encoded in bitstrings. At the remaining $d - 1$ levels, the problem is reduced to a simple bitstring containment search.

1. Calculate the module graph's characteristic function by encoding the properties of its modules in bitstrings $0 \ldots 010 \ldots 0$. Let r be the length of these bitstrings. Note, that r matches the number of different module properties.
2. Generate a new array R of dimension $(d-1)$ and size it to the slot graph's dilatation. R contains zero bitstrings of length r.
3. Perform the matching algorithm from section 2.2 under following adaptions:
   (a) If a pre-placement was given and the current index touches the pre-placement, accumulate the properties of pre-placement and pattern, else continue only with the pattern property.
   (b) If a module property matches a slot property set the appropriate bitstring in R to the logical or of itself and the module property bitstring.

Selecting a Permutation. As a rule, the quality of a solution is determined by the order in which the module graphs are being placed. Because the cost function is not specified in our abstract case, we enumerate the permutations in lexicographical order such that between two subsequent permutations a longest prefix remains constant. This means a reuse of a longest subsolution. In practice, we will stop the enumeration of the permutations after benefit or time limits have been exceeded. Frequently, the cost function consists of the dilatation of the placement. In this case, we use the heuristic to sort the module graphs by volume in descending order. So, we are placing hugest module graphs first and trying to use the gaps for smaller graphs.

Slot Graph Resizing. The first selected module graph M_{π_1} is to be placed in an empty slot graph. Note, that in general case, we have to check its properties nevertheless, because there may not exist always a solution. In this first step, we have to resize the slot graph to the size of M_{π_1}. If module graphs $M_{\pi_1} \ldots M_{\pi_{j-1}}$ have already been placed and we try to add M_{π_j}, the dilatation of the slot graph S determines the size of the search space in property containment procedure. It's obvious to keep the dilatation as small as possible in respect of runtime, but on the other hand to keep it broad enough to receive any solutions at all. For scaling the search space, we introduce a parameter δ, which represents a degree of overlapping between pre-placement and module graph to place. The most simple case is to set the parameter δ equal to the dilatation of M_{π_j}. Then we can always find a valid placement for M_{π_j} and the search space is probably too large. But, if we are able to estimate placement congestions in pre-placement area, we also could select δ dynamically, such that it is a measure of M_{π_j}'s dilatation and the estimated degree of overlapping the pre-placement.

3.3 Example

Some first steps in property containment search have been made by placing rectangular grids with integer numbers as properties. In the slot graph, the integer properties represented capacity bounds. The accumulation of module properties has been realized by simple adding the numbers. The implementability relation was established by the $\leq$-relation. Our example in figure 4 shows 15 placed module graphs of different sizes. The underlayed grid represents the slot graph and the usage of its slots. This solution was calculated from the first selected permutation. The (unparallelized) placement procedure took about one minute on a PC Linux PII 450 MHz with 512MB RAM.

A final remark to complexity: A survey on different variants of general floorplanning problems is given in Lengauer [Len90] or Sherwani [She99]. These problems have been proved to be NP-complete. However, the case of discrete floorplanning has not been researched so far. On the other hand, the complexity of the discrete variant will probably be the same because the special case of integer properties and module graphs with one node each, leads directly to the bin packing problem, which is a well–known NP-complete problem [GJ79].

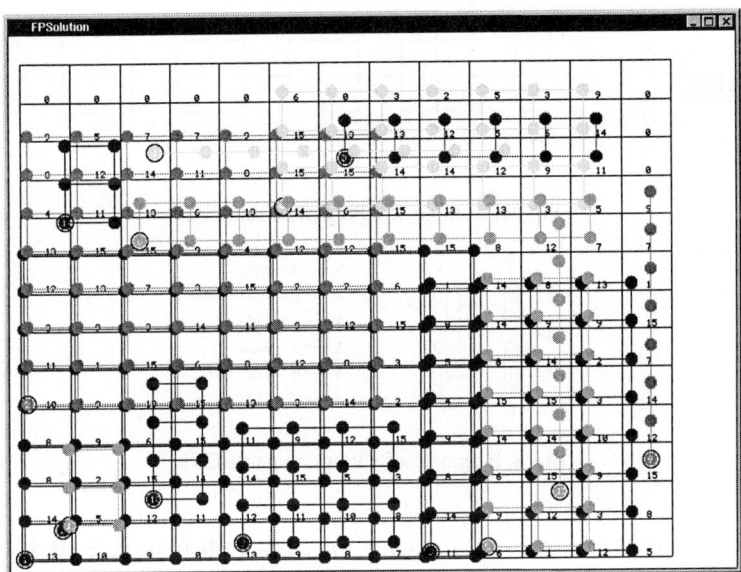

Fig. 4. Floorplanning Example

4 Application to FPGA Floorplanning

An adaption of our abstract method for FPGA floorplanning has already been drafted in section 1.1. Compared to common methods, our algorithm is more flexible in retargetability and predestinated for research in new architectures. The concept of periodic graphs and isomorphic subgraphs does not bind to fixed architecture decompositions as they are required in hierarchical methods. The subgraphs allow more flexible definitions of architecture segments because we can easily introduce cells of different functionalities. These degrees of freedom make our method workable for assignment problems of overlapable blocks on arbitrary regular architectural structures. An application of our method to FPGA design could work as follows:

In design process, we distinguish two types of macro blocks: prepared architecture–specific *subdesign macros* that are used in design entry step and *synthesized macros* that are generated based on the designed circuit and the architectural definition. At the technology mapping step after circuit synthesis, the programmable cells, i.e. the node types of the static graph, serve the technology. Then, critical paths and the structure of the static graph are used to form clusters fitting into one or more architecture segments. A subcircuit placement step generates macros from clusters and performs local routing of macro–internal signals. Now, our pattern matching based floorplanning method places the macros on the target architecture. The cost function considers the placement dilatation but also routability of signals between macro blocks. The inter–macro signals are routed in a final routing step.

We already mentioned, that it's possible to define cell properties by assignments of their programming bits. The characteristic function $K(p,q)$ of the compatibility relation

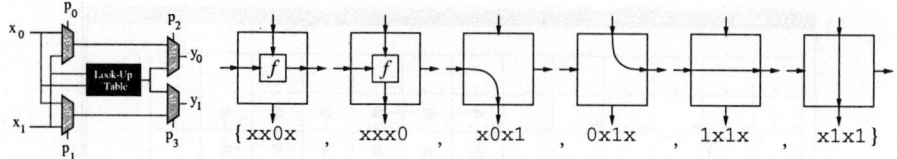

Fig. 5. Example of a Programmable Cell

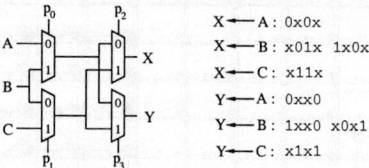

Fig. 6. Fragment of a Programmable Cell

for two assignments $p = (p_1 \ldots p_n)$ and $q = (q_1 \ldots q_n)$, where $p_i, q_i \in \{0, 1, x\}$, is:

$$K(p,q) = \overline{\bigvee_{i=1}^{n} (p_i \tilde{\oplus} q_i)}$$

Here, the symbol "$\tilde{\oplus}$" is the logical XOR, which in respect to *Don't Cares* has been defined as follows: $0\tilde{\oplus}x = 1\tilde{\oplus}x = x\tilde{\oplus}x = 0$. Figure 5 shows an example of a simple programmable cell. On the right side we see the possible basic functions and their programming assignments $(p_0 \ldots p_3)$ for this cell. Obviously, the cell can be configured for up to two different tasks, so the programming assignment 0011 realizes a knock–knee routing, for example. However, it is also possible, that a logic cell could be configured by more than one programming assignment for a special task. The property accumulation step in our floorplanning method could then be confronted with the problem, that some properties are compatible to only a subset of properties to accumulate. Figure 6 shows a fragment of a programmable cell as an example of such subset–compatibilities.

If we first required a routing of signal B to output X, we would have to select between the two assignments x01x and 1x0x. But this would cause a loss of either signal A or signal C. To preserve the functionality of the cell in this example, we have to use the set $\{$x01x, 1x0x$\}$ for property and calculate the compatibility relation for a property set $\{p^{(1)} \ldots p^{(k)}\}$ as followed:

$$K(\{p^{(1)} \ldots p^{(k)}\}, q) = \bigvee_{j=1}^{k} K(p^{(j)}, q)$$

What's an upper bound now for k? Let y be a primary output of a programmable cell, and let $S(y)$ be the set of all internal signals and signals on cell inputs, which can be routed to y. For a signal $s \in S(y)$ let $C_s(y)$ be the set of programming assignments, which routes s to y. Obviously, k is bounded by the total number of paths, that a signal could take through a cell:

$$k \leq \max_{y \in PO} \max_{s \in S(y)} \#C_s(y)$$

Note, that this is only an upper bound, because not all assignments in $C_s(y)$ do necessarily block signals, e.g. if alternative paths exist.

5 Conclusion and Future Works

In this paper we have introduced an abstract method for discrete floorplanning that places macro blocks on slot arrays of regular structures. Under consideration of compatibility and capacity constraints, we also allowed overlapping of macro blocks for using macro-internal gaps, i.e. free logic and/or routing resources. Our floorplanning method had only a few requirements to architectural definition so it surely could be applied to a wide range of problems. Especially, we suggested an application to FPGA design process, where macro blocks could be placed on FPGA architectures. This application should be of researchal interest, because almost only architecture-specific methods have been developed so far. Our new approach provides a high degree of freedom in architectural definition and forms a first basis for an universal design tool for architectural research on FPGAs. Our current investigations take care of the construction of retargetable macro generators and interactive routing tools. By realizing benchmark circuits on different architectures of various scaling, and evaluations of the designs, we hope to detect significant trends in the design of FPGA architectures. A synthesis of the results should help to design new efficient architectures and also specialized design tools.

References

[BR97] Vaughn Betz and Jonathan Rose: *VPR: A New Packing, Placement and Routing Tool for FPGA Research*, 7th Int'l Workshop for Field-Programmable Logic and Applications, LNCS 1304, pp. 213-222, 1997

[EB99] John M. Emmert, Dinesh Bhatia: *A Methodology for Fast FPGA Floorplanning*, ACM/SIGDA Int'l Symposium on Field-Programmable Gate Arrays, pp. 47-56, 1999

[GJ79] Michael R. Garey, David S. Johnson: *Computers and Intractability: A Guide to NP-Completeness*, Freeman, New York, 1979, p. 226

[HW95] Franz Höfting and Egon Wanke: *Minimum Cost paths in periodic paths*, SIAM Journal on Computing, Vol. 24, No. 5, pp. 1051-1067, October 1995

[KLP96] Zvi M. Kedem, Gad M. Landau and Krishna V. Palem: *Parallel Suffix-Prefix-Matching Algorithm and Applications*, SIAM Journal on Computing, Vol. 25, No. 5, pp. 998-1023, October 1996

[KMP77] D. E. Knuth, J. H. Morris and V. R. Pratt: *Fast Pattern Matching in Strings*, SIAM Journal on Computing, Vol. 6, 1977, pp. 323-350

[KRS97] H. Krupnova, C. Rabedaoro, G. Saucier: *Synthesis and Floorplanning for Large Hierachical FPGAs*, ACM/SIGDA Int'l Symposium on Field-Programmable Gate Arrays, pp. 105-111, 1997

[Len90] Thomas Lengauer: *Combinatorial Algorithms for Integrated Circuit Layout*, Teubner/Wiley, 1990, chap. 7.2, pp. 328-377

[SB97] Jianzhong Shi, Binesh Bhatia: *Performance Driven Floorplanning for FPGA Based Designs*, ACM/SIGDA Int'l Symposium on Field–Programmable Gate Arrays, pp. 112–118, 1997

[She99] Naveed Sherwani: *Algorithms for VLSI Physical Design Automation*, Kluwer Academic Publishers, 3rd Edition, 1999, chap. 6, pp. 191–218

[TSO94] Nozomu Togawa, Masao Sato, Tatsuo Ohtsuki: *Maple: A Simultaneuous Technology Mapping, placement, and Global Routing Algorithm for Field–Programmable Gate Arrays*, Int'l Conference on Computer–Aided Design, 1994

[YTK96] Takayuki Yamanouchi, Kazuo Tamakashi, Takashi Kambe: *Hybrid Floorplanning Based on Partial Clustering and Module Restructuring*, Int'l Conference on Computer–Aided Design, 1996

Efficient Self-Reconfigurable Implementations Using On-chip Memory*

Sameer Wadhwa and Andreas Dandalis

University of Southern California
{sameer, dandalis}@halcyon.usc.edu

1 Self-Reconfiguration

The limited I/O bandwidth in reconfigurable devices results in a prohibitively high reconfiguration overhead for dynamically reconfigured FPGA-based platforms. Thus, the full potential of dynamic reconfiguration can not be exploited. Usually, any attainable speed-up by executing an application on hardware is diminished by the reconfiguration overhead. The self-reconfiguration concept aims at drastically reducing the reconfiguration overhead by performing dynamic reconfiguration on-chip without the intervention of an external host. Thus, using self-reconfiguration, a configurable device can alter its functionality autonomously. Implementations based on self-reconfiguration promise significant speed-up compared with conventional approaches [7, 8].

Self-reconfiguration was first introduced in [4, 5]. In [7, 8] self-reconfiguration was proposed to be realized by altering the configuration bit-stream, that is, on-chip logic accesses and alters the configuration bit-stream to reconfigure the device. Compared with conventional implementations, significant speed-up was achieved for string matching and genetic programming problems [7, 8]. However, the proposed approach in [7, 8] can be realized only using multi-context configurable devices that allow on-chip manipulation of the configuration bit-stream. In state-of-the-art FPGAs, direct manipulation of the configuration bit-stream can only be performed by an external host. Moreover, the complexity depends on the structure of the configuration bit-stream and the on-chip configuration mechanism, and has not been analyzed thus far.

2 Our Approach

Our goal is to realize self-reconfiguration efficiently using state-of-the-art FPGAs. Since on-chip manipulation of the configuration bit-stream is not allowed, our key idea is to abstract the dynamic nature of a computation to embedded data memory (which is accessible on-chip). The dynamic nature of a computation corresponds to the dynamic features of its implementation, that is, features that are likely to be altered at runtime. Hence, instead of implementing logic that alters the configuration bit-stream, we implement logic that can control its functionality on-the-fly by altering on-chip data memory. Based on our ideas, we demonstrate efficient self-reconfigurable implementations for string matching, shortest path, and genetic programming.

---

* This research was performed as part of the MAARCII project. This work is supported in part by the DARPA Adaptive Computing Systems program under contract no. DABT63-99-1-0004 monitored by Fort Huachuca and in part by the National Science Foundation under grant no. CCR-9900613.

A self-reconfigurable implementation is problem-specific and consists of self-reconfigurable logic and the corresponding control circuit. The functionality of self-reconfigurable logic can be altered on-the-fly. The control circuit orchestrates the alteration of the underlying functionality.

Self-reconfigurable implementations can be abstracted as a set of *logiclets* and a programmable interconnection network as shown in figure 1. The *logiclets* are primitive logic elements. For example, a 16-bit arithmetic component can be realized as two 8-bit *logiclets* connected to each other. The functionality of a *logiclet* can

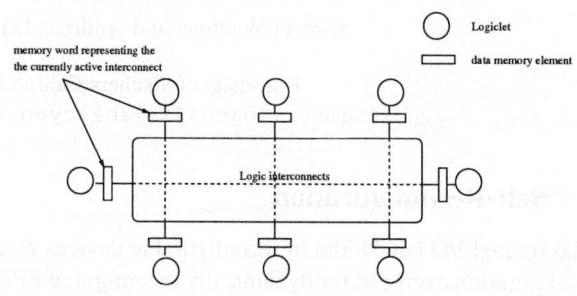

Fig. 1. Conceptual representation of logiclets connected by an addressable interconnect

also be determined by a memory-based look-up table (e.g. Finite State Machine). Thus, the functionality of an implementation can be altered by modifying the interconnection among *logiclets* and/or by altering the functionality of individual *logiclets*.

In a programmable interconnection network, each interconnection can be set "active" or "inactive" depending on the computation requirements. Hence, based on the runtime parameters, a new permutation of "active" interconnections can be derived. Such a permutation can be represented as a bit-pattern (interconnect address) as shown in figure 1. The bit-pattern can be stored in either embedded memory blocks or distributed memory. For example, if a distributed memory is used, each logiclet is associated with a memory element to store the "active" interconnect address. This "active" interconnect leads to the next logiclet in the function sequence. A number of such interconnects are configured on the device at compile-time and one of them is tagged as "active" during self-reconfiguration. As we demonstrate in the applications section, this functionaity can be easily realized using a multiplexer.

On the other hand, if shared memory is used, an interconnection is represented as a memory address. As a result, *logiclets* can exchange data by sharing the same memory address. As we demonstrate in the applications section, this functionality can be implemented using memory elements.

Self-reconfiguration is orchestrated by a control circuit. The control circuit is problem-specific and determines the permutation of "active" interconnections as well as the functionality of RAM-based *logiclets*. Thus, the underlying functionality is altered by modifying the bit-patterns stored in on-chip memory. The complexity of the control circuit is problem-specific and depends on the amount of dynamic modifications that are supported by the implementation. It is important to note that our approach to self-reconfiguration is significantly different from the approach adopted in [8,7]. In [8,7], the logic structures are adapted on the device to achieve self-reconfiguration. On the other hand, in our approach, pre-compiled logic structures are controlled on the device to self-reconfigure the logic functionality.

3 Application Demonstration

In this section, self-reconfigurable implementations for string matching, shortest path, and genetic programming are demonstrated. The implementations are based on the approach described in Section 2 and are realized using the Xilinx Virtex series of FPGAs.

3.1 String Matching

The string matching problem consists of finding all occurrences of a pattern in a text. In our implementation, we consider the KMP string-matching algorithm [2]. The algorithm begins by constructing an optimized finite state automata specific to the input pattern. The optimization involves constructing pattern-specific back-edges in the finite state automata. Then, the finite state automata performs the string matching on the input text.

The pre-processing phase can be realized efficiently using self-reconfiguration. As described in [8], the back-edges are constructed by using an OR-gate grid. By altering the configuration bit-stream, the OR-gate grid is adapted to the input pattern. On the contrary, in our implementation, the back-edges are abstracted as a look-up table. The look-up table is realized using the embedded RAM blocks of the Virtex FPGAs. Each state of the automaton corresponds to a memory address. Thus, a back-edge construction can be easily realized by altering the data contents of the corresponding address. In Figure 2, a high-level view of our implementation is shown.

Unlike the self-reconfigurable implementation in [8], our implementation can be realized using state-of-the-art FPGAs. The back-edge representation in our design results in simple control circuit for realizing self-reconfiguration. The simplicity of the control circuitry leads to reconfiguration time at least as fast as it is claimed in [8]. In addition, the clock rate achieved by our implementation outperforms the one achieved by [8]. This is because the OR-gate grid delay in[8] appears in the critical path of the design. On the contrary, in our design, look-up-table access occurs in parallel with character comparison and does not affect the critical path.

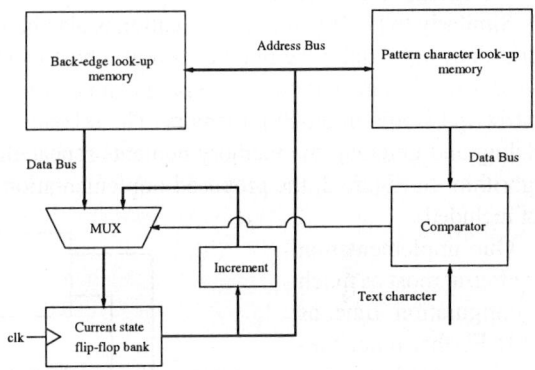

Fig. 2. Our proposed self-reconfigurable KMP implementation

For a pattern size of six characters, our implementation achieved a clock rate of $110MHz$ as opposed to $15MHz$ in [8]. However, the performance analysis in [8] was based on Xilinx 6200 series FPGAs. To make a fair comparison, we analyzed the performance of [8] on Xilinx Virtex series FPGAs and our proposed implementation still achieves a clock rate atleast twice as fast. Finally, our implementation requires less hardware area since it replaces the OR-gate grid by embedded RAM blocks and requires only one one comparator (in [8] the number of comparators required is proportional to the length of the input pattern).

3.2 Single-Source Shortest Path

The single source shortest path problem is a classical combinatorial problem that arises in numerous applications. For a given weighted, directed graph and a source vertex, the problem consists of finding the shortest paths from the source to all the vertices of the graph. In our implementation, we use the Bellman-Ford algorithm to solve the shortest path problem. The Bellman-Ford algorithm [2] relaxes the weights of the edges in an iterative fashion until the shortest paths to all the vertices of the graph are computed.

The key aspect of an FPGA-based implementation for solving the shortest path problem, is the time required to adapt the hardware to an input graph instance. For example, in [1], a very efficient implementation can be derived for a given graph instance by exploiting the massive parallelism inherent in the Bellman-Ford algorithm. However, a prohibitively high mapping time is also required to derive an efficient implementation. As a result, any consequent speed-up by executing Bellman-Ford using FPGAs is diminished by the reconfiguration overhead. In [3], a domain-specific approach was introduced that reduced significantly the reconfiguration overhead. Consequently, compared with software-based implementations, constant speed-up was achieved. In both [1] and [3], a host machine was used to adapt the hardware to the input graph instance by altering the configuration bit-stream.

Similarly to [1, 3], our implementation is also based on the Bellman-Ford algorithm but it does not require the intervention of a host machine to adapt to a graph instance. The dynamic characteristics of a graph can be efficiently represented by its adjacency matrix and stored in on-chip memory. The relaxation of the edges can be achieved by reading and updating the memory contents repeatedly according to the Bellman-Ford algorithm. In Figure 3, the proposed implementation is shown (the control circuitry is not included).

Our implementation requires at most as much reconfiguration time as in [3]. Furthermore, it requires less hardware area and can scale more efficiently that the implementation demonstrated in [3]. Regarding execution time on hardware, our implementation also outperforms the one proposed in [3] since it requires $O(n^2)$ less number of clock cycles while achieving a faster average edge relaxation rate. In Table 1, the indicated data correspond to a graph with weights of 16-bit precision. The average edge relaxation time for [3] is based on an implementation using Xilinx XC6200 FPGAs. However, we have implemented the same design as in [3] using Xilinx Virtex FPGAs, and our proposed implementation still achieves an average edge relaxation rate at least twice as fast.

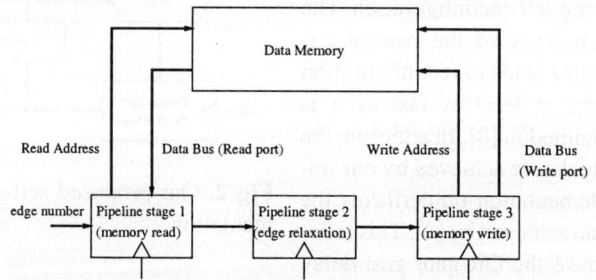

Fig. 3. Our proposed self-reconfigurable Bellman-Ford algorithm implementation

Table 1. Performance Comparison with [3]

Implementation	Avg. edge relaxation time	Number of clock cycles	Area
[3]	66.67ns	$O(n(n+e))$	$O(n+e)$
This paper	16.7ns	$O(ne)$	$O(e)$

3.3 Genetic Programming

Genetic Programming (GP) realizes a learning system by employing the Darwinian evolution principles to evolve a population of computer programs. GP consists of an evolution and a fitness evaluation phase that are executed repeatedly. The fitness evaluation phase decides which programs survive while the evolution phase evolve the survived programs. The fitness evaluation phase is the most computationally intensive phase in GP. By mapping the fitness evaluation phase onto reconfigurable hardware, significant speed-up is possible compared with software-based implementations [6].

In [7], self-reconfiguration was exploited to demonstrate a design where both the evolution and the fitness evaluation phases are executed on the reconfigurable device. Since both the phases of Genetic Programming algorithm were executed on the device, the reconfiguration overhead due to the limited I/O bandwidth was effectively eliminated from the critical path to the solution. The programs are represented as binary trees of fixed interconnection. During the evolution phase, the configuration bit-stream data corresponding to each tree-node is modified according to the evolution directives. As a result, the functionality of each tree-node can be switched based on a pre-defined function set.

In our implementation, each node of the binary tree is based on the conceptual model shown in figure 1. The binary tree-nodes are realized as shown in figure 4. The function set members for a GP application are realized as $logiclets$. Furthermore, each function set member is represented by a data word of length $\log m$ where m is number of members in the set. Each binary tree can thus be represented as a data word of length $n \log m$ where n is the number of nodes in the tree. This data word representation (i.e. bit-pattern) is stored in distributed memory and is used to alter the functionality of the tree-nodes. Thus, self-reconfiguration is realized by modifying the bit-pattern in accordance with the evolution semantics.

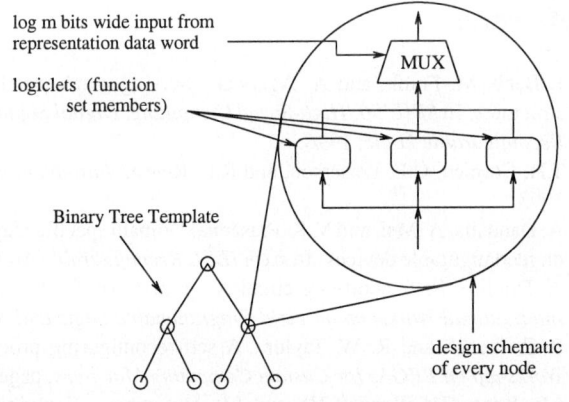

Fig. 4. Our proposed self-reconfigurable tree template and node implementation for Genetic Programming

Each tree-node in our design is more complex and requires more hardware area than in [7]. However, in our design, self-reconfiguration can be achieved by using state-of-the-art FPGAs and does not rely on specific device architectures. Finally, a preliminary performance analysis indicates that our implementation can be as fast as the one demonstrated in [7].

4 Conclusions

In this paper, we proposed an approach to realize efficient self-reconfigurable implementations using state-of-the-art FPGAs. Our key idea is to abstract the dynamic nature of a computation. Using our approach, we demonstrated self-reconfigurable implementations for string matching, shortest path and genetic programming. Our implementations outperformed the contemporary implementations for string matching and shortest path while performing atleast as well as the contemporary implementation for genetic programming.

The USC MAARCII project (http://maarcII.usc.edu) is developing novel mapping techniques to exploit dynamic reconfiguration and facilitate run-time mapping using configurable computing devices and architectures. The goal is to alleviate the long mapping time required by conventional CAD tools. Computational models and algorithmic techniques based on these models are being developed to exploit self-reconfiguration using FPGAs.

Acknowledgement

We would like to acknowledge the continued guidance and support of our research advisor, Prof. Viktor K. Prasanna, towards this work.

References

1. J. Babb, M. Frank, and A. Agarwal. Solving graph problems with dynamic computation structures. In *SPIE'96: High-Speed Computing, Digital Signal Processing, and Filtering using Reconfigurable Logic*, 1996.
2. T.H. Cormen, C.E. Leiserson, and R.L. Rivest. *Introduction to Algorithms*. The MIT Press, 1993.
3. A. Dandalis, A. Mei, and V. K. Prasanna. Domain specific mapping for solving graph problems on reconfigurable devices. In *sixth IEEE Reconfigurable Architectures Workshop*, April 1999.
4. A. Donlin. Self modifying circuitry - a platform for tractable virtual circuitry. In *Eighth International Workshop on Field Programmable Logic and Applications*, 1998.
5. P. C. French and R. W. Taylor. A self-reconfiguring processor. In *Proceedings of IEEE Workshop on FPGAs for Custom Computing Machines*, pages 50–59, April 1993.
6. J.R. Koza, F.H. Bennett III, and J.L. Hutchings. Evolving sorting networls using genetic programming and the rapidly reconfigurable xilinx 6216 field-programmable gate array. In *FPGA'98 Sixth International Symposium on Field Programmable Gate Arrays*, February 1998.
7. R. P. S. Sidhu, A. Mei, and V. K. Prasanna. Genetic programming with self-reconfigurable fpgas. In *International Workshop on Field Programming Logic and Applications*, August 1998.
8. R. P. S. Sidhu, A. Mei, and V. K. Prasanna. String matching on multicontext fpgas using self-reconfiguration. In *ACM/SIGDA International Symposium on Field Programmable Gate Arrays*, pages 217–226, Monterey, CA, February 1999.

Design and Implementation of an XC6216 FPGA Model in Verilog

Alexander Glasmacher and Kai Woska

University of Siegen, Institute of Technical Computer Science, 57068 Siegen, Germany
{glasmacher, woska}@ti.et-inf.uni-siegen.de

Abstract. Modeling in a hardware decription language offers the opportunity to experiment with various implementations of a design without regarding technological constraints. A model of an FPGA is a base for a very flexible design, allowing to add and remove any of its features. This paper describes the modeling of a special FPGA (Xlinx XC6216) in Verilog using only the Xilinx documentation. Some of the implementation details and problems are presented in this text.

1 An FPGA Verilog Model

The Xilinx XC6216 FPGA supports many interesting features and is usable for a wide range of applications. But to analyse all of its capabilities it is necessary to own some control over its interiors. The fact that the free documentation is sufficiently detailed enabled us to rebuild this device as a Verilog model. Verilog is a modular hardware description language, that allows to describe a hardware model at different abstraction levels in a behavioural and a structural view. A software simulation of this FPGA offers the opportunity to monitor and modify all of its components to adapt it to new tasks. The following two sections describe briefly the partitioning and implementation of the model. At the end an overview is given of the simulation circumstances and of further applications.

2 Partitioning into Modules

The Verilog model of the XC6216 is divided into modules. The partitioning of the FPGA model follows its logical structure. The *Chip* module is at the top level of the hierarchy. It connects the parts of the description and it is the interface of the model to the surrounding system. The array of 64x64 logic cells and the programmable routing resources between them are implemented by the cell array module hierarchy. This module hierarchy reflects the different levels of routing resources of the XC6216. The detailed description of the logic cells and the routing between them can be found in section 3.1. The cell array is surrounded by input/output blocks and IO Pads. They contain additional routing resources and connect the cell array with the environment of the FPGA. The programming and interface logic is described in the module *chipcontrol*. All data routing and cell addressing is processed here. It instantiates additional modules for the decoders and register access. They are described in section 3.2. Table 1.1 shows the basic modules of the model with their number of I/Os and lines of code.

Table 1-1: Basic Modules of the Verilog Model

Modul	I/Os	Lines of Code	Implementation
chip	4	3548	only wires, automat. generated
chiparray	62	489	only wires
Block16x16	36	614	Structural
Block4x4	31	537	structural/bevaioral
Cell	22	115	structural/bevaioral
chipcontrol	32	498	structural/bevaioral
mapcore, mapaddr	9	3260	structural, automat. generated
others	-	441	-

3 Implementation Details

3.1 The Logic Cell and the Cell Array

The logic cell contains logic for the cell function, the nearest-neighbour connections, and provides the configuration memory. The outputs of the four neighbour cells and the FastLANE 4 signals can be routed through multiplexers into the function unit. The outputs to the four neighbour cells are also controlled by multiplexers. They can be connected to the cell's neighbour inputs or to the output of the function unit. An additional multiplexer can route the function unit inputs to the switches at the 4x4 block border.

The function unit (FU) of the XC6200 can be configured as any two-input gate function, any kind of 2:1 multiplexer, constant 0 and 1, single input functions (buffer or inverter) or any of these in addition to a flipflop. The FU also contains the register access logic. The FU is described as a module, which instantiates the six multiplexer modules and the flip flop module. In addition to the three input signals and the output it also needs configuration signals from the cell memory, the register access wires and the Clk, Clr, and Reset signals for the flip flop.

The configuration for all multiplexers and the control logic is stored in 64 kbytes SRAM. 16 kbytes of the memory is reserved for the control unit. This part of the memory is implemented in the *chipcontrol* module of the Verilog description. The rest of the memory is located in the cells. Each of the 4096 cells stores 12 byte. This allows a parallel development of the control unit and the cell array and reduced the connections between the 4096 cells and the control unit. The 12 bytes of memory in each cell configure the function unit, the routing through the multiplexers and the IOBs. The memory is described as a 96 bit register. This allows to access individual bits of the memory with the hierarchical name of the register. This would not be possible, if the memory was defined as a 12x8 bit Verilog memory.

The cell array of the XC6216 consists of 4096 logic cells, 256 surrounding IOBs, and the programmable routing resources between them. The Verilog description of the cell array is divided into four modules instantiated in a hierarchical structure. The partitioning of the cell array into modules follows the logical structure of the real chip. At the bottom of the module hierarchy are the logic cells. In the next level are the *Block4x4* modules. They connect a 4x4 cell array and provide higher level routing resources and chip level signals. Above the *Block4x4* modules are *Block16x16* modules. They are similar to the *Block4x4* modules, but instead of connecting cells, they connect 16 *Block4x4* modules. At the top of the cell array module hierarchy is the *Cellarray* module. It connects all 16 *Block16x16* modules and is the interface to the control unit. The module *Chip* connects the cell array and the IOBs.

The module *Cellarray* is a pure connection module. It doesn't contain any logic functions. The 3402 signals in the interface to the module chip can be sorted into three groups. In the first group are the 2948 signals that connect the 256 IOBs with the 4096 logic cells. These signals are the FastLANEs, nearest neighbour connections, Magic wires, clock and clear. The second group are the 198 signals for the programming interface. It consists of the 32 bit bidirectional data bus and 32 bit mask register, 64 column select and 64 row select lines, and 6 control signals. The third group are 256 signals of the register access interface to the FU. This group includes the 192 selection and control signals and the 64 bit bidirectional register data bus. The *Cellarray* module distributes all this signals to the *Block16x16* modules and defines the connections between the 16 *Block16x16* modules.

The *Block16x16* module generates 64 FastLANE 16 outputs and 16 Clear signals. The *Block16x16* module also connects the *Block4x4* modules to module *Cellarray* and connect the 16 *Block4x4* modules.

The *Block4x4* module generates the 16 FastLANE 4 outputs, the nearest neighbour interconnects at the block border, the 4 clock signals for the flip flops in the function units, and instantiates 16 cell modules and connects them. The FastLANE 4 signals are the output signals of 16-to-1 multiplexers that are defined in the *Mux16* module. Not all inputs of this multiplexers are connected to a signal and are undefined. To generate the clock signals, it uses 4–to–1 and 2–to–1 multiplexers. It also generates the read and write signal for its 16 cells.

Normally each cell is connected directly to its neighbour cells through the nearest neighbour interconnections as shown in figure 1a. In the Verilog description it is necessary that this connection routes through the *Block4x4* module as shown in figure 1b, because Verilog allows only one interface per module. The same problem appears with the data bus and some of the global signals. They are only needed inside the cells, but they have to be routed through every module in the hierarchy to reach them. The consequences are huge module interfaces producing a simulation overhead.

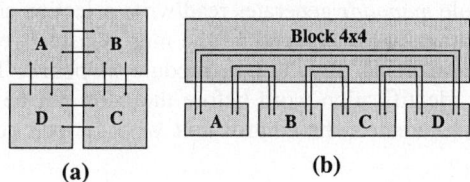

Fig.1. Neighbour connection on the chip (a) and in the model hierarchy (b).

Most of the programming signals for the logic cell memory are connected to each cell in a column or row. These signals are generated in the chipcontrol module. In this hierarchical Verilog model such signals have to travel through a large part of the module hierarchy to reach the *Cell* modules. To reach 64 cells in a line, the signal has to go through 4 *Block16x16* modules and 16 *Block4x4* modules. This also applies to the register access signals. Overall 437 signals have to be routed that way. This increases the size of the module interface and slows down the simulation.

Next to each border cell is an IOB. IOBs connect the routing structure of the cell matrix with the IO pads of the chip. The IOBs hold routing multiplexers for all routing levels that route signals back to the cell matrix. If its IO pad is configured as an input it can also route the input signals into the cell matrix. Not all IOBs are connected to IO pads. The IOBs are instantiated in the *Chip* module. This module is generated by a C program for a simple instantiation of the 256 IOB and IO pad modules.

3.2 The Control Unit

All accesses to the FPGA model are managed by the control unit. Serial or parallel configuration data is processed and routed to either the cell configuration memory or the programming control registers. Further the cell flipflops can be combined to registers and accessed via the control unit by a special mapping function. All addressing and data routing logic is located in the control unit. A 16 bit address word and an 8, 16, or 32 bit data word is necessary to program the FPGA. Wildcards help to program multiple cells simultaneously to implement regular patterns of logic. During programming a special mask function can be used to protect selected bits from being overwritten.

The programming control registers inside the control unit are used to configure the general FPGA functionality. These are an 8 bit device configuration register, two 6 bit wildcard registers, a 4 byte mask register, an 8 byte map register, and a 16 byte ID register. The device configuration register controls the serial loading speed, the data bus width and enables the clock signal for the cell array. The two wildcard registers are connected with the wildcard inputs of the row and column decoders at the boundaries of the cell array, but are only enabled during a write access to the cell memory. A detailed description of the wildcard decoder follows below. The outputs of the mask register are distributed to the cell memory similar to the internal data bus. For each data bit the respective bit from the mask register is routed to the cell memory. A memory bit can be protected from being overwritten by setting the appropriate bit of the mask register. The 64 bits of the map register are used to address rows of the cell array for a register access. In combination with the read/write signal, the module *mapaddr* generates read/write selection signals for each row of the cell array. Additionally the contents of the map register are used to trigger the 2080 switches of the mapping structure in module *mapcore*. The ID register must be written with an identification word before the pads can be used as outputs. Overall 454 internal wires connect the control unit with the cell configuration memory and flipflops.

Main component of the control unit is a synchronous mealy–type state machine. Besides controlling the serial programming it synchronizes the parallel interface of the FPGA. Therefore the original single parallel state of the FPGA is splitted into three substates - parallel idle, parallel sample and parallel read/write. The remaining states are adopted unmodified. State transition occur only at a rising edge of clock. To avoid timing conflicts in the simulation with further synchronous logic, the state register outputs are delayed. Two serial states are using a counter to hold the state for 9 resp. 16 clock cycles. After starting the simulation or applying an external reset, all registers and configuration memory of the control unit and the cell array are cleared. The first state after this reset state determines if the FPGA model is programmed serial or parallel.

By setting the signal *Serial* to „0" the state machine prepares the FPGA to be programmed with the serial interface. Then a sync pattern has to be loaded into the FPGA before programming data can be loaded serially. Loading occurs on rising edges of *SEClk*, a serial clock generated by the FPGA. The data/address pairs are shifted bitwise over a single Pin into an internal register until a complete pair is loaded. Then the address mode and column offset of the address are used to specify the destination of the data word, either the cell array memory, the programming control registers or the cell flipflops.

If the *Serial* signal is set on „1" the FPGA switches to parallel mode. Now the state machine waits in „parallel idle" state for an inactive *CS* Signal. On the next rising edge of clock a transition to state „parallel sample" occurs and the address signals are written into the address part of the same internal register that represents the serial shift chain. Additionally the *RdWr* value is stored into a flipflop. If this value is „0" the data register (data part of serial shift chain) is written with the supplied data bits. Now the same addressing/data routing logic is used as with the serial interface, but the writing event occurs only at the next transition of the state machine to „parallel read/write". A read access, which is not possible in serial mode, in this state routes the addressed data to the data pins and enables their outputs so the data is visible for peripheral logic.

To address the cells of the array, there is one select line for each row and column of cells. Two decoders, one for the row lines and one for the column lines, decode the row and column part of the address. The cell in the intersection of two active lines is addresses for a read or write access. With a wildcard decoder multiple lines can be activated, so more than one cell is addressed for writing the same data to its memory. To mark an address bit as a wildcard, the decoder holds one additional wildcard input for each address input. If a wildcard input is set to „1" the respective address bit is irrelevant for decoding and both possible values „0" and „1" are regarded. So two or more decoder outputs are active. The implementation of this wildcard decoder differs from normal decoders in a slight modification of its inputs. The AND gates of each output have all address bits as inputs, some unmodified, some inverted (s. Fig. 2). The wildcard decoder has the marked inputs on the left exchanged for the circuit on the right. A wildcard signal can now activate both the original address signal and its negation, so this address bit is irrelevant for decoding. The additional *Select* input disables the whole decoder, when no cells should be addressed.

The mapping architecture allows the user to combine flipflops in a single column to one register and access it through the external databus. The address word is used only to detect a register access and to address the concerned column with a decoder without wildcards. The single flipflops are addressed by the 64 map register bits of the control unit. The map register additionally controls a switching matrix, which connects the 64 flipflops on the right side with the internal data bus (32 bit) of the control unit on the lower left side. These switches are arranged so that only the upper left side is filled with switches to the respective diagonal. The lower right side is empty. All switches in a column are triggered by the same bit in the map register. The data paths now can be routed horizontally or be shifted up by one wire. The example in Fig. 3 shows how the data paths are routed through the matrix and, when reaching the diagonal, becoming unaffected by further switching. So all internal data bits are connected with the selected flipflops and information can be routed in both directions.

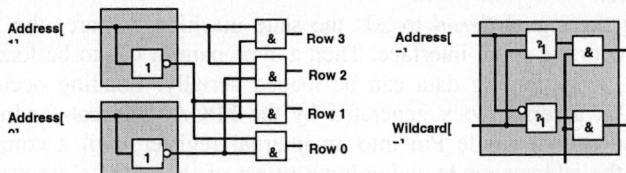

Fig.2. 2-to-4 decoder and modified input for the wildcard function

The Verilog model of module *mapcore* is generated automatically by a C program, which instantiates the 4160 transistors for the switching matrix. A second automatically generated module *mapaddr* provides the necessary addressing signals. Automatic generation has the advantage of easy modifications. With it only the short C source code has to be modified instead of the whole instantiation of about 5000 lines of Verilog code.

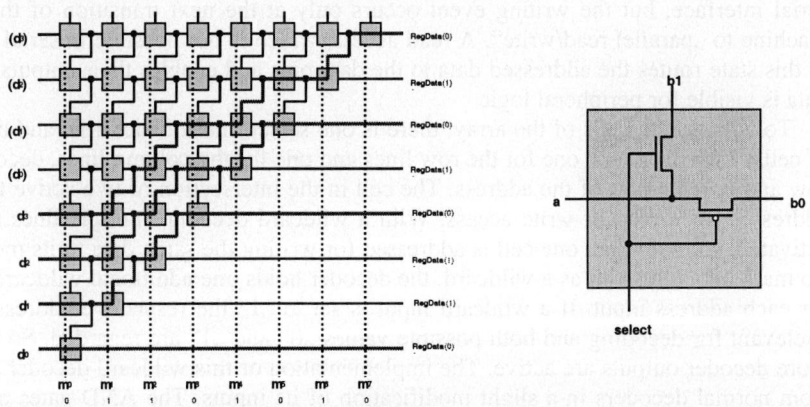

Fig. 3. Concept of a 4-to-8 mapping module and a single switch

4 Conclusions

The simulation time of the complete FPGA model with Cadence Verilog XL reaches over an hour on an Ultra Sparc 1. More than 100000 instantiated modules of the simulation need 800 MB of memory, so all of the 576 MB available RAM is consumed, and the rest is swapped to disc. So the NC–Verilog compiler has been used in later development. This tool stores the whole model in 70 MB of RAM. Compilation of the model takes only about 5 minutes and it was possible to start a compiled simulation within seconds. This has been an important step for using the model with genetic algorithms [4], because thousands of configurations must be loaded and analysed to gain any results. Genetic algorithms can be used to analyse and adapt initial random configurations to evolve circuits on FPGAs. By using a simulation instead of a real FPGA the technological characteristics of the FPGA are irrelevant and a pure digital circuit is evolved with no analogue side effects.

Altogether our model offers the opportunity to analyse all of its interior signals, which is not possible with real hardware. It can be used as a base to develop new FPGA models by modifying some or all of its features.

References

[1] *XC6200 Field Programmable Gate Array.* Xilinx Inc., 1997.

[2] Alexander Glasmacher: *Entwurf und Implementierung der Zellmatrix eines FPGAs als Verilogmodell.* Studienarbeit, Fachbereich Elektrotechnik und Informatik, Universität Siegen, 2000.

[3] Kai Woska: *Entwurf und Implementierung der Steuerlogik eines FPGAs als Verilogmodell.* Studienarbeit, Fachbereich Elektrotechnik und Informatik, Universität Siegen, 2000.

[4] Christine Bauer, Peter Zipf, H. Wojtkowiak: *System Design with Genetic Algorithms.* Submitted to FPL 2000.

Reusable DSP Functions in FPGAs

Jernej Andrejas and Andrej Trost

University of Ljubljana
Faculty of Electrical Engineering
Trzaska 25, 1000 Ljubljana, Slovenia

Abstract. In this article, we discuss various realizations of reusable DSP functions in FPGA devices. We have generated generic multipliers and dividers in VHDL code which can be used later for building more complex structures. We have simulated, implemented and verified presented functions within target Xilinx FPGA devices.

1 Introduction

The progress which has been made in FPGA technology over the last decade is forcing many digital structures and applications to change their physical environment from general purpose microprocessors and digital signal processors towards FPGA. Digital signal processing algorithms can be efficiently implemented with parallel structures in FPGA devices which can be used standalone or as specialized DSP co-processors.

The DSP functions can be implemented as hardware structures or as software algorithms. We focused on hardware implementations of two basic DSP operations: multiplication and division where a lot of speed improvement can be made in comparison to software implementations.

Multiplication is the most common function in many DSP algorithms. Hardware multipliers can be based on different binary multiplication algorithms. We begin with modified Baugh-Wooly algorithm [1] which is a fundamental structure for our implemented signed parallel-parallel and pipelined multipliers. Serial-parallel structures were also considered and we will present implementation results for signed serial-parallel multipliers. We also designed a 16 x 16 bit multiplier with exactly the same behavior as one in a commercial DSP.

Division is less common function in DSP and since it is more complex comparing to multiplication, we designed only parallel nonrestoring structures.

The multiplier and divider circuits were designed in VHDL as generic reusable IP components. The size of input vectors designates the circuit structure through generic parameters. Therefore, the optimal structures can be generated as required for specific applications.

2 Multiplication

Parallel signed multipliers can be made by direct realization of Baugh-Wooly algorithm where carry signal propagates through rows in CLA adders. We can take advantage of efficient adder realization by using the addition operator from *IEEE.std_logic_unsigned* library, while still maintaining reusable and device independent VHDL code.

The next multiplier is still based on Baugh-Wooly algorithm with a change in the direction of carry propagation from rows to columns, which we achieve by rotation of adders from horizontal to vertical axis. This structure, denoted as "carry-save" multiplier, is shown in Figure 1.

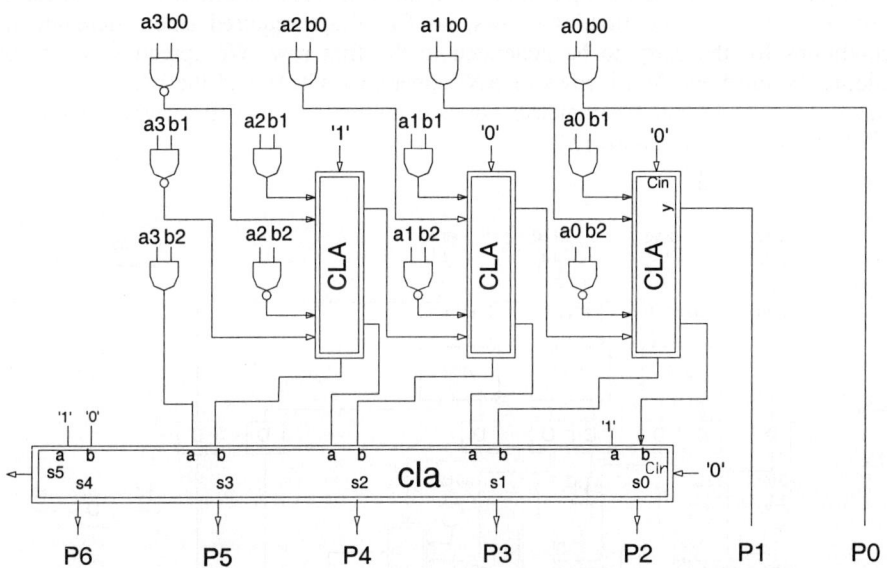

Fig. 1. 4 x 3 carry-save multiplier

The simplest way to implement the basic parallel multiplier is by using a multiplication operator, defined in libraries *IEEE.std_logic_signed* for signed numbers, and *IEEE.std_logic_unsigned* for unsigned multiplication. In this case, an optimized parallel multiplication macro will be instantiated by the synthesis tool.

We designed parametric VHDL components for parallel multipliers and performed synthesis and technology mapping with Synopsys Foundation Express and Xilinx Foundation F1.5 tools. The implementation results for Xilinx Spartan XCS40PQ208-4 FPGA device are presented in Table 1. The carry-save multipliers are generally the fastest, while the multipliers generated from the VHDL operator consume less area.

We can achieve higher frequency if we put additional registers in the parallel multiplier structure which break the long carry propagation path. These structures are called pipeline multipliers and can achieve much higher throughput when one of the inputs is held constant.

Table 1. Comparative results for basic parallel multipliers

Size	Baugh-Wooley		Carry-Save		VHDL Operator	
A x B	CLB	f [MHz]	CLB	f [MHz]	CLB	f [MHz]
4 x 4	26	29.2	21	41.9	16	31.9
8 x 4	43	29.9	38	30.9	32	23.8
8 x 8	81	18.6	85	21.0	60	23.8
12 x 8	115	16.8	126	20.2	92	17.3
16 x 8	149	15.5	165	18.5	124	13.9
16 x 16	273	10.3	297	13.6	244	12.8

Figure 2 presents the 4 x 4 pipeline multiplier which is a modified version of carry-save multiplier. In the first two rows, no CLAs are required since there are no conditions for the carry to be generated in the first row. We spread structure by adding the third and fourth rows of AND operators, CLAs and the whole row of D flip-flops. We designed parametric pipeline multipliers in VHDL which have the clock latency (Vector-B-size) / 2.

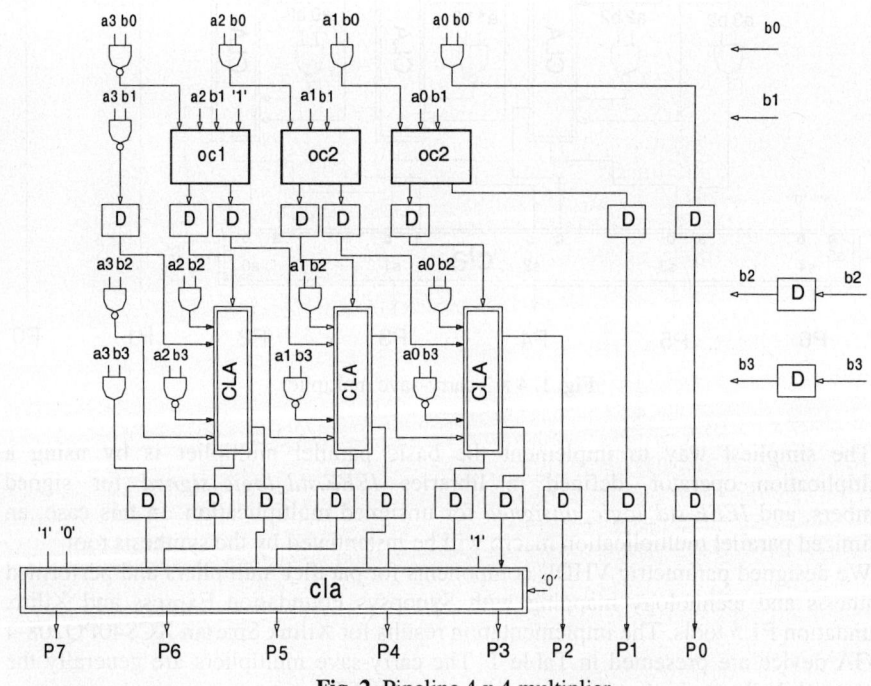

Fig. 2. Pipeline 4 x 4 multiplier

Pipeline multipliers in Xilinx FPGA devices can be very efficiently generated with LogiCore IP macro generator [4] which takes advantages of FPGA structure. The LogiCore produces device specific firm macro and VHDL component instantiation code. A disadvantage of this approach is that the VHDL code is device or at least vendor depended and cannot be reused in the further design process.

Parallel-serial multipliers consume the least area and can have serial or parallel outputs. The parallel-serial structures include shift registers and a control logic which provides signals for start and end of serial multiplication. Results for generic pipeline and parallel-serial multipliers implemented in XCS40PQ208-4 device are presented in Table 2.

Table 2. Results for pipeline and parallel-serial multipliers

Size	Generic Pipeline			LogiCore Macro			Parallel-Serial	
A x B	CLB	f[MHz]	Mb/s	CLB	f[MHz]	Mb/s	CLB	f[MHz]
4 x 4	18	82.2	78.4	-	-	-	8	80.0
8 x 4	36	44.6	63.8	-	-	-	16	46.0
8 x 8	91	42.7	81.4	54	69.3	132	18	46.0
12 x 8	138	47.6	113	76	64.9	155	22	26.1
16 x 8	183	39.9	114	98	58.5	167	30	24.4
16 x 16	429	32.1	122	213	33.0	126	34	21.8

The LogiCore macros outperform the generic pipeline solution, but cannot be generated for input vectors having less than 6 bits. We also do not have any control over the latency in LogiCore multiplier macros, which depend on the size of vector B. Since the pipeline multipliers are preferred solutions in DSP applications with high throughput, we calculated a serial data rate (Mb/s) for each implementation. Parallel-serial multipliers can be used in parallel signal processing structures due to their small size and relatively high clock frequency.

2.1 Special Multiplier Structures

Some applications may require special multiplier structures in order to minimize the cost of implementation. We designed a 16 x 16 multiplier which has the same behavior as one in a commercial DSP [5].

The multiplier in ADSP 2181 has a latency of 1 to 4 clock cycles, depending on the value of vector B. The latency is 1 clock cycle, when the upper 24 bits of the vector B are all zero or one; 2 cycles, when the upper 16 bits are all zero or one; 3 cycles, when the upper 8 bits are all zero or one or 4 cycles, in all other cases. This specification implies a pipeline multiplier with four rows of registers and a set of multiplexers for selecting the outputs which are available in less than 4 cycles.

In order to minimize the multiplier area, we use one 16 x 5 parallel multiplier with a row of D flip-flops and a feedback loop, as presented in Figure 3. The parallel multiplier has an additional CLA in the first row which calculates the equation $P = A*B + C$, where the value C is the feedback wired to D flip-flops at the top of the multiplier.

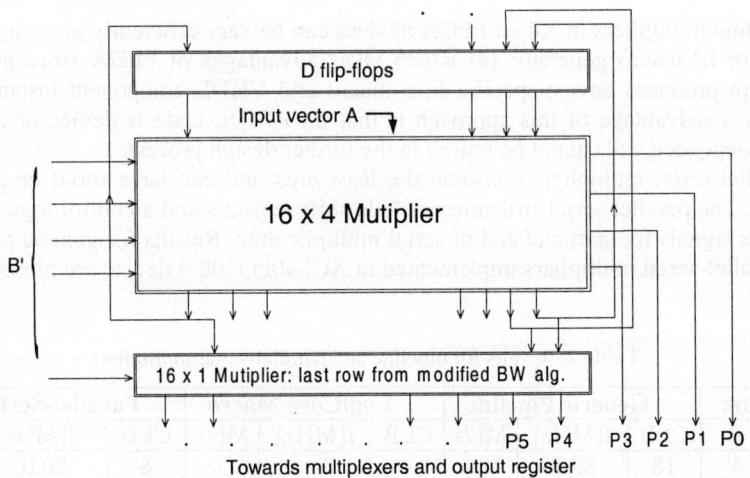

Figure 3. Multiplier from the specification of ADSP 2181

The same 16 x 5 multiplier structure is used from 1 to 4 times in one 16 x 16 bit multiplication, depending on the values of input vector B. The input B' of the parallel multiplier is composed out of 5 bits from the input vector B, as presented in Table 3.

Table 3. Input vectors B'

	\multicolumn{4}{c}{Input Vector B}			
Cycle	1	2	3	4
Input Vector B'	b_0	b_4	b_8	b_{12}
	b_1	b_5	b_9	b_{13}
	b_2	b_6	b_{10}	b_{14}
	b_3	b_7	b_{11}	b_{15}
	b_{15}	b_{15}	b_{15}	b_{15}

Additional control logic is provided for loading the D flip-flops and routing the outputs to 32 bit product vector. Comparative results from Table 4 show that we achieved drastic size-reduction in application from ADSP 2181. The multiplier also produces the output faster comparing to classic pipeline structure for the cases where the input vector B has the same value of the fifth and higher bits.

Table 4. Comparative results between multipliers

	16x16 BW	Pipeline 16 x 16	\multicolumn{2}{c}{ADSP 2181 Multiplier}	
Device	\multicolumn{3}{c}{Spartan XCS40-4}		XCV100-6
f_{MAX} [MHz]	10.3	30.1	15.3	28.2
CLB	273	429	135	85

3 Division

We designed a parametric VHDL component for standard nonrestoring divider for signed numbers [6]. The divider has a parallel structure composed of full adder cells, XOR gates and output multiplexers. The performances of the divider implemented in XCS40PQ208-4 device are shown in Table 5.

Additional speed improvement can be made by replacing each row of full adders with a single CLA adder, positioned like in multiplier's structure in Figure 1, where carry signal propagates through rows. The most significant carry bit in each row presents one bit of the division result.

Table 5. Parallel nonrestoring dividers

Vector A size	Vector B size	CLB	T_{DELAY} [ns]
8	4	19	73.8
12	4	36	115.2
12	8	43	147.0
16	4	52	151.7
16	8	74	227.0

4 Conclusions and Future Work

We designed different multiplier and divider structures as reusable generic VHDL components and implemented various circuits in Xilinx Spartan FPGA device. We tried to implement the structures in other FPGA devices (XC4000, Virtex) and found out that the timing results are only scaled in comparison to Spartan devices. The functions implemented in FPGA are certainly not so fast as they are in DSP processors, but on the other side, the presented approach offers additional flexibility. Future work will be focused on creating a general library of this functions.

References

[1] B. Glaser, Multipliers in digital integrated circuits, Faculty of Electrical Engineering, Ljubljana, 1993

[2] Xilinx Data Book, Xilinx Inc., 1998

[3] P. J. Ashenden, The Designer's Guide to VHDL, MKP Inc., 1996

[4] Parallel Multipliers – Area Optimized, Product Specification, Xilinx Inc., 1998

[5] ADSP-2100 Family EZ-KIT Lite Reference Manual, Analog Devices Inc., 1995

[6] J.F.Cavanagh, Digital Computer Arithmetic, McGraw Hill, 1985

A Parallel Pipelined SAT Solver for FPGA's *

M. Redekopp and A. Dandalis

University of Southern California, Los Angeles CA 90089, USA
{redekopp, dandalis}@halcyon.usc.edu

Abstract. Solving Boolean satisfiability problems in reconfigurable hardware is an area of great research interest. Originally, reconfigurable hardware was used to map each problem instance and thus exploit maximum parallelism in evaluation of variable assignments. However, techniques to greatly reduce the search space require dynamic reconfiguration, and make regular mappings more desirable. Unfortunately, using a regular mapping constrains the parallelism in assignment evaluation. The architectures that have emerged choose either custom mapping and maximum parallelism or regular mapping and the promise of significant decreases in the search space. We propose a framework that can exploit both. Our framework uses a regular mapping while introducing a scalable parallel architecture. Using our approach, speedups of up to one order of magnitude over current state-of-the-art reconfigurable hardware solvers have been obtained.

1 Problem

Boolean satisfiability (SAT) is a well-known NP-Complete problem that seeks to find an assignment to a set of boolean variables given a set of clauses as constraints. One way to represent SAT is using a binary decision tree (BDT) with each level corresponding to a decision and each node corresponding to a particular set of variable assignments. Decisions are made by assigning variables a specific value. Each new decision is checked for consistency with the set of clauses. During this process implications occur based on clause constraints. Backtracking occurs if a certain decision leads to a conflict in any clause. Backtracking is the process of unassigning or reassigning variables that were previously decided. A problem is satisfiable if there exists a node in the BDT that satisfies all clauses.

There are two main options to speedup standard backtrack search algorithms for solving SAT. The first is to decrease the evaluation time of each node in the search tree. This is easily done in hardware where all clauses can evaluate an assignment in parallel. The other option is to decrease the number of nodes visited in the search tree via sophisticated backtracking techniques and adding clauses dynamically [1]. FPGA implementations usually choose to exploit one option or the other. Choosing to decreasing the node evaluation time led to architectures

---

* This research was performed as part of the MAARCII project. This work is supported by the DARPA Adaptive Computing Systems program under contract no. DABT63-99-1-0004 monitored by Fort Huachuca

where all clauses were evaluated in parallel using an instance specific mapping of variables to clause circuits, as in [2]and [4]. However, to decrease the number of nodes visited requires dynamically adding clauses which is very time consuming for instance specific mappings. Instead a pipelined ring of clause circuits, or modules, with variables passing through the pipeline was proposed in [3] because it allowed fast dynamic reconfiguration times for new clauses by simply adding a new module to the end of the pipeline.

The main advantage of implementing SAT in hardware is the decrease in unit propagation time. Unit propagation time is defined as the time it takes for a decision to be checked and either move on to the next decision or backtrack. This corresponds to evaluating a node or nodes in the search tree. The main portion of this time is spent while clauses make implications or raise conflicts. Hardware solvers let clauses generate implications and conflicts in parallel, greatly reducing the unit propagation time. An instance specific mapping yields a propagation time proportional to the number of transitive implications, t, (the chain of implications that may result from implying or deciding a variable's value) made from a decision. A pipelined mapping yields unit propagation time proportional to $t \cdot e$, where t is again the number of transitive implications and e is the number of clauses.

2 Our Approach

2.1 Overview

Our design introduces a framework for fast node evaluation and dynamic learning to reduce the number of nodes visited. We propose a tightly integrated, parallel pipelined architecture for fast node evaluation while maintaining a regular pipelined mapping to simplify dynamic reconfiguration (see Figure 1). Dynamic learning requires maintaining data structures of information learned from earlier processing. Similar to [3], we envision FPGA's interacting with the host machine via a run-time assist running on the host to maintain and process the data structures for dynamic learning. Then using self-reconfiguration techniques, dynamic learning logic on the FPGA itself could add clauses dynamically. This remains a key part of our future work with the parallel architecture for fast node evaluation being the primary contribution of this work.

2.2 Parallel Pipelined Solver

Using a pipeline of clauses as our building block we split clauses into a set of parallel pipelines each with a set of variables cycling through the pipe and being merged when needed. For every decision or backtrack we run these pipelines separately and then merge their results until a consistent, global variable assignment is found. Our design of an efficient merging structure allows for tight coupling between pipelines and a high degree of parallelism. Since pipelines and merge units are regular in layout, fast compile times, fast clock speeds, and dynamic

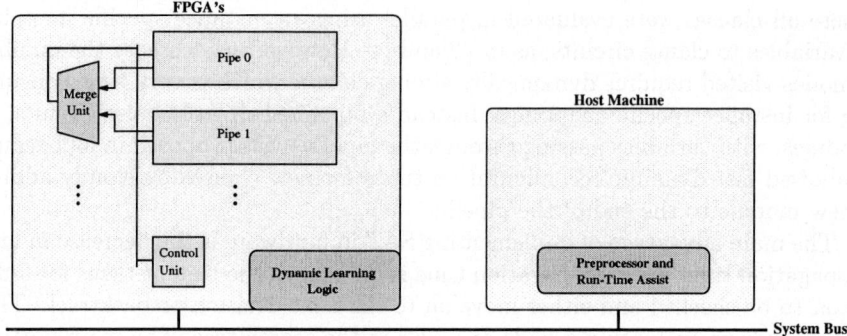

Fig. 1. Parallel Pipeline Framework

learning are possible. This design adds scalable parallelism by utilizing concepts similar to data parallelism, where multiple sets of data operate independently and are synchronized at certain points.

Given that a single pipeline has a unit propagation time of $t \cdot e$, our design decreases unit propagation time by shortening the pipeline. But, this action increases t since implications that could be found in one pass through the single pipeline may not be found by one pass through multiple pipelines. Also, creating independent sets of variables forces us to merge the results of the pipelines to update the implications or conflicts made in one pipeline to all the others before the pipelines can cycle again. This merge time must also be accounted for. Our unit propagation time is thus based on the number and cost of both merging and propagating variables through the pipelines. The unit propagation time of our design is:

$$UPT = t_p \cdot (\frac{e}{p} + \frac{v}{B}) + m_p \cdot (\log p + \frac{v}{B}) \quad (1)$$

where t_p is the average number of iterations per decision for p pipelines, e is the number of clauses, v is the number of variables, m_p is the number of merges per iteration, and B is the bus width in terms of variables.

Architecture. The basic architecture consists of a set of pipelines, operating in parallel. Each pipeline is similar in structure as that of current pipelined SAT solvers, such as the one in [3]. A single pipeline can be seen as a ring of clause modules pipelined together with a variable memory unit that cycles the variables through the clause modules. Clause modules are instance specific blocks that are based on a clause from the given SAT instance. Clause modules take a set of variables as input, generate implications or conflicts based on the input set, and produce an output set in a single cycle. Pipelines also have a variable memory that contains each variable's current value (0, 1, Undecided, or Conflicting). The variable memory is also responsible for implementing the state machine based on the given algorithm.

Fundamental to a tightly coupled approach is combining the information (implications or conflicts) from the pipelines into a consistent set of variable values. To do this we introduce a hardware block of merge units. Merging must be efficient to preserve the speedup gained from splitting the clauses into parallel pipelines. Therefore, we choose a tree structure of merging units. A subset of variables can thus be merged into their global state in $\log p$ steps. The actual merge hardware is simple as well. Using the standard two bit encoding of variables we can merge two variables through a simple bitwise OR'ing.

Algorithm. The basic algorithm must now be modified to accommodate multiple pipelines. For the problem to be proven satisfiable, a variable assignment must be found that satisfies all pipelines. Thus, we use the merge unit to assure the same variable assignment is being checked for all the pipelines. Our approach performs this merging during every decision so that the pipelines will update implications and conflicts to each other. When a decision or backtrack is made, each pipeline is at the same node and will thus make the same decision or backtrack. Using this technique also assures that the same decisions and backtracks will be made as in the standard single pipeline implementation since all implications will eventually be communicated to each pipeline. The basic algorithm for evaluating a new decision is as follows.

1. All pipelines make the same decision on their own set of variables.

2. Variables are cycled through the pipeline until all implications from that pipe are found.

3. If a conflict is found at anytime, the pipe informs the others and each pipe backtracks and the process starts again.

4. If no conflicts are found and all the pipelines have finished, a merge is performed. If the merge causes a conflict, all pipes will backtrack. If the merge caused a variable to be changed (e.g. Pipe 1 has v = 0 and Pipe 2 has v = U) the new set must be updated to all pipelines and they will now iterate with this new set by going back to step 2. If however no variables were changed in the process of merging, a consistent set has been found and a new decision can be made after updating each variable memory with this new set.

With this architecture and given the fact that we will make the same decisions and backtracks as the single pipeline we can now arrive at an approximate speedup equation by simply comparing unit propagation times:

$$Speedup = \frac{UPT_1}{UPT_p} = \frac{t_1 \cdot (e + \frac{v}{B})}{t_p \cdot (\frac{e}{p} + \frac{v}{B}) + m_p \cdot (\log p + \frac{v}{B})} \qquad (2)$$

Using this equation we can predict an optimal number of pipelines for speedup or area tradeoffs. The problem however is that t_1, t_p and m_p are intrinsic to the instance, the number of pipelines, and the partitioning of clauses. To find their exact values would require actually solving the problem, but if estimates can be found without running the entire problem, the equation can be used. Our future work will be to develop heuristics to find and use these estimates, and use self-reconfiguration to perform dynamic reconfigurations based on these parameters.

Another issue that needs to be addressed is the increase in area due to multiple pipelines. The number of clause modules is the same so the same area would be required in both our architecture and single pipeline architecture. The additional area comes from the variable memories and the merge units. If we have p pipelines the increase in area will be $p-1$ variable memories each consisting of $4 \cdot v$ bit registers (2 sets of 2 bits for each variable) and some control logic to implement the state machine. Each merge unit is made of B (B = bus width) OR gates. For a tree structure there would be $\frac{p}{2}-1$ such units. This increase in area is not prohibitive and thus allows for a reasonable number of pipelines.

3 Experimental Results

Using a C++ simulator that models a single pipeline and our parallel pipelined design to count cycles, we simulate both designs to solve specific instances. Using varying numbers of pipelines our parallel pipelined design showed speedups compared to the single pipeline. We have chosen problems from the DIMACS challenge set [5] and obtained the results shown in Table 1. The results show that moderate speedups can be obtained with even a few pipelines.

Table 1. Simulated Speedup over Single Pipeline Design

Problem	Simulated Speedup (No. of Pipelines)					
	2	4	8	16	32	64
par8-1-c	.94	1.32	2.21	2.64	2.99	3.21
hole6	1.23	2.08	3.32	4.69	5.88	6.73
aim-50-2_0-no-4	1.17	1.92	3.08	3.74	4.73	4.54
aim-50-1_6-yes1-1	1.32	1.88	2.96	3.67	3.73	3.34
aim-100-3_4-yes1-4	1.27	2.12	3.58	5.75	8.35	9.97

The nature of speedups can be characterized by accounting for two factors, the number of iterations per decision to find all implications and the number of merges per decision. Using equation (1) we see that when the number of pipelines is small the first term will dominate (i.e. most of the time is spent cycling the variable through the pipeline). This is the case with par8-1-c running with 2 pipelines. As the number of pipelines increases the merging time becomes the dominant term. This is the major reason why the speedups taper off after a certain number of pipelines. Also, as the pipeline length decreases to the point where it is always filled with variables, an increase in the number of pipelines will hurt performance (e.g. aim-50-1_6-yes1-1). Thus, if we can decrease the number of merges per decision, speedup will increase. It is also clear now that decreasing the number of iterations or passes per decision of the pipelines will yield greater speedups. This is difficult because the number of iterations per decision is primarily an intrinsic function of the instance itself. However, clause partitioning and ordering for each pipeline can make a difference. Unfortunately, to find an optimal ordering and partitioning requires solving the SAT instance. Alternately, certain heuristics could yield greater performance.

We also compared the speedups obtained from our simulator with the speedups predicted from equation (2). In all cases the predicted speedup was within a few percent of the actual speedup, but to find the intrinsic parameters t_1, t_p and m_p the simulator had to be run. However, estimates were found by running our simulator for a small number cycles. The resulting values for the parameters yielded at most 14% error after running only 20,000 cycles (less than

4 Future Work

Several key areas of our framework need to be explored. First and most important is a dynamic learning mechanism that can be integrated into our current framework. We thus plan to incorporate dynamic learning into our architecture and implement it using self-reconfiguration. Also researching possible heuristics for clause partitioning and optimal numbers of pipelines. Using learning techniques at runtime we plan to investigate the use of self-reconfiguration for increasing or decreasing the number of pipelines and better partitioning of clauses.

5 Conclusion

In conclusion, a new framework that exploits both fast node evaluation and regular mapping has been outlined. This parallel architecture and algorithm is unique in both hardware and software in that it uses a mechanism for tightly coupled data parallelism to solve SAT. We increased the amount of parallelism a pipelined design can attain by introducing multiple pipelines and developing efficient merge units to combine intermediate results. This yielded speedups of up to one order of magnitude over current state-of-the-art. Finally, we have presented a design that exploits parallelism and is still amenable to dynamic reconfiguration for dynamic learning.

The work reported here is part of the USC MAARCII project (http://maarcII.usc.edu). This project is developing novel mapping techniques to exploit dynamic reconfiguration and facilitate run-time mapping using configurable computing devices and architectures. Computational models and algorithmic techniques based on these models are being developed to exploit self-reconfiguration using FPGAs. Moreover, a domain-specific mapping approach is being developed to support instance-dependent mapping. Finally, the idea of "active" libraries is exploited to develop a framework for automatic dynamic reconfiguration.

Acknowledgments

A special thanks is extended to my advisor, Professor V. K. Prasanna for his leading and vision in this area.

References

1. J.M. Silva, *"GRASP - A New Search Algorithm for Satisfiability,"* Proc. Intn'l. Conf. on CAD, pp. 220-227, November 1996
2. P. Zhong, M. Martonosi, et al., *"Accelerating Boolean Satisfiability with Configurable Hardware,"* Proc. Symp. on Field-Programmable Custom Computing Machines, April 1998
3. P. Zhong, M. Martonosi, et al., *"Solving Boolean Satisfiability with Dynamic Hardware Configurations,"* Proc. Intn'l. Workshop on Field-Programmable Logic and Applications, Sept. 1998
4. Abramovici and Sousa, *"A SAT Solver Using Reconfigurable Hardware and Virtual Logic,"* Journal of Automated Reasoning, Vol 24, nos 1-2, pp. 5-36, Febr. 2000
5. DIMACS. Dimacs challenge benchmarks. Available at ftp://dimacs.rutgers.edu/pub/challenge/sat/benchmarks/cnf

A Multi-node Dynamic Reconfigurable Computing System with Distributed Reconfiguration Controller

Abdellah Touhafi

Vrije Universiteit Brussel,TW-INFO, Pleinlaan 2, 1050 Brussels Belgium
Atouhafi@info.vub.ac.be

Abstract. This paper reports the implementation of a multi-node dynamically reconfigurable computing system. The system is based on a scalable dynamic reconfigurable computing node which consists of three resource layers. Scalability of the system is introduced on some of those layers in order to deal with context synchronization aspects. This approach leads to a multi-node reconfigurable computing architecture with a distributed reconfiguration controller, which helps in hiding the reconfiguration and synchronization cost partially.

1. Introduction

Many multi-node reconfigurable computing systems have been built for special purpose computing tasks, software acceleration and circuit emulation. Those systems are mainly based on of the shelf FPGA's and in some cases special interconnect chips like FPIC's [1]. Those systems however, cope with an enormous performance drop once the circuit size grows and their mapping on the hardware can not be nicely pipelined and structured. The reason behind this performance drop is related to the fixed granularity of the used FPGA components and the interconnect latency at the system level. Out of Amdahls law we know that with each system-granularity point a certain maximum amount of resources can be used effectively for spatial parallelism. Ones over that ideal point more spatial resources will create an excessive communication cost such that the benefit gained by the extra components is back lost by the created communication overhead. When a circuit is mapped on a large multi-FPGA system, the number of processing elements that is required is directly related to the size of the circuit. This has as effect that for very large circuits which are mapped on systems with more nodes than the mentioned critical point might gain speed by using Dynamically Programmable Gate Array's instead of FPGA's. Those components give us the possibility to change the granularity of the system in a virtual manner by sequencing parts of the circuit such that the number of nodes is closer to the optimum and the interconnect cost diminishes. As an experimental platform, we have built a scalable multi-node dynamically reconfigurable computing system. The system is based on a scalable computing node such that a multi-node system can be built with a scalable distributed reconfiguration controller. In section two we will give an overview of the setup of such a scalable computing node and explain the different parts of it. Section three then details a four node dynamically reconfigurable computing board that is implemented in a scalable way such that a multi-board dynamic reconfigurable computing system can be built.

2 RTR Systems

The implementation of our scalable dynamically reconfigurable platform is based on a three layers architecture. Where scalability is introduced on different levels of the architecture in order to hide partially the reconfiguration-, communication-, scheduling- and synchronization cost inherent to the physical constraints of the used technology. The three layers characteristic for the architecture of a computing node are as denoted in figure one and consist of a scalable dynamic reconfigurable data-path layer, a scalable programmable reconfiguration controller layer and a distributed memory layer. A multi-node dynamic reconfigurable system can then be built using a set of interconnected computing nodes. Each of the computing nodes is organized around the scalable reconfiguration handler which has the ability to send and receive synchronization information from the other nodes. The reconfiguration controller has direct access to all its local resources and indirect access to the resources of the neighbor nodes through a set of four communication links. Its major task is to deal with the correct reconfiguration of its local dynamic reconfigurable data-path, to setup the state information and to save state information. Next to that, the controller also handles the data exchange between the active context and the memory. The dynamic reconfigurable data-path layer has four communication links. This for the contexts mapped on the data-path layer to exchange data. The memory layer contains four kinds of data: the configuration data of the different contexts, the state information of the contexts, the application data related to that context and the code of a reconfiguration handling program.

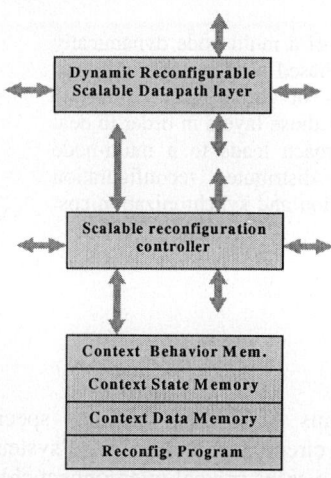

Fig. 1. Simplified Three layer architecture of one computing node.

2.1 The Scalable Reconfiguration Controller

The reconfiguration manager deals with the reconfiguration details, makes sure that the correct context is scheduled and computing resources are synchronized. A good reconfiguration controller should be able to manage the available computing resources efficiently among the tasks without introducing a lot of over-head in reconfiguration and scheduling time. Next to that the controller must be programmable and generally applicable. In order to achieve that we implemented the controller distributed among the dynamic reconfigurable nodes such that the amortized reconfiguration cost will diminish while available memory bandwidth and computing resources grow as the system grows. The scalable reconfiguration controller is implemented using a fast FPGA in stead of a RISC as the latter would require the implementation of additional communication link controllers. The scalability of the controller is achieved by providing communication busses and dedicated synchronization pins together with a dedicated memory- and reconfiguration interface. The control layer is organized as shown in figure two. For the programming of the control-layer we have foreseen a local controller which can be accessed through the local data-bus and four control-lines.

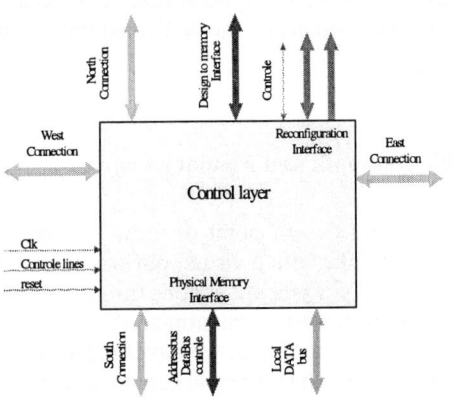

Fig. 2. The control layer.

As depicted in figure three the control layer is organized around this local controller and a reconfigurable logic plane. In the Reconfigurable Logic Plane the user can program a suitable controller extension for his application. The local controller contains a state-machine which gives the user (and/or programmer) of the system access to all the communication ports, the memory interface and the reconfiguration port of the controller. This way the user can trace the system and his application, even at runtime. It also creates the possibility to simulate or replace the controller extension by a software controller that runs on an external micro-processor. Remark that the local controller is connected to the reconfigurable part by a fast bi-directional local control-bus. The communication between the two parts is asynchronous and follows a predefined communication protocol. Normally the controller extension is programmed as a reconfiguration handler making the need of an external processor not necessary. If the designer of the controller extension follows the communication protocol he can make the registers of his design readable through the local controller. Four communication links are provided for the inter-controller communication. Remark, that the links are not used for the distribution of partial computing results that come from the computing layer. Instead, the individual node controllers send synchronization messages to each other for starting or stopping a computation, loading a new context or for checking the neighbors status registers and other aspects related to the dynamic reconfiguration control. It is also possible for neighbor nodes to exchange memory-data through the links. The designer of the controller extension, however, must implement a DMA-controller as part of the controller extension. The inter-node communication is

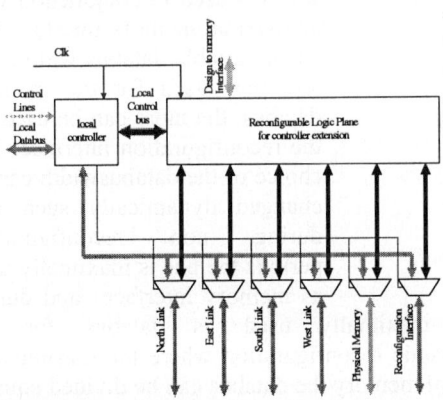

Fig. 3. Internal setup of control layer

message based and uses an asynchronous communication protocol. For synchronization purposes we have provided dedicated synchronization lines. The reconfiguration engines of interconnected nodes can synchronize the context switching and context activation by sending synch-signals on the dedicated lines or by sending synch-messages through the links.

2.2 The Scalable Dynamic Reconfigurable Datapath and Memory Layer

The Computing layer organization from a system design point of view is given in figure four. It consists out of four bi-directional links with a virtual pin size that goes from 16 pins to 256 pins. The control of the virtual pin-amount is done through virtual pin control lines. The virtual pin control lines are used to synchronize the data send through the virtual pins between neighbor nodes. Next to that, we have foreseen pins such that the context mapped into the computing layer has direct access to an external memory without occupying the reconfiguration interface. The reconfiguration interface has a dedicated clock pin and dedicated control pins, it further has a variable width bi-directional databus and a fixed address bus. The variable databus width is used in conjunction with an external memory interface that has a variable databus width. The less pins used for the memory databus, the more can be used for the reconfiguration interface. The choice of the databuswidth can be changed dynamically such that during non reconfiguration periods the bus is maximally used as memory interface and during reconfiguration-cycles the bus is maximally used as databus for the reconfigurationcontroller. During a dynamic reconfiguration where the non touched part of the circuit is accessing the external memory the databus can be divided equally between the memory interface and the reconfiguration controller. The implemented computing layer has four bi-directional communication links of each 16 bits. This gives the possibility to form meshes or other interconnect architectures among the computing nodes. There is also an interrupt line such that the active context can invoke a reconfiguration request by asserting the interrupt line and setting the reconfiguration bit of an interrupt register also located in the computing layer. Memory is used to store four kinds of data namely the configuration data (i.e. contexts), the state data, the application data and the reconfiguration code. The organization is such that we have a memory shared by the controller layer and the computing layer of the same node. An application specific interconnect that handles the memory sharing must be designed in the reconfigurable logic plane of the control layer. Note that this is the reason why the control layer has a *design-to-memory-bus* that is interconnected with the reconfigurable logic plane. The complexity of the

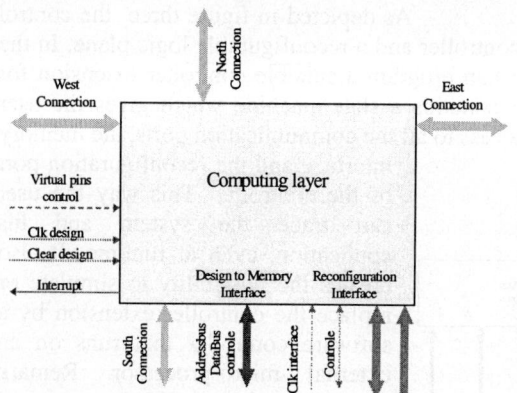

Fig. 4. The computing layer pin layout.

memory handler is rather low because there are no contention conflicts possible between the control layer and the computing layer. This because the system can be in only one of two states: a computing state during which the memory is accessed by the computing layer and a control state in which the controller needs access to the memory. In case related contexts are separated temporally as well as spatially on the computing system, the active context must have access to the memory plane of the node where the related node is located. That's why we have provided access to the memory through the communication links on the control layer. The use of a distributed memory has as advantage that the memory bandwidth scales up with the number of computing nodes and that the amortized reconfguration cost scales down with the number of computing nodes.

3 SUREsCA: A Scalable Multi-node Dynamically Reconfigurable Computing System

SUREsCA is a scalable dynamic reconfigurable computing system with four computing nodes and a master controller. As shown in figure five, the system has connectors on the four sides of the board such that large meshed multi-node systems can be formed. The master controller interconnects the board with a host by an EPP connection. The master itself is connected with its four neighbor masters such that synchronization between the masters can be accomplished. This is necessary for the system resource control as they all share the same parallel port. Note that the system is used as a standalone computing system and not as a co-processor for the host connected to it. The host is used only for the system setup and for system debugging. The master has control over two programmable clocks, the virtual pin control signals of the four nodes and the control signals of the control layer. The local data-busses of the four nodes share one bus which is also controlled by the master controller. The whole system is configured through the shared local databus. The computing layer of the four nodes is interconnected as a pipeline. When interconnecting two boards a large mesh or pipeline can be formed. The "design clock" pin of the computing layer is controlled by the master which can change the clock rate during a context switch. For the implementation of the computing layer we have used an XC6264 [3] RPU of XILINX. The control layer is implemented by an XC4013E FPGA [2] of XILINX. The Control Layer is interconnected the same way as the computing layer. The control signals are interconnected in a mesh while the

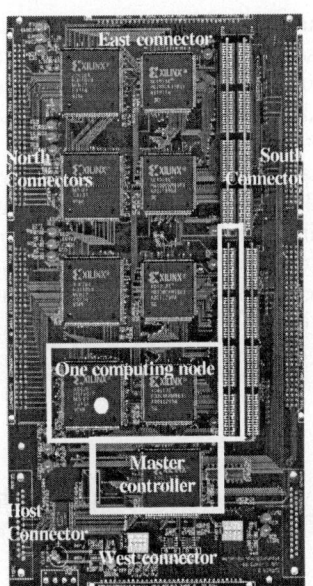

Fig. 5. Prototype board

programmation interface is interconnected as a common bus. Each controller has its individual set of control signals also interconnected with the master controller. We have implemented a scalable RISC-like reconfiguration engine into the controller extension for context control. The performance results of that specific controller can be found in [4]. The memory layer is based on fast 12 ns SRAM. Each node has four megabytes of Ram for the context storage, the application data storage, the state storage and the code of the reconfiguration handler.

The memory is accessible by the node resources and the reconfiguration controller of the near neighbor nodes. The system also provides three clock signals. One of them is a fixed non programmable clock signal which is used for the master controller and the control layer. The other two are programmable clocks which are used for the computing layer. One clock is used for the reconfiguration interface and the other clock is used for the loaded context. The two clock rates can be changed on demand of a local controller. The system is built on an eight-layer printed circuit board. The control layer is clocked with a 20 MHz clock while the dynamic control layer can be clocked from 2 MHz up to 100 MHz.

7 Summary

We've discussed the implementation issues of a multi-node dynamic reconfigurable computing system which is build, based on a scalable dynamic reconfigurable computing node. The implementation of the computing node is based on a three layer model which exists of a dynamic reconfigurable data-path layer, a programmable control layer and a memory layer. Scalability of the system is introduced on the control layer and on the dynamic reconfigurable datapath layer. This is necessary for context synchronization aspects. This approach leads to a multi-node system with a distributed reconfiguration controller which, helps in hiding the reconfiguration and synchronization cost partially. A multi-node system is built based on of the shelf FPGA's and DPGA's for proof of concept. On the build system a reconfiguration mechanism has been implemented which is reported in [4].

8 References

[1] M.Sliman Kadi et al,A fast FPGA prototyping system that uses inexpensive high peformance FPIC, proc. of ACM/SIGDA works Field Programmable Gate Array's 1994.
[2] XC4000E series, Xilinx, The programmable logic Databook
[3] XC6200 , Xilinx, Databook
[4] Abdellah Touhafi, W. Brissinck, E.F. Dirkx, A Scalable Run Time Reconfigurable Architecture, Proceedings of the X IFIP international conference on VLSI, VLSI 99, December 1999 Lisboa Portugal.

A Reconfigurable Stochastic Model Simulator for Analysis of Parallel Systems

O. Yamamoto[1], Yuichiro Shibata[2], Hitoshi Kurosawa[2], and Hideharu Amano[2]

[1] Tokyo Denki University, Dept. of Electronic Engineering
2-2 Kanda-Nishiki-cho Chiyoda-ku Tokyo 101-8457 Japan
[2] Keio University, Dept. of Computer Science,
3-14-1 Hiyoshi Kohoku-ku Yokohama 223 JAPAN

Abstract. Markov chain and queueing model are convenient tools with which to analyze parallel systems for architects. For a high speed execution and easy modeling, a reconfigurable Markov chain/queueing model simulation system called RSMS (Reconfigurable Stochastic Model Simulator) is proposed. A user describes the target system in a dedicated description language called Taico. The description is automatically translated into the HDL description of the Markov chain/queueing model simulator. Then, the simulator is implemented on the FPGA devices of the reconfigurable system, and directly executed. From the evaluation with analysis of example parallel systems, it appears that the analysis speed of the proposed system is much greater than that of common workstations.

1 Introduction

Various kinds of theoretical models including discrete time Markov chain(DTMC), queueing model, and Petri nets are used for analysis of parallel systems. In these models, DTMC and queueing models are familiar to architects who are not experts of theoretical analysis since they are easy to learn and apply to target systems. However, to analyze complicated large scale parallel systems, DTMC requires a huge number of states, and queueing model requires a large queueing network. So, it is really rare to construct models which can be solved analytically.

In such a case, stochastic analysis such as Monte Carlo method by the computer simulation can be applied. However, even with such methods, it takes a long time to solve systems which include events with very low probabilities. Although various techniques including the importance sampling[1],[2] are proposed to deal with such cases, these techniques are difficult to use for architects who are not experts of theoretical analysis.

By making the best use of recent advanced technologies on the SRAM-programmable FPGAs (Field Programmable Gate Array), a lot of novel computing systems which are classified into *reconfigurable systems* or *custom computing machines*[3]-[5] have been developed. In such systems, algorithms are translated into hardware logics on the FPGA, and directly executed more than hundred times faster than workstations. In this paper, we propose a reconfigurable DTMC and queueing model simulation system called RSMS(Reconfigurable Stochastic Model Simulator) for analysis of large parallel systems.

RSMS provides an easy-to-use simulation environment of DTMC and queueing network to parallel system architects who are not experts of theoretical analysis. RSMS only requires them to describe a target parallel system as a DTMC or queueing model in a simple language called Taico. RSMS consists of the following four components: the model description language Taico, the Taico-HDL translator, a commercial logic synthesis tool, and a reconfigurable machine called FLEMING[7].

The rest of the paper is organized as follows: Section 2 describes the model description language Taico, Section 3 describes the structures of simulation circuits, Section 4 presents application examples to analyzing practical parallel systems.

2 Model Description Language Taico

2.1 Description of DTMC in Taico

Generally, parallel systems consist of N elements $(E_1, E_2, \cdots, E_N)$ which operate in parallel with some interactions. Therefore, it is easy to describe a parallel system as a set of N state transition diagrams which correspond to the elements one-to-one and a set of interactions between them. When a state of each element $E_i, 1 \leq i \leq N$ can be represented by S_{E_i}, a state of the whole system is specified by a set of all the states:

$$(S_{E_1}, S_{E_2}, \cdots, S_{E_N}).$$

Description of DTMC in Taico accords to this policy. Taico provides methods for describing elements and interactions between them. A user divides the target parallel system into several elements and describes their state transition diagrams and interactions between them. In Taico, these interactions can be described in conditional expressions associated with descriptions of state transitions.

As an example, we show a simple system consists of two elements(E_1, E_2) in Figure 1. E_1 and E_2 have two states A, B and C, D, respectively. E_1 transits from A to B or from B to A with probabilities P_{ab}, P_{ba}, respectively. E_2 also transits between states C and D with probabilities P_{cd}, P_{dc}. Since the system is a DTMC model, every transition is synchronized to a system clock.

Where, we assume the following interaction between E_1 and E_2: E_1 can not make any state transition while E_2 stays on D. Figure 1 also shows a description of E_1 in Taico .

In the line 1, the name of the element E_1 is declared. And the line 2 is a declaration of states for $E1$. From line 3 to line 10 is a description of state transitions. For example, the line 3 describes that if E_1 is in state A and E_2 is in state D, E_1 must stay in A. And the line 5 and 6 describe that if E_2 is not in D, E_1 can transit to B with the probability P_{ba} and stays A with $1 - P_{ba}$.

To complete the description of the whole system, a description for E_2 which is a little modification of E_1 description is required. In RSMS, the following

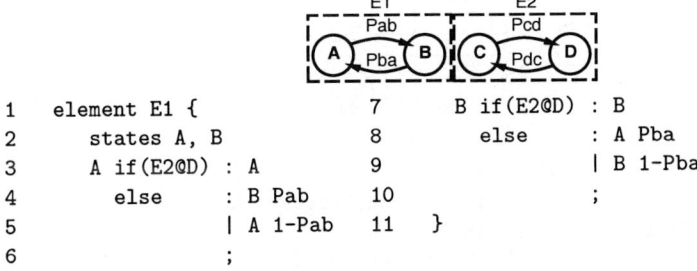

```
1   element E1 {                7       B if(E2@D) : B
2       states A, B             8         else     : A Pba
3       A if(E2@D) : A          9                  | B 1-Pba
4         else     : B Pab      10                 ;
5                  | A 1-Pab    11    }
6                  ;
```

Fig. 1. State transition diagram of a simple two elements system and description of element E_1 written in Taico

matters can be measured by automatic generated measurement circuits consist of 32-bit counters. (1)The number of times for which a target system arrives to the specified state(s). (2)The total length of target system's stay in the specified state(s). The former measurement is specified in Taico by the sentence reach(formula indicating state(s)) and the latter measurement is specified by the sentence stay(formula indicating state(s)). In the above example, the following specifies the measurement of the number of times for which E_1 reaches to B.

reach(E1@B)

In this case, a counter in a measurement circuit is incremented every time E_1 reaches to state B regardless of states of E_2.

2.2 Description of Queueing Network in Taico

Modeling a parallel system as a queueing model usually requires not a single queue but a network which consists of several queues and servers linked each other. In such a model, a call is generated by a source according to some probability distributions, and sometimes distinguished depending types to which it belongs. Calls move around the network, and also branch or join at junctions. Taico provides constructions for describing queue, call source, type of call, server, branch junction, and joining junction. Thus, users can easily describe queueing networks using these parts in Taico.

As an example, we show a simple queueing network in Figure 2. In this example, calls are generated by a call source named "S". Each call belongs to one of two types Type1 or Type2. At the junction B, each call branches to output o1 or o2 depending on its type. Where, a call which belongs to Type1 branches for o1 and enters the queue Q1, and a call which belongs to Type2 branches for o2 and enters the queue Q2. Calls queueing in Q1 and Q2 are served by servers SV1 and SV2, respectively, and removed from the network.

Figure 2 also shows a description of the example network. Where, source "S", branch "B", queue "Q1", "Q2", and server "SV1" and "SV2" are described in sequence. We omit details of the description due to space constraints.

During a simulation of a queueing network on FLEMING, the number of arrival of calls in each queue, the number of completion of service in each server,

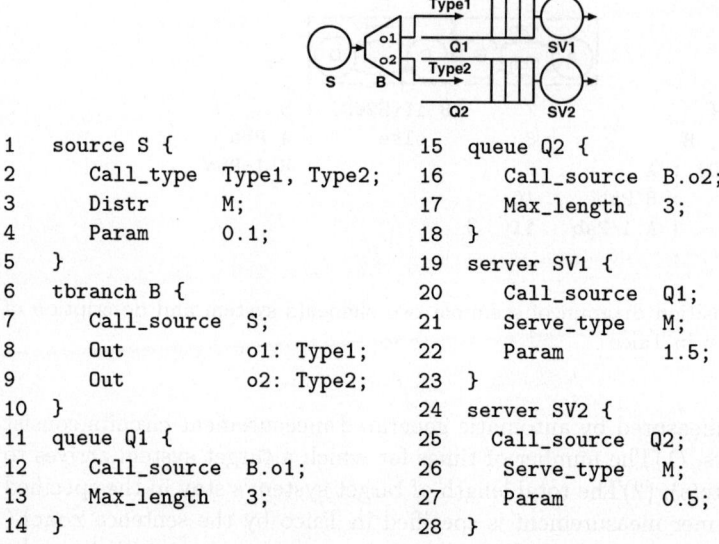

```
1   source S {                         15   queue Q2 {
2       Call_type  Type1, Type2;       16       Call_source  B.o2;
3       Distr      M;                  17       Max_length   3;
4       Param      0.1;                18   }
5   }                                  19   server SV1 {
6   tbranch B {                        20       Call_source  Q1;
7       Call_source  S;                21       Serve_type   M;
8       Out          o1: Type1;        22       Param        1.5;
9       Out          o2: Type2;        23   }
10  }                                  24   server SV2 {
11  queue Q1 {                         25       Call_source  Q2;
12      Call_source  B.o1;             26       Serve_type   M;
13      Max_length   3;                27       Param        0.5;
14  }                                  28   }
```

Fig. 2. Example of a simple queueing network and its description written in Taico

the average service time in each server, the average number of calls waiting for service in each queue, and the total simulation time are measured. These measurement are done by measurement circuits automatically added into each queue and servers in a Taico-HDL translation process.

3 Structures of Simulation Circuits

3.1 Structure of DTMC Simulation Circuit

In Taico the target parallel system is described in coordinate operating elements, and the behavior of each element is represented in a probabilistic state transition diagram. The hardware architecture of the proposed simulator is a direct translation of this representation. That is, state machines each of which is corresponding to each element are connected as shown in Figure 3.

Each state machine consists of a register holding the current state of the element, and combinatorial circuits for deciding the next state. The next state of each state machine is decided by the current states of relational state machines and the probabilistic condition for the state transition. The probabilistic condition is implemented with the comparison between a fixed number and the random number supplied from the attached Random Number Generator(RNG). The bit width of the register, combinatorial circuits and the connections between state machines are optimized for the target state transition. Since all blocks of this simulator work at a unique clock, the maximum frequency on the reconfigurable machine directly decides the analysis speed.

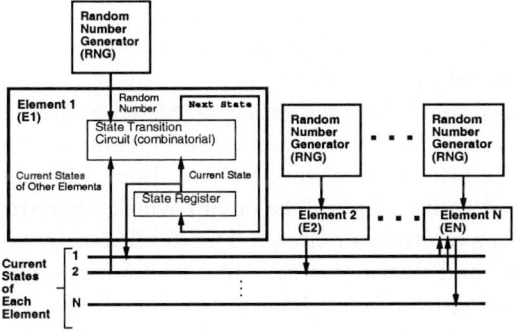

Fig. 3. Architecture of DTMC simulation circuit

For reporting the analysis results, measuring circuits which count the occurrence of particular states are also generated on demand. This measuring block usually consists of 32 bits counter and circuits for detecting whether the state machines to the particular states indicated with "reach" or "stay" in Taico description.

The HDL description of above simulator is translated from Taico description automatically with the Taico-HDL translator described in standard C language. Here, Verilog-HDL is used as a target HDL. This translator generates each state machine from the Taico description of each element, adds the RNGs and measuring circuits if necessary, and connects them each other.

3.2 Structure of Queueing Network Simulation Circuit

A queueing network is described in Taico as a collection of elements such as sources of call, branching/joining junctions, queues and servers. According to this policy of description, the structure of queueing network simulation circuit is a collection of small circuits each of which simulates each of elements one by one. And these circuits operate under a single system clock. The simulation speed (unit time/sec) depends on not only the system clock, but on an accuracy of simulation of Poisson distribution as described later. Same as the DTMC simulation circuits, random number generators are used to simulate probabilistic behavior of a model.

In the simulation circuit, a call is represented as a single pulse synchronized to the system clock. The circuit which simulates a source of call is constructed as a circuit which generates a pulse randomly in every clock cycle. Therefore, to simulate Poisson distribution accurately in such a case of continuous time analysis, a number of clock cycles is required. However, in most cases of parallel systems analysis using queueing network, all elements in target systems are assumed to be synchronized a single clock. In such a case, the clock corresponds directly to the clock of the simulation circuit, so the target system can be simulated without any degradation of speed.

The circuit which simulates a queue is constructed from FIFO memory. The circuit receives a call from the circuit linked to its input, and sends a call to the circuit linked to its output.

The circuit which simulates a server is constructed from a timer circuit. When the circuit receives a call from the circuit linked to its input, it starts to count the clock and after the service interval specified in a Taico description, sends the call to the circuit linked to its output. The circuit which simulates branch junction is constructed from a multiplexor circuit. The circuit receives calls from a circuit linked to its input, and distributes calls to outputs randomly or depending on types of call according to a Taico description. The circuit which simulates join junction is constructed form a de-multiplexor circuit. The circuit receives calls from circuits linked to its inputs and send the calls to its output one by one.

3.3 Random Number Generator

As a random number generator used in both DTMC and queueing model, we choose a generalized feedback shift register (GFSR) as a random number generator in our system. This algorithm generates random numbers according to the following formula.

$$X_n = X_{n-89} \oplus X_{n-38} \quad (X_n : 32bit\ vector, \oplus : bit\ by\ bit\ ExOR) \quad (1)$$

The period of sequence is 2^{89-1}. This generator can supply a random number with a clock by a simple circuit with shift-registers and exclusive-or, while a lot of flip-flops are required.

3.4 FLEMING: A Reconfigurable Testbed

A DTMC model or queueing network model described in Taico is translated into a HDL description of a simulation circuit by Taico-HDL translator. The HDL descriptions of these circuits are provided as a library in the translator. In the translation process, they are linked according to a model described in Taico and made into a simulation circuit. The simulation circuit is finally generated in a reconfigurable machine called FLEMING(Flexible Logic EMulatIon eNGine). Although FLEMING is originally developed as an emulation system for the virtual hardware WASMII[7], it is also useful as a general purpose reconfigurable testbed.

As shown in Figure 4, FLEMING consists of six *Reconfigurable Units (RUs)*, together with an *Interface Unit (IU)* that contains a conventional microprocessor. Each RU provides a Xilinx's XC5215 FPGA[8] and 128Kbyte local memory. These RUs are connected each other with *direct paths* and *reconfigurable paths*. The direct paths are permanently and cannot be changed; the reconfigurable paths can be modified by the *switching elements (SEs)*. Each SE consists of Lattice's ispLSI2032, an in-system programmable EEPROM-based PLD. The configuration of SEs is left in non-volatile memory and is down-loaded from the host computer via a dedicated cable.

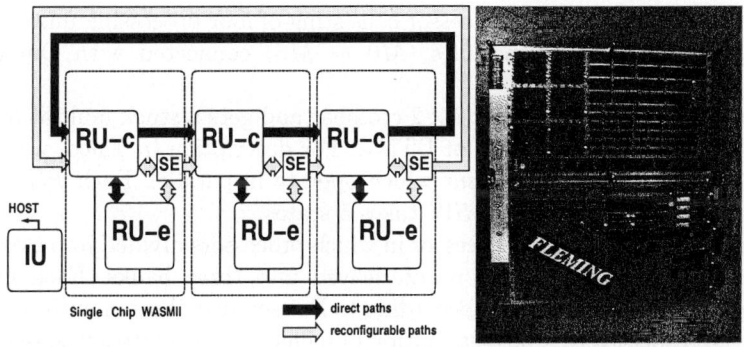

Fig. 4. Structure of FLEMING(left) and a photo of the FLEMING(right)

When the system begins operation, the host workstation automatically downloads the configuration data and the initial execution data into the RUs via the IU. As also shown in Figure 4, FLEMING is implemented on a 30 cm × 30cm bread board.

4 Evaluation

4.1 Target Parallel Systems

The following four actual parallel systems areanalyzed by RSMS:(1)the IEEE Futurebus arbiter, (2)a multiprocessor with 4-input Omega network with a fault, (3) a multiprocessor with multiple shared buses, and (4) a multiprocessor with 8-input Omega network. The target (1) and (2) are modeled as DTMC models, while the target (3) and (4) are modeled as queueing networks.

The target (1) is the arbitration protocol of IEEE Futurebus[9]. In this model, each element moves among six states as shown in the left of Figure 5.

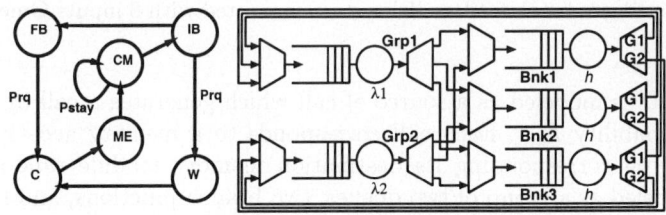

Fig. 5. State transition diagram of Futurebus bus arbitration protocol(left) and Queueing network for memory/bus access of multiple shared bus system(right)

The target (2) is a multiprocessor consisting of four processing units ($PU0 \sim PU3$) and four memory modules ($M0 \sim M3$) connected with Omega network[11].

Each switching element is a 2×2 crossbar and gets a stuck fault at a certain probability P_{down} in each step of DTMC. For description in Taico, we selected each PU and SW as an *element* which operate in parallel. Each PU takes 13 states alternatively while each SW takes 5 states.

The target (3) is a multiprocessor in which processors divided into two groups access a shared memory that is interleaved into three banks. Each group is assumed to access the memory according to Poisson distribution with parameter λ_1 and λ_2, respectively. The distribution of memory access latency is assumed to be a Poisson distribution with parameter h. The queueing network corresponding to the target system is shown in Figure 5.

Where, each processor group/memory bank is modeled as a pair of a queue and a server. Each memory access is represented as a call. In this model, there are two types of call, $Grp1$ and $Grp2$.

The target (4) is a multiprocessor same as the target (2) except the its size, but assumed to be fault free. This system consists of eight processing units ($PU0 \sim PU7$) and eight memory modules ($M0 \sim M7$) connected with Omega network[11]. The network consists of twelve switches $SW0 \sim SW11$. The queueing network of the target is shown in Figure 6.

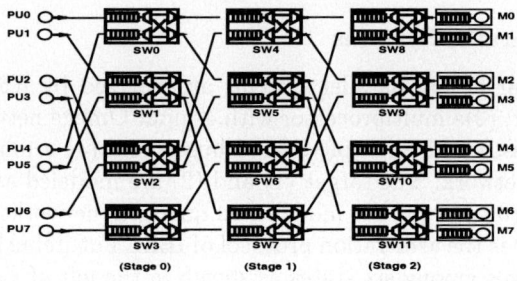

Fig. 6. Queueing network for Parallel system connected with 8 inputs Omega network

Each PU is modeled as a source of call which generates a call in every step with a probability P_{acc}. Each call corresponds to a memory access and is assigned a type corresponding its destination memory module randomly. Each SW is modeled as a group of two queues, two branch junctions, and two joining junctions. Each memory module is modeled as a pair of a queue and a server. The service distribution is uniform (3 steps). A call is served in a memory module then leaves the network.

4.2 Execution on FLEMING

Descriptions in Taico for the above four target systems are translated into Verilog-HDL, and the logic of the simulator is synthesized for FLEMING. Here, Mentor Graphics Autologic is used for the synthesis. It took a few seconds for translation and 20 minutes or up to 1 hour for logic synthesis.

The number of CLB(Configurable Logic Block)s and corresponding number of gates are shown in Table 1. Gates for the RNG is not counted since it allocated another RU because of its large hardware requirement. In FLEMING, six RUs are divided into three pairs. Since the required CLB of each block is less than that of CLB of each RU (XC5215), two RUs are used for each analysis, thus, an RU is used for the target simulator while the partner is used for the RNG.

Table 1. The maximum frequency and required CLBs

	Maximum Frequency	Num. of CLBs	Num. of gates
Futurebus	9.1 MHz	345	10350
4-in Omega	9.4 MHz	349	10470
8-in Omega	11.6 MHz	837	25110
Shared bus	15.3 MHz	302	9060
RNG	3.2 MHz	243	7290

As shown in Table 1, 3.2 MHz clock speed is achieved although the operation speed of the RNG bottlenecks the system. As described in section 3.1, the clock speed directly corresponds to simulation speed, thus, the above speed means 3.2 Msteps/sec of the simulation speed. When a small sized random number generator which provides a short period of sequence is used, both simulators work at 8 MHz clock.

For comparison, the simulation speed of a software simulator (written in C language) on a workstation (SUN Ultrasparc 300MHz) is shown in Table 2.

Table 2. Simulation speed with the workstation

	Simulation Speed (Steps/s)
Futurebus	46800
4 inputs MIN	29700
8 inputs MIN	6500
Shared bus	17100

Since the analysis of the 4-inputs Omega network requires 10^9 simulation steps, it takes more than 33000 seconds (about 9 hours) with software on the workstation. However, if the RSMSis used, only 330 seconds are required for analysis. This demonstrates the high performance of the simulator considering the time for logic synthesis and configuration. In addition, probabilistic parameters used in target can be modified via host workstation of FLEMING after the circuits are generated. So user need not to make a logic synthesis every modification of parameters.

5 Conclusion

A reconfigurable Markov chain and queueing model simulation system, RSMS is proposed and evaluated. In this system, a user describes the target parallel system in a dedicated description language called Taico. From the evaluation with analysis of example parallel systems, it appears that the analysis speed on a reconfigurable testbed is sometimes hundreds times than that of common workstations.

References

1. P. Shahabuddin, "Rare Event Simulation in Stochastic Models", Proc. of the Winter Simulation Conference, 1995, pp.178-185
2. M. and J. Villen-Altamarino, "RESTART: a straightforward method for fast simulation of rare events", Proc. of the Winter Simulation Conference, 1994, pp.282-289
3. J. Arnold, D. Buell and E. Davis, "SPLASH2 " Proc. of the 4th ACM Symposium on Parallel Algorithms and Architectures, pp.316-322, 1992.
4. M. Wazlowski, L. Agarwal, T. Lee, A. Smith, E. Lam, P. Athanas, H. Silverman and S. Ghosh, "PRISM-II Compiler and Architecture," Proc. of IEEE Workshop on FPGAs for Custom Computing Machines, IEEE Computer Society Press, pp.9-16, 1993.
5. R.Hartenstein, J.Becker, R.Kress, "Costum Computing Machines vs. Hardware/Software Co-Design: From a Globalized Point of View," Proc. of FPL'96, (LNCS 1142), pp.65-76, 1996.
6. P. L'Ecuyer, "Recent Advances in Uniform Random Number Generation", Proc. of the Winter Simulation Conference, 1994, pp. 176-183
7. Y. Shibata, X-P. Ling, H. Amano, "An Emulation System of the WASMII: Data Driven Computer on a Virtual Hardware", Proc. of FPL'96, (LNCS 1142), 1996, pp.55-64
8. XILINX Corp, Programmable Gate Array's Data Book, July 1996
9. IEEE, "IEEE Standard Backplane Bus Specification for Multiprocessor Architectures: Futurebus,", Jun. 1988
10. T. Terasawa, O Yamamoto, T. Kudoh, H. Amano: "A performance evaluation of the multiprocessor testbed ATTEMPT-0", Parallel Computing 21, 1995, pp.701-730
11. D.H. Lawrie: "Access and Alignment of Data in an Array Processor", IEEE Trans. Comput. Vol.C-24, No.12, Dec. 1975

A CORDIC Arctangent FPGA Implementation for a High-Speed 3D-Camera System

Stephen J. Bellis[1] and William P. Marnane[2]

[1] National Microelectronics Research Centre, Lee Maltings, Prospect Row,
Cork, Ireland
sbellis@nmrc.ucc.ie
http://www.nmrc.ie
[2] Department of Electrical Engineering,
University College Cork, Ireland
marnane@ucc.ie
http://www.ucc.ie

Abstract. This paper presents the design and FPGA implementation of a pipelined CORDIC arctangent unit suitable for use in a 3D camera system. The end use for this application is in the assembly of printed circuit boards where there is a need for high-speed 3D height inspection of solder paste. FPGAs are chosen as the implementation platform, firstly for their quick turnaround to a final prototype; secondly for their reprogrammability to meet advances in algorithm design via software rather than hardware; thirdly footprint compatible higher speed grade FPGAs can be used to adapt the system to improved sensor technologies as they become available; finally the latest FPGAs offer a wide range of resources, including SDRAM drivers, ZBT SRAM drivers, fast carry logic and interfaces such as LVTTL and LVDS.

1 Introduction

In printed circuit board assembly there is a need for accurate high-speed inspection [1]. IC packages are becoming increasingly intricate and the number of pins, for example on ball grid array packages, is also expanding [2]. To improve yield it is important to acquire 3D height images of the solder paste footprints quickly and accurately before soldering [3]. The 3DCam system makes this possible.

3DCam is based on the phase measurement triangulation algorithm [4]. Fringes are projected onto the solder paste to be measured using a liquid crystal modulator to filter a bright light source. A 2D camera is used to capture eight images consisting of fringes with two different wavelengths, each having four different phase shifts of 0, $\frac{\pi}{2}$, π and $\frac{3\pi}{2}$ radians. When projected on the object to be measured the fringes are distorted and the height of a particular pixel can be evaluated by applying the phase measurement triangulation algorithm to the same pixel in all eight images. Current systems use a PC to perform the processing for the evaluation, however, this method is slow as the PC has the heavy burden of controlling the movement of six cameras in parallel as well as performing their independent height evaluations.

This work aims to speed up the measurement process by instead performing the evaluation on a separate hardware platform. FPGAs offer the ideal solution to the hardware implementation. They offer a good turnaround rate to the final prototype compared to ASICs. Their reprogrammability can be used to adjust to developments in the evaluation process at any stage, an increase in the number of fringes for example. Fig. 1 shows the layout of the 3DCam system.

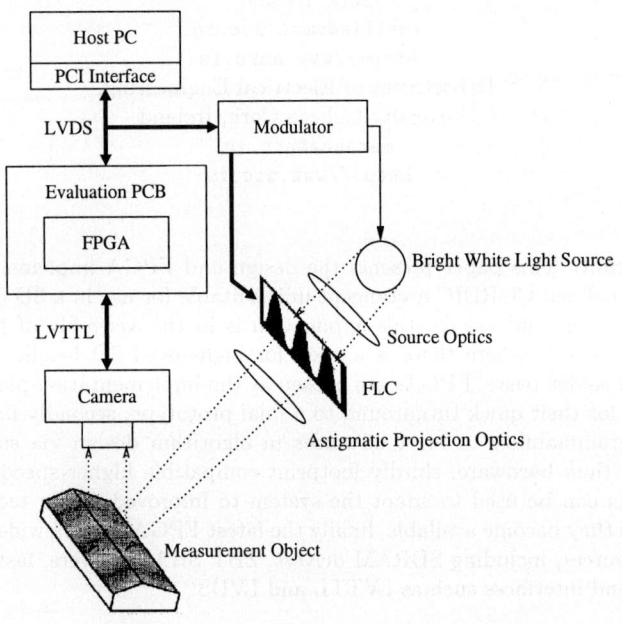

Fig. 1. Overview of the 3DCam system.

An area where rapid technological advances are being made is that of sensor development [5], [6]. Currently CCD technology is being used and this typically gives a pixel rate to 15.1875 MHz or 25 frames per second [4]. Image area is also small using such sensors at 752 horizontal by 582 vertical fringes and pixel resolution is noise limited to 8 bits. New sensor technologies offer advances in all areas, the sensor in this project has an image size of 1k by 1k pixels, 10 bit quantisation and pixel rates of 30 MHz are envisaged. The original specification for the 3DCam system predicted an 80 MHz pixel rate which could perhaps be achieved in the future with sensors which utilise multiple analogue to digital converters and multiple outputs. FPGAs also allow an upgrade path as different speed grade devices are footprint compatible.

Xilinx Virtex FPGAs [7] offer a wide range of resources to save hardware cost in the 3DCam system. The low voltage differential signaling (LVDS) IO drivers on Virtex-E [7] are of use for the long connection to the host PC and the LVTTL IOs are suitable for the camera communication. The 3DCam evaluation

PCB also requires external SDRAM for frame storage and external SRAM for table based computations. Zero Bus Turnaround SRAM (ZBT SRAM), can be used since this delivers a high throughput rate by eliminating dead cycles and it has a simplified user interface. Virtex devices also offer the necessary drivers to run these RAMs at their full potential speeds. Fast carry logic enables high-speed arithmetic and the flip-flop arrays allow large levels of pipelining.

2 Evaluation Algorithm

An overview of the evaluation algorithm is shown in fig. 2. The nature of the tasks involved in the 3DCam evaluation algorithm is highly repetitive, that is one million repetitions per frame, and in order to operate at the required throughput, it is necessary to implement parallel/pipeline processing schemes. These qualities of the algorithm are suited to FPGA implementation rather than a DSP software implementation which would be more suited to applications where functionality is more varied and less repetitive.

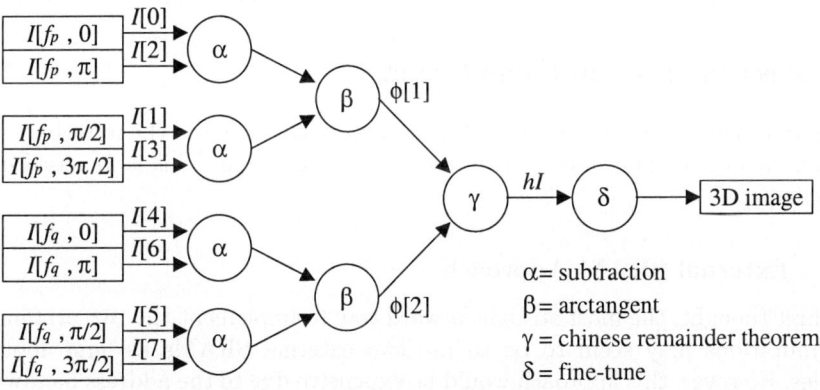

Fig. 2. Evaluation algorithm.

Initially, eight frames of data are stored one frame at a time in the SDRAM, the first four images having f_p fringes at the various phase shifts and the latter four having f_q fringes. Once this input data is captured then the evaluation begins on a pixel by pixel basis. All the arithmetic within the evaluation algorithm is computed using fixed point arithmetic. The first computational stage consists of four subtractions where pixels with the same co-ordinates, $I[0]$ to $I[7]$, from each of the eight frames are subtracted from each other. The sensor output requires the subtracters to work on 10 bit data to produce four 11 bit outputs which are fed into two arctangent stages. $I[0]$ to $I[3]$ result in angle $\phi[1]$:

$$\phi[1] = arctan \frac{I[1] - I[3]}{I[0] - I[2]} \qquad (1)$$

and $I[4]$ to $I[7]$ are used to compute angle $\phi[2]$:

$$\phi[2] = arctan\frac{I[5] - I[7]}{I[4] - I[6]} \tag{2}$$

Pipelining is used for maximum throughput such that, while performing the arctangent, a new set of subtractions on the next pixels are simultaneously computed. The 10 bit angles computed by the arctangent are resolved into a single height value in the Chinese remainder theorem stage which involves some modulo calculations and basic arithmetic which can be pipelined for high throughput:

$$daI = (f_q.\phi[1] + 2^9) \, mod \, 2^{10} - 2^9 \tag{3}$$

$$dbI = (f_p.\phi[2] + 2^9) \, mod \, 2^{10} - 2^9 \tag{4}$$

$$a = ((f_q.\phi[1]) - dbI + 2^9)/2^{10} \tag{5}$$

$$b = (f_p.\phi[2] + 2^9)/2^{10} \tag{6}$$

$$hI = (2^{10}(-f_p.a + f_q.b) + (daI + dbI)/2 + 2^{10} f_p.f_q) \, mod \, (2^{10} f_p.f_q) + 2^9 f_p.f_q \tag{7}$$

The final function in the evaluation chain is some fine-tuning which uses two external memories, to be implemented with 16 Mbit and 8 Mbit ZBT SRAM.

3 Arctangent Implementation

The arctangent stage is seen as the throughput bottleneck and the most hardware consuming of the four stages in the evaluation algorithm. This is focussed upon in this paper.

3.1 External SRAM Approach

At first thought, the most straightforward way to implement the two arctangent computations may seem to be to use two external SRAMs as large look up tables. However, this approach would be expensive due to the address bandwidth required. Fast SRAM such as ZBT SRAM could again be used for the storage, the cheaper SDRAM option being unsuitable as the refresh cycles could upset the synchronous operation of the system.

The two 11 bit inputs to the arctangent stage form the address bandwidth of 22 bits, which leads to a storage capacity of 64 Mbit for each of the two SRAM based arctangents required. Each of the arctangent memory tables could be made up from eight 512k x 18 bit ZBT SRAM modules using the three available chip enables on each module for depth expansion. The advantage of this approach is that the latency is quite low at several clock pulses. However, careful PCB design would be required for the enabling of the eight modules in order to run them at a high rate. The problems with this implementation are the expense of the SRAM modules and their high power consumption. The solution also puts a burden on FPGA resources such as delay locked loops and IO pins which need to be reserved for the fine-tune stage, where external memories are essential, and for the SDRAM frame storage control.

3.2 CORDIC Approach

An alternative approach to the arctangent implementation involves the use of COordinate Rotational Digital Computing CORDIC techniques [8]. This is a well established technique introduced by Volder [9] and later unified by Walther [10] and remains a powerful tool in the implementation of the trigonometric functions. A basic CORDIC processing element (PE) consists mainly of three recursively pipelined addition subtraction units and two scalers [8].

The CORDIC PE performs the rotation on X and Y:

$$\begin{bmatrix} x_{i+1} \\ y_{i+1} \end{bmatrix} = \begin{bmatrix} 1 & -m\sigma_i\delta_i \\ \sigma_i\delta_i & 1 \end{bmatrix} \begin{bmatrix} x_i \\ y_i \end{bmatrix} \quad (8)$$

where σ_i is the direction of rotation. δ_i is a positive set of constants decreasing with the index and these can be set to be a power of two so that the scaling operation becomes a binary shift. The metric $m = $ -1, 0 or 1 defines hyperbolic, linear or circular operation respectively. For the arctangent function the circular case, where $m = 1$ and Y tends to zero, is of interest. Therefore, some simplifications can be made to the unit, as the direction of rotation depends only upon changes in the sign of Y. In circular mode the initial vectors $[x_0, y_0]^T$ can be represented in polar notation $[R_0, \Phi_0]$ where:

$$R_0 = \sqrt{x_0^2 + y_0^2} \quad (9)$$

$$\Phi_0 = tan^{-1}(y_0/x_0) \quad (10)$$

After n rotations if y_n is reduced to zero then the new angle Φ_n is rotated through an angle α which is the arctangent result of interest, that is:

$$\Phi_n = \Phi_0 + \alpha \quad (11)$$

where:

$$\alpha = \sum_{i=0}^{n-1} \sigma_i \alpha_i = \sum_{i=0}^{n-1} \sigma_i tan^{-1}(\delta_i) \quad (12)$$

Z is an auxiliary variable, introduced to accumulate α_i on each iteration:

$$z_{i+1} = z_i + \sigma_i \alpha_i \quad (13)$$

where the α_i values are stored in the small look-up-tables (LUTs) within the configurable logic blocks (CLBs). After n iterations the arctangent result is stored in the Z register:

$$z_n = z_o + \alpha \quad (14)$$

Recursively, using one CORDIC PE the arctangent result can be obtained in n clock cycles where n has some dependence on the word lengths used. However, in order to obtain the throughput rate of 80 million pixels per second such a solution would be too slow. Instead a pipeline of these PEs can be formed to achieve the required throughput rate. The pipelined PE, as shown in fig. 3, has several modifications. The inclusion of the XOR gate, which compares the signs of X and Y, allows operation for angles to be computed in the full range from $-\pi$ to π. There is also the inclusion of a zero detect OR gate on Y to check if the result has been reached. If this is the case then rotations are stopped for the rest of the PEs in the pipeline so that the arctangent result can be preserved.

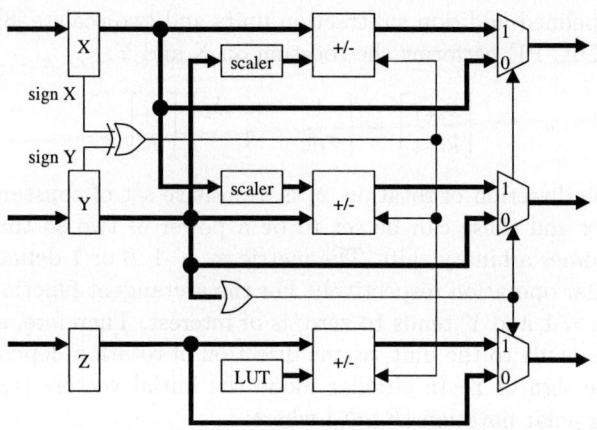

Fig. 3. Pipelined CORDIC processing element.

3.3 Low Contrast Detection

At the arctangent stage it is also necessary to check for a null-value corresponding to low contrast. Contrast C is defined as:

$$C = x_0^2 + y_0^2 \qquad (15)$$

and this is compared with a value, C_{min}, set by the 3DCam operator. If C is less than C_{min} then a null-value flag must be set and the angle result is replaced with a code representing the type of null-value, in this case low contrast.

One way to implement (15) is to use two pipelined multipliers to compute x_0^2 and y_0^2. The multipliers would have approximately the same number of pipelines as the CORDIC unit and could run in parallel to it. An adder computes the summation of the two squares and a subtracter compares this result with C_{min}. The null-value flag is then based on the sign of the subtraction output and is used as multiplexor control to replace the angle with a null-value code when the contrast is low.

An alternative is to again make use of the CORDIC unit to remove the multipliers and the adder thus saving some resources. On each rotation the magnitude on the polar vector gets scaled:

$$R_n = R_0 K_n \qquad (16)$$

where:

$$K_n = \prod_{i=0}^{n-1} K_i = \prod_{i=0}^{n-1} \sqrt{1+\delta_i^2} \qquad (17)$$

After n rotations, n being set if Y reaches zero or the end of the CORDIC pipeline is reached, an approximation to the modulus scaled by K_n is available from the X register at pipeline stage n. On FPGA initialisation, K_n and C_{min} are known. Hence a series of constants $K_n\sqrt{C_{min}}$ (one at each stage of the CORDIC pipeline) can be pre-computed using the PC host software and stored in the FPGA in a small BlockRAM. The pixels then have a low contrast on the following condition:

$$X < K_n\sqrt{C_{min}} \qquad (18)$$

which is equivalent to testing:

$$K_n\sqrt{x^2+y^2} < K_n\sqrt{C_{min}} \qquad (19)$$

If the input data has low contrast, this can then be easily computed by recording the values of n where Y zeroes out, using n to address a RAM whose data contains the appropriately scaled low contrast threshold and then subtracting the RAM data from the output X register content to compare. Fig. 4 shows the usage of a BlockRAM for low contrast detection.

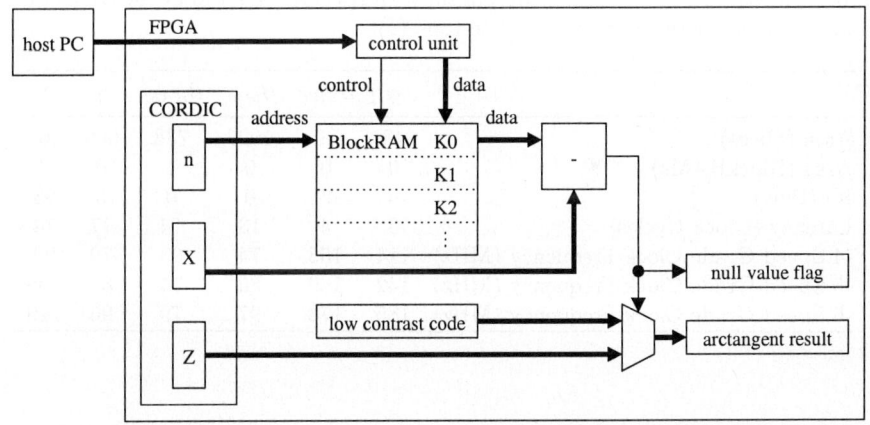

Fig. 4. Low contrast null-value computation using BlockRAM.

3.4 CORDIC Numerical Precision

Before producing FPGA implementation results for the CORDIC unit, the precision of the CORDIC logic, that is the word-length for each controlled addition-subtraction unit, and the number of CORDIC pipeline stages had to be decided.

To do so a parameterised VHDL description of the CORDIC arctangent unit was written. Functional VHDL simulation results were compared with those from the built-in C language function $atan2(y,x)$ with 11 bit quantised inputs and output rounded to 10 bits as required. Results showed that a 20 bit CORDIC word-length, which allowed 2 bits for expansion and 7 bits precision below the input data, and 10 CORDIC stages were necessary to reduce error to within a least significant bit compared with the C program. Rounding error can be eliminated with a 30 bit word-length and 28 pipeline stages. However, the increased FPGA resources required for such parameters cannot be justified since small rounding error can be corrected in the fine-tune stage.

4 Implementation Results

The results of the 3DCam module implementations, shown in table 1, include those for three arctangent solutions described in the previous section. The results were obtained from VHDL synthesis using Synopsys FPGA Express version 3.3 and Foundation 2.1i for place and route. The FPGA targeted for the comparison is the Virtex XCV400 -BG432 in the -4, -5 and -6 speed grades.

Table 1. Area, IO and timing implementation results for each subtraction (α), external ZBT SRAM arctangent and low contrast (β_{ZBT}), CORDIC arctangent with multiplier for low contrast (β_{Mul}), CORDIC arctangent with BlockRAM for low contrast (β_{RAM}), Chinese remainder theorem (γ) and fine-tune (δ).

	α	β_{ZBT}	β_{Mul}	β_{RAM}	γ	δ
Area (Slices)	43	89	1026	738	609	268
Area (BlockRAMs)	0	0	0	1	0	0
IO (Pins)	0	49	0	0	0	98
Latency (Clock Cycles)	3	4	13	14	17	14
-4 Speed Grade Clock Frequency (MHz)	114	153	74	63	79	92
-5 Speed Grade Clock Frequency (MHz)	142	169	85	74	87	105
-6 Speed Grade Clock Frequency (MHz)	185	178	97	79	96	119

Results show that the CORDIC unit using the BlockRAM method for low contrast measurement uses 28% less Virtex Slices (there are two Slices per CLB and a slice contains two each of four bit input LUTs, carry and control logic and 1 bit registers) compared with the version which uses the multipliers to determine low contrast. In comparison with the rest of the system blocks, described in more detail in [11], both of the CORDIC arctangent versions have the highest hardware burden. The arctangent ZBT SRAM controller performed very well in terms of area but each module increases the IO burden by 49 pins and the large added cost of eight ZBT SRAM modules per arctangent should also be taken into consideration.

The ZBT SRAM arctangent controllers showed excellent results under the Foundation implementation, giving over double the 80MHz pixel frequency goal and low latency. However, the results do not take into consideration PCB routing and ZBT SRAM delays which are likely to significantly reduce the throughput. In a timing comparison of the two CORDIC implementations, one more clock cycle is needed in the BlockRAM version but the multiplier version outperforms in terms of clock frequency. The Virtex-5 speed grade FPGA in the multiplier version reaches the original project goal of 80 MHz pixel rate and the -6 version even approaches 100 MHz. Although the BlockRAM version is slower, it is still fast enough for the current sensor technology with the cheapest FPGA -4 speed grade giving a throughput of 63 MHz compared to the required 30 MHz. In most cases the arctangent is the bottleneck on system throughput as expected. However, the CORDIC implementation has the advantage that heavier pipelining, with the cost of increased resources, could be used to further increase the throughput, if so required. This is not the case in the BlockRAM based approach where the BlockRAM memory access proved to be the limiting factor.

5 Conclusion

This paper has overviewed the design options and implementation of an arctangent unit, seen as the bottleneck computation in a 3D camera system for PCB inspection.

It was indicated that external ZBT SRAM memories would be required to store the arctangent results in a table based approach, as the capacity of the internal FPGA BlockRAM on Virtex devices was too small for this. Such an approach would be very expensive due to the address bandwidth and thus the number of external SRAM modules needed. This also meant that IO resources, much needed in other parts of the 3DCam system, were also used. High-speed ZBT SRAM interfaces for Virtex series FPGAs, gave a high throughput of 178MHz with a -6 speed grade device. However, using the necessary eight modules for each of the two arctangents, would slow down operation considerably due to the delays on the lengths of PCB tracks that would be required to route to all the SRAMs. Connecting each SRAM module to its own set of FPGA IO pins may alleviate this problem but such an approach is not practical due the IO burden that it would incur.

CORDIC logic was proposed as an alternative approach. This method allowed the arctangent to implemented directly on the FPGA making use of the fast carry chain and pipelining resources to obtain high throughput solutions. Two different designs based on the CORDIC processor were proposed, one using separate multipliers to detect low contrast and the other making further use of the CORDIC logic and a small BlockRAM within the Virtex FPGA. The results of implementation showed that the multiplier based designs were more expensive in area cost but gave a higher throughput. The Virtex-5 speed grade device reached the target goal of 80 MHz and the Virtex-6 speed grade exceeded this goal. The BlockRAM version showed lower slice cost but was still able to meet the requirements set by current sensor technology. An XCV400 device was targeted for the design, the unused resources available for the subtraction, Chinese remainder theorem and fine-tune sections of the algorithm. However, if the arctangent unit was to be solely implemented, the smaller XVC50 could be used for the memory based approach compared to the XCV100 for the multiplier based approach.

For the 3DCam evaluation system in general, FPGA's have a small lead time to prototype and it has been shown that that good use can be made of the wide variety of SRAM, SDRAM drivers and interface technologies available. FPGA reprogrammability and FPGA upgrade allow the design of a range of adaptable 3D cameras matched to different image sensors.

Acknowledgements

This work was carried out under financial support from the European Commission (Contract No. BRPR-CT98-0699, Project No. BE97-5071) and the authors would like to thank the 3DCam consortium for their efforts in this collaboration.

References

1. Clark, D.I., Melendez, C.A.: Inspection of Solder Paste Deposition for Chip Scale Assembly. National Electronic Packaging and Production Conference-Proceedings of the Technical Program (West and East), Vol 2. (1999) 981–983
2. Clark, D.I.: 'Tuning' the BGA Process. SMT Surface Mount Technology Magazine (1997) 15–16
3. Di Stefano, L., Boland, F.: Solder-Paste Inspection by Structured Light Methods Based on Phase Measurement, Proceedings of SPIE - The International Society for Optical Engineering, Vol. 2899. (1996) 702–713
4. Gruber, M., Häusler, G.: Simple, Robust and Accurate Phase-Measuring Triangulation Optik, Vol. 89, No. 3. Wissenschaftliche Verlagsgesellschaft mbH, Stuttgart (1992) 118–122
5. Mansoorian, B. Yee, H.-Y., Huang, S., Fossum, E.: 250mW, 60frames/s 1280$MUL@720 Pixel 9b CMOS Digital Image Sensor. Digest of Technical Papers - IEEE International Solid-State Circuits Conference (1999) 312–313
6. Malinovich, Y.: Ultra-High Resolution CMOS Image Sensors Electronic Product Design, Vol. 20, No. 7. IML Group plc Tonbridge England (1999)
7. Virtex 2.5V, Virtex-E 1.8V Field Programmable Gate Arrays. Xilinx, Inc. 2100 Logic Drive, San Jose, CA 95124 (2000)
8. Ahmed, H.M., Delosme, J.-M., Morf, M.: Highly Concurrent Computing Structures for Matrix Arithmetic and Signal Processing. IEEE Computer, Vol. 15. (1982) 65–82
9. Volder, J.E.: The CORDIC Trigonometric Computing Technique. IRE Transactions Electronic Computers, Vol. EC-8, No. 3. (1959) 330–334
10. Walther, J.S.: A Unified Algorithm for Elementary Functions. AFIPS Conference Proceedings, Vol. 38. (1971) 379–385
11. Bellis, S.J., Marnane, W.P.: FPGA Evaluation in a 3D Camera System. Irish Signals and Systems Conference 2000, Dublin, Ireland (2000)

Reconfigurable Computing for Speech Recognition: Preliminary Findings[*]

S.J. Melnikoff[1], P.B. James-Roxby[2], S.F. Quigley[1], and M.J. Russell[1]

[1] School of Electronic and Electrical Engineering, University of Birmingham, Edgbaston, Birmingham, B15 2TT, United Kingdom
S.J.Melnikoff@iee.org, S.F.Quigley@bham.ac.uk,
M.J.Russell@bham.ac.uk
[2] Xilinx, Inc., 2300 55th Street, Boulder, Colorado 80301, USA
Phil.James-Roxby@xilinx.com

Abstract. Continuous real-time speech recognition is a highly computationally-demanding task, but one which can take good advantage of a parallel processing system. To this end, we describe proposals for, and preliminary findings of, research in implementing in programmable logic the decoder part of a speech recognition system. Recognition via Viterbi decoding of Hidden Markov Models is outlined, along with details of current implementations, which aim to exploit properties of the algorithm that could make it well-suited for devices such as FPGAs. The question of how to deal with limited resources, by reconfiguration or otherwise, is also addressed.

1 Introduction

Techniques for performing speech recognition have existed since the late 1960s, and since then, these have been implemented in both hardware and software.

A typical speech recognition system begins with a signal processing stage which converts the speech waveform into a sequence of acoustic feature vectors, or "observations". That data is then passed through a decoder which computes the sequence of words or phones (sub-word units, e.g. vowels and consonants) which is most likely to have given rise to the data. Higher-level information about context and grammar can be used to aid the process.

What is being proposed here is an implementation of the decoder. This is highly computationally demanding, but has the advantage that it is also highly parallelisable, and hence an ideal candidate for application in programmable logic.

With such devices - FPGAs in particular - becoming available which can utilise an increasing number of processing resources at ever faster speeds, this paper describes preliminary findings in research aimed at implementing speech recognition on a programmable logic device, while also looking at how to deal with the eventuality that the device used does not have sufficient logic resources to perform all of the necessary calculations at each step, by use of run-time reconfiguration or otherwise.

---

[*] This research is funded by the UK Engineering and Physical Sciences Research Council

It is envisaged that such a decoder would act as a coprocessor in a larger system. This is advantageous both because it would free up resources for the rest of the system, and also because a dedicated speech processor is likely to be able to perform recognition faster than a general-purpose device.

This last point is particularly relevant here. At the time of writing, reconfigurable computing is still in its infancy, and so one of the aims of this research is to justify the use of this technology over conventional approaches (e.g. software implementations, ASICs, use of RAM, etc.).

The paper is organised as follows. Section 2 describes the theory of speech recognition based on the Hidden Markov Model. Section 3 then outlines some previous parallel implementations of this model, and describes a proposed structure for this implementation. This leads on to section 4, which discusses the findings of the current implementation, and looks at the problem of resource shortage. Section 5 describes the structure of the whole recognition system, and also looks at system performance. Section 6 then summarises the conclusions drawn so far, and section 7 outlines some of the tasks that will be carried out as the research continues.

2 Speech Recognition

The most widespread and successful approach to speech recognition is based on the Hidden Markov Model (HMM) [2], [8], [11], and is a probabilistic process which models spoken utterances as the outputs of finite state machines (FSMs).

2.1 The Speech Recognition Problem

The underlying problem is as follows. Given an observation sequence $O = O_1, O_2 ... O_T$, where each O_t is data representing speech which has been sampled at fixed intervals, and a number of potential models M, each of which is a representation of a particular spoken utterance (e.g. word or sub-word unit), we would like to find the model M which best describes the observation sequence, in the sense that the probability $P(M|O)$ is maximised (i.e. the probability that M is the best model given O).

This value cannot be found directly, but can be computed via Bayes' Theorem [11] by maximising $P(O|M)$. The resulting recognised utterance is the one represented by the model that is most likely to have produced O. The models themselves are based on HMMs.

2.2 The Hidden Markov Model

An N-state Markov Model is completely defined by a set of N states forming a finite state machine, and an $N \times N$ stochastic matrix defining transitions between states, whose elements $a_{ij} = P$(state j at time t | state i at time t-1); these are the *transition probabilities*.

With a Hidden Markov Model, each state additionally has associated with it a probability density function $b_j(O_t)$ which determines the probability that state j emits a particular observation O_t at time t (the model is "hidden" because any state could have emitted the current observation). The p.d.f. can be continuous or discrete; accordingly the pre-processed speech data can be a multi-dimensional vector or a single quantised value. $b_j(O_t)$ is known as the *observation probability*.

Such a model can only generate an observation sequence $O = O_1, O_2 \ldots O_T$ via a state sequence of length T, as a state only emits one observation at each time t. The set of all such state sequences can be represented as routes through the state-time trellis shown in Fig. 1. The $(j,t)^{th}$ node (a state within the trellis) corresponds to the hypothesis that observation O_t was generated by state j. Two nodes $(i,t$-$1)$ and (j,t) are connected if and only if $a_{ij} > 0$.

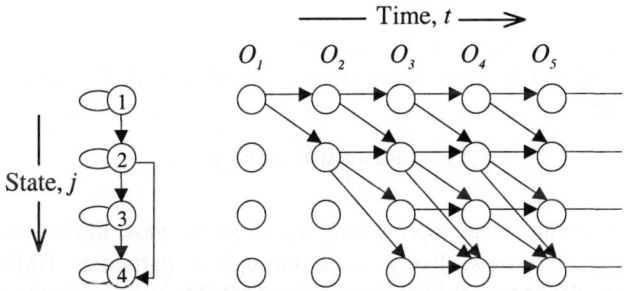

Fig. 1. Hidden Markov Model, showing the finite state machine for the HMM (*left*), the observation sequence (*top*), and all the possible routes through the trellis (*arrowed lines*)

As described above, we compute $P(M|O)$ by first computing $P(O|M)$. Given a state sequence $Q = q_1, q_2 \ldots q_T$, where the state at time t is q_t, the joint probability, given a model M, of state sequence Q and observation sequence O is given by:

$$P(O,Q|M) = b_1(O_1) \prod_{t=2}^{T} a_{q_{t-1}q_t} b_{q_t}(O_t), \quad (1)$$

assuming the HMM is in state 1 at time $t = 1$. $P(O|M)$ is then the sum of all possible routes through the trellis, i.e.

$$P(O|M) = \sum_{\text{all } Q} P(O,Q|M). \quad (2)$$

2.3 Viterbi Decoding

In practice, the probability $P(O|M)$ is approximated by the probability associated with the state sequence which *maximises* $P(O,Q|M)$. This probability is computed efficiently using Viterbi decoding.

Firstly, we define the value $\delta_t(j)$, which is the maximum probability that the HMM is in state j at time t. It is equal to the probability of the most likely partial state sequence $q_1, q_2 ... q_t$, which emits observation sequence $O = O_1, O_2 ... O_t$, and which ends in state j:

$$\delta_t(j) = \max_{q_1, q_2 ... q_t} P(q_1, q_2 ... q_t; q_t = j; O_1, O_2 ... O_t | M). \tag{3}$$

It follows from equations (1) and (3) that the value of $\delta_t(j)$ can be computed recursively as follows:

$$\delta_t(j) = \max_{1 \leq i \leq N}[\delta_{t-1}(i) a_{ij}] \cdot b_j(O_t), \tag{4}$$

where i is the previous state (i.e. at time t-1).

This value determines the most likely predecessor state $\psi_t(j)$, for the current state j at time t, given by:

$$\psi_t(j) = \arg\max_{1 \leq i \leq N}[\delta_{t-1}(i) a_{ij}]. \tag{5}$$

Each utterance has an HMM representing it, and so the most likely state sequence not only describes the most likely route through a particular HMM, but by concatenation provides the most likely sequence of HMMs, and hence the most likely sequence of phones uttered.

3 Parallel Implementation

3.1 Previous Implementations

Parallel implementations of speech recognition systems have been produced before, most using HMMs. In contrast to the approach described here, previous implementations have generally used multiple processing elements (PEs) of varying sophistication, either at the board or ASIC level, rather than a programmable logic device.

Typically, the recognition problem has been broken down with each PE dealing with one HMM node. For example, [4] has an array of PEs that mirrors the structure of the trellis. One issue that has arisen with some previous parallel implementations is the problem of balancing the workload among a limited number of PEs, which results in a speedup that is less than linear. Steps can be taken to avoid redundant calculations (e.g. "pruning" paths whose probabilities fall below a threshold [9]), but this is more difficult on parallel architectures than on serial ones [4]. Other approaches to parallel implementation include processor farms to automatically balance the load [1], [10], a more coarse-grained distributed computing model [3], [10], a tree-based architecture [9], or custom ICs with fine-grained PEs [7].

By using programmable logic, not only do we effectively have as many PEs as we want, but each PE can be optimised to handle the calculations for a single node. In addition, devices with (global) on-chip RAM are particularly suitable, as a buffer is needed to store the best predecessor states at each stage, for the purposes of backtracking.

Hence programmable logic, having not been applied to speech recognition in this way, has properties that may give it an edge over previous parallel implementations.

3.2 Proposed Structure

As described above, in order to perform Viterbi decoding, the trellis must be traversed forwards to find the best path, then once the observation sequence has ended, backtracking takes place, during which the best path is traced in reverse in order to extract the state sequence taken.

Forward Computation. Each node in the trellis must evaluate equations (4) and (5). This consists of multiplying each predecessor node's probability $\delta_{t-1}(i)$ by the transition probability a_{ij}, and comparing all of these values. The most likely is multiplied by the observation probability $b_j(O_t)$ to produce the result.

After a number of stages of multiplying probabilities in this way, the result is likely to be very small. In addition, without some scaling method, it demands a large dynamic range of floating point numbers, and implementing floating point multiplication requires more resources than for fixed point.

A convenient alternative is therefore to perform all calculations in the log domain. This converts all multiplications to additions, and narrows the dynamic range, thereby reducing all the arithmetic to (ideally) fixed point additions and comparisons, without in any way affecting the validity of the results obtained. Hence equation (4) becomes

$$\delta_t(j) = \max_{1 \le i \le N}[\delta_{t-1}(i) + \log a_{ij}] + \log[b_j(O_t)]. \tag{6}$$

The result of these changes mean that a node can have the structure shown in Fig. 2. The figure highlights the fact that each node is dependent only on the outputs of nodes at time $t-1$, hence all nodes in all HMMs at time t can perform their calculations in parallel.

The way in which this can be implemented is to deal with an entire column of nodes of the trellis in parallel. As the speech data comes in as a stream, we can only deal with one observation vector at a time, and so we only need to implement one column of the trellis. The new data values (observation vector O_t and maximal path probabilities $\delta_{t-1}(j)$) pass through the column, and the resulting δ_t values are latched, ready to be used as the new inputs to the column when the next observation data appears.

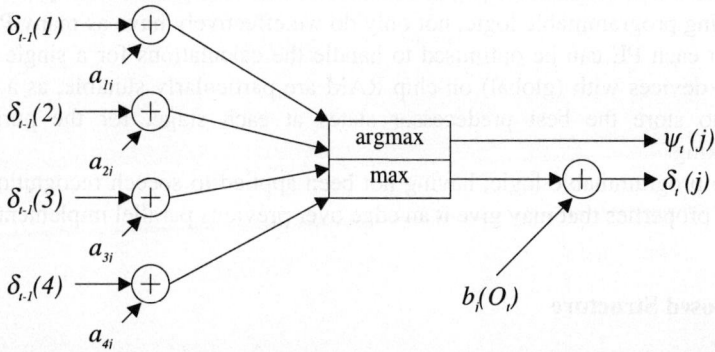

Fig. 2. Block diagram of a node representing state j in a 4-state finite state machine, with all calculations performed in the log domain. $\delta_{t-1}(i)$ are the outputs of previous nodes; O_t is the current observation vector. The transition probabilities a_{ij} and the observation probability distribution $b_j(O_t)$ are fixed for a specific node

Backtracking. Each node outputs its most likely predecessor state $\psi_t(j)$, which is stored in a sequential buffer external to the nodes. When the current observation sequence reaches its end at time T, a sequencer module reads the most likely final state from the buffer, chosen according to the highest value of $\delta_T(j)$. It then uses this as a pointer to the collection of penultimate states to find the most likely state at time T-1, and continues with backtracking in this way until the start of the buffer is reached. In the event that the backtracking buffer is filled before the observation sequence ends, techniques exist for finding the maximal or near-maximal path.

As the resulting state sequence will be produced in reverse, it is stored in a sequencer until the backtracking is complete, before being output. This state sequence reveals which HMMs have been traversed, and hence which words or sub-word units have been uttered. This information can then be passed to software which assembles the utterances back into words and sentences.

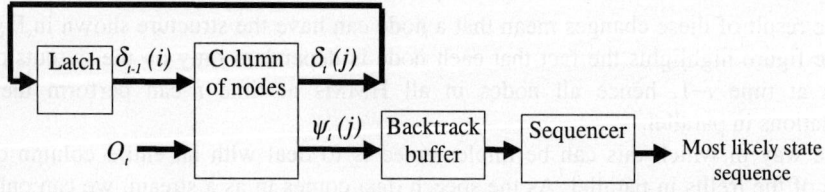

Fig. 3. Decoder structure. The nodes' outputs from time $t-1$ are supplied as their inputs at time t, along with the new observation vector O_t. The most likely predecessors of each state $\psi_t(j)$ are stored in the backtrack buffer until the speech data ends, then sent to the sequencer which traces the most likely path in reverse, before outputting it in the correct order

The structure of the decoder is shown in Fig. 3. Note that there will be additional logic in order to initialise the system, and to scale the values of δ_t in order to prevent overflow.

4 Implementation in Programmable Logic

4.1 Discrete HMM-Based Implementation

Parameters for a discrete HMM-based system have been obtained using speech recognition tools and real speech waveforms. In this case, each speech observation takes the form of an 8-bit value, corresponding to the address in a 256-entry table which describes the observation probability distribution $b_j(O_t)$ as a set of 15-bit vectors. Each node in the state-time trellis has a table associated with it. The transition probabilities are encoded in the same format.

We are using 49 HMMs, each one representing a monophone, i.e. an individual English vowel or consonant. Each HMM has 3 emitting states, so there are 3×49=147 nodes. Treating the speech observation data as an address, we need to obtain the value at this address for each node. If we do all this for each node in parallel, we need a 2205-bit-wide data bus.

The choice is therefore whether to store this data in on-chip RAM, use the LUTs as distributed RAM/ROM, or to store it off-chip.

Off-Chip RAM. If we were to store the data off-chip, we would have to perform several reads per observation vector, as the kind of data width required would not be realisable. In addition, off-chip RAM is likely to be slower than any on-chip alternative. However, dedicated RAM can provide more data storage than is available on an FPGA, which becomes particularly relevant as the recognition system is made more complex.

On-Chip RAM. On-chip RAM can offer increased speed, and very high data width. A trellis column containing 11 of the 49 HMMs has been implemented on a Xilinx Virtex XCV1000. It requires 31 of the 32 Block RAMs on the FPGA, plus around 4000 of the 24,500 LUTs (16%) for the addition and compare logic, and allows all 33 nodes to obtain their observation probabilities in parallel at an estimated clock frequency of 50MHz.

From these figures, we can predict that an XCV1000 could store around 70 HMMs. If more were required, we would have to use reconfiguration or off-chip RAM, and split the HMM column up, processing it in sections. At 50MHz, even allowing for a deep pipeline and access or reconfiguration delays, this would permit of the order of thousands of HMMs to be handled within the 10ms allowed for real-time speech processing.

While this gives a useful prediction of resource usage, clearly a larger FPGA is required for a full implementation, not least because the above figures do not include the resources needed for the backtracking buffer (which is likely to require on-board RAM as well), scaler, and other control logic.

Distributed RAM/ROM. LUTs can typically be configured as distributed RAM or ROM. While using these for storing the observation probabilities is likely to result in faster accesses than for Block RAM, it is at the expense of resources that need to be used for other parts of the system - whereas using Block RAM does not incur this penalty.

4.2 Reconfiguration vs. RAM [5]

A larger device may alleviate some of these problems, but speech recognition systems can easily be made more complex and so eat into any spare resources (explicit duration modelling [4], [6], [8] is one such resource-hungry improvement). It is therefore necessary to consider early on which of the above options should be used.

One possible solution is to use distributed ROM with run-time reconfiguration (RTR). Focussing on the observation probabilities, the only parts of the FPGA that need to be reconfigured are some of the LUTs; the associated control logic is identical for each node, and does not need to be changed (the transition probabilities would be different, but require significantly less data, and so could, in theory, be stored on-chip). In addition, the system control logic can remained fixed.

Given this situation, an FPGA which is too small to store all the required data could perhaps be repeatedly reconfigured at run-time by overlaying the LUTs holding the probabilities, so that each new observation vector is passed through all the HMMs in the system.

If on-chip RAM is too small, the only alternative is to perform a number of reads from off-chip RAM. A key deciding factor in whether to do this rather than RTR is the speed with which each can be performed. For RAM in particular, we are limited by the width of the data bus, which will obviously determine how many reads we need to do for each speech observation.

It remains to be seen which method will be the more suitable for this application.

5 Speech Recognition Systems

5.1 System Structure

At present, we are using an XCV1000-6 BG560, which resides on an ESL RC1000-PP prototyping board. The board is a PCI card which sits inside a host PC.

Recorded speech waveforms are pre-processed in software, and stored as quantised data. Once the initial system is completed, the speech data will be sent to the FPGA via the PCI bus; the FPGA will then perform the decoding and output a state sequence to the PC, which will map it back into phones.

In other words, the FPGA will be acting as a coprocessor, dealing with the most computationally-demanding part of the recognition process, thereby reducing the load on the PC's processor.

5.2 Performance

A significant and unique property of speech is that for the purposes of recognition, we can sample it at a mere 100Hz, giving us 10ms to process each piece of data - assuming that we are always aiming to do recognition in real-time. This means that whether we use RTR or off-chip RAM, there is a large period available to perform these operations, which provides a lot of flexibility when it comes to making the decoding algorithm more complex.

At this data rate, the pre-processing can be done in software in real-time. While this does not rule out eventually doing this on the FPGA as well, for the time being the FPGA will be used purely for the decoding.

6 Conclusion

So far, we have investigated Hidden Markov Model Viterbi decoding as a method of speech recognition, and have broken down the process in such as a way so as to take advantage of a parallel computing architecture.

Based on this analysis, we have begun work on an implementation of a real-time monophone speech decoder in programmable logic, which is expected to fit comfortably within an XCV1000, while utilising off-chip RAM. We believe that even if future FPGAs (or other similar devices) have the capacity to deal with a basic HMM-based algorithm, improvements can be made which, while making recognition more effective, would require off-chip RAM access or run-time reconfiguration in order to deal with the increase in processing resources needed.

7 Future Work

This research is clearly at an early stage, and so there are a number of issues which still need to be dealt with, including:

- **Integrate the recogniser into a complete system**: merely synthesising a recogniser will provide useful information on resource usage, but we need to able to test it! This will require using the FPGA prototyping board mentioned above, and writing software for the PC that houses it. It is envisaged that only recorded speech will be used for the time being. The results will then be tested against the output of an already completed software version of the recogniser.

- **Improve the recognition system**: once a monophone recogniser is completed, the next logical step is to move on to a bigram- and trigram-based system (pairs and triples of monophones). Whereas a monophone recogniser requires 49 HMMs, a bigram/trigram version uses around 500-600, another reason why being able to cope with limited resources is very important for this application.
- **Use of semi-continuous and continuous HMMs**: FPGAs are particularly well suited to dealing with discrete (quantised) speech data. However, use of continuous data has been shown to produce better results in terms of recognition accuracy. Implementing this requires computing sums of Normal distributions (Gaussian mixtures) on an FPGA.

References

1. Alexandres, S., Moran, J., Carazo, J. & Santos, A., "Parallel architecture for real-time speech recognition in Spanish," *Proc. IEEE International Conference On Acoustics, Speech And Signal Processing (ICASSP '90)*, 1990, pp.977-980.
2. Cox, S.J., "Hidden Markov models for automatic speech recognition: theory and application," *British Telecom Technology Journal*, 6, No.2, 1988, pp.105-115.
3. Kimball, O., Cosell, L., Schwarz, R. & Krasner, M., "Efficient implementation of continuous speech recognition on a large scale parallel processor," *Proc. IEEE International Conference On Acoustics, Speech And Signal Processing (ICASSP '87)*, 1987, pp.852-855.
4. Mitchell, C.D., Harper, M.P., Jamieson, L.H. & Helzerman, R.A., "A parallel implementation of a hidden Markov model with duration modeling for speech recognition," *Digital Signal Processing*, 5, No.1, 1995, pp.43-57 and http://purcell.ecn.purdue.edu/~speechg/
5. James-Roxby, P.B. & Blodget, B., "Adapting constant multipliers in a neural network implementation," *to appear in: Proc. IEEE Symposium on FPGAs for Custom Computing Machines (FCCM 2000)*, 2000.
6. Levinson, S.E., "Continuously variable duration hidden Markov models for automatic speech recognition," *Computer Speech and Language*, 1986, 1, pp.29-45.
7. Murveit, H. et al, "Large-vocabulary real-time continuous-speech recognition system," *Proc. IEEE International Conference On Acoustics, Speech And Signal Processing (ICASSP '89)*, 1989, pp.789-792.
8. Rabiner, L.R., "A tutorial on hidden Markov models and selected applications in speech recognition," *Proceedings of the IEEE*, 77, No.2, 1989, pp.257-286 *and* Waible, A. & Lee, K.F. (eds.), *Readings in Speech Recognition*, 1990, Morgan Kaufmann Publishers, Inc., pp.267-296.
9. Roe, D.B., Gorin, A.L. & Ramesh, P. "Incorporating syntax into the level-building algorithm on a tree-structured parallel computer," *Proc. IEEE International Conference On Acoustics, Speech And Signal Processing (ICASSP '89)*, 1989, pp.778-781.
10. Sutherland, A.M., Campbell, M., Ariki, Y. & Jack, M.A., "OSPREY: a transputer based continuous speech recognition system," *Proc. IEEE International Conference On Acoustics, Speech And Signal Processing (ICASSP '90)*, 1990, pp.949-952.
11. Young, S., "A review of large-vocabulary continuous-speech recognition," *IEEE Signal Processing Magazine*, 13, No.5, 1996, pp.45-57.

Security Upgrade of Existing ISDN Devices by Using Reconfigurable Logic

Hagen Ploog, Mathias Schmalisch, and Dirk Timmermann

Department of Electrical Engineering and Information Technology, University of Rostock
Richard-Wagner-Str. 31, 18119 Rostock, Germany
hp@e-technik.uni-rostock.de

Abstract. Integrated Services Digital Network (ISDN) is a de facto worldwide standard for wired digital telephony. Since ISDN was developed in 1984 as a public network it does not support modern sophisticated fraud detection systems. Indeed most current installations of ISDN are incapable of supporting encrypted transmission. Securing user information is therefore normally done outside the ISDN communication environment. In this paper we present our experience in using reconfigurable logic for securing existing ISDN devices against intruders in point to point communication.

1 Introduction

Many companies are using ISDN-based solutions for intranet or tele-applications, such as, tele-working or tele-conferencing. Since ISDN itself does not support secure transmission of data (phone, fax) securing user information is therefore normally done outside the ISDN communication environment. It can be realized either by dedicated hardware or a software package running on the data providing unit. The latter is not recommended for reasons of mobility since it is unwieldy to boot a computer just to make a secure phone call.

In this paper we present our experience in using reconfigurable logic for securing existing ISDN adapters against intruders in point to point communication. Instead of developing a completely new security device we expand the services of an existing least cost router (LCR) with a daughterboard containing a FPGA for speeding up the cryptographic processes. To ease the design, we focus on the implementation of the security device, so we do not reimplement the LCR-functionality. ISDN offers two B-channels for data transmission and one D-channel to control the communication. For secure phoning only one B-channel is used, but with different keys in each direction.

The paper is organized as follows: We briefly describe the structure of SECOM in chapter 2. In chapter 3 we focus on the protocol for key-exchange. In chapter 4 we present some implementation issues of the cryptographic algorithm. We finally close with the conclusion in chapter 6.

2 Architectural Description

The LCR we used contains a V25 microprocessor, RAM, EPROM and the complete ISDN-interface. To update the LCR and to reduce the number of additional wires to connect the board with the LCR, we built a piggy-pack board containing the FPGA (XC4020), boot-EPROM, RAM, some glue logic and the replaced EPROM of the LCR.

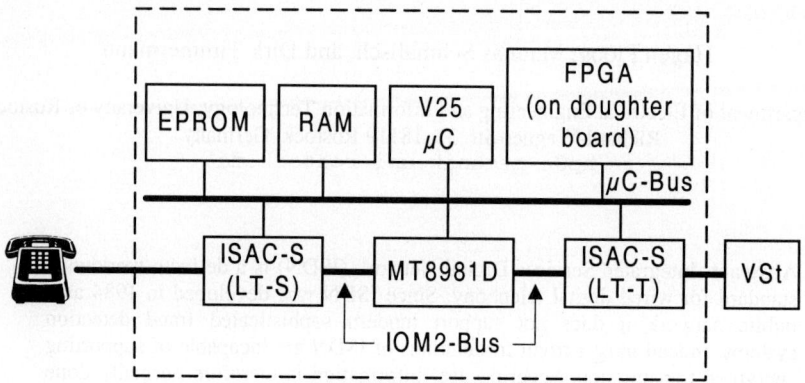

Fig. 1. Block diagram of the expanded LCR.

Generating a secure phone call is a three step process. During the first step we autodetect the existence of a corresponding encryption device. The second step is to exchange the session keys between both subscribers. The users input data is then encrypted and transmitted throughout the third step.

Autodetection is realized by transmitting a four byte sequence (0x00, 0x01, 0x02, 0x03) from the caller to the receiver. The probability that this sequence exists during regular communication is 2^{-32}, but it is only used during start up and can be easily expanded and modified for safety reasons. If the receiver detects this sequence, it also starts transmitting the same string several times to signal the existence of an encryption device. This process of repeating data sequences is often referred to as bit reiteration.

The controlling microprocessor decides whether the key exchange was successful in generating an optical feedback to the user and start the transmission of the encrypted session keys.

Since key exchange and data encryption are time-independent, we use the FPGA twice, but with different contents. Every time a phone call is going to be initiated the FPGA boots with an implementation of the public-key algorithm. After successfully encoding the session keys the FPGA is rebooted with the private-key algorithm.

3 Basic Security Model

We are using a hybrid system to secure telephone calls. A public key algorithm is used to encrypt the session key. The encrypted key is then transmitted via an insecure

ISDN-channel to the second subscriber, where it will be decrypted. The received key is used to decrypt the user data bytes with a fast private key algorithm. It is necessary to use a new session key each time, since static keys could be broken with an minor amount of time (and money) and hence the whole system would become insecure.

Using a hybrid system normally requires so called trustcenters for authorization of both sides' public keys, since both subscribers wants to be sure that the received key belongs to each other and not to an intruder. Planning our system just as a small point to point communication tool, we could replace the functionality of the trustcenter to an indoor operator, who is only signing the public keys. Therefore, an intruder can spy out the public keys of all subscribers but he is not able to generate a new list. Throughout it's usage, the public keys were read from a smart card, which is initialized by the operator. Alice, as the caller is signing the session key with her private key for authorization. She then encrypts the authorized key with Bobs public key to insure that only Bob can decipher the session key.

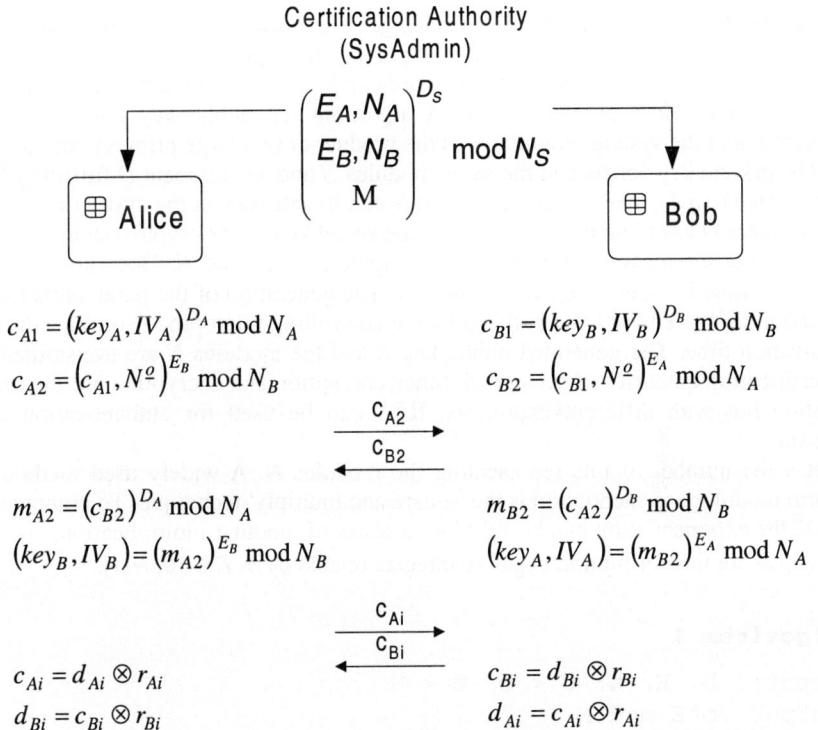

Fig. 2. Implemented protocol for key-exchange between two subscribers

4 Implementation Issues

4.1 Random Numbers

Some non time critical tasks such as the generation of random numbers can be done by the microcontroller during off line time. The system requires three 64 bit numbers for the triple DES core and one 64 bit number for the initialization vector (IV). These numbers are used as the session keys for the next phone call. We use a linear congruence generator for generating the numbers corresponding to

$$X_n = (2^{34} + 1) \cdot x_{n-1} + 1 \bmod 2^{64} \tag{1}$$

These keys each are encrypted inside the security device with it's private key.

4.2 Modular Exponentiation

We use the RSA algorithm 0 for key exchange. The most time consuming operation in the RSA algorithm is the modular exponentiation (ME) of long integers. To guarantee security, significantly greater wordlengths than in conventional computers are used (up to 2048 bits). In the RSA algorithm the public key consists of an exponent E and the system modulus N as the product of two large primes p and q, $N = p \cdot q$. The private key consists of the same modulus N and an exponent D fulfilling $D = E^{-1} \bmod (p-1) \cdot (q-1)$. The public key E and N can be released as the system modulus. The exponent D has to be hidden since it is the secret key of the cryptosystem.

To encrypt the message m one has to compute $c = m^E \bmod N$. Decryption of the cipher c is done by computing $m = c^D \bmod N$. The generation of the parameters (p, q, N, E, D) is software based and realized by the controlling microprocessor once during initialization time. The generated public key E and the modulus N are transmitted to the certification authority to get signed. Since encryption and decryption are the same operation but with different exponents, RSA can be used for authentication and ciphering.

Let n the number of bits representing the modulus N. A widely used method to perform modular exponentiation is the 'square and multiply'-technique. To compute $b^E \bmod N$, the exponentiation can be split into a series of modular multiplications, where b, E, and N are three n-bit non negative integers related by $b, E \in [0, N-1]$.

Algorithm 1

```
Input : b, E, N; 0 < b, E < N
Output: b^E mod N
Y = 1
For i = (n-1) down to 0 loop
    Y = Y * Y mod N
    Y = Y * B mod N if (E_i == 1)
```

Unlikely, due to the correlation of E and D, we do not profit by using short exponents during the decryption process so the algorithm takes 1.5 n modular multiplications in the average and 2 n in the worst case.

In 1985, P. L. Montgomery proposed an algorithm for modular multiplication $A \cdot B$ mod N without trial division 0.

Montgomery multiplication Let A, B be elements of Z_N, where Z_N is the set of integers between [0, N-1]. Let R be an integer relatively prime to N, e.g. gcd(R, N)=1, and $R > N$. Then the Montgomery algorithm computes

$$\text{MonProd}(A, B) = A \cdot B \cdot R^{-1} \bmod N. \qquad (2)$$

If R is a power of 2 the Montgomery algorithm performs a division by a simple shift, but it is working with any R being coprime to N.
For the computation of the Montgomery product we need an additional value N' satisfying $1 < N' < R$ and $N' = -N^{-1}$ (mod R). The algorithm for MonProd is given below:

Algorithm 2

```
Input   : ā, b̄, R⁻¹, N, N'
Output : ā·b̄·R⁻¹ mod N
t = ā·b̄
m = t N' mod R
u = (t + m·N) / R
if u ≥ N then u = u - N
```

MonProd using multiple-precision arithmetic To avoid brute force breaking of the cryptosystem the length of N should be at least 512 bits or more.

In multiple-precision (MP) arithmetic, large integers X, with x representing the length of X in bits (x=512, 768, or 1024 bits) are broken down into s quantities of length w, e.g., w=8, 16 or 32 bits. The arithmetic operations are implemented recursively, increasing the index from 0 to (s-1), with $s = \lceil x/w \rceil$. Any x-bit integer X can be interpreted as:

$$X = \sum_{i=0}^{x-1} x_i 2^i = \sum_{i=0}^{s-1} d_i (2^w)^i = \sum_{i=0}^{s-1} d_i W^i \qquad (3)$$

If $w \cdot s > x$ then X has to be padded with zeros on the left.

Dussè and Kalinski first noted that in the case of multiple-precision it is possible to use $N_0' = -N_0^{-1} \bmod W$ (N_0' and N_0 are the w least significant bits of N' and N' respectively) instead of N'. As a consequence, algorithm 2 can be written in the case of multiple precision as 0:

Algorithm 3

```
Input  : ā, b̄, W, N₀'
Output : ā·b̄·R⁻ˢ·ʷ mod N
t=0
n'_t = N'[0]
for i = 0 to s-1
   for j = 0 to i-1
      t = t + a[i-j]*b[j]
      t = t + n[i-j]*m[j]
   endfor
   t = t + a[0]*b[i]
   m[i] = t[0]*n'_t mod W
   t = t + m[i]*n[0]
   SHR(t,w)
endfor
for i = s to 2s-1
   for j = i-s+1 to s-1
      t = t + a[i-j]*b[j]
      t = t + n[i-j]*m[j]
   endfor
   m[i-s] = t[0]
   SHR(t,w)
endfor
```

The result will be found in t.

As shown here, the multiplication and accumulation are the heart of the algorithm. In each step j we have to compute $acc = acc + g \cdot h$, with g equals a or n and h equals b or m, depending on if we are in the multiplication or reduction part of the algorithm. It can be shown that the Montgomery multiplication can be performed without precalculation of N_0' 0. This is achieved by interleaving the multiplication with the accumulation, e.g. $t_j = t_{j-1} + g \cdot h_j$ and some modification on the LSB.

A VHDL description of an arithmetic co-processor for computing modular exponentiation based on the optimized Montgomery multiplication is given in 0. This model can be parameterized by w and N. Table 1 shows the required time to perform a modular exponentiation in milliseconds (f=16 MHz). In our implementation (n=256, W=16) the deciphering of the key is done in ~37 ms.

Table 1. Time [ms] for computing a modular exponentiation

w	$\log_2(n)$		
	256	512	1024
8	48.96	392.4	3143
16	12.24	98.1	785.6
32	3.06	24.5	196.4

4.3 Secure Phone Calls

After successfully decoding the session keys, the FPGA is re-booted with the private-key algorithm. Therefore the FPGA is reset and a dedicated IO-port controlled by the microprocessor selects the boot-area. As phone calls require real-time encryption we implement the block cipher in the so called cipher feedback mode (CFB) to achieve fast ciphering. Encryption in the CFB-mode is achieved by XOR-ing the plaintext with the m bit output of a key stream generator and feeding back the resulting cipher into a n bit shift register which was initialized with the initialization vector (IV).

Decryption is again a simple XOR-ing with the same output of the key stream generator since A = A xor B xor B. In that way the block cipher is used as a pseudo-random number generator. Any block cipher could be used to overcome export restrictions without changing the principle cryptographic process.

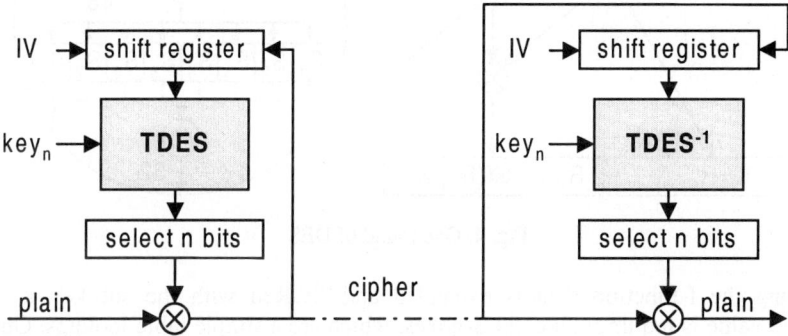

Fig. 3. CFB-mode

Besides real time encryption, the CFB-mode realizes self-synchronization which minimizes communication overhead. If a synchronization error occurs by corruption of the cipher during transmission, the decrypting unit generates wrong plaintext as long as the modified cipher is in the input shift register. For the case of telephony, synchronization is recovered after

$$\frac{n\, bit\, input\, register}{m\, bit\, feedback \cdot fclk} = \frac{64\, bits}{8\, bits \cdot 8\, kHz} = 1\, ms \qquad (4)$$

Unfortunately the CFB-mode enables intruders to insert faulty data into the stream without being detected if the data was taken from the actual call. So the intruder can retransmit recorded data, but since he is not able to decipher the transmitted cipher in real time he does not know *what* he is transmitting.

If someone tries to retransmit recorded data in a later phone call, the receiver just hears noise, since the session-key was changed.

4.4 DES Implementation

For the block cipher we use the Data Encryption Standard (DES) algorithm 0 with an expansion to triple DES to encrypt the user's data. In triple DES data is encrypted with the first key, decrypted with a second key and then encrypted again with a third key. In the DES algorithm the incoming data and key are passed through input and output permutations. Between these permutations the data is passed 16 times through a Feistel network, while 16 keys were generated simultaneously.

The data is split into two parts, L and R. R_{i-1} is modified by the function f and XORed again afterwards with L_{i-1} to build the new R_i. R_{i-1} is directly passed through to L_i. Fig. 4 is showing one round of the DES algorithm.

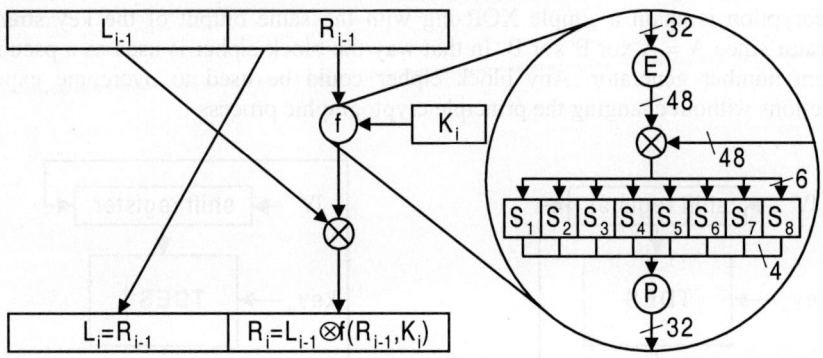

Fig. 4. One round of DES

During the f-function data is expanded and XORed with the sub-key k_i. The received value is fed through eight S-boxes, which are a simple table lookups. One S-box substitution is shown in Fig. 5. Each S-box takes about 10 configurable logic blocks (CLBs), eight for the LUTs and two for the mux.

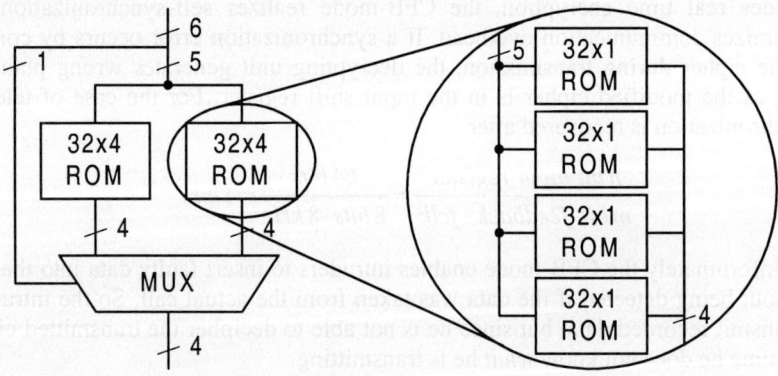

Fig. 5. Implementation of one S-box

Since ISDN clock-frequency is relatively low (8 KHz), we do not profit from loop unrolling, so we implemented an iterative version of the DES-algorithm, which leads consequently to a smaller architecture. The structure of the block diagram is shown in Fig. 6.

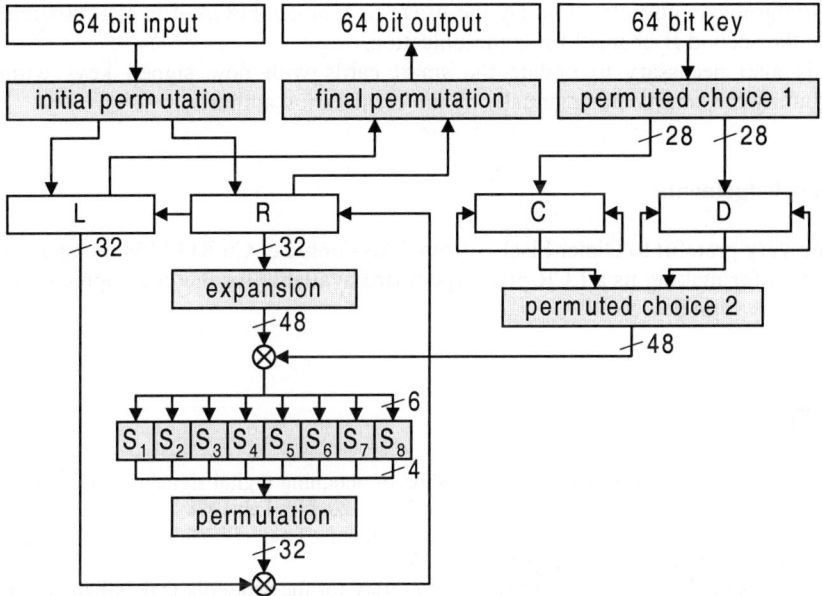

Fig. 6. Looped implementation of DES

It is widely known that the standard DES algorithm was broken with the help of the internet several months ago 0. Therefore, we expand our core from DES to triple DES by adding a key look-up table (LUT). This LUT can be written by the microprocessor to update the session key.

During online encoding, raw data is written into a dedicated address register belonging to the address space of the FPGA. The data is XORed inside the FPGA and moved to the same register again. Reading from that register automatically starts the controlling finite state machine to generate the next random number. Therefore key_1, key_2 and key_3 are successively read out of the LUT and fed into the DES core, where data is encrypted/decrypted with the key.

The implemented DES core takes 17 clock cycles to perform the DES algorithm. The modified version takes 51 clock cycles and three extra cycles to store the data during the reading of the keys from the LUT. Therefore, the generation of a new cryptographic secure random number takes 3.2 μs.

5 Conclusions and Future Work

We have shown that it is possible to protect ISDN communication. By the use of reconfigurable logic it is possible to implement different algorithms as the two we have used.

We use a small RSA key, because the encoding is fast. In order to increase the security during the key exchange, it is necessary to expand the RSA algorithm to 1024 bit or more. Therefore, a wider RAM has to be implemented. For fast encoding of such bit widths, it is necessary to use a larger FPGA to implement a larger multiplier for Montgomery multiplication. By the usage of a larger FPGA it is also possible to secure the second B-channel for communication.

It is also necessary to update the smart cards with new signed keys without distributing the smart cards manually by the certification authority.

Acknowledgements

We are very grateful to Dieter Fischer from TAS GmbH & Co KG Mönchengladbach, Germany, for making us a LCR prototype board available for the development of the ISDN encryption device.

References

Rivest, R.L., Shamir, A., Adleman, L.: A Method of obtaining digital signature and public key cryptosystems, Comm. Of ACM, Vol.21, No.2, pp.120-146, Feb.1978

Montgomery, P.L.: Modular Multiplication without Trial Division, Mathematics of Computation, Vol.44, No.170, pp.519-521, 1985.

Dusse, S.R, Kaliski Jr., B.S.: A Cryptographic Library for the Motorola DSP56000, Advances in Cryptology-Eurpcrypt`90 (LNCS 473), pp.230-244, 1991.

Ploog, H., Timmermann, D.: On Multiple Precision Based Montgomery Multiplication without Precomputation of $N_0' = -N_0^{-1} \bmod W$, accepted for presentation ICCD 2000

National Bureau of Standards FIPS Publication 46: DES modes of operation, 1977

Wienke, C.: Hardwareoptimale Implementierung der Montgomery-Multiplikation, University of Rostock, student work (in german), 1999
http://www.rsasecurity.com/rsalabs/des3/

The Fastest Multiplier on FPGAs with Redundant Binary Representation

Takahiro Miomo [1], Koichi Yasuoka [2], and Masanori Kanazawa [3]

[1] SANYO Electric Co.,Ltd.
574-8534, Daito, Japan, MIOM089614@dt.sanyo.co.jp
[2] Kyoto University, Institute for Research in Humanities
606-8265, Kyoto, Japan, yasuoka@kanji.zinbun.kyoto-u.ac.jp
[3] Kyoto University, Data Processing Center
606-8501, Kyoto, Japan, BWV147@i.kyoto-u.ac.jp

Abstract. In this paper, we propose the fastest binary multiplication algorithm on 4-LUT FPGAs. Our key idea is k-bit compaction, in which the n-bit multiplier is divided into n/k digits in 2^k-nary's, then the multiplicand is multiplied with each digit into a middle-product. And our second idea is one-minus-one encoding for the redundant binary representation. We've compared 2-bit, 3-bit and 4-bit compactions. And we have been able to construct 16-bit and 24-bit binary multipliers in 11 levels and 13 levels of 4-LUTs, respectively.

1. Introduction

Multiplication is one of the fundamental calculations on computers. Basically, multiplication consists of additions. If we realize multiplier on hardware directly as repetition of additions, the speed of calculation becomes slow. Many algorithms have ever been developed in order to realize high speed multipliers, such as Booth's algorithm [1,2,5], Wallace tree [4] and so on. Nowadays several VLSI chips [8,9] are available including hardware multipliers based on these algorithms. On the other hand, there is no optimum implementation of multipliers on 4-LUT FPGAs (Field Programmable Gate Arrays). Only Xilinx distributes some multipliers [10] on 4-LUT FPGA.

In this paper, we propose the fastest multiplication algorithm on 4-LUT FPGAs. Our key ideas are k-bit compactions and redundant binary representation. Our algorithm can compose the fastest multiplier on 4-LUT FPGAs. Binary and redundant binary representation is described in section 2. Algorithm is explained in section 3. Result and evaluation are shown in section 4 and section 5 concludes the paper.

2. Binary Representation and Redundant Binary Representation

We considered the multiplication of non-negative integers in this paper. We assumed the inputs and the outputs of the multiplier (the non-negative integers) are represented in binary representations (BR), where every digit of the number is a member of {0,1}. On the other hand, redundant binary representation (RBR), where every digit of the number is a member of {$\bar{1}$,0,1} ($\bar{1}$ denotes −1), is used inside the multiplier. The advantage of RBR over BR is "non-propagate carries" [3]. Namely in RBR addition, we can calculate carries independently on every digit of RBR.

We encode each digit of RBR by two bits,
   0 1 : $\bar{1}$ 1 0 : 1   0 0 : 0   1 1 : 0
that mean,
   $\bar{1} = 0 - 1$ $1 = 1 - 0$ $0 = 0 - 0 = 1 - 1$
The two bit encoding shown above for RBR is denoted as *one-minus-one encoding*.

3. The Algorithm

Our multiplication algorithm consists of three blocks namely: middle product generation, RBR-RBR-addition and RBR-BR-transformation. At first step, we multiply the multiplicand with the multiplier, digit by digit and get the middle products. Secondly, we add all the middle products and get their sum. Thirdly, we transform the sum into BR. The algorithm is explained in detail as under.

3.1. Middle Product Generation

When we calculate the multiplication of two BRs, a multiplicand

$$A = \sum_{i=1}^{n} a_i 2^{i-1} \ (a_i \in \{0,1\}) \text{ and a multiplier } B = \sum_{j=1}^{n} b_j 2^{j-1} \ (b_j \in \{0,1\}),$$

directly digit by digit, the number of generated middle products is as same as the number of digits of the multiplier. The fastest multiplier requires two techniques: (1) calculate every digit of every middle product independently (2) reduce the number of middle products. For the first requirement, we use RBR for the representation of the middle products. For the second requirement, we compact two, three or four digits of the multiplier (represented in BR) and consider the multiplier as quaternary, octal or hexadecimal number, respectively. The number of digits of the multiplier becomes half, one-third or quarter as many as in BR, respectively. We call the technique k-bit compaction. 2-bit compaction, 3-bit compaction and 4-bit compaction are described in the next sections in detail.

3.1.1. Using 2-Bit Compaction
Using 2-bit compaction, the multiplier B is treated as in quaternary representation (QR), that has half number of digits as many as in BR. Then we multiply the multiplicand A (represented in BR) with every digit in QR and generate middle products. Now we consider about the multiplication of A by a digit in QR. $A \times 0$ is 0. $A \times 1$ is A. $A \times 2$ is 1-bit shift of A. $A \times 3$ is $A \times (4-1)$, thus we subtract A from 2-bit shift of A. We can see all the middle products can be represented in RBR, in which every digit is a member of {$\bar{1}$,0,1}. For example, Fig. 1 shows the middle product generation of $1101101010 \times 1110010001$ using 2-bit compaction method.

Fig. 2 shows the FPGA circuit to generate every digit of the middle products by 2-bit compaction, according to Table 1. In order to make our FPGA circuit simple, we change $A \times 1$ into $A \times (2-1)$ in Fig.2 and Table 1. We can implement the middle product generation with 2-bit compaction in one level of 4-LUTs.

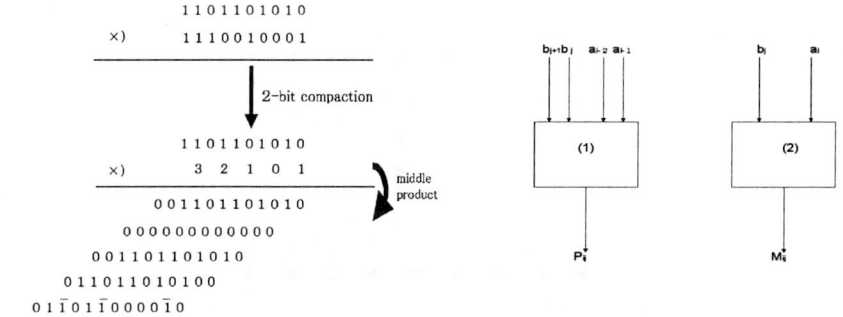

Fig. 1. 1101101010×1110010001 with 2-bit compaction example

Fig. 2. FPGA circuit for middle products by 2-bit compaction

Table 1. Logic function for 2-bit compaction

	$b_{j+1} \, b_j$	P_{ij}	M_{ij}
A×0	0 0	0	0
A×1	0 1	a_{i-1}	a_i
A×2	1 0	a_{i-1}	0
A×3	1 1	a_{i-2}	a_i

3.1.2. Using 3-Bit Compaction

Using 3-bit compaction, we consider the multiplier B as in octal representation (OR), that has one-third number of digits as many as in BR. Then we multiply the multiplicand A (represented in BR) with every digit in OR and generate middle products. For the multiplication of A by a digit in OR $A \times 0$, $A \times 1$, $A \times 2$ and $A \times 3$ can be calculated in the same way as mentioned in the previous section. $A \times 4$ is 2-bit shift of A. $A \times 6$ is $A \times (8-2)$, thus we subtract 1-bit shift of A from 3-bit shift of A. $A \times 7$ is $A \times (8-1)$, thus we subtract A from 3-bit shift of A. $A \times 5$ is $A \times (4+1)$, but it is not easy to calculate $A \times 5$ directly by this method. When we calculate $A \times 5$ by $A \times (4+1)$, every digit of the sum becomes a member of $\{0,1,2\}$. The sum does not belong to RBR format, so we need "carry stepping" to convert the sum into RBR, i.e.,
$\quad$ 0=0+0 $\quad$ 1=2+$\bar{1}$ $\quad$ 2=2+0

In the conversion shown above, the right $\{\bar{1},0\}$ side of the formulae stays in the digit, and the left $\{0,2\}$ side goes up to the next digit as a value $\{0,1\}$. Then each digit is converted by the addition of the staying value $\{\bar{1},0\}$ and the value $\{0,1\}$, thus it becomes a member of $\{\bar{1},0,1\}$. Fig. 3 shows the way of 101011×5 where the product 10202111 is converted into $1\bar{1}101100\bar{1}$.

Implementing $A\times 5$ on a logic circuit under one-minus-one encoding, we actualize $A\times 5$ as $A \times 5 = \sum_{i=1}^{n+3} ((a_{i-3} \vee a_{i-1}) - (a_{i-2} \oplus a_i))2^{i-1}$ with the conversion mentioned above. Now all the middle products, $A\times 0$ to $A\times 7$, can be represented in RBR, in which every digit is a member of $\{\overline{1},0,1\}$.

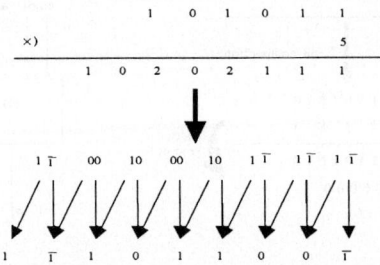

Fig. 3. 101011×5 with 3-bit compaction example

Fig. 4 shows the FPGA circuit to generate every digit of the middle products by 3-bit compaction, according to Table 2. We show the output logic functions of 4-LUTs in Fig. 4 below.

(1): $(a_{i-1}\cdot(\overline{b}_{j+1}\oplus b_j))\vee(a_{i-2}\cdot b_{j+1}\cdot b_j)$ (3): $(a_{i-2}\cdot \overline{b}_{j+1})\vee(a_{i-1}\cdot b_{j+1}\cdot \overline{b}_j)$

(2): $((1)\cdot(\overline{b}_{j+2}\vee \overline{b}_{j+1}))\vee(a_{i-3}\cdot b_{j+2})$ (4): $(a_i\cdot b_j)\oplus(b_{j+2}\cdot (3))$

In order to make our FPGA circuit simple, we change $A\times 4$ into $A\times(8-4)$ in Fig. 4 and Table 2. We can implement the middle product generation with 3-bit compaction in two levels of 4-LUTs.

Table 2. Logic function for 3-bit compaction

	$b_{j+2}\,b_{j+1}\,b_j$			P_{ij}	M_{ij}
$A\times 0$	0	0	0	0	0
$A\times 1$	0	0	1	a_{i-1}	a_i
$A\times 2$	0	1	0	a_{i-1}	0
$A\times 3$	0	1	1	a_{i-2}	a_i
$A\times 4$	1	0	0	a_{i-3}	a_{i-2}
$A\times 5$	1	0	1	$a_{i-3}\vee a_{i-1}$	$a_{i-2}\oplus a_i$
$A\times 6$	1	1	0	a_{i-3}	a_{i-1}
$A\times 7$	1	1	1	a_{i-3}	a_i

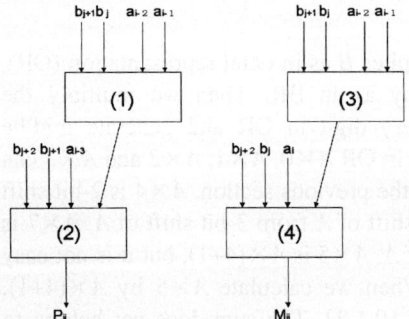

Fig. 4. FPGA circuit for middle products by 3-bit compaction

3.1.3. Using 4-Bit Compaction

Using 4-bit compaction, we consider the multiplier B as in hexadecimal representation (HR), that has quarter number of digits as many as in BR. Then we multiply the multiplicand A (represented in BR) with every digit in HR and generate middle products. Now we consider about the multiplication of the multiplicand A in BR by a digit in HR. $A\times 0$ to $A\times 7$ are the same way mentioned in the previous section. $A\times 8$ is 3-bit shift of A. $A\times 12$ is $A\times(16-4)$, thus we subtract 2-bit shift of A from 4-bit shift of A. $A\times 14$ is $A\times(16-2)$, thus we subtract 1-bit shift of A from 4-bit shift of A. $A\times 15$ is $A\times(16-1)$, thus we subtract A from 4-bit shift of A. $A\times 9$, $A\times 10$, $A\times 11$ and $A\times 13$ are $A\times(8+1)$, $A\times(8+2)$, $A\times(8+4-1)$ and $A\times(16+1-4)$, respectively. But it is not easy to calculate them directly in this way. When we calculate them directly digit by digit, every digit of the sum becomes a member of $\{\bar{1},0,1,2\}$. The sum does not belong to RBR, so we need "carry stepping" to convert the sum into RBR, i.e.,

$\bar{1}=0+1 \qquad 0=0+0 \qquad 1=2+\bar{1} \qquad 2=2+0$

With this method we can convert the sum into RBR by the same way as mentioned in the previous section for the conversion of $A\times 5 = A\times(4+1)$. Fig. 5 shows the FPGA circuit to generate every digit of the middle products by 4-bit compaction, according to Table 3. The output logic functions of 4-LUTs in Fig. 5 are:

(1): $\bar{b}_{j+3} \vee (a_{i-5} \cdot b_{j+2}) \vee (a_{i-4} \cdot \bar{b}_{j+2})$ (7): $(\overline{4}) \cdot ((5) \vee (a_{i-4} \cdot b_{j+3}))$
(2): $(b_{j,3} \cdot \bar{b}_{j,2} \cdot (a_{i-3} \vee \bar{b}_{j,1})) \vee (b_{j,2} \cdot (a_{i-3} \oplus \bar{b}_{j,3}))$ (8): $(a_i \cdot b_j) \vee (a_{i-1} \cdot b_{j+1} \cdot \bar{b}_j)$
(3): $(a_{i-1} \cdot \bar{b}_{j+1} \cdot b_j) \vee (\bar{a}_{i-1} \cdot b_{j+3} \cdot b_{j+1})$ (9): $b_{j+3} \cdot ((a_{i-2} \cdot b_{j+2}) \vee (a_{i-3} \cdot \bar{b}_{j+2}))$
(4): $(\bar{b}_{j,3} \cdot b_{j,2}) \vee (\bar{b}_{j,1} \cdot \bar{b}_{j,2}) \vee (b_j \cdot (\bar{b}_{j,1} \vee \bar{b}_{j,3} \cdot b_{j,2})))$ (10): $(b_{j,2} \cdot \bar{b}_{j,1} \cdot (\bar{b}_{j,3} \vee b_j)) \vee (b_{j,3} \cdot \bar{b}_{j,1} \cdot (b_{j,2} \vee b_j))$
(5): $a_{i-2} \cdot \bar{b}_{j+2}$ (11): $(a_{i-2} \cdot (\bar{b}_{j+3} \vee b_{j+1})) \vee (a_{i-4} \cdot b_{j+3} \cdot \bar{b}_{j+1})$
(6): $(4) \cdot ((① \cdot (2)) \vee ((① \vee (2)) \cdot (3)))$ (12): $(8) \oplus (9) \oplus ((10) \cdot (11))$

In order to make our FPGA circuit simple, we change $A\times 8$ into $A\times(16-8)$ in Fig. 5 and Table 3. We could not implement the circuit for P_{ij} in two levels of 4-LUTs but in three levels of 4-LUTs with a logical-OR-gate. The logical-OR-gate can be included in the next level of 4-LUTs in RBR-RBR-addition (cf. section 3.2), so we may consider the circuit in two levels of 4-LUTs.

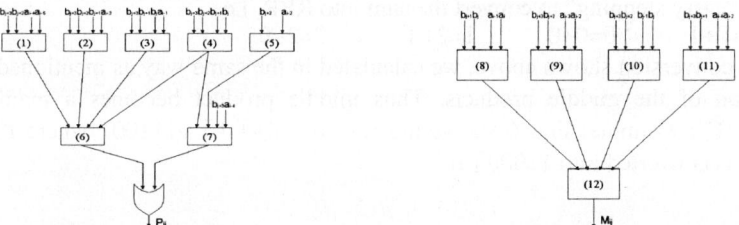

Fig. 5. FPGA circuit for middle products by 4-bit compaction

3.2. RBR-RBR-Addition

In this section, the addition of two RBRs (in short, RBR-RBR-addition) is explained to have the sum of the middle products. Using one-minus-one encoding, RBR-RBR-addition is represented as a combination of RBR-BR-addition and RBR-BR-subtraction. Here we mean "RBR-BR-addition" as an addition of an RBR and a BR, so as "RBR-BR-subtraction". Under one-minus-one encoding, an RBR is regarded as a representation of the difference of two BRs.

Table 3. Logic function for 4-bit compaction

	$b_{j+3}\ b_{j+2}\ b_{j+1}\ b_j$	P_{ij}	M_{ij}
$A \times 0$	0 0 0 0	0	0
$A \times 1$	0 0 0 1	a_{i-1}	a_i
$A \times 2$	0 0 1 0	a_{i-2}	a_{i-1}
$A \times 3$	0 0 1 1	a_{i-2}	a_i
$A \times 4$	0 1 0 0	a_{i-3}	a_{i-2}
$A \times 5$	0 1 0 1	$a_{i-3} \vee a_{i-1}$	$a_{i-2} \oplus a_i$
$A \times 6$	0 1 1 0	a_{i-3}	a_{i-1}
$A \times 7$	0 1 1 1	a_{i-3}	a_i
$A \times 8$	1 0 0 0	a_{i-4}	a_{i-3}
$A \times 9$	1 0 0 1	$a_{i-4} \vee a_{i-1}$	$a_{i-3} \oplus a_i$
$A \times 10$	1 0 1 0	$a_{i-4} \vee a_{i-2}$	$a_{i-3} \oplus a_{i-1}$
$A \times 11$	1 0 1 1	$(\bar{a}_{i-1} \cdot (a_{i-4} \vee a_{i-3})) \vee (a_{i-1} \cdot (a_{i-4} \cdot a_{i-3}))$	$a_{i-3} \oplus a_{i-2} \oplus a_i$
$A \times 12$	1 1 0 0	a_{i-4}	a_{i-2}
$A \times 13$	1 1 0 1	$(\bar{a}_{i-3} \cdot (a_{i-5} \vee a_{i-1})) \vee (a_{i-3} \cdot (a_{i-5} \cdot a_{i-1}))$	$a_{i-4} \oplus a_i \oplus a_{i-2}$
$A \times 14$	1 1 1 0	a_{i-4}	a_{i-1}
$A \times 15$	1 1 1 1	a_{i-4}	a_i

First we consider about RBR-BR-addition. Every digit of an RBR is a member of $\{\bar{1},0,1\}$, and every digit of a BR is a member of $\{0,1\}$. Thus, when we actualize RBR-BR-addition directly as the addition of each digit by digit, every digit of the sum of the addition becomes a member of $\{\bar{1},0,1,2\}$. The sum does not belong to RBR, so we need "carry stepping" to convert the sum into RBR, i.e.,

$\bar{1}=0+\bar{1}$ $0=0+0$ $1=2+\bar{1}$ $2=2+0$

In the conversion shown above, we calculated in the same way as mentioned in the conversion of the middle products. Thus middle product becomes a member of $\{\bar{1},0,1\}$. For example, Fig. 6 shows the way of $101\bar{1}1\bar{1}+111001$ where the sum $212\bar{1}10$ is converted into $11000\bar{1}0$.

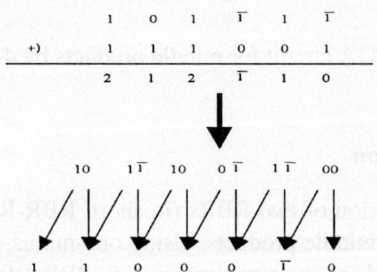

Fig. 6. RBR-BR-addition $101\bar{1}1\bar{1} + 111001$

On RBR-BR-subtraction, each digit of the difference becomes a member of $\{\bar{2}, \bar{1}, 0, 1\}$, and then it is converted in similar way:
$\bar{2} = \bar{2} + 0 \qquad \bar{1} = \bar{2} + 1 \qquad 0 = 0 + 0 \qquad 1 = 0 + 1$

Fig. 7 shows the implementation of the RBR-RBR-adder on FPGAs, based on the algorithm mentioned above. In Fig. 7 each 3-LUT (1) actualizes the RBR-BR-addition and (2) actualizes the RBR-BR-subtraction. We can implement the RBR-RBR-adder in two levels of 3-LUTs.

We also implement a 3-to-2 adder that calculates three RBRs into two RBRs with additions. Fig. 8 shows the 3-to-2 adder. We can implement the 3-to-2 adder in one level of 3-LUTs.

In order to include the logical-OR-gate of Fig. 5 (mentioned in 3.1.3) into the RBR-RBR-adder shown in Fig. 7, we need to modify the RBR-RBR-adder into the circuit as shown in Fig. 9. With the modification, we may as well regard that the circuit in Fig. 5 is in two levels of 4-LUTs as mentioned in 3.1.3.

We also implement a 5-to-1 adder that calculates five RBRs into one RBR with additions. Fig.10 shows the 5-to-1 adder. We can implement the 5-to-1 adder in four levels of 4-LUTs.

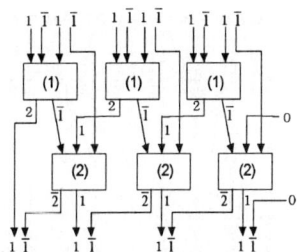

Fig. 7. RBR-RBR-adder

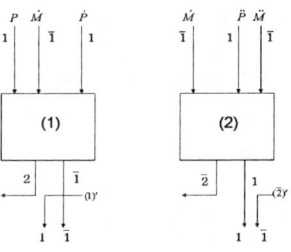

Fig. 8. 3-to-2 adder

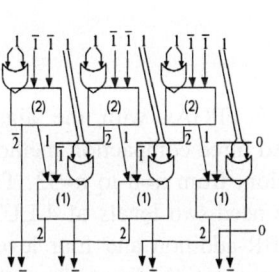

Fig. 9. Modified RBR-RBR-adder

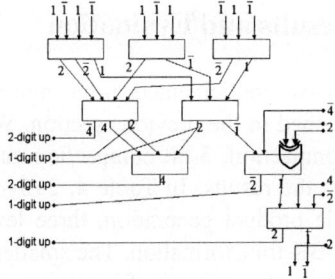

Fig. 10. 5-to-1 adder

3.3. RBR-BR-Transformation

The transformation of an RBR into a BR on one-minus-one encoding is a mere subtraction of two BRs. We show the example below.
$1\bar{1}100\bar{1} = 101000 - 010001 = 010111$

We use Unger method [6] for carry propagation on our FPGA circuit, just as a carry-look-ahead-subtractor. Fig. 11 shows the circuit to generate carries for the transformation of an 8-digit RBR into a 9-digit BR. In Fig. 11 each 4-LUT (1) actualizes the carry propagation, inputting two digits in the RBR. When the value of the more significant digit is $\bar{1}$ or 1, 4-LUT (1) outputs the more significant digit itself. When the value of the more significant digit is 0, 4-LUT (1) outputs the value of the less significant digit. In Fig.11 each 4-LUT (2) actualizes the generation of carries, inputting one digit in the RBR and a carry from less significant digits. When the digit in the RBR is $\bar{1}$, 4-LUT (2) outputs 1. When the digit in the RBR is 1, 4-LUT (2) outputs 0. When 0, 4-LUT (2) outputs the carry itself from less significant digits.

We can get the resulted digit X_i in the BR, making exclusive-OR of the corresponding carry C_i with two bits P_i and M_i which encode the corresponding digit in the RBR. Fig. 12 shows the circuit of RBR-BR-transformation of an 8-digit RBR into a 9-digit BR. We need $\lfloor \log_2 2n \rfloor$ levels of 4-LUTs to transform a 2n-digit RBR into a (2n+1)-digit BR.

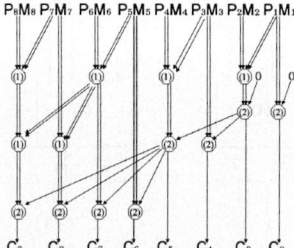

Fig. 11. The carry generation of RBR-BR-transformation

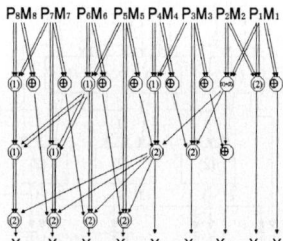

Fig. 12. FPGA circuit of RBR-BR-transformation

4. Results and Evaluation

We have implemented n-bit multipliers on 4-LUT FPGAs with the algorithm mentioned in the previous section. We have compared three compaction methods, 2-bit compaction, 3-bit compaction and 4-bit compaction, from n=8 to n=53. Table 4 shows the results. In Table 4, 2+3+4 means that we need two levels of 4-LUTs for middle product generation, three levels for RBR-RBR-addition and four levels for RBR-BR-transformation. The smaller the number of levels is, the faster the multiplier is. When the number of levels are the same in 2-bit, 3-bit or 4-bit compaction, we have compared the numbers of 4-LUTs to implement the whole multiplier. For example, the 18-bit multipliers in Table 4 have the same 13 levels with either compactions. We have compared the numbers of 4-LUTs of the 18-bit multipliers with 2-bit, 3-bit and 4-bit compactions as shown in Table 5, the multiplier with 3-bit compaction is the smallest among the 2-bit, 3-bit and 4-bit compactions. 3-bit compaction is most effective among the 18-bit multipliers.

In Table 4, the fastest n-bit multiplier is underlined. And when two or more fastest ones are found, the smallest one among the fastest ones is underlined.

For the floating-point numbers [7] we have examined the 24-bit multiplier, as shown in Table 6. The 24-bit multipliers have 14, 14 and 13 levels with 2-bit, 3-bit and 4-bit compactions, respectively. Thus, 4-bit compaction is the fastest on three compactions, but it is the largest on three compactions.

We have compared our 16-bit multiplier of 4-bit compaction with the latest 16-bit multiplier [10] distributed by Xilinx. Table 7 shows the results. In Table 4, we have used Xilinx Virtex-6 for 4-LUT FPGAs. Our 16-bit multiplier is about three times faster than the Xilinx multiplier.

Table 4. Results

n-bit	2-bit comp	3-bit comp	4-bit comp	n-bit	2-bit comp	3-bit comp	4-bit comp
8	1+4+4	2+3+4	2+2+4	31	1+8+6	2+7+6	2+6+6
9	1+4+4	2+3+4	2+3+4	32	1+8+6	2+7+6	2+6+6
10	1+4+5	2+4+5	2+3+5	33	1+8+6	2+7+6	2+6+6
11	1+5+5	2+4+5	2+3+5	34	1+8+6	2+7+6	2+6+6
12	1+5+5	2+4+5	2+3+5	35	1+8+7	2+7+7	2+6+7
13	1+5+5	2+4+5	2+4+5	36	1+8+7	2+7+7	2+6+7
14	1+6+5	2+4+5	2+4+5	37	1+8+7	2+7+7	2+6+7
15	1+6+5	2+4+5	2+4+5	38	1+8+7	2+7+7	2+6+7
16	1+6+5	2+5+5	2+4+5	39	1+8+7	2+7+7	2+6+7
17	1+6+5	2+5+5	2+4+5	40	1+8+7	2+7+7	2+6+7
18	1+6+6	2+5+6	2+5+6	41	1+8+7	2+7+7	2+7+7
19	1+6+6	2+5+6	2+5+6	42	1+8+7	2+7+7	2+7+7
20	1+6+6	2+6+6	2+5+6	43	1+8+7	2+7+7	2+7+7
21	1+7+6	2+6+6	2+5+6	44	1+8+7	2+7+7	2+7+7
22	1+7+6	2+6+6	2+5+6	45	1+8+7	2+7+7	2+7+7
23	1+7+6	2+6+6	2+5+6	46	1+8+7	2+8+7	2+7+7
24	1+7+6	2+6+6	2+5+6	47	1+8+7	2+8+7	2+7+7
25	1+7+6	2+6+6	2+6+6	48	1+8+7	2+8+7	2+7+7
26	1+7+6	2+6+6	2+6+6	49	1+8+7	2+8+7	2+7+7
27	1+7+6	2+6+6	2+6+6	50	1+8+7	2+8+7	2+7+7
28	1+7+6	2+6+6	2+6+6	51	1+9+7	2+8+7	2+7+7
29	1+7+6	2+6+6	2+6+6	52	1+9+7	2+8+7	2+7+7
30	1+7+6	2+6+6	2+6+6	53	1+9+7	2+8+7	2+7+7

Table 5. Number of 4-LUTs for 18-bit multipliers

	Middle product	RBR-RBR-add.	RBR-BR-trans.	Total
2-bit comp.	360	756	176	1292
3-bit comp.	504	484	176	1164
4-bit comp.	1380	444	176	2000

Table 6. Number of 4-LUTs for 24-bit multipliers

	Middle product	RBR-RBR-add.	RBR-BR-trans.	Total
2-bit comp.	624	1124	256	2004
3-bit comp.	864	832	256	1952
4-bit comp.	2088	660	256	3004

Table 7. The comparison of our 16-bit multiplier of 4-bit compaction and the Xilinx 16-bit multiplier

	Multiplier of 4-bit comp.	Xilinx multiplier
The number of 4-LUTs	1440	286
The number of levels	11	?
Speed of multiplier	6.6 (ns)	18.9 (ns)

5. Conclusion

In this paper, we have proposed the fastest multiplication algorithm on 4-LUT FPGAs. Our key ideas are k-bit compaction and redundant binary representation. The advantage of k-bit compaction is reducing the number of middle products. The advantage of RBR over BR is "non-propagate carries". Namely in RBR addition, we can calculate carries independently on every digit of RBR.

We have compared three compaction methods, 2-bit compaction, 3-bit compaction and 4-bit compaction. And the result indicates that for n-bit multipliers the fastest algorithm among 2-bit, 3-bit and 4-bit compactions is depending on the number of digits n. For example, for 16-bit multiplier 4-bit compaction is the fastest.

And we have compared our 16-bit multiplier of 4-bit compaction with the latest 16-bit multiplier distributed by Xilinx. Our 16-bit multiplier is about three times faster than the Xilinx multiplier. The results will develop the design of logic circuits on the field of FPGAs.

References

[1] A.D.Booth: A Signed Binary Multiplication Technique, The Quarterly Journal of Mechanics and Applied Mathematics, Vol.IV, Part2, pp.236-240, June 1951.
[2] O.L.MacSorley: High-Speed Arithmetic in Binary Computers, Proceedings of IRE, Vol.49, No.1, pp.67-91, January 1961.
[3] A.Avizienis: Signed-Digit Number Representations for Fast Parallel Arithmetic, IRE Transactions on Electronic Computers, Vol.EC-10, No.3, pp.389-400, September 1961.
[4] C.S.Wallace: A Suggestion for a Fast Multiplier, IEEE Transactions on Electronic Computers, Vol.EC-13, No.1, pp.14-17, February 1964.
[5] L.P.Rubinfield: A Proof of the Modified Booth's Algorithm for Multiplication, IEEE Transactions on Computers, Vol.C-24, No.10, pp.1014-1015, October 1975.
[6] S.H.Unger: Tree Realization of Iterative Circuits, IEEE Transactions on Computers, Vol.C-26, No.4, pp.365-383, April 1977.
[7] ANSI/IEEE Std 754-1985: IEEE Standard for Binary Floating-Point Arithmetic, The Standards Committee of the IEEE Computer Society, August 1985.
[8] S.Kuninobu, T.Nishiyama, H.Edamatu, T.Taniguchi and N.Takagi: Design of High Speed MOS Multiplier and Divider Using Redundant Binary Representation, Proceedings of the IEEE 8th Symposium on Computer Arithmetic, pp.80-86, May 1987.
[9] N.Takagi: Studies on Hardware Algorithms for Arithmetic Operations with a Redundant Binary Representation, Doctor Thesis, Faculty of Engineering, Kyoto University, August 1987.
[10] Xilinx Variable x Variable Multiplier RPMs for Virtex, Xilinx Inc, May 1999.

High-Level Area and Performance Estimation of Hardware Building Blocks on FPGAs

Rolf Enzler, Tobias Jeger, Didier Cottet, and Gerhard Tröster

Swiss Federal Institute of Technology (ETH), Electronics Laboratory
CH-8092 Zurich, Switzerland
enzler@ife.ee.ethz.ch

Abstract. Field-programmable gate arrays (FPGAs) have become increasingly interesting in system design and due to the rapid technological progress ever larger devices are commercially affordable. These trends make FPGAs an alternative in application areas where extensive data processing plays an important role. Consequently, the desire emerges for early performance estimation in order to quantify the FPGA approach and to compare it with traditional alternatives.
In this paper, we propose a high-level estimation methodology for area and performance parameters of regular FPGA designs to be found in multimedia, telecommunications or cryptography. The goal is to provide a means that allows early quantification of an FPGA design and that enables early trade-off considerations. We present our estimation approach as well as evaluation results, which are based on several implemented applications and prove the suitability of the proposed estimation approach.

1 Introduction

In the recent years, field-programmable gate arrays (FPGAs) have become increasingly important and have found their way into system design. FPGAs are used during development, prototyping and initial production and are for high-volume production replaced by hardwired gate arrays or application specific ICs (ASICs). This trend is enforced by the rapid technological progress, which enables the commercial production of ever larger devices. FPGAs with two million gates will be available soon, ten million gates are already planned.

The technology development together with the growing acceptance of FPGAs makes the implementation of more complex designs both possible and interesting. Especially for applications that require extensive data processing, FPGAs offer a valuable alternative [1, 2]. At the same time, the variety of devices is rapidly growing and the choice of the most suitable device for a given task is becoming increasingly difficult. Consequently, the desire emerges for a means that allows early area and performance estimation. The benefit of such an aid is twofold. On one hand, it allows to roughly quantify an FPGA design and therefore enables early comparisons to traditional approaches. On the other hand, it supports especially less experienced designers and thus, can help to make FPGAs more popular and regarded.

Several approaches for estimating area and performance parameters of FPGA designs have been proposed. The methodology proposed in [3] estimates area and timing based on models of the mapping process. Starting with a register transfer level (RTL) description, the area is estimated by predicting look-up table (LUT) mapping, configurable logic block (CLB) construction, and placement. The subsequent timing estimation is based on predicting CLB delay, wiring delay, and input-to-output delay. This approach is strongly integrated into the design flow since the placement information of the area estimation has to be taken into account by the placement tool. Another approach was enabled by the introduction of the PREP benchmarks [4, 5]. This benchmark suite consists of a set of circuits, which are implemented and measured on a variety of FPGAs. In order to predict area and performance of a certain application, it is partitioned into several components, which are substituted by the most similar benchmark circuits. Since the characteristics of the benchmark circuits are well known, estimations for the overall application can be derived. Unfortunately, the PREP effort was suspended three years ago and the benchmark circuits are not accurate anymore for todays FPGAs.

In this paper, we present a novel approach for area and performance estimation of FPGA designs. The methodology is targeted towards very regular and data-intensive tasks that can be found in multimedia, telecommunications or cryptography. The goal is to enable early estimation of performance characteristics of an algorithm. The proposed methodology is based on a non-formal design description, e.g. a data-flow graph (DFG) or a block diagram, which is early available in the overall design process. The estimation results are intended to give an idea of the implementation characteristics and to enable early design space exploration and trade-off considerations. As a benefit the tedious runs through the standard FPGA design flow (synthesis, mapping, placement and routing) are minimised.

2 Estimation Methodology

As Fig. 1 outlines, the proposed estimation methodology consists of four major steps: algorithm characterisation, FPGA mapping representation, parameter estimation, and design space exploration. The basic idea behind the concept is to separate the algorithm description from the influence of the FPGA architecture.

2.1 Algorithm Characterisation

This step characterises the algorithm on a high level, independent from any implementation issue. For that purpose, a DFG, a block diagram, or any comparable description is suitable. A task is characterised by its inputs and outputs, its operations, its extra registers (i.e. not pipeline registers), its inherent structure, and the number of iterations it is run through. The *Characterisation Vector* shown in Table 1 represents the characteristics of an algorithm, whereby several simplifications are used:

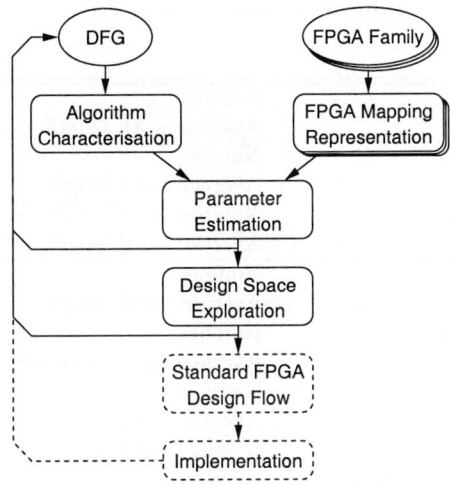

Fig. 1. Estimation methodology

- Not each element is considered separately. Elements of the same types are combined and the average word length over all the instances is used.
- The precise structure of the task is neglected. Instead, the *degree of parallelism* is defined, which provides a coarse idea of the task's composition. We propose the heuristic

$$\text{Degree of parallelism} = \frac{\text{Total number of operations}}{\text{No. of operations in the longest data path}}. \quad (1)$$

- Some types of operations are substituted by similar operations. Subtracters for example are replaced by adders. Table 2 summarises the substitution scheme. The basic operations that our methodology supports are adders, array multipliers, multiplexers (MUX), bit-wise logic operations and look-up tables (LUTs). Multipliers play a special role, since they can be implemented in rather different ways. We consider three alternatives: array multipliers, constant coefficient multipliers (KCMs) [6], and word-serial multipliers.

2.2 FPGA Mapping Representation

This step considers the influence of the FPGA architecture, especially on the mapping of the operations. Therefore, a mapping model is specified for each type of operation, from which the area and timing parameters are derived. The individual models are not given here, but they are implicitly used in (2) and (3), where they are combined for the estimation step. Instead, we outline the adder operation as an example. An adder is mapped onto a Xilinx XC4000E device, so that two bits are processed in one CLB. The area in terms of number of CLBs corresponds therefore to half of the adder's word length. For the timing, the combinatorial and the ripple line delay of the CLBs are taken into account.

Table 1. Characterisation Vector

Description		Element
Data inputs	Number	C_1
	Average word length	C_2
Data outputs	Number	C_3
	Average word length	C_4
Control I/Os	Number	C_5
	Average word length	C_6
Adders	Number	C_7
	Average word length	C_8
Array multipliers	Number	C_9
	Average input word length	C_{10}
Multiplexers	Number	C_{11}
	Average fan-in	C_{12}
	Average word length	C_{13}
Bit-wise logic operations	Number	C_{14}
	Average fan-in	C_{15}
	Average word length	C_{16}
LUTs	Number	C_{17}
	Average fan-in	C_{18}
	Average word length	C_{19}
Extra registers	Number	C_{20}
	Average register length	C_{21}
Inherent degree of parallelism		C_{22}
Number of iterations		C_{23}

2.3 Parameter Estimation

Based on the antecedent steps of algorithm characterisation and FPGA mapping representation, the parameters area, timing (propagation delay), number of iterations, and number of I/O pins are estimated for the overall task. The following equations show the calculation rules.

Area [CLBs]:

$$A = \frac{C_7 C_8}{2} + 2 C_9 C_{10}^2 + \frac{C_{11} C_{12} C_{13}}{4} + \frac{C_{14} C_{15} C_{16}}{8} + \frac{C_{17} C_{18} C_{19}}{8} + \frac{C_{20} C_{21}}{2} \quad (2)$$

Timing (propagation delay) [s]:

$$T = \frac{1.5}{C_{22}} \left(C_7(d_r C_8 + d_c) + 2 d_c C_9 C_{10} + d_c C_{11} \log_2(C_{12}) + d_c \frac{C_{14} C_{15}}{4} + d_c C_{17} \right) \quad (3)$$

Number of iterations:

$$I = C_{23} \quad (4)$$

Number of I/O pins:

$$P = P_{\text{Din}} + P_{\text{Dout}} + P_{\text{Ctrl}} = C_1 C_2 + C_3 C_4 + C_5 C_6 \quad (5)$$

Table 2. Substitution scheme for a simplified algorithm characterisation

Operation	Substitution
Subtracter	Adder
Comparator	Adder
Shifter	Multiplexer
Barrel-shifter	neglected (since hard-wired)
Multiplier	▷ Array multiplier ▷ KCM[a]: 1 LUT (fan-in ρ), $2^{log_2(\rho)-2} - 1$ adders (word length 2ρ) ▷ Serial: 1 adder, 1 MUX (fan-in 4), 1 logic operation (fan-in 2)

[a] ρ: word length of the original multiplier

For area and timing the approach is basically the same: the contributions of each operation type are summed up and for the latter divided by the degree of parallelism. For the timing an empirical correction factor of 1.5 is introduced in order to reflect the routing influence. The constants d_c and d_r refer to the CLB's combinational and ripple line delay, which can be derived from the data sheet. For an XC4000E-3 device, the values are 3 ns and 0.4 ns, respectively [7].

2.4 Design Space Exploration

The presented estimation methodology allows to investigate area vs. performance trade-offs on a high level. The standard methods for that purpose are pipelining, replication and decomposition. Pipelining inserts S registers into the data path in order to shorten the critical path length. Replication intends to copy the building block R times. Decomposition breaks up the building block into a sequence of D identical subtasks, which are then iteratively reused D times.

Table 3 shows the final estimation metrics for a building block as well as the extension for design space exploration. Due to the FPGA's CLB structure, pipelining can be taken into account rather accurately. Similar to area and timing, the number of potential pipeline stages can be predicted to

$$S = \frac{1}{C_{22}} \left(C_7 + C_9 C_{10} + C_{11} \log_4(C_{12}) + \frac{C_{14} C_{15}}{8} + C_{17} \right) . \qquad (6)$$

Based on our design experience, we have introduced an empirical performance degradation factor of 25% for the pipelining case. For replication and decomposition, the given estimation figures have to be viewed as an upper limit.

3 Examples

In this section, the estimation methodology is discussed on the basis of two example implementations, a FIR filter and motion estimation. The implementation results are compared to the estimated area and performance parameters. For our investigations, we have chosen the Xilinx XC4000E family due to its popularity.

Table 3. Area and performance estimation for a building block (column 2) with extensions for design space exploration (columns 3 to 5)

		Estimation Building Block	Design Space Exploration Pipelining	Replication	Decomposition
Area	[CLBs]	A	A	$R \cdot A$	$\frac{1}{D} \cdot A$
Frequency	[Hz]	$\frac{1}{T}$	$\frac{S}{1.3} \cdot \frac{1}{T}$	$\frac{1}{T}$	$D \cdot \frac{1}{T}$
Throughput	[bit/s]	$\frac{P_{Din}}{T \cdot I}$	$\frac{S}{1.3} \cdot \frac{P_{Din}}{T \cdot I}$	$R \cdot \frac{P_{Din}}{T \cdot I}$	$\frac{P_{Din}}{T \cdot I}$
Latency	[cycles]	I	$S \cdot I$	I	$D \cdot I$
I/O	[pins]	P	P	$R \cdot P$	P

3.1 FIR Filter

A FIR filter is composed of several tap stages where each tap multiplies a data sample with a constant coefficient and sums up the result with the value from the previous stage. Figure 2 outlines an efficient implementation, which uses a constant coefficient multiplier (KCM) [6]. From that description, the characterisation vector (7) can be derived. There is a 16-bit input, a 32-bit output, an adder, and the KCM is represented by a LUT and three adders (see Table 2). The degree of parallelism is according (1) calculated to 1.25.

$$c_{FIR} = [1, 16, 1, 32, 0, 0, 4, 32, 0, 0, 0, 0, 0, 0, 0, 0, 1, 16, 20, 0, 0, 1.25, 1] \qquad (7)$$

Table 4 shows the results for estimation and implementation. For the estimation results we consider the pipelining case with four stages, according to the chosen implementation.

3.2 Motion Estimation

The main task in motion estimation is to compare two image blocks of 16×16 pixels. The distortion of two blocks is computed by accumulating the absolute differences between according pixels [8]. The implementation outlined in Fig. 3 processes the computations for one image line, i.e. 16 pixel pairs, in parallel. The final adder accumulates the partial sums, so that every 16 clock cycles a distortion computation is produced. Not shown are the multiplexed inputs.

While deriving the characterisation vector, the problem arises that the circuit cannot be characterised properly, because one part is iterating (the final accumulator) while the rest is not. As a work-around, the implementation can be partitioned into the tree-like adder structure (*subcircuit 1*) and the accumulator (*subcircuit 2*). Thus, subcircuit 1 is characterised by (8), subcircuit 2 by (9).

$$c_{ME_1} = [32, 4, 1, 12, 0, 0, 47, 9, 0, 0, 16, 2, 8, 0, 0, 0, 0, 0, 0, 0, 10.5, 1] \qquad (8)$$
$$c_{ME_2} = [\ 1, 12, 1, 16, 0, 0, 1, 16, 0, 0, 1, 2, 16, 0, 0, 0, 0, 0, 0, 0, 1, 16] \qquad (9)$$

Table 4. Estimation and implementation results for the FIR tap

FIR tap		Estimation	Implementation
Area	[CLBs]	104	83
Frequency	[MHz]	38.7	40
Throughput	[Mbit/s]	620	640
Latency	[cycles]	4	4
I/O	[pins]	48	48

Table 5. Estimation and implementation results for the motion estimation algorithm

Motion Estimation		Estimation			Implementation
		Subcircuit 1	Subcircuit 2	Combined	
Area	[CLBs]	276	16	292	260
Frequency	[MHz]	75.2	53.8	53.8	40
Throughput	[Gbit/s]	19.2	0.40	13.8	10.2
Latency	[cycles]	5	16	21	21
I/O	[pins]	140	28	144	144

The estimations can then be combined intuitively: the area is added up, the lower frequency is chosen, the latencies are added up, the throughput of subcircuit 1 is scaled to the lower frequency of subcircuit 2, and the pin count is derived with the input pins from subcircuit 1 and the output pins of subcircuit 2. Table 5 summarises the results of the combined estimation and the implementation.

4 Evaluation

Besides the two examples discussed in the previous section, four more algorithms have been implemented and evaluated:

- a fast Fourier transform (FFT),
- a Viterbi decoder,
- CDMA despreading, and
- Twofish [9].

Figure 4 summarises the results. The evaluation proves that the estimations are suitable for high-level design quantification. However, the results indicate as well the limits of the methodology:

- Routing effects are not taken into account. Thus, the methodology serves well for regular designs with mainly local interconnections. For less regular designs this will lead to an underestimated CLB count and an optimistic timing estimation.
- Control overhead is not taken into account. Again, this serves well for regular designs with few control requirements, but will lead as well to an underestimated CLB count and an optimistic timing estimation.

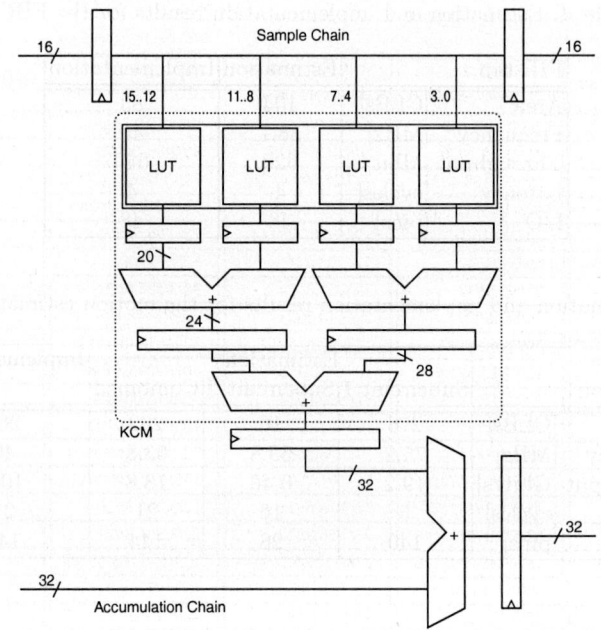

Fig. 2. Implementation of one tap stage of a FIR filter

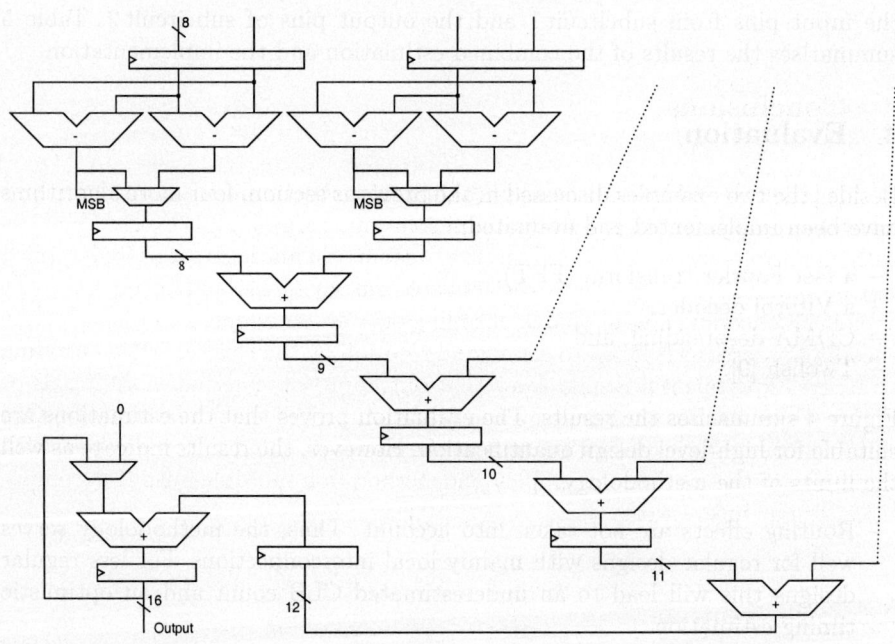

Fig. 3. Implementation of the motion estimation algorithm

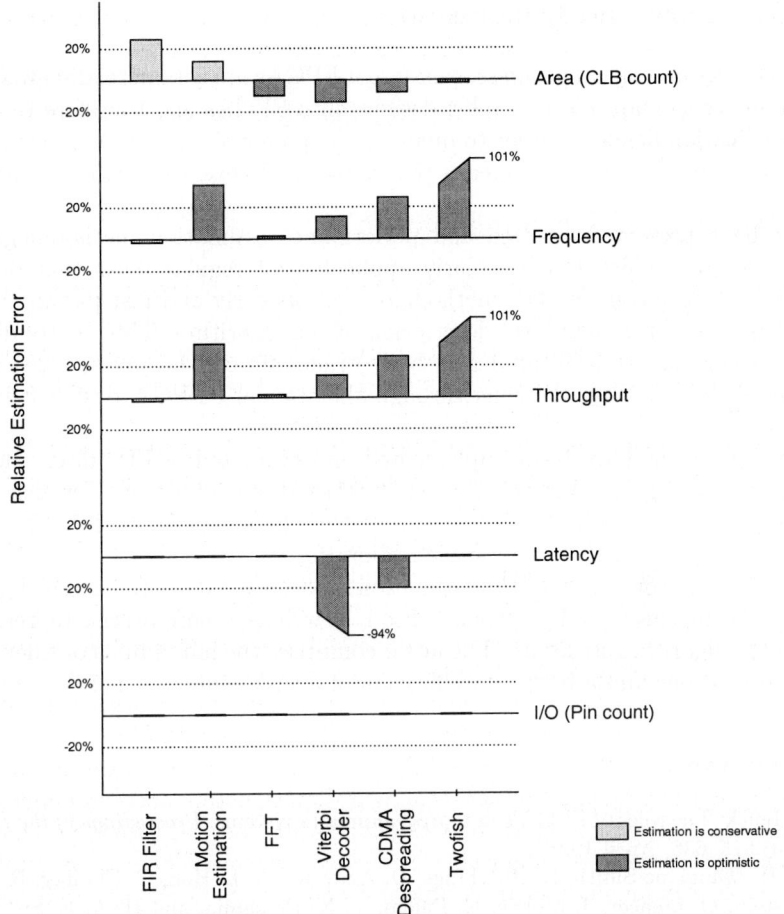

Fig. 4. Evaluation results of the six investigated algorithms

- For pipelined designs the estimation model assumes uniformly partitioned pipeline stages. For designs with irregular pipeline stages this will lead to an optimistic timing estimation, as the Twofish example shows.
- The latency estimation is based on the number of predicted pipeline stages. However, latency might not arise due to pipelining, but due to a design's functionality. In such a case, latency is underestimated, as the Viterbi decoder and CDMA despreading show.
- Novel FPGA architectures show the trend to integrate significant memory resources on-chip, e.g. the Virtex device [7]. This opens alternatives in the algorithm design which the proposed methodology might not fully cover. However, it is conceivable to extend the methodology with such additional functionality.

5 Summary and Conclusion

Due to the technological progress, ever larger FPGAs are commercially available, which allows to map more complex designs onto FPGAs and therefore to enter new application fields. In order to quantify the power of an FPGA implementation, the desire emerges for a means that allows high-level estimations of FPGA designs.

We have presented an area and performance estimation methodology for FPGA designs, which is particularly applicable for regular tasks that do not require extensive control. The methodology allows early and fast parameter estimation based on a high-level description of the algorithm. Thus, early design space exploration is facilitated and basic trade-offs can be investigated on a high level. Beneficially, the runs through the standard FPGA design flow are minimised.

Six algorithms have been implemented and evaluated: a FIR filter, motion estimation, an FFT, a Viterbi decoder, CDMA despreading and Twofish. The results prove the suitability of the proposed methodology for high-level design estimation and for early design space exploration.

Possible improvements of the estimation model are a more thorough elaboration of routing effects and control overhead, as well as a more precise representation of the algorithm structure. The latter comprises the individual consideration of the operations and a better specification of a task's inherent parallelism.

References

1. S. Hauck. The roles of FPGA's in reprogrammable systems. *Proceedings of the IEEE*, 86(4):615–638, April 1998.
2. W. H. Mangione-Smith, B. Hutchings, D. Andrews, A. DeHon, C. Ebeling, R. Hartenstein, O. Mencer, J. Morris, K. Palem, V. K. Prasanna, and H. A. E. Spaanenburg. Seeking solutions in configurable computing. *IEEE Computer*, 30(12):38–43, December 1997.
3. Min Xu and F. J. Kurdahi. Accurate prediction of quality metrics for logic level designs targeted toward lookup-table-based FPGA's. *IEEE Transactions on Very Large Scale Integration (VLSI) Systems*, 7(4):411–418, December 1999.
4. W. Miller and K. Owyang. Designing a high performance FPGA – using the PREP benchmarks. In *Wescon'93 Conference Record*, pages 234–239, 1993.
5. S. Kliman. PREP benchmarks reveal performance and capacity tradeoffs of programmable logic devices. In *Proceedings of the IEEE International ASIC Conference and Exhibit (ASIC'94)*, pages 376–382, 1994.
6. K. Chapman. Constant coefficient multipliers for the XC4000E. Xilinx Application Note XAPP054, Xilinx, Inc., December 1996.
7. Xilinx. Data Book 2000.
8. V. Bhaskaran and K. Konstantinides. *Image and Video Compression Standards: Algorithms and Architectures*. Kluwer Academic Publishers, 2nd edition, 1997.
9. B. Schneier, J. Kelsey, D. Whiting, D. Wagner, and C. Hall. Twofish: A 128-bit block cipher. Technical report, Counterpane Systems, June 1998.
   http://www.counterpane.com/twofish.html

Balancing Logic Utilization and Area Efficiency in FPGAs

Russell Tessier and Heather Giza

Department of Electrical and Computer Engineering
University of Massachusetts
Amherst, MA. 01003.
tessier@ecs.umass.edu

Abstract. In this paper we outline a procedure to determine appropriate partitioning of programmable logic and interconnect area to minimize overall device area across a broad range of benchmark circuits. To validate our design approach, FPGA layout tools which target devices with less that 100% logic capacity have been developed to augment existing approaches that target fully-utilized devices. These tools have been applied to FPGA and reconfigurable computing benchmarks which range from simple state machines to pipelined datapaths. In general, it is shown that the minimum *area* point for architectures similar to those available from Xilinx Corporation falls below the 100% *logic* utilization point for many circuits.

1 Introduction

Traditionally, the capacity of FPGA devices has been completely identified by the quantity of logic gates available inside the devices. In practice, however, it is accepted that 100% logic utilization of FPGAs is frequently impractical due to a limited supply of programmable routing resources. Clearly, the individual nature of a specific logic design defines the amount of interconnect needed to complete device routing. If the routing allocated to a device is at a high level relative to its available logic, unused *routing* area will be wasted and the design can be defined as *logic limited*. If the level of routing resources is at a low level relative to its available logic, the logic device will be *routing-limited*, thus requiring the user to select an FPGA with a larger amount of routing and logic resources in order to successfully complete place and route. Since the additional logic resources will likely be unused, this leads to wasted *logic* area. An area-efficient FPGA family can be designed by allocating routing resources to a given logic capacity so that area wastage across a collection of designs with similar amounts of logic is minimized and the mapping for most designs is *balanced*.

The issue of balancing FPGA resources to minimize area was first explored by Dehon in [10]. In this previous work, the interconnect of reconfigurable devices is modelled as a hierarchical binary tree with individual LUTs located at tree leaves. A collection of benchmark designs was applied to devices of varying interconnect richness and it was determined that for an FPGA family the

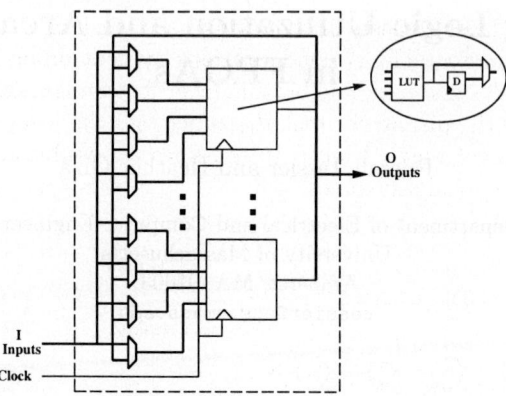

Fig. 1. Basic Logic Element and Logic Cluster

optimal area point supports 85% logic utilization across all designs. While this initial work clearly identifies area and logic utilization tradeoff issues, it has two significant limitations. In general, a binary tree is a limiting interconnect structure that leads to severe routing inefficiencies [16]. In this paper we consider lower-dimensional interconnect that more accurately reflects *island-style* routing structures found in XC4000 and Virtex devices from Xilinx Corporation [3]. Secondly, the previously-analyzed benchmarks are primarily oriented toward small state machines rather than the data paths commonly implemented in contemporary FPGAs. In this paper we consider a sampling of these benchmarks in conjunction with MCNC benchmarks and circuits from the RAW reconfigurable computing benchmark suite [5] to better represent the benchmark design space.

In performing our analysis of area efficiency it was often necessary to target designs to devices with less than 100% logic utilization. To perform this mapping accurately, new FPGA clustering and placement techniques were developed that specifically assume that some FPGA logic resources will be left unpopulated. It will be shown that these CAD techniques reduce overall required routing area by 40% versus previously-reported clustering and placement approaches when applied to designs mapped to devices with less than 100% logic utilization.

2 Background

In developing an area efficient FPGA design methodology, an effort has been made to match switch populations to existing commercial devices and to use available benchmark circuits from a spectrum of design suites.

2.1 Island-Style FPGAs

While early FPGA architectures typically contained simple logic blocks containing one or two LUT/flip-flop pairs, more recent devices [2] [3] have grouped multiple LUT/FF pairs together into a single *cluster* to take advantage of design locality and to reduce FPGA place-and-route time. A key action in designing these architectural families has been the determination of logic cluster granularity. As previously described by Betz and Rose [7], if logic clusters contain insufficient logic resources, the amount of inter-cluster routing resources needed for routing will be great. Conversely, if clusters contain excessive amounts of logic, much of these resources will be wasted. Figure 1 shows a generalized model of a cluster-based FPGA device. Each cluster contains N basic logic elements (BLEs), each possessing a single look-up table/flip-flop pair. The cluster has a total of I inputs and O outputs which connect cluster logic to the surrounding interconnection matrix. In [7] it was determined that the appropriate relationship between N and I is $I = 2N + 2$. To provide parallels to the Xilinx Virtex [3] architecture, a cluster size of $N = 4$ and cluster input count of $I = 10$ is used in experimentation. The routing structure of an *island-style* architecture is created by replicating a logic and routing *cell* in two dimensions to form a uniform, flat logic and routing substrate. The fraction of cluster I/Os that connect to tracks in each routing channel ($F_c = 0.3$) and the connectivity of each routing track to other tracks in a switchbox ($F_s = 3$) have been set to values determined by previous work [8].

Often, FPGA companies use the same logic and routing cell (with associated proportion of tracks per channel) to make numerous logic block arrays of differing logic block counts. If a logic design does not meet the routing constraints of a specific device in the family, it is often possible to meet routing constraints by migrating the design to a larger device in the family and leaving the added logic resources unused.

2.2 Design Requirements

For a given design, a known relationship exists between the amount of logic (or number of logic blocks) and the number of wires associated with the design. This relationship, Rent's Rule [12]:

$$\textbf{Rent's Rule}: \quad N = KG^p \tag{1}$$

where N is the number of wires emanating from a region, G is the number of circuit components (or logic blocks), K is Rent's constant, and p is Rent's exponent, characterizes the routing density in a circuit. Most circuits, except for linear arrays with primarily local communication, have been shown to have Rent exponents of $p > 0.5$ indicating that as a quantity of logic scales, the amount of interconnect emanating from it grows faster than its perimeter, which is directly proportional to $G^{0.5}$. As stated previously in [10], it is possible to characterize the relationship between a design and a target FPGA relative to their corresponding p values assuming sufficient logic capacity is present in the FPGA. If $p_{interconnect} > p_{design}$ the design is effectively *logic limited* since some routing will be unused and if $p_{interconnect} < p_{design}$ the design is *routing limited* since some logic resources will have to be left unused in order for the design to route. Generally, FPGAs that have interconnect levels most closely aligned with the majority of target benchmarks will have the least area wastage.

While the Rent exponent p of an FPGA based on a binary tree is generally easy to determine [10] given the centralized nature of hierarchical routing, the determination of p for island-style arrays must be determined experimentally. In general, if a design with Rent exponent p successfully routes on an FPGA device with no unused logic or routing resources (e.g. the design is balanced), the device may be characterized as having an interconnect capable of supporting other designs with Rent exponent p. It should be noted that full utilization of interconnect indicates that the device *track count* is the minimum needed for routing the array, not that every wire track is used. In Section 5 it will be shown that this procedure of calibrating the Rent exponent of given array sizes and track widths can be performed prior to experimentation to determine the capability of an array to route a specific group of designs (e.g. those with similar Rent exponents). It is interesting to note that while the *absolute* value of island-style track count relative to p is difficult to determine with accuracy analytically, the *growth rate* of track count relative to logic block count in devices with Rent exponent p can be determined analytically [14] through the use of average design wire length.

3 Related Work

With the exception of [9] and [10], most FPGA architectural evaluations [4] [8] have assumed that FPGA designers and consumers desire *full* device logic utilization for *all* designs, even at the cost of extreme amounts of routing area that is unused for *most* designs. As mentioned in [10], for most previous FPGA architectural evaluations, following assignment of design logic to programmable logic resources, device track counts and switch patterns are varied to find the lowest-cost solution from a routing area standpoint. In our evaluation, both routing *and* logic utilization are allowed to vary to permit a minimum overall area solution.

In [9], an FPGA architecture is described that allows logic blocks to be used either for logic or routing. While this approach allows for area tradeoffs, the fine-grained nature of the device architecture makes routing impractical for large, macro-based designs frequently implemented in practice today. As previously mentioned, in [10], a bifurcator-based binary tree model for routing is used to evaluate area utilization. While providing a flexible, scalable model for area experimentation, the bifurcator interconnect model is generally too restrictive for commercial development due to performance and locality limitations. A more complete discussion of previous work in FPGA architecture evaluation for island-style devices and others can be found in [8] and [10].

4 Experimental Methodology

In order to determine the area-minimizing ratio of logic to interconnect for an FPGA logic family, it is necessary to map a collection of benchmarks of approximately the same logic block count to a variety of FPGA arrays with varying logic block counts and interconnect richness (e.g. Rent exponents p). One mapping issue encountered in performing this evaluation was a lack of documented FPGA clustering and placement tools that can be applied to designs with less than 100% logic block utilization. Before describing our complete methodology, several novel approaches for mapping logic designs to FPGA devices with less than 100% utilization are described.

4.1 Clustering

A key aspect of mapping LUT-based designs to FPGAs with logic clusters is the process of clustering. In previous, full-utilization clustering approaches [7] [13], each cluster is packed as full as possible in an attempt to reduce the overall number of required device clusters. In our new approach, an attempt is made to *spread the logic evenly across all clusters in the device* while limiting the number of inputs that logically drive each cluster to be less than the number of pins physically available. The motivation for this approach is apparent if one considers the need for subsequent routing. Since each cluster input can drive any LUT input, underassigning logical inputs to physical cluster input pins gives a router much more flexibility in routing wires. For example, consider a cluster that has ten input pins, but only six that are to be used. The six logical inputs can be assigned to any of the ten available pins. If all ten inputs needed to be used, the number of possible input pin permutations would be greatly reduced. Another advantage of the modified clustering approach is that it distributes logic evenly across the chip. Generally, this helps the router avoid routing hot spots.

In the new clustering algorithm, the number of LUTs to be held in each cluster (N_{high}, N_{low}) is first determined. These utilization numbers reflect the overall LUT utilization of the device and differ by only one LUT. Following this step the number of device clusters that hold each quantity of LUTs (C_{high} and C_{low}, respectively) is determined. Clustering is then performed for the two types of clusters with cluster inputs in each case, $I_{cluster}$, set to limit cluster fanin. Additional details about the clustering algorithm can be found in [15].

4.2 Placement

Simulated annealing is by far the most popular placement algorithm used for FPGAs [8]. This hill-climbing approach requires a cost function that closely models the costs likely to be faced during a subsequent routing phase. Prior to developing new clustering techniques, several new placement techniques were tested for use in conjunction with the original greedy clustering algorithm described in [7]. For designs targeted to devices with less than 100% logic utilization, greedy clustering leads to a number of both fully-populated clusters and some clusters that are completely empty. Both of the following placement techniques attempt to distribute the empty clusters inside the target device to minimize routing congestion. Each technique involves the use of a modified simulated annealing cost function that has been augmented to include costs in addition to wire length.

Bin Utilization. While wire length minimization has been shown to be an effective technique for promoting routability in fully-populated designs, the use of wire length alone in partially-populated devices can lead to routing congestion in one area of the device while other areas are completely empty. A way to overcome congestion in specific regions of the device is to penalize local region congestion in the annealing cost function.

To promote congestion-free routing, a bin-based placer was developed that considers the device as a collection of placement regions. Prior to placement, an *occupancy limit* for each region is set to be the percentage of populated clusters in the entire device. The net effect of a utilization factor is that populated clusters are spread evenly throughout the device. If the population of a bin exceeds the occupancy limit at a given time, a penalty factor is added to the annealing wire length cost function.

The efficiency of the placement approach is directly related to the size of the bin used. If the bin size is too small, not only is computation time increased, but also overall placement wirelength may be adversely affected. If the bin size is too large, the benefits of binning may be reduced. We have found that a bin size containing approximately 25-36 clusters leads to the best placement results.

Non-linear Congestion. An alternate binning approach, first described in [6], abandons the wire length cost model for simulated annealing in favor of a cost model based on wiring track demand within specific bins. In this case, the cost of the logic in each bin is characterized as:

$$Max\left(\frac{D_x}{\rho * S_x}, \left(\frac{D_x}{\rho * S_x}\right)^2\right) + Max\left(\frac{D_y}{\rho * S_y}, \left(\frac{D_y}{\rho * S_y}\right)^2\right) \quad (2)$$

where D_x (D_y) is the demand for horizontal (vertical) routing tracks within the region, S_x (S_y) is the supply of available horizontal (vertical) tracks within the region and ρ is a scaling factor. This approach is much more time consuming than the utilization-based binning approach since demand values must be updated by examining the routing bounding box of each net affected by a potential block move.

4.3 Experimental Procedure

To demonstrate how an area-efficient FPGA family can be determined, the ten benchmarks listed in Table 1 were mapped to a set of island-style FPGAs of various logic block counts and channel densities. The Rent exponents listed in Table 1 were determined through recursive bipartitioning using a KLFM mincut

Table 1. Benchmark Design Statistics

Circuit	Source	LUTs	Rent Exp. (p)
switch	Ind	1860	.62
r4000	PREP	1825	.65
alu4	IWLS93	1522	.63
apex2	IWLS93	1878	.70
ssp16	RAW	1798	.54
bsort	RAW	1653	.48
spm4	RAW	1892	.52
bigkey	MCNC	1707	.56
des	MCNC	1591	.57
seq	MCNC	1750	.65

partitioner [11]. These similarly-sized benchmarks were taken from the MCNC benchmark suite [17], the RAW benchmark suite [5], and the PREP FPGA benchmark suite [1]. One design, a small network switch, was obtained from a commercial company.

The following steps were performed to determine the appropriate amount of routing tracks for a logic family to achieve minimum area across all benchmarks:

1. The Rent parameters of grids containing 22x22 logic blocks (clusters) were determined for assorted channel track counts using the procedure listed in Section 2.2. Since all benchmarks achieve exactly or nearly 100% logic utilization at this logic block count, the largest track count required for a grid of this size represents an upper area bound for these benchmarks.
2. Designs were mapped to grids with additional logic blocks compared to those used in step 1. Mapping was performed using the clustering and placing approaches outlined in Section 4. In many cases a design mapped to a larger logic grid required a lower track count to route successfully, thus requiring less routing area at the cost of additional logic area.
3. The minimum area point across all designs, track counts, and logic array sizes was determined through area summation of both logic block and routing switch transistor counts.

The VPR tool set [8] was used to perform all design routing with routing segment length distributions the same as those found in Xilinx Virtex devices. The **trans_count** tool from the University of Toronto was used to evaluate island-style FPGA area. As mentioned in Section 2, all clusters were assumed to contain four LUTs.

5 Results

The first step in the design procedure was to determine which of the clustering and placement algorithms were best suited to mapping designs to FPGAs with

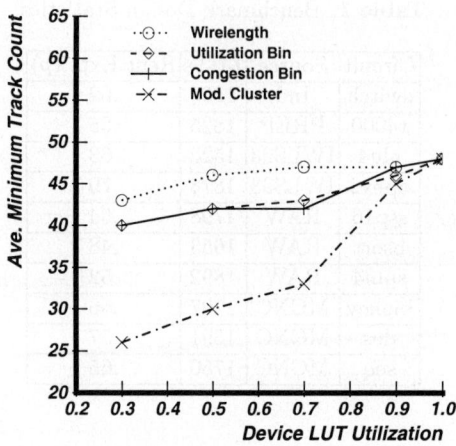

Fig. 2. Ave. minimum tracks based on device utilization

less than 100% logic utilization. All techniques, except the modified clustering approach described in Section 4, used the greedy clusterer described in [7]. Clusters created by the modified clustering algorithm were placed in the FPGA using simulated annealing based solely on wire length minimization. As can be seen in Figure 2, the modified clustering approach was most effective at distributing logic around the device for a variety of LUT logic utilization levels. Even though in many cases the total number of inter-cluster nets that needed to be routed *increased*, the additional routing flexibility obtained through reduced LUTs and inputs per cluster helped achieve lower-area placements. While utilization and congestion bin-based costs performed better than wire-length only based cost, the improvements were minimal.

The second part of the design analysis was to determine the number of clusters required per device to map the benchmark designs to devices with a fixed number of tracks per channel. As seen on the left side of Figure 3, as the number of available tracks per channel was reduced, the number of clusters required per device increased dramatically indicating low logic utilization per device for these cases. On the right side of the graph it can be seen that beyond a certain interconnect point (about 50 tracks per channel) adding extra tracks does not reduce average cluster count. This point indicates 100% routability for all benchmark designs. The dashed lines in the graph will be explained below.

The final step in the analysis was to add the transistor area consumed by logic clusters and routing for the design curves illustrated cumulatively in Figure 3 to determine the area for designs mapped to various levels of logic and interconnect. As shown in Figure 4, the minimum area point for all designs occurred for a track count of about 38. From experimentation, this value roughly corresponds to a Rent exponent p of approximately 0.55. In Figure 3 it can be seen that a track count of 38 corresponds roughly to an average logic utilization of about 80%.

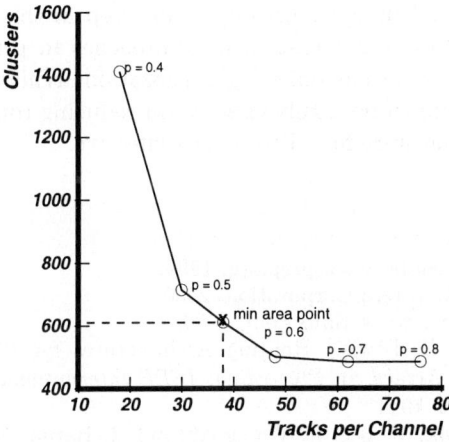

Fig. 3. Ave. clusters required for logic devices versus track counts

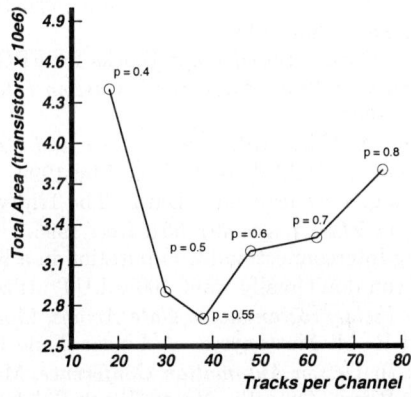

Fig. 4. Combined logic and routing area required for logic devices versus track counts

Two observations can be noted. First, a Rent exponent of 0.55 is in the range of the Rent values of the benchmarks, as one would expect. Secondly, the p value of 0.55 and utilization value of 80% are close to the 0.6 and 85% found by Dehon for the binary tree model [10].

6 Conclusions

In this paper we have outlined a procedure by which an area-efficient FPGA family can be designed. By evaluating a series of benchmark circuits, it is possible to determine routing track counts that will lead to reduced overall logic *and* routing area across all designs. An important step in this work was the analysis of several clustering and placement approaches to promote routability in FPGA designs with less than 100% logic utilization. While improved clustering techniques were found to be highly effective in reducing routing area, bin-based placement approaches were found to be less effective.

References

1. *Prep Benchmark Suite.* www.prep.org, 1999.
2. *Altera Data Book.* Altera Corporation, 2000.
3. *Xilinx Corporation.* www.xilinx.com, 2000.
4. A. Agarwal and D. Lewis. Routing Architectures for Hierarchical Field Programmable Gate Arrays. In *Proceedings IEEE International Conference on Computer Design*, Oct. 1994.
5. J. Babb, M. Frank, V. Lee, E. Waingold, and R. Barua. The RAW Benchmark Suite: Computation Structures for General Purpose Computing. In *Proceedings, IEEE Workshop on FPGA-based Custom Computing Machines*, Napa, Ca, Apr. 1997.
6. V. Betz and J. Rose. On Biased and Non-Uniform Global Routing Architectures and CAD Tools for FPGAs. *University of Toronto Department of Electrical Engineering, Technical Report*, June 1996.
7. V. Betz and J. Rose. Cluster-Based Logic Blocks for FPGAs: Area-Efficiency vs. Input Sharing and Size. In *Proceedings, IEEE Custom Integrated Circuits Conference*, pages 551–554, 1997.
8. V. Betz, J. Rose, and A. Marquardt. *Architecture and CAD for Deep-Submicron FPGAs.* Kluwer Academic Publishers, Boston, Ma, 1999.
9. G. Borriello, C. Ebeling, S. Hauck, and S. Burns. The Triptych FPGA Architecture. *IEEE Transactions on VLSI*, pages 491–501, Dec. 1995.
10. A. Dehon. Balancing Interconnect and Computation in a Reconfigurable Computing Array (or, why you don't really want 100% LUT utilization). In *7th International Workshop on Field-Programmable Gate Arrays*, Monterey, Ca, Feb. 1999.
11. C. M. Fiduccia and R. M. Mattheyses. A Linear Time Heuristic for Improving Network Partitions. In *Design Automation Conference*, May 1984.
12. B. Landman and R. Russo. On a Pin Versus Block Relationship For Partitions of Logic Graphs. *IEEE Transactions on Computers*, C-20(12), Dec. 1971.
13. A. Marquardt, V. Betz, and J. Rose. Using Cluster-Based Logic Blocks and Timing-Driven Packing to Improve FPGA Speed and Density. In *International Symposium on Field Programmable Gate Arrays*, Monterey, Ca., Feb. 1998.
14. R. Tessier. *Fast Place and Route Approaches for FPGAs: Chapter 6*. PhD thesis, Massachusetts Institute of Technology, Department of Electrical Engineering and Computer Science, 1999. available at www.ecs.umass.edu/ece/tessier/tessier.html.
15. R. Tessier and H. Giza. Balancing Logic Utilization and Area Efficiency in FPGAs. *University of Massachusetts Department of Electrical and Computer Engineering, Technical Report TR-CSE-00-5*, June 2000.
16. W. Tsu, K. Macy, A. Joshi, R. Huang, N. Walker, T. Tung, O. Rowhani, V. George, J. Wawrzynek, and A. Dehon. HSRA: High-Speed Synchronous Reconfigurable Array. In *7th International Workshop on Field-Programmable Gate Arrays*, Monterey, Ca, Feb. 1999.
17. S. Yang. Logic Synthesis and Optimization Benchmarks. *Microelectronics Centre of North Carolina Tech. Report*, 1991.

Performance Penalty for Fault Tolerance in Roving STARs

John M. Emmert[1], Charles E. Stroud[1],
Jason Cheatham[2], Andrew M. Taylor[2], Pankaj Kataria[2], and Miron Abramovici[3]

[1] Dept of Electrical and Computer Engineering
University of North Carolina at Charlotte
emmert@ieee.org
[2] Dept of Electrical Engineering
University of Kentucky
[3] Bell Labs - Lucent Technologies
Murray Hill, NJ

Abstract. In this paper we analyze the performance penalty of a fault-tolerant (FT) adaptive computing system (ACS) that implements the roving Self Testing AReas (STARs) approach for on-line testing and fault tolerance for FPGAs[1, 5]. For most benchmarks, the presence of the STARs increases the critical path delay by 4.6% to 22%, and preallocating spare cells for fault tolerance causes an additional increase of up to 37%. We also present a procedure for estimating the worst case performance penalty caused by an incremental change of an already placed and routed FPGA. This estimate can be used to guide the selection of fault-tolerant reconfigurations to minimize their impact on the system timing. Our results show that the estimate is within 10% of the real delay values [1].

Key Words: FPGA, Fault Tolerance, Adaptive Computing System

1 Introduction

A fault-tolerant (FT) adaptive computing system (ACS) is a system that continues to operate correctly in the presence of faults. FPGAs provide a good platform for fault tolerance because of their fine-grain regular structure and inherent redundancy. Several methods for FT FPGAs have been presented in the recent past [2–4, 6, 7, 10–14]. FPGAs featuring partial run-time reconfiguration offer additional benefits, first used in our roving Self-Testing AReas (STARs) approach for on-line fault detection/location [1] and for multi-level fault tolerance [5].

Our approach targets logic and interconnect faults that may appear during the lifetime of an FPGA device. (For transient faults, our FT ACS combines concurrent error detection with a checkpointing and roll-back strategy.) The roving STARs approach provides many unique features, such as complete on-line testing of both logic and interconnect without stopping the system function, complete testing of spare resources, diagnosis with maximum diagnostic resolution, reuse of defective cells whenever possible, and uninterrupted system operation even when a fault is detected.

---

[1] this work is supported by the DARPA ACS program under contract number F33615-98-C-1318

Figure 1 illustrates an FPGA with a vertical STAR (V-STAR) and an horizontal STAR (H-STAR) dividing the working area where the application logic resides. The STARs are off-line and being tested while the rest of the device is on-line, continuing normal system operation. Run-time partial reconfiguration via the FPGA boundary-scan interface allows configurations used by STARs to be downloaded and the test activity to proceed without interrupting the normal system operation. When testing a STAR is complete, the STAR moves to a new location (roving), by exchanging places with an adjacent slice of the system logic. After faults are detected in a STAR, the system function continues to execute, because it is spatially separate from the STAR. However, before a slice of the system logic is relocated over the current STAR position where faults have been diagnosed, the slice may have to be incrementally reconfigured to avoid these faults. More information on roving STARs can be found in [1, 5].

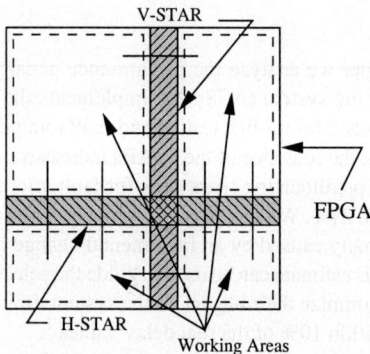

Fig. 1. *FPGA with roving STARs*

In this paper, we analyze the effect of the roving STARs approach on the system performance, and we present a procedure for estimating the worst-case performance penalty caused by incrementally changing an already placed and routed FPGA. Our procedure is based on a FPGA model with varying lengths of wiring segments available for routing and on predicting the programmable resources a router will use to route segments of critical paths. We also introduce the idea of using a programmable system clock and adjusting its period for fault tolerance. If the circuit changes done for fault tolerance increase the delays of critical paths, the system clock will be adjusted based on a post-routing timing analysis. Without such an adjustment, the clock speed must be slow enough that the system will work for any possible sequence of FT reconfigurations. This setting would be done initially and the system would always work at this reduced speed even if no faults ever occur. In contrast, adjusting a programmable clock period will introduce timing penalties only when needed, as a result of new faults.

The paper is organized as follows. In section 2 we describe our methodology for mapping circuits to our FT ACS. In section 3 we analyze the performance penalty for seven benchmark circuits mapped to our FT ACS. In section 4 we describe the model we use to represent FPGAs with different lengths of routing segments, and we describe our delay estimation technique. In section 5 we present our conclusions.

2 System Mapping

In this section we describe our methodology for mapping applications to the working area of our FT ACS. We start with a system function described by an HDL like Verilog or VHDL. We use a commercial tool package, like Synopsys, to synthesize our HDL design description to an EDIF netlist. Using vendor software tools, we map the functionality of the logic in the EDIF netlist to the logic available in the programmable logic blocks (PLBs) for the target architecture. We then reserve two rows and two columns of PLBs for the roving STARs.

We preallocate the spare PLBs by distributing them evenly within the FPGA, with the goal of having one spare as close as possible to every PLB that may implement part of the application logic. This strategy attempts to make the timing effects of replacing faulty PLBs with their designated spare cells relatively small and of the same order of magnitude. Then standard FPGA tools are used to place and route the application in the non-spare PLB locations on the FPGA, leaving aside the initial area for the STARs. Once all logic cell functions in the application have been placed and all FT spare PLB locations have been determined, we assign a spare cell to each functional PLB used in the application. In general, we may have several spare cells that can be used to replace a functional PLB, and the same spare may be designated as replacement for several functional PLB. We attempt to assign the spares with the goal of minimizing a cost function that reflects the performance penalty caused by the FT replacement of functional PLBs with spare cells. The estimation technique used for this will be described in section 4.

3 Performance Penalty

There are three ways performance is affected by our roving STARs approach. The first performance penalty is introduced because the application logic is often split by the roving STARs (see Figure 1). In the worst case, a signal in the circuit's critical path may be split by one or two STAR widths. The presence of preallocated spare cells that cannot be used for the application logic extends the length of signal nets compared to an unconstrained placement, and thus causes a second detrimental effect on performance. In general, the timing impact of preallocated spares increases with the number of spares. The third cause of performance degradation occurs when logic cell functions are moved from their original PLB locations to spare PLBs as a result of FT reconfiguration. This penalty can be minimized by the spare assignment technique described in the previous section.

In the remainder of this section, we investigate the first and second penalty for seven benchmark circuits mapped to our FT ACS. First we map the circuit as a non-FT FPGA design using commercial CAD tools, with options set for performance optimization. Then we map the same set of circuits to the FT ACS with STARs but without preallocated FT spares. This will allow us to evaluate the first performance penalty caused by the presence of the STARs. Next we map the circuits with STARs and with preallocated FT spares. The method we use to place the spares is described in [5].

The results presented in Table 1 are based on implementing the seven benchmarks using the ORCA2C15 FPGA. Two of the benchmark circuits we implemented were from the DARPA ACS program. We relied on the the ORCA Foundry Trace tool to calculate the worst-case propagation delay through the combinational logic for each circuit. Table 1 shows the worst-case delay for the critical paths in the seven circuits we implemented. Column **Type** indicates the type of the circuit - S for sequential and C for combinational. The column **Optimized System** gives the delays for the circuits mapped to a non-FT design without STARs or spares. This provides the base data for the implementation with no performance penalty. The column **System w/STARs** shows the maximum delays computed for the 10 positions of the V-STAR, with no preallocated FT spares. Similarly, the column **System w/STARs & FT Spares** gives the same delays computed for an FPGA with preallocated FT spares.

Table 1. *Benchmark circuit delay information.*

Circuit	Type	#PLBs	Optimized System (ns)	System w/STARs (ns)	%diff	System w/STARs & FT Spares (ns)	%diff
Huffman	S	40	93.6	114.4	22%	156.3	37%
Fibonacci	S	70	120.8	136.3	13%	130.8	-4%
Wallace Tree Mult	S	65	143.1	149.7	4.6%	166.8	11%
Dig Single SB Mod	S	229	73.5	78.1	6.3%	84.7	8.4%
Hilbert	S	192	76.2	87.5	15%	94.5	8%
Random	S	134	59.0	121.0	105%	148.3	23%
Mono-FFT	C	62	111.6	120.8	8%	123.9	3%

We can see that for five circuits the delay increase caused by the insertion of the roving STARs is between 4.6% and 15%, while for "Huffman" is 22%. The only circuit where the delay penalty is much larger (105%) is "Random," which has a large number of flip-flops using direct connections between PLBs. It should be noted that for the "Random" only two positions of the V-STAR (columns 17-18 and 19-20) caused the large discrepancy. The other eight positions showed results similar to the other circuits. We are currently performing further investigation on the cause of the discrepancy for Random. For six circuits, the use of preallocated spares causes an additional increase of up to 23%. Only for "Huffman" we have a larger increase of 37%. The fact that for one circuit the presence of the spares results in slightly better delay is due to "quirks" in the place and route tools.

We emphasize that better results can be obtained with more control over the place and route tools. When we compute the roving configurations, we start with the basic timing-optimized system, and we incrementally modify it to account for the insertion of the STARs at different positions. The problem is that when the tools are used in the incremental mode, we can no longer set the options for timing optimization.

4   Performance Penalty Estimation

In this section we describe the generic model we use to represent FPGA architectures that have multi-length, programmable interconnect segments, and we present our performance penalty estimation technique. This model can be mapped to most commercially available FPGA architectures. The model is based on an $N \times N$ array of PLBs. The PLBs are connected through a programmable interconnect network made up of N horizontal and N vertical wiring channels. Each wiring channel is composed of a number of wiring segments. The wiring segments can have different lengths, and we describe each segment length using the parameter $\times i$ where $i = 1$ describes a distance spanning two adjacent PLBs and i is an element of the set of possible segment lengths, SL. The elements in the set SL are defined by the FPGA manufacturer, and SL varies from FPGA architecture to architecture. For example, $SL = \{1, 4, \frac{N}{2}, N\}$ for the ORCA2C architecture we use in our implementation.

In the model, each wiring channel is composed of sets of wiring segments. The segments in each set all have the same length and the sets are numbered from 1 to n where n is the number of elements in the set SL. Relative to interconnect delays, we define the delay through a programmable interconnect point (PIP) as D_{pip}. As stated earlier, the length and type of interconnects described by the model is dependent on the FPGA manufacturer and the specific part. Here we attempt to generically categorize the type and length of some commonly found programmable interconnects. First we have a direct connection that is capable of supporting high speed logic chaining for applications like addition and counting. This type of connection is supported in most FPGA architectures [9, 8]. We define the delay of this connection as D_{chain}. Second we have a direct connections between the outputs of one PLB and inputs of an adjacent PLB. We can lump any external switches required for this connection in with the delay of the segments used for the connection. We define the delay of this connection as D_{dir}. Third we have several lengths of routing segments based on the minimum distance between switch matrices. We define the delay of these segments as $D_{\times i}$ where $i \in SL$ is a multiple of the minimum distance between switch matrices. We lump the delay between the I/O of the PLB to each type of connecting segment into the delay $D_{pin \times i}, i \in SL$.

Relative to interconnect delay prediction, Xu et al. presented a method for predicting the interconnect delay (prior to routing) for the Xilinx 4000 series of FPGAs[15]. They model the programmable interconnect network using different delays for different length interconnect segments. Using circuit placement data, they estimate delay between connected logic block pins by predicting the segments the router will use to connect the pins. In their implementation, they use a combination of the shorter segments to connect any pins that are less than 8 PLBs apart and long segments to connect the others. For our method we assume the delay through a programmable interconnect point (PIP) will dominate the delay through shorter segments, and excess delay is introduced with every PIP. For the upper bound, we assume the shortest length segments (most PIPs) will be used to reconnect the broken signal. In datapath circuits, the delay is usually dominated by propagation delay of an adder or a counter. FPGA manufacturers have attempted to minimize this delay by introducing specialized high speed connections between PLBs, for example high speed carry chaining between PLBs. Thus, the critical path of a circuit often includes many such chained connections, and if any of these direct connects are split and rerouted using other routing segments, additional delay is introduced in the critical circuit paths.

Our analysis is limited to splitting of these chained direct connections, however, it can easily be extended to include all types of routed signal connections found in FPGAs. We describe a procedure to estimate the additional delay introduced when two adjacently placed logic cell functions in a circuit critical path are separated. The delay of a signal routed through the programmable interconnect network of an FPGA is based on the number of wiring segments, the length of the wiring segments, and number of programmable switches in the signal's route. Our Δdelay calculations are based on several assumptions:

- A1. The interconnect delay is dominated by the delay of the PIPs.
- A2. Pins are available on all sides of a PLB.
- A3. The delays for horizontal interconnects are the same as the delays for the corresponding vertical interconnects.
- A4. Changes in delay due to moving logic cell functions are additive.

Using our model we can estimate an upper bound for the delay introduced to the critical path when the distance between two logic cell functions in the critical path is changed. The upper bound provides a worst-case estimate for reduction in system clock speed due to reconfiguration of circuit placement for fault tolerance. It should be noted that before the system clock speed is actually adjusted for fault tolerance, the actual required delay should be calculated using actual timing data from the routed circuit. Our method is strictly for guiding incremental FT reconfiguration.

We use ΔX and ΔY to represent the distance between two logic cell functions in the x-axis and y-axis directions respectively. For each break between logic cell functions in the circuit critical path, we estimate the upper bound for the **change** in the critical path delay using the ΔD_upper_est procedure in figure 4.

ΔD_upper_est($\Delta X, \Delta Y$)
  begin
    let D = - original delay between logic cells;
    $D = D + 2 \times D_{pin \times 1}$;
    $D = D + (\Delta X + \Delta Y + 1) \times D_{\times 1}$;
    $D = D + (\Delta X + \Delta Y) \times D_{pip}$;
    if $\Delta X > 0$ AND $\Delta Y > 0$ then
      $D = D - (D_{\times 1} + D_{pip})$;
    end if;
    return D;
  end;

Fig. 2. *Procedure for estimating the upper bound for change in delay.*

In the procedure, we initially set the change in the delay to *the original delay between logic cell functions*. For two adjacent logic cell functions that make use of either the fast *chained* connection or another direct connection between the two logic blocks, we can

Performance Penalty for Fault Tolerance in Roving STARs   551

set this value to D_{chain} or D_{dir} respectively. Otherwise, the original delay can be set using data from actual circuit routing information.

The critical path can be split by one, two, or more STAR widths[2]. In the event that the configuration is changed, we look at any nets in the critical path to see if their delays change the worst case propagation delay, and we look at other changed nets to see if a new critical path is created. Knowing the number of folds in the critical path and the maximum clock frequency of an application mapped as a non-FT design, we can estimate the maximum clock frequency for the same application mapped to our FT FPGA using procedure ΔD_upper_est. Additionally, if a logic cell function in the middle of a chain is moved to a FT spare location, our procedure must be used twice to estimate the additional path delay.

Figures 3 and 4 show an example of how we model a one-axis and dual-axis split in a chained logic cell function respectively. If the the signal initially routed through the fast *chained* connection is in the critical path before and after the move, we can estimate the worst case performance degradation due to the move with ΔD_upper_est. In Figure 3, we break the initially *chained* connection between A and B, by moving the function of B into C. We apply procedure ΔD_upper_est with $\Delta X = 0$ and $\Delta Y = 3$. This gives $\Delta Delay = 2 \times D_{pin \times 1} + 4 \times D_{\times 1} + 3 \times D_{pip} - D_{chain}$. Similarly for the example in figure 4 with $\Delta X = 3$ and $\Delta Y = 3$, we get $\Delta Delay = 2 \times D_{pin \times 1} + 6 \times D_{\times 1} + 5 \times D_{pip} - D_{chain}$.

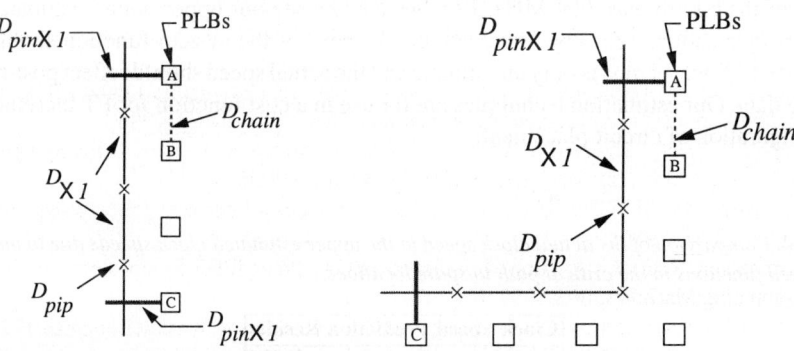

Fig. 3. *Moving to different row, same column.*

Fig. 4. *Moving to different row and column.*

The examples in Figures 3 and 4 can also be used to predict the worst-case effect on performance of splitting a system function by one or both of the roving STARs respectively.

To test our worst-case estimator, we simulate the effect on system clock speed of moving system logic cell functions to FT spare locations. We picked direct connected logic cell functions in the application critical path(s) and moved them to spare locations

---

[2] if the critical path folds back on itself it may be broken multiple times

at various distances from their original locations. We compare the upper bound estimate to the actual change in the system clock speed.

The parameters for the model used in the delay estimator ΔD_upper_est can be determined using manufacturing data or backed out of static timing analysis for specifically routed test circuits. The data in tables 2 and 3 show the values we determined for the parameters in the delay estimator for the ORCA2C FPGA.

Table 2. *Delay statistics.*

ΔDelay Statistics for the ORCA2C FPGA (ns)		
D_{chain}	D_{dir}	D_{pip}
0.5	1.5	1.3

Table 3. *Delay statistics for pins and segments.*

ΔDelay Statistics for the ORCA2C FPGA (ns)				
	$i=1$	$i=4$	$i=10$	$i=20$
$D_{\times i}$	0.2	0.8	2.0	4.0
$D_{pin \times i}$	1.0	1.3	1.6	1.6

In table 4, we see the actual maximum system clock speed (S_max) as determined by `trace` and the upper bound estimation ($\Delta D\_upper\_est \rightarrow$ S_upper) and percent difference for moving a logic cell function in the critical path to a spare location various Manhattan distances (ΔM) from its original location. The original maximum clock speed of the circuit was 7.54 MHz. For this data we see our upper bound estimate is a conservative estimate for how much the clock speed of the system function should be decreased. However, this is only an estimate and the actual speed should reflect post-route timing data. Our estimation techniques are for use in a cost function for FT incremental reconfiguration of circuit placement.

Table 4. *Comparison of the actual clock speed to the upper estimated clock speeds due to moving logic cell functions in the critical path to spare locations.*

Clock Speed Prediction Results			
ΔM	S_max (MHz)	S_upper (MHz)	%diff
1	7.44	7.90	6.0
2	7.41	7.11	-4.1
3	6.89	6.97	1.2
4	7.17	6.82	-5.0
5	7.06	6.55	-7.5
6	7.01	6.42	-8.8
7	6.95	6.31	-9.7
8	6.72	6.19	-8.2

5 Conclusions

We have described the procedure for mapping system functions and applications to our FT ACS, and the relative performance cost between mapping system functions to a non-FT FPGA and a FT ACS that uses our roving STARs approach[1, 5]. For most cases we showed only a slight performance penalty due to the introduction of roving STARs and little additional penalty for preallocating low numbers of FT spares.

We have presented a procedure for estimating an upper bound on the performance cost of relocating logic cell functions for fault tolerant applications. We have tested our method by reconfiguring several benchmark circuits and comparing the estimated performance change to the actual change. Our method can be used in conjunction with [3] for quickly reconfiguring multiple faulty logic cell locations. Our method of prediction can also be used as a quick estimate to predict the affects on system performance when a circuit is mapped to our FT ACS.

We have introduced the idea of adjusting the system clock for Fault Tolerance. In the event a system function must be reconfigured for fault tolerance, post place and route circuit analysis is used to adjust the speed of the system clock. In this way system performance is gradually degraded as more faults occur, rather than designed with a performance penalty or cushion to cover any reduction caused by reconfiguring circuit mapping for fault tolerance.

References

1. M. Abramovici, C. Stroud, S. Wijesuriya, C. Hamilton, and V. Verma. Using Roving STARs for On-Line and Diagnosis of FPGAs in Fault-Tolerant Applications. *Proceedings of the 1999 International Test Conference*, pages 973–982, October 1999.
2. S. Dutt, V. Shanmugavel, and S. Trimberger. Efficient Incremental Rerouting for Fault Reconfiguration in Field Programmable Gate Arrays. *ACM/IEEE International Conference on Computer-Aided Design (ICCAD)*, November 1999.
3. J. M. Emmert and D. K. Bhatia. Reconfiguring FPGA Mapped Designs with Applications to Fault Tolerance and Reconfigurable Computing. In *Lecture Notes in Computer Science, 7th International Workshop on Field Programmable Logic (FPL97)*, volume 1304, pages 141–150. Springer-Verlag, August/September 1997.
4. J. M. Emmert and D. K. Bhatia. Incremental Routing in FPGAs. In *11th Annual IEEE International ASIC Conference*, pages I302–I305, September 1998.
5. J. M. Emmert, C. E. Stroud, B. Skaggs, and M. Abramovici. Dynamic Fault Tolerance in FPGAs via Partial Reconfiguration. In *Eighth Annual IEEE Symposium on Field-Programmable Custom Computing Machines*, April 2000.
6. F. Hanchek and S. Dutt. Methodologies for Tolerating Cell and Interconnect Faults in FPGAs. *IEEE Transactions on Computers*, 47:15–33, January 1998.
7. F. Hatori, T.Sakurai, K. Sawada, M. Takahashi, M. Ichida, M. Uchida, I. Yoshii, Y. Kawahara, T. Hibi, Y. Sacki, H. Muraga, and K. Kanzaki. Introducing Redundancy in Field Programmable Gate Arrays. In *Proceedings of the IEEE International Conference on Custom Integrated Circuits*, pages 7.1.1–7.1.4, 1993.
8. Lucent Inc. *http://www.micro.lucent.com/micro/fpga*.
9. Xilinx Inc. *http://www.xilinx.com*.

10. J. L. Kelly and P. A. Ivey. A Novel Approach to Defect Tolerant Design for SRAM Based FPGAs. In *ACM Second International Workshop on Field-Programmable Gate Arrays*, pages 1–11, Feburary 1994.
11. J. Lach, W. H. Mangione-Smith, and M. Potkonjak. Efficiently Supporting Fault Tolerance in FPGAs. In *International Symposium on Field Programmable Gate Arrays*, 1998.
12. V. Lakamraju and R. Tessier. Tolerating Operational Faults in Cluster-based FPGAs. In *ACM International Symposium on Field-Programmable Gate Arrays*, 2000.
13. K. Roy and S. Nag. On Routability for FPGAs under Faulty Conditions. *IEEE Transactions on Computers*, 44:1296–1305, November 1995.
14. G. Tempesti, D. Mange, and A. Stauffer. A Robust Multiplexer-Based FPGA Inspired By Biological Systems. In *The Euromicro Journal*, volume 43, September 1997.
15. M. Xu and F. J. Kurdahi. Accurate Prediction of Quality Metrics for Logic Level Designs Targeted Toward Lookup-Table-Based FPGAs. *IEEE Transactions on Very Large Scale Integration (VLSI) Systems*, 17:411–418, December 1999.

Optimum Functional Decomposition for LUT-Based FPGA Synthesis

Jian Qiao[1], Makoto Ikeda[2], and Kunihiro Asada[2]

[1] Graduate School of Electrical Engineering, University of Tokyo
[2] VLSI Design and Education Center, University of Tokyo
Hongo 7-3-1, Bunkyo-ku, Tokyo 113-8656, Japan

Abstract. In general, Partially Dependent Functions(PDFs) are meaningful for sharing multiple-output CLBs or an LUT. In this paper, we present a novel encoding algorithm for detecting PDFs during functional decomposition. To exploit all solution space, we have introduced pliable encoding to supplement the classical rigid encoding as the latter failed to catch a satisfactory solution. We show that the best solution can only be found by pliable encoding in some cases, and hence the classical encoding strategy should be modified to take account of pliable encoding. Experimental results on a set of MCNC91 benchmarks are quite encouraging.

1 Introduction

Functional decomposition was first explored systematically in the early 60's [1-3], and found applications in numerous areas(e.g. artificial intelligence, learning theory, reliability theory, and VLSI design). Recently, with its rapid growing applications to logic emulation and reconfigurable computing, LUT-based FPGA synthesis has aroused wide research interests; and functional decomposition becomes a noticeable approach to mapping logic design onto LUT-based FPGAs.

There exist two open problems as functional decomposition is used to LUT-based FPGA synthesis: one is how to select a good bound set such that the number of compatibility classes is minimal; the other is how to encode the compatibility classes such that the implementation is minimal in terms of the LUT or CLB count. Research work so far has led to many effective approaches to the problems. The methods proposed in [4,7] address the bound set selection problem; while the algorithms appeared in [6-11] deal with the encoding problem. Generally, methods for class encoding can be classified into two categories according to optimization criteria. The first category [6,7] focuses on the ease of re-decomposition of the image function g; while the second[8-11] concentrates on producing the decomposition function $\vec{\alpha}$ which are partially dependent or of minimal support such that these PDFs can be merged into a minimal number of multiple-output CLBs. Algorithms suggested in [7,9,11] have also made attempts to share logic functions among the multiple outputs of a network; however, only a set of t PDFs, which satisfy some conditions and relate to each other in a certain way, are meaningful for sharing a multiple-output CLB and/or an

LUT. On the other hand, encoding algorithms proposed so far have adopted only rigid encoding strategy, to the best of our knowledge, that rules out some feasible PDFs and may result in a sub-optimum in some cases. For instance, the function given in Fig. 1 a is decomposed by rigid encoding($t = 2$) as shown in Fig. 1 b; and we need 3 5-LUTs/CLBs to implement it; anyway, if we instead take $t = 3$(pliable encoding), it can be decomposed as shown in Fig. 1 c, and we need only 2 5-LUTs/CLBs to implement it.

$$\begin{aligned}\{8\} = {} & x_1x_2x_3x_4x_5 + x_1x_2x_3\overline{x}_4\overline{x}_5x_6 + x_1x_2\overline{x}_3x_4\overline{x}_5\overline{x}_6 + x_1x_2\overline{x}_3\overline{x}_4x_5x_6 \\ & + x_1\overline{x}_2x_3x_4\overline{x}_5x_6 + x_1\overline{x}_2x_3\overline{x}_4x_5 + x_1\overline{x}_2\overline{x}_3x_4x_5x_6 + x_1\overline{x}_2\overline{x}_3\overline{x}_4\overline{x}_5\overline{x}_6 \\ & + \overline{x}_1x_2x_3x_4\overline{x}_5x_6 + \overline{x}_1x_2x_3\overline{x}_4x_5 + \overline{x}_1x_2\overline{x}_3x_4x_5x_6 + \overline{x}_1x_2\overline{x}_3\overline{x}_4\overline{x}_5\overline{x}_6 \\ & + \overline{x}_1\overline{x}_2x_3x_4x_5 + \overline{x}_1\overline{x}_2x_3\overline{x}_4\overline{x}_5x_6 + \overline{x}_1\overline{x}_2\overline{x}_3x_4\overline{x}_5\overline{x}_6 + \overline{x}_1\overline{x}_2\overline{x}_3\overline{x}_4x_5x_6 \end{aligned}$$

(a)

$$\begin{aligned}\{8\} = {} & x_5\overline{\langle 2\rangle}\langle 3\rangle + \overline{x}_5\langle 2\rangle\overline{\langle 3\rangle} \\ \langle 2\rangle = {} & x_1x_2x_3\overline{x}_4x_6 + x_1x_2\overline{x}_3x_4\overline{x}_6 + x_1\overline{x}_2x_3x_4x_6 + x_1\overline{x}_2\overline{x}_3\overline{x}_4\overline{x}_6 \\ & + \overline{x}_1x_2x_3x_4x_6 + \overline{x}_1x_2\overline{x}_3\overline{x}_4\overline{x}_6 + \overline{x}_1\overline{x}_2x_3x_4x_6 + \overline{x}_1\overline{x}_2\overline{x}_3x_4\overline{x}_6 \\ \langle 3\rangle = {} & x_1x_2x_3x_4 + x_1x_2\overline{x}_3\overline{x}_4x_6 + x_1\overline{x}_2x_3\overline{x}_4 + x_1\overline{x}_2\overline{x}_3x_4x_6 \\ & + \overline{x}_1x_2x_3\overline{x}_4 + \overline{x}_1x_2\overline{x}_3x_4x_6 + \overline{x}_1\overline{x}_2x_3x_4 + \overline{x}_1\overline{x}_2\overline{x}_3x_4x_6 \end{aligned}$$

(b)

$$\begin{aligned}\{8\} & = x_3x_5\langle 4\rangle + x_3\overline{x}_5x_6\overline{\langle 4\rangle} + \overline{x}_3x_5x_6\overline{\langle 4\rangle} + \overline{x}_3\overline{x}_5\overline{x}_6\langle 4\rangle \\ \langle 4\rangle & = x_1x_2x_4 + x_1\overline{x}_2\overline{x}_4 + \overline{x}_1x_2\overline{x}_4 + \overline{x}_1\overline{x}_2x_4 \end{aligned}$$

(c)

Fig. 1. Decompositions by different encoding strategies: (a) A 6-variable function to be decomposed; (b) Decomposition by rigid encoding strategy; (c) Optimum decomposition by pliable encoding strategy.

In this paper, we focus on the compatible class encoding problem. Our target is Xilinx 3090 series FPGAs [13], whose CLB is of 2-outputs and can implement either one function of at most 5 inputs, or two functions of at most 4 inputs with a total at most 5 inputs. We present an approach to produce a set of t PDFs which can be merged into a 2-output CLB or an LUT, in order to get an optimal decomposition in terms of the number of CLBs and/or LUTs. To exploit all design space during encoding, pliable encoding strategy has been introduced to supplement the classical rigid encoding when the latter failed to find a satisfactory decomposition.

The remainder of this paper is organized as follows. Section 2 introduces some background about functional decomposition. Section 3 formulates the compatibility class encoding problem. Section 4 explains our new encoding approaches. Experimental results and discussions are reported in Section 5.

2 Preliminaries

Definition 2.1 *Functional decomposition is a procedure that decomposes a complex function $f(\mathbf{X})$ into several simpler functions $\vec{\alpha}$ and g in terms of the number of input variables, and it can be expressed as*

$$f(\mathbf{X}) = g(\vec{\alpha}(\mathbf{x}_b), \mathbf{x}_f) \qquad (1)$$

where $\mathbf{X}(\mathbf{X} = \{x_1, x_2, \ldots, x_n\}$, $\mathbf{X} \in \{0,1\}^n$) is the input variable set; $\mathbf{x}_b(\mathbf{x}_b = \{x_1, x_2, \ldots, x_s\}$, $\mathbf{x}_b \in \{0,1\}^s$) is called the bound set *(BS); and $\mathbf{x}_f(\mathbf{x}_f = \{x_{s-i+1}, \ldots, x_n\}(i \geq 0)$, $\mathbf{x}_f \in \{0,1\}^{n-s}$) the* free set *(FS). The function $\vec{\alpha}$ ($\vec{\alpha} = (\alpha_1, \alpha_2, \ldots, \alpha_t)$, $\vec{\alpha} \in \{0,1\}^t$) is called the* encoding function *or* decomposition function; *and g the* base function *or* image function. *Equation 1 gives a disjunctive decomposition if $\mathbf{x}_b \cap \mathbf{x}_f = \phi$; and it gives a* Non-Disjunctive Decomposition *(NDD) if $\mathbf{x}_b \cap \mathbf{x}_f \neq \phi$; besides, it is a simple decomposition if $\|\vec{\alpha}\| = 1$; otherwise, it is a complex decomposition.*

In the following, we introduce briefly some basic concepts about functional decomposition. The details can be found in [6-8,10-11].

Definition 2.2 *Any two different BS vertices $\mathbf{x}_i$ and $\mathbf{x}_j$ ($\mathbf{x}_i, \mathbf{x}_j \in \{0,1\}^s$, $i \neq j$) are said to be* compatible, *denoted as $\mathbf{x}_i \sim \mathbf{x}_j$, if and only if the equation*

$$f(\mathbf{x}_i, \mathbf{x}_f) = f(\mathbf{x}_j, \mathbf{x}_f) \qquad (2)$$

holds for any a given FS vertices $\mathbf{x}_f$. The set of all mutually compatible BS vertices forms a compatibility class.

Theorem 2.1 *For any two different BS vertices $\mathbf{x}_i$ and $\mathbf{x}_j$, and the decomposition function $\vec{\alpha}$, if the expression*

$$\mathbf{x}_i \not\sim \mathbf{x}_j \Longrightarrow \vec{\alpha}(\mathbf{x}_i) \neq \vec{\alpha}(\mathbf{x}_j) \qquad (3)$$

holds, the decomposition defined in Equation 1 always exists.

Theorem 2.1 gives the necessary and sufficient condition for the existence of a decomposition. Let t be the size of $\vec{\alpha}$, and M be the number of the compatibility classes under partition $\mathbf{P}(\mathbf{x}_b/\mathbf{x}_f)$, Equation 3 can be transformed as

$$t \geq \lceil log_2 M \rceil \qquad (4)$$

The encoding is said to be *rigid* if the equal sign is taken; otherwise it is said to be *pliable*. In addition, if each compatibility class is assigned just one $\vec{\alpha}$ code, it is called *strict encoding*; otherwise, if the BS vertices in one compatibility class are assigned more than one $\vec{\alpha}$ code, it is called *non-strict encoding*.

Definition 2.3 *If a function defined on the BS space is independent of some its input variables, it said to be a* partially dependent function *on the BS space, and denoted as PDF; besides, if some components of the decomposition function $\vec{\alpha}$ are PDFs, the decomposition is called a* partially dependent decomposition, *and denoted as PDD.*

Similarly, if a function depends on only one variable in the bound set, we called it a single variable function, and denoted it as SVF. Notice that a SVF is just a special PDF whose fan-in is 1, and that a PDD can be treated as an NDD in a sense. In this paper, we mean NDD specially for a PDD of which at least one $\vec{\alpha}$ component is a SVF.

3 Compatible Class Encoding

We formulate the compatibility class encoding problem as follows:

Definition 3.1 *Given a function $f(\mathbf{X})$ and partition $P(\mathbf{x}_b, \mathbf{x}_f)$, the generalized encoding problem is to find the $\vec{\alpha}$ and g such that the function can be decomposed as Equation 1, and the cost to implement it is a minimum in terms of the CLB or LUT count.*

Note that the size t of $\vec{\alpha}$ is determined by Formula 4. Theorem 2.1 says that the BS vertices of different compatibility classes should have different $\vec{\alpha}$ codes, but it says nothing about the BS vertices of the same compatibility class. To exploit all design space, we may assign different $\vec{\alpha}$ codes to one class(non-strict encoding), and/or let t be greater than $\lceil log_2 M \rceil$(pliable encoding).

In general, for a given t, a PDD is a better solution in terms of CLB count if the $\vec{\alpha}$ components can be merged into 2-output CLBs in pairs; and an NDD is among the best solutions for a SVF needs no additional LUT and/or CLB; so it is important to detect all SVFs and PDFs which can serve as an $\vec{\alpha}$ component.

Definition 3.2 *A group of 2^r BS vertices, which are different just at certain r variables $x_{j1}, x_{j2}, \cdots, x_{jr}$, is called a r-adjacent group with respect to variables $x_{j1}, x_{j2}, \cdots, x_{jr} (j1, j2, \cdots, jr \in [0, s-1], r \in [0, s-2])$.*

Notice that the group of BS vertices forms a $n - r$ cube of the n-dimensional Boolean space. For instance, 4 BS vertices $\{(00100), (00101), (00110), (00111)\}$ are different only at x_0 and x_1 bits, and form a 2-adjacent group with respect to x_0 and x_1(or a 3 cube).

Given the BS size s is 5, there are totally 5 sets of 1-adjacent groups with respect to 1 variable $x_i (i \in [0,5])$; 10 sets of 3-adjacent groups with respect to 3 variables x_{j1}, x_{j2}, and x_{j3}; 10 sets of 2-adjacent groups with respect to 2 variables x_{j1} and x_{j2}; and 5 sets of 4-groups with respect to 4 variables x_{j1}, x_{j2}, x_{j3}, and x_{j4}(where $j1, j2, j3, j4 \in [0,4]$). In Figure 2, we have shown a part of the sets of the r-adjacent groups($r \in [1,4]$).

Each function defined on the BS space corresponds to a bipartition of the BS vertices: with one part of BS vertices assigned to the on-set; and the remainder to the off-set. The correspondence is an one-to-one, so we can get all PDFs which are independent of certain r variables by a bipartition of the r-adjacent groups; but not all the PDFs can serve as an $\vec{\alpha}$ component.

Proposition 3.1. *Given an encoding problem: $f(\mathbf{X})$, $P(\mathbf{x}_b/\mathbf{x}_f)$, and t, a Boolean function defined on the BS space divides all the BS vertices into two parts. If the*

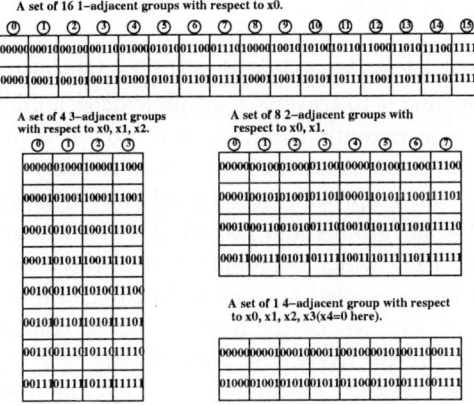

Fig. 2. Some sets of r-adjacent groups($r = [1, 4]$).

number of compatibility classes in each part is not greater than 2^{t-1}, the function is feasible to be an $\overrightarrow{\alpha}$ component; namely, there exists at least a decomposition in which the function is an $\overrightarrow{\alpha}$ component. *Proof. Trivial.* □

Definition 3.3 *Any m functions($m \in [1,t]$) defined on the BS space partition the BS vertices up to 2^u parts; if the number of the compatibility classes in each part is not greater than 2^{t-m}, we say the m functions are mutually compatible with respect to the encoding problem.*

Proposition 3.2. *There exists at least a decomposition in which the m functions serve as the m $\overrightarrow{\alpha}$ components($m \leq t$) if and only if the m functions are compatible mutually with respect to the encoding problem.* *Proof. Trivial.* □

According to Proposition 3.2, to get an optimum decomposition, half the battle is to find a set of t PDFs which are feasible, and compatible mutually with respect to the given problem.

4 Finding an Optimum Decomposition

4.1 Bound Set Selection

The problem of bound set selection is often a bottleneck of functional decomposition. We use here an approximate approach which bases on an stepwise enumerative search over the input variable space. At first, input variables are divided into groups up to 9 or 10 variables; then an enumerative search on each group is performed for a good bound set [12].

4.2 Detection of all PDFs

We use a tailor-made backtracking algorithm [14] to detect all feasible PDFs. The basic idea of backtracking is to traverse a graph lexicographically, and treat each path from the root as a potential solution; the process is advanced recursively along a tree until the constraints are met where a backtracking is made. For LUT-based FPGAs, the graph can be reduced to a tree which is constructed for each set of r-adjacent groups and rooted at 1: each temporary path in the tree corresponds to a PDF which is independent of the r variables. Suppose we assign the r-groups corresponded to each path to the on-set(the remainder to the off-set), and let M_1 and M_2 be the numbers of the compatible classes in the on-set and the off-set, respectively, the Formula $M_1 \leq 2^{t-1}$ can be treated as the constraint on backtracking: all branches beyond the points will be pruned, which reduces considerable execution-time(as illustrated in Figure 3). Formula $M_i \leq 2^{t-1} (i = [1,2])$ serves the criterion to check the feasibility of a potential PDF according to Proposition 3.1 .

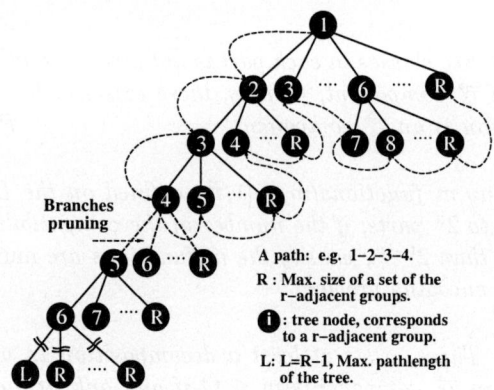

Fig. 3. Detection of all feasible PDFs: the path from the root corresponds to a potential PDF; and all the branches beyond the constraints are pruned.

The time bound of backtracking depends on the number of nodes in the graph to be traversed, and is generally exponential. However, the graph to be traversed is a tree in our encoding problem; besides, the BS size s is 5, and hence the maximal length of a reasonable path is 15(for a 4-input PDF); so the algorithm is practical and effective for detection of all feasible PDFs.

4.3 Encoding Strategy

We set the BS size s to 5, and try to produce a set of t PDFs which can be maximally merged into 2-output CLBs, and/or an LUT; so, what we should do is to pick over a set t PDFs which are compatible mutually from a large set of feasible PDFs. The mutually compatibility checking can be done easily according to Definition 3.3 .

A. Rigid encoding. In general, rigid encoding strategy is adopted to guide the detection and selection of the set of PDFs. In this case, t takes the value $\lceil log_2 M \rceil$. Generally, an encoding process is dominated by the feasible SVFs if there are ones: because a SVF needs no additional CLB or LUT, it is always the best choice; and the resulting decomposition is an NDD. For instance, we can get the optimal NDD of a SVF-ALPHA, a 2SVF-ALPHA, and even a 3SDF-Alpha(Alpha means an arbitrary 5-input function, which is feasible and compatible mutually with the others) when t is 2, 3 and 4, respectively. A set of pairs of mutually compatible PDFs, which forms a PDD, is a better solution next to an NDD.

B. Pliable Encoding. As the size of newly resulting g is less than 5, pliable encoding strategy should be considered to take over the encoding process if the classical rigid encoding process above failed to reach a satisfactory solution: no an NDD and/or PDD solution. In such case, we should release t such that t is greater than $\lceil log_2 M \rceil$, and still less than 5(that makes no change of the cost to implement g). Pliable encoding mostly occurs as the function to be decomposed is of 6 or 7 input variables. According to Proposition 3.1 , all the PDFs are feasible in this case; so the number of PDFs may be very large(Max. over 167000). To manipulate the large set of PDFs effectively, we take the internal representation of a PDF as an **int**, and use bitwise operations on all the PDFs. In some case, pliable encoding may be recursively applied once to catch an optimum decomposition(for 6-input functions).

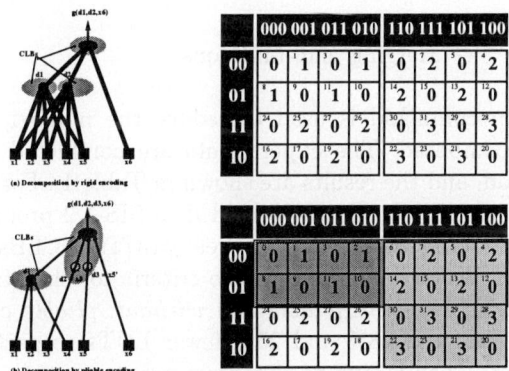

Fig. 4. Example of optimum encoding: there is no an NDD or a PDD by rigid encoding($t = 2$); anyway, we can get an NDD by pliable encoding($t = 3$).

To take an example, let us re-examine the function of Figure 1 . As in Fig. 4 , the number of the compatibility classes is 4. In the case of rigid encoding: $t = 2$, we have to pick over an Alpha-Alpha decomposition as there are no feasible PDFs(also refer to Figure 1b); and we need 3 LUTs/CLBs to it. However, we can get an NDD(2SVFs-Alpha) if we take pliable encoding:$t = 3$(also refer to Figure 1c), and we instead need just 2 LUTs/CLBs to implement it.

5 Experimental Results

Our algorithm has been implemented in language C, and incorporated into SIS-1.2 program developed in UC Berkeley [15]. To assess our decomposition method, we arranged two experiments on a large set of mcnc91 logic synthesis benchmarks. One takes account of pliable encoding, and denoted as *with-pliable*; the other adopts the classical rigid encoding strategy, and denoted as *without-pliable*; both *with-pliable* and *without-pliable* use our new encoding approach.

In technology-independent stage, the following script is used to prepare the initial network for a two-level network; and the standard script provided in SIS-1.2 program is used for a multi-level network.

collapse
simplify -d -m nocomp

In technology-dependent stage, the script for decomposition and FPGA mapping is shown as

xl_partition -n 9 -tm
decomposition   ← Various decomposition algorithms used here
xl_partition -n 5 -tm
xl_cover
xl_merge -l   ← Merging sub-functions

where *xl_partition* command is used to reduce the number of nodes in the network to be decomposed. The experiments are conducted on Sun SPARC ultra-60 workstation, and the results are shown in Table 1. For comparison, the results from *xl_k_decomp* command provided in SIS-1.2 program are given in column 2, and denoted as $SIS\_1.2$. The area(#LUTs/#CLBs), depth(#level) and computational time(sec) are used as the criteria for the evaluation.

As shown in table 1, *with_pliable* and *without_pliable* can produce 26% and 21% fewer CLBs, and 28% and 25% fewer LUTs respectively, than that in SIS-1.2 program. That is due to our approach focuses on finding a set of PDFs which can be maximally merged into multiple-output CLBs or an LUT. Table 1 also shows that the results from *with_pliable* is better than that from *without_pliable*, that means that using pliable encoding strategy, we can get the optimum decomposition(generally, an NDD) which cannot be reached by the classical rigid encoding. However, the search for an effective PDD is expensive, even very difficult as the number of feasible PDFs are large(≤ 5000); so our approach need much computational time. Pliable encoding strategy may find application to performance-oriented synthesis by introducing SVFs on the critical path during decomposition.

Table 1. *Experimental Results*

Benchmarks	SIS-1.2 #LUT/#level/sec//#CLB	without_pliable #LUT/#level/sec//#CLB	with_pliable #LUT/#level/sec//#CLB	#PI/#PO
9symml	7/3/0.4//7	6/3/18.7//6	8/3/662.2//5	9/1
alu2	91/21/28.9//76	89/30/26.2//75	89/30/97.6//75	10/6
alu4	296/39/198.4//243	237/25/690.4//216	226/22/1628.6//206	14/8
apex2	198/16/301.3//168	109/13/768.0//98	99/11/1698.2//88	39/3
apex6	232/20/10.5//189	172/7/281.2//144	171/7/628.6//143	135/99
apex7	59/7/3.3//47	57/7/2.9//44	57/7/3.0//44	49/37
b9	52/5/2.8//42	39/5/39.8//34	38/3/525.6//32	41/21
clip	36/5/2.6//29	22/3/40.5//21	20/3/144.//19	9/5
duke2	149/8/6.3//137	133/8/780.5//125	129/7/1838.6//121	22/29
example2	129/7/13.6//106	107/5/10.4//84	102/6/296.8//68	85/66
frg1	39/14/10.4//38	32/7/29.6//31	30/8/169.6//29	28/3
i7	103/2/6.4//102	103/2/13.2//102	103/2/14.8//102	199/67
misex2	49/3/1.4//41	34/4/68.8//30	32/5/1268.6//26	25/18
misex3c	260/11/18.3//216	143/9/126.0//134	135/10/1628.0//110	14/14
rd84	13/3/1.2//13	12/3/16.6//11	12/3/466.8//10	8/4
sao2	52/5/2.0//51	23/5/56.8//22	22/3/201.8//21	10/4
too_large	184/31/568.9//166	138/11/305.5//114	133/11/1265.6//108	38/3
vda	260/11/18.9//156	206/10/286.6//156	197/9/510.8//147	17/39
vg2	27/6/1.8//25	21/6/6.2//19	20/6/46.2//17	25/8
t481	14/4/8.5//13	5/3/26.8//5	5/3/26.9//5	16/1
Total(LUT/CLB)	2250/1865	1688/1471	1525/1376	793/436

6 Conclusions

In this paper, we addressed the classical functional decomposition, and proposed a novel approach for finding an optimum solution. Targeting LUT-based FPGAs with a multiple-output CLB architecture, we focus on finding a set of PDFs which can be maximally merged into the multiple-output CLBs and/or an LUT. To exploit all encoding space, pliable encoding strategy is adopted to take over the encoding process as it failed to get a good solution by the classical rigid encoding strategy. Experimental results show that our approach can find more NDDs or PDDs which cannot be found by the traditional rigid encoding strategy. Our algorithm may find application to a performance-oriented decomposition with slight modifications. We will employ our method in a multiple-output decomposition as our future work.

Acknowledgements

We thank Dr. Murgai for providing us with SIS-1.2 program, and for his many helpful discussions.

References

1. R. L. Ashenhurst, "The Decomposition of Switching Functions," Proc. Int'l Symp. on Theory of Switching Functions, 1959.
2. J. P. Roth, and R. M. Karp, "Minimization Over Boolean Graphs," IBM Journal of Research and Development, pp.227-238, April 1962.
3. H. A. Curtis, "A Generalized Tree Circuit," Journal of the ACM, Vol.8(4), pp.484-496, 1961.
4. W. Z. Shen, J. D. Huang, and S. M. Chao, "Lambda Set Selection in Roth-Karp Decomposition for LUT-Based FPGA Technology Mapping," in 32nd ACM/IEEE Design Automation Conference, pp.65-69, June 1995.
5. Jie-Hong Jiang, Jing-Yang Jou, Juinn-Dar Huang, and Jung-Shian Wei, "A Variable Partitioning Algorithm of BDD for FPGA Technology Mapping," IEICE Trans. Fundamentals, Vol.E80-a, No.10,pp.1813-1819, 1997.
6. Rajeev Murgai, Robert K. Brayton, and Alberto Sangiovanni-Vincentelli, "Optimum Functional Decomposition Using Encoding," in Proc. 31th ACM/IEEE Design Automation Conference, pp.408-414, June 1994.
7. Jie-Hong R. Jiang, Jing-Yang Jou, and Juinn-Dar Huang, "Compatible Class Encoding in Hyper-Function Decomposition for FPGA Synthesis," in 35th ACM/IEEE Design Automation Conference, pp.712-717, June 1998.
8. Juinn-Dar Huang, Jing-Yang Jou, and Wen-Zen shen, "Compatible Class Encoding in Roth-Karp Decomposition for Two-Output LUT Architecture," in Proc. ICCAD, pp.359-363, Nov. 1995.
9. Hiroshi Sawada, Takayuki Suyama, and Akira Nagoya, "Logic Synthesis for Look-Up Table based FPGAs using Functional Decomposition and Support Minimization," in Proc. ICCAD, pp.353-358, Nov. 1995.
10. Jason Cong, and Yean-Yow Hwang, "Partially Dependent Functional Decomposition with Applications in FPGA Synthesis and Mapping," in Proc. ACM/SIGDA Int'l Symp. on FPGAs, pp.35-42, Feb. 1997.
11. Christian Legl, Bernd Wurth, and Klaus Eckl, "Computing Support-Minimal Subfunctions During Functional Decomposition," in IEEE Trans. on VLSI, Vol.6, No.3, pp.354-363, Sep. 1998.
12. Jian Qiao, Makoto Ikeda, and Kunihiro Asada, "Functional Decomposition for LUT-based FPGA synthesis," Proc. of 13th IEICE Circuits and Systems Workshop, pp.119-124, April 2000.
13. Xilinx Inc., 2069, Hamilton Ave. San Jose, CA-95125, The Programmable Gate Array Data Book.
14. Edward M. Reingold, Jurg Nievergelt, and Narisingh Deo, Combinatorial Algorithms, pp.107-130, 1977.
15. E. Sentovich, K. Singh, L. Lavagno, C. Moon, R. Murgai, A. Saldanha, H. Savoj, P. Stephen, R. Brayton, and A. Sangiovanni-Vincentelli, "SIS: A System for Sequential Circuit Synthesis," U. C. Berkeley Technical Report UCB/ERL M92/41, May 1992.

Optimization of Run-Time Reconfigurable Embedded Systems

Michael Eisenring and Marco Platzner

Swiss Federal Institute of Technology (ETH) Zurich, Switzerland
{eisenring|platzner}@tik.ee.ethz.ch

Abstract. Run-time reconfigurable approaches for FPGAs are gaining interest as they enlarge the design space for system implementation by sequential execution of temporally exclusive system parts on one or several FPGA resources. In [7], we introduced a novel methodology and a design tool for communication synthesis in reconfigurable embedded systems. In [5], this work was extended by a hierarchical reconfiguration structure that implements reconfiguration control. In this paper, we describe techniques that are employed to optimize the reconfiguration structure and its communication requirements. The optimizations reduce the required FPGA area and I/O pins.

1 Introduction

Embedded systems are the backbone for a wide range of application domains: simple home appliances, PDAs (personal digital assistants), portable phones, and complex autopilots in airplanes. The rising design complexity of such systems is tackled by sophisticated computer-aided design (CAD) tools [8, 10, 12] that guide the designer from system specification to implementation. Examples for decisions to be taken during design are component selection, i.e., selecting computing resources among different types of processors and programmable hardware devices, and communication type selection, e.g., using standard protocols such as the CAN bus or dedicated links based on built-in facilities such as DMA channels.

Run-time reconfiguration (RTR) of FPGAs is gaining interest for embedded system design as it enlarges the design space by allowing to execute time-exclusive system parts sequentially [9, 14] on a moderately sized FPGA device. The challenge is to design efficient RTR systems in terms of reconfiguration time (system performance) and area overhead (implementation cost). A further important issue is the synthesis of communication channels between heterogeneous components [11, 12] on one hand and between time-exclusive system parts on the other hand (interconfiguration communication [9, 7, 6]).

Most current approaches for reconfigurable system design focus on aspects such as optimal partitioning [3], scheduling [4, 13], or communication synthesis [12]. We learned through our previous work [7] that dynamic reconfiguration of FPGAs sometimes leads to remarkable overheads in terms of FPGA area and memory. Consequently, we now consider communication and reconfiguration issues at the same time to reflect their strong interdependence.

In this paper, we propose two optimization techniques that are employed to minimize the overhead added by the reconfiguration structure and its communication requirements.

2 Hierarchical Reconfiguration

In our framework [5], an application is captured by a problem specification consisting of (i) a problem graph PG, (ii) an architecture graph AG, and (iii) a mapping M. The problem graph PG represents the application's behavior in form of communicating tasks and buffers. Each problem graph node has an associated control port for receiving control commands (e.g., *start*) and replying status messages (e.g., *done*). The architecture graph AG describes the target that may consist of connected computing resources (general- and special-purpose processors, ASICs, FPGAs), and memories. The mapping M determines the implementation of the problem graph on the target architecture. A mapping includes spatial partitioning (assignment of tasks and buffers to computing resources and memories), temporal partitioning (assignment of tasks and buffers to FPGA configurations), scheduling of tasks and buffers inside configurations, and the scheduling of complete configurations.

In our work, we assume that a mapping has been derived by a set of front-end tools specific to the used specification model (task graphs, SDF graphs, etc.) or by user intervention. We focus on the back-end which is formed by the subsequent steps of generating an appropriate reconfiguration structure and communication channels. In [7], we presented the CORES/HASIS tool set providing communication synthesis for reconfigurable embedded systems. These tools establish the required communication infrastructure and automatically generate device drivers and interface circuitry for each FPGA configuration and the host. In [5], we extended CORES/HASIS by a hierarchical reconfiguration structure.

In this paper, we discuss optimizations that can be applied to save FPGA area and I/O pins. These optimizations are based on the sharing of objects and reduce the overhead caused by the automatic generation of reconfiguration control. The added reconfiguration structure is hierarchical and consists of two layers:

1. a top layer, where one or several *configurator* tasks cfg supervise a set of dynamically reconfigured FPGAs by downloading and starting complete configurations, and

2. a bottom layer, where each configuration c_{ij} for each FPGA F_i includes a *dispatcher* task d_{ij} that starts and stops the nodes of the configuration using their control ports.

Example 1 (Hierarchical reconfiguration structure). Figure 1a) shows the hierarchical reconfiguration structure for an FPGA F_1 with two configurations c_{11}

and c_{12}. The top layer consists of the configurator task cfg running on the host that supervises the two FPGA configurations by controlling the corresponding dispatcher tasks d_{11} and d_{12}. The bottom layer for configuration c_{11} is shown in Figure 1b) where the dispatcher task d_{11} supervises the local nodes b, q_3, c, and d using their control ports. Figure 1c) outlines a possible dispatcher function that implements a local schedule.

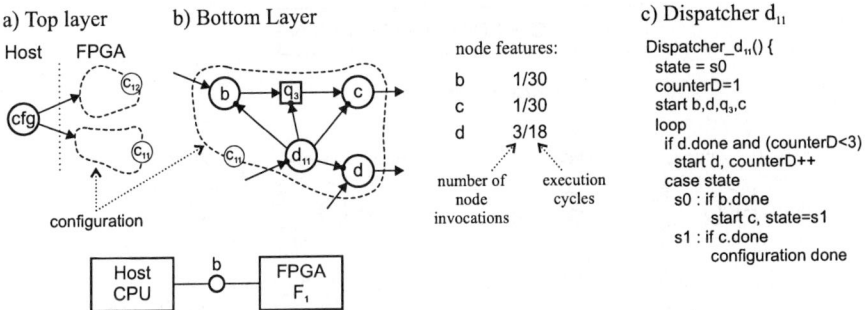

Fig. 1. Hierarchical reconfiguration structure.

Our tool inserts edges (communication channels) $cfg - d_{ij}$ to connect all dispatcher tasks to the configurator on the host. For FPGAs not directly connected to the host, routing nodes have to be inserted on intermediate FPGAs: $cfg - r_{klm} - d_{ij}$. Our framework supports both off-line and on-line scheduling techniques. The actual schedule is implemented in a distributed manner by the configurator and all the dispatcher tasks. Each FPGA executes only one of its configurations at any given time. However, the configuration schedule, i.e., the total order of all the configurations, may not be known at compile time. In this case, we have to add a routing node r_{klm} for each communication channel m into each configuration c_l on each intermediate FPGA F_k. This process is called *routing node distribution* and inserts $n \cdot c$ routing nodes for an intermediate FPGA in the problem graph [7], where n is the number of communication channels that must be routed and c the overall number of configurations for the FPGA. If the configuration schedule is known, the number of inserted routing nodes can be reduced.

Example 2 (Routing node distribution). Figure 2a) shows an architecture graph with a host and two FPGAs. Two different configuration schedules that lead to different routing node distributions are shown in Figure 2b) and Figure 2c), respectively. In both mappings, FPGA F_1 has two configurations c_{11} and c_{12}, and FPGA F_2 implements three configurations c_{21}, c_{22}, and c_{23}. The configuration schedule in Figure 2b2) gives the order of configurations for each FPGA. As there is no information about the relative timing of configurations on F_1 and F_2, 6 routing nodes are inserted on FPGA F_1. These 6 routing nodes require

12 I/O ports on FPGA F_1 and 6 I/O ports on FPGA F_2. Figure 2c2) shows a configuration schedule with an additional dependency. Configuration c_{12} will only be executed when configurations c_{11} and c_{22} have completed. Consequently, the configurations on FPGA F_1 do not have to implement all communication channels. Only 3 routing nodes are required, leading to 6 and 3 I/O ports for FPGAs F_1 and F_2, respectively.

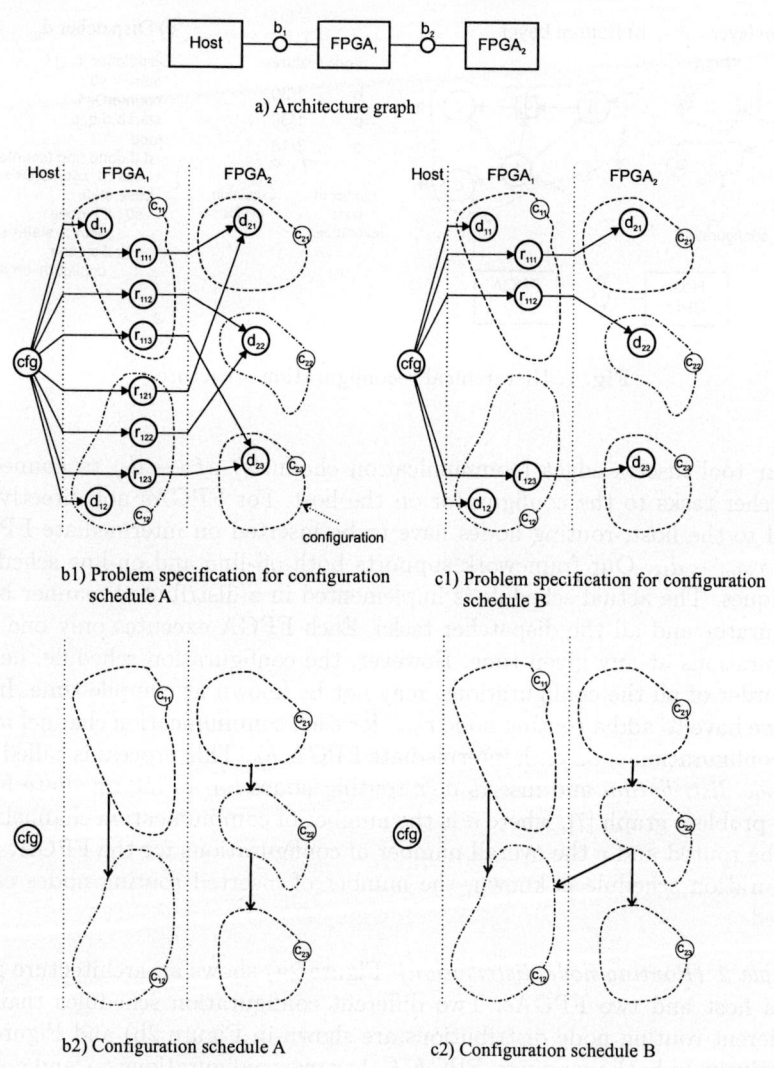

Fig. 2. Routing node distribution.

Our back-end tools analyze the configuration schedule and try to insert routing nodes into configurations only if necessary to reduce the required FPGA area and I/O pins. For the remaining routing nodes and I/O ports, optimization strategies are applied to reduce the number of routing nodes and required I/O ports even further.

3 Optimization by Object Sharing

Objects that can be shared comprise problem graph nodes and I/O ports. Although we consider here only routing nodes that have been added by our back-end tools, object sharing could be applied to the original nodes of the problem graph as well. Nodes can be divided into three groups that demand for different interface circuitry (see Figure 3). Nodes of type a are connected only to nodes in the same configuration and are thus not amenable to the proposed optimizations. Nodes of type b are connected to nodes in the same configuration as well as to nodes on other computing resources. Nodes of type c have only connections to nodes bound to other computing resources. Node types b and c require I/O ports and are the main targets of object sharing. The routing nodes, which are of type c, benefit most from object sharing optimizations. The optimizations are split into two groups:

1. *Port sharing:* Several communication channels are routed over the same FPGA I/O pins in order to save pins.

2. *Node sharing:* The implementation of a routing node is shared between several communication channels in one configuration. This reduces the required FPGA area and routing resources.

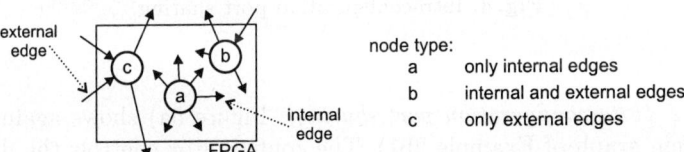

Fig. 3. Node types.

3.1 Port Sharing

A port is a set of I/O pins that enable data communication between two connected computing resources. Sharing ports among several channels defuses the problem of limited I/O pin resources. Port sharing applies to external edges of the node types b and c and has been extensively used in the Virtual Wire project [2, 1]. We extend port sharing to time-exclusive configurations of run-time reconfigurable systems. Therefore, we differentiate between two types of port sharing:

- *Intraconfiguration* port sharing allows communication channels in the same configuration to share I/O ports by adding multiplexing and demultiplexing interface circuitry [1]. This technique can be applied to both CTR and RTR systems.

- *Interconfiguration* port sharing allows communication channels in different configurations of one FPGA to share I/O ports. These channels would otherwise be mapped to different ports as configurations of other FPGAs could require that both channels exist at the same time. Interconfiguration port sharing applies only to RTR systems.

Example 3 (Intraconfiguration port sharing). Figure 4a) shows part of the problem graph of Example 2b1). Applying intraconfiguration port sharing to edges $cfg - r_{111}, cfg - r_{112}$, and $cfg - r113$ implies the multiplexing/demultiplexing interface circuits i_3 and i_4 (see Figure 4b).

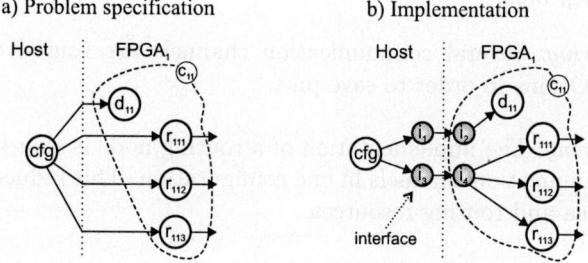

Fig. 4. Intraconfiguration port sharing.

Example 4 (Interconfiguration port sharing). Figure 5a) shows again a part of the problem graph of Example 2b1). The configurator controls the dispatchers via the edges $cfg - d_{11}$ and $cfg - d_{12}$. As the dispatchers reside in time-exclusive configurations, the corresponding ports can be shared. In Figure 5b) this is implemented by the interface circuits i_1 and i_2.

3.2 Node Sharing

Node sharing is a technique where several identical problem graph nodes assigned to the same configuration share a single physical implementation on the target architecture. Generally, node sharing can be applied to all three node types a, b, and c. Node sharing to original problem graph nodes allows to trade-off between required FPGA area and execution time and could require additional buffers.

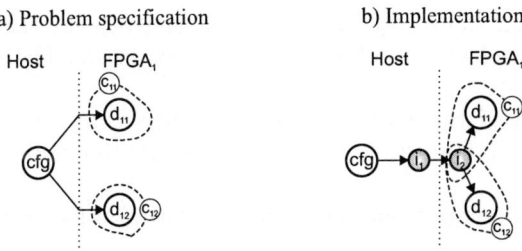

Fig. 5. Interconfiguration port sharing.

Node sharing for original problem graph nodes actually means to modify the mapping determined by front-end tools. Hence, we consider node sharing only for routing nodes (nodes of type c), which is extremely valuable if combined with port sharing.

Example 5 (Node and port sharing for routing nodes). Figure 6a) shows a problem specification including FPGA F_1 with one configuration and FPGA F_2 with three configurations. The communication channels $cfg - r_{111} - d_{21}, cfg - r_{112} - d_{22}$, and $cfg - r_{113} - d_{23}$ are routed over FPGA F_1. The three routing nodes can share one physical implementation as the three configurations of FPGA F_2 never exist at the same time. This sharing of nodes can be combined with intraconfiguration port sharing of the three channels between the host and FPGA F_1 and interconfiguration port sharing between FPGA F_1 and FPGA F_2 (see Figure 6b).

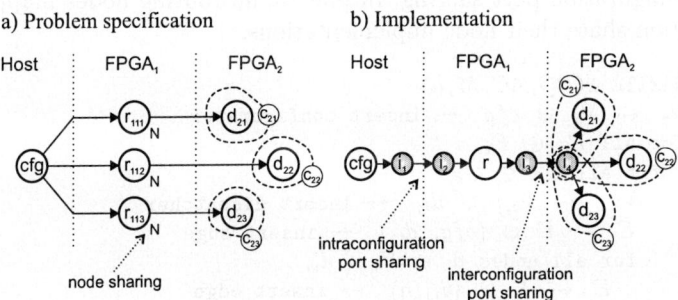

Fig. 6. Node and port sharing.

4 DYNAMITE Algorithm

The proposed optimization techniques have been implemented in our synthesis tool CORES/HASIS [6]. The corresponding algorithm *DYNAMITE* (**DYNAMIc sysTem implEmentation**) consists of two parts:

- DYNAMITE_1 is executed for each host and extends the original problem graph with the hierarchical reconfiguration structure. The procedure has two main steps:
  (i) extension of the problem graph by introducing configurator and dispatcher tasks and inserting routing tasks by routing node distribution (lines 1 ... 10) and
  (ii) application of port and node sharing optimizations (lines 11 ... 17).

- DYNAMITE_2 performs the actual communication synthesis, i.e., introduces interface circuits, by executing the HASIS tool set for each configuration (lines 18 ... 21).

The pseudo-code shown below outlines the basic steps of the DYNAMITE algorithm and is based on following assumptions: A host h supervises a set of FPGAs F_h. Single FPGAs are denoted by F_i. The problem graph PG consists of nodes and edges. The nodes are further split into subsets, depending on where they are mapped to. For example, V_h denotes the problem graph nodes mapped to the host, $V_{c_{ij}}$ denotes nodes mapped to configuration c_{ij}. C_{f_i} is the set of configurations of FPGA F_i. All edges between the dispatchers of an FPGA and the configurator on the host are routed over the same set of FPGAs.

Lines 2-8 insert and connect the configurator and dispatcher nodes. In lines 9-10, routing node distribution is performed for FPGAs that are not directly connected to the host. This step inserts routing nodes into several configurations, depending on information that is extracted from the configuration schedule. Lines 11-17 perform port and node sharing optimizations. In line 12, all edges connecting to dispatcher nodes share their ports. This includes intra- as well as interconfiguration port sharing. In line 15, all routing nodes mapped to one configuration share their node implementations.

```
1.  DYNAMITE_1(PG, AG, M, h)
2.    V_h ← V_h ∪ cfg            -- insert configurator
3.    for all F_i ∈ F_h
4.      for all c_ij ∈ C_{F_i}
5.        V_{c_ij} ← V_{c_ij} ∪ d_ij   -- insert dispatcher
6.        E ← E ∪ (cfg, d_ij)        -- insert edge
7.        for all nodes n ∈ V_{c_ij} \ d_ij
8.          E ← E ∪ (d_ij, n)         -- insert edge
9.      if non_adjacent(F_i, h)
10.       routing_node_distribution(PG,AG,M,F_i,h)
11.     E_temp ← {(x, d_ij) | j = 1 ... |C_{F_i}|}
12.     share_ports(E_temp)
13.     while (((x,y) ∈ E_temp), x ≠ cfg)
14.       V_routing ← {v| source(e), e ∈ E_temp}
15.       share_nodes(V_routing)
16.       E_temp ← {(x,y)|y ∈ V_routing}
17.       share_ports(E_temp)
```

```
18. DYNAMITE_2(PG, AG, M)
19.    for all F_i ∈ F_h
20.        for all c_ij ∈ C_{f_i}
21.            HASIS.start(V_{c_ij}, AG, M)
```

Figure 7 shows the optimized implementation for Figure 2b1) after DYNA-MITE has been applied. The hierarchical reconfiguration structure consists of a configurator node on the host, one dispatcher node per FPGA configuration, and two routing nodes on FPGA F_1. Overall, three I/O ports are required on FPGA F_1 and one I/O port on FPGA F_2 to implement the reconfiguration structure.

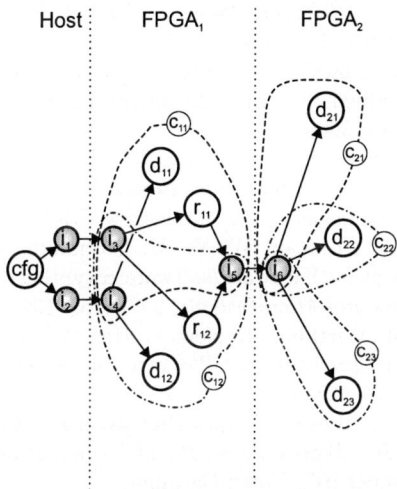

Fig. 7. Object sharing optimizations.

5 Conclusions

The paper discussed optimization strategies for the hierarchical reconfiguration structure introduced in [5]. The optimizations are based on object sharing and include port sharing and node sharing. Port sharing saves I/O pins by multiplexing several communication channels over one physical channel. Node sharing saves FPGA area by reusing one physical node implementation for several routing nodes.

References

1. J. Babb, R. Tessier, and A. Agarwal. Virtual Wires: Overcoming Pin Limitations in FPGA-based Logic Emulators. In *IEEE Workshop on FPGA-based Custom Computing Machines*, pages 142–151, Napa, CA, April 1993.

2. J. Babb, R. Tessier, M. Dahl, S. Hanono, D. Hoki, and A. Agarwal. Logic emulation with virtual wires. *IEEE Transactions on Computer-Aided Design of Integrated Circuit and Systems*, 16(6):609–626, June 1997.
3. K. Chatha and R. Vemuri. Hardware-Software Codesign for Dynamically Reconfigurable Architectures. In *9th International Workshop on Field-Programmable Logic and Applications, FPL'99, Lecture Notes in Computer Science, 1673*, pages 175–184, Glasgow, UK, August/September 1999.
4. R. Dick and N. Jha. CORDS: Hardware-Software Co-Synthesis of Reconfigurable Real-Time Distributed Embedded Systems. In *IEEE/ACM International Conference on Computer-Aided Design*, pages 62–68, 8-12 November 1998.
5. M. Eisenring and M. Platzner. An Implementation Framework for Run-time Reconfigurable Systems. In *The Second International Workshop on Engineering of Reconfigurable Hardware/Software Objects, ENREGLE 2000*, Monte Carlo Resort, Las Vegas, Nevada, USA, June 26-29 2000.
6. M. Eisenring and M. Platzner. Synthesis of Interfaces and Communication in Reconfigurable Embedded Systems. *To appear in IEE Proceedings - Computers and Digital Techniques*, 2000.
7. M. Eisenring, M. Platzner, and L. Thiele. Communication Synthesis for Reconfigurable Embedded Systems. In *9th International Workshop on Field-Programmable Logic and Applications*, pages 205–214, Glasgow, UK, August/September 1999.
8. R. Ernst, J. Henkel, T. Benner, W. Ye, U. Holtmann, and D. Herrmann. The COSYMA environment for hardware/software cosynthesis of small embedded systems. *Microprocessors and Microsystems*, 20(3):159–166, May 1996.
9. B. Hutchings and M. Wirthlin. Implementation Approaches for Reconfigurable Logic Applications. In *International Workshop on Field-Programmable Logic and Applications*, pages 419–428, 1995.
10. A. Kirschbaum and M. Glesner. Rapid Prototyping of Communication Architectures. In *8th IEEE Int. Workshop on Rapid System Prototyping*, pages 136–141, June 24-26 1997, Chapel Hill, North Carolina.
11. M. O'Nils and A. Jantsch. Communication in Hardware/Software Embedded Systems - A Taxonomy and Problem Formulation. In *15th NORCHIP Seminar, Copenhagen, Denmark*, pages 67–74, November 1997.
12. R. Ortega and G. Borriello. Communication Synthesis for Distributed Embedded Systems. In *IEEE/ACM Int'l Conf. on Computer-Aided Design*, pages 437–444, San Jose, CA, November 1998.
13. K. Purna and D. Bhatia. Temporal Partitioning and Scheduling Data Flow Graphs for Reconfigurable Computers. *IEEE Transactions on Computers*, 48(6):556–564, June 1999.
14. E. Sanchez, M. Sipper, J. Haenni, J. Beuchat, A. Stauffer, and A. Perez-Uribe. Static and Dynamic Configurable Systems. *IEEE Transactions on Computers*, 48(6):556–564, June 1999.

It's FPL, Jim - But Not as We Know It!
Opportunities for the New Commercial Architectures

Tom Kean

Algotronix Consulting, PO Box 23116, Edinburgh EH8 8YB, United Kingdom
tom@algotronix.com

Abstract. Following the simple Programmable Logic Device (SPLD) and Field Programmable Gate Array (FPGA) generations a third generation of programmable logic technologies is now reaching the marketplace. These new architectures are driven by the move to system level integration and fast expanding markets such as networking and wireless communications which are not addressed adequately by mainstream FPGA's. This paper considers the technologies, business models and chances of success of the third generation companies using the Triscend CSoC and Systolix Pulse DSP architectures as examples.

1 Introduction

The 25 year history of commercial programmable logic shows two important technical generations: simple PLD (SPLD) sum-of-products (PAL) technology and Field Programmable Gate Array (FPGA) technology. Today, we are seeing the beginning of a third-wave of programmable architectures with distinctive features focussed on the challenges of high volume embedded applications (figure 1).

Although PAL technology was introduced more than 20 years ago and there have been few significant architectural improvements in the last ten years it is still an important niche component in the marketplace. No single player managed to dominate the simple PLD (SPLD) market and SPLD's quickly became a commodity component until improvements in process technology made them irrelevant.

Today, FPGA technology is, after 16 years of development, also reaching maturity. Product generations now serve to tune the architecture for improvements in process technology rather than to introduce fundamentally new structures. The last significant improvement in mainstream FPGA architecture was, arguably, the introduction of block RAM by Altera in 1995 which allowed FPGA's to address applications which required medium sized memories. In contrast to SPLD's, the FPGA business has come to be dominated by two strong players Xilinx and Altera and has remained highly profitable.

Given this background of incremental development of a highly profitable but apparently mature technology it is, perhaps, not surprising that a wave of radical new architectures have emerged from start-up companies. These companies are vying to define a third-generation of programmable logic. This surge of architectural development is pulled by demand from emerging markets which the established second generation companies have chosen not to address and fuelled by the recent flood of venture capital into technology companies.

An important technical theme underlying the new FPL architectures is the merging of FPGA technology with ideas from computer architecture - including DSP processors, parallel computers and VLIW machines. Since many of the new architectures are directed at computational applications it is not surprising to see direct support in the silicon for arithmetic operations and multi-bit words.

Influences from the academic FPL community and research funded by DARPA are clear (notably the context switching proposals of Andre de Hon [1], the processor like operators of the Kress Array [2] and the combination of FPL with microprocessor in OneChip [3] and Napa [4]) as are influences from research on non-mainstream FPGA architectures by the second generation companies [5][6].

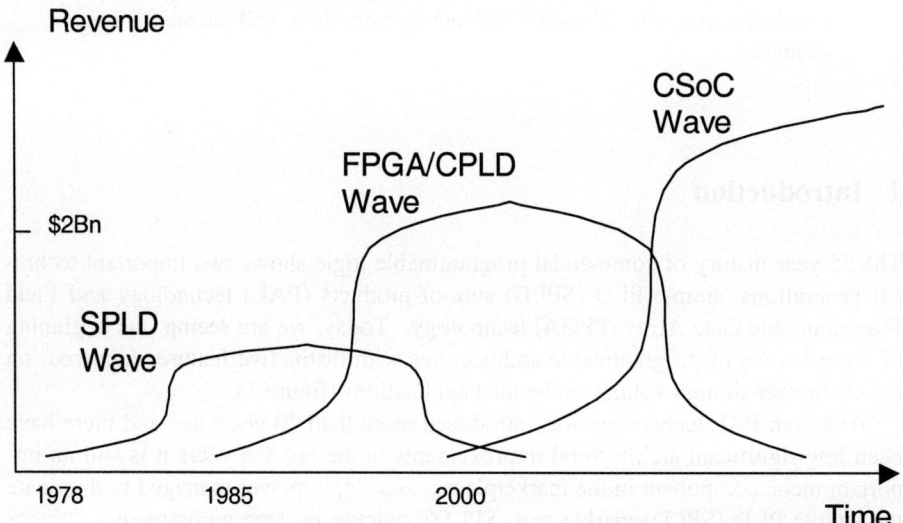

Fig. 1. The history of programmable logic can be viewed as a sequence of waves of development driven by major changes in architectural style

2 Market Drivers

While academic research has largely concerned itself with applying FPL to general purpose computing the explosive growth in the networking, mobile communications and multimedia markets is driving the commercial architectures. These embedded applications demand raw computational performance without sacrificing flexibility, power consumption or time to market. Dataquest estimated the market for function specific signal processing as $6.3 billion in 1999. Table 1 shows some of the third generation FPL companies and their target markets.

Table 1. The new FPL companies

Company	Architecture	Business Model	Markets
Adaptive Silicon	Not disclosed	Sell Cores	Embedded DSP
Chameleon Systems	Array of 32 bit processors	Sell Chips	Voice over IP, Software Radio, networking
Malleable	Not disclosed	Sell Chips	Voice over IP
Morphics	Not disclosed	Sell Solutions (chips and software)	Cellular Communications / Software Radio
Systolix	Systolic Array	Sell Cores	Signal Conditioning, Embedded DSP
Triscend	System on Chip	Sell Chips	Communications, Embedded Systems

2.1 Software Download

A key driver for third generation architectures is the move away from programming the PLD once, during manufacture to downloading improved designs in the field. This ability to upgrade product features after the initial sale is a fundamental benefit of reconfigurable technologies over ASIC's and changes the economics of embedded equipment - moving it to a model more like the computer industry. The majority of software currently running on personal computers was not available on the day they were purchased.

Smith [7] illustrates the economic impact of time to market in ASIC design by showing how a 1 month lead in time to market can result in a 70% difference in product lifetime revenue. Figure 2 updates this analysis to show the effect of software download. Firstly, if a manufacturer has an option to download software in the field he can ship a product at an earlier stage of development. Thus, the product with software download reaches market first (illustrated by the upper curve). Some time later, the competing product reaches market (the lower curve). By this time the first product has established itself and the competing product never gains the same market acceptance. So far this mirrors Smith's analysis of time to market benefits: however, the important difference is that using software download the manufacturer of the first product can extend the functionality of the product and thus its life span in the marketplace. These updates are a further source of revenue from existing customers. Thus, the revenue curve in the case of software download can have multiple peaks.

Today, software download is a compelling technology for embedded products with a communications capability. The largest scale deployment of software download to date was in the 56K bit modem market where two groups of competing companies shipped large numbers of modems before the V90 international standard was approved. Both groups knew that their modem's would eventually have to be standard compliant but neither could afford the time-to-market disadvantage of waiting until the standard was finalized. When the standard appeared both groups supplied downloadable patches via their web sites that upgraded their modems to be standard compliant.

Although time to market and upgrade revenues are more than sufficient reason in themselves to use software download there are three other important applications:

1. Bug fixes. Software download allows serious problems to be fixed in the field without an expensive product recall. This substantially reduces the risk of market introduction and may allow a less expensive and time consuming beta-test program.

2. Customization. Download of small amounts of data can be used to enable product features or securely install customer specific information. When the equipment has a limited user interface it may be convenient for customers to deal with a call center or website which then downloads personal or configuration information rather than input it directly.

3. Remote diagnostics and monitoring. A special version of the FPL configuration which stresses the system and checks for common symptoms can be downloaded allowing more effective product support.

3 Business Models

The second generation FPL companies distinguished themselves over first generation companies not only through new architectures but also by a new business model: the fabless semiconductor company. It is interesting to speculate whether these FPGA companies could have built sustainable businesses based only on the architectural breakthrough or whether their commercial success was determined as much by the new business model which allowed easier access to the marketplace.

Third generation FPL companies are entering the market with innovative architectures which combine aspects of DSP and VLIW processors with FPL technology. These architectures seem 'prima-facie' better suited to the DSP challenges of the target markets than 'conventional' programmable logic. However, there is also a step change in business model as we enter the era of system-on-chip. System on chip represents an opportunity for the new companies and a challenge to the business practices of their competitors.

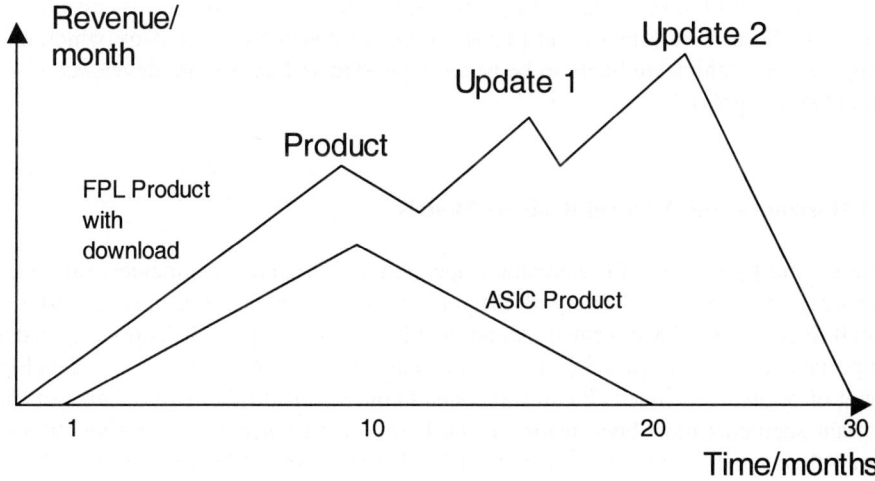

Fig. 2. Economic benefit of software download.

Some of the new companies are reacting to System on Chip by becoming chip-less as well as fabless: that is they offer Intellectual Property (IP) cores to be integrated onto their customers System on Chip designs rather than physical components. The move to IP cores dramatically lowers the barriers to entry into the marketplace: a typical IP vendor may require only a few tens of employees, where a fabless vendor may require a few hundred and a vendor with its own manufacturing facility more than a thousand. Thus, using this model a venture funded startup company can compete and win sales from a billion dollar a year established company. What is less clear is whether this model will eventually result in a small number of high profit companies as did the fabless-model or whether the low barriers to entry will create a cluttered playing field of small companies in cut-throat competition with each other. The second outcome might benefit the large systems companies who will create the System on Chip IC's at the expense of the FPL companies.

A second group of companies are keeping the model of selling chips rather than IP but are producing Configurable System on Chip (CSoC) IC's as standard products. These devices contain micro-controllers, memory and configurable logic so they can efficiently implement all aspects of a customer design. Thus, these companies are bringing the benefits of deep sub-micron SoC technology to companies and projects which could otherwise not justify it financially. This is closely analogous to the way the FPGA companies brought the benefits of ASIC gate array technology to companies which could not justify the associated tooling charges and design risk. Historically, this has been a very successful business model. Clearly, this model requires more investment than the IP cores model and it is possibly more vulnerable to competition from established second generation companies.

Of course, there is no reason why a company should not adopt both business models: selling CSoC chips and IP cores. In fact, the technology developed for the CSoC marketplace is directly applicable to the IP cores business. Selling IP cores can be seen as a way of leveraging extra profit from technology whose costs are already covered. From a customer point of view cores provided by a company which also supplies CSoC chips are likely to be better supported and have more developed CAD and library support.

3.1 Horizontal and Vertical Business Models

The second generation FPL companies operated as 'horizontal' companies, supplying the same component to a variety of different industry segments. Recently, a cluster of small IP companies have formed around the FPL vendors to provide 'cores' targeted at important segments (figure 3 (a)). Vendors have also begun some in-house development of segment focussed IP cores and small concessions to the requirements of important segments have been made on the base silicon (such as the introduction of carry-chains and shift register mode for LUT RAM to help DSP applications). However, the second generation companies are not producing distinct product families for industry segments. Instead there are generic 'high performance' and 'low cost' product ranges which are roughly synonymous with 'this years' and 'last years' architectures.

New entrants to the market must show significantly improved price/performance over the mainstream architectures and may have difficulty persuading customers to invest engineering time in creating complex designs for untried architectures. They do not yet have the sales to foster an infrastructure of third party IP companies in the same way as the second generation vendors. One approach to address these competitive difficulties is to focus the architecture on a particular industry segment (figure 3(b)). This allows tailoring of the architecture more closely to that segments requirements - possibly improving price/performance. More importantly, segment focus allows the product vendor to develop a comprehensive supporting range of IP for the programmable architecture. Thus customers can be presented with packaged solutions for their applications which can be compared directly on price and performance with existing solutions: customers are not forced to 'buy-in' to the underlying architecture or to commit engineering resource to designing for it.

4 Systolix Pulse-DSP

The Systolix Pulse DSP is a third generation FPL architecture aimed at digital filtering and signal conditioning. The architecture is described in [8] and consists of an array of bit-serial arithmetic processors coupled by a special interconnect framework which transfers multi-bit wide words and error correction information (figure 4). Targeting the architecture at a narrow - but very important - class of signal processing algorithms has allowed the high level textual Pulse Programming Language and the graphical Filter Express design tools to be developed. These allow the customer to capture their design in terms of DSP algorithm parameters without compromising implementation efficiency.

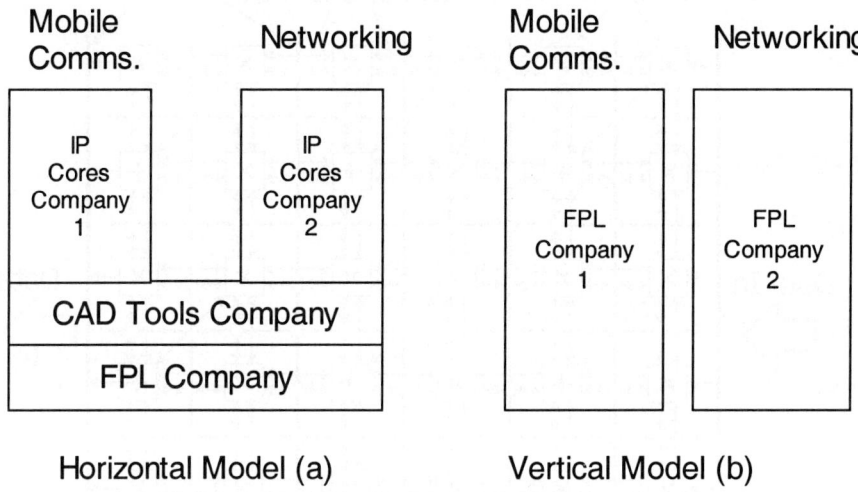

Fig. 3. Horizontal (a) and Vertical (b) Business Models

The first product to use the Systolix Pulse-DSP technology is the AD7725 sigma-delta A/D converter from Analog Devices [9]. The Systolix array provides flexible user specified signal conditioning of the converted data. Systolix offers cores of various sizes and performance ratings for integration into third party System on Chip ASIC's. Thus in our categorization Systolix is an example of a fabless, chipless and vertically targeted FPL vendor.

5 Triscend E5-Configurable System on Chip

Unlike Systolix, Triscend sells chips directly to end-users. Triscend's focus is to bring the benefits of system on chip technology to companies or projects for which an ASIC based SoC is not viable - for example, because of low volume requirements. The FPL component of Triscend's System on Chip technology - termed Configurable System Logic (CSL) is itself a parameterisable FPL-core.

Triscend's CSL technology [10] is more general purpose than many third generation FPL architectures. For example, in figure 4, the Triscend chip is shown in a wireless communications application [11] implementing 'glue logic' functions such as display interfaces as well as computational functions like channel filtering and Viterbi.

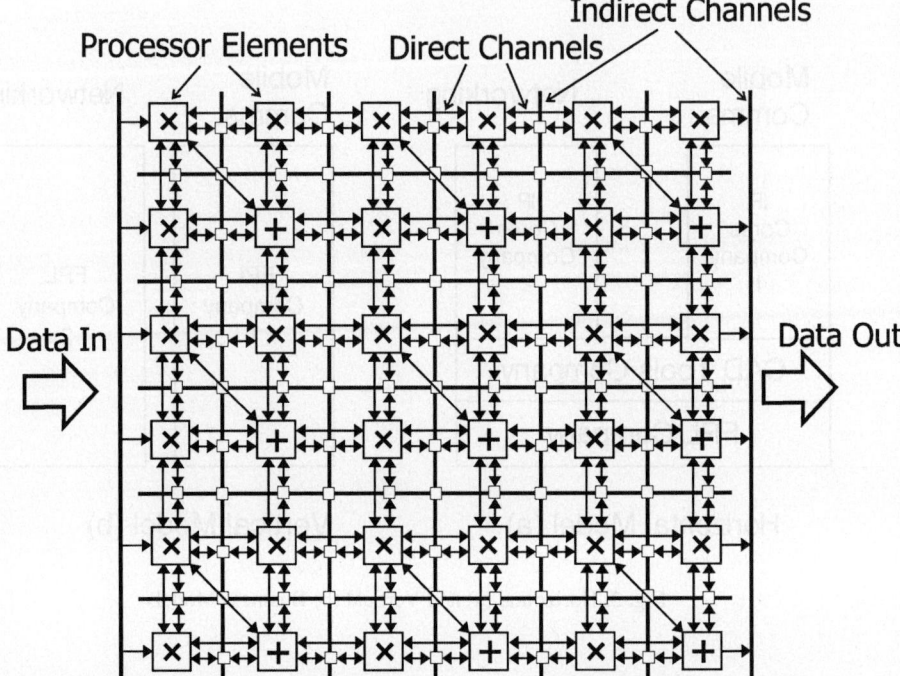

Fig. 4. Systolix PULSE-DSP Architecture (figure courtesy of Systolix Ltd.)

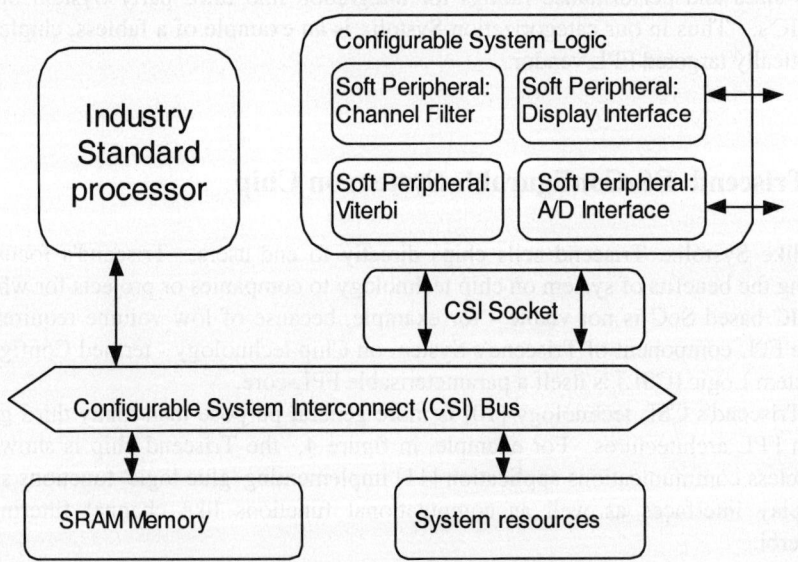

Fig. 5. Triscend CSoC in Wireless Communications (figure courtesy of Triscend Inc.)

Triscend has targeted its first family of devices (the 8032 based E5) at microcontroller users. The Triscend FastChip software provides a drag-and-drop user interface through which customers can add peripherals to the central core. Thus the E5 could be viewed as providing the world's largest catalogue of 8032 variants! Naturally, customers can also make use of standard FPGA tools such as Synopsys and OrCad to create their own custom peripherals as required. Triscend's second generation technology will feature the ARM7 TDMI processor and is directed at networking and communications applications [12].

A particularly important feature of the E5 given its target market is the close coupling between the microcontroller core and the programmable logic: the microcontroller can manage the reconfiguration of the programmable logic and directly address registers within the user logic. A header file for C or assembly language programmers containing symbolic references to the resources provided by the design mapped onto the CSL array is generated automatically by the CAD tools.

6 Summary

The central driving force in programmable logic architecture is, as it has always been, the ability of silicon to implement more and more functionality each year. As this happens a programmable chip can map larger and larger sections of the system and it must address different challenges (table 2).

First wave, sum of products architectures were efficient for small amounts of glue logic but did not scale as the process technology improved and more complex sections of the system had to be mapped to the programmable logic device. Complex PLD (CPLD) architectures borrowed some of the features of FPGA's and managed to delay the inevitable for some time but as process technology improved the underlying deficiencies became more and more apparent.

Table 2. Characteristics of FPL generations

	First Wave	Second Wave	Third Wave
Defining Company	Monolithic Memories	Xilinx	TBD
Defining Architecture	22V10 PAL	XC4000 FPGA	TBD
Programming Model	Write Once	Write Many	Download in Field
Functionality provided	Glue Logic	Subsystems	Systems
Business Structure	Own Fab. Sell chips	Fabless, Sell chips	Fabless, Sell IP cores and chips
Business Model	Horizontal	Horizontal	TBD

Similarly, second generation FPGA devices can efficiently map large blocks of logic within a system but do not scale to map entire systems as demanded in the era of-system on chip. Processors, their associated program memories and busses and purely computational functions (such as filter acceleration) do not map efficiently to general purpose FPGA architectures.

Third generation FPL devices, now coming on to the market, address the requirements of system on chip integration. As with earlier generations of programmable logic there is a step change in business model from chip vendor to IP core vendor. This change addresses the market requirement for lower cost of programmable components and allows easier market entry for small companies. The lower revenues achievable with this model also make competition from established second generation companies less likely.

It will be interesting to see whether the combination of the new architectures, the chipless business model and the rapidly growing application areas constitute a strategic inflection point which reshapes the FPL industry to the same extent as the FPGA architecture and fabless model did 16 years ago.

References

1. de Hon, Andre : Reconfigurable Architectures for General Purpose Computing, PhD Thesis, MIT Artificial Intelligence Laboratory 1996, AITR1586
2. Kress, R. : A fast Reconfigurable ALU for Xputers, PhD Thesis, Universitaet Kaiserslautern, 1996, D-386
3. Wittig R. et al : OneChip: An FPGA Processor with Reconfigurable Logic, , Proc. IEEE Symposium on Custom Computing Machines, FCCM 97, Napa CA 1996
4. Rupp C.R. et al : The NAPA Adaptive Processing Architecture, Proc. IEEE Symposium on Custom Computing Machines, FCCM 98, Napa CA 1998
5. Churcher S. et al : The XC6200 FastMap™ Processor Interface. Proceedings FPL95, Springer LNCS 975
6. Trimberger, S. et al : A Time-Multiplexed FPGA, Proc. IEEE Symposium on Custom Computing Machines, FCCM 97, Napa CA 1997
7. Smith M. J. : Application-specific Integrated Circuits, Addison Wesley Longman 1995
8. Jones, G. : PulseDSP - A Signal Processing Oriented Programmable Architecture, Field Programmable Logic and Application, Proceedings FPL99, Glasgow UK, Springer LNCS 1673
9. Analog Devices Inc. : AD7725 16-bit Sigma-Delta ADC with Programmable Post Processor, Preliminary Technical Data, Norwood MA, Feb 2000
10. Triscend Inc. : Triscend E5 Configurable System on Chip Family, Mountain View CA, January 2000
11. Kean, T. : Soft RF: new frontier for hackers, Focus on Software Radio, EE Times, August 16 1999
12. Triscend Inc. : Triscend Announces Industry's First 32-bit Configurable Processor will be ARM based, Press Release, November 1998

Reconfigurable Systems: New Activities in Asia

Hideharu Amano, Yuichiro Shibata, and Masaki Uno

Department of Information and Computer Science, Keio University
3-14-1 Hiyoshi Yokohama 223-8522, Japan
wasmii@am.ics.keio.ac.jp

Abstract. Systems and researches on reconfigurable systems in Asia and South Pacific are picked up and introduced. Like Northern America and European countries, various platforms and application specific systems have been proposed and developed. Recently, novel reconfigurable devices which provide dedicated functions for reconfigurable systems have been also developed.

1 Introduction

Recent dynamic reconfigurable FPGAs (Field Programmable Gate Array) or CPLDs (Complex Programmable Logic Devices) have made possible new varieties of *reconfigurable systems* and *custom computing machines*. In these systems, total or partial hardware configuration is changed so as to fit the target application or surrounding conditions. A large part of works on such machines are done in U.S.A. where most of reconfigurable devices are produced, Canada and European countries. However, there are also a lot of research projects on reconfigurable systems in Asia and south pacific countries.

Like activities in other countries, general reconfigurable engines have been developed as well as specialized systems for many application areas. Novel reconfigurable devices which provide dedicated functions for reconfigurable systems have been also developed. In this paper, activities are listed and introduced as possible [1].

2 Reconfigurable Platforms

Table 1 shows reconfigurable platforms developed in Asia and South Pacific. Although these systems have been designed for a specific application or research interest, they can be used for various types of applications.

FPGA-based Parallel Machine RASH[2] by Mitsubishi Electric Corp. consists of six boards each of which carries eight 100,000 gates class CPLD chips and a 2MB-SRAM module connected with local buses. Cooperation of these boards through the Compact-PCI backplane, RASH performs an exhaustive key search

---

[1] A part of this survey is duplicated with our previous survey report in 1998[1], but a lot of new activities are added. Regardless the title, activities in south pacific countries are also listed.

Table 1. Reconfigurable Platforms

Name	Institute	FPGA	Structure	Main target
RASH[2]	Mitsubishi(J)	FLEX10K100A ×8/BD	Buses	DES encryption
RM-I [5]	Kobe U.(J)	XC3090×4	Shared bus	Logic/Fault simulation
RM-II [5]	Kobe U.(J)	XC4005×9	Cross bus	Logic/Fault simulation
RM-III [6]	Kobe U.(J)	XC4005×6	FPIC	Logic/Fault simulation
RM-IV [6]	Kobe U.(J)	XC4006×16	FPIC	Logic/Fault simulation
SPACE [7]	U. South Australia (A)	CAL1024×16	Grid bus	Text searching
FLEMING [8]	Keio U.(J)	XC5215×6	Circular network	Virtual Hardware emulation, Queuing/Markov analysis
SOP [13]	NEC(J)	XC4010	Aptix board	General purpose (Data flow control)
RiSP/MEB200-A250 [18]	NAIST(J)	FLEX10K130V	Direct connection	Queueing network emulation
OPERL [15]	Nagoya U.(J)	OR2C40	PCI bus board	General purpose
Camereon [17]	Execute system(J)	XC3030	PC98 bus board	Function test

of DES code with 2,000 times high speed operation as that of Pentium-PC with 400MHz. A new key search algorithm is also developed for RASH[3].

RM-I – IV [4][5][6] by Kobe University are prototypes of a general purpose reconfigurable machine. A flexible connection based on the FPICs (Field Programmable Interconnect Chips) is used in recent models (RM-3 and RM-4), while earlier models are based on the bus connection or the cross-bus connection. On these platforms, design CAD programs (gate level logic simulation and logic diagnosis), and image processing (wave transform and blind de-convolution) are implemented. Most of these applications work 10 – 100 times faster than the current common workstations.

SPACE by University of South Australia [7] is another experimental platform for developing custom computing machines. Unlike other platforms, it consists of Algotronix CAL FPGA chips which are randomly and rapidly reconfigurable. 16 CAL chips are connected in 2-dimensional (4×4) mesh structure. Transputer T425 and 4 MB DRAM are connected through the port interface. On this platform, exact and error-tolerant text searching are implemented.

FLEMING [8] by Keio University was developed as a hardware emulator system of a virtual hardware with data flow mechanism called WASMII [9][10]. In this system, an application is described in a data flow language, and translated into a set of data flow graphs which are directly executed. When required hardware of the application exceeds the system size, the configuration data is replaced also by data-driven manner. A continuous system simulator and Hopfield style neural networks are implemented based on this mechanism. FLEMING is also used as a general platform. Two kinds of simulators for system analysis, using queuing networks Markov chains [11], Power flow analysis electric circuit simulation and robot arm control program[12] have been developed on it. SOP (Sea Of Processors) [13] by NEC works also in data-driven manner. In this system, C language with few restrictions is used for describing applications. Instead of the virtual hardware mechanism in FLEMING/WASMII, a large amount of mesh-connected FPGAs supports *sea of processors* on which most of applications can be implemented. Reconfigurable synchronous dataflow computer is also studied in Tohoku university[14].

The rest of platforms [15][17] [?] are small systems with a single FPGA implemented on a card which can be attached into the PC bus. On the OPERL card, an accelerator for subgraph isomorphism problems has been implemented[16]. On MEB200-A250 by Mitsubishi Elec. Micro-Comp. Application Software, a reconfigurable queuing network emulator RiSP is developed[18]. In RiSP, a graphic user interface is used for drawing the target queuing network, and the configuration logic for the emulator is generated automatically. These systems can be easily used for research on new applications of custom computing.

3 Application Specific Systems

Although there are a lot of systems which use SRAM-type FPGAs as their components, they are not be classified as reconfigurable systems if the configuration is fixed. We picked up systems which can replace the configuration for adapting to applications or surrounding conditions, and show them in Table 2.

As this table demonstrates, various reconfigurable systems are applied to a wide range of fields. The first application field is communication/network control. YARDS [19] by NTT realizes a high-speed ATM (Asynchronous Transfer Mode) network control function. Remote reconfiguration via ATM networks is possible. NTT also developed enhanced reconfigurable system called ATTRACTOR[20]. It adopts a board-level modularity concept that allows different functions to be implemented on different boards individually. A board consists of 12 FPGAs, SRAM modules and RISC card which are connected both with Compact PCI bus and high speed serial links.

A reconfigurable network switch or interface has been developed for flexible configuration of PC clusters. In Maestro[21], switch box uses FLEX10K devices for flexible packet switching, while communication primitives are changed by loading configurations of FPGA on the network interface boards in RHiNET-1/NI[22].

Wireless LAN demodulator [23] implemented on the PCI Pamette platform developed by DEC is another example of applications in the field of communications. In this system, C++ language is used for describing adaptive demodulator algorithms. Reconfigurable systems with FPGAs are also used in software radio which adapts radio parameters, such as mode, band, antenna configuration, code and encryption[24]. Dynamic reconfiguration algorithms for encryption are also studied[25].

The second major target application is image and signal processing used for multimedia applications. Although it is a growing field of reconfigurable systems, it is sometimes difficult to overcome high performance dedicated system LSIs. In this field, simple parallel processing on an array of FPGAs is effective for performance enhancement. A lot of systems including Color Image Processing [26],

Table 2. Special Purpose/Application Specific

Name	Institute	Target	FPGA	Structure
ATTRACTOR [12]	NTT Labs(J)	Telecommunication control	FLEX10K ×12/board	MPU, ATM-SW and memory modules
YARDS[19]	NTT Labs(J)	Telecommunication control	XC4010×2 MAX9K×2	FPGA/MPU cooperation
Maestro/SW[21]	Tsukuba U.(J)	Switch for PC cluster	FLEX10K	Based on the IEEE 1394 protocol
RHiNET-1/NI [22]	RWCP(J)	Network I/F for PC cluster	FLEX10K	Dynamic changing primitives
WLAN demodulator[23]	Macquarie U.(A)	Wireless LAN demodulation	XC4010×4	Implemented on PCI Pamette
XE/55V[26]	IBM Japan(J)	Color Image Processing	XC3090	FPGA/MPU cooperation
IQ demodulator[27]	Nanyan U.(S)	In-phase /Quadrature-phase demodulation	XC4010	PC card
HAB2[34]	U. Tokyo(J)	Animation	XC4085×11	Connected via SCSI I/O
FPGA Array[28]	Oita U.(J)	Digital Signal Processing	XC3142×9	3×3 Mesh structure
FPGA based Systolic Array[30]	La Trobe U.(A)	DFT	XC4010	2-D Array
DCT on CC[32]	U. South Australia (A)	DCT	Xilinx FPGA	Efficient implementation of DCT network
Reconfigurable Sensor[37]	Keio U.(J)	Robotics	EPF81500×2	Mounted on a personal robot
GA engine[38]	U. Tokyo(J)	GA algorithm	XC4010×8 XC4005	Connected to PC
SIMD GA machine[39]	Tokushima U.(J)	GA algorithm	XC4013	Under development
Neuron Emulator[40]	Nippon Bunri U.(J)	Boltzmann machine emulation	XC4010	SIMD control
Device simulation engine[41]	Meiji U.(J)	Solving Poisson's equation	XILINX	Under development
ANET[43]	Utsunomiya U.(J)	Multiprocessor with reconfigurable network	Altera CPLD	Available with 16 nodes
ATTEMPT-1 [44]	Keio U.(J)	Multiprocessor testbed	FLEX8000	Flexible cache/bus structure
Mi-con builder[45]	Kumamoto Technopolice(J)	Design platform	Altera CPLD	Bus connected modules
Processor emulator[46]	Waseda U.(J)	Design platform	EPF81500×2 EPF81188×2	Card
CCSimP[47]	Auckland U.(NZ)	Custom processor	FLEX8820	Instruction set is reconfigurable
Silicon TRON[49]	Toyohashi I.T.(J)	Real time OS	XC4010	Co-processor

IQ Demodulation [27], FFT [28][29], DFT [30] [31] and DCT [32] have been developed. On the runtime reconfigurable MPEG Video encoder[33], various algorithms such as motion estimation, DCT/IDCT and quantization/dequantization are executed during encoding. HAB2[34] is a testbed board for management of animation with run-time reconfiguration of hardware. Marine navigation system[35] has been also implemented on an FPGA by making the best use of built-in RAM. Although most of them are implemented on a card attached to PC, the reconfigurable sensor [37] is mounted on a personal robot.

GA (Genetic Algorithm) [38][39][36] or neural networks emulation [40] is another hopeful target since massively parallel processing of simple operations is also required. Although the floating point operation is too heavy even for the current FPGA, the device emulation engine which treats only fixed point short data is developed [41]. Heuristic search algorithms for constraint satisfaction problems are solved by a runtime reconfigurable implementation using Xilinx XC6216[42].

ANET [43] and Attempt-1 [44] are reconfigurable multiprocessors. In ANET, the network configuration can be changed so as to fit the target application. Attempt-1 is designed for investigating a cache structure and control in a single chip multiprocessor. The operation speed, consistency control, bus bandwidth and the cache structure can be changed by reconfiguration for emulating the situation of a single chip multiprocessor. Mi-con builder [45] and the processor emulator[46] have been developed as platforms for designing and investigating a new processor architecture.

Since it is hard to compete the performance with recent microprocessors, there are a few projects on a reconfigurable microprocessor itself. CCSimP [47] is a research processor whose instruction set is changeable for applications. The core is implemented on Altera's FLEX8820, and works at 20MHz. Using multi-thread and speculative execution techniques, Maruyama and his colleagues achieves better performance compared with a recent workstations for treating recursive calls and loops[58]. Silicon TRON [49] is a co-processor which performs a part of real time operating systems.

4 Novel Devices and Approaches

In order to overcome the limitation of reconfigurable systems with common FPGA/CPLD devices, novel reconfigurable devices have been researched and developed.

DRL is a dynamically and partially reconfigurable multi-context logic device implemented by NEC [50]. Eight context each of which provides 9,216 of usable gates at maximum can be switched at 4.6 ns. DES algorithms are implemented efficiently using partial multi-context facilities[51]. As described later, a virtual hardware mechanism with data-driven mechanism is also implemented on this chip[52].

NEC also developed an embedded DRAM-FPGA chip[53] for using a large amount of memory both for the context and data. Unlike DRL, 256 contexts can be hold inside the chip, while time for context switching is extended.

Plastic Cell Architecture (PCA)[54][55] is a novel element for dynamic reconfigurable computing. A cell each of which consists of the variable part (plastic part) and the routing switch (built-in part) are repeated and arranged in an orthogonal array. By communicating messages asynchronously between cells, target circuits are configured dynamically and autonomously in the chip. Multiple chips can be easily connected with serial I/O links. The first prototype using 0.25μm CMOS process technology will be available in the first quarter of 2000.

The arithmetic computing speed of the reconfigurable systems is handicapped by the fine grain logic configuration units used in general purpose FPGAs/CPLDs. To address this problem, coarse-grain FPGA architectures have been investigated. FPAccA[56] provides nine adders and three multipliers which can be connected each other freely. FPAccA model 2.0 chip achieves 300MFLOPS at 100MHz clock using 0.35μ process. An ALU based reconfigurable adaptive device by RWCP[57] consists of two dimensional ALU array. In this project, two prototype chips have been developed using 0.35μ process.

An FPGA structure for word-oriented data path which can form full adders efficiently is also studied in Fudan Univ[59]. University of Newcastle proposes cell structures for pipelined multipliers [60].

University of Tsukuba has been investigating a new architecture consisting of multiple operation units, cache memories with a high bandwidth, a data interconnect and a PLD block[58]. A reconfigurable logic in the PLD block controls the high speed data manipulation enabling the chip to efficiently operate pipeline processing of multi-thread execution.

Although there is no actual implementation in the current stage, interesting activities on reconfigurable machines have be done.

The major disadvantage of the reconfigurable machines is that it cannot be solve the problem which exceeds the size of the system. It is like a computer without virtual memory. To address this problem, WASMII [9][10] and Rotary Computer [61] uses an extended FPGA device called MPLD (Multifunction Programmable Logic Device) [62] proposed by Fujitsu. This device provides multiple configuration RAM sets which can be quickly replaced by a multiplexor. By a combination with the MPLD, data driven control, and static scheduling of configuration data transfer from/to outside the chip, WASMII is implemented on above described DRL chip by NEC[52]. S-machine [63] and HOSMII [64] also address this problem based on a technology on FPGA-DRAM integration. Compared with a MPLD, a large number of contexts can be implemented inside the chip.

Integration of FPGA and processor core in a single chip is another new field of reconfigurable machines. Iida and his colleagues propose a single chip multiprocessor with custom area [65]. Multithread library is implemented on this area for high speed thread management.

5 Summary

Systems and researches on reconfigurable systems in Asia and South Pacific are picked up and introduced. This survey is based on reports presented in FPGA-related international symposiums such as FCCM[2], FPGA[3], ASP-DAC[4], ASICON[5] and FPL[6]. Japanese activities are also picked up from internal workshops including FPGA/PLD Conference and Exhibition and IEICE/IPSJ technical reports. We believe that there are also a lot of activities in Korea, Taiwan and other countries, which we could not catch up. Since most of FPGA-related international symposiums/workshops are held in North America or European countries, it is somehow difficult to investigate activities in Asia and South Pacific country. Making other opportunities of easy international presentation for researchers in this area will be a powerful contribution for the circulation of their activities.

References

1. H.Amano, Y.Shibata, "Reconfigurable Systems: Activities in Asia and South Pacific," Proc. of ASP-DAC, pp. 453–457, 1998.
2. K.Nakajima, H.Mori, H.Sato, T.Takahashi, H.Asami, Y.Mizukami, M.Iida, K.Shindome, "FPGA-based Parallel Machine RASH," Proc. of JSPP'99, pp.222. (in Japanese)
3. H.Asami, M.Iida, K.Nakajima, H.Mori, "Improvement of DES circuit on FPGA-based Parallel Machine RASH," Tech. Rep. of IEICE. CPSY99-111. (in Japanese)
4. N. Suganuma, Y. Murata, S. Nakata, S. Nagata, M. Tomita, K. Hirano, "Reconfigurable Machine and Its Application to Logic Diagnosis," ICCAD-92, pp. 373–376, 1992.
5. M. Tomita, N. Suganuma, K. Hirano, "Reconfigurable Machine and Its Application to Logic Simulation," IEICE Trans. Fundamentals, Vol. E76-A, No. 10, pp. 1705–1712, 1993.
6. M. Numa, "Reconfigurable Machines: RM-I to RM-IV and Their Applications," IEICE Technical Report CPSY96-92, 1996 (in Japanese)
7. B. Gungher, G. Milne, L. Narasimhan, "Assessing Document Relevance with Run-Time Reconfigurable Machines," Proc. of the IEEE Symposium on FPGAs for Custom Computing Machines, pp. 10–17, 1996.
8. X.-P. Ling, Y. Shibata, H. Miyazaki, H. Amano, "Total System Image of the Reconfigurable Machine WASMII," Proc. of International conference on Parallel Distributed Processing Techniques and Applications, pp. 1092–1096, 1997.
9. X.-P. Ling, H. Amano, "WASMII: a Data Driven Computer on a Virtual Hardware," Proc. of the IEEE Symposium on FPGAs for Custom Computing Machines, pp. 33–42, 1993.
10. X.-P. Ling, H. Amano, "WASMII: an MPLD with Data-Driven Control on a Virtual Hardware," Journal of Supercomputing, Kluwer Academic Publishers, Vol. 9, No. 3, pp. 253–276, 1995.

[2] IEEE Symposium on FPGAs for Custom Computing Machines
[3] ACM/SIGDA International Symposium on Field Programmable Gate Arrays
[4] Asia and South Pacific Design Automation Conference
[5] IEEE International conference on ASIC
[6] International Workshop on Field-Programmable Logic and Applications

11. O. Yamamoto, Y. Shibata, H. Kurokawa, H. Amano, "A Reconfigurable Markov Chain Simulator for Analysis of Parallel Systems," Proc. of IEEE the Innovated System in Silicon, 1997.
12. H.Miyazaki, Y.Shibata, A.Takayama, X-P.Ling, H.Aamano, "Emulation of Multichip WASMII on Reconfigurable System Testbed FLEMING," Proc. of PACT98 workshop on reconfigurable computing, pp.47-52, 1998.
13. T. Yamauchi, S. Nakaya, N. Kajihara, "SOP: A Reconfigurable Massively Parallel System and Its Control-Data-Flow based Compiling Method" Proc. of the IEEE Symposium on FPGAs for Custom Computing Machines, pp. 148–156, 1996.
14. H.Sasaki, H.Maruyama, H.Tsukioka, S.Shoji, H.Kobayashi, T.Nakamura, "An Architecture of the Reconfigurable Synchronous Dataflow Computer and its Software Development Environment," Proc. of the 7th FPGA/PLD Design conference and exhibit., pp.9-14, 1999. (in Japanese)
15. S. Ichikawa, T. Shimada, "Design and Implementation of Reconfigurable PCI Card," IEICE Technical Report, CPSY96-97, 1996 (in Japanese)
16. S. Ichikawa, L.Udorn, K.Konishi, "Hardware Accelerator for Subgraph Isomorphism Problems," Proc. of FCCM 2000.
17. M. Satachi, A. Kanomata, "Microcomputer-FPGA Cooperation Board Camereon," Proc. of the 5th Japanese FPGA/PLD Conference and Exhibit, pp. 259–267, 1997 (in Japanese)
18. Y.Noguchi, K.Saisho, A.Fukuda, "A Reconfigurable Simualtion System with Programmable Devices," IPSJ Tech. Rep. 98-ARC-131, 1998 (in Japanese)
19. A. Tsutsui, T. Miyazaki, "YARDS: FPGA/MPU Hybrid Architecture for Telecommunication Data Processing," Proc. of the ACM/SIGDA International Symposium on Field Programmable Gate Arrays, pp. 93–99, 1997.
20. T. Miyazaki, K.Shirakawa, M.Katayama, T.Murooka, A.Takahara, "A Transmutable Telecom System," Proc. of the International Workshop on Field-Programmable Logic and Applications, (LNCS 1482), pp.366–375, 1998.
21. S.Yamagiwa, M.Ono, T.Yamazaki, P.Kulkasem, M.Hirota, K.Wada, "Maestro-Link: A High Performance Interconnect for PC Cluster," Proc. of the International Workshop on Field-Programmable Logic and Applications, (LNCS 1482), pp.421–425, 1998.
22. H.Nishi, K.Tasho, T.Kuhoh, J.Yamamoto, H.Amano, "A Local area system network RHiNET-1: a network for high performance parallel computing," Proc. of IEEE High Performance Distributed Computing 2000.
23. T. McDermott, P. Ryan, M. Shand, D. Skellern, T. Percival, N. Weste, "A Wireless LAN Demodulator in a Pamette: Design and Experience," Proc. of the IEEE Symposium on FPGAs for Custom Computing Machines, pp. 40–45, 1997.
24. M.Cummings, S.Haruyama, "FPGA in the Software Radio," IEEE Communications Magazine, Feb. pp.108-112, 1999.
25. T.Yamaguchi, Y.Hashiyama, S.Okuma, "A Study on Reconfigurable Computing System for Encryption," IEICE Tech. Rep. CPSY99-82. (in Japanese)
26. H. Nakano, "Flexible Image Processor Board XE/55V," Proc. of the 2nd Japanese FPGA/PLD Conference and Exhibit, pp. 365–371, 1994 (in Japanese)
27. C. C. Jong, Y. Y. H. Lam, L. S. Ng, "FPGAs Implementation of a Digital IQ Demodulator," Proc. of the International Workshop on Field-Programmable Logic and Applications, (LNCS 1304), pp. 410–417, 1997.
28. H. Hikawa, K. Sato, H. Iwabuchi, "Reconfigurable Array-Processor Based on FPGA," Proc. of the 3rd Japanese FPGA/PLD Conference and Exhibit, pp. 493–504, 1995 (in Japanese)

29. Z-h. Liu, Y-q.Han, "Implementation of FFT in FPGA Technology," Proc. of IEEE ASICON98, pp.28–31, 1998.
30. C. H. Dick, "Computing the Discrete Fourier Transform on FPGA Based Systolic Arrays," Proc. of the ACM/SIGDA International Symposium on Field Programmable Gate Arrays, pp. 129–135, 1996.
31. C. H. Dick, "Computing 2-D DFTs Using FPGAs," Proc. of the International Workshop on Field-Programmable Logic and Applications, (LNCS 1142), pp. 96–105, 1996.
32. N. W. Bergmann, Y. Y. Chung, B. K. Gunther, "Efficient Implementation of the DCT on Custom Computers," Proc. of the IEEE Symposium on FPGAs for Custom Computing Machines, pp. 244–245, 1997.
33. A.Oue, T.Isshik, H.Kunieda, "MPEG Video Encoder Based on Run-Time Reconfigurable Architecture," Proc. of IEEE ASICON98, pp.83–91, 1998.
34. M.Sekiyama, M.Nomura, K.Hiraki, "Validity of Run-time Reconfigure at Treatment of Animation with Hardware," IPSJ Tech. Rep. 98-ARC-130-23, 1998. (in Japanese)
35. X-y. Meng, J. Liang, "The New Application of Built-in RAM of FPGA in Marine Navigation System," Proc. of IEEE ASICON98, pp.8–11, 1998.
36. T.Maruyama, T.Funatsu, T.Hoshino, "Field-Programming Gate-Array System for Evolutionary Computation," Proc. of the International Workshop on Field-Programmable Logic and Applications, (LNCS 1482), pp.356–365, 1998.
37. K. Nukata, Y. Shibata, H. Amano, Y. Anzai, "A Reconfigurable Sensor-Data Processing system for Personal Robots," Proc. of the International Workshop on Field-Programmable Logic and Applications, (LNCS 1304), pp. 491–500, 1997.
38. Y. Ohsima, T. Matsumoto, K. Hiraki, "Reconfigurable GA Engine," Proc. of the 3rd Japanese FPGA/PLD Conference and Exhibit, pp. 541–548, 1995 (in Japanese)
39. M. Sano, Y. Takahashi, "SIMD GA Machine Based on FPGA," Proc. of the 5th Japanese FPGA/PLD Conference and Exhibit, pp. 241–248, 1997 (in Japanese)
40. Y. Kitamura, M. Sasaki, T. Kanokogi, "Neuro Processor Implementation Based on FPGA," Proc. of the 3rd Japanese FPGA/PLD Conference and Exhibit, pp. 531–539, 1995 (in Japanese)
41. K. Bando, Y. Iguchi, T. Yamada, "Design of a Device Simulation Engine Based on FPGA," Proc. of the 3rd Japanese FPGA/PLD Conference and Exhibit, pp. 563–567, 1995 (in Japanese)
42. C.K Chung and P.H.W.Leong, "An Architecture for solving boolean satisfiaability using runtime configurable hardware," Proc. of ICPP Workshop, pp. 346–351, 1999.
43. T. Yoshinaga, T. Baba, "A Local Operating System for the A-NET Parallel Object Oriented Computer," Journal of Information Processing, Vol. 14, No. 4, pp. 415–422, 1991.
44. K. Inoue, T. Kisuki, M. Okuno, E. Shimizu, T. Terasawa, H. Amano, "ATTEMPT-1: A Reconfigurable Multiprocessor Testbed," Proc. of the International Workshop on Field-Programmable Logic and Applications, (LNCS 1142), pp. 200–209, 1996.
45. S. Mitsugi, Y. Sawayama, "Mi-con builder: Design Support System for Development of Microcomputers," Proc. of the Altera PLD World 96, pp. 87–92, 1996 (in Japanese)
46. W. Ogata, "Reconfigurable Computer Architecture Evaluation System Based on FLEX8000," Proc. of Altera PLD World 96, pp. 101–114, 1996 (in Japanese)
47. Z. Salcic, B. Maunder, "CCSimP — An Instruction-Level Custom-Configurable Processor for FPLDs," Proc. of the International Workshop on Field-Programmable Logic and Applications, (LNCS 1142), pp. 280–289, 1996.

48. T.Maruyama, M.Takagi, T.Hoshino, "Hardware Implementation Techniques for Recursive Calls and Loops," Proc. of the International Workshop on Field-Programmable Logic and Applications, (LNCS 1673), pp. 451–461, 1999.
49. T. Nakano, A. Utama, M. Itabashi, A. Shiomi, M. Imai, "The Evaluation of Silicon TRON Design," IEICE Technical Report, CPSY93-62, 1993 (in Japanese)
50. T.Fujii, K.Furuta, M.Motomura, M.Nomura, M.Mizuno, K.Anjo, K.Wakabayashi, Y.Hirota, Y.Nakazawa, H.Ito, M.Yamashina, "A Dynamically Reconfigurable Logic Engine with a Multi-Context Multi-Mode Unified-Cell Architecture," Proc. Intl. Solid-State Circuits Conf., pp.360–361 (1999).
51. M.Yamashina, M.Motomura, "Reconfigurable Computing: Its concept and practical embodiment using newly developed DRL LSI," Proc. ASP-DAC 2000, pp.329–332, (2000).
52. M.Uno, Y.Shibata, H.Amano, K.Furuta, T.Fujii, M.Motomorura, "A Virtual Hardware System on a DRL device," IEICE Tech. Rep. CPSY99-113, 2000. (in Japanese)
53. M.Motomura, Y.Aimoto, A.Shibayama, Y.Yabe, M.Yamashina, "'An Embedded DRAM-FPGA Chip with Instantaneous Logic Reconfiguration," Proc. Intl. Conf. on VLSI Circuits, pp. 55–56 (1997).
54. K.Nagami, K.Oguri, T.Shiozawa, H.Ito, R.Konishi, "Plastic Cell Architecture: Towards Reconfigurable Computating for General Purpose," in Proc. of FCCM'98, pp.68–77, 1998.
55. H.Nakada, K.Oguri, N.Imlig, M.Inamori, R.Konishi, H.Ito, K.Nagami, T.Shiozawa, "Plastic Cell Architecture: A Dynamically Reconfigurable Hardware-based Computer," in Proc. of IPPS/SPDP99 LNCS1586, pp.679–687, 1999.
56. Y.Kawano, H.Ochi, T.Tuda, "Design of FPAccA model 2.0 Chip - Reconfigurable Floating-Point-Unit Array-," IEICE Tech. Rep. CPSY99-112, 2000. (in Japanese)
57. N.Kajihara, S.Nakaya, T.Yamauchi, T.Inuo, "The Design and Implementation of an ALU Based Reconfigurable Adaptive Device," Proc. of 2000 RWC Symposium (TR-99-002), pp.237–242, 2000.
58. T. Maruyama, T. Hoshino, "A Reconfigurable Architecture for High Speed Computation by Pipeline Processing," Proc. of the International Workshop on Field-Programmable Logic and Applications, (LNCS 1673), pp.514–519, 1999.
59. Z-h. Huang, J-r. Tong, "An Efficient FPGA Logic Block for Word-oriented Datapath," Proc. of IEEE ASICON98, pp.20–23, 1998.
60. M.Wojko, "Pipelined Multipliers and FPGA Architectures," Proc. of the International Workshop on Field-Programmable Logic and Applications, (LNCS 1673), pp. 347–352, 1999.
61. S. Mitsugi, "Rotary Computer and Virtual Circuit," Proc. of the IPSJ 44th Annual Convention, 6-109, 1992.
62. S. Yoshimi (Fujitsu Inc.), "Multi-function Programmable Logic device," Japan Patent (A), Hei2-130023, 1990.
63. T. Sueyoshi, "Present Status and Problems of the Reconfigurable Computing Systems — Toward the Computer Evolution —," IEICE Technical Report, CPSY96-91, 1996 (in Japanese)
64. Y. Shibata, H. Miyazaki, X.-P. Ling, H. Amano, "HOSMII: a Virtual Hardware System Based on an FPGA Embedded with DRAM," IEICE Technical Report, CPSY97-45, 1997 (in Japanese)
65. M. Iida, M. Kuga, T. Sueyoshi, "On Chip Multi-processor Using Multithread Control Library Implemented as Hardware," Proc. on Joint Symposium on Parallel Processing, pp.337–344, 1997 (in Japanese)

StReAm: Object-Oriented Programming of Stream Architectures Using PAM-Blox

Oskar Mencer, Heiko Hübert, Martin Morf, and Michael J. Flynn

Computer Systems Laboratory, Department of Electrical Engineering
Stanford, CA 94305, USA
{oskar, heiko, morf, flynn}@arith.stanford.edu

Abstract. Simplifying the programming models is paramount to the success of reconfigurable computing. We apply the principles of object-oriented programming to the design of stream architectures for reconfigurable computing. The resulting tool, **StReAm**, is a *domain specific compiler* on top of the object-oriented module generation environment PAM-Blox. Combining module generation with a high-level programming tool in C++ gives the programmer the convenience to explore the flexibility of FPGAs on the arithmetic level and write the algorithms in the same language and environment.

Stream architectures consist of the pipelined dataflow graph mapped directly to hardware. Data streams through the implementation of the dataflow graph with only minimal control logic overhead. The main advantage of stream architectures is a clock-frequency equal to the data-rate leading to very low power consumption. We show a set of benchmarks from signal processing, encryption, image processing and 3D graphics in order to demonstrate the advantages of object-oriented programming of FPGAs.

1 Introduction

In this paper we present **StReAm**, a domain specific compiler for programming FPGAs. **StReAm** is build on top of the module generation environment PAM-Blox[6] and PamDC[1]. FPGAs offer reconfigurability on the bit-level at the cost of larger VLSI area and slower maximal clock frequency compared to custom VLSI. Simplifying the programming models is paramount to the success of reconfigurable computing with FPGAs.

FPGAs are programmable devices. Yet, programming FPGAs, or writing compilers for FPGAs, is much more complex than writing compilers for microprocessors. Because FPGAs offer programmability of the logic and the interconnect, compiling a program into an FPGA is similar to a VLSI CAD system. On the other hand the CAD design flow is not practical for programming FPGAs.

HandelC[3] is a hardware (FPGA) programming language based on communicating sequential processes[2]. Every expression implies a latency of one clock cycle. Area-time tradeoffs can be explored by rewriting expressions. JHDL[7] and Pebble[5] are examples for structural languages for FPGAs on the PAM-Blox

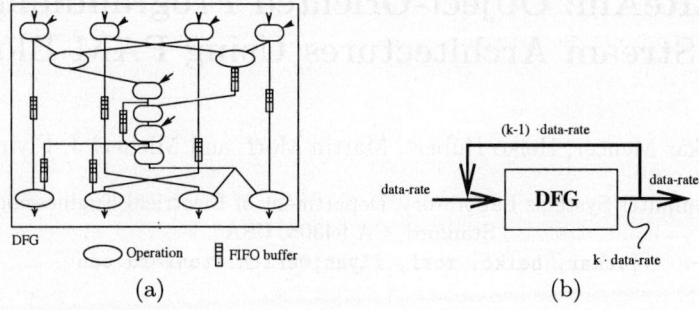

Fig. 1. (a) shows an acyclic dataflow graph (DFG) with operations and distributed FIFO buffers. (b) shows a DFG with a loop(1...k), and the associated clock frequencies based on the data-rate.

level. JBITS[8] is an object-oriented environment on the FPGA configuration bitstream level. Neither JHDL nor Pebble offer operator overloading. Instead, expressions are constructed by nesting function calls. Novel architectures combining a microprocessor with reconfigurable logic are natural targets for hardware compilation using software languages. For example, Callahan[12] compiles C for the Garp processor including a reconfigurable datapath.

1.1 Stream Architectures

General purpose microprocessors are designed to deliver low latency computation with maximal clock frequencies leading to high power consumption. In terms of performance and power consumption, latency tolerant applications can be efficiently implemented with architectures that provide high throughputs, such as Imagine[14], Score[11], RaPiD[15], and the PCI-PipeRench[10].

Figure 1 (a) shows the execution model of the stream architecture with completely unrolled loops. In a microprocessor the data goes from the register-file to the arithmetic unit. The result of the arithmetic operation can be forwarded to another arithmetic unit and is finally written back to the register file. In a stream architecture the role of the register file is taken over by distributed FIFO buffers with a delay equal to the time between production of the value and consumption of the value by the following operation. The distributed FIFO buffers enable us to exploit temporal data locality, while streaming data through pipelines exploits spatial data locality.

2 StReAm: Programming FPGAs

StReAm is a domain specific tool build on top of PAM-Blox. Figure 2 shows the "city-model" for programming FPGAs. PAM-Blox simplify the design of datapaths for FPGAs by implementing arithmetic module-generators in object-oriented C++. With PAM-Blox, hardware designers can benefit from all the advantages of object-oriented system design such as:

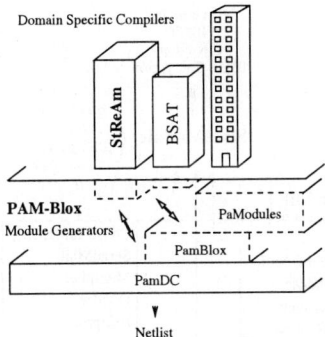

Fig. 2. The figure shows the "city-model" for programming FPGAs. Vertical domain specific compilers such as **StReAm** and BSAT[19] sit on top of a horizontal foundation of PAM-Blox layers for module-generation.

- *Inheritance:* Code-reuse is implemented by a C++ class hierarchy. Child objects inherit all public methods (function) and variables (state). For example, all objects with a carry-chain, such as adders, counters, and shifters, inherit the absolute and relative placement functions from their common parent.
- *Virtual Functions and Function Overloading:* Function overloading enables selective code-reuse. Part of the parent object can be redefined by overloading of inherited (virtual) methods. For example, a two's complement subtract unit can be derived from an adder by forcing a carry-in of one, and inverting one of the inputs.
- *Template Class:* The template class feature of C++ enables us to efficiently combine C++ objects and module-generation. In case of an adder, the template parameter is the bit-width of the adder. The instantiation of a particular object based on the template class creates an adder of the appropriate size.
- *Operator overloading and template functions* are used by **StReAm** described below.

StReAm uses operator overloading and template functions in C++ to create dataflow graphs which are consecutively scheduled to obtain a stream architecture. The nodes of the stream architecture are mapped to PAM-Blox modules, to create a netlist file for the Xilinx place-and-route tools. Figure 3 shows the details of the class hierarchy of the system.

StreaModule is a subclass of PaModule. Applications are written as subclasses of StreaModule. **StReAm** enables high-level programming on the expression level. **StReAm** includes automatic scheduling of stream architectures, hierarchical wire naming and block placement. In addition, **StReAm** supports structural programming and allows the designer to combine structural descriptions with expressions. Thus, **StReAm** simplifies the design of complex stream architectures to just a few lines of code.

A hardware integer (HWint) data type supports the common operators +,-,*,/,%. The user can define other operators and functions by utilizing operator

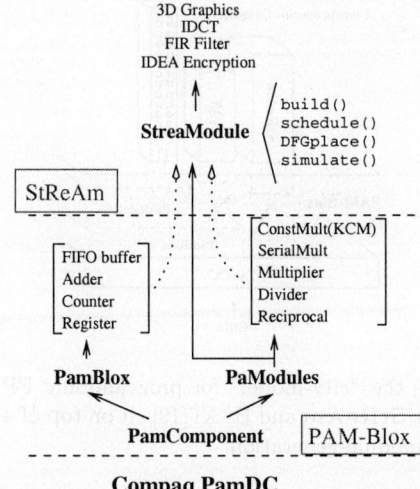

Fig. 3. The figure shows **StReAm**'s class hierarchy on top of PAM-Blox. Arrows (→) denote a subclass, or a set of subclasses. The dotted and curved arrows denote operator overloading. Applications (stream architectures) are implemented as subclasses of StreaModules.

overloading and template functions in C++. Extending the set of operators and functions requires manual design of optimized PamBlox or PaModules. Thus, the designer can adapt the arithmetic units to the specific needs of the application.

StReAm currently supports arrays of the hardware integer type `HWint`, expressions with `HWint`'s and C++ integers resulting in hardware constants, and static `'for'` loops. In addition, more complex hardware units with possibly multiple inputs and outputs are implemented as template functions.

One of the advantages of using FPGAs for computing is the flexibility on the arithmetic level. We define families of arithmetic units that are compatible with each other. As an example, the 4-bit digit-serial family consists of a 4-bit wide datapath with arithmetic units for addition, constant addition, and constant multiplication. The arithmetic family can be specified as a global parameter (used in the examples in section 4), or at the equation level.

3 Scheduling Stream Architectures

StReAm automatically schedules the arrival of input data for each arithmetic component. The scheduling algorithm creates FIFO buffers and component start signals (for sequential components). The scheduler also calculates overall latency and data-rate for a given stream architecture. Our initial implementation utilizes "as soon as possible" (ASAP) scheduling, which is optimized for minimum-latency and resource unconstraint problems [4] without resource sharing.

Operator overloading creates a dataflow graph with arithmetic units as nodes. The scheduling algorithm traverses the dataflow graph including the components, data dependencies and scheduling information such as latency and

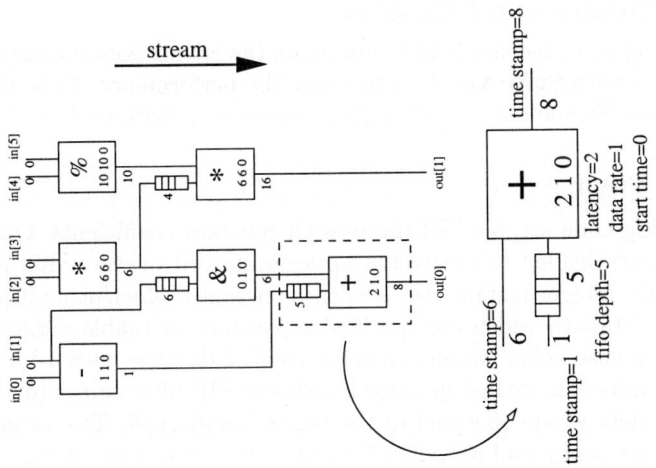

Fig. 4. The figure shows the scheduled data-flow graph implementing the equations: $out[0] = (in[0] - in[1]) + in[1] \& (in[2] * in[3])$; $out[1] = in[2] * in[3] * (in[4]\%in[5])$. Sequencing information is given in the nodes (component latency, data-rate and start time) and interconnections include time stamps.

throughput of each component. The scheduler retrieves the scheduling information from the state of the hardware objects. A sequencing graph is given in figure 4.

The scheduling algorithm performs the following four tasks:

– *Determine time stamps:* For each component, the time stamp (t_s) of the component output is set according to: out t_s = max(in t_s)+comp_latency
– *Global latency and data rate:* Global latency is determined by the sum of latencies in the longest path of the design which is equal to the maximal time stamp of global StreaModule outputs. The data rate describes the time interval in which components consume and produce data. For sequential components the data rate is determined by the latency, whereas for pipelined components the data rate is usually higher. Global data rate is determined by the minimal data rate of all components in the design.
– *Distributed FIFO buffers:* The scheduler ensures equal arrival times of component inputs by inserting delays with distributed FIFO buffers. The delay or FIFO depth results from differences of time stamps.
– *Supplying components with start signals:* Sequential and serial components require a start signal each time new input data can be applied to the component. Start signals depend on time stamps and global data rate.

In addition to the values mentioned above, each hardware object includes a precision value and an overflow bit as part of the state of the hardware object. The precision value inside the hardware object can be used at compile time to evaluate error propagation through the dataflow graph.

4 Benchmarks and Results

The following three benchmarks demonstrate the advantages of designing stream architectures with **StReAm**. Results show the performance of the final circuits for the Xilinx XC4000 family after Xilinx place and route tools.

4.1 FIR Filter

The following code creates FIR filters with constant coefficients. Operators '+' and '*' are overloaded to create the appropriate arithmetic units. Multiplying by a constant integer instantiates efficient constant-coefficient multipliers. Data width and datapath width are specified separately to enable digit-serial arithmetic. In the case below we implement a 16-bit FIR filter with 4-bit digit serial arithmetic units. The `delay` operator inserts the FIR filter delays (deltas) similar to the way dela ys are specified in the Silage language[4]. The variables `in[]`, `out[]` are the inputs and outputs of the stream architecture, defined by setting NUM_BLOCK_INPUTS, NUM_BLOCK_OUTPUTS:

```
const int NUM_BLOCK_INPUTS=1;
const int NUM_BLOCK_OUTPUTS=1;
const int BITS = 16;
const int COMP_MODE = DIGIT_SERIAL;
const int STAGES=4;
const int coef[STAGES]={23,45,67,89};
HWint<BITS> delayOut;
HWint<BITS> adderOut;

void Filter::build(){
  delayOut=in[0];
  adderOut=delayOut*coef[0];
  for (i=1;i<STAGES;i++){
    delayOut=delay(delayOut,1);
    adderOut=adderOut+delayOut*coef[i];
  }
  out[0]=adderOut;
}
```

Table 1 shows the results for four variations of the 4-tap FIR filter. The results show a 4-stage FIR filter implemented with combinational arithmetic units, and three pipelined versions. As expected the bit-serial design takes the smallest area with the longest latency. The parallel, pipelined version has higher throughput but requires most area. The lower part of the table shows the maximal number of stages that **StReAm** can fit on a Xilinx XC4020 FPGA with 800 CLBs. All designs are created with the same few lines of code shown above by simply setting the compiler parameter COMP_MODE.

4.2 IDEA Encryption

IDEA (International Data Encryption Algorithm)[13] was developed by Xuejia Lai and James Massey. IDEA is a strong encryption algorithm developed for

Table 1. FIR Filter Results

	combi-national	pipelined parallel	pipelined digit-serial	pipelined bit-serial
4 stage FIR				
Area[CLB]	246	293	210	184
Cycle Time(CT)	70.1ns	20.8ns	21.2ns	24.2ns
Latency	3	9	17	52
Throughput	16bits/CT	16bits/CT	4bits/CT	1bit/CT
FIR Stages	6	6	14	17
Area[CLB]	332	432	678	635
Latency	5	11	57	260
Cycle Time(CT)	88.7ns	25.1ns	27.3ns	28.0 ns
Throughput	16bits/CT	16bits/CT	4bits/CT	1bit/CT

DSP microprocessors. IDEA encrypts or decrypts 64-bit data blocks, using symmetric 128-bit keys. The 128-bit keys are expanded further to 52 sub-keys, 16 bits each. The kernel loop (or round) is generally executed 8 times for either encryption or decryption. Hand crafted results for a stream architecture implementation of IDEA are presented in [17]. One IDEA round can be mapped to a four-input, four-output stream architecture. In order to fit two loops onto one Xilinx XC4020E FPGA we use digit serial arithmetic with a datapath width of 4 bits. The following code shows the four-input, four-output IDEA::build implementation of one round of IDEA encryption:

```
const int NUM_BLOCK_INPUTS=4;
const int NUM_BLOCK_OUTPUTS=4;
const int BITS = 16;
const int COMP_MODE=DIGIT_SERIAL;
const int key[10]={9277,98,237,4,978,122,723,3654,24,1536};
HWint<BITS> t[9];
HWint<BITS> temp;

void IDEA::build(){
  t[1] = ideaKCM16(in[0] , key[0]);
  t[2] = (in[1] + key[1]);
  t[3] = (in[2] + key[2]);
  t[4] = ideaKCM16(in[3] , key[3]);
  tmp = t[1] ^ t[3];
  tmp = ideaKCM16(tmp , key[4]);
  t[7] = (tmp + (t[2] ^ t[4]));
  t[8] = ideaKCM16(t[7] , key[5]);
  tmp = (t[8] + tmp);
  out[0] = t[1] ^ t[8];
  out[3] = t[4] ^ tmp;
  tmp = tmp ^ t[2];
  out[1] = t[3] ^ t[8];
  out[2] = tmp;
}
```

The resulting stream architecture with 14 arithmetic units and 8 automatically generated and scheduled FIFO buffers is shown in figure 1. In addition to operator overloading, IDEA requires a special mod $2^{16}+1$ constant multiplier implemented as a PaModule with fixed bitwidth, which is instantiated by the function ideaKCM16(). Final results are shown in Table 2.

4.3 Inverse Discrete Cosine Transform (IDCT)

The IDCT is used in signal and image processing (e.g. MPEG, H.263 standards). We implement an 8x8 1-dimensional IDCT. The actual code for this example is beyond the space constraints of this paper and can be obtained from the authors. The resulting stream architecture consists of 98 arithmetic units and 4 FIFO buffers. The final results are shown in Table 2.

4.4 3D Motion: Real-Time Translation and Rotation

In 3D graphics, a common problem is the translation and rotation of a large set of points in 3D. This stream of points is transformed by a translation vector and two 2D rotation angles obtained from one 3D rotation. The following implementation uses 2D CORDIC modules (ROTATE()) implemented as PaModules[18]. The **StReAm** program looks as follows:

```
const int NUM_BLOCK_INPUTS=3;
const int NUM_BLOCK_OUTPUTS=3;
const int BITS = 12;
const int COMP_MODE=PARALLEL;
HWint<BITS> x_in,y_in,z_in;      //inputs
HWint<BITS> x0,y0,z0,phi1,phi2;//rotation
HWint<BITS> dx,dy,dz;            //translation
HWint<BITS> x[2],y[2],z[2];      //temp coords

MOTION3D::build(){
  x_in = in[0];
  y_in = in[1];
  z_in = in[2];
  x0 = configReg[0];
  y0 = configReg[1];
  z0 = configReg[2];
  phi1 = configReg[3];
  phi2 = configReg[4];
  dx = configReg[5];
  dy = configReg[6];
  dz = configReg[7];
  (x[0],y[0])=ROTATE((x_in-x0),(y_in-y0),phi1);
  (y[1],z[1])=ROTATE(y[0],(z_in-z0),phi2);
  out[0]=x[0] + x0 + dx;
  out[1]=y[1] + y0 + dy;
  out[2]=z[1] + z0 + dz;
}
```

The StreaModule above takes 3 input coordinates (x_in, y_in, z_in). representing a point in space. The result is a rotated and translated point (out[0...2]). The center of rotation (x0, y0, z0), angles phi1, phi2) and translation vector (dx, dy, dz) are stored in configuration registers (configReg). The value of the configuration registers can be changed without reconfiguration of the FPGAs. Writing these eight configuration values to the FPGA configures the stream architecture to perform a particular 3D motion.

Table 2. Benchmark Results

	IDEA	IDCT	3D MOTION
Area[CLB]	460	463	320
Cycle Time(CT)	24.1ns	27.9ns	33.9ns
Throughput(bits/CT)	$4 \cdot (16/4) = 16$	12.4	36
Total Latency	17	15	27
Arithmetic	digit-serial 16-bit data	parallel* 14-bit	parallel 12-bit data

*sequential multiply

This example demonstrates a template function:ROTATE. C++ instantiates the ROTATE function to create CORDIC units[18] with the appropriate bitwidth based on the types of the input variables. In addition, the rotate function demonstrates a multi-input, multi-output module instantiation by overloading the "," operator in (x[0],y[0]) leading to the efficient program above. The code above results in 9 add/sub units, 2 CORDIC units and 1 FIFO buffer. The final results of a fully pipelined 3D rotation and translation module are shown in Table 2.

5 Conclusions and Future Work

StReAm applies an object-oriented design methodology to programming FPGAs. FPGAs offer the flexibility to adapt the number representation, precision, and arithmetic algorithm to the particular needs of the application. Yet, in general it is difficult to explore completely different arithmetic solutions. Combining module generation with a high-level programming tool in C++, shown in this paper, gives the programmer the convenience to explore the flexibility of FPGA on the arithmetic level and write the algorithms in the same language and environment.

For **StReAm** the key enabling C++ technologies are dynamic operator overloading and template functions. Furthermore, just as in PAM-Blox, the class hierarchy, inheritance, template classes and method overloading enable efficient code-reuse and code-management.

Future work needs to address the problem of debugging, simulation, and verification of module generators. Ideally, a compiler for combined processor/FPGA systems would be able to explore parallelism and pipelining on the algorithm level, instruction level, arithmetic level and bit level.

Acknowledgments

We would like to thank W. Luk, J. Wawrzynek, and Arvind for helpful discussions on module-generation and the programming approach to hardware design. Thanks to Compaq Systems Research Center for support of this work, and M. Shand for maintaining PamDC. Thanks to L. Séméria for discussions on the draft of this paper. The second author thanks his advisor Prof. H. Klar for support of this research.

References

1. P. Bertin, D. Roncin, J. Vuillemin, *Programmable Active Memories: A Performance Assessment*, ACM FPGA, February 1992.
2. C.A.R. Hoare *Communicating Sequential Processes*, Prentice Hall Int., 1985.
3. Embedded Solutions *Handel C*, http://www.embeddedsol.com/
4. G. DeMicheli *Synthesis and Optimization of Digital Circuits*, McGraw-Hill, 1994.
5. W. Luk, S. McKeever, *Pebble: A Language for Parametrised and Reconfigurable Hardware Design*, FPL, Tallinn, Aug. 1998.
6. O. Mencer, M. Morf, M. J. Flynn, *PAM-Blox: High Performance FPGA Design for Adaptive Computing*, IEEE FCCM, Napa Valley, CA, 1998.
7. P. Bellows, B. Hutchings, P. Bellows, J. Hawkins, S. Hemmert, B. Nelson, M. Rytting, *A CAD Suite for High-Performance FPGA Design*, IEEE FCCM, Napa Valley, CA, 1999.
8. S. A. Guccione, et.al., *JBits: A Java-based Interface for Reconfigurable Computing*, 2nd Annual Military and Aerospace Applications of Programmable Devices and Technologies Conference (MAPLD), Laurel, Maryland, 1999.
9. M.B. Gokhale, J.M. Stone, *NAPA C: Compiling for a Hybrid RISC/FPGA Architecture*, IEEE FCCM, Napa Valley, CA, 1999.
10. R. Laufer, R. Reed Taylor, H. Schmit *PCI-PipeRench and SWORDAPI: A System for Stream-based Reconfigurable Computing*, IEEE FCCM, Napa Valley, CA, 1999.
11. Berkeley Brass Project, *SCORE: Stream Computations Organized for Reconfigurable Execution Fast Module Mapping and Placement for Datapaths in FPGAs*, http://www.cs.berkeley.edu/Research/Projects/brass/SCORE/
12. T.J. Callahan, J. Wawrzynek, *Instruction-Level Parallelism for Reconfigurable Computing*, FPL, Tallinn, Estonia, Aug-Sep 1998.
13. X. Lai, et. al., *Markov Ciphers and Differential Cryptanalysis*, EUROCRYPT '91, Lecture Notes in Computer Science 547, Springer-Verlag, 1991.
14. S. Rixner, et. al., *A Bandwidth-Efficient Architecture for Media Processing*, MICRO, Dallas, Nov. 1998.
15. C. Ebeling, et. al., *Mapping Applications to the RaPiD Configurable Architecture*, IEEE FCCM, Napa Valley, CA, 1997.
16. S. Bakshi, D.D. Gajski, *Partitioning and Pipelining for Performance-Constrained Hardware/Software Systems*, IEEE Transaction on VLSI Systems, Dec. 1999.
17. O. Mencer, M. Morf, M. Flynn, *Hardware Software Tri-Design of Encryption for Mobile Communication Units*, ICASSP, Seattle, May 1998.
18. O. Mencer, L. Séméria, M. Morf, J.M. Delosme, *Application of Reconfigurable CORDIC Architectures*, The Journal of VLSI Signal Processing, Special Issue: VLSI on Custom Computing Technology, Kluwer, March 2000.
19. O. Mencer, M. Platzner, *Dynamic Circuit Generation for Boolean Satisfiability in an Object-Oriented Design Environment*, HICSS (ConfigWare), Jan. 1999.
20. O. Mencer, *Rational Arithmetic Units in Computer Systems*, PhD Thesis (with M.J. Flynn), E.E. Dept., Stanford, March 2000.

Stream Computations Organized for Reconfigurable Execution (SCORE)
Extended Abstract

Eylon Caspi[1], Michael Chu[1], Randy Huang[1], Joseph Yeh[1],
John Wawrzynek[1], and André DeHon[2]

[1] University of California at Berkeley, Berkeley, CA 94720, USA,
http://www.cs.berkeley.edu/projects/brass/
[2] California Institute of Technology
Department of Computer Science, 256-80, Pasadena, CA 91125, USA
andre@acm.org

Abstract. A primary impediment to wide-spread exploitation of reconfigurable computing is the lack of a unifying computational model which allows application portability and longevity without sacrificing a substantial fraction of the raw capabilities. We introduce SCORE (Stream Computation Organized for Reconfigurable Execution), a stream-based compute model which virtualizes reconfigurable computing resources (compute, storage, and communication) by dividing a computation up into fixed-size "pages" and time-multiplexing the virtual pages on available physical hardware. Consequently, SCORE applications can scale up or down *automatically* to exploit a wide range of hardware sizes. We hypothesize that the SCORE model will ease development and deployment of reconfigurable applications and expand the range of applications which can benefit from reconfigurable execution. Further, we believe that a well engineered SCORE implementation can be efficient, wasting little of the capabilities of the raw hardware. In this abstract, we highlight the key components of the SCORE system.

1 Introduction

A large body of evidence exists documenting the raw advantages of reconfigurable hardware such as FPGAs over conventional microprocessor-based systems on selected applications. Yet reconfigurable computing remains in limited use, popular primarily in application-specific domains or as a replacement for ASICs for rapid prototyping and fast time-to-market. This limited popularity is not due to any lack of raw hardware capability, as million-gate devices are readily available [18] [1], and as we have seen recent advances in high clock rates [15], rapid reconfiguration [8] [6], and high-bandwidth memory access [10] [13]. Rather, we believe that the limited applicability of reconfigurable technology derives largely from the lack of any unifying compute model to abstract away the fixed resource limits of devices which otherwise restrict software expressiveness and longevity across device generations.

Existing targets are non-portable. Software for reconfigurable hardware is typically tied to a particular device (or set of devices), with limited source compatibility and no binary compatibility even across a vendor-specific family of devices. Redeploying a program to a bigger, next-generation device, or alternatively to a smaller, cheaper or lower-power device typically requires substantial human effort. At best, it requires a potentially expensive pass through mapping tools. At worst, it requires a significant rewrite to fully exploit new device features and sizes. In contrast, a program written for microprocessor systems can automatically run and benefit from additional resources on any ISA-compatible device, without recompilation.

Existing targets expose fixed resource limitations. The exposure of fixed resource limitations in existing programming models tends to impair their expressiveness and applicability. In such programming models, an application's choice of algorithm and spatial structure is restricted at compile time by the size of available hardware. The typical lack of dynamic resource allocation makes it difficult to express algorithms with data-dependent structure or potentially unbounded resource usage.

The SCORE compute model addresses the issue of fixed resource limits by virtualizing the computational, communication, and memory resources of reconfigurable hardware. FPGA configurations are partitioned into fixed-size, communicating pages that, in analogy to virtual memory, are "paged-in" or loaded into hardware on demand. Streaming communication between pages that are not simultaneously in hardware may be transparently buffered through memory. This scheme allows a partitioned program to run on arbitrarily-many physical pages and to automatically exploit more available physical pages without recompilation. With proper hardware design, this scheme permits binary compatibility and scalability across an architectural family of page-compatible devices.

Section 2 of this paper highlights other systems and compute models which have influenced the formulation of SCORE. Section 3 presents the key components of the SCORE model. Section 4 discusses the hardware requirements for a SCORE implementation and why they are reasonable in today's technology. Section 5 shows results from a JPEG encoder in SCORE as an example of our early experience implementing a SCORE system.

2 Related Work

By hand-partitioning a particular design (motion-wavelet video coder) into a graph of FPGA-sized "pages" and manually reconfiguring each device with those pages, Villasenor *et al.* [16] were able to run the design on one third as many devices (*i.e.* physical pages) as were originally required with only 10% performance overhead. The key to this approach's efficiency was to amortize the cost of reconfiguration by having each page process a sizable stream of data (buffered through memory) before reconfiguring. SCORE aims to automate the partitioning and efficient dynamic reconfiguration performed manually by Villasenor.

The ease and success of such automation depends on appropriate models for program description and dynamic reconfiguration. In this regard SCORE builds on prior art developing ISA, data flow, distributed, and streaming computation models. Owing to space limitations, this abstract cannot give proper credit to all of the influences.

The first attempts to define a "compute model" for reconfigurable computing devices were focussed on augmenting a traditional processor ISA with *reconfigurable instructions*. PRISC [14], Chimæra [7], GARP [8], and OneChip [10] provide different levels of functionality within an ISA model. They all have the limitation that the reconfigurable array configuration must be smaller than the available, physical logic, and that reconfigurable instructions must be composed sequentially in the ISA. Consequently, these architectures do not support transparently scaling array size and automatically exploiting the additional parallel hardware.

WASMII [12] and Brebner's SLUs [2] partition designs into page-like entities. However, in these models, inter-page communication is buffered through a small, *fixed* set of device registers. With such a small communication buffer, a page can operate for only a short time before depleting available inputs or output space and triggering reconfiguration. Hence when running a design which is larger than available hardware, execution time may be dominated by reconfiguration time. CMU's PipeRench [6] uses virtual *stripes* that communicate through input-output registers as in WASMII. PipeRench's stripe-sequential, pipelined reconfiguration scheme hides the excessive reconfiguration overhead seen in WASMII. This scheme may, however, waste available parallelism since it is limited to loading a single, fixed-width stripe's worth of configuration data on each cycle.

Traditional and hybrid data flow formulations [5] [4] expose more parallelism than control-flow ISAs. Nevertheless, these models have the same problem of fixed communication buffers as in WASMII. Streaming formulations of data flow remove the limitation of fixed input-output buffers, allowing arbitrarily many tokens to queue up along an arc of a data flow graph. Lee's synchronous data flow (SDF) [11] uses streaming for the restricted case of static flow rates, while Buck's integer-controlled data flow (IDF) [3] incorporates data-dependent control flow by adding to SDF a set of canonical dynamic-rate operators (*e.g. switch, select*). SCORE permits a dynamic-rate model with data-dependent control flow inside any operator. Once assembled, the expressiveness of SCORE program graphs is essentially equivalent to IDF.

In many ways, the SCORE computational model is similar to Hoare's Communicating Sequential Processes (CSP) [9]. Buffering between operators (processes) is implicit in the SCORE model, whereas it must be explicit in the CSP model. SCORE operators, unlike CSP processes, must be deterministic.

3 SCORE Compute Model

A compute model defines the computational semantics that a developer expects the hardware to provide. For convenience, the SCORE compute model is best viewed at two levels of abstraction. The *execution model* defines the run-time view of a SCORE computation, *i.e.* the run-time data structures that define a SCORE computation as well as how the hardware will dynamically interpret that description. The *programming model* provides a higher level view of SCORE application composition and execution, suitable for the programmer. It abstracts away some of the hardware size details visible in the execution model, focusing the programmer on algorithmic style and structure.

3.1 Execution Model

The key idea of a computer architecture is that it defines the computational description that a machine will run and the semantics for running it (*e.g.* the x86 ISA is a popular architectural definition for processors). Someone building a conforming device is then free to implement any detailed computer organization that reads and executes this computational description (*e.g.* i80286, i80386, i80486, Pentium, and K6 are all different implementations that run the same x86 computational description). Following this technique, the execution model for SCORE defines the run-time computational description for an architecture family and the semantics for executing this description.

The SCORE execution model defines all computation in terms of three key components:

- A *compute page* (CP) is a fixed-size block of reconfigurable logic which is the basic unit of virtualization and scheduling.
- A *memory segment* is a contiguous block of memory which is the basic unit for data page management.
- A *Stream link* is a logical connection between the output of one page (CP, segment, processor, or IO) and the input of another page. Stream implementations will be physically bounded, but the execution model provides a logically unbounded stream abstraction.

A computational description in this execution model is independent of the size of the reconfigurable array, admitting architectural implementations with anywhere from one to a large number of compute pages and memories. The model provides the semantics of an unlimited number of independently operating physical compute pages and memory segments. Compute pages and segments operate on stream data tagged with input presence and produce output data to streams in a similar manner. The use of data presence tags provides an operational semantics that is independent of the timing of any particular SCORE-compatible computing platform.

Hardware Virtualization Compute pages, segments, and streams are the fundamental units for allocation, virtualization, and management of the hardware resources. At run time, an operating system manager schedules virtual pages and streams onto the available physical resources, including page assignment and migration and inter-page routing.

If there are enough physical resources, every page of a computation graph may be simultaneously loaded on the reconfigurable hardware, enabling maximum-speed, *fully-spatial* computation. Figure 1 (top right) shows this case for the video processing operator shown on the left of the same figure. If hardware resources are limited, a computation graph will be time-multiplexed onto the hardware. Streams between virtual pages that are not simultaneously loaded will be transparently buffered through on-chip memory. Figure 1 (bottom right) shows this case for the video processing operator. Each component operator is loaded into hardware in sequence, taking its input from one memory buffer and producing its output to another.

3.2 Programming Model

A programming model gives the programmer a framework for describing a computation in a manner independent of device limits, along with guidelines for efficient execution on

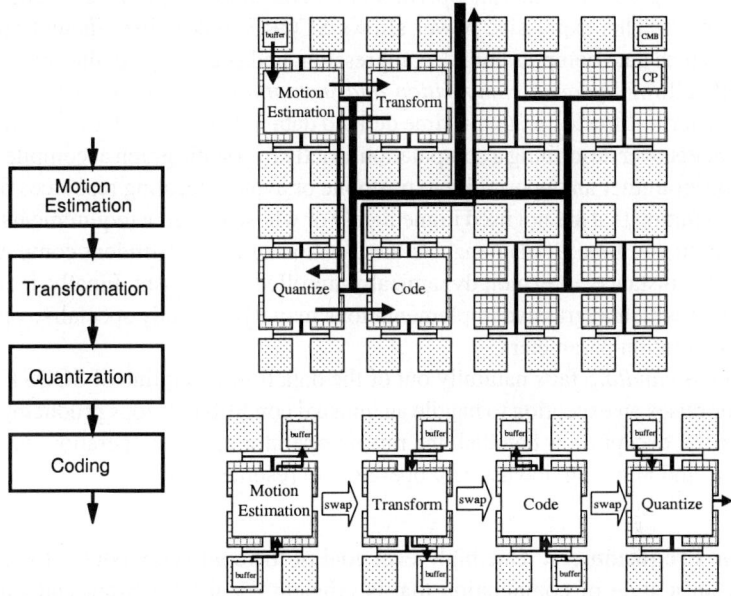

Fig. 1. Example computation (left) and implementation on different sized hardware (right)

any hardware implementation. A compiler is typically used to translate the abstracted, higher level description into the details needed for execution. The key abstractions and mechanisms of the SCORE programming model are *operators*, *streams*, and *memory segments*.

Basic Components. An *operator* represents a particular algorithmic transformation of input data to produce output data (*e.g.* multiplier, FIR filter, FFT). Operators may be behavioral primitives or hierarchical graph compositions of other operators. Figure 1 shows an example video processing operator composed from a *motion estimation* operator, an image *transformation* operator, a data *quantization* operator, and a *coding* operator. Operators are more abstract than compute pages in that their size is not fixed or limited.

Inter-operator communication uses a streaming data flow discipline, as in the execution model.

A *memory segment* is a contiguous block of memory, as in the execution model. Memory segments may be any size.[1] To use a memory segment, it is placed into a specific operating mode (*e.g.* FIFO, read-only, random read-write) and linked into a data flow graph in a compositional operator like any other operator.

Dynamic Features. On top of these basic components, SCORE supports a number of important dynamic features.

---

[1] The segment size will be limited by an architecturally defined maximum.

SCORE supports *dynamic rate operators* that consume and produce tokens at data-dependent rates. This expressive power allows SCORE to describe efficient operators for tasks such as data compression, decompression, and searching or filtering.

SCORE allows *dynamic composition and instantiation* wherein operators can be instantiated at run-time to create run-time defined data flow graphs. This mechanism has several benefits over describing a computation strictly by a static graph at compile time. It gives the programmer an opportunity to postpone or avoid allocating resources for parts of the computation that are not used immediately or whose resource requirements cannot be bound until run time. It also enables the creation of data-dependent computational structures, for instance, to exploit dynamically-unrolled parallelism. Finally, it creates a framework in which aggressive implementations may dynamically specialize operators around instantiation parameters.

Exception handling falls naturally out of the data flow discipline of SCORE. When an operator raises an exception to handle an unusual condition, it stops producing output data. Once the exception is handled, the raising operator resumes operation, producing output data, and allowing downstream operators to resume in turn.

Advice for Programmers. One high-level goal of the compute model is to focus the developer on a style of computation that is efficient for the hardware and execution model. To better utilize scalable reconfigurable hardware, SCORE developers should:

- *describe computations as spatial pipelines with multiple, independent computational paths.* A hardware implementation will attempt to concurrently execute as many of the specified, parallel paths as possible.
- *avoid or minimize feedback cycles.* Cyclic dependencies introduce delays that cannot be pipelined away and hence increase total run time or lead to page-thrashing in small hardware implementations.
- *expose large data streams to SCORE operators.* Large data sets help amortize the overhead of loading computation into reconfigurable hardware, especially with small, time-multiplexed hardware implementations.

4 Hardware Requirements

SCORE assumes a combination of a sequential processor and a reconfigurable device. The reconfigurable array must be divided into a number of equivalent and independent compute pages.[2] Multiple, distributed memory blocks are required to store intermediate data, page state, and page configurations.

The interconnect among pages is critical to achieving high performance and supporting run-time page placement. It should support high bandwidth, low latency communication among compute pages and memory, allowing memory pages to be used concurrently. The interconnect must buffer and pipeline data as well as provide back-pressure signals to stall upstream computation when network buffer capacity is exceeded. Routing resources should be sufficiently rich to facilitate rapid, online routing.

---

[2] In a degenerate case, there can be only one page, but this sacrifices many of the strengths of the SCORE model.

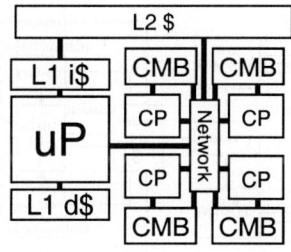

Fig. 2. Hypothetical, single-chip SCORE system

The compute pages themselves may use any reconfigurable fabric that supports rapid reconfiguration, with provision to save and restore array state quickly. The BRASS HSRA subarray design [15] is a feasible, concrete implementation for a compute page. It provides microsecond reconfiguration and high-speed, pipelined computation.

Each *configurable memory block* (CMB) is a self-contained unit with its own stream-based memory port and an address generator. CMBs may be accessed independently and concurrently in a scalable system. The memory fabric may use external RAM or on-chip memory banks (*e.g.* BRASS Embedded DRAM [13]), with additional logic to tie into the data flow synchronization used by the interconnect network. The memory controllers need to support a simple, paged segment model including address relocation within a memory block and segment bounds. Streaming data support obviates the need for external addressing during reconfiguration and stream buffering.

The sequential processor plays an important part in the SCORE system. It runs the page scheduler needed to virtualize computation on the array, and it executes SCORE operators that would not run efficiently in reconfigurable implementation. Consequently, the processor must be able to control and communicate with the array efficiently. A single-chip SCORE system (*e.g.* see Figure 2) integrating a processor, reconfigurable fabric, and memory blocks could provide tight, efficient coupling of components.

5 Example: JPEG Encode

We have implemented a complete SCORE runtime system and simulator on top of Linux and are developing several sample applications. As an early exercise and demonstration vehicle, we have implemented a complete JPEG (Joint Photographic Experts Group) image compression algorithm [17] in TDF[3] and C++ and have performed basic scaling experiments where we vary the number of computational pages in the system.

Application Figure 3 shows the data flow in our JPEG encoder implementation. The TDF implementation uses thirteen 512-LUT pages in order to realize a fully spatial JPEG compressor which is capable of processing one image sample per cycle. For smaller hardware, the SCORE scheduler automatically manages, at run time, the reconfiguration necessary to share the physical CPs among the thirteen virtual CPs.

---

[3] TDF is an experimental intermediate form for describing SCORE operators and their composition.

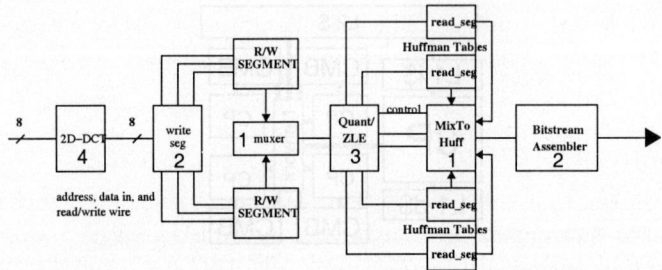

Fig. 3. JPEG Data Flow including Page and Segment Decomposition (large numbers on computational blocks indicate number of 512-LUT pages required)

System Assumptions For these experiments, we assume a single-chip system as described in Section 4 and external secondary memory. System parameters are based on our experience with the HSRA [15] and embedded DRAM memory [13] (Figure 4). Page decomposition is performed manually. The scheduler is list based and operates in a time-sliced fashion. The scheduler manages CP and segment placement, including reconfiguration and all data transfer on and off the component, including data segment swapping. We assume that scheduling time is overlapped with computation and takes 50,000 cycles. We do not currently model any limitations on routability among pages. The simulator accounts for all time required to reconfigure pages, store state, and transfer data among memories.

Results To study the scalability, performance, and efficiency of the SCORE system, we ran our JPEG implementation on a series of simulated, architecture-compatible SCORE systems with a varying number of compute pages. Figure 4 shows the results, plotting total runtime (makespan) versus the number of CPs used by the system. This shows that: (1) the problem can be automatically scheduled onto less hardware, realizing a reasonable area-time curve (CP-makespan); and, (2) the computation can often be time-multiplexed, automatically, onto less hardware than the original, fully spatial implementation without a large loss in overall performance.

Our present scheduler exhibits several anomalies. The shallowness of the CP-makespan curve for the unlimited memory experiment indicates a performance benefit from additional memory. This suggests that there may be benefit to increasing the memory-to-logic area balance, as well as to tuning the memory management code. The current CMB requirement is an artifact of our manual page decomposition and is something we hope to reduce with smarter, automatic page decomposition.

This experiment represents a single set of SCORE system parameters. As ongoing work, we are exploring many of the system parameters to gain insight into the regions of operation where SCORE scheduling is most robust, and to determine the parameters that provide the most efficient and balanced design.

Simulator Parameters	Value Assumed
Reconfiguration Time	5,000 cycles
Schedule Time Slice	250,000 cycles
Compute Page (CP) size	512 LUTs
Config. Mem. Block (CMB) size	2Mbits
External Memory Bandwidth	2GB/s

Fig. 4. JPEG CP vs. Makespan

6 Summary

Reconfigurable computation, defined simply as computation performed on a collection of FPGA or FPGA-like hardware, has shown remarkable promise on point applications but has not achieved wide-spread acceptance and usage. One must make a large commitment to a particular FPGA-based system to develop an application. Industry steadily produces newer, larger, and faster hardware. Unfortunately, without a unifying computational model that transcends the particular FPGA implementation on which the application is first developed, one is stuck redoing significant work to port the application to newer hardware. This is particularly onerous when the established, alternative technology, the microprocessor, offers users steady performance improvements with little or no time investment to adapt to new hardware.

Overcoming this liability requires a computational model that abstracts computational resources, allowing application performance to scale automatically, adapting to new hardware as it becomes available. The computational model must expose and exploit the strengths of reconfigurable hardware, help users understand how to optimize applications for reconfigurable execution, deal efficiently with dynamic and unbounded resource requirements and program characteristics, and support the efficient composition of solution components.

In this paper, we have introduced a particular computational model which attempts to address these needs. SCORE uses a paging model to virtualize all hardware resources including computation, storage, and communication. It allows dynamic instantiation of dynamically sized computational operators and supports dynamic rate applications. We have implemented a complete SCORE run-time system and simulator. Initial experiments suggest that we can achieve the desired scalability on sample applications. With this initial success, we are now attempting to broaden the range of applications, to automate more of the SCORE tool flow, and to systematically explore the design space for SCORE compatible architectures.

References

1. Altera Corporation, 2610 Orchard Parkway, San Jose, CA 95134-2020. *APEX Device Family*, March 1999. ¡http://www.altera.com/html/products/apex.html¿.
2. Gordon Brebner. The Swappable Logic Unit: a Paradigm for Virtual Hardware. In *Proceedings of the 5th IEEE Symposium on FPGAs for Custom Computing Machines (FCCM'97)*, pages 77–86, April 1997.
3. Joseph T. Buck. *Scheduling Dynamic Dataflow Graphs with Bounded Memory using the Token Flow Model*. PhD thesis, University of California, Berkeley, 1993. ERL Technical Report 93/69.
4. David E. Culler, Seth C. Goldstein, Klaus E. Schauser, and Thorsten von Eicken. TAM — A Compiler Controlled Threaded Abstract Machine. *Journal of Parallel and Distributed Computing*, June 1993.
5. Jack B. Dennis. Data Flow Supercomputers. *Computer*, 13:48–56, November 1980.
6. Seth C. Goldstein, Herman Schmit, Matthew Moe, Mihai Budiu, Srihari Cadambi, R. Reed Taylor, and Ronald Laufer. PipeRench: a Coprocessor for Streaming Multimedia Acceleration. In *Proceedings of the 26th International Symposium on Computer Architecture (ISCA'99)*, pages 28–39, May 1999.
7. Scott Hauck, Thomas Fry, Matthew Hosler, and Jeffery Kao. The Chimaera Reconfigurable Functional Unit. In *Proceedings of the IEEE Symposium on FPGAs for Custom Computing Machines*, pages 87–96, April 1997.
8. John R. Hauser and John Wawrzynek. Garp: A MIPS Processor with a Reconfigurable Coprocessor. In *Proceedings of the IEEE Symposium on Field-Programmable Gate Arrays for Custom Computing Machines*, pages 12–21. IEEE, April 1997.
9. C. A. R. Hoare. *Communicating Sequential Processes*. International Series in Computer Science. Prentice-Hall, 1985.
10. Jeffery A. Jacob and Paul Chow. Memory Interfacing and Instruction Specification for Reconfigurable Processors. In *Proceedings of the 1999 International Symposium on Field Programmable Gate Arrays (FPGA'99)*, pages 145–154, February 1999.
11. Edward A. Lee. *Advanced Topics in Dataflow Computing*, chapter Static Scheduling of Data-Flow Programs for DSP. Prentice Hall, 1991.
12. X. P. Ling and H. Amano. WASMII: a Data Driven Computer on a Virtual Hardware. In *Proceedings of the IEEE Workshop on FPGAs for Custom Computing Machines (FCCM'93)*, pages 33–42, April 1993.
13. Stylianos Perissakis, Yangsung Joo, Jinhong Ahn, André DeHon, and John Wawrzynek. Embedded DRAM for a Reconfigurable Array. In *Proceedings of the 1999 Symposium on VLSI Circuits*, June 1999.
14. Rahul Razdan and Michael D. Smith. A High-Performance Microarchitecture with Hardware-Programmable Functional Units. In *Proceedings of the 27th Annual International Symposium on Microarchitecture*, pages 172–180. IEEE Computer Society, November 1994.
15. William Tsu, Kip Macy, Atul Joshi, Randy Huang, Norman Walker, Tony Tung, Omid Rowhani, Varghese George, John Wawrzynek, and André DeHon. HSRA: High-Speed, Hierarchical Synchronous Reconfigurable Array. In *Proceedings of the International Symposium on Field Programmable Gate Arrays*, pages 125–134, February 1999.
16. John Villasenor, Chris Jones, and Brian Schoner. Video Communications using Rapidly Reconfigurable Hardware. *IEEE Transactions on Circuits and Systems for Video Technology*, 5:565–567, December 1995.
17. Gregory K. Wallace. The JPEG Still Picture Compression Standard. *Communications of the ACM*, 34(4):30–44, April 1991.
18. Xilinx, Inc., 2100 Logic Drive, San Jose, CA 95124. *Virtex Series FPGAs*, 1999. ¡http://www.xilinx.com/products/virtex.htm¿.

Memory Access Schemes for Configurable Processors

Holger Lange and Andreas Koch

Tech. Univ. Braunschweig (E.I.S.), Gaußstr. 11, D-38106 Braunschweig, Germany
lange,koch@eis.cs.tu-bs.de

Abstract. This work discusses the Memory Architecture for Reconfigurable Computers (MARC), a scalable, device-independent memory interface that supports both irregular (via configurable caches) and regular accesses (via pre-fetching stream buffers). By hiding specifics behind a consistent abstract interface, it is suitable as a target environment for automatic hardware compilation.

1 Introduction

Reconfigurable compute elements can achieve considerable performance gains over standard CPUs [1] [2] [3] [4]. In practice, these configurable elements are often combined with a conventional processor, which provides the control and I/O services that are implemented more efficiently in fixed logic. Recent single-chip architectures following this approach include NAPA [5], GARP [6], OneChip [7], OneChip98 [8], Triscend E5 [9], and Altera Excalibur [10]. Board-level configurable processors either include a dedicated CPU [11] [12] or rely on the host CPU for support [13] [14].

Design tools targeting one of these hybrid systems such as GarpCC [15], Nimble [16] or Napa-C [17] have to deal with software and hardware issues separately as well as with the creation of interfaces between these parts. On the software side, basic services such as I/O and memory management are often provided by an operating system of some kind. This can range from a full-scale general-purpose OS over more specialized real-time embedded OSes down to tiny kernels offering only a limited set of functions tailored to a very specific class of applications. Usually, a suitable OS is either readily available on the target platform, or can be ported to it with relative ease.

This level of support is unfortunately not present on the hardware side of the hybrid computer. Since no standard environment is available for even the most primitive tasks such as efficient memory access or communication with the host, the research and development of new design tools often requires considerable effort to provide a reliable environment into which the newly-created hardware can be embedded. This environment is sometimes called a *wrapper* around the custom datapath. It goes beyond a simple assignment of chip pads to memory pins. Instead, a structure of on-chip busses and access protocols to various resources (e.g., memory, the conventional processor, etc) must be defined and implemented.

In this paper, we present our work on the Memory Architecture for Reconfigurable Computers (MARC). It can act as a "hardware target" for a variety of hybrid compilers, analogously to a software target for conventional compilers. Before describing its specifics, we will justify our design decisions by giving a brief overview of current configurable architectures and showing the custom hardware architectures created by some hybrid compilers.

2 Hybrid Processors

Static and reconfigurable compute elements may be combined in many ways. The degree of integration can range from individual reconfigurable function units (e.g., OneChip [7]) to an entirely separate coprocessor attached to a peripheral bus (e.g., SPLASH [4], SPARXIL [18]).

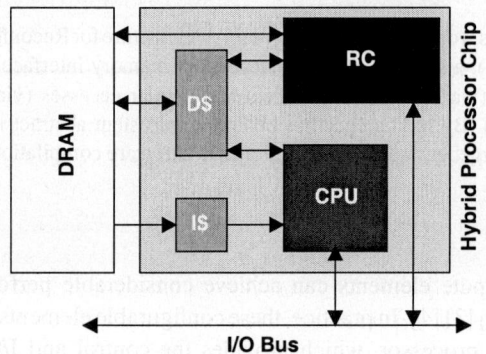

Figure 1. Single-chip hybrid processor

Figure 1 sketches the architecture of a single-chip hybrid processor that combines fixed (CPU) and reconfigurable (RC) compute units behind a common cache (D$). Such an architecture was proposed, e.g., for GARP [6] and NAPA [5]. It offers very high bandwidth, low latency, and cache coherency between the CPU and the RC when accessing the shared DRAM.

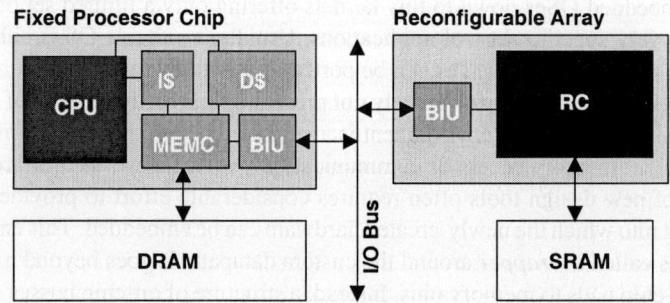

Figure 2. Hybrid processor emulated by multi-chip system

The board-level systems more common today use an architecture similar to Figure 2 . Here, a conventional CPU is attached by a bus interface unit (BIU) to a system-wide I/O bus (e.g., SBus [18] or PCI [11] [12]). Another BIU connects the RC to the I/O bus. Due to the high communication latencies over the I/O bus, the RC is often attached directly to a limited amount of dedicated memory (commonly a few KB to a few MB of

SRAM). In some systems, the RC has access to the main DRAM by using the I/O bus as a master to contact the CPU memory controller (MEMC). With this capability, the CPU and the RC are sharing a logically homogeneous address space: Pointers in the CPU main memory can be freely exchanged between software on the CPU and hardware in the RC.

Table 1 shows the latencies measured on [12] for the RC accessing data residing in local Zero-Bus Turnaround (ZBT) SRAM (latched in the FPGA I/O blocks) and in main DRAM (via the PCI bus). In both cases, one word per cycle is transferred after the initial latency.

Operation	Cycles
ZBT SRAM read	4
ZBT SRAM write	4
PCI read	46-47
PCI write	10

Table 1. Data access latencies (single word transfers)

It is obvious from these numbers that any useful wrapper must be able to deal efficiently with access to high latency memories. This problem, colloquially known as the "memory bottleneck", has already been tackled for conventional processors using memory hierarchies (multiple cache levels) combined with techniques such as pre-fetching and streaming to improve their performance. As we will see later, these approaches are also applicable to reconfigurable systems.

3 Reconfigurable Datapaths

The structure of the compute elements implemented on the RC is defined either manually or by automatic tools. A common architecture [6] [16] [18] is shown in Figure 3.

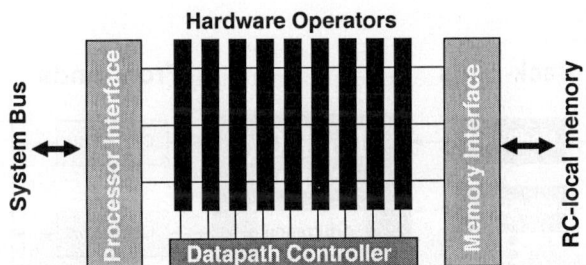

Figure 3. Common RC datapath architecture

The datapath is formed by a number of hardware operators, often created using module generators, which are placed in a regular fashion. While the linear placement shown in the figure is often used in practice, more complicated layouts are of course possible. All hardware operators are connected to a central datapath controller that orchestrates their execution.

In this paper, we focus on the interface blocks attaching the datapath to the rest of the system. They allow communication with the CPU and main memory using the system bus or access to the local RC RAM. The interface blocks themselves are accessed by the datapath using a structure of uni- and bidirectional busses that transfer data, addresses, and control information.

For manually implemented RC applications, the protocols used here are generally developed ad-hoc and heavily influenced by the specific hardware environment targeted. (e.g., the data sheets of the actual SRAM chips on a PCB). In practice, they may even vary between different applications running on the same hardware (e.g., usage of burst-modes, fixed access sizes etc.).

This approach is not applicable for automatic design flows: These tools require pre-defined access mechanisms to which they strictly adhere for all designs. An example for such a well-defined protocol suitable as a target for automatic compilation is employed on GARP [6], a single-chip hybrid processor architecture. It includes standardized protocols for sending and retrieving data to/from the RC using specialized CPU instructions and supported by dedicated decoding logic in silicon. Memory requests are routed over a single address and four data busses that can supply up to four words per cycle for regular (streaming) accesses.

None of these capabilities is available when using off-the-shelf silicon to implement the RC. Instead, each user is faced with implementing the required access infrastructure anew.

4 MARC

Our goal was to learn from these past experiences and develop a single, scalable, and portable memory interface scheme for reconfigurable datapaths. MARC strives to be applicable for both single-chip and board-level systems, and to hide the intricacies of different memory systems from the datapath. Figure 4 shows an overview of this architecture.

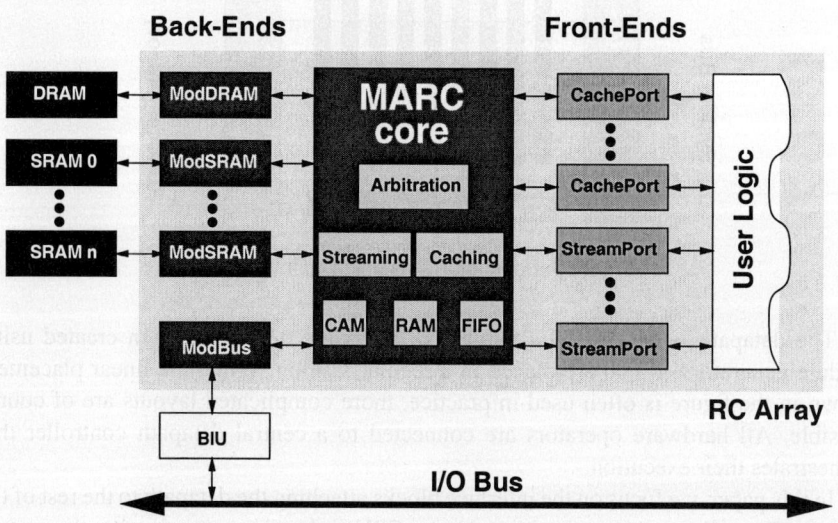

Figure 4. MARC architecture

Using MARC, the datapath accesses memory through abstract front-end interfaces. Currently, we support two front-ends specialized for different access patterns: Caching ports provide for efficient handling of irregular accesses. Streaming ports offer a non-unit stride access to regular data structures (such as matrices or images) and perform address generation automatically. In both cases, data is pre-fetched/cached to reduce the impact of high latencies (especially for transfers using the I/O bus). Both ports use stall signals to indicate delays in the data transfer (e.g., due to cache miss or stream queue refill). A byte-steering logic aligns 8- and 16-bit data on bits 7:0 and 15:0 of the data bus regardless of where the datum occurred in the 32-bit memory or bus words.

The specifics of hardware memory chips or system bus protocols are implemented in various back-end interfaces. E.g., dedicated back-ends encapsulate the mechanisms for accessing SRAM or communicating over the PCI bus using the BIU.

The MARC core is located between front- and back-ends, where it acts as the main controller and data switchboard. It performs address decoding and arbitration between transfer initiators in the datapath and transfer receivers in the individual memories and busses. Logically, it can map an arbitrary number of front-ends to an arbitrary number of back-ends. In practice, though, the number of resources managed is of course limited by the finite FPGA capacity. Furthermore, the probability of conflicts between initiators increases when they share a smaller number of back-ends. However, the behavior visible to the datapath remains identical: The heterogeneous hardware resources handled by the back-ends are mapped into a homogeneous address space and accessed by a common protocol.

4.1 Irregular Cached Access

Caching ports are set up to provide read data one cycle after an address has been applied, and accept one write datum/address per clock cycle. If this is not possible (e.g., a cache miss occurs), the stall signal is asserted for the affected port, stopping the initiator. When the stall signal is de-asserted, data that was "in-flight" due to a previous request will remain valid to allow the initiator to restart cleanly.

Table 3(a) describes the interface to a caching port. The architecture currently allows for 32-bit data ports, which is the size most relevant when compiling software into hybrid solutions. Should the need arise for wider words, the architecture can easily be extended.

Arbitrary memory ranges (e.g., memory-mapped I/O registers) can be marked as non-cacheable. Accesses to these regions will then bypass the cache. Furthermore, since all of the cache machinery is implemented in configurable logic, cache port characteristics such as number of cache lines and cache line length can be adapted to the needs of the application. As discussed in [19], this can result in a 3% to 10% speed-up over using a single cache configuration for all applications.

4.2 Regular Streamed Access

Streaming ports transfer a number of data words from or to a memory area without the need for the datapath to generate addresses. After setting the parameters of the transfer (by switching the port into a "load parameter" mode), the port presents/accepts one data item per clock cycle until it has to refill or flush its internal FIFOs. In that case, the stall

Table 2. Port interfaces

Signal	Kind	Function
Addr	in	Address.
Data	in/out	Data item.
Width	in	8, 16, 32-bit access.
Stall	out	Asserted on cache miss.
OE	in	Output enable
WE	in	Write enable
Flush	in	Flush cache.

(a) Caching port interface

Sig/Reg	Kind	Function
Addr	reg	Start address.
Stride	reg	Stride (increment).
Width	reg	8,16,32-bit access.
Block	reg	FIFO size.
Count	reg	Length, transfer.
R/W	reg	Read or write.
Data	i/o	Data item.
Stall	out	Wait, FIFO flush/refill.
Hold	in	Pause data flow.
EOS	out	End of stream reached.
Load	in	Accept new parameters.

(b) Streaming port interface

signal stops the initiator using the port. When the FIFO becomes ready again, the stall signal is de-asserted and the transfer continues. The datapath can pause the transfer by asserting the hold signal. As before, our current implementation calls for a 32-bit wide data bus. Table 3(b) lists the parameter registers and the port interface.

The 'Block' register plays a crucial role in matching the stream characteristics to the specific application requirements. E.g., if the application has to process a very large string (such as in DNA matching), it makes sense for the datapath to request a large block size. The longer start-up delay (for the buffer to be filled) is amortized over the long run-time of the algorithm. For smaller amounts of data (e.g., part of a matrix row for blocking matrix multiplication), it makes much more sense to pre-fetch only the precise amount of data required. [20] suggests compile-time algorithms to estimate the FIFO depth to use.

The cache is bypassed by the streaming ports in order to avoid cache pollution. However, since logic guaranteeing the consistency between caches and streams for arbitrary accesses would be very expensive to implement (especially when non-unit strided streams are used), our current design requires that accesses through the caching ports do not overlap streamed memory ranges. This restriction must be enforced by the compiler. If that is not possible, streaming ports cannot be used. As an alternative, a cache with longer cache lines (e.g., 128 bytes), might be used to limit the performance loss due to memory latency.

4.3 Multi-threading

Note that all stall or flow-control signals are generated/accepted on a per-port basis. This allows true multi-threaded hardware execution where different threads of control are assigned to different ports. MARC can accommodate more logical ports on the frontends than actually exist physically on the back-ends. For certain applications, this can be exploited to allow the compiler to schedule a larger number of memory accesses in parallel. The MARC core will resolve any inter-port conflicts (if they occur at all, see Section 5) at run-time. The current implementation uses a round-robin policy, later versions might extend this to a priority-based scheme.

4.4 Flexibility

A separate back-end is used for each memory or bus resource. For example, in a system with four ZBT SRAM memories, four instances of the ZBT SRAM back-end would be instantiated. The back-ends present the same interface as a caching port (Table 3(a)) to the MARC core. They encapsulate the state and access mechanisms to manage each of the physical resources. E.g., a PCI backend might know how to access a PCI BIU and initiate a data transfer.

In this manner, additional back-ends handling more memory banks can be attached easily. Analogously, MARC can be adapted to different FPGA technologies. For example, on the Xilinx Virtex [24] series of FPGA, the L1 cache of a caching port might be implemented using the on-chip memories. On the older XC4000XL series, which has only a limited amount of on-chip storage, the cache could be implemented in a direct-mapped fashion that has the cache lines placed in external memory.

5 Implementation Issues

Our first MARC implementation is targeting the prototyping environment described in [12]. The architecture details relevant for this paper are show in Figure 5 .

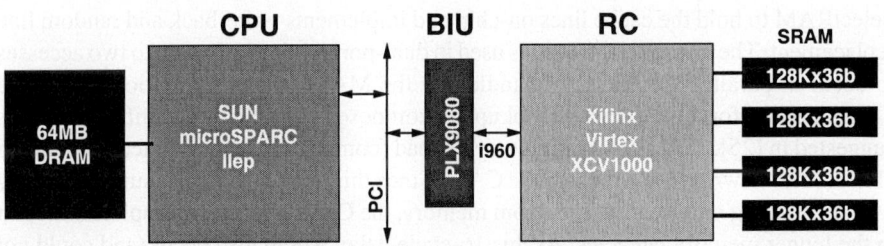

Figure 5. Architecture of prototype hardware

A SUN microSPARC-IIep RISC [21] [22] is employed as conventional CPU. The RC is composed of a Xilinx Virtex XCV1000 FPGA [24].

5.1 Status

At this point, we have implemented and intensively simulated a parameterized Verilog model of the MARC Core and back-ends. On the front-end side, caching ports are already operational, while streaming ports are still under development. The design is currently only partially floorplanned, thus the given performance numbers are preliminary.

5.2 Physical Resources

The RC has four 128Kx36b banks of ZBT SRAM as dedicated memory and can access the main memory (64MB DRAM managed by the CPU) over the PCI bus. To this end, a PLX 9080 PCI Accelerator [23] is used as BIU that translates the RC bus (i960-like) into PCI and back. The MARC core will thus need PLX and ZBT SRAM back-ends. All of their instances can operate in parallel.

5.3 MARC Core

The implementation follows the architecture described in Section 4 : An arbitrary number of caching and streaming ports can be managed. In this implementation (internally relying on the Virtex memories in dual-ported mode), two cache ports are guaranteed to operate without conflicts, and three to four cache ports may operate without conflicts. If five or more cache ports are in use, a conflict will occur and be resolved by the Arbitration unit (Section 4.3). This version of the core currently supports a 24-bit address space into which the physical resources are mapped.

5.4 Configurable Cache

We currently provide three cache configurations: 128 lines of 8 words, 64 lines of 16 words, or 32 lines of 32 words. Non-cacheable areas may be configured at compile time (the required comparators are then synthesized directly into specialized logic). The datapath can explicitly request a cache flush at any time (e.g., after the end of a computation).

The cache is implemented as a fully associative L1 cache. It uses 4KB of Virtex Block-SelectRAM to hold the cache lines on-chip and implements write-back and random line replacement. The BlockSelectRAM is used in dual-port mode to allow up to two accesses to occur in parallel. Conflicts are handled by the MARC Core Arbitration logic. The CAMs needed for the associative lookup are composed from SRL16E shift registers as suggested in [25]. This allows a single-cycle read (compare and match detection) and 16 clock cycles to write a new tag into the CAM. Since this operation occurs simultaneously with the loading of the cache lines from memory, the CAM latency is completely hidden in the longer memory latencies. As this 16-cycle delay would also occur (and could not be hidden) when reading the tag, e.g., when writing back a dirty cache line, the tags are additionally stored in a conventional memory composed from RAM32x1S elements that allow single-cycle reading.

For each caching port, a dedicated CAM bank is used to allow lookups to occur in parallel. Each cache line requires 5 4-bit CAMs, thus the per-port CAM area requirements range from 160 to 640 4-LUTs. In addition to the CAMs, each cache port includes a small state-machine controlling the cache operation for different scenarios (e.g., read hit, read miss, write hit, write miss, flush, etc.). The miss penalty c_m in cycles for a clean cache line is given by

$$c_m = 7 + c_{be} + w + 4,$$

where c_{be} is the data transfer latency for the back-end used (Table 1) and w is the number of 32-bit words per cache line. 7 and 4 are the MARC Core operation startup and shutdown times in cycles, respectively. For a dirty cache line, an additional w cycles are required to write the modified data back.

For comparison with [19], note that according to [26], the performance of 4KB of fully-associative cache is equivalent to that of 8KB of direct-mapped cache.

5.5 Performance and Area

The performance and area requirements of MARC Core, the technology modules and two cache ports are shown in Table 3.

Table 3. Performance and area requirements

Configuration	4LUTs	FFs	RAM32X1Ss	BlockRAMs	Clock
32x32	2844	976	12	8	31 MHz
64x16	4182	1038	26	8	30 MHz
128x8	7132	1531	56	8	29 MHz
XCV1000 avail.	24576	24576	(each uses 2 4LUTs)	32	—

For the three configuration choices, the area requirements vary between 10%-30% of the chip logic capacity. Since all configurations use 4KB of on-chip memory for cache line storage, 8 of the 32 512x8b BlockSelectRAMs are required.

5.6 Scalability and Extensibility

As shown in Table 3, scaling an L1 on-chip above 128x8 is probably not a wise choice given the growing area requirements. However, as already mentioned in Section 4.4, part of the ZBT SRAM could be used to hold the cache lines of a direct mapped L2 cache. In this scenario, only the tags would be held inside of the FPGA.

A sample cache organization for this approach could partition the 24-bit address into a 8-bit tag, 12-bit index and 4-bit block offset. The required tag RAM would be organized as 4096x8b, and would thus require 8 BlockSelectRAMs (in addition to those used for the on-chip L1 cache). The cache would have 4096 lines of 16 words each, and would thus require 64K words of the 128K words available in one of the ZBT SRAM chips. The cache hit/miss determination could occur in two cycles, with the data arriving after another two cycles. A miss going to PCI memory would take 66 cycles to refill a clean cache line and deliver the data to the initiator.

6 Related Work

[19] gives experimental result for the cache-dependent performance behavior of 6 of the 8 benchmarks in the SPECint95 suite. Due to the *temporal configurability* we suggest for the MARC caches (adapting cache parameters to applications), they expect a performance improvement between 3% to 10% over static caches. [27] describes the use of the

configurable logic in a hybrid processor to either add a victim cache or pre-fetch buffers to an existing dedicated direct-mapped L1 cache on an per-application basis. They quote improvements in L1 miss rate of up to 19%. [28] discusses the addition of 1MB of L1 cache memory managed by a dedicated cache controller to a configurable processor. Another approach proposed in [29] re-maps non-contiguous strided physical addresses into contiguous cache line entries. A similar functionality is provided in MARC by the pre-fetching of data into the FIFOs of streaming ports. [30] suggests a scheme which adds configurable logic to a cache instead of a cache to configurable logic. They hope to avoid the memory bottleneck by putting processing (the configurable logic) very close to the data. The farthest step with regard to data pre-fetching is suggested in [31], which describes a memory system that is cognizant of high-level memory access patterns. E.g., once a certain member in a structure is accessed, a set of associated members is fetched automatically. However, the automatic generation of the required logic from conventional software is not discussed. On the subject of streaming accesses, [20] is an exhaustive source. The 'Block' register of our streaming ports was motivated by their discussion of overly long startup times for large amounts of pre-fetched data.

7 Summary

We presented an overview of hybrid processor architectures and some memory access needs often occurring in applications. For the most commonly used RC components (off-the-shelf FPGAs), we identified a lack of support for even the most basic of these requirements.

As a solution, we propose a general-purpose Memory Architecture for Reconfigurable Computers that allows device-independent access both for regular (streamed) and irregular (cached) patterns. We discussed one real-world implementation of MARC on an emulated hybrid processor combining a SPARC CPU with a Virtex FPGA. The sample implementation fully supports multi-threaded access to multiple memory banks as well as the creation of "virtual" memory ports attached to on-chip cache memory. The configurable caches in the current version can reduce the latency from 46 cycles (for access to DRAM via PCI) down to a single cycle on a cache hit.

References

1. Amerson, R., "Teramac – Configurable Custom Computing", *Proc. IEEE Symp. on FCCMs*, Napa 1995
2. Bertin, P., Roncin, D., Vuillemin, J., "Programmable Active Memories: A Performance Assessment", *Proc. Symp. Research on Integrated Systems*, Cambridge (Mass.) 1993
3. Box, B., "Field-Programmable Gate Array-based Reconfigurable Preprocessor", *Proc. IEEE Symp. on FCCMs*, Napa 1994
4. Buell, D., Arnold, J., Kleinfelder, W., "Splash 2 – FPGAs in Custom Computing Machines", *IEEE Press*, 1996
5. Rupp, C., Landguth, M., Garverick, et al., "The NAPA Adaptive Processing Architecture", *Proc. IEEE Symp. on FCCMs*, Napa 1998
6. Hauser, J., Wawrzynek, J., "Garp: A MIPS Processor with a Reconfigurable Coprocessor", *Proc. IEEE Symp. on FCCMs*, Napa 1997

7. Wittig, R., Chow, P., "OneChip: An FPGA Processor with Reconfigurable Logic", *Proc. IEEE Symp. on FCCMs*, Napa 1996
8. Jacob, J., Chow, P., "Memory Interfacing and Instruction Specification for Reconfigurable Processors", *Proc. ACM Intl. Symp. on FPGAs*, Monterey 1999
9. Triscend, "Triscend E5 CSoC Family", http://www.triscend.com/products/IndexE5.html, 2000
10. Altera, "Excalibur Embedded Processor Solutions", http://www.altera.com/html/products/excalibur.html, 2000
11. TSI-Telsys, "ACE2card User's Manual", *hardware documentation*, 1998
12. Koch, A., "A Comprehensive Platform for Hardware-Software Co-Design", *Proc. Intl. Workshop on Rapid-Systems Prototyping*, Paris 2000
13. Annapolis Microsystems, http://www.annapmicro.com, 2000
14. Virtual Computer Corp., http://www.vcc.com, 2000
15. Callahan, T., Hauser, J.R., Wawrzynek, J., "The Garp Architecture and C Compiler", *IEEE Computer*, April 2000
16. Li, Y., Callahan, T., Darnell, E., Harr, R., et al., "Hardware-Software Co-Design of Embedded Reconfigurable Architectures", *Proc. 37th Design Automation Conference*, 2000
17. Gokhale, M.B., Stone, J.M., "NAPA C: Compiling for a Hybrid RISC/FPGA Machine", *Proc. IEEE Symp. on FCCMs*, 1998
18. Koch, A., Golze, U., "Practical Experiences with the SPARXIL Co-Processor", *Proc. Asilomar Conference on Signals, Systems, and Computers*, 11/1997
19. Fung, J.M.L.F., Pan, J., "Configurable Cache", *CMU EE742 course project*, http://www.ece.cmu.edu/ ee742/proj-s98/fung, 1998
20. McKee, S.A., "Maximizing Bandwidth for Streamed Computations", *dissertation*, U. of Virginia, School of Engineering and Applied Science, 1995
21. Sun Microelectronics, "microSPARC-IIep User's Manual", http://www.sun.com/sparc, 1997
22. Weaver, D.L., Germond, T., "The SPARC Architecture Manual, Version 8", Prentice-Hall, 1992
23. PLX Technology, "PCI 9080 Data Book", http://www.plxtech.com, 1998
24. Xilinx, Inc., "Virtex 2.5V Field-Programmable Gate Arrays", http://www.xilinx.com, 1999
25. Xilinx, Inc. "Designing Flexible, Fast CAMs with Virtex Family FPGAs", *Xilinx Application Note 203*, 1999
26. Hennessy, J., Patterson, D., "Computer Architecture: A Quantitative Approach", *Morgan-Kaumann*, 1990
27. Zhong, P., Martonosi, M., "Using Reconfigurable Hardware to Customize Memory Hierarchies", *Proc. SPIE, vol. 2914*, 1996
28. Kimura, S., Yukishita, M., Itou, Y., et al., "A Hardware/Software Codesign Method for a General-Purpose Reconfigurable Co-Processor", *Proc. 5th CODES/CASHE*, 1997
29. Carter, J., Hsieh, W., Stoller, L., et al., "Impulse: Building a Smarter Memory Controller", *Proc. 5th Intl. Symp. on High. Perf. Comp. Arch. (HPCA)*, 1999
30. Nakkar. M., Harding, J., Schwartz, D., et al., "Dynamically programmable cache", *Proc. SPIE, vol. 3526*, 1998
31. Zhang, X., Dasdan, A., Schulz, M., et al., "Architectural Adaptation for Application-Specific Locality Optimizations", *Proc. Intl. Conf. on Comp. Design (ICCD)*, 1997

Generating Addresses for Multi-dimensional Array Access in FPGA On-chip Memory

A.C. Döring and G. Lustig

Medizinische Universität zu Lübeck
Institut für Technische Informatik
Ratzeburger Allee 160
23538 Lübeck, Germany
{doering,lustig}@iti.mu-luebeck.de

Abstract. Multidimensional arrays are among the most common data types. Their use in configurable hardware requires the injective translation of the index tuple into a memory address. This problem is considered in the paper, searching for a balance between speed and waste of memory. The basic idea is to divide one of the index ranges such that one part is a power of two. In this way the indices can be concatenated with fewer loss. To combine both resulting parts into one memory, several techniques are used.
The integration of the proposed method into libraries and tools allows efficient description of algorithms on a higher abstraction level.

1 Introduction

The tremendous growth in density and speed of programmable logic devices opens new application areas for configurable hardware. Algorithms can be much more complex and larger data volumes can be processed. For an efficient use of the capabilities of these devices a high data rate is implied. Since the number of pins and the clock frequency on the pins is limited, bandwidth at the chip boundary is expensive and thus some data structures have to be stored in on-chip memory. Consequently, many newer families of high-end programmable logic devices include dedicated memory blocks [9, 2, 1]. These blocks are distributed over the device and can be used independently allowing a high internal data rate. Recent research [8] has concentrated on optimal routing and appropriate dimensions of the memory. All models and devices share the assumption that the number of memory words is a power of 2 and furthermore that the memory is accessed with a binary address.

Typical advanced algorithms use complex data structures like trees or multi-dimensional arrays. Hence, these data structures have to be organized in the on-chip memory blocks. The problem of accessing such data structures is essentially a problem of access scheduling and generating the right address. The latter problem can be manifold. Incremental accesses are typically easier than random ones. A powerful reconfigurable architecture for regular successive accesses is given in [4].

Random access pattern require the fast generation of the right memory address directly from the array identification and the indices. For the problem of merging several arrays into one memory, [6] proposes an elegant solution requiring only a permutation of index bits and possibly an inverter and a multiplexer. However, only VLSI systems without configurability were intended. By the simplicity of the approach in most cases only the multiplexer remains: the permutation represents just a different routing and the inversion can be integrated into the logic cell generating the address bit.

The problem of configurable address generation from several indices for multi-dimensional array access has not been covered so far. This work introduces techniques which can be combined with the memory itself in future programmable logic device families or can be applied in existing devices with some loss in speed. They could be included as library elements (macros) in current tools while future tools can synthesize multidimensional arrays directly this way. By permitting some unused memory positions, the presented techniques preserve the high speed of on-chip memory while requiring only a small amount of logic.

Emphasis is put on space-speed relations rather than synthesis algorithms. The paper is organized as follows. In the next section the problem is defined in detail and initial observations as well as an example are given. In the third section several methods for index generation are presented along with corresponding architectures.

2 Addresses for Multidimensional Arrays

Algorithms in hardware (ASIC or FPGA) are similar to those implemented in software. Hence, the same type of data structures can be found in both worlds. One of the most important data types are multi-dimensional arrays. Examples for their use are dynamic programming techniques or handling of objects with a geometric relationship like 2D or 3D images. In a multidimensional array data objects are identified by a tuple $\mathbf{i} = (i_1, \ldots, i_k)$ of indices. Different tuples refer to different objects, i.e. memory cells.

Continuous index ranges i.e. $i_j \in \{0, \ldots, D_j - 1\}$ are very frequent, hence most programming languages only allow the use of arrays in this way. Here, only continuous arrays are considered. D_j is the number of elements for the jth index. In consequence, the problem is stated as follows:

Definition 1. *A k-ary indexing function f is an injective function from*

$$\{0, \ldots, D_1 - 1\} \times \ldots \times \{0, \ldots, D_k - 1\}$$

into $\{0, \ldots, S-1\}$. *The number of unused memory locations* $L(f) = S - \prod_{j=1}^{k} D_j$ *is called loss.*

S is the required memory size. Note that, only the generation of the address and not the access of the memory is defined.

In software, compilers translate the array access into the generation of a memory address. This translation typically uses a linear combination with constant coefficients a_j:

$$m_i = a_0 + \sum_{j=1}^{k} i_j * a_j$$

While in software implementations an absolute offset (start address) a_0 is needed, the distinct memory blocks in a chip can be independently accessed starting with address 0.

For the design of an ASIC optimizing the indexing function is in most cases the wrong way. Any method (like concatenation) can be used and afterwards the decoder for activating the word lines can be reduced to those memory lines actually used. Hence, in the following configurable implementations are emphasized.

Obviously, the linear combination from software is optimal (allows loss $L = 0$) with the following coefficients:
$a_0 = 0$ and $a_i = \prod_{j=1}^{i-1} D_j$ for $i \in \{0, \ldots, k\}$.

However the implementation of several circuits for multiplication with constants is costly. For larger indices use of the Chinese remainder theorem(see [5]) allows the reduction of the size of the individual multipliers. Such a circuit would still be slower than the memory access itself.

In contrast to the multiplication techniques, concatenation represents an implementation without any delay but with a high loss. It can be regarded as linear combination too. Let $B_j = 2^{\lceil \log_2 D_j \rceil}$ be the smallest power of 2 larger than D_j. If D_j is replaced by B_j in the coefficient computation injectivity is not destroyed and only multiplications by powers of two occur. These multiplications can be neglected as they only determine the routing of signals to the memory address pins. The loss of this method is
$\sum_{i=1}^{k}(D_i - 1) \prod_{j=1}^{i-1} B_j + 1 - \prod_{i=1}^{k} D_i$.

In the worst case (D_j is just a power of two plus 1) it is nearly 2^{k-1}.

It is sufficient to investigate the case $k = 2$ because higher dimensions can be treated by tree-like nesting 2-ary functions.

If one index has an even range, its lowest bit can be extracted and fed directly to the memory address. Assume $D_1 = 2 * D_1'$ and f be an indexing function for $\{0, \ldots D_1' - 1\} \times \{0, \ldots D_2 - 1\}$. Then $2 * f(i_1/2, i_2) + (i_1 \mod 2)$ is an indexing function for indices with D_1 and D_2 values. This resulting function has the same affort as f. Consequently all factors of 2 in the D_j can be eliminated. Thus, only odd values of D_j are of interest.

Hence, in the following indexing functions with 2 arguments and an odd range are considered. For brevity the range of the indexing function is given by "$D_1 \times D_2$".

The following example is a proposal from a news group discussion of the topic [3]. It illustrates the low effort for the methods discussed in this paper. Especially it shows that the reduction to odd ranges saves hardware.

$D_1 = 24, D_2 = 20$

$$f(i_1, i_2) = \begin{cases} 384 + 4 * i_1 + (i_2 \mod 4) & \text{if } i_2 > 15 \\ 16 * i_1 + (i_2 \mod 16) & \text{if } i_2 < 16 \end{cases}$$

It is illustrated in figure 1. The dashed rectangle spans the original array. After partitioning a new rectangle results with one power-of-two side length.

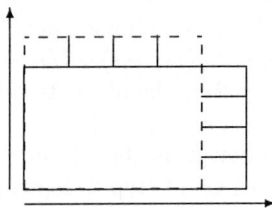

Fig. 1. Illustration of the example index function

In total two OR gates and five 2-to-1 multiplexers are needed. The datails (adress bit inversion) will be shown in the next section. Cancelling powers of two, the problem 24×20 is identical to the 3×5 problem. Using the same technique as in the example, two OR gates and two multiplexers suffice. For this example the loss is 0.

3 2-ary Indexing Functions

In the following it is assumed that both indices are odd and larger than one. In consequence, $B_j/2 < D_j < B_j$. The number R_j resulting by stripping the highest one in the binary representation of D_j is the remainder: $R_j = D_j - B_j/2$. It is clear that the whole index range can be divided into the regions $D_1 \times B_2/2$ and $D_1 \times R_2$. The separation is easy because only the highest address bit of i_2 has to be tested. Both present another instance of the index generation problem. However, the address generation for the first partition is straight forward since one index is a power of two. If there were an efficient solution for the second partition, the methods from [6] or addition can be applied to combine both parts.

Using concatenation for the second partition is a promising option since the second index range is much smaller compared to the original problem and in consequence the loss is smaller, too. For instance, the example from the previous section can be regarded as concatenation together with bit inversion [6].

Altogether the solution of a given indexing problem can be done with the following decisions:

1. how many and which partitions are done, and
2. which method is used for each partition to combine the parts into one address space.

A partition is always done at a power of two such that the address for one part can be done by concatenation without loss. The indices of the other part have odd ranges. Finally, either concatenation is used or one of the ranges has been reduced to just one element, eliminating the need for index combination. The total loss has two sources: the loss of the concatenation and the loss of the method for uniting the parts.

If two indices are combined by concatenation there are two options with respect to the sequence. If index i_1 gets higher significance, i.e. is put in front of i_2, the highest resulting value is $B_2(D_1 - 1) + (D_2 - 1)$; otherwise it is $B_1(D_2 - 1) + (D_1 - 1)$. Since $D_j < B_j < 2D_j$ the absolute difference between the loss in both cases is less than $D_1 D_2 + \max(D_1, D_2)$.

As techniques for array union from [6] rely on the possible increase of one or both index ranges, the decisions of step 2 depend on each other. The use of a technique with less loss on a lower level may or may not lead to a low loss on a higher level in total. For practical important address ranges the number of partitions is small so the elaboration of an optimal solution is computationally feasible.

At this point it is necessary to give a short review of the techniques presented in [6]. Their aim is to avoid additions. Clearly, addition is the most convenient method for combining two arrays into one address space. The argument for avoiding addition is speed: an adder takes as much time as the memory access itself in some target architectures. Hence, in the following these methods are called 'adder-less'.

The basic approach is to provide several methods which allow the combination of two arrays into one memory without loss. They can only be applied for certain size combinations. Other combinations need the increase of one or both indices. There are three different methods with different conditions for their applicability. All three methods rely on a multiplexer that feeds the address generated from the corresponding index to the output. The correctness is proven in [7].

The following table gives a summary. Two one-dimensional arrays with indices m and n respectively and ranges $\{0, \ldots, M-1\}$, $\{0, \ldots, N-1\}$ have to be combined into one array of size $M + N$. $\wedge$ denotes logical AND, $\oplus$ exclusive OR, period . concatenation of bit vectors, $/, \%$ integer division and remainder, and x_i is the i-th bit of x in binary presentation.

Name	1st address	2nd address	condition
Banking	$m.0$	$n.1$	$M = N$ or $M - 1 = N$
Address Bit Inversion 1	$m \oplus N$	$n \oplus M$	$M \wedge N = 0$
Address Bit Inversion 2	$m \oplus N$	$n \oplus (M - 1)$	$(M - 1) \wedge N = 0$
Address Bit Inversion 3	$m \oplus (N - 1)$	$n \oplus M$	$M \wedge (N - 1) = 0$
Rotation and Inversion	$m_y.m_x.\cdots.m_{y+1}.m_{y-1}.\cdots.m_0$	$n \oplus (2^x - 1)$	$(M/2^{y+1})2^y + \min(2^y, M\%2^{y+1}) + N = 2^x$

As shown, there are many options with different conditions. Therefore, as reported in [6], for small sizes only a minimal increase is necessary to fulfill one of them. For the problem discussed here the sizes M and N result from the concatenation (at the lowest level) or a combination from lower levels and from one partition which is the product of a power of two and one index range. Hence, most of them are derived directly from the given indices and do not have a special form.

Since the loss for some cases with the adder-less method is quite high, it may be worth trading depth for speed by using an adder. This trade-off can be tuned by choosing an appropriate size for the adder. All adders occurring have only a small length, determined by the maximal possible memory depth. For a Virtex-type FPGA this is 4K, hence maximum 12 Bit. As in FPGAs ripple-carry adders dominate for this size, delay grows linearly with adder length. Using an adder with a shorter length than the occurring values requires rounding up the increment.

Formally, assume two arrays of size M and N and indices m and n respectively shall be united by addition with restricted length l. Hence, the address m or n for one access is unchanged and the other is incremented by the upper bound of the former index into $m + N$ or $n + M$ respectively. Let us assume the second way (m and $n + M$). If $l < \log_2(M + N)$ the full addition $n + M$ can not be performed. In consequence M has to be replaced by a number M' such that the lower $k := \lceil \log_2(M + N) \rceil - l$ bits are zero. The expression $n + M' = (M'/2^k + b/2^k).b\%2^k$ results from concatenating the l bits from the sum of the topmost bits of n and M' and the lower bits of n. The loss of this method results from the rounding of M to M'. Obviously, this technique also increases the possible index range for one of the two arrays. Which of the two arrays gets the lower address can be chosen in a way to reduce the loss, i.e. if $M' - M$ or $N' - N$ is smaller. It may be added that the addition does not need to be left adjusted. In some cases no carries can occur in the top bits of the addition. This can be observed especially if the array sizes differ strongly. This allows the reduction of the rounding because the addition can start with lower bits.

4 Evaluation

In this section the proposed methods are rated. Focus is the achievement of a low loss. The speed and cost (in terms of gate/look-up-table count) are less dependent on the array ranges but rather on the method applied. Most of these facts are therefore straight-forward. Throughout this section index range combinations are investigated where both indices are odd and smaller than 128. This scope is motivated by the typical size of on-chip memories.

In the first place it is interesting to see in which cases there is no loss at all. This is shown on the left hand side of Figure 2. The absence of loss implies that there is neither a loss by concatenation nor by combination of the parts. The first fact reduces the investigated cases to those situations where one index is the sum of two powers of two. Since it was demanded that the indices shall be odd, only cases where one index is a power of two plus one can occur. Certainly, the

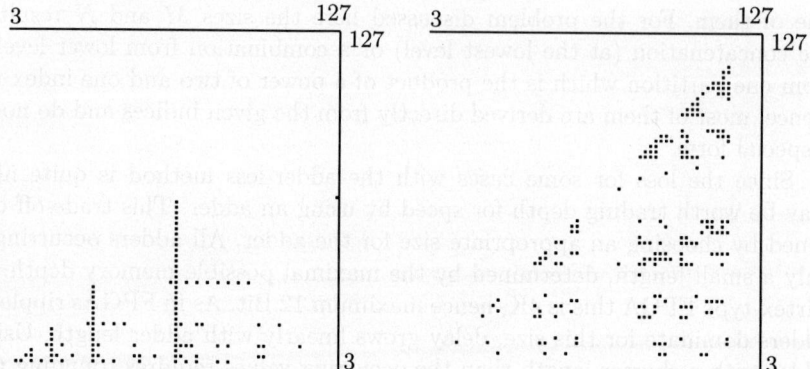

Fig. 2. Combinations without loss (left) and less then 10% loss (right) with adder-less methods

second condition is not satisfied in all these cases. Beside it those combinations where the loss is larger than 10% are shown. It can be seen that this is only a small fraction: 42 out of 2016 cases fall in this range. Only one case has a loss of about 20% (Figure 3 left).

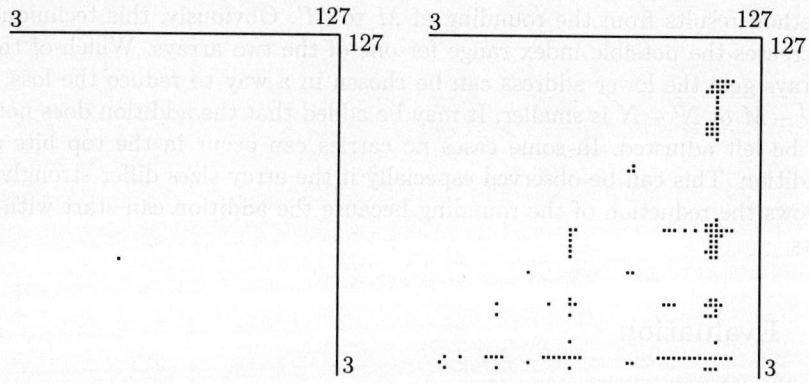

Fig. 3. Cases with more than 20% loss without adders (left), cases where a 3-bit adder is better than the adder-less methods (right)

To investigate the influence of structure, the case 43 × 43 is considered in more detail. It represents the worst one among all those which were investigated ($D_i < 128$, D_i odd). This is no surprise since this case is near $\sqrt{2} \cdot 32$. The other cases near this number and near $\sqrt{2} \cdot 64$ namely 45 × 45, 87 × 87 and 89 × 89 have a high loss, too. Besides this difficulty, they are of special interest since their good treatment can decide a factor of two of memory usage, if memory depth is available in powers of two only.

The adder-less solution with one multiplexer requires 2219 elements, though only $43 \cdot 43 = 1849$ places are used. The index space is divided into two segments of 32×43 and 11×43. Concatenation for the second part requires 683 memory cells implying a loss of 210. The combination with the (loss-less) part 32×43 with 1376 cells without adder results in another loss of 160. Using an adder of 4 or 6 bits length (in contrast to the 7 bits nominally required) reduces the second loss to 32 and 0 by rounding up to 704 and 688 respectively. The binary representation of $681 = 1010101011_2$ shows, why reduction is only achieved in steps of two bits for the adder.

Since the larger portion of the loss is due to the concatenation of the second part another concatenation step is suggesting. Dividing the second part into 8×43 and 3×43 results in a loss of 42 while the alternative cut into 11×32 and 11×11 has a lost of 50. Hence, the fact that another partition is made has a superior influence than its choice. Combining these three parts results in a total loss of 114.

An overview impression for the relative merits of the use of limited-length adders is given in Figure 3, right. It shows for which cases the application of a 3-bit adder saves loss in comparison to the adder-less methods with one partition step.

As demonstrated by this exemplary case the origin of the loss is important to know. Hence in Figure 4 a histogram is shown which illustrates the distribution of the fraction of the loss incurred by concatenation by the total loss over the investigated range (as before). Of course, only those cases are accounted, where a loss is observed.

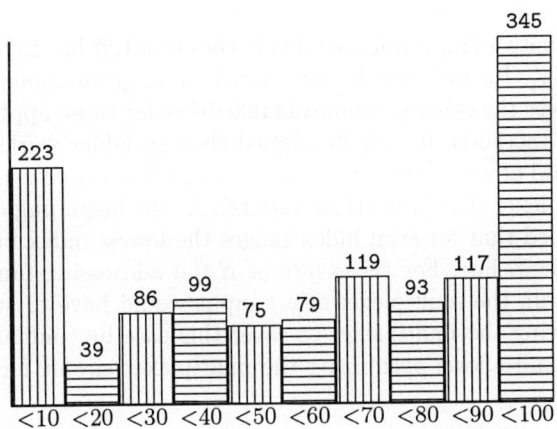

Fig. 4. Distribution of the fraction of the loss by concatenation to the total loss

5 Architecture

By the evaluation it turned out that for most cases for two-dimensional arrays one multiplexer is sufficient. For some cases a second partition step allows another considerable reduction of the loss. This second multiplexer can be used for three-dimensional arrays as well. Hence an architecture with two multiplexer stages covers a wide range of applications, while it is considerably cheap – it has only the width of the addresses of the internal memory.

In any case one input to the array is fed directly by the index inputs up to inversion. As mentioned before inversion can be ignored in a LUT-based FPGAs as it nearly always can be included in the generation of the affected signal. For those cases where the reduced adder is used, circuitry between the two multiplexers would be needed (see Figure 5, left). However, such an arrangement would imply the delay for the adder when it is not needed, too.

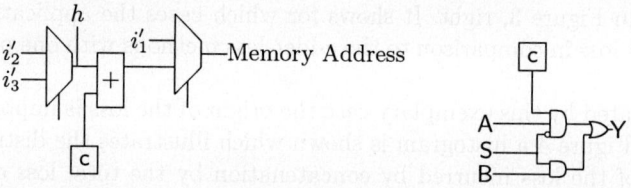

Fig. 5. Architecture for loss-minimization(left), and maskable 2-to-1 multiplexer(right), $\boxed{c}$ is a configurable constant

If this intermediate adder is not included in the circuit, it has to be duplicated at both inputs i'_2, i'_3. Its task can be performed by programmable logic in the usual way. This saves the otherwise unavoidable delay for those applications that use the adder-less methods. It may be argued that an adder works faster with one constant addend of zero than usually. If the adder is omitted everything that remains is a multiplexer (here with three inputs). At the beginning of the second section it was argued that for even index ranges the lowest index bit can be fed directly to an address line. For those bits or if the addressing functionality is not to be used at all, the multiplexer select input would have to supplied with a constant. Modifying the multiplexer to cover this case by configuration saves routing resources and allows optimizing the multiplexer circuit for this crucial situation.

6 Conclusion

In this paper methods for the generation of a memory address for the access of multidimensional arrays have been investigated. The results are promising as the hardware effort and the speed penalty as well as the memory loss by unused cells are rather low. The computational effort for the generation of a particular circuit can be made acceptably low, as in [7] an efficient method for the computation of the concatenation (`Minimal_grow`) is mentioned. For many cases the results are so good that probably no significantly better method exists with a comparable space/time trade-off. The difficulty of the address generation problem differs, and for the harder cases better methods may exist, e.g for index ranges $\{0, \ldots, 42\} \times \{0, \ldots, 42\}$. While investigating methods, which are based on linear algebra, it turned out that linear functions are not better than concatenation. A linear function generates the address bits by exclusive or from index bits. Applications with wide memories, e.g. for cryptographic keys or high precision numbers have stronger loss requirements. In these and similar cases another indirection for a lossless implementation can be considered too.

The question whether it is worth integrating dedicated configurable circuits into future configurable VLSI architectures depends strongly on the expected applications. The speed overhead for applications not using such a feature is very low – just passing one multiplexer. Since the proposed structure can be used for other purposes like alternating accesses to the memory, it is worth being considered.

Acknowledgment

This work has been funded by the German science foundation DFG under contract MA1412/3-2.

References

1. Actel Corporation. *ProASIC 500K Family Datasheet*, advanced v.3 edition, December 1999.
2. Altera Corporation. *APEX 20K Programmmable Logic Device Family*, November 1999.
3. Andreas Gieriet. Re: Indexing functions. Usenet Newsgroup contribution, January 2000. comp.lang.vhdl,comp.lsi,comp.arch.fpga.
4. R.W. Hartenstein, M. Herz, T. Hoffmann, and U. Nadeldinger. Exploiting contemporary memory techniques in reconfigurable architectures. In *Field Programmable Logic and Applications '98*, number 1482 in LNCS, pages 189–198. Springer, 1998.
5. John D. Lipson. *Elements of Algebra and Algebraic Computing*. Addison Wesley, 1981.
6. Herman Schmit and Donald E. Thomas. Address generation for memories containing multiple arrays. In *Proceedings of the 1995 IEEE/ACM international conference on Computer-aided design*, pages 510 – 514, 1995.
7. Herman Schmit and Donald E. Thomas. Address generation for memories containing multiple arrays. *IEEE Transactions on Computer-Aided Design of Integrated Circuits and Systems*, 17(5):377–385, May 1998.
8. Steven J. E. Wilton, Jonathan Rose, and Svonko G. Vranesic. The memory/logic interface in fpga's with large embedded memory arrays. *IEEE Transactions on Very Large Scale Integration Systems*, 7(1):80–91, March 1999.
9. XILINX Inc. *Virtex-E Field Programmable Gate Arrays*, January 2000.

Combining Serialisation and Reconfiguration for FPGA Designs

Arran Derbyshire and Wayne Luk

Department of Computing
Imperial College of Science, Technology and Medicine
180 Queen's Gate
London SW7 2BZ
United Kingdom

Abstract. This paper describes a tool framework and techniques for combining serialisation and reconfiguration to produce efficient designs. Convolver and matrix multiplier designs are examined. Several optimisation techniques, such as restructuring and pipeline morphing, are presented with an analysis of their impact on performance and resource usage. The proposed techniques do not require the basic processing element to be modified. An estimate of the performance of the serial designs is given when mapped using distributed arithmetic and constant multiplier cores onto a Xilinx Virtex FPGA.

1 Introduction

Serialisation is a method that enables the behaviour of a large array of processing elements to be emulated by fewer processing elements, usually at the expense of increasing latency and reducing throughput. Reconfiguration allows the serialisation of an array of non-identical processing elements, such as a convolver with constant-coefficient multipliers.

Our approach can be seen as an extension of previous work on systolic array synthesis [5] to cover partially-pipelined designs which are reconfigurable at run time. This paper illustrates its application to convolver and matrix multiplier designs. The novel aspects include: (a) a proposed tool framework that will automate the derivation and composition of readable, generic serial reconfigurable designs; (b) combining serialisation and reconfiguration techniques in developing designs with different levels of pipelining – unlike the Locally Parallel Globally Sequential(LPGS) and Locally Sequential Globally Parallel(LSGP) serialisation schemes [3], our designs do not require additional registers in processing elements; (c) analysing three optimisation techniques: multiplexing, restructuring and morphing [4]; and (d) evaluating implementations in Xilinx Virtex devices, demonstrating the potential of the proposed approach for implementing very long filters [7] and large matrix multipliers using a relatively small amount of logic resources.

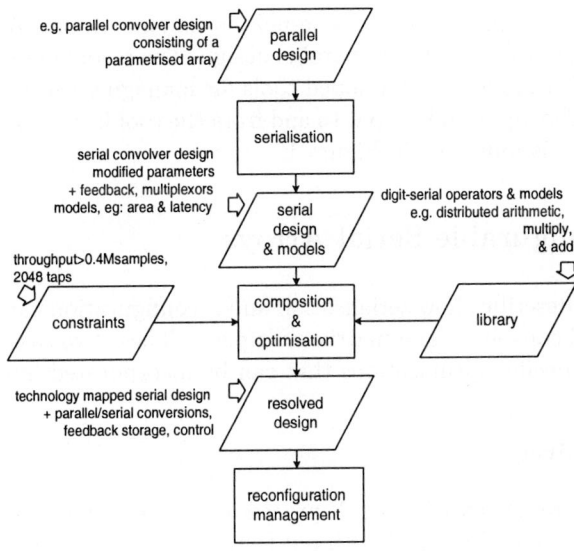

Fig. 1. Serialisation and reconfiguration tools framework.

2 A Framework for Reconfigurable Serial Designs

Parallel designs match the behaviour of the algorithm more closely than serial designs. The control of a serial array, its temporary storage and determining the correct area/time tradeoffs are the additional complexities. For these reasons, it is often more convenient to automatically serialise complex parallel designs. Figure 1 shows a framework of tools currently under development that facilitate, in particular, the serialisation of regular designs . The tools are divided into three main functions: serialisation, composition and optimisation, and reconfiguration management. The serialisation tool takes a structural description of the parallel design and produces a serial design with equivalent behaviour. It uses a syntax-directed approach that results in a serial design that is readable and generic. Both the parallel and serial designs are expressed with the Pebble language [2], which is also used by the tool during the serialisation process. Parallel structures to be serialised within the parallel design must be given in a particular syntactical form.

Models of latency, area and throughput are generated to allow serialised blocks to be composed and optimised. Composition involves inserting delays and parallel-serial convertors into the datapath to schedule the serial blocks and resolve data widths. Serial blocks may be either those derived by serialisation or serial library blocks, both may be combined in a design. Examples of these respectively are the multiply-accumulate processing elements of a convolver and a digit-serial multiplier. Optimisation resolves the degree of serialisation given the application constraints and the block models. Examples of the application constraints are minimum latency, throughput and maximum area. These are supplied by the user along with the parallel design. The reconfiguration management integrates with previously developed tools for managing run-time reconfigurable designs [1]. The input and output to and from the tool framework for the example of a convolver is indicated in Figure 1.

3 Reconfigurable Serial Arrays

This section describes how serialisation and reconfiguration can be combined for parametrised convolvers and matrix multipliers. These two case studies highlight application specific optimisations that can be incorporated into the tools.

3.1 Convolver

Consider a parallel array having N processing elements and a serial array having K elements, where $N = uK$. The input to the serial array is multiplexed between the feedback path and the external input. In this design, a particular part of the parallel array is emulated by the serial array for vK cycles; a single store is included in the feedback path and the array is reconfigured when the store is filled. The parameters u and v respectively determine, in terms of K, the degree of serialisation and the number of compute cycles between reconfiguration. Figure 2 shows a convolver design and the order the input values x would normally move through the registers D at different instants of time. This parallel array has eight processing elements ($N = 8$).

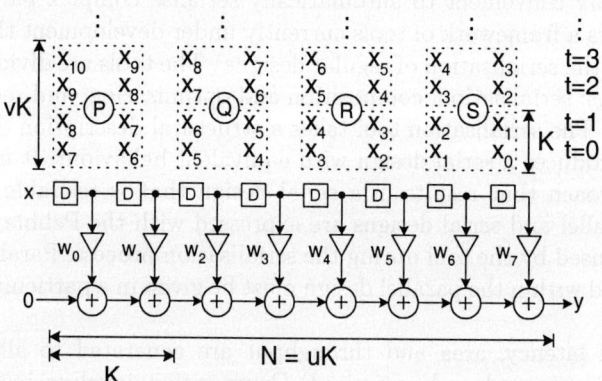

Fig. 2. Parallel convolver: each row of x are the values in the shift register at time $t = 0, 1, 2, \ldots$ The parameter N is its number of processing elements, K is the number of processing elements in the corresponding serial convolvers (Figure 3), u is the degree of serialisation, and v is the number of compute cycles between reconfiguration ($N = 8, K = 2, u = 4, v = 2$).

Figure 3 shows the corresponding (a) non-pipelined serial design and (b) pipelined serial design, each with two elements ($K = 2$). The serial design first processes the input values x_6, x_7, x_8, x_9 and x_{10} in block P in Figure 2, with the constant-coefficient multipliers configured to w_0 and w_1. They are then reconfigured to w_2 and w_3 and the input values in block Q are processed. The remaining input values are processed in the same way with the coefficients corresponding to the parallel array. This order is indicated in Figure 2 by the labels P, Q, R and S. The parameter v determines the number of cycles between reconfiguration and the size of the feedback storage.

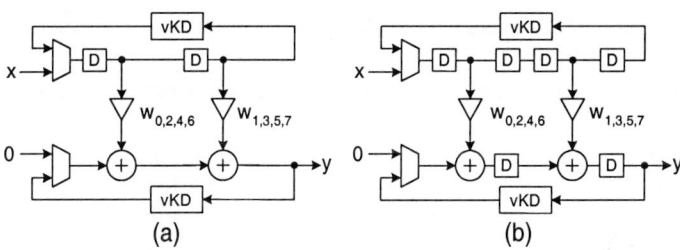

Fig. 3. Serial convolvers ($N = 8, K = 2, u = 4$): (a) non-pipelined design, (b) pipelined design.

There are three possible optimisation strategies to reduce latency of the serial design. First, multiplexing: the registers in the serial array are replaced by loadable registers in which the correct input values x are loaded when the constant-coefficient multipliers are reconfigured. This removes any latency involved in changing the x values which occurs when, for instance, block Q follows block P. The input values are stored in another shift register connected to the array via a row of multiplexors. Second, restructuring: since addition is commutative and associative, the order of computation can be reversed: S first, then R, Q and P (Figure 2). Third, pipeline morphing [4]: the array must first be pipelined (Figure 3b), increasing latency but reducing combinational delay. Latency is then reduced by overlapping computation and reconfiguration. This technique is applicable to both fully-pipelined and also partially-pipelined designs [3].

Table 1 shows a comparison of the convolver designs in terms of their parameters (the expressions have been simplified). The pipelined and morphed designs are the same except that the morphed design has a lower latency because of overlapping reconfiguration and computation. Both are based on the non-restructured serial design, but corresponding versions can be derived from the restructured design. The pipelined designs have the largest number of registers, followed by the multiplexed designs and then the restructured designs. The multiplexed designs have the lowest latency, followed by the restructured designs and then the pipelined designs. The pipelined and the morphed designs, how-

Table 1. Comparison of convolver designs. R is the time in cycles to reconfigure a constant multiplier. Latency corresponds to the number of cycles for an x value to move through the entire shift register.

Design	Number of Registers	Number of Multiply Adds	Cycles between Reconfiguration	Latency (cycles)
parallel	uK	uK	–	uK
serial	$2(u+v-1)K$	K	$(u+v-1)K$	$(u^2+uv-u-v)K$ $+uKR$
serial-multiplexed	$(u+2v+1)K$	K	vK	$(u-1)vK+uKR$
serial-restructured	if $u>v$ then $(u+v)K$ else $2vK$	K	$(v+1)K$	$(u+1)vK+uKR$
serial-pipelined	$2(u+v)K$	K	$(2u+v-2)K$	$(2u^2+2uv-2u-v)K$ $+uKR$
serial-morphed	$2(u+v)K$	K	$(2u+v-2)K$ then 1 during refill	$(u^2+uv-u-v)K$ $+uR$

ever, have a lower combinational delay than the multiplexed and restructured designs.

3.2 Matrix Multiplier

Consider a parallel array having M by N processing elements (Figure 4) that can be serialised as either a row or a column. A row serial array will have K elements where $N = uK$ and a column serial array will have J elements where $M = eJ$. For a row serial design, a particular column in the parallel array is emulated by the serial array for vK cycles; a single store is included in each of the M feedback paths and the array is reconfigured when the store is filled (Figure 5). A column serial design will behave in the same way but for fJ cycles with N feedback paths and stores. The parameters e and u respectively determine the degree of serialisation for row and column serial designs. Similarly, parameters f and v respectively determine the number of compute cycles between reconfiguration.

The matrix multiplier shown in Figure 4 implements the function $\mathbf{A}\underline{x} = \underline{y}$ and is pipelined in the row direction. Column pipelining would not provide any parallelism since the datapath in the column only distributes the input data x_j. Pipeline morphing can be used to reduce the latency of the row serial-pipelined design (Figure 5(a)); by letting R=0 it can be seen from Table 2 that the morphed design would have the same latency plus the latency due to pipelining K, as the serial design. This ideal situation would have a higher throughput at the expense of latency but require zero reconfiguration overhead. Assuming the same processing element implementation, this throughput advantage would not be gained for a column pipeline-morphed design.

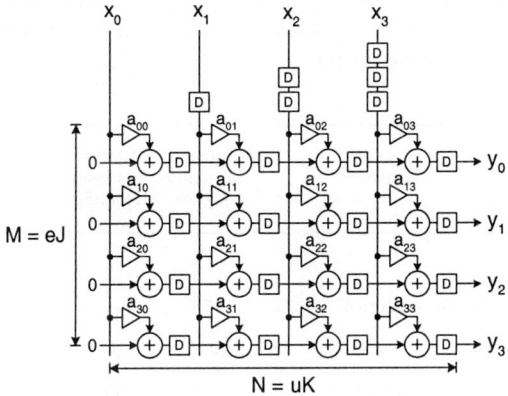

Fig. 4. Row parallel-pipelined matrix multiplier ($M = 4, N = 4$), where $\mathbf{A}\underline{x} = \underline{y}$, $\mathbf{A} = (a_{ij})$, $i,j = 0,1,2,3$, $\underline{x} = (x_0\ x_1\ x_2\ x_3)^T$, $\underline{y} = (y_0\ y_1\ y_2\ y_3)^T$.

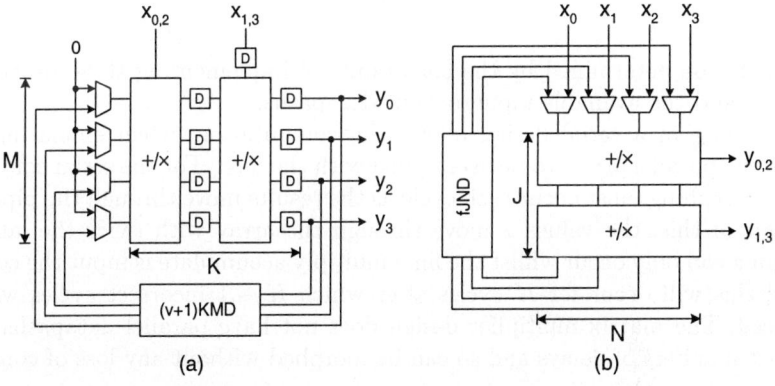

Fig. 5. Serial matrix multipliers: (a) row serial-pipelined design ($M = 4, K = 2, u = 2$), (b) column serial design ($N = 4, J = 2, e = 2$).

3.3 Design Summary

The convolver can be optimised by multiplexing and restructuring because these techniques optimise the latency of loading the correct values into the input datapath shift register after each reconfiguration. The matrix multiplier does not have a registered input datapath and so these optimisations do not apply to serial matrix multiplier designs. In comparison to the convolver, there is the additional flexibility to serialise in either the row or column directions or even both. The row serial processing elements are a parallel accumulate whereas the column serial processing elements are a series accumulate. The choice of serial-

Table 2. Comparison of matrix multiplier designs. R is the time in cycles to reconfigure a constant multiplier. Latency corresponds to the number of cycles between a particular input x and the corresponding output y.

Design	Number of Registers	Number of Multiply Adders	Cycles between Reconfig.	Latency (cycles)
parallel	0	MN	–	0
row parallel-pipelined	$uKM + uK(uK-1)/2$	MN	–	uK
column serial	fJN	JN	fJ	$(e-1)(R+f)J+1$
row serial	vKM	KM	vK	$(v-1)(R+v)K+1$
row serial-pipelined	$(v+1)KM + K(K-1)/2$	KM	$(v+1)K$	$(v-1)(R+v+1)K+K$
row serial-morphed	$vKM + K(K-1)/2$	KM	$(v-1)K$	$(v-1)(R+v)K+(R+1)K$

isation can be determined by the constraints of implementing these processing elements and the available input/output datapaths.

Morphing in a serial design allows the computation, when emulating one part of the parallel array, to be overlapped with the next. For the serial convolver design, morphing must occur each cycle as the results move through the pipeline. In terms of this, the values x move through the array with twice the latency. Morphing can only occur whilst the final multiply accumulate is input the correct values; this will occur for K cycles after which $K-1$ incorrect cycles will be produced. The matrix multiplier design does not have parallel datapaths with different numbers of delays and so can be morphed without any loss of compute cycles.

The inclusion of multiplexors, feedback, storage and control can be automated during the serialisation with library components for the delays, arithmetic operators and memory control circuits. Given some prior knowledge of the technology constraints, the tools could analyse the input and output datapaths of an array like the convolver to determine how optimisation can be applied. An analysis of the delays can determine the suitability and control of morphing. An analysis of commutativity and associativity of operators in the path can determine the suitability of restructuring.

4 Implementation

This section provides an estimate of the size and performance of re-structured serial designs when mapped onto Xilinx Virtex devices. Virtex devices have on-chip RAM and 16-stage lookup table (LUT) based shift-registers, which can be used to optimise serial designs. The reconfiguration time for an entire Virtex device is in the order of microseconds: for example, 200μs for a Virtex XCV300 FPGA.

4.1 Convolver

It has been shown that convolver designs can be implemented efficiently using the Distributed Arithmetic (DA) algorithm in the LUT-based architecture [6]. Since the core of our serial convolver design is itself a convolver, so it can be implemented using DA with additional feedback, storage and control. The feedback store is implemented in Block SelectRAM, dedicated memory blocks which eliminate system complexity involved in having external RAM. The maximum number of 12-bit data that can be stored in the Block SelectRAM of a Virtex XCV300 device is 2048.

A Xilinx bit-serial DA convolver (FIR filter) core has a throughput of 9×10^6 samples per second at a clock speed of 107MHz, adopting 12-bit arithmetic and a length of 128 taps ($K = 128$); it occupies around 20% of the logic resources of a Virtex XCV300 (speed grade -6) device [8]. The time to reconfigure this core is approximately 100μs, assuming run-time partial reconfiguration can be used.

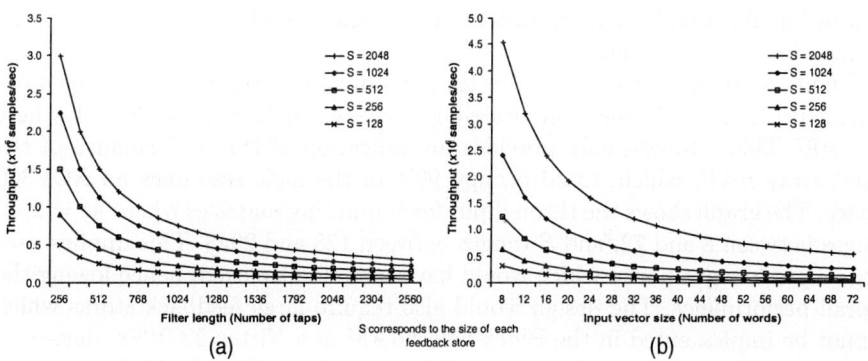

Fig. 6. Throughput of (a) serial convolver and (b) row serial-pipelined matrix multiplier designs.

Figure 6(a) shows the estimated throughput of serial convolver designs utilising the above characteristics. Each curve represents the throughput against number of taps for convolvers with a given size of feedback store S, where $S = vK$ (Figure 2). Latency increases with the storage size. Delay and area overheads from the feedback and control circuitry are assumed to be insignificant compared to the core delay and area.

As an example, when $S = 2048$ the graph indicates that a convolver of 1024 taps can process 750,000 samples per second using 20% of the logic resources of a Virtex XCV300 device and fully utilising its Block SelectRAM. In contrast, a parallel implementation has a throughput of 6×10^6 and requires 40% of an XCV1000 device. A non-reconfigurable serial implementation based on a multiply-accumulator providing the same throughput would consume the area of an entire XCV300 for one seventh the number of taps in the corresponding DA-based implementation.

If partial reconfiguration is not used, then throughput of the designs will drop by 20% due to the additional reconfiguration overhead. However, if the additional area is used by further DA cores increasing K by a factor of 4, then the throughput will double.

4.2 Matrix Multiplier

The processing elements in a column serial matrix multiplier design are made up of multiply-accumulates in series that can be implemented using the DA algorithm as used for the convolver. A row serial design cannot, so it must be implemented as separate multiplications and additions. Xilinx constant coefficient multiplier cores [9] are suitable for this. A 12-bit pipelined constant coefficient multiplier core can be clocked at 148MHz with a latency of 3; for the row serial design this latency will increase the feedback storage for each datapath by 3 and increase the overall latency by $3(u-1)$. This will not occur if pipeline morphing is used but for a real implementations, the latency due to pipelining morphing itself, is likely to be greater.

Figure 6(b) shows the estimated throughput of row serial matrix multiplier designs using the multiplier core described above when $M = 9$ and $K = 4$, where $S = vK$. This estimate only provides an indication of the performance of the serial array itself, which would occupy 90% of the logic resources an XCV300 device. The graph shows the throughput for computing matrices where $M = 9$, N ranges between 8 and 72, and S ranges between 128 and 2048. This implies very large input/output ports, which would have to be multiplexed, hence lowing the overall performance. The design would also require large feedback stores which cannot be implemented in the Block SelectRAM of a Virtex XCV300 device.

The XCV300 has 8 independent dual-port Block SelectRAM banks, each with a maximum depth of 256 for 12bit words. A realistic row serial-pipelined design where $M = 4$, $N = 4$, $K = 2$, $u = 2$, $v = 128$ and using the maximum rate of reconfiguration will have a throughput of approximately 630 000 samples per second and occupy 25% of the logic resources. An equivalent parallel design would have throughtput of 67×10^6 samples per second unpipelined, 89×10^6 samples per second pipelined an would occupy 48% of the logic resources. A column serial design using a DA-based implementation would use 30% of the logic resources with a throughput of 1.5×10^6 samples per second.

5 Summary

We have described a tool framework and techniques for combining serialisation and reconfiguration. The techniques have been applied to convolver and matrix multiplier designs with different tradeoffs in performance and resource usage. Current and future work includes integrating the optimisation techniques, constraints resolution and reconfiguration into the existing tools, and extending our framework to cover less regular designs.

Acknowledgements

Many thanks to Seng Shay Ping and Steve McKeever for comments and assistance. The support of Embedded Solutions Limited, UK Engineering and Physical Sciences Research Council (Grant number GR/54356 and GR/59658), and Xilinx, Inc. is gratefully acknowledged.

References

1. W. Luk, N. Shirazi and P.Y.K. Cheung, "Compilation tools for run-time reconfigurable designs", in *Proc. IEEE Symposium on Field-Programmable Custom Computing Machines*, IEEE Computer Society Press, 1997, pp. 56–65.
2. W. Luk and S. McKeever, "Pebble: a language for parametrised and reconfigurable hardware design", in *Field-Programmable Logic and Applications*, LNCS 1482, Springer, 1998, pp. 9-18.
3. W. Luk, A. Derbyshire, S. Guo and D. Siganos, "Serial hardware libraries for reconfigurable designs", in *Field-Programmable Logic and Applications*, LNCS 1673, Springer, 1999, pp. 185-194.
4. W. Luk, N. Shirazi, S. Guo and P.Y.K. Cheung, "Pipeline morphing and virtual pipelines", in *Field Programmable Logic and Applications*, LNCS 1304, Springer, 1997, pp. 111–120.
5. D.I. Moldovan and J.A.B. Fortes, "Partitioning and mapping algorithms into fixed size systolic arrays", in *IEEE Transactions on Computers*, Vol. 35, No. 1, 1986, pp. 1–12.
6. L. Mintzer, "FIR filters with Field-Programmable Gate Arrays", in *Journal of VLSI Signal Processing*, Vol. 6, No. 2, 1993, pp. 119-127.
7. B. Mulgrew, P. Grant and J. Thompson, *Digital Signal Processing: Concepts And Applications*, http://www.ee.ed.ac.uk/~pmg/SIGPRO/#s4, 1998.
8. Xilinx Inc., *Distributed Arithmetic FIR filter*, Product Specification Data Sheet, 1999.
9. Xilinx Inc., *Constant (k) Coefficient Multiplier Generator for Virtex*, Reference Design, Application Note, 1999.

Multiple-Wordlength Resource Binding

George A. Constantinides[1], Peter Y.K. Cheung[1], and Wayne Luk[2]

[1] Department of Electrical and Electronic Engineering,
Imperial College, London SW7 2BT, U.K.
{g.constantinides, p.cheung}@ic.ac.uk

[2] Department of Computing, Imperial College,
London SW7 2AZ, U.K.
wl@doc.ic.ac.uk

Abstract. This paper describes a novel resource binding technique for use in multiple-wordlength systems implemented in FPGAs. It is demonstrated that the multiple-wordlength binding problem is significantly different for addition and multiplication, and techniques to share resources between several operations are examined for FPGA architectures. A novel formulation of the resource binding problem is presented as an optimal colouring problem on a resource conflict graph, and several algorithms are developed to solve this problem. Results collected from many sequencing graphs illustrate the effectiveness of the heuristics developed in this paper, demonstrating significant area reductions over more traditional approaches.

1 Introduction

This paper describes a novel resource binding technique used by the Synoptix high-level synthesis system for FPGAs [1]. Synoptix synthesizes designs using multiple-wordlength resources, in an effort to minimize the total resource utilization required to implement a given Digital Signal Processing algorithm. The use of multiple-wordlength resources has an impact on the resource allocation and binding problem of high-level synthesis. This paper introduces algorithms for optimal and heuristic resource-binding for such multiple-wordlength systems. The nature of the binding problem is analyzed, and the suitability of current FPGA architectures is assessed.

Traditionally the wordlength problem for DSP applications has been to find a single uniform system wordlength, which satisfies both the conflicting requirements of design area/speed and acceptable rounding and truncation signal distortion. The idea of a single uniform wordlength is consistent with the DSP processor model of computation, where a single, or multiple, pre-designed fixed-wordlength computational units are responsible for all operations. When synthesizing a circuit for FPGA implementation, we are freed from such constraints. It is possible to use different wordlength functional units at different locations within the array, in order to minimize the overall logic utilization requirements. It is this approach that is taken by the Synoptix system, as described in [1].

Of the several recent approaches to wordlength optimization [2–4], few have considered in detail the resource binding problem when wordlength information is known. One approach described in [2] is to modify a standard clique partitioning algorithm on the compatibility graph [5]. In the compatibility graph, nodes represent operations, and edges represent two operations that do not conflict, and so could possibly be implemented in the same resource. The standard high-level synthesis problem of resource allocation is to find the fewest resources to implement the graph. This is equivalent to partitioning the compatibility graph into the fewest cliques possible. In a standard approach described in [5], cliques are extracted by sorting nodes in descending order of degree. This is modified by the authors of [2] to sort nodes in descending order of wordlength.

In contrast, our approach operates by formulating a cost function on the conflict graph. In the conflict graph, nodes represent operations, and edges represent two operations that cannot be bound to the same resource. This paper demonstrates how an appropriate cost function can be used to achieve optimal colourings of the conflict graph, and therefore minimal area implementations of multiple-wordlength systems. We introduce optimal and heuristic approaches to the colouring problem, and demonstrate that a surprisingly simple heuristic can achieve highly successful results.

Section 2 of this paper introduces the problem of multiple-wordlength binding, and illustrates the effectiveness of current FPGAs for implementing such designs. Section 3 introduces optimal and heuristic solutions to the binding problem, the effectiveness of which is illustrated in Sect. 4. Finally some conclusions are drawn in Sect. 5.

2 Wordlength Binding

2.1 Addition and Multiplication

The multiple-wordlength resource binding problem is somewhat different for the two operators of multiplication and addition. In this discussion it is worth remembering that adders are typically small, and efficiently implemented in FPGA devices, while parallel multiplier resources are generally large and inefficiently implemented [6].

Consider the circuit shown in Fig. 1, where two 2-bit additions can be performed during a single clock cycle, and a single 4-bit addition can be performed during another clock cycle. By chaining together the carry-chains of two 2-bit adders, it is possible to produce a single ripple-carry computational unit, able to perform both operations. For adders, this is discussed in more detail in [7, 8].

We now demonstrate that the same is not true for multiplication operations. Consider the 4×4-bit multiplication arrangement shown in Fig. 2(a) [9]. As shown by the multiplexers in Fig. 2(b), in order to perform a 4×3-bit and a 4×2-bit multiplication using a single 4×4-bit multiplier, it is necessary to break the sum/carry chaining and insert alternative operands at internal points within the multiplier array. It soon becomes clear that any general design will suffer

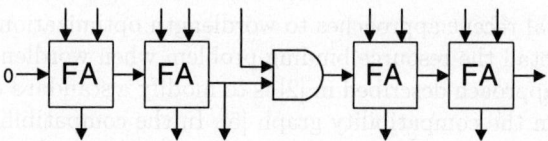

Fig. 1. Two adders chained to produce a single large adder

greatly from routing congestion, as all operands must be fed into their appropriate locations deep within the multiplier array, and there must be similar routing paths for the results. One possible solution to this problem is to limit the type of resource-sharing that can take place for multipliers. Figure 2(c) illustrates the use of a single 5×5-bit multiplier to implement a 2×3-bit and a 2×2-bit multiplier on one clock cycle, and a 5×5-bit multiplier on another cycle. Note that unlike the arrangement in Fig. 2(b), during a single cycle each row or column belongs to at most one multiplier. This allows existing vertical and horizontal-running wires to be used both for passing inputs to multiplier arrays, and for collecting results from them. Using this approach data need only be fed into, and collected from, the boundaries of the multiplier array.

If multiplier resources are to be reused in this way, an efficient implementation of the basic cell, shown in Fig 2(d) is necessary. For FPGA implementations, we propose three possible approaches to provide the necessary control signals to the multiplexers and gates inside the array: use of globally distributed signals,

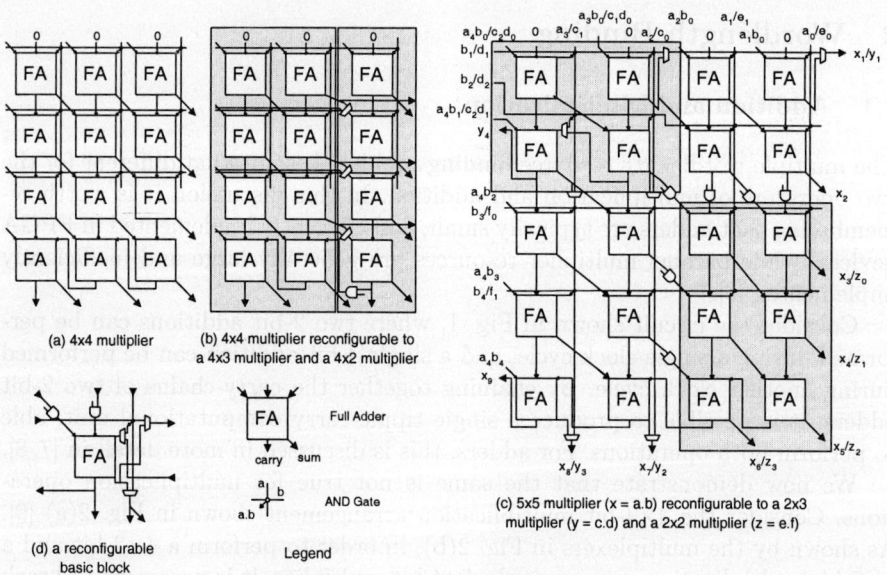

Fig. 2. Sharing a large multiplier resource

static 'scan-path' implementation, or dynamic reconfiguration. Many FPGAs have the ability to globally distribute a handful of signals. While this is certainly a possible solution, use of such signals is expensive, as it denies their use to any other circuits within the FPGA. Also for a multiplier array shared by several multipliers, several signals would be needed. An alternative method is to use a scan-path technique to reconfigure the multiplier array - each basic cell (Fig. 2(d)) can be in one of four states: 'outside multiplier', 'inside multiplier', 'right-edge', or 'bottom edge', indicating where in a multiplier the specific cell lies. Each cell therefore needs two state bits, which can be loaded using a scan-path mechanism [10] with two scan-paths, one horizontal and one vertical. Thus an entire n by m array can be reconfigured within $\max(n,m)$ cycles. Clearly the key problem of such an implementation is the significantly increased complexity of the basic cell over that of a simple multiplier array, which may outweigh the area gain from sharing the resource. Indeed the problem is compounded by the fact that each output of a basic cell is now driven by logic within that cell, whereas for the original multiplier array, several outputs were simply routing constructs on their respective inputs. This is confirmed by a Xilinx XC4k implementation of a 16×16-bit array of multiplier cells, which uses 938 CLBs for the cells in Fig. 2(d), but only 290 CLBs for a more traditional basic cell - the costs clearly outweighing the advantages.

We believe that the only feasible approach to sharing a single multiplier between several smaller multipliers within an FPGA is to use dynamic reconfiguration. However the Xilinx XC6200 and Virtex, two existing FPGA architectures offering partial dynamic reconfiguration, are clearly not suited to this task. The Virtex reconfiguration is too coarse grained - we estimate it would take approximately 400 cycles to completely reprogram a 16x16 multiplier array. This rules out Virtex for all but the longest of schedules. By contrast the XC6200 has the fine-grained architecture necessary, including features such as wild-carding. The problem is that by using the new basic cell, all routing must be local, unlike a more traditional design, where inputs can be fed through non-local routing to all participating cells. However the XC6200 has a relative paucity of local routing, leading in our estimation to an area growth of over two times.

It it therefore clear that for current FPGAs, while the use of multiple wordlength resources is a useful technique to minimize utilization [1], it is unlikely that sharing a single multiplier between two or more multipliers *on the same cycle* is an efficient approach. For adders, this is not necessarily true [8], and in any case adders consume significantly fewer FPGA resources than multipliers [6]. We therefore concentrate in the rest of this paper on formulating and solving a multiple-wordlength resource binding problem, wherein a large multiplier array can be used as a *single* multiplier on each clock cycle (though it may have different sizes at different cycles).

2.2 Problem Formulation

The *resource conflict graph* $G_-(V,E)$ is a graph whose vertex set $V = \{v_i, i = 1, 2, ..., n_{ops}\}$ is in one-to-one correspondence with the operations, and whose edge set $E = \{\{v_i, v_j\} \ i, j = 1, 2, ..., n_{ops}\}$ denotes conflicting operation pairs [5]. We define the *annotated multiplier conflict graph* to be the graph $G_-(V, E)$ together with an annotation (n_i, m_i) for each vertex v_i. Each annotation consists of an ordered pair of wordlengths, representing the two input wordlengths for the multiplier in question, ordered such that $n_i \geq m_i$ for all i. A *colouring* on the annotated multiplier conflict graph is a labelling $C : V \to L$ of the vertices by a set of labels L such that no edge in E connects two vertices with the same label. Approximating the area of an n-bit by m-bit parallel multiplier resource by nm, we may associate with each feasible colouring C a cost K_C defined in (1).

$$K_C = \sum_{\ell \in L} \left(\max_{i:C(v_i)=\ell} \{n_i\} \max_{i:C(v_i)=\ell} \{m_i\} \right) . \quad (1)$$

The multiple-wordlength multiplier resource binding problem can then be defined as finding a feasible colouring C^* such that K_{C^*} is minimal. Note that if $n_i = n$ and $m_i = m$ for all i, this problem reduces to minimum colouring, since K_C becomes proportional to the number of colours. It is important to note that the *optimal* colouring may not always be a *minimal* colouring. Figure 3 illustrates a simple annotated multiplier conflict graph consisting of four multipliers. The graph can be coloured with two colours (Fig. 3(a)) with a cost of 1024. However, increasing the number of colours to three (Fig. 3(b)) allows a lower cost of 768 to be achieved. Three multipliers have been used (two 16×8-bit and one 32×16-bit) and yet the overall resource requirement is less than with two multipliers (two 32×16-bit). This a key difference between the multiple-wordlength binding problem and the more traditional binding problem, where a minimal colouring (minimum number of multipliers) is the aim.

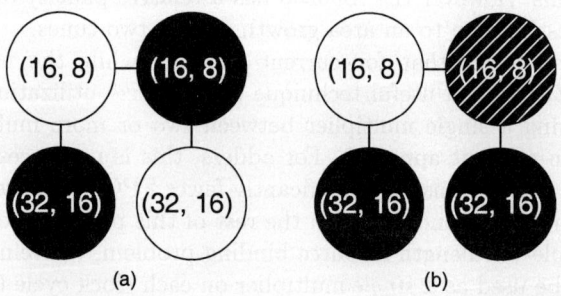

Fig. 3. (a) Minimal and (b) optimal colourings for an annotated conflict graph

3 Binding Algorithms

Having formulated the problem as a form of optimal colouring on an annotated graph, in this section of the paper we present several algorithms to perform the colouring. Three algorithms are presented: a simulated annealing heuristic, a fast effective application-specific heuristic 'swap and inherit', and a branch and bound algorithm, which produces a solution optimal with respect to the cost function. For comparative purposes, and to form a starting point for some of the algorithms, a standard left-edge colouring algorithm was also created, which colours the graph constructively by a sequential scan of the vertex set ordered by schedule start-time [5]. Also for comparative purposes, a simple 'sort by label' heuristic was implemented, which also colours the graph constructively by a sequential scan of the vertex set, but the ordering is by decreasing wordlength. The idea behind this is to 'hide' the cost of smaller nodes behind pre-coloured larger nodes.

3.1 Simulated Annealing

A simulated annealing based heuristic has been developed to solve the optimal colouring problem. Three annealing moves are provided: swap node colours, inherit node colour, and new node colour. Given two nodes of different colour, the 'swap node colours' move swaps the colours of the two nodes. The total number of colours in the graph is unchanged. The 'inherit node colour' also operates on a pair of nodes: node v_1 inherits the colour of node v_2, and the colour of node v_2 is unchanged. Thus if before the move there is only one node of colour $C(v_1)$, the overall number of colours in the graph will decrease. Otherwise it will remain unchanged. Finally, the 'new node colour' move operates on a single node, which must not be the only node of its colour. This node is re-coloured to a currently unused colour, increasing the total number of colours in the graph by one.

This framework of moves provides a structured way to move from one feasible graph colouring to another, by excluding infeasible moves. The starting point of the annealing is a left-edge colouring of the graph, as this provides a reasonable quality solution for the case when resources are limited (see Sect. 4 of this paper).

Our simulated annealing heuristic has several features. Due to the highly nonlinear nature of the cost function (1), if nodes were selected in a purely random manner for the moves described above, the vast majority of moves would have zero cost, since the maximum within each class would remain unchanged in these cases. The standard Metropolis algorithm for simulated annealing would always perform these moves [11]. This would lead to many moves giving little feedback to the cost-estimation process - it is hard to know whether these moves are 'good' or 'bad' until they become non-zero cost. If these moves were considered by the annealing algorithm it would therefore take many times more iterations to come to a result which cannot be known to be better than a result achieved by excluding these operations.

For pairwise operations, a necessary condition for a change in the cost function (either positive or negative) is that one of the nodes is has either the maximum n or maximum m value of its colour. By maintaining two lists of nodes, sorted in descending order of n and m respectively, our algorithm efficiently chooses only pairwise annealing moves where this condition is satisfied.

3.2 Branch and Bound

An exact method for finding an optimal solution to the colouring problem has also been implemented using a branch and bound technique, as illustrated in the pseudo-code below.

```
optimum_colouring( vertex, best_cost, num_colours ) {
  if( vertex = NULL ) {   // No more vertices to colour
    if( evaluate_cost() < best_cost )
      best_cost = evaluate_cost();
  } else {
    if( partial_cost() < best_cost ) { // Worth continuing (*)
      for c = 1 to num_colours {
        if( colouring vertex with c is feasible ) {
          colour( vertex ) := c
          optimum_colouring( vertex->next,best_cost,num_colours );
        }
      }
      colour( vertex ) = num_colours+1; // Always feasible
      optimum_colouring( vertex->next, best_cost, num_colours+1 );
    }
  }
}
```

Without the line marked (*) in the pseudo-code, this would provide a complete enumeration of all possible colourings. This line contains the bound, using a function `partial_cost()`, which evaluates the cost up to the colouring of the current vertex. The key point here is that the cost function (1) can never decrease by adding more vertices, only remain the same or increase. This forms the basis of the branch and bound.

3.3 Swap and Inherit

A fast and effective heuristic, 'swap and inherit', has also been developed to solve this colouring problem. From an analysis of the optimal colouring of realistic small graphs (fewer than 40 nodes can be coloured using the branch and bound algorithm in reasonable time), it was observed that non-minimal optimal colourings are, in reality, quite rare. In fact, never more than about 15% of those graphs generated by the TGFF algorithm [12]) required non-minimal colourings for optimality. If the range of possible graph colourings is restricted to minimal colourings, the search space is significantly reduced and other, faster algorithms become plausible candidates.

The swap and inherit heuristic operates as a steepest-descent local search, starting from a left-edge colouring. At each iteration, every feasible non-zero cost swap and inherit operation is considered in turn. At worst case this is a total of $n_{ops}(n_{ops} - 1)$ ordered pairs of vertices. However, using the condition on non-zero cost operations described in Sect. 3.1 significantly reduces the number of vertex pairs that need to be considered. The operation providing the biggest pay-off in cost-function reduction is then performed, before proceeding to the next iteration. This loop is repeated until no pairwise operation will result in a cost-reduction, at which point the algorithm terminates. Note that the cost-function does not need to be recalculated from scratch at each operation, since the nature of (1) shows that post-operation cost can be easily derived from pre-operation cost using only local information about the annotation of each node taking part in the operation, together with the two largest n and m values for each of the twos colours.

The swap and inherit heuristic has the advantage over simulated annealing that it will quickly and efficiently find minima in the cost function. It clearly has the disadvantage that these minima may be local, due to both the greedy nature of the search performed, and the lack of an 'add new colour' move, which always has positive cost and would therefore be rejected anyway by a greedy algorithm. It is our contention that these disadvantages are relatively unimportant for realistic problems, as will be demonstrated in Sect. 4.

4 Results

The algorithms described in Sect. 3 have been implemented and tested on a set of randomly generated conflict graphs with varying properties. Firstly random sequencing graphs were generated using the method described in [12]. Nodes in these graphs were identified as adders or multipliers (the two types of operation node generated by our high level synthesis environment [1]). Each adder was assigned a latency of one clock cycle, and each multiplier a random latency uniformly distributed in the range 4–8 clock cycles. The wordlengths of each multiplier were then assigned in the range 16–32 bits, such that operations with a longer latency have larger wordlengths. Each sequencing graph was scheduled using the list-scheduling algorithm [5], with a constraint on the maximum number of multiplier and adder resources. From the scheduled sequencing graph, the conflict graph for each resource-type/latency was produced: two nodes are connected in the graph if their scheduling intervals intersect. Finally, these graphs were processed by the multiple-wordlength binding algorithms presented in this paper, in addition to the 'left-edge' and 'sort by label' algorithms mentioned in Sect. 3.

Shown in Fig. 4(a) is a plot of the difference between the cost using each algorithm and that using a random-order sequential scan of the vertex set [5], as a proportion of the random-order cost. Each point on the graph represents the average of 200 random sequencing graphs. The swap and inherit heuristic consistently out-performs all algorithms except simulated annealing, which marginally outperforms the heuristic by at most 5% even for very large sequencing graphs. Interestingly, the left-edge algorithm outperforms sort-by-label for a large number of sequencing nodes. This is because as the graph complexity increases, it becomes more important to consider the internal structure of the graph, a factor ignored by the sort-by-label algorithm.

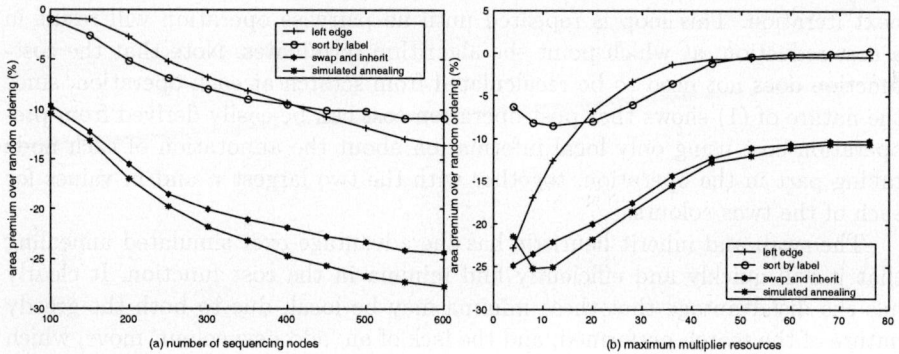

Fig. 4. Variation of multiplier area premiums (a) with number of nodes (for fixed resource constraints) (b) with resource constraints (for fixed number of nodes)

Figure 4(b) illustrates how the performance of the algorithms changes as resource constraints on the scheduling algorithm are relaxed. Left-edge shows a significant advantage for tight resource constraints, however this advantage is rapidly lost as the constraints are relaxed, as the importance of the internal structure of the graph is reduced. The swap and inherit algorithm lies consistently beneath all curves curves except simulated annealing, which marginally outperforms it, illustrating the robust performance of the heuristic. Indeed, for very tight resource constraints the swap and inherit outperforms simulated annealing, illustrating that the same annealing schedule and parameters are not optimal over the entire problem parameter space. By contrast, since the swap and inherit heuristic has left-edge as its starting point and is greedy, left-edge area gives a upper-bound on swap and inherit area.

5 Conclusions

After consideration of multiple-wordlength resource sharing, we conclude that for current FPGAs the multiple-wordlength multiplier resource binding problem should be defined such that a multiplier array is used to implement a single multiplier on each clock cycle. This problem has been formulated as an optimal colouring on an annotated conflict graph, and several algorithms have been developed to solve the colouring problem. It has been shown that while a simulated annealing solution provides good quality solutions, for the price of a small area premium a fast steepest descent algorithm can be substituted. Both algorithms show significant area reductions over the use of more traditional approaches for the case of multiple-wordlength datapaths.

Our current work on this problem includes integrating the scheduling and binding problems to produce sharing between multiple-wordlength resources of different natural latency, and the investigation of the interaction between the wordlength optimization scheme described in [1] and the high-level synthesis techniques presented in this paper.

Acknowledgements

The authors would like to acknowledge the support of Hewlett-Packard Laboratories and the Engineering and Physical Sciences Research Council, U.K.

References

1. Constantinides, G.A., Cheung, P.Y.K., Luk, W.: Multiple precision for resource minimization. To appear in Proc. FCCM 2000
2. Kum, K., Sung, W.: Word-length optimization for high-level synthesis of digital signal processing systems. Proc. IEEE Int'l. Workshop on Signal Processing Systems SIPS'98 (1998) 569–678
3. Willems, M., Bürgsens, V., Keding, H., Grötker, T, Meyer, M.: System-level fixed-point design based on an interpolative approach. Proc. 34th Design Automation Conference (1997) 293–298
4. Cmar, R., Rijnders, L., Schaumont, P., Vernalde, S., Bolsens, I.: A methodology and design environment for DSP ASIC fixed point refinement. Proc. Design Automation and Test in Europe '99 (1999)
5. DeMicheli, G.: Synthesis and optimization of digital circuits. New York: McGraw-Hill (1994)
6. Haynes, S.D., Cheung, P.Y.K.: Configurable multiplier blocks for use within an FPGA. IEE Electronics Letters 34 (1998) 638–639
7. Landwehr, B., Marwedel, P., Dömer, R.: OSCAR: Optimum simultaneous scheduling, allocation and resource binding based on integer programming Proc. European Design Automation Conference (1994) 90–95
8. Ercegovac, M., Kirovski, D., Potkonjak, M.: Low-power behavioral synthesis optimization using multiple precision arithmetic. Proc. 36th Design Automation Conference (1999)
9. Hwang, K.: Computer arithmetic: principles, architecture and design. New York: Wiley and sons (1979)
10. Weste, N.H.E., Eshraghian, K.: Principles of CMOS VLSI design. Reading, MA: Addison-Wesley (1993)
11. Press, W.H., Flannery, B.P., Teukolsky, S.A., Vetterling, W.T.: Numerical Recipes in C. Cambridge, UK: Cambridge University Press (1988)
12. Dick, R.P., Rhodes, D.L., Wolf, W.: TGFF: Task graphs for free. Proc. CODES/CASHE'98 (1998) 97–101

Automatic Temporal Floorplanning with Guaranteed Solution Feasibility

Milan Vasilko and Graham Benyon-Tinker

Microelectronic Systems Research Group
School of DEC, Bournemouth University, Talbot Campus
Fern Barrow, Poole, Dorset BH12 5BB, UK

M.Vasilko@computer.org

Abstract. This paper presents an automatic design synthesis technique for Dynamically Reconfigurable Logic (DRL) systems. Given an input behavioural algorithm, a target technology library server and a set of design constraints, the synthesis algorithm will generate a DRL design solution in a form of a 3D floorplan and a design schedule. The technique optimises the design solution in a multiple-objective design search space, while making realistic assumptions about the implementation reconfiguration overheads. Partial reconfiguration is considered if such a feature is available in the target technology.

Simultaneous consideration of the multiple design objectives at various abstraction levels, together with a realistic estimation of the reconfiguration overheads, guarantees the feasibility of the automatically generated solutions. The presented approach is based on generic algorithms with problem-specific coding and operators. The performance of the algorithm was tested using a selection of small benchmarks within the DYNASTY Framework.

1 Introduction

The practicality of using DRL technologies for a real-time implementation of a specific system is determined by two primary factors:

- ability of such a system to tolerate the overheads associated with the dynamic reconfiguration
- capabilities of the target reconfigurable technology; in particular its support for high-speed and partial reconfiguration

Several approaches have been proposed to address the problem of the automatic synthesis for Dynamically Reconfigurable Logic (DRL) systems (e.g. [1–4]). However, the usability of these techniques for practical DRL applications is often limited. Many of these techniques either ignore partial reconfiguration, or use simplified models of the target DRL technology in order to reduce the complexity of a design search space. Such simplifications require post-processing steps or numerous iterations in order to produce even a single feasible design solu-

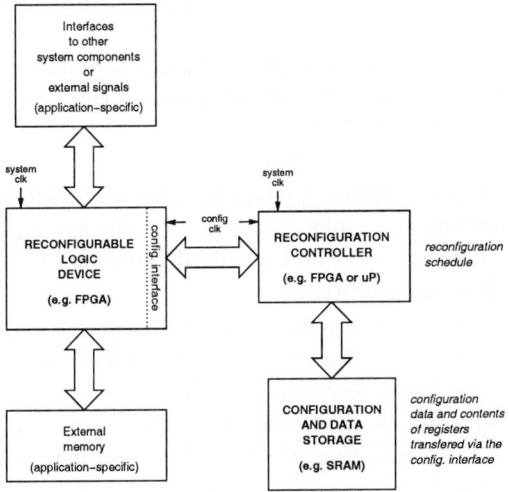

Fig. 1. Model of the target reconfigurable system.

tion[1] (problems involve: placement conflicts, routing problems, data-dependency violations due to prohibitive reconfiguration overheads, etc.).

In [5] we have proposed a manual temporal floorplanning design methodology aimed to produce feasible reconfigurable design solutions with the help of a target technology library server . This paper presents an example of an automatic synthesis technique working within the framework of this methodology. Our approach is based on an adaptive evolutionary optimisation algorithms (genetic algorithms), and is capable of generating design solutions with guaranteed implementation feasibility.

2 Problem Model

In the algorithm presented in this paper, we use a simple model of a reconfigurable system with one global configuration controller (Fig. 1). This model is common for most of the presently known reconfigurable FPGA technologies.

It is further assumed that:
- an input design problem is fully specified prior to the temporal floorplanning
- a system (or its part) designed using the proposed method is non-reactive, i.e. its behaviour cannot be changed through the external control signals. Such an operation is typical for signal-processing applications.

---

[1] We use the term *feasible solution* here in its traditional meaning known from the field of combinatorial optimisation. In the context of the presented DRL synthesis problem, a design solution is feasible if and only if its implementation is possible in the selected target DRL technology and this implementation provides a behavioural functionality identical to that of an input problem model. The solution feasibility alone does not imply that the solution satisfies all the design constraints.

- the target reconfigurable system is synchronous with one common system clock signal
- the configuration controller is external to the dynamically reconfigurable logic array and all array resources are available for the design implementation
- an external memory is available for storage of the configuration data and the data shared between the configurations
- data between blocks in different configurations is transfered either via registers shared between the configurations or via the external memory. In the latter case, the data is stored and retrieved from the external memory as a part of the configuration process.

An input to the synthesis algorithm is a behavioural model of the design problem in a form of a Control/Data Flow Graph (CDFG). The synthesis process will generate a design solution containing the final 3D floorplan and an execution and configuration schedule for the design (Fig. 2).

The information extracted from the final 3D floorplan can be used to generate the configuration data needed for the implementation of the design in the target DRL technology. The reconfiguration schedule can be executed by the external reconfiguration controller, which will control the system execution and reconfiguration process.

The following tasks are performed on the input design model during the automatic temporal floorplanning:

- *Module allocation:* each node in a CDFG is assigned to a module selected from one of the libraries available in the technology library server.
- *Scheduling:* execution period for each of the CDFG nodes is scheduled within the overall design schedule.
- *3D floorplanning:* design modules are positioned in a 3D floorplan. The coordinates in the horizontal plane represent spatial positions of design modules. The vertical module coordinates provide a temporal dimension, which is measured in the schedule control steps.
- *Cost evaluation:* an on-line cost evaluation function is used to evaluate the overall quality of the generated solutions. The cost function forces rejection of solutions violating either design constraints (overall latency, solution spatial size, data-dependency violations) or target technology constraints (module spatial overlaps in a 3D floorplan, configuration dependency violation). Configuration latency is also recalculated as a part of the cost evaluation.

3 Synthesis Algorithm

Solution search for the problem of temporal floorplanning has to produce a design satisfying multiple design and technological constraints. Several optimisation techniques exist, which can cope with the optimisation in a multiple-objective search space.

Genetic algorithms [6] have been shown to be successful for a variety of multiple-objective design problems, including those of traditional ASIC synthesis. These optimisation algorithms model the process of the natural evolution

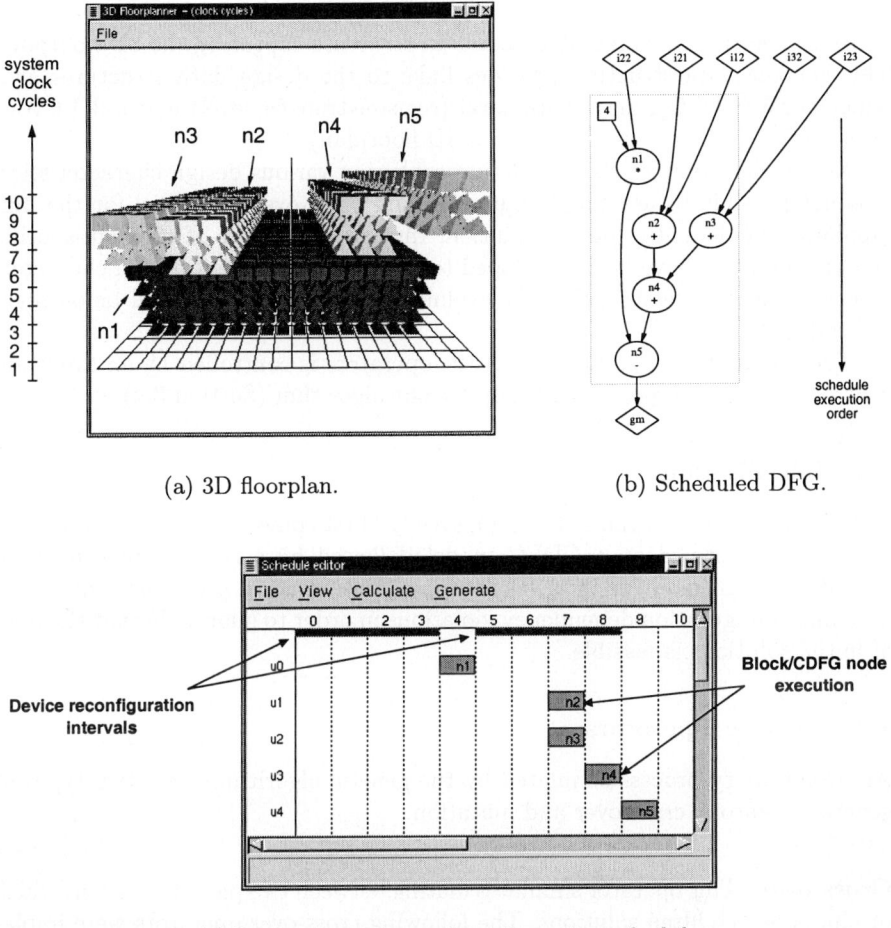

Fig. 2. A Laplace operator mask 3D floorplan and data-flow graph during temporal floorplanning. Each layer in the 3D floorplan represents one *system clock cycle*; a pyramid indicates that a block is being reconfigured and a cube denotes its execution.

using mathematical models for natural selection, reproduction, cross-over and mutation.

We have developed a variation of a genetic algorithm adapted to the problem of temporal floorplanning. The MIT GAlib library [7] was used to implement the algorithm core. Our approach uses a steady-state generic algorithm with tournament selection. A problem-specific genome, genetic operators, cost function and evolution control routine were developed for this synthesis problem and these are briefly outlined in the following sections.

3.1 Genetic Solution Representation (Genome)

A design solution is represented as a data structure capturing the 3D floorplan. This genome data structure provides links to the design data structures at a behavioural (CDFG), an architectural (register-transfer level) and a 3D layout level (netlist of blocks positioned in a 3D floorplan).

As this is a complex data structure capturing various design characteristics, it is not possible to use simple mutation and cross-over operators for the manipulation of the entire design solution. Instead, a number of problem-specific generic operators have been developed to manipulate different design characteristics at different stages during the evolutionary process. These will be outlined in Section 3.3.

The probability of application of the operators is controlled by an evolution control strategy designed specifically for our algorithm (Section 3.4).

3.2 Initialisation

A design solution is initialised using a greedy "first come - first serve" allocation algorithm performed on a CDFG model, followed by a random placement of allocated design modules in a 3D floorplan. Initialisation procedure checks for data and configuration dependency violations in order to guarantee that the pool of initial solutions is feasible.

3.3 Genetic Operators

An evolutionary process simulated by the genetic algorithms uses two types of genetic operators: cross-over and mutation.

Cross-over. This operator simulates mating between two parent solutions which produces two children solutions. The following cross-over operators were implemented in our approach:
- *module allocation cross-over* exchanges modules allocated to identical CDFG nodes in parent solutions
- *random-sized 2D floorplan cross-over* exchanges X-Y (i.e. horizontal only) positions between the two module groups in one floorplan layer
- *random-sized 3D floorplan cross-over* exchanges a randomly-sized group of modules between the two parent 3D floorplans. This will copy the X-Y-Z positions of the selected modules (both horizontal and vertical placement).

Mutation. This operator simulates random changes to one or more individual solutions. The following mutation operations were designed:
- *module allocation mutation* changes the module allocated to a given CDFG node to a module of a different type, but with the same functionality (e.g a ripple-carry adder can be swapped for a carry-lookahead adder)
- *2D floorplan mutation* changes X-Y coordinates of the selected module in a 2D floorplan layer

- *3D floorplan mutation* changes X-Y-Z coordinates of the selected module in a 3D floorplan layer
- *3D floorplan "shaking"* produces an effect of a randomised "shaking" of the entire 3D floorplan. This is a greedy algorithm, which generates new X-Y coordinates for all randomly selected modules in the solution. This may lead to further compaction of the 3D floorplan.

3.4 Evolution Control Strategy

The simulated evolution is being controlled by a core steady-state generic algorithm. A supplementary monitoring algorithm is implemented, which controls the frequency of application of the selected genetic operators. These probabilities change dynamically in the response to the population divergence changes during the course of the evolution. The control function and the individual probabilities can be changed by the designer.

The overall strategy is to apply the operators which produce big changes in the design solution early during the evolution (when the population divergence is large). As the confidence in the generated solutions increases (observed as decreasing population divergence) the probability of the fine-tuning operators (e.g. 2D floorplan mutation) increases at the expense of operators producing big changes. The evolution terminates once a solution satisfying the design objectives was generated or at a request from the designer.

Solution correction algorithm. is invoked on a design solution after application of each generic operator. This checks for data dependencies, evaluates configuration overhead and calculates the overall design latency. Dependency violations are resolved by gradual increase of the design latency until all such violations are removed.

Configuration time is calculated using a technology-specific algorithm from the target technology library server. Depending on the capabilities of the target technology, this algorithm may consider partial reconfiguration and resource sharing at fine granularity.

Cost (fitness) function. used in our algorithm evaluates the overall design execution latency. This is a composite metric measured in the system clock cycles, and includes both execution and reconfiguration delays. Other criteria (e.g. memory size required for the configuration storage) could be also incorporated in the cost function.

4 Design Experiments

The temporal floorplanning algorithm presented in this paper was tested using three small design benchmarks. Our goal was to compare the results against the benchmarks, for which good manually-optimised solutions are known.

A model FPGA device based on the Xilinx XC6200 [8] was used for the experiments. All experiments were conducted within the DYNASTY Framework [5] and its XC6200 technology library server.

The XC6200 library server implemented in the DYNASTY Framework provides an estimation algorithm suitable for the calculation of the reconfiguration overhead in a given 3D floorplan. The algorithm uses a detailed model of the XC6200 architecture and its configuration interface. In its present implementation, the XC6200 configuration estimation algorithm does not use the wildchar feature of the XC6200 configuraion interface.

The following benchmarks were used for our experiments (Fig. 3):
- *HAL differential equation solver [9]* was used to test the algorithm in a scenario when a large problem needs to be mapped on an area-limited reconfigurable architecture. This is achieved by "folding" the algorithm execution across a series of configurations.
- *Laplace transform spatial filter mask [10]* was used to test the case when sharing between two configuration has to be maximised in order to minimise the reconfiguration overhead. Two masks with different coefficients were used for this evaluation.
- *Pattern matcher comparator circuit [11]* was used to test whether the algorithm will be able to identify that configuration of only one logic cell needs to be modified in order to change between the two versions of a circuit.

5 Conclusions

For the pattern matcher circuit an identical result to the manually-optimised design was achieved leading to configuration overhead of only one system clock cycle. For the "folded" implementation of the Laplace transform and HAL differential equation benchmarks, the average latency of the automatically generated results was higher than for the manually-optimised solution by 19% and 27% respectively. Individual results approaching the qualities of the manually-optimised design were observed in many synthesis trials.

These results demonstrate that the presented automatic technique is *not* able to achieve results identical to those optimised manually. This, however, is an expected result as the behavioural/RTL synthesis techniques for static systems suffer from the similar inefficiencies. Similarly to our preliminary results, these techniques cannot achieve the efficiency identical to the manually-optimised solutions for most, but very simple cases.

The accuracy of the presented synthesis method depends also on the accuracy of the estimation algorithms provided by the library server. Within the DYNASTY framework, designers can choose the type of estimation algorithm used for configuration overhead estimation. This provides an opportunity to select the desired tradeoff between the algorithm execution time and the accuracy of the generated design solutions

The presented automatic design exploration tool can be used to synthesise a DRL design for a given problem within a very short time. While manual optimisation of the above benchmarks may take several hours or even days,

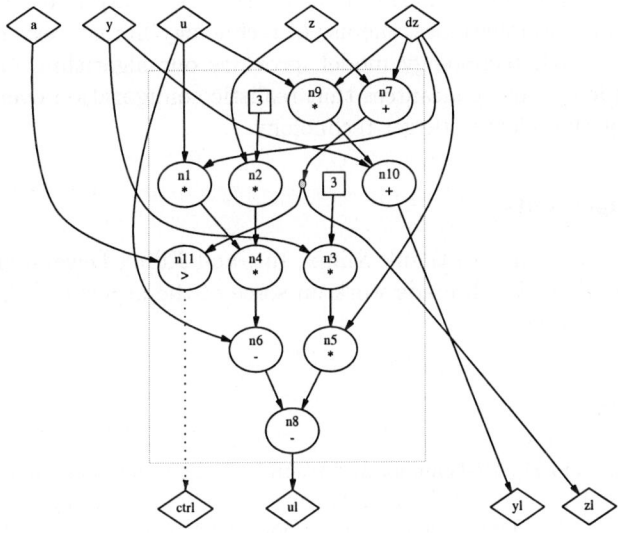

(a) HAL differential equation solver (loop body).

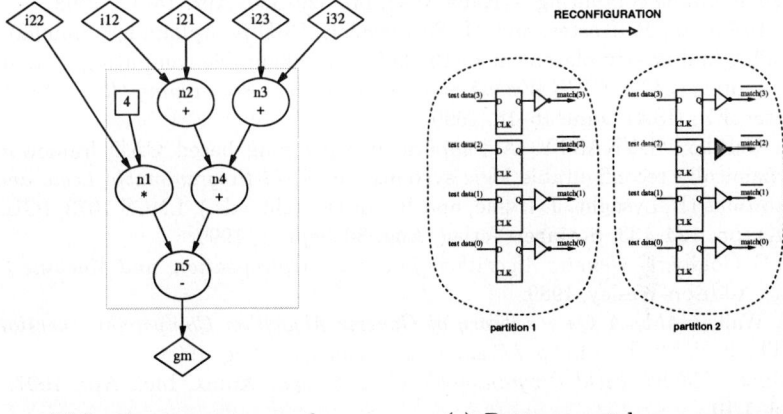

(b) Laplace operator mask.

(c) Pattern matcher comparator circuit.

Fig. 3. Benchmark design problems.

our algorithm can produce solutions with about 50% inefficiency within several minutes (Pentium 450MHz PC). Such an approximate result can be used to estimate the feasibility of the implementation of the input design problem using the selected DRL technology.

In most real-world scenarios, designers wish to explore the design implementation tradeoffs in different target technologies. With the approach presented in this paper it is possible to perform such a tradeoff analysis using different design constraints. Furthermore, the use of technology library servers rather than a generalised DRL technology model, provides our algorithm with a technology independence, and guarantees that realistic configuration overheads will be estimated for the selected target technology.

Acknowledgements

The authors would like to thank Xilinx, Inc. and Xilinx Development Corporation. for donations which made work on some of the aspects of the DYNASTY Framework possible.

References

1. M. Vasilko and D. Ait-Boudaoud, "Architectural synthesis techniques for dynamically reconfigurable logic," in Hartenstein and Glesner [12], pp. 290–296.
2. M. Kaul and R. Vemuri, "Optimal temporal partitioning and synthesis for reconfigurable architectures," in *Design, Automation and Test in Europe Conference*, (Paris, France), Feb. 23–26, 1998.
3. K. M. GajjalaPurna and D. Bhatia, "Temporal partitioning and scheduling for reconfigurable computing," (Napa, CA), pp. 329–330, Apr. 15–17, 1998.
4. K. Bazargan, R. Kaster, and M. Sarrafzadeh, "3-D floorplanning: Simulated annealing and greedy placement methods for reconfigurable computing systems," in *Proceedings of the IEEE Workshop on Rapid System Prototyping (RSP'99)*, (Clearwater, FL, USA), June 16–18, 1999.
5. M. Vasilko, "DYNASTY: A temporal floorplanning based CAD framework for dynamically reconfigurable logic systems," in *Field-Programmable Logic and Applications* (P. Lysaght, J. Irvine, and R. Hartenstein, eds.), LNCS 1673, (Glasgow, UK), pp. 124–133, Springer-Verlag, Aug. 30–Sept. 1, 1999.
6. D. E. Goldberg, *Genetic Algorithms in Search, Optimisation, and Machine Learning*. Addison-Wesley, 1989.
7. M. Wall, *GAlib: A C++ Library of Generic Algorithm Components, version 2.4*. MIT, available from http://lancet.mit.edu/ga/, Aug. 1996.
8. Xilinx, *XC6200 Field Programmable Gate Arrays*. Xilinx, Inc., Apr. 1997. Version 1.10.
9. P. G. Paulin and J. P. Knight, "Algorithms for high-level synthesis," *IEEE Design and Test of Computers*, vol. 6, pp. 18–31, Dec. 1989.
10. J. P. Heron and R. F. Woods, "Architectural strategies for implementing an image processing algorithm on XC6200 FPGA," in Hartenstein and Glesner [12], pp. 317–326.
11. P. Foulk and I. Hodson, "Data folding in SRAM configurable FPGAs," in *IEEE Workshop on FPGAs for Custom Computing Machines* (D. A. Buell and K. L. Pocek, eds.), Napa, CA, USA: IEEE Comput. Soc. Press, Apr. 5–7, 1993.
12. R. W. Hartenstein and M. Glesner, eds., *Field-Programmable Logic: Smart Applications, New Paradigms and Compilers, (FPL '96 Proceedings)*, LNCS 1142, Springer-Verlag, 1996.

A Threshold Logic-Based Reconfigurable Logic Element with a New Programming Technology

Kazuo Aoyama[1], Hiroshi Sawada[1], Akira Nagoya[2], and Kazuo Nakajima[3]

[1] NTT Communication Science Laboratories, 2-4, Hikaridai, Seika-cho, Soraku-gun, Kyoto 619-0237, Japan
[2] NTT Network Innovation Laboratories, 1-1, Hikarinooka, Yokosuka-Shi, Kanagawa 239-0847, Japan
[3] Department of Electrical and Computer Engineering, University of Maryland, College Park, Maryland 20742, USA

Abstract. We introduce a new reconfigurable logic element. Its operations are based on threshold logic and it can store its own configuration data. The element is composed of threshold gates which are implemented in a two-level feed-forward neuron MOS circuit. We present a effective method of switching and storing the values of two variable thresholds in a neuron MOS transistor so as to reconfigure the element without requiring any additional memory circuit or device. Circuit simulation results are provided to verify the correct operations of the reconfigurable element in the following four function modes: symmetric function modes with/without configuration data storage, and multiplexer function modes with/without control data storage.

1 Introduction

The demands for configurable elements such as Field Programmable Gate Arrays (FPGAs) have rapidly increased in recent years. Configurability of such devices comes from the flexibility of both logic blocks and interconnection resources. In this paper we focus on a configurable logic element.

There are three basic types of configurable elements [1]. The first type is based on a look-up table (LUT) that directly implements a truth table. In this type, SRAMs are mainly used as a programming technology. The second type uses a programmable logic array (PLA) that realizes logic functions expressed in sum-of-products form using an AND-plane followed by an OR-plane. The programming element is an EEPROM that utilizes wired-AND and wired-OR implementations. The third type is based on cascaded multiplexers (MUXs). Anti-fuse programming technologies are used to form a low resistance connection.

In this paper, we apply threshold logic as a new principle for reconfigurability of devices. In particular, we show that any symmetric function of k variables is realized by a combination of $(k + 2)$ threshold gates. Note that symmetric functions appear in most parts of arithmetic processing elements.

A threshold gate is easily implemented in a neuron MOS (νMOS) inverter that consists of two νMOS transistors [2]. A logic circuit with νMOS transistors, which can alter its function according to external control signals, has also been proposed in the past [3], [4], [5]. However, no programming technology has ever been utilized in νMOS circuits.

In this paper, we propose a reconfigurable νMOS circuit shown in Table 1 which can store its own configuration data *in itself* without additional memory circuits and devices. Reconfigurability of the νMOS circuit is explained by comparing the circuit with a combination of threshold gates.

In the next section, we briefly review threshold logic and a logic circuit with νMOS transistors. In Sect. 3, we explain the reconfigurability of the circuit using a combination of threshold gates at the logic level and the νMOS circuit at the circuit level. Section 4 presents a circuit and a procedure for storing configuration data in a νMOS transistor as the programming technology. In Sect. 5, a design of a two-level feed-forward circuit is described so as to demonstrate its reconfigurability and an operation for storing its own configuration data. Circuit simulation results are also provided for the correctness of its circuit operations. Section 6 concludes the paper with some remarks and future work.

Table 1. Comparison of reconfigurable elements

Logic Block Type	Principle of Reconfigurability	Programming Technology
LUT	Truth Table	SRAM
PLA	Sum of Products	EEPROM
MUX	Cascaded Multiplexers	Anti-fuse
Proposed Element	*Threshold Logic*	νMOS

2 Preliminaries

2.1 Threshold Logic

A *threshold gate* is a generalization of certain conventional switching gates such as AND, OR, NAND, NOR and NOT gates [6]. It has two-valued inputs represented by variables x_i ($i = 1, 2, \cdots, k$) of the *input vector* X and a single two-valued output y. Its internal parameters are a *threshold th* and weights $w_1, w_2, \cdots, w_k$ that constitute the *weight vector* W. Each weight w_i is associated with *input variable* x_i. The values of the threshold th and the weights w_i ($i = 1, 2, \cdots, k$) may be positive or negative real numbers. The output y of the gate is given as

$$f(X) = \begin{cases} 1 & \text{if } \sum_{i=1}^{k} w_i x_i \geq th \\ 0 & \text{if } \sum_{i=1}^{k} w_i x_i < th \end{cases} \quad (1)$$

As indicated above, certain conventional gates are special cases of threshold gates. For example, when $w_i = 1$ ($i = 1, 2, \cdots, k$) and $th = 1$ in (1), the threshold gate represents an OR gate with k inputs. Threshold logic is a unified theory of such threshold gates based on the threshold decision principle as expressed in (1).

2.2 Neuron MOS Inverter: Structure and Operation

The νMOS transistor is different in structure from a conventional MOS transistor. It has an electrically-floating gate electrode called a *floating gate* and a number of gate electrodes that are capacitively coupled to the floating gate [2].

The complementary νMOS inverter (simply called νMOS inverter) consists of a series connection of a p-type and an n-type νMOS transistor, as shown in Fig. 1(a). A circuit diagram and a logic diagram for an n-input νMOS inverter are shown in Fig. 1(a) and 1(b), respectively.

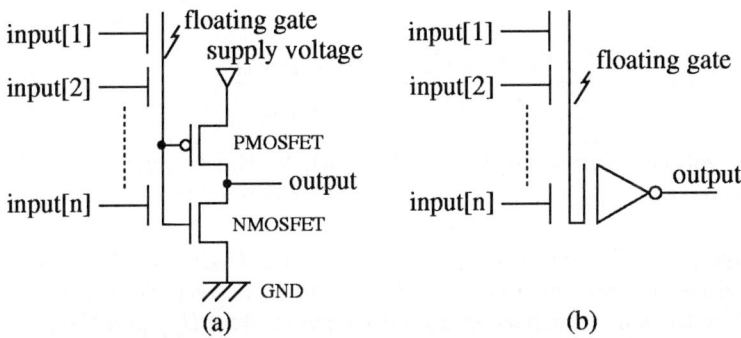

Fig. 1. Circuit symbols for a complementary ν MOS inverter. (a) Circuit diagram. (b) Logic diagram.

The operation of the νMOS inverter can be interpreted as that of a threshold gate. Let us assume that a "1" represents output voltages higher than the switching voltage of the νMOS inverter and a "0" represents lower output voltages. We call the switching voltage a *floating gate threshold voltage* and denote it by V_{fth}. The output voltage (U_{out}) represented by 1 or 0 is obtained by using the voltage of the floating gate (V_{fg}) and V_{fth} as follows.

$$U_{out} = \begin{cases} 0 & \text{if } V_{fg} > V_{fth} \\ 1 & \text{if } V_{fg} < V_{fth} \end{cases} \quad (2)$$

Furthermore, let us assume that

$$\sum_{i=1}^{n} C_i \gg \sum_{i=1}^{3} C_{p(i)} + \sum_{i=1}^{3} C_{n(i)}, \quad (3)$$

where C_i denotes the input gate capacitance between the i-input gate (input[i] in Fig. 1(a)) and the floating gate, $C_{p(i)}$ the capacitance between the floating gate and the terminals: source, drain and bulk of the p-type νMOS transistor, and $C_{n(i)}$ the capacitance between the floating gate and any terminal of the n-type νMOS transistor. Under this assumption, we have

$$V_{fg} = \frac{\sum_{i=1}^{n} C_i \cdot V_i}{\sum_{i=1}^{n} C_i}, \quad (4)$$

where V_i is the voltage of the i-input gate. The typical input-output characteristics of the νMOS inverter are given by (2) and (4).

Some input gate electrodes are used for the input variables, but others are used for controlling the threshold. In the latter case, *variable thresholds* are generated in the νMOS inverter [4]. A diagram for such a νMOS inverter is depicted in Fig. 2(a). There are three different types of input gate electrodes: 1) input1[i] for the i-th input variable ($i = 1, 2, \cdots, k$), 2) input2 for the signal that switches the two thresholds, and 3) two gate electrodes, one connected to the supply voltage terminal and the other connected to the ground terminal, for adjusting thresholds. The value of the floating-gate voltage V_{fg} of the inverter is given as

$$V_{fg} = \frac{\sum_{i=1}^{k} C_i \cdot V_i + C_v \cdot V_v + C_{vdd} \cdot V_{dd}}{\sum_{i=1}^{k} C_i + C_v + C_{vdd} + C_{gnd}}, \quad (5)$$

where V_i is the voltage of input1[i] ($i = 1, 2, \cdots, k$), V_v the voltage of input2, V_{dd} the supply voltage, and C_i, C_v, C_{vdd}, and C_{gnd} denote the capacitances described in Fig. 2(a).

In order to simplify (5), we use new parameters U_i, U_v, U_{vdd}, and U_{gnd}. They represent the values of capacitances C_i, C_v, C_{vdd}, and C_{gnd}, respectively, which are normalized by the sum of capacitances. Other parameters U_{fg} and U_{fth} are also utilized instead of V_{fg} and V_{fth}. More specifically, U_{fg} denotes the value of V_{fg} normalized by a maximum of V_{fg}, which is the supply voltage V_{dd} that appears in (5), and U_{fth} is the value of V_{fth} normalized by the same value. Finally, we define a new parameter Z, called an *input status*, as follows.

$$Z = \frac{\sum_{i=1}^{k} C_i \cdot V_i}{V_{dd} \sum_{i=1}^{k} C_i / k}. \quad (6)$$

Using the above parameters, (5) and (2) are modified as follows:

$$U_{fg} = \left(\frac{\sum_{i=1}^{k} U_i}{k}\right) \cdot Z + U_v \cdot \left(\frac{V_v}{V_{dd}}\right) + U_{vdd} \quad (7)$$

$$U_{out} = \begin{cases} 0 & \text{for } U_{fg} > U_{fth} \\ 1 & \text{for } U_{fg} < U_{fth} \end{cases}. \quad (8)$$

Characteristics of the new parameter U_{fg} are illustrated in Fig. 2(b). In the figure, two lines denoted by *line0* and *line1* plot the values of U_{fg} for the cases of $V_v = 0$ and $V_v = V_{dd}$, respectively. These lines intersect the horizontal line of value U_{fth} at $Z = z_{ith0}$ and $Z = z_{ith1}$, respectively, as shown by dots. We call these points *input thresholds* to distinguish them from U_{fth}. Consequently, the νMOS inverter has two different *input thresholds* depending on the value of V_v.

Comparing (7) and (8) for the νMOS inverter and (1) for the threshold gate, we can observe that the νMOS inverter is expressed by a series combination of the threshold gate and the inverter.

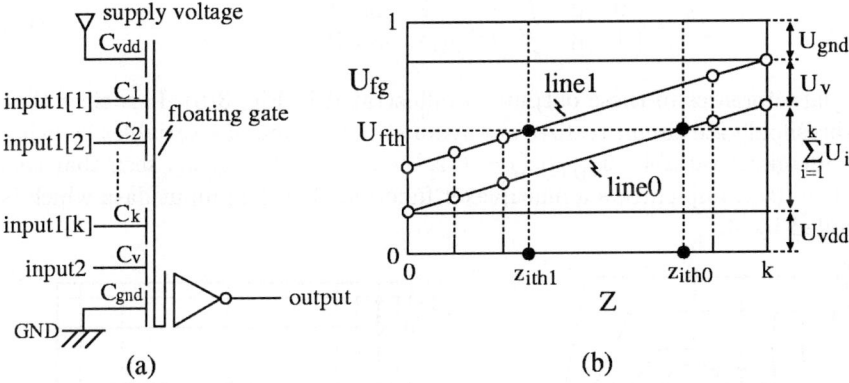

Fig. 2. Structure and characteristics of variable-threshold νMOS inverter. (a) Basic structure. (b) Diagram representing normalized floating gate voltage (U_{fg}) as function of *input status (Z)*.

3 Reconfigurability Based on Threshold Logic

3.1 Logic Level

A Boolean function of k variables is called *symmetric* if its output remains unchanged for any permutation of certain input variables contained in a subset of the k variables. Such functions are frequently used in arithmetic and/or logic circuits. It is known that a single threshold gate as expressed by (1) cannot realize all Boolean functions but that a combination of such gates can. In this section, we show that any symmetric function can be implemented very easily by a combination of threshold gates.

To realize such a function of k input variables, we use a two-level feed-forward circuit consisting of $(k+2)$ threshold gates as shown in Fig. 3(a). We denote the $(j+1)$-st threshold gate ($0 \leq j \leq k$) at the first level by THG1[$j+1$] and the one at the second level by THG2.

Each gate THG1[$j+1$] ($j = 0, 1, \cdots, k$) has k input variables of the same weight, namely, $w = 1$, and a control variable denoted by $x_{2[j+1]}$ for two variable thresholds as shown in Fig. 2(b). The higher and lower threshold values for THG[$j+1$] are ($j+1/2$) and ($j-1/2$), respectively, by setting $x_{2[j+1]}$ as "0" and "1", respectively. The inputs to the last gate THG2 are the same k input variables as mentioned above and the outputs from all THG1 gates. The threshold value for THG2 is ($k + 1/2$).

Threshold gates THG1[$j+1$] and THG2 operate as follows. The output of THG1[$j+1$], denoted by $f^{(j+1)}$, depends on the value of $x_{2[j+1]}$ and input status Z, which represents the number of input variables whose values are "1". The output f^0 of THG2 depends on $x_{2[Z+1]}$. More specifically, these outputs are expressed as:

$$f^{(j+1)} = \begin{cases} 0 & \text{if } j < Z \text{ or } (j = Z \text{ \& } x_{2[j+1]} = 1) \\ 1 & \text{if } j > Z \text{ or } (j = Z \text{ \& } x_{2[j+1]} = 0) \end{cases} \quad (9)$$

$$f^0 = \begin{cases} 0 & \text{if } f^{(Z+1)} = 1 \quad \text{for } Z \\ 1 & \text{if } f^{(Z+1)} = 0 \quad \text{for } Z \end{cases} \tag{10}$$

The characteristics of these outputs are illustrated in Fig. 3(b). It is clear that this threshold gate circuit realizes any symmetric function of k variables by using a set of control variables $x_{2[j+1]}$ $(j = 1, 2, \cdots, k)$. It is also easily seen that this circuit, in fact, implements a multiplexer function of $(k+1)$ input data which is controlled by Z.

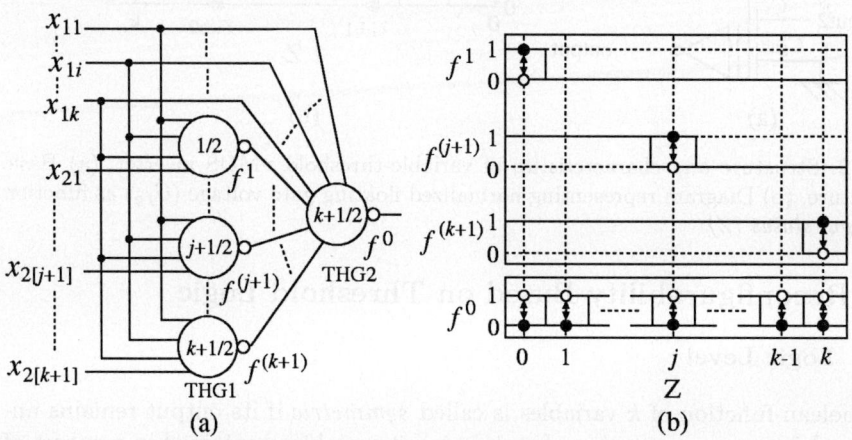

Fig. 3. (a) Structure of a combination of threshold gates. Large and small circles designate threshold and NOT gates, respectively. Threshold values are specified inside large circles. (b) Output functions with respect to Z. A pair of black and white circles indicates variable values by controlling signals.

3.2 Circuit Level

By substituting the νMOS inverters of Fig. 2(a) for the threshold gates described above in Sect. 3.1, we obtain the νMOS circuit depicted in Fig. 4(a). The equal weight of input variables in the threshold gate corresponds to an equal value of input gate capacitances of the νMOS inverter which are described by (4) and (6), where Z in (6) is modified as:

$$Z = \sum_{i=1}^{k} \left(\frac{V_i}{V_{dd}} \right). \tag{11}$$

Note that the input status Z represents the number of input variables whose values are "1" in logic.

The two variable threshold values of gate THG1$[j+1]$ correspond to the *input thresholds*: z_{ith0} and z_{ith1} in the variable-threshold νMOS inverter of Sect. 2.2. We now call threshold gate THG1$[j + 1]$ the $(j+1)$-st *pre-inverter* and THG2 the *main inverter* at the circuit level. Furthermore, the value of U_{fth} is adjusted to 1/2 in the pre-inverters and the main inverter. As a result, U_{fg} in the main inverter is expressed as a function of Z and is shown in Fig. 4(b). A logical inversion of U_{fg} in Fig. 4(b) corresponds to f^0 in Fig. 3(b). Thus, the νMOS circuit corresponds to the threshold gate circuit presented in the preceding section.

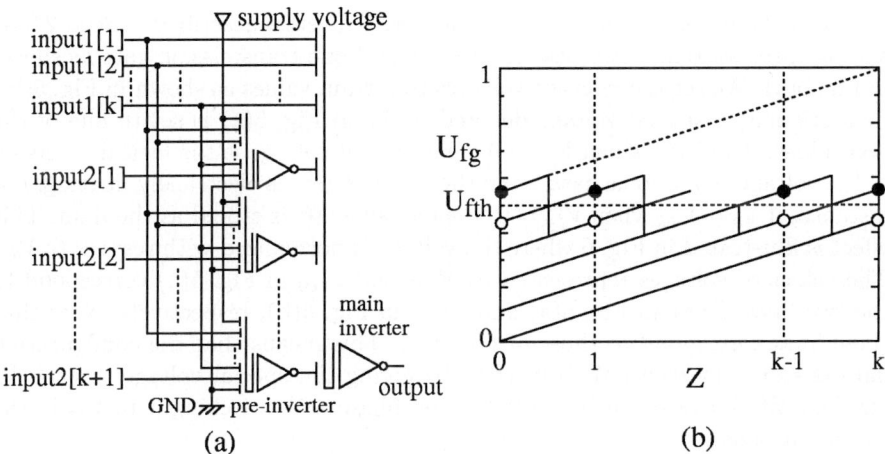

Fig. 4. (a) Structure of a two-level feed-forward νMOS circuit. (b) U_{fg} as function of Z. A pair of black and white circles indicates variable values by controlling signals.

4 Programming Technology

Configuration data is said to be stored in a νMOS circuit such as the one shown in Fig. 4(a) when either line0 or line1 of Fig. 2 (b) which is associated with each νMOS inverter is realized without external continuous signals. In this section, we present an innovative method of storing configuration data without any additional memory circuit or device such as an SRAM, latch circuit, and EEPROM for each input2[j+1]. We achieve this by controlling the relation between the charge and the voltage of the floating gate in the νMOS inverter.

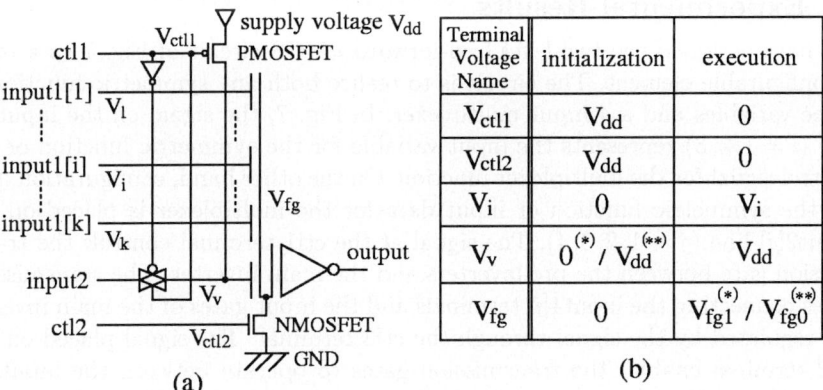

Fig. 5. (a) Structure of a νMOS circuit for storing configuration data. (b) Voltage conditions for initialization phase and for execution phase.

For this purpose, we first enhance the νMOS inverter described in Sect. 2.2 by adding three switches: two pass transistors and one transmission gate as shown in Fig. 5(a). We set the relevant voltages to certain values as shown in Fig. 5(b). In particular, a special voltage denoted by V_v in Fig. 5(a) is set to one of the two values, 0 and V_{dd} when $V_{fg} = 0$. This special voltage is the logical inversion of the voltage required as data when the floating gate is electrically floating. For instance, if $V_v = V_{dd}$ when $V_{fg} = 0$, then a value "0" is stored as the data. This effect is illustrated in Fig. 6 where the voltage is normalized with respect to V_{dd}. The values of voltages represented by V_{fg1} and V_{fg0} in Fig. 5(b) correspond to the two lines: $line1$ in Fig. 6(a) and $line0$ in Fig. 6(b), respectively. Note that these lines correspond to those of Fig. 2(b). This means that the configuration data is stored in each νMOS inverter by giving the special voltage to each V_v for the νMOS inverter in the initialization phase and switching it to V_{dd} in the execution phase.

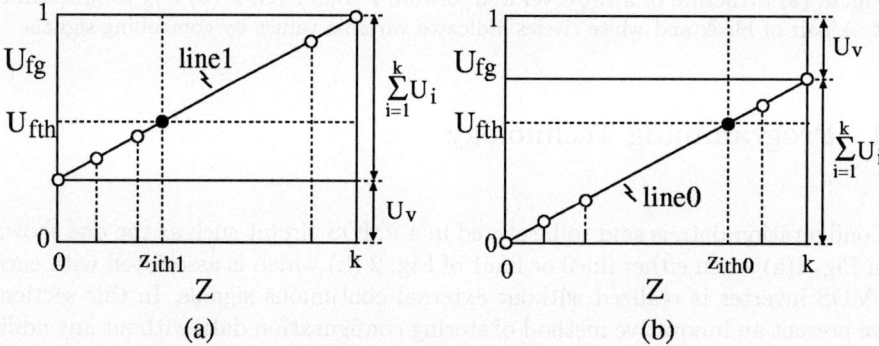

Fig. 6. U_{fg} as function of *input status* Z. (a) A value "1" is stored by initially setting $V_v = 0$. (b) A value "0" is stored by initially setting $V_v = V_{dd}$.

5 Experimental Results

We have designed the two-level feed-forward νMOS circuit of Fig. 7 as a basic reconfigurable element. The circuit is to realize both any symmetric function of three variables and a 4-input multiplexer. In Fig. 7, the signal on the input1[i] line ($i = 1, 2, 3$) represents the input variable for the symmetric function or the control signal for the multiplexer function. On the other hand, configuration data for the symmetric function or input data for the multiplexer is placed on the input2[j] line ($j = 1, 2, 3, 4$). The signal at the ctl1 terminal controls the transmission gate between the pre-inverters and the main inverter. The transmission gates connecting the input1[i] terminals and the input gates of the main inverter are regulated by the signal through the ctl3 terminal. The signal placed on the ctl2 terminal enables the transmission gates to operate between the input2[j] terminal and the input gate of the pre-inverter. Initial values of the charges and voltages of floating gates in the pre-inverters and the main inverter are given when the signal through the ctl4 terminal is "1" in logic.

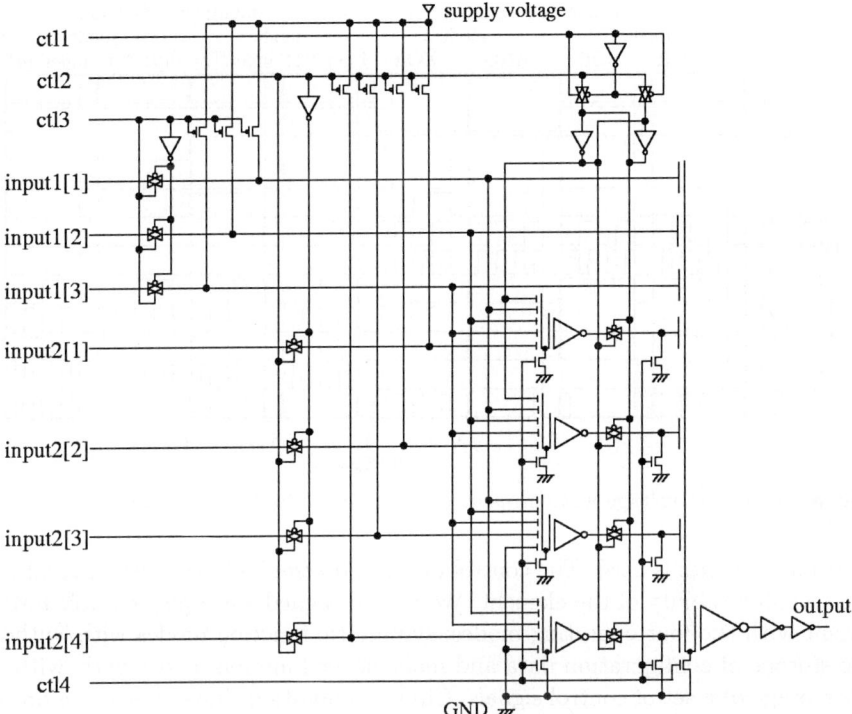

Fig. 7. νMOS circuit realizing four modes: a symmetric function with/without configuration data storage and a multiplexer function with/without control data storage.

Figure 8 shows the results obtained by circuit simulations. Two representative functions in each of the four operating modes are executed consecutively. When a function is realized, the first 0.2μsec is the period of setting up the initial conditions for the charge and voltage of the floating gate of each νMOS inverter. In the first 2μsec (*mode1*), XNOR and NOR, as examples of a symmetric function, are realized without configuration data storage. In 2-4μsec (*mode2*), the AND and XOR operations are performed with configuration data storage. Note that any input2[j] terminal is fixed to the ground voltage in the execution period. In 4-6μsec (*mode3*), the voltages of input2[1] and input2[2] are selected without control data storage. In 6-8μsec (*mode4*), the voltages of input2[3] and input2[4] are applied with control data storage. Note that *mode4* can also be utilized as a wire that connects any input2[j] and the output. The proper operations of the circuit are verified for all functions listed in Fig. 8.

6 Conclusions and Future Work

We have presented a new reconfigurable logic element using a combination of threshold gates. It is implemented in a two-level feed-forward νMOS circuit. The circuit realizes any symmetric function and a multiplexer function. As for the programming technology, a νMOS inverter with two pass transistors and one

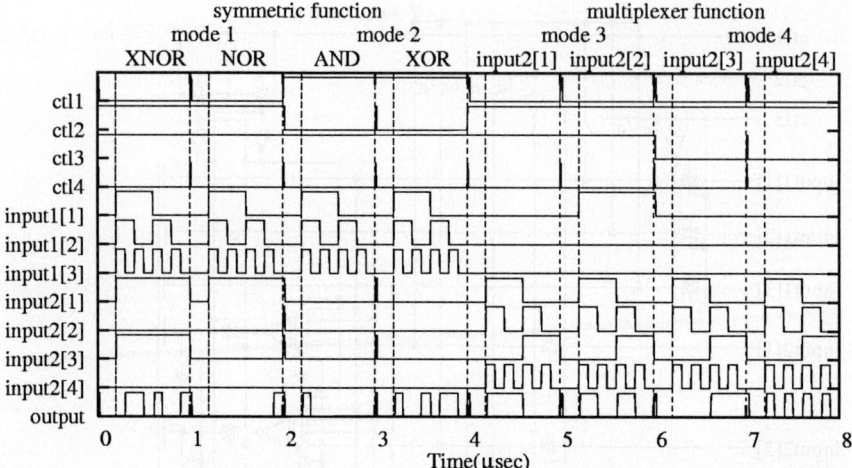

Fig. 8. Operation voltage waveforms at the terminals obtained by circuit simulation.

transmission gate is used. The control of *input thresholds* in the circuit results in the reconfigurability of the element. We have designed a 3-input variable νMOS circuit with the four operating modes: symmetric function modes with/without the storage of configuration data and multiplexer function modes with/without the storage of a set of control signals. Circuit simulations have shown the proper operations in the four function modes.

We plan to fabricate a chip for the νMOS circuit and compare the circuit performances such as area, execution and reconfiguration speeds with those for a conventional LUT using SRAMs. Furthermore, we will explore basic logic block architecture so as to effectively utilize features of the reconfigurable element.

Acknowledgements
The authors would like to thank Prof. T. Shibata of The University of Tokyo in Japan for informative discussions about circuits with neuron MOS transistors.

References

1. Brown, S.D., Francis, R.J., Rose, J., Vranesic, Z.G.: Field-Programmable Gate Arrays. Kluwer Academic Publishers (1992)
2. Shibata, T., Ohmi, T.: A Functional MOS Transistor Featuring Gate-Level Weighted Sum and Threshold Operations. IEEE Trans. ED. **39** (1992) 1444-1455
3. Shibata, T., Kotani, K., Ohmi, T.: Real-Time Reconfigurable Logic Circuits Using Neuron MOS Transistors. IEEE ISSCC93 **FA 15.3** (1993) 238-239
4. Shibata, T., Ohmi, T.: Neuron MOS Binary-Logic Integrated Circuits-Part I: Design Fundamentals and Soft-Hardware-Logic Circuit Implementation. IEEE Trans. ED. **40** (1993) 570-576
5. Shibata, T., Ohmi, T.: Neuron MOS Binary-Logic Integrated Circuits-Part II: Simplifying Techniques of Circuit Configuration and their Practical Applications. IEEE Trans. ED. **40** (1993) 974-979
6. Muroga, S.: Threshold Logic and Its Applications. John Wiley & Sons, Inc. (1971)

Exploiting Reconfigurability for Effective Detection of Delay Faults in LUT-Based FPGAs

Andrzej Krasniewski

Institute of Telecommunications, Warsaw University of Technology
Nowowiejska 15/19, 00-665 Warsaw, Poland
andrzej@tele.pw.edu.pl

Abstract. We present an extension of a procedure for self-testing of an FPGA that implements a user-defined function. This extension, intended to improve the detectability of FPGA delay faults, exploits the reconfigurability of FPGAs and is based on modifying the functions of LUTs in the section under test. A modification procedure replaces a user-defined function of each LUT with a specific function that preserves the blocking capability and input-output transition pattern of the original function. We show that the proposed method significantly increases the susceptibility of FPGA delay faults to random testing.

1 Introduction

The proposed testing techniques for reprogrammable FPGAs can be classified into:
- external techniques that exploit regular internal structure and reconfigurability of an FPGA to concurrently examine its individual components - programmable logic blocks, interconnection segments and interconnection switching arrays [1], [2];
- BIST-based techniques that exercise an FPGA in a number of self-test sessions, so that during each session a selected part of the FPGA is examined using the remaining portions of the device, temporarily configured into test pattern generators and test response compactors [3].

The techniques of both categories examine, as exhaustively as possible, all possible operation modes of programmable components, so that to give a reasonable chance that after programming the device will correctly operate in the field, regardless of a specific function implemented by the user. Such a test strategy, normally employed by the FPGA manufacturer, can be referred to as application-independent testing.

The application-independent testing, even if run at-speed (with normal operation clock frequency), is unlikely to effectively detect timing-related faults. To explain that, it must be observed that FPGA delay faults are mainly associated with interconnections: interconnection delays can account for over 70% of the FPGA clock cycle period [4] and programmable interconnections are the primary source of large variations in propagation delays. Testing for delay faults should, therefore, focus on excessive delays in the interconnection structure. During the application-independent testing, it is however impossible to examine a significant fraction of all possible FPGA interconnection patterns and therefore it is impossible to check a significant fraction of interconnections that occur in a particular user-defined circuit.

To deal with FPGA delay faults effectively, the concept of application-dependent testing (also referred to as user test [2]) has been proposed. The idea is to exercise only one configuration of the FPGA - corresponding to the user-defined function.

The application-dependent self-testing of a reconfigurable FPGA can be performed by decomposing the user-defined logic into a number of sections and exercising each section using the remaining components of the FPGA temporarily configured into BIST modules, similarly as proposed for application-independent FPGA testing [3]. This way, FPGA self-testability is obtained at no circuitry or performance overhead.

In [5], we proposed a technique for application-dependent testing of FPGAs, called C-exhaustive testing (combinationally-exhaustive testing); we also presented the corresponding BIST scheme. This scheme provides for at-speed testing of the FPGA components configured in the same or very similar way as in the normal system operation. Therefore, it is quite suitable for the detection of timing-related problems.

As shown in [6], the basic C-exhaustive self-test scheme can be extended to improve the effectiveness of detection of delay faults. The first step is to satisfy the *timing preservation requirement*, i.e. to make the conditions of testing identical or very close to those that occur in the normal circuit operation. The next step is to replace the function of each LUT included in the section under test with a XOR function. In this paper, we first recall this method and discuss its advantages and drawbacks. Then, we present a different procedure for the modification of the LUT functions which overcomes the drawbacks of the XOR-based replacement procedure.

2 XOR-Based Modification of LUT Functions

We consider a LUT-based FPGA in which a programmable logic block is includes one or more single-output SRAMs, each of which implements a look-up-table (LUT).

A combinational logic block in a circuit implemented with such an FPGA can be thought of as a network of interconnected LUTs, each of which implementing a user-defined function.

Consider a pair of vectors applied to the input of the combinational logic block (network of LUTs). We say that a *transition* occurs at a given interconnection (output of some LUT) if the logic value at that interconnection corresponding to the first vector differs from the logic value corresponding to the second vector.

The propagation delay of a path in the network of LUTs is associated with the propagation of a transition that occurs on the input of the path. It must, however, be noted that unlike in a network of NOT, AND, NAND, OR and NOR gates, for a path in a network of LUTs, the polarity of a transition at the input of the path (rising or falling) may not determine the polarity of transitions at the interconnections along the path. To illustrate this statement, consider a path which includes a LUT that implements a XOR function. A rising transition on the on-path input of such a LUT may produce either a rising or a falling transition on the LUT output, depending on the state of the other inputs of the LUT.

As the propagation delay of an interconnection may, in general, differ for a rising and falling transition, the propagation delay of a path can only be defined for a given *transition pattern* (*path transition pattern*) which specifies the polarity of a transition at each interconnection along the path. It is sufficient to consider only *feasible transition patterns*; for each feasible transition pattern, there exists a pair of vectors that, if applied to the input of the considered network, produces that transition pattern.

To detect a path delay fault associated with a particular transition pattern, a pair of vectors must be applied to the input of the network. This pair must produce an appropriate transition on the input of the path and propagate this transition, so that at each interconnection along the path a transition defined by the transition pattern occurs.

Assuming that during the self-test a random sequence of vectors is applied to the considered network of LUTs, the detectability of delay faults can be increased by modifying the functions implemented by the LUTs. Clearly, such a modification can only be made if the propagation delay of a SRAM that implements a LUT does not depend on the SRAM content. We assume that this condition is satisfied.

In [6], we proposed a straightforward modification of the network under test - a user-defined function of each LUT is replaced with a XOR function. We showed that such a modification quite effectively increases the detectability of delay faults. In particular, we showed that for the modified network in which the longest path includes no more than 8 LUTs, for a test session of 2^{22} clock cycles (approximately 42 ms with a 100 MHz clock), the coverage of path transition patterns which translates, under some assumptions, into the coverage of path delay faults, exceeds 0.9999999.

A more detailed analysis of the method of replacing a user-defined function of each LUT with a XOR function reveals, however, several potential problems with this straightforward solution. These include:

- introducing zero-activity (redundant) nodes. After modifying the network, it may happen that a zero-activity node (a node at which no transition occurs regardless of input changes) is created in an originally non-redundant network. Clearly, for a path that includes such a node, no test exists for any delay fault associated with that path. Fortunately, it has been shown that zero-activity nodes are very unlikely to occur in real circuits designed for implementation with LUT-based FPGAs [7].
- introducing untestable path delay faults. After modifying the network, a detectable path delay fault may become undetectable. It happens when the effect of the propagation of a local extra delay is cancelled by the effect of the propagation of the same extra delay along another path which, because of the specific properties of XOR gates, cannot be "unsensitized" [7].
- occurrence of false transition patterns. After modifying the network, path transition patterns that do not occur in the original circuit can be generated during the self-test session. As a result, a user-defined circuit which would operate correctly can fail the test [8].

To alleviate these problems, another modification of LUTs is proposed.

3 Proposed Modification of the LUT Functions

The idea of the proposed modification of the combinational logic block under test is to change the user-defined content (function) of some or, in many cases, all LUTs, so that for each modified LUT the blocking capability is preserved, the input-output transition pattern is preserved, and the output activity in response to random input vectors is higher than in the original LUT.

The preservation of the blocking capability means that in the case when in the original LUT a transition at some input can be blocked by appropriate state of the other inputs (a stable 0 or 1 can occur at the LUT output, regardless of the state the considered input), then such a possibility exists also in the modified LUT.

The preservation of the input-output transition pattern means that in the modified LUT, for each single-input transition, the set of possible output transitions is the same as in the original LUT. This means, for example, that for a LUT that implements an AND function, the modified LUT never produces a falling transition on its output in response to a rising transition on one of its inputs.

By preserving of the blocking capability and the input-output transition pattern of the LUTs, the problems associated with XOR-based modification of LUTs, described in Section 2, are eliminated.

The proposed procedure for LUT modification is an extension of the procedure presented in [8], which guarantees no false transition patterns, but does not protect against introducing zero-activity nodes and untestable path delay faults.

3.1 Preserving LUT Blocking Capability and Input-Output Transition Pattern

To introduce the concept of the preservation of blocking capability and input-output transition pattern, consider a LUT that implements a single-output Boolean function F of N input variables. Let X be the set of input variables and z be the output variable of F. Function F is represented by its on-set, F_{ONSET}, i.e. the set of input vectors for which z = 1 (after FPGA programming, the LUT content is completely specified; therefore, z = 0 for input vectors not included in F_{ONSET}). For a LUT represented by function F, for each input $x \in X$, we define:

$S0_F(x)$:   the set of input vectors, such that z = 0 regardless of the state of input x;
$S1_F(x)$:   the set of input vectors, such that z = 1 regardless of the state of input x;
$TSP_F(x)$:   the set of input vectors, such that a transition on input x results in a Transition of the Same Polarity on the output z;
$TOP_F(x)$:   the set of input vectors, such that a transition on input x results in a Transition of the Opposite Polarity on the output z.

For input vectors included in all these sets, the value of variable x is represented by *.

$S0_F(x) = \emptyset$ ($S1_F(x) = \emptyset$) implies that the LUT output cannot be forced to 0 (to 1) disregarding input x (by setting appropriate values of all the other inputs). $TSP_F(x) = \emptyset$ or $TOP_F(x) = \emptyset$ implies that the polarity of a transition on input x determines the polarity of the output transition (if such an output transition occurs) regardless of the state of all the other inputs; such an input is called a *polarity-controlling input*.

Assuming that the original and modified LUTs are represented by functions F and FM, respectively, the preservation of blocking capability and input-output transition pattern can formally be defined as follows.

A LUT modification preserves the blocking capability if for each $x \in X$

$$(S0_{FM}(x) = \emptyset \text{ only if } S0_F(x) = \emptyset) \text{ and } (S1_{FM}(x) = \emptyset \text{ only if } S1_F(x) = \emptyset).$$

A LUT modification preserves the blocking capability if for each $x \in X$

$$(TSP_{FM}(x) = \emptyset \text{ iff } TSP_F(x) = \emptyset) \text{ and } TOP_{FM}(x) = \emptyset \text{ iff } TOP_F(x) = \emptyset).$$

3.2 Increasing LUT Output Activity

The output activity of an N-input LUT represented by function F in response to changes on input $x \in X$ is represented by a pair of probabilities:

$psp_F(x)$: probability that, for a random state of the N-1 remaining inputs, a transition on input x produces a transition of the same polarity on the output z,

$pop_F(x)$: probability that, for a random state of the N-1 remaining inputs, a transition on input x produces a transition of the opposite polarity on the output z.

It is clear that

$$psp_F(x) = |TSP_F(x)|/2^{N-1} \text{ and } pop_F(x) = |TOP_F(x)|/2^{N-1}.$$

where $|A|$ denotes the cardinality of set A.

A geometric average of all non-zero psp's and pop's is used as a global indicator of the LUT output activity, OA_F, i.e.

$$OA_F = [(\Pi_{x \in XPSP} psp_F(x)) \cdot (\Pi_{x \in XPOP} pop_F(x))]^{1/(|XPSP| + |XPOP|)}$$

where XPSP is the set of all $x \in X$, such that $psp_F(x) \neq 0$, and XPOP is the set of all $x \in X$, such that $pop_F(x) \neq 0$.

A modification of a function implemented by the LUT, in particular a modification that preserves the blocking capability and input-output transition pattern, can significantly change the output activity of the LUT, as illustrated by the following Example.

Example 1. Consider a 4-input LUT represented by $F_{ONSET} = \{0111, 1011\}$. For this LUT we have

$S0_F(x1) = \{*000, *001, *010, *100, *101, *110\}, \quad S1_F(x1) = \emptyset;$
$S0_F(x2) = \{0*00, 0*01, 0*10, 1*00, 1*01, 1*10\}, \quad S1_F(x2) = \emptyset;$
$S0_F(x3) = \{00*0, 00*1, 01*0, 10*0, 11*0, 11*1\}, \quad S1_F(x3) = \emptyset;$
$S0_F(x4) = \{000*, 001*, 010*, 100*, 110*, 111*\}, \quad S1_F(x4) = \emptyset;$

and

$TSP_F(x1) = \{*011\}, \quad TOP_F(x1) = \{*111\};$
$TSP_F(x2) = \{0*11\}, \quad TOP_F(x2) = \{1*11\};$

$TSP_F(x3) = \{01*1, 10*1\}$, $TOP_F(x3) = \emptyset$;
$TSP_F(x4) = \{011*, 101*\}$, $TOP_F(x4) = \emptyset$.

The output activity measures for individual inputs are:

$psp_F(x1) = psp_F(x2) = 0.125$, $psp_F(x3) = psp_F(x4) = 0.25$;
$pop_F(x1) = pop_F(x2) = 0.125$, $pop_F(x3) = pop_F(x4) = 0$;

and, hence, $OA_F = 0.176$.

Assume that the LUT has been modified, so that $FM_{ONSET} = \{0011, 0101, 0110, 0111, 1001, 1010, 1011, 1111\}$. For the modified LUT, we have:

$S0_{FM}(x1) = \{*000, *100\}$, $S1_{FM}(x1) = \{*011, *111\}$;
$S0_{FM}(x2) = \{0*00, 1*00\}$, $S1_{FM}(x2) = \{0*11, 1*11\}$;
$S0_{FM}(x3) = \{00*0, 11*0\}$, $S1_{FM}(x3) = \{01*1, 10*1\}$;
$S0_{FM}(x4) = \{000*, 110*\}$, $S1_{FM}(x4) = \{011*, 101*\}$;

and

$TSP_{FM}(x1) = \{*001, *010\}$, $TOP_{FM}(x1) = \{*101, *110\}$;
$TSP_{FM}(x2) = \{0*01, 0*10\}$, $TOP_{FM}(x2) = \{1*01, 1*10\}$;
$TSP_{FM}(x3) = \{00*1, 01*0, 10*0, 11*1\}$, $TOP_{FM}(x3) = \emptyset$;
$TSP_{FM}(x4) = \{001*, 010*, 100*, 111*\}$, $TOP_{FM}(x4) = \emptyset$.

It can easily be seen that the considered modification preserves both the blocking capability and the input-output transition pattern of the LUT.

The output activity measures for individual inputs are:

$psp_{FM}(x1) = psp_{FM}(x2) = 0.25$, $psp_{FM}(x3) = psp_{FM}(x4) = 0.5$;
$pop_{FM}(x1) = pop_{FM}(x2) = 0.25$, $pop_{FM}(x3) = pop_{FM}(x4) = 0$;

and, hence, $OA_{FM} = 0.315$, which means that the modified LUT has significantly higher output activity than the original LUT.

3.3 LUT Replacement Procedure

A procedure for finding the best replacement for a given LUT relies on a "library" of functions with optimal output activity characteristics. The functions stored in the library correspond to *basic input-output transition patterns*. For a function of N input variables, we define N+1 basic input-output transition patterns, TP(0), ..., TP(N):

TP(0): $TSP(x) \neq \emptyset$ and $TOP(x) = \emptyset$, for each $x \in X$;
TP(n), for n = 1, ..., N-1: $TSP(x) \neq \emptyset$ and $TOP(x) \neq \emptyset$, for $x \in \{x_1, ..., x_n\}$
 $TSP(x) \neq \emptyset$ and $TOP(x) = \emptyset$, for $x \in \{x_{n+1}, ..., x_N\}$;
TP(N): $TSP(x) \neq \emptyset$ and $TOP(x) \neq \emptyset$, for each $x \in X$.

For a LUT represented by TP(n), $x_1, ..., x_n$ are non-polarity-controlling inputs, whereas $x_{n+1}, ..., x_N$ are polarity-controlling inputs. It can be seen, for example, that an AND function has input-output transition pattern TP(0), a 4-input XOR function has input-output transition pattern TP(4), and the 4-input functions of Example 1 (original F and modified FM) have input-output transition pattern TP(2).

If, for a function Fopt with optimal output activity characteristics found for a given input-output transition pattern, we have $S0_{Fopt}(x) \neq \emptyset$ and $S1_{Fopt}(x) \neq \emptyset$ for each $x \in X$, then the optimal function preserves the blocking capability regardless of the original user-defined function. If, however, for some $x \in X$, $S0_{Fopt}(x) = \emptyset$ or $S1_{Fopt}(x) = \emptyset$, then other functions, in particular a maximum output activity function for which $S0_{Fopt}(x) \neq \emptyset$ and $S1_{Fopt}(x) \neq \emptyset$ for each $x \in X$, must also be included in the library. This discussion is illustrated by the following example.

Example 2. Consider a 4-input LUT and the basic input-output transition pattern TP(4). The maximum output activity function for TP(4) is a 4-input XOR function with $OA_{Fopt} = 0.5$. However, for this function, we have $S0_{Fopt}(x) = \emptyset$ and $S1_{Fopt}(x) = \emptyset$ for each $x \in X$. Therefore, the XOR function can be used as a replacement for other (user-defined) function F only if $S0_F(x) = \emptyset$ and $S1_F(x) = \emptyset$ for each $x \in X$.

To satisfy the preservation of blocking capability requirement for other functions, we have found other three functions of high output activity:

$F1_{ONSET} = \{0000, 0011, 0101, 0110, 1001, 1100, 1111\}$,
$F2_{ONSET} = \{0000, 0011, 0101, 0110, 1000, 1001, 1110, 1100, 1111\}$,
$F3_{ONSET} = \{0010, 0011, 0101, 1000, 1010, 1100, 1111\}$,

with the following characteristics

$S0_{F1}(x) \neq \emptyset$ and $S1_{F1}(x) = \emptyset$ for each $x \in X$, $OA_{F1} = 0.433$;
$S0_{F2}(x) = \emptyset$ and $S1_{F2}(x) \neq \emptyset$ for each $x \in X$, $OA_{F2} = 0.433$;
$S0_{F3}(x) \neq \emptyset$ and $S1_{F3}(x) \neq \emptyset$ for each $x \in X$, $OA_{F3} = 0.306$.

In the case when the user-defined function has some specific blocking capability characteristics, Fopt, F1 or F2 can be used. Otherwise, F3 which preserves the blocking capability for any function, must be used as a replacement.

We have developed a library of functions with optimal output activity for all basic input-output transition patterns and specific blocking capability characteristics for functions (LUTs) of up to 5 inputs. With such a library, a two-step procedure similar to that described in [8] can be applied for the replacement of a given LUT.

4 Estimation of Improvement in Susceptibility to Random Testing

In our study, the effectiveness of the proposed method for the modification of a combinational logic block composed of LUTs is demonstrated by calculating the potential improvement in the susceptibility of specific path delay faults to random testing.

In our experiments, a network composed of 4-input LUTs is examined. We consider a critical path π that includes k LUTs; path π is critical in the sense that, for each LUT, a transition on its on-path input is the latest of all its input transitions. We assume that all the LUTs along path π are characterised by the same input-output transition pattern - in our experiments, basic input-output transition patterns TP(0), TP(2), and TP(4) are examined. We assume also that the logic state of each off-path input to the LUTs along path π is random (in particular, independent of the other inputs).

It must be observed that, for a 4-input LUT characterized by TP(0) or TP(4), all 4 inputs have the same polarity-controlling characteristics, which is not the case for TP(2), where x1 and x2 are non-polarity-controlling (nPC) inputs, whereas x3 and x4 are polarity-controlling (PC) inputs. Therefore, for TP(2), when defining path π, the type of inputs on the path must be specified. Two cases are considered: (1) all on-path inputs of LUTs are nPC inputs, and (2) all on-path inputs of LUTs are PC inputs.

For each LUT along path π, two types of functions are examined: the worst-case function, i.e. function with the worst output activity characteristics, and the optimal function, i.e. function with the optimal output activity characteristics.

For TP(0), there are several optimal functions, but they do not differ with regard to the output activity measures for individual inputs. For TP(2), there are two different optimal functions; one of these two functions (FM of Example 1) is examined. For TP(4), the optimal function and its output activity depends on the assumed blocking pattern; three functions, denoted as Fopt, F1 and F3 in Example 2, are examined.

Two simple path transition patterns are considered: (1) the rising pattern for which rising transitions occur on all interconnections along the path, and (2) the alternate pattern for which rising transitions occur on the input of the first, third, ... LUT, and falling transitions occur on the input of the second, fourth, ... LUT.

For a path delay fault associated with a given path transition pattern, the susceptibility to random testing is measured by

P: probability of detection of the considered fault by a randomly generated test, i.e. probability that a randomly generated pair of input vectors produces the appropriate path transition pattern,

L: length of a random test sequence (number of pairs of input vectors) required to detect the fault with a given probability δ which can be calculated as

$$L = \lceil \log(1-\delta)/\log(1-P) \rceil$$

where $\lceil x \rceil$ denotes the least integer greater than or equal to x [9].

The maximum improvement in susceptibility of a path delay fault to random testing, resulting from the modification of the LUTs along the path, can be measured by

$$\alpha = P(Fopt)/P(Fwc), \alpha \geq 1$$
$$\beta = L(Fwc)/L(Fopt), \beta \geq 1$$

where P(Fopt), L(Fopt) and P(Fwc), L(Fwc) denote the values of P and L for the LUT functions with optimal and worst-case output activity characteristics, respectively.

As for $P \ll 1$, $\lceil \log(1-\delta)/\log(1-P) \rceil \approx \log(1-\delta)/\log(1-P)$ and $\ln(1-P) \approx -P$, we obtain $\beta \approx \alpha$. This means that α can be considered as a "universal testability improvement factor", and $L(Fopt) \approx L(Fwc)/\alpha$.

In Table 1, we present simple formulas derived in [7], that show the dependence of the worst-case probability of fault detection, P(Fwc), and the testability improvement factor, α, on the length of the path, k (number of LUTs along the path), for the path delay faults considered in our experiment.

It can be seen that no improvement in susceptibility of the considered faults to random testing ($\alpha = 1$) is obtained only for the case when the worst-case probability of fault detection is high. In other cases, the improvement is significant. To illustrate the scale of the improvement, the length of a random test sequence required to detect the fault with the probability $\delta = 0.999$, obtained for the worst-case and optimal LUT functions, for $P(Fwc) = 2^{-(3k+2)}$ and the values of the testability improvement factor, α, from Table 1 and the selected values of the path length, k, is given in Table 2.

Table 1. Dependence of the worst-case probability of fault detection and the testability improvement factor on the length of the path

input-output transition pattern	blocking pattern	type of on-path inputs	path transition pattern	worst-case probability of fault detection $P(Fwc)$	testability improvement factor α
TP(0)	-	-	rising	$2^{-(3k+2)}$	3^k
TP(2)	-	PC	rising	$2^{-(2k+2)}$	2^k
TP(2)	-	nPC	rising	$2^{-(3k+2)}$	2^k
TP(2)	-	nPC	alternate	$2^{-(3k+2)}$	3^k
TP(4)	$S0=\varnothing, S1=\varnothing$	-	-	$2^{-(k+2)}$	1
TP(4)	$S0\neq\varnothing, S1=\varnothing$	-	rising	$2^{-(3k+2)}$	3^k
TP(4)	$S0\neq\varnothing, S1=\varnothing$	-	alternate	$2^{-(3k+2)}$	4^k
TP(4)	$S0\neq\varnothing, S1\neq\varnothing$	-	rising	$3^k \cdot 2^{-(3k+2)}$	1
TP(4)	$S0\neq\varnothing, S1\neq\varnothing$	-	alternate	$2^{-(3k+2)}$	2^k

Table 2. Length of a random test sequence required to detect the path delay fault with the probability $\delta = 0.999$

path length k	L(Fwc) corresponding to $P = 2^{-(3k+2)}$	L(Fopt) ($\alpha = 2^k$)	L(Fopt) ($\alpha = 3^k$)	L(Fopt) ($\alpha = 4^k$)
4	113173	7074	1398	443
6	7243306	113177	9936	1769
8	463576621	1810847	70657	7074

The data in Table 1 and Table 2 should be interpreted as follows. Consider a path that includes 6 LUTs (k=6), each characterized by the input-output transition pattern TP(2), which passes through nPC inputs of the LUTs. For a fault associated with the alternate path transition pattern, from Table 1 we obtain $P(Fwc) = 2^{-(3k+2)}$ and $\alpha = 3^k$. Thus, from Table 2, we obtain, for a random test sequence required to detect the considered fault with the probability $\delta = 0.999$, its worst-case length L(Fwc) = 7243306 and its minimum length L(Fopt) = 9936 (improvement factor $\alpha = 729$).

The following observations can be made regarding the enhancement of testability of delay faults by such a modification of the LUT functions that preserves the LUT blocking capability and input-output transition patterns:

- Although the data in Table 1 and Table 2 are derived assuming the worst-case functions implemented by original LUTs, such worst-case functions (e.g. AND, OR, NAND, NOR) quite frequently occur in real designs. Therefore, in practice, the range of improvement in the detectability of path delay faults can be close to that given in Table 1 and Table 2.
- The testability improvement factor α increases as the length of the path grows. It can also be shown that α grows with the number of LUT inputs. Thus, the improvement in detectability of path delay faults resulting from the circuit modification grows as the circuit becomes more difficult to test.

5 Conclusion

We show how to increase the detectability of FPGA delay faults. The proposed method is based on a modification of the LUTs in the combinational logic under test - for each LUT, its function is replaced with a function that preserves the blocking capability and input-output transition pattern of the original user-defined function.

The proposed method significantly enhances the susceptibility of FPGA path delay faults to random testing and, at the same time, eliminates the problems that occur when the earlier proposed XOR-based LUT replacement procedure is used.

References

1. Huang, W. K., Meyer, F. J., Chen, X.-T., Lombardi, F.: Testing Configurable LUT-Based FPGA's. IEEE Trans. on VLSI Systems (1998) 276-283
2. Renovell, M., Figueras, J., Zorian, Y.: Test of RAM-based FPGA: Methodology and Application to the Interconnect. Proc. 15th VLSI Test Symp. (1997) 230-237
3. Stroud, C., Konala, S., Chen, P., Abramovici, M.: Built-In Self-Test of Logic Blocks in FPGAs (Finally, a Free Lunch: BIST Without Overhead!). Proc. 14th VLSI Test Symp. (1996) 387-392
4. Leeser M. et al.: Rothko - A Three-Dimensional FPGA. IEEE Design & Test of Computers 1 (1998) 16-23
5. Krasniewski, A.: Design for Application-Dependent Testability of FPGAs. Proc. Int'l Workshop on Logic and Architecture Synthesis (1997) 245-254
6. Krasniewski, A.: Application-Dependent Testing of FPGA Delay Faults. Proc. EUROMICRO'99 (1999) 260-267
7. Krasniewski, A.: Self-Testing of FPGA Delay Faults in the System Environment. Tech. Report, Warsaw Univ. of Technology, Inst. of Telecommunications (2000)
8. Krasniewski, A.: Enhancing Detection of Delay Faults in FPGA-Based Circuits by Transformations of LUT Functions, Preprints IFAC Workshop on Programmable Devices and Systems – PDS2000 (2000) 127-132
9. David R.: Random Testing of Digital Circuits - Theory and Applications, Marcel Dekker, Inc. (1998)

Dataflow Partitioning and Scheduling Algorithms for WASMII, a Virtual Hardware

Atsushi Takayama, Yuichiro Shibata, Keisuke Iwai, and Hideharu Amano

Department of Computer Science, Keio University
3-14-1 Hiyoshi Yokohama 223-8522 Japan
{takayama,shibata,iwai,hunga}@am.ics.keio.ac.jp

Abstract. This paper presents a new dataflow graph partitioning algorithm for a data driven virtual hardware system called WASMII. The algorithm divides a dataflow graph into multiple subgraphs so as not to cause a deadlock. Then the subgraphs are translated into an FPGA configuration and executed on WASMII in a time-multiplexed manner. The experimental results show the proposed algorithms can achieve 13% to 39% improvement of execution performance compared to other existing graph partitioning algorithms at the most.

1 Introduction

Although FPGAs have made new varieties of *custom computing machines* possible, two major obstacles have limited the use of these systems. First, there are hardly any standard and practical methods of translating an algorithm into an FPGA configuration. Second, the size of available FPGAs has restricted their applications.

To address these problems, we have designed a data-driven virtual hardware system called WASMII [1] based on a multi-context FPGA. An algorithm to be executed on WASMII is written in a dataflow language and then translated into a collection of FPGA contexts. WASMII executes these contexts in a time-multiplexed manner with a data driven control mechanism.

One of key technologies to execution on WASMII is a compiler that generates FPGA configuration data from a dataflow language description. In this paper, a new graph partitioning algorithm called *ITT* is proposed and implemented in the WASMII compiler. The performance is evaluated using real applications and compared with traditional partitioning algorithms.

2 WASMII Architecture

The WASMII architecture is based on a dataflow paradigm of computation. In this paradigm, a program is written in a dataflow language and then translated into a dataflow graph. Nodes and links of a graph are directly represented on a reconfigurable device. This direct representation distinguishes WASMII from most other dataflow machines.

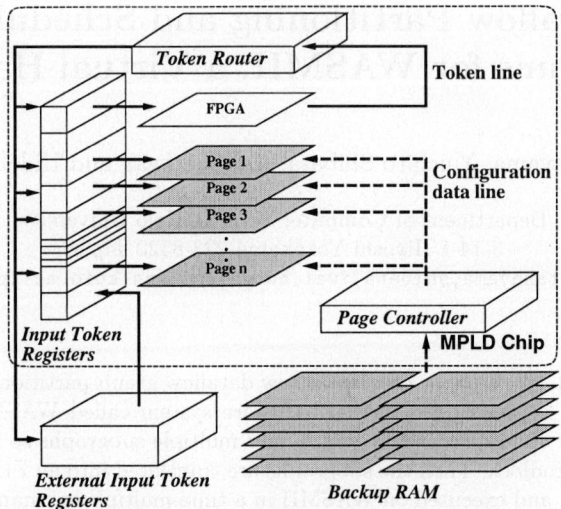

Fig. 1. WASMII architecture

A direct representation of a dataflow graph in hardware limits the size of the graph to the size that the hardware can represent. WASMII bypasses this limitation by reconfiguring the hardware dynamically, using a multi-context FPGA and additional memory to store the requisite configurations. We call this mechanism virtual hardware, in analogy to virtual memory.

When the current configuration page of WASMII is replaced by another one, all state information held in the logic circuits are invalidated. Therefore we use a set of token registers per configuration page, to store the states of the computation as shown in Fig. 1.

When an activated page produces an output token, it is sent to the token register of the appropriate configuration page by a token router. A page is ready to be activated when all its input tokens are present. When the current activated page has completed its computation and dispatched its all of output tokens, one of ready pages is selected to be replaced.

3 WASMII Compiler and Dataflow Partitioning

3.1 WASMII Compiler

First of all, an application program written in a common programming language is translated into a dataflow graph by the frontend of the compiler. DFC-Compiler which was developed for ETL's dataflow machine Sigma-I[2] is available as a frontend. This compiler translates an application written in a C-like language into an intermediate form which represents a dataflow graph. It uses techniques which are established for dataflow machines.

Then the backend of WASMII compiler applies the following steps to an intermediate code produced by the frontend.

1. Graph Analysis:
   The interconnection between nodes is analyzed first. Node names, port names and required bit width are extracted from the input netlist of a dataflow graph.
2. Graph partitioning:
   The dataflow graph is divided into some pages so that each SRAM context is able to store a whole page. As described later, it is the most difficult part of this backend.
3. Input token registers assignment:
   Input token registers are assigned into every token transferred over between subgraphs.
4. VHDL translation:
   An operator suited for each node is picked up from the VHDL library, and each subgraph is translated into a VHDL module description. Here, hardware resources required for each node and execution time are picked up from the node library.

WASMII compiler executes all above steps automatically. Once the HDL description is generated, the configuration data is obtained by using a commercial synthesis tool and a place-and-route tool dedicated to the target FPGA. The backend is implemented with perl5, a highly polished language for text manipulation.

3.2 Requirements for the Partitioning Algorithm

The most awkward step in the WASMII compiler is partitioning of the dataflow graph. In this process, the followings must be considered:

- Deadlock:
  Deadlocks caused by mutual subgraph dependency must be avoided.
- Fitting:
  In order to reduce the overhead caused by the page switching, the subgraph should include as many nodes as possible within the limitation of a page.
- Parallelism and time efficiency:
  A page should include nodes which are able to fire at the similar time. In other words, nodes which are fired different time must be excluded as possible.
- Tokens transferred over between subgraphs:
  In order to reduce the overhead caused by token transfer, edges across the boundaries of pages should be reduced as possible.

Fig. 2 shows an example of a deadlock caused by an improper partitioning. In this figure, Page2 is waiting for a token from Page1, and Page1 is also waiting for

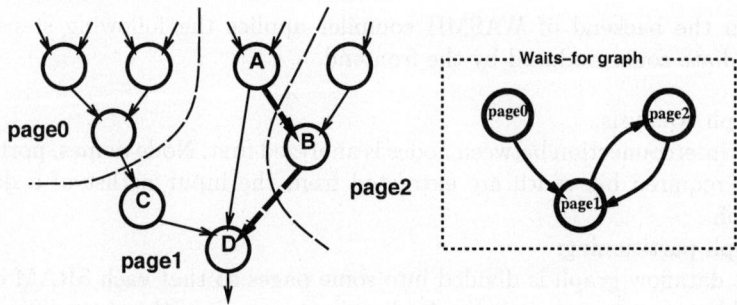

Fig. 2. An example of deadlocked partitioning

a token from Page2. This mutual dependency, ignoring precedence constraints of nodes, causes the deadlock.

The situation can also be expressed using WFG (waits-for graph) as shown in the lower part of Fig. 2. Each node in the WFG corresponds to a page, and the edge from the node labeled Page1 to Page2 shows that Page2 waits for a token from Page1. When WFG has a cycle, a deadlock occurs. In other words, a graph has to be divided so that the corresponding WFG does not have a cycle for deadlock avoidance.

3.3 Dataflow Partitioning Algorithm: ITT

Our partitioning method called *ITT* avoids the deadlock by considering the waits-for dependency between pages. The basic idea of this method is to assign a node into a page along the flow of a token.

Based on this idea, ITT introduces a simple rule of partitioning: when a node is assigned into a page, all the nodes providing tokens to that node have to have already been assigned into each page. A node whose all precedence nodes have been assigned into each page is called a *ready node*. According to the rule, nodes are successively assigned into a page until the sum of the hardware size of the nodes comes up to the limit. Then the page is fixed and other nodes start being assigned into another new page. Therefore, as far as the rule is obeyed, a page waits for tokens only from the pages that have already been fixed and never waits for a token from any pages that will be created after that. This means that the partitioned pages have a partial order with respect to waits-for dependency and WFG never has a cycle.

3.4 Node-Choosing Algorithms

When there are some ready nodes in the step of choosing a node to assign into a page, which node should be selected? This node-choosing algorithm influences the total execution time. It must extract parallelism considering both time efficiency and communication costs between subgraphs. To effectively extract parallelism in the dataflow graph, some nodes which are able to be fired simultaneously should be assigned into the same subgraph. However, this means increasing communication costs between subgraphs because of its dividing edge of the graph. Also, decreasing communication costs between subgraphs causes poor parallelism in a subgraph. There is a trade-off between these two subjects.

We show two node-choosing algorithms considering following two parameters assigned to each node $v_i \in V$; $Rsd\_time(v_i)$ and $Upto\_time(v_i)$, where V is a set of nodes in a given dataflow graph. Let $V_s \subset V$ and $V_e \subset V$ be a set of the start nodes and the terminal nodes of the graph, respectively. Let $Exec\_time(v_i)$ be a time for which v_i requires to complete its execution. Given a path P in the graph, let *path length* of P be the sum of $Exec\_time(v_p)$ such that $v_p \in P$. $Rsd\_time(v_i)$ denotes the longest *path length* from v_i to $v_e \in V_e$, and $Upto\_time(v_i)$ denotes the longest *path length* from v_i to $v_s \in V_s$.

Choosing the ready nodes into subgraphs in order of the value of their $Rsd\_time(v_i)$ extracts parallelism in the dataflow graph effectively (**CF-node choosing algorithm**). On the other hand, assigning the nodes into subgraphs according to $Upto\_time(v_i)$ decreases the number of tokens which are transferred between subgraphs and communication costs (**DF-node choosing algorithm**). The effect of two algorithms can be combined by using them selectively when choosing a node in a graph.

4 Evaluation

4.1 Evaluated Application

The following programs written in the intermediate language form are given to the backend for evaluation:

- test_array(98 nodes, 4816 CLBs):
  A small scale graph consisting of a tandem connected pairs of an adder and a multiplier.
- random_nodes(512 nodes, 26680 CLBs):
  A graph consisting of an array of 3 kinds of nodes arranged randomly so as to form a tree structure.
- edge_extraction(2176 nodes, 66752 CLBs):
  A graph used for 8 × 8 pixels edge extraction. Its critical path length is only 4 and graph lies vertically to dataflow direction.
- power_normal(101 nodes, 9720 CLBs):
  A graph used for a power current dynamics analysis which solves simultaneous equations with fixed point complex numbers. In this graph, a real part and an imaginary part of a complex number are computed in different nodes.
- power_complex(53 nodes, 8240 CLBs):
  A graph for the same application as "power_normal" but uses a large granularity nodes which compute both the real part and imaginary part of the complex number in a single clock cycle.
- robot(89 tasks, 27313 CLBs):
  A program for Stanford manipulator[4] which controls a robot arm by solving ordinary differential equations.

Table 1. Simulation parameters

System clock:	20 MHz
Context switching overhead (page hit):	30 ns
Context switching overhead (page fault):	1 μs
Number of context memory:	8

- fpppp(335 tasks, 21387 CLBs):
  A kernel routine of Fpppp in SPEC benchmark programs[4].
- sparse(97 tasks, 21296 CLBs):
  A sparse matrix solving program for an electric circuit simulation[4].

These programs are executed on HDL level simulator for WASMII. Data width of each token is set to be 8 bit. The target FPGA is XC5215[5] by Xilinx, which is used in FLEMING, a WASMII emulator[3]. It consists of 1,936 CLBs, 15,000 usable gates. Other simulation parameters are set as shown in Table 1. In this table, "page hit" means that the configuration data activated at the next cycle is on the configuration memory, while "page fault" means that the target configuration data needs to be loaded from the external memory.

4.2 Effects of the Graph Partitioning Algorithm

Fig. 3 shows the total execution time at HDL simulations. The explanatory notes show used graph partitioning algorithm. According to the current implementation of WASMII, every token is transfered and written into the input token registers one by one in this simulation.

In this figure, 'CF' and 'DF' are corresponding to cases that all nodes are selected with the CF and DF algorithms, respectively. 'CF7' means that the CF algorithm is used randomly with 70% probability, while the rest of nodes are chosen according to the DF algorithm. In 'CF3', the CF is applied to 30% nodes randomly. In the figure, all graphs in every program are standardized to the case that all nodes are selected with the CF algorithm.

In this situation, higher DF probability achieves better results. This is directly caused from token transfer overhead between token registers and execution part in a WASMII unit. Fig. 4 shows the serial token transfer time in this evaluation, that is, a token is serially transferred per 1 clock.

Using the CF, graph cut directions tend to be vertically to the dataflow direction, so there are many graph cuts. On the other hand, using the DF, there tend to be fewer cuts compared to the CF. Thus, the DF that decreases tokens transfer between pages achieves better results.

Fig. 5 shows a pure calculation time. It shows that the CF is superior to the DF at the point of extracting parallelism among nodes. Thus, in the case of setting no limit for token transfer bandwidth('parallel token transfer'), the total execution time changes as shown in Fig. 6.

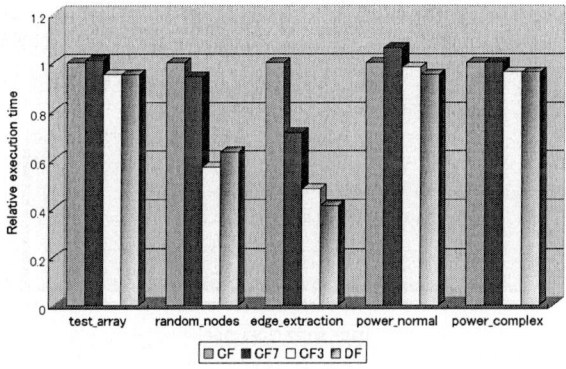

Fig. 3. Total execution time

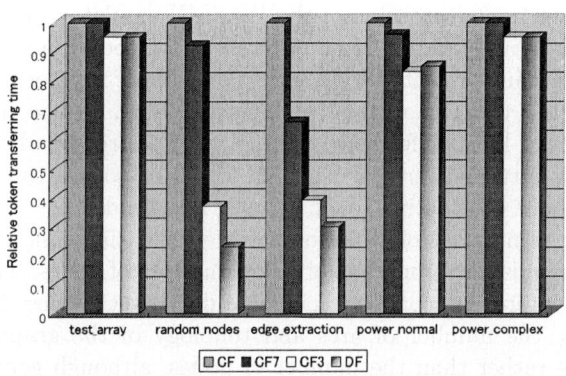

Fig. 4. Token transfer time

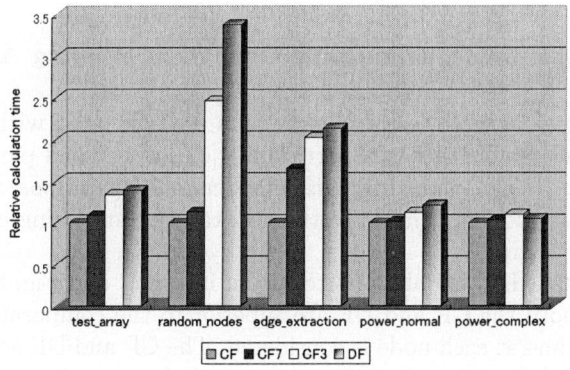

Fig. 5. Pure calculation time

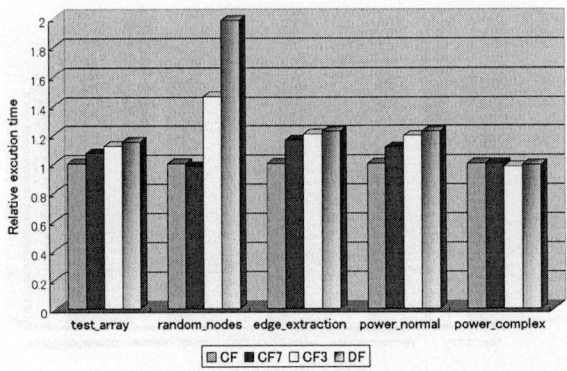

Fig. 6. Virtual execution time(parallel token transfer)

In the current implementation of the WASMII emulator, the transfer of the token written back into input token registers is processed serially, since the input token registers are implemented with a simple one-port register file. In this case, it is better to use the DF at the graph partitioning. In the future WASMII system, tokens can be transferred in parallel with a large bandwidth inside the chip or a multi-port register file. Thus, it is better to use the CF to extract parallelism without considering token transfer overhead.

Considering complexity of partitioning, the increasing time required for the graph partitioning is not proportional to the number of nodes. This comes from that analyzing inter-node connection is time dominant process in partitioning. In this process, the number of arcs and topology of the graph influence the processing time rather than the number of nodes, although generally the time increases as the size of the graph grows up. However, since the analyzing time is limited by the size of context, time for partitioning is not beyond the practical boundary.

4.3 Comparison with Traditional Graph Partitioning Algorithms

Here, the proposed graph partitioning results are compared with a level based partitioning and clustering based partitioning[6]. Level based partitioning, similar to the CF, targets extracting parallelism among operations, while the clustering based partitioning, similar to the DF, targets decreasing communication costs between subgraphs.

Results of the HDL simulation are shown in Fig. 7 and Fig. 8. As shown in these figures, both the CF and DF are superior to the comparative ones, since the execution time at each node is considered. The CF and DF achieve 13% and 39% performance improvement at most respectively.

In these figures, the CF partitioning is sometimes superior to the DF even with the serial token transfer at 'robot', 'fpppp' and 'sparse'. This comes from

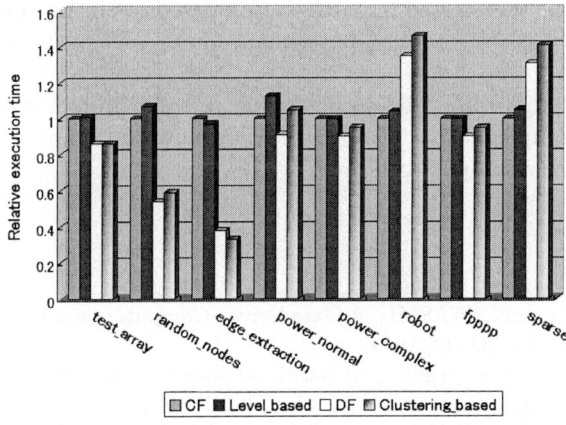

Fig. 7. Compared to other graph partitioning algorithm

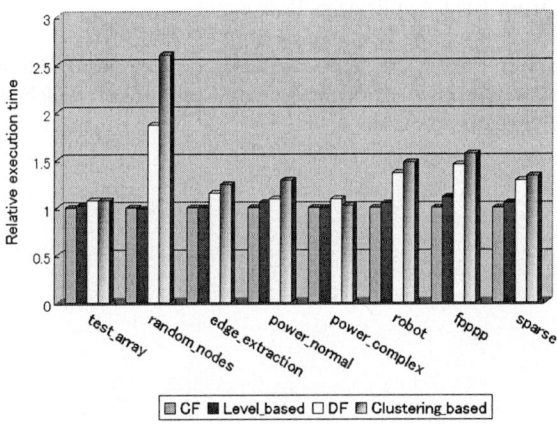

Fig. 8. Compared to other graph partitioning algorithm (parallel token transfer)

that the size of nodes are large in these applications and token transfer between pages does not degrade the performance so much.

5 Conclusion

A new graph partitioning algorithm called *ITT* which uses two node choosing algorithms, the DF and CF, is proposed and implemented in the WASMII compiler. Evaluation results with some test programs show that the DF node choosing algorithm is useful in the current configuration of WASMII in which tokens are serially transferred, while the CF node choosing algorithm works efficiently when tokens can be transferred in parallel. Compared to the proposed algorithm with traditional ones, 13% to 39% performance improvement is achieved at the most.

The proposed algorithms should be further refined through evaluations with a lot of practical applications. Design of more powerful frontend system and entry language are also our future work.

References

1. X.-P. Ling, H. Amano: "WASMII: A Data Driven Computer on a Virtual Hardware" Proc. FCCM '93, pp. 33–42, 1993.
2. K.Hiraki, T.Shimada, K.Nishida: "A hardware design of the SIGMA-1: A data flow computer for scientific computations" Proc. ICPP 1984.
3. H.Miyazaki, Y.Shibata, A.Takayama, X.Ling and H.Amano: "Emulation of Multi-chip WASMII on Reconfigurable System Testbed FLEMING" PACT'98 Workshop on Reconfigurable Computing, pp.47–52(1998)
4. http://www.kasahara.elec.waseda.ac.jp/schedule/apply_pe.ht ml (Prototype Task Graphs Generated from Real Application Programs)
5. Xilinx Inc.: "The Programmable Logic Data Book" 1996.
6. Karthikeya M. Gajjala Purna and Dinesh Bhatia: "Temporal Partitioning and Scheduling Data Flow Graphs for Reconfigurable Computers" IEEE Trans. Computers, Vol.48, pp.579–590, June, 1999.

Compiling Applications for ConCISe: An Example of Automatic HW/SW Partitioning and Synthesis

Bernardo Kastrup[1], Jeroen Trum[1,2], Orlando Moreira[1,3], Jan Hoogerbrugge[1], and Jef van Meerbergen[1,2]

[1] Philips Research Laboratories, Prof. Holstlaan 4 (WL11), 5656 AA Eindhoven, The Netherlands. Tel.: +31 40 274 4421, Fax: +31 40 274 4004.
Bernardo.Kastrup@philips.com
[2] Eindhoven University of Technology, 5600 MB Eindhoven, The Netherlands.
[3] Aveiro University, Campo Universitário Santiago, 3810 Aveiro, Portugal.

Abstract. In the ConCISe project, an embedded programmable processor is augmented with a Reconfigurable Functional Unit (RFU) based on Field-Programmable Logic (FPL), in a technique that aims at being cost-effective for high volume production. The target domain is embedded encryption. In this paper, we focus on ConCISe's programming tool-set. A smart assembler, capable of automatically performing HW/SW partitioning and HW synthesis, generates the custom operations that are implemented in the RFU. Benchmarks carried out with ConCISe's simulators show that the RFU may speed up off-the-shelf encryption applications by as much as 50%, for a modest investment in silicon, and with no changes in the traditional application programming flow.

1 Introduction

In traditional programmable architectures, instructions in the native Instruction Set Architecture (ISA) are designed to operate on fixed bit-width quantities in the data-path as coherent values (i.e. numbers to be added, multiplied, etc.). Instructions that operate on numbers are generally applicable. The price of generality is that traditional ISAs are inefficient when memory or register contents are to be processed as a set of independent bits.

Figures 1 and 2 illustrate examples of irregular bit manipulations from encryption algorithms. In both cases, the MIPS assembly instruction sequence necessary to implement the manipulations, as generated by an optimising compiler, is shown alongside the corresponding custom hardware. Note that those bit manipulations are simple, and could be implemented in a functional unit with a few logic gates. However, the resulting custom instruction would be specific (and therefore only useful) to the DES algorithm. When some degree of generality is required, this is not a cost-effective alternative. This is particularly important in the embedded encryption and domain, where bit manipulations are a major part of the computation, and cost and power budgets are limited.

Field-Programmable Logic (FPL) could be used to address the generality versus efficiency contest illustrated above. An FPL-based functional unit could be reconfigured per application, thus implementing a different set of custom operations for each given program. This paper reports on an approach, called ConCISe, for enhancing a programmable processor's capability to perform irregular bit manipulations in a fast, and yet cost-effective way. Section 2 presents ConCISe's hardware architecture. Sections 3 introduces ConCISe's software tool-set, the heart of the approach. Section 4 presents benchmark results obtained using the prototype tool-set. Finally, section 5 concludes this paper.

```
srl     $13, $2, 20
andi    $25, $13, 1
srl     $14, $2, 21
andi    $24, $14, 6
or      $15, $25, $24
srl     $13, $2, 22
andi    $14, $13, 56
or      $25, $15, $14
sll     $24, $25, 2
```

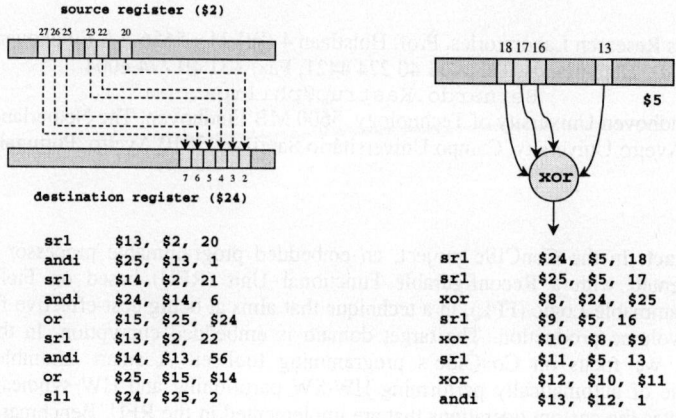

Fig. 1. Example of bit manipulation in the DES encryption algorithm.

```
srl     $24, $5, 18
srl     $25, $5, 17
xor     $8, $24, $25
srl     $9, $5, 16
xor     $10, $8, $9
srl     $11, $5, 13
xor     $12, $10, $11
andi    $13, $12, 1
```

Fig. 2. Example of bit manipulation in the A5 encryption algorithm.

2 ConCISe Architecture

ConCISe, initially described in [1], was *not* conceived as a general-purpose technique. It targets the embedded encryption domain, where bit-level manipulations are significant and power dissipation is a limitation (i.e., high clock frequencies are not desirable). The architecture was developed to be a commercially sound alternative for the specific requirements of those domains, which include low cost, simplicity, testability, reliability, and ease of programming.

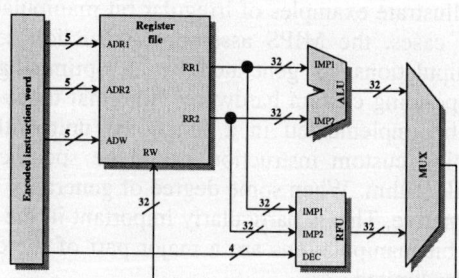

Fig. 3. ConCISe microarchitecture overview.

ConCISe's basic idea is fairly simple, as illustrated in Figure 3 for a 32-bit RISC data-path. An extra FPL-based Reconfigurable Functional Unit (RFU) is added parallel to the ALU, receiving the same source operands from the register file. The ALU and RFU cannot execute concurrently (the RFU is not a VLIW or super-scalar extension). Like the ALU, the RFU must compute its result in a single clock cycle. It can be configured differently for each particular application program, in order to implement different custom operations. The executables for this architecture not only contain a list of instructions and program data, but also hardware configuration bits for the RFU. At load-time, the OS loads instructions and program data into memory, and the configuration bits into the RFU. The processor itself is used to load its RFU configuration bits prior to the execution of the application.

The RFU concept in Figure 3 is *not* new. Previous studies have used the same idea [2][3]. In ConCISe, however, the RFU is based on a Complex Programmable Logic Device (CPLD) hard core, embedded in the processor's layout. Also differently from [2], because a single custom operation does not increase the performance enough, and because of the complexity and overhead of run-time reconfiguration, we statically encode several custom operations in a single CPLD configuration. This allows for cross-minimisation of the logic of different custom operations [9]. It also opens compiler issues entirely different from, and considerably more sophisticated than, the ones addressed in [2], as it will be shown in section 3. The way ConCISe's compiler detects, selects, and instantiates custom operations in the program code is its main contribution to the field.

Let us now define an Application-Specific Instruction (ASI) as the one instruction that calls the RFU at run-time. There will be a single ASI corresponding to each particular application program. The ASI is encoded as a normal register to register instruction, in which all three operands, plus one 4-bit immediate field called DEC, are present (See Figure 3). The operands encode two source and one destination register; DEC identifies the custom operation within the RFU configuration that is to be executed (such as the input signals in the ALU responsible for selecting an add, sll or xor operation). As dec is 4 bits wide, there can be up to 16 custom operations per ASI (i.e. per application program).

Figure 4 illustrates the internal architecture of the CPLD core. It is a stripped down, slightly modified version of commercial, SRAM-based XPLA2 devices [4]. Four logic blocks receive 40 input signals each from a virtual cross-point switch. The inputs for the cross-point come from two sets of 32 input signals (the two source operands of the RFU) and a set of four input signals for DEC. Each logic block has eight outputs, making up the 32 output bits of the result.

The internal architecture of the logic block is shown in Figure 5. The combination of PAL and PLA arrays allows complex logic functions to be built with a single pass through the arrays. Each output signal has four dedicated Product Terms (PTs) from the PAL array connected to it and, optionally, up to 32 PTs from the PLA array. A total of 36 PTs can therefore be used to produce a single result bit. The PAL/PLA combination enables PLA PT sharing among different result bits (through different Sum Terms, or STs). This increases the effective density of the device and allows yet larger and more complex functions to be implemented. The architecture is ideal for bit manipulations. The cross-point and the PAL/PLA arrays render arbitrary combinations of input bits available to any PT, facilitating random logic functions. The configured circuits are always purely combinatorial.

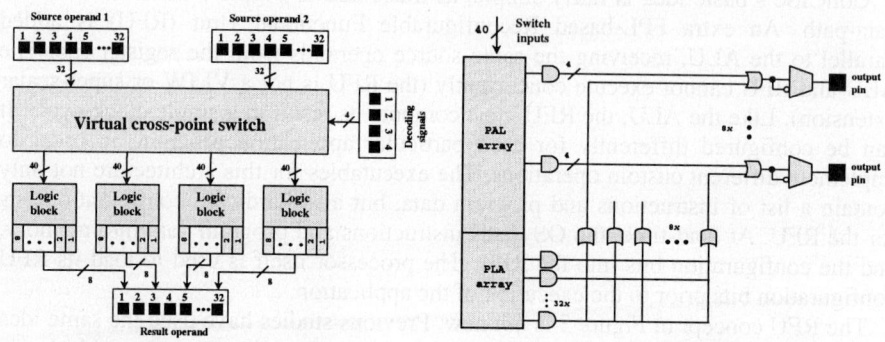

Fig. 4. The RFU architecture.   **Fig. 5.** A logic block.

Another feature of this CPLD architecture is its predictable timing model. The delay depends solely on whether or not PTs from the PLA are used, and it is a constant in both cases. Using 1998 technology and a 0.35μm process, the maximum delay is approximately 5.0ns. Therefore, the RFU can comfortably execute in a single cycle for clock frequencies of 100MHz or slightly more. We estimate its size to be between 4 and 5 mm^2, which is about 20% the size of a Philips PR3930 5-stage MIPS CPU, in the same 0.35μm process.

3 Compiling and Simulating ConCISe Applications

The following detailed description of ConCISe's tool-set is the main contribution of this paper, and represents the core of our progress with respect to our previously reported work [1]. The tools target a MIPS R3000 as basis platform, and perform the following steps (Figure 6):
1. Source code is processed by a core compiler, generating *optimised* MIPS assembly code;
2. A simulator runs the assembly and produces profile data (basic block execution counts);
3. The assembly code is read by a cluster detection/selection module, which looks for data-flow segments potentially suitable for hardware synthesis (henceforth called *candidates*). This module will be explained in detail in sections 3.1 and 3.2. Up to 16 candidates are selected in the critical parts of the code (based on the profile data) and become custom operations. They are then encoded together in a *cluster*. All custom operations within a cluster are to be implemented in a single RFU configuration;
4. The cluster is then sent to a translator, where the operations of its data-flow segments are converted into a hardware description in HDL. Decoding logic (a multiplexer) is added, such that the different custom operations may be executed independently. Details of the translation module are given in Section 3.3;
5. The resulting circuit description is processed by a commercial hardware synthesis tool where a fitting report is generated, as well as a circuit netlist;

6. If the cluster does not fit in the available CPLD resources, the maximum number of custom operations allowed in the cluster is reduced by one, and an entirely new selection starts. The cycle repeats until the cluster fits or no custom operation is left;
7. The data-flow segments in the assembly code that are part of the finally selected cluster are replaced with their equivalent ASI instances;
8. The resulting assembly is sent to a modified assembler that recognises the newly added ASI instances. The netlist generated by the hardware synthesis tool is combined with the assembly, producing the final executable;
9. The executable is then run by the ConCISe simulator. When an ASI instance is to be executed, the logic operations specified in the hardware netlist are simulated at logic gate level. Finally, benchmark results are produced.

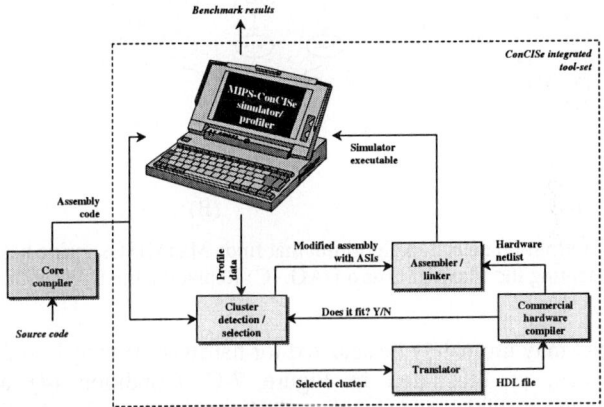

Fig. 6. ConCISe's tool-set, featuring automatic HW/SW partitioning and HW synthesis.

3.1 The Detection of Candidates

The detection mechanism starts by performing a simple control-flow analysis to identify the basic blocks of the input assembly. A bottom-up detection algorithm is applied to each basic block, to look for 'MaxMISOs' ("Maximal Multiple Input Single Output graph", introduced in [5]). MaxMISOs are Direct Acyclic Graphs (DAGs) in which nodes represent instructions and edges represent data dependencies. A MaxMISO may have multiple inputs, but only a single output. The following MIPS assembly instructions are currently allowed in a MaxMISO: and, andi, lui, nor, or, ori, sll, sra, srl, xor, and xori. They are *called synthesisable instructions*, as they are the only ones the tool-set considers to be valid for hardware synthesis in the RFU. Instructions with carry chains (e.g. add, mult) are too complex for 1-level logic, and are not considered valid for synthesis. Multiplications by a power of two are translated into slls. The RFU does not have memory access, and cannot implement loads and stores. Figure 7-A illustrates the detection algorithm. Figure 7-B, illustrates the corresponding MaxMISO.

In the example in Figure 7-A, starting from the bold-faced or, the detection proceeds upwards along the data dependencies until: (1) the next instruction is non-synthesisable (e.g. a lw or an add); (2) the next instruction is part of a previously detected MaxMISO; (3) there is an attempt to read beyond the beginning of the basic block; or (4) the next instruction read has its output read more than once. This is repeated for every instruction in the basic block.

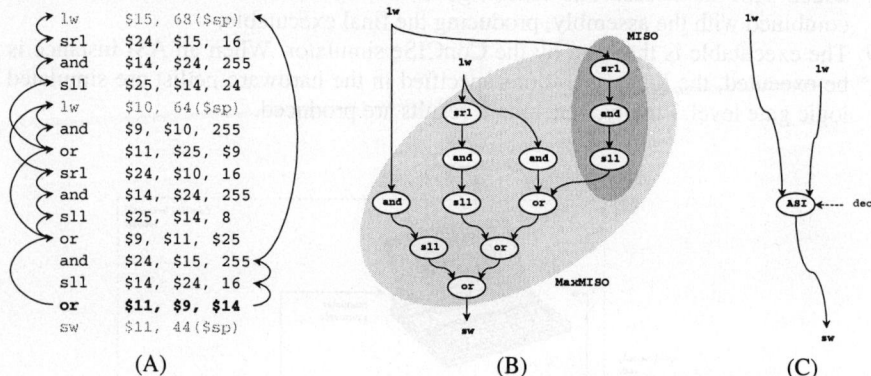

Fig. 7. (A) Bottom-up detection algorithm that finds MaxMISOs inside basic blocks. (B) Representing the MaxMISO as a DAG. (C) Replacing the DAG with an ASI.

A MaxMISO may ultimately be selected for hardware synthesis and be replaced by an ASI instance, as illustrated in Figure 7-C. Condition (4) above prevents MaxMISOs with multiple outputs, i.e. ASIs with multiple results, from being detected. However, if the output of an instruction in a certain MaxMISO is read more than once, but only by other instructions which are themselves part of the same MaxMISO, condition (4) above should not be considered, because the MaxMISO would still be a 1-ouput DAG. In spite of this, in the current version of our tool-set, we adopt the simplistic approach to stop before adding an instruction that would lead to a node in the MaxMISO with multiple output edges. As a result, instead of DAGs, our MaxMISOs become *directed trees*. Furthermore, our approach, and the benchmark results reported, are conservative.

After detecting the MaxMISOs in every basic block, the algorithm extracts every sub-tree that can be derived from each MaxMISO. The sub-trees are called MISOs [4]. Figure 7-B illustrates a MISO that can be derived from the shown MaxMISO. A list of trees is formed, containing all detected MaxMISOs and all derived MISOs. Each tree in the list then goes through a filtering process. Trees with more than two inputs are discarded, since no more than two source operands are allowed in the R3000 pipeline. Trees formed by a single instruction are also discarded, since no speed-up is achieved if a single native instruction is replaced by an ASI instance. The final list contains only validated trees which can be replaced by an ASI instance. These trees are then called *candidates*.

3.2 The Selection of Candidates

The input code can be subdivided into two parts: MaxMISOs and the remaining code. Candidates can only appear in MaxMISOs, so in order to optimise the entire code using a set of candidates, it is sufficient to only look at MaxMISOs. An *occurrence* of a candidate is one specific appearance of a candidate within a certain MaxMISO, so it is a specific sub-tree of a MaxMISO equal to a candidate. For example, figure 8 shows three MaxMISOs and 3 candidates. Candidate 2 has two occurrences, one in MaxMISO A and one in MaxMISO B. Note that candidate MISOs may have occurrences in MaxMISOs other than the ones they were originally derived from. Candidates may also have occurrences in MaxMISOs that are themselves not valid candidates.

A *tiling* of a MaxMISO is a set of candidate occurrences within the MaxMISO, such that none of the occurrences overlap. See MaxMISO A in figure 8 for an example. The set containing the shown occurrences of candidates 1 and 2 is not a tiling, because they overlap. The set containing the shown occurrences of candidates 2 and 3 is a tiling, because they do not overlap. A tiling can be translated back to assembly code. Candidate occurrences in the tiling are replaced by their corresponding RFU ASI instances. All other instructions are preserved. The *tiling cost* of a MaxMISO with a given tiling equals the number of occurrences in the tiling plus the number of instructions that are not covered by any occurrence in the tiling. Given a set of selected candidates, the task of the *tiler* is to find a tiling of minimal cost for all MaxMISOs.

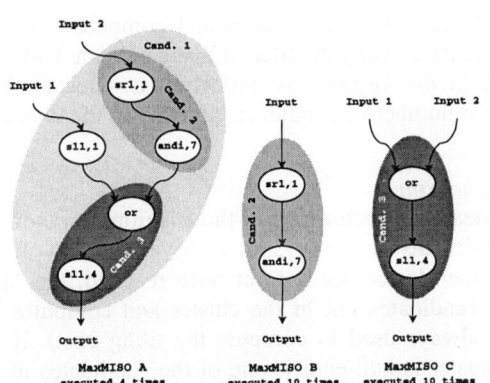

Fig. 8. An example program consisting of three MaxMISOs.

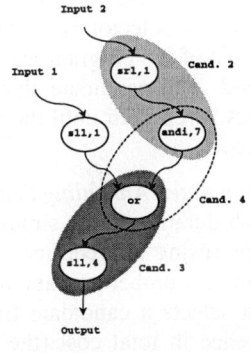

Fig. 9. A MaxMISO showing occurrences of three candidates.

The Tiler

Given a set of candidates, the tiler uses a dynamic programming algorithm to find a tiling with minimal tiling cost. For each node n in a MaxMISO tree T, the cost of an optimal tiling for the sub-tree with root n (the largest sub-tree of T with root n, thus including all the leaves that are descendants of n) is the minimum of:

1. The summed cost of the optimal tilings of the direct descendant sub-trees of n plus 1 (the cost 1 is for the node n itself). Note that, in this case, n is not the root of a candidate; and

2. For candidate occurrences *r* with root in *n*, the cost of the optimal tiling of the direct descendant sub-trees of *r* plus 1 (where 1 is the cost of *r*).

See figure 9 for an illustration. The cost of the srl, 1 instruction is 1. For the cost of the sub-tree with root andi, 7, we can choose between the cost of andi, 7 plus the cost of the optimal tiling of its children (cost 1); or the cost of candidate 2, which has its root in andi, 7, plus the cost of its children (none). The optimal tiling for the sub-tree starting in or is either: the cost of or (1) plus the cost of its children, which is 1 (for sll, 1) plus 1 (for candidate 2); or the cost of candidate 4 plus the costs of its children (1 for srl, 1 and 1 for sll, 1). The cost of an optimal tiling for the sub-tree starting in or equals 3, regardless of whether candidate 2 or 4 is chosen. In the same way, we can compute the optimal tiling of the tree with root sll, 4. The minimal tiling cost equals 3, using candidates 2 and 3.

Selection Mechanisms

The limited set of candidates ultimately selected to be synthesised is called a *cluster*. The aim of the selection process is to come up with a cluster from which maximum speed-up can be achieved. We examined two heuristic search mechanisms to do this: a "greedy" selector and a selector using simulated annealing. Both mechanisms try to find a solution with minimal *total cost*, where *total cost* is defined as the summed execution count of all MaxMISOs. The execution count of a MaxMISO equals the number of times the MaxMISO is executed, multiplied by the number of instructions in the MaxMISO (which, after tiling, is the tiling cost). The search mechanisms try to select candidates for the cluster such that the total cost of all MaxMISOs is as small as possible after tiling. Selected candidates become RFU operations.

The Greedy Search Mechanism

The greedy selector runs through all unselected candidates and computes the new total cost of the program for each candidate (using the tiler) if that candidate had been selected. The candidate that results in the largest cost reduction is selected. This process is repeated until the maximum number of candidates allowed in the cluster is selected.

The Simulated Annealing Search Mechanism

In each iteration of the simulated annealing selector, one of three actions is randomly chosen (using a predefined probability distribution): add, remove or swap. If the maximum number of candidates in the cluster has not yet been reached, the 'add' action selects a candidate from the candidates not in the cluster and computes the difference in total cost (the tiler is always used to compute the tiling cost). If the 'remove' action is chosen and the cluster is non-empty, one of the candidates in the cluster is randomly chosen and the cost difference of removing this candidate is computed. If 'swap' is chosen, a candidate randomly chosen from the cluster is replaced by a candidate not in the cluster, and the difference in cost of this replacement is computed. If the action resulted in a cost reduction, the action is accepted; if it resulted in a cost increase, the action is only accepted if $exp(-\Delta cost/t) > rand$, where $\Delta cost$ is the cost difference, *rand* is a random number between 0 and 1, and t is the 'temperature', which slowly decreases throughout the iterations. If the temperature is high, large cost increases are accepted. The probability of acceptance of an action that increases cost, reduces with the temperature. In the end, only cost reductions are accepted.

The annealing algorithm can give better results than the greedy algorithm, because annealing can try more possible combinations of candidates, whereas greedy inspects only one combination. Figure 8 shows the three MaxMISOs of an example program. MaxMISO A is executed four times, B and C are executed ten times. The figure shows three candidates. Candidates 2 and 3 both have two occurrences, one as a subtree in MaxMISO A, and one covering either the entire MaxMISO B or C. Note that many more sub-trees of MaxMISO A are candidates, but they are not shown here.

Assume that we are allowed to select two candidates. The greedy algorithm first selects the candidate with the highest cost reduction. It can choose between candidates 1, 2 and 3, and all candidates which are sub-trees of A but are not shown in figure 8. Candidates 2 and 3 are both executed 10+4=14 times, and could give a cost reduction of 14 (two instructions are replaced by one). The selected candidate is candidate 1, with a cost reduction of 16, which is the number of executions (4) times the number of saved instructions (five minus one instruction to replace candidate 1). The greedy algorithm can then choose between the remaining candidates 2 and 3. Candidates 2 and 3 have occurrences in MaxMISO A, but the tiler will decide that it is cheaper to tile MaxMISO A with candidate 1, instead of using candidate 2 or 3 and leaving the remaining instructions untouched. Both candidates 2 and 3 result in an equal additional cost reduction of 10, so the greedy algorithm just picks one of them. The greedy algorithm finishes with a total cost reduction of 26. Annealing has more freedom to select combinations of candidates and could also try a cluster of candidates 2 and 3 (although no guarantee is given). This would give a cost reduction of 28, better than the result of the greedy algorithm.

3.3 The Assembly to HDL Translation

The logic functions in the selected custom operations are translated into equivalent statements in HDL. Different custom operations in a cluster lead to different *intermediate results* in the hardware description. A multiplexer is added, controlled by the external dec signals, which are responsible for run-time selection of the operation within the cluster that is to be executed. Depending on the value of dec, one of the intermediate results is forwarded to the output. The architecture of the hardware module for the cluster at the HDL level is presented in figure 10.

The architecture in figure 10 is not necessarily preserved during hardware synthesis. All custom operations in the cluster (and the multiplexer) are logically minimised by the hardware synthesis tool. Cross-minimisation may occur when different custom instructions share a common PT in the same output bit. Also note that, although we do not use flip-flops or other state-holding elements in our CPLD-based RFU (as shown in figures 4 and 5), the approach poses no constraints for doing so. Future versions of ConCISe may well implement multi-cycle custom operations, where intermediary results are stored in RFU internal registers.

4 Benchmark Results

We used five well-known encryption algorithms to benchmark our approach: Eric Young's DES implementation [6]; Bruce Schneier's A5 implementation [7]; a Philips in-house benchmark derived from the RSA Data Security Inc. MD5 message-digest algorithm; and Brian Gladman's implementations of Loki97 and Magenta [8]. All five codes were taken off-the-shelf, without changes. In every case, the assembly was produced by an optimising compiler. Note that a skilled programmer could re-write the algorithms to take advantage of ConCISe's RFU, and encryption algorithm developers could also use bit-level manipulations more freely in their algorithms, with fewer concerns about their performance on a programmable microprocessor. In addition, the core compiler is unaware of the existence of the RFU, which wastes further optimisation opportunities.

The results are shown in figure 11. In every case, we assume that the clock frequency is such that the RFU can execute in a single clock cycle (comfortably up to 100MHz). A speed-up of 100% means that the Instruction eXecution Count (IXC) is halved. Programmer intervention is *never* used to generate code for the RFU version. Results obtained with both search mechanisms are shown, and are compared to the results we would obtain if we could use an ASI in every position where a candidate could be tiled. As expected, we can see that the annealing search mechanism obtains slightly better results than the greedy mechanism. Figure 2 illustrates one of the custom operations actually synthesised in our test, which partly computes one of A5's Linear Feedback Shift Registers. Figure 1 illustrates an actually detected but not selected (not in the critical path) DES candidate. Figure 7 illustrates a detected MaxMISO of Magenta that was also a selected and synthesised candidate.

Figure 12 shows ConCISe's RFU speed-up when a progressively higher number of custom operations is encoded in the RFU. The point at which the curve levels off represents the limit of hardware synthesis opportunities, given the conservative assumptions of our detection module. The grey ellipse over each curve shows the number of custom operations we can actually encode before the RFU circuit no longer fits in the available CPLD resources. We can see that A5 is already close to levelling-off, while there is a long way to go before we exhaust synthesis opportunities for Loki97. Finally, figure 13 illustrates the IXC distribution for different kinds of instructions. Note that many synthesisable instructions may only occur in trees that do not pass the filtering criteria and, therefore, cannot be replaced by an ASI anyway. Assuming that an RFU operation in the CPLD takes the same amount of power as an ALU operation (the CPLD used is known for its low-power dissipation [4]), figure 13 gives a rough idea of how much less power dissipation ConCISe would allow for, to the extent that power dissipation is proportional to the IXC. We have no data, though, to confirm (or discard) that assumption.

In order to investigate the run-time effects of ConCISe, we have also used another assembler/simulator package capable of simulating an entire system (caches, memories, buses, I/O, etc.). The simulator is cycle-accurate, except for a few minor assumptions. A system made up of a ConCISe-MIPS R3000 with 16K of data cache, a Philips PI bus, embedded flash-ROM, and DRAM was simulated. Figure 14 illustrates the RFU speed-up for different sizes of instruction cache. The peak seen at 512B of cache is due to the fact that the assembly code with ASI instances already fits in a 512B instruction cache, while the original assembly does not. This can be seen in figure 15. For an instruction cache of 1KB or higher, both codes fit in the cache, and the speed-up converges to the IXC speed-up (slightly different from the value in figure 11 due to differences in the assemblers used). The results illustrate the (side-effect) reduction of code size that results from the use of ASIs.

FPL run-time reconfiguration could be used to encode as many custom operations in the RFU as necessary to reach the point at which the curves in figure 12 level off. However, run-time reconfiguration does have its shortcomings. The reconfiguration latency implies an overhead every time a new configuration is to be loaded. In previous, similar studies, the FPL resources had to be reconfigured each time a new custom operation was needed at run-time [2][3]. We can minimise this effect by encoding several custom operations in a single hardware configuration. In spite of this, we believe we can still avoid the use of run-time reconfiguration by experimenting with other alternatives to increase the logic density of our RFU circuits.

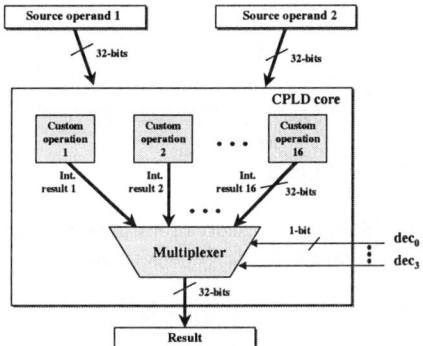

Fig. 10. Encoding multiple custom operations in one CPLD configuration.

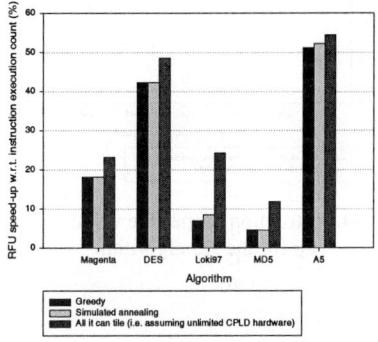

Fig. 11. ConCISe speed-up for different encryption algorithms.

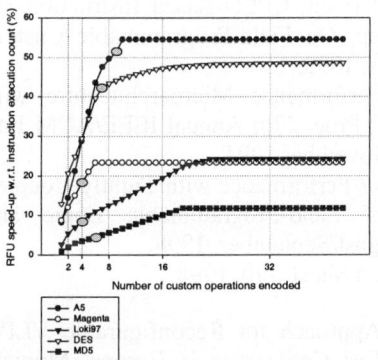

Fig. 12. ConCISe speed-up for different numbers of custom operations.

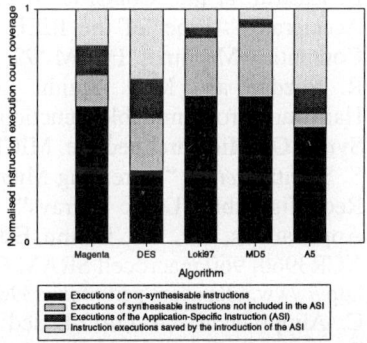

Fig. 13. Normalised instruction execution count coverage showing the RFU savings.

5 Conclusions

We have developed a complete tool-set for ConCISe, in which all hardware/software partitioning and hardware synthesis steps are done automatically. Our compiler approach provides a powerful and general framework that can be modified and extended to different architectures. Benchmarks show that, for a small investment in silicon, ConCISe can speed-up off-the-shelf embedded encryption algorithms by as much as 50%, while preserving the traditional application programming flow. Better results can be achieved if the programmer adopts RFU-aware coding styles. In addition, the elimination of some conservative assumptions in our tool-set will, eventually, improve the results.

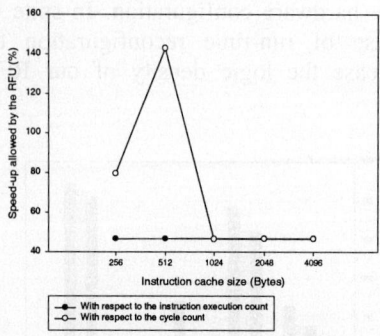 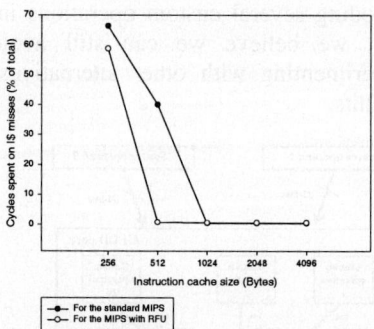

Fig. 14. Instruction cache size versus speed-up for the A5 algorithm.

Fig. 15. Relative penalty of instruction cache misses for the A5 algorithm.

References

[1] B. Kastrup et al. "ConCISe: A Compiler-Driven, CPLD-Based Instruction Set Accelerator". Proc. of the IEEE Intl. Symp. On Field-Programmable Custom Computing Machines, FCCM '99, Napa, CA, 1999.
[2] R. Razdan and M.D. Smith. "A High-Performance Microarchitecture with Hardware-Programmable Functional Units", Proc. 27th Annual IEEE/ACM Intl. Symp. On Microarchitecture, MICRO-27, November 1994.
[3] S. Sawitzki et al. "Increasing Microprocessor Performance with Tightly-Coupled Reconfigurable Logic Arrays", Proc. of Field-Programmable Logic and Applications, FPL '98, Tallinn, Estonia, August/September, 1998.
[4] XCR3960, 960 macrocell SRAM CPLD. Data Sheet, July 1998. http://www.xilinx.com/partinfo/xcr3960.pdf
[5] C. Alippi et al. "A DAG-Based Design Approach for Reconfigurable VLIW Processors", Proc. Of IEEE Design and Test Conference in Europe, Munich, March 1999.
[6] ftp://ftp.psy.uq.oz.au/pub/Crypto/DES/
[7] B. Schneier. "Applied Cryptography: Protocols, Algorithms and Source Code in C", Second Edition, John Wiley & Sons, Inc., 1996.
[8] http://www.btinternet.com/~brian.gladman/cryptography_technology/aes/index.html
[9] B. Kastrup and O. Moreira. "A Novel Approach to Minimising the Logic of Combinatorial Multiplexing Circuits in Product-Term-Based Hardware", Proc. of EUROMICRO Symp. On Digital Systems Design (IEEE Computer Society Press), Maastricht, September 2000.

Behavioural Language Compilation with Virtual Hardware Management

Oliver Diessel[1] and George Milne[2]

[1] School of Computer Science and Engineering
University of New South Wales, Australia
odiessel@cse.unsw.edu.au

[2] Advanced Computing Research Centre
School of Computer and Information Science
University of South Australia, Australia
milne@cis.unisa.edu.au

Abstract. High-level, behavioural language specification is seen as a significant strategy for overcoming the complexity of designing useful and interesting reconfigurable computing applications. However, appropriate frameworks for the design of behaviourally specified systems are still being sought. We are investigating behavioural language and compiler design based on the Circal process algebra, which is a natural framework within which to describe the concurrent activity of reconfigurable logic circuits. In this paper we describe an FPGA interpreter that exploits the inherent concurrency, hierarchy, and modularity of Circal and its circuit realization to automatically manage hardware virtualization. The techniques employed by the interpreter may be used to overcome resource limitations and adapt circuits to changing application needs at run time.

1 Introduction

One of the attractions of reconfigurable computing systems based on field programmable gate array (FPGA) technology is that the circuit realizing a design may change during the run time of an application to achieve better performance, to reflect changes in the application model, or to make better use of the underlying hardware.

This capability has been difficult to realize in practice due to: a lack of suitable languages in which to describe the attributes of applications that can profit from and exploit reconfigurable logic; the complexity of the steps that need to be taken in designing reconfigurable computing applications; and the perception that users need to be highly skilled in both software and hardware engineering to design applications that achieve performance or cost benefits over application specific integrated circuits and/or microprocessors. For these reasons, reconfigurable technology has not attracted systems designers who would like to program reconfigurable systems in an abstract, technology-independent manner using high-level language concepts.

Traditionally, the specification of reconfigurable computing applications has been attempted with the aid of inherently structural hardware description languages (HDLs) such as VHDL [2] and Verilog [18], (augmented) programming languages such as C++ [1], and schematic design entry, none of which are ideal since they take a low-level view of systems and their implementation. It is therefore difficult to describe systems at a more abstract behavioural level as we do with high-level programming languages that are oriented towards the function of a program rather than its realization on the underlying hardware.

To bring reconfigurable computing to the mainstream, to make it more accessible, and to permit faster prototype turnaround, we shall need to allow design entry via suitable high level languages (HLLs). Such languages will allow people more versed in algorithms and applications and less experienced with the underlying hardware details to apply and experiment with reconfigurable computing.

We have adopted the Circal [9] process algebra as the basis of such a language for a number of reasons. First, process algebras (PAs) such as Circal, CSP [7], and CCS [13] are formal languages developed for the purpose of describing concurrent systems. We believe them to be appropriate for describing FPGAs since, as with all VLSI digital logic, they are designed to represent highly concurrent systems. As such, there is a good match between language concepts and hardware realization vis-a-vis the expression of parallelism and the inherent parallelism of digital logic. Second, PAs are elegant, simple, yet powerful formalisms in which it is easier to explore fundamental language issues than with HDLs and programming languages. Third, traditional applications of reconfigurable logic such as prototyping and system control, even the design of the control part of data-oriented applications, are modelled as interacting finite state machines (FSMs) — PAs have essentially been created for the purpose of describing assemblies of interacting FSMs at a behavioural level. Fourth, there is the hope that a top-down, hierarchical, and modular focus, as emphasized by a PA such as Circal, will aid synthesis because ever more complex structures may be built through assembly, while the effort required to design each module (the unit of design) remains relatively constant.

This research is related to earlier work in compiling Occam to FPGAs [15, 17, 8, 16]. The Occam language was seen as a natural language for design input due to its simplicity and its facility for expressing parallelism. There was also a belief that the constructive approach used to translate Occam into digital logic and the formal semantics of the language could lead to the development of a verifiably correct hardware compiler.

The results reported here extend this research direction and investigate how to express and control dynamic reconfiguration through the use of a language that supports the description of changing hardware structures, such as occurs during reconfiguration, to overcome resource limitations or to adapt circuits to the changing needs of an application. This paper reports on the techniques we have developed to overcome resource limitations and applied to an interpreter for such a language, based on the Circal process algebra. We believe the ideas presented here will form the basis for the design of a language for reconfigurable computing modelled on a process algebra that supports the direct description of dynamically changing hardware structure [11].

In [5] we described an FPGA compiler for Circal that synthesizes complex systems from high-level behavioural descriptions. In this paper, we describe new features of a Circal interpreter that exploits language features in order to reconfigure hardware to overcome resource limitations. This scheme allows the necessary circuitry to be loaded as dictated by execution flow at run time.

2 Description of the Circal language

This section presents Circal as a descriptive medium for reconfigurable computing. We describe the key language concepts and how they are used to describe concurrent systems. We also introduce a simple example that serves to illustrate these concepts, the presentation of the Circal translation scheme, and our hardware management strategies later in the paper.

Circal is a formal language used to model the behaviour of complex, concurrent systems in a constructive, modular, and hierarchical manner by (1) modelling the behaviour of its component processes, and (2) by modelling the interaction of these component processes in terms of how they communicate events or actions between themselves. Systems, and the processes that model their behaviour, are described hierarchically and in a modular fashion. The description of a system thus typically proceeds in a top-down manner with the elaboration of component processes leading to further decomposition until the desired level of description is reached [10].

Circal is an event–based language and processes interact by participating in the occurrence of events. For an event to occur, all processes that include the event in their specification must be in a state that allows them to participate in the event. The Circal language primitives are:

State Definition $P \leftarrow Q$ defines process P to have the behaviour of term Q. Process Q is given the name P.

Termination Δ is a deadlock state from which a process cannot evolve.

Guarding $a\,P$ is a process that synchronizes to perform event a and then behaves as, or evolves to, P. $(a\,b)\,P$ synchronizes with events a and b simultaneously and then behaves as P.

Choice $P + Q$ is a term that chooses between the actions in process P and those in Q, the choice depending upon the environment in which the process is executed. Usually the choice is mediated through the offering by the environment of a guarding event.

Non–determinism $P \& Q$ defines an internal choice that is determined by the process without influence from its environment. Either branch might be taken by the process, the reason for the choice being unobservable.

Composition $P * Q$ runs P and Q in parallel, with synchronization occurring over similarly named events. When P and Q share a common event, both must be in a state in which they can accept that event before the event and synchronous state evolution can occur. P and Q may independently respond to events that are unique to their specification. Should such independent events occur simultaneously, the processes respond simultaneously.

Abstraction $P - a$ hides event set a from P, the actions in a becoming encapsulated and unobservable. Unobservable events internal to a process lead to non-deterministic behaviour.

Relabelling $P[a/b]$ replaces references to event b in P with the event named a. This feature is similar to calling procedures with parameter substitution.

Circal differs from most Process Algebras in that it has a strict interpretation of the response of processes to the simultaneous occurrence of events and is therefore well-suited to modelling synchronous devices such as FPGAs.

Circal has been used extensively to describe systems composed of interacting finite state machines, to describe control paths for digital systems, to describe asynchronous logic and to specify cellular automata for FPGA implementation [10]. To demonstrate the approach to modelling adopted in a Circal descriptive framework, consider a mobile phone system that is also capable of receiving and recording television or radio broadcast signals. We shall examine the description and composition of parts of the broadcast receiver subsystem B and the phone subsystem P. Consider a mode of operation in which the user initiates broadcast reception by the s action used to select a channel. Should an urgent phone call arrive, the system is able to buffer reception of the broadcast while the user answers the phone with action a. When the user hangs the phone up, the broadcast may be resumed from the time it was interrupted, by use of event r, and the remainder of the reception is buffered until the user flushes the buffer by selecting a new channel or terminates reception with another r event.

In this presentation, we depict a block diagram of the structure of the composed subsystems of the mobile phone M in Figure 1. The following Circal

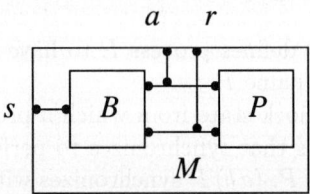

Fig. 1. Mobile phone system comprising broadcast and phone subsystems.

definitions describe the broadcast component B in terms of the four distinct states it may take.

$$B_i \leftarrow s\,B_r + a\,B_i + r\,B_i, \text{ when } B \text{ is inactive,} \tag{1}$$

$$B_r \leftarrow a\,B_s + s\,B_r + r\,B_i, \text{ when } B \text{ is receiving,} \tag{2}$$

$$B_s \leftarrow r\,B_b, \text{ when } B \text{ is storing, and} \tag{3}$$

$$B_b \leftarrow s\,B_r + r\,B_i, \text{ when } B \text{ is buffering.} \tag{4}$$

The phone component may be defined as

$$P_i \leftarrow a\,P_a + r\,P_i, \text{ when } P \text{ is inactive, and}$$
$$P_a \leftarrow r\,P_i, \text{ when } P \text{ is answering.}$$

Finally, we define the mobile phone system M as the composition or synthesis of the two components B and P by $M \leftarrow B * P$.

Such Circal expressions define the behaviour when in a given state in terms of the occurrence of permitted events, that in this example model the interaction between the system and the user.

The focus of this paper is on describing and managing finite FPGA resources to create a larger virtual resource using Circal as the descriptive medium. In terms of the example of Figure 1, we provide techniques for automatically swapping active subcomponents of M into hardware when there is insufficient resource to implement all components of the system at once.

3 Description of the Compiler

In [5] we described a compiler that derives and implements a digital logic representation of high-level behavioural descriptions of systems specified using Circal.

Significantly, this compiler structures the derived circuits so as to reflect the design hierarchy and interconnection of process modules given in the specification. This approach simplifies the composition of modules since the majority of interconnections that are to be implemented are between co-located blocks of logic and the replacement or exchange of system modules is facilitated by the replacement of a compact region rather than of distributed logic. At the topmost design level, the circuit is clustered into blocks of logic that correspond to the processes of a system. These are wired together on similarly labelled ports to effect event broadcast and to allow process state transitions to be synchronized. Our strategy for virtual hardware management makes use of an interpreter that follows a similar translation philosophy.

An overview of the realization of Circal expressions in digital logic is depicted in Figure 2(a). The process logic blocks individually implement circuits with behaviours corresponding to the component processes of the specification — see Figure 2(b). Each block is provided with inputs corresponding to the events in its sort. Events are realized by the presence or absence of signals that are generated by the environment on similarly named wires. The response of process logic blocks to an event is determined by the global acceptability of an event. Processes independently assert a request signal when acceptable events for the current state are offered by the environment. Synchronized state evolution occurs upon the next clock edge if all processes agree on the acceptability of the event.

Below the process level in the hierarchy, the circuits are partitioned into component circuit modules that implement combinational logic functions of minor complexity. A typical example of such a module generates a minterm that recognizes an acceptable event combination; another forms the disjunction of several

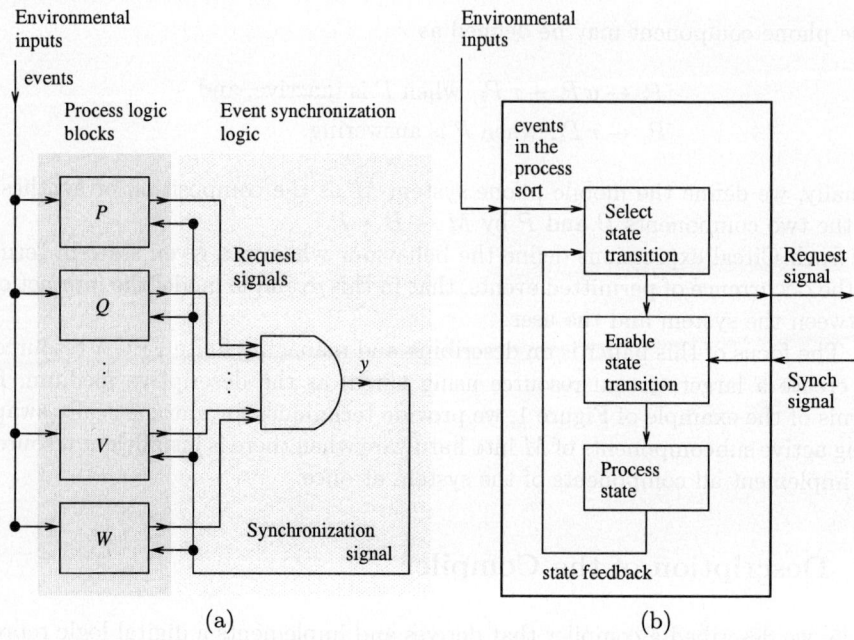

Fig. 2. (a) Circuit block diagram, and (b) Circal process logic block.

such minterms in order to recognize those event combinations that are acceptable in a particular state. Modules are rectangular in shape and are laid out onto abutting regions of the array surface. Signals flow from one module to another via aligned ports. The partitioning of the system circuit into component circuit modules is fixed during the analysis phase of the compiler, which is programmed with a particular arrangement of the modules in mind — the module types and their relative position is thus directed by the compilation process [6].

The component circuit modules are each specified by a number of parameters, the derivation of which represents the goal of the analysis phase of the compiler. The following synthesis phase applies each set of module parameters to a corresponding module generator that maps its functional and spatial requirements to FPGA resources and produces a bitstream fragment for the circuit component. Circuit module generators perform the physical mapping of the circuit to FPGA resources in order to obtain quick physical designs and to control the layout. These factors simplify reconfiguration by allowing precise changes to be carried out quickly.

For example, to implement the process logic for the broadcast component B, the Circal definitions (1) through (4) in Section 2 are translated into a set of boolean equations over similarly labelled literals. One equation describes the logic for the request signal r_B that should be generated for the block,

$$r_B = (s.\bar{a}.\bar{r} + \bar{s}.a.\bar{r} + \bar{s}.\bar{a}.r + \bar{s}.\bar{a}.\bar{r}).B_i + (\bar{s}.a.\bar{r} + s.\bar{a}.\bar{r} + \bar{s}.\bar{a}.r + \bar{s}.\bar{a}.\bar{r}).B_r$$
$$+ (\bar{s}.\bar{a}.r + \bar{s}.\bar{a}.\bar{r}).B_s + (s.\bar{a}.\bar{r} + \bar{s}.\bar{a}.r + \bar{s}.\bar{a}.\bar{r}).B_b$$

The rest describe the input functions for the (D-type) flip-flops implementing the 4 states of the process within the "Enable state transition" block of Figure 2(b). These equations include a literal for the synchronization signal y.

$$D_{B_i} = y.([\overline{s}.a.\overline{r} + \overline{s}.\overline{a}.r + \overline{s}.\overline{a}.\overline{r}].B_i + \overline{s}.\overline{a}.r.B_r + \overline{s}.\overline{a}.r.B_b) + \overline{y}.B_i$$
$$D_{B_r} = y.(s.\overline{a}.\overline{r}.B_i + [s.\overline{a}.\overline{r} + \overline{s}.\overline{a}.\overline{r}].B_r + s.\overline{a}.\overline{r}.B_b) + \overline{y}.B_r$$
$$D_{B_s} = y.(\overline{s}.a.\overline{r}.B_r + \overline{s}.\overline{a}.\overline{r}.B_s) + \overline{y}.B_s$$
$$D_{B_b} = y.(\overline{s}.\overline{a}.r.B_s + \overline{s}.\overline{a}.\overline{r}.B_b) + \overline{y}.B_b$$

Note that most of the terms in these equations are formed from the conjunction of a minterm defined over the events the process can respond to and a process state. In fact the terms in r_B are covered by the parenthesized terms of the flip-flop input functions. Thus r_b is implemented as the disjunction of these latter terms. Each minterm, the disjunction of minterms that combine with a state, and the disjunction of terms that combine with y in a flip-flop input function, as well as the disjunction of terms to form r_B are encoded as parameterized modules and implemented as rectangular circuit fragments within the logic block for a process.

4 A Circal Interpreter

The Circal compiler described above, and in more detail in [5,6], produces a static design prior to circuit loading and execution. Using the same philosophy for realizing Circal in FPGA logic, the Circal interpreter described in this paper is, in contrast, able to finalize physical designs and modify designs at run time either in order to better manage limited reconfigurable resources or to realize dynamically reconfigurable systems specified in dynamically structured Circal (dsCircal), a development of Circal that permits the direct description of systems whose structure changes through time [11,12].

There are several reasons for using an interpreter rather than a compiler to manage the implementation of a Circal design. First, we could compile and temporally partition the system off-line, but we may not know in advance of running the system which Circal processes need to be simultaneously active. If the partitioning is unsuitable, the performance of the system will be affected. Second, we need to be prepared to adapt to time-varying resource availability such as in distributed (networked) or multitasking reconfigurable computing environments. A static design may be held up or may hold up other applications due to allocation conflicts. Third, we cannot use a static compilation approach if the behaviour and/or circuit structure is permitted to change over time, as may be described in the dsCircal language.

The Circal interpreter pre-processes a system description until functional module parameters such as the number of variables in minterm blocks are known. Some spatial parameters, such as sizes of modules and relative offsets are also determined at the pre-processing stage. At run time, the interpreter looks after loading modules on an as needs basis, employing techniques for managing the reconfigurable resource as described in Section 5. This involves finalizing module locations on the underlying FPGA substrate and generating the bitstream fragments for the modules as they are to be loaded. Bitstream generation at run time does not represent a significant overhead because the time to generate and emit the bitstream is proportional to its size. The interpreter suspends the application clock for the duration of the reconfiguration.

5 A Strategy for Virtual Hardware Management

The implementation of a system described in Circal exhibits both coarse and fine grained parallelism. A process logic block is a relatively large unit of computation or circuit that can be viewed as a "grain of large size", while the circuit module subcomponents of a process are small units of computation, typically no larger than a few gates, and may therefore be viewed as being of a much finer grain size. Realistic systems will be composed of multiple processes, while within individual processes high degrees of parallelism may exist between small subcomponents.

We exploit the two extremes of grain size to manage hardware use in three ways:

1. We sequentialize deployment and execution of circuitry by repeated reconfiguration when streams could be executed concurrently but there is insufficient resource to do so. This strategy is applied at the coarse grain size of individual processes.

2. We deploy circuit modules as signals advance through the circuit so as to allow concurrent execution yet reduce demand on resource. This strategy is intended to be employed at a fine grain size on time-multiplexed chips [4, 19] and relies upon allocating the subcomponents of processes to successive context layers so as to keep the cost of reconfiguration low.

3. We load logic as processes evolve when the choice of logic to be executed is determined at run time. This strategy is applied at both the coarse process and fine module grain sizes. On the one hand, the deployment of processes or assemblies of process logic may be guarded by events that will control the loading of circuitry should such an event occur. On the other hand, the need for certain modules, such as those to detect specific event combinations, only arises in particular states. To save on resources, we thus only implement those modules that are needed given the current state of the system.

Apart from allowing large systems to run on limited FPGA resources, the benefit of dynamic circuit loading is that it saves loading unnecessary circuitry, which saves on load time and lowers demand for the resource. However, such a scheme requires very efficient techniques for loading circuitry to minimize reconfiguration overheads. We tackle this problem by primarily relying upon fast module generators that produce circuitry in time proportional to the time needed to load it. The overheads of the interpreter are thus kept low.

To illustrate the use of these techniques, we contrast the runtime control of the reconfigurable resource performed by the compiler with that carried out by the interpreter. The host program of the compiler that loads and runs the fixed, static circuits executes the following loop:

```
repeat {
  wait until event occurs
  present events to system
  allow system to determine its response and evolve state
} until system halts
```

The interpreter takes one of two alternative approaches depending upon whether the design, as described in Circal, is static or dynamic. If the design is static, it can be partitioned before execution, and all we need do at run time is cycle between the partitions. Thus the above loop becomes:

```
partition system by packing components into available area
repeat {
  wait until event occurs
  for each partition and while event still acceptable
    load partition and determine acceptability of event
  if event acceptable to entire system
    for each partition
      load partition and allow state to evolve
} until system halts
```

If on the other hand the design or the amount of available resource is dynamic, or we wish to employ the third strategy above, then partitioning is done at run time during the execution phase. The loop then becomes:

```
repeat {
  wait until event occurs
  while event acceptable and components remain to be processed
    compute partition by packing components into available area
    load partition and determine acceptability of event
  if event acceptable to system as a whole
    for each partition
      load and evolve state
} until system halts
```

In the mobile phone example pictured in Figure 1, these techniques would be employed if the circuit to implement M were too large, but B and P on their own fit into the available FPGA resource.

When a process can assume one of many states, as for process B in our example, rather than implementing the logic for all possible states in a single block, strategy 3 suggests we just implement the logic corresponding to the definition of the current state. As the state changes, the behaviour of the new state is implemented by reconfiguring the subcomponents that recognize acceptable events for this new state. We thus initially implement the boolean equations corresponding to the definition for state B_i,

$$B_i \leftarrow s\, B_r + a\, B_i + r\, B_i,$$

that is,
$$r_{B_i} = (s.\bar{a}.\bar{r} + \bar{s}.a.\bar{r} + \bar{s}.\bar{a}.r + \bar{s}.\bar{a}.\bar{r}),$$
and
$$D_{B_i} = y.(\bar{s}.a.\bar{r} + \bar{s}.\bar{a}.r + \bar{s}.\bar{a}.\bar{r}).B_i + \bar{y}.B_i, \text{ and}$$
$$D_{B_r} = y.s.\bar{a}.\bar{r}.B_i.$$

Should an s event occur, for example, the logic for B would be reconfigured to implement equations corresponding to the definition for state B_r.

6 Conclusions

In this paper, we have described a behavioural specification language for reconfigurable computing together with techniques for managing hardware use at run time by exploiting the hierarchy and modularity in the language and its implementation using FPGA technology. The techniques used have been described in the context of overcoming resource limitations. However, they are equally applicable to the implementation of systems whose circuit structure changes during execution.

Current work is being carried out to complete the implementation of the Circal interpreter and the testing of its performance. We are also investigating techniques and language constructs appropriate for the description and management of run-time, dynamically changing circuit structures such as described in [12].

Acknowledgement

This research was funded by the Australian Research Council.

References

1. P. Bertin and H. Touati. PAM programming environments: Practice and experience. In Buell and Pocek [3], pages 133 – 138.
2. D. C. Blight and R. D. McLeod. VHDL for FPGA design. In Moore and Luk [14], pages 246 – 254.
3. D. A. Buell and K. L. Pocek, editors. *Proceedings IEEE Workshop on FPGAs for Custom Computing Machines (FCCM'94)*, Los Alamitos, CA, Apr. 1994. IEEE Computer Society Press.
4. A. DeHon. DPGA–coupled microprocessors: Commodity ICs for the early 21st Century. In Buell and Pocek [3], pages 31 – 39.
5. O. Diessel and G. Milne. Compiling process algebraic descriptions into reconfigurable logic. In J. Rolim, editor, *Parallel and Distributed Processing, 15 IPDPS 2000 Workshops Proceedings*, volume 1800 of *Lecture Notes in Computer Science*, pages 916 – 923, Berlin, Germany, 2000. Springer–Verlag.

6. O. Diessel and G. Milne. A hardware implementation of the Circal process algebra and compiling HCircal. Technical report ACRC–00–013, Advanced Computing Research Centre, School of Computer and Information Science, University of South Australia, Mawson Lakes, SA, 2000.
7. C. A. R. Hoare. *Communicating Sequential Processes*. Prentice-Hall International series in computer science. Prentice–Hall, Inc., Englewood Cliffs, NJ, 1985.
8. H. Jifeng, I. Page, and J. Bowen. Towards a provably correct hardware implementation of Occam. In G. J. Milne and L. Pierre, editors, *Correct Hardware Design and Verification Methods, IFIPWG10.2 Advanced Research Working Conference, CHARME'93 Proceedings*, volume 683 of *Lecture Notes in Computer Science*, pages 214 – 225, Berlin, Germany, May 1993. Springer–Verlag.
9. G. Milne. CIRCAL and the representation of communication, concurrency and time. *ACM Transactions on Programming Languages and Systems*, 7(2):270–298, 1985.
10. G. Milne. *Formal Specification and Verification of Digital Systems*. McGraw–Hill, London, UK, 1994.
11. G. Milne. A model for dynamic adaptation in reconfigurable hardware systems. In A. Stoica, D. Keymeulen, and J. Lohn, editors, *Proceedings of the First NASA/DoD Workshop on Evolvable Hardware*, pages 161 – 169, Los Alamitos, CA, July 1999. IEEE Computer Society Press.
12. G. Milne. Modelling dynamic structures. Technical report ACRC–99–01, Advanced Computing Research Centre, School of Computer and Information Science, University of South Australia, Adelaide, Australia, Jan. 1999.
13. R. Milner. *Communication and Concurrency*. Prentice–Hall, Inc., New York, NY, 1989.
14. W. R. Moore and W. Luk, editors. *FPGAs, Edited from the Oxford 1991 International Workshop on Field Programmable Logic and Applications*, Abingdon, England, 1991. Abingdon EE&CS Books.
15. I. Page and W. Luk. Compiling Occam into FPGAs. In Moore and Luk [14], pages 271 – 283.
16. P. Shaw. *A Generic Approach to Compiling Occam into Circuits*. PhD thesis, Department of Computer Science, University of Strathclyde, Dec. 1994.
17. P. Shaw and G. Milne. A highly parallel FPGA–based machine and its formal verification. In H. Grünbacher and R. W. Hartenstein, editors, *Field–Programmable Gate Arrays: Architectures and Tools for Rapid Prototyping, Second International Workshop on Field–Programmable Logic and Applications*, volume 705 of *Lecture Notes in Computer Science*, pages 162–173, Berlin, Germany, Sept. 1992. Springer–Verlag.
18. D. Soderman and Y. Panchul. Implementing C algorithms in reconfigurable hardware using c2verilog. In K. L. Pocek and J. M. Arnold, editors, *The 6th Annual IEEE Symposium on FPGAs for Custom Computing Machines (FCCM'98)*, pages 339 – 342, Los Alamitos, CA, Apr. 1998. IEEE Computer Society Press.
19. S. Trimberger, D. Carberry, A. Johnson, and J. Wong. A time–multiplexed FPGA. In K. L. Pocek and J. M. Arnold, editors, *The 5th Annual IEEE Symposium on FPGAs for Custom Computing Machines (FCCM'97)*, pages 22 – 28, Los Alamitos, CA, Apr. 1997. IEEE Computer Society Press.

Synthesis and Implementation of RAM-Based Finite State Machines in FPGAs

Valery Sklyarov

Department of Electronics and Telecommunications
University of Aveiro
Portugal
skl@inesca.pt

Abstract. This paper discusses the design and implementation of finite state machines (FSM) with combinational circuits that are built primarily from RAM blocks. It suggests a novel state assignment technique, based on fuzzy codes, that is combined with the replacement (encoding) of the FSM input vectors. It also shows how FSMs with dynamically modifiable functionality can be constructed and then implemented in commercially available FPGAs. The results of experiments have shown that FSMs with the proposed architecture can be implemented using less hardware resources, such as the number of FPGA configurable logic blocks (CLB), while at the same time extending their functional capabilities.

1 Introduction

The primary architectures (models) of FSMs usually have simple and regular structures at the top level [1]. They are considered to be a composite of a combinational scheme and memory. The former calculates new states in state transitions and forms outputs, and the latter is used to store states.

The top-level architecture can generally be reused for different applications. However, the combinational scheme is typically very irregular, and its implementation depends on the particular unique behavioral specification for a given FSM. Since such specifications vary from one implementation to another, we cannot construct a reusable FSM circuit. Note that there are some techniques (for example, microprogramming) and technology dependent design methodologies (for instance, those aimed at dynamically modifiable field programmable devices such as the Xilinx XC6200 family) that do allow reusable parameterizable templates to be built for FSM-based applications. However these approaches have many limitations, such as restricting the number of inputs that can affect state transitions in the FSM, requiring a considerable amount of RAM (ROM) for the combinational circuit, and necessitating rather complex circuits and time-consuming procedures for dynamic modifications to the logic and interconnections.

This paper presents an approach to the design of FSMs that is based on the use of RAM blocks, but of a modest size. It eliminates many of the restrictions that apply to traditional FSM architectures and current methods for FSM synthesis. Since very fast RAM-based CLBs are available within widely used and relatively cheap FPGAs such as the XC4000XL of Xilinx, we can apply the proposed technique directly to the design of FPGA-based circuits. Such an implementation is very efficient. Since each CLB can be configured to be 16x2 or 32x1 RAM (ROM), and its speed is comparable with ordinary logic, with the aid of the proposed technique we can implement very regular and very fast dynamically modifiable circuits, something which is generally impossible using traditional approaches.

2 The Architecture of RAM-Based FSMs

The set of state transitions for any FSM can be presented in the form: $a_{to} = a_{from}X(a_{from},a_{to})$, where a_{from} and a_{to} are the initial and next state in the state transition, $X(a_{from},a_{to})$ is a product of the input variables from the set $X=\{x_1,...,x_L\}$ that cause the transition from a_{from} to a_{to}, L is the number of FSM inputs, $a_{from}, a_{to} \in A=\{a_0,...,a_{M-1}\}$, A is the set of FSM states, and M is the number of states. The FSM generates outputs from the set $Y=\{y_1,...,y_N\}$ where N is the number of FSM outputs.

The structural model of a FSM assumes that all states are coded, and the size R of the code varies from the value $intlog_2 M$ (for binary state encoding) to M (for one-hot state encoding). Thus a RAM-based combinational circuit has R+L inputs and R+N outputs, and the size of RAM is equal to $2^{R+L}(R+N)$ bits. Even for binary state encoding and modest values of L and N, except for some trivial cases this size becomes very large.

Let's consider an example. Fig. 1,a shows a state transition graph for a FSM where M=5, $R_{min}=3$, and L=2. Fig. 1,b depicts a trivial RAM-based implementation of this FSM, and the RAM size is equal to $2^5(3+N)$. One way to decrease the memory required is to split the conditional state transitions using two additional intermediate states. However, any conditional state transition will then require twice the time, and the RAM required is still $2^4(3+N)$. We will also need additional hardware to multiplex the input variables x_1 and x_2 to the same RAM input.

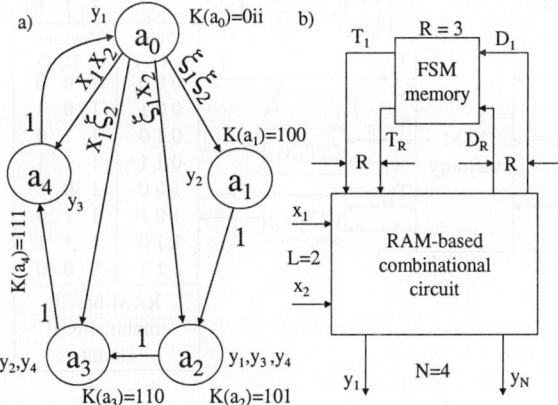

Fig. 1. State transition graph (a) and a feasible top-level structure of a RAM-based FSM (b)

The proposed approach is based on the so-called *fuzzy state encoding technique*, and it enables us to improve the implementation of FSMs, even for the trivial case we have just considered.

Let us define $K(a_m)$ as the code for the state a_m. A code is *fuzzy* if its size is not fixed for all m. For example, the code of the state a_m might be 0ii, where the character "i" indicates that the bit must be ignored and is considered in a specific way. Note that "i" does not denote "don't care", which is designated as "-".

In order to distinguish the codes for different states, these codes must be orthogonal. This means that for any two codes, there is at least one bit position that is equal to 1 (0) in one code and 0 (1) in the other. For example, all the codes $K(a_0),...,K(a_4)$, shown in fig. 1,a are orthogonal. The size of the code $K(a_0)$ is equal to 1 and the size of all the other codes is equal to 3. Since bits 2 and 3 in the code $K(a_0)$ are not used for representing the code, we can employ them to identify transitions from the state a_0 in such a way that they are (see fig. 1): $a_0(T_1\xi_1\xi_2) \Rightarrow a_1$, $a_0(T_1\xi_1x_2) \Rightarrow a_2$, $a_0(T_1x_1\xi_2) \Rightarrow a_3$, $a_0(T_1x_1x_2) \Rightarrow a_4$. Now if the FSM is set in one of the states $\{a_1,a_2,a_3,a_4\}$, we can use the bits T_2 and T_3 from the FSM memory (see fig. 1,b) to identify the corresponding code. If the FSM is in the state a_0, the code $K(a_0)$ can be identified by just one bit T_1, and since the remaining bits are not needed in a_0 we can use the corresponding RAM inputs to distinguish conditional state transitions. Fig. 2 presents the complete implementation of the FSM scheme with the behavior given in fig. 1,a. Two extra blocks, $C(T_2,x_1)$ and $C(T_3,x_2)$, provide predefined selections of the signals between the parentheses, and send them to the RAM inputs T_2^* and T_3^*.

The idea that we considered above can be used to design RAM-based FSMs, and the synthesis of such FSMs involves the following two steps: 1) the replacement of input variables (encoding of input vectors) such that the number of inputs, L, for the RAM-based circuit is reduced; 2) state encoding that defines fuzzy codes for the FSM states that satisfy our requirements.

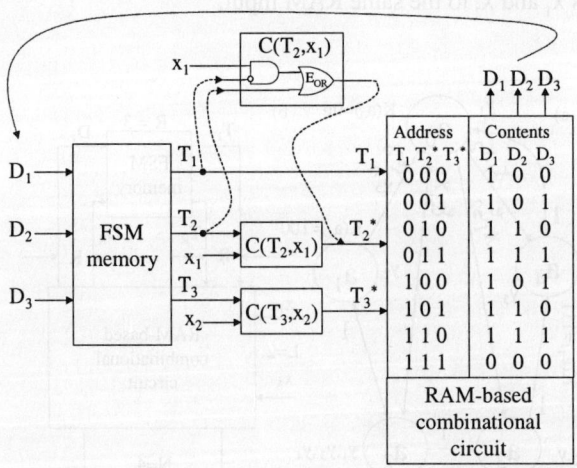

Fig. 2. Implementation of the FSM with fuzzy state codes

3 Replacement of Input Variables

The primary method for input variable replacement was considered in [2]. In this case, the combinational scheme of a FSM is composed of two sub-schemes. The first sub-scheme makes it possible to replace external input variables from the set X with new variables from the set $P = \{P_1,...,P_G\}$, and for many applications $G \ll L$. It performs the following function:

$$P(a_{from}, a_{to}) = \rho(a_{from}, X(a_{from}, a_{to})),$$

where $P(a_{from}, a_{to})$ is the vector which can be used in the state a_{from} instead of the input vector $X(a_{from}, a_{to})$, and ρ is a conversion function [2]. Since this is presented in detail in [2,3], we will just consider an example here that will be used later to illustrate our approach (see table 1, where for the sake of clarity we have omitted the output variables and they can be generated just as for the Moore FSM). The column $P_B(a_{from}, a_{to})$ contains the variables P_1, P_2, P_3 that can be used instead of the variables $x_1,...,x_8$ after applying the method [2]. The conversions required are represented by the following Boolean functions: $P_1 = a_1 x_1 \vee a_2 x_6 \vee a_5 x_6$, $P_2 = a_1 x_2 \vee a_2 x_7 \vee a_5 x_4$, $P_3 = a_1 x_3 \vee a_2 x_8 \vee a_5 x_5$. Such a replacement enables very efficient implementations of functions such as P_1, P_2, and P_3, to be provided on multiplexers [3]. Another kind of replacement (which differs from [2,3]) is based on an encoding technique (see the column $P(a_{from}, a_{to})$). However in this case the circuit that implements the Boolean functions $P_1,...,P_G$ would be less regular.

4 State Encoding

Consider the main idea of state encoding. Suppose that the code $K(a_1)$ of the state a_1 is 01ii. Since in table 1 there are three transitions from a_1, to different states a_3, a_2 and a_4, we can code these transitions as $[01(i=0)(i=0)] \Rightarrow a_3$, $[01(i=0)(i=1)] \Rightarrow a_2$, and $[01(i=1)(i=0)] \Rightarrow a_4$. If the results of replacement are presented in the column $P(a_{from}, a_{to})$ of table 1, then the 3rd and the 4th outputs of the FSM memory will be mixed with the variables $P_3 P_4$ by means of OR gates (see elements E_{OR} in fig. 2). In this case if the FSM is in the state a_1, the outputs T_3 and T_4 must be set to zero. However, if we replace E_{OR} with E_{XOR}, which performs an XOR function, the outputs T_3 and T_4 could also be set to non zero values and we would obtain the same results by a trivial reprogramming of the RAM.

Let us designate $A(a_{from})$ as the subset of states that follow the state a_{from} and suppose that $k_{from} = |A(a_{from})|$. For our example in table 1 we have $A(a_0) = \{a_1\}$, $k_0 = 1$, $A(a_1) = \{a_3, a_2, a_4\}$, $k_1 = 3$, $A(a_2) = \{a_1, a_5, a_6, a_9\}$, $k_2 = 4$, etc. If $k_{max} = \max(k_0, k_1, k_2,...)$, then $G_{min} = \text{intlog}_2 k_{max}$, where G_{min} is the minimum number of variables from the set P that affect individual transitions. For our example in table 1 $G_{min} = 2$ (see column $P(a_{from}, a_{to})$).

Consider any subset $A(a_m) = \{a_{m1}, a_{m2},...\}$, $m=0,...,M-1$, such that $k_m > 1$. If $k_m = 1$ then the code, $K(a_m)$, of a_m can be considered to be the RAM address and it can be directly used for the unconditional transition from a_m to $A(a_m)$. We want to generate codes for the states $a_{m1}, a_{m2},...$ on the outputs of the FSM RAM so we can set the following correspondence: $c_m^{m1} \Rightarrow a_{m1}$, $c_m^{m2} \Rightarrow a_{m2},...$, where c_m^{m1}, c_m^{m2},... are the symbols that correspond to the respective RAM address codes (AC) that will be designated as

Table 1. Structural table of FSM

A_{from}	$K(a_{from})$	$a_{to} \Leftarrow AC$	$K(a_{to})$	$K(c_{from}^{to})$	$X(a_{from}, a_{to})$	$P_B(a_{from}, a_{to})$	$P(a_{from}, a_{to})$
A_0	0000	a_1	01 00	0000	1	not valid	not valid
a_1	01ii	$a_3 \Leftarrow c_1^3$ $a_3 \Leftarrow c_1^3$ $a_2 \Leftarrow c_1^2$ $a_4 \Leftarrow c_1^4$	00 01 00 01 10 00 00 11	0100 0100 0101 0110	ξ_1 $x_1\xi_2\xi_3$ $x_1 x_2$ $x_1\xi_2 x_3$	Π_1 $P_1\Pi_2\Pi_3$ Π_3 $P_1 P_2$ $P_1\Pi_2 P_3$	$\Pi_3\Pi_4$ $\Pi_3\Pi_4$ $\Pi_3 P_4$ $P_3\Pi_4$
a_2	10ii	$a_1 \Leftarrow c_2^1$ $a_5 \Leftarrow c_2^5$ $a_6 \Leftarrow c_2^6$ $a_9 \Leftarrow c_2^9$	01 00 10 01 00 10 11 10	1010 1001 1000 1011	ξ_7 $\xi_6 x_7 \xi_8$ $x_7 \xi_8$ $x_6 x_7 x_8$	Π_2 $\Pi_1 P_2 P_3$ $P_2\Pi_3$ $P_1 P_2 P_3$	$P_3\Pi_4$ $\Pi_3 P_4$ $\Pi_3\Pi_4$ $P_3 P_4$
a_3	0001	a_7	01 11	0001	1	not valid	not valid
a_4	0011	a_5	10 01	0011	1	not valid	not valid
a_5	1ii1	$a_5 \Leftarrow c_5^5$ $a_7 \Leftarrow c_5^7$ $a_8 \Leftarrow c_5^8$ $a_9 \Leftarrow c_5^9$	10 01 01 11 11 00 11 10	1001 1101 1111 1011	$x_4\xi_5\xi_6$ ξ_4 $x_4 x_5$ $x_4\xi_5 x_6$	$\Pi_1 P_2\Pi_3$ Π_2 $P_2 P_3$ $P_1 P_2\Pi_3$	$\Pi_2\Pi_3$ $P_2\Pi_3$ $P_2 P_3$ $\Pi_2 P_3$
a_6	0010	a_0	00 00	0010	1	not valid	not valid
a_7	0111	a_8	11 00	0111	1	not valid	not valid
a_8	1100	a_0	00 00	1100	1	not valid	not valid
A_9	1110	a_0	00 00	1110	1	not valid	not valid

$K(c_m^{m1}), K(c_m^{m2}),\ldots$. Let us also agree to call $c_m^{m1}, c_m^{m2},\ldots$ ACs when there is no possible ambiguity. Finally we can build new subsets, which are $C(a_m) = \{c_m^{m1}, c_m^{m2},\ldots\}$, m=0,...,M-1. It is obvious that the following correspondence exists: $[A(a_m)=\{a_{m1}, a_{m2},\ldots\}] \Leftrightarrow [C(a_m)=\{c_m^{m1}, c_m^{m2},\ldots\}]$, i.e. for each element a_{mi} there exists an

Synthesis and Implementation of RAM-Based Finite State Machines in FPGAs   723

address code c_m^{mi} and RAM provides the conversion $c_m^{mi} \Rightarrow a_{mi}$. In fact a_{mi} is the code written at address c_m^{mi} in RAM. Now we can formulate the target requirements for the encoding:

1. All ACs $c_m^{m1}, c_m^{m2}, \ldots$ (m=0,...,M-1) with different superscripts must be unique (because they cause transitions to different states). As a result we can formulate the following requirement: $\forall A(a_m) \cap A(a_s) = \emptyset \ \exists \ \{K(c_m^{m1}), K(c_m^{m2}), \ldots\}$ ort $\{K(c_s^{s1}), K(c_s^{s2}), \ldots\}$, where ort is the relationship of orthogonality considered above and any element of the first set must be orthogonal to any element of the second set. Here $K(c_{from}^{to})$ is the binary code of c_{from}^{to} (see table 1). ;

2. ACs with the same superscript could be the same (because they cause transitions to the same states). Hence, if $A(a_m) \cap A(a_s) \neq \emptyset$, $\{K(c_m^{m1}), K(c_m^{m2}), \ldots\}$ ins $\{K(c_s^{s1}), K(c_s^{s2}), \ldots\}$ is allowed, where ins is the relationship of intersection (or non-orthogonality): $\{c_m^{m1}, c_m^{m2}, \ldots\}$ ins $\{c_s^{s1}, c_s^{s2}, \ldots\} \Leftrightarrow \{c_m^{m1}, c_m^{m2}, \ldots\}$ ~~ort~~ $\{c_s^{s1}, c_s^{s2}, \ldots\}$;

3. The predefined size, S, of the resulting codes is equal to R (S=R). In some cases S may be greater then R but we want to find the minimum value of S (S≥R).

4. Variables $c_m^{m1}, c_m^{m2}, \ldots$ in each individual subset $C(a_m)$, $k_m > 1$, m=0,...,M-1, must be encoded in such a way that a maximum number of their bits with coincident indexes have constant values that are the same for all variables $c_m^{m1}, c_m^{m2}, \ldots$ from $C(a_m)$.

The ACs that satisfy the requirements considered above can be obtained with the aid of a slightly modified encoding algorithm [3], which allows for a combinational circuit of a FSM to reduce the functional dependency of outputs on inputs. This is based on the iterative placement of the symbols that must be coded in special tables that look like Karnaugh maps. This method permits the encoding procedure to be carried out for quite complicated FSMs. The results of this step for our example (see table 1) are shown in fig. 3,a. Next we find the codes for the states a_m, such that $k_m > 1$. They are: $K(a_1)$=01ii (see the squares c_1^3, c_1^2, c_1^4), $K(a_2)$=10ii (see the squares $c_2^6, c_2^5, c_2^9, c_2^1$), $K(a_5)$=1ii1 (see the squares $c_5^7, c_5^5, c_5^9, c_5^8$). Here $A(a_1) \cap A(a_2) = \emptyset$ and $A(a_1) \cap A(a_5) = \emptyset$. That is why $\{K(c_1^3), K(c_1^2), K(c_1^4)\}$ ort $\{K(c_2^6), K(c_2^5), K(c_2^9), K(c_2^1)\}$ and $\{K(c_1^3), K(c_1^2), K(c_1^4)\}$ ort $\{K(c_5^7), K(c_5^5), K(c_5^9), K(c_5^8)\}$ (see fig. 3,a). Since $A(a_2) \cap A(a_5) = \{a_5, a_9\} \neq \emptyset$, it is allowed $\{K(c_2^6), K(c_2^5), K(c_2^9), K(c_2^1)\}$ ins $\{K(c_5^7), K(c_5^5), K(c_5^9), K(c_5^8)\}$. That is why the segments $c_2^6, c_2^5, c_2^9, c_2^1$ and $c_5^7, c_5^5, c_5^9, c_5^8$ of the map in fig. 3,a have two shared squares marked with c_2^5/c_5^5 and c_2^9/c_5^9 and $\{K(c_2^6), K(c_2^5), K(c_2^9), K(c_2^1)\}$ ins $\{K(c_5^7), K(c_5^5), K(c_5^9), K(c_5^8)\} = \{1101, 1111\}$ (note that each shared square contains symbols c_m^s with equal superscripts s).

All non-encoded states just cause unconditional transitions (k_m=1), and they can be assigned any unused codes that are available in the second step. This is feasible because an address code for any unfilled square in fig. 3,a does not exist. It follows from the predefined requirements to be established for the encoding of input variables (see column $P(a_{from}, a_{to})$ of table 1). Let us consider, for example, the unused square 0111 of the map in fig. 3,a. It is easy to verify that this code cannot be generated on any transition from the state a_1 (see table 1) as well as on any other transition except the specified unconditional transition from the state a_7 (see fig. 3,b). If the map does not have sufficient room, the size, S, of the codes must be incremented and the map must be enlarged [3]. Thus the resulting value of S could be greater then R (which is, of course, undesirable). The final results of state encoding are shown in fig. 3, b.

Now the RAM has 4 inputs and 4+N outputs, and it must be programmed as follows (see columns $K(c_{from}^{to}) \Rightarrow K(a_{to})$): 0000⇒0100; 0100⇒0001; 0101⇒1000;

0110⇒0011; 1010⇒0100; 1001⇒1001; 1000⇒0010; 1011⇒1110; 0001⇒0111; 0011⇒1001; 1101⇒0111; 1111⇒1100; 0010⇒0000; 0111⇒1100; 1100⇒0000; 1110⇒0000. The Boolean functions $C(T_2,P_2)$, $C(T_3,P_3)$, $C(T_4,P_4)$ for additional blocks such as those shown in fig. 2, can be obtained directly from the columns a_{from}, $X(a_{from},a_{to})$, $P(a_{from},a_{to})$ of table 1. After trivial minimization they will be the following: $P_2=T_1T_2(\xi_4 \vee x_5)$, $P_3=T_1T_2x_4(x_5 \vee x_6) \vee T_1T_2(\xi_7 \vee x_6 x_8) \vee T_1T_2x_1\xi_2x_3$, $P_4=T_1T_2x_1x_2 \vee T_1T_2x_7x_8$. Note that these functions are very simple and they are well suited to being implemented in widely used FPGAs, such as the Xilinx XC4000XL.

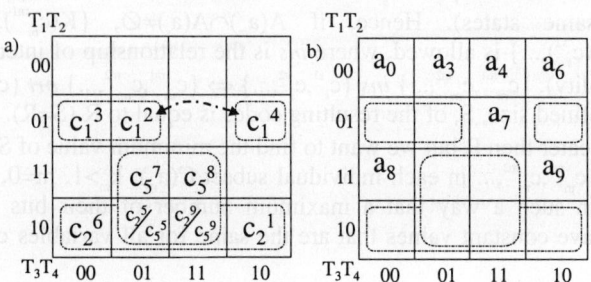

Figure 3. Maps that present the results of state encoding

The technique considered above includes many heuristic operations. Let us consider a method that enables us to solve this problem more formally. Consider the graph Λ, which reflects two following relationships α and β:

$$(c_m^s \ \alpha \ c_e^f) \Leftrightarrow (m = e); \quad (1)$$
$$(c_m^s \ \beta \ c_e^f) \Leftrightarrow (s = f). \quad (2)$$

Vertices of Λ correspond to symbols from the set $C(a_0),..., C(a_{M-1})$ Two vertices c_m^s and c_e^f are connected with an edge if and only if $(c_m^s \ \alpha \ c_e^f)$ or $(c_m^s \ \beta \ c_e^f)$. We will call the relationship (1) a hard relationship (because it strongly affects the results of state encoding) and the relationship (2) – a soft relationship (because it affects the quality of encoding but does not influence much to target requirements). That is why β edges will be shown in Λ with less thickness than α edges. Graph Λ for our example is shown in fig. 4,a. Let us designate $c_m=C(a_m)=\{c_m^{m1}, c_m^{m2},...\}$. All the vertices in each group c_m must be coded in such a way that permits our target requirements to be satisfied (see points 1-4 above). If $k_m = |\{c_m^{m1}, c_m^{m2},...\}| = |A(a_m)|$ is the number of elements in c_m, then we have to use $h_m = \text{intlog}_2 k_m$ bits of code in order to distinguish all superscripts m1, m2,..., which cause transitions to different states. As a result we can consider h_m-cubes, which enables us to find out the address codes indicated by fuzzy positions of state codes that are designated by symbols i. For example, $c_1 = \{c_1^2, c_1^3, c_1^4\}$, $k_m = |\{c_1^2, c_1^3, c_1^4\}| = 3$, $h_m = \text{intlog}_2 k_m = \text{intlog}_2 3 = 2$ and we have to consider 2-cubes, such as that can be represented by 4 squares of a Karnaugh map (or by 4 nodes of a 2-cube). If for a group c_m, $k_m < 2^{hm}$, we will insert $2^{hm}-k_m$ dummy vertices and will connect them with the other vertices of c_m by dashed lines. For example, for the group c_1 in fig, 4,a ($k_m=3$)<($2^{hm}=2^2=4$). That is why we need to add $2^{hm}-k_m=4-3=1$ vertex, as shown in fig.4,b.

Now let us group all the vertices of Λ that correspond to symbols $c_m^{m1}, c_m^{m2},...$ with the same subscript m, i.e. to the set c_m (see fig. 4,b, where the groups are encircled by dotted closed curves). Some groups may be connected (by edges) and other groups may be isolated. Fig. 4,c shows the new graph Γ that depicts the number of connections between the groups of Λ (see the number enclosed to the edge) and the number of vertices in each group of Λ (see the numbers enclosed to vertices).

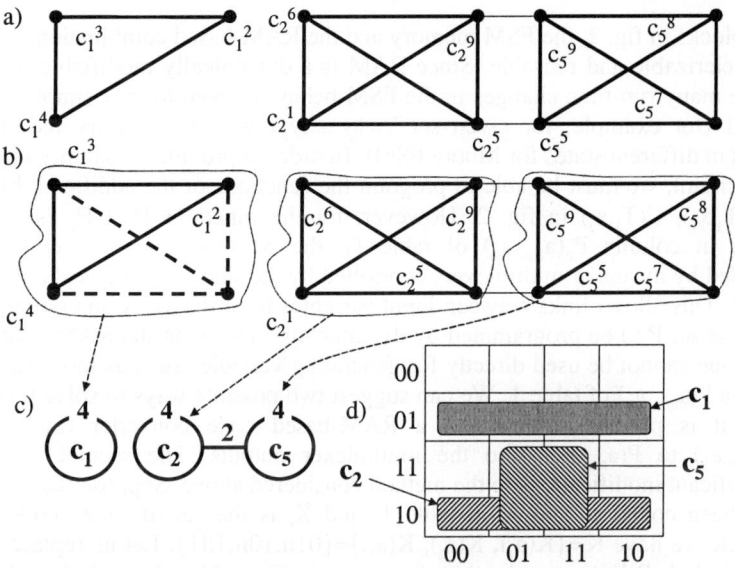

Figure 4. Graph Λ (a), extended graph Λ (b), graph Γ (c) and encoding map (d)

Let us analyze the graphs Λ and Γ in more detail. Each vertex of Γ represents the respective group c_m of Λ, i.e. the group that has to be coded by the corresponding h_m-cube. If two groups c_m and c_s (two vertices c_m and c_s of Γ) have been connected by an edge then they represent transitions to the same states and ACs for such transitions may be the same. The number $N(c_m,c_s)$ near the respective edge specifies the number of such transitions. So, if vertices c_m and c_s of Γ have been connected by an edge with $N(c_m,c_s)$ we need to accommodate c_m and c_s in such a way that: c_m is coded by h_m-cube; c_s is coded by h_s-cube; h_m-cube and h_s-cube have $N(c_m,c_s)$ intersecting (shared) squares. This is shown in fig.4,d, where c_1 is an isolated h_1-cube (i.e. 2-cube), c_2 and c_5 cubes that are intersecting by 2 squares, because $N(c_m,c_s)=2$ (see fig. 4,c). Finally we have to accommodate symbols c_i^j in the map (see fig. 4,d) in such a way that symbols with the same superscript will occupy the same square. This is trivial and we will obtain finally our previous table shown in fig. 3,a.

The method considered above is based on formal steps. A problem arises when we want to construct very complicated FSMs. In such cases the size of RAM becomes very large, and the circuit has a lot of redundancy. This problem can be overcome through a modular hierarchical specification of the FSM behavior such as that considered in [4]. This enables the description of the FSM to be decomposed into relatively autonomous fragments (sub-descriptions). Each fragment (module) can then be implemented in hardware using the approach we have discussed. The interaction mechanisms between the autonomous fragments were also considered in [4], and are based on the model of communicating FSMs with common stack memory.

5 Reusable Templates for RAM-Based FSM

Two blocks in fig. 2, the FSM memory and the RAM-based combinational circuit, are parameterizable and reusable. Since RAM is a dynamically modifiable unit, we can realize many run-time changes in the FSM behavior, even for our simple example in table 1 (for example, for given set Y={$y_1,...,y_N$} we can arbitrary redefine output values in different states for Moore FSM). In order to provide reusability for the entire FSM circuit, we must be able to program the functions of the additional blocks such as $C(T_2,x_1)$, $C(T_3,x_2)$ in fig. 2. However, for the functions $P_1,...,P_G$ (such as those shown in column $P_B(a_{from},a_{to})$ of table 1), the corresponding conversions can be provided by means of multiplexers controlled by the same RAM-based combinational circuit. This allows links between input variables from the set X and output variables from the set P to be programmed by dynamically modifying the RAM contents. This technique cannot be used directly for generating variables such as those shown in the column $P(a_{from},a_{to})$ of table 1. We can suggest two possible ways to solve this problem. First, it is possible to connect a RAM-based code converter (that transforms $P_B(a_{from},a_{to})$ to $P(a_{from},a_{to})$) to the multiplexer outputs. The second way assumes insignificant modifications to the method considered above. Suppose that all the states have been coded as shown in table 1, and K_f is the set of fuzzy codes. For our example we have K_f={$K(a_1)$, $K(a_2)$, $K(a_5)$}={01ii,10ii,1ii1}. Let us replace symbols i with symbols P_t having such t that shows the position of i in the code from left to right (starting from 1). For our example we can write the following sets of characters $01P_3P_4$, $10P_3P_4$ and $1P_2P_31$. Now we can change the indexes in the column $P_B(a_{from},a_{to})$ of table 1 in such a way that they will fit the respective bit positions in the subsets considered. For example, the symbols P_1,P_2,P_3 for the set $P_B(a_1,a_{to})$={ $P_B(a_1,a_2)$, $P_B(a_1,a_3)$, $P_B(a_1,a_4)$ } could be re-indexed as follows $P_1 \Rightarrow P_3$, $P_2 \Rightarrow P_4$, $P_3 \Rightarrow P_5$. Thus new symbols P_3 and P_4 fit the third and fourth positions in the set $01P_3P_4$. The new symbol P_5 can be used as a new bit for ACs. Unfortunately, in this case the size of the ACs has to be increased. This is the price of flexibility. Finally we will get: $P_B(a_1,a_2)=P_3P_4$, $P_B(a_1,a_3)=\Pi_3 \vee P_3\Pi_4\Pi_5$, $P_B(a_1,a_4)=P_3\Pi_4P_5$, $P_B(a_2,a_1)=P_4$, $P_B(a_2,a_5)= \Pi_3P_4P_5$, $P_B(a_2,a_6)=P_4\Pi_5$, $P_B(a_2,a_9)=P_3P_4P_5$, $P_B(a_5,a_3)=\Pi_2P_3\Pi_5$, $P_B(a_5,a_7)=\Pi_3$, $P_B(a_5,a_8)= P_3P_5$, $P_B(a_5,a_9)= P_2P_3\Pi_5$. Now we can implement our FSM based on RAM with the size of ACs equal to 5. The RAM becomes larger but we have been able to construct a dynamically modifiable circuit for the replacement of input variables. This circuit can be realized on programmable multiplexers [3] controlled by FSM RAM. Note that we still have two problems. Firstly, we might lose the flexibility of replacing non-encoded states, such as appeared in fig. 3,b. Since the size of the encoding map will be increased we could conceivably cope with this problem. Secondly, the outputs of a multiplexer-based circuit can be connected to the inputs of primary RAM in a different manner. This problem can be also solved in several ways. On the one hand we can build a RAM-based demultiplexer. On the other hand we can use pre-fixed connections by providing full set of multiplexers for the circuit that replaces variables. It is also possible to avoid flexible connections by setting up trivial constraints [3] for state encoding (for example, we can fix the number of bits with symbols i and their positions in all codes).

Thus the scheme of the FSM becomes fully dynamically reconfigurable, i.e. the functionality of the FSM can be changed after it has been implemented in hardware, even during run-time, by reloading the RAM blocks. Of course, each particular template has some constraints. However there are parameters for the template that can be altered. Thus the constraints can be changed by parameterization for the desired range of applications, much the same as changes of input/output numbers for RAM and ROM. Finally a library of templates can be created for FSMs having different characteristics, such as the values of L, N, M, $\max(k_m | m=0,...,M-1)$, etc.

6 Experimental Results

The proposed technique has been analyzed in several contexts. Firstly, we examined FSMs that are used in a variety of practical systems. This enabled us to estimate some parameters, such as the expectable range of G, the potential for behavioral specifications to be decomposed into smaller parts, and so on. Secondly, we compared the results of synthesis of the RAM-based FSM proposed in this paper, with the results obtained using known methods based on both binary and one-hot state encoding techniques.

All the experiments were performed with XS40 boards (XStend V1.2) of XESS that contain the Xilinx XC4010XL FPGA and the Xilinx Development System (series 1.5). Combinational circuits for FSMs were constructed from FPGA CLBs configured as RAM and ROM. For dynamic modifications we used dual port RAM library components, such as RAM 16X4D. Thus the first port took part in the FSM state transitions whilst the second port was used to reprogram RAM from the PC via the parallel port. Run-time modifiability is supported by software developed in Visual C++. Finally, FSMs with dynamically alterable behavior were implemented on statically configured FPGAs, such as the XC4010XL.

The reports of the experiments are summarized in table 2. The columns "Binary" and "One-hot" show the results obtained using the Xilinx Foundation Software. The average value of G from more than 50 practical FSMs is 2.7. Most of the FSMs were decomposed into relatively autonomous modules to which we applied the proposed technique. In fact this granulation is quite natural, and arises from the modular nature of the specifications of the various operations controlled by the FSM [4]. We found that even in the case of partially hardwired circuits the majority of modifications that were needed in practice could be provided without redesigning the circuits. Note that in spite of the extended facilities, for all the examples the number of CLBs needed for the FSM circuits (see table 2) was less than that for the other methods of synthesis.

For each column "binary" and "one-hot" we synthesized the respective circuits using both available criteria (such as "optimized for area" and "optimized for speed") and chose the best result. For some examples we could not obtain the final scheme using Xilinx synthesizers because the results of placement were negative. On the other hand in case of the proposed technique we were able to construct final circuits for all the examples.

7 Conclusion

We have described an approach to the design of RAM-based FSMs. It combines the state assignment technique proposed in the paper that allows the code for the states to be *fuzzy*, with the replacement (encoding) of input vectors. As a result, the structure of the FSM becomes well suited to implementation in commercially available FPGAs and the FSM acquires capabilities for dynamic modification. The latter can be achieved even when statically configured FPGAs such as the Xilinx XC4000XL are used.

Table 2. The results of experiments

Name of example	Parameters of FSM (L/N/M/R/G)	Number of CLBs for FPGA XC4010XL		
		RAM-based FSM	Binary	One-hot
Proc.	15/10/47/6/3	60	96	166
Plot.	11/25/24/5/2	41	42	53
Telea v.	14/17/33/6/4	68	86	137
Tech C	22/18/55/6/3	82	114	172
Conv	6/5/23/5/2	24	33	32
Vend.	7/4/18/5/2	22	30	28
Traf L.	3/7/11/4/2	9	15	12
LProc.	19/8/36/6/4	33	50	38
Abstr 1.	8/0/10/4/2	8	14	10
Abstr 2.	8/9/10/4/2	11	22	15

References

1. Giovanni De Micheli: Synthesis and Optimization of Digital Circuits: McGraw-Hill, Inc., (1994)
2. Baranov, S.: Logic Synthesis for Control Automata. Kluwer Academic Publishers, (1994)
3. Sklyarov, V.: Synthesis of FSMs based on matrix LSI. Science and Technique, Minsk (1984)
4. Sklyarov, V.: Hierarchical Finite State Machines and Their Use for Digital Control. IEEE Transactions on VLSI Systems. Vol. 7, No 2 (1999) 222-228

Evaluation of Accelerator Designs for Subgraph Isomorphism Problem

Shuichi Ichikawa[1], Hidemitsu Saito[1,2], Lerdtanaseangtham Udorn[1,3], and Kouji Konishi[1,4]

[1] Department of Knowledge-based Information Engineering,
Toyohashi University of Technology, Toyohashi 441-8580, Japan
ichikawa@tutkie.tut.ac.jp
[2] Presently with Toshiba Corp.
[3] Presently with Toyota Caelum Inc.
[4] Presently with NTT Software Corp.

Abstract. Many applications can be modeled as subgraph isomorphism problems. However, this problem is generally NP-complete and difficult to compute. A custom computing circuit is a prospective solution for such problems. This paper examines various accelerator designs, and compares them quantitatively from two points of view: cost and performance. An algorithm that is suited for hardware implementation is also proposed. The hardware for the proposed algorithm is much smaller on logic scale, and operates at a higher frequency than Ullmann's design. The prototype accelerator operates at 16.5 MHz on a Lucent ORCA 2C15A, which outperforms the software implementation of Ullmann's algorithm on a 400 MHz Pentium II.

1 Introduction

Many applications, including scene analysis and chemical structural formula databases, are modeled as subgraph isomorphism problems. However, a subgraph isomorphism problem is generally NP-complete [1] and difficult to compute in practical time. There is a strong desire among application developers to shorten the processing time of subgraph isomorphism detection.

Many such hard computation problems are heavily computation intensive. The amount of data is small and communication time is negligible in comparison to computation time. All these properties would seem preferable for acceleration of the process by custom computing machinery.

In this paper, various aspects of hardware accelerators for subgraph isomorphism problems are discussed. Design alternatives are examined mainly from two points of view: cost and performance. A prototype accelerator that is implemented on FPGA is then described.

2 Related Work

There are few studies on custom hardware for graph isomorphism problems, including the subgraph isomorphism problem.

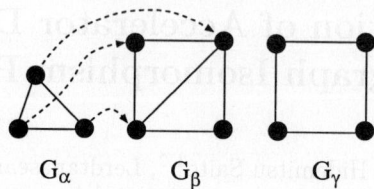

Fig. 1. Subgraph Isomorphism

Ullmann [2] introduced an algorithm for subgraph isomorphism that has been very popular in recent years. Ullmann showed that the *refinement procedure* of his algorithm can be implemented by parallel hardware for faster execution, but neither a detailed discussion nor real implementation was included.

The graph isomorphism problem can be formulated as a constraint satisfaction problem (CSP). Swain and Cooper [3] presented a parallel hardware design for CSP with arc consistency. They mentioned graph matching as a possible application for their circuitry, although their design is not optimized for graph isomorphism. In addition, no real implementation was described in their work.

There are some more studies on custom computing engines for CSP. However, some have been neither implemented nor evaluated [4] [5]. The DRA chip by Gu [6] is a VLSI implementation of a discrete relaxation algorithm (DRA), which is implemented with a 3μ NMOS process. DRA is a general computational technique and is applicable to subgraph homeomorphism problems. However, no more detailed discussion or evaluation of graph problems is found in Gu's work.

In this paper, various implementations of Ullmann's algorithm are examined in detail. Then, a new algorithm is proposed that requires much less in the way of hardware resources. This new algorithm is implemented using a Lucent OR2C FPGA.

3 Subgraph Isomorphism Problem

First, let us define the problem. A graph G is defined by (V, E), in which V is the set of vertices and E is the set of edges. $G_\alpha = (V_\alpha, E_\alpha)$ is the *subgraph* of $G_\beta = (V_\beta, E_\beta)$, if both $V_\alpha \subseteq V_\beta$ and $E_\alpha \subseteq E_\beta$ hold. G_α is *isomorphic* to G_β, if and only if there is 1:1 correspondence between V_α and V_β that preserves adjacency.

A subgraph isomorphism problem is a decision problem to determine whether G_α is isomorphic to a subgraph of G_β. For example, see Figure 1. G_α is isomorphic to a subgraph of G_β. On the other hand, G_γ has no subgraph that is isomorphic to G_α.

3.1 Enumeration Algorithm

As is easily seen, subgraph isomorphism can be determined by brute-force enumeration with a depth-first tree-search algorithm. Figure 2 shows an example

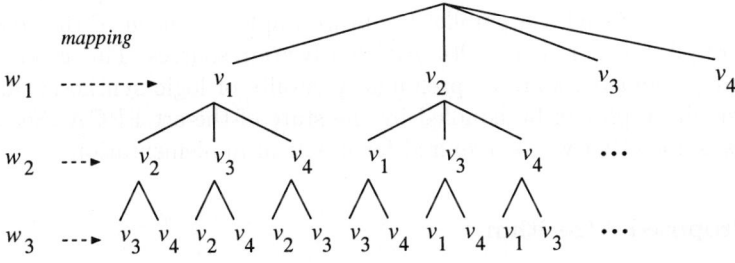

Fig. 2. Search Tree

of a search tree. Assume that $V_\alpha = \{w_1, w_2, w_3\}$ and $V_\beta = \{v_1, v_2, v_3, v_4\}$. At the i-th stage of the search tree, w_i is mapped to a possible vertex in V_β. At each leaf, the adjacency condition is checked by examining the correspondence of the edges from E_α to E_β. Subgraph isomorphism is found when all adjacency is preserved at a leaf.

3.2 Ullmann's Algorithm

The naive tree-search algorithm described in the previous section requires an impractical execution time due to the vast search space. The number of leaves is $_{p_\beta}P_{p_\alpha}$, where $p_\alpha = |V_\alpha|$ and $p_\beta = |V_\beta|$. This grows quickly as p_α and p_β grow. Thus, some procedure is required to prune unnecessary sub-trees to shorten the execution time.

The most popular algorithm is the one proposed by Ullmann, which is a smart tree-search algorithm with a *refinement procedure* for pruning [2]. For G_α to be isomorphic to a subgraph of G_β, adjacent vertices in G_α must be mapped to adjacent vertices in G_β. If this condition is not satisfied, there is no chance of finding subgraph isomorphism. The central idea of the refinement procedure is to check this requirement recursively.

In Ullmann's algorithm, the refinement procedure is invoked at every node (including internal nodes). This involves some overhead in each internal node, but the performance gain is drastic because the expansion of the search tree is repressed effectively. Ullmann formulated the refinement procedure as follows. Let $A = [a_{ij}](1 \leq i, j \leq p_\alpha)$ and $B = [b_{ij}](1 \leq i, j \leq p_\beta)$ be the adjacency matrices of G_α and G_β, respectively. Matrix $M = [m_{ij}](1 \leq i \leq p_\alpha, 1 \leq j \leq p_\beta)$ is defined as follows: If the mapping from $v_{\alpha i} \in V_\alpha$ to $v_{\beta j} \in V_\beta$ is possible, $m_{ij} = 1$. Otherwise, $m_{ij} = 0$. Then, the following procedure is applied until no element of M is updated. The $r_{xj}(1 \leq x \leq p_\alpha, 1 \leq j \leq p_\beta)$ are temporal variables.

$$r_{xj} = (\exists y)(m_{xy} \cdot b_{yj}) \tag{1}$$

$$m_{ij} = m_{ij} \cdot (\forall x)(\bar{a}_{ix} \vee r_{xj}) \tag{2}$$

For more details of the refinement procedure, see Ullmann's paper [2].

Ullmann discussed the parallel hardware implementation of the refinement procedure [2], but it requires $O(p_\alpha p_\beta^2)$ hardware resources. This grows rapidly for larger p_α and p_β, and our preliminary results of logic synthesis show that only a small graph can be handled by the state-of-the-art FPGA (See Section 5). Thus, some other way is required for practical implementation.

3.3 Proposed Algorithm

A problem of the refinement procedure is that it checks not only mapped vertices but also not-yet-mapped vertices. This involves huge resources. In this study, we examine a simplified pruning procedure that only handles mapped vertices. See Figure 1 again. At the i-th level of the search tree, only vertices $w_1, ..., w_i (1 \leq i \leq p_\alpha)$ are mapped. Here, we only check the adjacency of these i vertices at the i-th level. For G_α to be isomorphic to a subgraph of G_β, it is necessary that any subgraph of G_α is isomorphic to a subgraph of G_β. Our simplified pruning procedure checks this necessary condition. A complete description of this algorithm is found in another paper [8].

The adjacency check of this algorithm is simply realized by referring to the adjacency matrix of G_β, instead of an expensive refinement procedure. Thus, this method reduces hardware resources to $O(p_\beta^2)$, which is small enough to fit into state-of-the-art hardware for acceleration of subgraph isomorphism. On the other hand, the search space reduction with this algorithm is modest, because the ability to prune is inferior to that of Ullmann's refinement procedure. This can make execution time longer. The overall balance is dependent on the mixture of various implementation factors.

In the next section, some design alternatives are presented and examined in detail.

4 Implementation Issues

Ullmann's idea [2] is to calculate $M = [m_{ij}]$ $(1 \leq i \leq p_\alpha, 1 \leq j \leq p_\beta)$ in parallel, as described in Section 3.2. The element circuit to calculate m_{ij} is shown in Figure 3. Let us call this element *sub_comb*. The whole circuit is implemented by the $p_\alpha \times p_\beta$ matrix of sub_comb. Note that the $r_{kj}(1 \leq k \leq p_\alpha)$ of Figure 3 can be shared among $m_{ij}(1 \leq i \leq p_\alpha)$. Therefore, the required hardware resource would be $O(p_\alpha p_\beta^2)$. This combinatorial implementation is referred to as *comb* in the following discussion.

Combinatorial implementation is too costly. It is possible to reduce the amount of hardware needed by designing a sequential circuit, in exchange for increased processing time. The following are three trivial ways to reduce the number of sub_combs.

sub_i Modify M row by row, using p_β units of sub_comb.
sub_j Modify M column by column, using p_α units of sub_comb.
sub_i_j Modify M element by element, using a single unit of sub_comb.

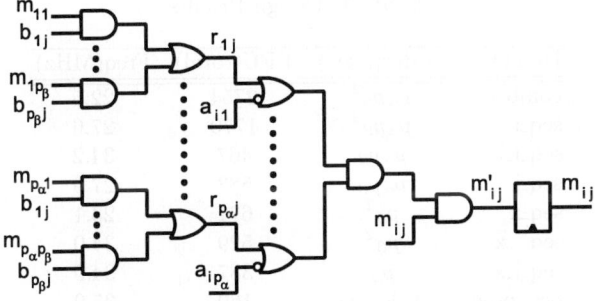

Fig. 3. Combinatorial Circuit for m_{ij}

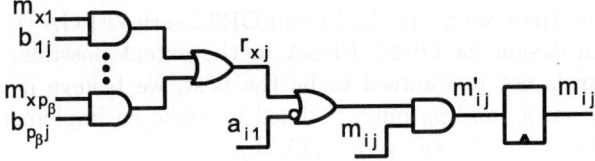

Fig. 4. Sequential Circuit for m_{ij}

Another possible design is to make sub_comb sequential. The p_α-input AND of sub_comb can be implemented sequentially. This idea is illustrated in Figure 4. Let us name this circuit *sub_comb_x*. The followings are sequential implementations which use sub_comb_x.

sub_x Modify all m_{ij} in parallel, using $p_\alpha p_\beta$ units of sub_comb_x.
sub_i_x Modify M row by row, using p_β units of sub_comb_x.
sub_j_x Modify M column by column, using p_α unit of sub_comb_x.

There are pros and cons of sequential circuits. Additional costs can emerge from an input multiplexer and sequence controller in a sequential circuit. Memory cost sometimes decreases because the number of read/write ports can be smaller in a sequential implementation than in a combinatorial implementation.

5 Evaluation

This section presents the various aspects of design, which include Ullmann's original circuit (*comb*), the proposed circuit (*proposed*), and sequential circuits described in the previous section. We do not have enough space to describe each design in detail, so we limit ourselves to the summary shown in Table 1. Please note that the logic scale shown in Table 1 only counts logic gates. In addition to them, $O(p_\beta^2)$ memory cells are required in each design for adjacency matrices.

The order of resources is important, because it limits the scalability. However, the real resource count for a certain technology is also important in understanding the constant factor. Even the designs that require the same order of resources can show big differences in real resource count.

Table 1. Design Results

Design	Order(logic)	PFU(total)	Freq(MHz)
comb	$p_\alpha p_\beta^2$	2754	22.5
seq_i	$p_\alpha p_\beta^2$	1770	27.6
seq_i_j	$p_\alpha p_\beta$	467	34.2
seq_j	$p_\alpha p_\beta$	583	27.9
seq_x	p_β^2	671	23.1
seq_i_x	p_β^2	529	34.0
seq_j_x	p_β	387	34.0
proposed	$p_\alpha \log p_\beta$	160	35.9

To investigate the constant factor, we have to assume some technology or implementation. Here, we adopt the Lucent OR2C series FPGA [7] as a measure. We tuned each design for OR2C FPGA to the extent possible. Though each implementation is not guaranteed to be the best, we believe it is not too far away. In addition, p_α and p_β must be fixed to make an implementation. Here, we designed the circuit for $(p_\alpha, p_\beta) = (15, 15)$.

The logic of each design is described in VHDL, embedding native OR2C macro library. VHDL description is then processed by Synopsys FPGA Compiler to derive a netlist. The logic synthesis system provides very sophisticated features that we could have utilized. However, we did not use most of its features to exclude the influences from logic synthesis tool. There are still many tips and tricks in logic synthesis, which can affect much to the results. The characteristics of each design becomes clearer by evaluating gate-level designs.

The derived netlist is mapped onto OR2C technology to extract the logic scale and gate delay. The PFU count is summarized in Table 1. PFU (programmable function unit) is a basic logic component of OR2C FPGA [7]. The PFU count in the table includes both logic gates and memory cells. The operating frequency in Table 1 is based on an estimated gate delay. Thus, the routing delay is not counted here.

As seen in Table 1, PFU count varies much according to design, even if the order of resources is the same. As the largest chip of OR2C FPGA is OR2C40A, which contains 900 PFU, comb and seq_i do not fit in a single OR2C FPGA chip. PFU count is strongly related to cost, so we use PFU count as a measure of implementation cost in the following discussion.

Another point is performance. Operating frequency alone is insufficient as a performance measure. Even for the same set of input graphs, each design requires a different number of cycles, because the sequence and configuration are different in each design. Therefore, we have to count the number of cycles using hardware simulators, in addition to estimating the operating frequency.

We have to pay close attention to the nature of input data (graphs), because cycle count is strongly data-dependent. Here, we examine four sets of edge density [1] $(ed_\alpha, ed_\beta) = (0.2, 0.2)$, $(0.2, 0.4)$, $(0.4, 0.2)$, and $(0.4, 0.4)$. The average of

---

[1] Let us consider a graph with p vertices and q edges. The edge density ed is defined by the following equation: $ed = 2q/p(p-1)$. That is, ed is the ratio of the number

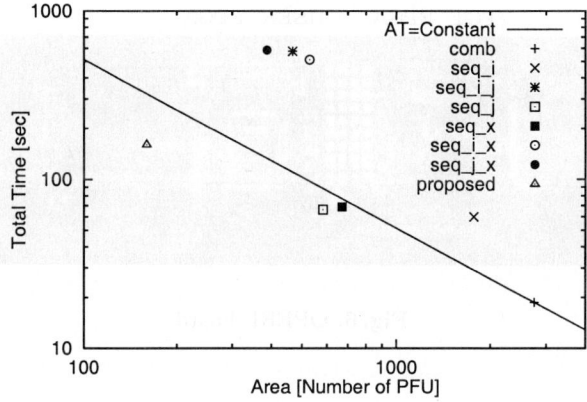

Fig. 5. Area vs. Time

100 trials on randomly generated connected graphs are measured for each set of (ed_α, ed_β).

The execution time can be estimated with operating frequency and cycle counts. Figure 5 summarizes the relationship between the area and the time of each design. The slanting line in the figure is the $AT = constant$ line that corresponds to Ullmann's original design. Cost is regarded to be almost proportional to PFU count (area), and performance is defined by the reciprocal of the execution time. Therefore, the AT product is regarded as a measure of the ratio of cost to performance. Figure 5 shows that *seq_j*, *seq_x*, and *proposed* designs turn out to be cost-effective solutions to the subgraph isomorphism problem.

It seems a little odd that the proposed algorithm is very cost-effective. The first reason is that it is very small and fits well to OR2C FPGA. This makes the AT product better. Conversely, its ineffectiveness in pruning can make the AT product worse. In fact, a worse AT product is seen in the cases of $(p_\alpha, p_\beta) = (0.2, 0.2)$, $(0.4, 0.2)$, and $(0.4, 0.4)$. However, the proposed algorithm works very well in the case of $(p_\alpha, p_\beta) = (0.2, 0.4)$, where the average execution time is far bigger than that of other three cases. The result in Figure 5 is the sum of all four cases, so the case $(0.2, 0.4)$ dominates.

Why does the proposed algorithm do well when the average execution time is large? Notice that subgraph isomorphism would be very likely if $ed_\alpha < ed_\beta$ holds. In such cases, pruning does not work well even with a refinement procedure, because there are numerous isomorphisms in many subtrees. If the execution time does not differ as much, the proposed algorithm can be more cost-effective, because it is smaller than Ullmann's circuitry.

The lesson is that we have to choose a suitable design, considering the nature of the application and input graphs. In some cases, the proposed algorithm would

---

of edges to that of the perfect graph K_p. It is obvious that the following relationship holds: $0 \leq ed \leq 1$.

Fig. 6. OPERL board

be very effective. In more general cases, seq_j would be reasonable. Seq_x also seems good, but the logic scale of seq_x would be $O(p_\beta{}^2)$ instead of the $O(p_\alpha p_\beta)$ of seq_j. As $p_\alpha \leq p_\beta$ holds generally and $p_\alpha \ll p_\beta$ holds in some applications, seq_j would scale better than seq_x for bigger graphs.

6 Prototype Hardware

In this section, the FPGA implementation of the proposed algorithm is outlined. We chose this design mainly because it is the smallest and simplest. The details of this prototype are described in other papers [8] [9].

The prototype was implemented on an OPERL board [10], which is a run-time reconfigurable PCI card with two Lucent OR2C FPGAs [7] (see Figure 6). USER FPGA (OR2C15A) contains an application circuit that is programmed and accessed from the host computer via PCI bus. Another is PCI FPGA (OR2C15A), which contains PCI interface circuitry and a run-time reconfiguration controller for USER FPGA. The host computer is a personal computer with AMD K6-III (400 MHz) and FreeBSD 2.2.8R. USER FPGA can be programmed in less than 5 ms. The application program can transfer data using system call (read/write/mmap) or I/O instructions.

The key to utilizing SRAM-based FPGA is the extensive use of mapping RAM in logic. Subgraph isomorphism problems naturally fit this scheme, as it is implemented by a tree-search with adjacency matrices. We implemented a unit that can handle up to $(p_\alpha, p_\beta) = (15, 15)$, which fits well to the basic component of OR2C FPGA (16 × 4 bit SRAM). This unit operates at 16.5 MHz, which is half of the PCI clock. The unit could have been pipelined for 33 MHz operation to derive twice the performance, but we chose to make things simple for this prototype.

Even this simple prototype outperforms an off-the-shelf microprocessor. An OR2C15A chip that contains two units of our proposed algorithm shows about 20 times better performance than the software implementation of Ullmann's algorithm on a 400 MHz Pentium II processor. For the performance details of this prototype, see another paper [8].

The performance can be boosted easily by (1) pipelining hardware, (2) implementing several units that work in parallel, and (3) using a larger FPGA chip. For example, the largest chip of OR2C FPGA (OR2C40A) contains 900 PFUs. Using OR2C40A, four independent units of the proposed algorithm can be implemented on one chip. In this case, the performance gain would scale up four times of a single unit.

7 Conclusion

Though the prototype hardware can handle only small graphs, it is easy to implement an accelerator for larger graphs. For example, seq_j requires only an $O(p_\alpha p_\beta)$ logic gates. This is not so much for a VLSI implementation. The real problem is the explosion of execution time. Remember that this problem is NP-complete. Pruning alleviates the problem, but never solves it.

The key is to design an application specific circuit. In this paper, we treated algorithms and designs for general subgraph isomorphism problems. However, as mentioned at the end of Section 5, the algorithm and architecture should be customized for the application in order to maximize performance, considering the nature of the data.

Take, for example, the case of a chemical structural database. In such an application, the data structure is not a general graph. Each vertex has attributes to represent its class: H, C, benzene ring, etc. The edges can also have attributes: single bond, double bond, etc. Such attributes help to make execution time shorter, if such information is used for pruning.

It is not always cost-effective to design such special circuitry, but the evolution of FPGA and logic synthesis will make it feasible in the near future.

Acknowledgment

This work was partially supported by the Hori Information Science Promotion Foundation and the Ministry of Education, Science, Sports and Culture of Japan.

References

1. M. R. Garey and D. S. Johnson. *Computers and Intractability.* Freeman, 1979.
2. J. R. Ullmann. An algorithm for subgraph isomorphism. *J. ACM*, Vol. 23, No. 1, pp. 31–42, 1976.
3. M. J. Swain and P. R. Cooper. Parallel hardware for constraint satisfaction. In *Seventh National Conference on Artificial Intelligence (AAAI '88)*, pp. 2:682–686. Morgan Kaufmann, 1988.
4. C. Cherry and P. K. T. Vaswani. A new type of computer for problems in propositional logic, with greatly reduced scanning procedures. *Information and Control*, Vol. 4, pp. 155–168, 1961.
5. J. R. Ullmann, R. M. Haralick, and L. G. Shapiro. Computer architecture for solving consistent labelling problems. *Computer Journal*, Vol. 28, No. 2, pp. 105–111, May 1985.

6. J. Gu, W. Wang, and T. C. Henderson. A parallel architecture for discrete relaxation algorithm. *IEEE Trans. Pattern Analysis and Machine Intelligence*, Vol. PAMI-9, No. 6, pp. 816–831, Nov. 1987.
7. Lucent Technologies Inc. *ORCA OR2CxxA (5.0 V) and OR2TxxA (3.3 V) Series FPGAs Data Sheet*, 1996.
8. S. Ichikawa, L. Udorn, and K. Konishi. An FPGA-based implementation of subgraph isomorphism algorithm. *IPSJ Transactions on High Performance Computing Systems*, 2000 (to appear, in Japanese).
9. S. Ichikawa, L. Udorn, and K. Konishi. Hardware accelerator for subgraph isomorphism problems. In *Proc. IEEE Symp. FPGAs for Custom Computing Machines (FCCM '00)*. IEEE Computer Society, 2000 (to appear as extended abstract).
10. S. Ichikawa and T. Shimada. Reconfigurable PCI card for personal computing. In *Proceedings of the 5th FPGA/PLD Design Conference & Exhibit*, pp. 269–277, Tokyo, 1997. Chugai (in Japanese).

The Implementation of Synchronous Dataflow Graphs Using Reconfigurable Hardware

Martyn Edwards and Peter Green

Department of Computation, UMIST, PO Box 88, Manchester M60 1QD, United Kingdom
{M.Edwards, P.Green}@co.umist.ac.uk

Abstract. The paper explores a number of possible hardware architectures for implementing synchronous dataflow (SDF) models of digital signal processing (DSP) applications in reconfigurable logic components, for example, Field Programmable Gate Arrays (FPGAs). The objective is to produce efficient hardware implementations of SDF graphs by exploiting the parallelism inherent in most graphs whilst taking advantage of the reconfigurable aspects of the target architecture. Classic area/performance tradeoffs can be made in order to meet the requirements of DSP applications.

1 Introduction

The SDF model of computation was developed to handle regular computations that operate on "infinite" streams of data [1, 2]. In an SDF model, an application is represented by a directed graph, where the vertices of the graph, known as *actors*, symbolise data computations and the edges depict data communications between actors. The general dataflow model [3] defines the behaviour of an application as a sequence of actor firings and SDF is a special case with the useful property that deadlock and boundedness are decidable. Furthermore, the schedule of actor *firings* is computable statically, making SDF an extremely useful specification formalism for multirate DSP applications [4], which incorporate real-time software and hardware. SDF models are popular in the domains of speech, image, and video processing, consumer products, personal mobile telephony, and data compression/encryption.

A significant amount of research has been undertaken in the development of algorithms for translating SDF models into efficient software implementations for DSP processors, which contain a limited amount of on-chip memory. The bulk of the work has concentrated on minimising the amount of memory required for the program code and the data communications buffers for specific DSP processor targets [1, 2, 5, 6]. Whereas there is a large body of work concerned with the rapid prototyping (emulation and implementation) of SDF applications on heterogeneous target platforms consisting of DSP processors and FPGAs, for example, Ptolemy II [7], GRAPE-II [8] and COSSAP [9], there are surprisingly few concrete details available concerning the synthesis of optimised hardware implementations.

A major reason for choosing a hardware-based implementation for all, or part, of an SDF model is the ability to vary the numbers and types of execution units used to implement the actors. Solutions can vary between those which maximise parallelism (performance) by having multiple or separate execution units for each actor to those which minimise area by having a single execution unit shared by all the actors [10, 11]. These area/performance tradeoffs are especially important for FPGA implementations due to their restricted hardware resources in terms of the available reconfigurable logic elements, signal routing resources, and numbers of registers available for data buffering. Some researchers have investigated "efficient" FPGA implementations of SDF models in the past [12, 13, 14], but they do not appear to have taken full account of the extra degree of freedom which arises if an FPGA can be reconfigured at system run-time. This paper explores a number of possible hardware architectures for implementing SDF models in reconfigurable logic components. The objective of the work is to produce efficient hardware implementations of SDF graphs by exploiting the parallelism inherent in most graphs whilst taking advantage of the reconfigurable aspects of the target architecture. Such an approach allows classic area/performance tradeoffs in order to meet the requirements of an application.

The next section reviews the basic concepts of synchronous dataflow and identifies some of the techniques employed for the synthesis of software implementations of SDF models. Section 3 presents a number of alternative architectural styles for reconfigurable FPGA-based hardware implementations of such models. Finally, we present our conclusions and plans for future work.

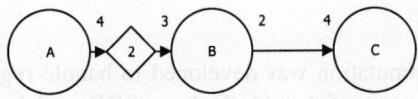

Fig. 1. Synchronous Dataflow Graph

2 Synchronous Dataflow Systems

A synchronous dataflow system is represented by a directed graph, whose vertices (*actors*) represent computations of arbitrary complexity, and whose edges specify data buffers. Fig. 1 illustrates an SDF graph containing three actors (A, B, and C) and two edges connecting the actors. Each actor produces (consumes) a fixed number of data values (known as *tokens*) onto (from) each output (input) edge each time it is executed (*fired*). For example, actor B consumes 3 tokens and produces 2 tokens. The inputs to actor A (the *source* actor) and the outputs from actor C (the *sink* actor) are normally not shown. The number of tokens needed for an actor to fire, together with the number of tokens it produces, is fixed at the design time of an application, and the granularity of a token is arbitrary, for example, it could be a single bit or a bit vector. A further parameter on each edge specifies the number of initial tokens (known as *delays*) residing on that edge. For example, the edge between actor A and actor B contains two initial tokens – the default condition is that an edge does not contain any initial tokens.

Tokens are buffered at the input of an actor until a *threshold* is reached, the actor is then *fired*. For example, actor C can only fire when at least four tokens are present at its inputs. In the corresponding abstract model of computation, the output tokens are produced when an actor fires with zero delay. In reality, however, an actor produces its output tokens after a determinate, fixed delay which is dependent on the complexity of its computation. Each actor can operate concurrently provided the requisite number of tokens are present at each of their inputs and the required computational resources are available. An actor operates on signals which contain an infinite stream of values, for example, the data from a CDROM player. Furthermore, actors must consume the tokens on their inputs in the same order as they were generated by the corresponding producer actors, that is, on a first-in-first-out (FIFO) basis.

2.1 SDF Graph Scheduling

A *schedule* is a sequence of actor firings which is bounded and static for a specific SDF graph G. A *valid schedule* S is one that fires each actor at least once, does not produce deadlock[1] in the graph, and does not produce a net change in the number of tokens on each edge of the graph [2]. A valid schedule is repeated ad infinitum to produce a continuous sequence of actor firings and specifies the minimum number of firings q_G of each actor G during each iteration of the schedule.

For the SDF graph of Fig. 1, a *periodic schedule* is produced if $q_A = 3$, $q_B = 4$, and $q_C = 2$. A valid schedule indicates an ordering of the actor firings in each iteration, for example, $S_1 = $ (A A A B B B B C C). Other valid schedules may be generated [5], for example, $S_2 = $ (A A A B B C B B C) and $S_3 = $ (A B B C A B A B C). The chosen schedule will affect the characteristics of software and hardware implementations, for example, the sizes of the token buffers required at the inputs of each actor.

2.2 Buffer Memory Requirements for an SDF Graph

Given an SDF graph $G = (V, E)$, a valid schedule S, and an edge e in G, then *MaxTokens(e, S)* denotes the maximum number of tokens that are queued on e during the execution of S. In hardware and software implementations of graphs it is advisable to minimise the number of tokens that need to be buffered. For DSP processors with limited on-chip memory, and FPGAs with restricted numbers of flip-flops, determining the optimum sizes of the token buffers is an application critical problem. The buffer memory requirement[2] for a schedule S is given by [5]

$$\text{BufferMemory}(S) = \sum_{e \in E} \text{MaxTokens}(e, S) \quad (1)$$

The maximum size buffer for an edge e in a graph G is determined by [5]

$$\text{MaxBufferSize}(e) = n_{source} \times q_{source} + \text{InitialTokens} \quad (2)$$

---

[1] Deadlock occurs when all actors have an insufficient number of input tokens to fire.
[2] It is assumed that each edge of an SDF graph has its own separate token buffer.

where n_{source} is the number of tokens produced by the firing of the source actor, q_{source} is the number of times the source actor is fired in one iteration of a valid schedule, and *InitialTokens* are the number of initial tokens on the graph edge. For the SDF graph of Fig. 1, MaxBufferSize(e_{AB}) = 14 and MaxBufferSize(e_{BC}) = 8, which corresponds to the buffer requirements of schedule S_1. For schedule S_3, however, MaxTokens(e_{AB}, S_3) = 6 and MaxTokens(e_{BC}, S_3) = 4. The size of the token buffer memory is related to the schedule, and techniques exist for computing the "smallest close-to-possible buffer memory size and guarantee a deadlock free schedule" [12].

2.3 Software Synthesis of SDF Graphs

For the software synthesis of an SDF model it is necessary to execute the code block corresponding to the functionality of each actor at the times specified by the schedule. The code blocks for each actor, which are normally obtained from a predefined library, are executed in-line and the resulting sequence of code blocks is enclosed in an infinite loop[3]. A *single appearance schedule (SAS)* is one where each actor's code block only needs to be executed once per loop iteration. This approach is usually adopted because the performance overhead associated with implementing in-line code blocks is small compared to that related to the management of sub-programs [6].

For the SDF graph given in Fig.1, the valid schedule S_2 contains nested loops and can be represented by a SAS: ((3A) (2 ((2B) C))). The parentheses in the schedule are used to denote repetitive patterns of actor invocations, for example, ((2B) C) = (B B C). Note that S_1 is also a SAS: ((3A) (4B) (2C)), but that S_3 is not. A SAS may not result in a minimum size token buffer memory, for example, schedules S_1 and S_2 require a larger memory than S_3.

The amount of code memory required for an SDF application is normally much greater than the size of the associated token buffer memory. Software synthesis techniques, therefore, tend to favour minimising code size. For our example, S_2 would be chosen because it is a SAS and needs a smaller token buffer memory than S_1. Joint code and buffer memory minimisation for a single processor is an NP-complete problem, but heuristics been developed which produce acceptable solutions [5, 6, 12].

3 Synthesis of SDF Graphs in Reconfigurable Hardware

Whereas similar techniques to those employed for software synthesis can be applied to hardware synthesis, the main advantage of implementing an SDF graph in hardware is that it is possible to have concurrent activations of the same and/or different actors. In order to achieve this it is necessary to derive the *dependency graph* [11] associated with a scheduled SDF graph. Fig. 2(a) repeats the example SDF graph and specifies the number of times each actor is fired in one iteration of a valid schedule(q_A, q_B, and q_C). Figure 2(b) shows the associated dependency graph.

---

[3] It is assumed that each code block is executed on a single DSP processor.

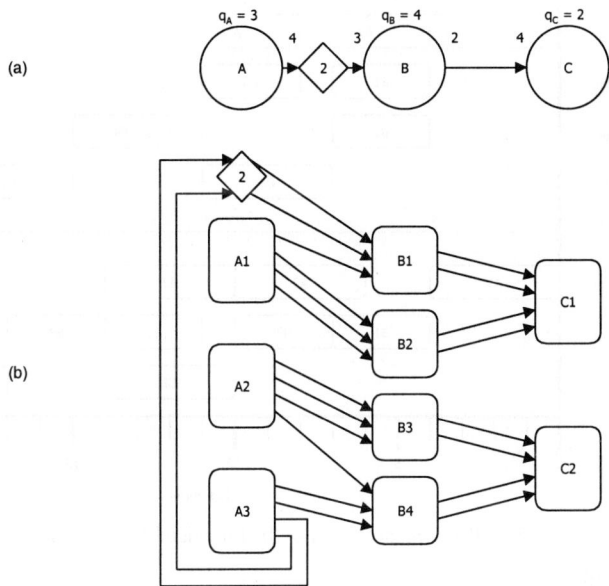

Fig. 2. (a) Synchronous Dataflow Graph (b) Dependency Graph

The dependency graph indicates that there are three firings of actor A (A1 to A3) four firings of actor B (B1 to B4) and two firings of actor C (C1 and C2). Firing A1 produces four tokens, which are consumed by the firings of B1 and B2 – the remaining actor firings produce and consume tokens in a similar manner. The initial tokens are consumed by the firing of B1 and are "refreshed" when A3 is fired in order to keep the number of tokens in balance before and after a single iteration of the schedule. The size (number of nodes) of a dependency graph is at least an exponential function of the size of the corresponding SDF graph [11]. In order to contain this problem for hardware synthesis, SDF graphs should be limited to ones with a small number of vertices, which implies that "coarse" grain actors are better than "fine" grain ones. For example, an actor implementing a FIR filter or image edge detection operation is preferred to one performing a simple ADD function.

The hardware implementation of an SDF graph implies the usual tradeoffs between area and performance. Firstly, we would favour the schedule S_3 as it results in a minimum size token buffer memory. Additionally, we will assume each actor has its own execution unit and that a firing of actors A and C takes 4 system clock cycles, and a firing of actor B takes 3 cycles. For our purposes, the number of clock cycles is related to the number of tokens produced/consumed by an actor. Note that the values of the input tokens for an actor firing are held constant for the duration of the firing.

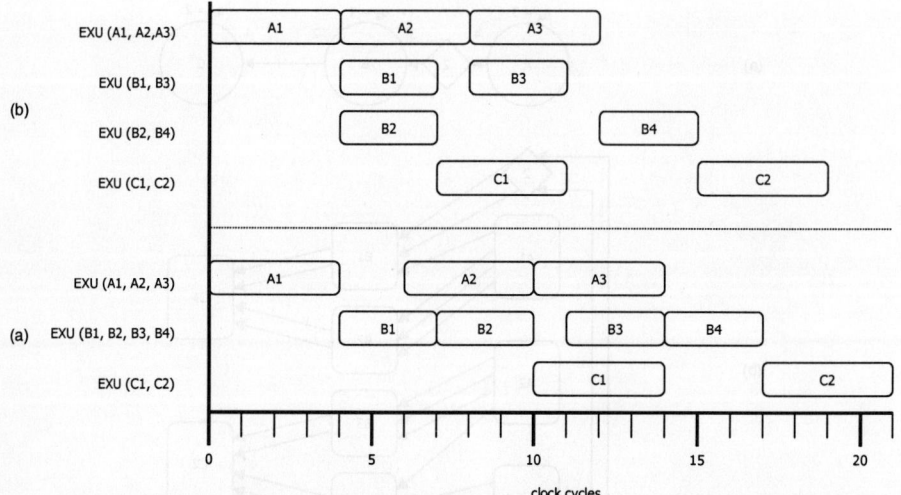

Fig. 3 (a) Schedule Performance Profile (b) Enhanced Performance Profile

Fig. 3 (a) indicates that the execution time for a single iteration of the schedule S_3 is 21 clock cycles – if all actors shared a single execution unit the same schedule would take 32 clock cycles. Further examination of this schedule indicates that a one clock cycle performance improvement can be achieved by having an additional execution unit which allows B1 and B2 to be executed in parallel as shown in Fig. 3 (b). In general, allocating additional execution units to actors should improve performance at the expense of increased hardware resources, albeit by a minimal amount in this case. Unfortunately, both of these implementations indicate that the execution units are idle for long periods during the schedule which leads to an inefficient use of hardware resources [1]. This problem may potentially be alleviated by reconfiguring an actor's execution unit to perform multiple functions, as discussed below.

3.1 Token Buffer Memory

The classic way to implement buffered communications where tokens are consumed in the order they are produced is to use a FIFO, and software implementations of SDF graphs on a single processor normally rely on the efficient implementation of memory-based queues. Hardware implementations of FIFOs, however, are notoriously inefficient, which is largely due to the high area and performance overheads in the associated controller and data path. Furthermore, due to the inherent parallelism in a hardware implementation with multiple execution units, it would be necessary to have multiple FIFOs corresponding to a single graph edge or concurrent read/write paths from a single FIFO, either of which would further increase the implementation overheads. For these reasons, the use of FIFOs was not considered further. An array of registers can, however, be used as an efficient token buffer on an FPGA. The inputs and outputs of an array can easily be routed in parallel to and from the appropriate

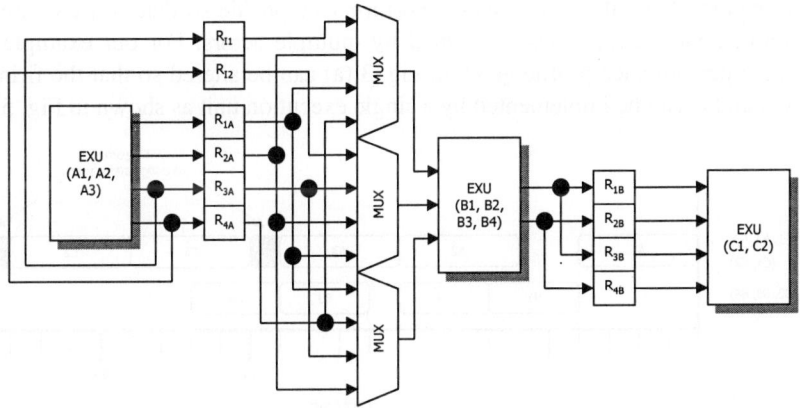

Fig. 4. SDF Graph Hardware Architecture

actor execution units. Care must be taken, however, when allocating tokens to registers in order to minimise the complexity of the interconnections between the actor execution units. These problems and their solutions are similar to those encountered during the "scheduling" and "allocation" operations in high-level synthesis [15].

Consider a hardware architecture developed for our example SDF graph, given in Fig. 4, which corresponds to the schedule performance profile given in Fig. 3 (a).

The architecture consists of three execution units and two token register arrays: array R_{IA} to R_{4A} corresponds to edge e_{AB} of the SDF graph; and array R_{IB} to R_{4B} corresponds to edge e_{BC}. The additional registers R_{II} and R_{I2} relate to the two initial tokens on the edge e_{AB} and are refreshed at the end of each iteration of the schedule – the two registers must be preset with the initial token values. The three 4-to-1 multiplexers on the inputs of the execution unit for actor B are responsible for routing the correctly ordered tokens produced by the 3 firings of actor A onto the 3 inputs of actor B's execution unit. In this case, multiplexers are not required on the inputs of the execution unit for actor C. In general, however, depending on the allocations of actor firings to execution units and tokens to the individual registers of the array it may be necessary to introduce multiplexers on the inputs and outputs of each execution unit.

For an Atmel AT40K series reconfigurable FPGA [16], a token register requires 1 logic cell/bit and a 4-to-1 multiplexer requires 3 cells/bit. The communications structure for our hardware architecture example, with 8 bits per token, is 152 cells. The cell count could be reduced if on-chip RAM was used for the token arrays. There are 29 datapath signals and 16 control signals required for loading the registers and controlling the multiplexers. The clock rate is estimated to be in excess of 40 MHz. The equivalent structure using two sequential access FIFOs is estimated at 215 logic cells.

3.2 Reconfigurable Logic Architecture

As previously indicated, the chosen schedule is not efficient in terms of the utilisation of hardware resources. By exploiting the potential of a partially reconfigurable FPGA

[16] it is possible to alter the schedule performance profile so that an execution unit may implement the functions performed by multiple actors. For our example SDF graph, the performance profile given in Fig. 3 (a) can be altered so that the firings of actors A and C can be implemented by a single execution unit as shown in Fig. 5.

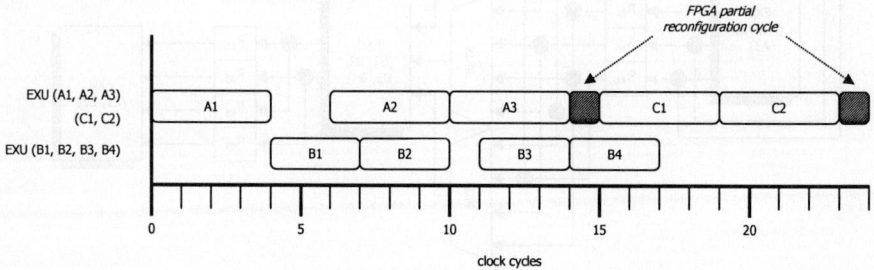

Fig. 5. Reconfigured Schedule Performance Profile

At clock cycle 15 the first execution unit is reconfigured to implement actor C and at clock cycle 24 it must be reconfigured again to implement actor A ready for the next iteration of the schedule. These reconfigurations have increased the latency of a single iteration of the schedule by three clock cycles, which has been offset by the increased utilisation of the remaining two execution units. The latency of the schedule could be reduced by a further clock cycle if the second execution unit is reconfigured to implement the firing C2 of actor C at clock cycle 18, thus allowing the firings of C1 and C2 to be overlapped. Whichever reconfiguration option is adopted, it would appear that a single system clock cycle is insufficient time to partially reconfigure an FPGA. However, it is envisaged that a typical application would have system clock rates of the order of tens of kHz, for example, speech processing, thus allowing sufficient time for the partial reconfiguration of the FPGA, using a high speed configuration clock, during a single system clock cycle. Multiple system clock cycles may, of course, be used for reconfiguration so long as the overall latency of an iteration of the valid schedule does not exceed that of a purely sequential sequence of actor firings on a single execution unit, otherwise, no performance improvement will accrue.

A snapshot of the hardware architecture corresponding to the reconfigured schedule performance profile at system clock cycle 16 is given in Fig. 6. The diagram indicates that architecture reconfiguration consists of disconnecting the inputs to the token register array corresponding to edge e_{AB} and feeding back the outputs of the register array corresponding to the edge e_{BC} to the inputs of the execution unit for actors A and C. Furthermore, because firing C1 has been delayed, the size of the token register array for edge e_{BC} must be increased from four to eight registers, and four 2-to-1 multiplexers employed to correctly route the tokens to the inputs of the execution unit for actor C. Delaying the firings of B4 by one cycle would, however, reduce the size of the token array by one register and remove two of the multiplexers.

It is evident that whilst area reductions can be achieved by reconfiguring an execution unit to perform multiple actor functions, the area required for actor communications may increase as a result of altering the timings of the actor firings in a schedule.

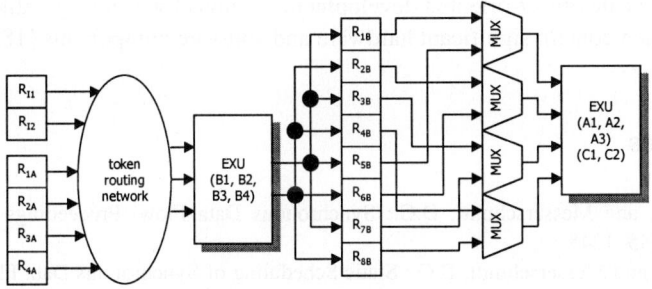

Fig. 6. Snapshot of Reconfigured Hardware Architecture

It is implicit that the implementation of an execution unit would include a controller which manages the loading of the token register array, and the switching of the multiplexers on its input and output communication paths for an actor firing. Whereas a separate controller could be dedicated to this task, it is likely that it would be integrated with the controller responsible for executing the functionality of the actor. Reconfiguring an execution unit implies changing the functionality of not only an actor's data path but also the associated controller.

Finally, the execution of an actor firing may either be scheduled by a global controller or determined locally within the associated execution unit. A global controller would instruct the execution unit to perform its actor's functions by asserting a *START* signal. When the execution unit has completed in a determinate number of system clock cycles and written the tokens to its register array(s), it can assert a *DONE* signal which indicates that the firing has terminated. Any run-time reconfiguration of execution units would also be managed by the global controller, which may be implemented in software on a single chip that integrates a microcontroller, FPGA configuration memory, and FPGA, for example, the Atmel FPSLIC [17].

4 Conclusions and Further Work

This paper has described our initial work on the implementation of SDF models in reconfigurable hardware. We have shown that when selecting a hardware architecture for the implementation of an SDF graph, a designer should aim to minimise the number of token buffer registers, use the minimum number of execution units consistent with the parallelism inherent in the chosen schedule, perform actor-to-execution-unit and token-to-buffer-register allocations so as to minimise the interconnection overhead between execution units and buffer registers, and reconfigure the operation of individual execution units to perform multiple actor functions in order to increase the utilisation of the FPGA hardware. Whereas the route to the implementation of an SDF model in an FPGA is reasonably clear, more work is required in order to understand the full implications of reconfiguring the FPGA at run-time. The next stage is to provide tool support for this methodology. This work forms part of a much larger project which is to create object-oriented development methods for reconfigurable computing systems which contain significant hardware and software components [18].

References

1. Lee, E.A. and Messerschmitt, D.G.: Synchronous Data Flow. Proceedings of the IEEE (1987) 1235–1245
2. Lee, E.A. and Messerschmitt, D.G.: Static Scheduling of Synchronous Data Flow Programs for Digital Signal Processing. IEEE Transactions on Computers (1987) 24–35
3. Lee, E.A. and Parks, T.M.: Dataflow Process Networks. Proceedings of the IEEE (1995) 773–801
4. Ifeachor, E.C. and Jarvis, B.W.: Digital Signal Processing: A Practical Approach. Addison-Wesley (1993)
5. Bhattacharyya, S.S., Murthy, P.K. and Lee, E.A.: Software Synthesis from Dataflow Graphs. Kluwer Academic Publishers (1996)
6. Teich, J., Zitzler, E. and Bhattacharyya, S.S.: 3D Exploration of Software Schedules for DSP Algorithms. In: Proceedings of the 7th. International Workshop on Hardware/Software Co-design, Rome, Italy (1999)
7. Davis, J., et al.: Overview of the Ptolemy Project. ERL Technical Report UCB/ERL No. M99/37, Department of Electrical Engineering and Computer Sciences, University of California at Berkeley (1999)
8. Lauwereins, R., Engels, M., Adé, M., and Peperstraete, J.A.: Grape-II: A System-Level Prototyping Environment for DSP Applications. IEEE Computer, February (1995)
9. Synopsys: COSSAP Design Environment. Synopsys Inc, Mountain View, USA (1999)
10. Lavenier, D. and McConnell, R.: A Component Model for Synchronous VLSI System Design. Internal Publication Number 822, IRISA, Rennes, France (1994)
11. Williamson, M.C.: Synthesis of Parallel Hardware Implementations from Synchronous Dataflow Graph Specifications. Ph.D. Thesis, Department of Electrical Engineering and Computer Sciences, University of California at Berkeley (1998)
12. Adé, M., Lauwereins, R. and Peperstraete, J.A.: Data Memory Minimisation for Synchronous data Flow Graphs Emulated on DSP-FPGA Targets. In: Proceedings of the Design Automation Conference, Anaheim, USA (1997)
13. Dalcolmo, J., Lauwereins, R. and Adé, M.: Code Generation of Data Dominated DSP Applications for FPGA Targets. In: Proceedings of the 9th. International Workshop on Rapid System Prototyping, Leuven, Belgium (1998)
14. Horstmannshoff, J., Grotker, T., and Meyr, H.: Mapping Multirate Dataflow to Complex RT Level Hardware Models. In: Proceedings of Application Specific Systems, Architectures and Processors, Zurich, Switzerland (1997)
15. Gajski, D.D., Dutt, N.D., Wu, A.C-H., and Lin, S.Y-L.: High-Level Synthesis: Introduction to Chip and System Design. Kluwer Academic Publishers (1992)
16. Atmel: AT40K FPGA Data Sheet. Atmel Corporation, San Jose, USA (1999)
17. Atmel: AT94K Series FPSLI Data Sheet. Atmel Corporation, San Jose, USA (1999)
18. Edwards, M., and Green, P.: An Object Oriented Design Method for Reconfigurable Computing Systems. In: Proceedings of DATE 2000, Paris, France (2000)

Multiplexer Based Reconfiguration for Virtex Multipliers

Tim Courtney, Richard Turner, and Roger Woods

School of Electrical and Electronic Engineering
The Queen's University of Belfast, Stranmillis Road, Belfast, N. Ireland
{t.courtney, r.h.turner, r.woods}@qub.ac.uk

Abstract. A novel approach, based on a radix-4 Booth encoding, is presented for constant coefficient multipliers. The major advantage of this approach is that it reduces the amount of reconfiguration time needed to switch between multipliers when compared to the Xilinx constant coefficient multiplier (KCM) core. The approach utilises an existing radix-4 Booth encoding system and gives reductions in the reconfiguration data required to switch multiplier coefficient by an average of 59% and a worst case of 34%. The proposed structure is 4 CLBs smaller and 4% faster than the KCM approach. The approach exploits the MUXes in the Virtex routing network to perform the reconfiguration of the radix-4 Booth encoded multiplier

1. Introduction

Programmable logic has been used to accelerate complex software by allowing the highly parallel parts of the algorithm to be implemented on an FPGA. This can result in considerable speed-ups. As well as uses in software acceleration, it has been suggested that FPGA technology can also be used in remote processing e.g. signal processing at mobile telecommunication base stations[1] where the processing capability needs to be fast and adaptable. This requires the availability of fast FPGAs whose function can be quickly changed as required.

Techniques such as the constant coefficient multiplier (KCM) can be used to accelerate the performance of a number of DSP filtering and transforms. Currently, the biggest problem with this approach is the time taken to reconfigure the hardware when a new coefficient i.e. multiplier, is required. This "downtime" represents the time that the processor is unavailable for processing data. If we look at systems such as the mobile telecommunications signal processing units, it is easy to see that long downtime will result in unacceptable performance.

Currently, we are looking at the effects of this downtime in the design of a totally adaptive filter[2]. One of the aims of this work is to develop constant coefficient multipliers with low reconfiguration times. The multiplier implementation proposed in the paper uses the 28 to 1 routing multiplexors (MUXes)[α] in the Virtex device. This allows greater flexibility in the implementation of adaptive algorithms as it is now

---

[α] In the Virtex architecture there are 28 to 1 routing MUXes placed immediately before each of the slice inputs. We change these MUXes as a method of reconfiguration.

possible to change the adaptation algorithm more frequently and so gain an improvement in system performance.

Previous work has examined the effect of the choice of the multiplier structure on the relationship between area and reconfiguration time[3]. This paper looks at how a 2-bit modified Booth algorithm[4] multiplier can be used to match the performance of a look up table based KCM produced by Xilinx[5] whilst reducing the reconfiguration time. The Xilinx design is a hybrid LUT-adder tree multiplier that exploits the fast carry logic and the 4-input LUT cell of the Virtex family. This design has been used as a benchmark for this reconfiguration method since it is a small and fast core and fully documented on the Xilinx web site[5].

2. Implementation of Modified Booth Encoding on an FPGA

The advantage of using this modified Booth encoding is well known and is illustrated in Table 1. For an n-bit word, up to n operations are required to perform the multiplication using Booths original algorithm[6]. Using the modified Booth encoding scheme, this is reduced to $n/2$ as either one addition, one subtraction or no operation is required for every 2 bits of the original data word. This means that only half the normal number of operations, and therefore half the logic, is required to perform the multiplication. This gain is easy to achieve in software as it involves manipulation of the data between subtraction and addition operations and power of 2 multiplication. However in a hardware implementation it is not possible to have a variable power of 2 offset without the use of a MUX, also only logic for fast addition is available in the Virtex architecture, these factors present three difficulties that must be overcome for this system to be implemented. Each of these are dealt with in the following three sub-sections.

Table 1. 2-bit modified Booth encoding system

Bits of Coefficient word K			Booth encoding of K		Modified Booth encoding of K	
K_n	K_{n-1}	K_{n-2}	K_n	K_{n-1}	K_n	K_{n-1}
0	0	0	0	0	0	0
0	0	1	0	+	0	+
0	1	0	+	−	0	+
0	1	1	+	0	+	0
1	0	0	−	0	−	0
1	0	1	−	+	0	−
1	1	0	0	−	0	−
1	1	1	0	0	0	0

2.1. The Double Subtract Problem

Both the bit-level functions, $A_i - B_j$ and $A_i + B_j$ can be implemented using 3 to 2 compressors. (How we attain the subtraction is dealt with in sections 2.2 below.) In a strictly Booth encoded multiplier these are the only bit-level operations required.

With a 2-bit modified Booth coding system it is necessary to be able to implement the function $-A_i - B_j$, which cannot be done using a simple 3 to 2 compressor and would appear to require additional hardware. In a Virtex device there is fast carry hardware available that can be used for the $A_i + B_j$ and $A_i - B_j$ blocks but for this to be used for the $-A_i - B_j$ block would require a change in the number system for this block. Since it must connect to subsequent adders in the multiplier tree this is not a sensible option. Thus a $-A_i - B_j$ block will use a larger chip area then the other 2. Given that both the $A_i + B_j$ and $A_i - B_j$ blocks will fit into the same area, this inability to perform a 'double subtract' would appear to be a major problem as it results in needing a larger floorplan to accommodate these $-A_i - B_j$ operations. This would result in larger area and longer reconfiguration streams being required to move between coefficients.

A reasonably simple solution to this problem is to defer the subtraction down to the next level (figure 1). This works for all coefficients except "–85" (for the 8-bit case) which encodes to 0 – 0 – 0 – 0 –. The problem with this coefficient is that deferring subtractions ends up with a double subtraction in the last level of the adder tree. There is only a single coefficient for any word-length that ends up in this form (i.e. 0 – 0 – 0...) no matter how long the coefficient word-length.

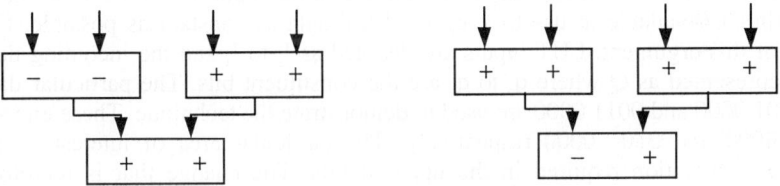

Fig. 1. 2 functionally identical tree segments produced through deferring of subtract operations

There are two ways of solving this problem. The first, and preferred, option is to exploit the fact that this system is designed for filters (be they adaptive or not). Since there is an accumulate stage following a multiply stage there is another adder block after the multiply stage which can be modified to achieve the final subtraction. In this way, it is possible to build the multiplier up as a pure adder tree and then subtract instead of add this result in at the accumulation stage as shown in figure 2.

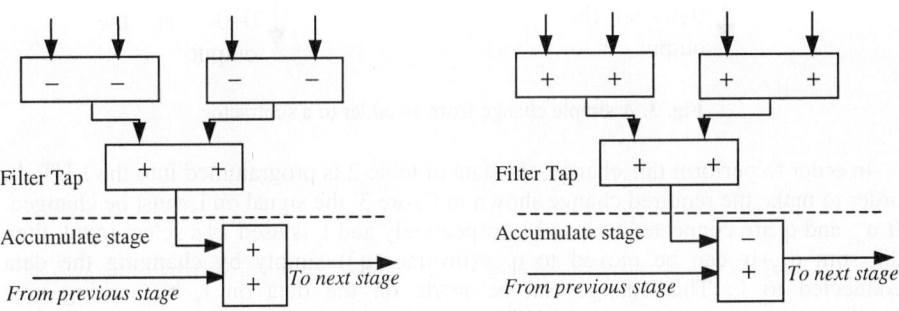

Fig. 2. Deferment of subtractions to the accumulator

The second option is to approximate the unrepresentable coefficient to a near neighbour. As this system is designed for adaptive filters where the coefficients are estimates at any one time in the system, then this would result only in a least significant bit error.

With the Xilinx hybrid LUT KCM[5] the adder tree structure remains the same for all coefficients and the only change is in the LUT data. For this modified Booth structure the adder tree does change between coefficients. This will result in longer configuration streams unless it is possible to keep the LUT data constant and only change the routing MUXes, which is the approach we have adopted here.

2.2. Changing an Adder to a Subtractor

In either a Booth or a modified Booth coding system, there is the additional problem of changing from adder to subtractor with the minimum amount of reconfiguration on a specific FPGA. In the Virtex FPGA, a 4-input look up table (LUT) is used as the programmable block where inputs come via a routing matrix with the direct connections coming from 28 to 1 routing MUX units.

Given that both $A_i + B_j$ and $A_i - B_j$ only require 2 of the inputs of the LUT, we have 2 further inputs available to use to keep the LUT data as constant as possible. For purposes of this argument, LUT inputs are denoted as l_1 to l_4 and the incoming data word is represented as Q where q_0 to q_7 are the constituent bits. The particular data values 0101 0000 and 0011 0000 are used to demonstrate the technique. These encode to 0+0+ 0000 and 0+0− 0000 respectively. The particular area of interest is the addition or subtraction required in the upper 4 bits. The change that is therefore required is fully explained in figure 3 below.

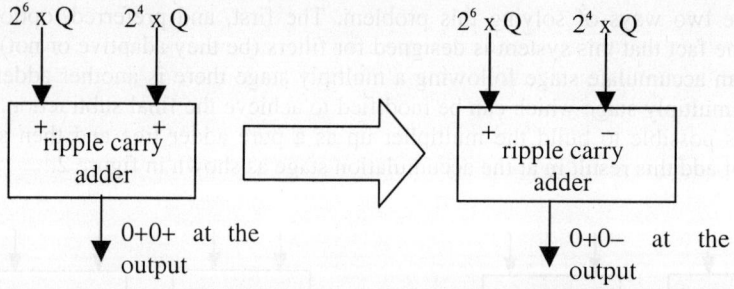

Fig. 3. A simple change from an adder to a subtractor

In order to perform this change, the data of table 2 is programmed into the LUT. In order to make the required change shown in figure 3, the signal on l_3 must be changed. If q_{i+2} and q_i are connected to l_1 and l_2 respectively and l_3 is used as a select input, then the sum $q_{i+2}+q_i$ can be moved to $q_{i+2}+$(inverse (q_i)) simply by changing the data connected to l_3. This change can be made on the data on l_3 by writing new configuration data to the routing MUX connecting to l_3 or by using a control line. The process of writing the configuration data to the routing MUX is preferred as this does not require further logic over that of the straightforward adder and can be performed using the JBits[7] program. By connecting one of the inputs to the 28 to 1 routing MUX for l_3, to a logic zero, the configuration of the MUX can then be set such that logic zero is fed to the output. If the MUX is set to its off position, a logic one is set to its output (the LUT input l_3). In this way, the LUT data can be kept constant and change made from an adder to a subtractor unit. The hot-1 required to complete the change from adder to subtractor is easily injected into the bottom of the ripple carry chain, this is also performed using JBits.

Table 2. LUT data for change from adder to subtractor

Input l_1	Input l_2	Input l_3	Output
0	0	0	0
0	0	1	1
0	1	0	1
0	1	1	0
1	0	0	1
1	0	1	0
1	1	0	0
1	1	1	1

Logic function resulting from LUT data in Table 2

2.3. Getting the Correct Data to the LUT

The above work allows one example of conversion from a unit performing the sum 0+0+ to one performing 0+0−, but how can this be applied generally? Once again, this is achieved using JBits[7] to control the 28 to 1 routing MUXes. Use of JBits in this manner is simple since the 28 to 1 MUX units are accessible using the JBits class Mux28to1. In total, there are 25 combinations of operations that might appear in a 4-bit section of the modified Booth encoded coefficient. For an operation of +00−, it is necessary to connect q_i to l_2 and q_{i+3} to l_1. For 0−+0 q_{i+1} connects to l_1 and q_{i+2} connects to l_2. To allow for all 25 combinations it is necessary to allow q_i to q_{i+3} or logic '0' to connect to l_1 and l_2. The logic '0' is required to allow combinations such as +000, this can be a +00+ block with one of its inputs set to '0'. LUT input l_3 only requires to be a logic '0' or '1', this is achieved by connecting the logic '0' on a single MUX input and using the 'off' state of the MUX to produce the logic '1'. LUT input l_4 is not used and so its MUX is left with all 18 inputs open.

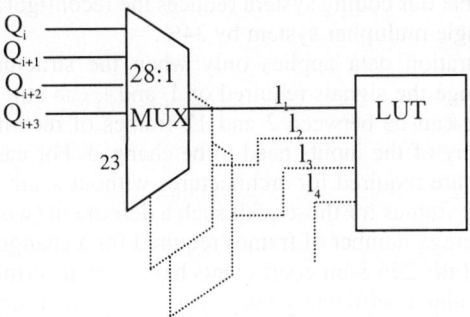

Fig. 4. Diagram of 28:1 MUX and LUT connections

3. Configuration Comparison with Xilinx LUT Based Multiplier

The use of 4 input Look Up Tables (LUTs) in a hybrid LUT-adder tree multiplier is an alternative method of reducing the amount of logic in a multiplier, as used in the Xilinx KCM case. The main disadvantage of this approach is that it is necessary to change the contents of every LUT to change the coefficient within a LUT based system. For example, look at the change from 121_{10} to -103_{10} (encoded as +00− +00+ and−00+ +00+). With the hybrid LUT system, it is necessary to change all the LUTs, with our approach, it is only necessary to change the connections to a single subtractor. One point counting in favour of the hybrid LUT system is that it is only ever necessary to change the top-level LUTs as there is no need for deferred operations. A brief analysis of the reconfiguration requirement follows.

3.1. The Reconfiguration Required

From an analysis of the bitstream for a Virtex device, the bits in the frames that control the settings of the input MUXes were identified. To do this JBits was used to read in a configuration stream, make changes to a particular MUX and then generate the new bitstream. This new bitstream was then compared with the "read-in" bitstream and the frames that changed were identified. This yielded the result that it is possible to switch a MUX between up to 10 of its 28 input lines using 2 frames of data. The exact number of lines that can be selected using 2 frames varies between 7 and 10 from MUX to MUX. It was found that if a configuration bit of one of the 28 to 1 MUXes for the F LUT in a slice is in a particular frame, then the corresponding bit for the G LUT is also in that frame. To change the bits of Q that are connected to l_1 and l_2 therefore requires 4 frames to be written (2 each for the MUX for l_1 and l_2). Another 2 frames control l_3 (it requires 2 frames since some MUXes do not have any input lines that can be selected using only a single frame) and a 7th frame is used to control the addition of a hot-1 into the bottom end of the ripple carry chain.

Figure 5 shows the Reconfiguration State Graph[8] (RSG) for an 8-bit (square) modified Booth encoded multiplier. This RSG shows the number of frames required for partial reconfiguration between the various configurations required by a system. This graph shows that the maximum number of Virtex configuration frames that must be changed to reconfigure is 21. For the Xilinx KCM, 32 frames must be changed in order to perform a reconfiguration (2 of 16-bit LUTs must change - each requiring 16 frames[9]). This means that our coding system reduces the reconfiguration overhead that must be built into a single multiplier system by 34%.

The above configuration data applies only when the structure changes, if the structure does not change the signals required on l_1 and l_2 can still change (e.g. +00+ to 0++0) for this there can be between 2 and 12 frames of reconfiguration required depending on how many of the inputs need to be changed. For ease of analysis, it is assumed that 8 frames are required for architectures without a subtraction deferred to the second level and 12 frames for those with such a deferment (worst cases).

To determine an average number of frames required for a change of coefficient, the architectures of each of the 256 8-bit coefficients have been determined. From this the probability of a particular coefficient change can be found. From this the average number of frames required to change the multiplier coefficient was determined and found to be 13·2 frames (Note that this is an overestimate since it assumes a worst case situation for all coefficient changes in which the architecture of the multiplier does not change.) Simple analysis shows that for any coefficient change all 32 of the frames containing LUT data must change for a coefficient change in the Xilinx LUT based KCM. This gives us an improvement in the average case of some 59%.

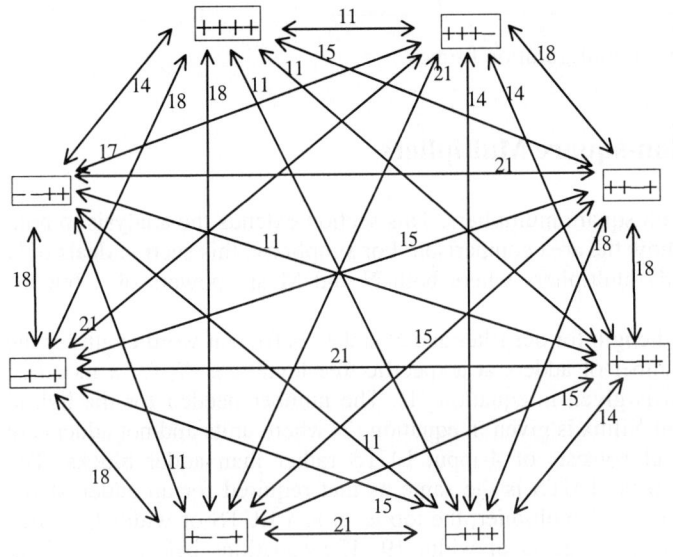

Fig. 5 The Reconfiguration State Diagram[7] for an 8-bit multiplier built using modified Booth encoding.

To decode the symbols at the nodes please refer to figure 5b below.

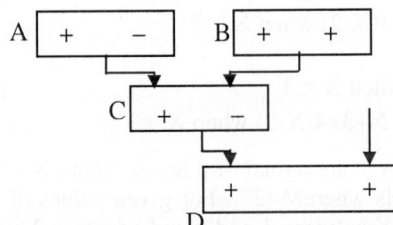

Fig. 5b In the RSG nodes this structure would be –+–+. The initial – relates to subtractor A, the following + to adder B, the following – to subtractor C and the final + to adder D. The 8 nodes in the RSG represent all the required structures for an 8-bit multiply accumulate. The first symbol always relates to unit A and so on for B, C, and D.

3.2. A System Perspective

A swift glance might suggest that a filter system would have to allow for the maximum reconfiguration (in our case 21 frames per tap) to be accomplished. In reality, given that this re-coding system is designed for filter situations with many taps, there will be many coefficients to change at a given time, each with a different transition. In this case, an average configuration distance, along with an error margin, would be a more appropriate allowance. If it is assumed that leaving enough time for 90% of the possible transitions to be accomplished, it is necessary to allow 18 frames per tap to be written. This is a saving of 44% over the hybrid LUT KCM.

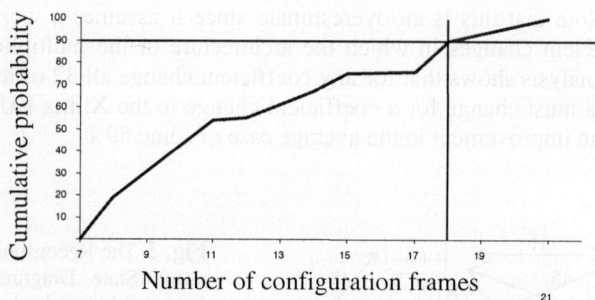

Fig. 6. Graph demonstrating that over 90% of reconfiguration streams are 18 frames or shorter

4. The Case of Non-square Multipliers

Section 3 dealt only with square multipliers. This section extends the analysis to non-square multipliers to show the area comparison. For simplicity, this section deals only with non-square (NxM) multipliers where both N and M are powers of 2 but the results apply generally.

If M is the data wordlength for our filter and N is the coefficient wordlength for the multiplier, then the number of adders at a specific tree level, e.g. X, for a modified Booth encoded system is given in equation (1). The number needed for the hybrid LUT based system from Xilinx is given in equation (2) where units and not adders are used since the top-level consists of 4-input LUTS rather than adder blocks. The resources required for these LUTS is the same as that required for an adder of the same width. Thus for a 16x16 multiplier, the top level is 4 LUTS of width 19 which uses the same resource as 4 adders of width 19. The equations below come from analysis of the tree structures obtained using each of the multiplier techniques.

$$\frac{N}{2^{X+1}} \text{ adders of width } \begin{cases} M+3 \text{ when } X < 3 \\ M+3+4(X-2) \text{ when } X \geq 3 \end{cases} \quad (1)$$

$$\frac{M}{2^{X+1}} \text{ units of width } \begin{cases} N+3 \text{ when } X < 3 \\ N+3+4(X-2) \text{ when } X \geq 3 \end{cases} \quad (2)$$

With the modified Booth encoded system there are a total of p levels where $N=2^{p+1}$. With the hybrid LUT method there are q levels where $M=2^{q+1}$. For given values of M and N, it is possible to sum equation (1) over X between 1 and p and equation 2 over X between 1 and q. If M>N, then equation (1) gives a lower result and so a modified Booth encoded system will have the smaller area. If N>M then a hybrid LUT style multiplier is smaller. This is a simple area analysis showing potential for gain when using a modified Booth encoding system. Analysis of the reconfiguration gain or loss has not yet been performed.

5. Layout & Speed Comparison with Xilinx LUT Based Multiplier

Size and speed measurements of the Xilinx KCM core has been determined from the KCM generator data sheet[10] and compared with a 16-bit pipelined multiplier that uses the proposed new structure. This multiplier has been written structurally using VHDL, synthesised using Synplify© 5.2.2a from Synplicity Inc and tested using ModelSim© from Mentor Graphics. The final implementation toolset was the Xilinx Foundation 2.1i series. To verify the Xilinx KCM core a multiplier was created using the downloadable software[10] and this was then implemented using Xilinx Foundation for schematic entry, placement, routing and timing analysis.

From figure 7, it can be seen that the proposed multiplier is smaller than the Xilinx core, which was expected from our simple analysis. One hypothesis for the reason that the Xilinx core looks to be larger than our core is that we have not been able to verify that our core can be placed and routed for all 32768 possible 16-bit coefficients. It has been checked for a number of randomly generated coefficients and these all prove place and routable. Given that there is plenty of routing resource available in the Virtex device, it is probable that our design can be placed and routed in the same area (or less) as the Xilinx KCM core. The only reason that there might be an issue is in the routing of the data inputs to the top-level of the tree. This is a potential problem as there are 4 lines that must come in over 4 out of 7 to 10 physical wires on the FPGA (the number of inputs that can be accessed using only 2 frames of data to configure the 28 to 1 MUXes varies from 7 to 10 between different MUXes). This has not proved to be a problem with the randomly selected coefficients.

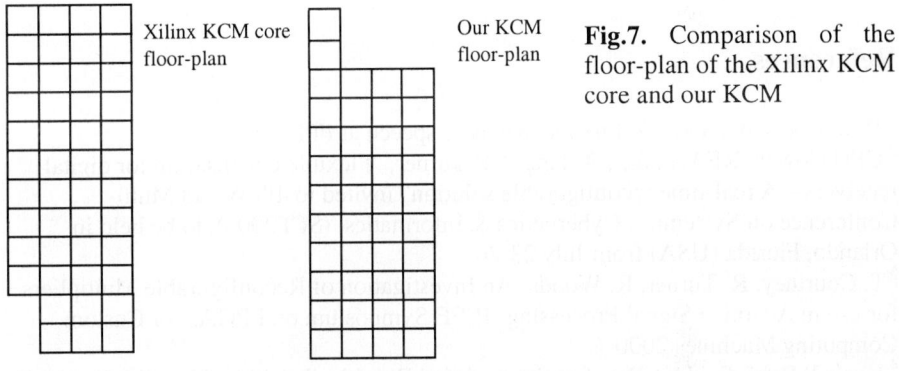

Fig.7. Comparison of the floor-plan of the Xilinx KCM core and our KCM

The only difference between a pipelined and a non-pipe-lined version of either design is the use of flip-flops on the outputs of the LUTs, adders and subtractors. Given that the flip-flops are an integral part of the Virtex architecture, it would seem reasonable to suggest that a combinatorial will have the same floorplan as a pipelined version.

The speeds of both designs are very similar. Speed analysis from the Xilinx Flow Engine version 2.1i_sp5 (from the Foundation suite) indicates that proposed new design will run at 148Mhz. In this design the critical path has a routing delay of 2.3ns (34%) which would suggest that further effort on manual routing is unnecessary. The Xilinx core attains a speed of 142Mhz[10], which corresponds to a period of 7.04ns compared to 6.76ns in the proposed design. Assuming that the logic delays are the same (since they have the same adder requirements) this is a routing delay of 37% for the Xilinx core, which is comparable to ours. The variation is likely to be due to differences in the exact routing used.

6. Conclusions

One of the conclusions from this work is that there are 'better' multiplier architectures than the 'normal' LUT based multiplier for filter systems. This is not surprising but it seems to have been largely ignored by library developers. Part of this conclusion is a statement that the choice of number system makes a difference to the system both in terms of the area required and also in terms of the attainable speed. It is necessary to qualify this conclusion with the statement that the input widths of a multiplier have as much bearing on the optimum structure as factors such as the number system chosen.

Careful observation of the underlying FPGA architecture can greatly assist in reduction of the required re-configuration data. In the proposed multiplier, this was shown to be as much as 50%. In the case of the Virtex FPGAs, the use of the input MUXes for reconfiguration for some designs can significantly reduce the required configuration data. This suggests that future work should look at both the logic resources within a given FPGA and also at the surrounding circuitry.

Whether the overall objective is design for reconfiguration or not, our proposed multiplier results in an improved performance when compared with LUT based systems for a multiplier with a coefficient word-length shorter than the data word-length.

References

[1] Wim Roelandts, CEO Xilinx inc. Keynote speech at FPL'99

[2] CFN Cowan, RF Woods, LK Ting & R Turner, "Flexible equalisation for digital receivers – A real-time reconfigurable solution" invited to 4th World Multi-Conference on Systemics, Cybernetics & Informatics. (SCI'2000), to be held in Orlando, Florida (USA) from July 23-26.

[3] T. Courtney, R. Turner, R. Woods 'An Investigation of Reconfigurable Multipliers for use in Adaptive Signal Processing' IEEE Symposium on FPGAs for Custom Computing Machines 2000.

[4] Louis P Rubinfield "A Proof of the modified Booth's algorithm for multiplication" IEEE transactions on Computers October 1975 pp1014-1015

[5] Xilinx KCM download material at
http://www.xilinx.com/ipcenter/reference_designs/#Math

[6] A D Booth "A Signed Binary Multiplication Technique" Quarterly journal of Mechanics and Applied Mathematics Vol4, part 2,1951 pp236-240

[7] JBITS Application Program Interface (API) into the Xilinx Virtex FPGA family bitstream. ©Xilinx Inc.

[8] 'Design and Implementation of Reconfigurable DSP Circuit Architectures' pp145-146, PhD thesis, J-P Heron 12/1998 The Queen's University of Belfast.

[9] Virtex Series Configuration Architecture User Guide published on-line by Xilinx. http://www.xilinx.com/xapp/xapp151.pdf

[10] http://www.xilinx.com/ipcenter/reference_designs/kcm_vgen_v1_2.pdf

Efficient Building of Word Recognizer in FPGAs for Term-Document Matrices Construction

Christophe Bobda and Thomas Lehmann

Heinz Nixdorf Institute, Paderborn University
Fuerstenallee 11,
D-33102 Paderborn, Germany
{bobda, torkin}@upb.de
http://www.upb.de/cs/ag-rammig

Abstract. FPGAs are a flexible system for the implementation of finite state machines. In this paper a optimized architecture for word recognition is discussed. In the introduction the advantages and disadvantages of other approaches are shown. From this starting-point approaches for optimization and the resulting structure are described. The paper ends with a real life performance test.

1 Introduction

One of the commonly used document representation is the so called vector space. This model represents one document as a vector of key words present in the document. A complete collection of n documents over a list of m target words is then represented by a words by documents matrix $A \in R^m \times R^n$. An entry a_{ij} in A is the frequency of the word i in the document j. The words by documents matrix is then used for indexing purpose or statistical analysis like LSI (Latent Semantic Indexing)[3]. Building a terms by documents matrix is done by scanning the documents of the given collection in order to find the appearance of key words (Pattern Matching) and return the corresponding entry in the matrix for each document. This construction is an inherently parallel problem, since many different words can be search in parallel. Although pattern matching have been shown to be one of the applications to benefit from the reconfigurable and parallel structure of FPGAs[2, 4, 6, 9, 5, 10], the overhead need to implement a search engine is still high. It can be balanced if the capacity of the search engine (that we define as the number of words to be search in parallel) which is also the complexity of the function implemented, is big enough and the amount of data to process allow a maximum utilization of a configuration before reconfiguring the circuitry[5]. In this paper we target the Xilinx FPGAs for pattern matching, which are made as a collection of CLBs (Configurable Logic Blocks). Resources in CLBs are dominated by flip-flops and LUTs (look-up tables). Our evaluation will take in consideration the number of flip-flops, look-up tables and in some extend the number of CLBs need to implement a particular search engine.

2 Related Work

2.1 The Sliding Windows Approach

One approach of text searching is the so called sliding window (SL)[4, 9]. In this method, a sliding window recognizer stores a target word in a register A and stream the text through a shift register B with the same length as A. For each character of the target word stored in a byte, an 8-bit comparator is used to compare this character with the corresponding character of the text which streams through the shift register. A hit occurs when all the comparators return the value true. The sliding window can be extended to check a match of multiple patterns in parallel. Each target word will then be stored in one register and will have as many comparators as required. The length of the window (the number of characters in the windows) is defined by the segment of the text to be processed. Words with length bigger than the length of the window can not be handled. To overcome this problem one can define the length of text to be considered as the maximum length over all the target words. In this case, all the words with a length smaller than the maximum length should be filled with don't care characters to be handled correctly.

Redundancy in the SL reduce the capacity of such implementation, thus making its use not competitive. In the case of the Xilinx Virtex FPGA XCV300 with a maximum of 6144 flip-flops, a sliding windows of length 10 needs $10 \times 8 = 80$ flip-flops to store one target word in the device. Consider that the device placement and routing permits an utilization of 80 %. The number of words which can be folded in such an FPGA will theoretically be in the range of 60, which is small compared to the number of words which can be folded in the same divide with a more efficient implementation.

2.2 Hashed Table-Based Text Searching

This algorithm has been implemented on the SPLASH System[10]. The text to be processed is streamed in a pair of consecutive characters called "superbyte". An incoming superbyte is mapped on one character of the "target alphabet". Each non alphabet character is mapped to a delimiter. To determine whether or not a word is in the target list, a hashing technique is used. A hash table in memory is used to store the value of a presence bit for a particular target word. An entry zero in this table means that the word is not present and a value one means that the word will probably be present. A hash register (with a length of 22 bit in the SPLASH implementation), which is initially set to zero, is incrementally modified by the incoming "superbytes". At the end of a word marked by a delimiter, the hash register is set to zero to allow the next word to be processed. The hash register is used to address a hash table of 2^{22} pseudo-random mappings of words. The modification of the hash register happens as follows: When a non delimiter superbyte is encountered the contents of the 22-bit hash register is updated by first XOR-ing the upper 16-bit of the register with the incoming superbyte and a value of a hash function. The modified value of the hash register is then circularly shifted by a fixed number of bits. Upon reaching the end of a word, the content of the register is used to address the hash table and determine the value of the presence bit. To reduce the likelihood of false hits a number of independent hash functions is calculated for each word of the text, with the stipulation that each hash function lookup of a word must result in a hit for that word to be counted as a target word.

Estimations on performance of the SPLASH text searching have been done mainly on the basis of the critical path length returned by the place and route tool. Communication between the host computer and the boards like memory latency have not been taken in consideration.

2.3 Automaton-Based Text Searching

It is well known that any regular grammar can be recognized by a deterministic finite state machine (FSM). In an automaton-based search algorithm, a finite state machine is built on the basis of the target words. The target words define a regular grammar which is compiled in an automaton acting as a recognizer for that grammar. When scanning a text, the automaton changes its state with the appearance of characters. Upon reaching an end state, a hit occurs and the corresponding word is set to be found. One advantage of the FSM-based search machine is the elimination of the preprocessing step done in many other methods to remove stop words (like 'the', 'to', 'for' etc., which does not affect the meaning of statements) from documents. In the Foulk[2] implementation of the hardware based retrieval machine a memory is used to store the transition table. Two registers hold the current state and the incoming character. The logic is only used to decode the address of the next state in memory and to set the correct values in the registers.

The performance (speed) of such an implementation is governed by the path (RAM output → state register → RAM address → RAM output) which can considerably slow down the search process, because of the multiple memory accesses. To increase the speed of an FSM implementation, memory accesses can be suppressed by compiling the transition table in hardware and having a mechanism to execute the state machine. Folding big transition tables in FPGAs can be difficult because of the limited capacity of those devices. Transition tables for word recognizers are often full of backtracking edges and crossing edges (edge which connects two nodes on different paths in the FSM-tree). With the sequential structure of the memory based recognizer, it is almost impossible to eliminate the backtracking edges which constitute in most case the biggest part of the transition table.

The SPACE (Scalable Parallel Architecture for Concurrency Experiments) machine[6, 7] makes use of the parallel structure of FPGAs to eliminate backtracking edge from the FSM. This search machine is a FSM like implementation for text searching capable of handling a search over a list of almost 100 target words. The search is performed simultaneously on a board with 16 CAL1024 FPGAs without using a memory to store the transition table. Each word in the grammar is compiled in a FSM which is mapped to the hardware device (Fig. 1).

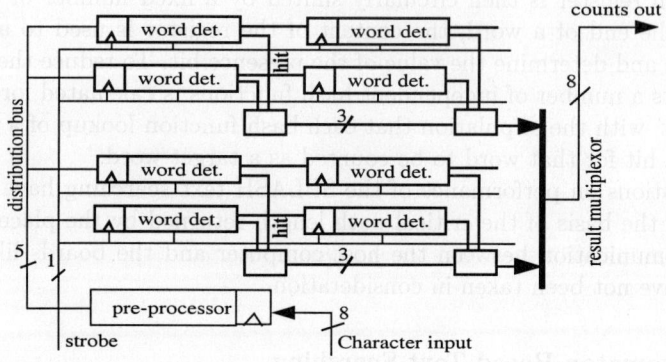

Fig. 1. Organization of the search machine on SPACE: Example of a two levels word detectors with 4 target words per level

A transputer is used to stream characters in ASCII form into the machine. For the case insensitivity purpose the 8-bit characters are mapped by the preprocessor to 5-bit characters. With the incoming characters, which clock the flip-flops, all the FSM move simultaneously to their next state. Upon reaching an end state, the corresponding accumulator is incremented and the result is returned. The backtracking edges appearing in the formal representation of the FSM become redundant and will not be take in consideration. Figure 2a) shows a transition graph of an FSM. The transition table requires 5×6 memory locations to be stored (Fig. 2b)). For the same FSM the hardware representation will need only 4 flip-flops and 4 AND gates (Fig. 2c)).

While having the advantage of replacing a word already folded in the FPGA with a new target word of the same length, the SPACE implementation present two major inconveniences: First, it does not take into consideration words which share a common prefix. Second, it uses one comparator for each character of a target word.

Those two factors lead to redundancy in flip-flop and look-up table utilization, like in the sliding window recognizer. On the SPACE board, with a total of 8192 flip-flops it has been possible to implement a list of only 96 target words with average length 12.

When taking in consideration the common prefix of words, it is possible to save a considerable amount of flip-flops. For this purpose, the search machine should be implemented as an automaton recognizer common to all the target words. The resulting structure is a tree (Fig. 3) in which a path from the root to a leaf determines the appearance of a corresponding target word in the streamed text. Words which share a common prefix uses a common path from the root corresponding to the length of their common prefix. A split occurs at the node where the common prefix ends. In the hardware implementation of a group of words with a common prefix, common flip-flops will be used to implement the

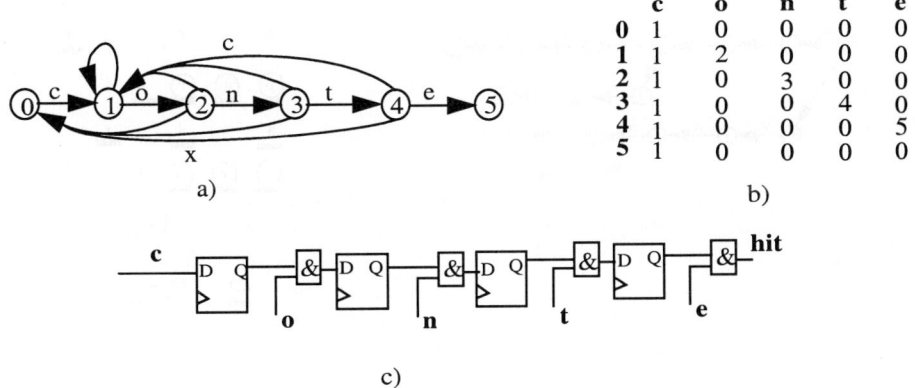

Fig. 2. FSM recognizers for the word "conte": a) sate diagram, b) transition table, c) basis structure the hardware implementation: 4 flip-flops will be need to code a 5 × 6 transition table

common path (Fig. 3a)). An attempt to implement each word on his own path will lead to redundancy in flip-flops utilization (Fig. 3b)).

For each character in the target alphabet only one comparator is needed. The comparison can occur once at a particular location in the device. Incoming characters can be directly send to a set of all possible comparators. Upon matching a particular one, a corresponding signal will be send to all the ports which need the result of that comparison. This method will reduce the number of comparators needed almost by the sum of the length of all target words. Comparison are implemented in FPGAs in LUT (look-up table). A Virtex CLB contains four flip-flops and four 4-LUTs. Although one CLB can be used to code four states it isn't used in SPACE. One 5-bit or 8-bit comparator needs three 4-LUTs. With the SPACE implementation three of the 4-LUTs will be use to code one comparator. Because each state is connected to his own comparator, only one state can be coded on one CLB with one 4-LUT left. For three CLBs there will be three 4-LUTs left which can be used to code another comparator, thus allowing four CLBs to be used to code only three states and three comparators. This is not a good utilization of the available resources. Lets see why: For a Virtex FPGA XCV300 with 1536 CLBs and a resource utilization of 80 % there will be a total of 1229 CLBs available which can be used to code 1639 states and 1639 comparators. If we consider that the average length of target words is 10, each FSM (corresponding to a target word) will be coded on 10 states. That means 1639 states can be used to code a maximum of 163 target words of average length 10. Consider now that we are using only one comparator for each character of the target alphabet, we need only one CLB to code one comparator together with one state and there will be one 4-LUT left. That means four comparators will be coded on three CLBs together with three states. With this we only need

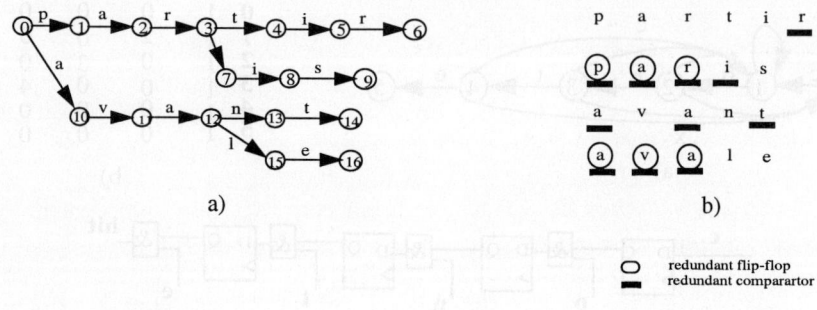

Fig. 3. a) Use of the common prefix to reduce the number of flip-flops of the common word detector for "partir", "paris", "avale","avant". b) implementation without use of common prefix and common comparator set

|alphabet|·3/4 CLBs to code the alphabet and the first |alphabet|·3/4 states of the FSM. With an alphabet of 256 letters (a character is coded on 8 bit) we need 192 CLBs to code the alphabet and the first 192 states. Lets consider the same device (Virtex FPGA XCV300) with 1536 CLBs. As mentioned before, if the device utilization is 80 % there will be 1229 available CLBs. If we remove 192 CLBs to code the alphabet and the first 192 states we still left with 1184 CLBs. Because each of the CLBs left can be used to code four states, it will be possible to code $1037 \times 4 = 4148$ states on the rest of CLBs. The total amount of states which can then be coded on the device will be $4148 + 192 = 4340$. With the same assumption as before it will be possible to compile 434 target words of average length 10 in the same device. Lets consider now that the use of the common prefix of words can increase the capacity of the search machine by 10 %[1], then it will be possible for us to compile 477 words in the same device. To achieve this performance, we propose the following architecture.

3 System Architecture

The proposed search engine consists of an array of comparators to decode the characters of the FSM alphabet, a state decoder which moves the state machine in the next states and a preprocessor to map incoming 8-bit characters to 5-bit characters (Fig. 4). Since case insensitivity is considered in most application in information retrieval, the preprocessor is designed to map upper and lower case characters to the binary code of 1 to 26 and the rest of character to 0[6]. Characters are streamed to the device in ASCII notation. An incoming 8-bit character triggers the clock and is mapped to a 5-bit character which is sent to

---

[1] we have observe an increase of 10 % to 20 % in the capacity when taking the common prefix of words in consideration

the comparator array. All the 5-bit signals are distributed to all the comparators which operate in parallel to check if a match of the incoming character occurs. If a match occurs for the comparator k, the output signal k is set to one and all the other are set to zero. If no match occurs, all the output signal are set to be zero (Fig. 5 c).

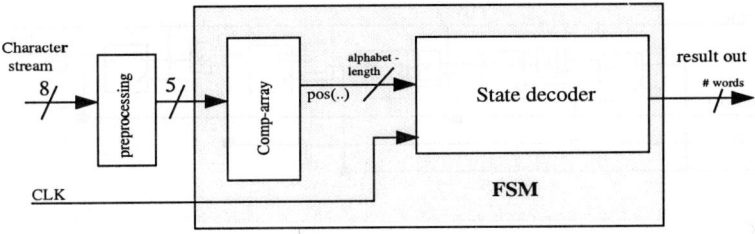

Fig. 4. Basis structure of our FSM-based words recognizer

3.1 State Decoder

The one-hot approach (Fig. 5 c) has been chosen first because it takes a major advantage toward the regular structure of the FPGA and it is the fastest way to implement FSM in hardware[8]. Second because there is no need to incorporate backtracking edges in a suitable hardware representation. To implement a set of different words, the resulting tree structure (Fig. 3) of the common FSM is mapped in hardware. All the leafs corresponding to target words are connected to the hit port. The width of the hit port is determined by the number of positions needed to code the number of target words. Upon matching a particular word, one leaf of the automaton is reached and the hit output is set as to the index of the matched target word.

3.2 Automaton Generation

One of the major problem that prevent FPGAs to be used is the difficulty for software programmers of mapping algorithm in hardware. This process is usually done by experienced hardware designer with the help of CAD (Computer Aided Design) tools and can takes few minutes to hours or days. Because of the lack of hardware know-how of the information retrieval people, we have developed a tool set which permit anyone with no experience in hardware programming to automatically generate a term by document matrix form a document collection with a given list of target words. Our program automatically generates a VHDL description of the search machine, the synthesis is done trough the Synopsys compiler which generates a netlist file for the Xilinx place and route tool. We

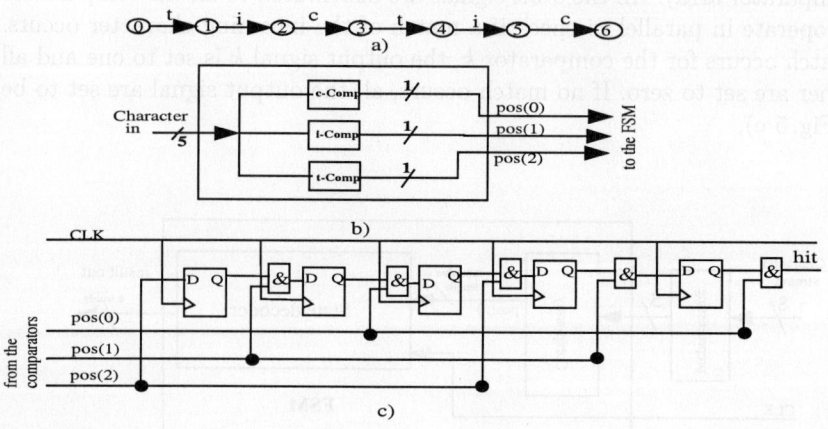

Fig. 5. Processing steps of the FSM for the word "tictic"

use the algorithm described in [1] to generate the corresponding tree structure which is then mapped in hardware. The resulting state machine is optimized (in terms of number of states) and is able to solve the Mississippi problem[2] for a set of target words. With the Union, concatenation, kleen Huelle operations all the basic FSMs (FSM related to one word) are used to build one FSM capable of recognizing all the target words. A set of final states is linked to the appearance of target words in a streaming text. The resulting transition table is then translated into VHDL code in such a way that no backtracking and crossing edges appear in the configuration. The resulting VHDL code is then synthesized, mapped, placed, routed and configured to be downloaded into the FPGA with the help of the generated scripts. The document collection is then scanned and a column vector representing the weigh of target words in this document is returned for each document.

4 Performance Test

For performance evaluation we used a Xilinx Virtex XCV300 on a Spyder Virtex board by FZI Karlsruhe[11]. The FPGA on the Spyder board is coupled with the PCI bus of a 333MHz Pentium II by the Plextor PCI bridge PLX 9080. The FPGA works synchronously with the PCI bus, thus the FPGA clock frequency is 33MHz (Fig. 6). The operation system is Linux 2.2.12.

The test word list consist of 330 words with an average of 10 characters each. This leads to a automaton with 2370 states. The utilization of the FPGA is 1817

---
[2] Can the state machine recognize the word 'issip' in a file containing the word Mississippi?[2]

CLB slices, including bus interface. The XCV300 contains 3072 slices. Thus the total utilization is 59 %.

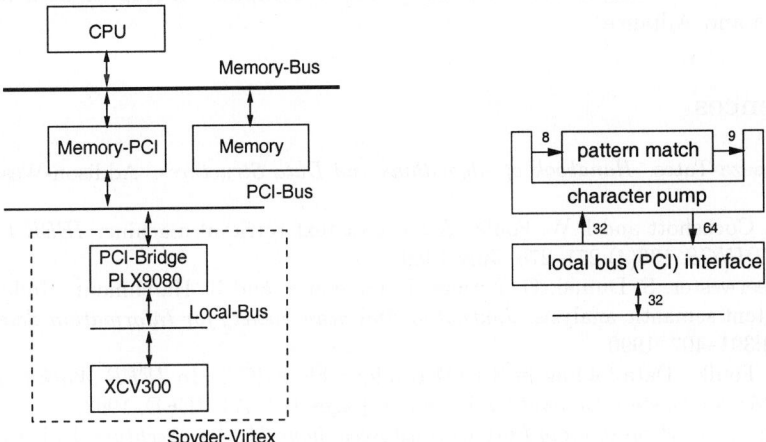

Fig. 6. System architecture   **Fig. 7.** Entity hierarchy

The bottleneck of the system is the PCI bridge PLX 9080. A direct slave write cycle of a 32 bit data word takes 15 PCI cycles. Thus the theoretical data transfer rate is 8Mbyte/s. To enhance the performance four 8 bit coded characters are combined in one 32 bit data word and pump the character one by one through the word recognizer (Fig. 7). The results are collected and stored in a 64 bit result register[3]. Hence three 32 bit accesses to the FPGA are needed to match four characters by more than 255 words checked in parallel. So the stream rate is estimated by 3 million[4] characters per second.

In practice we have measured a cycle time of about $16\mu s$ for one single write and two single read operations due to the bottleneck of system calls and the PCI-interface. Hence we are able to match about 240K characters per second (8 bit coded characters, four characters per data word). In the future the PCI-interface will be enhanced by burst read and write operations to step towards the theoretical limit.

5 Conclusion and Future Work

In this paper an optimized architecture for FPGA-based word recognition was shown. The system structure uses redundancies due to common prefixes in the word list and sharing of comparator results. Real life performance tests have shown the practicability and the recognition speed of 240K characters per second.

---

[3] 32 bit if less than 255 words are compiled into the word recognizer.
[4] 4 million if less than 255 words are compiled into the word recognizer.

In the future the device interface should be enhanced to reduce the influence of this bottleneck on the total stream rate. Furthermore the FPGA-based indexing will be integrated into a parallel search engine on a Linux-cluster. This includes a fast reconfiguration with an optimized compilation step without using Synopsys and Alliance.

References

1. R. Baeza-Tates. *Handbook of Algorithms and Data Structures*. Addison-Wessley, 1991.
2. W.P. Cockshott and P.W. Foulk. A low-cost text retrieval machine. *IEEE PROCEEDINGS*, 136(4):271–276, July 1989.
3. S. Deerwester, S. Dumai, G. Furnas, T. Landauer, and R. Harshmann. Indexing by latent semantic analysis. *Journal of American Society for Information Science*, 41(6):391–407, 1990.
4. P.W. Foulk. Data-folding in SRAM configurable FPGA. In *IEEE Workshop on FPGAs for Custom Computing Machines*, pages 163–171. IEEE, 1993.
5. S. Guccione. *Programming Fine-Grained Reconfigurable Architechture*. PhD thesis, The University of Texas at Austin, May 1995.
6. B. Gunther and G. Milne. Accessing document relevance with run-time reconfigurable machines. In *IEEE Workshop on FPGAs for Custom Computing Machines*, pages 9–16, Napa California, 1996. IEEE.
7. B. Gunther and G. Milne. Hardware-based solution for message filtering. Technical report, school of computer and information science, 1996.
8. P. Kurup and T. Abbasi. *Logic Synthesis Using Synopsys*. Kluwer Akademic publisher, 1997.
9. S.H-M. Ludwig. *Hades-Fast Hardware Synthesis Tools and a Reconfigurable Coprocessor*. PhD thesis, Swiss Federal Institute of Technologie, Zürich, 1997.
10. D.V. Pryor, M.R.Thisle, and N.shirazi. Text searching on splash 2. In *IEEE Workshop on FPGAs for Custom Computing Machines*, pages 172–177. IEEE, 1993.
11. Karlheinz Weiss, Thorsten Steckstor, Carsten Ötker, Igor Katchan, Carsten Nitsch, and Joachim Philipp. *Spyder - Virtex - X2 User's Manual*, 1999.

Reconfigurable Computing between Classifications and Metrics – The Approach of Space/Time-Scheduling

Christian Siemers

University of Applied Sciences Heide, Rungholtstr. 9, D-25746 Heide (Germany)
christian.siemers@computer.org

Abstract. Reconfigurable computing receives its merits from scheduling time-based into space-based execution. This paper reviews some common parameters and introduces an additional metric for eventhandling. The focus is set on event-bound applications, and a novel architecture is introduced enabling runtime scheduling between time-based and space-based execution.

1 Motivation

Software-programmable and configurable hardware do not have the same roots, but the user-programmable hardware types seem to converge in their usability. One indicator for this is the origination of common classification systems and metrics. Are there mixed architectures possible, and what should be the main characteristics?

This paper attempts to survey common as well as different characteristics between reconfigurable and sequential executing hardware systems. For this purpose, approach [1] is discussed in chapter 2 highlighting the distinction between both system types. Chapter 3 introduces then a system capable of scheduling between time- and space-based type of execution.

2 Classification of Computing Hardware Systems

The hardware of all computing system implementations show some comparable characteristics concerning design space, binding and programming times and architectural space [1][2]. Fig. 1 shows a coarse design space overview resulting in the well-known "Computing in Time – Computing in Space".

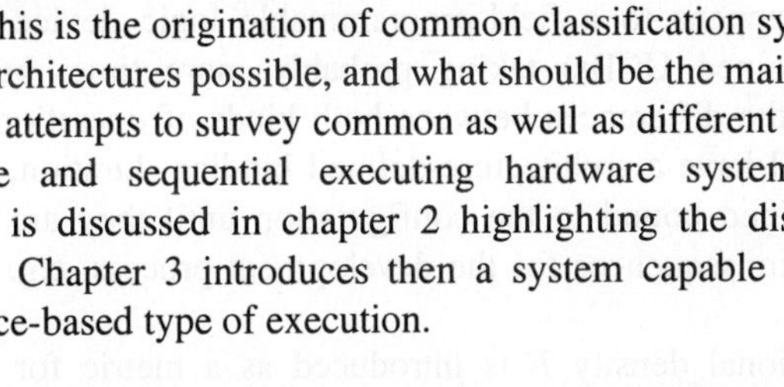

(Distribution of computation)		*(Time of definition of computation)*	
		pre-fabrication (Hardware)	post-fabrication (Software)
	Space	ASIC	FPLD
	Time-sequential Space		Universal Configurable Blocks
	Time		Processor

Fig. 1. Coarse Design Space for Computing Implementations

Compared with [2] a new class of design space called time-sequential space is added. This class shall contain all demanded architectures capable of scheduling between space- and time-based execution. The Universal Configurable Blocks [3], which will be reviewed in chapter 3, will fit into this class.

The figure 2 derived from [2] with some additions uses characteristic times for identifying the several kinds of hardware for computation. Any processor, which definitely belongs to the class of sequential executing hardware, fetches an instructions, interprets it, and configures the internal hardware for operation.

	(Hardware)			(Software)		
	Custom VLSI	ASIC	FPLD, one-time progr.	FPLD	UCB	μP
Binding time	- fabrication - first mask metal mask		fuse program	load config.	load config.	cycle
Binding duration	- infinite -		infinite	user-defined	user-defined	cycle
Programming time	- fabrication -		seconds	μs - ms	cycle	cycle

Fig. 2. Binding and programming times for computing hardware

Exactly the same happens to a field-programmable logic device (FPLD) (and inside the below explained UCBs) taking probably more time, but this is not significant. Where are the differences between both kinds of operations? Sequential executing hardware will have a architecture-defined binding duration, while FPLDs will be application-defined bound to the configuration until they are reconfigured. This results in drastic consequences for the development process, e.g. the modeling language.

Inside [1] the functional density F is introduced as a metric for performance-related systems and applications. It is defined as averaged number of gate evaluations per area and time, measured in $N_{ge}/\lambda^2 s$ with λ as half of the minimum structure size. As maximum values, $F = 2 .. 20$ are reported for microprocessors, $100 .. 300$ for FPLDs.

For i/o-dominated systems this metric appears to be not suitable. Whenever the latency time is more important than computing time itself – e.g. embedded systems are often outside world driven –, it is suggested to define the event density E as the metric to meet these constraints. As a first approach, E is defined as the average availability of the eventhandler per area and time, measured in $N_{event}/\lambda^2 s$.

Table 1. Preliminary results for event density E

Devicetype	$E [N_{event}/\lambda^2 s]$
Microprocessor	0.01 .. 0.1
UCB (dedicated)	0.5 .. 5
FPLD	350 .. 500

The here reported values for E are measured without any dependence to the operating system but will decrease in real systems. For the purpose of this paper, a standard event is defined as an interrupt request from any device outside to be serviced by the microprocessor or FPLD and includes just the interrupt response time and the time to leave the service routine and return to normal without any internal computation. Table 1 summarizes the results for microprocessor and FPLDs.

Please note that the results are derived from pre-simulation calculations and subject to further research but nevertheless show the general aspect. How should this be interpreted, and why is this important?

E just quantifies how many events may be handled by a system. In this way, an eventhandler is interpreted simply as a reaction of the system to any external request. Implementation in space means that the reactive part is always available, while in time it must be loaded when requested. As long as a microprocessor may service one interrupt request per time, the values must be low compared with those of an FPLD.

The UCBs as introduced in [3] may act like a sequential executing hardware and receives therefore E values like those for the microprocessor reported. In reconfigurable (dedicated) mode the values for E increase significantly, and this mode is applicable inside multi-UCB machines [3]. As soon as computations will be included for determining E the values for the dedicated UCBs will rise significantly towards FPLD values.

3 Universal Configurable Blocks and Machines

To switch any executing system from sequential to reconfigurable mode, this system must hold some characteristics:
- The binding time of a configuration/instruction must be machine-defined in the sequential mode and requests for a configuration/instruction flow and a sequencer.
- In reconfiguration mode, the binding time must be application-definable, and the maximum value might be infinite. Therefore the configuration must contain a complete operation (with exits for further proceeding).

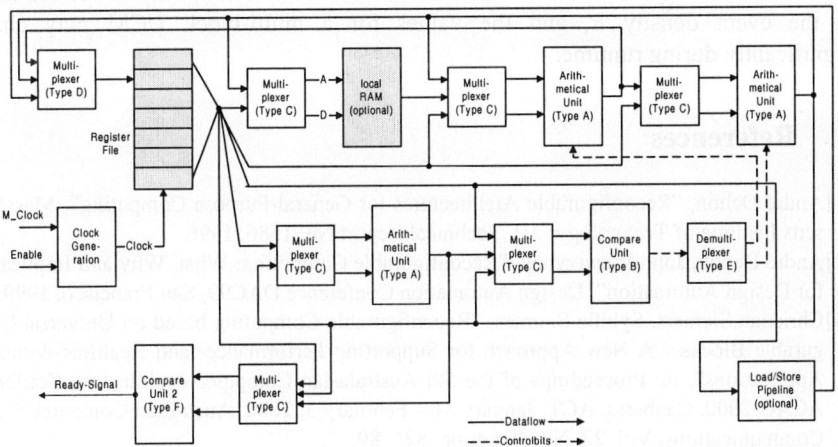

Fig. 3. Architecture of Universal Configurable Blocks (UCB)

- To enable runtime switching, the description for both modes should be made using the same programming language and even one sourcecode, and optimally there should be no restrictions inside the source code.

The Universal Configurable Blocks (UCB) [3] show significant relationships to processor kernel including register file, a reconfigurable ALU (rALU) and optionally local data memory. The rALU itself is configurable in the sense that datapaths are connectable between registers and sub-units, while reconfigurable operations may be added to receive more flexibility. High speed reconfiguration is supported by the comparable small size of a configuration stream.

As the preconfigured sub-units shall correspond to the operations defined in the microprocessor model (instruction set), the translation of an instruction flow into the necessary configuration is much simplified. The algorithm is called procedural driven structural programming (PDSP) [3] and integrates data forwarding as well.

The PDSP algorithm will translate only parts of the instruction flow (so-called hyperblocks) into configurations, so that UCBs request for a higher machine called Universal Configurable Machine (UCM, [3]). The UCM may contain a hyperblock sequencer (this enables the machine to execute in the sense of any microprocessor) and a UCB scheduler, which actually schedules flows of hyperblocks to the UCBs as executing units (space/time-scheduling).

4 Conclusion

It was the purpose of this paper to review some metrics and classifications, to introduce space/time-scheduling and to integrate a novel kind of executing hardware into these systems. For the purpose of performance-dominated systems, the scheduling during compiletime appears as the best solution for best overall optimization.

Runtime space/time-scheduling on the other side may show its merits inside event-dominated systems, e.g. inside embedded systems. The UCM architecture enables now runtime scheduling between space- and time-based execution. The related metric is the event density E, and the values for a multi-block UCM may change significantly during runtime.

5 References

[1] André Dehon, "Reconfigurable Architectures for General-Purpose Computing". Massachusetts Institute of Technology, A.I. Technical Report No. 1586, 1996.
[2] André Dehon, John Wawrzynek, "Reconfigurable Computing: What, Why and Implications for Design Automation". Design Automation Conference DAC99, San Francisco, 1999.
[3] Christian Siemers, Sybille Siemers, "Reconfigurable Computing based on Universal Configurable Blocks - A New Approach for Supporting Performance- and Realtime-dominated Applications", in: Proceedings of the 5th Australasian Computer Architecture Conference ACAC-2000, Canberra, ACT, January 31 – February 3, 2000. Australian Computer Science Communications, Vol. 22, Number 4, pp. 82 .. 89.

FPGA Implementation of a Prototype WDM On-Line Scheduler

Winnie W. Cheng, Steven J.E. Wilton, and Babak Hamidzadeh

Department of Electrical and Computer Engineering
University of British Columbia,
Vancouver, B.C., Canada
wcheng@ieee.org, {stevew|babak}@ece.ubc.ca

Abstract. Message sequencing and channel assignment are two important aspects to consider in optimizing the performance of Wavelength Division Multiplexing (WDM) networks. A scheduling technique, Multiple-Messages-per-Node with Shortest Job First priority (MMN-SJF), has been proposed to tackle these two areas simultaneously and offers a globally optimizing approach to scheduling. In this paper, a reconfigurable testbed consisting of several interconnected FPGAs for analyzing such scheduling algorithms is introduced and in particular, a prototype scheduler is developed to investigate the implementation and hardware complexity associated with MMN-SJF. We find that the MMN-SJF scheduling technique can be implemented cost effectively and with only simple logic blocks.

1. Introduction

Wavelength Division Multiplexing (WDM) is an effective way of utilizing the large bandwidth of an optical fiber. By allowing multiple messages to be transmitted in parallel, on a number of channels, this technique has the potential to significantly improve the performance of optical networks. However, efficient access protocols and scheduling algorithms are needed to fully unleash this potential by allocating and coordinating system resources optimally. Simulation results and analytical modelling have shown the Multiple-Messages-per-Node scheduling with Shortest-Job-First priority (MMN-SJF) to be a promising scheduling technique. Nonetheless, it is crucial to evaluate the complexities of the algorithm when implemented on hardware. Prototypes can be built around a reconfigurable testbed using Field Programmable Gate Arrays (FPGA) to study the complexities involved. In this paper, a design of such testbed is presented and is used in examining the MMN-SJF scheduling scheme.

2. WDM On-Line Scheduler

The MMN-SJF technique [1] assumes N nodes, each connected to the network through its own Network Interface Unit (NIU). The bandwidth of this network is divided into C channels; thus, up to C messages can be sent across the network simultaneously. Only *C-1* of these channels are actually used to send data; these channels are referred to as *data channels*. The remaining channel is called the *control channel*, and is used to exchange information about messages to be scheduled.

Messages from the local node are buffered in each NIU until they can be sent over the network. The operation of the network consists of two phases. In the first phase, the NIUs broadcast, in turn, information about the top *l* messages in their SJF-prioritized queue. Once all *N* nodes have broadcast information about their top *l* messages, each NIU has a consistent view of what messages are waiting to be sent. In the second phase, each NIU then performs the same scheduling on these *l*N* messages. The scheduling algorithm handles channel assignment and message sequencing. It determines which of the *C-1* data channels will be used for each message using the Earliest-Available Time Scheduling (EATS) scheme, and which order the messages assigned to each channel will be sent using the Shortest Job First (SJF) scheme. All nodes will arrive at the same schedule. The messages are then queued for their respective channels for the actual transmission and the first phase starts again with a new set of *l*N* messages.

Note that this is only one possible scheduling algorithm that can be implemented by the NIU. In [1] [2], an analytical model is used to compare this algorithm to other possible algorithms. Since we wish to create a testbed where we can implement these various algorithms, we have chosen to use FPGAs as the network interface units. The implementation described in this paper is specifically for the MMN-SJF algorithm, but clearly the interface could be reconfigured to implement other algorithms.

3. FPGA Implementation

The main functional blocks of the prototype scheduler are illustrated in Figure 1. The scheduler is sub-divided into two sections that run in parallel.

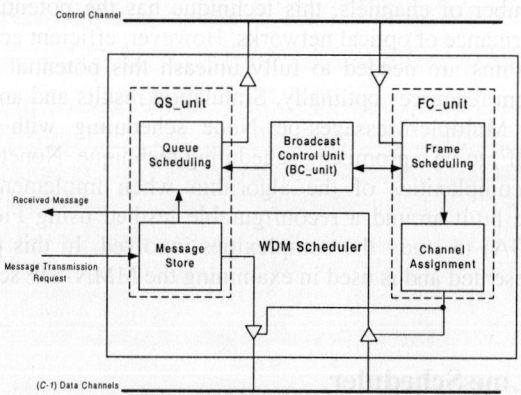

Fig. 1. Block diagram of Network Interface Unit.

The Queue Scheduling and the Message Store unit (QS_unit) can execute concurrently with the Frame Scheduling and Channel Assignment unit (FC_unit) to increase throughput. The Broadcast Control unit (BC_unit) deals with synchronization issues with other nodes and coordinates the broadcast of control packets.

The QS_unit interfaces primarily with the message generator and can present two SJF-sorted headers when requested by the BC_unit. The FC_unit is heavily pipelined to schedule the control packets as they are received from the control channel. Once all the control packets have been received, all nodes will have the same schedule and channels can then be assigned for the actual transmission.

The QS_unit operates independently from the other units of the scheduler. It waits for a message request from the local node. Then it stores the message and queues the header using the SJF priority scheme. At the same time, the FC_unit and the BC_unit loops through the two phases and are synchronized by a start signal.

A testbed for evaluating WDM network scheduling techniques is constructed with four interconnected Altera EPF10K20 FPGAs as shown in Figure 2. Three of the four FPGAs are used to simulate three network nodes running the same algorithm, each with a message generator to supply test vectors. A separate FPGA generates synchronization signals for automated testing and data capture. In our prototype, we replaced the optical interconnecting network with an electrical interconnect, and used separate lines for each channel. The reprogrammable nature of the FPGAs allows other scheduling implementations to be downloaded and tested in this environment in the future.

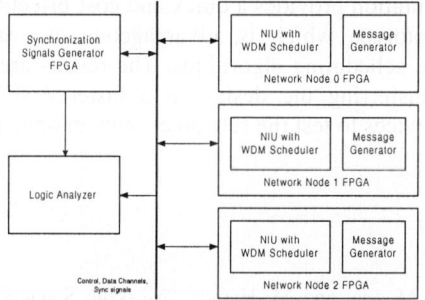

Fig. 2. Testbed for WDM Scheduling Algorithms.

Our current testbed consists of three nodes. We have assumed l, the number of messages from each node that is scheduled at once, to be two (i.e. 6 messages are scheduled at one time). We have also assumed the interconnect fabric consists of 3 data channels and 1 control channel. Although this is a small system, the design can be easily scaled.

4. Performance Analysis

The design was simulated using Altera MaxplusII CAD tools. A simulated performance of 26.80 MHz was obtained. Each NIU fits on one Altera EPF10K20 FPGA with a 93% utilization of logic cells and uses 3 embedded array blocks.

The design is tested using Altera UP1 Education Boards. Each NIU has a unique ID but runs the same scheduling algorithm. The channels are monitored by logic analyzers and the circuits are clocked with a 25MHz oscillator. The observed results are as predicted by correct message sequencing and channel assignment.

The throughput of the prototype scheduler is approximately 60Mbit/s and is scalable along with other design parameters. The number of nodes, the number of messages and the number of bits in a message can be increased to achieve greater throughput without much compromise on the area required.

Overall, the algorithm does not require any complex and computationally intensive hardware architecture. The sub-blocks of the scheduler are composed of mainly simple comparators, small adders, multiplexors and registers. Three embedded array blocks (EAB) are used for storage to implement two FIFOs and one RAM. The Altera EPF10K20 FPGA has 1152 logic units and 6 EABs which are equivalent to approximately 20000 gates [3].

5. Conclusions and Future Work

This paper has presented a hardware implementation of a Wavelength Division Multiplexing On-Line scheduling algorithm on an Altera's EPF10K20 FPGA. The circuit was tested at 25MHz in a network configuration of 3 nodes. This prototype can be easily scaled to accommodate different design parameters.

The FPGA implementation provides a quick and cost-effective solution to building a proof-of-concept prototype which is advantageous in evaluating the hardware complexity of proposed scheduling algorithms. The results are promising and future work may include transferring the design to a faster ASIC implementation and incorporating optical devices to test the scheduler with an optical physical layer.

References

1. B. Hamidzadeh, M. Maode, and M. Hamdi, "Message Sequencing Techniques for On-Line Scheduling in WDM Networks," *Proc. IEEE Globecom '97*, June 1997.
2. B. Hamidzadeh, M. Maode, and M. Hamdi, "Efficient Sequencing Techniques for Variable-Length Messages in WDM Networks" *Journal of Lightwave Technology*, Vol. 17, No. 8, pp. 1309-1319, August 1999.
3. Altera Corporation, *Datasheet: FLEX 10K Embedded Programmable Logic Family version 4.01*, June 1999.

An FPGA Based Scheduling Coprocessor for Dynamic Priority Scheduling in Hard Real-Time Systems

Jens Hildebrandt and Dirk Timmermann

University of Rostock, Institute of Applied Microelectronics and Computer Science,
Richard-Wagner-Str.31, D-18119 Rostock, Germany
{hil, dtim}@e-technik.uni-rostock.de

Abstract. In this paper we present a scheduling coprocessor device for uniprocessor computer systems running a real-time operating system (RTOS). The coprocessor shortens the scheduling time of the operating system by performing dynamic priority computation for all tasks in parallel and making a task selection according to these priorities at a higher speed than a software solution would do. This paper starts with a survey of related work and gives a motivation for the development of the proposed coprocessor architecture. We describe the architecture of our deterministic scheduling coprocessor and an efficient FPGA implementation and give a performance evaluation.

1 Introduction

In multitasking real-time operating systems (RTOS) the scheduler has a twofold impact on system performance. By determining the order of task execution according to a specific scheduling algorithm the scheduler of an RTOS bears a huge part of responsibility for the timeliness of the whole real-time system. Furthermore, the scheduler belongs to the most often called operating system functions. Thus, scheduler function execution time makes up a considerable share of overall operating system overhead. One way to decrease system overhead while using powerful scheduling methods is to support scheduling by dedicated hardware benefiting from higher execution speed and excessive parallelism.

In recent years, some work has been done in the area of hardware based scheduling or, more generally, hardware implemented operating system functions. In [1] and [3] an entire real-time kernel implemented in hardware is described for use in single- and multiprocessor systems. The scheduler incorporated in that device uses static priority preemptive scheduling. A scheduling coprocessor for multiprocessor real-time systems is presented in [2]. This device supports static as well as online scheduling and is designed to accelerate scheduling in the Spring operating system kernel [6]. The architecture proposed in [5] is aimed at a different field of application.. This work describes a scalable Earliest-Deadline-First (EDF) scheduler for ATM networks. Here, the scheduler inserts incoming data packets into an output queue according to deadlines derived form the guaranteed bandwidth of the input channel.

2 The Scheduling Coprocessor Architecture

The scheduling coprocessor proposed in this paper is intended for use in single-processor real-time systems running a real-time operating system (RTOS). The coprocessor supports dynamic priority scheduling and uses the same basic architecture for a whole class of scheduling algorithms by changing only minor functional blocks specific to the desired scheduling method. The coprocessor can easily be adapted to actual requirements (number of tasks, parameter resolution) via design parameters during synthesis. The device periodically computes task priorities and performs a selection by these values of the next task to run. Task switching itself has to be done by software as this operation is very processor specific and depends on the operating system as well. This split of the scheduler ensures a high degree of independence from the hardware and software environment the coprocessor works in.

The basic architecture of the scheduling coprocessor is given in [Fig. 1.]. Task parameters and task state information are loaded into internal registers via a simple interface with data and address lines, chip select, and read/write control lines. A scheduling operation is started by a trigger pulse on the *tck* input. End of operation and hence the availability of a valid scheduling result is signaled by an active interrupt output *sched_int* . A second interrupt output, *err_int*, gets active whenever a deadline violation by one ore more tasks is detected. Following an interrupt a read access to the coprocessor delivers the number of either the next task to execute or, in case of an error interrupt, of a task that will miss or already has missed its deadline.

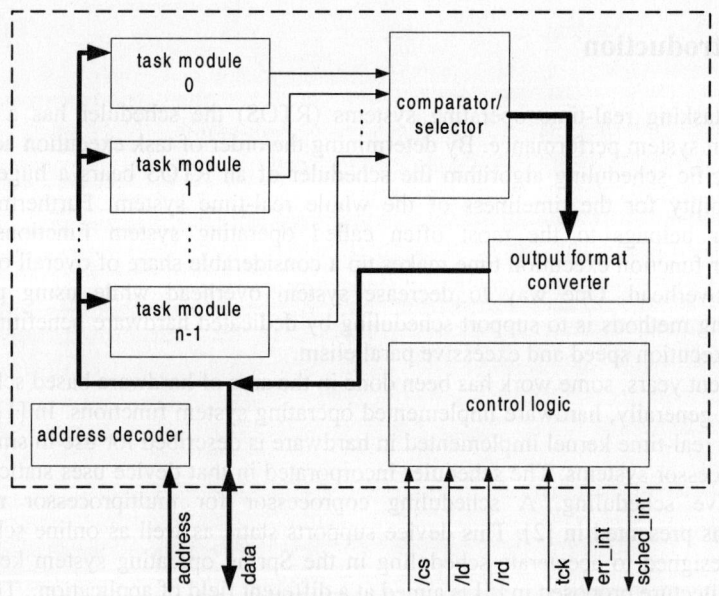

Fig. 1. Basic architecture of the scheduling coprocessor

The main components of the coprocessor are the *task modules* and the *comparator/selector* unit.

Each *task module* represents one task and contains registers for task parameters and task state. Based upon this information the dynamic priority of the task is computed inside the *task module* according to the implemented scheduling algorithm. The computation is started by the external *tck* signal. The result is shifted out of the *task module* serially under control of the *comparator/selector* module.

The maximum number of tasks that can be scheduled is determined by the number of *task modules* contained inside the coprocessor device. Task parameters can be changed during run time. Thus, a time multiplexed usage of one *task module* for two or more tasks which are not active at the same time is possible although this requires a careful system analysis and some additional operating system overhead at run time.

The *comparator/selector* module compares the priority values of tasks computed inside the *task modules* and selects, according to the particular scheduling algorithm, either the smallest or the biggest value. The information which *task module* outputs that value is coded in the output vector of the *comparator/selector*.

The *comparator/selector* works bit-serially, i.e. it compares the priority values of all tasks in parallel by reading them bit by bit. By this, execution time of a compare-and-select operation is independent of the number of tasks actually taking part in the scheduling process. Instead, execution time is determined by the bit-width of priority values which is constant for a given implementation of the coprocessor. This deterministic behavior is important for real-time systems as it eases exact timing analysis of a system.

3 Implementation

The coprocessor architecture described in the previous section was realized in several versions using different scheduling algorithms in a XILINX Virtex FPGA. The most advanced one implements the Enhanced Least-Laxity-First (ELLF) [4] scheduling algorithm. Therefore, *task modules* comprise two preloadable downward counters, one of them for the remaining run time of the task and the other one for the remaining time until deadline. The difference of these values is loaded into a shift register and shifted out to the *comparator/selector* bit by bit. Alternatively, the remaining time until deadline can be loaded into the shift register which is required in a second phase of the compare/select process. Thus, as these two parameters have to be shifted out consecutively, a complete scheduling operation for this implementation of ELLF takes

$$N = 2w+2 \tag{1}$$

clock periods, where w is the bit-width of the laxity and time-until-deadline values. The two extra clock cycles are needed for decreasing the counters and loading the new laxity value into the shift register. In Table 1. execution times and resource requirements for different combinations of maximum number of tasks and parameter resolution of this ELLF implementation are given.

Table 1. Resource requirement and execution time for ELLF implementations with different maximum task numbers and parameter resolutions (using Xilinx Virtex 1000)

Max. tasks	Parameter resolution, bit	Equiv. gate count	Execution time at max. clock rate, μs	Max. clock rate, MHz
16	12	70199	0.750	34.650
16	16	76849	1.005	33.838
20	12	78234	0.774	33.575
20	16	86540	1.019	33.340
32	16	116852	1.079	31.488

4 Conclusions

The scheduling coprocessor architecture described in the previous sections is suitable for implementations of different dynamic priority scheduling algorithms. It provides a fast and deterministic means for dynamic priority computation and hence makes this algorithms effectively usable for real-time operating systems. Usage of FPGA devices makes it even possible to configure the scheduling coprocessor at run time for different algorithms according to the actual requirements of the operating system. Due to the universal architecture, this can be done without changing the software routines that access the coprocessor.

References

1. Adomat, J. et al.: Real-Time Kernel in Hardware RTU: A Step Towards Deterministic and High-Performance Real-Time Systems. Proceedings of the Euromicro RTS'96 Workshop. IEEE Computer Society, Los Alamitos (1996) 164-168
2. Burleson, W. et al.: The Spring Scheduling Coprocessor: A Scheduling Accelerator. IEEE Transactions on Very Large Scale Integration (VLSI) Systems, Vol. 7, No. 1, (March 1999) 38-47
3. Furunäs, J. et al.: RTU94 – Real Time Unit 1994 – Reference Manual. Technical Report, Mälardalens Real-Time Research Centre (1998)
4. Hildebrandt, J., Golatowski, F., Timmermann, D.: Scheduling Coprocessor for Enhanced Least-Laxity-First Scheduling in Hard Real-Time Systems. Proceedings of the 11th Euromicro Conference on Real Time Systems. IEEE Computer Society, Los Alamitos (1999) 208-215
5. Kim, B.K., Shin, K.G.: Scalable Hardware EDF Scheduler for ATM Networks. Proceedings of the 18th IEEE Real-Time Systems Symposium. IEEE Computer Society, Los Alamitos (1997) 210-218
6. Stankovic, J., Ramamritham, K.: The spring kernel: A new paradigm for real-time systems. IEEE Transactions on Software Engineering. IEEE Computer Society, Los Alamitos (May 1992) 54-71

Formal Verification of a Reconfigurable Microprocessor

Sergej Sawitzki[1], Jens Schönherr[2], Rainer G. Spallek[1], and Bernd Straube[2]

[1] Institute of Computer Engineering, Department of Computer Science, TU Dresden,
D-01062 Dresden, Germany, {sawitzki, rgs}@ite.inf.tu-dresden.de,
[2] Fraunhofer Institut Integrierte Schaltungen (IIS), EAS Dresden, Zeunerstraße 38
D-01069 Dresden, Germany, {schoenherr, straube}@eas.iis.fhg.de

1 Introduction

The increasing acceptance of reconfigurable logic in form of FPGAs or CPLDs has caused new research activities in the field of processor architecture, the reconfigurable processors. The basic idea consists in combining the flexibility of reconfigurable logic with the transparent and well-known instruction set programming model. In this way critical parts of the application can be implemented directly in hardware. It has been shown that reconfigurable microprocessors are able either to achieve speed-ups or to improve the cost/performance ratio for a broad range of applications [1].

The correctness of processors is a key for their application. Simulation methods, that are used traditionally to verify processor designs, do not guarantee the absence of design errors. Formal verification methods, instead, use proofs in the mathematical sense and, therefore, check the design completely. We assume a processor description at the register transfer (RT) level as design under verification. To represent the structure and behavior of the processor, we use a quantifier-free, i.e. implicit all quantified, first-order logic with equality. Arithmetic functions are represented by their symbol only, i.e. those functions are uninterpreted. The validity of formulas in quantifier-free first-order logic can be checked automatically by decision procedures like SVC (Stanford Validity Checker [2]). In addition, SVC contains algorithms to solve linear inequalities, linear algebra, propositions about bit vectors and about infinite arrays.

Many publications deal with the verification of the correct handling of hazards by the pipeline control [3]. In contrary, this paper demonstrates the verification of the data path including the non-pipeline-specific control.

Formal verification was not considered as a design check approach for most reconfigurable processors. In the following sections, a case study of the formal verification of CoMPARE (Common Minimal Processor with Reconfigurable Extension, [4]) is described. A long version of this paper could be found in [5].

2 The Subject of the Study: CoMPARE

CoMPARE is a RISC-like architecture with a reconfigurable extension that maintains close compatibility with the usual programming model. To simplify the design neither caches nor FPU and only 16 instructions and 16 registers on 8 bit wide, three-stage-pipelined data paths were implemented. CoMPARE uses a reconfigurable processing unit (RPU), which is a conventional ALU augmented by an LUT-based configurable array unit (CAU) used to implement additional, customized instructions. The architecture differs from the conventional RISC processor structure only in the use of a reconfigurable processing unit in the place of the standard ALU. The hardwired instructions of the ALU are always available, but it only needs to provide the most basic instructions. Additional operations useful to accelerate different applications are provided by the CAU. CoMPARE executes the instructions in a 3-stage pipelined manner. In the first phase the Fetch-and-Decode-Unit (FDU) accesses the instruction memory to fetch the next instruction. In the second stage the operands are fetched from the register file and processed corresponding to the OP-Code, i.e. an ALU/CAU operation or a memory access. Data memory is separated from the instruction memory, so no pipeline hazards can occur at this point. The third stage finally composes the results from the hardwired and reconfigurable logic and writes them back into the register file. Since the pipeline is only 3 stages deep and no control circuit for pipeline hazards is required we desist from a check for pipeline hazards. Instead, we focus to the verification of the data path and the logic that controls it.

3 Formal Verification of the Data Path

Verification Approach. In this paper we describe the verification of the data path, whereby the arithmetic functions and the CAU-behavior are abstracted by uninterpreted functions. The proof of correctness of the implementation of the arithmetic functions and the circuit implemented by the CAU is another verification task that is not explained here.

Correctness Condition. The desired behavior of each instruction is often given in hardware description notation (HDN) [6]. The HDN represents the programmers view of the processor and describes for each instruction the change of the registers and memories that are caused by this instruction. The registers and memories that are mentioned in the HDN are called visible (for the programmer) while all the other registers of the processor are called invisible. The behavior of all invisible registers of the processor is not specified and depends on the implementation only.

To check the correctness of the processor implementation it must be checked that for each instruction the visible registers and memories change (or keep) their values as described in the HDN. More formally, for each instruction it is to check that the description of the instruction word (iw), the configuration of the CAU ($ccau$), and the description of the circuit behavior (cb) projected to the visible registers implies the expected behavior of the visible registers (ib) of the instruction. The correctness condition for each instruction is summarized in formula (1) where v represents values of the visible registers and memories and

i represents values of the wires and invisible registers.

$$\forall v.\exists i(iw(v) \land ccau(i) \land cb(v,i)) \rightarrow ib(v) \tag{1}$$

Formula 1 can be transformed into the equivalent formula 2.

$$\forall v.\forall i.(iw(v) \land ccau(i) \land cb(v,i)) \rightarrow ib(v) \tag{2}$$

As it will be shown in the next subsections, the formulae for iw, $ccau$, cb, and ib are in quantifier-free first-order logic. Hence, the verification can be carried out by proving the validity of (2) using decision procedures like SVC.

Description of the Circuit Behavior. In our approach, the behavior of the processor is derived from the RT level description. The values of the registers and wires of the processor are represented by variables. To distinguish between the values of the visible registers before and after execution of the instruction for each visible register x an additional variable x_after is necessary. To abstract from the overlapped execution of instructions in the pipeline the circuit is unrolled by replacing the latches between pipeline-stages by wires.

For each output of a functional block an equation between the variable that is assigned to this output and an expression, that describes the behavior of the functional block depending on its inputs, is created. The behavior of the whole processor is described by the conjunction of the equations for each variable.

Specification of the Instruction Word. For each instruction it has to be described which bits of the instruction word contain source and destination registers, immediate values, and the OP-Code. In our approach dedicated variables are assigned to the parts of the instruction word. These variables are used to describe the specified behavior.

Specification of the CAU Configuration. In case of instructions which use the CAU it must be specified, which operation is executed in the CAU, which of the inputs is used for this operation and which part of the CAU output register contains the results.

Specification of the Expected Behavior. The expected behavior of each instruction is described by the values of the visible registers after the execution of the instruction. For the formal verification it is important that this description is complete. Therefore the value of all visible registers and memories after the execution of the instruction must be specified, even if they are not expected to change. Additionally, all aspects of the behavior must be written explicitly, even if they are given in HDN implicitly.

4 Results and Conclusion

The verification was carried out for each instruction of CoMPARE with SVC used as decision procedure. During the verification of CoMPARE some problems could be detected. While specified behavior is usually implemented correct formal verification was able to find mainly undesired side-effects of instructions:

- The reconfigurable ADDC (add then compare) instruction changes a register that is not specified as a destination register.

Table 1. Verification Runtime Values (CPU-time/h:min:s)

	Number	Min	Max	Sum	Avg
Hardwired Instructions	16	0:1:29.0	5:08:49.0	21:31:51.0	1:20:44.4
Reconfigurable Instructions	9	1:13:14.0	47:10:57.0	116:24:35.0	12:56:03.9

- The jump instruction does increment PC instead of load the PC by the destination address.
- The STOR, BE, BLU, and BL instructions write to the register specified as a source operand location.

The runtime on a Sun Enterprise 450 (250 MHz) for the verification is summarized in Table 1. As reconfigurable instructions only those were verified, that were used in the algorithms mentioned in [4]. The experiences in the verification of CoMPARE have shown that accuracy of specification in conventional design flows is not sufficient. From the formal verification point of view HDN is not correct because it makes implicit assumptions about the behavior of visible registers. In case of CoMPARE these are:

- if nothing is said about the PC, then the PC is incremented
- all registers and memory cells that are not destinations do not change
- GPR 0 never changes its value (zero), even if it is used as a destination

Besides of that, for the verification of the instructions which use the CAU the configuration of the CAU must be considered as well.

To sum up it can be stated that conventional methods for formal verification could be adapted in context of reconfigurability. Although the verification took a plenty of time, it is a useful approach for reconfigurable processors.

References

1. Rupp, C.R., Landguth, M., Garverick, T., Gomersall, E., Holt, H., Arnold, J.M., Gokhale, M.: The NAPA Adaptive Processing Architecture. In Proc. of FCCM'98, pp. 28–37, Napa, CA, 1998.
2. Barrett, C.W., Dill, D.L., Levitt, J.R.: Validity Checking for Combinations of Theories with Equality. In Proc. of FMCAD'96, Springer-Verlag, 1996.
3. Burch, J.R., Dill, D.L.: Automatic verification of pipelined microprocessors control, In Proc. of CAV '94, pp. 68–80, Stanford, CA, Springer-Verlag, 1994.
4. Sawitzki, S., Gratz, A., Spallek, R.G.: CoMPARE: A Simple Reconfigurable Processor Architecture Exploiting Instruction Level Parallelism. In Proc. of PART'98, pp. 213–224, Springer-Verlag, 1998.
5. Sawitzki, S., Spallek, R.G., Schönherr, J., Straube, B.: Formal Verification for Microprocessors with Extendable Instruction Set. In Proc. of ASAP 2000, IEEE, 2000.
6. Hennessy, J.L., Patterson, D.A.: Computer Architecture: A Quantitative Approach, 2nd ed., Morgan Kaufmann Publishers, San Francisco CA, 1996.

The Role of the Embedded Memories in the Implementation of Artificial Neural Networks

Rafael Gadea[1], Vicente Herrero[2], Angel Sebastia[1], and Antonio Mocholí[1]

[1] Department of Electronic Engineering, Universidad Politecnica de Valencia
46022 Valencia, Spain
{rgadea, asebasti, amocholi}@eln.upv.es
[2] Department of Electronic Engineering, Universidad Politecnica de Valencia
46022 Valencia, Spain
vherbos@teleco.upv.es

Abstract. The paper describes the implementation of a systolic array for a multilayer perceptron on different FPGA architectures with a hardware-friendly learning algorithm: Pipelined On-line Backpropagation. By exploiting the embedded memories of certain families alongside the projection used in the systolic architecture, we can implement very large interconnection layers. These physical and architectural features – together with the combination of FPGA reconfiguration properties with a design flow based on generic VHDL – permit us to create an easy, flexible and fast method of designing a complete ANN on a single FPGA. The result offers a high degree of parallelism and fast performance.

1 Introduction

In recent years it has been shown that neural networks are capable of providing solutions to many problems in the areas of pattern recognition, signal processing, time series analysis, etc. While software simulations are very useful for investigating the capabilities of neural network models and creating new algorithms, hardware implementations are essential for taking full advantage of the inherent parallelism of neural networks.

Traditionally, ANNs have been implemented directly on special-purpose digital and analogue hardware. More recently, ANNs have been implemented with reconfigurable FPGAs. Although FPGAs do not achieve the power, clock rate, or gate density, of custom chips; they do provide a speed-up of several orders of magnitude compared to software simulation [1]. A principal restriction of this approach until now has been the limited logic density of FPGAs.

This paper presents an advance in one basic respect with regard to previously reported neural implementations on FPGA – that is, the use of embedded RAM memories to store the synaptic weights. This type of solution is determined by the projection used in the systolic architecture and it is chosen because it considerably improves the number of Processing Elements (PE) mapped on a single FPGA. However, the design of memory and arithmetic resources of the synaptic nodes is complicated by the fact that forward and backward passes of on-line pipeline backpropagation algorithm for different training patterns must be processed in parallel [2][3]. In [4] and [5] we show that this parallelism, referred to as "forward-backward parallelism", performs well in convergence time and generalisation rates. The better hardware performance of on-line pipeline backpropagation is shown in terms of speed of learning. These results were obtained through RTL models of RAM memories, and therefore independent of the technology. In this paper, our main purpose will be to implement these synaptic weights with embedded RAM memories of different FPGAs. These must be read and written simultaneously by the forward and backward phases of our algorithm.

In Section 2 we show the different solutions for the implementation of synapses and weights in Xilinx and Altera devices.

2. Weight Memory

Possibilities in FPGAs

We study the following alternatives for implementing the weight memory of the synapses of a multilayer perceptron:

Table 1. Alternatives for implementation

FAMILY	Recourse	Organization
XILINX	CLB o Slices	16x1 (4000 &Virtex)
	Block SelecRAM+	256x16 (VIRTEX)
ALTERA	EAB	256x8 (FLEX10K)
	EAB	256x16 (FLEX10KE)

All these alternatives (except for the case of EAB of FLEX10K) can implemented with synchronous dual-port RAM.

Limitations in FPGAs

When we want to give a real solution for the weight storage in multilayer perceptrons with the on-line pipeline backpropagation algorithm we can make the following conclusions:

CLB or Slices (XILINX): If we employ the DP_RAM Macro from LogiBLOX we can implement our dual-port RAM for the weight storage without functional limitations. The worse case, when the forward and backward addresses are the same, is resolved without conflicts in data storage.

The only problem with this solution is the inherent problem of using distributed RAM blocks. These small RAM blocks must be connected together to make weight storage of manageable size. For example, if we want to implement a memory module of a vertical synapse of our "alternating orthogonal systolic array", we need N1O CLBs for weight storage (being N1O the number of neurons in the first hidden layer). These CLBs are connected together using multiplexers implemented with more logic blocks. These extra multiplexers cause extra delay and extra routing problems, which slow down the weight storage block. In contrast, non-distributed resources from the following can be used to implement large, dedicated blocks of RAM that eliminate these timing and routing concerns.

Block SelecRAM+(XILINX-Virtex): If we employ Block SelecRAM+ we cannot implement our dual-port RAM for the weight storage in one cycle. This dual-port RAM can perform two operations simultaneously (read-read, read-write, write-write), but in the last two cases, the address for these two operations cannot be the same. Evidently, the case write-write is not relevant for our problem, but the case of read-write is fundamental for a one-cycle solution.

Our contributed solution works in two cycles. In the first, we perform the forward and backward read operations. In the second, we perform the update write operation.

Embedded Array Block (ALTERA): If we employ EAB we must distinguish between the flex10K family, and the flex10E family. The embedded array blocks of flex10KE cannot implement our dual-port RAM for the weight storage in one cycle. This RAM can perform only one operation (read or write) in each cycle, and therefore we need three cycles to perform the necessary operations.

The FLEX10KE EAB can act in dual-port or single-port mode. When in dual-port mode, separate clocks can be used for EAB read and write sections, which allows the EAB to be written and read, as well as different rates. Additionally, the read and write sections can work with the same address, which is the main issue for our application.

To perform the second read operation we propose one of two solutions: either using another cycle and multiplexing in time; or storing the weights in duplicate. Of course, this second solution requires two EABs for synapse: one for the forward phase and another for the backward phase.

Resource Usage in FPGAs

The results of the above alternatives for the implementation of weight memory are summarised in Table 2, assuming that the number of storage weights is 20 and the resolution of these weights is 16 bits.

Table 2. Resource usage of synapse memory.

Dual Port RAM, two cycles,		Dual Port RAM, one cycle,		
Flex10KE	Virtex	XC4000E	Virtex	Flex10KE
10K30E	XCV300	XC4010E	XCV300	10K30E
28 Logic cells + 1 EAB	8 Slices + 1 Block RAM	28 CLB + 32 CLB	25 Slices + 32 Slices	21 Logic cells + 2 EAB

3. Conclusions

The role of the embedded array memories of FPGAs for the implementation of the synaptic weights in ANNs has been summarized. The future of the FPGAs is linked to the increase in the number of embedded memories in the new devices. Therefore, it is important to understand and delimit their possibilities, especially for weight storage in our pipelined on-line backpropagation algorithm.

References

[1] S. Hauck, "The Roles of FPGAs in Reprogrammable Systems" *Proceedings of the IEEE*, 86(4), April 1998, pp. 615-638.
[2] C.R. Rosemberg, and G. Belloch, "An Implementation of Network Learning on the Connection Machine", *Connectionist Models an their Implications*, D. Waltz and J Feldman, eds., Ablex, Norwood, NJ. 1988
[3] A. Petrowski, G. Dreyfus, and C. Girault, "Performance Analysis of a Pipelined Backpropagation Parallel Algorithm", *IEEE Transaction on Neural Networks*, Vol.4 , no. 6, November 1993, pp. 970-981.
[4] R. Gadea, A. Mocholí, "Systolic Implementation of a Pipelined On-Line Backpropagation", *Proc.of the NeuroMIcro'99*, April 1999, pp. 387-394.
[5] R. Gadea, A. Mocholí, "Forward-backward Parallelism in On-Line Backpropagation", *International Work- Conference on Artificial and Natural Neural Networks*, June 1999, pp. 157-165.

Programmable System Level Integration Brings System-on-Chip Design to the Desktop

Guy Lecurieux Lafayette

ATMEL European Marketing Manager - Programmable Logic
2, Allee Maryse Bastie, Orlytech
91781 Wissous Cedex, France

Abstract. This paper introduces a new family of standard products, called FPSLIC FPSLIC (Field Programmable System Level Integration Circuits), and associated design tools for programmable SoC.

1. Introduction

By 1985 the first Field Programmable Gate Arrays (FPGAs) were introduced. Xilinx developed a family of standard user-configurable products utilizing industry standard SRAM technology, and a (relatively) low cost design tool that for the first time made Gate Array technology available to virtually any design engineer who had access top a desktop computer.

Today the chip industry has progressed from putting thousands of gates of logic into a single chip to putting an entire system on a chip (SOC). This means integrating not only the programmable and ASIC logic on a single IC, but also including the processor, memory and analog functions as well.

A new family of standard products, called FPSLIC (Field Programmable System Level Integration Circuits) and associated design tools have been introduced by ATMEL to address programmable SOC.

2. FPSLIC Architecture

A single FPSLIC (shown in figure 1) contains embedded 10K or 20K or 40K gates FPGA, a high performance 30+ MIPS AVR® RISC microcontroller with hardware multiplier; a 36K byte block of selectable instruction code/data SRAM; a 2-wire serial interface, two UARTs, two 8 bits timer/counters, one 16 bits timer/counters, a watchdog timer and a real-time clock and interrupts.

2.1 High-Performance Embedded RISC AVR Microcontroller

FPSLIC devices contain Atmel's 8-bit RISC AVR MCU with throughput in excess of 30 MIPS. The AVR has 127 16-bit fixed-length instructions that have been optimized so that 90% of all MCU operations can be handled by a single instruction. A two-stage pipeline and separate addresses for load and store operations enable single cycle instruction execution. Thirty-two 8-bit registers allow the CPU to access multiple data simultaneously, eliminating the need for most data transfer operations, thereby enabling much smaller code size.

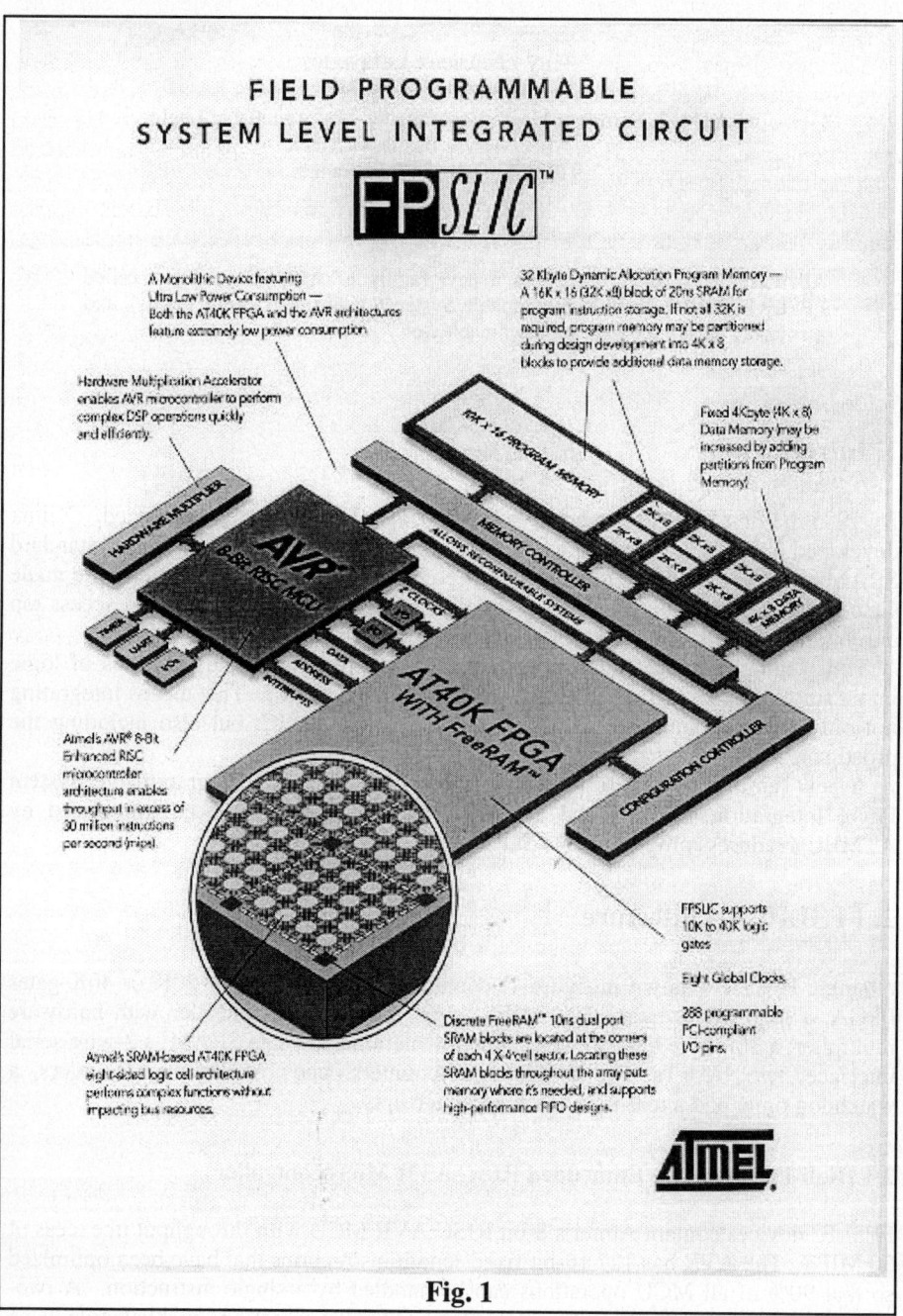

Fig. 1

The AVR can actually reconfigure the entire contents of the FPGA, as well as individual elements of the FPGA doing partial reconfiguration. These FPSLIC features enable reconfigurable peripherals on-demand, as well as adaptive hardware including logic acceleration, adaptive filters for DSP, reconfigurable cross point switches and reconfigurable network processors, and many other possibilities

2.2 The Embedded FPGA Contains All of the Features of Atmel's AT40K FPGA.

The AT40K FPGA architecture consists of symmetrical blocks of four logic cells on a side (16 cells per block). AT40K logic cells have eight sides and allow direct orthogonal and diagonal connection to contiguous cells on all eight sides. This effectively doubles the number of cells that can be directly connected to each other.

The AT40K logic cell consists of two 3-input look-up tables (LUTs), a fourth input, an upstream AND gate, a register, a clock and preset, and a registered or non-registered internal feedback. Output can be registered or tri-stated. AT40K FPGAs can be partially or fully reconfigured without affecting system operation. Using Atmel's patented CacheLogic®

2.3. 32Kbyte Dynamic Allocation SRAM

FPSLIC devices have a 16K x 16 block (32K x 8) of 20 ns SRAM for program instruction storage. If all 32K bytes of SRAM is not required for instruction SRAM, instruction memory space can be allocated to the data memory space in 4K x 8 blocks. The SRAM is partitioned during design development into instruction and data memory. There is an additional 4K x 8 of data memory available in the FPSLIC devices in addition to the 32K byte dynamic allocation memory.

In addition, the interface between the FPGA and the AVR has been implemented The same is true of the memory interface and controller. Peripheral functions implemented in the FPGA can be directly mapped into 16 addresses into the AVR I/O map.

The data memory is analogous to dual port RAM, in that both the FPGA and the AVR can access it.

3. FPSLIC Design Tools

System Designer includes a system design manager, synthesis, hardware and software simulation, and Co-verification.

The design manager seamlessly integrates all the design tools, databases and flows required for FPSLIC implementation. The design manager steps the user through each stage of the design process, from Verilog/VHDL design entry for the hardware (FPGA), through synthesis, place & route, and simulation, as well as guiding the user through the microcontroller design process and verification, as well as co-simulation and verification between the software and hardware aspects of the system.

Included in the FPSLIC design suite are the AT40K series FPGA design software, Exemplar synthesis compiler, Model Technology hardware simulator, AVR studio and Seamless co-verification tools, powered by Mentor Graphics. In addition, the tools can be adapted to work with addional microcontroller and processor cores, as well as different variations of the FPSLIC architecture.

3.1 Co-verification

FPSLIC System Designer incorporates a co-verification back plane, effectively connecting the FPGA hardware simulator to the microcontroller instruction set simulator. The use of co-verification effectively eliminates the need for an in-circuit emulator (ICE) by facilitating the verification process. This is possible by allowing the designer to make changes to the hardware/software and seeing the resultant interaction and effect on the software/hardware. This is all done on a desktop PC operating under Windows or NT.

3.2 FPSLIC Configuration

The entire FPSLIC device is SRAM-based, which brings the benefit of unlimited reconfiguration and update capability – for both the FPGA hardware and AVR microcontroller software. The AVR microcontroller can actually reprogram all, or parts of the FPGA – in system, on-the-fly, in real time. In order to support this programming ability, it is necessary to store the FPSLIC configuration data (instruction set for the AVR and FPGA) in a non-volatile external configuration memory.

On Applying Software Development Best Practice to FPGAs in Safety-Critical Systems

A. Hilton and J. Hall

The Open University

Abstract. New standards for developing safety-critical systems require the developer to demonstrate the safety and correctness of the programmable logic in such systems. In this paper we adapt software development best practice to developing high-integrity FPGA programs.

1 Introduction

Programmable logic devices are increasingly important components of complex and safety-critical systems. Standards such as the emerging UK Defence Standard 00-54 [6] and IEC 61508 [3] now require developers to reason about the safety and correctness of programmable logic devices in such systems. In addition, programming such devices is becoming more like programming conventional microprocessors in terms of program size, complexity, and the need to clarify a program's purpose and structure.

This paper looks at existing best practice in software development and shows how it might be adapted to programmable logic devices without incurring undue overhead in system development time. It does not consider the issue of testing programmable logic programs.

2 Safety Standards

A *safety-critical system* is a collection of components acting together where interruption of the normal function of one or more components may cause injury or loss of life. The *integrity* of such a system is measured in terms of the probability of total or partial failure. [3] defines four integrity levels, SIL 1, SIL 2, SIL 3 and SIL 4, with the highest level (SIL 4) specifying a frequency of less than 1 failure per 10^8 hours of operation.

Since many safety-critical systems affect public safety, governmental and associated oversight agencies have drawn up standards documents for the development of safety-critical systems. Newer standards are starting to require the rigorous demonstration of safety for programmable logic components that has been required for software for many years.

UK Defence Standard 00-54 [6] is a new interim standard for the use of safety-related electronic hardware (SREH) in UK defence equipment. It relates to systems developed under a safety systems document such as IEC 61508 [3].

Def Stan 00-54 is appropriate if an electronic component of the system is identified as having a safety integrity level of SIL 1 or greater. The techniques described in the document are to be used to analyse complex electronic designs for systematic failures. The standard contains the following recommendations which are of particular interest to us.

> (§12.2.1) A formally defined language which supports mathematically based reasoning and the proof of safety properties shall be used to specify a custom design;
> (§13.4.1) Safety requirements shall be incorporated explicitly into the Hardware Specification using a formal representation; and
> (§13.4.4) Correspondence between the Hardware Specification and the design implementation shall be demonstrated by analytical means, subject to assumptions about physical properties of the implementation.

where 'custom design' refers to the non-standard components of the electronic component under examination, and in particular to an FPGA's program data.

Def Stan 00-54 also notes that widely used standard HDLs without formal semantics, such as VHDL and Verilog, present compliance problems if used as a design capture language: Z [7] is suggested as an example of a suitable language.

Def Stan 00-54 is interim, and may well change at formal issue as did Def Stan 00-55. Nevertheless, the concerns which it expresses about existing practices and its suggestions for process improvements are worth careful scrutiny. A formal language which supports reasoning about programmable logic behaviour will assist developers to comply with this standard; without the ability to reason formally, it is not possible to meet the requirements of §12.2.1, §13.4.1 and §13.4.4.

3 Applying Software Best Practice to Programmable Logic

Programmable logic devices, FPGAs in particular, may be built into safety-critical systems when the system is first designed or as part of a re-engineering of an older system. Such incorporation brings with it a need to be able to reason formally about safety and correctness of programs executing on the FPGA; as noted above, Def Stan 00-54 requires this analytic reasoning. Here we have three distinct needs for a semantics of FPGA programs, to be able to:

- demonstrate that programs satisfy their specifications;
- refine high-level designs into code while demonstrating semantic equivalence between them; and
- reason about behaviour at the interface between software and programmable logic.

We develop these points in the rest of this section, with the objective of outlining a method to produce a correct FPGA program from a high-level specification.

3.1 Demonstrating FPGA Program Correctness

There are two choices for showing that a FPGA's program satisfies its specification. The more common, *verification*, is 'show that the implementation does what the requirements say'. One possibility is to use 'model-checking', automatic checking of finite state specifications against a given implementation. The key weakness of model checking is that it is time-consuming, and usually will only be able to tell you *whether* your system is correct, not where it is weak.

In this paper we adopt the second strategy which is often initially harder: 'develop the requirements into an implementation'. This development is the process of *refinement*; step-by-step application of a set of laws which transform an abstract specification into a concrete implementation. This approach requires more 'up-front' investment of time and effort. However, the correctness of the implementation with respect to the specification is guaranteed, excepting the possibility of human error in the refinement steps.

Both of these approaches require the ability to reason analytically about FPGA programs. We address this in the following section.

3.2 Analytical Reasoning

Synchronous Receptive Process Theory (SRPT), described in [1], was developed from Josephs' Receptive Process Theory [4] with the motivation of being able to reason about synchronous (clocked) events. It specifies a system as a set of events Σ, and a set of processes P_X each of which has a set of inputs $I \subseteq \Sigma$ and output events $O \subseteq \Sigma$ where $I \cap O = \emptyset$. Processes are defined in terms of output events in reaction to input events. SRPT has a denotational semantics expressed in terms of the *traces* of each process. Each trace $t : \mathbb{N} \to \mathbb{P}(I \cup O)$ specifies a possible sequence of sets of events for the process at each tick of the global clock.

The structure of a FPGA can be considered as a collection of small SRPT processes reacting to input signals to produce output signals, when cells are viewed as processes and their routing is viewed as describing which signals pass to which process. In our work to date we have demonstrated a method of proof that a FPGA cell (modelled by an SRPT process) satisfies a specification in terms of event sequences in its traces.

3.3 Design Refinement

We wish to refine a FPGA program design from the Z specification language to an implementation, maintaining demonstrable correctness. Refining the specification directly to SRPT is possible but hard work. A useful stepping stone would be a software language that could act as the target of refinement from Z and then be compiled into SRPT processes. One candidate is SPARK Ada [2], a subset of the Ada language. SPARK Ada has a formal semantics defined in Z, tool support from the SPARK Examiner static analysis tool, and the strong type system of Ada. SPARK Ada is also strongly recommended for use in developing SIL 4 systems.

Given an SRPT description of the program, we could attempt to compile it into VHDL, but maintaining correctness would be hard. VHDL lacks a semantics, with vendor implementations differing significantly. FPGA netlists will vary in semantics depending on the target device. One intermediate option is to use a language such as Pebble [5]. Pebble is synchronous, low-level enough to compile to VHDL or netlist format without too high a probability of serious compiler error, and high-level enough to abstract away from device dependencies. SRPT could be mapped directly onto Pebble with minimal effort.

This development process is illustrated in Figure 1.

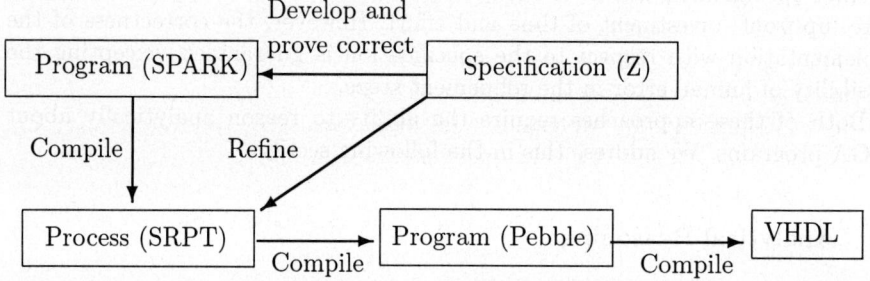

Fig. 1. Development Process

3.4 Conclusion

We have seen how a forthcoming safety standard places requirements for analytical demonstration of the safety of systems incorporating programmable logic. We have identified key technologies and methods for such analysis, and proposed a process for developing programs for PLDs to a high standard of integrity.

References

1. Janet E. Barnes. A mathematical theory of synchronous communication. Technical report, Oxford University Computing Laboratory, 1993.
2. Jonathan Garnsworthy and Bernard Carré. SPARK - an annotated Ada subset for safety-critical systems. *Proceedings of Baltimore Tri-Ada Conference*, 1990.
3. International Electrotechnical Commission. *Functional Safety of Electrical / Electronic / Programmable Electronic Safety-Related Systems, IEC Standard 61508*, March 2000.
4. Mark Josephs. Receptive process theory. *Acta Informatica*, 29:17–31, 1992.
5. Wayne Luk and Steve McKeever. Pebble — a language for parametrised and reconfigurable hardware. In R. Hartenstein and A Keevallik, editors, *Proceedings of the 8th International Workshop on Field Programmable Logic (FPL'98)*, number 1482 in Lecture Notes In Computer Science, pages 9–18. Springer-Verlag, September 1998.
6. Requirements for safety related electronic hardware in defence equipment, March 1999. Interim Defence Standard 00-54 Issue 1.
7. J. M. Spivey. *The Z Notation: A Reference Manual*. Prentice-Hall, 2nd edition, 1992.

Pre-route Assistant:
A Routing Tool for Run-Time Reconfiguration

Brandon Blodget

Xilinx Inc.
2100 Logic Drive
San Jose, California 95124
Brandon.Blodget@xilinx.com

Abstract. *Pre-Route Assistant* is a web utility that helps pre-route *JBits* [1] Run-Time Parameterizable Cores (RTPCores). Given the connection points, it produces the *JBits* calls to turn on the corresponding wires, that the user can cut and paste into their *JBits* code. Pre-Routed cores are useful for Run-Time Reconfigurable (RTR) applications, for they can be written directly to a device bitstream without additional routing overhead. Having a library of Parameterizable, Pre-Routed cores gives RTR applications much more flexibility and power. This paper introduces *Pre-Route Assistant*, explores why pre-routing is useful for RTR.

1 Introduction

Run-Time Reconfiguration (RTR) is part of the Reconfigurable Computing Field, which performs circuit logic and routing customization at run-time [2]. The traditional approach to RTR using FPGA's is to pre-generate bitstreams and then swap them in and out at run time. Since the bitstreams are pre-generated this limits the ability of the RTR application to adapt. Another RTR strategy, sometimes called Dynamic RTR, is to hold off making the bitstream until it is actually needed. Thus, these bitstreams are generated at run time and therefore can make the application more adaptable. The faster these bitstreams can be generated the more useful Dynamic RTR becomes. *Pre-Route Assistant* assists the Dynamic RTR designer by making it easier to pre-route *JBits* [1] RTPCores. Pre-routed cores can be implemented faster at run-time.

Pre-Route Assistant is a web utility that generates *JBits* code to route RTPCores together. It uses *JRoute* [3] as a backend engine to generate the *JBits* code. *Pre-Route Assistant* allows the user to specify the points they want routed together by entering Java and *JRoute* statements into a HTML textarea field. The users then clicks a button and *Pre-Route Assistant* generates *JBits* calls that will route these points without contention. The user can then cut and paste these calls directly into their *JBits* code.

Section 2 gives a brief overview of *JBits* and *JRoute*. Section 3 introduces *Pre-Route Assistant*. Section 4 elaborates on the benefits of *Pre-Route Assistant*. Section 5 compares *Pre-Route Assistant* to using the *JRoute* API directly in RTR designs. Finally, Section 6 contains ideas for improving *Pre-Route Assistant* and concluding remarks.

2 Background

2.1 JBits

The Xilinx *JBits* bitstream interface is a set of Java classes that provide an application program interface for the Xilinx FPGA bitstream. This interface operates on either bitstreams generated by Xilinx design tools, or on bitstreams read back from actual hardware. This provides the capability of designing, modifying and dynamically modifying circuits in Xilinx Virtex$^{(tm)}$ FPGA device series.

2.2 JRoute

JRoute [3] provides an application programming interface (API) for routing of Xilinx FPGA devices. This API is built on top of *JBits*. Unlike the standard Xilinx tools, *JRoute* can perform the routing at run-time. This is because *JRoute* is a point to point router. *JRoute* routes each route one at a time, avoiding contention as it goes.

It is possible to specify routing directly with *JBits*, but this requires that the designer set every routing pip explicitly. *JRoute* offers a higher level abstraction. With *JRoute* the designer need only specify the source pin and the sinks and JRoute figures out which resources to use. *JRoute* can also route port to port connections between RTPCores. *JRoute* has a resource database which it uses to avoid contention.

3 Pre-route Assistant

Pre-Route Assistant is a web utility that generates *JBits* code to route RTPCores. It uses *JRoute* [3] as a backend engine to generate the *JBits* code. *Pre-Route Assistant* allows the user to enter Java and *JRoute* statements into a HTML textarea field.

There are two main types of *JRoute* statements, pin definitions, and routing statements. Pin definitions define end points. Routing statements define connections between endpoints. The following are examples of pin definition statements:

```
Pin src  = new Pin(5, 5, Wires.S1_YQ);
Pin sink = new Pin(6, 5, Wires.S0F1);
```

In the above example src and sink are defined to be of type Pin. Src is initialized to be the Slice 1 YQ output of the CLB in row 5, col 5. Sink is initialized to be the Slice 0 F1 input of the CLB in row 6, col 5. These two pins can be routed together with the following routing statement:

```
router.route(src, sink);
```

When the user clicks on the "Try It!" button, *Pre-Route Assistant* outputs the following:

```
jbits.set( 5, 5, OUT2.OUT2, OUT2.S1_YQ );
jbits.set( 5, 5, OutMuxToSingle.OUT2_TO_SINGLE_NORTH6,
           OutMuxToSingle.ON );
jbits.set( 6, 5, S0F1.S0F1, S0F1.SINGLE_SOUTH6 );
```

The above are low level *JBits* commands which set specific routing resources that will route from src to sink. They can be copied directly into *JBits* RTPCore source code.

4 Benefits of Pre-route Assistant

Pre-Route Assistant can be used in conjunction with *JBits* to create pre-routed run-time parameterizable cores (RTPCores). These pre-routed RTPCores can be thought of as hardmacros that contain both placement and routing information. These RTPCores are not really "hard" however, since they can be moved and stretched based on parameters specified at run-time.

Routing is a non-trivial problem for traditional static FPGA design. Large designs sometimes run out of routing resources or cannot meet timing requirements. When they route successfully, it often takes them a long time. Dynamic RTR demands for routing are even stricter than for static design. In short, Dynamic RTR demands instantaneous, guaranteed routing. Design time routing via *Pre-Route Assistant* meets these seemingly irreconcilable demands and has some additional benefits.

Fast Routing. The most time consuming part of routing is figuring out what routing patterns to use. Using *Pre-Route Assistant* this search is done at design time. Thus at run-time all the RTR application has to do is flip bits to generate the routing. This bit flipping is done by the generated *JBits* calls and can be done very fast at run time.

Guaranteed Routing. Failure to route is not an option. Failure to route means application failure in many RTR applications. Using Pre-Route Assistant the routing is done at design time. This means the routing is guaranteed at run-time since the designer has pre-specified it.

Automated Routing. Routing a design by hand is a very tedious task. Pre-Route Assistant helps make this task easier by allowing the user to specify routes at a high level and outputs the appropriate low level *JBits* code. This code can then be copied directly into the RTPCore source code.

Flexible Routing. Pre-routing does not have to mean ridged, inflexible routing. Do to the regular routing architecture in the Virtex$^{(tm)}$ architecture the low level *JBits* code that does the routing can be moved or put into Java looping statements. This allows designers to create "parameterizable" cores that can be placed anywhere on the chip.

5 Pre-route Assistant Compared with JRoute Standalone

The main advantage of *Pre-Route Assistant* over using the *JRoute* API directly, is speed. *Pre-Route Assistant* converts the JRoute calls into low level *JBits* calls. This frees the application from having to do this extra processing at run-time. Tests have shown that the low level *JBits* calls run 4.6 times faster than the corresponding point to point *JRoute* calls in low density designs. As routing densities increase the performance improvement of pre-routing increases. Another advantage that *Pre-Route Assistant* gives you over *JRoute* is guaranteed routing. If *JRoute* can not perform a route it throws and exception at run-time. Pre-routing using *Pre-Route Assistant* avoids this.

One advantage of JRoute standalone is it guarantees there will be no contention. *Pre-Route Assistant* places this burden on the designer. Other advantages of *JRoute* standalone are, it allows for quicker development of RTR applications, and it allows these applications to be more flexible.

These two methodologies compliment each other well. During development the designer can use the *JRoute* API directly for rapid development. Once the application is working, if further performance is necessary, *Pre-Route Assistant* can be used to pre-route low level RTPCores. *JRoute* provides access to its resource database so the pre-routed cores can mark the resources they use. This way *JRoute* can "stitch" pre-routed cores together without contention.

6 Future Work and Conclusions

The *Pre-Route Assistant* is built of off the *JRoute* package for *JBits*. To make *JRoute* fast it only does one route at a time, avoiding contention as it goes. This means that success in routing a set of routes can be dependent on the order of the routes. If *Pre-Route Assistant* fails on a group of routes, often switching the order of the routes can make it succeed. One possible improvement for *Pre-Route Assistant* would be to have it try other route orderings automatically if a route failed.

In conclusion, the Pre-Router Assistant is a useful tool for run-time reconfiguration and design-time routing. It allows you to specify high level routes and it outputs low level *JBits* code which will do the routes. This allows and RTR designer to create pre-routed parameterizable cores which can be written directly to a bitstream at run-time.

Acknowledgements

This work is partially funded by DARPA contract DABT63-99-3-0004 in the ACS program.

References

1. Steven A. Guccione and Delon Levi. XBI: A java-based interface to FPGA hardware. In John Schewel, editor, *Configurable Computing: Technology and Applications, Proc. SPIE 3526*, pages 97–102, Bellingham, WA, November 1998. SPIE – The International Society for Optical Engineering.
2. Steven A. Guccione and Delon Levi. Design advantages of run-time reconfiguration. In John Schewel, editor, *Reconfigurable Technology: FPGAs for Computing and Applications, Proc. SPIE 3844*, pages 87–92, Bellingham, WA, September 1999. SPIE – The International Society for Optical Engineering.
3. Eric Keller. Jroute: A run-time routing api for fpga hardware. In J. Rolim et al., editor, *7th Reconfigurable Architectures Workshop RAW 2000, Lecture Notes in Computer Science 1800*, pages 874–882, Cancun, Mexico, May 2000. Springer-Verlag.

High Speed Computation of Lattice Gas Automata with FPGA

Tomoyoshi Kobori, Tsutomu Maruyama, and Tsutomu Hoshino

Institute of Engineering Mechanics and Systems, University of Tsukuba
1-1-1 Ten-nou-dai Tsukuba Ibaraki 305-8573 JAPAN
kobori@darwin.esys.tsukuba.ac.jp

Abstract. Lattice gas automata are a class of cellular automata, and are used for simulating fluid dynamics. In the cellular automata, a single update rule is applied simultaneously to each cell on the lattice. Therefore, many approaches with parallel systems have been researched.
In this paper, we propose a computation method of cellular automata for small systems with limited memory bandwidth. We implemented the method on a FPGA board (ADC RC1000 with one Virtex XCV1000). The speed gain for a lattice gas FHP-III model with 2048 × 1024 lattice is 143 times compared with Pentium-III 700MHz.

1 Introduction

Lattice gas automata are a class of cellular automata, and are used for simulating fluid dynamics. In the lattice gas models, a single update rule which consists of integer operations with small bit-width is applied simultaneously to each cell on the lattice. Therefore, lattice gas models have been widely studied, and many approaches using parallel systems and FPGA systems have been proposed [2][3].

The size of FPGAs have been drastically improved in the last several years, and with one latest FPGA, it becomes possible to apply the simple rules of the lattice gas models to more than one hundreds cells on the lattice in parallel. However, internal memory size of FPGAs is still too small for storing whole lattice (the number of the cells is more than one million in general), and the memory bandwidth of the FPGA becomes the bottleneck for the parallel processing.

In this paper, we propose a computation method of the lattice gas models for small systems with limited memory bandwidth. In this procedure, status of some cells become invalid because the status of their neighborhood are not given correctly owing to the limited memory bandwidth. In order to reduce the invalid computation in the method, we need memories which have very high bandwidth on the FPGA. The distributed RAMs of Xilinx FPGAs are very suitable for this method. We implemented the method on a FPGA board (ADC RC1000 with one Virtex XCV1000, which has 128 bit width memory interface), and the speed gain for a FHP-III model with 2048 × 1024 lattice is more than one hundred times compared with Pentium-III 700MHz. This method can also be applied to other cellular automata.

2 Lattice Gas Model

Many of lattice gas models are based on FHP model[1], and hexagonal grids shown in figure 1 are used. In the figure, bold lines show the borders of each cell, and the dots show particles on the cells. The particles travel at unit speed, and collide on the center of each cell, and then change their directions. Only one particle is allowed to travel in each direction from a cell (six directions in the figure). This means that only six particles (and one particle which remains on the cell) can arrive at a cell at a time.

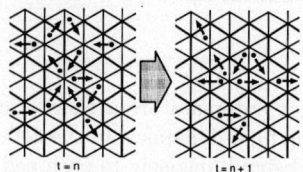

Fig. 1. Hexagonal Grids for FHP models

FHP-III models have the most complex collision rules in FHP models, which conserve mass and momentum at each cell. When we run simulation, eight bits are used for each cells. The seven bits are the status of each cell in FHP-III model. The one extra bit is used for representing objects on the lattice.

3 Overview of the Computation Method

In this section, we introduce the basic strategy of the computation method.

When the width (k cells) of the lattice is not larger than the I/O width of the FPGA (k cells), the FPGA can read one line (k cells) of the lattice at a time, and the update rule can be applied to k cells on the line in every clock cycle by storing three lines in the circuit on the FPGA (Figure 2 (a)). By pipelining the circuit and storing data for $3 \times n$ lines in the circuit(Figure 2 (b)), we can process $k \times n$ cells at a time (n is the depth of the pipeline).

In the figure 2(c), suppose that the circuit can only hold for $k \times w$(width)$\times 3 \times$ n(lines) cells, and the I/O width of the FPGA is k cells. FPGA reads $k \times w$ cells in w clock cycles, and each $k \times n$ cells on FPGA are processed as soon as each k cells are read in. In this case, status of neighborhood can not be given on the both edge on the circuit, and status of n cells on each edge become incorrect at the depth n on the pipeline (Black parts in the figure 2 (c)). Therefore, outputs only for $k \times w - 2n$ cells are correct, and the effective parallelism is $n(k - 2n/w)$ with the circuit which can process $n \times k$ cells at a time. In order to scan all the lattice using this method, the part which results become invalid have to be processed twice as shown in the figure 2 (c). In the figure, data for the area surrounded by bold-lines have to be read in twice. In the figure 2 (c), the boundary conditions for upper rectangles (Black parts) are once calculated during the computation of lower rectangles of the upper $k \times w$ rows. If we can store the boundary conditions, we can obtain correct status for the upper rectangles. In this case, effective parallelism becomes $n \times (k - n/w)$.

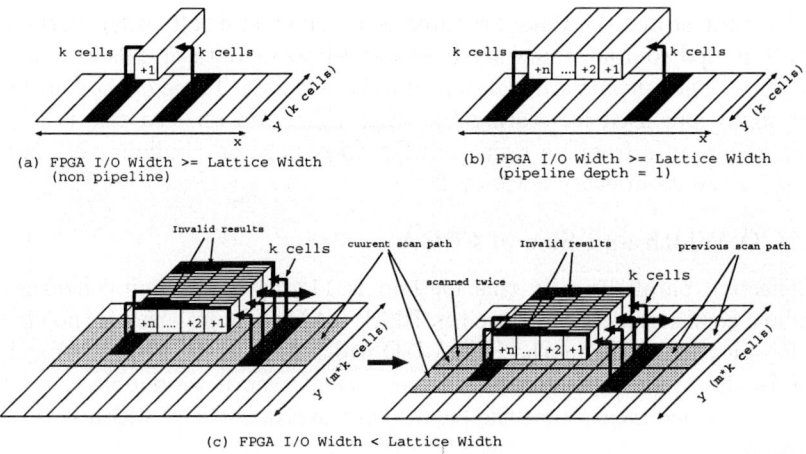

Fig. 2. Basic Strategy of the Computation Method

4 Circuit for the XCV1000 on the RC1000 Board

4.1 Details of the Circuit

We implemented the method on the FPGA board (ADC RC1000). It has one Virtex XCV1000, and four 2MB SRAM banks with 32 bit width (8MB and 128 bit width in total). Figure 3 shows the block diagram of the circuit. There are 8 × 16 units in the computation array, and each unit computes next status of each cell. The right of the figure 3 shows the structure of the unit. Each unit has four buffers which consist of distributed RAMs. These distributed RAMs are used to store the data for 16 computation planes.

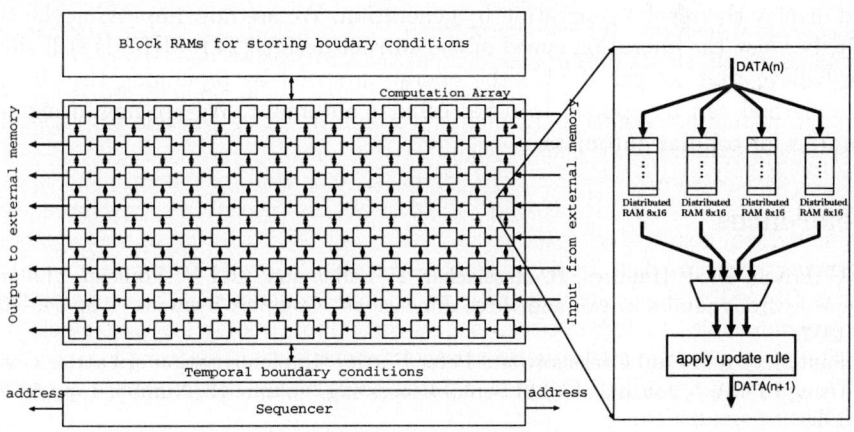

Fig. 3. Overview of the Circuit

Each unit stores the data for three cells (right and left cells) of the same generation, and computes new status of the cell using data of cells in upper and lower units. The outputs are transferred to its left unit. Three of the four buffers in the figure are used for storing the three cells, and another one is used for storing the results from its right unit. By preparing four buffers, the unit can process its inputs in every clock cycle.

4.2 I/O Width and Size of FPGA

The effective parallelism by this method is 112 with 128 units, because the boundary conditions can be stored in Block RAMs. Table 1 shows the effective parallelism when changing the FPGA I/O width (size of the FPGA is fixed). As shown in the table, the speed gain is very small even if we double the current I/O width, which means that the balance of the size and I/O width is the most important.

Table 1. Effective Parallelism

I/O width (bits)	32 + 32	64 + 64	128 + 128
Effective Parallelism	64	112	124

5 Conclusions

In this paper, we proposed a new computation method of cellular automata for small systems with limited memory bandwidth. We implemented the method on a FPGA board (ADC RC1000 with one Virtex XCV1000), and the speed gain for a lattice gas FHP-III model with 2048 × 1024 lattice is 143 times compared with Pentium-III 700MHz.

In the method, we can only display the results every 16 generations. Therefore, we need some circuits that reduce the size of the outputs on the FPGA, and display the results generation by generation. We are now improving the circuit, because the operation speed of the current design (24.6 MHz) is still slow. We believe that we can double the operation speed by pipelining the circuit. The method can be applied to other cellular automata. We are now designing libraries for cellular automata.

References

1. U. Frisch, D. d' Humires, B. Hasslacher, P. Lallemand, and Y. Pomeau. "Lattice gas hydrodynamics in two and three dimensions" Complex Systems, 1 pp.649-707, 1987.
2. Paul Shaw and Paul Cockshott and Peter Barrie, "Implementation of Lattice Gases Using FPGAs", Journal of VLSI Signal Processing, Volume 12, Number 1, pp.51-66, 1996.
3. C. Adler, B. M. Boghosian, E. G. Flekkoy, N. Margolus and D. H. Rothman, "Simulation Three-Dimensional Hydrodynamics on a Cellular-Automata Machine", Journal of Statistical Physics, 1995

An Implementation of Longest Prefix Matching for IP Router on Plastic Cell Architecture

Tsunemichi Shiozawa[†], Norbert Imlig[†], Kouichi Nagami[†], Kiyoshi Oguri[††],
Akira Nagoya[†], and Hiroshi Nakada[†]

[†]NTT Network Innovation Laboratories
1-1 Hikari-no-oka, Yokosuka-shi, Kanagawa 239-0847 Japan
shiozawa@exa.onlab.ntt.co.jp
[††]Department of Computer and Information Sciences, Nagasaki University
1-14 Bunkyo, Nagasaki-shi 852-8521, Japan

Abstract. In this paper, we introduce an implementation of the longest prefix matching operation by using the reconfigurable computer architecture called Plastic Cell Architecture (PCA). By using the characters of PCA, it is possible to build the computing mechanism, which suits the granularity of the problem and the structure of it. We apply them to design the longest prefix matching operation that is one of the key issues for the high-throughput Internet Protocol (IP) routers.

1 Introduction

From the improvement in the degree of the integration of LSI, and the viewpoint of reuse of design property, the new layer of the scalable and homogeneous resource to be prepared on a silicon chip, and use of design property needs to be aimed at by separating a physical layer and a logic layer like software. As one of the candidates of such a layer, we position the reconfigurable hardware and have proposed the Plastic Cell Architecture [1-4].

From the beginning, the Plastic Cell Architecture is the architecture, which aimed at realization of a general-purpose computing mechanism on the homogeneous resource. We consider the application [3] that can expand a throughput to scalable as the size of it. Therefore, the PCA chip architecture such as function and structure is determined so that the high throughput-oriented application might suit it.

2 Longest Prefix Matching in IP Router

Because of a rapid expansion of Internet, it will demand more throughputs by the network. In the Internet, communication is based on the packet including the IP address in the header, and a packet is transmitted to relay to the next router (*next hop*) with reference to this IP address. If the IP address is regularly assigned in consideration of the structure of the whole network, the determination of the next hop within a router is realizable with reference of a small table and simple processing. The large table for determining next hop is needed in a router by the regularity of an IP address having collapsed, and complicated table lookup processing is required for routing packets. The example of the table used for routing is shown in Table 1. In this example, "0" is chosen an IP address as next hop to the packet of "53.11.10.10", and "3" is chosen an IP address as next hop to the packet of "53.12.0.255". Thus, the table reference which chooses the longest matched entry of the pattern which is in agreement using mask bit length is called the *longest prefix matching*.

The processing capability between terminals and the throughput of a network will be restricted by the processing capability of the router in the packet communication and routing table as shown in Table 1 must be modified adapting to change of a network. So in addition to the improvement in reference capability of a router, it needs to realize the programmability for corresponding to these changes.

Table 1. The example of routing table

prefix	mask bits	next hop
112.0.0.0	F0.00.00.00	0
53.0.0.0	FF.00.00.00	3
53.10.0.0	FF.FF.00.00	2
53.11.0.0	FF.FF.00.00	0
else	FF.FF.FF.FF	1

There are the following two methods as main technology of realizing the longest prefix matching operation inside a router. The first method is the technique of decreasing the number of times which a processor refers to by devising the data structure of the routing table stored in a memory [5-6]. The second method is the technique of searching the contents of a table with using the pattern matching hardware like content-addressable memories (CAMs) [7]. However, these methods using processor or the pattern matching hardware aim at the improvement in a throughput by decreasing latency to one processing of a packet. Thus, in spite of being the application with which a high throughput is essentially demanded, having used fixed hardware such as a processor or CAMs which can perform only one processing simultaneously is generating a performance bottleneck. The merits that realize a router which is demanded the high throughput and programmability is achieved on the reconfigurable hardware are as follows.
(a) It is possible to avoid the collision about data access and decrease the latency of data access by locating the individual data in the near of processing.
(b) It is possible to fit the size of the processing subject for the processing demand.

3 Plastic Cell Architecture (PCA)

Fig. 1 shows the PCA which we are proposing. PCA is composed of the homogeneous cell connected mutually, and each cell consists of the *Built-in part (BP)* and the *Plastic part (PP)*. The BP and PP of each cell are also connected via the connection path to its same type neighbors.

The BP takes charge of routing messages and configuration of the PP. The BP is designed as a high-speed processor with limited functions. It accepts instructions in the message and is controlled by several finite state machines. To set the route and transport messages, the BP has input buffers with a decoder for the message and selectors to set the direction of forwarding.

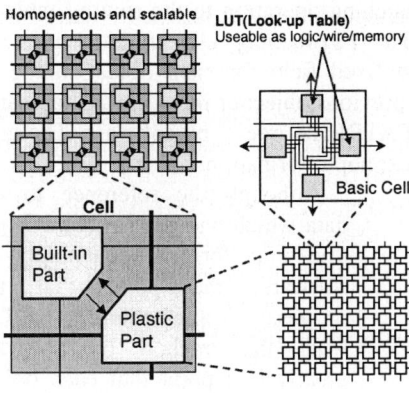

Fig 1. Structure of PCA

The PP which consists of a *Basic Cell* behaves as a data processing circuit and a memory in which data is stored. The Basic Cell consists of four Look-Up Tables (LUT) which configured as the circuit primitive, such as a combinatorial logic, latch or wire. The circuits on the PP and the BP are asynchronous circuit [4] in order to eliminate a clock for scalability.

Making the prototype chip (PCA-1) has been completed in our research group. In the prototype chip, the BP execute 12 types of commands be executed and each PP is composed of 8x8 Basic Cell.

4 Implementation

4.1 Design Policy

Based on the following methodology, we implement an Internet Protocol router on PCA using a pipeline structure.
(a) Data processing performed within an object and the controls between objects are separated.
(b) Variables particular to processing is embedded in a message, and BPs are used also as a buffer which it not only considers the communication path between objects as wiring, but buffering variables temporarily.

We call these design methodology *Communicating Logic* [4]. Above (a) means that it is possible to change the control between objects (order and dependency) dynamically by selecting routing commands inside the source object at the time of execution. Above (b), by raising the locality of variables, the performance down by the difference of the processing speed between objects is decreased, and the reusability of an object is increased. It means that BPs are used as a part of function of the object created on PPs.

A pipeline is constituted from making the object which operates independently and communicates using BPs. Since the BP has the function to arbitrate the message which arrived from the different input port, without adding a particular circuit between objects, the exclusion control to a share object is realizable performing communication between objects by the atomic message using BPs. On the other hand, inside an object, the control signal to confirm transfer between the PP and the BP is needed. In PCA prototype chip, it is premised on the asynchronous circuit [8] using the timing control gate and the data latch achieved by combining adjacent Basic Cell.

4.2 Implementation of the Longest Prefix Matching

The objects and communication path between the objects when implementing the circuit which performs the longest prefix matching operation to the routing table of Table 1 on PCA are shown in Fig. 2. The *Forwarding Object* determines the destination object referring to the specified fixed field for each object in the IP address of the message which received from previous object or input port. This search will become equivalent to the search using PATRICIA tree [5] by software. The gray objects are *Terminal Objects* with hold the next hop information.

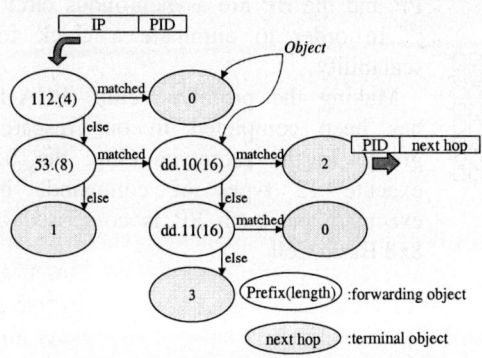

Fig 2. Longest Prefix Matching on PCA

Although the reference to the data which had the structure like a tree is performed sequentially by software, the point that the proposal implementation differs from the method by software greatly is a point that each object can operate simultaneously in parallel. That is, the upper left object will send the message to the lower object, if the first four bits of an IP address in the message are "0111" (112=b01110000), otherwise, it will transmit to the right object and when transmission of the message is completed, it starts processing of a following message. Thus, by using a large number of objects which execute a simple address matching and message forwarding, pipeline of tree structure is composed by forwarding the processing result of these objects through the BPs. Both Forwarding Object and Terminal Object are implemented on the prototype chip by the size of 2x3 cells.

By the above, the usage rate of the upper left object is the highest, and usage rate of right-hand side and bottom objects are lower. In other words, an upper left object is considered to be a bottleneck in this operation. To such bottleneck objects, a duplicate object is created if necessary, and the load is distributed. By using PCA, the duplicate of the bottleneck object can be created to suite the traffic pattern of IP address contained in the arrived packet, and the throughput can be enhanced.

5 Conclusion

We describe the design methodology and concept by which the throughput-oriented application is implemented on PCA and applied to an IP router. The performance of the high throughput oriented application is extensible and scalable by designing pipeline structure using the BP on PCA. The asynchronous circuit design, which has been adopted with the prototype chip, is suitable for designing the pipeline structure.

We are now evaluating the performance of above application and implementing a high-level description language and CAD tools for PCA object synthesis.

References

[1] K. Nagami, K. Oguri, T. Shiozawa, H. Ito and R. Konishi, "Plastic Cell Architecture: Towards Reconfigurable Computing for General-Purpose," Submitted to FCCM'98, 1998.
[2] H. Ito, K. Oguri, K. Nagami, R. Konishi, and T. Shiozawa, "The Plastic Cell Architecture for Dynamic Reconfigurable Computing," Proc. of RSP'98, pp39-44, 1998.
[3] T. Shiozawa, K.Oguri, K.Nagami, H.Ito and R.Konishi, "A Hardware Implementation of Constraint Satisfaction Problem Based on New Reconfigurable LSI Architecture," Proc of FPL'98, pp426-430 (1998).
[4] N. Imlig, R. Konishi, T. Shiozawa, K. Oguri, K. Nagami, H. Ito, M. Inamori, H. Nakada, "Communicating Logic: An Alternative Embedded Stream Processing Paradigm," Proc. of Conf. on ASP-DAC2000, pp317-pp.322, 2000.
[5] D.Morrison, "PATRICIA- Practical Algorithm To Retrieve Information Coded in Alphanumeric," Journal of the ACM, vol. 15, No. 4, pp. 514-535, October 1968.
[6] Gene Cheung and Steve McCanne, "Optimal Routing Table Design for IP Address Lookups Under Memory Constraints," Proceedings of INFOCOM'99 ,pp.1437-1444, 1999.
[7] A. Moestedt and P. Sj'odin, "IP address lookup in hardware for high-speed routing," in Hot Interconnects VI, Aug. 1998.
[8] I.E. Sutherland, "Micropipelines, The 1988 Turing Award Lecture," Comm. ACM, vol. 32, no. 6, pp.720-738, June, 1989.

FPGA Implementation of an Extended Binary GCD Algorithm for Systolic Reduction of Rational Numbers

Bogdan Mătăsaru and Tudor Jebelean

RISC-Linz, A–4040 Linz, Austria
bmatasar@risc.uni-linz.ac.at

Abstract. We present the FPGA implementation of an extension of the binary *plus–minus* systolic algorithm which computes the GCD (greatest common divisor) and also the normal form of a rational number, without using division. A sample array for 8 bit operands consumes 83.4% of an Atmel 40K10 chip and operates at 25 MHz.

1 Introduction

Arbitrary precision (or exact) arithmetic is necessary in various computer algebra applications (e. g. solving of systems of polynomial equations [2]) or cryptography and it may consume most of the computing time.

Reduction of rational numbers occurs very often in exact arithmetic: sooner or later, the reduction of the result is required in order to avoid an unacceptable increase in size of its numerator and denominator. The usual approach is to use the GCD (greatest common divisor) once (or twice on shorter operands [3]) and some divisions (or better exact divisions [7]). Alternatively, one can use the extended GCD algorithm [6], but this will probably be less efficient for sequential implementations.

In this paper we present the systolic implementation of an extension of the binary GCD algorithm [9], more precisely of the plus-minus algorithm [1] as improved in [4]. Extensions of the original binary algorithm have been considered by Penk [6], and also in [10]. Our algorithm has a different flavor [8] because it is designed for systolic implementation.

Since it avoids the division, and it is also based on simple operations like shifts and additions/subtractions, our algorithm may be interesting even for classical implementations on some sequential computers. In this paper we demonstrate the usefulness of this approach on a systolic architecture, by designing a systolic version of the algorithm and by implementing it on an Atmel FPGA circuit. We use a very fine grained parallelism, that is at bit level:this has the advantage of time-overlapping of many arithmetic operations. The systolic algorithm is an extension of the systolic GCD presented in [4] which avoids global broadcasting by pipelining the "command" through the array. This in turn has the disadvantage that *wait* states have to be introduced, because of the two-way flow of the information. Our algorithm takes advantage of these *wait* states: the computations required by the extended algorithm are done instead of wait. Hence, the speed is the same as the one of the previous algorithm, but additionally we obtain the reduced fraction.

The circuit is presented as a systolic array, enjoying the properties of uniform design (many identical cells) and local communications (only between adjacent cells). The input of the operands is done in parallel manner, while the output can be organized serially or in parallel, depending on the application.

The sample implementation of an array for 8 bit operands on the Atmel FPGA part 40K10 consists of 968 elementary macros and consumes after layout 83.4% of the area. The longest delay is 40 ns, thus operation at 25 MHz is possible, which rivals the speed of the best software implementations on sequential machines for words of 32 bits, but it will probably gain considerably in speed in a special device for more words.

2 The Algorithm

The input of the binary (plus-minus) GCD algorithm consists of 2 n-bit operands a and b. The operations executed on the operands are additions, subtractions and shifts and they are decided by inspecting the least significant two bits of each operand.

Let us denote by a_k, respectively b_k, the values of the operands at step k. The extended GCD algorithm computes also the sequences of cofactors of u_k, v_k, t_k, and w_k such that at each step k:

$$u_k \cdot a + v_k \cdot b = a_k \cdot 2^k, \quad t_k \cdot a + w_k \cdot b = b_k \cdot 2^k. \qquad (1)$$

The algorithm ends when $b_k = 0$. Then, a_k equals the GCD and $t_k \cdot a + w_k \cdot b = 0$, hence $a/b = -w_k/t_k$.

The sequence of cofactors is defined recursively starting from the initial values: $u_0 = 1, v_0 = 0, t_0 = 0, w_0 = 1$. (We denote by $x[1], x[0]$ the least significant bits of an operand x.)

Shift both: ($a_k[0] = 0$, $b_k[0] = 0$): the cofactors remain unchanged.
Interchange and shift b: ($a_k[0] = 0$, $b_k[0] = 1$):
$u_{k+1} := 2 \cdot t_k, \ v_{k+1} := 2 \cdot w_k, \ t_{k+1} := u_k, \ w_{k+1:} = v_k.$
Shift b: ($a_k[0] = 1$, $b_k[0] = 0$):
$u_{k+1} := 2 \cdot u_k, \ v_{k+1} := 2 \cdot v_k, \ t_{k+1} := t_k, \ w_{k+1} := w_k.$
Plus-minus: ($a_k[0] = 1$, $b_k[0] = 1$), **plus** if $a_k[1] \neq b_k[1]$, otherwise **minus**:
$u_{k+1} := 2 \cdot t_k, \ v_{k+1} := 2 \cdot w_k \ t_{k+1} := u_k \pm t_k, \ w_{k+1} := v_k \pm w_k.$

One can easily verify that the relations (1) are preserved at each step, and one can prove that t_k and w_k remain relatively prime and at least one of them is not null. Thus, when b_k becomes null, $-w_k/t_k$ is the reduced form of the initial fraction a/b. (For the proofs and a more detailed description of the algorithm see [8].)

3 The Systolic Array

The systolic array is organized as in [4]: the operands are fed in parallel, one digit of each in each processor, the rightmost processor (P_0) corresponds to the least-significant bit – see Fig. 1. An array of $N+1$ processors will accommodate operands up to N bits long. (The leftmost processor and the ones above the significant bits of the operands will contain the sign bit). All the intermediate values are kept in complement representation: therefore additions/subtractions can be performed without knowing the actual sign of the operands.

Each processor communicates only with its neighbors: the commands (states) and the carries propagate right-to-left, while the intermediate values of the operands propagate left-to-right. All the processors except P_0 are identical. P_0 computes at each step a command code (depending on $a[1], a[0], b[1], b[0]$) which is then propagated to the other processors and controls their operations.

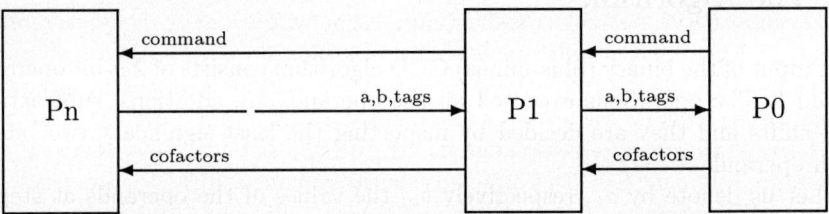

Fig. 1. The systolic array for the extended binary algorithm.

Each processor has a memory of 16 one-bit registers. 8 registers are necessary for the *plus-minus* GCD array and they have the same meaning as in [4]: s_1, s_2, s_3 contain the command code (or *state*), a, b are bits of the operands, ta, tb (*tags*) indicate their significant bits, and sa stores the sign of a.

Additionally, 8 registers are used by the extended algorithm: u, v, t, w keep the values of the cofactors, ct and cw are carries needed for the plus-minus operations, and u', v' keep intermediate values needed for left-shifts.

Note that the data used to build the cofactors flows from right to left, either as a carry in the plus/minus steps, or by shifting in the shift steps. That is, the partial value of a cofactor kept in the registers of the processor P_k depends only on the previous values in the processors $P_0, \ldots, P_k$. Moreover, the cofactors are less or equal to the correspondent input operands, so their length is less or equal to n. Therefore, the number of processors needed for the GCD computation is sufficient also for obtaining the reduced form of the rational number.

The termination of the systolic GCD algorithm is detected by P_0 when the value of b is 0 and the tag of b is 1. Sometimes, the extended algorithm requires several additional steps to finish the propagation of the "command" to the most significant bits of the cofactors. However, this is not a problem if the result is retrieved in a LSF way because after b_k becomes 0 the circuit pipelines only **B** operations which do not change the values of the cofactors t_k and w_k.

4 FPGA Experiments

We implemented the array on an ATMEL FPGA using the Atmel IDS environment from Cadence Systems and Workview Office from Viewlogic Systems. However, the circuit is not related to a specific FPGA architecture and could be also implemented as ASIC.

For a circuit containing 9 processors (accommodates operands up to 8 bits), the netlist phase reports a number of 968 elementary blocks, which is smaller than the area used by the GCD together with division presented in [5]. Some of the intermediate values between the GCD algorithms and the two exact divisions are not needed anymore; this simplifies the function that updates the operands. The function that computes the cofactors requires 31 elementary gates per processor. Thus, the circuit for computing the extended gcd is also simpler than a circuit which computes the gcd followed by two exact divisions. The longest delay path passes through 13 ports and it is determined by the original GCD array - the computation of the cofactors does not increase the computing time. The automatic layout was successful on a Atmel AT40K10 chip, and consumes 384 logical cells (83.4% of the total). The longest delay through our the circuit is 40 ns – corresponding to a speed of 25 MHz. This gives an estimated time of 0.005 ms for computing the reduced fraction of 32 bit operands, which rivals the best current sequential processor (Ultra SPARC 60 at 300 MHz with the GMP library we obtained an average of 0.006 ms). However, a special device constructed on the bases of this implementation for longer operands (e. g. 4 to 10 words) will gain in speed by a considerable factor, because the computing time of the systolic array increases only linearly with the length of the operands.

References

1. R. P. Brent and H. T. Kung, *A systolic algorithm for integer GCD computation*, Symp. on Computer Arithmetic (K. Hwang, ed.), IEEE Computer Society, 1985.
2. B. Buchberger, Grö bner Bases: *An Algorithmic Method in Polynomial Ideal Theory*, Recent trends in Multidimensional Systems (Bose and Reidel, eds.), D. Reidel Publishing, 1985, pp. 184-232.
3. P. Henrici, *A subroutine for computations with rational numbers*, Journal of the ACM 3 (1956), 6-9.
4. T. Jebelean, *Systolic normalization of rational numbers*, ASAP'93 (L. Dadda and B. Wah, eds.), IEEE Computer Society, 1993, pp. 502-513.
5. _ *Rational arithmetic using FPGA*, More FPGAs (W. Luk and W. Moore, eds.), Abingdon EE&CS Books, Oxford, 1994, pp. 262-273.
6. D. E. Knuth, *The art of computer programming*, vol. 2, Addison-Wesley, 1981.
7. W. Krandick and T. Jebelean, *Bidirectional exact integer division*, Journal of Symbolic Computation 21 (1996), 441-455.
8. B. Mătăsaru, *An extension of the binary GCD algorithm for systolic parallelization*, Tech. Report 99-47, RISC-Linz, 1999, http://www.risc.uni-linz.ac.at.
9. J. Stein, *Computational problems associated with Racah algebra*, J. Comp. Phys. 1 (1967), 397-405.
10. K. Weber, *The accelerated integer GCD algorithm*, ACM Trans. on Math. Software 21 (1995), no. 1, 111-122.

Toward Uniform Approach to Design of Evolvable Hardware Based Systems

Lukáš Sekanina and Azeddien M. Sllame

Brno University of Technology, Czech Republic
sekanina@dcse.fee.vutbr.cz, sllame@dcse.fee.vutbr.cz

Abstract. The paper tries to establish the uniform design concept for evolvable hardware based applications. Evolvable circuit is understood as a system component with ability to evolve. As demo example, a component "evolvable pixel predictor" is presented.

1 Introduction

Evolvable hardware (EHW) can be considered as a technology, which enables to establish some evolvable system with ability of hardware on-line adaptation to dynamically changing environments [1]. Circuit connection, encoded to chromosome, of the fast *reconfigurable circuit* (RC) is autonomously synthesised by *genetic algorithm* (GA). Nature of genetic algorithm does not guarantee that 100% quality of resulting connection will be achieved in all cases. This problem has to be considered during system design and potentially influences the class of *evolvable hardware based applications* (EHBA). In case of *open-ended evolution* [2], dynamically changing environment is reflected by dynamically changing fitness function. Then evolution must not be ever stopped since known high quality solution could be unsatisfactory in a new environment.

Available papers about evolvable hardware usually describe ad hoc design for a given task, e.g. [3–5]. This paper is the first attempt to establish the *uniform approach* for design of EHBA. Section 2 introduces our concept of *evolvable component*. As an example, the component "evolvable pixel predictor" is presented in Section 3 and its design and implementation in Section 4. From discussion in Section 5, conclusions are derived.

2 Conceptual View

Evolvable digital system may be viewed as a collection of interacting components where at least one of them is under evolution. *Common components* (e.g. processors, decoders or interfaces) with well known function and structure, are used through their inputs, outputs and the control signals by other components. In our concept, the evolvable component consists of the reconfigurable circuit and the implementation of genetic algorithm. Everything surrounding the evolvable component (meaning other components) is called *application*. The RC in the evolvable component interacts with application in the same way as common component, but its function and internal structure is unknown. Furthermore, application must specify how current circuit (configuration of the RC) is successful. From application point of view, the evolvable component is a black box, which can perform some important system function, and quality of this function is influenced by numbers (fitness values) given from application. From the evolvable component point of view, the application is dynamically changing environment and the evolvable component tries to adapt to changes. The process of genetic learning is controlled by application which still asks for better connection. This separation leads to clear interface among components (see Fig. 1). All genetic operations, fitness and population memories are carried out on the evolvable component, only fitness calculation is the part of application. When the fitness calculation is out of evolvable chip, then it is easy to support the concept of open-ended evolution (from a view of the component designer).

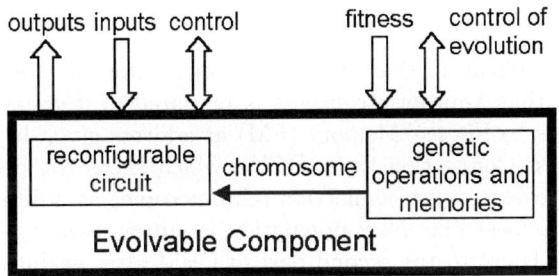

Fig. 1. Evolvable component and its interface.

3 An Example: Evolvable Component for Pixel Prediction

As demo example, we describe our evolvable component (i.e. *evolvable chip*) for pixel prediction. That is a simple evolvable combinational circuit with four 8bit inputs *X0-X3* and single 8bit output *Y*. A pixel value *Y* is predicted from its neighbours *X0-X3*. Then application—*image compression* [4, 5, 7]—performs the rest of actions in the compression algorithm. Evolution leads to optimal prediction in block of pixels, which ensures high compression ratios, and hardware implementation allows feasible time of compression.

Internal structure and interface of evolvable chip are depicted in Fig. 2. After *RESET*, Initial Population Unit (IPU) generates initial population to the lower part of the Chromosome Memory (CHM). If the application wants to calculate fitness for the new connection, activates *NC* (New Connection) signal and Fitness Calculation Control Unit (FCCU) takes the first non-evaluated chromosome and downloads it to the RC. Activation of *CP* (Connection is Prepared)

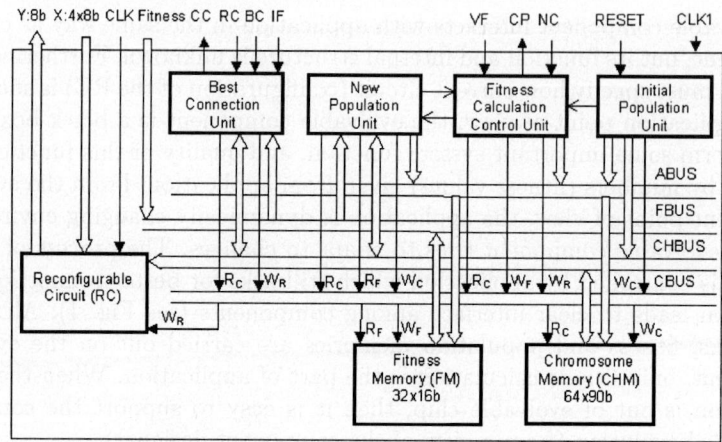

Fig. 2. Block structure of the evolvable chip for pixel prediction.

which tells the application that evaluation can be started. *VF* (Valid Fitness) signal indicates that appropriate fitness is prepared at *Fitness* inputs. FCCU stores this fitness to Fitness Memory (FM) at address given by address of the chromosome. Best Connection Unit (BCU), which keeps the best chromosome and its fitness, saves current connection (chromosome) as well as fitness if current fitness is the best one. New population is automatically generated (using New Population Unit) to the second part of CHM after evaluation of all chromosomes. Using *BC* (Best Connection) activation, the application asks for the best connection. Signal *IF* (Invalidate Fitness) is to invalidate the fitness of the best chromosome and thus the new environment may be announced. Signal *RC* (Read Connection) and data pin *CC* (Current Connection) are considered for reading of the best chromosome outside the evolvable chip.

4 Design, Implementation and Results

First, evolvable component as well as application were modelled using C++ at higher level of abstraction. In case of evolvable component, architecture of reconfigurable circuit (e.g. the number and function of programmable elements, connectivity rules), suitable genetic operators and chromosome to architecture mapping were looked for in simulations. Reaching satisfactory performance, resulted architecture of the evolvable component was carried out to hardware. Entire evolvable chip is described using VHDL. Our design methodology is based on communicating VHDL modules which allowed us to validate each module (e.g. cellular automata for random number generation, memories) alone.

The RC, genetic operations and memories are implemented in the same Xilinx Virtex chip. Note that the RC has a unique architecture (i.e. circuit elements, configuration style) which satisfies just designer requirements. To implement RC, we have used special technique initially proposed in [6]. According to VHDL description of the RC, special architecture—including configuration logic and configuration memory—is implemented on the top of a normal FPGA. Such a simple RC occupies about 500 Virtex-slices and its configuration (90 bits) takes a clock cycle (*WR* signal) because only 9 nine functional blocks per 10 configuration bits are used. Pipelined implementation of the RC enables one prediction per a clock cycle at frequency up to 60MHz (*CLK* in Fig. 2) [6].

5 Discussion and Conclusions

Considering previous example, our uniform approach to design of EHBA is based on decomposition of the system into components and consequent definition of interfaces among them. In case of evolvable component, simulations are used to determine its architecture. Internal mechanism of the component (e.g. appropriate chromosome have to be downloaded into RC after *NC* signal) and interface are the same for all evolvable components. Thus it is possible to define a *generic evolvable component*. Taking such component, only determination of the RC's architecture, chromosome encoding and genetic operations will be a designer task for a given application. Of course, fitness calculation and the communication interface have to be defined in some common component. We have software and hardware images of the generic evolvable component which may be used as templates for future projects. Thus the code reusability is ensured. It is the first step toward uniform approach to design of EHBA.

This research was performed with the CEZ: J22/98:262200012 and the GACR 102/98/0552.

References

1. Sanchez, E., Tomassini, M. (Eds.): Towards Evolvable Hardware: The Evolutionary Engineering Approach. LNCS 1062, Springer-Verlag, Berlin (1996)
2. Sanchez, E. et al.: Phylogeny, Ontogeny, and Epigenesis: Three Sources of Biological Inspiration for Softering Hardware. In: Evolvable Systems: From Biology to Hardware, LNCS 1259, Berlin, Springer-Verlag (1997) 35–54
3. Kajitani, I. et al: A gate-level EHW chip: Implementing GA operations and reconfigurable hardware on a single LSI. In: Evolvable Systems: From Biology to Hardware, LNCS 1478, Springer Verlag (1998) 1–12
4. Salami, M., Murakawa, M., Higuchi, T.: Data Compression Based on Evolvable Hardware. In: Evolvable Systems: From Biology to Hardware, LNCS 1259, Berlin, Springer-Verlag (1997) 169–179
5. Tanaka, M., et al.: Data Compression for Digital Color Electrophotographic Printer with Evolvable Hardware. In: Evolvable Systems: From Biology to Hardware, LNCS 1478, Springer Verlag (1998) 106–114
6. Sekanina, L., Ruzicka, R.: Design of the Special Fast Reconfigurable Chip Using Common FPGA. In: Proc. of the Design and Diagnostic of Electronic Circuits and Systems IEEE DDECS'2000, Polygrafia SAF Bratislava, Slovakia (2000) 161–168
7. Sekanina, L: Evolvable Hardware as Non-Linear Predictor for Image Compression. In: 2nd Prediction Conference Nostradamus'99, Zlin, Czech Rep. (1999) 87–92

Educational Programmable Hardware Prototyping and Verification System

Andrej Trost, Andrej Zemva, and Baldomir Zajc

University of Ljubljana
Faculty of Electrical Engineering
Trzaska 25, 1000 Ljubljana, Slovenia

Abstract. This paper describes our hardware prototyping and verification system for teaching digital circuits. The system is composed of FPGA modules and a general hardware verification interface which supports utilizing any combination of different FPGA devices within the same design flow. For the most demanding designs, additional boards can be connected to create an FPGA-DSP system or even a multi-FPGA custom computing engine. We describe some typical applications and student projects implemented on the presented programmable prototyping system.

1 Introduction

Programmable prototyping systems are used extensively in digital design practice courses where students can experience the complete design process from initial circuit specification to the physical implementation and system integration [1]. The FPGA technology significantly reduces the time and the cost of the prototyping realization of the design and enables completion of large ASIC designs in the educational process [2].

In this paper, we present a modular prototyping and verification system which is used in the laboratory practice courses covering topics of digital design, integrated circuits and embedded systems. In the next section, we present hardware of the prototyping system and software support for the hardware verification. Design cycle and the required time schedule for the specific subtasks is described next and a set of typical applications is presented in Section 4.

2 Prototyping and Verification System

Basic building blocks of our hardware prototyping and verification system are presented in Figure 1. The system consists of an FPGA module, a CPLD interface connected to the PC, and additional I/O modules or a DSP board.

We use different generations of FPGA modules based on Xilinx XC4000E, Spartan and Virtex devices. The modules also contain some fast static RAM and one or two test and configuration connectors for the CPLD interface which performs configuration of the FPGA device and hardware verification of the design. The I/O modules are used for standalone operation of the designed digital system and they typically consist of LED displays, keyboard, system clock generators and A/D or D/A converters. With the Virtex module we can create an FPGA-DSP prototyping system by connecting the I/O signals to the expansion connector on ADSP-2181 board [3]. Some of the FPGA and I/O modules were designed by students for their final projects.

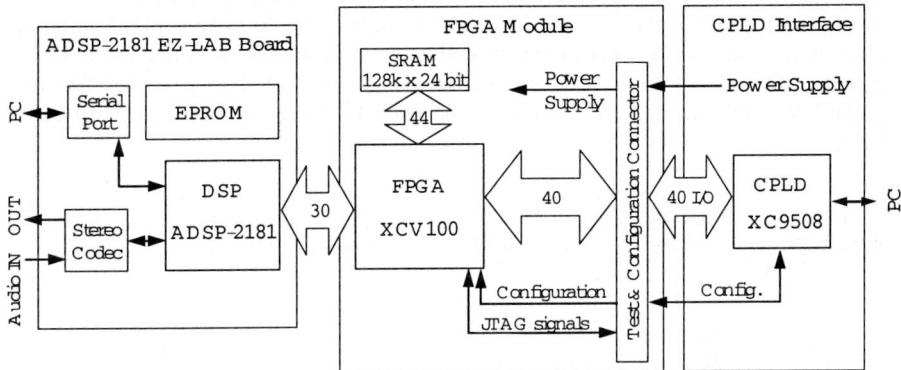

Fig. 1. Hardware prototyping and verification system

In order to further increase logic capacity of the modular prototyping system, we connected the FPGA modules on the main board, as presented in Figure 2. The main board contains one Spartan (XCS40) FPGA used as a configuration engine for up to six FPGA modules, DRAM controller and verification interface. The board is connected to the PC which is used for configuration and testing of FPGA modules.

FPGA modules are interconnected with a 16-bit control bus driven by the Spartan FPGA on the main board and a 24-bit data bus. The data bus is composed of local data paths with bidirectional 3-state buffers. The buffers enable simultaneous data transfer between 3 pairs of FPGA modules at any given time. This interconnection scheme is best used when large amount of local communication between neighbor modules is required which is the case for designs in the pipeline architecture.

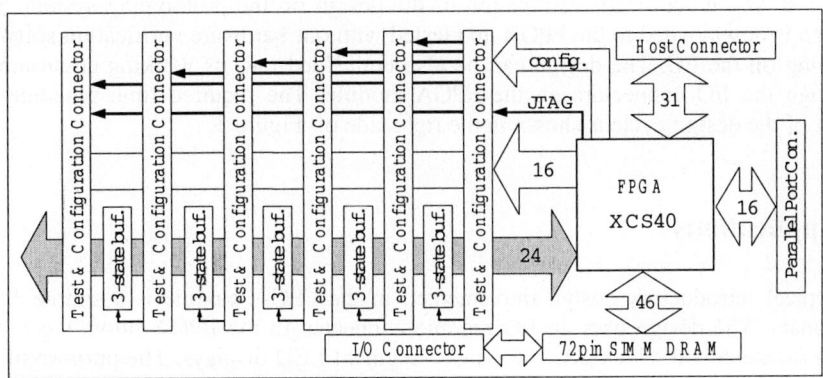

Fig. 2. Main board of the custom computing engine

3 The Design Cycle

Figure 3 presents the design cycle on the prototyping and verification system. The first step is a circuit specification phase, where the circuit functions or even the whole system is simulated in C++ or Java environment. For example, the operation of a digital filter can be simulated and tested in the C++ program, before we actually begin with the circuit design. Another example are image processing applications, where we can test algorithms in the Java environment on some sample images [4]. The circuit design and simulation is performed in VHDL environment with Aldec Active-HDL simulator. Results of high level simulation can be exported to a vector file in a standard WAVES format [5] which can be used later during hardware verification phase.

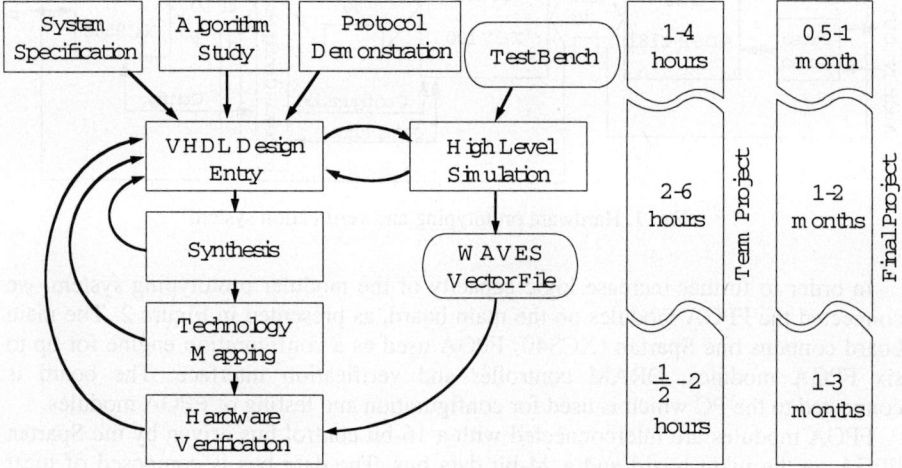

Fig. 3. Typical design cycle and time schedule

Synthesis and technology mapping are performed automatically with Synopsys FPGA Express and Xilinx Foundation tools with no or very little user interaction. The last step is hardware verification of the design on the prototyping system. The design is downloaded to the FPGA and tested with our hardware verification software running on the PC. The design can be also embedded into its working environment through the I/O connectors on the FPGA module. The required time schedule for steps of the design cycle is shown in the right side of Figure 3.

4 Applications

A typical introductory design implemented in the FPGA module is a simple finite automata. The design uses an I/O module connected to the FPGA providing inputs from the keyboard, clock generator and 7-segment LED displays. The purpose of the design is to demonstrate students the complete prototyping design cycle and to outline some problems and solutions during transition from computer simulator to the real world. Most of implementation errors occur due to the wrong assumptions on polarity, timing dependency and duration of input and output signals. Students are later encouraged to choose a project and to implement the design on the prototyping module. Some common digital design projects are: serial communications controller (UART), cipher circuit [6] and simple 4-bit or 8-bit microprocessor [7].

The next project exploits FPGA module simultaneously with the DSP board. A signal processing algorithm is first implemented as a C++ program and tested on the DSP development board. The critical timing parts of the algorithm are then implemented in hardware. By solving this type of a project, students get familiarized with the concept of HW/SW co-design [8].

Multi-FPGA applications are required for larger designs due to insufficient logic or memory resources on a single FPGA module. Typical applications are implementations of real-time image processing algorithms, for example Canny and nonlinear Laplace edge detection circuits [9].

5 Conclusions

We have presented programmable hardware prototyping and verification system which we extensively use in educational process at our University. The presented system supports a broad scope of digital design applications. Our future work will be based on seamless integration of hardware and software design in our design flow for embedded systems. We will also continue to upgrade our FPGA modules and I/O boards in order to support the newest FPGA devices and design techniques.

References

[1] J.O. Hamblen, H. L. Oven, S. Yalamanchili and B. Dao, *An Undergraduate Computer Engineering Rapid Systems Prototyping Design Laboratory,* IEEE Transactions on Education, Vol 42, No. 1, pp. 8-14, Feb. 1999

[2] A. Zemva, A. Trost and B. Zajc, *Educational Programmable System for Prototyping Digital Circuits,* International Journal of Electrical Engineering Education, Vol. 35, No. 3, pp. 236-244, March 1998

[3] *ADSP-2100 Family EZ-KIT Lite Reference Manual,* Analog Devices Inc., 1995

[4] *Digital Image Processing in Java,* http://www.dic3.fe.uni-lj.si/courses/mt-sp.html

[5] IEEE. *IEEE Standard for Waveform and Vector Exchange,* IEEE Standard 1029.1-1991

[6] B. Schneier. *Applied Cryptography,* John Willey & Sons, 1996

[7] D. Van den Bout. *The Practical Xilinx Designer Lab Book,* Prentice Hall, 1997

[8] G. de Micheli, R. K. Gupta. *Hardware/Software Co-Design,* Proc. IEEE, vol. 82(3), pp. 349-365, 1997

[9] A. Trost, B. Zajc. *Design of Real-Time Edge Detection Circuits on Multi-FPGA Prototyping System,* International Conf. on Electrical and Electonics Engineering, pp. 385-389, Bursa, Turkey, 1999

A Stream Processor Architecture Based on the Configurable CEPRA–S

Rolf Hoffmann[1], Bernd Ulmann[2],
Klaus–Peter Völkmann[1], and Stefan Waldschmidt[1]

[1] Darmstadt University of Technology, 64283 Darmstadt, Germany,
{hoffmann,voelk,waldsch}@informatik.tu-darmstadt.de
[2] Raven Information Technologies GmbH,
ulmann@raven-infotech.de

Abstract. Stream processing is a very efficient method to process large amounts of data. In contrast to vector architectures, stream processing involves instruction stream which are associated with data streams instead of a single instruction operating on data streams (vectors) thus facilitating individual processing of stream elements. Furthermore, operators in the arithmetic/logic unit can be configured to meet special processing requirements of an application. In the following article an architecture which can be configured as a stream processor is described.

1 Preliminary Work

In projects on Cellular Processing at the Darmstadt University of Technology (partly supported by the DFG) some configurable coprocessors based on FPGA technology have been developed (eg. [1]) to speed up cellular processing. The last processor built was the CEPRA-1X [2] which used the memory of a host computer for storing the cell field. The cell states were streamed via a PCI interface through a highly pipelined calculation unit. At present a more universal configurable coprocessor, the CEPRA-S, is being implemented. This machine and stream processing as an application is described in the following.

2 The Architecture of the CEPRA-S

The CEPRA-S (Fig. 1) is designed as a configurable coprosssor PCI plug-in card for special applications, especially cellular processing and stream processing. The block transfer rate is near to 132 MByte/s (33 MHz PCI clock, 32 bit). It consists of two Xilinx XC-4025 and eight memory banks, each of size 256k 16 bit words. One FPGA acts as a control unit (CU) to which a memory PM is connected which can be used as program or data memory. The PM may also be used to store global data or control information. The CU generates eight addresses for the data memory banks DM0 to DM7 which are connected to the second FPGA acting as a generalized ALU (also called execution unit EU) thereby allowing eight data accesses in parallel. An additional memory unit (TM) can be used as a look up table, as scratch pad memory, etc. Both FPGAs are connected by the IBUS for the exchange of data and control information.

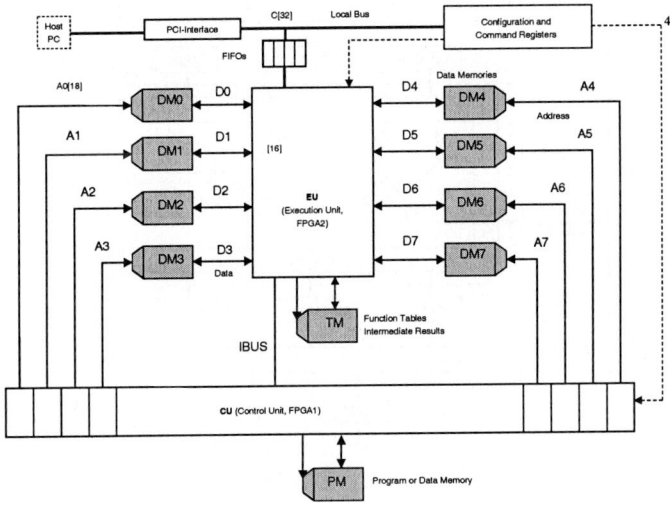

Fig. 1. The CEPRA-S

3 Stream Processing

Introduction. A stream processor is a specialized computer architecture (Fig. 2) consisting of several distinct units: A *stream control unit* SCU which controls the data flow through the computational element of the machine, *control memory* CMEM containing the global instructions to be executed by the SCU, a *stream processing unit* SPU (this is some type of a generalized arithmetic logic unit which is fed with data and instructions from the stream memory units under the control of the SCU) and finally the *stream memory* SMEM which is connected to the SPU and is used as the main data source and drain as controlled by the SCU.

The main difference between stream processors and vector machines is that the SPU does not operate on data streams under the total control of the SCU which controls only the streams itself. Instead a stream can be interpreted as data or instruction stream, so each processing element of the SPU receives three streams: Two input data streams and a third stream which is used as control instruction stream. Thus each pair of input data has an instruction assigned from a corresponding instruction stream.

The First Stream Processor. The very first roots of stream processors reach back to the early 50s when Konrad Zuse invented the "Feldrechner" [3]. The main parts of the Feldrechner were a drum memory which was used as data/instruction supply and data take up (this implies the address generation functionality of the

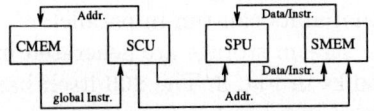

Fig. 2. General structure of a stream processor

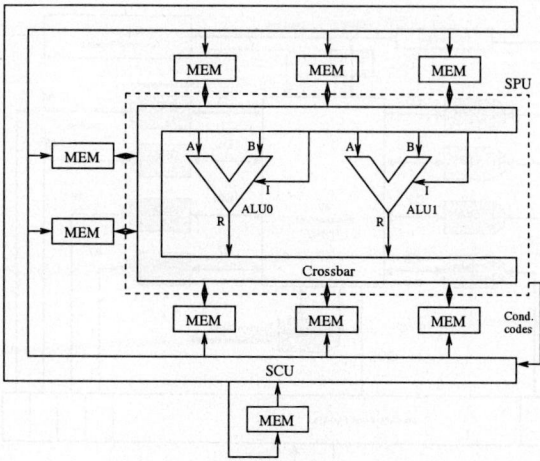

Fig. 3. The CEPRA-S/Stream

SCU since the memory addresses are generated implicitly by the drum revolutions), an arithmetic unit, data selectors and a control unit for conditional execution. A separate instruction track on the magnetic drum corresponded in an element wise fashion with the data streams.

The Feldrechner was thought of as a matrix-/vector-accelerator which is one of the main applications stream processors can be used for. Technological problems made the idea of stream processing quite difficult to implement since such architectures rely extremely on fast memory systems. With the advent of fast, small and cheap high speed semiconductor memory the idea of stream processing is capable to gain more interest.

4 The CEPRA-S as Stream Processor

The configuration of the CEPRA-S as a stream processor (called CEPRA-S/Stream) is shown in Fig. 3. Its main component is the SPU consisting of two special arithmetic logic units (ALU0 and ALU1) which can be configured accordingly to the requirements of the actual application and a lookup table (LT) (not shown here for clarity). These units are surrounded by a crossbar unit which is used as the main interconnect to the stream memory banks. Each of the ALUs operates on three input streams (data and instruction) while generating one output stream (data or instruction).

The stream memory consists of eight distinct memory chips – each is capable of holding 2^{18} machine words. Using the crossbar structure, it is possible to select four memory banks as data sources, two for providing the instruction streams and two banks as destination ensuring a well balanced data throughput so that in most cases all functional units can run in parallel.

The addresses for the stream storage are generated by the SCU which is surrounding the memory banks in Fig. 3. The SCU itself has its own local memory which is used for storing the *global instructions* to be executed. These instructions are quite VLIW-like, as can be found in machines like the Multiflow TRACE or the Nanodata QM-1 for example, since they consist of three *subinstructions* to control all data streams and the global program flow through the SCU independently at the same time.

Theory of Operation. Prior to performing calculations, the stream and global instruction memory subsystems of the CEPRA-S/Stream are loaded with the appropriate data by the host computer. As soon as the machine starts running, the SCU reads global instructions from its associated memory.

Each subinstruction contains four register parts – three load/one store register for both of the ALUs. Each register description consists of three parts:

- The number of the selected register (memory bank) to control the crossbar,
- the start address of the stream to be processed and
- the stride for the vector (possibly zero or negative).

Both subinstructions share the same length specification for the streams which are to be processed. The third subinstruction is used to control the global program flow which the SCU executes and other housekeeping functions. To process two and more dimensional data structures, it is necessary to use the contents of special SCU registers as start addresses for the registers specified in the subinstructions. During the execution of a global instruction the SCU can modify the contents of those address registers being controlled by additional instructions to provide new start addresses for subsequent SPU instructions.

5 Conclusion

The stream processor CEPRA-S/Stream can be used as a powerful attached processor. Due to its very flexible nature and its high data bandwidth it is ideally suited for tasks which are compute intensive such as signal processing or tasks in the fields of number theory and cryptography. Since the processing of data streams is controlled by associated (but randomly selectable) instruction streams, the resulting architecture is highly flexible and can be easily adapted to a variety of applications.

References

1. Rolf Hoffmann, Klaus-Peter Völkmann, and Marek Sobolewski. The cellular processing machine CEPRA-8L. *Mathematical Research*, 81:179–188, 1994.
2. Christian Hochberger, Rolf Hoffmann, Klaus-Peter Völkmann, and Jens Steuerwald. The CEPRA-1X cellular processor. In Rainer W. Hartenstein and Viktor K. Prasanna, editors, *Reconfigurable Architectures, High Performance by Configware*. IT Press, Bruchsal, 1997.
3. Konrad Zuse. *Der Computer – mein Lebenswerk*. Springer-Verlag, Berlin Heidelberg, 1986.

An Innovative Approach to Couple EDA Tools with Reconfigurable Hardware

Uwe Hatnik, Jürgen Haufe, and Peter Schwarz

Fraunhofer Institute for Integrated Circuits
Design Automation Department EAS Dresden, Germany

Abstract. The integration of real hardware components into simulation environments requires a suitable interface. There are a variety of simulators with unique specific vendor dependent interfaces, which are not compatible in general and some of them cannot support features that are required by modern design tools. To overcome the resulting insufficience, the Open Model Interface (OMI) was defined. This paper shows that the OMI, developed for complex digital software models, can also be used to couple hardware with simulators, whereby all advantages of the OMI (e.g. vendor independence, IP protection) are preserved.

1 Motivation

Usually simulators provide an interface, which allows to integrate third party models and which can also be used to include real hardware components. Most of the existing interfaces, e.g. CLI (VSS/Synopsys), are provided by the simulator vendors and are not compatible to other tools. Some of them, e.g. SWIFT [2], even have a hidden implementation. The great number of interfaces forces independent model providers to adapt their model implementations to the different simulators. The adaptation consumes much of time and money. The probability that errors occur is also raised up. Important problems are the different interface concepts and necessary functions, which are not supported by all interfaces. The Open Model Interface (OMI), since 1999 an IEEE standard, was developed for complex digital software models [3]. We examined the possibility of the OMI to include not only pure software models into a simulation environment, but also reconfigurable hardware as an implementation platform for hardware prototypes.

This paper is organized as follows. Section 2 gives a short introduction of the OMI and shows main advantages. The object oriented simulation approach, we have used for our realization, is explained in section 3. Implementation aspects are described in section 4.

2 Approach and Advantages

The OMI is an open standard interface, which allows interoperability between an application (e.g. a simulator) and functional models, which are presented in a binary form. The models can be developed in a variety of languages, for example

VHDL, Verilog HDL, and C. To generate a binary form, a suitable compiler is necessary. Because models are only supplied in a binary form, a simple but effective IP (intellectual property) protection is possible. Furthermore, a single model library may contain models of different model providers. These multiple models may be used concurrently during one session.

A separate software component exists between application and models, the OMI model manager. The model manager connects the application with the models and provides built-in or external models. If the application wants to use a model, the model manager creates and manages a unique customized instance, derived from the demanded model. Figure 1 shows the resulting structure. Only the interface between application and model manager is defined by the OMI specification. The connection between model manager and models as well as instances is unrestricted. This allows a very high flexibility as well as easy model generation and reuse. The model manager mainly provides routines to realize the functionality of the models and to provide model information. Furthermore the model manager may implement additional functions, for example version and licence management. A model query mechanism may be used by the application to get model information, e.g. ports, parameters, supported data types, viewports etc. Viewports are model-internal ports, visible from the outside to simplify verification and test. They have to be provided by the model developer and allow to control the internal visibility with respect to IP protection.

The interaction between the model and the application is not fixed but can be adapted dynamically during runtime. A so-called callback mechanism allows to register and remove model function calls (named callbacks), dependent on the required interaction. More information about the goals and advantages of the OMI can be found in [4].

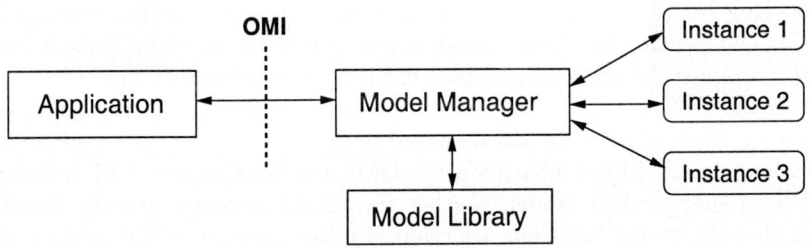

Fig. 1. OMI Basic Components

Because the OMI is a young IEEE standard, only the latest releases of EDA tools (e.g. BONeS/Cadence) support this interface. Therefore, we have developed an OMI adaption for the simulators VSS and Fusion to gain experiences with the OMI. Additional, we have developed an own model manager to use some test models and include a FPGA board. As soon as more OMI compliant tools are available, the FPGA board can also be used with these tools.

A disadvantage of the OMI approach is the overhead, caused mainly by the data conversion and the callback management. The overhead depends on the data transfer rate and the model complexity. Increasing model execution time causes a smaller relative overhead and vice versa.

3 Object Oriented Simulation

In the last years, the object oriented simulation approach has been established and also the OMI follows this idea. Object oriented simulation means that a system consists of subsystems, which are simulated autonomously. Such a subsystem is named "object" and may contain other objects, so that an object hierarchy may be built. All implementation details are encapsulated by the object, only an interface allows data exchange and simulation control.

The OMI follows this approach because it is customized for functional models, which may contain own simulation algorithms. Furthermore, each object encapsulate its implementation (IP protection) and may use other models, so that a model hierarchy is possible.

For our work the encapsulation of all implementation details is the most important feature of this approach. It allows to couple hardware components without influence of the OMI application. The application uses an OMI model, which can be realized via software or hardware components.

4 Implementation

In [5], we have shown the possibility to include real hardware into simulation environments via the OMI, exemplary based on the interface board SimConnect. This board controls the data transfer between a host computer and a FPGA prototyping board. An application programming interface (API) realizes data transfer and control functions, which are executed by the SimConnect board. The SimConnect board realizes data exchange between host and FPGA and controls the FPGA prototyping board according to the called API commands. A more detailed description can be found in [5].

To include the FPGA board via the OMI, the SimConnect API is encapsulated by a special OMI model. Neither the model manager nor the simulator knows that the model functions are realized using hardware. During the evaluation phase the model registers all necessary simulator callbacks and initializes the SimConnect board as well as the FPGA on the prototyping board. The FPGA design is loaded from the host file system. To protect the design IP it is possible to integrate the design directly into the model or to encrypt the design file. In this case the model must contain a decrypt algorithm. The registered callbacks are called during the simulation phase, e.g. when an input port has changed. In that case the called instance function reads the signal value from the simulator, transforms the data format, and uses the SimConnect API functions to transfer the data to the FPGA on the prototyping board. If all needed data are available, the FPGA can be enabled for a predefined number of clocks or until an stop

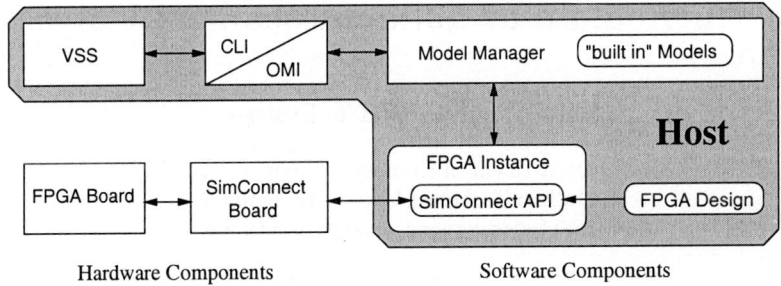

Fig. 2. Basic Components

signal occurs (e.g. an output signal changes its value). After that SimConnect propagates the output data to the instance. The instance converts these data into an OMI format and gives it to the simulator, using OMI functions.

Besides the FPGA instance the simulator may also create other model instances. If the host provides several I/O-ports, also several FPGA boards can be used at the same time.

5 Conclusion

We have shown that the OMI standard is not only suitable for models written in software, but the standard can also be used to include real hardware components into simulation environments. Thereby it is possible to substitute hardware components for software models, which opens new application fields, e.g. the combination of simulation and hardware prototyping in a common environment. Our approach supports all OMI advantages like application independency, IP protection, dynamic interaction control, model information query, control of internal visibility etc.

References

[1] Open Model Forum Home Page, http://www.eda.org/omf
[2] Synopsys Inc.: SWIFT Interface Specification
[3] IEEE P1499 Technical Committee: IEEE P1499 – Standard Interface for Hardware Description Models of Electronic Components. IEEE Standard Department
[4] Hobbs, W.: Model Availability, Portability, and Accuracy – An IC Vendor's Perspective, Effort and Vision for the Future. Computer Simulation, special issue on "Simulation Software Development" (1995) vol. 4, pp. 155–182
[5] Haufe, J., Schwarz, P., Berndt, T., Große, J.: Accelerated Logic Simulation by Using Prototype Boards. Design, Automation and Test in Europe DATE 1998, Paris, 23.–26.2.98, 183–189 (Designer Track)

FPL Curriculum at Tallinn Technical University

K. Tammemäe and T. Evartson

Department of Computer Engineering
Tallinn Technical University, Estonia
nalle@cc.ttu.ee, teet@pld.ttu.ee

Abstract. This paper describes reconfigurable logic in education at Tallinn Technical University (TTU) in the light of rapid changes of country's economical structure and information technology environment. A logical set of courses has been introduced at every educational direction of Computer Engineering (CE) along with the set of design tools, prototyping boards and reconfigurable platforms. The courses, hardware and design tools, utilized for educating the field programmable logic and mixed hardware/software systems are described.

1 Introduction

Field programmable logic is one of the most rapidly evolving digital electronics technology areas, and expectations for future integration with digital system-on-chip design are high. During recent years, the reconfigurable logic has proved to fit almost every application domain, not to mention its historical use for prototyping of digital systems [1]. The technology of reconfigurable logic keeps the evolution pace of mainstream semiconductor technology, and although the peak frequency difference remains the order of magnitude is not worsening. The same is true about the amount of logic in VLSI and reconfigurable logic technology. Moreover, the reconfigurable logic enables to use wider range of trade-offs where designing the hardware/software interface. The expansion of design space freedom comes at price of additional education. The gain is availability of more flexible devices, which have longer life-span then those, designed with rigid hardware/software boundary in mind.

During recent years we have seen the rise of Estonian digital synthesis enterprises. So far, these are quite small ones, around ten designers, but rapidly expanding and searching for educated workers. All of them have been established by foreign design companies, which were attracted by Estonia's cheap infrastructure and low running costs. In several cases, the initial designs were accomplished in analog field. Because of the initial sucess more complex design tasks were issued and more decision freedom was allowed. There is a clear tendency toward pure digital and/or mixed digital/analog designs. First time the students of TTU have had an opportunity to find employment in hardware design area at homeland. This is a remarkable positive feedback encouraging university to accept more students, to improve courses and to issue specific diploma or Master thesis tasks.

2 Hardware and Tools

There are two programmable logic prototyping platforms in use:

1. XESS XC4010XL development boards with embedded Intel 8051 family microcontroller [4].
2. Virtual Computer Corporation HOT Works development system (DS) [5].

The number of prototyping boards can be expanded with XC4010XL+ boards in future, which have an integrated keyboard/mouse interface and larger SRAM memory. Also, some of the courses will use Spartan and Virtex prototyping boards ordered through Insight Memec, Finland.

Our department applied for Xilinx University Program donation and received five Foundation Express 2.1 floating licenses for PC platform. From high-end, there are nine Synopsys SECP licenses for Unix platform obtained through EUROPRACTICE. There are three computer classes, which can be used for design courses. One is equipped with Sun UltraSparc 5 workstations, another with older Sparc 2 workstations and third with multiboot PC-s (Linux and Microsoft Windows). Our high-end processing server is a dual-processor Sun UltraSparc 60.

3 Curricula

The programmable logic devices (PLD) are used in three study programs in CE education:

- *Bachelor Program (4 years)*: IAF3930 Programmable Logic Design, IAY3710 VLSI design, IAY5750 HW/SW Codesign.
- *Diploma Program (5 years)*: IAF3933 Programmable Logic, IAF3934 Programmable Logic - Project, IAY3714 VLSI Synthesis and HDL, IAY5750 HW/SW Codesign.
- *Master Program (4 + 2 years)*: IAF5930 Programmable Logic, IAY3750 HW/SW Codesign.

3.1 Practical Works in Field Programmable Logic Course

We describe a PLD course, which has been set up at the Tallinn Technical University with cooperation with Darmstadt University of Technology, supported by TEMPUS JEP-4772-92/1 Project in 1992 and later prolonged.

The theoretical part of PLD course consists of eight lectures to discover the world of different FPGA architectures, programming technologies and design specific methods.

The practical part of PLD course consists of sixteen practical works in PC laboratory supported by specific hardware and software. On the basis of Xess Corporation XS Board V1.2, XStend Board V1.2 and Xess Foundation 2.1 environment along with Xess Corporation XSTOOLS 2.0 software, an advanced laboratory course has been developed to teach and train students to design and implement digital circuits. Xess prototyping board incorporates Xilinx 4010XL FPGA, Oki MSM80C154S microcontroller, 32kB RAM, 7-segment LED display, VGA RGB analog display connector, and Centronics interface to PC for configuration and I/O operations. "In-house" made teaching boards [8] may be little cheaper but that depends on the board manufacturing technology at the spot. Additionally, a unique "user friendly" software has to be developed.

The list of lab works the students should pass is as follows:

1. LED control with register (FPGA circuit design).
2. LED control with decoder (FPGA circuit design).
3. LED control with 4-bit BCD counter (FPGA circuit design).
4. Traffic Light Control (FPGA circuit design).
5. RGB signal generator for VGA (FPGA ABEL).
6. XStend keyboard and LED connection with decoding (FPGA ABEL).
7. LED control with 4-bit counter (FPGA circuit design and i8031 ASM).
8. LED control with 4-bit counter (FPGA ABEL and i8031 ASM).
9. XStend keyboard and LED connection with decoding (FPGA ABEL and i8031 ASM).

3.2 Practical Works in Hardware/Software Codesign Course

Advanced practical works have been developed for HW/SW codesign course, which will start in reviewed form in fall 2000. The first half of the practical works is planned on XESS boards, another half on Spartan/Virtex boards. For hardware design, VHDL is used. The software part depends on the tools and boards, and can be assembler or C.

The work flow for XESS boards is planned to be as follows:

1. Fixed microprocessor/FPGA cooperation on base of XESS XC4010XL board.
2. Partitioning functions between microcontroller and FPGA.

Unfortunately the components on XESS XC4010XL board are too tightly interconnected, which leaves not enough opportunities to play around with HW/SW interface. The memory lines are shared and although the access to common memory can be organized in interleaved way, the added complexity of such a solution is high and unnecessary. The board is designed to fulfill one crisp goal - RGB video signal generation for VGA displays. The on-board memory is dedicated as video memory, whereas the FPGA implements the necessary memory scannings and video signal timings. Microcontroller can be used for image processing but the program space is very limited. A much better solution would be to use separate dual-port video and program memories.

We were highly impressed by the features of HOT Works development system, which enables remote programming and feedback. Although the production of Xilinx 6200 family chips is phased out by Xilinx, Inc., the systems are still available by VCC, along with support and drivers for various platforms and applications. Still, the concept would be truly interesting only in the case of contemporary FPGA technology. From the remote education or virtual laboratory point of view, the prototyping boards have to be connected to a server PCI bus. This makes it possible to share the access for programming and usage over the Internet. The possibilities of remote usage of VCC HOT Works DS have been investigated in [6], [7].

The following assignment sets can be included into HW/SW codesign curriculum:

1. *Autonomous tasks.* An area in memory will be dedicated to virtual screen which can be controlled over the Internet.
2. *Hardware/software interaction.* The task is to implement an HW/SW accelerator of simplified cryptographic function where our department has remarkable research experience [2], [3].
3. *Internet server layer.* At this level, additional software layer will be built which enables adjusting and launching of accelerated cryptographic functions over the Internet.

The complexity of the second and third tasks is high and those works are considered to be a part of Master program course only. The goal is to let students to get an idea of hardware/software design trade-offs. It is important to reach a conclusion that there are several opportunities to define hardware/software interface, and to understand that there is always a reason to reconsider the current trade-off if the design parameters are changing.

4 Conclusion

An overview of reconfigurable logic education in TTU has been given in this paper. The courses have not run long enough to get a sufficient feedback from students and digital design industry. Anyway, the first opinions have been good and we keep courses open for improvements.

References

1. J. Becker, F. M. Renner, M. Glesner, "Perspectives of Reconfigurable Computing in Education", In *Microelectronics Education*, Kluwer Academic Publishers, 1998.
2. Juri Põldre, Kalle Tammemäe, "Reconfigurable Multiplier for Virtex FPGA Family", *FPL'99*, Glasgow, 1999, pp. 369–364.
3. Juri Põldre, Ahto Buldas, "A VLSI Implementation of RSA and IDEA encryption engine", *NORCHIP'97*, 1997.
4. http://www.xess.com
5. http://www.vcc.com
6. Stuart Nisbet, Steven A. Guccione, "The XC6200DS Development System", *FPL'97*, London, 1997.
7. Reiner W. Hartenstein, Michael Herz, Frank Gilbert, "Designing for Xilinx XC6200 FPGAs", *FPL'98*, Tallinn, 1998.
8. T. Vassileva and V.Tchoumatchenko, "FPGA as Educational ASIC", In *Proceedings of the European Workshop Microelectronics Education*, Grenoble, France, 1996.

The Modular Architecture of SYNTHUP, FPGA Based PCI Board for Real-Time Sound Synthesis and Digital Signal Processing

Jean-Michel Raczinski and Stéphane Sladek

CEMAMu
France Télécom R&D - B403
38-40, rue du Général Leclerc
92794 Issy-Les-Moulineaux Cedex 9 France

raczinski@cemamu.asso.fr, sladek@cemamu.asso.fr

Abstract. SYNTHUP is a standard PCI plug-in board based on Xilinx FPGAs. It has been designed at CEMAMu for real-time sound synthesis and can be used for general purpose digital signal processing. Its modular architecture features a PCI interface, seven identical cells dedicated to computing, each made-up of one FPGA that drives two independent 4M×16 SDRAM with separate address and data buses. An array of five FPGAs is dedicated to data exchange between the cells and also drives five 12 bit ports. An eight cell is used for processing control, synthesis parameters update for example. PCI bus mastering (scatter-gather DMA) and a total of 128M bytes of dual port SDRAM allow the synthesizer to function independently of the host. The paper introduces our first results in additive synthesis and the implementation of adaptive FIR filters with distributed arithmetic.

1 Introduction

When we started the design of SYNTHUP as the foundation of our new workstation for real-time sound synthesis, we based the board on FPGAs in order to achieve a high degree of both performance and programmability: additive synthesis of several hundreds of oscillators, programmability of both synthesis and its control, implementation of digital signal processing functions (FFTs, filters, etc.) running in parallel, good decoupling from the host and a large amount of on board memory, all this for the lowest price.

2 SYNTHUP Architecture

The board is made up of a PCI interface, seven identical cells dedicated to computing, an array of five FPGAs dedicated to data exchange and one cell for control (Fig. 1).

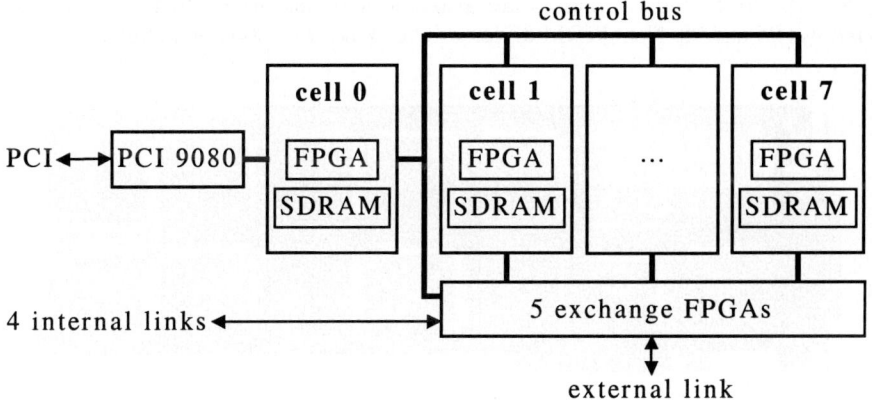

Fig. 1. SYNTHUP architecture

The basic cell is made up of one FPGA that drives two independent 4M×16 SDRAM (Fig. 2). This allows two accesses (read and/or write) to take place simultaneously. The memory can also be configured as a plain 4M×32. It is possible to upgrade the cell with two 16M×16 SDRAM.

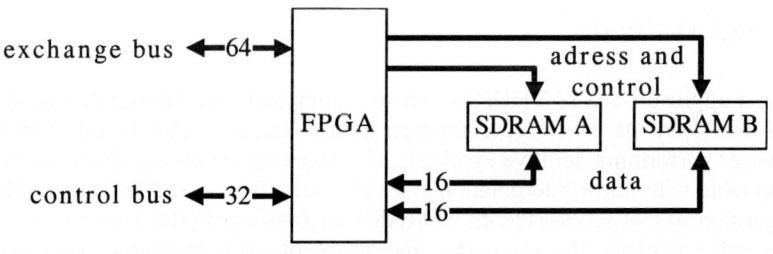

Fig. 2. SYNTHUP cell

Each cell can exchange 64 bits with the other cells through an array of five exchange FPGAs that work as a crossbar switch. Thanks to the FPGA technology, each bit can be programmed individually as input or output or general I/O.

The exchange FPGAs are also responsible for the communication with other boards. They drive five 12 bit ports: one link is available on a 37 pin connector on the card bracket, the four others are intended for communication with other boards in the PC. Here also, each bit is programmable as input, output or general I/O with data or control functionality.

The PCI interface is handled by a standard chip from PLX (PCI 9080). It features full PCI V2.1 compliance (32 bit, 33 MHz) including 5 volts and 3,3 volts compatibility; true Plug and Play installation and configuration as well as bus mastering for high speed transfer between the board and the host memory (scatter-gather DMA).

Applications are downloaded from the host via PCI into the logical resources of the FPGAs in few milliseconds. This makes the system fully re-configurable at will.

A VxD driver and C++ classes are available allowing access to the board under Windows 95 and 98. Next WDM driver will be Windows 2000 compatible.

Fig. 3. SYNTHUP PCB

The board works with a single 40 MHz clock. The footprint of the FPGAs (PQ240) allows installation of any component of the 4000XL or 4000XLA family, starting with 4013 (10K-30K gates equivalent) up to 4085 (75K-200K gates equivalent). A fully equipped board with 4044XLA devices is available for 5000 •.

3 Sound Synthesis

As a first application, SYNTHUP is part of a computer-aided music composing tool named UPIC by its inventor, composer Iannis Xenakis. The board works as a synthesizer performing additive synthesis of 800 simultaneous oscillators (waveform look-up table with linear interpolation at 48 kHz sampling rate). We have parallelized the algorithm so that accesses to the SDRAMs are optimized (100% activity).

One cell calculates the frequency and phase of each oscillator. Two cells are dedicated to waveform read and interpolation, each handling 400 tables. Another cell calculates the envelopes (linear interpolation) and a fifth cell gathers the contributions of each oscillator to the output channels. The output audio samples are sent to an external module for Digital to Analog conversion. It is also possible to output the samples to a standard sound card through PCI.

Pitch data, which represent a large amount of data and don't need a fast update rate, are stored in the PC RAM while all other objects (waveforms, envelopes, etc.) are stored on board. The main role of the control cell is to update synthesis parameters. Pitch of each oscillator is updated every 10,7 ms (512 samples) with bus master DMA. Envelopes are updated every 0,7 ms (32 samples). These update rates are programmable. As both synthesis and its control function on the same clock, it is possible to synchronize all the oscillators with the precision of one sample.

We currently use Xilinx Foundation Series software for design entry (schematic, VHDL) and simulation.

4 Adaptive Filter Implementation

We have studied Distributed Arithmetic implementation of FIR filters on SYNTHUP [2]. Serial implementation allows us to filter 48 audio channels in real time (16 bit input data sampled at 48 kHz, 16 bit coefficients). Each channel gets its own filter. A 100 taps filter fits into a 4036XLA device. One can also build a 4800 taps filter for one channel.
The same RAM based look-up table is used for the different channels. The FPGA receives successive frames of audio samples, one frame per channel. Filtering a channel starts after initialization of its data input FIFO and initialization of the coefficients table. In order to keep this period of time as short as possible, the size of the frames has to be much larger than the sizes of the filter and the coefficients table. Doubling the input FIFO and the coefficients table (one for filtering, the other for initialization) allows us to reach the maximum number of channels. As new coefficients are loaded at each frame, we can implement adaptive filters that are capable of self-adjustment.

5 Conclusion

We have demonstrated the efficiency of the modular architecture of SYNTHUP and its FPGAs for additive synthesis and filtering in digital audio applications. Future developments include other types of sound synthesis and DSP functions. The authors would like to thank Gérard Marino and Vincent Fontalirant for their help all along this work. CEMAMu is a research center sponsored by the French ministry for culture (DMDTS). The works presented here have been realized with the help of France Telecom R&D at Issy-les-Moulineaux.

References

1. Raczinski, J.-M., Marino, G., Sladek, S., Fontalirant, V.: A Flexible Architecture for Real-Time Sound Synthesis and Digital Signal Processing. AES 108th Convention. Paris (2000)
2. Raczinski, J.-M., Sladek, S., Chevalier, L.: Filter Implementation on SYNTHUP. Proceedings of the 2nd COST G-6 Workshop on Digital Audio Effects, DAFx99, NTNU, Trondheim, December 9-11 (1999)
3. Raczinski, J.-M., Marino, G., Sladek, S., Fontalirant, V.: SYNTHUP Carte PCI pour la Synthèse du Son et le Traitement de Signal en Temps Réel. Proceedings of the JIM99. Paris (1999) 75-82
4. The Fastest Filter in the West. Xilinx Publication (1997)
5. The Role of Distributed Arithmetic in FPGA-based Signal Processing. Xilinx Publication (1997)
6. Goslin, G. R.: A Guide to Using Field Programmable Gate Arrays (FPGAs) for Application-Specific Digital Signal Processing Performance. Xilinx publications (1995)
7. Mintzer L.: FIR Filters with Field Programmable Gate Arrays. Journal of VLSI Signal Processing, No. 6 (1993) 120-127
8. Xilinx DSP Overview: http://www.xilinx.com/dsp/

A Rapid Prototyping Environment for Microprocessor Based System-on-Chips and Its Application to the Development of a Network Processor[*]

André Brinkmann, Dominik Langen, and Ulrich Rückert

Department of Electrical Engineering and Heinz Nixdorf Institute
Paderborn University, 33102 Paderborn, Germany.
{brinkman, langen, rueckert}@hni.uni-paderborn.de.

Abstract. The rapid advances in microelectronic circuit design have dramatically increased the design complexity of modern integrated devices. One approach to fit the time-to-market requirements is the use of rapid prototyping environments. In this paper we introduce a new FPGA based prototyping environment, on which a full functional embedded system can be implemented. The main distinction to other environments is the incorporation of a synthesizable and configurable microprocessor core into the design space. Furthermore we present the application of this environment to the development of a network processor which consists of a processor core and an Ethernet controller.

1 Introduction

During the last decade the rapid advances in microelectronic circuit design led to an increase in transistor count and clock speed. Today's deep submicron fabrication technologies enable design engineers to put an impressive number of components like microprocessors and coprocessors on a single chip. These so called system on chips (SOCs) lower the power consumption and the total fabrication cost of embedded systems while increasing performance and reliability. The complexity of SOCs is outpacing the capabilities of modern design tools and verification methodologies, resulting in long and expensive design cycles. To meet the time-to-market requirements has become a formidable challenge for SOC design engineers. The use of rapid prototyping systems could ease this task [4,3,6]. Prototyping environments are normally based on a standard microprocessor, surrounded by a large amount of memory and interfaces to the outside world. Only the add-on hardware is realized on field programmable devices (*FPGAs*). Improvements of the processor core itself or the interfaces are not possible. This may be sufficient for a wide number of applications, but excludes the processor core from the design space. In this paper we will present a new approach which

---

[*] Research partially supported by the DFG-Sonderforschungsbereich 376, Project C5 and Infineon Technologies AG

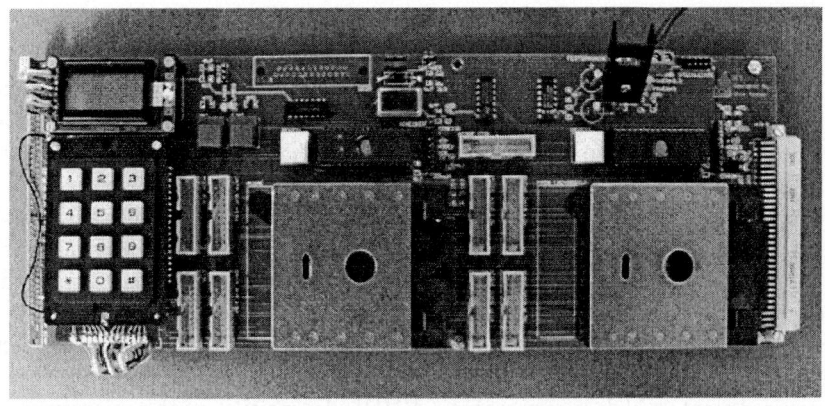

Fig. 1. The rapid prototyping board.

includes a configurable microprocessor core in the design space. In the next section we will introduce our rapid prototyping environment and the implemented interfaces. In section 3, we describe the integration of an Ethernet controller into our prototyping environment. Finally we will draw some conclusions and describe the next steps.

2 Rapid Prototyping Environment

Our rapid prototyping environment consists of three main parts: a FPGA board, a microprocessor core with software support and an Amba AHB interface for the core. The main distinction to other prototyping environments is the incorporation of the configurable microprocessor core. The core is described in the hardware description language VHDL and can be used both as a black box or as part of the design space by altering e.g. the architecture, the instruction set, or the interface depending on the requirements of the currently developed system.

The FPGA board includes two Xilinx XC4085 re-programmable FPGAs, 256 KByte SRAM, 128 KByte EPROM, a LCD display, a keypad, and off-board connectors for extension cards. The whole FPGA board has 6 layers and an area of 130 x 350mm^2 (Fig. 1). In this figure the memory subsystem is covered by the keypad. The two FPGAs are connected via 196 wires with each other, 80 of these wires can be observed by a logic analyzer. The microprocessor core and the Amba interface are mapped to the left FPGA. The other FPGA is used for the implementation of the application specific part, in this case for the Ethernet controller. The right FPGA is directly connected to a connector with 96 pins. This connector can be used for extension boards which can provide additional hardware for the system on the FPGA board. In our case we put the physical layer of the Ethernet on such an extension board.

The unmodified version of the microprocessor core is fully binary compatible to the Motorola M-Core processor and can be programmed with a number of

C/C++ environments. The M-Core is a 32-bit RISC one-address machine with a load/store architecture. Every opcode has a fixed length of 16 bit and every instruction except of the load and store instructions works only on registers. Fourteen percent of its opcode space is unoccupied and a hardware accelerator interface is supported. So the core can be easily enhanced. A detailed description of the architecture can be found in [7, 8].

The simple bus interface of the M-Core described in [8] has several disadvantages which disqualifies it for advanced applications. The main drawback is, that the simple bus interface does not support multiple bus masters, e.g. required by advanced network switches consisting of multiple DMA capable modules [2]. In a standard rapid prototyping environment, it would not be possible to efficiently exchange this simple microprocessor bus against a more suitable interface. In our environment, which incorporates a VHDL description of the microprocessor core and the bus interface, this drawback could be fixed by a *simple* rewriting of the bus interface. This new bus interface could be directly connected to the microprocessor core without any glue logic. For our application, we have chosen the *Amba Advanced High-performance Bus AHB* [1]. The Amba bus supports an arbitrary number of masters like processor cores and DMA units.

3 Integration of an Ethernet Controller

As Ethernet networks become more and more widespread, their importance as a means of communication for (embedded) computer systems grows accordingly [9]. Therefore, we present the design of an Ethernet medium access control (MAC) layer [5] for an embedded system and its integration into our rapid prototyping environment. The logic of the controller is mapped onto the right FPGA of our prototyping board (see Fig. 1) and it is connected to the M-Core processor via the Amba AHB bus interface. In the following, we describe the main modules of the Ethernet controller, the bus interface, the receive module, and the transmit module, and their integration into our rapid prototyping environment.

The transmit and receive unit of the Ethernet controller have to transfer data packets between the bus interface and the physical layer and to handle the Ethernet layer 2 protocol stack. To handle the communication, we use dualported SRAMs between the bus interface and the transmit and receive unit, respectively. In the following, we will call them fifo memories, because we use them in a very similar manner. One unit pushes data packets into the memory and the other unit reads packets out of it.

The bus interface is connecting the microprocessor core with the receive and transmit unit of the Ethernet controller via the Amba AHB bus. In this implementation with a single Ethernet controller we have chosen a simple slave interface without DMA capabilities. This involves that the microprocessor core is fully responsible for the transfers to and from the fifo memories. The transfers can either be triggered by interrupts or the processor polls the status of the memories. The controller is programmed by a memory mapped register set. An interface to the MII management register set is also incorporated.

The prototyping board itself does not contain the necessary physical Ethernet layer and the buffer memory of the controller. To test the Ethernet controller in a real environment, we have developed an extension card, which contains the physical Ethernet layer. This card is connected to the prototyping board via the offboard connectors. The entire system has been tested with a transfer rate of 10 MBit/s in a heterogeneous environment of workstations and personal computers. Ping, arp and reverse arp were successfully performed. The Ethernet controller and the physical layer are also capable to support 100 MBit/s. In our case, the system speed is limited by the speed of the microprocessor core.

4 Conclusion

We have presented a rapid prototyping environment including a configurable microprocessor core in the design space. The VHDL description of the core enables the designer to configure the core according to the requirements of his current project. In our example, we have exchanged the standard bus interface against a multimaster capable Amba AHB bus to couple the M-Core processor with an Ethernet controller. Together with the extension card, the prototyping environment is able to simulate a whole SOC. In future work we will use Xilinx Virtex FPGAs to support an increased amount of logic and on-chip RAM. This will enable us to integrate additional modules like a simple cache or additional peripheral devices. We also plan to alter the instruction set of the microprocessor core to increase the resource efficiency (more speed and/or less power) of our system.

References

1. ARM: AMBA^{TM} Specification (Rev. 2.0) (1999).
2. P. Berenbrink, A. Brinkmann, C. Scheideler: Design of the PRESTO Multimedia Data Storage Network, Proc. of the Workshop on Communication and Data Management in Large Networks (INFORMATIK 99) (1999).
3. W. B. Gardner and M. Serra: An Object-Oriented Layered Approach for Hardware/Software Codesign of Embedded Systems, Proc. of the 31st Hawai'i Conference on System Science (1998).
4. W. Hardt and W. Rosenstiel: Speed-Up Estimation for HW/SW-Systems, Proc. of the 4th ACM Workshop on Hardware/Software Codesign (1996).
5. IEEE: IEEE Standard 802.3: Carrier Sense Multiple Access with Collision Detection (CSMA/CD) Access Methods and Physical Layer Specifications, The Institute of Electrical and Electronics Engineers, Inc. (1998).
6. H. Kalte, M. Porrmann, U. Rückert: Rapid Prototyping System für dynamisch rekonfigurierbare Hardwarestrukturen, Proc. of the AES2000 (2000).
7. Motorola: M-Core Reference Manual (1998).
8. Motorola: MMC2001 Reference Manual (1998).
9. S. Rüping, E. Vonnahme, J. Jasperneite: Analysis of Switched Ethernet Networks with different Topologies used in Automation Systems, Fieldbus Technology (1999).

Configuration Prefetching for Non-deterministic Event Driven Multi-context Schedulers*

Juanjo Noguera[1] and Rosa M. Badia[2]

[1] Dept. Computer Science, Universitat Autònoma de Barcelona
Edifici C, Campus UAB, E08193 Bellaterra, SPAIN
juanjo@cnm.es

[2] Dept. Computer Architecture, Universitat Politècnica de Catalunya, SPAIN

Abstract. Reconfiguration overhead minimization is one of the major matters of concern in Reconfigurable Computing. In this paper we address the problem of configuration prefetching for multi-context reconfigurable devices in order to minimize reconfiguration overhead. We present a novel non-deterministic event driven multi-context scheduler, and how it is applied to a case study of software acceleration.

1. Introduction and Motivation

Many of the most existing applications developed nowadays with reconfigurable devices involve run-time reconfiguration during application execution. However, benefits offered by run-time reconfiguration highly depend on configuration latency.

Several approaches address this problem of minimizing reconfiguration overhead, which can be classified into five different groups: (1) configuration compression, (2) relocation/defragmentation in partially reconfigurable systems, (3) configuration caching, (4) temporal partitioning, and (5) configuration prefetching.

Configuration prefetching techniques are based on the idea of loading the next reconfiguration context before it is actually required, hence overlapping device reconfiguration and application execution. The challenge in configuration prefetching is determining far enough in advance which configuration will be required next.

S. Hauck firstly introduced configuration prefetching in [1], where a single-context prefetching technique is presented. However, new approaches and possibilities are possible since configuration prefetching techniques for multi-context Dynamically Reconfigurable Logic (DRL) devices have not been widely explored. In this paper, we address this topic and present a novel multi-context prefetching technique for non-deterministic event driven *multi-context schedulers* (sometimes referred as *configuration controller*, too). Furthermore, the presented configuration controller is assumed

---

* This work have been founded by CICYT project TIC98-0410-C02-01. Authors acknowledge Altera support within its Programmable Hardware Development program.

to be part of a run-time hardware-software codesign methodology for dynamically reconfigurable architectures, which is explained in detail in [4].

2. Run-Time Event-Driven Multi-context Scheduler

In this section we present a run-time event-driven DRL multi-context scheduler. The presented scheduler assumes an *Event Stream* which has been sorted following any policy (earliest deadline first, shortest tag first, etc). We also assume that only the first event of the event stream is being processed on a DRL cell or CPU at same time.

The key idea of the scheduler is to minimize DRL context switch overheads, in order to minimize the total application execution time. This objective is accomplished using a lookahead strategy into the event stream memory (see fig. 1). Event Window (EW) is left as a parameter of our scheduler, and it describes the number of events that are observed in advance. From the DRL array state (that is, which contexts are active) and the EW, the DRL scheduler must decide which context should be replaced from the DRL array, and which context must be loaded into.

The pseudo-code for the proposed run-time DRL scheduling algorithm is shown in figure 2. The basis for the behavior of the proposed algorithm is the use of an array (*DRLArrayUtilization*), which represents the expected state (active contexts) for the DRL array within the EW. This array is obtained from the actual DRL array state and from the EW, using the function *ObtainDRLArrayUtilization*. Afterwards the algorithm calculates the number of DRL cells that will not be used within the EW (variable K). These K DRL cells (if there are anyone) are available for a context switch.

If there are not any available DRL cell for a context switch, the algorithm will select the DRL cell which has an active context that would be required latest (note that this is not a typical LRU replacement policy). The algorithm will also select a context to be placed as active in this DRL cell. The first context in the event stream which is not active within the DRL array will be selected. Finally, it performs the context switch with function *DRL_Behavior(DRL_cell, Context)*. On the other hand, if there are K DRL cells available for a context switch, the algorithm enters into a loop that goes through all EW. If it finds a context (associated with an event) which is not active within the DRL array, the algorithm selects the first available DRL cell to be set as active. Finally, the algorithm performs the context switch.

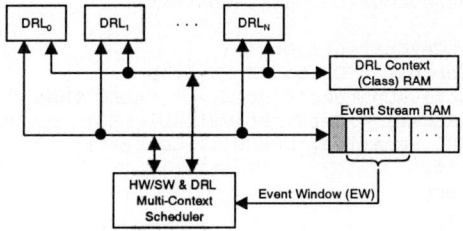

Fig. 1. DRL Multi-Context Scheduler Lookahead Strategy

Two different alternatives are possible for the explained DRL multi-context scheduler depending on the event window type: (1) static EW, and (2) dynamic EW.

A static EW based DRL multi-context scheduler assumes that the size of the EW will not change during the application execution. On the other hand, a dynamic EW based DRL multi-context scheduler assumes that the EW size can change its value during the application run-time execution. This dynamic EW size is calculated off-line (at compile time) for each event type. The key point in the dynamic EW multi-context scheduler is to look far enough in advance into the EW such that the sum of execution times for all events found in the EW equals the device reconfiguration time. Thus, each event type present in the system specification has an optimal EW size, which is given by the following expression:

$$EW_{Dynamic}^{C_i} = \left\lfloor \frac{T_{RECONFIG}}{T_{EXEC\{HW,SW\}}^{C_i}} \right\rfloor \quad (1)$$

where: (1) T_{EXEC} stands for the execution time (hardware or software) required by Context C_i, and (2) $T_{RECONFIG}$ stands for the DRL cell reconfiguration time.

3. A Case Study: Broadband Telecom Networks Simulation

In this section, we present a case study of our proposed DRL multi-context scheduler, and how it can be applied to a real life open problem: software acceleration of broadband telecom networks simulation [3].

An important point is that to perform these experiments we need event traces (event stream, in our methodology). For this application case study, we used two types of event traces: (1) a *real-case event trace*, that has a sequence of events where a maximum of two events belonging to the same context can be found (i.e. 1, 2, 2, 3, 4, 4, ...); and (2) a *best-case event trace, that* can be derived from the real-case event

```
DynamicDRLSchedulingAlgorithm (EW) {
  ObtainDRLArrayUtilization(EW);
  K = NumberOfAvailableDRL();
  if K = 0 then
    DRLCell = GetLatestRequiredContext();
    Context = GetFirstContextNotInDRLArray(EW);
    DRL_Behaviour(DRLCell, Context);
  else
    CE = GetCurrentEvent();
    for Context = CE to CE+EW loop
      if ActiveContext(Context) = FALSE then
        DRLCell = GetFirstAvailableDRL(Context);
        DRL_Behaviour(DRLCell, Context);
      end if;
    end loop;
  end if;
}
```

Fig. 2. DRL Multi-Context Scheduler Algorithm

trace if it is ordered by context (as a second ordering factor, as the event stream is firstly ordered by tag). Thus, the best-case event trace for our system would be such that several sequential events belong to the same context could be found (i.e. 1, 1, 1, 1, 2, 2, 2, 2, 3, 3, ...).

Figure 3 shows the results for simulation execution time when increasing the number of DRL. It can be clearly seen that dynamic EW is only useful when there are event repetitions in the trace. Our experiments show that at least four repetitions should be found in the event trace. With the best-case event trace and using the dynamic EW an improvement of 33% is obtained.

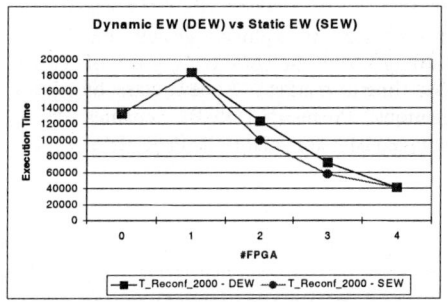 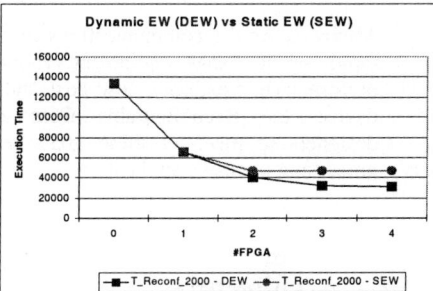

Fig. 3. Execution time results. The figure on the left corresponds to the real-case event trace and the one on the right corresponds to the best-case event trace.

4. Conclusions

In this paper, we have presented a major contribution: a novel approach to dynamic DRL multi-context scheduling addressed to discrete event systems [2], that uses a lookahead mechanism (event window, EW) in order to minimize reconfiguration overhead. Two versions of this context scheduler have been presented: static and dynamic EW.

We have studied the concrete application of software acceleration of broadband telecom networks simulation. Real-case and best-case event traces have been used in order to test both schedulers. Results demonstrate the benefits of our approach.

References

1. S. Hauck, "Configuration Prefetch for Single Context Reconfigurable Coprocessors", ACM/SIGDA International Symposium on FPGA, pp. 65-74, 1998.
2. E. A. Lee, "Modeling Concurrent Real-Time Processes using Discrete Events". Annuals of Software Engineering, Special Volume on Real-Time Software Engineering. 1998.
3. J. Noguera, R. M. Badia, J. Domingo, J. Sole, "Reconfigurable Computing: an Innovative Solution for Multimedia and Telecommunication Network Simulation". IEEE Proc. of the 25th Euromicro Conference. Milan, Italy. 1999.
4. J. Noguera, R. M. Badia, "Run-Time HW/SW Codesign for Discrete Event Systems using Dynamically Reconfigurable Architectures", Accepted for publication in the International Symposium on System Synthesis (ISSS'2000). Madrid, Spain. 2000.

Wireless Base Station Design Using a Reconfigurable Communications Processor

Chris Phillips

Chameleon Systems, Incorporated, 161 Nortech Parkway, San Jose, CA 95134, USA
chris@cmln.com

Abstract. As the communications market continues its explosive growth and rapid rate of change, equipment vendors struggle with the conflicting goals of performance, flexibility, low cost and fast time-to-market. A new class of device, the Reconfigurable Communications Processor (RCP), enables designers to meet all these goals simultaneously for multi-channel, data-processing intensive applications.

1 RCP Architecture

Chameleon Systems' CS2112 RCP, built using a 0.25-micron CMOS process, provides 24,000 MOPs and 3,000 MMACS processing power – about ten times that of a high-performance DSP.

2 Design of a cdma2000 Base Station

2.1 Wireless Base Station Infrastructure

The need for performance, flexibility, fast time-to-market, and low cost are especially critical in wireless base stations. Performance demands for next-generation systems are radically increased by the greater signal processing requirements of new standards, and the new features required by users. In the physical layer, for example, aggressive signal processing, such as beamforming and multi-user detection techniques are required to increase capacity and coverage.

Flexibility is required to handle the varying levels and quality of traffic from old and new protocols simultaneously. In CDMA base receivers, processing resources are allocated to received signals depending upon their signal quality. Additional rake fingers, for example, are directed towards those channels suffering severe multipath interference.

In the access layer, service providers overlay different 2G and 3G protocols. Voice, data and video are expected to co-exist. This means that hardware and software resources must be dynamically allocated to users depending upon their bandwidth requirement.

2.2 Implementation

Figure 1 shows a block diagram of a typical cdma2000 base station. On the receive side, the antenna receives data which is sampled as parallel words. These samples, or chips, represent the basic unit of data in the wireless symbol domain.

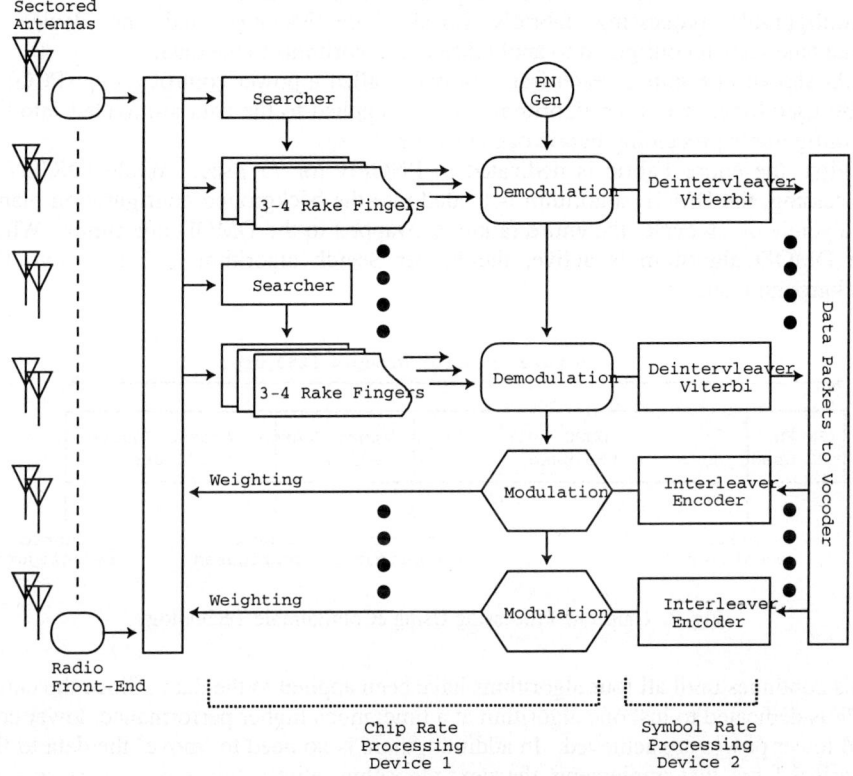

Fig. 1. cdma2000 Base Station

Once the signal is received, the rake receiver searches through the signal's sample-time window and looks for sets of transmitted original and delayed versions. Each 'finger' of the rake searches for a given delayed version of the transmitted signal.

The demodulator processes the data and recovers the transmitted signal. Each finger of the rake receiver multiplies the received sample by a delayed version of the specific pseudo random number that was used to encode the data. This delay factor compensates for the multipath effects of the wireless channel.

In Chameleon Systems' CS2112 device, the Pseudo-Random Number Sequence Generator (PNGEN) is implemented using a pre-computed polynomial look-up-table and delay-line technique that achieves a throughput of 64 chips per clock. The signal is decoded using a match-filter technique that interpolates the received data. The derived data is then passed to a set of filter stages whose outputs are used to locate the best match based on a PN sequence.

The chip-rate and symbol-rate processors for a system with 50 user channels can be implemented in two Chameleon CS2112 RCP devices. As shown in the following figure, the chip-rate processor is implemented in one device and the symbol-rate processor is implemented in the second device.

In Chameleon Systems' implementation of the wireless base station, eConfigurable technology is used to dramatically increase performance of the Reconfigurable Communications Processor. In this implementation, a frame of data is stored in the reconfigurable processing fabric's Local Store Memory and the device is instantaneously reconfigured to apply different algorithms to the data.

As shown in Figure 2, each frame of data, called a power control group (PCG) is 1250 μsec long. The four algorithms that are applied to the data are loaded into the reconfigurable processing Fabric one at a time.

First, the entire Fabric is dedicated to PNGEN for 77 μsec. While PNGEN is processing, the DMOD algorithm is loaded into the background configuration plane. In a single clock cycle, the entire fabric is swapped to the DMOD algorithm. While the DMOD algorithm is active, the Finger Search algorithm is loaded into the background plane.

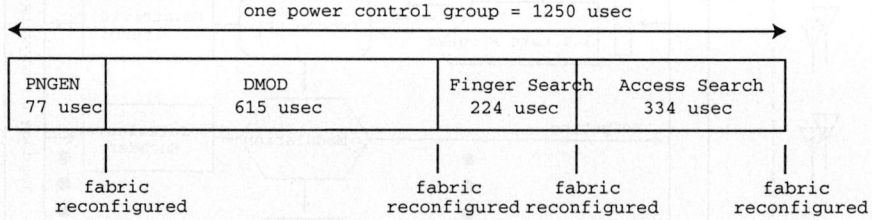

Fig. 2. Chip-rate Processing Using eConfigurable Technology

This continues until all four algorithms have been applied to the data. Since the entire RPF is dedicated to just one algorithm at a time, much higher performance, lower cost and lower power are achieved. In addition, there is no need to 'move' the data to the physical logic that implements the next algorithm, eliminating typical performance bottlenecks found in ASICs and FPGAs.

eConfigurable technology enables the entire chip-rate processing for a 50 channel system to be implemented in one Chameleon CS2112 device. Traditional approaches implement each of the four chip-rate processing algorithms as separate hardware modules in ASICs or FPGAs.

3 Summary

In the race to deploy next-generation wireless protocol systems, equipment vendors must overcome the challenges of performance, flexibility, cost and time-to-market. Chameleon Systems' Reconfigurable Communications Processor meets all four of these goals enabling vendors to be first to market with the highest performance, most flexible products at the lowest cost.

Placement of Linear Arrays

Erwan Fabiani and Dominique Lavenier

IRISA, Campus de Beaulieu,
35042 Rennes Cedex, FRANCE
{efabiani, lavenier}@irisa.fr

Abstract. This paper presents a methodology for mapping linear processor arrays onto FPGA components. By taking advantage of regularity and locality properties of these structures, a placement is pre-defined, allowing vendor tools to skip this phase and produce fast and optimized routing.

1 Introduction

In many compute intensive applications such as image or signal processing, time is mostly spent in executing loops. Speeding-up these applications leads to hardware implementations which directly benefit from the inherent loop parallelism. The resulting architecture is a regular array, often a systolic array, made of simple processing elements dedicated to efficiently performing the body of the inner loops [1]. The structure can either be uni or bi-dimensional, but in the following we will restrict to linear arrays only.

Implementing such nested loops onto FPGA components presents many advantages. First, the regular nature of FPGA component matches perfectly with the architecture we focus on: replication of identical regularly interconnected processing elements. Second, the best uses of FPGA boards (from a performance point of view) have been demonstrated on many compute intensive applications, as illustrated by the numerous applications implemented on the PAM boards [2]. Third, new advanced microprocessor architectures tend to incorporate reconfigurable resources in their data-path. Parallelizing loops on these specific areas is a very attractive way to efficiently exploit reconfigurable computing. Globally, there are three steps as described in [3]:

- **Parallelization:** This step consists in deriving regular array architectures from loop specifications or equivalent formal description such as systems of *affine recurrence equations*. The ALPHA language, developed at IRISA allows the programmer to explore transformations needed for systematic derivation of regular arrays and for automatic parallelization [4].
- **Partitioning:** Since the available reconfigurable resources may not support the entire array, transformation of the architecture is required : splitting the array into sub-arrays or clustering groups of processing elements. The automating of this task is still ongoing research and is not yet fully resolved.

- **Physical Mapping:** This last step maps the architecture on the reconfigurable support. From a RTL description (provided by the previous stages), one must find the best mapping both in term of speed performance and area occupation. This is actually a very time-consuming step which tends to become longer as the FPGA components grow in complexity.

The work presented in this paper deals with the last stage. It focuses on reducing the place-and-route process involved in the physical mapping task by taking advantage of the regular nature of the array we want to map.

2 Regular Place-and-Route Foundation

Place-and-Route steps are very time consuming, especially with the larger FPGA components. This is mainly due to the algorithmic techniques (such as simulated annealing) used for finding reasonable solutions. The advantage of these techniques are their generality: they provide relatively good solutions whatever the structure of the designs. In our case, as we try to shift towards software compilation requirement, the major drawback is definitely the computation time.

One way to limit this time is to provide a pre-defined placement and, of course, the best as possible to optimize the routing phase. The methodology we developed for mapping regular arrays onto FPGA components is mainly based on this idea. Our thesis is that placing an array of processing elements according to its regular and locality properties brings three major improvements over usual place-and-route techniques: (1) the placement time is drastically reduced; (2) the routing time is optimized; (3) the frequency is increased. Our placement strategy for taking advantages of these improvements is based on the following rules:

1. Signals which belong to a same processor have their sources placed in a same restricted area. This implies a reduction of the placement, the routing and the delay time.
2. Identical processors have identical placement: the placement focuses only on one processing element and is replicated over the FPGA component. The time is thus independent of the number of processing elements.
3. Neighboring processing elements are close to each other. Again, the expected benefits are a reduction of the placement, the routing ant he delay time.

A few experiments have been carried out to validate this thesis. Basically, we compare the time to place-and-route a design with and without placement directives. Several linear array designs have been tested using the PPR Xilinx router tool for the XC4000 family. We observe that the placement phase is more time consuming than the routing phase, and shortening this step results in a significant speed-up (3 on average), even if the routing phase, in some cases increases. We also observe that it does not lead to degraded clock frequency.

3 Regular Place-and-Route Strategy

Figure 1 details the place-and-route environment for mapping regular arrays onto FPGA components. The input and output of FRAP are written in a same structural description, respectively without and with placement directives. The regular placement is performed with the FRAP tool and acts in three steps:

1. All possible shapes for a processing element are generated by combining all shapes of its sub-components.
2. A full *snake* placement of the linear array is determined using the processing element shapes previously computed.
3. The final placement of the processing elements are performed according to their shapes.

From the output of FRAP an EDIF file is generated and input to the vendor place-and-route tools. Since the placement is fully specified, the computation time is reduced to roughly the time for routing the FPGA component.

Steps 1 and 3 deal with processing element placement. We consider those elements rather small, that is a few operators essentially coming from a library, and that finding a good placement is a fast and non critical process.

In step 2, the problem is to place a linear array on a bi-dimensional FPGA structure. The only way to keep two neighbor processing elements close to each other is to implement a snake-like arrangement of the array. The determination of the snake-like arrangement proceeds in two phases [5]: (1) divide the FPGA area in sub-areas that we call *convenient areas*, and (2) for each convenient area, place a maximum number of processing element in a snake-like fashion.

The second phase is solved using the knapsack metaphor [6] allowing the use of different kind of shapes for the processing elements.

Figure 2 is an illustrating example of the result of the FRAP placement. The full FPGA area has been partitioned into three convenient areas. In the convenient area 1, an horizontal snake is made of two different segments, segment of shape A and segment of shape B. The convenient area 2 is also an horizontal snake made only with a processing element of shape A. The convenient area 3 is a vertical snake made of processing elements of shape C. The overall placement requires of determining placements for the 3 different shapes of the processing element.

4 Conclusion and Future Works

We have presented a strategy for placing linear regular arrays onto FPGA components. This strategy uses the knapsack technique and provides fast placement compared to the vendor tools. The speed-up comes mainly from the regular nature of the architecture we focus on, that is, linear arrays of identical processors on which a two-level placement is achieved: (1) a cell-level placement and (2) an array-level placement.

Even if we can drastically shorten the placement step, the overall place-and-route process remains too long to be included into a compiling framework. It may takes a few tens of minutes up to a few hours to achieved a suitable routing, that is definitely too long for programmers who are used to a faster compiling process. Consequently, the next step is to shorten the routing phase.

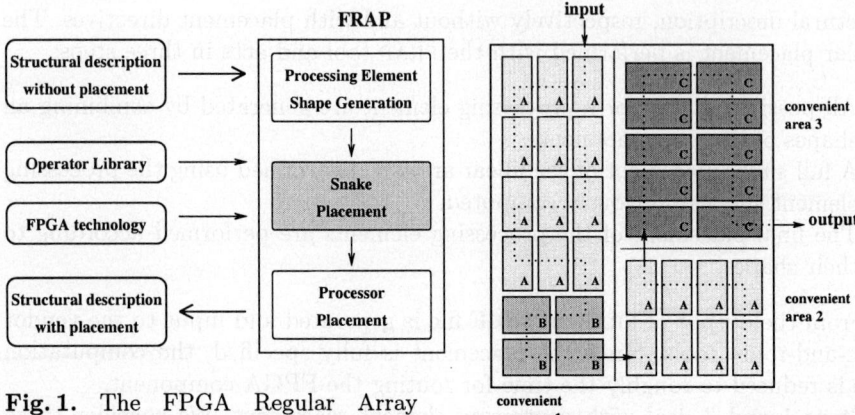

Fig. 1. The FPGA Regular Array Placer (FRAP): the description given as an input is processed and output with placement directive annotations.

Fig. 2. illustrating placement produced by FRAP

As for placement, this step can benefit from regular architecture by duplicating routing pattern of the processor cells. Unfortunately, unlike for placement, this strategy cannot be implemented through a few "routing" directives. It requires a detailed knowledge of the routing resources of the target FPGA as well as direct access to the programming of the routing switches.

References

1. P. Quinton and V. V. Dongen. The mapping of linear recurrence equations on regular arrays. *Journal of VLSI Signal Processing*, 1(2), 1989.
2. J. Vuillemin, P. Bertin, D. Roncin, M. Shand, H. Touati and P. Boucard. Programmable Active Memories: Reconfigurable Systems Come of Age. *IEEE Transactions on VLSI Systems*, 4(1), 1996.
3. E. Fabiani, D. Lavenier and L. Perraudeau. Loop Parallelization on a Reconfigurable Coprocessor. In *WDTA'98 : Workshop on Design, Test and Applications*, Dubrovnik, Croatia, 1998
4. P. LeMoenner, L. Perraudeau, P. Quinton, S. Rajopadhye, T. Risset Generating Regular Arithmetic Circuits with ALPHARD. *MPPS'96: Massively Parallel Computing Systems*, Ischia, Italie, 1996.
5. E. Fabiani and D. Lavenier. Using knapsack technique to place linear arrays on FPGA. Research report 1335, IRISA, June 2000.
6. S. Martello and P. Toth. Knapsack Problems: Algorithms and Computer Implementation. *John Wiley and Sons*, 1990.

Author Index

A

Aalsma, M. 29
Abke, J. 191
Abramovici, M. 545
Amano, H. 475, 585, 685
Anderson, J. 211
Andrejas, J. 456
Antonakopoulos, T. 39
Aoyama, K. 665
Arias-Estrada, M. 270
Asada, K. 555

B

Badia, R.M. 842
Barke, E. 191
Bartzick, T. 151
Bauer, C. 250
Becker, J. 58, 312
Bellis, S.J. 485
Benyon-Tinker, G. 656
Blaickner, A. 322
Blodget, B. 797
Bobda, C. 759
Brinkmann, A. 838

C

Cabestany, J. 87
Cantó, E. 87
Casadevall, F. 332
Caspi, E. 605
Chandra Jain, S. 201
Cheatham, J. 545
Cheng, W.W. 773
Cheung, P.Y.K. 96, 646
Chu, M. 605
Constantinides, G.A. 646
Cottet, D. 525
Courtney, T. 749

D

Dandalis, A. 443, 462
DeHon, A. 605

Derbyshire, A. 636
Diessel, O. 707
Ditmar, J. 19
Domínguez, M.A. 175
Döring, A.C. 626

E

Edwards, M. 739
Eisenring, M. 565
ElGindy, H. 379
Emmert, J.M. 545
Enzler, R. 525
Evartson, T. 830

F

Fabiani, E. 849
Fallside, H. 48
Fernández, P.G. 342
Flynn, M.J. 595

G

Gadea, R. 785
García, A. 342
García, J.L. 332
Gause, J. 96
Gelonch, A. 332
Giza, H. 535
Glasmacher, A. 449
Glesner, M. 58, 312
Govindarajan, S. 7
Green, P. 739
Grover, R.S. 422
Grünbacher, H. 322
Guccione, S.A. 352

H

Hall, J. 793
Hamidzadeh, B. 773
Hartenstein, R. 389
Hatnik, U. 826
Haufe, J. 826
Havinga, P.J.M. 400
Henze, M. 151

Herrero, V. ... 785
Herz, M. ... 389
Heysters, P.M. ... 400
Hildebrandt, J. ... 777
Hilton, A. ... 793
Hoffmann, R. ... 822
Hoffmann, Th. ... 389
Hoogerbrugge, J. ... 695
Hoshino, T. ... 240, 801
Huang, R. ... 605
Hübert, H. ... 595

I

Ichikawa, S. ... 729
Ikeda, M. ... 555
Iliopoulos, M. ... 39
Imlig, N. ... 805
Insenser, J.M. ... 87
Iwai, K. ... 685

J

James-Roxby, P.B. ... 495
Jantsch, A. ... 19
Jayaraman, R. ... 211
Jebelean, T. ... 810
Jeger, T. ... 525
Jou, R. ... 29

K

Kanazawa, M. ... 515
Kastrup, B. ... 695
Kataria, P. ... 545
Kean, T. ... 575
Kickler, J. ... 151
Kobori, T. ... 801
Koch, A. ... 615
Kolla, R. ... 432
Konishi, K. ... 729
Krasniewski, A. ... 675
Kress, R. ... 78
Krishnamoorthy, S. ... 181
Kropp, H. ... 221
Krupnova, H. ... 68
Kumar, A. ... 201

Kumar, S. ... 201
Kurosawa, H. ... 475

L

Lacadena, I. ... 87
Lafayette, G.L. ... 789
Lange, H. ... 615
Langen, D. ... 838
Lavenier, D. ... 849
Lehmann, T. ... 759
Levinson, L. ... 121
Li, Q. ... 422
Lías, G. ... 175
Lloris, A. ... 342
Luk, W. ... 96, 361, 636, 646
Lustig, G. ... 626
Lysaght, P. ... 141

M

Mătăsaru, B. ... 810
Madabhushi, C. ... 211
Makimoto, T. ... 1
Männer, R. ... 121
Marnane, W.P. ... 485
Martonosi, M. ... 412
Maruyama, T. ... 240, 801
Maya, S. ... 270
McCaskill, J.S. ... 286
McCready, R. ... 157
McMillan, S. ... 352
Meerbergen, J. van ... 695
Mei, A. ... 106
Melnikoff, S.J. ... 495
Mencer, O. ... 595
Middendorf, M. ... 379
Milne, G. ... 260, 707
Miomo, T. ... 515
Miyashita, A. ... 240
Mocholí, A. ... 785
Moreira, O. ... 695
Moreno, J.M. ... 87
Morf, M. ... 595
Moure, M.J. ... 175

N

Nag, S. 211
Nagami, K. 805
Nageldinger, U. 389
Nagoya, A. 665, 805
Nagy, O. 322
Nakada, H. 805
Nakajima, K. 665
Ng, K.-w. 361
Niittylahti, J. 371
Noguera, J. 842

O

Oguri, K. 805

P

Parilla, L. 342
Pfeifer, P. 163
Phillips, C. 846
Pionteck, T. 312
Platzner, M. 565
Ploog, H. 505
Prasanna, V.K. 106
Pyttel, A. 78

Q

Qiao, J. 555
Quigley, S.F. 495

R

Rabaey, J.M. 277
Raczinski, J.-M. 834
Ramírez, J. 342
Redekopp, M. 462
Renner, F.-M. 58
Renovell, M. 300
Reuter, C. 221
Revés, X. 332
Reynoso, R. 270
Rissa, T. 371
Robinson, D. 141
Rückert, U. 838
Russell, M.J. 495

S

Saito, H. 729
Saucier, G. 68
Saunders, J. 211
Sawada, H. 665
Sawitzki, S. 781
Schmalisch, M. 505
Schmeck, H. 379
Schmidt, B. 379
Schönherr, J. 781
Schwarz, P. 826
Sebastia, A. 785
Sedlmeier, A. 78
Sekanina, L. 814
Shang, W. 422
Shibata, Y. 475, 585, 685
Shiozawa, T. 805
Sidhu, R. 106
Siemers, C. 769
Simmler, H. 121
Sklyarov, V. 718
Sladek, S. 834
Sllame, A.M. 814
Smit, G.J.M. 400
Smit, J. 400
Smith, M.J.S. 48
Spallek, R.G. 781
Stefanoviĉ, D. 412
Straube, B. 781
Stroud, C.E. 545
Swaminathan, S. 181

T

Takayama, A. 685
Tammemäe, K. 830
Tang, X. 29
Taylor, A.M. 545
Tessier, R. 181, 535
Timmermann, D. 505, 777
Tomaszewicz, P. 169
Torkelsson, K. 19
Torres, C. 270
Torresen, J. 230
Touhafi, A. 469

Trost, A. 456, 818
Tröster, G. 525
Trum, J. 695
Turner, R. 749

U

Udorn, L. 729
Ulmann, B. 822
Uno, M. 585

V

Valdés, M.D. 175
Vasilko, M. 131, 656
Vemuri, R. 7
Völkmann, K.-P. 822

W

Wadhwa, S. 106, 443
Wagler, P. 286
Waldschmidt, S. 822
Wawrzynek, J. 605

Wilton, S.J.E. 773
Wojtkowiak, H. 250
Wolz, F. 432
Woods, R. 749
Woska, K. 151, 449

Y

Yamaguchi, Y. 240
Yamamoto, O 475
Yasuoka, K. 515
Yeh, J. 605

Z

Zajc, B. 818
Zemva, A. 818
Zhang, X.-j. 361
Zhu, J. 260
Zipf, P. 250

Lecture Notes in Computer Science

For information about Vols. 1–1804
please contact your bookseller or Springer-Verlag

Vol. 1805: T. Terano, H. Liu, A.L.P. Chen (Eds.), Knowledge Discovery and Data Mining. Proceedings, 2000. XIV, 460 pages. 2000. (Subseries LNAI).

Vol. 1806: W. van der Aalst, J. Desel, A. Oberweis (Eds.), Business Process Management. VIII, 391 pages. 2000.

Vol. 1807: B. Preneel (Ed.), Advances in Cryptology – EUROCRYPT 2000. Proceedings, 2000. XVIII, 608 pages. 2000.

Vol. 1809: S. Biundo, M. Fox (Eds.), Recent Advances in AI Planning. Proceedings, 1999. VIII, 373 pages. 2000. (Subseries LNAI).

Vol. 1810: R.López de Mántaras, E. Plaza (Eds.), Machine Learning: ECML 2000. Proceedings, 2000. XII, 460 pages. 2000. (Subseries LNAI).

Vol. 1811: S.W. Lee, H.. Bülthoff, T. Poggio (Eds.), Biologically Motivated Computer Vision. Proceedings, 2000. XIV, 656 pages. 2000.

Vol. 1813: P.L. Lanzi, W. Stolzmann, S.W. Wilson (Eds.), Learning Classifier Systems. X, 349 pages. 2000. (Subseries LNAI).

Vol. 1815: G. Pujolle, H. Perros, S. Fdida, U. Körner, I. Stavrakakis (Eds.), Networking 2000 – Broadband Communications, High Performance Networking, and Performance of Communication Networks. Proceedings, 2000. XX, 981 pages. 2000.

Vol. 1816: T. Rus (Ed.), Algebraic Methodology and Software Technology. Proceedings, 2000. XI, 545 pages. 2000.

Vol. 1817: A. Bossi (Ed.), Logic-Based Program Synthesis and Transformation. Proceedings, 1999. VIII, 313 pages. 2000.

Vol. 1818: C.G. Omidyar (Ed.), Mobile and Wireless Communications Networks. Proceedings, 2000. VIII, 187 pages. 2000.

Vol. 1819: W. Jonker (Ed.), Databases in Telecommunications. Proceedings, 1999. X, 208 pages. 2000.

Vol. 1820: J.-J. Quisquater, B. Schneier (Eds.), Smart Card Research and Applications. Proceedings, 1998. XI, 381 pages. 2000.

Vol. 1821: R. Loganantharaj, G. Palm, M. Ali (Eds.), Intelligent Problem Solving. Proceedings, 2000. XVII, 751 pages. 2000. (Subseries LNAI).

Vol. 1822: H.H. Hamilton, Advances in Artificial Intelligence. Proceedings, 2000. XII, 450 pages. 2000. (Subseries LNAI).

Vol. 1823: M. Bubak, H. Afsarmanesh, R. Williams, B. Hertzberger (Eds.), High Performance Computing and Networking. Proceedings, 2000. XVIII, 719 pages. 2000.

Vol. 1824: J. Palsberg (Ed.), Static Analysis. Proceedings, 2000. VIII, 433 pages. 2000.

Vol. 1825: M. Nielsen, D. Simpson (Eds.), Application and Theory of Petri Nets 2000. Proceedings, 2000. XI, 485 pages. 2000.

Vol. 1826: W. Cazzola, R.J. Stroud, F. Tisato (Eds.), Reflection and Software Engineering. X, 229 pages. 2000.

Vol. 1827: D. Bert, C. Choppy, P. Mosses (Eds.), Recent Trends in Algebraic Development Techniques. Proceedings, 1999. X, 477 pages. 2000.

Vol. 1829: C. Fonlupt, J.-K. Hao, E. Lutton, E. Ronald, M. Schoenauer (Eds.), Artificial Evolution. Proceedings, 1999. X, 293 pages. 2000.

Vol. 1830: P. Kropf, G. Babin, J. Plaice, H. Unger (Eds.), Distributed Communities on the Web. Proceedings, 2000. X, 203 pages. 2000.

Vol. 1831: D. McAllester (Ed.), Automated Deduction – CADE-17. Proceedings, 2000. XIII, 519 pages. 2000. (Subseries LNAI).

Vol. 1832: B. Lings, K. Jeffery (Eds.), Advances in Databases. Proceedings, 2000. X, 227 pages. 2000.

Vol. 1833: L. Bachmair (Ed.), Rewriting Techniques and Applications. Proceedings, 2000. X, 275 pages. 2000.

Vol. 1834: J.-C. Heudin (Ed.), Virtual Worlds. Proceedings, 2000. XI, 314 pages. 2000. (Subseries LNAI).

Vol. 1835: D. N. Christodoulakis (Ed.), Natural Language Processing – NLP 2000. Proceedings, 2000. XII, 438 pages. 2000. (Subseries LNAI).

Vol. 1836: B. Masand, M. Spiliopoulou (Eds.), Web Usage Analysis and User Profiling. Proceedings, 2000, V, 183 pages. 2000. (Subseries LNAI).

Vol. 1837: R. Backhouse, J. Nuno Oliveira (Eds.), Mathematics of Program Construction. Proceedings, 2000. IX, 257 pages. 2000.

Vol. 1838: W. Bosma (Ed.), Algorithmic Number Theory. Proceedings, 2000. IX, 615 pages. 2000.

Vol. 1839: G. Gauthier, C. Frasson, K. VanLehn (Eds.), Intelligent Tutoring Systems. Proceedings, 2000. XIX, 675 pages. 2000.

Vol. 1840: F. Bomarius, M. Oivo (Eds.), Product Focused Software Process Improvement. Proceedings, 2000. XI, 426 pages. 2000.

Vol. 1841: E. Dawson, A. Clark, C. Boyd (Eds.), Information Security and Privacy. Proceedings, 2000. XII, 488 pages. 2000.

Vol. 1842: D. Vernon (Ed.), Computer Vision – ECCV 2000. Part I. Proceedings, 2000. XVIII, 953 pages. 2000.

Vol. 1843: D. Vernon (Ed.), Computer Vision – ECCV 2000. Part II. Proceedings, 2000. XVIII, 881 pages. 2000.

Vol. 1844: W.B. Frakes (Ed.), Software Reuse: Advances in Software Reusability. Proceedings, 2000. XI, 450 pages. 2000.

Vol. 1845: H.B. Keller, E. Plöderer (Eds.), Reliable Software Technologies Ada-Europe 2000. Proceedings, 2000. XIII, 304 pages. 2000.

Vol. 1846: H. Lu, A. Zhou (Eds.), Web-Age Information Management. Proceedings, 2000. XIII, 462 pages. 2000.

Vol. 1847: R. Dyckhoff (Ed.), Automated Reasoning with Analytic Tableaux and Related Methods. Proceedings, 2000. X, 441 pages. 2000. (Subseries LNAI).

Vol. 1848: R. Giancarlo, D. Sankoff (Eds.), Combinatorial Pattern Matching. Proceedings, 2000. XI, 423 pages. 2000.

Vol. 1849: C. Freksa, W. Brauer, C. Habel, K.F. Wender (Eds.), Spatial Cognition II. XI, 420 pages. 2000. (Subseries LNAI).

Vol. 1850: E. Bertino (Ed.), ECOOP 2000 – Object-Oriented Programming. Proceedings, 2000. XIII, 493 pages. 2000.

Vol. 1851: M.M. Halldórsson (Ed.), Algorithm Theory – SWAT 2000. Proceedings, 2000. XI, 564 pages. 2000.

Vol. 1852: T. Thierauf, The Computational Complexity of Equivalence and Isomorphism Problems. VIII, 135 pages. 2000.

Vol. 1853: U. Montanari, J.D.P. Rolim, E. Welzl (Eds.), Automata, Languages and Programming. Proceedings, 2000. XVI, 941 pages. 2000.

Vol. 1854: G. Lacoste, B. Pfitzmann, M. Steiner, M. Waidner (Eds.), SEMPER — Secure Electronic Marketplace for Europe. XVIII, 350 pages. 2000.

Vol. 1855: E.A. Emerson, A.P. Sistla (Eds.), Computer Aided Verification. Proceedings, 2000. X, 582 pages. 2000.

Vol. 1857: J. Kittler, F. Roli (Eds.), Multiple Classifier Systems. Proceedings, 2000. XII, 404 pages. 2000.

Vol. 1858: D.-Z. Du, P. Eades, V. Estivill-Castro, X. Lin, A. Sharma (Eds.), Computing and Combinatorics. Proceedings, 2000. XII, 478 pages. 2000.

Vol. 1860: M. Klusch, L. Kerschberg (Eds.), Cooperative Information Agents IV. Proceedings, 2000. XI, 285 pages. 2000. (Subseries LNAI).

Vol. 1861: J. Lloyd, V. Dahl, U. Furbach, M. Kerber, K.-K. Lau, C. Palamidessi, L. Moniz Pereira, Y. Sagiv, P.J. Stuckey (Eds.), Computational Logic – CL 2000. Proceedings, 2000. XIX, 1379 pages. (Subseries LNAI). .

Vol. 1862: P.G. Clote, H. Schwichtenberg (Eds.), Computer Science Logic. Proceedings, 2000. XIII, 543 pages. 2000.

Vol. 1863: L. Carter, J. Ferrante (Eds.), Languages and Compilers for Parallel Computing. Proceedings, 1999. XII, 500 pages. 2000.

Vol. 1864: B. Y. Choueiry, T. Walsh (Eds.), Abstraction, Reformulation, and Approximation. Proceedings, 2000. XI, 333 pages. 2000. (Subseries LNAI).

Vol. 1865: K.R. Apt, A.C. Kakas, E. Monfroy, F. Rossi (Eds.), New Trends Constraints. Proceedings, 1999. X, 339 pages. 2000. (Subseries LNAI).

Vol. 1866: J. Cussens, A. Frisch (Eds.), Inductive Logic Programming. Proceedings, 2000. X, 265 pages. 2000. (Subseries LNAI).

Vol. 1867: B. Ganter, G.W. Mineau (Eds.), Conceptual Structures: Logical, Linguistic, and Computational Issues. Proceedings, 2000. XI, 569 pages. 2000. (Subseries LNAI).

Vol. 1868: P. Koopman, C. Clack (Eds.), Implementation of Functional Languages. Proceedings, 1999. IX, 199 pages. 2000.

Vol. 1869: M. Aagaard, J. Harrison (Eds.), Theorem Proving in Higher Order Logics. Proceedings, 2000. IX, 535 pages. 2000.

Vol. 1872: J. van Leeuwen, O. Watanabe, M. Hagiya, P.D. Mosses, T. Ito (Eds.), Theoretical Computer Science. Proceedings, 2000. XV, 630 pages. 2000.

Vol. 1876: F. J. Ferri, J.M. Iñesta, A. Amin, P. Pudil (Eds.), Advances in Pattern Recognition. Proceedings, 2000. XVIII, 901 pages. 2000.

Vol. 1877: C. Palamidessi (Ed.), CONCUR 2000 – Concurrency Theory. Proceedings, 2000. XI, 612 pages. 2000.

Vol. 1878: J.P. Bowen, S. Dunne, A. Galloway, S. King (Eds.), ZB 2000: Formal Specification and Development in Z and B. Proceedings, 2000. XIV, 511 pages. 2000.

Vol. 1879: M. Paterson (Ed.), Algorithms – ESA 2000. Proceedings, 2000. IX, 450 pages. 2000.

Vol. 1880: M. Bellare (Ed.), Advances in Cryptology – CRYPTO 2000. Proceedings, 2000. XI, 545 pages. 2000.

Vol. 1881: C. Zhang, V.-W. Soo (Eds.), Design and Applications of Intelligent Agents. Proceedings, 2000. X, 183 pages. 2000. (Subseries LNAI).

Vol. 1883: B. Triggs, A. Zisserman, R. Szeliski (Eds.), Vision Algorithms: Theory and Practice. Proceedings, 1999. X, 383 pages. 2000.

Vol. 1886: R. Mizoguchi, J. Slaney /Eds.), PRICAI 2000: Topics in Artificial Intelligence. Proceedings, 2000. XX, 835 pages. 2000. (Subseries LNAI).

Vol. 1889: M. Anderson, P. Cheng, V. Haarslev (Eds.), Theory and Application of Diagrams. Proceedings, 2000. XII, 504 pages. 2000. (Subseries LNAI).

Vol. 1892: P. Brusilovsky, O. Stock, C. Strapparava (Eds.), Adaptive Hypermedia and Adaptive Web-Based Systems. Proceedings, 2000. XIII, 422 pages. 2000.

Vol. 1893: M. Nielsen, B. Rovan (Eds.), Mathematical Foundations of Computer Science 2000. Proceedings, 2000. XIII, 710 pages. 2000.

Vol. 1896: R. W. Hartenstein, H. Grünbacher (Eds.), Field-Programmable Logic and Applications. Proceedings, 2000. XVII, 856 pages. 2000.

Vol. 1897: J. Gutknecht, W. Weck (Eds.), Modular Programming Languages. Proceedings, 2000. XII, 299 pages. 2000.

Vol. 1899: H.-H. Nagel, F.J. Perales López (Eds.), Articulated Motion and Deformable Objects. Proceedings, 2000. X, 183 pages. 2000.

Vol. 1900: A. Bode, T. Ludwig, W. Karl, R. Wismüller (Eds.), Euro-Par 2000 Parallel Processing. Proceedings, 2000. XXXV, 1368 pages. 2000.

Vol. 1912: Y. Gurevich, P.W. Kutter, M. Odersky, L. Thiele (Eds.), Abstract State Machines. Proceedings, 2000. X, 381 pages. 2000.

Vol. 1913: K. Jansen, S. Khuller (Eds.), Approximation Algorithms for Combinatorial Optimization. Proceedings, 2000. IX, 275 pages. 2000.